THE OXFORD HANDBOOK OF
GANGS AND SOCIETY

THE OXFORD HANDBOOK OF

GANGS AND SOCIETY

Edited by
DAVID C. PYROOZ,
JAMES A. DENSLEY
and
JOHN LEVERSO

OXFORD
UNIVERSITY PRESS

Oxford University Press is a department of the University of Oxford. It furthers the University's objective of excellence in research, scholarship, and education by publishing worldwide. Oxford is a registered trade mark of Oxford University Press in the UK and certain other countries.

Published in the United States of America by Oxford University Press
198 Madison Avenue, New York, NY 10016, United States of America.

© Oxford University Press 2024

All rights reserved. No part of this publication may be reproduced, stored in a retrieval system, or transmitted, in any form or by any means, without the prior permission in writing of Oxford University Press, or as expressly permitted by law, by license, or under terms agreed with the appropriate reproduction rights organization. Inquiries concerning reproduction outside the scope of the above should be sent to the Rights Department, Oxford University Press, at the address above.

You must not circulate this work in any other form
and you must impose this same condition on any acquirer.

Library of Congress Cataloging-in-Publication Data
Names: Pyrooz, David, C. editor. | Densley, James A. (James Andrew), 1982– editor. | Leverso, John, editor.
Title: The Oxford handbook of gangs and society / [edited by] David C. Pyrooz, James A. Densley, and John Leverso.
Description: New York, NY : Oxford University Press, [2024] | Includes bibliographical references and index.
Identifiers: LCCN 2023032620 (print) | LCCN 2023032621 (ebook) | ISBN 9780197618158 (hardback) | ISBN 9780197618172 (epub) | ISBN 9780197618189 (online)
Subjects: LCSH: Gangs. | Gang members.
Classification: LCC HV6437 .O94 2024 (print) | LCC HV6437 (ebook) | DDC 364.106/6—dc23/eng/20230929
LC record available at https://lccn.loc.gov/2023032620
LC ebook record available at https://lccn.loc.gov/2023032621

DOI: 10.1093/oxfordhb/9780197618158.001.0001

Printed by Integrated Books International, United States of America

Contents

List of Editors — xi
List of Contributors — xi

1. Introduction to the OUP Handbook of Gangs and Society — 1
   DAVID C. PYROOZ, JAMES A. DENSLEY, AND JOHN LEVERSO

SECTION 1: REVISITING DEFINITIONS IN THE TWENTY-FIRST CENTURY

2. The Eurogang Definition: Context, Development, Scrutiny, and Debate (Including a Conversation with Malcolm Klein) — 15
   FRANK M. WEERMAN AND SCOTT H. DECKER

3. What Gangs Aren't: Contrasting Gangs with Other Collectives — 36
   MARTIN BOUCHARD, KARINE DESCORMIERS, AND ALYSHA GIRN

4. A Relational Approach to Street Gangs — 54
   ANDREW V. PAPACHRISTOS, JOHN LEVERSO, AND DAVID HUREAU

5. Gangs in Practice: Violence Prevention, Law Enforcement, and the Received Idea of the "Gang" — 74
   DAVID M. KENNEDY

6. The Social Construction of the American Street Gang — 89
   PATRICK LOPEZ-AGUADO

7. Gang Identity across the Life Course — 106
   SOU LEE AND BRYAN F. BUBOLZ

8. Place Matters: Geographers and Gang Members — 122
   STEFANO BLOCH

SECTION 2: APPROACHES TO THE EMPIRICAL STUDY OF GANGS

9. The History and Evolution of Gang Scholarship:
   A Topic Modeling and Change Point Detection Approach — 139
   JASON GRAVEL

10. Funding Gang Research to Advance Policy and Practice — 207
    PHELAN A. WYRICK, BARBARA TATEM KELLEY, AND
    MARY POULIN CARLTON

11. The National Youth Gang Survey: Past, Present, and Future — 235
    MEAGAN CAHILL, JAMES C. HOWELL, AND ARLEN EGLEY, JR.

12. Historical Gang Research Methods: An Overview — 256
    MITCHEL P. ROTH

13. Critical Approaches to Gangs — 269
    TILMAN SCHWARZE AND ALISTAIR FRASER

14. Women in Gang Research: An Overview — 287
    MARTA-MARIKA URBANIK AND SANDRA M. BUCERIUS

15. Indigenous Gangs and Gang Research — 312
    ADRIENNE FRENG AND HANNAH ST. CLAIR

16. Studying Gangs in Central and South America:
    Reflections on Gender and Researcher Positionality — 329
    MARÍA JOSÉ MÉNDEZ AND ELLEN VAN DAMME

17. Gang Research in the Caribbean — 351
    EDWARD R. MAGUIRE

SECTION 3: CORE AND EMERGING ISSUES

18. What Is Gang Culture? Three Conceptualizations of
    an Elusive Concept — 375
    CAYLIN LOUIS MOORE AND FORREST STUART

19. Masculinities and Respect in the Group Context of Gangs — 395
    LORINE A. HUGHES AND LISA M. BROIDY

20. Birds of a Feather? Individual Differences and Gang Membership 413
    JENNIFER J. TOSTLEBE AND JOSE ANTONIO SANCHEZ

21. Rational Choice, Gang Membership, and Crime:
    Moving Actors and Choice to Center Stage 444
    KYLE J. THOMAS

22. Psychopathology as a Cause or Consequence of
    Youth Gang Involvement 470
    PATRICIA K. KERIG, LUCYBEL MENDEZ,
    AVA R. ALEXANDER, AND SUSAN CHEN

23. The Emerging Frontier: Gangs in Developing Countries 499
    HERBERT C. COVEY

24. Gang Ecological Diversity in the Hollenbeck Area of
    Los Angeles, 1978–2012 518
    P. JEFFREY BRANTINGHAM AND MATTHEW VALASIK

SECTION 4: GANGS IN INSTITUTIONAL CONTEXT

25. Storming the Capital: The Place of Street Capital and
    Social Capital within Gangs 543
    SIMON HARDING AND ROSS DEUCHAR

26. On Gangs and Family: Primary, Secondary, and Surrogate Family 560
    GABRIEL T CESAR, D'ANDRE WALKER, AND TIFFANY FERNANDEZ

27. Linking Education and Criminology Research to Understand
    the Schooling Experiences of Gang Youth and Adults 577
    ADRIAN H. HUERTA

28. Religion and Gangs: An Introduction to the Isolated and
    Integrated Affiliation Models 599
    TIMOTHY R. LAUGER AND HALEIGH KUBINIEC

29. Re-examining the Literature on Social Media and Gangs:
    Critical Race Theory as a Path for New Opportunities 618
    CAITLIN ELSAESSER AND DESMOND PATTON

30. Comparative Approaches to the Study of Prison Gangs and
    Prison Order   638
    DAVID SKARBEK AND KAITLYN WOLTZ

31. Transnational Gangs? Understanding Migration and Gangs   659
    JOSÉ MIGUEL CRUZ AND JONATHAN D. ROSEN

SECTION 5: LEGACIES OF SECOND-GENERATION RESEARCHERS

32. The Legacy of Scott H. Decker   677
    DAVID C. PYROOZ AND RICHARD K. MOULE JR.

33. The Legacy of Finn-Aage Esbensen   696
    DENA C. CARSON, ADRIENNE FRENG, CHRIS MELDE, AND
    DANA PETERSON

34. The Legacy of John M. Hagedorn   714
    ROBERTO R. ASPHOLM

35. The Legacy of Cheryl L. Maxson   732
    SHANNON E. REID

36. The Legacy of Joan W. Moore   744
    JAMES DIEGO VIGIL

37. The Legacy of James Diego Vigil   753
    MIKE TAPIA AND E. MARK MORENO

SECTION 6: RESPONDING TO GANGS

38. Clinical Intervention for Gang-Involved Youth:
    Toward an Empirically Validated Model   773
    PAUL BOXER, JOANNA KUBIK, AND STEPHANIE MARCELLO

39. No Public Benefit: The Placentia Gang Injunction
    Opposition Campaign   787
    SEAN GARCIA-LEYS AND JESSE ENGEL

40. "Somebody's Watching Me": Surveying Police Surveillance
    of Gangs   809
    MATTHEW VALASIK AND P. JEFFREY BRANTINGHAM

41. Policing Gangs: Five Reasons Why Traditional Strategies Fail 832
    MADELEINE NOVICH

42. Defund the Police? Considerations for Reducing Gang Violence 849
    ANTHONY A. BRAGA, JOHN M. MACDONALD, AND GEORGE TITA

43. Making Sense of the Models: Continuities and Differences across
    Prominent Gang/Group Gun Violence Intervention Models 870
    JESSE JANNETTA, PAIGE S. THOMPSON, AND LILY ROBIN

Index 895

Editors

David C. Pyrooz, PhD, University of Colorado Boulder

James A. Densley, DPhil, Metro State University

John Leverso, PhD, University of Cincinnati

Contributors

Ava R. Alexander, MS, University of Utah

Roberto R. Aspholm, PhD, University of St. Thomas

Stefano Bloch, PhD, University of Arizona

Martin Bouchard, PhD, Simon Fraser University

Paul Boxer, PhD, Rutgers University

Anthony A. Braga, PhD, University of Pennsylvania

P. Jeffrey Brantingham, BA, PhD, University of California, Los Angeles

Lisa M. Broidy, PhD, University of New Mexico

Bryan F. Bubolz, PhD, Northern Michigan University

Sandra M. Bucerius, PhD, University of Alberta

Meagan Cahill, PhD, Police Executive Research Forum

Mary Poulin Carlton, PhD, US Department of Justice

Dena C. Carson, PhD, Indiana University–Purdue University Indianapolis

Gabriel T. Cesar, PhD, Florida Atlantic University

Susan Chen, University of Utah

Herbert C. Covey, PhD, Retired

José Miguel Cruz, PhD, Florida International University

Scott H. Decker, PhD, Arizona State University

Karine Descormiers, PhD, Combined Forces Special Enforcement—British Columbia

CONTRIBUTORS

Ross Deuchar, PhD, University of the West of Scotland

Arlen Egley, Jr., PhD, Truman State University

Caitlin Elsaesser, PhD, University of Connecticut

Jesse Engel, Peace and Justice Law Center

Tiffany Fernandez, MS, Florida Atlantic University

Alistair Fraser, PhD University of Glasgow

Adrienne Freng, PhD, University of Wyoming

Sean Garcia-Leys, Esq., Peace and Justice Law Center

Alysha Girn, MA, Simon Fraser University

Jason Gravel, PhD, Temple University

Simon Harding, PhD, University of West London

James C. Howell, PhD, National Gang Center

Adrian H. Huerta, PhD, University of Southern California

Lorine A. Hughes, PhD, University of Colorado, Denver

David Hureau, PhD, University of Albany, SUNY

Jesse Jannetta, MPP, Urban Institute

Barbara Tatem Kelley, MA, MEd, US Department of Justice

David M. Kennedy, John Jay College of Criminal Justice

Patricia K. Kerig, PhD, University of Utah

Joanna Kubik, PhD, Rider University

Haleigh Kubiniec, MS, Niagara University

Timothy R. Lauger, PhD Niagara University

Sou Lee, PhD, Gonzaga University

Patrick Lopez-Aguado, PhD, Santa Clara University

John M. MacDonald, PhD, University of Pennsylvania

Edward R. Maguire, PhD, Arizona State University

Stephanie Marcello, PhD, Rutgers University

Chris Melde, PhD, Michigan State University

Lucybel Mendez, PhD, University of Tennessee-Knoxville

María José Méndez, PhD, University of Toronto

Caylin Louis Moore, MA, Stanford University

E. Mark Moreno, PhD, Texas A&M University—Commerce

Richard K. Moule Jr., PhD, University of South Florida

Madeleine Novich, PhD, Manhattan College

Andrew V. Papachristos, PhD, Northwestern University

Desmond Patton, PhD, University of Pennsylvania

Dana Peterson, PhD, University at Albany School of Criminal Justice

Shannon E. Reid, PhD, University of North Carolina at Charlotte

Lily Robin, MPP, Urban Institute

Jonathan D. Rosen, PhD, New Jersey City University

Mitchel P. Roth, PhD, Sam Houston State University

Jose Antonio Sanchez, MS, University of Colorado Boulder

Tilman Schwarze, PhD, University of Glasgow

David Skarbek, PhD, Brown University

Hannah St. Clair, University of Wyoming

Forrest Stuart, PhD, Stanford University

Mike Tapia, PhD, Texas A&M University—Commerce

Kyle J. Thomas, PhD, University of Colorado Boulder

Paige S. Thompson, MA, Urban Institute

George Tita, PhD, University of California, Irvine

Jennifer J. Tostlebe, PhD, University of Nebraska Omaha

Marta-Marika Urbanik, PhD, University of Alberta

Matthew Valasik, PhD, University of Alabama

Ellen Van Damme, PhD, University of California, Los Angeles and University of Leuven

James Diego Vigil, PhD, University of California, Irvine

D'Andre Walker, PhD, University of Mississippi

Frank M. Weerman, PhD, Netherlands Institute for the Study of Crime and Law Enforcement (NSCR)/Erasmus University Rotterdam

Kaitlyn Woltz, PhD, California State University San Marcos

Phelan A. Wyrick, PhD, US Department of Justice, Office of Justice Programs

CHAPTER 1

INTRODUCTION TO THE OUP HANDBOOK OF GANGS AND SOCIETY

DAVID C. PYROOZ, JAMES A. DENSLEY, AND JOHN LEVERSO

THE *Oxford Handbook of Gangs and Society* is designed to be the premier resource for practitioners, policymakers, researchers, and students concerned with gangs. It contains 42 chapters written by the very best minds in the field. These chapters are organized into six sections that reflect the central theme of the handbook: "looking back, moving forward." This appreciates the longstanding and at times contentious history of research on gangs, while also aiming to advance the field of study squarely into the twenty-first century.

Looking back means reflecting on the large-scale cultural, economic, political, and social changes that have occurred since Thrasher's (1927) groundbreaking monograph, *The Gang*. When that book was written nearly a century ago, gangs were considered a normative component of adolescence and conflicts between gangs were rarely lethal. Immigration to the United States was almost exclusively from European countries, and family livelihoods were sufficiently supported by manual labor. The child-savers movement was in full swing, commercial radio was in its infancy, and movies did not have sound. The first baccalaureate degree in criminology was less than a decade old.

How times have changed. Demographics are different, the economy is different, technology and media are different, and so too are our systems of academia and criminal justice. Major structural changes have contoured the forms and functions of gangs and our understanding of them. Yet even in the presence of these shifts, there is continuity in what are considered core issues, such as definitions and views of gangs, the emergence of groups and their transitions, the nature of the gang and ebb and flow of violence, group processes within gangs, and how to best respond to gangs and gang members.

Moving forward means considering the future of the field of study. New challenges await. Technology has always influenced the world of gangs, but the rise of 3D-printed firearms and auto sears or switches that can make any semiautomatic gun automatic, synthetic drugs, generative artificial intelligence, and even the metaverse present new challenges. Automation, digital currencies, remote learning and working, changing views on the nature of work, entry-level wage increases, and demographic declines in births and immigration in high-income countries will also affect the economy and "enterprise" of the gang (Padilla 1992). Disaster and displacement under global climate change will disrupt social order in communities, with consequences for gang membership and formation.

Legal and political forces are also at work. Abolitionists and reformists have called for the undoing of the police state and mass incarceration, which includes specialized gang policing and anti-gang legislation. Political polarization could define the gang as we know it out of existence, reifying groups as social movements or criminal enterprises. Fragile democracies could see an increase in ideological gangs or gang-like quasi-institutions serving the broader aims of governance. Economic, political, and social forces will at the same time shape the academy and research enterprise, from sources of data and funding to disciplinary priorities, which could alter the study of gangs. These are just some of the issues foreshadowed in this volume.

Why This Book? And Why Now?

There is no central body responsible for the production and organization of knowledge on gangs. And there is a lot of it—more books, reports, articles, and essays than ever before (see **Chapter 9** in this volume). The fact that we can refer to "gang research" or "gang studies" is a testament to a field devoted to the subject matter. Such specialization typically brings about ways to support knowledge production and organization, but this has not been embraced by scholars who conduct basic and applied research on gangs. There is no academic journal, division in an international society, funding agency, or research center to which the field turns for guidance and support. If anything, the field is highly fractured with much dissensus, in part owing to the retirements and, sadly, deaths of leading figures. Edited volumes, journal special issues, and synthesizing texts have long occupied a place of prominence in scholarship on gangs, from Ron Huff's *Gangs in America* trilogy, to the six (and counting) Eurogang volumes, to prior handbooks, which is perhaps somewhat distinct from other fields. Part of the motivation for this volume is to address this void in the literature by offering the most compelling and comprehensive compilation of works on gangs extant, which takes on added significance considering the incredible growth of the literature in the 2010s.

No single perspective on gangs dominates this volume. Our strategy from the outset was to cast the widest net possible. We sought to assemble a list of contributors who were representative of the community who studies gangs. We sought to curate content that represented the most timely and important topics in the field. We believe we were successful on both fronts, as readers will quickly see from perusing the table of contents.

Over 80 different authors contributed to this handbook, and the result is truly interdisciplinary. At times for better and at other times for worse, the study of gangs has long been dominated by criminologists, a source of some ingrained tensions in the field owing to disciplinary orientations. A core goal of ours was to incorporate a broader range of perspectives, which is something we believe we accomplished: anthropologists, geographers, historians, legal scholars, psychologists, and sociologists are all represented in this volume. A related goal was to reflect the diversity of the field, from demographics to geography to seniority.

The scholars represented as authors include a blend of domestic and international; early, mid-career, as well as senior scholars; and there are more female voices here than in any other comparable volume on gangs.

Another core aim of ours was to be comprehensive in scope. There is no one truth about gangs, although some will claim otherwise. The chapters in this volume capture perspectives that often give rise to different viewpoints on understanding and responding to gangs, ranging from an academic discipline to researcher positionality to epistemology and methodology.

How Should Readers Approach This Handbook?

This is not a book to read in one sitting. Every chapter is authoritative and integrative in coverage, by design. We solicited chapters from the very best scholars in the field—the people who initiated, shaped, or redefined a particular area of study. They each had a stake in the production and organization of knowledge. We gave authors the license to make the point they wanted or needed to make, but also held them accountable for ensuring their chapter offered a state-of-the-art review of the literature. Therefore, chapters can be read standalone to understand the progress or direction of issues, but they can also be read collectively within sections. Some sections, such as gang definitions or gang responses, naturally appeal to sequential reading, and readers who do this will be rewarded with breadth and depth of coverage on the issues. Other sections, such as studying gangs or core and emerging issues, reflect a broader range of topics with less interconnectedness.

To this end, we offer readers a snippet of the key issues covered in the chapters, organized by the six themes of the handbook, as follows: (1) revisiting definitions of gangs; (2) the empirical study of gangs; (3) core and emerging issues in gang research; (4) the integration of gangs in predominant institutions; (5) legacies of second-generation gang researchers; and (6) responding to gangs. If we are to look back to move forward, these are the areas in which we can learn and advance the most. The following gives readers a sense of why we solicited the chapters we did, the significance of the issues covered, and the implications of this work for their field.

Section 1: Revisiting Definitions in the Twenty-First Century

Few issues have animated the literature on gangs with as much energy and for such duration as the questions "What is a gang?" "What is a gang member?" The purpose of this section is not to relitigate "old" issues, such as the tautology of criminal involvement or whether organization matters, but instead to engage in substantive conversations occurring at the boundaries of social groups; advances in geography, identity, and network theory and research; consensus definitions; and the various conceptualizations of gangs.

Frank Weerman and Scott Decker kick off the section in Chapter 2 by tracing the development of the Eurogang definition of gangs. Arguably the most prominent research-based gang definition, they pull back the curtain with untold stories on how the "consensus definition" came to be. They speak from their memories as regular participants in the Eurogang program of research, including the meetings when the definition was formulated, as well as those of the late Malcolm Klein, the intellectual force behind Eurogang who died in 2023, just before the publication of this volume. They elaborate on the five defining properties of the definition, its widespread adoption and application, and consider how the internet and social media challenge a core component of the definition, street orientation.

In Chapter 3, Martin Bouchard, Karine Descormiers, and Alysha Girn move the discussion from what gangs are to what gangs are not (i.e., peer groups or organized criminal groups). They begin with the postulation that deviant groups span a continuum from peer groups to organized crime: "Our work is aimed at shedding light on the gray areas in between those extremes—the space where 'gangs' tend to belong." In short, this is boundary work. The authors propose that gangs can be distinguished from peer groups and organized crime along seven dimensions and elaborate on ways to measure each of them.

Gangs are groups, but they are also networks. In Chapter 4, Andrew Papachristos, John Leverso, and David Hureau argue for the (re)centering of relational thinking in gang research. They posit that the gang world is not built through individual actions alone but shaped by relationships and social networks among groups and gang members. In making this argument, the authors review the definitional debate underscoring how gang dynamics and relations are an essential part of gangs. To spur future research, the authors also review qualitative and quantitative data and methods that can be used to conduct studies of gangs via a relational perspective.

David Kennedy takes readers on a journey through the received idea of the gang in Chapter 5. Whereas scholars have long bickered over definitions, no such efforts have been made to unpack "the gang" from the perspectives of outreach workers and other frontline practitioners. The idea that gangs are conspiratorial, monolithic, organized, structured, and rule-bound is misleading and stubbornly resistant to facts. It is also an impediment to meaningfully understanding and responding to violence. Kennedy calls for a scholarly agenda devoted to the practitioner's received idea of the gang—from foundations to consequences—comparable to the attention scholars have aimed at legal and academic gang definitions.

In Chapter 6, sociologist Patrick Lopez-Aguado provides a critical perspective on gang definitions. He argues that the gang problem is a social construction because the meanings ascribed to gangs change and are contingent on the definer. In this chapter, he investigates the role of the media and state, as well as moral panics, in defining gangs. The social construction perspective provides an alternative and much-needed critical viewpoint on the gang definition debate.

Sou Lee and Bryan Bubolz suggest in Chapter 7 that gang membership should be viewed as a situated identity performance rather than a fixed state. In essence, they suggest that a more granular conception of gang membership is advantageous (e.g., gang identity salience is more likely in some situations than others) over static conceptions of being a gang member versus not being a gang member. Drawing off symbolic interactionism, they show how joining, persistence in, and disengagement from gangs are closely related to identity mechanisms such as reflected appraisals, identity salience, and depersonalization in specific contexts. The authors also provide specific guidelines for incorporating and measuring identity in both qualitative and quantitative studies. Thus, this chapter offers an additional vantage point rarely examined in the gang definition debate.

In Chapter 8, cultural geographer and graffiti writer Stefano Bloch infuses cultural geography with critical criminology to advocate for the inclusion of gangs and gang members in geographical theories of space and place. He contends that a deeper understanding of notions of territoriality and neighborhood would benefit geography generally and gang research specifically. This compelling autoethnographic chapter charts the path forward for how to make "geography a home for gang studies."

Section 2: Approaches to the Empirical Study of Gangs

As the field of gang research approaches its centennial, it is important to document its origin, growth, and evolution. The nine chapters in this section focus on a variety of issues concerning the production of knowledge in gang research. The coverage is striking. The object of study ranges from a corpus of the literature to entire portfolios of scholarship to methods to specialized populations. The epistemological foci should guide the next generation of scholarship.

Jason Gravel opens this section with a remarkable account of the history of gang scholarship in Chapter 9. He revisits Pyrooz and Mitchell's (2015) "Little Gang Research, Big Gang Research." Similarly, he turns the tools of science on itself to facilitate a systematic review of the literature on gangs. Differently, he uses change point detection methods to identify eras when the literature underwent shifts in growth and topic modeling to determine shifts in the subject matter of interest. "Big" gang research appears here to stay. The quantity of scholarly output now clocks in around 250 works annually, and the corpus of gang scholarship rose to 6,500 works, up from 5,000 in 2013. There was also the emergence of a large cohort of researchers in the 2010s who regularly contribute to the literature. Gravel thoughtfully considers the implications of these changes in the literature for the science of gangs and the increasing diversity of gang scholarship.

Universities and institutes subsidize a fair amount of research and evaluation on gangs (through salaries, computing, internal grants, etc.), but many of the cornerstone projects in gang research could never have been completed without external funding. Few organizations have done more to support gang research than the US Department of Justice's Office of Justice Programs, which funded the Causes and Correlates of Delinquency studies, Gangs Resistance Education and Training (G.R.E.A.T.), the National Youth Gang Survey (NYGS), and the Comprehensive Gang Model (also known as the Spergel Model), among many other projects. And few people are as intimately knowledgeable of the Office of Justice Program's funding efforts as Phelan Wyrick, Barbara Tatem Kelley, and Mary Poulin Carlton, the authors of Chapter 10. They describe how priorities concerning gangs are established and the types of solicitations that appeal to gang scholarship. They summarize the portfolios of research and evaluation supported by the National Institute of Justice and Office of Juvenile Justice and Delinquency, which includes $32 million distributed to 44 proposals between 2010 and 2021.

Few researchers have done (or will do) more to paint a national portrait of gangs and violence than the trio who authored Chapter 11. Meagan Cahill, James (Buddy) Howell, and Arlen Egley share with readers the past, present, and future of the National Youth Gang

Survey (NYGS). Howell and Egley were principally responsible for generating 17 annual waves of national data on the number of gangs, gang members, and gang homicides—among other factors—based on surveys of law enforcement agencies until the NYGS was discontinued in 2013. When the National Institute of Justice relaunched the survey in 2020, the baton was officially passed to Meagan Cahill. The chapter examines the knowledge contribution of the NYGS and details its future directions.

Historical criminologist Mitchel Roth argues in Chapter 12 for a more inclusive research strategy in the study of gangs. He provides an overview of the value historical research brings to gang research, along with the methods used by historians that would appeal to scholars who study gang membership. He contends that engaging with newspaper archives, oral histories, dictionaries, and other materials would offer a deeper, richer, and more accurate understanding of gangs, including their origins and evolutions, topics often missed or skimmed over in the literature.

In Chapter 13, Tilman Schwarze and Alistair Fraser provide an overview of the intellectual history of critical gang studies in sociology and criminology. To foreground how critical scholars have developed new and innovative theoretical and methodological approaches to gang research, they examine key studies on gangs across geographical contexts and call for a deeper appreciation of the historical, structural, political, and economic factors that contribute to gang formation and evolution.

Research led by women has changed the way gangs are thought about today. This goes well beyond studies into the prevalence and roles of girls and women in gangs and extends to research about group dynamics and the application of gender theory and feminist and queer methodologies in criminology. These contributions are documented in Chapter 14 by Marta-Marika Urbanik and Sandra Bucerius. They examine 20 female gang ethnographies and their many contributions to the field of gang scholarship. The authors further discuss the process of conducting gang research as a woman, including issues such as gaining access and navigating risks.

Adrienne Freng and Hannah St. Clair provide a detailed historical and contemporary account of Indigenous gangs in the United States and Canada in Chapter 15. They examine the legacies of structural racism, marginalization, and mistreatment that underlie gang formation and gang membership in Indigenous communities and explore the utility of mainstream gang theory and research for understanding the experiences of Indigenous populations. The authors conclude that more research and rigorous evaluation are needed before we can definitively argue that culturally specific programming will work above and beyond general gang prevention and intervention programming for Indigenous youth.

In Chapter 16, we turn to the topic of researching gangs in Central and South America. María José Méndez and Ellen Van Damme provide a personal and powerful reflection on positionality in (qualitative) gang research and the challenges and opportunities associated with scholarship performed in typically hypermasculine and patriarchal spaces. The authors call on readers to better understand and appreciate the role of gender and sexuality in gang research, especially gang research conducted in Central and South America, emphasizing the traditional marginalization of women's perspectives, the privileging of a male gaze, and the reinforcement of gender stereotypes.

From Central and South America, we move to the Caribbean. While the Caribbean region is glamorized as a tourist destination, it is also known to be one of the most violent areas in the world. With a strong focus on research methodologies, which may be useful in other settings, Edward Maguire lays out in great detail the history of studying gangs in the Caribbean in Chapter 17. Studying gangs in the Caribbean contributes insights into organized gangs that are involved in the political process, as compared to studying street-oriented youth in other contexts, which is less able to inform research and policy in this area of the world. After detailing both twentieth-century and contemporary research on gangs in the Caribbean, the author also charts a path forward for future research to aid Caribbean governments and non-governmental organizations in addressing gang violence.

Section 3: Core and Emerging Issues

Core issues are those that have long captured the attention of gang researchers, warranting synthesis, integration, or perhaps rethinking. Emerging issues, in contrast, are those that have not been subject to much attention from the research community or have operated on the fringes of the field (see Decker, Pyrooz, and Densley 2022). Each of the chapters in this section offers a fresh perspective, reflecting tremendous advances in theory and research and new ways of thinking about gangs.

The first issue is gang culture. Over the past century the term "gang culture" has become monolithic in representing just about any aspect of gang behavior and organization. Although culture is a fundamental concept, it falls short in comprehensively explaining the diversity and causal factors behind gang behaviors. To improve the theoretical and methodological value of the gang culture concept, in Chapter 18, Caylin Moore and Forrest Stuart synthesize and organize extant research into three themes: culture-as-values, culture-as-toolkit, and culture-as-products. Each conception generates differing frameworks for understanding gang culture and its influence on phenomena such as attitudes, behaviors, and the social organization of the gang, offering conceptual clarity to a core issue in gang research.

Masculinity has been a core issue in gang research for over a half-century. In Chapter 19, Lorine Hughes and Lisa Broidy provide an in-depth review of the rich history of gang masculinity. While several excellent reviews of this topic exist, the authors offer a new take on the issue—how group processes and gang dynamics enact and enable masculinity performances. When masculinity is accomplished in the gang context, typically through involvement in violence, it is done so in a group context. The authors argue that more attention to the group level in masculinity studies can enhance our understanding of the connection between masculinity and violence.

Debates over non-random selection into gangs have long animated the field owing to its relevance to the causal question "Is the gang/offending link a product of types of people (i.e., selection) or contexts (i.e., group influence)?" This question has been the subject of considerable empirical inquiry, and while the evidence favors the group context, individual differences still matter. In Chapter 20, Jennifer Tostlebe and Jose Sanchez, both sociologists, take an inventory of possible individual differences, including what they are, their origins and stability in the life course, how they are relevant to gangs and offending, and the current state of the evidence.

Kyle Thomas calls for moving actors and choice to the center stage of gang research in Chapter 21. There are many instances of scholars taking choice and decision making seriously, but Thomas offers what is certainly the most developed application in the annals of gang research. He contrasts the externalist view, where forces are exerted upon actors, with the internalist view, where forces are acted upon—people reflect, deliberate, imagine, and act purposefully based on expectations and preferences. He outlines the six core assumptions of a rational choice theory of gangs and details the subjective expected utility model. Thomas then applies the model to four areas that have commanded the attention of researchers: gang joining, the enhancement effect, the collective behavior of the group, and disengagement from gangs. His proposal is ripe for empirical testing.

In Chapter 22, Patricia Kerig, Lucybel Mendez, Ava Alexander, and Susan Chen explore psychopathology as a cause and consequence of gang membership. Recent research has found gang members are at heightened risk of mental health problems before, during, and after gang membership. The chapter provides an expert review of this emerging topic by synthesizing research on gangs and mental health, discussing whether mental health is a cause of gang membership, a consequence of gang membership, or both. The authors go beyond extant research and discuss novel ideas for future research to investigate this topic, such as identifying the underlying developmental processes that might serve as risk factors, protective mechanisms, and targets for intervention.

Herb Covey contends in Chapter 23 that gang research must expand to developing countries. He provides a strong case that the conditions that give rise to gangs are either present or destined to worsen in upcoming years, including population growth, rapid urbanization, the inequitable distribution of wealth, globalization and internet usage, civil conflicts, armed groups, and politicization and radicalization. He questions the relevance of applying existing concepts and methods to study these issues in the emerging frontier of gang research.

Jeffrey Brantingham and Matthew Valasik round out the section. In Chapter 24, they use a case study of gang cliques in Los Angeles over 35 years to provide descriptive evidence of gang continuity and change as well as the ecological diversity of gang cliques. Specifically, they document how most cliques are short lived and violence is mainly concentrated among a small number of cliques. After documenting the diversity of gangs in Los Angeles, the authors put forth important next steps in the study of gang diversity that has implications for both Los Angeles and other cities with long histories of gang activity.

Section 4: Gangs in Institutional Context

Crime and violence have occupied a central place in the study of gangs. This is due, in part, to the orientations of criminologists who research and evaluate the etiology of (and responses to) crime and delinquency. This section aims to expand the boundaries of independent and dependent variables, so to speak, that are relevant to gang research. It does so through the consideration of gangs in the context of key socializing institutions.

In Chapter 25, British gang scholars Simon Harding and Ross Deuchar apply social capital theory to life in the gang. The authors draw on both European and North American research traditions to develop further the concept of "street capital" and explain the motivations for joining gangs, the incentives for crime and violence while in gangs, and the gaps in current policy and practice when it comes to engaging gang members and diverting them away from gang life.

The family institution plays a multifaceted role in gang membership, where the nuclear family is correlated with gang joining and family formation is related to gang disengagement. Despite families playing such an important role in the gang, research has rarely explored the link directly. Drawing on life course and attachment theories in Chapter 26, Gabriel Cesar, D'Andre Walker, and Tiffany Fernandez provide a comprehensive review of the role of family throughout the gang trajectory, highlighting how the family as a socializing institution both pulls individuals toward and away from the gang.

School is another key socializing institution. In Chapter 27, Adrian Huerta takes a critical look at the school, pointing out that gang members face both increased risk of victimization from rival groups in school and heightened gaze from educators who assume these adolescents are fully committed to criminal behavior. Under the backdrop of the school-to-prison pipeline/nexus (e.g., zero-tolerance policies), he explores the complicated relationship between adolescent gang membership and educational pathways through an examination of primary, secondary, and postsecondary education. He also embeds quotes from former gang members to show how they overcome mistreatment throughout the educational pipeline, humanizing the gang experience and reframing gang-associated youth to being at-promise rather than at-risk.

Chapter 28 examines the emerging topic of religion and gangs. Tim Lauger and Haleigh Kubiniec explore two models of religious affiliation among gang members—isolated and integrated. The former highlights the contradiction and conflict between gang membership and orthodox religion, wherein religious adherence can facilitate gang disengagement and criminal desistance. The latter explores the reality that many active gang members are expressly religious, and many gangs include elements of religion, like rituals or symbols, as part of their collective identity. The chapter concludes by exploring the complex relationship between gang crime and religious adherence.

Social media increasingly influences adolescent lives, and in Chapter 29 Caitlin Elsaesser and Desmond Patton demonstrate how critical race theory can assist gang scholars to understand the dynamics of gang activity online. The authors review the existing literature on gang and gang member uses of social media, reminding readers to center anti-racism whenever they interpret the everyday activities of marginalized and racialized youth who are labeled gang-involved by control agents. In so doing, the authors provide a timely critique of gang scholarship that examines social media outside of its local and structural context.

David Skarbek and Kaitlyn Woltz survey the literature on prison gangs in Chapter 30. They argue that the inventory of theories of prison gang activity needs revising since they cannot explain variation in time and place, and they also lack clear empirical propositions lending themselves to falsifiability. Skarbek and Woltz distinguish between thin and thick theory and how qualitative and quantitative evidence appeals to each. They then turn to their preferred governance theory, which they argue offers the most compelling account of variation in prison gang activity in the United States and internationally.

José Miguel Cruz and Jonathan Rosen examine the "transnational gang" in Chapter 31. They detail how migration contributes to the movement of people and ideas, resulting in the global recycling of gang identities, cultures, and customs. Drawing on an extensive body of research on Central American gangs, the authors explore different theoretical explanations for the emergence of transnational gangs with implications for future research, policy, and practice.

Section 5: Legacies of Second-Generation Researchers

In the 2015 Wiley *Handbook of Gangs*, Scott Decker and David Pyrooz included four chapters devoted to the legacies of first-generation pioneers in gang research: Malcolm Klein, Jim Short, Walter Miller, and Irving Spergel. These chapters were written by their academic progeny or those who knew their work intimately.

Chapters 32 through 37 of the present *Oxford Handbook of Gangs and Society* follow this tradition and pay tribute to the legacies of the succeeding generation of leading gang researchers. David Pyrooz and Rick Moule first detail the life and work of the most cited gang researcher in history, Scott Decker. Finn-Aage Esbensen's massive contribution to the field is then outlined by Dena Carson, Adrienne Freng, Chris Melde, and Dana Peterson. Roberto Aspholm next offers his account of the impact of the critical ethnographer, John Hagedorn. Shannon Reid follows in conversation with Eurogang co-founder Cheryl Maxson. Finally, Diego Vigil talks about his mentor Joan Moore, before Vigil himself gets the legacy treatment from Mike Tapia and E. Mark Moreno. These chapters provide little-known personal insights and stories from the past, in addition to detailed reflections on pioneering and pivotal gang scholarship.

Section 6: Responding to Gangs

Few questions in gang research attract as much controversy as "how do we respond to gangs?", partly because the politics far outpace the science. Much has changed since Klein and Maxson (2006) concluded that most responses to gangs appear promising because they have not been subject to rigorous evaluation. This section provides in-depth accounts and overviews of individual, group, and community responses to gangs.

To what interventions should case managers refer gang-involved youth? Paul Boxer, Joanna Kubik, and Stephanie Marcello identify a critical problem: No validated treatments exist. In Chapter 38 they describe three "starting points" for providing evidence-based interventions to gang populations: cognitive behavioral, family centered, and ecologically oriented. They then detail the promises and perils of two recent applications of leading, name-brand interventions: functional family therapy and multisystemic therapy, the latter of which the chapter authors led. They integrate insights from developmental and clinical-intervention research to offer several critical pieces of guidance for intervening with gang-involved youth.

Legal scholars Sean Garcia-Leys and Jesse Engel contend in Chapter 39 that controversial civil gang injunctions, court orders that place certain restrictions and prohibitions on individuals associated with a particular gang within a specific geographic area or community, offer "no public benefit." They share a narrative account of the stages of an injunction that was attempted in Latino neighborhoods in Placentia (Orange County), California, from its conception in 2015 to its (in this case) defeat in 2018. They argue that civil gang injunctions are futile because they either unnecessarily target people who have disengaged from gang involvement or superfluously target people already under criminal justice supervision. Suppression-oriented strategies to reduce gang activity must involve police oversight and community voices, especially by the people most likely to be impacted.

In Chapter 40, Matt Valasik and Jeff Brantingham provide a timely exploration of police surveillance of gangs and gang members. Using the Los Angeles Police Department as a case study, the chapter examines the core controversies of data-driven and predictive policing strategies. It concludes that despite fears of a rise in increasingly invasive, potentially unconstitutional, and unethical "big data" policing, the policing of gangs remains a low-tech process focused primarily on reaction to and investigation of crimes.

There are five reasons why traditional policing strategies fail to reduce gang activity, Madeleine Novich argues in Chapter 41. First, police intelligence gathering does not establish desired networks since they are gathered through biased strategies. Second, police behavior is racially motivated, seeding distrust in communities. Third, police behavior is disrespectful, creating negative perceptions in communities. Fourth, suppression-oriented policing does not reduce gang violence. Finally, suppression-oriented policing backfires by labeling, stigmatizing, and incarcerating. Instead, Novich argues, responses to gangs must be proactive, not just reactive; involve multiple community and government stakeholders, not just law enforcement; and include prevention and intervention, not just suppression.

In Chapter 42, Anthony Braga, John MacDonald, and George Tita offer a timely and critical reflection on the reported increase in gang and gun violence in the post-pandemic United States. They explore how a movement to defund the police that grew in the aftermath of the 2020 murder of George Floyd, a Black man, by Minneapolis police, may have unintentionally undermined the evidence-based focused deterrence gang violence reduction strategy by eroding community trust and cooperation and changing the certainty, swiftness, and severity of criminal sanctions. The authors examine what we know about the dynamics of gang and group violence to make a compelling theoretical case against knee-jerk policies that may further harm the poor minority neighborhoods suffering the brunt of everyday gun violence.

Finally, Chapter 43 is dedicated to comparing and contrasting the three most prominent models for addressing youth gun violence connected to gangs and groups: focused deterrence, public health, and the Comprehensive Gang Model. The Urban Institute's Jesse Jannetta, Paige Thompson, and Lily Robin highlight the considerable overlap in intervention components across these three violence reduction models, including their data-driven and community-oriented approaches. But where they differ is their orientations to enforcement and suppression, and the quantity and quality of evidence supporting their success.

Acknowledgments

There are many people to thank. The first are the contributors. It has been a privilege to read your work and we are extremely grateful that you trusted us with your ideas, which have tested and shaped our thinking in ways both small and large. We recognize that undertaking this endeavor amid a global pandemic was no small commitment, and we are thankful for the trust placed in us. We also recognize that the pandemic affected some of our colleagues more than others. Several contributors had to drop out or could not participate owing to personal or professional demands; you know who you are, and we remain grateful for your consideration.

Second, the team at Oxford University Press (OUP). Michael Tonry and Sandra Bucerius, co-editors of the *Oxford Handbook* series in criminology, invited us to produce this volume, and we are thrilled to be joining the pantheon of other editors in this stellar series. Thanks also to Meredith Keffer and Lacey Harvey at OUP for their patience and responsiveness throughout this three-year endeavor, as well as the anonymous reviewers of our proposal.

Third, thank you to our colleagues at our respective universities for their feedback and support—University of Colorado Boulder (David), Metro State University (James), and University of Oklahoma (John). Fourth, to our families. Thank you to Natty, Cyrus, and Addy (David); Emily, Alex, and Andrew (James); and Kailee, Lorrayne, and Henry (John). Two months into a global pandemic, signing on to edit a massive handbook with 80 different authors probably seemed like insanity, but hopefully the result makes clear why we did it.

And, finally, as co-editors of this volume, over four years and scores of Zoom meetings and phone calls, some of the greatest joys of collaboration come from children barging into virtual meetings, pets blocking video cameras, out-of-the-blue text messages and phone calls, documents conflicting on Dropbox, and other unforeseen events that come to define the shared history of volumes like this.

REFERENCES

Decker, Scott H., David C. Pyrooz, and James A. Densley. 2022. *On Gangs*. Philadelphia, PA: Temple University Press.

Klein, Malcolm W., and Cheryl L. Maxson. 2006. *Street Gang Patterns and Policies*. New York: Oxford University Press.

Padilla, F. 1992. *The Gang as an American Enterprise*. New Brunswick, NJ: Rutgers University Press.

Pyrooz, David C., and Meghan M. Mitchell. 2015. "Little Gang Research, Big Gang Research." In *The Handbook of Gangs*, edited by Scott H. Decker and David C. Pyrooz, 28–58. Chichester, UK: Wiley-Blackwell.

Thrasher, Frederic M. 1927. *The Gang: A Study of 1,313 Gangs in Chicago*. Chicago, IL: University of Chicago Press.

SECTION 1

REVISITING DEFINITIONS IN THE TWENTY-FIRST CENTURY

CHAPTER 2

THE EUROGANG DEFINITION
Context, Development, Scrutiny, and Debate (Including a Conversation with Malcolm Klein)

FRANK M. WEERMAN AND SCOTT H. DECKER

I am done with gangs. Malcolm Klein, 1971.
I've had it with gang definitions. David Curry, 2015.
Ain't no gangster. Kiing Khash, 2020.

FROM its inception, the study of gangs has had vivid debate about definitions. Throughout the history of gang research, numerous definitional approaches have been proposed and debated, and the influence of various established gang definitions have waxed and waned over time (see, e.g., Ball and Curry 1995; Curry 2015).[1] Finding a formulation that is applicable and acceptable to multiple researchers appears to be, not only in the United States but also in other countries, in Europe, and the rest of the world, fraught with multiple challenges. Some of those challenges are political while others are cultural (including language), and all are overlaid with methodological considerations and longstanding academic traditions. A definition that is acceptable to researchers from different backgrounds and strongly varying perspectives must be a relatively neutral scientific proposition rather than a statement of values. At the same time, it should be clear and coherent—able to distinguish both what *is* a gang as well as what *is not*.

This chapter describes how a group of researchers, gathered under the umbrella of the Eurogang Program of Research (also known as the Eurogang network or the Eurogang project), attempted to navigate these challenges and arrive at a "consensus definition." As such, this is a history of how fundamental steps in research (conceptual and operational definitions) are negotiated, contested, and resolved. The aim was to arrive at a definition that was methodologically adequate and enabled comparisons between countries that were highly different in gang traditions, culture, and politics. It was also needed to be (and it turned out to be) politically acceptable. The challenges of agreeing on adequate definitions to fit gangs in multiple countries, each with their social and political context, youth cultures, and justice system, are even more complicated than previous attempts in the United States only.

The Eurogang network was composed of members from Europe (including the United Kingdom) and the United States. Differences in methods and traditions of study within the group of researchers were noticeable from the start. There was a heavier qualitative and reflexive component in the research designs of most of the Europeans that also included a concern about the political uses of such a definition, and a more quantitative and rigorous component in the designs of most of the Americans. There was also a dogged insistence of American gang researchers, led by Malcolm Klein who had researched gangs since the 1960s, for a definition built on the foundations of decades of work in the United States. Nevertheless, the Eurogang Program of Research succeeded in finding a compromise in the form of a consensus definition that was acceptable to most members of the group at the time it was arrived at.

This definition was formulated as follows: *A gang (or a troublesome youth group) is any durable street-oriented youth group whose involvement in illegal activity is part of its group identity.*

Over the years, this consensus definition achieved success beyond what was originally expected. It was increasingly applied in research, not only by the members of the Eurogang network but also by others, and it enabled and stimulated comparisons between countries and social categories. It became a sort of standard in gang research, required by reviewers and to a certain extent immune to adaptation. However, at the same time, there have always been debates and fractures in the consensus about the definition. Some researchers contested the definitional approach and dropped out of the group or provided critiques on the group in a variety of forums.

In this chapter, we sketch the context in which the consensus definition evolved and describe its inception and development. We draw on the memories of Malcolm Klein, famous gang researcher and initiator of the Eurogang project, as well as previous publications and our own memories about various meetings of the Eurogang network.[2] Next, we describe how the Eurogang definition has been increasingly used in comparative research on gangs around the world and review a number of studies that focused on the methodological characteristics and peculiarities of the definition itself as well as potential alternatives. At the end of the chapter, we discuss whether the Eurogang definition is still suitable in the current times in which young people and groups increasingly manifest and interact on the internet and social media.

THE POLITICS OF GANG DEFINITIONS

The politics of gang definitions has been an issue since the study of gangs began in the United States in the early part of the twentieth century. One of the first attempts to define gangs was in Thrasher's seminal work on gangs in Chicago (1927). In this period, European immigrants were largely the focus of studies of gang membership in the east and Midwest, and Mexican-Americans were the focus in the west (particularly California). Later, studies on gangs shifted their focus to Black communities in deprived urban areas. The disproportionate assignment of gang status to ethnic and racial minorities led to concerns about the consequences of such labels for social opportunities and the use of punitive sanctions, including prison (e.g., Lee and Bubolz 2020; Moore 1985; Woods 2011).

This is clearly at the basis of the nascent movement in the United States to "de-stigmatize" many youths by identifying them as "group" members rather than gang members. Similar concerns fueled a debate about the use of the term "gang" in the 1980s. In some US cities there were public claims that youth in groups who wear similar clothes and shoot at their rivals were not "real" gang members but belonged to a group of urban youths that bonded together in deprived circumstances. In other contexts, members of violent youth groups weren't seen as genuine gang members but as local imitations because they were not from Los Angeles or Chicago. Part of that observation was correct, because many of the emerging gangs in this period did imitate the behavior of gangs in other cities, through movies, music, and television shows (Decker and Van Winkle 1996; Huff 1998).[3] However, the "gang as group" movement (which still plays out today; see Ervin et al. 2022) ignored one important and consistent finding about gang members: they are victimized at substantially higher rates than non-gang members matched on race/ethnicity, age, socioeconomic status, and neighborhood, and also higher than members of non-gang delinquent groups (see Battin et al. 1998; Carson, Wiley, and Esbensen 2017; Pyrooz, Moule, and Decker 2014). As such, gang members are exposed to far more negative consequences than one would expect if they were only name bandied by groups of researchers. In this context, using the "G" word (gang) would be important to identify individuals at elevated risks for becoming victims of violent crime.

The desire not to stigmatize marginalized youth whose rates of offending and victimization are substantially higher than their non-gang counterparts has led to concern among some European practitioners and scholars to not repeat the American experience in the identification of youth groups engaged in offending or non-conforming behavior. The late 1990s was a time of increasing reliance on suppression, particularly the use of imprisonment in the United States, to address gangs and gang members' behavior. The use of suppression-based interventions to deal with gangs in the United States fell disproportionately on racial and ethnic minorities. Many European academics during this period were openly critical of US-based policies that had suppression as a foundation. Similarly, the perception of what American gangs were like among many European scholars and policymakers was based on sensationalized media representations. They were not alone; much of American law enforcement shared these misrepresentations, seeing gangs as highly organized, disciplined groups capable of executing sophisticated crimes (see **Chapter 5** by Kennedy in this volume). Both groups were wrong, and to their own peril.

In Europe and the United Kingdom, there has also been some historic controversy over identifying and defining gangs. For example, the respected British criminologist David Downes (1966), later joined by Campbell and Muncer (1989), argued that the lack of British gang research was owed to the fact that there "simply weren't gangs" in the UK (Decker, Pyrooz, and Densley 2022). This point of view ignored Patrick's (1971) work in Glasgow on Scottish "gangs." The tension about the existence of gangs in Britain is further captured in the juxtaposition of Bennett and Holloway's (2004) study based on interviewing arrestees from gangs and Pitts' (2008) ethnographic work on gangs with critical commentaries from Hallsworth and Young (2008) and Hagedorn (2008). The latter authors argue that gangs and the definition of groups as gangs are reflections of race-based social circumstances and global pressures rather than neighborhood or individual characteristics. An even more provocative (and perhaps sinister) view is that gangs are the creations of criminologists (Katz and Jackson-Jacobs 2004), based largely on secondary records and an absence of direct contact with so-called gang members themselves.

Similar discussions about whether "gangs" exist or not have been held in other European countries, although the debates have been less polarized than in the United Kingdom. In the Netherlands, for example, various researchers have reported on groups they called *bendes* or *jeugdbendes*, Dutch synonyms for a gang (like the French synonym *bande*). Others denied the existence of gangs and emphasized the differences with the American gang context (for an overview, see Van Gemert 2012). Those who characterized the groups they study as (synonyms for) gangs reported features like leadership, organization, and roles but do not provide an explanation of what they mean by these words. Those who were opposed to using words like *bendes* argued that gangs like those in America cannot be found in the Netherlands, apparently having a clear but perhaps distorted image of these groups in their head. Interestingly, the government in the Netherlands has also been reluctant to characterize groups as gangs. They argue that using such words can lead to panic and overreactions and generally prefer the phrase "troublesome youth group" for a large variety of groups with young people that get attention from the police.

The Eurogang project (which began during the second half of the 1990s) stepped into the middle of these debates. At the heart of this effort to bring science to the international comparative study of gangs was Malcolm Klein, perhaps the leading authority on gangs in the world. It is important to point out that Klein was a long-time critic of suppression-based efforts to respond to gang behavior. He seemed an unlikely target for critics of the suppression-based American response to gangs since he expressed such criticism himself for decades. Indeed, he was well-known among Los Angeles Police Department (LAPD) and Sheriff's Department (LASD) commanders as a critic who pressed hard about the lack of meaningful responses to gangs other than arrest. At a public presentation in 1999 by an LAPD district commander touting violence reductions in her district, Klein stood up and shouted "Bully for you. Why don't you have someone do a real evaluation of this so-called gang intervention?" Klein was so stridently public in his criticism of the LAPD's treatment of gangs that the department publicly repudiated him.

A Short Interview with Malcolm Klein (March 9, 2022)

Malcolm ("Mac") was the intellectual force behind the Eurogang Program of Research. In his frequent travels to Europe in the 1980s and 1990s he saw increasing evidence of groups that resembled American-style gangs (from graffiti to public youth behavior and styles). Working closely with Cheryl Maxson (his long-time collaborator), Klein decided to discuss this observation with researchers from Europe. In 1997, he convened a small a group of American gang researchers with scholars from Europe that were already attending a conference on restorative justice to discuss the issue of gangs in a post-conference workshop in Leuven (see Weerman et al. 2009). Later that same year he held another explanatory meeting in San Diego. In 1998, he initiated a full workshop of four days with American, European, and British "gang" and youth researchers, considering the question of whether there was evidence of American-style gangs in Europe and Great Britain. The group gathered at a conference center in Schmitten, Germany, in 1988. The mythic image of American gangs as portrayed in popular media (on the web, in music videos, and through public behavior) dominated the conversation. The meeting concluded with a broad understanding that gangs in America bore little resemblance to the infamous Chicago gangsters of the Prohibition era or the exaggerated media images of the late-twentieth-century American gangs like the Los Angeles Bloods and the Crips. The group met again one year later (1999) in Oslo, and the meetings featured much debate between Jim Short and Malcolm Klein about the definition of a gang—specifically whether a definition with crime in it was tautological. After four days of frustrating discussion (and some walking out of the meeting in protest by both American and European researchers), it was determined that to move forward a series of five subcommittees would be formed, one of which was on "Gang Definitions" chaired by Malcolm Klein.

> MK: The issue is comparable definitions. How do we know if what we (Americans) are talking about (gangs) is the same thing as when Europeans/British are talking about gangs. (This was complicated even more by the inclusion of non-English-speaking nations). It was at the second meeting, in Oslo, that things really crystallized. Subcommittees were formed: definitions, instruments, methods (particularly ethnography: "the ethnographer is the instrument!"), policy, sources of data.

Malcolm Klein presented a first attempt for a definition at Leuven the following year, followed by a large meeting at Egmond aan Zee in the Netherlands in 2000, in which the subcommittees further discussed the issues. In the early days of this work, Klein was the only member of the definitions subcommittee. The goal of reaching a definition of gangs that was acceptable to all was still not reached. There was considerable outcry from the critical criminologists in the crowd, including John Hagedorn and Simon Hallsworth. Their primary objections centered on the political implications of the gang label, being imposed as it was by the powerful upon less powerful people, typically young people of color in marginalized communities. They found some support from Jim Short, whose disagreements with Klein over the definition of a gang are well documented (Esbensen and Maxson 2020). This issue was scientific at its foundation and not political.

> MK: Common definitions are needed. They are essential if there is to be a scientific study of gangs. Good definitions are needed, common definitions. Crime, delinquency, misbehavior, all of these must be a part of the definition of a gang. They are necessary elements, though not sufficient by themselves. The distinction between *defining* and *descriptive* characteristics is crucial to a scientific definition.[4] Descriptive characteristics such as ethnicity and race can be used to show variation in types of gangs or gang members, but the defining elements (durability, street orientation, youthfulness, illegal activity, and identity) are necessary characteristics of gangs that must be present. This is (too often) a source of confusion. *Gang organization* is a good example. It is a descriptor, not a definer, and as such is not central to the definition of a group. [Though it must be pointed out that along with his colleague Cheryl Maxson, Mac has conducted extensive research on gang typologies, a key element of which is organizational structure.]
>
> The history of gangs and the methods we use to understand them is scattershot. It is important that we understand what the commonalities are among gangs and what they share in common with groups. There has been an unfortunate conflation of groups with gangs.

This happened in two specific sites (Russia and Israel) where it was a stretch to call the groups being studied "gangs" in a sense that was consistent with the Eurogang consensus definition.

FORMULATING A CONSENSUS DEFINITION

After the seeds were planted by Malcolm Klein, the definition was further developed during the meetings of the Eurogang network in Egmond aan Zee, the Netherlands (in 2000) and in Straubing,[5] Germany (2002 and 2003). The development of the other instruments was beneficial to this process, because decisions had to made about which elements should be included in the youth survey, expert survey, and in a protocol for ethnographic research. Recognizing that not all topics could be included by every researcher, a discussion was initiated to clarify which topics or items fell within a first level of "must" include (i.e., items that captured the more definitional elements of a street gang), a second level of "should" include (i.e., elements that prior research revealed were common descriptors of gangs), and a third level of variables that would be "useful" to include (based on prior research on the correlates of gang involvement). The discussion of what should be in these different levels was intense, in particular surrounding the differences between the first and second level. A particular issue that was discussed was the element of territoriality. This was perceived as a defining characteristic for some (mostly American) researchers, while it was seen as more descriptive for others. In the end, it was decided that it should be placed in the second level, because many gangs and youth groups that were studied within European countries were not territorial or defending a particular neighborhood.

Initial drafts of the research instruments were already introduced and discussed at the 2000 Eurogang meeting in Egmond aan Zee. The drafts were translated into languages other than English by collaborating researchers of the group and pre-tested in various countries before the consecutive meetings in Straubing. These developments helped to clear out the most essential elements of a definition that could be adopted within the group as a basis for multi-method and multisite research and cross-national comparisons.

A final agreement on a definition was still not reached at the start of the first meeting in Straubing, despite the development of various research instruments. During this meeting, a group of around 15 attendants came together in a session that was meant to propose a final formulation that could be adopted by researchers within the Eurogang network. This session was assiduously and persistently led by Finn Esbensen, who did not want to stop before a proposal was reached to formulate a complete and unambiguous definition. Although the elements that should be part of such a definition were clear from the existing list of first-level items that instruments "must" include, reaching a consensus was a strenuous process, with lengthy discussions about the choices and the exact wordings of necessary elements. The discussion continued in a second session by gathering all attendants to the meeting, of which some were walking in the woods, calling back home, or just lollygagging over an extra cup of coffee. In this second session, choices had to be made between alternative formulations of elements and actual votes were cast, some of them by show of hands. In the end, those that were present accepted the final wordings that were presented on an overhead sheet, and this text became the "Eurogang consensus definition."

The adoption of this consensus definition reflected the hard work and intellect of the involved researchers, but also personal machinations of group processes. The final decisions were based on discussions and votes by researchers who were present at a specific meeting at a specific time. The result of such a democratic process should be seen as a consensus definition and not *the* definitive answer and delineation, if that is ever possible. But to some extent, it is also rather coincidental who was present and which words were chosen in the end. If other people would have been around, or if the discussion would have lasted one hour longer, the definition could have turned out differently. It is also good to keep in mind that not everyone in the group was completely happy with the result, and one of the involved researchers even asked whether they "had" to use the definition and what would happen if they did not. As it turned out, a few researchers who voted for the definition later neglected or adapted the consensus definition in their own work. Nevertheless, over time the definition found its way into research and became so commonly used that it grew to become the standard it is now.

THE MEANING OF THE CONSENSUS DEFINITION ELEMENTS

The complete definition, as it was adopted during the meetings of the Eurogang project, is now officially phrased in the following way (see Decker and Weerman 2005; Klein, Weerman, and Thornberry 2006; Weerman et al. 2009): "a street gang (or troublesome youth group corresponding to a street gang elsewhere) is any durable, street-oriented youth group whose identity includes involvement in illegal activity." Various elements can be discerned in this sentence, and below we provide a short explanation of the considerations behind them.

First of all, the definition is about a *street* gang. This expresses the initial focus of interest of the Eurogang Program of Research to investigate the existence and characteristics of groups outside the United States that resembled the phenomenon of street gangs that Klein and other gang researchers were familiar with from their home country. During the formulation of the definition, it was discussed whether it was also possible to use the word "gang" itself, or the phrase "youth gang." However, in the end it was decided that the main interest was in groups that were visible in public and that were associated with problems and deviance in public places, and the term "street gang" was seen as being closest to this interest. It was also clear from the start that the definition should not include organized crime groups, which usually operate more in hiding and for which the group (or a network) is merely a vehicle for crime and not an entity in itself. Similarly, it was made clear from the start that gangs are something else and more than just a group of co-offenders.

The addition of a synonym between parentheses "or troublesome youth groups corresponding to a street gang elsewhere" was added to serve researchers from countries in which the word "gang" (or similar terms like *bande* or *jeugdbende*) were uncommon or associated with images or stereotypes that were far beside reality (like associating a gang with a mafia type of organized crime group). The word that would be used in publication was left to the researcher to decide. This was expressed by the phrase "for those preferring not to use the word gang (bande, etc.), the phrase 'troublesome youth group' can be substituted." "Troublesome youth groups" was a term that has been used in other countries (like the Netherlands) to name groups of young people in public places that cause problems to the public and the police, but for which words like "gangs" and *bandes* were deemed as not (or not always) viable.

The element "durable" was included to distinguish the groups of interest from temporary or spontaneous groups, like groups of young people that only gather in public during a limited period (e.g., during holidays or the summer), or spontaneous "mobs" of protesters, vandalizers, or street fighters (like the groups that are formed during riots). How long a group should be in existence to be called "durable" remained a bit ambiguous, but at least several months was seen as a rough guideline (in the Eurogang survey instrument, the minimum duration required to be recognized as a gang is at least three months). It is also important to note that durability refers to the group as an entity. In practice, there is often a high turnover within informal groups like street gangs, and individuals can come and go within groups that nevertheless remain durable as a distinguishable entity over time.

The element "street oriented" was included to ensure that the focus would be on groups that were visible in public places, like the street gangs that manifest themselves in neighborhoods in the United States. It was acknowledged that the word "street" in street gangs should not be taken literally, since gangs also often meet and hang out in places other than streets, sometimes intentionally to keep hidden or out of trouble. What would distinguish street gangs from other criminal or deviant groups, however, would be their presence in public. Therefore, it was decided that "street oriented" would mean that people in the group would need a lot of their group time to be outside home, work, and school, not only in the street but also in public places like malls, parks, cars, and so on.

The element "youth group" was included to distinguish the groups of interest from organizations and groups that exist primarily of adults (or children). For example, motorcycle gangs, which also sometimes manifest themselves in public places, are intentionally left out of the scope of the definition, even though there may be similarities and overlap. The street gangs in which the Eurogang Program of Research was interested consisted mainly of young people. Nevertheless, it was decided that the element of "youth" could remain somewhat ambiguous, since some of the street gangs that were already studied in the past also included members in their 20s and even 30s. It was decided that the majority of the group participants should be either in their adolescence or young adulthood, up to the age of mid-20s. With regard to the second part of this element, the "group," no clear boundaries were set, but it was clear that dyads would not suffice to constitute a group. At least three members should be present (see Esbensen and Maxson 2012). In practice most groups that are considered gangs or troublesome youth groups have more than a few members, but the sizes vary considerably.

Finally, the element *whose identity includes involvement in illegal activity* was meant to ensure that the focus of research is on deviant groups and not on groups that are primarily social collectives without a special meaning to their members or participants. There should be a sense of "we-ness" in the group, an own identity (Esbensen and Maxson 2012). In this sense, the word "identity" really refers to the group as a whole and not to an individual's self-image: Members should see their group as an entity of its own with a special meaning that includes breaking the law and committing offenses or other substantial rule violations. This element was strongly debated during the meetings, with several scholars arguing that including illegal activity might lead to tautological reasoning, and at the same time several others seeing illegality as the core characteristic of a gang. In the end, focusing on identity and not behavior was a solution to avoid the tautology problem, since participants do not necessarily have to behave delinquently themselves to see illegality as part of their group's identity.

Using the Consensus Definition in Research

Soon after its inception the definition was employed by various researchers from the Eurogang network. In particular, it was applied by researchers who wanted to compare the groups they found in Europe with gangs that were already known from the United States. As a helping tool, other instruments that were developed by the group of researchers from the Eurogang Program of Research were employed to gather research data that was in line with the consensus definition. In particular, the Eurogang survey was developed in such a way that all the necessary elements to meet the definition (the "definers") were covered in a precise and rigorous way, and that various "descriptors" could also be included to compare the characteristics of gangs and troublesome youth groups in different countries. But the definition was also processed into ethnography guidelines that helped qualitative researchers guide their work and collect information that could be used to define the groups they studied as gangs and compare their characteristics with groups elsewhere.

In the early period after reaching an agreement, the definition and the instruments that were based on it were mainly applied in Europe to investigate to what extent the groups and group members in that continent resembled those from gangs in the United States. For example, it was used in a study by Esbensen and Weerman (2005) that compared the characteristics of street gangs and youths in such groups in the United States and Europe. This study used two surveys among adolescents, one across the United States and one in the Netherlands. The Dutch survey had incorporated the Eurogang survey instrument to define gang membership based on the consensus definition, but the American part of the comparison was based on an already existing survey in which respondents were simply asked whether they were in a street gang. Other studies, first primarily from researchers who were part of the research network, also adopted the consensus definition (sometimes with small alterations). These included studies using survey methods (e.g., Sharp, Aldridge, and Medina-Ariza 2006; Alleyne and Wood 2012; Melde and Esbensen 2012; Peterson and Carson 2012; Pedersen and Linstad 2012), an expert survey developed by the research network (Van Gemert 2005), and qualitative methods like interviews and ethnographic observations (e.g., Aldridge, Medina-Ariza, and Ralphs 2008; Sela-Shayovitz 2012).

There were also researchers connected to the Eurogang network who continued to use the self-definition method or other operationalizations of what constitutes a gang member (e.g., Feixa et al. 2008; Hennigan and Spanovic 2012; Pyrooz et al. 2012; Vandenbogaerde and Van Hellemont 2016). These studies were published in various volumes of the research network, demonstrating a certain tolerance within the network toward alternative approaches. The use of the definition was not seen as mandatory or necessary in this phase—it was more like a preferred method for comparisons than a basic requirement to do research within the

Eurogang group. At the same time, the definition slowly found its way toward the academic world outside the Eurogang network.

A major step in the global adoption of the definition came when the International Self-Reported Delinquency (ISRD) group adopted the Eurogang definition for its second round of comparative research in four large regions of the world (Gatti, Haymooz, and Schadee 2011). These regions include all parts of Europe, Great Britain, the Mediterranean, and Latin America (Decker et al. 2022). No doubt this adoption by the ISRD group happened in part because of the friendship between Josine Junger-Tas (who led the ISRD along with fellow Dutch scholar Ineke Marshall) and Mac Klein. It is perhaps the most significant adoption of the definition thus far as it was used in over 20 countries. The results of the ISRD work have set a baseline for many countries' measure of gang prevalence and characteristics. There is still concern over the use of a single definition in cross-country, cross-cultural settings. In particular, the extremely high prevalence of gangs that was found in the Republic of Ireland still begs an explanation. Collectively, the works using the Eurogang definition in the ISRD have resulted in nearly 700 citations reflected across more than a dozen countries. Further, the ISRD questionnaire that included the items about gangs were used in a survey in China (Webb et al. 2011), which ensures that the definition of a gang measured by the Eurogang approach will continue to be applied in the burgeoning research in that country.

In short, while the adoption of the definition has been uneven, it has had great impact on research throughout the world and has now become widely known among gang researchers and scholars in the fields of juvenile delinquency in general. Apparently, the definition has become standardized to such an extent that sometimes reviewers of manuscripts (or grant proposals) demand use of the definition or at least reference to it.

Methodological Studies on the Consensus Definition

Next to descriptive and comparative research on gangs that adopted the consensus definition, several studies appeared that were focused on the methodological qualities and peculiarities of the definition itself and its application in the Eurogang survey instrument. These studies often provide a comparison with other measures of gang membership or distinguish different meanings that can be applied to the various elements of the definition.

A first relevant study (Weerman, 2005) was based on a preliminary version of the consensus definition and the Eurogang survey (drafted before final consensus about the wording of the definition was reached). This study focused on how helpful the "definers" in the Eurogang survey were in identifying gang members among Dutch youths, and to what extent it differed from the way in which young people in the Netherlands self-identify as member of a *jeugdbende*, a Dutch translation of "youth gang." It appeared that the majority of respondents classified as being in a delinquent youth group (according to the preliminary Eurogang instrument) also self-identified as being in a gang (*jeugdbende*) more than other youths in less troublesome groups. However, there was also a considerable proportion that did not self-identify as a member of a *jeugdbende*. Interestingly, a relevant proportion of the youths that were not in a group that met the preliminary consensus definition saw themselves as member of a *jeugdbende*, even when their group was not involved in delinquent behavior at all. This means that the two indicators of gang membership partly overlap (demonstrating validity of the Eurogang instrument), but also partly measure different phenomena.

A more extensive methodological study comparing membership of gangs according to the Eurogang definition with other measures was published by Matsuda et al. (2012) in a volume of the Eurogang Program of Research that was partly devoted to definitional issues (Esbensen and Maxson 2012). This study compared findings from survey research that was based on three different measures and definitional approaches: one that was based on the Eurogang consensus definition, one based on self-identification as a gang member, and one based on whether youth report that their friends are gang members. Interestingly, these three measures resulted in largely different groups of respondents that only partly overlapped with each other. No more than 9% of all survey participants were a gang member according to all three definitions. At the same time, the three groups looked much like each other in terms of delinquent behavior. Regardless of the used indicators, those who counted as gang members were involved in much more offending than non-gang members. The same was true for alcohol and drug use and various attitudinal correlates of delinquency: The average scores of youths in gangs according to the Eurogang definition, self-identification, and peer identification looked much like each other and differed from other youths. This suggests that the exact definition and measurement of gang membership perhaps matters less in practice. It also means that the Eurogang definition has enough validity and potential to select a group of individuals with relatively high levels of problems and problem behavior.[6]

In the same volume, Aldridge, Medina-Ariza, and Ralphs (2012) reported on validity problems they encountered when applying the definition and instruments that were based on it in various studies. In an ethnographic study on recognized gangs in an English city, they found that most gangs had meeting places and hangout spots that were not in public and, as such, these gangs did not seem to be "street oriented" as would be required by the Eurogang definition. Further, they found that some groups in the city were involved in illegal behavior as part of their group identity but clearly were not regarded as street gangs. Examples were groups of young people that evolved an identity around using drugs in public places and a group that organized illegal rave parties. According to a literal interpretation of the definition, these groups would be regarded as a gang. Further applying the Eurogang instrument in a survey in Madrid, the authors found that illegal activity as part of the group identity often involved the forbidden use of alcohol or drugs in public places. These groups also qualify as gangs when the definition is applied literally, but their behavior might have been legal in other countries, where they would only count as an informal youth group.

In a follow-up paper, Medina et al. (2013) conducted a latent class analysis on data from a survey in England and Wales that resulted in four types of troublesome youth groups according to the definition. The group members of three of these types were often involved in delinquent behavior and violence. However, in one of the types, recreational drug use was the only "illegal behavior" present. This suggests that the term "illegal behavior" may be too broad to capture what was originally intended with the consensus definition as it may include a variety of minor infractions.

In another volume of the Eurogang research network (Maxson and Esbensen 2016), several other studies were published in which qualities of the Eurogang consensus definition were investigated. Roman, Cahill, and Eidson (2016) conducted a study among a community-based sample of youths that were involved in "street groups" in two cities and focused on the element of illegal group identity. They found that a considerable portion of respondents either reported that illegal behavior was considered normal in their group (without actual lawbreaking) or that group members committed offenses together (while illegal behavior was not seen as normal). Further, several respondents agreed that members of their group committed illegal behavior together or found illegal behavior normal, while other criteria of the Eurogang definition were not met. At the same time, many respondents who did not completely meet the criteria of the Eurogang definitions had various other characteristics that were similar to those who met all the criteria, in particular being a member of a territorial group and being involved in violence with a weapon. This suggests that the definition might miss groups of interest that have a lot in common with gangs as defined by the various criteria.

Melde, Esbensen, and Carson (2016) used a large longitudinal survey to investigate whether the Eurogang definition yields findings about changes in a sophisticated measure of offending propensity and violent behavior over time that are comparable to two other measures of gang membership (self-reports and whether friends are in a gang). The results appeared to be quite similar, in line with the cross-sectional results of Matsuda et al. (2012). However, gang members according to the Eurogang definition appear to increase less in violence than gang members according to the other measures. Carson and Esbensen (2016) used the same dataset to compare motivations for gang disengagement among former members of a gang according to the following delineations: the Eurogang consensus definition only, self-reported gang membership only, and being a member according to both definitions. Overall, various reasons for gang disengagement were mentioned similarly across definitional groups. In all groups, moving was a common reason to leave a gang, and other reasons (adult interventions, direct or indirect experiences with violence, change in friendships) were mentioned equally often. This again confirms that the consensus definition yields similar results as other definitional approaches of gangs.

These similarities between the correlates and outcomes of gang membership according to the Eurogang definition and other definitions are in line with studies that did not use the consensus definition but compared other common measures of gang membership. For example, these studies found that self-reported gang membership is highly correlated with measures of gang membership based on friend reports and official registries (Esbensen et al. 2001; Decker et al. 2014). In all, the evidence thus far shows that the Eurogang consensus definition seems to be as useful as other definitional approaches of gang membership, and there is no evidence that the instruments using the Eurogang definition produce results with low validity or reliability. But it is important that attention to definitions continues to evolve, as new countries and continents attempt to assess whether they have a gang problem and what its dimensions are.

DISCUSSING ONLINE APPLICABILITY

The Eurogang project and the consensus definition emerged in a time when social media were in its beginning stages and smartphones were not yet invented. The internet had already started to play an important role in the lives of adolescents, providing a new context of "virtual peers" (Warr 2002). However, online activity was far from what it is today. Gangs and youth groups were primarily visible on the street and in other public places, but not so much yet on the internet. Since then, however, the role of the online world has increased tremendously. Social media, like Facebook, Instagram, Snapchat, and TikTok, emerged and evolved with the introduction of affordable smartphones in 2010, which has made the internet available and reachable at almost any place and any moment of the day. As a result, the daily activities and lives of young people have changed dramatically (see boyd 2014; Lenhart 2015; Twenge 2019; Valkenburg and Peter 2009).

This development also changed the activities of gangs and the lives of gang members. Gang members now commonly use the internet and social media to express their gang identity and features of their gang life. The internet has become a place to promote gangs, to do "internet banging," and to perform a "gangsta" life in public (Morselli and Décary-Hétu 2013; Patton et al. 2016; Van Hellemont 2012). Social media are used for expressive reasons, but also to reach instrumental goals (e.g., to promote drug selling) (Storrod and Densley 2017). As a result, the street and the internet have become intertwined, and gang researchers increasingly add "netnography" to their methods to understand what gangs do on "the digital street" (Urbanik and Roks 2020; Roks and Van den Broek 2021).

Interestingly, gang members appear to spend even more time on social media than their non-gang counterparts do (McCuddy and Esbensen 2020; Pyrooz, Decker, and Moule 2015). One study found that the more organized gangs are, the greater the chance that they have their own website and that they post videos to recruit new members online (Moule et al. 2014). These findings illustrate the importance of the online context as a venue for gang activity and visibility.

The profound changes in the daily lives of gang members may raise the question of whether the consensus definition of the Eurogang is still feasible. In particular, whether the element of street orientation also captures the meeting places and activities of gangs in the modern age of the internet and social media. In 2018, during a meeting of the Eurogang network in Almen, the Netherlands, a session was devoted to discuss the applicability of the consensus definition to the online world. This was done in concert with an attempt to expand the survey instrument and ethnography guidelines with items that were focused on online activities of gangs and troublesome youth groups. The issue was shortly revisited a year later at a meeting in Canterbury, UK, and again in 2022 in Neustadt an der Weinstrasse, Germany. Several substantive and methodological issues were raised during these discussions.

One issue was whether online visibility of gangs counts as a "presence in public." In general, the internet can be seen as a public place par excellence, as it is focused on general visibility and easy accessibility and availability of information and content. Websites and social media posts can be viewed by people around the globe, and in principle this means that online posts of gangs and gang members may also be seen as public. However, personal online messages, email, and chats can also be directed to one other person or a secluded group of receivers. Also, online places like group websites and chat boxes can have limited access, and young people are increasingly using modes of communication that are very volatile, with posts visible only for a short period of time or only visible to a limited group of friends. To be visible in public, it would be necessary that gangs and gang members either have a website, chat box, or other online place where they regularly post messages or content, or post content on social media accounts that are accessible to everyone.

As mentioned, many contemporary gangs are online, engaging in activities in which they show their existence and perform a gang image. In this sense, they may be seen as "present in a public place" as required by the explanation of the consensus definition. On the other hand, it can be debated whether this would also count as "street oriented." Originally, the idea behind expanding "street" to public places like parks, cars, and malls was that gangs and troublesome youth groups usually gather at physical places in inhabited areas but not necessarily on a street. Street orientation also implied that gangs and gang members are committed to a particular area in a city or town, often with their own territory or a group identity that is connected to a neighborhood context or to a "life on the street." Clearly, the internet is not a physical street or a neighborhood. But at the same time, many gang members and other young people express their connectedness to the neighborhood they live in, and to "street life" in general (Ilan 2017; Roks and Van den Broek 2021). In that sense, online communication of gang members and presences of street gangs on the internet may still be "street oriented" despite the fact that it does not take place in a physical space.

Another issue that has been debated is the sheer possibility that gangs or troublesome youth groups are publicly visible online only while not meeting regularly in a physical space. During the debates at the Eurogang meetings, some researchers argued that this is merely a theoretical option, and that online presence and communication necessitates social encounters and interaction in real life. Only this will provide a real group identity and enough material to enable meaningful content to be posted online. Other researchers argued that the social lives of young people have changed so much that they often spend more time online than hanging on the streets. Online interaction is as "real" to young people now as meeting each other physically, and this also seems to be true for gang members, as demonstrated by the many accounts of vivid online interactions within gangs that have recently occurred (for overviews, see Urbanik et al. 2020; Fernández-Planells, Orduña-Malea, and Pàmpols 2021). It is not hard to imagine gangs and other youth groups that are mainly active online, while seldom seeing each other in real life. Unfortunately, no studies have yet focused on this possibility or investigated the prevalence of such groups and their characteristics. This would be helpful in our understanding of the applicability of the Eurogang consensus definition in online contexts.

Another element that played a role in the discussions about potential adaptations in the consensus definition is the methodological issue of continuity and comparability in the Eurogang Program of Research. If the definition is altered in any way, the results of new studies on gangs are no longer completely comparable with studies before the change. This would mean a break in the already long chain of research using the consensus definition from 2005 onwards. It would also mean that communication between researchers may be hampered by ambiguity about exactly which version of the Eurogang definition has been used. It would necessitate extra information in the method sections of publications, stating that either the original definition was followed or the consensus definition 2.0 (and so on). These considerations strengthen hesitations toward altering or even discussing the exact wording of the consensus definition. At the same time, their weight may be regarded as relative, since methodological studies have shown that different definitions of gangs usually result in similar findings. Given the already existing heterogeneity in gang definitions and measurement approaches, it is questionable whether a change in the consensus definition would be a heavy problem.

The discussions about the applicability of the definition to the online world demonstrate again the problems and pitfalls connected to reaching consensus. The current state of affairs is that the definition and its explanation is not yet changed, but that the issue will be revisited again once more research is available about whether online only gangs really exist, and if so whether they have characteristics that are similar or comparable to gangs and troublesome youth groups that are only active offline or visible in both the physical world and on the internet. It seems that the final word about this definition has not been spoken.

Concluding Remarks

In their article "Core Controversies and Debates in the Study of Gangs," Esbensen and Maxson (2020) deal with "definitions" as the first topic in their chapter. They note that definitions, measurement, and methods remain the three core issues in the study of gangs. Despite the quarter century that has passed since the first Eurogang meeting in 1998, controversy remains. Nevertheless, it has been possible to arrive at a definition that became widely accepted among gang researchers, in particular those in Europe but also elsewhere. This consensus definition was formulated after an initial period of controversy and lengthy discussions. On the one hand, this means that the definition was the result of a careful process in which "definers" and "descriptors" of gangs were distinguished, but on the other hand it was "forced" in two workshop sessions by the researchers who were present at that time and with the exact wording that was proposed and agreed upon. The final definition of a gang or troublesome youth group includes the young age characteristic of the group, the public/street character of it, its durable nature, and the presence of an "identity that includes involvement in illegal behavior."

Nowadays, the use of the Eurogang consensus definition has spread across gang researchers, in particular among the scholars that are connected to the Eurogang network of research but also increasingly outside this group. This was stimulated by the adoption of the definition by the International Self-Report Delinquency Study. The most important achievement of the definition is that it truly enabled comparative research of gangs in multiple countries and locations. By adopting a minimalistic approach, the definition enabled communication about gangs and gang-like groups with strongly varying appearances. This made it possible to conduct empirical research on the similarities and differences between gangs and gang members in different countries. Adding more elements to the definition (like territoriality, which is not always present in gangs outside the United States) or using words that make the application of the definition narrower would devalue the usefulness of the definition.

After adoption of the definition, researchers connected to the Eurogang network started to use it in research and also made methodological comparisons of its characteristics. In general, empirical and methodological studies using the Eurogang definition demonstrate its validity and usefulness. However, similar results about delinquent behavior, deviance, and potential causes and correlates were obtained using different definitional approaches and measurements. This suggests that results of correlational studies (in contrast with comparative studies) are not necessarily dependent on the Eurogang definition.

Recently, researchers have begun to discuss the applicability of the definition in the age of social media and the internet. In particular, the possibility that gangs today are predominantly active online and not visible on the streets anymore led to the question of whether the definition should be adapted. There may be good reasons to modernize and further sharpen the definition, not only with regard to its applicability in the online world but also to further resolve unclarities and confusion. In the end, the definition was the result of a discussion held at a particular time with a particular and limited set of participants. On the other hand, the process of reaching consensus was so difficult that changing the exact wording and explanation of the current definition also comes with a cost. It would mean a break with the definition that has been used in the past and thus would make comparisons over time more difficult.

In the end, a common understanding between gang researchers about the topic of their study remains crucial, and a consensus definition is particularly helpful in comparing countries and periods. The Eurogang definition was meant to provide a stable and widely used instrument to enable comparisons among countries and over time. At the same time, it should not be chiseled in stone, but tailored to the peculiarities and dynamics of the gang phenomenon itself.

Postscript

Malcolm Klein passed away on August 1, 2023 at the age of 92. During the interview, about one year earlier with the second author of this chapter (Decker), he was eager to catch up on current controversies in gang research. Of course, he was particularly concerned about definitions and measurement of gang membership. While his contributions to gang research in the area of definitions is important, his dogged determination to bring researchers together in diverse settings to discuss the key issues of gang structure, criminal involvement of gangs and gang members, and criminal justice system responses to gangs are foundational issues in our understanding of these key issues. Beginning with his work on the Ladino Hills project (1967) and "Chasing After Street Gangs" (1971), he has dedicated over 50 years to the study of gangs. On the phone call, he was the same dedicated, irascible scholar we all knew, and he will remain a giant in the field of gang research.

Notes

1. Some may claim that criminology has a "fetishism" when it comes to definitions of gangs.
2. The first author joined the Eurogang network in 2000 and attended most of the meetings since then, including the ones where the consensus definition was formulated; the second author attended various meetings in the years when the consensus definition was discussed and established, including the very first one in 1998.
3. And nowadays, through varieties of social media.

4. Indeed, the distinction between descriptives and definers has gained additional importance as comparative studies of gangs, extremist groups, and other groups requires a means of distinguishing among them. This is particularly important in the comparison between street gangs and right-wing groups, a comparison whose importance has grown in recent years.
5. Ironically, the meetings in Straubing were held at a residential training facility for the German federal prison system.
6. Nevertheless, it would be interesting to investigate further what kinds of groups these measures are indicating and why they are similar in behavior and correlates. This probably requires in-depth qualitative research to understand what each of these measures is really tapping into.

References

Aldridge, Judith, Juanjo Medina-Ariza, and Rob Ralphs. 2008. *Youth Gangs in an English City: Social Exclusion, Drugs and Violence*. Manchester, UK: University of Manchester Press.

Aldridge, Judith, Juanjo Medina-Ariza, and Rob Ralphs. 2012. "Counting Gangs: Conceptual and Validity Problems with the Eurogang Definition." In *Youth Gangs in International Perspective*, edited by F. Esbensen and C. L. Maxson, 35–51. New York: Springer.

Alleyne, Emma, and Jane L. Wood. 2012. "Gang Membership: The Psychological Evidence." In *Youth Gangs in International Perspective*, edited by F. Esbensen and C. L. Maxson, 151–168. New York: Springer.

Ball, Richard A., and G. David Curry. 1995. "The Logic of Definition in Criminology: Purposes and Methods for Defining 'Gangs.'" *Criminology* 33 (2): 225–245.

Battin, Sara R., Karl G. Hill, Robert D. Abbott, Richard F. Catalano, and J. David Hawkins. 1998. "The Contribution of Gang Membership to Delinquency beyond Delinquent Friends." *Criminology* 36 (1): 93–115.

Bennett, Trevor, and Katy Holloway. 2004. "Gang Membership, Drugs and Crime in the UK." *British Journal of Criminology* 44 (3): 305–323.

Boyd, Danah. 2014. *It's Complicated: The Social Lives of Networked Teens*. New Haven, CT: Yale University Press.

Campbell, Anne, and Steven J. Muncer. 1989. "Them and Us: A Comparison of the Cultural Context of American Gangs and British Subcultures." *Deviant Behavior* 10 (6): 271–288.

Carson, Dena C., and Finn-Aage Esbensen. 2016. "Motivations for Leaving Gangs in the USA: A Qualitative Comparison of Leaving Processes across Gang Definitions." In *Gang Transitions and Transformations in an International Context*, edited by Cheryl L. Maxson, and Finn-Aage Esbensen, 139–155. New York: Springer.

Carson, Dena C., Stephanie A. Wiley, and Finn-Aage Esbensen. 2017. "Differentiating between Delinquent Groups and Gangs: Moving beyond Offending Consequences." *Journal of Crime and Justice* 40: 297–315.

Curry, G. David. 2015. "The Logic of Defining Gangs Revisited." In *The Handbook of Gangs*, edited by Scott H. Decker and David C. Pyrooz, 7–27. Chichester, UK: Wiley-Blackwell.

Decker, Schott H., and Barrik van Winkle. 1996. *Life in the Gang: Family, Friends, and Violence*. Cambridge, UK: Cambridge University Press.

Decker, Scott H., David C. Pyrooz, and James A. Densley. 2022. *On Gangs*. Philadelphia, PA: Temple University Press.

Decker, Scott H., and Frank M. Weerman, eds. 2005. *European Street Gangs and Troublesome Youth Groups*. Lanham, MD: AltaMira Press.

Decker, S. H., D. C. Pyrooz, G. Sweeten, and R. K. Moule. 2014. "Validating Self-Nomination in Gang Research: Assessing Differences in Gang Embeddedness across Non-, Current, and Former Gang Members." *Journal of Quantitative Criminology*, 30 (4): 577–598.

Downes, D. 1966. *The Delinquent Solution: A Study in Subcultural Theory*. New York: Routledge.

Ervin, S., et al. 2022. *Implementing Youth Violence Reduction Strategies: Findings from a Scan of Youth Gun, Group, and Gang Violence Interventions*. Washington, DC: Urban Institute.

Esbensen, Finn-Aage, and Cheryl L. Maxson. 2012. "The Eurogang Program of Research and Multimethod Comparative Gang Research: Introduction." In *Youth Gangs in International Perspective*, edited by Finn-Aage Esbensen and Cheryl L. Maxson, 1–14. New York: Springer.

Esbensen, Finn-Aage, and Cheryl L. Maxson. 2020. "Core Controversies and Debates in the Study of Gangs." In *Social Bridges and Contexts in Criminology and Sociology*, edited by Lori Hughes and Lisa Broidy, 83–99. New York: Routledge.

Esbensen, Finn-Aage, and Cheryl L. Maxson, eds. 2012. *Youth Gangs in International Perspective: Results from the Eurogang Program of Research*. New York: Springer.

Esbensen, Finn-Age., and Frank M. Weerman. 2005. "Youth Gangs and Troublesome Youth Groups in the United States and the Netherlands: A Cross-National Comparison." *European Journal of Criminology* 2 (1): 5–37.

Esbensen, Finn-A, L. Thomas Winfree Jr., Ni He, and Terrance J. Taylor. 2001. "Youth Gangs and Definitional Issues: When Is a Gang a Gang, and Why Does It Matter?" *Crime & delinquency* 47 (1): 105–130.

Fernández-Planells, Ariadna, Enrique Orduña-Malea, and Carles Feixa Pàmpols. 2021. "Gangs and Social Media: A Systematic Literature Review and an Identification of Future Challenges, Risks and Recommendations." *New Media & Society* 23 (7): 2099–2124.

Gatti, Uberto, Sandrina Haymoz, and Hans M. A. Schadee. 2011. "Deviant Youth Groups in 30 Countries: Results from the Second International Self-Report Delinquency Study." *International Criminal Justice Review* 21 (3): 208–224.

Hagedorn, John. 2008. *A World of Gangs: Armed Young men and Gangsta Culture*. Minneapolis: University of Minnesota Press.

Hallsworth, Simon, and Tara Young. 2008. "Gang Talk and Gang Talkers: A Critique." *Crime, Media, Culture* 4 (2): 175–195.

Hennigan, Karen, and Marija Spanovic. 2012. "Gang Dynamics through the Lens of Social Identity Theory." In *Youth Gangs in International Perspective*, edited by Finn-Aage Esbensen and Cheryl L. Maxson, 127–149. New York: Springer.

Huff, C. Ronald. 1998. "Criminal Behavior of Gang Members and At-Risk Youth." Office of Justice Programs. Accessed July 31, 2023. https://www.ojp.gov/ncjrs/virtual-library/abstracts/criminal-behavior-gang-members-and-risk-youths

Ilan, J. 2017. *Understanding Street Culture: Poverty, Crime, Youth and Cool*. Bloomsbury Publishing.

Kash, Kiing. 2020. Ain't no gangster. Youtube. https://www.youtube.com/watch?v=uBwZzTOzy_g

Katz, Jack, and Curtis Jackson-Jacobs. 2004. "The Criminologists' Gang." In *The Blackwell Companion to Criminology*, edited by Colin Sumner, 91–124. Chichester, UK: Wiley-Blackwell.

Klein, Malcolm W. 1967. *Juvenile Gangs in Context*. Englewood Cliffs, NJ: Prentice Hall..

Klein, Malcolm W. 1971. *Street Gangs and Street Workers*. Englewood Cliffs, NJ: Prentice-Hall.

Klein, Malcolm W., Frank M. Weerman, and Terence P. Thornberry. 2006. "Street Gang Violence in Europe." *European Journal of Criminology* 3 (4): 413–437.

Lee, Sou, and Bryan F. Bubolz. 2020. "The Gang Member Stands Out: Stigma as a Residual Consequence of Gang Involvement." *Criminal Justice Review* 45 (1): 64–83.

Lenhart, Amanda. 2015. *Teens, Social Media, and Technology Overview*. Washington, DC: Pew Research Center.

McCuddy, Timothy, and Esbensen, Finn-Aage. 2020. "The Role of Online Communication among Gang and Non-gang Youth." In *Gangs in the Era of Internet and Social Media*, edited by C. Melde and F. Weerman, 81–104. New York: Springer.

Matsuda, Kristy N., Finn-Aage Esbensen, and Dena C. Carson. 2012. "Putting the 'Gang' in 'Eurogang': Characteristics of Delinquent Youth Groups by Different Definitional Approaches." In *Youth Gangs in International Perspective*, edited by Finn-Aage Esbensen and Cheryl L. Maxson, 17–33. New York: Springer.

Maxson, Cheryl L., and Finn-Aage Esbensen, eds. 2016. *Gang Transitions and Transformations in an International Context*. New York: Springer.

Medina, Juanjo, Judith Aldridge, Jon Shute, and Andy Ross. 2013. "Measuring Gang Membership in England and Wales: A Latent Class Analysis with Eurogang Survey Questions." *European Journal of Criminology* 10 (5): 591–605.

Melde, Chris, and Finn-Aage Esbensen. 2012. "The Onset of (Euro) Gang Membership as a Turning Point in the Life Course." In *Youth Gangs in International Perspective*, edited by Finn-Aage Esbensen, and Cheryl L. Maxson, 169–187. New York: Springer.

Melde, Chris, Finn-Aage Esbensen, and Dena C. Carson. 2016. "Gang Membership and Involvement in Violence among US Adolescents: A Test of Construct Validity." In *Gang Transitions and Transformations in an International Context*, edited by Cheryl L. Maxson and Finn-Aage Esbensen, 33–50. New York: Springer.

Moore, Joan W. 1985. "Isolation and Stigmatization in the Development of an Underclass: The Case of Chicano Gangs in East Los Angeles." *Social Problem* 33 (1): 1–12.

Morselli, Carlo, and Décary-Hétu, David. 2013. "Crime Facilitation Purposes of Social Networking Sites: A Review and Analysis of the 'Cyberbanging' Phenomenon. *Small Wars & Insurgencies* 24(1): 152–170.

Moule, Richard K., Jr., David C. Pyrooz, and Scott H. Decker. 2014. "Internet Adoption and Online Behaviour among American Street Gangs: Integrating Gangs and Organizational Theory." *British Journal of Criminology* 54 (6): 1186–1206.

Patrick, J. 1971. *A Glasgow Gang Observed*. Scotland: Neil Wilson Publishing.

Patton, Desmond U., Jeffrey Lane, Patrick Leonard, and Jamie Macbeth. 2016. "Gang Violence on the Digital Street: Case Study of a South Side Chicago Gang Member's Twitter Communication." *New Media & Society* 19 (7): 1–19.

Pedersen, Maria Libak, and Jonas Markus Lindstad. 2012. "The Danish Gang-Joining Project: Methodological Issues and Preliminary Results." In *Youth Gangs in International Perspective*, edited by Finn-Aage Esbensen and Cheryl L. Maxson, 239–250. New York: Springer.

Peterson, Dana, and Dena C. Carson. 2012. "The Sex Composition of Groups and Youths' Delinquency: A Comparison of Gang and Nongang Peer Groups." In *Youth Gangs in International Perspective*, edited by Finn-Aage Esbensen and Cheryl L. Maxson, 189–210. New York: Springer.

Pitts, John. 2008. "Intervening in Gang-Affected Neighbourhoods." In *Prevention and Youth Crime*, edited by Maggie Blyth and Enver Solomon, 21–40. Bristol, UK: Policy Press.

Pyrooz, David C., Richard K. Moule, Jr., and Scott H. Decker. 2014. "The Contribution of Gang Membership to the Victim Offender Overlap." *Journal of Research in Crime and Delinquency* 51 (3): 315–348.

Pyrooz, David C., Scott H. Decker, and Richard K. Moule Jr. 2015. "Criminal and Routine Activities in Online Settings: Gangs, Offenders, and the Internet." *Justice Quarterly* 32 (3): 471–499.

Roks, Robert A., and Jeroen van den Broek. 2021. "Digital Streets, Internet Banging, and Cybercrimes: Street Culture in a Digitized World." In *Routledge Handbook of Street Culture*, edited by Jeffrey Ian Ross, 357–367. New York: Routledge.

Roman, Caterina, Meagan Cahill, and Jillian L. Eidson. 2016. "Street Gang Definitions across Two US Cities: Eurogang Criteria, Group Identity Characteristics, and Peer Group Involvement in Crime." In *Gang Transitions and Transformations in an International Context*, edited by Cheryl L. Maxson and Finn-Aage Esbensen, 15–32. New York: Springer.

Sela-Shayovitz, Revital. 2012. "Gangs and the Web: Gang Members' Online Behavior." *Journal of Contemporary Criminal Justice*, 28 (4): 389–405.

Sharp, Clare, Judith Aldridge, and Juanjo Medina-Ariza. 2006. *Delinquent Youth Groups and Offending Behaviour: Findings from the 2004 Offending Crime and Justice Survey*. London, UK: Home Office.

Storrod, Michelle L., and James A. Densley. 2017. "'Going Viral' and 'Going Country': The Expressive and Instrumental Activities of Street Gangs on Social Media." *Journal of Youth Studies* 20 (6): 677–696.

Thrasher, Frederic M. 1927. *The Gang: A Study of 1,313 Gangs in Chicago*. Chicago, IL: University of Chicago Press.

Twenge, Jean M. 2019. "More Time on Technology, Less Happiness? Associations Between Digital-Media Use and Psychological Well-Being." *Current Directions in Psychological Science*, 28(4): 372–379.

Urbanik, Marta-Marika, and Robert A. Roks. 2020. "GangstaLife: Fusing Urban Ethnography with Netnography in Gang Studies." *Qualitative Sociology* 43 (2): 213–233.

Urbanik, Marta-Marika, Robert A. Roks, Michelle L. Storrod, and James A. Densley. 2020. "Ethical and Methodological Issues in Gang Ethnography in the Digital Age: Lessons from Four Studies in an Emerging Field." In *Gangs in the Era of Internet and Social Media*, edited by Chris Melde and Frank M. Weerman, 21–41. New York: Springer.

Valkenburg, P. M., and J. Peter. 2009. "Social Consequences of the Internet for Adolescents: A Decade of Research." *Current Directions in Psychological Science* 18(1): 1–5.

Vandenbogaerde, Ellen, and Elke van Hellemont. 2016. "Fear and Retaliation: Gang Violence in Brussels and Caracas." In *Gang Transitions and Transformations in an International Context*, edited by Cheryl L. Maxson and Finn-Aage Esbensen, 51–63. New York: Springer.

Van Gemert, Frank H. M. 2005. "Youth Groups and Gangs in Amsterdam: An Inventory Based on the Eurogang Expert Survey." In *European Street Gangs and Troublesome Youth Groups: Findings from the Eurogang Research Program*, edited by Scott H. Decker and Frank M. Weerman, 147–168. Lanham, MD: AltaMira Press.

Van Gemert, Frank. 2012. "Five Decades of Defining Gangs in the Netherlands: The Eurogang Paradox in Practice." In *Youth Gangs in International Perspective: Results from the Eurogang Program of Research*, edited by Finn-Aage Esbensen and Cheryl L. Maxson, 69–83. New York: Springer.

Van Hellemont, Elke. 2012. "Gangland Online: Performing the Real Imaginary World of Gangstas and Ghettos in Brussels." *European Journal of Crime, Criminal Law and Criminal Justice* 20 (2): 165–180.

Warr, Mark. 2002. *Companions in Crime: The Social Aspects of Criminal Conduct*. Cambridge, UK: Cambridge University Press.

Webb, Vincent J., Ling Ren, Jihong Solomon Zhao, Ni Phil He, and Ineke Haen Marshall. 2011. "A Comparative Study of Youth Gangs in China and the United States: Definition, Offending, and Victimization." *International Criminal Justice Review* 21 (3): 225–242.

Weerman, Frank M. 2005. "Identification and Self-Identification: Using a Survey to Study Gangs in the Netherlands." In *European Street Gangs and Troublesome Youth Groups*, edited by Scott H. Decker and Frank M. Weerman, 129–146. Lanham, MD: AltaMira Press.

Weerman, Frank M., Cheryl L. Maxson, Finn-Aage Esbensen, Judith Aldridge, Juanjo Medina, and Frank van Gemert. 2009. *Eurogang Program Manual*. St. Louis: University of Missouri Press.

Woods, Jordan B. 2011. "Systemic Racial Bias and RICO's Application to Criminal Street and Prison Gangs." *Michigan Journal of Race & Law* 17 (2): 303–358.

CHAPTER 3

WHAT GANGS AREN'T
Contrasting Gangs with Other Collectives

MARTIN BOUCHARD, KARINE DESCORMIERS, AND ALYSHA GIRN

ALL gang scholars have encountered and potentially struggled with the problem of defining gangs. Many settle on being practical about it ("here we use X definition"), others creatively avoid it ("we don't use a definition, but a set of criteria"), and yet most still approach the study of gangs and groups with no specific definition in mind, relying on an implied understanding of what gangs are and what gangs aren't. We personally are guilty of having done all three across a number of publications.

The reasons to pay attention to what gangs are and aren't are numerous. For one, there appears to be a "gang effect"—becoming a gang member has been shown to increase one's criminal involvement beyond what would have been otherwise expected (e.g., Bouchard and Spindler 2010; Pyrooz et al. 2016; Thornberry et al. 1993). The gang environment provides a series of additional encouragements and resources that are decidedly criminogenic and that are specific to these types of collectives. This group process also appears to be more intense for "gangs" compared to peer groups (e.g. Bouchard and Spindler 2010). If this is something about "what gangs are," then being able to determine whether a collective is indeed a gang and not a peer group that dabbles in delinquency becomes extremely valuable.

For another, considerable resources are invested in tackling the "gang problem" in most jurisdictions (Klein and Maxson 2006). Budgets, of course, directly depend on counting gangs—the size of the problem. And the size of the problem depends on how one defines and measures "gangs." A jurisdiction could decide that any collective involved in some form of criminality would constitute a gang and could proceed to design interventions that target gangs at large. Yet, if applying broad definitions, time and resources could be invested in tackling groups that are not involved in serious crime or otherwise pose a significant threat (see **Chapter 6** by Lopez-Agaudo in this volume). In addition, the differences between the different types of collectives may not be obvious. Properly diagnosing the nature of a jurisdiction's gang problem, then, is of paramount importance to appropriate resource investment and deployment.[1]

The study of *what* gangs are cannot be detached from *why* they exist in the first place. From the perspective of the prospective member, gangs may provide an outlet for fostering friendships, shaping identity, responding to a variety of threats, and providing the opportunities and resources to earn money for thrill-seeking adolescents. Gangs, in short, provide a perceived subcultural solution to several human needs (Cohen 1955).

The specific form and flavor that gangs take help to determine whether youths remain embedded in gangs through adulthood and whether they preserve some stakes in conformity. It impacts the extent to which they will experience violent victimization (Pyrooz et al. 2012) and the risks of premature death (Pauls 2017; Pyrooz et al. 2020). Youths involved in peer groups who like to dabble in minor drug dealing and property crime may get out unscathed. But those who are involved in gangs that routinely enter conflict with others may experience victimization and trauma at levels that would be challenging to recover from (Beresford and Wood 2016; Kerig et al. 2016).

The problem is that a broad definition may treat these distinct and different groups and experiences as the same. If all delinquent youth collectives are considered gangs, then we risk designing interventions that completely miss the mark. We risk throwing the book at a simple manifestation of adolescence instead of carefully teasing out the elements that make some of these potentially more harmful and consequential. It is normal, then, that criminologists have been interested in defining and measuring what gangs are.

But this chapter is named what gangs "aren't." Part of the exercise is to be able to tell, when one encounters a group, whether we are dealing with a peer group, a gang, or a criminal organization. At the extreme of the continuum, the differences may be obvious; there are no mistaking high schoolers at the local park who sometimes get into trouble with members of the La Cosa Nostra. It is, however, much more challenging to distinguish between that peer group and another that some would consider to be a local gang. Both, after all, could be formed of teenagers who may belong to the same school, getting together in groups of the same size, and be involved, in the aggregate, in many of the same legal and illegal activities. What, then, can help distinguish between the two?

Our work is aimed at shedding light on the gray areas in between those extremes—the space where "gangs" tend to belong. Doing so requires an inquiry beyond how gangs differ from peer groups, but also at the other end of the spectrum to consider how gangs differ from criminal organizations.

This premise comes with a few assumptions about how we approach the study of gangs. First, we see groups, gangs, and criminal organizations as loosely belonging to the same spectrum of collectives involved in crime, even if the nature of their involvement and the presence of organizational features vary widely. In essence, we adopt the same approach as others have done before in seeing these collectives not necessarily as distinct species but as manifestations of collectives being observed at a different stage (Ayling 2011; Densley 2012), or simply at a different point on the continuum of organization (Bouchard and Spindler 2010; Decker and Pyrooz 2014). Through this process, we build on the foundation laid out a long time ago by Thrasher:

> There is no hard and fast dividing line between predatory gangs of boys and criminal groups of younger and older adults. They merged into each other by imperceptible gradations, and the latter have their real explanation, for most part, in the former. (Thrasher 1963, 281)

Yet, even if this approach helps resist adopting rigid labels, we recognize the benefit of identifying the stage a collective is at (e.g., the "recreational" versus the "crime" stage;

Densley 2012), or where it fits on the spectrum of organization (e.g., from "informal-diffuse" to "instrumental-rational" organization; Decker and Pyrooz 2014). In this chapter, we refer to the low organization, recreational stage collectives as "peer groups," the slightly more organized and crime-focused entities as "gangs," and the more structured, criminal enterprise-focused collectives as "criminal organizations."[2] From Densley (2012), we preserve the concept of evolutionary phases: Most gangs would have first started as peer groups, and then a minority of gangs would further evolve into bona fide criminal enterprises. The evolution can be observed in the intensity of a collective's delinquent involvement and perhaps how much of their identity, as a group, revolves around crime, both symbolically and economically[3] (Densley 2014).

This does not imply that we see clear-cut distinctions between them. In fact, part of the chapter will demonstrate how, on some dimensions, some gangs may appear more similar to peer groups whereas other gangs may be indistinguishable from criminal organizations. Some "gangs" may indeed be gangs and yet be disorganized, while others will adopt more organizational features without necessarily qualifying as criminal organizations. While there is room for variation within categories, we believe that a number of dimensions effectively help to distinguish gangs between either peer groups, criminal organizations, or both.

Aims

Our goal was to comb through the existing evidence on gangs to establish the various dimensions upon which these collectives may be assessed. We found that gangs can be distinguished from either peer groups or criminal organizations along seven dimensions:

1. The willingness to use violence or its threat
2. The group's commitment to crime
3. The importance of economic goals
4. The scope of criminal activity
5. The group organization/structure
6. The age structure of membership
7. The social structure of cooperation in and outside the group

As summarized in Table 3.1, we divide the dimensions into two broad categories: the dimensions that belong to "crime" and those that belong to how collectives are "organized." These two dimensions have been at the core of gang definitional debates for a long time (Curry 2015; Klein and Maxson 2006; Pyrooz and Densley 2018). Here, however, we use these dimensions inspired by research invested in describing the different types of gangs (Klein and Maxson 2006; Spindler and Bouchard 2011), recognizing that both categories need to be considered to do justice to the variations in gang behavior.

The vast majority of dimensions are amenable to measurement on a scale or a continuum from "low" for peer groups to "high" for criminal organizations. In general, we avoided dimensions that were so specific to one type of collective that it would not make sense to evaluate how that dimension plays out in others. For instance, criminal organizations may

Table 3.1 Seven Dimensions to Differentiate Groups from Gangs and Gangs from Criminal Organizations

Dimension	Measurement	Peer Groups	Gangs	Criminal Organizations
CRIME				
Willingness to use violence or its threat	Discrete	No	Yes	Yes
Group commitment to crime	Continuum	Small	Increasingly important	Very important
Importance of economic goals	Continuum	Small	Increasingly important	Essential
Scope of criminal activity	Continuum	Micro-local	Mostly local	Beyond local
ORGANIZATION				
Group organization/structure	Continuum	No to little organization	Some organization	Relatively organized
Age-graded membership structure	Continuum	Homogenous	Limited range	Wide range
Cooperation in and outside the group	Continuum	In	Mostly in, some out	In and out

be the only collectives invested in criminal governance or widespread corruption of public officials. The more generic dimension of "scope of criminal activity" is meant to capture these types of scenarios. Yet the dimension of willingness to use violence or its threat is not as easily amenable to scaling. Instead, when used on its own,[4] it is meant as a discrete marker to differentiate between groups and gangs; the proportion of violence in a collective is not assumed to increase as we move from gangs to criminal organizations. For all other dimensions, it is reasonable to expect a continuum where a measure that captures the dimension increases in some way from peer groups to criminal organizations. The bulk of the chapter provides an overview of each dimension with some of the research that informs it.

The distinctions we made between cells in Table 3.1 are simplifications. We have done enough research on gangs, groups, and organizations to know that there is wide variation within each category. Yet for minds that can imagine an "average" or typical entity within this range, the table may help make some basic distinctions clearer. Ideally, we hope that the proposed dimensions inspire gang scholars to integrate some of these measures into their empirical research. From there, we will be able to propose quantitative ranges to go along with the qualitative labels provided here.

In proposing these dimensions, we always had measurement in mind: Researchers or practitioners who encounter individuals who belong to collective entities should be able to tell, by locating the group along these dimensions, whether it is dealing with a group, a gang, or a criminal organization.[5] An added bonus is to help us think through definitions: Could it be that by being able to locate where gangs fit along these dimensions we would be able to get close to a definition that can fairly represent the range of gangs that exist? We aim to make clear statements and, where appropriate, clear recommendations to capture each dimension.

SEVEN DIMENSIONS TO TELL GROUPS, GANGS, AND CRIMINAL ORGANIZATIONS APART

Crime Dimensions

The Willingness to Use Violence or Its Threat

A common difficulty in trying to distinguish between peer groups and gangs is that both groups tend to be involved in similar types of crimes. For instance, in a sample of self-nominated gang and peer group members, Spindler and Bouchard (2011) found as many as 16 combinations of structure and criminal behavior within the data, with individuals from different categories being represented in every single combination.

Yet some aspects of their criminal involvement still differed. Part of it is the importance that crime takes generally (i.e., how much are members thinking about committing crimes and getting involved in criminal activities?), including the importance of economic aims (i.e., how much is making money from crime a central concern of the group?). Another aspect has to do with the scope of crime, especially when it comes to market crimes: Many types of collectives may be involved in drugs, but involvement beyond the local market gets us closer to criminal organizations rather than gangs or groups.

In this section, we are focused on another dimension that, for us, is at the core of what a gang is: the willingness to use violence. In countless studies, both qualitative and quantitative, scholars have found at least some general overlap in the nature of crimes committed by collectives that considered themselves to be peer groups and those that self-nominated as gangs, as both were involved in crimes such as drug dealing, vandalism, and burglary. Yet, being involved in violence, especially in collective violence in the name of the group, was something that stood out as a marker of difference between groups. Violence is a resource that is not necessarily accessible to all collectives or to all members within a collective (Densley 2012). This point is well articulated in Aldridge et al.'s (2012) research study that focused on testing different aspects of the Eurogang definition. The authors begin their argument by pointing out that a general concept such as "involvement in illegal activity as part of its group identity" was too broad a dimension to truly define gangs (Aldridge et al. 2012). Instead, a feature of gangs that separated them from other youth group formations was whether the group had a reputation or a willingness to resort to violence. Through this criterion, the gang is not required to *specialize* in violence; it was only required to be a recognized possibility.

Similar findings were reported in Ashton and Bussu's (2020) study of how adolescents at risk of gang involvement define gangs and other groups. Respondents saw peer groups as involved in a variety of criminal acts, but only perceived gangs and more organized groups to go deeper into violent crimes. Lopez et al. (2006) reported similar findings in their comparisons of "gangs" versus "crews." Gangs were defined by participants as organized groups with long histories of existence and initiation rituals, while crews were described more loosely as friends who had common interests, with shorter periods of existence and no explicit initiation rituals. Like others, the study by Lopez et al. (2006) showed how gangs and crews differed primarily in terms of violence. Crews shared many characteristics with gangs, but engagement in shooting and serious assaults were not among them. Carson et al.'s (2017) use of the G.R.E.A.T. (Gang Resistance Education and Training) study confirmed that periods of delinquent group involvement were marked with increases in nonviolent offending, but it was only periods of actual gang membership that were associated with increases in violent behavior.

This is not a surprise, of course. The fact that violence is central to what gangs are has often been at the heart of theories of gang behavior (Decker 1996) or gang definitions at large (Curry 2015). But we see it as an essential distinction between peer groups and gangs, emphasizing its importance for future work on gangs, especially for scholars and practitioners who hope to exclude peer groups from consideration.

Violence is also ubiquitous for criminal organizations. We see no large enough difference between gangs and criminal organizations' willingness to use violence to consider this dimension along a continuum. Violence or its threat (Reuter 1983) has been part of the definitions of organized crime for a long time (Varese 2017). This is because violence is often a necessary aspect of managing illegal business. In the absence of legal dispute resolution mechanisms, violence becomes part of the portfolio of strategies used to settle disputes or overtake the competition (Bouchard et al. 2021; Chung 2008; Reuter and Tonry 2020). We also do not believe that measuring the willingness to use violence on a continuum, or quantifying it, would reveal that this dimension increases as we go from peer groups to gangs and finally to criminal organizations. Gangs, in other words, may be just as willing to use violence as criminal organizations.

The nature of violence, however, may differ between groups. Instrumental violence may be more frequent in criminal organizations than in street gangs due to the importance of economic goals (Decker and Pyrooz 2014), and this more specific distinction in ways that violence is used may prove fruitful in distinguishing gangs from other collectives in many jurisdictions. Yet we stopped short of identifying gangs specifically with expressive or symbolic violence and criminal organizations with instrumental violence as we find too many instances of instrumental violence in street gangs (e.g., turf wars) and symbolic violence in criminal organizations.[6]

But this distinction may help tell groups from gangs in cases where data on involvement in violence, or willingness to use it, would be available. From a measurement perspective, this dimension requires access to data on the diversity of crimes committed in the context of the gang. Data that are not amenable to make a direct connection between criminal activity and whether and how it is associated with a collective entity would not be suitable for this task. Data extracted from police files where motive can be determined (Papachristos

2009) can be used to measure this dimension. Interviews with gang members, ethnographic observations, as well as self-reported data on criminal involvement in the name of a group may be better suited to tackle the "willingness" aspect of this dimension (e.g., Ashton and Bussu 2020; Decker 1996; Descormiers and Morselli 2011; Pyrooz et al. 2012).

The Group's Commitment to Crime

A clear distinction between peer groups and gangs is the increased importance of criminal involvement. Contrary to the willingness to use violence, this more generic category is quantifiable. And the generic aspect is key here: It matters little, in this dimension, what specific criminal activity members commit.[7] What matters is the amount of time they spend thinking about crime and doing crime.

Nowhere is this distinction clearer than in Densley's (2012) analysis of the organization of London gangs. Densley's paper is especially useful in its representation of the full spectrum of gang organization we are tackling in this chapter. The article describes the natural progression of gangs from recreational neighborhood groups to delinquent collectives and finally to full-scale criminal enterprises. Densley argues that crime and enterprise are not specific gang "types," but rather represent sequential stages in the evolutionary cycle of gangs. In the early "peer group" stages, crime is recreational, opportunistic, and irregular. It is when crime evolves to be slightly more regular, requiring some planning and organization, that entities are said to have reached the next "gang" stage. Once fully evolved into a criminal enterprise, the group's commitment to crime is so strong, that it requires more structure and organization than at any other stage. Ashton and Bussu's (2020) study on the differences in criminal involvement for various types of collectives confirms that a group's commitment to crime tends to increase as one moved from groups to gangs to organized crime groups, with the latter being the most clearly focused on "serious" money making and firearms. Similar findings were uncovered in studies of gang typologies (e.g., Klein and Maxson 2006; Spindler and Bouchard 2011): Criminal involvement increases with organizational level for most types of collectives.

In considering group commitment to crime, it is important not to lose sight of the fact that most collectives, even the most organized ones, do not exist solely for the purpose of committing crimes. While the commission of crime may be essential to include in members' motives to belong, there is typically more to membership than simply access to criminal opportunities. Table 3.1 summarizes it as "very important" but not necessarily the only dimension of importance for criminal organizations. For instance, mafia scholars have demonstrated in numerous ways how "crime" is but one aspect of what belonging to La Cosa Nostra means (Haller 1990; Paoli 2002), and the same is true for many outlaw motorcycle gangs (Quinn and Koch 2003; Von Lampe and Blokland 2020).

Indeed, the question for this dimension is a matter of degree. For each collective, one could ask the following question: If we removed criminal involvement from the portfolio of activities committed by the group, would the group dissolve completely? We can imagine that many peer groups and gangs would survive this test, but few, if any, criminal organizations would. Peer groups and gangs are often described first as groups of friends (e.g., Ashton and Bussu 2020; Densley 2012). While criminal organizations embrace values of brotherhood, it is only a secondary portion to the glue that bonds these collectives together.

We can easily imagine ways to quantify this. A measure that taps into the proportion of time spent planning and committing crime appears to be a suitable way to operationalize a group's commitment to crime. We also see how qualitative approaches may be incorporated to capture how members speak to the role of crime within the group and how it exists potentially alongside other functions and collective interests.

The Importance of Economic Goals

A focus on the importance of economic goals can help distinguish groups, gangs, and criminal organizations. In their paper on gangs and organized crime, Decker and Pyrooz (2014) emphasize the symbolic aspects of gangs as a key dimension separating gangs from organized crime. Indeed, less tangible aims like the need to belong or gaining respect or protection are common motives expressed by gang members when joining gangs (Descormiers and Corrado 2016). We understand the intention, but we see so much symbolism in criminal organizations that we resist the temptation to classify them as entirely focused on the economics of crime. Economic goals are indeed more important in organized crime—after all, criminal organizations offer their members the possibility of an alternative criminal career. Within criminal organizations, the allure of membership is highly tied to the prospects of economic wealth (Augustyn et al. 2019) Membership needs to be worth their financial while or else they would move on as independent traffickers. However, economic aims alone do not entirely explain an individual's decision to join a criminal organization (Levitt and Venkatesh 2000). Symbolism is also a key element of almost any sustainable criminal organization, from the colors and vests worn by motorcycle gangs to the long process and customs associated with becoming a "man of honor" in La Cosa Nostra (e.g., Paoli 2002; Quinn and Koch 2003).

Given this, we formulated this dimension not as a fight between symbolic or economic, but as a continuum measuring the importance of economic goals for a group. In Densley's (2012) stages but also in research comparing peer groups and gangs (e.g., Ashton and Bussu 2020; Bouchard and Spindler 2010), we can see a clear tendency for economic goals to increase in importance. Spindler and Bouchard's (2011) comparison of group and gang members' criminal involvement, for instance, found that 51% of group members could be classified as falling under the "minor crime" category, with the most prevalent activity being "regular cannabis use." Self-reported gang members, for their part, clustered mainly in the "Market" and "Serious" categorizations (Spindler and Bouchard 2011). Yet the authors still found that 25% of gang members could be classified as being involved in minor delinquency, reminding us of the variation that exists within each category but also that economic goals tend to increase as we go from groups to gangs (Spindler and Bouchard 2011).

The importance of economic goals is likely to reach its peak within criminal organizations that are largely involved in profit-related crimes, such as drug trafficking. This will manifest itself in criminal organizations formulating plans for economic growth at the group level, such as expanding and diversifying markets. These plans are absent from peer groups and not consistently present in gangs.

Measuring the importance of economic goals can be done from surveying gang members about their group's commitment to profit-making activities. It is one thing to collect data on crimes committed by members of the same group and another to ask about perceptions and intentions. A group may be caught by the police when they are involved in shootings, robberies, or assaults, but they may otherwise be highly focused on the business side of operations. An ideal research design would include both components: digging through police data and interviewing gang members on their approach to the business aspects of criminal involvement.

The Scope of Criminal Activity

One dimension that is more rarely touched upon is the difference in the scope of criminal activity between groups, gangs, and criminal organizations. For us, scope is important to distinguish collectives based on the mere consideration of the types of crimes they are involved in. Anyone, at any stage, may be involved in drug dealing and drug supplying at large; yet only the most advanced forms of collectives will be involved in drug dealing beyond the retail level, de facto excluding peer groups who tend to be constrained to their own neighborhoods. And when it comes to transactions at the importation or exportation level, further distinctions between gangs and criminal organizations emerge, with only the latter having the resources and breadth of activity to be players on the international scene. Only criminal organizations, in other words, may demonstrate true market power and political influence (Curry and Mongrain 2009; Varese 2017). Only criminal organizations may be involved in corrupting law enforcement officials and customs agents.

This dimension is particularly helpful in distinguishing between collectives that are involved in illegal markets. Broadly speaking, it is entirely possible to find all versions of the collectives we consider in this chapter to be involved in drug supply in some form. The type of crime they are involved in, then, wouldn't be helpful in differentiating between groups, gangs, and criminal organizations. Yet the scope of criminal activity may be performed at entirely different levels, making this aspect potentially useful to tell the groups apart. Groups are generally local in scope, local in the "micro places" sense of the term. Taking their typically young age into account, and the rather opportunistic and sporadic criminal involvement they exhibit, we should not expect their crimes to go beyond their immediate environment. The scope of criminal activity tends to increase as groups evolve to the gang and criminal organization stages—neighborhood, retail-level deals turn into city-level deals and beyond. Yet some of these boundaries may be blurred where the involvement of gangs goes beyond the local level, without necessarily implying the involvement of criminal organizations. For example, Robinson et al. (2019) described the contemporary drug dealing practices of "county lines," an illicit drug supply model where gangs use young people or vulnerable individuals to cross police borders and courier drugs. This has been viewed as a form of gang evolution as gangs establish themselves as brokers between national wholesale and local street dealing (Harding 2020; Robinson et al. 2019).

From a measurement perspective, encountering a collective involved in transactions beyond the retail level is a sign that we are beyond the peer group, recreational level. Scholars don't always have to decide on what the cut-off points are for retail, mid-level, and wholesale transactions. Bouchard and Ouellet (2011), for instance, use a continuous measure of transaction size (in dollar amounts) to control for market level in their study of drug dealers and detection. The scope of criminal activity can also be measured by the size of drug transactions, the number of areas in which the group is active, or the relative distance between the source of the illegal products they buy and their destination (Bouchard and Ouellet 2011).

Organizational Dimensions

The Group Organization/Structure

We now move to the dimensions that relate more to the organizational aspects of collectives. In many ways, organizational components can hardly be separated from the criminal dimensions of gangs. They arguably have a symbiotic relationship or, at the very least, influence each other. In which direction? Some, like Densley (2012), argue that external threats and the necessities of the crimes themselves—especially those with financial stakes like drug supplying—create incentives to organize, build systems, and become predictable. However, Densley meant this in the evolutionary sense, going from one stage to the other. We can also appreciate how gangs may come up with some organizational features that may not be attached to any specific criminal needs.

Gangs vary in their levels of organization. Most show very low levels of organization (Decker et al. 2008; Bjerregard 2010), but it is not uncommon to find gangs with a moderate degree of organizational structure (Bouchard and Spindler 2010; Decker 2001; Decker and Curry 2000; Esbensen and Weerman 2005; Pyrooz et al. 2012) such as having a leader and some form of hierarchy. Bjerregaard (2002) studied "organized gangs" and described them as possessing the characteristics typically associated with traditional street gangs but having names, leaders, regular meetings, a stash of guns, and an association with a particular territory. Within the literature on criminal organizations, we see criminal organizations as seemingly highly structured, with governance systems, rules, charts, and promotional ladders (Finckenauer 2005; Varese 2017; Von Lampe 2016).

At what point do "organized gangs" become "criminal organizations"? And where do peer groups fit into all of this? Our reading of the literature suggests that peer groups do not typically adopt any organizational features (see Table 3.1). This is, for us, an important marker of the difference between groups and gangs. Some characteristics of almost any group, like convergence in time and space, for instance, are not a sign of organization. The first, early attempts at organization for crime will determine if the group successfully transitions into a gang. Most will scatter before they reach that stage.

As for the difference between gangs and criminal organizations, examining the literature from the point of view of "organized crime" reveals some convergence in the way that scholars describe the groups they study. Decker and Pyrooz's (2014) distinction between the instrumental-rational and the informal-diffuse perspectives is useful to illustrate the difference between gangs and criminal organization in this dimension. The instrumental-rational perspective suggests that gangs have a vertical structure, enforce discipline among their members, and are successful in defining and achieving group values. Furthermore, the instrumental-rational perspective states that gangs include age-graded levels of membership, leadership roles, coordinated drug sales, and ties and influence in the political process. Conversely, the informal-diffuse perspective posits that gangs are diffuse, self-interested, and self-motivated aggregations of individuals, most of whom sell drugs for themselves. The informal-diffuse perspective also states that leadership is functional and situational, membership is transitory, codes of conduct are limited to secrecy and loyalty, and most importantly, gang members distribute drugs for individual reasons as opposed to collective purposes. With these perspectives, Decker and Pyrooz (2014) argue that it is more useful to conceptualize gangs along a continuum, with informal-diffuse at one end and instrumental-rational at the other end. Once individuals become extremely organized and institutionalized, groups depart from the "street gang" criteria and enter the definitional parameters of an organized crime group.

Another angle to distinguish gangs from criminal organizations refers to governance. While both groups can be heavily involved in the drug trade, only criminal organizations have the power to regulate and control the production and distribution of drugs (Decker et al. 2022; McLean et al. 2019). Campana and Varese (2018) state that criminal organizations use an extralegal governance structure, which they define as the ability to generate fear within a community, coerce legal businesses, and influence official figures. McLean et al. (2019) expand on this and suggest that although criminal organizations set rules on product control, they also set the rules within the underworld and have the power to regulate access. That said, we believe governance is too specific a dimension to properly differentiate between the three types of collectives considered here and instead prefer to treat it as one aspect of the broader dimension of organization.

How do we measure "organization"? Scales are provided in Bouchard and Spindler (2010) as well as in Decker et al. (2008) and other work on the organizational structure of gangs. We would argue to maintain the idea of scales. But we also believe that close attention needs to be paid to which items make it on the scale. We need to make sure, in short, that all items do indeed inform on gang organization, as opposed to behaviors that any group is likely to display simply by virtue of forming a group. In Bouchard and Spindler (2010), for instance, few "group" members reported their group having organizational features, but as many as 22% reported having a meeting location. While informative to know that a group has a regular meeting point, this item may not help us distinguish groups from gangs. We prefer Decker et al.'s (2008) variation in that regard: "Does the gang have regular meetings?" an item that shows a willingness to plan.

The scales would need to be applied and validated on criminal organizations to be used in this spirit of considering all collectives as variations of one large family and in the spirit of this chapter. This could mean expanding the list of items to include features that may be found in the most organized forms of collective, like the existence of promotional ladders or of layers of protection between leaders and lower-level members. More importantly, we need to be careful in making inferences about group organization based on a single member's perceptions of an organization. Young or recent members may not be aware of many of the organizational aspects of the gang, especially for larger gangs (see Pyrooz and Decker 2019 for an extended treatment of these issues).

The Age Structure of Membership

A clear distinction between gangs and criminal organizations has to do with the age of their members. There is tendency for the age range of members to increase as we move from peer groups to criminal organizations. The wider the age range, the more likely we are dealing with a more fully developed collective entity. Peer groups tend to have young members of the same age; gangs may also show little variation in age, but many will show a tendency for age-graded structures. Within criminal organizations, veterans are present to provide guidance and mentorship to young recruits, perhaps also to run the business aspects of the gang while younger members do lower-level jobs and perhaps take more risks in terms of police detection. When these differences stay within a three-to-four-year "cycle" of one another (Tremblay et al. 2016), or even within a decade, we may still be dealing with gangs. Yet when a collective entity starts to show even wider ranges, often with veterans pushing into their 40s or 50s and recruits who are 20 or 30 years younger, we may be dealing with a collective that evolved into a criminal organization.

It is not uncommon for Mafiosi or Hells Angels full patch members to be well over 50 or 60 years old, while younger recruits are in their 20s and 30s. Not adolescents by any means, and yet still rookies and newbies in the context of the collectives to which they belong. The participants in Ashton and Bussu's (2020) study described organized crime groups as having elders, where the organization had a clear hierarchy with an inner circle at the top where elders acted to "groom" younger members. In addition, people were associated with organized crime groups through family connections, a sustainability mechanism that betrays the "established" or "resilient" status of organization.

Measuring the age range of members of criminal collectives is of utmost importance to understand the relative complexity of their organization. Members that belong to youth groups and gangs with a limited age range would be less likely to experience a long and successful criminal career, due to the lack of mentorship. Those who are mentored by veterans are most likely to receive the training and criminal opportunities necessary to continue beyond adolescence (Ouellet et al. 2022).

The Social Structure of Cooperation in and outside the Group

Our last dimension is not as well researched by gang scholars as the others. Instead, it recently emerged as gang scholars paid more attention to the social networks in and around gang members (Ouellet et al. 2019; Papachristos 2006). There is something fundamentally social about gangs—from the reasons why members join, why they stay, and why they leave gangs. The higher stakes involved in many gang crimes and the requirement for continuity imply a higher need for secrecy and trust in one's associates as a driver of action. And the mechanisms of trust—how it is created as well as its effects—are best understood when paying attention to the social relations among members.

This is what we refer to as the social structure of cooperation—the patterns in the social interactions of members of collectives in the context of planning and committing crimes. Membership to a specific group or gang shapes who and how many partners are available to cooperate with. For our purposes, we focus on a single aspect of cooperation, the relative frequency with which members of collectives cooperate with outsiders, that is, with individuals who are not considered to be actual members of their own collective.

Here we argue that the social structure of cooperation will differ as we move from peer groups to gangs to criminal organizations. All require social networks, but all use networks differently. To understand how we go back to a concept that has been used to describe gangs for a very long time—cohesion (Papachristos 2013; Short and Strodtbeck 1965). Cohesion refers to how close and connected the members of a group are to each other. Not all members of a group necessarily interact on a consistent basis, and not everyone may collaborate for crimes; variations in patterns of interactions for criminal collaboration have important implications for the resilience and criminal productivity of gangs (Ouellet et al. 2019).

We propose that collectives will move from a structure of criminal cooperation that is mostly closed in on itself in peer groups to one that opens gradually to outsiders as groups evolve into gangs and then into criminal organizations. This measure is focused not so much on the interactions that qualify as social in nature; rather, it is focused on co-offending—cooperation for criminal activities. We believe the patterns would apply to criminal activities at large; criminal organizations are more likely to forge alliances than gangs in the drug trade, and gangs themselves would risk these alliances with outsiders more often than peer group members (whose involvement in the drug trade may never even require considering cooperation with outsiders). Contracted violence would follow a similar pattern; while gangs may be just as likely as criminal organizations to be involved in violent conflicts, criminal organizations would be more likely to cooperate with outsiders to achieve their goals.

How do we measure this? Ideally, social network data would be available. Network data allow researchers to better model the mechanisms that explain recruitment into gangs, the movement of individuals in and out of these organizations, and the decisions to collaborate with certain individuals over others (Bouchard 2020). Yet patterns of ingroup versus outgroup cooperation have been studied by social psychologists for a long time despite the absence of detailed network data. Regardless of the nature of the data available, the first step in studying ingroup and outgroup cooperation is to determine the boundaries of the collectives themselves—who is a member of this group and who isn't? Ouellet et al. (2019) proposed a network-based approach to determine gang boundaries, but traditional lists based on criminal intelligence (Malm et al. 2011) or detailed police incident data may also work (Papachristos 2009), unless the validity of membership attributions is questionable or appears to be biased (see Densley and Pyrooz 2020 for the value of valid gang police data and suggestions on improving them).

Then we need data on collaboration that will tell us if cooperation occurs within or outside the gang. With network data, scholars can provide specific measures such as the E-I index of each collective—a score that captures a group's pattern of collaboration on a scale of mostly external to mostly internal (Ouellet et al. 2019). Without network data, but with membership data or detailed interviews with gang members, we can still measure the proportion of collaboration that occurs outside rather than inside the gang. Opening up to outsiders is, for us, both a risk that a collective takes but also a sign that the business is done at a higher level, a level that supersedes considerations for limiting interactions solely to internal members.

Concluding Thoughts: Putting It All Together

Taken as a whole, we believe the seven dimensions we propose can help make sense of gangs encountered in developed nations. We hope the list brings some level of clarity to what could be important to investigate in trying to understand the nature of a gang landscape in any jurisdiction, and also help frame expectations. For instance, observing that a group is involved in selling drugs is not on its own "organized crime" or "gang behavior" simply because there are, say, three or more individuals are involved. And, at the risk of stating the obvious, a gang is not a gang because it has been labeled at some point as a gang. It could be a group still, or it could have started as a gang but eventually evolved into a criminal organization. Resilient gangs that survive the initial challenges of turnover in membership and in leadership have, one way or another, found a way to create sustainability and attract new recruits while preserving veteran leadership (Ouellet et al. 2019). But they may not be "gangs" anymore, a realization that has important implications for the type of interventions that are practical and reasonable for them (Gravel et al. 2013).

The dimensions in Table 3.1 may interact in non-linear ways. For instance, we argued that the willingness to use violence may not help differentiate gangs from criminal organizations when considered in isolation. Yet the fact that criminal organizations are better organized and potentially have more resources may lead to a higher degree of sophistication in carrying out violent acts. They are more likely to have the resources to hire contract killers, to aim for high-level targets, to penetrate legitimate businesses, and to travel, if needed, to execute a plan. Scoring similarly on one dimension, then, does not imply similarity in all regards. Developing a scoring system and validating it against police or self-reported gang data would be the natural next steps from the ideas proposed in this chapter.

Applying the dimensions to some of the well-known groups, gangs, and criminal organizations is another logical next step. And it may lead to surprises. Levitt and Venkatesh's (2000) gang, with its large size and layers of organization, would score more points in the "criminal organization" category than in the "gangs" one. The same would happen for many gangs active where we are from, British Columbia, Canada. Groups like the Red Scorpions gang and the United Nations gang (Bouchard and Hashim 2017), for instance, are often referred to as "gangs" but would score most of their points in the criminal organization column. And this is exactly the way it should be. We believe that the term "gangs" may be overused to describe collectives that should sometimes be referred to simply as peer groups while at other times these collectives have fully made the transition to organized crime. Defining concepts that are meant to capture a wide variety of styles, structures, and behaviors such as "gangs" and "organized crime" are bound to fail, one way or another. However, in the process of going through the exercise, there were some aspects of what gangs are, and what gangs aren't, that started to emerge.

Our point is not to say that measuring collectives along these seven dimensions would change most of what we know about what is a gang and what isn't. There will be some definitional puzzles remaining for the next generation of gang scholars to sort out. Instead, we argue that at least some of the assumptions of what constitutes a group, a gang, and a criminal organization may be shaken up once looked at under the scrutiny of specific dimensions like the ones we propose in this chapter. We may "know" that the presence of adult mentors and gang veterans within the same collective signals a higher degree of sophistication while failing to realize that this attribute would also qualify them under the label of criminal organization. If we are serious about the business of defining and labeling gangs, then we need to look closely at the collectives we encounter for what truly set them apart.

Notes

1. We also encountered the opposite issue—jurisdictions assuming there were no "gang issues" when there were. Neither of these contexts is amenable to appropriate gang interventions.
2. We prefer the latter term as opposed to "organized criminal group" (OCG) or other similar terms as it avoids adding the qualifier "organized" to label these collectives. While many may show signs of organization, this aspect of their structure can be measured and the qualifier "organized" may or may not apply. We do use OCG when we summarize a study that uses it.
3. For Densley (2012), the level of organization adopted by a gang will help serve the nature of the criminal involvement of their members. For us, the relationship between organization and crime may be less rational, at times. Some organizational features may be adopted for symbolic reasons, with no implications for criminality.
4. It is possible to distinguish the violence used by gangs from the violence used by criminal organizations when merging this category with another dimension, such as organization. The more sophisticated the use of violence, the more likely an entity is to be a criminal organization.
5. Notable by its absence is the often-mentioned dimension that would capture specialization: the extent to which collectives tend to focus on a single activity. While it could very well be that there is a stronger tendency for gangs to be more involved in cafeteria-style offending than peer groups, the evidence for criminal organizations is not as strong. There are examples of organizations that specialize in one activity (e.g., Reuter 2014) and others that don't (e.g., Tremblay et al. 2009), but to our knowledge there are no strong patterns either way. Without clear evidence, we prefer to keep the dimension out of Table 3.1. We would expect a U-shaped curve on the specialization scale where both peer groups and criminal organizations are more likely to specialize than gangs.
6. Examples of symbolic or expressive violence in criminal organizations include outlaw motorcycle gangs using the "power of the patch" to intimidate law enforcement agencies or citizens (Von Lampe and Blokland 2020; Tremblay et al. 2009) and Mexican criminal organizations using symbolism such as "narco-messages" after a murder (Atuesta 2017).
7. This is also why this dimension is treated separately from economic aims; we encountered many collectives that qualify as gangs, are almost fully committed to crime, but only engage in violent crime or assaults. This aspect makes them gangs more than groups, but the lack of economic motives makes them more like groups.

References

Aldridge, J., J. Medina-Ariz, and R. Ralphs. 2012. "Counting Gangs: Conceptual and Validity Problems with the Eurogang Definition." In *Youth Gangs in International Perspective*, edited by F.-A. Esbensen and C. L. Maxson, 35–51. New York: Springer.

Ashton, S. A., and A. Bussu. 2020. "Peer Groups, Street Gangs and Organised Crime in the Narratives of Adolescent Male Offenders." *Journal of Criminal Psychology* 10 (4): 277–292.

Atuesta, L. H. 2017. "Narcomessages as a Way to Analyse the Evolution of Organised Crime in Mexico." *Global Crime* 18 (2): 100–121.

Augustyn, M. B., J. M. McGloin, and D. C. Pyrooz. 2019. "Does Gang Membership Pay? Illegal and Legal Earnings through Emerging Adulthood." *Criminology* 57 (3): 452–480.

Ayling, J. 2011. "Gang Change and Evolutionary Theory." *Crime, Law and Social Change* 56 (1): 1–26.

Beresford, H., and J. L. Wood. 2016. "Patients or Perpetrators? The Effects of Trauma Exposure on Gang Members' Mental Health: A Review of the Literature." *Journal of Criminological Research, Policy and Practice* 2 (2): 148–159.

Bjerregaard, B. 2002. "Self-Definitions of Gang Membership and Involvement in Delinquent Activities." *Youth and Society* 34 (1): 31–54.

Bjerregaard, B. 2010. "Gang Membership and Drug Involvement: Untangling the Complex Relationship." *Crime and Delinquency* 56 (1): 3–34.

Bouchard, M. 2020. "Collaboration and Boundaries in Organized Crime: A Network Perspective." *Crime and Justice: An Annual Review of Research* 49: 425–469.

Bouchard, M., Hashimi, S. (2017). When is a "war", a "wave"? Two approaches to detecting waves of gang violence. Canadian Journal of Criminology and Criminal Justice 59: 198–226.

Bouchard, M., and A. Spindler. 2010. Groups, Gangs, and Delinquency: Does Organization Matter? *Journal of Criminal Justice* 38 (5), 921–933.

Bouchard, M., F. Ouellet. 2011. "Is Small Beautiful? The Link between Risks and Size in Illegal Drug Markets." *Global Crime* 12: 70–86.

Bouchard, M., M. Soudijn, and P. Reuter. 2021. "Conflict Management in High-Stakes Illegal Drug Transactions." *British Journal of Criminology* 61 (1): 167–186.

Campana, P., and F. Varese. 2018. "Organized Crime in the United Kingdom: Illegal Governance of Markets and Communities." *British Journal of Criminology* 58 (6): 1381–1400.

Carson, D. C., S. A. Wiley, and F. A. Esbensen. 2017. "Differentiating between Delinquent Groups and Gangs: Moving beyond Offending Consequences." *Journal of Crime and Justice* 40 (3): 297–315.

Chung, A. 2008. "The Big Circle Boys: Revisiting the Case of the Flaming Eagles." *Global Crime* 9 (4): 306–331.

Cohen, A. K. 1955. *Delinquent Boys: The Culture of the Gang.* New York: Free Press.

Curry, G. D. 2015. "The Logic of Defining Gangs Revisited." In *The Handbook of Gangs*, edited by S. H. Decker and D. C. Pyrooz, 7–27. New York: Wiley.

Curry, P. A., and S. Mongrain. 2009. "What Is a Criminal Organization and Why Does the Law Care?" *Global Crime* 10 (1–2): 6–23.

Decker, S. H. 1996. "Collective and Normative Features of Gang Violence." *Justice Quarterly* 13 (2): 243–264.

Decker, S. H. 2001. "The Impact of Organizational Features on Gang Activities and Relationships." In *The Eurogang Paradox*, edited by M. W. Klein et al., 21–39. Dordrecht: Springer.

Decker, S. H., and G. D. Curry. 2000. "Addressing Key Features of Gang Membership: Measuring the Involvement of Young Members." *Journal of Criminal Justice* 28 (6): 473–482.

Decker, S. H., C. M. Katz, and V. J. Webb. 2008. "Understanding the Black Box of Gang Organization: Implications for Involvement in Violent Crime, Drug Sales, and Violent Victimization." *Crime and Delinquency* 54 (1): 153–172.

Decker, S., J. Densley, and D. Pyrooz. 2022. *On Gangs.* Philadelphia, PA: Temple University Press.

Decker, S. H., and D. C. Pyrooz. 2014. Gangs: Another Form of Organized Crime? In *Oxford Handbook of Organized Crime*, edited by L. Paoli, 270–287. New York: Oxford University Press.

Densley, J. A. 2012. "The Organisation of London's Street Gangs." *Global Crime* 13 (1): 42–64.

Densley, J. A. 2014. "It's Gang Life, but Not as We Know It: The Evolution of Gang Business." *Crime and Delinquency* 60 (4): 517–546.

Densley, J. A., and D. C. Pyrooz. 2020. "The Matrix in Context: Taking Stock of Police Gang Databases in London and Beyond." *Youth Justice* 20 (1–2): 11–30.

Descormiers, K., and R. Corrado. 2016. "The Right to Belong: Individual Motives and Youth Gang Initiation Rites." *Deviant Behavior* 37 (11): 1341–1359.

Descormiers, K., and C. Morselli. 2011. "Alliances, Conflicts, and Contradictions in Montreal's Street Gang Landscape." *International Criminal Justice Review* 21 (3): 297–314.

Esbensen, F. A., and F. M. Weerman. 2005. "Youth Gangs and Troublesome Youth Groups in the United States and the Netherlands: A Cross-National Comparison." *European Journal of Criminology* 2 (1): 5–37.

Finckenauer, J. O. 2005. "Problems of Definition: What Is Organized Crime?" *Trends in Organized Crime* 8 (3): 63–83.

Gravel, J., M. Bouchard, K. Descormiers, J. Wong, and C. Morselli. 2013. "Keeping Promises: A Systematic Review and a New Classification of Gang Control Strategies." *Journal of Criminal Justice* 41: 228–242.

Haller, M. H. 1990. "Illegal Enterprise: A Theoretical and Historical Interpretation." *Criminology* 28 (2): 208–236.

Harding, S. 2020. *County Lines: Exploitation and Drug Dealing among Urban Street Gangs*. Bristol, UK: Policy Press.

Hashimi, S., and M. Bouchard. 2017. "On to the Next One? Using Social Network Data to Inform Police Target Prioritization." *Policing: An International Journal* 40 (4): 768–782.

Kerig, P. K., S. D. Chaplo, D. C. Bennett, and C. A. Modrowski. 2016. "'Harm as Harm': Gang Membership, Perpetration Trauma, and Posttraumatic Stress Symptoms among Youth in the Juvenile Justice System." *Criminal Justice and Behavior* 43 (5): 635–652.

Klein, M. W., and C. L. Maxson. 2006. *Street Gang Patterns and Policies*. Oxford, UK: Oxford University Press.

Levitt, S. D., and S. A. Venkatesh. 2000. "An Economic Analysis of a Drug-Selling Gang's Finances." *Quarterly Journal of Economics* 115: 755–789.

Lopez, E. M., A. Wishard, R. Gallimore, and W. Rivera. 2006. "Latino High School Students' Perceptions of Gangs and Crews." *Journal of Adolescent Research* 21 (3): 299–318.

Malm, A., G. Bichler, and R. Nash. 2011. "Co-offending between Criminal Enterprise Groups." *Global Crime* 12 (2): 112–128.

McLean, R., R. Deuchar, S. Harding, and J. Densley. 2019. "Putting the 'Street' in Gang: Place and Space in the Organization of Scotland's Drug-Selling Gangs." *British Journal of Criminology* 59 (2): 396–415.

Ouellet, M., Bouchard, M., and Charette, Y. 2019. "One Gang Dies, Another Gains? The Network Dynamics of Criminal Group Persistence. *Criminology* 57 (1): 5–33.

Ouellet, F., M. Bouchard, and V. Thomas. 2022. "The Intangible Benefits of Criminal Mentorship." *Global Crime*. Online First.

Paoli, L. 2002. "The Paradoxes of Organized Crime." *Crime, Law and Social Change* 37 (1): 51–97.

Papachristos, A. V. 2006. "Social Network Analysis and Gang Research: Theory and Methods." *Studying Youth Gangs*, edited by J. Short and L. Hughes, 99–116. Toronto, ON: Altamira.

Papachristos, A. V. 2009. "Murder by Structure: Dominance Relations and the Social Structure of Gang Homicide." *American Journal of Sociology* 115 (1): 74–128.

Papachristos, A. V. 2013. "The Importance of Cohesion for Gang Research, Policy, and Practice." *Criminology and Public Policy* 12: 49.

Pauls, N. 2017. *Pathways to Early Mortality for Serious and Violent Young Offenders.* Unpublished Master's Thesis, Simon Fraser University.

Pyrooz, D. C., and Decker, S. H. 2019. *Competing for Control: Gangs and the Social Order of Prisons.* Cambridge University Press.

Pyrooz, D. C., and J. A. Densley. 2018. "On Public Protest, Violence, and Street Gangs." *Society* 55 (3): 229–236.

Pyrooz, D. C., A. M. Fox, C. M. Katz, and S. H. Decker. 2012. Gang Organization, Offending, and Victimization: A Cross-National Analysis. In *Youth Gangs in International Perspective*, edited by F.-A. Esbensen and C. L. Maxson, 85–105. New York: Springer.

Pyrooz, D. C., R. K. Masters, J. J. Tostlebe, and R. G. Rogers. 2020. "Exceptional Mortality Risk among Police-Identified Young Black Male Gang Members." *Preventive Medicine* 141: 106269.

Pyrooz, D. C., J. J. Turanovic, S. H. Decker, and J. Wu. 2016. "Taking Stock of the Relationship between Gang Membership and Offending: A Meta-Analysis." *Criminal Justice and Behavior* 43 (3): 365–397.

Quinn, J., and D. Shane Koch. 2003. "The Nature of Criminality within One-Percent Motorcycle Clubs." *Deviant Behavior* 24 (3): 281–305.

Reuter, P. 1983. *Disorganized Crime, Illegal Markets and the Mafia.* Cambridge, MA: MIT Press.

Reuter, P. 2014. "Drug Markets and Organized Crime." In *The Oxford Handbook of Organized Crime*, edited by L. Paoli, 359–381. Oxford, UK: Oxford University Press.

Reuter, P., and M. Tonry. 2020. "Organized Crime: Less Than Meets the Eye." *Crime and Justice* 49: 1–14.

Robinson, G., R. McLean, and J. Densley. 2019. "Working County Lines: Child Criminal Exploitation and Illicit Drug Dealing in Glasgow and Merseyside." *International Journal of Offender Therapy and Comparative Criminology* 63 (5): 694–711.

Short, J. F., and F. L. Strodtbeck. 1965. *Group Process and Gang Delinquency.* Chicago, IL: University of Chicago Press.

Spindler, A., and M. Bouchard. 2011. "Structure or Behavior? Revisiting Gang Typologies." *International Criminal Justice Review* 21 (3): 263–282.

Thornberry, T. P., M. D., Krohn, A. J., Lizotte, and D. Chard-Wierschem. 1993. "The Role of Juvenile Gangs in Facilitating Delinquent Behavior." *Journal of Research in Crime and Delinquency* 30 (1): 55–87.

Thrasher, F. M. 1963. *The Gang: A Study of 1,313 Gangs in Chicago.* Chicago, IL: University of Chicago Press.

Tremblay, P., M. Bouchard, and S. Petit. 2009. "The Size and Influence of a Criminal Organization: A Criminal Achievement Perspective." *Global Crime* 10: 24–40.

Tremblay, P., C. Mathieu, C. Yanick, and M. Tremblay-Faulkner. 2016. *Le délinquant affilié: La sous-culture des gangs de rue haïtiens de Montréal.* Montreal: Liber.

Varese, F. 2017. *What Is Organised Crime?* Oxford, UK: Hart Publishing.

Von Lampe, K. 2016. "The Ties That Bind: A Taxonomy of Associational Criminal Structures." In *Illegal Entrepreneurship, Organized Crime and Social Control*, edited by G. A. Antonopoulos, 19–35. Cham, Switzerland: Springer.

Von Lampe, K., and A. Blokland. 2020. "Outlaw Motorcycle Clubs and Organized Crime." *Crime and Justice: An Annual Review of Research* 49: 521–578.

CHAPTER 4

A RELATIONAL APPROACH TO STREET GANGS

ANDREW V. PAPACHRISTOS, JOHN LEVERSO, AND DAVID HUREAU

DONTE joined LIVES, a gun violence intervention program, nearly 10 months *before* he was shot.[1] Like many other program participants, Donte felt like he was living on borrowed time. His crew, T-Street, were in a heated dispute with their rivals, X-Town. When outreach workers from LIVES offered Donte a lifeline, he grabbed it with both hands.

This is why many were shocked when he was shot.

To some, Donte's victimization signaled programmatic "failure." After all, the explicit goal of the program is to reduce gun violence. But for Donte and the outreach staff, victimization was not necessarily an indictment of failure. Instead, the victimization of any single participant—even those deeply engaged in the program, like Donte—underscores the limitations of individual approaches to reducing gang violence. Gang violence is *relational* by nature, even though most programs tend to focus almost exclusively on gang-involved individuals or specific groups within a community. Ignoring the underlying group dynamics of violence as well as the social networks that make up gangs themselves can lead to negative—and even deadly—consequences.

The gang world is built not through individual actions alone; it is shaped by larger forces of relationships and social networks among groups and gang members. Focusing on only one group (or one member) overlooks this deceivingly complex fact of gang life. In this case, LIVES was able to get Donte and his crew to "play defense" (to stop carrying guns and to let their dispute with X-Town soften or at least cool down). But LIVES was less successful in reaching members of X-Town, meaning that crew was still playing "offense." Such a situation was untenable and, as Donte mentions, makes system failure feel like an individual failure:

> Man, I'm out here doing everything right. You feel me? I'm here. I'm doing the program. I'm on the straight, for real. So they (LIVES) got me doing all this, right, and me and my boys we trying to do what's right. I ain't even carrying [a gun] like that anymore. They got me playing defense. And that's what I gotta do. But, like, just because I'm playing defense out here doesn't mean the "opps" [opposition] stop playing offense. They just keep coming at me, no matter what I do. It's like I can't escape the game, no matter what I'm doing. Eventually, the line is going to break.

Donte's observation about playing defense versus offense is a theme emerging from gang-affiliated young people who are part of these sorts of programs. They understand that even when they try to change themselves, even if they take steps to disarm or change their own thinking, they live in a deadly swirl of volatile relationships that are much larger than their immediate social network or their crew (Stuart 2020). These relationships among groups, especially antagonistic ones, are so intertwined in the raison d'être of gangs that even the most earnest individual efforts, like Donte's, make it seem impossible to escape the tangle of dangerous relations, conflicts, and situations (Papachristos 2009).

This chapter outlines a relational understanding of gangs and gang behaviors that is grounded in group processes *and* social networks. While prior research—especially during the "Golden Age" of gang research (Pyrooz and Mitchell 2015)—firmly noted the importance of group processes in understanding gangs, contemporary methodological approaches to gangs, as well as the dominant criminal justice and behavioral science approaches informing policy responses to gang violence, often ignore the fundamentally relational nature of gangs and gang behaviors (Sierra-Arévalo and Papachristos 2015). Recent developments in network analysis and relational approaches to ethnography open new avenues in understanding gangs and gang behaviors that have implications for research and practice.

The Definitional Debate

No subject has spilled more ink within the field of gang research than the debate about how to define the very object of study, the "gang." The various definitions of a "gang" or "street gang" tend to include some element of the following characteristics:[2]

- Some explicit dimension of *groupness* or extra-individual identity, often including (but not necessarily) a name or use of unique symbols or identifying traits
- *Durability*; that is, the group has some identity as opposed to a group coming together for a singular event or short/task-specific purpose
- *Communication* (including online communications) that expresses group identity, relationships, and membership
- An orientation toward *street culture*, identity, and status
- Some involvement in *crime or delinquency* as part of the group's identity

The center of the definitional debate pivots on the last point: whether or not "crime" (or delinquency or violence) should be included in the definition (Curry 2015). On one hand, involvement in crime and delinquency is the very reason most scholars and non-scholars are interested in gangs in the first place: They are creating enough of a racket in the real world that they are deemed "problematic" (or at least drawing attention from external non-gang actors, like community members or the police). On the other hand, including it in the definition of the object of study itself creates a tautology—we are defining gangs by the very outcomes we hope to explain by studying the gang and gang processes.

What is not debated, however, is that gangs are *groups* and that understanding group identity and group processes is foundational to understanding the behavior of gangs (as groups) and gang members (as individuals). Even if gangs started spontaneously, they are not groups of random individuals lumped together by accident, but some (quasi-)intentional grouping of peers or associates that come together in time and space (most often in disenfranchised or underserved communities) for mutual protection, socialization, and so on.

A relational or group-process-oriented approach to gangs—such as the one advanced here—centers this group nature in favor of understanding how internal and external processes of the gang shape behaviors (Short and Strodtbeck 1965). Importantly, some types of crime and violence—especially conflict with other groups—are intimately tied to group processes themselves, so much so that even early definitions, such as Thrasher's (1927), listed conflict and positionality as defining traits of gangs. For Thrasher, gangs were defined by their positionality in the city, larger society, and life-course development:

> Gangs [are] interstitial groups, a product of the in-between areas where formal institutions failed to take hold and flourish in ways that made sense to youth and a manifestation of the period of adjustment between childhood and adulthood (37).

Gangs were "in-between" formal and informal institutions, not in some abstract way, but in concrete ways within their neighborhoods. Gangs are gangs precisely because a neighborhood scout troop or a sports team or the local church youth clubs either did not exist or were inaccessible to some part of the community, in many cases because of various neighborhood boundaries created by patterns of segregation, housing policy, discrimination, and racism. Gangs' "street" orientation is thus a defining element (Klein and Maxson 2010) precisely because they are tied to particular pieces of neighborhood turf, corners, or public spaces and not formal institutions like recreation centers, churches, or schools.

What's more, from a relational perspective, gangs often define themselves in opposition to other groups or gangs, a property that is often reflected in the language (quasi-communication) gangs use to define themselves. Many gangs, for instance, use derogatory remarks against their rivals interchangeably with their own gang name. The Latin Kings, one of Chicago's largest Latinx gangs, uses the phrase "2-6 Killer" (a slander against one of their longest rivals) interchangeably with "King Love" (a praise to their own identity) (Conquergood 1993). Recent critical perspectives also align with such a relational interpretation by framing gangs not simply as a form of protection against other gangs or neighborhood threats, but as a form of resistance against external entities such as the police, failing schools, and even the state (Brotherton and Barrios 2004; Durán 2013).

We extend previous processual and relational thinking by adding explicit elements of social network theory (and methods). Although understanding gangs as networks begins from a deeply relational perspective, it simultaneously complicates the very notion of "groupness." A social network perspective is, of course, relational, starting by identifying "actors" and seeking to define "relationships" among them (Wasserman and Faust 1995). From the perspective of relational social science, the network perspective requires that the social analyst provide evidence of a gang's groupness, rather than simply assume it from the outset (Morselli 2009). This is especially important in a social and research domain where (often problematic) labeling processes can influence notions of groupness as much as—if not more than—individual identification (Rios 2011). Drawing on the theory of network science as much as its method, we caution against *analytic groupism*—the idea that one can simply accept gangs as groups based on unscientific definitions (Decker and Van Winkle

1996; Desmond 2014; McGloin 2005). Instead, we urge analytically constructing "the gang" in ways that capture how these complex, evolving, and overlapping social networks are consequential for individual and collective outcomes of importance.

From a network perspective, gangs cannot be reduced to simply another "variable." The boundaries of gangs as groups are frequently fluid and, as with other social groups, contain multiple subgroupings, cliques, and pairings that might complicate definitions of the "group" or "gang" yet deeply impact individual and group behaviors. Just as a city's "gang problem" is often disproportionately built upon the violent actions associated with a small number of gangs (see **Chapter 24** in this volume), network theory prompts a question regarding how much the actions of a "violent" gang can be attributed to actions associated with subnetworks within it. The overarching insight is that the same relational perspective that has been so fruitful in the investigation of relations *between* gangs should also be extended to relations *within* them.

Figure 4.1 summarizes a network-informed relational approach to gangs. Groups are often defined by neighborhoods and tied to particular locations. So, in this case, Gangs A and B are associated with Neighborhood X, whereas Gangs D and E are associated with Neighborhood Y. Each gang has a set of "members" (the darker nodes in Figure 4.1) who are largely, but not entirely, tied more closely to members of their own crews with fewer (but not zero) ties to members of other crews. Yet not all members of a gang are strongly tied to each other; indeed, there are smaller cliques and crews within each gang. There are also ties to other cliques and crews outside of the gang that look quite "gang-like" but might not be labeled as "gangs" (e.g., the small triads above Gang A or even the small triads that are directly between Gang A and Gang B). When we look at gangs (especially groups such as Gang A or Gang E) in this way, we see the limits of analytic groupism: Group A might not be a singular, cohesive group (though an analyst might treat it as such) while, at the

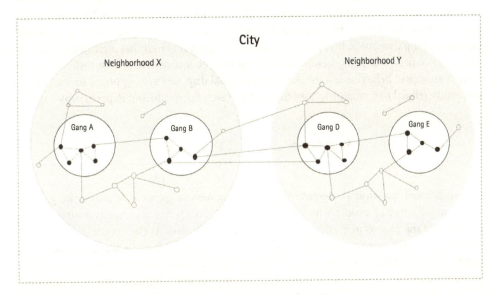

FIGURE 4.1 A Network-Informed Relational Approach to Gangs

same time, there are other "groups" not defined as gangs that can influence group behavior (like those clusters not defined as gangs but sitting in strategic positions within the neighborhood).

Still, even within this fictitious example, group boundaries (and likely group processes) do matter. Gang D and Gang E are not strongly linked (though some members have direct and indirect boundaries); they are also likely defined in opposition to each other. Similarly, there are fewer cross-neighborhood ties; yet those cross-neighborhood ties between Gang B and Gang D might very well be important sources of gang behaviors, including violence. And finally, labeling and public signaling of group status are likely to influence treatment from law enforcement, as well as rival gangs.

Our objective is not to offer yet another definition of "street gangs" but to underscore that group dynamics are an essential element of gangs. When extending group process thinking, however, we must also be cautious that we are not simply reducing gangs to a "group-level" variable analytically or theoretically. A focus on relations—especially, but not exclusively, from a network perspective—offers one productive way of understanding the gang world that is true to the behaviors of gangs and gang members themselves. Group and gang boundaries are probably much more fluid and amorphous than most social science research has given them credit for, but the group still matters. The rest of this chapter more fully explores these group processes by integrating recent research insights into the discussion.

The Dynamic Nature of Gangs

The relational nature of gangs—the idea that one gang's behaviors or identity are intertwined with those of other groups and actors—implies that gangs are dynamic rather than static phenomena. Gangs (as groups) ebb and flow over time in response to their environs and other actors in their social field, and gang members (as individuals) ebb and flow throughout gang life and behaviors.[3] While research has only recently started to apply formal relational models to gang dynamics, there is a rich history of gang research that attempts to unpack the dynamic nature of gang membership, going back to a core debate about whether gang participation and behavior is a product of individual disposition as opposed to something inherently related to group processes themselves (Sierra-Arévalo and Papachristos 2015).

Gangs as Networks

A foundational question in determining the groupness of gangs is whether the gang is simply a collective of people with certain types of characteristics or predispositions who opt into a gang (a *selection* effect) or whether the gang itself is the correlate or cause of the observed behavior (a *facilitation* effect). Added to this debate between selection and facilitation is a third possible explanation, the *enhancement* effect: that group processes amplify behaviors regardless of individual predispositions. Evidence from longitudinal studies of the facilitation and enhancement models underscores the dynamic nature of gang behaviors. When controlling for individual factors, both gang membership and levels of gang behaviors (including offending and victimization) are higher during periods of gang involvement (Pyrooz et al. 2016). In other words, gangs—and presumably some group processual element of gangs—amplify levels of such behavior. Whatever a person's "normal" levels of offending might be, they increase substantially during periods of heightened gang involvement, even when controlling for prior non-gang activity.

The groupness of gangs that likely drives facilitation and enhancement effects, we argue, rests in large part on the constellation of relationships among individuals and groups within and outside of the gang—precisely the sorts of structures and ties in the hypothetical Figure 4.1. That is, the "gang" is created, maintained, and dissolved through the relationships of (1) individuals inside and outside of the gang, and (2) groups as collective entities with each other and other groups and institutions. Such a set of network and relational ties sets the stage for gang behaviors by shaping with whom gang members interact, the sorts of situations they find themselves in, and the microprocesses that guide opinions, attitudes, and behaviors.

The gang is nothing if not the social product of the relationship among its members and the ways gang members (and non-members) are connected. The ties that bind gang members together include friendship, kinship, shared neighborhood residence, and school boundaries, and even animosity and rivalry. These ties are often what attract gang members to each other in the first place and define the boundaries of the group (however amorphous those boundaries might be). An individual, for example, joins this or that particular gang (as opposed to some other group or crew) precisely because their neighborhood peers or classmates or family members are associated with it. Such basic social boundaries often create significant network and relational boundaries within and between gangs and other actors.

Here it is useful to contrast the behavioral influence of gang relationships with school relationships. Who attends which school is influenced by both selection and facilitation. Most students have very little choice in selecting their neighborhood public schools—they simply inherit the school of the local district where they live (though their parents may have chosen a particular neighborhood *because* of its schools, i.e., selection). Other students might have been selected or applied to a specific school (if the community or city has such a "choice" process). Regardless, once a student is in a school, the pool of other students, teachers, and administrators shapes students' social networks, peer groups, activities, and so on. One's friends, classmates, teammates, and romantic partners tend to come from those school-centered networks, in part because school structures the time and interactions of young people with each other.[4] Students, for example, are much more likely to be friends with peers from the same school in large part because schools create points of socialization for similarly aged peers to interact both inside and outside the classroom.

The gang operates in a similar but differently oriented way. Just as a new student inherits a potential pool of peers, so too does a new gang associate inherit a set of relationships, friendships, and peers based on the gang and its identity and activities. Since the typical gang is smaller than school classrooms, the networks of gang members are perhaps even more densely connected, meaning members are more likely to know and interact with each other. This sort of "cohesion," as we discuss below, can be associated with deviance. But, at a minimum, it means there exists a set of relationships that can easily provide social support or surveillance, camaraderie or conflict, and status or stress, all of which can be associated with behaviors such as drug use, sexual behaviors, bullying, and deviance.

Shaping Group and External Relationships through Conflict

Gang networks also shape the relationships of individuals and groups with other individuals, institutions, and groups. Although gang boundaries are often amorphous, membership more strongly associates an individual with one group over others—which explicitly means they are *not* a part of another group (Garot 2010). One's peers and associates tend to be part of, or more closely aligned with, one's own group and the definition of group boundaries, especially neighborhood boundaries. Once again, think back to Figure 4.1: Although most gang members have ties to other gang and non-gang actors within and across neighborhood boundaries, a large share of any members' ties appear within their own group. At times, this can also mean associations with members from other groups might be fraught—especially if the group is a rival. There are whole sets of relationships that are "off limits" or at least possibly detrimental to the existing set of gang-influenced ties.

Group and external relationships within and between gangs can take different forms, including alliances, neutrality, avoidance, or indifference. But perhaps the most salient and studied relational type for the gang is *conflict*. Like Thrasher (1927), we take conflict to include conflict between gangs themselves as well as the broader notion of conflict with larger society or other social institutions within society (such as the police, schools, or formal clubs). While not necessarily the same as "violence," conflict in this context generally means conflict "with" someone or some other real or symbolic entity.

Ironically (or, perhaps, tragically), conflict—or threat of conflict—is one of the primary reasons cited for joining gangs. Perhaps the most common response to why gangs form (or why one joins a gang) is for protection. This implies a need for protection from someone or something; often other gangs are sources of neighborhood violence. A key element in gang formation, then, is not necessarily some *internal* drive but an *external* push in which groups form in response to the actions of other groups. The gang becomes the manifestation of the Musketeer-like promise of mutual protection of "all for one, and one for all"—we will come to your aid, and, in return, you will come to ours as well. This further generates a classic collective action problem that ensures a group will continue to exist, but only if members can be seen or experienced as trying to fulfill that promise (though fulfillment need not be required as much as the attempt to fulfill it) (Gould 2004).

One growing line of network-based research has demonstrated that violent acts between gangs create social ties and relational patterns that are enduring and shape future behavior (Papachristos 2009). In line with our argument here, this research shows that relational patterns of violence among gangs are durable and, at an extreme, can structure violence between groups. Our research in Chicago and Boston (Papachristos, Hureau, and Braga 2013), as well as research in Los Angeles (Tita and Radil 2011), New Jersey (McGloin 2005), and multiple cities in Canada (Airola and Bouchard 2020; Ouellet and Bouchard 2018) demonstrates that conflict between groups can generate a network structure of alliances and disputes that are associated with violence. The idea is straightforward but powerful: The animosity between groups, be they active gang wars or lingering disputes from years past, generates a set of relationships between individuals. While individuals come and go through the group, these networks of conflict (and alliances) endure—it is part of the "durability" of the gang—and is inherited by the next cohorts of gang associates. This underlying network structure, as just described, shapes identity and subsequent behaviors and activities.

Such conflict need not be real, nor need it occur in the real world. Street talk and rumor can become truth as gang mythology is used to create and exaggerate violent propensities (Felson 2006; Lauger 2012). For example, Katz (1988) posits that gangs can create "dread" to bolster the perception of themselves as violent, and recent network-oriented research by Lewis and Papachristos (2020) implies that gangs in Chicago engage in "generalized" violence that is not directly tied to a specific threat as a form of posturing to ensure their position in the larger pecking order of gangs in a particular neighborhood or social space, or at least to avoid being the bottom of the pecking order (Papachristos 2009).

Perhaps nowhere is the strategic presentation of dread more evident than in social media interactions. Research demonstrates that the online posturing and performing of gang identities is an important form of online behavior of gang members (Hsiao, Leverso and Papachristos;2023Lane 2018; Lauger and Densley 2018; Leverso and Hsiao 2021). For example, in a case study of Chicago Latinx gangs, Leverso and Hsiao (2021) observed high-level performances of exaggerated gang identities that included threatening behavior. Gang members use "the digital street" (Lane 2018) to enact performative violence; often following many of the same group-related and conflict-driven principles already discussed.

Online threats are significant on their own, even if they do not lead to real-world violence. They are manifestations of gang identity—again, frequently explicitly relational and conflictual—that likely boosts internal group feelings and sentiment. The ethnographic work of Stuart (2020) provides rich details of how one Chicago gang uses social media to bolster its own group's reputation. And while such online taunts and jabs can turn into offline violence, most often they do not. Thus, while some researchers are extremely interested in how online and offline violence relate—and research into the online–offline connections is an important area of investigation—understanding online gang behaviors independently from offline violence also provides rich insights into group processes, especially the creation of new relational forms and possibilities.

Group Dynamics and Microprocesses

Gang networks provide situations and opportunities that enhance social processes related to crime and violence, including access to weapons like firearms (Ciomek, Braga, and Papachristos 2020; Hureau and Braga 2018; Roberto, Braga, and Papachristos 2018) and even a list of enemies and allies (Conquergood 1993; Hagedorn 2015). Although individuals have agency and make decisions (see **Chapter 20**), the gang context structures situations and opportunities and, at the same time, amplifies group processes that can generate individual and corporate behavior. We argue that this emergent gang effect comes (in part) from how the gang as a collective entity structures the relationships of its associates, generates opportunities for certain types of individual and group behavior, and boosts group processes. To advance our argument we build on McGloin and Collins' (2015) review of gang group processes but advance a relational approach to understanding the group process.[5]

Opportunities and Situations

When someone is involved in a gang, the facilitation or enhancement effect simply isn't a large button saying "gang member" that one presses, releasing a host of negative outcomes, but more of a dimmer switch that activates all sorts of pathways influencing the behaviors and actions of its members. Most directly, gang involvement changes the situations one might find oneself in and the social processes that shape interactions in those situations. We argue that some of the traditional distinctions between internal and external, which rely on solidified group boundaries, might matter less than the actual patterning of social ties among individual gang actors or groups. Harkening back to Figure 4.1, there are "non-gang" ties between Gangs A and B that might drive behavior but would not be defined as either internal or external group processes.

Association with a gang and its networks generates situations that heighten possible risky interactions. In the theoretical sense, gang association changes the *routine activities* and *opportunities* of gang members by influencing the people they associate with and the situations they are in. For example, gang association might involve situations that increase one's exposure to violence or crime-heightened situations. Importantly, recent network-related research shows that some of the possible impacts of gang association extend beyond traditional group boundaries. For example, research in both Chicago (Roberto et al. 2018) and Boston (Ciomek et al. 2020) found that "social distance" to gang members (even if one is not defined as a part of a formal group boundary) correlates with access to firearms and even gunshot victimization. This is to say, gangs as collective entities shape behavior for those who might not be directly subject to either internal or external processes through the patterning of social ties.

Microprocesses and Collective Behavior

Gang involvement leads to situations where group structures and processes are activated that would not (necessarily) happen in individual contexts. Once in those situations, there are certain rules of engagement or group-level processes that shape micro- and group-level dynamics and behaviors (Lewis and Papachristos 2020). Following McGloin and Collins (2015), we consider "microprocesses" as situational mechanisms that "exist between individual-level and macro-level risks and are often the plane of intersection between the two; dynamic, situated social interactions were pivotal for understanding behaviors within and between gangs" (277).

Social Support, Mutual Protection, and Cohesion

Social support is perhaps the most foundational internal process within the gang (and many peer groups)—the sense that those in an immediate social circle understand, relate, and care for each other (Decker, Pyrooz, and Densley 2022; Vigil 1988). Social support is foundational in adolescent peer groups, friendships, co-worker and classmate ties, neighboring relationships, and kinship (Warr 2002). Those in your crew are, in theory, your "friends," or at least people you can count on for emotional and social support.

Yet social support in a more formalized group setting also carries with it obligations. For gangs, this might include expectations to hang out, be "on the block," attend certain gatherings (like meetings or parties), and so on (Garot 2010; Harding 2010). Related to exposure, such social support can morph into "peer pressure" that might make certain activities (like drinking or drug use) a part of the social experience, intertwined with social support and social status.

Mutual protection is one of the strongest sources of internal group processes (which then spill out to external ones). As discussed above, one of the most pervasive reasons for joining a gang is for protection. This fact generates a basic collective action problem that is hardwired into the gang: If a group fails to protect its members—if members fail to rally to each other's call for protection—then the group in the aggregate fails to deliver on its collective reason for existing. Threats, whether real or perceived, thus generate instances where group processes can heighten and threaten the existence and identity of the group itself (Decker and Van Winkle 1996; Thrasher 1927).

Both social support and mutual protection are related to a third core principle: *cohesion*. Broadly, the idea of cohesion refers to a sense that members believe their group is densely connected and well supported; and, in the gang context, this has been described as "the quintessential group process" shaping the social interactions of gang members and potentially the group (Klein 1997). In theory, more cohesive groups have a stronger sense of "togetherness"; members are "down" and can be counted on to, say, have your back in a fight or provide support with a problem. Following this logic, more cohesive gangs might be better able to protect their members or provide social support. They are "tighter" and potentially more dangerous. Importantly, the very same set of densely connected ties that lend a sense of "tightness" might also lead to stricter supervision of member behavior and monitoring of adherence to gang norms.

Although there is consensus that cohesion is important for gangs, the evidence as to cohesion's impact on group behavior—especially violence—is inconsistent. On one hand, scholars theorize that cohesion makes group identification stronger and, in so doing, further amplifies group processes associated with delinquency (Hennigan and Spanovic 2012; Klein 1971; Klein and Crawford 1967). On the other hand, scholars argue that low cohesion among gangs makes them less able to regulate group member behavior, rendering the group unable to control individual members from fighting with other gangs—and each other (Decker and Curry 2017; Felson 2006; Hughes 2013). Most recently Hughes (2013) was unable to find any relationship between cohesion and delinquency; rather, Hughes found prestige to be positively associated with violence, highlighting another important microprocess, the attainment of status.

Social Status

Social status, or the relative social standing of an individual or group vis-à-vis others, is another central organizing principle in the gang. The idea of status broadly aligns with other concepts such as "honor" or "respect." Regardless of the specific term, the idea refers to a social currency that is associated with "higher" or "lower" social value or position within a group or social field. Theories and empirical studies abound that link acts of violence, aggression, or other behaviors within and between gangs to a struggle for social status or standing (Anderson 2019; Gould 2004; Horowitz 1983; Short and Strodtbeck 1965). Social status is entirely relational, group based, and extremely specific to the context or a given social field (Gould 2004). This means that maintaining or achieving one's relative honor vis-à-vis a group is largely done through actions: One is perceived as "honorable" because one consistently acts in such a way that others in their social field perceive as honorable.

The gang context—and, indeed, the larger street context—contains an array of written and unwritten rules about what is or is not honorable/respectable behavior that affords social status. While these can include style, dress, language, and even the way one walks (Anderson 2000 Katz 1988), one of the most central honor-bestowing behaviors in the gang context is the willingness to defend one's reputation and that of their crew, especially through violence (Densley 2012). Such status contests can occur *within the gang*, as individuals struggle for influence among their own crew, or *between gangs*, as groups jockey for relative social standing in a particular setting (e.g., prison or the community). One of the earliest empirical examples can be found in Whyte's classic "bowling" scene in *Street Corner Society* in which the Corner Boys' relative social standing largely plays out in the ranking of bowlers: The best bowlers also happen to be the most influential leaders (Whyte 1943). Internal status seeking need not be based on violence or the threat of violence, but can also be based on various valued traits or resources. For example, Stuart's (2020) recent ethnography of a Chicago gang involved in making drill music shows that the social standing of various group members relates to different aspects they bring to the group. The person who is the actual rapper—the actual face of the group online—tends to get higher status because of his rapping skill, while a "shooter" might have relative offline standing because of a willingness to use violence. Other members with resources, such as music or computer skills, might be seen as more influential, while other "hangers-on" might just be seen as "one of the guys," part of the crew but of mediocre or general status.

Similar status struggles play out between gangs as collectives to avoid looking "weak" or to garner a tough reputation. From this perspective, struggles between gangs can be seen as dominance contests to create hierarchies or pecking orders (Lewis and Papachristos 2020; Papachristos 2009). The crucial element here is that violence is not simply dyadic, occurring between two gangs, but rather an interaction that takes place within a larger network or social field. What one gang does (or does not do) is viewed and judged by other gangs or groups in its environs. Failure to respond to a threat, for instance, is not simply viewed by the original aggressor, but also by other gangs, as weak.

METHODS

Throughout this chapter, we have attempted to stress that a relational approach to gangs is both conceptually and empirically a way of seeing and analyzing the world. Gangs are not a collection of atomized individuals acting divorced from their context but rather inhabit a world in which action, identity, and other processes emerge and feedback on a complex web of other relationships, affiliations, and actions. There is no single method that holds a monopoly over different ways of capturing the relational aspect of gangs. In fact, like approaches to other societal and scientific problems, understanding the relational aspects of gangs demands a multitude of methods.

Any relational approach to the understanding of gangs must consider several dimensions. First, nearly all network and relational studies must consider what is commonly referred to as the "boundary specification problem," the fundamental decision made by the researcher about what constitutes the (1) actors and (2) relationships in the network under investigation (Wasserman and Faust 1995). More plainly put: What are the boundaries of the network, who is eligible to be in the network, and who is not?

In a graphical sense, studying a network of any sort requires establishing a unit of analysis (the actors) and a set of relationships that can be defined on those actors: students in a school, employees at businesses, organizations in a field, and so on. The relational focus pivots on that decision. The same circumscription should apply to gang studies. One might study, for example, the sets of relationships among members of the same gang (Stuart 2020) or gangs in the same neighborhood (Vargas 2016). Or one might be interested in the conflict among all gangs in a single city (Ouellet and Bouchard 2018) or gang members in a prison (Kreager et al. 2017). Regardless, defining a single unit of analysis and then defining the system of relationship among them—that is, boundary specification—is a vital first step when considering appropriate methods.

A second key methodological (and theoretical) decision is to determine whether the analytic focus is on *global*, as opposed to *local*, processes, outcomes, or dynamics. Global network studies seek to focus on the "system as a whole," such as all the students in a school, all the inmates in a prison, or all the street gangs in a city. The focus tends to be on elucidating the structure itself—that revealing the actual structure of the entire system affords key insights into gang dynamics and processes (Morselli 2009). Here, studies of gang dynamics in entire cities fit the bill, including those in Los Angeles (Tita and Radil 2011), Newark (McGloin 2005), Boston (Papachristos et al. 2013), Toronto (Ouellet and Bouchard 2018), and Chicago (Papachristos 2009).

In contrast, network studies of *local*—or what is often called "ego-centric" analysis—focus on how an individual actor's (or unit's) immediate social network influences an outcome or process of interest. The classic version of this in network science is the importance of one's "social support" network on outcomes on a range of opinions, attitudes, and behaviors (Burt 1984). As described below, very few studies have used this approach in studying gang members, but the possibilities are many. For example, Roman, Cahill, and Mayes (2021) used a longitudinal survey approach in neighborhoods in Washington, DC, and Philadelphia to understand the ways gang members' social networks impact offending and gang desistance.

As with any study, the research question should guide the use of methods, though sometimes the availability of data also plays a role in shaping the question as well as boundary specification. For instance, reliance on official criminal justice data likely has geopolitical boundaries drawn into the data itself: Arrest records tend to cover only a particular agency, often "stopping" at geopolitical rather than social or spatial boundaries. Likewise, traditional survey data are bounded by the sample population, which may or may not allow a more in-depth examination of specific geographies or subpopulations. Conversely, any single ethnographic study likely focuses on the depth of analysis in a smaller number of locations as opposed to generalizability across multiple locations. Each of these various types of studies is, of course, needed, and results should be examined across studies of different methods and samples. The remainder of this chapter will (briefly) focus on some key methodological approaches that can be used to advance a relational understanding of gangs.

Social Surveys

Network studies have a long history of using what are known as "name generators" to construct the local networks (aka, "ego-networks") around individual survey respondents. The most common of these questions is the "important matters" question, which asks respondents to list "up to five people with whom they have discussed important matters over the last six months" (Burt 1984). After listing their responses, the respondent is then asked another series of questions about the "alters" they have listed, including sociodemographic information about alters and the relationships among alters (e.g., does person A know person B?). The result is fairly detailed information about the respondent's first-order (think, one handshake) discussion network.

Two examples of ego-network generation applied to gangs are worth noting: a survey of recently released gun offenders in Chicago (Papachristos, Meares, and Fagan 2012) and a study of gang members in two neighborhoods in Washington, DC, and Philadelphia (Roman et al. 2021).

In a survey of N = 141 individuals recently released from prison with a recent gun charge, Papachristos et al. (2012) asked respondents a series of ego-network-generating questions, including questions about possible deviant ties among individuals (e.g., "Who would have your back in the fight?" and "Who might you turn to if you needed a gun?"). The focus of this study was to understand the impact of one's ego-network (local network) on opinions toward the law. Results showed differences not only between being a gang member or not being a gang member, but also having more or fewer gang members in anyone's network (net of individual membership). Not only did gang members (in general) have more negative views of the law and its agents as "legitimate forms of authority," any respondent with a saturation of gang members in their networks (regardless of gang membership) also had more negative views.

The Connect Survey collected ego-network data on 229 gang members in Philadelphia and Washington, DC, to examine whether the networks of gang members overlapped with neighborhood networks, related to levels of delinquency, and possibly influenced desistence from crime and gang involvement (Roman et al. 2021). The survey asked a single network-generating question, a form of the "important matters" question, allowing respondents to name up to 20 people. The name generator was followed by a series of "alter questions" that asked the respondent information on the people listed, including the strength of the relationship; the alters' known gang involvement, criminal involvement, and gun-carrying behavior; and whether the respondent engaged in specific behaviors with the alter such as drinking or using drugs. There appear to be considerable changes in network composition over time relating to both pro-social and gang-related network ties. Some of these network changes were associated with reductions in criminal behavior and increases in pro-social relationships, especially for those who disengaged from gang participation. Furthermore, some suggestive evidence shows that involvement in violence reduction programs that hope to create or develop pro-social relationships might foster desistance from crime and violence.

Social Media Data

Social media data contain posts and responses associated with individual users that might readily lend themselves to relational and network analyses. Individuals comment and reply selectively based on others' posts and comments, generating networks of relationships between posters and responders. This sort of data can illuminate online relationships and dynamics among and between gangs and how/if those relationships may spill over into the real world. Leverso and Hsiao (2021) used such an approach to understand relationships between gangs on the digital street and how those interactions relate to geographic proximity. Using digital trace data, this study created relationships between users based on positive and negative gang phrases in comments and created networks of gangs' online interactions. The authors found that online interactions among gangs are conditional on the type of post. For example, posts about performances of gang identity increased negative interactions between gangs, while posts about broader street culture decreased negative interactions between gangs. Therefore, even in generally hostile spaces, interactions are still situationally dependent. The authors also found that online interactions only modestly correlated with the geographic proximity of gangs in the real world. That is, gangs that interacted online were not necessarily spatially close offline.

Administrative Records

Within the current gang research literature, a common source of networked administrated data derives from criminal justice databases, especially police or victimization records. The general premise of such data is to identify unique individuals or gangs within records and then use specific events or relationships to link them. So, for example, two individuals arrested for committing a crime together would be linked through an instance of joint arrest; in this case, the individuals are considered "co-offenders," where the units are unique individuals and the ties are joint involvement in an arrest (or simply, a co-arrest). Research by Papachristos, Wildeman, and Roberto (2015) in Chicago has relied heavily on co-offending ties such as these, and one such study demonstrated that gang members' exposure to gunshot victimization was three times higher than non-gang members, which, in turn, elevated risks of subsequent non-fatal shooting victimization. Related research also demonstrated that gang members' position within networks in both Chicago (Roberto et al. 2018) and Boston (Ciomek et al. 2020) increases their access to firearms. That is, gang members are closer to firearms than non-gang members—and increased proximity might be related to elevated levels of victimization.

A Relational Approach to Qualitative Research on Gangs

Some of the most detailed data on the relationships between gang members and gangs come from ethnographic, observational, and interview data. With deep roots in the fields of anthropology and sociology, early gang studies, including those by Thrasher (1927), Whyte (1943), Suttles (1968), as well as more contemporary ethnographers like those of Venkatesh (1997), Vargas (2016), and Patillo (2013), have provided insights into the complex and often contradictory relationships between gang members, gangs, and even their communities.

Central to ethnographic research's potential for relational insight derives from how scholars define their object of analysis (Desmond 2014). That is, scholars that set out to study "a gang" or "a corner" will develop different kinds of data and perhaps markedly different conclusions from those who seek to study the unfolding process of ongoing gang conflicts or the processes by which neighborhood people differentially come to hang and out and leave the corner. More importantly, these researchers will be endowed with very different resources for the *explanation* of the behavior they seek to study; one set of data is drawn principally from within a bounded social or geographic unit, while the other is intentionally drawn from the relations between such units. The latter represents an example of what Desmond (2014) refers to as *relational ethnography*, an ethnography built from "studying fields rather than places, boundaries rather than bounded groups, processes rather than processed people, and cultural conflict rather than group culture" (547).

Although much of the early qualitative research into gangs—especially that associated with the Chicago School of Sociology—was explicitly relational in its simultaneous focus on spatial ecology and social relations (Abbott 1997), there can be little doubt that much classic and contemporary qualitative gang research has largely accepted "the gang" as a social or geographic starting unit for analysis. We see no reason to criticize these studies, especially as many of them brought forward textural insights on gangs afforded by proximity, with several following the vectors of the groups they studied as they extended into various domains of social life (e.g., Whyte 1943). Yet to keep up with the relational turn in the social sciences, and more importantly the increased concern with gang *processes*, including the role of gangs in criminalization, maintaining boundaries, embedding members, and shaping fields of social media engagement and violence, we encourage qualitative researchers to train their analyses less on "the gang" and more on the spaces in between it and other social fields.

Conclusion

Before anything else, gangs are collective entities created through constellations of complex, overlapping social ties among and between members, their groups, and their communities. While the purposes, behaviors, and characteristics of gangs vary tremendously, most gang scholars—and gang members—recognize the primacy of "the group." This is as true of members' sociopsychological needs as it is for explaining behaviors such as crime and violence. The last several decades have seen the expansion of relational thinking and network science across the sciences, including criminology. We have argued for the (re)centering of relational thinking in gang research, which should be accounted for by an expansion and integration of methods that capture the dynamics of groups and their members. At the same time, we caution against overly reifying "the group" and, rather, encourage the use of appropriate methods to capture the dynamic, interconnected nature of the networks that create what people call "gangs."

Part of such a relational shift requires constantly remembering that gangs and gang members exist and act within larger systems and social fields. Yes, there is individual choice (see **Chapter 21** for rational choice perspectives on gangs). People have free will. But the networks of gangs and the social field of gang relations can constrain and condition behavior as much as, if not more than, the physical or invisible walls of segregation, racism, and inequality. Theories or analyses that ignore such systems or fields should at least consider how their particular findings are situated within such contexts.

This is not to say, of course, that all research should be relational or network focused. But it is meant to say that very little of the real gang behavior happens "net of everything else." In both a statistical and real-world sense, we should attend to the ways we perceive the behavior as interdependent, relational, and situated. Studies that focus on individual behavior should consider how their results might be situated within such real-world contexts or how, for instance, they might otherwise operate under conditions of interdependence. Relational thinking suggests stitching together such research with findings from other contexts to build a richer set of insights about group processes and behaviors—we have attempted to start such an effort here.

Epistemological debates are central to the sciences and the humanities. And they should be central to the field of gang research, especially as new methods, data, and empirical spaces emerge. The burgeoning world of online gang space is an excellent case in point. Expanding knowledge and fine-tuning theory is essential for good (and practical) science.

As the vignette that opened this chapter underscores, the real-world costs of ignoring relational thinking might be greater in the study of gangs than in many other social science spaces. To the extent that criminologists believe that science should inform policy and practice, ignoring the power of networks and relational thinking when designing gang interventions and policies is myopic at best. We need to advance our theories and methods for the sake of science as well as practice. Some scholars have already begun the task of translating such relational thinking into policy and programmatic frameworks. This is a crucial next step for gang research. While proceeding with caution, we hope that seeing the connection among and between gangs and gang members might lead to new approaches to reducing problematic gang behaviors that both attend to the needs of individual gang members while also navigating the tangled web of gang relations.

Notes

1. All of the names (including those of organizations) have been anonymized.
2. For a recent summary of this extensive debate, see *On Gangs* (Decker, Pyrooz, and Densley 2022).
3. Here we lean on the idea of a "social field" as offered by Bourdieu (1984) and others. Broadly, the idea of a social field refers to social environments within which conflict and competition between individuals and groups occurs within quasi-bounded social spaces (e.g., markets, art spaces, intellectual disciplines). An application of field theory to the study of gangs is a worthy area of future research that aligns with our argument here. For an example of how gangs might fit within the larger field of violence prevention or neighborhood crime, see the work of Vargas (2016) or Harding (2010).
4. This does not, of course, negate the importance of out-of-school or non-school ties. But the likelihood of forming certain ties is related most directly to whom one interacts with frequently during those structured times.
5. Our approach extends and augments McGloin and Collins (2015) in two ways. First, McGloin and Collins emphasize normative orientations, collective behavior, and status

considerations, whereas we stress how the constellation of social ties among actors shapes opportunities and situations. Second, McGloin and Collins draw somewhat clearer distinctions between internal and external processes, whereas we have problematized the boundary issues (as in Figure 4.1). We see these approaches as complementary and both in need of empirical testing, an important area of future research.

REFERENCES

Abbott, Andrew. 1997. "Of Time and Space: The Contemporary Relevance of the Chicago School." *Social Forces* 75 (4): 1149–1182.

Airola, Alice, and Martin Bouchard. 2020. "The Social Network Consequences of a Gang Murder Blowout." *Social Sciences* 9 (11): 204. doi: 10.3390/socsci9110204.

Anderson, Elijah. 2019. "Code of the Street." In *The Wiley Blackwell Encyclopedia of Urban and Regional Studies*, edited by Anthony M. Orum, 1–3. Chichester, UK: Wiley-Blackwell.

Anderson, Elijah. 2000. *Code of the Street: Decency, Violence, and the Moral Life of the Inner City*. WW Norton & Company.

Bourdieu, Pierre. 1984. *A Social Critique of the Judgement of Taste*. Translated by Richard Nice. London: Routledge.

Brotherton, David C., and Luis Barrios. 2004. *The Almighty Latin King and Queen Nation: Street Politics and the Transformation of a New York City Gang*. New York: Columbia University Press.

Burt, Ronald S. 1984. "Network Items and the General Social Survey." *Social Networks* 6 (4): 293–339.

Ciomek, Alexandra M., Anthony A. Braga, and Andrew V. Papachristos. 2020. "The Influence of Firearms Trafficking on Gunshot Injuries in a Co-Offending Network." *Social Science & Medicine* 259: 113–114. doi: 10.1016/j.socscimed.2020.113114.

Conquergood, Lorne Dwight. 1993. *Gang Communication and Cultural Space*. Evanstan, IL: Northwestern University.

Curry, G. David. 2015. "The Logic of Defining Gangs Revisited." In *The Handbook of Gangs: Wiley Handbooks in Criminology and Criminal Justice*, edited by Scott H. Decker and David C. Pyrooz, 7–27. Oxford, UK: Wiley Blackwell.

Decker, Scott H., and G. David Curry. 2017. "Gangs, Gang Homicides, and Gang Loyalty: Organized Crimes or Disorganized Criminals." *Journal of Criminal Justice* 30 (4): 343–352.

Decker, Scott H., David C. Pyrooz, and James A. Densley. 2022. *On Gangs*. Philadelphia, PA: Temple University Press.

Decker, Scott H., and Barrik Van Winkle. 1996. *Life in the Gang: Family, Friends, and Violence*. Cambridge, UK: Cambridge University Press.

Densley, James A. 2012. "Street Gang Recruitment: Signaling, Screening, and Selection." *Social Problems* 59 (3): 301–321.

Desmond, Matthew. 2014. "Relational Ethnography." *Theory & Society* 43 (1): 547–579.

Durán, Robert. 2013. *Gang Life in Two Cities: An Insider's Journey*. New York: Columbia University Press.

Felson, Marcus. 2006. "The Street Gang Strategy." In *Crime and Nature*, 305–324. Thousand Oaks, CA: Sage Publications.

Garot, Robert. 2010. *Who You Claim*. New York: New York University Press.

Gould, Roger V. 2004. *Collision of Wills*. Chicago, IL: University of Chicago Press.

Hagedorn, John M. 2015. *The Insane Chicago Way*. Chicago, IL: University of Chicago Press.

Harding, David J. 2010. *Living the Drama: Community, Conflict, and Culture among Inner-City Boys*. Chicago, IL: University of Chicago Press.

Hennigan, Karen, and Marija Spanovic. 2012. "Gang Dynamics through the Lens of Social Identity Theory." In *Youth Gangs in International Perspective*, edited by Finn-Aage Esbensen and Charyl L. Maxson, 127–149. New York: Springer.

Horowitz, Ruth. 1983. *Honor and the American Dream: Culture and Identity in a Chicano Community*. New Brunswick, NJ: Rutgers University Press.

Hsiao, Yuan, John Leverso, and Andrew V. Papachristos. 2023. "The Corner, the Crew, and the Digital Street: Multiplex Networks of Gang Online-Offline Conflict Dynamics in the Digital Age." *American Sociological Review* 88 (4): 709–741.

Hughes, Lorine A. 2013. "Group Cohesiveness, Gang Member Prestige, and Delinquency and Violence in Chicago, 1959–1962." *Criminology* 51 (4): 795–832. doi: 10.1111/1745-9125.12020.

Hureau, David M., and Anthony A. Braga. 2018. "The Trade in Tools: The Market for Illicit Guns in High-Risk Networks." *Criminology* 56 (3): 510–545.

Katz, Jack. 1988. *Seductions of Crime: Moral and Sensual Attractions in Doing Evil*. New York: Basic Books.

Klein, Malcolm W. 1997. *The American Street Gang: Its Nature, Prevalence, and Control*. New York: Oxford University Press.

Klein, Malcolm. 1971. *Street Gangs and Street Workers*. Englewood Cliffs, NJ: Prentice-Hall.

Klein, Malcolm W., and Lois Y. Crawford. 1967. "Groups, Gangs, and Cohesiveness." *Journal of Research in Crime and Delinquency* 4 (1): 63–75.

Klein, Malcolm W., and Cheryl L. Maxson. 2010. *Street Gang Patterns and Policies*. Oxford, UK: Oxford University Press.

Kreager, Derek A., Jacob T. N. Young, Dana L. Haynie, Martin Bouchard, David R. Schaefer, and Gary Zajac. 2017. "Where 'Old Heads' Prevail: Inmate Hierarchy in a Men's Prison Unit." *American Sociological Review* 82 (4): 685–718. doi: 10.1177/0003122417710462.

Lane, Jeffrey. 2018. *The Digital Street*. New York: Oxford University Press.

Lauger, Timothy R. 2012. *Real Gangstas*. New Brunswick, NJ: Rutgers University Press.

Lauger, Timothy R., and James A. Densley. 2018. "Broadcasting Badness: Violence, Identity, and Performance in the Online Gang Rap Scene." *Justice Quarterly* 35 (5): 816–841. doi: 10.1080/07418825.2017.1341542.

Leverso, John, and Yuan Hsiao. 2021. "Gangbangin on the [Face]Book: Understanding Online Interactions of Chicago Latina/o Gangs." *Journal of Research in Crime and Delinquency* 58 (3): 239–268. doi: 10.1177/0022427820952124.

Lewis, Kevin, and Andrew V. Papachristos. 2020. "Rules of the Game: Exponential Random Graph Models of a Gang Homicide Network." *Social Forces* 98 (4): 1829–1858. doi: 10.1093/sf/soz106.

McGloin, Jean Marie. 2005. "Policy and Intervention Considerations of a Network Analysis of Street Gangs." *Criminology & Public Policy* 4 (3): 607–635. doi: 10.1111/j.1745-9133.2005.00306.x.

McGloin, Jean M., and Megan E. Collins. 2015. "Micro-Level Processes of the Gang." In *The Handbook of Gangs: Wiley Handbooks in Criminology and Criminal Justice*, edited by Scott H. Decker and David C. Pyrooz, 276–293. Oxford, UK: Wiley Blackwell.

Morselli, Carlo. 2009. *Inside Criminal Networks*. Vol. 8. Springer.

Ouellet, Marie, and Martin Bouchard. 2018. "The 40 Members of the Toronto 18: Group Boundaries and the Analysis of Illicit Networks." *Deviant Behavior* 39 (11): 1467–1482. doi: 10.1080/01639625.2018.1481678.

Papachristos, Andrew V. 2009. "Murder by Structure: Dominance Relations and the Social Structure of Gang Homicide." *American Journal of Sociology* 115 (1): 74–128. doi: 10.1086/597791.

Papachristos, Andrew V., David M. Hureau, and Anthony A. Braga. 2013. "The Corner and the Crew: The Influence of Geography and Social Networks on Gang Violence." *American Sociological Review* 78 (3): 417–447. doi: 10.1177/0003122413486800.

Papachristos, Andrew V., Christopher Wildeman, and Elizabeth Roberto. 2015. "Tragic, but Not Random: The Social Contagion of Nonfatal Gunshot Injuries." *Social Science & Medicine* 125: 139–150.

Papachristos, Andrew V., Tracey L. Meares, and Jeffrey Fagan. 2012. "Why Do Criminals Obey the Law? The Influence of Legitimacy and Social Networks on Active Gun Offenders Criminology." *Journal of Criminal Law and Criminology* 102 (2): 397–440.

Pattillo, Mary. 2013. *Black Picket Fences: Privilege and Peril among the Black Middle Class*. Chicago, IL: University of Chicago Press.

Pyrooz, David C., and Meghan M. Mitchell. 2015. "Little Gang Research, Big Gang Research." In *The Handbook of Gangs: Wiley Handbooks in Criminology and Criminal Justice*, edited by Scott H. Decker and David C. Pyrooz, 28–58. Oxford, UK: Wiley Blackwell.

Pyrooz, David C., Jillian J. Turanovic, Scott H. Decker, and Jun Wu. 2016. "Taking Stock of the Relationship between Gang Membership and Offending: A Meta-Analysis." *Criminal Justice and Behavior* 43 (3): 365–397.

Rios, Victor M. 2011. *Punished: Policing the Lives of Black and Latino Boys*. New York: New York University Press.

Roberto, Elizabeth, Anthony A. Braga, and Andrew V. Papachristos. 2018. "Closer to Guns: The Role of Street Gangs in Facilitating Access to Illegal Firearms." *Journal of Urban Health* 95 (3): 372–382. doi: 10.1007/s11524-018-0259-1.

Roman, Caterina G., Meagan Cahill, and Lauren R. Mayes. 2021. "Changes in Personal Social Networks across Individuals Leaving Their Street Gang: Just What Are Youth Leaving Behind?" *Social Sciences* 10 (2): 39. doi: 10.3390/socsci10020039.

Short, James F., and Fred L. Strodtbeck. 1965. *Group Process and Gang Delinquency*. Chicago, IL: University of Chicago Press.

Sierra-Arévalo, Michael, and Andrew V. Papachristos. 2015. "Social Network Analysis and Street Gangs." In *The Handbook of Gangs: Wiley Handbooks in Criminology and Criminal Justice*, edited by Scott H. Decker and David C. Pyrooz, 157–177. Oxford, UK: Wiley Blackwell.

Stuart, Forrest. 2020. *Ballad of the Bullet*. Princeton, NJ: Princeton University Press.

Suttles, Gerald D. 1968. *Social Order of the Slum: Ethnicity and Territory in the Inner City*. Chicago, IL: University of Chicago Press.

Thrasher, Frederic Milton. 1927. *The Gang: A Study of 1,313 Gangs in Chicago*. Chicago, IL: University of Chicago Press.

Tita, George E., and Steven M. Radil. 2011. "Spatializing the Social Networks of Gangs to Explore Patterns of Violence." *Journal of Quantitative Criminology* 27 (4): 521–545. doi: 10.1007/s10940-011-9136-8.

Vargas, Robert. 2016. *Wounded City: Violent Turf Wars in a Chicago Barrio*. New York: Oxford University Press.

Venkatesh, Sudhir Alladi. 1997. "The Social Organization of Street Gang Activity in an Urban Ghetto." *American Journal of Sociology* 103 (1): 82–111. doi: 10.1086/231172.

Vigil, James Diego. 1988. "Group Processes and Street Identity: Adolescent Chicano Gang Members." *Ethos* 16 (4): 421–445.

Warr, Mark. 2002. *Companions in Crime: The Social Aspects of Criminal Conduct*. Cambridge, UK: Cambridge University Press.

Wasserman, Stanley and Katherine Faust. 1995. *Social Network Analysis: Methods and Applications*. Cambridge, UK: Cambridge University Press.

Whyte, William Foote. 1943. *Street Corner Society: The Social Structure of an Italian Slum*. Chicago, IL: University of Chicago Press.

CHAPTER 5

GANGS IN PRACTICE
Violence Prevention, Law Enforcement, and the Received Idea of the "Gang"

DAVID M. KENNEDY

THE last several decades have seen the emergence of "evidence-based" violence prevention, meaning a portfolio of interventions that meet formal scholarly evidentiary standards for effectiveness (Braga, Weisburd, and Turchan 2019; National Academies of Sciences 2018; Branas et al. 2020). That development has, in the United States, risen to the level of being recognized and supported at the highest policy levels, including recently being highlighted by the Biden Administration in a national initiative supported by unprecedented levels of federal funding (White House 2021). The most prominent interventions in this portfolio, and the ones with the strongest evidence base and broadest range of field experience, are the focused deterrence "group violence intervention" (Braga, Weisburd, and Turchan 2019; National Academies of Sciences 2018) and street outreach (Pugliese et al. 2022).[1] Both of these interventions are built around what is perhaps the most salient empirical fact about what is currently being called "community violence" that has also emerged over the last several decades: that it is driven by dynamics involving a remarkably small number of people at extraordinarily high risk for both violent victimization and violent perpetration, most often operating not primarily as individuals but in groups and networks, and involved in patterns of retaliation and vendetta embedded in those groups and networks (Braga and Kennedy 2021).

Notably absent from those findings about violence, its underlying presentation and dynamics, and what works to prevent it is any mention of gangs. The Biden Administration's initiative refers to material citing the most salient facts about community violence, which states that it "takes place in under-resourced neighborhoods," "disproportionately impacts Black and Hispanic/Latino communities, specifically young Black and Hispanic/Latino men," "usually occurs outside of the home in a public setting," "occurs between individuals who are not intimately related," "often is sparked by a dispute between individuals or groups and may be retaliatory as a result of long-standing conflicts," and is "sometimes referred to as 'urban violence' or 'group violence'" (Educational Fund to Stop Gun Violence 2021). The concentration of violence is such that:

> Analyses in a variety of cities have found that small networks of individuals—sometimes as few as a couple hundred—are involved in most of the city's shootings. In Oakland, for instance, just 0.1% of the population was responsible for the majority of the city's homicides, while in New Orleans, networks of 600 to 700 individuals are linked to most of the city's murders. Even within Chicago's highest violence neighborhoods, those who have a social network in which someone was murdered are 900% more likely to die of homicide than neighboring residents. (Educational Fund to Stop Gun Violence 2021)

The absence of gangs and gang talk in this context will seem, to many, peculiar in the extreme: High levels of violence in poor minority neighborhoods driven by very small, very active groups of young men locked in lethal cycles of retaliation and vendetta is, after all, essentially the definition of a gang problem. But the focused deterrence group violence intervention uses the term "group" in an explicit rejection of the term "gang,"[2] and a review of the website for CureViolence, perhaps the most nationally prominent street outreach organization, reveals no references to gangs: This despite the fact that the group violence intervention has its roots in Boston's Operation Ceasefire, which was explicitly aimed at gang violence (Braga, Hureau, and Papachristos 2014, 113–139), and street outreach has its roots in the "detached streetworker" gang intervention tradition dating back to the mid-twentieth century (National Council on Crime and Delinquency 2009).[3]

This can be seen as in keeping with a long history of difficulty with, and controversy over, the term. It's no secret that within gang scholarship the idea and definition of a "gang" have been essentially impossible to pin down, to the degree that the study of the history of definitions of gangs has become itself a subspecialty (Ball and Curry 1995, 224–245). Definitions have ranged from the largely innocuous early observation by Puffer that boys inhabit "the family, the neighborhood, and the play group; but for the normal boy, the play group is the gang" (Ball and Curry 1995, 233) to the positively baroque. Spergel suggested drawing on the definition developed by the Eurogang Program of Research as it studied youth group violence in the European context (Esbensen and Maxson 2012, 1–14), to wit:

> A youth gang is any durable and variably organized street-oriented group of juveniles, mainly adolescents, and young adults, located in, perceived to be, and deriving from socioeconomically and culturally marginalized community and institutional contexts, which may include the presence and influence of adult criminal organization. (Spergel 2009, 672)

The result has been that "at no time has there been anything close to consensus on what a gang might be—by scholars, by criminal justice workers, by the general public" (Miller 1975, 115, quoted in Ball and Curry).

It may be, however, that this is more true for scholars—for whom it certainly is true—than it is for criminal justice practitioners and for the public. There, experience would suggest, there is very much a sense of what "gang" means, and that same experience would suggest that that sense is very powerful and, in its own way, very much a problem. Scholars have paid a great deal of attention to the academic definitions of "gang"—where they come from and how they do and don't work—but there has been no such tradition of unpacking the same issues for practitioners and the public. I attempt here the beginning of that project.

THE RECEIVED IDEA OF THE GANG

Working in the field reveals very clearly that there is a quite well-articulated, powerful, and consequential sense of what "gang" means. Scholars may not know exactly what a gang is, but the Federal Bureau of Investigation (FBI) is clear and typifies these mainstream ideas: "Some 33,000 violent street gangs, motorcycle gangs, and prison gangs are criminally active in the U.S. today," the FBI says. "Many are sophisticated and well organized; all use violence to control neighborhoods and boost their illegal money-making activities, which include robbery, drug and gun trafficking, prostitution and human trafficking, and fraud" (Federal Bureau of Investigation 2016). Gangs, in this mainstream sense, are large, purposeful organizations; often with national and even transnational spans of activity; with leadership, hierarchy, and structure; with rules for entry and exit and mechanisms to recruit new members; committed to making money and exercising territorial, market, and other kinds of control; and using violence in pursuit of all those ends.

Something very close to this is sometimes articulated explicitly, as with the FBI, but more often it can be found as astrophysics found Pluto: through evidence of the influence of invisible but powerful forces. I have written elsewhere how the Boston Gun Project team picked up the "gang" framing from our practitioner partners in Boston, who used it to refer to the small, fluid drug crews that had developed in Boston with the advent of crack-era street drug markets. We used that framing without issue in Boston; it was uncontroversial in Minneapolis, the first replication site for the strategy; in Baltimore, the next stop, it was catastrophic. There, "gang" meant something quite specific to the police we were working with: large, structured, criminal enterprises with leadership, rules, and purpose, which, as they saw it, Baltimore and its superheated street drug scene did not have. Our use of the word was itself enough to undermine our credibility and even integrity, since officers saw it as playing to out-of-touch department leadership and politicians, who also used "gang" language (Kennedy 2011).

We found ourselves in a defensive crouch, explaining that in Boston the word hadn't meant "structured and organized" at all, but rather small, usually disorganized, usually leaderless, largely chaotic neighborhood networks. What would you call what you are dealing with, we asked? "Neighborhood networks," the line cops said, and that's the term we used in the Baltimore project. The use of the term "gang" turned out to be a major impediment to clear thinking and action around violence. In city after city and setting after setting, the received idea of a gang stopped actual analysis and work cold: "We don't have real gangs," people said; "we do have real gangs, so those programs that worked for not-real gangs won't work here"; "our gangs don't look like that other city's gangs"; "we have 'hybrid' gangs, so we need a different approach"; "we used to have real gangs but there's no structure now"; and on and on and on.

But, at the same time, in literally every setting in which we worked in the United States and internationally, if we began with an examination of violence, that examination led to a concentration of perpetration and victimization involving groups. They might be Chicago "gangs" or factions, or Sureno and Norteno cliques in Los Angeles, or the loose drug crews we were used to from Boston, or small sets of older guys supplying weight drugs to neighborhood sets, or the rare but real organized crime network. But they were always groups, and just punting on the "gang" question lost the applied work absolutely nothing and made it immeasurably easier to see, document, analyze, and act around those facts. Our work going forward defaulted to the simpler and obvious "groups."

That usage is not now uncommon, but even so is often used in ways that underscore the salience and staying power of key notions about "gangs." A criminal justice official in Kalamazoo, Michigan, spoke to the distinction between those that are "real" gangs and those that aren't:

"There's no Vice Lords or Crips. Those are gangs. In L.A., they have gangs," says Boysen, the assistant chief of the Kalamazoo Department of Public Safety. "We don't have gangs in Kalamazoo. But we have street groups. We have cliques. We have North Side groups. We have South Side groups. We have East Side groups. And we know who they are." (Jones 2020)

It may be possible to trace the origins and development of this core practitioner and public idea of what a "gang" is. Anything like that is beyond the scope of this chapter. In practice, the basic idea is deeply entrenched and fits neatly with the other two core received ideas about how crime is organized: the dangerous solo offender on the low end, "gangs" in the midfield, and "organized crime" on the high end. The FBI, again, formalizes this view in the Supplementary Homicide Reports (SHRs) that are submitted by reporting law enforcement agencies as part of the Uniform Crime Reporting Program (UCR), which contain expanded information about homicides. The category appropriate to this discussion is "gangland killings," evoking the tommy-gun-era of Prohibition gangs at issue when the UCR was instituted in 1929, but already well out of date when the SHR was added in the early 1960s (Regoeczi et al. 2014, 1).

The two US cities generally recognized as major "gang" centers, Los Angeles and Chicago, contributed to the notions of categorizing homicide and other crimes as "gang related" and "gang motivated," respectively (Maxson and Klein 1990, 70). The first counted a crime if it was committed by a gang member, the second only if "it exhibits qualities of a gang motive, such as retaliation, initiation, or defending gang turf" (Rosenfeld, Bray, and Egley 1999, 498). This led to lively debates in both scholarly and practitioner circles about which definition was most realistic and how to interpret the picture of gang crime each produced. Less obvious was the fact that *both* definitions imported the core idea that "gang" meant something sufficiently defined, structured, and purposeful that determining membership and motive were both coherent and possible, and that "motive" in this usage imported ideas of both a more or less corporate structure and coherent interests linked to that structure and its interests.

The power of this image of the gang as a structured, purposeful entity was clearly visible in the position of police departments in other US cities that they had little or no gang problems, because they did not have what they saw as Los Angeles- or Chicago-style gangs. When the US Department of Justice established the Strategic Approaches to Community Safety Initiative (SACSI) to replicate the Boston Gun Project's action-research approach to public safety (Dalton 2002, 16), participating federal prosecutors from member city New Haven, Connecticut, were vociferous that they had eliminated gang activity in their city through a statewide federal takedown of the Latin Kings (Mahony 1995). Urged by SACSI technical advisors to ask front-line New Haven Police Department officers what was driving gun crime in the city, they came back with the answer: small, disorganized neighborhood drug crews, for which neither they nor the New Haven Police Department had any language to describe and to which neither had been paying, as such, any official attention. The New York Police Department had long held that it had no meaningful gang problem when, in 2012, then-commissioner Ray Kelly announced a focus on "crews." The "Crew Cut" initiative, Kelly said, would target:

> [not] large, established gangs such as the Bloods and Crips, but [the] looser associations of younger men who identify themselves by the block they live on, or on which side of a housing development they reside. Their loyalty is to their friends living in a relatively small area and their rivalries are based not on narcotics trafficking or some other entrepreneurial interest, but simply on local turf. (Esposito 2012)

These not-gangs, Kelly said—previously given neither formal recognition nor any concerted attention by the department—were responsible for nearly a third of the city's shootings (Esposito 2012).

These core ideas about gangs—that *real* gangs were typified by those found in Los Angeles and Chicago and meant size, structure, and purpose—were steadily marketed to police departments, corrections agencies, and schools throughout at least the latter part of the last century and the early years of this century by a cottage industry of self-styled "gang experts." These were mostly current and ex-law enforcement, with a sprinkling of former gang members, who sold "trainings" that presented a coherent, terrifying, and utterly factitious picture of gangs, always with the explicit message that the recipients, whoever they might be, were losing an invisible war with an organized and malevolent enemy and that Armageddon was looming.[4] These "trainings" generally took the form of caricatured accounts of Bloods, Crips, Latin Kings, People, Folk, MS-13, and other "national" and "transnational" gangs; terrifying photographs of alleged gang members—invariably Black or Brown men—murders, crime scenes, tattoos, graffiti, heaps of drugs, stacks of weapons, and the like; breathless explanations of alleged gang methods of secret communications—colors, crowns, stars, pitchforks, hats, socks, numbers, words with dropped or added letters, hand gestures, and on and on; and the twin messages that these gangs were coming for your community and your kids, and that one of the kids they had recruited could be standing right next to you and planning to kill you *right now* and you'd never know it, because you didn't understand the deadly significance of his one sock being rolled down. Nearly always there was the message that any sort of local delinquency would inexorably grow into organized gang structures if it wasn't caught early, and the weary message that "if we'd stopped this early in Los Angeles/Chicago/wherever we wouldn't have lost the war, so don't do what we did then and *act now*." Not one of the countless such briefings I've experienced ever offered any practical advice about what the locals could actually *do* about the looming terror.

The impact of these presentations was often profound, with officials and parents essentially convinced that they were engaged in and losing an invisible war. I came to have particular sympathy for police school resource officers, who were particular targets for this industry and not surprisingly often believed what they were told, and as a result frequently became fevered messengers that gangs were coming to wreak havoc by turning junior high school students into a secret army, and that they could stop what was otherwise inevitable if only someone—their own department, the schools, parents, somebody—would listen. The deluge, of course, never actually came.

The focus on young people—juveniles, with whatever local legal meaning that term carried, and the more generalized "youth"—is another important aspect of the received idea of the "gang." Whether explicit, as in the common construction of "youth gang," or implicit, "gang" in this common sense carries the connotation of being composed of and being about young people. This fits with, adds to, and is furthered by the public perception that homicide and serious violence, particularly in communities of color, is driven by juveniles—a perception that is profoundly inaccurate but has tremendous staying power.[5] The city studies that have informed the development of evidence-based violence prevention typically show less than 10% of homicide and non-fatal shootings to be associated with juveniles as victim, offender, or both; and yet criminal justice and community participants in such cities routinely believe, before seeing those findings, that most such violence involves juveniles, and generally that it is worsening.[6] Experience has shown that where genuinely dangerous juveniles are in fact found, they nearly always are associated with groups composed largely of adult men; actively violent standalone groups of juveniles are nearly unheard of. The local conviction that "gangs" are a juvenile issue can be aggregated into national "findings," as when agency self-reporting conveys it as a fact, for example, to the FBI's National Gang Intelligence Center (NGIC). The 2011 National Gang Threat Assessment from the NGIC reported "that juvenile gangs are responsible for a majority of crime in various jurisdictions in Arizona, California, Connecticut, Florida, Georgia, Illinois, Maryland, Michigan, Missouri, North Carolina, New Hampshire, South Carolina, Texas, Virginia, and Washington" (Federal Bureau of Investigation 2011). "Facts" like these are dramatically, ludicrously wrong but serve to perpetuate the framing of "gangs" as about juveniles.

It's also the case that there is a clear and irreconcilable contradiction between the other aspects of the received idea of "gangs" and the identification of "gangs" with juveniles. It is obviously nonsensical to hold that gangs are organized, hierarchical, purposeful, focused on profit and territory, and expansionist—and that they are composed of kids. That this is self-evidently ludicrous does not keep it from being routinely believed in practice.

Finally, for these purposes, the received idea of a "gang" holds that violence is used in furtherance of core gang interests: to make money, to gain and protect turf, and the like. To quote NYPD Commissioner Kelly again, "narcotics trafficking or some other entrepreneurial interest." This fits neatly with the central idea that gangs are organized and purposeful. The FBI's 2011 National Gang Assessment reported that:

> many gangs have advanced beyond their traditional role as local retail drug distributors in large cities to become more organized, adaptable, and influential in large-scale drug trafficking. Gang members are migrating from urban areas to suburban and rural communities to recruit new members, expand their drug distribution territories, form new alliances, and collaborate with rival gangs and criminal organizations for profit and influence. (Federal Bureau of Investigation 2011)

Working with local police and prosecutors—and with front-line community groups—shows how routine this understanding is. It is absolutely contradicted by the city studies that have supported evidence-based violence prevention. The overwhelming preponderance of group-related violence is driven by respect issues, retaliation, vendetta, and the like; typically, under one-fifth of homicides and non-fatal woundings have anything to do with money, even when robberies, retaliation for drug robberies and bad deals, and similar situations are included in that category. The Oakland example is again illustrative; the city "knew" that the violence there was driven by the drug trade, but actual analysis showed that only 13% of incidents had any connection to drugs, and the violence was actually driven by "specific running group/gang conflicts and personal disputes between group members" (California Partnership for Safe Communities 2021).

As with other aspects of the idea of a "gang," notions of economic and turf competition are often imported into interpretation and then become known "facts." When the New Jersey State Police were running violence prevention operations in Irvington, adjacent to Newark, a team leader took me to what was then the hottest spot, a public housing area. "It's a turf war between two drug groups," he told me. Asked how he knew it was a turf war, his puzzled answer was that the violence was between the drug groups. Such assumptions are both driven by and sustain the core idea that gangs use violence for clear economic and related purposes, even as actual analysis consistently shows otherwise.

Consequences of the Received Idea

Perhaps the most important result of the received idea of a "gang" is that it has made practitioners, policymakers, reporters, and the like blind to what has, all along, been there for the seeing. Evidence-based violence prevention, as has been noted, has built over the last several decades on readily ascertainable facts on the ground: that community violence is driven by groups, that those groups are composed of both perpetrators and victims of violence, and that violence is overwhelmingly driven not by economic motives but by the street code, social friction, group dynamics like peer pressure, retaliation and vendettas between groups, the sustaining of "beef" even as groups largely or completely turn over at the level of individual membership, and the like. None of this was in any way obscure; as I've written elsewhere, that picture (and an associated form of effective intervention) was delivered by front-line practitioners in literally the first meeting of the Boston Gun Project in 1995 (Kennedy 2011). It has invariably been borne out since then by extremely simple research methods, which consist primarily of systematic mixed-method reviews of groups and violent incidents (Kennedy, Braga, and Piehl 1997, 219–262). Beyond that, those decades have shown that simply asking knowledgeable law enforcement, community, social service, and group-involved people the question "Is what is going on in your community driven by extremely active groups, who do some violence and an awful lot of other crime, and is it mostly about respect, retaliation, and vendetta?" invariably gets a response in the affirmative.

This should have been obvious to both scholars and practitioners. Scholars can find its roots in, among others, Wolfgang, Filgio, and Sellin (1987), Matza (1964), Klein (1984, 185), and Anderson (2000). Practitioners don't need a bibliography; it is what they deal with every day and it is there simply for the seeing. It was not seen and understood, by either party, in large part because of the power of the received idea of the gang and the way it has been worked into what we look for, what we see, how we understand it, and how that becomes reified in our institutions, our discourse, our research, our reporting, and—not at all least—our laws and our interventions. It should not have taken a National Institute of Justice–funded research project to bring to the surface that groups representing 1% of their age group were associated with 60% of the youth homicide in Boston (Kennedy, Braga, and Piehl 2001) any more than it should have taken the invention of the notion of a "crew" to allow the NYPD to see what was driving a third of the shootings in New York. In this, as in many other things, it turns out that one has to be pretty sophisticated to be this stupid.

Beyond that, the real world of high-risk groups and networks, and those in them, are in many important ways not what we think they are—something that can usually be ascertained simply by looking at easily available facts. Local groups are not colonizers sent by shadowy figures in Chicago, Los Angeles, and El Salvador to take over drug markets and murder mothers in their sleep. Juveniles are not the issue here mostly at all; they are certainly not at the heart of any gang or violence problem, and they are emphatically not "getting younger and younger" (I've been hearing this for some 30 years now, making the core of the gang problem mathematically prenatal). Gangs are (overwhelmingly) not structured, purposeful, and predatory; they do not use violence predominantly to make money or "in the interest of" the gang—in fact, most of their violence is bad for any business they do, since it is the one thing most likely to bring legal and public attention. They are not monolithic or disciplined, and most people in them are not particularly dangerous or committed to violence. The Boston practitioners who first taught the Boston Gun Project team these essentials reckoned that perhaps one or two people per "gang" were what they called "impact players," which has generally held out over many cities and groups since.[7] The mythmaking about even the storied "real" gangs in Los Angeles and Chicago is wrong, according to those who were there: "'A lot of people think that there's a level of sophistication within the gang culture like the Mafia,' says Aqeela Sherrills, an original LA Crip and now a nationally prominent violence prevention practitioner. 'Not at all. There's no organization, there's no nothing'" (Duane 2006).

These misrepresentations have real consequences. In one direction, we can look for something—the received idea of a "gang"—not find it, and thus miss entirely what is really going on. Since the last decades have in fact shown that groups that are not like the "gangs" people are looking for are the prime locus for both perpetration and victimization in community violence, when we miss that we miss something critically important.

In the other direction, we can see something real and misunderstand what it is, as is the case when groups as they really are have our presumptions about "gangs" mapped onto them. In the aftermath of the NYPD's discovery of "crews," for example, the NYPD and New York City prosecutors undertook a series of legal conspiracy cases against what they regarded as criminal organizations in the city's public housing projects. Speri describes one of them:

> In total, some 700 officers from an array of local and federal agencies, as well as helicopters and armored vehicles, swarmed the Eastchester Gardens projects and other public housing buildings in this section of the Bronx in the early hours of April 27. Officers from the NYPD gang squad, as well as the Drug Enforcement Administration, Immigration and Customs Enforcement, and the Bureau of Alcohol, Tobacco, Firearms, and Explosives, were targeting two rival gangs. (Mattison said there are actually three gangs, and officials conflated two in their indictment.) Eighty-eight people were arrested in the blitz, which also led to new, federal charges against several people who were already serving time. In two separate indictments, the defendants, identified by their names and a variety of street names, were charged with racketeering conspiracy, narcotics conspiracy, narcotics distribution, and firearms offenses. (Speri 2016)

These operations were expressly framed around violence prevention. By contrast, the evidence-based violence prevention strategies that employ deterrence and law enforcement—informed by the recognition that "gangs" are not in fact monolithic and most of those involved are not particularly violent—have pared that element down to the degree that in Oakland, for example, operations frequently restrict arrest and prosecution to actual shooters, with other group members receiving supportive interventions (Crandall 2023).

Even as the understanding of groups, group dynamics, and their connection to violence has taken root, one can see the old, dominant framing playing out. One regularly encounters a kind of reverse origin story: Having taken, for the first time, a careful look at a city's groups, local people will respond with a narrative about how things have changed since the (imaginary) time when gangs were *real* gangs. "This may be what it's like *now*," they'll say, "but it *used* to be different . . ." Given the chaos that in fact characterizes group violence, this is often cast as a kind of golden age, when gangs had structure, they observed decencies ("we'd never shoot somebody in front of their mother"), violence was *for a good reason* rather than some nonsense about disrespect, and the like. This kind of thing is prevalent even in "gang" cities like Chicago, where both law enforcement and gang members will bemoan the good old days when the gangs had real leadership and structure, apparently oblivious to the fact that in those "good old days" the homicide counts were dramatically high (Chicago saw nearly 1,000 homicides in 1974, over 900 in 1992, and slightly more than 400 in the early years of the last decade, well into the time of the alleged "decay" of Chicago's gangs; even the city's current homicide spike does not reach those earlier levels).

The same thing played out nationally as the FBI and other clearinghouse sources of gang information reported on a steadily worsening national gang picture. The Department of Justice's National Gang Center's National Youth Gang Survey showed an ominous growth in gangs and gang membership between 2003 and 2012, from 20,100 gangs to 30,700, and from about 710,000 gang members to 850,000 (National Gang Center 2022). Over that time homicide *fell* nationally, from 16,503 to 14,168 (Federal Bureau of Investigation 2003; Federal Bureau of Investigation 2012).

There has in fact been time enough for a sort of reverse origin story to emerge about the Boston Gun Project's Operation Ceasefire and the analytical and operational portfolio that emerged from it. That work showed the concentration of violence in "gangs," which weren't what people thought of as gangs because they were in no way organized, structured, and purposeful, and developed an effective intervention for that fact pattern. In the new cities we work in, we now not infrequently hear that *that* intervention won't work *here*, because our groups are in no way organized, structured, and purposeful, and Boston had *real* gangs . . .

Gang Scholarship and the Front Lines

None of this is to say that the vast body of gang scholarship is beside the point if one important body of applied violence prevention work is to focus on "groups" and group dynamics in conscious distinction from a focus on gangs. To the contrary, since that applied focus indeed is on groups, and all gangs are groups, all of gang scholarship is of potential interest. That has been the fact in practice. That portfolio of applied work has drawn widely from gang scholarship. A partial roster would include the Boston Gun Project's attention to Miller's seminal early research on Boston gangs (in which gang dynamics at work in the 1990s are clearly evident; Miller 2011); classic scholarship on patterns of gang criminality and violence (Klein 1984, 185); Matza's brilliant application of social psychology to gang dynamics (Matza 1964); examinations of how both gang-involved and non-gang-involved youth navigate gang neighborhoods (Garot 2010); ethnographies of the drug gangs that arose in the crack era (Bourgois 2003; Williams 1990); scholarship on how those drug gangs changed generationally in response to the era's tsunami of addiction and violence (Johnson, Golub, and Dunlap 2000, 164–206); research on the economics of street-level drug dealing (not a good career choice, mythology to the contrary notwithstanding; MacCoun and Reuter 1992, 477–491); research into the norms that shape violence dynamics (Anderson 2000; Wilkinson 1998); research showing that the movement of gangs to new cities is overwhelmingly driven by ordinary social processes rather than purposeful, malign expansion strategies (Maxson 1997); research into the phenomenon of thoroughly local groups "claiming" national affiliation (Sullivan 2005); research into levels of violence of groups regarded as gangs and groups not so regarded (Sullivan 2005); research into how gang dynamics are being adapted to and affected by social media and digital communication (Upton, Eschmann, and Butler 2013), and literally on and on and on. There is a small but important literature on the misconceptions that dominate popular ideas about gangs, with responses rooted in gang scholarship (Howell 2007). Beyond that, since the "group" focus is inclusive of such things as motorcycle gangs, organized crime, much white-collar crime, and a wide range of criminal networks, the vast literatures in those areas can all be pertinent, depending on the particular violence issue in question and its connection to such group dynamics.

From the other direction, law enforcement actors can and frequently do carry with them the received idea of what a gang is, which is misleading and confounding in an endless variety of ways. But they also carry with them insight into actual groups and group dynamics that are better than anyone else's except for actual group members, and sometimes better than theirs. It was, remember, gang officers in Boston who began all this by giving away their transformative understanding of violence and violent groups in Boston, an insight earned entirely through their own work and experience. The now conventional wisdom that community violence is rooted in groups and that those groups and everybody in them is a tiny subset of the larger population has been built up from mixed-methods research with front-line law enforcement personnel, with the most important information coming from qualitative research (Kennedy, Braga, and Piehl 2017; Braga, McDevitt, and Pierce 2006; Braga and Hureau 2012; Corsaro 2018; Lurie 2019). The experience and knowledge of front-line officers is often the most powerful and readily accessible counter to dominant misrepresentations of "gangs." In one LAPD area (LAPD nomenclature for "precinct"), the statewide CalGang system held that there was a terrifyingly large, 5,000-strong Sureno gang; however, local officers, when asked, concluded that there were in fact about 150 active members. As has worked with violence prevention itself, if the question put to officers is what they know about violence, and then about any groups associated with violence, the received idea of a gang will often be put aside and genuine information and insight emerges. As Kalamazoo Assistant Chief Boysen says, police (and others on the front lines, including many community members) really do know who they are.

Conclusion

All of this is to say that the received idea of a "gang" is tremendously potent, stubbornly resistant to facts, and is a core impediment to understanding and acting against violence. Those working in both scholarship and practice around public safety and the dynamics that produce violence should keep front of mind that we are engaged with that phantasm and how assiduously that phantasm is nourished by powerful energies and agencies. I noted above the FBI's statement:

> Some 33,000 violent street gangs, motorcycle gangs, and prison gangs are criminally active in the U.S. today. Many are sophisticated and well organized; all use violence to control neighborhoods and boost their illegal money-making activities, which include robbery, drug and gun trafficking, prostitution and human trafficking, and fraud.

This is frankly and outrageously false. It is absolutely not the case that, to rephrase the FBI, each and every one of the 33,000 violent street gangs across the United States uses violence to control neighborhoods and further drug trafficking, prostitution, and other organized crime. It is in fact the case that this is not even remotely true, and that "gangs" that meet that description are so rare as to be the next best thing to non-existent. It is absolutely the case that very large proportions of law enforcement, the media, and the public believe that this or something like this is true, and that belief stands in the way of understanding what is true, what works around the very real violence and other harms "gangs" do, and why what does work in fact works, since it seems unlikely to most people that it would work with respect to the phantasm they take as real.

As one last data point, it could be noted that the Trump Administration made much of MS-13, casting it as a top threat to US national security. "MS-13 is a violent transnational criminal organization, whose criminal activities respect no boundaries," said John Durham, director of the Department of Justice's Joint Task Force Vulcan. "The only way to defeat MS-13 is by targeting the organization as a whole, focusing on the leadership structure, and deploying a whole-of-government approach against a common enemy" (Department of Justice 2020). The larger picture being portrayed was ludicrous; in the United States MS-13 is very serious in the several fairly small areas across the country where it is a problem, but it is essentially completely absent elsewhere and makes a tiny overall contribution to the nation's violent crime problem (Garcia-Navarro 2018). Despite this, public opinion surveys during this time showed that 85% of Trump voters thought that MS-13 posed a "somewhat serious" or "very serious" threat to the nation; more than half thought it posed "a direct threat to their community"; and 51% were at least "somewhat" worried that they were personally at risk (Barnes 2018). Given Trump's vote count in the 2016 presidential election, that last means that some 32 *million people* thought they were personally at risk from MS-13. Such a thing would be impossible without the deeply spurious, but socially and culturally influential, received idea of what a "gang" is. It doesn't seem too much, then, to suggest that that idea gets as much thoughtful attention as the scholarly attention to the scholarly equivalent has long gotten.

Notes

1. These interventions go by various names, including "street outreach," "interventionists," "interrupters," "credible messengers," the branded "CureViolence," and others. This chapter will use the term "street outreach" as inclusive of all such interventions.
2. See, for example, Kennedy 2009.
3. It should be noted that the rejection of an explicit "gang" focus among outreach work organizations is not universal; the Los Angeles Urban Peace Institute, for example, continues to use the term and associated framing. See Urban Peace Academy 2022.
4. I'm aware of no formal study of this industry and its impact on policing, corrections, education, and other institutions. Such a study would be an important addition to our understanding of the creation of the meaning of "gang" and of the actions of those institutions. The account here is drawn from my own exposure from the mid-1980s to the present.
5. See, for example, Lotke 1996.
6. A standout example of this is Oakland, California, which before the equivalent study was done "knew" that that city's extreme levels of violence were driven by juveniles; the actual average age of victims was 30 (California Partnership for Safe Communities 2021)
7. On this point, see, for example, Pitts 2013.

References

Anderson, Elijah. 2000. *Code of the Street: Decency, Violence, and the Moral Life of the Inner City*. New York: WW Norton & Company.

Ball, Richard A., and G. David Curry. 1995. "The Logic of Definition in Criminology: Purposes and Methods for Defining 'Gangs.'" *Criminology* 33 (2): 225–245.

Barnes, Luke. 2018. "A New Poll Shows Just How Effective Trump's MS-13 Propaganda Is." ThinkProgress, July 17. https://thinkprogress.org/trumps-ms-13-propaganda-poll-threat-2a8aee60be99/.

Bourgois, Philippe. 2003. *In Search of Respect: Selling Crack in El Barrio*. Cambridge, UK: Cambridge University Press.

Braga, Anthony A., and David M. Hureau. 2012. "Strategic Problem Analysis to Guide Comprehensive Gang Violence Reduction Strategies." In *Looking beyond Suppression: Community Strategies to Reduce Gang Violence*, edited by Erika Gebo and Brenda Bond, 129–152. Lanham, MD: Lexington Books.

Braga, Anthony A., David M. Hureau, and Andrew V. Papachristos. 2014. "Deterring Gang-Involved Gun Violence: Measuring the Impact of Boston's Operation Ceasefire on Street Gang Behavior." *Journal of Quantitative Criminology* 30 (1): 113–139.

Braga, Anthony A., and David M. Kennedy. 2021. *A Framework for Addressing Violence and Serious Crime: Focused Deterrence, Legitimacy, and Prevention*. Cambridge, UK: Cambridge University Press.

Braga, Anthony A., Jack McDevitt, and Glenn L. Pierce. 2006. "Understanding and Preventing Gang Violence: Problem Analysis and Response Development in Lowell, Massachusetts." *Police Quarterly* 9 (1): 20–46.

Braga, Anthony A., David Weisburd, and Brandon Turchan. 2019. "Focused Deterrence Strategies Effects on Crime: A Systematic Review." *Campbell Systematic Reviews* 15 (3).

Branas, Charles, Shani Buggs, Jeffrey A. Butts, Anna Harvey, Erin M. Kerrison, Tracey Meares, Andrew V. Papachristos et al. 2020. "Reducing Violence Without Police: A Review of Research Evidence." CUNY Academic Works.
California Partnership for Safe Communities. 2021. *Understanding Serious Violence and Identifying Highest Risk Populations.* The Council on Criminal Justice Violent Crime Working Group, September. https://counciloncj.org/wp-content/uploads/2021/09/CPSC-Brief-PA-overview-for-VCWG-REV.pdf.
Corsaro, Nicholas. 2018. "More than Lightning in a Bottle and Far from Ready-Made." *Criminology & Public Policy* 17: 251.
Crandall, Vaughn (California Partnership for Safe Communities). 2023. Personal communication to author.
Dalton, Erin. 2002. "Targeted Crime Reduction Efforts in Ten Communities—Lessons for the Project Safe Neighborhoods Initiative." *US Attorneys Bull* 50: 16.
Department of Justice. 2020. "The Department of Justice Announces Takedown of Key MS-13 Criminal Leadership." July 15. https://www.justice.gov/opa/pr/department-justice-announces-takedown-key-ms-13-criminal-leadership.
Duane, Daniel. 2006. "Straight Outta Boston." *Mother Jones*, January/February. https://www.motherjones.com/politics/2006/01/straight-outta-boston/.
Educational Fund to Stop Gun Violence. 2021. "Community Gun Violence." Accessed August 2. https://efsgv.org/learn/type-of-gun-violence/community-gun-violence/.
Esbensen, Finn-Aage, and Cheryl L. Maxson. 2012. "The Eurogang Program of Research and Multimethod Comparative Gang Research: Introduction." In *Youth Gangs in International Perspective*, edited by F.-A. Esbensen and C. L. Maxson, 1–14. New York: Springer.
Esposito, Richard. 2012. "New York's Kelly Plans 'Crew Cut' for Gang Members." *ABC News*, October 1. https://abcnews.go.com/Blotter/nypd-plans-crew-cut-gang-members/story?id=17370903.
Federal Bureau of Investigation. 2011. "2011 National Gang Threat Assessment." https://www.fbi.gov/stats-services/publications/2011-national-gang-threat-assessment.
Federal Bureau of Investigation. 2003. "Crime in the United States 2003, Federal Bureau of Investigation, Section II—Offenses Reported, p. 15." https://ucr.fbi.gov/crime-in-the-u.s/2003/03sec2.pdf.
Federal Bureau of Investigation. 2013. "Crime in the United States 2012: Table 12." https://ucr.fbi.gov/crime-in-the-u.s/2012/crime-in-the-u.s.-2012/tables/12tabledatadecpdf.
Federal Bureau of Investigation. 2016. "What We Investigate: Gangs." Accessed May 3. https://www.fbi.gov/investigate/violent-crime/gangs.
Garcia-Navarro, Lulu. 2018. "The Realities of MS-13." National Public Radio, June 3. https://www.npr.org/2018/06/03/616552016/the-realities-of-ms-13.
Garot, Robert. 2010. *Who You Claim: Performing Gang Identity in School and on the Streets*, Vol. 3. New York: New York University Press.
Howell, James C. 2007. "Menacing or Mimicking? Realities of Youth Gangs." *Juvenile and Family Court Journal* 58 (2): 39–50.
Johnson, Bruce, Andrew Golub, and Eloise Dunlap. 2000. "The Rise and Decline of Hard Drugs, Drug Markets, and Violence in Inner-City New York." In *The Crime Drop in America*, edited by Alfred Blumstein and Joel Wallman, 164–206. Cambridge, UK: Cambridge University Press.

Jones, Al. 2020. "Kalamazoo Police Look to Violence Intervention Program and Community Partnerships to Halt Shootings." *Southwest Michigan's Second Wave*, October 13. https://www.secondwavemedia.com/southwest-michigan/features/Police-look-to-violence-intervention-program-and-community-partnerships-to-halt-shooting-101220.aspx.

Kennedy, David M. 2009. "Gangs and Public Policy: Constructing and Deconstructing Gang Databases." *Criminology & Public Policy* 8: 711.

Kennedy, David M. 2011. *Don't Shoot: One Man, a Street Fellowship, and the End of Violence in Inner-City America*. London: Bloomsbury Publishing.

Kennedy, David M., Anthony A. Braga, and Anne M. Piehl. 1997. "(Un)Known Universe: Mapping Gangs and Gang Violence in Boston." In *Crime Mapping and Crime Prevention*, edited by David Weisburd and Tom McEwen, 219–262. Monsey, NY: Criminal Justice Press.

Kennedy, David M., Anthony A. Braga, and Anne M. Piehl. 2001. *Reducing Gun Violence: The Boston Gun Project's Operation Ceasefire*. Washington, DC: US Department of Justice.

Kennedy, David M., Anthony A. Braga, and Anne M. Piehl. 2017. "The (Un) Known Universe: Mapping Gangs and Gang Violence in Boston." In *Quantitative Methods in Criminology*, edited by David Weisburd, 327–370. New York: Routledge.

Klein, Malcolm W. 1984. "Offence Specialisation and Versatility among Juveniles." *British Journal of Criminology* 24: 185.

Lotke, Eric R. 1996. "Youth Homicide: Keeping Perspective on How Many Children Kill." *Valparaiso University Law Review* 31: 395.

Lurie, Stephen. 2019. "There's No Such Thing as a Dangerous Neighborhood." Bloomberg Citylab, February 25. https://www.citylab.com/perspective/2019/02/broken-windows-theory-policing-urban-violence-crime-data/583030/.

MacCoun, Robert, and Peter Reuter. 1992. "Are the Wages of Sin $30 an Hour? Economic Aspects of Street-Level Drug Dealing." *Crime & Delinquency* 38 (4): 477–491.

Mahony, Edmund. August 18, 1995. "Prosecution Rests Case against Latin Kings." *Hartford Courant*. August 18. https://www.courant.com/news/connecticut/hc-xpm-1995-08-18-9508180410-story.html.

Matza, David. 1964. "Delinquency and Drift." New York: John Wiley & Sons.

Maxson, Cheryl L., and Malcolm W. Klein. 1990. "Street Gang Violence: Twice as Great, or Half as Great." *Gangs in America* 1: 70.

Maxson, Cheryl Lee. 1997. *Gang Members on the Move*. Washington, DC: US Department of Justice.

Miller, Walter B. 1975. *Violence by Youth Gangs and Youth Groups as a Crime Problem in Major American Cities*. Washington, DC: Department of Justice.

Miller, Walter Benson. 2011. *City Gangs*. Tempe, AZ: Arizona State University School of Criminology and Criminal Justice.

National Academies of Sciences, Engineering, and Medicine. 2018. *Proactive Policing: Effects on Crime and Communities*. Washington, DC: National Academies Press.

National Council on Crime and Delinquency. 2009. *Developing a Successful Street Outreach Program: Recommendations and Lessons Learned*. Washington, DC: Office of Justice Programs.

National Gang Center. 2022. "National Youth Gang Survey Analysis: Measuring the Extent of Gang Problems." Accessed May 16. https://nationalgangcenter.ojp.gov/survey-analysis/measuring-the-extent-of-gang-problems.

Pitts, John. 2013. *Reluctant Gangsters: The Changing Face of Youth Crime*. London: Willan.

Pugliese, Katheryne, Paul Odér, Talib Hudson, and Jeffrey A. Butts. 2022. *Community Violence Intervention at the Roots (CVI-R)—Building Evidence for Grassroots Community Violence Prevention*. New York: City University of New York.

Regoeczi, Wendy C., Duren Banks, Michael Planty, Lynn Langton, and Margaret Warner. 2014. "The Nation's Two Measures of Homicide." Office of Justice Programs.

Rosenfeld, Richard, Timothy M. Bray, and Arlen Egley. 1999. "Facilitating Violence: A Comparison of Gang-Motivated, Gang-Affiliated, and Nongang Youth Homicides." *Journal of Quantitative Criminology* 15 (4): 498.

Spergel, Irving. 2009. "Gang Databases—To Be or Not to Be." *Criminology & Public Policy* 8: 672.

Speri, Alice. July 12, 2016. "In New York Gang Sweeps, Prosecutors Use Conspiracy Laws to Score Easy Convictions." *The Intercept*, July 12. https://theintercept.com/2016/07/12/in-new-york-gang-sweeps-prosecutors-use-conspiracy-laws-to-score-easy-convictions/.

Sullivan, Mercer L. 2005. "Maybe We Shouldn't Study 'Gangs': Does Reification Obscure Youth Violence?" *Journal of Contemporary Criminal Justice* 21 (2): 170–190.

Upton Patton, Desmond, Robert D. Eschmann, and Dirk A. Butler. 2013. "Internet Banging: New Trends in Social Media, Gang Violence, Masculinity and Hip Hop." *Computers in Human Behavior* 29 (5): A54–A59.

Urban Peace Institute. 2022. "Our Work." Accessed May 15. https://www.urbanpeaceinstitute.org/our-work-urban-peace-academy.

White House. 2021. "Fact Sheet: More Details on the Biden-Harris Administration's Investments in Community Violence Interventions." Accessed August 2, 2023, https://www.whitehouse.gov/briefing-room/statements-releases/2021/04/07/fact-sheet-more-details-on-the-biden-harris-administrations-investments-in-community-violence-interventions/.

Wilkinson, Deanna Lyn. 1998. *The Social and Symbolic Construction of Violent Events among Inner City Adolescent Males*. New Brunswick, NJ: Rutgers University Press.

Williams, Terry Tempest. 1990. *The Cocaine Kids: The Inside Story of a Teenage Drug Ring*. Lebanon, IN: Da Capo Press.

Wolfgang, Marvin E., Robert M. Figlio, and Thorsten Sellin. 1987. *Delinquency in a Birth Cohort*. Chicago, IL: University of Chicago Press.

CHAPTER 6

THE SOCIAL CONSTRUCTION OF THE AMERICAN STREET GANG

PATRICK LOPEZ-AGUADO

IN his 2015 ethnography *No Way Out*, Waverly Duck introduces readers to the community of Bristol Hill,[1] a poor and predominantly Black city with underperforming schools and a heavy police presence. With so few economic opportunities available, the drug trade takes a prominent role in the community, shaping the neighborhood's reputation as well as the economic prospects for many of the young men and boys who grow up here. In this context, drug dealing is a common although largely individualistic endeavor—dealers here "function as independent entrepreneurs with direct connections to suppliers" (Duck 2015, 13) who have autonomy and control over their own operations and can leave when they choose.[2]

Despite working independently, local dealers on Lyford Street—Bristol Hill's primary open-air drug market—often have various relationships with one another by virtue of living in a tight-knit community in which most residents know each other. This connects them to a shared loose network of relatives and neighbors, but when the killing of a prominent government official in the community generated media attention and put pressure on local authorities to solve the crime, these ties were framed as something much more sinister. In the subsequent investigation, gun records and a plea deal testimony gave detectives information on four additional murders committed over the previous three years. A range of circumstances and conflicts shaped these respective killings, but authorities quickly claimed that the murders were all united by a common cause, and before long legal indictments and media reports began collectively referring to the young men implicated in these violent events as the Lyford Street Gang.

Authorities argued that the connections and relationships between the accused characterized the structure of a drug dealing gang that was willing to commit violence "to protect its territory and . . . to silence anyone who threatened the neighborhood drug enterprise" (Duck 2015, 85), ultimately using this explanation to prosecute five homicides in three separate trials. But this assessment was in stark disagreement with how local residents understood the killings; long-time residents and even local law enforcement officers knew that no such gang existed in the community. The young men prosecuted as members were competing drug dealers rather than gang colleagues, and the family ties that did connect some of these young men differed from gang ties because they would have existed regardless of anyone's gang involvement. Residents were also skeptical of characterizing the homicides as gang violence—let alone as violence driven by a collective effort to protect the "gang's" drug business—because of what they knew of the parties involved and the conflicts between them: One homicide involved a teenage boy who shot his mother's physically abusive boyfriend, another was a vengeance killing against a man who had previously murdered the assailant's cousin, and yet another was an act of self-defense following an argument over a dice game.

Regardless, a narrative framing these acts as the work of a drug gang emerged for specific reasons. Law enforcement and prosecutors advanced the view that these crimes were gang driven because it aided in convicting the suspects in court (Duck 2015, 83). News media outlets generated considerable public attention and pressure on state authorities to respond (especially after the murder of a government official) and had a hand in creating and popularizing the Lyford Street Gang name that would be used to prosecute the suspects as gang members (Duck 2015, 86). By defining this imposed collective through such authoritative channels, social structures outside the community were able to legally and socially invent a gang that did not actually exist on the neighborhood's streets, complete with a territory, a set of members, a history of offenses, and a status that could be punished. This construction legitimized a narrative that was useful for both institutional contexts because both the courtroom and the newsroom are ultimately tasked with explaining crime and violence to community outsiders, and gangs represent a popular explanation that appeals to many common preconceptions of violence in poor communities of color.

If we understand social constructions as the processes in which social meanings are built, Duck's ethnography describes at least three such processes at work in this case:

1. Institutional powers named and created the Lyford Street Gang specifically by grouping individuals together in media reports and legal filings.
2. Court officials identified the resulting group as a gang, and in so doing applied the meanings popularly attributed to gangs as a type of group to the defendants themselves.
3. The convictions and punishments given to the defendants subsequently validated and confirmed popular understandings of gangs as criminal groups.

It is critical to recognize that these constructions serve the direct function of facilitating criminal convictions, because prosecuting defendants as the Lyford Street Gang allowed authorities to tie multiple incidents and suspects together, and to present these incidents as an ostensibly organized campaign of violence that makes each event seem more deliberate and each suspect appear more dangerous and powerful. But even more instrumental to this function is how framing defendants as a gang taps into an established set of motives, norms, and values generally (and often mistakenly) assumed to drive gang crime. Gang accusations essentially entail using such assumptions and descriptions to characterize the accused, and therefore rely on a popular recognition of gangs and gang members as criminal types for this characterization to be effective. In the United States, this recognition has long been shaped by the institutional processes that state, media, and academic authorities have used to define gangs as criminal groups, and the relative ability of these forces to distribute or enforce their particular definitions.

In the sections that follow I examine how the range of social meanings ascribed to gangs varies based on the interests and needs of the definer, and how some meanings are given more power and influence than others. I begin by discussing how group insiders build their own understandings of what gangs and gang membership mean. Specifically, I review how ethnographic studies of gangs have long illustrated the ways in which members build group meanings tied to identity, ethnicity, place, or experiences within local power dynamics. I then explore how these constructions contrast with how external social structures define gangs and what it means to be part of one. These external definitions—articulated in media depictions or state legislation—ultimately shape the stigmas and punishments that come to define group membership. Finally, I discuss the social construction of the gang member as a criminal trope, and argue that the identification of people of color with this trope has defined its function in the era of mass incarceration. I conclude this chapter with some closing thoughts on how the dominant institutions that define gangs can resist or mitigate this carceral function.

Gangs as Social Groups

The most fundamental form of gangs' social construction takes place through the organic formation of the group and the subsequent social meanings that members give to that formation. Gangs exist as (usually) small social groups not unlike other networks of close relationships like families, cliques, fraternities, work groups, or teams; such groups are the elementary components of a society—"tiny publics" that make engagement in the broader society possible by providing individuals with a venue for collaborating with known others to learn, create, and react to particular understandings of how the self and the collective relate to other social groups and forces (Fine 2012). These tiny publics, then, not only exist as interactional arenas capable of socializing members to shared norms and expectations, but as cultural fields in which the meanings attributed to group identities, membership, interaction, relationships, conflicts, symbols, values, and embodiment are crafted, negotiated, and agreed upon (Fine 2012).

These internal constructions and understandings of group identity and membership are fundamentally tied to the social contexts within which such groups form and exist. Place in particular is consequently important for gang identity (Lopez-Aguado and Walker 2021; Papachristos and Hughes 2015; Fraser 2013; Maxson 2011), so much so that gang names are oftentimes interchangeable with the respective neighborhoods, streets, parks, or landmarks where groups congregate (Vigil 1988). This conflation runs so deep that gangs are even commonly referred to as "neighborhoods," or membership as being "from a neighborhood." Place gives meaning to group processes and experiences through its role as the unique spatial context in which these interactions and relationships occur, and where identities are enacted, embodied, and accomplished (Fraser 2013). This place attachment can be even more intense for marginalized youth with limited spatial mobility—the case for most gang-involved youth—due to limited access to other spaces and peer networks that are therefore largely shaped by proximity (Harding 2010). Place attachment (see **Chapter 8**, this volume), then, informs the meanings that gang members ascribe to their groups, shaping essential aspects like rivalries, kinship, collective values, and self-perception (Maxson 2011).

The structural characteristics of gang-identified places even impact the structures of gang formations, and consequently the meanings that members see in their own involvement. For example, when a changing drug trade, the demolition of public housing complexes, and a series of federal indictments severely weakened the organizational structures of Chicago's largest gangs, these organizations effectively splintered and dissolved into myriad hyperlocal clusters (Aspholm 2020). As these changes unfolded, young gang members began to view and enact membership in very different terms than their counterparts a generation before, staunchly prioritizing local and individual autonomy over centralized authority or discipline (Aspholm 2020). The intricacies of a given place can therefore shape a gang's size or how power is internally distributed, and thus inform how members construct and socialize group norms, expectations, values, culture, and identity.

The significance that gang members find in accessing, navigating, and occupying public spaces is situated in the social power dynamics that shape everyday life in their respective communities. These local power hierarchies consequently shape the meanings that members attach to the groups that oftentimes make this access possible. In her work with gang-involved Mexican and Chicana girls, Norma Mendoza-Denton (2007) found that these young women composed their groups as vehicles for navigating male-dominated public spaces in contexts where racial and patriarchal forms of control largely confined them to the home or restricted them from moving safely and freely. As such, these young women valued gang membership as a means of reconstructing feminine gender performances in ways that claimed space and power while resisting expectations of passive domesticity. Vanessa Panfil (2017) has similarly found that gang-affiliated queer youth—often unwelcome or closeted within predominately straight gangs—use personal networks to build their own "gay gangs" based in sexual identity as supportive groups that protect collective access to a limited number of contested queer-friendly spaces. Gang ethnographies that critically examine membership and participation as gendered experiences have revealed much about how members ascribe meaning to their groups relative to their everyday experiences navigating broader systems of power (see also Miller 2001; Miranda 2003; Durán 2013).

Such works also illustrate how young people in marginalizing contexts commonly construct gangs as instrumental venues for making sense of how one is positioned within local struggles, understanding that position as one shared by others like oneself, and negotiating how one can experience or manage that positionality. The girls in Mendoza-Denton's (2007) work valued their groups not only as vehicles for feminist resistance and spatial mobility, but also as venues for performing Mexican and Chicana identities within predominately white school and community settings. For them, gangs serve as important contexts for validating, practicing, and embodying ethnic identity, and subsequently for building these identities as members collaborate on what it means to be one of them and what distinguishes them from the rest of society. Consequently, gangs can serve as a means for members to understand such differences through an empowering rather than deficient lens—one in which members can see group rivalries as symbolic of local racial, ethnic, linguistic, or cultural conflicts (Katz 1996; Mendoza-Denton 2007), and one's significant relationships and supportive networks rearticulated as affiliations (Miranda 2003; Durán 2013).

Because the significance of group belonging is tied to (and often in reaction to) social context, the meaning-making processes within gangs not only inform how members see themselves and their environments, but can also allow for the construction or promotion of a particular worldview from members' shared positions. For example, Robert Durán (2013) argues that barrio gangs in Colorado and Utah emerged within subordinated communities as adaptations to colonial control, structural neglect, and racist victimization, to the point that initiation into membership "serves the important function of changing victims into protagonists" (151). Membership can help insiders feel that they are protected from the violence or degradation of oppression, or that they are actively fighting back against it, thus attaching social meanings to their groups that are based in ideologies of political or subaltern resistance. In some instances, the resulting worldview can even transform the group into something resembling a politicized social movement,[3] encouraging members and outsiders to understand the group as a vehicle for personal empowerment and community improvement. In these instances, the means used by such "street organizations" (Brotherton & Barrios 2004) to distribute their political message or address community conditions can also become the meaning-making processes that produce the group's reputation and perception of what they represent.[4]

Gangs' relationship with oppressive or marginalizing social environments often establish these groups as sources of empowerment or validation for their members (Rios and Lopez-Aguado 2012), a powerful contrast to the stigmatization and victimization they routinely experience in the dominant society (Durán 2013). This contrast is fundamental to gang formation itself, as conflict with external forces—not just with rival groups but just as frequently with immediate power structures and authority figures—is what drives gang cohesion and fosters collective identity (Thrasher 1927). The solidarity resulting from this us-versus-them dynamic can express itself in politicized terms, as discussed above, but more commonly materializes as broadly oppositional identities. However, this opposition can be just as political even if never articulated as such, because for youth impacted by multiple marginalities (see Vigil 1988) gang identity is an accessible means of resisting authority structures or social systems that stigmatize or exclude them. For example, even though they knew that their appearances exposed them to profiling and police stops, Rios and Lopez-Aguado (2012) found that it was important for gang-involved youth to adopt the recognized aesthetics of gang membership—to look like a gang member; participants valued this image not only for identifying themselves to an audience of other members, but also to a public audience, as it emphatically disqualified them from a racialized local labor market that exploited their neighbors and relatives.

Like other groups of marginalized youth who are ostracized from broader society, these youth recognized that the "gang member" exists as a popularly feared image that they could adopt and perform as a powerful way of signaling their opposition to a system that subjugated them. Ironically, much of the rebellious allure of this figure is itself constructed by the very moral panics that have consistently vilified gangs as a social threat requiring control.[5] The more that an identified group is publicly vilified and criminalized as a public threat, the more its value as a form of symbolic resistance is heightened; this becomes visible in the "franchising" or appropriation of well-known affiliations by local gangs who begin calling themselves Crips, Bloods, or Maras to associate themselves with notorious groups perceived as dangerous, violent, or powerful (Durán 2013; Zilberg 2011).

Gangs as Social Threat

Regardless of the many various meanings that gang members attach to their own groups, the definitions that external social structures ascribe to gangs have a more significant role in shaping popular understandings of gangs, as well as the implications of being identified as part of one. Simply put, such structures have much more power to distribute their definitions than any gang defining itself does. Working together, social systems coalesce around a consistent "truth" about gangs that can offer simplified and orderly (and at times self-serving) explanations for urban crime or juvenile delinquency that are easy for non-members to understand: "Despite the fact of gang phenomena taking a diffuse form, theoreticians, social workers, the police, the press, and the public [inaccurately] distort gangs and gang behavior toward a gestalt of clarity" (Yablonsky 1959, 112). Much like the case with the Lyford Street Gang (Duck 2015) discussed in the introduction, news media plays a central role in shaping public perceptions of gangs by framing local crime or violence as the work of a cohesive group or set of groups, even when the reality may be much more complicated or disorganized (Durán 2013; Tovares 2002; Thompson, Young, and Burns 2000). This can work to reify a particular group through documentation and subsequent legal action—as is visible in the works of both Duck (2015) and Yablonsky (1959)—while also attaching a primarily criminal interpretation to the group. But as Yablonsky describes, the press does not work alone in this process, but rather works in concert with academic researchers and state agencies to craft a public understanding of gangs as an identifiable type of group, one that generally attaches similar criminal interpretations to any collective labeled as a gang.

The dynamic between media and state forces in times of moral panic are particularly revealing of how social structures collaborate to shape the social meanings ascribed to gangs, as panics facilitated by media outlets have consistently informed state efforts to criminalize gangs. Often motivated by their own financial incentives to attract consumers, news media have regularly sensationalized gangs as folk devils the public should be fearful of (Thompson et al. 2000; Durán 2013). In the United States this threat has historically been constructed as a criminal risk posed by exploited or marginalized communities of color, and as home to the reputed "gang capital" of the nation, California has long held an outsized influence in defining young cohorts in these communities as criminal groups. Coverage of the Zoot Suit Riots, for example, largely obscured the role of military personnel in instigating the violence and rationalized the mass arrests and beating of Latinx youth that ensued; subsequent reporting began emphasizing the pachuco/a as a racialized criminal archetype (Romero 2001)—enough so to successfully outlaw the clothing styles associated with this figure (Cosgrove 1984; Ramírez 2009). More significantly, local newspapers across the country soon began publishing reports of gangs of pachucos and zoot suiters spotted "moving east" from Los Angeles into smaller cities and towns in middle America, prompting local authorities in many of these communities to implement their own anti-gang policing efforts (Durán 2013).

This narrative of migrating gangs and subsequent crackdowns on local youth of color would repeat itself over four decades later with fears of Crip and Blood gang violence in the late 1980s and early 1990s. At the height of this panic, gang reporting commonly comprised multiple stories each day in many local media outlets, mostly characterizing gangs as violent criminal threats (Thompson et al. 2000). Much like the pachuco panic decades before, the media fixation on Crips and Bloods began with local crime reporting in Los Angeles, where this coverage was also contextualized by a civic culture that encouraged state antipathy toward gangs and facilitated more aggressive anti-gang policing compared to other large cities (see Sánchez-Jankowski 1991). The concentration of media infrastructure in LA and the sheer gravity of its market size helped spread these stories to distant outlets who were again anxious of West Coast gang feuds spreading to local communities. This time the narrative of migrating gangs was also buttressed by gang "experts" from the Los Angeles Police Department who would tour departments in smaller cities as paid consultants, teaching officers and community leaders how to identify local youth of color as Crip and Blood gang members (Durán 2013). In both periods, the specter of gangs offered a language for describing the visible presence of Black and Brown youth as a collective threat to the public good, and in both instances this language provided a means for classifying local youth of color as criminal while also legitimizing these classifications as ostensibly colorblind.[6]

Sensationalized gang reporting can generate public interest in ways that spur state actions that articulate the government's own constructions of gang meanings. State and law enforcement officials even use the same media platforms to distribute and produce their own interpretations of gangs and gang members as criminal threats requiring control (Hu & Dittman 2019); this happens through gang reporting that defines gangs through legal statutes, state press conferences to declare gang crackdowns, op-ed articles from police chiefs, or advertisements for electoral campaigns vowing law and order. Growing public fears of gangs can present opportunistic politicians with an issue they can use to establish their own legitimacy as tough-on-crime candidates, and the resulting organizational responses that the state puts into place to control gangs subsequently generate statistical evidence for the existence of local gangs (Meehan 2000). This happens because the organizational responses that the state dedicates to responding to gangs (such as gang policing units or task forces) triggers the classification of some reported incidents as gang related; determining which incidents are classified as such is influenced by how members of the public perceive the events they report, how dispatchers interpret and relay calls to officers, and how officers document their own activities throughout their shifts (Meehan 2000). The end result of this process is a certain number of ostensibly gang-related crimes and occurrences that come to be pointed to as statistical proof of a gang problem.

The counting of newly categorized "gang offenses" subsequently drives and legitimizes the drafting and passage of anti-gang legislation, such as when California's Street Terrorism Enforcement and Prevention (STEP) Act passed in 1988 with an introductory section citing the rising numbers of gangs and gang homicides reported by law enforcement.[7] Such pieces of legislation are the most significant way that the state constructs what the term "gang" means. This is true not only because legislation requires governing bodies to define what a gang is so as to identify applicable instances of policy enforcement, but also because it is through such legislation that the state defines gangs as fundamentally criminal entities. Much like how the legal construction of racial categories has historically created the differences in rights, protections, status, and mobility that define what it means to be racialized in the United States (Alexander 2010), laws implemented to facilitate the control of gangs—typically with enhanced punishments or expanded authority to police and surveil gang suspects—ultimately define the lived experiences and social implications of gang identification or membership. Local governments repeat this process each time states pass their own gang laws or cities and counties pass injunctions or other policing directives, reinforcing the broad criminalization of gangs by both designating additional restrictions and punishments for gangs while also strengthening the public's perceptions of gangs as groups defined by criminality.[8] This criminalization also of course shapes the realities that researchers and journalists encounter as they study gangs and attempt to construct their own definitions and interpretations.

While the drafting of legislation does force the state to define gangs, the definitions generated in this process can be absurdly shallow, in that they often feature seemingly infinite breadth with minimal depth; state definitions of gangs will generally limit these definitions to purely criminal descriptions of group motive or function while describing group structures in impossibly broad terms, creating definitions that are designed to be as widely applicable as possible for prosecuting criminal cases. For example, California's STEP Act defines gangs as an "organized association or group of three or more persons, whether formal or informal, having as one of its primary activities the commission of one or more of [several enumerated criminal offenses], having a common name or common identifying sign or symbol, and whose members engage in, or have engaged in, a pattern of criminal gang activity" and makes membership in such a group a felony. Noteworthy in this definition is that crime is mentioned twice as a defining principle of what constitutes a gang, and the only other qualifiers are that the group has at least three members and a common name or symbol (which doesn't even necessarily have to come from the members themselves). This is not a useful definition for describing or understanding groups who identify as gangs, but it is useful for convicting and incarcerating people; as of 2019, 11,484 people held in California's state prison system were incarcerated with enhanced sentences for gang convictions using the definition above (Clayton 2019).

When prosecutors use such shallow definitions to charge defendants as members of gangs, they effectively name specific peer networks as groups matching the legal standard of a gang, thus tying these networks to a bundle of social meanings ascribed to gangs. This designation works to authoritatively define the accused as criminal while also associating them with all the fears historically generated through past and present moral panics. Labeling theory explains that the accusation alone can be sufficient to influence how others interpret one's actions or motives (Becker 1963), incentivizing prosecutors to emphasize defendants as gang members[9] even when it is irrelevant to the offenses in question (Hagedorn 2022). The process of arguing that particular defendants are gang affiliated also opens the door for the construction and legitimation of more detailed bodies of knowledge about gangs that reaffirm their criminality and help secure convictions (Rios and Navarro 2010). Prosecutors accusing defendants of gang-related offenses must argue that the evidence against them signifies gang activity, motivating them to argue that a broad range of behaviors are gang driven or motivated. Able to aid them in this endeavor are myriad law enforcement gang "experts" available to verify and confirm that the evidence does indeed indicate gang activity or that suspects meet state gang standards. In testifying to this effect, such police witnesses often interpret signs of urban youth culture as evidence of gang membership (Rios and Navarro 2010) and present popular myths about gangs as facts (Hagedorn 2022); claims that one's gang is a priority over all else, that members only understand respect as fear, or that members are obligated to violently retaliate against any perceived disrespect, for example, are crafted and authenticated through courtroom attempts to describe defendants as driven by gang criminality in innumerable ways. Such an approach reduces defendants to one-dimensional criminal figures and redefines their close or familial relationships as gang associations. It also contributes to constructing narratives about gangs that become legitimized and shared at professional conferences, law enforcement training workshops, and informational sessions that teach community members to identify gang members in local contexts.

Reflecting this common legal standard, academic definitions have increasingly emphasized group criminality over time (Brotherton 2008). For example, in one of the first comprehensive sociological studies of gangs, Frederic Thrasher (1927) defined them as childhood play groups that come of age together and build a cohesive identity (along with several other group characteristics) through years of conflict with outsiders. Thrasher focuses on group dynamics in his description, but crime was not something fundamental to how he defined gangs. Decades later, however, one of the most prevalent contemporary academic definitions of gangs (see **Chapter 2** for an elaboration on the Eurogang definition) now centers crime, describing gangs as "durable and street-oriented youth groups whose involvement in illegal activity is part of their group identity" (Klein, Weerman, and Thornberry, 2006). Gangs have not necessarily become *more* criminal in purpose or function in this time,[10] but they have become more prominent symbols of urban, juvenile, or non-white criminality, particularly in the era of mass imprisonment. In these evolving academic constructions, we can see how the meanings attached to gangs through scholarly research have shifted with the escalating criminalization and punishment that has increasingly accompanied gang identification over the decades. Even when conducting original research on gangs, researchers may still premise or build their analyses upon preconceived understandings of gangs that are largely constructed by state and media interests invested in criminalizing young people of color.

IMAGINING AND IDENTIFYING GANG MEMBERS

Moral panics and legal constructions of gangs as criminal threats culminate in the passage of anti-gang legislation that facilitates their social control through enhanced surveillance, policing, prosecution, or social exclusion. However, any policy measure or enforcement effort directed against gangs still relies on the categorization of representative individuals to control or punish: the identification of suspected gang members or affiliates. What state constructions and legal definitions of gangs ultimately accomplish then is the establishment of gang membership as an identifiable—and ultimately punishable—status, one that is premised less on one's actions than a condemnation of one's relationships, networks, or community.

Gang membership can be notoriously difficult to determine, however, especially for outsiders. While membership as a social role or identity can be inconsistent, fluid, and contextual (see Garot 2010), state efforts to define gang membership as a legal category attempt to standardize its characteristics, leading to assessments that often differ significantly from local, on-the-ground understandings of gang involvement (Rios and Navarro 2010). The results of this standardization are often vague or subjective standards for gang validation that are better suited for broad legal applicability than they are for accurate identification. For example, the state of California uses criteria such as "associating with documented gang members," "frequenting gang areas," or "wearing gang dress" to determine membership for the purposes of adding people to state databases (California State Auditor 2016) or prosecuting them with sentencing enhancements. These gang validation criteria are primarily designed to implicate local networks (Parenti 2000), but this means many neighbors and relatives with no gang history or involvement are falsely identified as gang members because of their relationships with past or present members; in my own courtroom observations for example, unaffiliated cousins and spouses have been charged with potential life sentences under the argument that their relationships constituted gang association, and therefore made them criminal conspirators to their loved ones' deeds. Gang databases are similarly plagued with ongoing scandals over falsified additions (Chabria, Rector, and Chang, 2020) or failures to remove inactive persons (California State Auditor 2016), reflecting broader inaccuracies and corruptions in how the state classifies people as gang-involved subjects. But even when individuals don't identify or affiliate with a gang, the "membership" constructed through such legal processes becomes real through the state's power to punish it as such, and to document this assessment as legal precedent for future prosecutions.

Many of the criteria the state uses to validate gang members could potentially apply to almost any group of people, so legal definitions rely on the assessments of individual officers to interpret which clothing or locales are gang involved or not. Consequently, most of those who are validated as gang involved are people who match racialized stereotypes, live in stigmatized communities, or have familial relationships with people already identified as gang members. This is because subjective assessments often reflect the racial biases of police officers or other authority figures (Rios 2011) or default to popular myths about gangs (Hagedorn 2022) that are similarly racist. The reliance on individual discretion to identify gang members—especially within vague legal standards that do not narrow this identification down in any meaningful way—requires the existence of the gang member as an imagined ideal type (Weber 1949) that can serve as a comparative reference to the individuals that officers classify as gang members or non-members. This ideal type functions as an image widely accepted as generalizable to all gang members, composed of the characteristics commonly presumed to make gang members who they are. This abstract construction then provides much of the basis for identifying gang affiliation or involvement in the field, but in the United States this construction cannot be separated from the nation's histories of racialized criminalization. Colonial domination of Black and Brown populations often relied on claims of wanton criminality to legitimize systems of labor exploitation and social control (Romero 2001; Kelley 2000; Smiley and Fakunle 2016), and over time gangs have provided a popular frame or language for conceptualizing these communities' young people as criminal threats. These histories have so thoroughly shaped popular conceptions of gang members that—as a punishable legal category—this status essentially only exists for people of color, such that in California 86% of validated gang members (California State Auditor 2016) and 92% of individuals sentenced to prison with gang enhancements (Clayton 2019) are Black or Latinx.

Mary Romero (2001) argues that the social and legal construction of the Latino gang member descends directly from the politicized caricature of the Mexican bandido, a trope used to elicit public support for the military conquest of the American southwest in the late 1840s. This trope framed invading and annexing the region as a civilizing project necessary for making the west safe for national expansion by depicting Mexican residents and military personnel as lawless bandits quick to victimize anyone. In doing this, state officials popularized the racialized image of the bandido as a scheming, quick-tempered, and irrationally violent figure who was representative of Mexicans living in the region. This figure was instrumental for justifying the violence of conquest, claiming that state violence was necessary to control the threat posed by roving criminals. This construction was powerful enough to far outlive the war itself, evolving over time into the urbanized stereotypes of the pachuco, cholo, and gang member; in Romero's analysis, the gang member is simply the latest iteration of the same racialized profile, one that still functions to rationalize state violence and punitive social control by painting Latino men as exceptionally dangerous subjects requiring said control.

Smiley and Fakunle (2016) document a similar history behind the constructed image of the "thug," tracing it to the Reconstruction era figure of the "brute." Much like the bandido, the brute was a racialized caricature that depicted Black men as naturally aggressive and prone to violence. In the context of the postbellum south, this construction framed recently emancipated Black residents as incapable of the political and economic mobility that their new legal rights promised. Beyond this, however, it functioned to justify terrorizing and intimidating Black communities into disenfranchised and exploitable caste positions by describing Black men as violent criminal threats to white women (Smiley and Fakunle 2016; Kelley 2000). This same dehumanizing image, updated and repackaged as the contemporary thug, still informs how Black men are routinely characterized as violent drug dealers and gang members, and still rationalizes—even posthumously—the extralegal violence regularly carried out against them (Smiley and Fakunle 2016).

The historical legitimizing functions of these racialized criminal tropes have helped establish gang membership as a broadly recognized articulation or explanation of non-white criminality. This gives authoritative declarations of gang membership a similar legitimizing power, and makes the poor young people of color who are most vulnerable to criminal justice targeting susceptible to accusations of gang involvement as justification for ongoing control and punishment. In California, correctional staff and administrators often center gang conflicts—using racial classifications as proxies for gang affiliation—when distributing housing assignments within segregated carceral facilities and institutions (Lopez-Aguado 2018; Walker 2022). This is ostensibly done to prevent violence in facilities by keeping rivals separated, but structuring entire facilities around these divisions compels staff to categorize all individuals in the facility—regardless of whether they have any history of gang involvement or not[11]—into one racialized faction or another, and to separate them as such.

This sorting process represents an example of the institutional creation of large groups that are policed as extended criminal affiliations: a carceral construction of gangs. But the discursive framing of these categorical identities as criminal gangs also influences how state agencies construct punishable groups and designate individuals as gang involved beyond the walls of the prison or jail. When the Supreme Court ruled that this state-mandated racial segregation must stop, they still permitted the separation of gang members or "disruptive groups" who posed risks to the security of the institution (Savage and Warren 2005), creating an incentive for prison authorities to insist that segregated racial groups are indeed composed of criminal gangs and their associates. Not surprisingly, the classifications and socialization that result from the racial sorting process are now commonly recorded in parole and probation files as evidence of gang affiliation—creating additional restrictions and barriers to re-entry—and the penal housing categories themselves are frequently described as criminal organizations in gang validation records and criminal indictments (Lopez-Aguado 2018). The institutional logic of categorizing criminalized people within a rigid typology of racialized "gang" affiliations also comes to inform labeling practices in juvenile justice settings and policing within local communities as well. For example, when young people living in neighborhoods impacted by gang violence are stopped by police, they are often ascribed with criminalized affiliations or gang ties through a "polarized labeling" that follows the same process as prison sorting; how officers racially identify an individual determines the gangs they accuse one of supporting, following the institutional presumption that youth of color must either affiliate with one racially defined gang in the community or its rival (Lopez-Aguado 2018).

Considering the Carceral Functions of Gang Constructions

To make a point about how language is always changing, and that because of this words could have evolving or even multiple definitions, an old teacher of mine once explained that a word is ultimately defined by its use; whatever people use it to explain or describe, that's what it means. In considering what the term "gang" means, and how these meanings have been constructed over time, one can see that this word is similarly bound by what the term itself is principally used to do—isolate and punish people of color by describing them as violent criminal threats.[12] Given the nation's history of racial domination and its current context of mass imprisonment, it is impossible to separate the criminality generally associated with gangs from the means and processes of colonial and carceral control. In both past and present, the "gang" has been socially constructed as a punishable status that rationalizes state violence and social control.

People who do identify with gangs build social meanings for their own groups and collective identities, meanings that are often contextualized by the communities they reside in and the social orders that structure everyday life in these spaces. But this power to define themselves is also largely limited to constructing meanings within their own networks or communities; in the public sphere, these nuanced and multi-layered self-constructions are often overshadowed by media depictions and legal definitions that generally collapse gangs into purely criminal groups. The United States' history of using gangs as racialized folk devils has associated a range of fearmongering social meanings and myths to this term, and has informed the heavily lopsided identification of people of color as criminal gang members.

Criminalizing gangs is ultimately about establishing gang membership as a punishable legal category, one that solely exists to facilitate criminal convictions—in addition to the presumption of criminality that the term itself commonly evokes, defendants are accused of gang membership to make them eligible for longer prison sentences, which prosecutors can then use to coerce them into guilty pleas. In this respect, gang membership functions much like Foucault's (1977) description of delinquency—a criminalized status[13] that doesn't reduce or remedy gang crime so much as it categorizes and depoliticizes defendants in ways that alienate them from the public. This is not because all or even most gangs are explicitly political groups, but because depoliticization functions to strip away any possible meanings to the accused's actions other than those construed as strictly antithetical to the legitimacy of state order. Said another way, it works to frame the actions of identified gang members as purely criminal and nothing more.

Recognizing the socially constructed gang as a tool for legitimizing racial domination and mass imprisonment makes clear the need for the social institutions discussed in this chapter to critically evaluate and address the ways they contribute to this end. State and local governments need to repeal and amend legislation that criminalizes gang membership or association, as these laws are almost always selectively enforced against communities of color and essentially function to give Black and Brown defendants longer prison sentences than white folks convicted of the same crimes (Lopez-Aguado 2021). When reporting on crime or violent incidents, journalists should question police or prosecutors who offer simplified explanations of "gang activity" and assess the interpersonal or communal factors that contextualize a given reported event. Finally, scholars and researchers must exercise caution in how they may reify gang constructions in their own work, to always question the use of this label as it is frequently applied to people and communities, and to only describe research participants as gang members when participants use this same language to describe themselves.

Notes

1. Bristol Hill, Lyford Street, and the Lyford Street Gang are all pseudonyms from Duck 2015.
2. Duck describes dealers working together, and younger dealers learning from or apprenticing under older dealers. However, dealers were also free to work with whomever they wished, or on their own, and Duck is explicit about the lack of gang organizations in this community.
3. See Brotherton and Barrios' (2004) work on the Almighty Latin King and Queen Nation as an example.
4. It is important to note that some gangs become politicized, while in other instances political movements are also labeled as gangs as a means of delegitimizing them.
5. See Van Hellemont and Densley 2019 for more on how fictional depictions of gang violence contribute to this allure.
6. Contemporary reporting on gangs still reproduces many of these same constructions of gangs as racialized threats. In their extensive review of newspaper reports on gangs, Hu and Dittman (2019) found that gang reporting still usually characterizes gang members as Black or Latino men from poor neighborhoods, disproportionately ties gang crime or violence to immigrants and refugees, and still regularly discusses gangs as dangers flowing from diverse urban settings into predominately white suburban and rural spaces. Recent moral panics about Mara Salvatrucha in particular have made these constructions especially visible, as the broad characterization of Latinx migrants as gang members bolstered efforts by the Trump Administration to restrict and further criminalize migration from Latin America.
7. Specifically, the bill claims that 600 gangs existed across the state and that gang homicides rose 80% over the previous year. This dramatic rise is likely a result of the increased use of newly incorporated gang classifications, as described by Meehan (2000). The designation

of violent crimes as gang driven can also be based in the subjective interpretations of community outsiders who don't understand local dynamics, as described by Duck (2015).
8. In their review of gang legislation across the United States, Decker, Pyrooz, and Densley (2022) found a dramatic lack of non-punitive legal policies; with the exception of some federal legislation that included prevention programming, gang legislation is almost entirely focused on criminalizing gangs and gang members.
9. Because states define gangs as fundamentally or primarily criminal groups, gang membership is also frequently described as a master status in which one's membership, and therefore one's criminality, is depicted as one's defining characteristic over any other social roles or identities.
10. As Densley, Pyrooz, and Decker 2021 argue, the essence of street gangs has remained consistent over time while the social contexts around them—particularly access to firearms—have changed in ways that have made gang conflicts and interpersonal violence in general more lethal.
11. The vast majority of incarcerated peoples are not gang involved, and on average prison systems only recognize about 15% of their residents as gang members (Pyrooz and Mitchell 2020). However, racial sorting like that practiced in California houses everyone as potential affiliates, and in doing so generates and assigns the very associations that states use as criteria for gang validation (Lopez-Aguado 2018). This process formally validates many penal residents as gang involved, producing about a quarter of all registered gang members in the state (California State Auditor 2016). But even for those not formally labeled as gang members, one's housing assignment still creates documentation of suspected gang involvement that can be used against them later: Residents can be charged with gang enhancements for offenses committed in supposedly gang-specific housing units, have gang restrictions on personal items or associations attached to their parole conditions, or see in-custody incidents and parole violations used in court to establish a history of gang involvement if charged with future offenses.
12. Recent calls to police far-right groups as gangs accurately highlight how these groups' whiteness shields them from the same criminalization that confronts similarly violent Black or Latinx groups (see Valasik and Reid 2021). However, demanding that white groups be treated "as gangs" to address their criminality—or as a matter of racial fairness—still invokes the "gang" as a racialized construction deserving of aggressive policing and social control. Arguing that some white groups are equally criminal to the scores of Black and Brown folks policed and punished as gang members may legitimize the criminalization of the former, but it does so by endorsing the generations of ongoing carceral violence visited upon the latter.
13. Not to be confused with the term commonly used to describe juvenile criminality, Foucault (1977) describes "delinquency" as a recognizable and exploitable social status that the state ascribes to individuals by incarcerating them. He argues that governments construct and ascribe this status because it moralizes lawbreaking in ways that condition the broader public toward state obedience.

REFERENCES

Alexander, Michelle. 2010. *The New Jim Crow: Mass Incarceration in the Age of Colorblindness*. New York: The New Press.

Aspholm, Roberto R. 2020. *Views from the Streets: The Transformation of Gangs and Violence on Chicago's South Side*. New York: Columbia University Press.
Becker, Howard S. 1963. *Outsiders: Studies in the Sociology of Deviance*. New York: Free Press.
Brotherton, David C. 2008. "Beyond Social Reproduction: Bringing Resistance Back in Gang Theory." *Theoretical Criminology* 12 (1): 55–77.
Brotherton, David C., and Luis Barrios. 2004. *The Almighty Latin King and Queen Nation: Street Politics and the Transformation of a New York City Gang*. New York: Columbia University Press.
California State Auditor. 2016. "The CalGang Criminal Intelligence System." State of California.
Chabria, Anita, Kevin Rector, and Cindy Chang. 2020. "California Bars Police from Using LAPD Records in Gang Database. Critics Want It Axed." *Los Angeles Times*, July 14.
Clayton, Abené. 2019. "92% Black or Latino: The California Laws that Keep Minorities in Prison." *The Guardian*, November 26. https://www.theguardian.com/us-news/2019/nov/26/california-gang-enhancements-laws-black-latinos.
Cosgrove, Stuart. 1984. "The Zoot-Suit and Style Warfare." *History Workshop Journal* 18 (1): 77–91.
Decker, Scott H., David C. Pyrooz, and James A. Densley. 2022. *On Gangs*. Philadelphia, PA: Temple University Press.
Densley, James, David Pyrooz, and Scott Decker. 2021. "The Real Cultural Significance of 'West Side Story'? It Spread Powerful Myths about Gangs." *The Los Angeles Times*, December 10. https://www.latimes.com/opinion/story/2021-12-10/west-side-story-gang-myths-spielberg.
Duck, Waverly. 2015. *No Way Out: Precarious Living in the Shadow of Poverty and Drug Dealing*. Chicago, IL: University of Chicago Press.
Durán, Robert J. 2013. *Gang Life in Two Cities: An Insider's Journey*. New York: Columbia University Press.
Fine, Gary Alan. 2012. *Tiny Publics: A Theory of Group Action and Culture*. New York: Russel Sage Foundation.
Foucault, Michael. 1977. *Discipline & Punish: The Birth of the Prison*. New York: Vintage Books.
Fraser, Alistair. 2013. "Street Habitus: Gangs, Territorialism and Social Change in Glasgow." *Journal of Youth Studies* 16 (8): 970–985.
Garot, Robert. 2010. *Who You Claim: Performing Gang Identity in School and on the Streets*. New York: New York University Press.
Hagedorn, John M. 2022. *Gangs on Trial: Challenging Stereotypes and Demonization in the Courts*. Philadelphia, PA: Temple University Press.
Harding, David. 2010. *Living the Drama*. Chicago, IL: University of Chicago Press.
Hu, Xiaochen, and Layne Dittmann. 2019. "How Does Print Media Describe Gang Members? Analysis of Newspaper Reports and Policy Implications." *Journal of Criminal Justice and Popular Culture* 19 (1): 19–36.
Katz, Susan Roberta. 1996. "Where the Streets Cross the Classroom: A Study of Latino Students' Perspectives on Cultural Identity in City Schools and Neighborhood Gangs." *Bilingual Research Journal* 20 (3–4): 603–631.
Kelley, Robin D. G. 2000. "Slangin Rocks . . . Palestinian Style: Dispatches from the Occupied Zones of North America." In *Police Brutality: An Anthology*, edited by Jill Nelson, 21–59. New York: WW Norton.
Klein, Malcolm, Frank Weerman, and Terence Thornberry. 2006. "Street Gang Violence in Europe." *European Journal of Criminology* 3 (4): 413–437.

Lopez-Aguado, Patrick. 2018. *Stick Together and Come Back Home: Racial Sorting and the Spillover of Carceral Identity*. Berkeley: University of California Press.

Lopez-Aguado, Patrick. 2021. "The Case for Restricting Gang Enhancements in California." *The Appeal*, June 28.

Lopez-Aguado, Patrick, and Michael Walker. 2021. "'I Don't Bang, I'm Just a Blood': Situating Gang Identities in Their Proper Place." *Theoretical Criminology* 25 (1): 107–126.

Maxson, Cheryl. 2011. "Street Gangs." In *Crime and Public Policy*, edited by J. Q. Wilson and J. Petersilia, 158–182. New York: Oxford University Press.

Meehan, Albert J. 2000. "The Organizational Career of Gang Statistics: The Politics of Policing Gangs." *Sociological Quarterly* 41 (3): 337–370.

Mendoza-Denton, Norma. 2007. *Homegirls: Language and Cultural Practice among Latina Youth Gangs*. Malden, MA: Blackwell Publishing.

Miller, Jody. 2001. *One of the Guys: Girls, Gangs, and Gender*. New York: Oxford University Press.

Miranda, Marie. 2003. *Homegirls in the Public Sphere*. Austin: University of Texas Press.

Panfil, Vanessa R. 2017. *The Gang's All Queer*. New York: New York University Press.

Papachristos, Andrew V., and Lorine A. Hughes. 2015. "Neighborhoods and Street Gangs." In *The Handbook of Gangs*, edited by Scott H. Decker and David C. Pyrooz, 98–117. Chichester, UK: Wiley-Blackwell.

Parenti, Christian. 2000. *Lockdown America: Police and Prisons in the Age of Crisis*. New York: Verso.

Pyrooz, David C., and Meghan M. Mitchell. 2020. "The Use of Restrictive Housing on Gang and Non-Gang Affiliated Inmates in U.S. Prisons: Findings from a National Survey of Correctional Agencies." *Justice Quarterly* 37 (4): 590–615.

Ramírez, Catherine S. 2009. *The Woman in the Zoot Suit: Gender, Nationalism, and the Cultural Politics of Memory*. Durham, NC: Duke University Press.

Rios, Victor. 2011. *Punished: Policing the Lives of Black and Latino Boys*. New York: New York University Press.

Rios, Victor, and Karlene Navarro. 2010. "Insider Gang Knowledge: The Case for Non-Police Gang Experts in the Courtroom." *Critical Criminology* 18: 21–39.

Rios, Victor, and Patrick Lopez-Aguado. 2012. "Pelones y Matones: Chicano Cholos Perform for a Punitive Audience." In *Performing the US Latina and Latino Borderlands*, edited by Arturo J. Aldama, Chela Sandoval, and Peter J. García, 382–401. Bloomington: Indiana University Press.

Romero, Mary. 2001. "State Violence, and the Social and Legal Construction of Latino Criminality: From El Bandido to Gang Member." *Denver University Law Review* 78: 1081–1112.

Sánchez-Jankowski, Martin. 1991. *Islands in the Street: Gangs and American Urban Society*. Berkeley: University of California Press.

Savage, David G. and Jenifer Warren. 2005. "Justices Reject Segregation in State's Prisons." *Los Angeles Times*, February 24.

Smiley, Calvin John, and David Fakunle. 2016. "From 'Brute' to 'Thug:' The Demonization and Criminalization of Unarmed Black Male Victims in America." *Journal of Human Behavior in the Social Environment* 26 (3–4): 350–366.

Thompson, Carol Y., Robert L. Young; and Ronald Burns. 2000. "Representing Gangs in the News: Media Constructions of Criminal Gangs." *Sociological Spectrum* 20 (4): 409–432.

Thrasher, Frederic M. 1927. *The Gang: A Study of 1,313 Gangs in Chicago*. Chicago, IL: University of Chicago Press.

Tovares, Raúl Damacio. 2002. *Manufacturing the Gang: Mexican American Youth Gangs on Local Television News*. Ann Arbor, MI: Greenwood Publishing.
Valasik, Matthew, and Shannon E. Reid. 2021. "Classifying Far-Right Groups as Gangs." *Contexts* 20 (4): 74–75.
Van Hellemont, Elke, and James A Densley. 2019. "Gang Glocalization: How the Global Mediascape Creates and Shapes Local Gang Realities." *Crime, Media, Culture* 15 (1): 169–189.
Vigil, James Diego. 1988. *Barrio Gangs*. Austin: University of Texas Press.
Walker, Michael L. 2022. *Indefinite: Doing Time in Jail*. New York: Oxford University Press.
Weber, Max. 1949. *Max Weber on the Methodology of the Social Sciences*, translated by Edward A. Shils and Henry A. Finch (1st ed.). Glencoe, Illinois: Free Press.
Yablonsky, Lewis. 1959. "The Delinquent Gang as a Near-Group." *Social Problems* 7 (2): 108–117.
Zilberg, Elana. 2011. *Space of Detention*. Durham, NC: Duke University Press.

CHAPTER 7

GANG IDENTITY ACROSS THE LIFE COURSE

SOU LEE AND BRYAN F. BUBOLZ

IN a general sense, identity refers to "the shared social meanings that persons attribute to themselves in a role" (Burke and Reitzes 1991, 242). Research demonstrates that individuals maintain numerous identities simultaneously, such as being a parent, political activist, or gang member (Bubolz and Simi 2015; Simi, Futrell, and Bubolz 2016; Stryker 2000). Historically, the role of identity in gang membership has been largely overlooked in favor of descriptive and easily measurable predictors of gangs (e.g., income, residence, prior criminal record, race, and ethnicity). However, more recently identity has gained significant attention from criminologists when researching various aspects of gang involvement (see Bubolz and Lee 2019; Lauger 2012; Leverso and Matsueda 2019).

Two identity frameworks have been used among gang scholars: (1) identity theory (IT), which focuses on interpersonal role interactions (Stets and Burke 2000); and (2) social identity theory (SIT), which emphasizes intergroup dynamics and expectations (Tajfel and Turner 1979). Despite where they situate identity (interpersonal versus group), the mechanisms in which these identities are performed are similar and may occur simultaneously (see Stets and Burke 2000); however, some key distinctions warrant discussion. With IT, "behavior between two or more individuals is ... determined by their interpersonal relationships and individual characteristics" (Hennigan and Spanovic 2012, 130). Expressions of identity are important because they serve as attempts to verify authenticity in identity claims (Lauger 2012). In gangs and other violent subcultures, individuals are constantly challenged to prove and defend their individual claims of elevated status and skills at fighting (Anderson 1999; Lauger 2012).

With SIT, individuals maintain collective identities that focus on intergroup dynamics (Stone 1962; Tajfel and Turner 1979). Social identities result from identification with groups and refer to the emotional value that an individual attaches to those groups. This attachment influences how a person will act within and toward other groups; that is, "the behavior between two or more individuals is ... determined by their membership in a particular group" (Hennigan and Spanovic 2012, 130). Tajfel and Turner (1979) describe three pivotal steps involved in the creation of a social or collective identity: (1) identifying with a social group and having a sense of belonging; (2) using a process of categorization to distinguish and differentiate between themselves and other groups; and (3) making comparisons to outgroups, which can be either a source of pride or motivation to improve conditions within their group. In- and outgroup comparisons influence motivation in part because individuals view their respective group as better and more deserving of favorable conditions.

In view of the extant literature, we argue that advancing identity is necessary to a global understanding of gang membership. While conceptually distinct, both IT and SIT configure identity as "soft" and dynamic—that is, identity is a situational resource used to "do" gang membership. This interactional perspective requires acknowledgment of situational circumstances as precipitants to gang-like behaviors (e.g., physical violence and verbal disputes). Furthermore, symbolic interactionism has not been explicitly incorporated into much of the gang research (Decker, Melde, and Pyrooz 2013). This is especially problematic given that identity mechanisms—reflected appraisals, commitment, identity salience, and depersonalization—influence situational behaviors; that is, when an individual decides to "do" their gang identity. For these reasons, we believe that an explicit incorporation and measurement of identity concepts is integral to understanding the situational dynamics that influence gang performance as well as how identity encourages persistence and, ultimately, disengagement from gangs. The following sections locate identity as a central feature of gang involvement, life, and the disengagement process. We conclude with directions for future research and policy implications that place identity at the forefront.

Identity, Gang Involvement, and Gang Life

The process of becoming a gang member is closely tied to identity mechanisms. For instance, joining a gang occurs over an extended period of time among adolescent groups with a shared social history (Fleisher 2000). Gangs provide individuals with a shared sense of structure, values, goals, and social identity that are missing from other conventional outlets (Cohen 1955; Goldman, Giles, and Hogg 2014; Horowitz 1983; Vigil 1988). Through continued interactions among neighborhood cliques, a collective identity is formed that defines the core values of the gang (Lauger 2012). The values and goals incorporate specific ethnic and cultural aspects of significance, such as demonstrating soul (intense level of dedication or devotion) among Black gangs (Keiser 1969), honor (deferential treatment) among Chicano gangs (Horowitz 1983), and communality among Asian gangs (Lee 2020); however, there are general values that transcend ethnic and cultural boundaries such as respect, status, and legitimacy that often requires violence (Hughes and Short 2005; Lauger 2012; Stretesky and Pogrebin 2007).

The gang also becomes an important avenue for disenfranchised youth to find acceptance and success in a culture that often rejects mainstream institutions (Cohen 1955; Vigil 2002). The children of immigrants and refugees also struggle with the tension that exists between maintaining their ethnic and cultural traditions and full assimilation into American society. This tension and the feeling of isolation makes the gang an appealing option for many youth searching for a shared sense of collective identity (Lee 2020; Vigil 2002). Though these motivations may appear disconnected or unrelated to identity, Goldman et al. (2014) provide a compelling account of how social identity and other identity-related concepts qualify many of these factors, including the pursuit of status and respect as well as experiences with multiple marginalization (Vigil, 1988).

Although gangs are an appealing source of social support and structure, they are not an open society where everyone is welcomed. Interested members must demonstrate their legitimacy and meet the standards established by other members of the gang (Densley 2012). Although the exact criteria for inclusion is not always clear and explicit, becoming a member demarcates a symbolic boundary between gang and non-gang individuals (Lauger 2012). One way that gangs make in- and outgroup distinctions is through violent rituals. These initiation ceremonies signify group inclusion and the final stage of acceptance into the gang, cementing the identity as part of an individual's self-concept (Murer and Schwarze 2020; Padilla 1992; Stretesky and Pogrebin 2007).

Fighting and violence are also important aspects of gang life and play a significant role in the advancement of street reputation and identity (Bubolz and Lee 2019; Hughes and Short 2005; Stretesky and Pogrebin 2007). Regarding potentially violent encounters, Garot (2007) captured the interactional dynamics associated with gang identity by assessing the situational context of being "banged on, sweated, or hit up" (55) and how and when one's gang identity would be explicitly announced or performed. These exchanges involve various "turns" or ritualized understandings by which members choose to activate their gang identity and engage in a violent encounter. However, gang members also avoid violence by "ranking out" (i.e., not claim one's gang) or through other strategic verbal maneuvers (e.g., appearing incompetent, inquiring on females, presenting faith). Garot's (2010) notion of "soft" gang membership is especially salient given that individuals are not locked into "doing" their version of gang identity in every possible instance. Essentially, a gang member "could embody every variety [of gang involvement] at different times, or represent himself as embodying different varieties [of gang involvement] with different people" (Garot 2010, 101).

Though not discussed by Garot (2007), it is possible that such actions (i.e., "doing" gang in these situations) may be informed by signaling theory and gang embeddedness. By drawing on Densley (2012) and Pyrooz and Densley's (2016) work on gang selection and criminal offending, we can see that gang members may strategically send out signals of involvement (i.e., verbal acclamation of affiliation) to communicate their unobservable qualities such as toughness, capacity for violence, and loyalty to their gang. These signals are likely encouraged and pursued among highly embedded members whose gang affiliation is of upmost importance to their self-concept and "extends throughout gang membership as individuals continue to cultivate and communicate their reputations" (Pyrooz and Densley 2016, 453). As such, given the potential for victimization, an affirmative response to the question "where you from?" is an "honest" signal that communicates these qualities and strengthens both personal and collective gang reputations among highly embedded individuals. Indeed, high degrees of signaling behavior are significantly related to offending, including criminal assaults (an item that partially constitutes gang embeddedness; Pyrooz and Densley 2016; Pyrooz, Sweeten, and Piquero 2013).

Likewise, gang members may choose not to disclose their affiliation when they have weaker levels of embeddedness; that is, they may be less susceptible to the group processes that facilitate these behaviors (e.g., verbal confirmation of one's affiliation despite the dangers associated with doing so). These individuals may be "low-quality" recruits with marginal signaling behaviors prior to joining and thus are less likely to engage in situations where violence and victimization are at their greatest potential (Pyrooz and Densley 2016). However, it is possible that the gang itself disavows claiming one's set in these emotionally tense situations (Garot 2007), therefore qualifying the parameters for signaling behaviors and thus the necessity and appropriateness of "doing" gang in these encounters. Additionally, the "receiver" in these exchanges is most often a rival gang member who is unlikely to retell of the individual's transgression directly to his gang peers. Because of this, the individual who "ranks out" or otherwise chooses not to claim risks little damage to their reputation within their own gang.

Furthermore, drawing on SIT, Stretesky and Pogrebin (2007) explored the socialization process in producing gang identity and how it fosters criminal violence and gun use. They found that through repeated interactions with their gangs, participants described a shift in their self-perception, one that aligned with the values of their respective gangs (e.g., violence and loyalty), and subsequently encouraged violence to sustain one's identity. Study participants identified their gangs as the most important primary group, highlighting their deeply entrenched gang identities, embeddedness, and continual quest for reputation, respect, and masculine capital including the possession, display, and use of firearms.

Though many individuals join gangs primarily for brotherhood and camaraderie, others also use gangs and violent conflicts for status enhancement. Gang life involves the constant threat and enactment of violence to demonstrate and protect one's collective and individual group identities. In our previous work (Bubolz and Lee 2019), we explicitly used IT to demonstrate the relationship between identity standards, reflected appraisals, commitment, and violence. Notably, we found that "gang members" were tied to the gang primarily through socioemotional forms of identity commitment and relied heavily on reflected appraisals concerning social ties and emotional support. These members engaged in violence only if the act required little effort and the associated costs were minimal. These individuals primarily derived their gang identity from the brotherhood they felt through group inclusion. In contrast, "gangbangers" primarily achieved or performed their gang identity through violence ("putting in work") by engaging in activities such as stabbings, shootings, and robberies. These individuals used violence to demonstrate their cognitive commitment to the gang, thus affirming their own identity as hardened members (Bubolz and Lee 2019). Indeed, "for the gang member, violence is the currency of life and becomes the currency of the economy of the gang" (Jankowski 1991, 139).

Other scholars have documented the nexus between gang identity, violence, and persistence. Relying on measures of group identification (items related to the importance of the group to one's self-concept), Hennigan and Spanovich (2012) found that among gang members (but not other members of neighborhood peer groups such as crews or posses), social identity fully mediated the effects between group cohesiveness (i.e., frequency of meeting as a group) and criminal activity and violence. In other words, the more individuals identified with their gangs, the stronger their connections to the gang's normative expectations and thus a greater likelihood that they engaged in criminal activity and violence—so much so that they were less likely to be deterred by concerns of police apprehension and punishment when compared to individuals in other neighborhood peer groups. Additionally, using measures of social identity, Leverso and Matsueda (2019) found that one's degree of gang identity (i.e., awareness of group membership, self-esteem, and affective commitment to the gang) was a significant contributor to gang persistence (i.e., decreased rate of leaving), even after accounting for self-control and prior offending and victimization.

Research demonstrates that there is considerable variation across gang membership. Drawing on this axiom, one concept that has gained attention in the literature is Pyrooz et al.'s (2013) notion of "gang embeddedness," which they defined as the "adhesion of the gang member to the gang" (243). In practice, this refers to a member's degree of involvement, identification, and status within the gang and highlights the complexities associated with gang involvement, namely the stagnancy and diminishment of social and human capital in conventional arenas (e.g., education, employment). The current configuration of gang embeddedness captures one key aspect of identity—the affective evaluation of the gang and, thus, social identity. This item asks, "How important is the gang/posse to you?" and unsurprisingly is one of the strongest measures of gang embeddedness. Though this item is the only direct tie to identity, it is a welcomed advancement over previous conceptualizations of gang membership (namely the gang and non-gang dichotomy).

Altogether, extant research suggests that gang membership is riddled with violence and unconventional normative expectations. However, members are not always "doing" gang identity at all times; that is, gang identity is *one* of many important resources that individuals draw upon in various situations and circumstances. As such, the fluidity of gang identity is paramount to understanding street gangs. Recently, Lauger's (2020) propositions of gang identity, performance, and violence supports our call for a situated or "soft" conceptualization of gang identity (Garot 2010). First, a gang's collective identity informs an individual's conceptualization of the gang through social interactions. Through these interactions, subtle distinctions between members emerge and influence the unique role they assume. Second, an individual's identity salience influences the activation of their gang identity in various social situations. Third, the performance of gang identity is a function of the situation and context that involves reflected appraisals from a relevant audience (e.g., rivals, peers) and challenges to one's gang identity. Lastly, gang violence is likely influenced by the salience of one's gang identity and their commitment to the group as well as their specific role within the gang. In short, we believe that incorporating these propositions into research as testable hypotheses, interview questions, and theoretical frameworks (see Lauger 2020 for specific examples) would catalyze identity as a fundamental consideration of gang life and related behaviors (criminal and non-criminal) and provide valuable context for robust concepts such as gang embeddedness.

GANG IDENTITY AND DISENGAGEMENT

Identity is central to the disengagement process, as highlighted by the literature on criminal desistance (e.g., Copp et al. 2020; Giordano, Cernkovich, and Rudolph 2002; Healy 2014; Maruna et al. 2004; Paternoster and Bushway 2009). Indeed, as a salient feature of gang membership, shifts in identity have real-life impact. As Pyrooz and Decker (2011) remind us, "cessation of gang membership involves both cognitive or identity shifts *and* restructured routine activities" (423, emphasis in original). There are numerous reasons for gang exit, but pull factors such as parenthood and religious or spiritual awakening illustrate the role of identity most clearly, namely the shuffling of an individual's identity salience (or hierarchy), which in turn alters the emotional attachment to the gang (as a social identity) or commitment as a gang member (as a role identity). Though parenthood may not always promote gang exit (see Pyrooz, McGloin, and Decker 2017), qualitative accounts have highlighted the importance of identity transformations within this life event (e.g., Berger et al. 2017; Bubolz 2014; Forkby, Kuosmanen, and Örnlind 2020; Lee 2020; Moloney et al. 2011; Moloney et al. 2009). While there is undoubtedly some change in routine activities in response to new parental duties, parenthood also engenders new identities and as such, new identity standards associated with that role and group affiliation. Studies have found that parenthood can provide new scripts for achieving masculine and feminine identities, which can result in social distancing from one's gang and adoption of new behaviors to affirm these new identities (i.e., congruence between actual and reflected appraisals and identity standards). For instance, Moloney et al. (2009) found that fatherhood offered "alternative scripts of masculinity—the breadwinner and good provider, the protector and teacher" (317). Indeed, the transformation of masculine identity standards (or masculinity maturation; Leverso and Hess 2021) has been widely acknowledged within gang interventions (see Deuchar and Weide 2019). Similarly, Moloney et al. (2011) found that young female gang mothers altered their behaviors (including leaving the gang) to achieve adult femininity. They found that while demonstration of personal autonomy and sexual reputation characterized femininity among gang-involved girls, financial and emotional independence and being seen as "good mothers" became central features of young gang mothers' identities.

In addition to parenthood, religious or spiritual awakening also invokes ideas of identity change (Decker and Pyrooz 2020; Hallett and McCoy 2015). Importantly, religious or spiritual discoveries allow gang members to realize their existential self—their "view of self with respect to the meaning and purpose of his or her own existence" (Jang and Johnson 2017, 82). By attending to this dimension of one's self-concept, gang members organize their actions and behaviors accordingly to bestow meaning into their lives. In doing so, these individuals may pursue lifestyles that are consistent with these newfound awakenings, namely leaving the gang. For example, nearly one-third of Bubolz's (2014) sample of former gang members identified spiritual or religious awakening as an important motive for disengagement. While some participants identified supernatural consequences of gang involvement (i.e., a fear of going to Hell), embedded within other responses were concerns with identity or role conflict (Lauger and Rivera 2022; Merton 1957; Stryker and Macke 1978). Specifically, these conflicts emerge when two or more identities involve incompatible expectations. When asked about his process of leaving, one participant (Dan) in Bubolz's (2014) study explained:

> I got saved and I knew that there was a greater purpose for me, you know ... I was going to church in the midst of being a part of a gang and I felt like I was living a double life. Like I was going to church, but I would have a pocket full of money from the drugs that I sold and I felt like I was living a double life. I felt like I had to make a choice.

As illustrated by Dan's narrative, his existential identity (informed by his religious awakening), role conflict, and other features of gang life reinforced his decision to leave. In brief, it is necessary that we consider identity mechanisms as they relate to reported motivations for leaving. It is precisely these identity shifts that help us understand why these motivations trigger and sustain disengagement as well as the credible commitments (consistency of these actions) individuals use to signal the authenticity of their former status (Densley and Pyrooz 2019).

Recently, scholars have developed or applied frameworks that highlight identity for understanding gang disengagement, including Decker, Pyrooz, and Moule's (2014) application of Ebaugh's (1988) role-exit theory and Berger et al.'s (2017) desistance process among core gang members. Of notable importance is Bubolz and Simi's (2015) cognitive-emotional theory of gang exit. What makes this theory particularly relevant to our discussion is the primacy of identity in understanding why disillusionment (the most frequently cited reason for exit; see Carson and Vecchio 2015; Decker and Pyrooz 2020) is such a powerful motivator for leaving. They posit that when individuals become gang involved, members develop an inflated identity standard. This is due to the glamorized aspects of membership in broader society—notably protective, familial, and economic expectations. However, the gang fails to meet these expectations (i.e., identity incongruence), resulting in disillusionment and ultimately social stress and anger. In turn, anger contributes to social distancing from the gang, which motivates changes in self-concept. Through repeated episodes of incongruence and anger, a shift in identity salience occurs by which the importance of the gang identity is reduced and other identities filter and inform action and behavior. It is precisely this shuffling of identities that leads to gang exit. In short, Bubolz and Simi (2015) demonstrate how identity processes (e.g., identity standards and salience, incongruence, and social stress) explain why disillusionment is such a frequent motivator for gang exit.

The processual nature of disengagement involves identity transitions and is extremely complex. While identity shifts do occur, the shedding of a former (gang) identity is difficult as remnants of former identities can linger and permeate into current conceptualizations of self (Ebaugh 1988). Despite denouncing gang affiliation, former gang members may experience ongoing role residual while transitioning into new roles. Ebaugh (1988) defined role residual as "the identification that an individual maintains with a prior role such that the individual experiences certain aspects of the role after he or she has in fact exited from it" (173). This "hangover identity" permeates into current conceptualizations of the self and can manifest as specific attitudes, behaviors, and preferences associated with former identities.

Our recent study explored the existence of role residual among former gang members (Bubolz and Lee 2021). We found that nearly all participants described some form of role residual (83% of the sample), namely the persistence of former gang symbols, demeanor, and worldview. First, participants reported an ongoing preference for certain colors, apparel, and logos associated with their former gangs. Second, participants also described continued displays of aggression and violent posturing that characterized their demeanor while involved. Third, residual worldview emerged as a continued predilection for former gang codes of conduct and values. Additionally, role residual was enacted in passive and strategic ways. The former manifested unintentionally, without a specified goal, and was not situationally conditioned or induced. In contrast, the latter was enacted strategically as a situational resource to achieve a particular outcome, such as fending off victimization. In short, lingering aspects of one's former gang identity is expected given that they "continually have to deal with society's reaction to their once having been a part of a previous role" (Ebaugh 1988, 5).

In summary, identity and its various mechanisms for performance (e.g., depersonalization, reflected appraisals, identity salience, self-categorization) is central to understanding all aspects of gang life, from involvement to disengagement. While other social and structural mechanisms may also facilitate entry, persistence, and exit from the gang, identity mechanisms undoubtedly underlie much of these observable processes and events (e.g., violence, parenthood, spiritual awakening) and illuminate the complexities associated with gang disengagement (e.g., role residual).

CONCLUSION AND DISCUSSION

While studies on gangs have invoked the concept of identity by drawing distinctions to various degrees of membership (Lauger 2012; Pyrooz et al. 2013; Vigil 1988), participation in violence (Bubolz and Lee 2019; Hughes and Short 2005), and disengagement (Bubolz and Lee 2021; Decker et al. 2014), much of the existing research has not made significant use of identity processes in understanding a variety of gang-related outcomes. If we wish to prioritize identity as a theoretical framework rather than a nebulous concept, scholarship needs to focus on identity dynamics within the gang life course.

We agree with Garot (2010) that it is necessary to conceptualize gang identity as performative (or fluid, soft, and situational), rather than essentialist (or fixed, stable, and static). As Garot (2010) reminds us, "when it comes to understanding gang membership, most of the gang literature is mired in notions from the 1950s that identity simply *is*, rather than is artfully created and contingent on circumstances and audience" (14, emphasis in original). Specifically, additional work is needed to move our current efforts on classifying gang membership beyond self-nomination and gang embeddedness to be more inclusive of identity-specific measures. Such efforts will allow us to better understand the process of internalizing one's gang identity and consequently the patterns associated with "doing" gang. Indeed, drawing on his own experiences, Bolden (2020) tells us that "the more known you become as a core member, the less ability and desire you [have] to turn gang identity on and off" (55).

While self-nomination is considered one of the most robust indicators of gang involvement, it fails to capture the heterogeneity of gang membership. As countless studies have illustrated, there is no prototypical "gang member" given the various etic and emic classifications (e.g., hardcore, gangbangers, regular, peripheral, situational, and wannabe's). We should not abandon self-nomination, but rather move beyond this binary measure to better capture the textures of gang involvement. One way in which this has been advanced was through the work of Pyrooz et al. (2013), specifically their development of gang embeddedness. While it furnishes a more complex measurement of gang immersion, there is still a need for additional and more nuanced identity-specific measures. As noted earlier, scholars have prioritized these identity mechanisms and revealed the very real impact that gang identity can have on various outcomes, including criminal and violent conduct as well as sustained membership (Hennigan and Spanovich 2012; Leverso and Matsueda 2019). Both studies measured social identity by using Luhtanen and Crocker's (1992) subscale of collective self-esteem (e.g., "The [group] is an important reflection of who I am," "In general, belonging to [the group] is an important part of my self-image"), with Leverso and Matsueda (2019) furthering this inquiry by including additional items that tap into gang identity (e.g., "Being in the gang makes me feel important," "Being in the gang makes me feel like I really belong somewhere").

For quantitative gang scholars, we encourage the continued use of Luhtanen and Crocker's (1992) subscale and Leverso and Matsueda's (2019) six itemed identity measure. We believe that employing these measures in future research can better pinpoint the influence of gang identity on a variety of behaviors (e.g., violence, gang-motivated criminal activities, responses to identity challenges) as well as add nuance to existing approaches, namely self-nomination and gang embeddedness. For instance, how do these identity measures relate to variations in gang embeddedness, the length of membership, and the disengagement process, including lingering socioemotional ties, role residual, and resistance to traditional hooks for change (e.g., children, marriage, employment)? These are questions that we firmly believe benefit from an identity-specific approach.

Furthermore, to capture an individual's identity salience (or hierarchy), we propose a three-step process informed by previous efforts (see Callero 1985; Hooper 1976; Mulford and Salisbury 1964; Thoits 1992) in which a global portrait of one's identities are obtained, followed by demarcation of importance, and concluding with a specific salience score for each identity. To achieve this, we recommend the following: First, individuals are asked to respond to the question "Who am I?" and are instructed to list any of their social roles or descriptions to establish an identity inventory. Second, they are asked to rank these identities into three categories of importance ("most important to you," "second most important to you," and "third most important to you"), with a maximum of three identities per category. Third, to further specify the salience or rank of each role within each strata of importance, individuals are asked the following statements for each identity: (1) "Being a [identity] is something I always think about," (2) "I would feel a loss if I were forced to give up being a [identity]," (3) "I have strong and clear feelings about being a [identity]," (4) "[identity] is an important part of who I am," and (5) "I am committed to being a [identity]." These items can be rated and summed on a Likert scale (e.g., "I strongly agree" to "I strongly disagree"), with higher scores indicating greater salience. This process would reveal important insights about an individual's identity salience and provide useful information to supplement existing measurements such as gang embeddedness and social identity measures.

In addition to incorporating quantitative identity measures into interview protocols, as noted above, we agree with Garot (2010) that gang identity is fluid and used as a strategic (and at times unintentional) and situated resource. It is within qualitative methodologies that we believe these situations are best examined given the open-ended and semi-structured nature of interviews and ability to probe for additional response and detail. This point is especially salient given that individuals are not locked into "doing" their version of gang identity in every possible instance (Garot 2010). While prior research has confirmed the use of gang identity in potentially violent confrontations (Garot 2007), research has seldom examined how gang identity can appear strategically and passively (Bubolz and Lee 2021) in nonrelevant social situations, such as when seeking employment, attending a family event, or interacting with law enforcement. "Doing" gang in these instances may be unnecessary and even counterproductive. Relatedly, understanding when one decides to enact gang identity in these non-gang social situations requires that we also examine the extent to which gang members define or understand when their identity is stigmatized and glamorized.

It is also possible that gang identity can take on a "trans-situational" quality (Stryker 2000), where its activation is likely to occur in both gang and non-gang social situations. To be clear, we view gang identities as "soft" and engaged only when situational dynamics are appropriate; however, the number of situations that are interpreted as appropriate is not static and can change based on a variety of other factors including time in the gang, rank, emotional attachment, and commitment. According to symbolic interactionism, definitions of situations determine action, are created through shared meanings in interactive settings, and develop cognitive schemas "predisposing [individuals] to perceive and act in situations in line with extant identities" (Stryker 2000, 28). Trans-situational identities explain how roles may persist and be enacted across different social venues that may not appear relevant to an outsider's perspective (Stryker 2000). In these situations, the cognitive schemas (lens of interpretation) have become more permanent and resilient to alternate lines of action.

As such, qualitative approaches should inquire on specific situations and factors that precipitate or discourage the likelihood that one's gang identity (and versions of it) is enacted as well as the extent to which a gang identity has become trans-situational. General research questions such as "Do members continue to express their gang identity when outside a social arena that values gang behavior?" and "How often do members engage in identity activation and deactivation and to what extent is this a viable strategy for the most committed members?" are important starting points. Additionally, interview protocols should include questions such as "In what situations might you claim your gang (or not)?", "What might prevent you from hitting up a rival?", "Are there situations (specific places and people) in which you might not claim your gang or color up?", and "In what situations (when, where, and why) do you dress and act like a gang member?" These are a few examples of how we can advance this line of research, with the understanding that these topics and questions are further probed to reveal relevant situational and non-situational factors (e.g., emotional considerations, audience members, physical and virtual settings, presence of firearms and weapons, and length of involvement).

It is equally important to assess how gang identity adapts or evolves over time in response to important life events, such as receiving status or positive appraisals from the gang, attending a gang party for the first time, and feeling abandoned or disillusioned. For example, if joining gangs is a lengthy process, how does gang identity change as individuals gain more acceptance into the group and subsequently impact their internalization of gang identity? Cumulative and incremental experiences in a gang career can have either subtle or significant influence on the importance of the gang identity. If possible, these experiences and their impact on the activation of the gang identity should be explored and measured using longitudinal data. The collection of longitudinal data would open avenues for gang intervention and identify when individuals feel most vulnerable and turn to the gang for support. If longitudinal options are not feasible, then retrospective life history interviews should be considered as an alternative research approach.

In short, advancing identity as a central feature of gang membership necessitates the inclusion of identity-specific measures in both quantitative and qualitative research. Doing so allows scholars to: (1) move beyond self-nomination and gang embeddedness in assessing the heterogeneous nature of gang membership; (2) reveal the situationally relevant features that encourage and repress the performance of one's gang identity; (3) and examine the evolution of identity in response to important and critical life events. While there "is no concrete rule about the degree to which a gang member embraces or internalizes his or her gang identity" (Lauger 2020, 7), in these ways we inch closer to advancing gang identity as an evolving and situated resource for identity accomplishment.

Policy Implications

Those interested in reducing or preventing gang violence should focus on the situational dynamics that encourage gang members to choose violence as a desired response. For instance, while the current approach typically used by law enforcement has some predictive power for violent victimization (Papachristos, Wildeman, and Roberto 2015; Pyrooz et al. 2020), it does a poor job of capturing the nuances of gang membership. Gang databases rely on superficial and highly subjective criteria, namely a non-weighted inclusion standard such as associating with known gang members, dressing like a gang member, using gang signs, possessing gang paraphernalia, and having gang tattoos. Law enforcement agencies typically use a simple counting approach to determine whether an individual should be included as a member in the database (e.g., meeting two or three criteria; Barrows and Huff 2009; Densley and Pyrooz 2020; Leyton 2003). As the number of criteria observed or reported increases in a suspected gang member, so does their documented status in the gang. Having an elevated status of a "shot caller" or "hardcore" member is viewed as being more dangerous than someone who is classified as a "peripheral" or "regular" member (Simi and Hoffman 2012).

Identifying these nuances can be challenging given that gang identities are created and fostered during the formative years of adolescence. Additionally, there are robust and residual aspects that can remain and be signaled even after gang exit. Given that former gang members may experience role residual (Bubolz and Lee 2021), it is easy to understand how others may not recognize their former status (Densley and Pyrooz 2019). These individuals may continue to find themselves on gang databases and be the recipient of actual and anticipated stigma from law enforcement and members of the broader community (Lee and Bubolz 2020). Classification systems should use a weighted set of criteria, where subjective indicators such as physical appearances and associating with other gang members are given less weight while others are weighted more heavily. For instance, involvement in a known gang crime (ideally gang motivated as opposed to gang related) would serve as a better predictor of gang membership and violence when compared to style of dress. Indeed, what is most alarming about gang involvement is not membership but the violence that may accompany such identity. As such, attending to these distinctions are important because they can increase the predictive capability of these systems by distinguishing between members involved for fraternal and social reasons from those who seek status through violence (Bubolz and Lee 2019).

In acknowledging that violence is situationally induced, street-level gang interventionists may be an important resource to collaboratively monitor suspected gang members and the situational dynamics that can lead to gang activity. Interventionists likely have an intimate understanding of the precursors to violence among gang members (e.g., how "hitting up" looks and sounds, variations in posturing and words exchanged before violence ensues). Ideally, this information would be shared with law enforcement to improve their databases, but we recognize this may be difficult and can create distrust toward interventionists as they may be viewed as a double agent or snitch (Simi and Hoffman 2012). We agree with Densley and Pyrooz (2020) that law enforcement agencies are also able to collect data on gang membership and violence given their systematic measurement protocols and resources. These data serve as an important tool to ensure officer safety and as an avenue for criminal investigations. Therefore, we do not advocate for the elimination of gang databases, but rather the improvement in how data are collected, maintained, and used. Indeed, the "opposite of bad data is not no data, but good data" (Densley and Pyrooz 2020, 24). In short, the goal of these efforts is to have a granular understanding of gang membership by considering various aspects of gang identity, particularly the situational dynamics of violence through street-level interventionists and a reduced emphasis on subjective indicators of involvement currently used in gang databases.

REFERENCES

Anderson, Elijah. 1999. *Code of the Street: Decency, Violence, and the Moral Life of the Inner City*. New York: WW Norton & Company.

Barrows, Julie, and C. Ronald Huff. 2009. "Gangs and Public Policy: Constructing and Deconstructing Gang Databases." *Criminology and Public Policy* 8 (4): 675–703.

Berger, Rony, Hisham Abu-Raiya, Yotam Heineberg, and Philip Zimbardo. 2017. "The Process of Desistance among Core Ex-Gang Members." *American Journal of Orthopsychiatry* 87 (4): 487–502. https://doi.org/10.1037/ort0000196.

Bolden, Christian. 2020. *Out of the Red: My Life of Gangs, Prison, and Redemption*. New Brunswick, NJ: Rutgers University Press.

Bubolz, Bryan F. 2014. *Once a Gang Member Always a Gang Member? A Life History Study of Gang Desistance*. Doctoral Dissertation, University of Nebraska—Omaha.

Bubolz, Bryan F., and Sou Lee. 2019. "Putting in Work: The Application of Identity Theory to Gang Violence and Commitment." *Deviant Behavior* 40 (6): 690–702.

Bubolz, Bryan, and Sou Lee. 2021. "'I Still Love My Hood': Passive and Strategic Aspects of Role Residual among Former Gang Members." *Criminal Justice and Behavior* 48 (6): 846–863. https://doi.org/10.1177/0093854820959115.

Bubolz, Bryan F., and Pete Simi. 2015. "Leaving the World of Hate: Life-Course Transitions and Self-Change." *American Behavioral Scientist* 59 (12): 1588–1608.

Burke, Peter J., and Donald C. Reitzes. 1991. "An Identity Theory Approach to Commitment." *Social Psychology Quarterly* 54 (3): 239–251. https://doi.org/2786653.

Callero, Peter L. 1985. "Role Identity Salience." *Social Psychology Quarterly* 48 (3): 203–215. https://doi.org/10.2307/3033681.

Carson, Dena C., and J. Michael Vecchio. 2015. "Leaving the Gang: A Review and Thoughts on Future Research." In *The Handbook of Gangs*, edited by Scott H. Decker, and David C. Pyrooz, 257–275. Chichester, UK: Wiley-Blackwell.

Cohen, Albert K. 1955. *Delinquent Boys: The Culture of the Gang*. New York: Free Press.

Copp, Jennifer E., Peggy C. Giordano, Monica A. Longmore, and Wendy D. Manning. 2020. "Desistance from Crime during the Transition to Adulthood: The Influence of Parents, Peers, and Shifts in Identity." *Journal of Research in Crime and Delinquency* 57 (3): 294–332. https://doi.org/10.1177/0022427819878220.

Decker, Scott H., Chris Melde, and David C. Pyrooz. 2013. "What Do We Know about Gangs and Gang Members and Where Do We Go from Here?" *Justice Quarterly* 30 (3): 369–402. https://doi.org/10.1080/07418825.2012.732101.

Decker, Scott H., and David C. Pyrooz. 2020. "The Role of Religion and Spirituality in Disengagement from Gangs." In *Gangs in the Era of Internet and Social Media*, edited by Chris Melde and Frank Weerman, 225–249. Cham: Springer.

Decker, Scott H., David C. Pyrooz, and Richard K. Moule Jr. 2014. "Disengagement from Gangs as Role Transitions." *Journal of Research on Adolescence* 24 (2): 268–283. https://doi.org/10.1111/jora.12074.

Densley, James A. 2012. "Street Gang Recruitment: Signaling, Screening, and Selection." *Social Problems* 59 (3): 301–321. https://doi.org/10.1525/sp.2012.59.3.301.

Densley, James A., and David C. Pyrooz. 2019. "A Signaling Perspective on Disengagement from Gangs." *Justice Quarterly* 36 (1): 31–58. https://doi.org/10.1080/07418825.2017.1357743.

Densley, James A., and David C. Pyrooz. 2020. "The Matrix in Context: Taking Stock of Police Gang Databases in London and Beyond." *Youth Justice* 20 (1–2): 11–30. https://doi.org/10.1177/1473225419883706.

Deuchar, Ross, and Robert D. Weide. 2019. "Journeys in Gang Masculinity: Insights from International Case Studies of Interventions." *Deviant Behavior* 40 (7): 851–865. https://doi.org/10.1080/01639625.2018.1443761.

Ebaugh, Helen R. F. 1988. *Becoming an Ex: The Process of Role Exit*. Chicago, IL: University of Chicago Press.

Fleisher, Mark S. 2000. *Dead End Kids: Gang Girls and the Boys They Know*. Madison: University of Wisconsin Press.

Forkby, Torbjörn, Jari Kuosmanen, and Henrik Örnlind. 2020. "Leaving Gangs: Failed Brotherhood and Reconstructed Masculinities." In *Gangs in the Era of Internet and Social Media*, edited by Chris Melde and Frank Weerman, 155–174. Cham: Springer.

Garot, Robert. 2007. "'Where You From!' Gang Identity as Performance." *Journal of Contemporary Ethnography* 36 (1): 50–84.

Garot, Robert. 2010. *Who You Claim: Performing Gang Identity in School and on the Streets*. New York: New York University Press.

Giordano, Peggy C., Stephen A. Cernkovich, and Jennifer L. Rudolph. 2002. "Gender, Crime, and Desistance: Toward a Theory of Cognitive Transformation." *American Journal of Sociology* 107 (4): 990–1064. http://www.jstor.org/stable/10.1086/343191.

Goldman, Liran, Howard Giles, and Michael A. Hogg. 2014. "Going to Extremes: Social Identity and Communication Processes Associated with Gang Membership." *Group Processes & Intergroup Relations* 17 (6): 813–832. https://doi.org/10.1177/1368430214524289.

Hallett, Michael, and J. Stephen McCoy. 2015. "Religiously Motivated Desistance: An Exploratory Study." *International Journal of Offender Therapy and Comparative Criminology* 59 (8): 855–872. https://doi.org/10.1177/0306624X14522112.

Healy, Deirdre. 2014. "Becoming a Desister: Exploring the Role of Agency, Coping and Imagination in the Construction of a New Self." *British Journal of Criminology* 54 (5): 873–891. https://doi.org/10.1093/bjc/azu048.

Henningan, Karen, and Marija Spanovich. 2012. "Gang Dynamics through the Lens of Social Identity Theory." In *Youth Gangs in International Perspective: Results from the Eurogang Program of Research*, edited by Finn-Aage Esbensen and Cheryl L. Maxson, 127–149. New York: Springer.

Hooper, Michael. 1976. "The Structure and Measurement of Social Identity." *Public Opinion Quarterly* 40 (2): 154–164. https://doi.org/10.1086/268284.

Horowitz, Ruth. 1983. *Honor and the American Dream: Culture and Identity in a Chicano Community*. New Brunswick, NJ: Rutgers University Press.

Hughes, Lorine A., and James F. Short Jr. 2005. "Disputes Involving Youth Street Gang Members: Micro-Social Contexts." *Criminology* 43 (1): 43–76. https://doi.org/10.1111/j.0011-1348.2005.00002.x.

Jang, Sung J., and Byron R. Johnson. 2017. "Religion, Spirituality, and Desistance from Crime: Toward a Theory of Existential Identity Transformation." In *The Routledge International Handbook of Life-Course Criminology*, edited by Arjan Blokland and Victor van der Geest, 74–86. Oxford: Routledge.

Jankowski, Martin S. 1991. *Islands in the Streets: Gangs and American Urban Society*. Berkeley: University of California Press.

Keiser, R. Lincoln. 1969. *The Vice Lord: Warriors of the Streets*. New York: Holt, Rinehart, and Winston.

Lauger, Timothy R. 2012. *Real Gangstas: Legitimacy, Reputation, and Violence in an Intergang Environment*. New Brunswick, NJ: Rutgers University Press.

Lauger, Timothy R. 2020. "Gangs, Identity, and Cultural Performance." *Sociology Compass* 14 (4): e12772. https://doi.org/10.1111/soc4.12772.

Lauger, Timothy R., and Craig J. Rivera. 2022. "Banging while Believing: The Intersection of Religiosity, Gang Membership, and Violence." *Social Problems*: 1–19. https://doi.org/10.1093/socpro/spac027.

Lee, Sou. 2020. *Menyuam Laib: Entry, Persistence, and Exit Among Hmong Gang Members*. Doctoral Dissertation, Southern Illinois University—Carbondale.

Lee, Sou, and Bryan F. Bubolz. 2020. "The Gang Member Stands Out: Stigma as a Residual Consequence of Gang Involvement." *Criminal Justice Review* 45 (1): 64–83. https://doi.org/10.1177/0734016819867385.

Leverso, John, and Chris Hess. 2021. "From the Hood to the Home: Masculinity Maturation of Chicago Street Gang Members." *Sociological Perspectives* 64 (6): 1206–1223. https://doi.org/10.1177/07311214211040844.

Leverso, John, and Ross L. Matsueda. 2019. "Gang Organization and Gang Identity: An Investigation of Enduring Gang Membership." *Journal of Quantitative Criminology* 35 (4): 797–829. https://doi-org.gonzaga.idm.oclc.org/10.1007/s10940-019-09408-x.

Leyton, Stacey. 2003. "The New Blacklists: The Threats to Civil Liberties Posed by Gang Databases." In *Crime Control and Social Justice: The Delicate Balance*, edited by Darnell F. Hawkins, Samuel L. Myers Jr., and Randolph N. Stone, 109–174. Westport, CT: Greenwood Press.

Luhtanen, Riia, and Jennifer Crocker. 1992. "A Collective Self-Esteem Scale: Self-Evaluation of One's Social Identity." *Personality and Social Psychology Bulletin* 18 (3): 302–318. https://doi.org/10.1177/0146167292183006.

Maruna, Shadd, Thomas P. Lebel, Nick Mitchell, and Michelle Naples. 2004. "Pygmalion in the Reintegration Process: Desistance from Crime Through the Looking Glass." *Psychology, Crime & Law* 10 (3): 271–281. https://doi.org/10.1080/10683160410001662762.

Merton, Robert K. 1957. "The Role-Set: Problems in Sociological Theory." *British Journal of Sociology* 8 (2): 106–120. https://www.jstor.org/stable/587363.

Moloney, Molly, Geoffrey P. Hunt, Karen Joe-Laidler, and Kathleen MacKenzie. 2011. "Young Mother (in the) Hood: Gang Girls' Negotiation of New Identities." *Journal of Youth Studies* 14 (1): 1–19. https://doi.org/10.1080/13676261.2010.506531.

Moloney, Molly, Kathleen MacKenzie, Geoffrey Hunt, and Karen Joe-Laidler. 2009. "The Path and Promise of Fatherhood for Gang Members." *British Journal of Criminology* 49 (3): 305–325. https://doi.org/10.1093/bjc/azp003.

Mulford, Harold A., and Winfield W. Salisbury II. 1964. "Self-Conceptions in a General Population." *Sociological Quarterly* 5 (1): 35–46. https://doi.org/10.1111/j.1533-8525.1964.tb02254.x.

Murer, Jeffrey S., and Tilman Schwarze. 2020. "Social Rituals of Pain: The Socio-Symbolic Meaning of Violence in Gang Initiations." *International Journal of Politics, Culture, and Society* 35: 95–110. http://doi.org/10.1007/s10767-020-09392-2.

Padilla, Felix M. 1992. *The Gang as an American Enterprise.* New Brunswick, NJ: Rutgers University Press.

Papachristos, Andrew V., Christopher Wildeman, and Elizabeth Roberto. 2015. "Tragic, but Not Random: The Social Contagion of Nonfatal Gunshot Injuries." *Social Science & Medicine* 125: 139–150. https://doi.org/10.1016/j.socscimed.2014.01.056.

Paternoster, Ray, and Shawn Bushway. 2009. "Desistance and the 'Feared Self': Toward an Identity Theory of Criminal Desistance." *Journal of Criminal Law and Criminology* 99 (4): 1103–1156. https://www.jstor.org/stable/20685067.

Pyrooz, David C., and Scott H. Decker. 2011. "Motives and Methods for Leaving the Gang: Understanding the Process of Gang Desistance." *Journal of Criminal Justice* 39 (5): 417–425. https://doi.org/10.1016/j.jcrimjus.2011.07.001.

Pyrooz David C., and James A. Densley. 2016. "Selection into Street Gangs: Signaling Theory, Gang Membership, and Criminal Offending." *Journal of Research in Crime and Delinquency* 53 (4): 447–481. https://doi.org/10.1177/0022427815619462.

Pyrooz, David C., Ryan K. Masters, Jennifer J. Tostlebe, and Richard G. Rogers. 2020. "Exceptional Mortality Risk among Police-Identified Young Black Male Gang Members." *Preventive Medicine* 141: 106–269. https://doi.org/10.1016/j.ypmed.2020.106269.

Pyrooz, David C., Jean M. McGloin, and Scott H. Decker. 2017. "Parenthood as a Turning Point in the Life Course for Male and Female Gang Members: A Study of Within-Individual Changes in Gang Membership and Criminal Behavior." *Criminology* 55 (4): 869–899. https://doi.org/10.1111/1745-9125.12162.

Pyrooz, David C., Gary Sweeten, and Alex R. Piquero. 2013. "Continuity and Change in Gang Membership and Gang Embeddedness." *Journal of Research in Crime and Delinquency* 50 (2): 239–271. https://doi.org/10.1177/0022427811434830.

Simi, Pete, and Dennis Hoffman. 2012. *2011-2012 Omaha Gang Assessment.* Omaha: University of Nebraska.

Simi, Pete, Robert Futrell, and Bryan F. Bubolz. 2016. "Parenting as Activism: Identity Alignment and Activist Persistence in the White Power Movement." *Sociological Quarterly* 57: 491–519. https://doi.org/10.1111/tsq.12144.

Stets, Jan E., and Peter J. Burke. 2000. "Identity Theory and Social Identity Theory." *Social Psychology Quarterly* 63 (3): 224–237. http://doi.org/2695870.

Stone, Gregory P. 1962. "Appearance and the Self." In *Human Behavior and Social Processes*, edited by Arnold M. Rose, 94–116. Boston, MA: Houghton Mifflin.

Stretesky, Paul B., and Mark R. Pogrebin. 2007. "Gang-Related Gun Violence: Socialization, Identity, and Self." *Journal of Contemporary Ethnography* 36 (1): 85–114. https://doi.org/10.1177/0891241606287416.

Stryker, Sheldon. 2000. "Identity Competition: Key to Differential Social Movement Participation?" In *Self, Identity, and Social Movements*, edited by Sheldon Stryker, Timothy J. Owens, and Robert W. White, 21–40. Minneapolis: University of Minnesota Press.

Stryker, Sheldon, and Anne S. Macke. 1978. "Status Inconsistency and Role Conflict." *Annual Review of Sociology* 4 (1): 57–90. https://doi.org/10.1146/annurev.so.04.080178.000421.

Tajfel, Henri, and John Turner. 1979. "An Integrative Theory of Intergroup Conflict." In *Social Psychology of Intergroup Relations*, edited by William G. Austin and Stephen Worchel, 33–47. Monterey: Brooks/Cole Publishing.

Thoits, Peggy A. 1992. "Identity Structures and Psychological Well-Being: Gender and Marital Status Comparisons." *Social Psychology Quarterly* 55 (3): 236–256. https://doi.org/10.2307/2786794.

Vigil, James D. 1988. *Barrio Gangs: Street Life and Identity in Southern California*. Austin: University of Texas Press.

Vigil, James D. 2002. *A Rainbow of Gangs: Street Culture in the Mega-City*. Austin: University of Texas Press.

CHAPTER 8

PLACE MATTERS
Geographers and Gang Members

STEFANO BLOCH

I came to geography by way of gang affiliation and graffiti writing (Bloch 2019). This trajectory from the streets to the classroom should come as no surprise to those who know the history of geography as a real-world endeavor and academic discipline forged from the exploits of place-takers and place-makers (Livingstone 1992). Geography is an interdisciplinary field of study whose adherents have analyzed the world and its myriad social and natural environments from both a humanistic and structuralist perspective, using both quantitative and qualitative methods, and at scales ranging from the universal to the particular. But what unites over two centuries of formal geographical praxis and theory is that above all else, "place matters" (Buttimer and Seamon 1980; Massey 2005; Soja 1989; Tuan 1977).

Definitions and explanations for the distinction between space and place abound (Cresswell 2014; Lefebvre 1991), but I offer one that, hopefully, captures the essence of their difference for use in the present chapter. That is, "space" is the Euclidian and abstract notion of the location to which ideological intent is ascribed from afar, whereas "place" is space once imbued with meaning upon encounter. As Massey (1994) argues in her influential conceptualization of a "sense of place," all places range from the reactionary to the progressive, just as the communities and social formations that inhabit all places necessarily rely on inclusive principles as well as exclusionary practices (Bloch 2022b). "Gang space," in turn, can be thought of as the outsiders' conceptualization and notion of a gang's hood, whereas "gang places" are those socially produced locations that self-identified gang members physically inhabit, demarcate, and fight for. The former is the stuff of mythmaking (Katz 2000), while the latter is the stuff of experience (Conquergood 1993). Complicating my distinction is the colloquial use of "space" to indicate a specific aspect, node, or surface of the built environment, such as the space of the wall, the space of the street corner, or public spaces more generally. But in such usage, spaces in aggregate constitute a particular place (Bloch 2012b).

Despite the salience of place in geographical thinking, geographers have not adequately studied gangs as geographically oriented social entities. Perhaps the lack of gang research in geography is because sociologists and criminologists were first to take up the mantle of gang research almost a century ago, beginning in earnest with the work of Thrasher (1927). Following Thrasher's study of "1,313 gangs in Chicago" and later works studying the socially produced "life space of the gang" throughout the mid-twentieth century (Klein 1995; see also Anderson 1976; Liebow 1967; Short and Strodtbeck 1965; Whyte 1943), geographers continued to divert their attention away from gangs even as street gangs came to prominence in cities across the United States by the 1980s.

Rather than focus on gang members who were assertively inhabiting the very places that geographers used as case-study sites, geographers gravitated toward exceedingly esoteric and structurally abstract discussions of "space" (Lefebvre 1991). From focusing on landscape morphology (Sauer 1925) and urban economic restructuring (Harvey 1973) to developing "geographical epistemologies" (Lowenthal 1961) borrowed from continental philosophy and metaphysics, geographers can rightly be criticized for "neglecting facets of human experience" in favor of theoretical conceptualization (Buttimer 1976, 277). But, to be sure, gangs have found their way into the geographical literature, albeit sparingly. In addition to providing a review of what geographers have said about gangs, as well as a nod to the work by non-geographer gang researchers who have employed geographical thinking and spatial methods (e.g., Weisburd et al. 2016), I conclude with a modest case for what geographers still have to offer gang studies moving forward. My discussion is situated within an interspersed autoethnographic account of growing up gang affiliated and how it led me to geography.

GANGS IN GEOGRAPHY

By the time we were in our early teens, my friends and I could draw a map of the more than 500-square-mile city of Los Angeles with enough accuracy to sell to commuters at local gas stations. We were not aspiring cartographers or budding real estate speculators; rather, for us, possessing an intimate knowledge of neighborhood boundaries—both real and imagined—was a matter of survival. As graffiti writers growing up during the turbulent 1990s, we traversed the city as part of our goal to "go all city," that is, be the most prolific "taggers" whose names could be seen adorning "spots" from the north side of the San Fernando Valley to the South Bay, and from the beaches to the inland reaches of the LA basin.

While a century of socioeconomic preoccupation with race and class helped planners and politicians carve up Los Angeles into a mosaic of differentiation facilitated by top-down segregation and bottom-up congregation, it was gang members, like property owners, who became entrenched in those locations and sometimes violently laid claim to those places. As graffiti writers, just as we knew how to navigate around police patrols and roving vigilantes in the tonier enclaves throughout the city's west side, we also had to know whose hood we were entering on the city's equally exclusionary working-class east side. As vandals, we were *persona non grata*, and we had to know the lay of the land more completely and acutely than anyone else. But also, as graffiti writers, we saw the city as a container for the light poles, curbs, walls, and freeway signs on which we would write our names, often in a seemingly cryptic scrawl that no less expressed an insider language full of meaning.

We did not lay claim to any one specific place. For us, the entirety of the city was ours. It was through this lens that we viewed gangs as distinctly different despite our superficial aesthetic commonalities. We dressed like them, did graffiti like them, and lived in the same neighborhoods as them. For police who either could not or would not see beyond these outward indicators, we were them for purposes of categorization and criminalization (Bloch 2020b, 2020c). We also knew them as friends and sometimes foes. They were our brothers and sisters, and sometimes even our parents or partners. Sometimes we even led dual lives as gang members and graffiti writers ourselves. But as a social formation, gangs, even more than graffiti writers for whom spaces served as a canvas, were obsessed with the contours of particular places and place identity.

Gang members' preoccupation with place as a social construct imbued with cultural meaning is evidenced by their collective embrace of neighborhood namesakes and focus on territoriality as their raison d'être. While "gang-related activity" certainly signals their geographical embeddedness and emplacement, gang members' preoccupation with place is most overtly and visually displayed in their graffiti. Gang graffiti is nothing less than a geographical expression of both *place-making* and *place-taking*. Most gang namesakes, particularly those in Los Angeles, the so-called "gang capital of the world," are derived from local streets, neighborhoods, and even whole regions: 18th Street, North Hollywood Boys, and Mid City Crips, to name a few. When written on walls as part of the demarcation of their declared hoods, gang members often include cardinal points in their graffiti, indicating a specific "West Side" (WS) klik, or to distinguish themselves geographically from "sets" on the East Side (ES) of the city. In addition to cardinal points, gangs often express place specifically with the use of spraypainted arrows pointing to "set space" (Tita, Cohen, and Engberg 2005) or a stylized and underlined V or B demarcating the Barrio or Varrio (Spanish for "neighborhood"). Gang names written on walls also often possess a preceding 13, indicating *sureño* (southern California) identity and affiliation, or 14 for *norteño* if the klik claims territory north of the California city of Bakersfield. Further, place identifiers do not just remain on the walls, as gang members often tattoo place names and area codes onto their bodies as part of a prideful place identification and solidarity. When I was younger, closely reading the writing on the walls, as well as on people's bodies, was a consequential lesson in geographical thinking. It also became the lens through which I would read and review scholarly writing on gangs to this day. But in my home discipline of geography, those writings are regrettably far and few between.

David Ley (1974, 1975) was the first and remains one of the few geographers to take gangs seriously as a subject of research. While exploring how urban environments are structured and residents navigate places as motivated by human agency, Ley (1975) challenged work on urban ecologies coming out of the Chicago school of sociology to "show sensitivity" to the fact that place is a not a constant, and that "causal explanations" for gangs and delinquency "must include variables and ideologies which are national, and not simply local, in their range" (249). Invoking spatial scales in his discussion, Ley (1975) stressed that "gangs cannot be discussed independently of their milieu." In making this claim, he sought to merge sociological thinking with geographical contextualization to depict "gang space" as more dynamic than had been discussed in the literature to that point. He argued that "there is a spatial ecology which leads to the formation of the gang, and then an ongoing social ecology which lends a meaning to space" (Ley 1975, 248), thereby articulating a brand of highly localized human-centered research at the scale of the block.

However, Ley's work on "gang space" was not to be replicated because the dominant strands of the discipline were already tending toward structuralist thinking in which any potential study of how gang members socially produce place would be supplanted by economic investigations into the large-scale ravages of capitalism and more localized processes of "ghetto formation" (Harvey 1972). Even David Harvey, whose work otherwise constituted a paradigm shift in sociospatial thinking and more critically accounted for marginalized and maligned communities, limited his investigation into gangs to seemingly dismissive postulations about their "persistent appropriations of space" (Harvey 1987, 268). Nowhere else in Harvey's work is a spatially conscious social entity—from communards to capitalists—so easily glossed over despite being so persistent and policed as place-makers. Such a glossing-over of gang identity and behavior was to be the status quo in the discipline for decades, even by the most critical of scholars for whom gangs should have been a ripe territory for investigation.

I came to Ley's work as a master's student interested in scholarly discussions about graffiti. Initially, I had checked Susan Phillips' (1999) book on "wallbangin'" out of the UCLA library, but it was so true to our story as gang-adjacent "bombers" (prolific graffiti writers) that I felt I needed something more well-steeped in a spatial theory that brought needed generalizability to the specificity of neighborhood demarcation. I moved from Phillips' anthropological work to an even more geographical-adjacent scholar in Mike Davis (1990). His work on oppressive political regimes in Los Angeles provided the perfect frame to help explain how "gang neighborhoods" were policed and graffiti disparaged in the context of a moral panic and what Iveson (2010) identifies as new military urbanism. I found Davis' radical formulations to be just what I needed as a nascent scholar of urban geography, and placing his analysis in Los Angeles helped ground what other scholars of graffiti were likewise providing elsewhere (Ferrell, 1993). But it was an article in the flagship geography journal by Ley and Cybriwski (1974) that allowed me to truly merge my passion for wall writing with my newfound academic preoccupation with scholarly writing. It was in Ley and Cybriwski's (1974) research that I saw the earliest and most nuanced research on graffiti in which a distinction between gang graffiti and wall writing by "graffiti kings" was made. As they show, graffiti by individual "kings" is intended to announce "I was here," whereas gang graffiti is far more likely to suggest "stay out." Though in both cases "wall graffiti offer an accurate indicator of turf ownership" (Ley and Cybriwski 1974, 495), with one being ephemeral, the other vying for permanence.

Finding Ley and Cybriwsky's article perhaps naively made me think geography was the perfect home for my interests and experience. I completed my master's degree in urban planning and moved to a PhD program in geography. I found myself unable to stay within the geographical literature if I was to continue writing about graffiti and gangs. As my dissertation took shape (Bloch 2012a), I was praised (and funded) for embracing interdisciplinarity, but in my mind, I had no other choice. Despite one of the most sophisticated discussions of graffiti as a form of transgression waged against "moral geographies" being produced by a human geographer (Cresswell 1996), the discipline as a whole seemed to look over the heads of the people in my community to theorize oppression far afield and from a God's eye view. I attributed this, perhaps correctly, to the fact that geographers, no matter how critical or engaged, lacked the personal experience needed to investigate place-making by gang members and graffiti writers in a nuanced and grounded way. For Pulido (2002) this may have something to do with the class and race composition of geography as a "white discipline," but for me, it seems to be because geographers relegated the study of subcultures to sociologists and cultural anthropologists as part of the discipline's mission to prove its hard-sciences chops. That is, geographers were too busy measuring and theorizing space to take the time or employ the methods needed to observe spatial relations as practiced by a criminalized urban underclass.

There have, however, been attempts to bring gangs into discussions of poverty, displacement, criminalization, and marginalization, but they have most often been mentioned by geographers as the amorphous objects of oppression rather than as place-making agents. When not theorized as such within discussions of security politics, or what geographer Dugan Meyer (2021) insightfully identifies as a "security symptom" in the context of displacement by gentrification, gangs are included among a litany of other overpoliced sources of neighborhood disorder such as prostitution, drug dealing, and homelessness. In the large geographical literature on the conflictual politics and policing of public space, gangs are wholly unrepresented even though they are a public-facing and place-claiming social formation whose membership of mostly impoverished young men of color is estimated to be in the hundreds of thousands in the United States alone (Decker et al. 2022). Rather than reproduce the long list of geographers who omit gangs despite the opportunity to include gang formation and activity in their research, I will include those works that have brought gangs into the conversation.

Writing about the formation of Black gangs in Los Angeles, Alonso (2004) argued "to fully understand the dynamics of these gangs, we must view them from a historical perspective that illuminates the roles of race, place and social structure in early gang formation" (663). Based in part on his reading of the "multiple marginality" thesis offered by Vigil (1988) in his analysis of Chicano gangs in LA, Alonso argues that "race is central as an etiological factor" (669) in gang formation, but that the racialized production of segregated places, as well as racist policing by both local and federal law enforcement agencies, creates a sociopolitical and economic environment in which gangs flourish. Similarly, in addition to my own review of gangs and geographical thinking (Bloch 2022a) and an analysis of racialized prison gangs (Bloch and Olivares-Pelayo 2021), Susan Phillips and I (Bloch and Phillips 2022) have examined how in the wake of residential redlining schemes, "street gangs have laid claim to neighborhood spaces throughout Los Angeles since the at least the 1940s, creating a quasi-autonomous geography of enmity and alliance that authorities and the public simplistically see as having been produced unidirectionally, from the bottom up" (752).

Gang in Place

Outside geography, there are criminological and sociological treatments of gang research that are decidedly spatial in scope and often far more mindful of the importance of place in gang research than that which has been produced by geographers proper. For example, in their effort to "situate gang identities in their proper place," Lopez-Aguado and Walker (2021) argue that gang members "consistently tether place to identity" (109). Referencing qualitative work on gangs by Maxson (2011), Moore, Vigil, and Garcia (1983), and Vigil (1988) to name a few, they point out that "criminalized identities are nested geographically, so that the smaller the social geographic area, the more meaningful the identity in terms of gang-involvement." "Place," they argue, is therefore not just a background element but "a distinguishing feature of every encounter, as well as a key resource in the situational 'activation' of any gang identity." "The rivalries, kinship, and meanings tied to a particular gang identity," they argue, "are all shaped, in part, by place" (108).

Earlier work likewise incorporated a geographical perspective in the analysis of gangs, seeking, for example, to explore gang "set space" (Tita et al. 2005) to "demonstrate the primacy of 'place' in shaping the identity of the gang as a social group" (Brantingham et al. 2012, 852; see also Curry and Spergel 1988). But such geographical framing and nuanced spatial approaches are employed to better understand, identify the location of, and even predict fear and violence (see Papachristos, Hureau, and Braga 2013; Valasik and Tita 2018; Radil, Flint, and Tita 2010; Tita and Radil 2010; Curtis et al. 2014). While gang members as a group often evoke fear and disproportionately contribute to violent crime rates including homicide (Cohen and Tita 1999; Sanchez, Decker, and Pyrooz 2022; Valasik 2018; Valasik et al. 2017; Valasik and Reid 2021; see also Aspholm 2022), it is only one, relatively outsized, aspect of what they do, who they are, and how they claim places and identities as their own (Kontos, Brotherton, and Barrios 2003). As Decker, Melde, and Pyrooz (2013) acknowledge, "understanding other forms of criminal behavior is important to create a fuller understanding of what gangs are and what their members do. The lack of focus on group process in non-criminal behavior among gangs and gang members is an even larger omission from the inventory of gang research" (386). In reality, as Luis J. Rodriguez (1993; Rodriguez, Martínez, and Rodriquez 2000) puts it, 90% of what gang members do is "kick it," with the vast majority of gang life spent engaging in non-violent, mundane place-making and "hanging around" (Brotheron and Barrios 2004; Klein 1995; Moore 1991; Vigil 1988).

The importance of understanding place when both theorizing and policing gangs is without question. The loss of geographical specificity is not just an inconsequential oversight; rather, it allows for the blanket application of the gang identifier in the broad conceptualization and criminalization of mostly young men of color who spend a disproportionate amount of time in public space relative to their more affluent and white counterparts and age cohort. The displacement of territory and movement away from place as a defining feature of gang activity can allow for gang members to be "tied to the much more abstract terrain of 'the street'" (Lopez-Aguado and Walker 2021, 111), thereby allowing for the increased criminalization of places vis-à-vis unwanted populations. Whereas gangs used to be thought of as place-based, their place attachment has in recent years been replaced by symbolic and appropriated "brands of gang culture" (Lopez-Aguado and Walker 2021) that fall under the placeless monikers and horizontal leadership structure of, for example, "transnational gangs" such as the Crips, Bloods, Latin Kings, and Mara Salvatrucha, each of which have been targeted under RICO (Racketeer Influenced and Corrupt Organizations Act) statutes in addition to being surveilled via "community policing" efforts and local civil injunctions (Durán 2013; Muñiz 2015; Bloch and Meyer 2019). This loss of place as a defining component of gang activity has, in short, increased the scale at which "gang members"—both real and imagined—can be targeted by law enforcement.

Adding to the erosion, or at least distortion, of physical place as a defining characteristic and necessary component for identifying gangs is the movement of gang "activity" to online platforms. So-called "cyber banging" (Patton, Eschmann, and Butler 2013) has "respatialized" gang activity according to Roberts (2021), creating yet another scale at which to analyze and better understand gang activity as well as the tools the justice system may use to investigate and prosecute gang members (Pyrooz and Moule 2019). While there remains much work to be done in terms of researching the contours and characteristics of such virtual spaces, it is clear that the internet is not a replacement for gang places, but an additional venue through which gang interaction takes place in ways akin to, for example, online dating and attending art openings in the metaverse. In each case, the virtual world is not a substitute for place, but an extension and even enhancement of already existing places. Nevertheless, one of the primary questions being asked in regard to cyber banging is the degree to which it is spilling over into the "real world" and contributing to violent confrontation (Irwin-Rogers, Densley, and Pinkney 2018; Leverso and Hsiao 2021; Melde and Weerman 2020; Stuart 2020). As Moore and Stuart (2022) put it "there remains a significant debate as to the exact relationship between online representations of gang violence and offline physical violence" (310). But the same questions can and have been asked about the space of the wall on which "callouts," "cross-outs," "roll calls," and "disses" have been spraypainted for generations. So important is wall space in the expression of a gang and its antagonisms and alliances, I cannot conceive of a discussion about online spaces that do not directly evoke the role walls have played in precipitating gang interaction, identity, and place-making.

PLACE MATTERS

As this chapter demonstrates, I tend to review and hold accountable the qualitative literature while admittedly giving short shrift to the quantitative studies. But, in full disclosure, quantitative data elude me, and not for the reasons one may think. It is not because I question the utility of reducing gang members to data points, or that I find fault in using aggregate data to generalize about a subculture that is so very complex, conflictual, and contradictory. It is far simpler than that.

North Hollywood Boyz (NHBZ) and North Hollywood Locos (NHLS) were bitter rivals. NHBZ was much larger but had fewer allies in neighboring communities. NHLS was a smaller klik, but Vineland Boys (VBS), Radford Street (RST), Boys From The Hood (BFTH), Runnymede Street Locas (RSLS), and the local 18th Street set all had their back. The school I was attending at the time, one of many I would enroll in and leave due to chronic displacement and homelessness with my mother (Bloch 2020a; 2022c), had about 15 members of NHBZ and only one member of NHLS. But he made up for being alone by being fierce and always ready to fight. In my pre-algebra class, he turned to me and asked to see my hands. I held them out, knuckles up because I knew what he was looking for, and right then and there he asked me if I wanted to "get down" with NHLS. I felt excited to be asked. Some of the guys in my burgeoning graffiti crew were members of NHBZ, so I wanted to turn him down. I told him I would let him know the next day in class. I went home, and with a Magnum marker I covered the bedroom walls in the tiny apartment we were renting with NHLS block letters. I knew how to construct traditional *placas* since I was able to hold a pencil. In each letter, I drew stylized cracks and ornate spider webs in the corner, as well as a perfect drop shadow making the letters appear 3D. I also placed little Xs in the N and the H to exhibit requisite antipathy for that other North Hollywood–based set.

My older brother, who was already in a gang whose hood was located where we had previously lived (Moore et al. 1983), came in and told me I was making a big mistake. If I got down with NHLS I wouldn't have a chance at going all city. Besides, most of the best graffiti writers in the area were affiliated with NHBZ through friends, neighbors, and older brothers. As a member of NHLS, I might be able to rely on my "tagger" status when getting hit up and asked where I "was from" by individual NHBZ who didn't know me personally, but as soon as a fellow writer called me out for being an NHLS I would have to either "claim my set" or "rank out" (Garot 2010). More importantly, it meant that much of the city would be cut off from me.

The alliances that NHLS maintained with other hoods were not geographically contiguous. I would have to cross in and out of friendly and rival territory every time I went out writing. I could go north on Laurel Canyon Boulevard from where I lived, but not south. I could go west on Burbank Boulevard and then north up Coldwater Canyon to Vanowen Street, and then make my way back east, cutting through Vineland Boys' and RST's hood, but I couldn't complete the circle by going back south on Laurel Canyon because of the one NHBZ klik that had a small hood near Victory Boulevard. Vineland Avenue was fine in both directions, but Van Nuys Boulevard was not. The geography of gang enmity and alliance was too complex for someone who just wanted to hit "spots" and get fame (Ferrell and Weide 2010).

I decided that being in a gang was too limiting, socially as well as spatially. But I also couldn't turn down my classmate. So I never went back. The day I showed him my knuckles was my last day of junior high school and the last day I would ever be enrolled in a math class. Just under a year later, I enrolled myself at North Hollywood High School, and by then I was already known as an all-city graffiti writer who had garnered enough street cred to not even be asked to join a gang (see Pyrooz and Densley 2016). Looking back, I had already become a geographer by then as well, though it would take me a few years to realize it. Before completing my senior year, I was kicked out of school for writing on the bathroom wall, which I didn't do. It freed me up to write even more graffiti on city walls, which I did do, before enrolling at a local community college a few years later, where my academic life began.

Conclusion

Like Papachristos and Hughes (2015) before me, I acknowledge that the "intersection of social and geographic space represents a new area of inquiry worthy of both theoretical and methodological consideration" for criminologists (109). But I am likewise asserting that this intersection has been well traveled by generations of geographers whose research has ignored gangs and gang members for untold reasons. Therefore, the question remains about how to "spatialize" research on gangs beyond acknowledging the geographical truism, as Papachristos and Hughes (2015) do, "that gangs are both the by-product and creators of their communities" (107). Furthering Papachristos and Hughes's "call-to-arms," which "requires traversing methodological trenches and debates in order to see how different methods and data sources might build upon our current knowledge of the gang-neighborhood relationship" (110), while simultaneously borrowing from Soja's (1989) rhetorical formulation, I offer a few ways to begin thinking about "reasserting space" in gang studies.

For the non-geographer, this "reassertion" includes borrowing methods and theory from geographers on how to observe and think about the co-constitutive nature between people and places, as well as observing how social ideals and practices manifest ideologically and therefore physically within the built environment. Moving beyond "gangs are both by-product and creator of their communities," although certainly true, scholars of gangs would be well served to more actively take into consideration how normative concepts and expressions of identity are both part and parcel of how urban spaces act, feel, look, and function. The importance of the built environment and its attributes has been acknowledged by those who seek to abate gang activity through so-called "crime prevention through environmental design" as well as the implementation of civil gang injunctions (see Valasik and Tita 2018), but an acknowledgment that "place matters" must also be used to better inform those who seek to understand not simply police gang activity. In short, places occupied by gangs are rife with meaning above and beyond criminality, and it is those meanings, processes, and manifestations of economic, cultural, and political power at all scales, from the global to the local, that are as crucial to take into consideration when otherwise analyzing gangs as criminalized social groups (Harvey 2000).

Beyond the rather trite encouragement to simply "think spatially," geographers are most well positioned to contribute to the literature on gangs by relying on place-based methodologies that contribute to greater inclusion. In addition to "place-based elicitation" and "on the ground" methods that I have advanced elsewhere (Bloch 2018; 2020c)—methods that allow for the collection of "unrehearsed" interview data "at the scene of the crime" and where members of criminalized and transgressive subcultures live and operate—it is through autoethnographic research and writing used by former gang members that I see as capable of contributing the most insightful content for geographical gang studies (see Bloch 2022c). There is already a model for this in sociology, where self-identified former gang members and gang-affiliated scholars, as well as the formerly incarcerated, have carved out a space in the literature with real-world research and reflections on identity and place-making (Bolden 2020; Contreras 2013; Durán 2013; Ortiz 2022; Rios 2011; Walker 2022; Weide 2022). Each of these works has been produced by insiders and "complete member researchers" engaged in ethnographic and autoethnographic reflection and writing that owes, in part, to the demands for reflexivity and positionality made by feminist geographers over the past three decades (Adler and Adler, 1987; Rose 1997).

While insider knowledge of place and identity is no more or less complete, objective, or omniscient than excellent outsider studies of gangs, it is experiential in a way that allows scholars to contribute to what Butz (2010) sees as the utility in autoethnographic research in geography. For Butz, autoethnography—that analytical and evocative style of writing (graphy) about culture (ethnos) from the perspective of personal experience (auto)—is adept at producing a "knowledgeable perspective on the metropolis from the margins that is emotionally invested, grounded in place, saturated with local specificity, the ebb and flow of daily life, and what is going on behind the scenes" (152). I add to this geographical description of autoethnography the work of a criminologist for whom the method is likewise "a way of living in and knowing the world" (Ferrell 2018, 147), which is requisite for rigorous studies of marginalized places and the criminalized people who produce and inhabit them. As Ferrell (2018) reminds us in his advocacy for increased criminological ethnography, it is insiders, including (former) gang members and other criminalized populations, who are more likely to possess "a form of situated knowledge, an ability to read, reference, and make sense of particular situations that mostly remain opaque to those outside them" (150). Such a place-based perspective held by former gang members and gang-affiliated scholars can, I argue, enhance, and complicate gang studies moving forward.

References

Adler, P. A., and Adler, P. 1987. *Membership Roles in Field Research*. Thousand Oaks, CA: Sage.
Alonso, Alejandro A. 2004. "Racialized Identities and the Formation of Black gangs in Los Angeles." *Urban Geography* 25 (7): 658–674.
Anderson, Elijah. 1976. *A Place on the Corner*. Chicago, IL: University of Chicago Press.
Aspholm, Roberto R. 2022. "Deaths of Despair: Gang Violence after the Crack Crisis." *Critical Criminology* 30 (1): 49–69.
Bloch, Stefano. 2012a. "The Changing Face of Wall Space: Graffiti-Murals in the Context of Neighborhood Change in Los Angeles." PhD Diss., University of Minnesota.
Bloch, Stefano. 2012b. "The Illegal Face of Wall Space: Graffiti-Murals on the Sunset Boulevard Retaining Walls." *Radical History Review* 113: 111–126.
Bloch, S. Stefano. 2018. "Place-Based Elicitation: Interviewing Graffiti Writers at the Scene of the Crime." *Journal of Contemporary Ethnography* 47 (2): 171–198.
Bloch, Stefano. 2019. *Going All City: Struggle and Survival in LA's Graffiti Subculture*. Chicago, IL: University of Chicago Press.
Bloch, Stefano. 2020a. "An Autoethnographic Account of Urban Restructuring and Neighborhood Change in Los Angeles." *Cultural Geographies* 27 (3): 379–394.
Bloch, Stefano. 2020b. "Broken Windows Ideology and the (Mis)Reading of Graffiti." *Critical Criminology* 28 (4): 703–720.
Bloch, Stefano. 2020c. "Are You in a Gang Database?" *New York Times*, February 3. https://www.nytimes.com/2020/02/03/opinion/los-angeles-gang-database.html.
Bloch, Stefano. 2022a. "For Autoethnographies of Displacement Beyond Gentrification: The Body as Archive, Memory as Data." *Annals of the American Association of Geographers* 112 (3): 706–714.
Bloch, Stefano. 2022b. "Aversive Racism and Community-Instigated Policing: The Spatial Politics of Nextdoor." *Environment and Planning C: Politics and Space* 40 (1): 260–278.
Bloch, Stefano. 2022c. "Gangs, Gang Members, and Geography." *Geographical Compass* 16 (8): e12651.
Bloch, Stefano. and Dugan Meyer. 2019. "Implicit Revanchism: Gang Injunctions and the Security Politics of White Liberalism." *Environment and Planning D: Society and Space* 37 (6): 1100–18.
Bloch, Stefano, and Enrique Alan Olivares-Pelayo. 2021. "Carceral Geographies from Inside Prison Gates: The Micro-politics of Everyday Racialisation." *Antipode* 53 (5): 1319–1338.
Bloch, Stefano, and Susan A. Phillips. 2022. "Mapping and Making Gangland: A Legacy of Redlining and Enjoining Gang Neighbourhoods in Los Angeles." *Urban Studies* 59 (4): 750–770.
Bolden, Christian L. 2020. *Out of the Red: My Life of Gangs, Prison, and Redemption*. New Brunswick, NJ: Rutgers University Press.
Brantingham, Jeffrey P., George E. Tita, Martin B. Short, and Shannon E. Reid. 2012. "The Ecology of Gang Territorial Boundaries." *Criminology* 50 (3): 851–885.
Brotherton, David C. and Luis Barrios. 2004. *The Almighty Latin King and Queen Nation*. New York: Columbia University Press.
Buttimer, Ann. 1976. "Grasping the Dynamism of Lifeworld." *Annals of the Association of American Geographers* 66 (2): 277–292.
Buttimer, Ann, and David Seamon. 1980. *The Human Experience of Space and Place*. London: Routledge.

Butz, David. 2010. "Autoethnography as Sensibility." In *The Sage Handbook of Qualitative Geography*, edited by Dydia DeLyser, Steve Herbert, Stuart Aitken, Mike Crang, and Linda McDowell, 138–155. Thousand Oaks, CA: Sage.

Cohen, Jacqueline, and George Tita. 1999. "Diffusion in Homicide: Exploring a General Method for Detecting Spatial Diffusion Processes." *Journal of Quantitative Criminology* 15 (4): 451–493.

Conquergood, Lorne D. 1993. *Homeboys and Hoods: Gang Communication and Cultural Space*. Evanston, Il: Center for Urban Affairs and Policy Research, Northwestern University.

Contreras, Randol. 2013. *The Stickup Kids: Race, Drugs, Violence, and the American Dream*. Berkeley: University of California Press.

Cresswell, Tim. 1996. *In Place/Out of Place: Geography, Ideology, and Transgression*. Minneapolis: University of Minnesota Press.

Cresswell, Tim. 2014. *Place: An Introduction*. New York: John Wiley and Sons.

Curry, G. David, and Irving A. Spergel. 1988. "Gang Homicide, Delinquency, and Community." *Criminology* 26 (3): 381–406.

Curtis, Jacqueline W., Ellen Shiau, Bryce Lowery, David Sloane, Karen Hennigan, and Andrew Curtis. 2014. "The Prospects and Problems of Integrating Sketch Maps with Geographic Information Systems to Understand Environmental Perception: A Case Study of Mapping Youth Fear in Los Angeles Gang Neighborhoods." *Environment and Planning B: Planning and Design* 41 (2): 251–271.

Davis, Mike. 1990. *City of Quartz: Excavating the Future of Los Angeles*. London: Verso.

Decker, Scott H., Chris Melde, and David C. Pyrooz. 2013. "What Do We Know about Gangs and Gang Members and Where Do We Go from Here?" *Justice Quarterly* 30 (3): 369–402.

Decker, Scott. H., David C. Pyrooz, and James A. Densley. 2022. *On Gangs*. Philadelphia, PA: Temple University Press.

Durán, Robert J. 2013. *Gang Life in Two Cities*. New York: Columbia University Press.

Ferrell, Jeff. 1993. *Crimes of Style: Urban Graffiti and the Politics of Criminality*. Boston, MA: Northeastern University Press.

Ferrell, Jeff. 2018. "Criminological Ethnography: Living and Knowing." In *Doing Ethnography in Criminology*, edited by Stephan K. Rice and Michael D. Maltz, 147–161. Cham: Springer.

Ferrell, Jeff, and Robert D. Weide. 2010. Spot Theory. *City* 14 (1–2): 48–62.

Garot, Robert. 2010. *Who You Claim: Performing Gang Identity in School and on the Streets*. New York: New York University Press.

Harvey, David. 1972. "Revolutionary and Counter-revolutionary Theory in Geography and the Problem of Ghetto Formation." In *Geography of the Ghetto: Perceptions, Problems, and Alternatives*, edited by Harold M. Rose, 75–97. DeKalb: Northern Illinois University Press.

Harvey, David. 1973. *Social Justice and the City*. Athens: University of Georgia Press.

Harvey, David. 1987. "Flexible Accumulation through Urbanization: Reflections on Post-Modernism." *Antipode* 19(3): 260–286.

Harvey, David. 2000. *Spaces of Hope*. Berkeley: University of California Press.

Irwin-Rogers, Keir, James Densley, and Craig Pinkney. 2018. "Gang Violence and Social Media." In *Routledge International Handbook of Human Aggression*, edited by Roxanna Short, 400–410. London: Routledge.

Iveson, Kurt. 2010. "The Wars on Graffiti and the New Military Urbanism." *City* 14 (1–2): 115–134.

Katz, Jack. 2000. "The Gang Myth." In *Social Dynamics of Crime and Control*, edited by Susanne Karstedt and Kai Bussmann, 171–187. London: Bloomsbury.

Klein, Malcolm W. 1995. *The American Street Gang: Its Nature, Prevalence, and Control.* Oxford: Oxford University Press.

Kontos, Louis, David C. Brotherton, and Luis Barrios, eds. 2003. *Gangs and Society: Alternative Perspectives.* New York: Columbia University Press.

Lefebvre, Henri. 1991. *The Production of Space.* Translated by Donald Nicholson-Smith. Oxford: Blackwell.

Leverso, John, and Yuan Hsiao. 2021. "Gangbangin on the [Face] book: Understanding Online Interactions of Chicago Latina/o Gangs." *Journal of Research in Crime and Delinquency* 58 (3): 239–268.

Ley, David. 1974. *The Black Inner City as Frontier Outpost Images and Behavior of a Philadelphia Neighborhood.* Washington DC: Association of American Geographers.

Ley, David. 1975. "The Street Gang in Its Milieu." In *The Social Economy of Cities*, edited by Gary Gappert and Harold M. Rose, 247–273. Beverly Hills, CA: Sage.

Ley, David, and Roman Cybriwsky. 1974. "Urban Graffiti as Territorial Markers." *Annals of the Association of American Geographer* 64 (4): 491–505.

Liebow, Elliot. 1967. *Tally's Corner: A Study of Negro Streetcorner Men.* New York: Little, Brown, and Company.

Livingstone, David. 1992. *The Geographical Tradition.* Oxford: Blackwell.

Lopez-Aguado, Patrick, and Michael L. Walker. 2021. "'I Don't Bang: I'm Just a Blood': Situating Gang Identities in Their Proper Place." *Theoretical Criminology* 25 (1): 107–126.

Lowenthal, David. 1961. "Geography, Experience, and Imagination: Towards a Geographical Epistemology." *Annals of the Association of American Geographers* 51 (3): 241–260.

Massey, Doreen. 1994. *Space, Place and Gender.* Minneapolis: University of Minnesota Press.

Massey, Doreen. 2005. *For Space.* London: Sage.

Maxson, Cheryl L. 2011. "Street Gangs." In *Crime and Public Policy*, edited by James Q. Wilson and Joan Petersilia, 158–182. Oxford: Oxford University Press.

Melde, Chris, and Frank Weerman. 2020. *Gangs in the Era of Internet and Social Media.* Cham: Springer.

Meyer, Dugan. 2021. "Security Symptoms." *Cultural Geographies* 28 (2): 271–284.

Moore, Caylin Louis, and Forrest Stuart. 2022. "Gang Research in the Twenty-First Century." *Annual Review of Criminology* 5: 299–320.

Moore, Joan. 1991. *Going Down to the Barrio: Homeboys and Homegirls in Change.* Philadelphia, PA: Temple University Press.

Moore, Joan, Diego Vigil, and Robert Garcia. 1983. "Residence and Territoriality in Chicano Gangs." *Social Problems* 31 (2): 182–194.

Muñiz, Anna. 2015. *Police, Power, and the Production of Racial Boundaries.* New Brunswick, NJ: Rutgers University Press.

Ortiz, Jennifer. 2022. "From East New York to the Ivory Tower: How Structural Violence and Gang Membership Made Me a Critical Scholar." In *Survivor Criminology: A Radical Act of Hope*, edited by Kimberly J. Cook, Jason M. Williams, Reneé D. Lamphere, Stacy L. Mallicoat, and Alissa R. Ackerman. New York: Rowman and Littlefield.

Papachristos, Andrew V. and Lorine A. Hughes. 2015. "Neighborhoods and Street Gangs." In *The Handbook of Gangs*, edited by Scott H. Decker and David C. Pyrooz, 98–117. New York: John Wiley and Sons.

Papachristos, Andrew V., David M. Hureau, and Anthony A. Braga. 2013. "The Corner and the Crew: The Influence of Geography and Social Networks on Gang Violence." *American Sociological Review* 78 (3): 417–447.

Patton, Desmond Upton, Robert D. Eschmann, and Dirk A. Butler. 2013. "Internet Banging: New Trends in Social Media, Gang Violence, Masculinity and Hip Hop." *Computers in Human Behavior* 29 (5): A54–A59.

Phillips, Susan A. 1999. *Wallbangin': Graffiti and Gangs in LA*. Chicago, IL: University of Chicago Press.

Pulido, Laura. 2002. "Reflections on a White Discipline." *The Professional Geographer* 54 (1): 42–49.

Pyrooz, David C., and Densley, James A. 2016. "Selection into Street Gangs: Signaling Theory, Gang Membership, and Criminal Offending." *Journal of Research in Crime and Delinquency*, 53 (4): 447–481.

Pyrooz, David C., and Richard K. Moule Jr. 2019. "Gangs and Social Media." In *Oxford Research Encyclopedia of Criminology and Criminal Justice*, edited by Henry N. Pontell. New York: Oxford University Press.

Radil, Steven M., Colin Flint, and George E. Tita. 2010. "Spatializing Social Networks: Using Social Network Analysis to Investigate Geographies of Gang Rivalry, Territoriality, and Violence in Los Angeles." *Annals of the Association of American Geographers* 100 (2): 307–326.

Rios, Victor M. 2011. *Punished: Policing the Lives of Black and Latino Boys*. New York: New York University Press.

Roberts, Ryan J. 2021. "Re-spatializing Gangs: An Exponential Random Graph Model of Twitter Data to Analyze the Geospatial Distribution of Gang Member Connections." *International Journal of Cyber Criminology* 15 (2): 18–43.

Rodriguez, Joseph A., Ruben Martínez, and Luis J. Rodriquez. 2000. *East Side Stories: Gang Life in East LA*. New York: PowerHouse.

Rodriguez, Luis J. 2005. *Always Running: La Vida Loca: Gang Days in LA*. New York: Simon and Schuster.

Rose, Gillian. 1997. "Situating Knowledges: Positionality, Reflexivities and Other Tactics." *Progress in Human Geography* 21 (3): 305–320.

Sanchez, Jose Antonio, Scott H. Decker, and David C. Pyrooz. 2022. "Gang Homicide: The Road so Far and a Map for the Future." *Homicide Studies* 26 (1): 68–90.

Sauer, Carl. 1925. *The Morphology of Landscape*. Berkeley: University of California Press.

Short, James F., and Fred L. Strodtbeck. 1965. *Group Process and Gang Delinquency*. Chicago, IL: University of Chicago Press.

Soja, Edward W. 1989. *Postmodern Geographies: The Reassertion of Space in Critical Social Theory*. London: Verso.

Stuart, Forrest. 2020. "Code of the Tweet: Urban Gang Violence in the Social Media Age." *Social Problems* 67 (2): 191–207.

Thrasher, Frederic Milton. 1927. *The Gang: A Study of 1,313 Gangs in Chicago*. Chicago, IL: University of Chicago Press.

Tita, George E., Jacqueline Cohen, and John Engberg. 2005. "An Ecological Study of the Location of Gang Set Space." *Social Problems* 52 (2): 272–299.

Tita, George E., and Steven M. Radil. 2010. "Making Space for Theory: The Challenges of Theorizing Space and Place for Spatial Analysis in Criminology." *Journal of Quantitative Criminology* 26 (4): 467–479.

Tuan, Yi-Fu. 1977. *Space and Place: The Perspective of Experience*. Minneapolis: University of Minnesota Press.

Valasik, Matthew. 2018. "Gang Violence Predictability: Using Risk Terrain Modeling to Study Gang Homicides and Gang Assaults in East Los Angeles." *Journal of Criminal Justice* 58: 10–21.

Valasik, Matthew, Michael S. Barton, Shannon E. Reid, and George E. Tita. 2017. "Barriocide: Investigating the Temporal and Spatial Influence of Neighborhood Structural Characteristics on Gang and Non-gang Homicides in East Los Angeles." *Homicide Studies* 21 (4): 287–311.

Valasik, Matthew, and Shannon E. Reid. 2021. "East Side Story: Disaggregating Gang Homicides in East Los Angeles." *Social Sciences* 10 (2): 48.

Valasik, Matthew, and George Tita. 2018. "Gangs and Space." In *The Oxford Handbook of Environmental Criminology*, edited by Gerben Bruinsma and Shane D. Johnson, 839–867. Oxford, UK: Oxford University Press.

Vigil, Diego J. 1988. *Barrio Gangs: Street Life and Identity in Southern California*. Austin: Texas University Press.

Walker, Michael L. 2022. *Indefinite: Doing Time in Jail*. Oxford, UK: Oxford University Press.

Weide, Robert D. 2022. *Divide and Conquer: Race, Gangs, Identity, and Conflict*. Philadelphia, PA: Temple University Press.

Weisburd, David, John E. Eck, Anthony A. Braga, Cody W. Telep, Breanne Cave, Kate Bowers, Gerben Bruinsma, et al. 2016. *Place Matters: Criminology for the Twenty-First Century*. Cambridge, UK: Cambridge University Press.

Whyte, William Foote. 1943. *Street Corner Society: The Social Structure of an Italian Slum*. Chicago, IL: University of Chicago Press.

SECTION 2

APPROACHES TO THE EMPIRICAL STUDY OF GANGS

CHAPTER 9

THE HISTORY AND EVOLUTION OF GANG SCHOLARSHIP
A Topic Modeling and Change Point Detection Approach

JASON GRAVEL

In 1834, James Arthur Robert Stevenson published an account of the Phansigar—a group of about 60 men of "the most deliberate and decided villains that stain the face of the earth" (Stevenson 1834, 280). The Phansigar (meaning strangers in Urdu, a close language relative of Hindi) were described by British colonial officers in nineteenth-century India as gangs of murderers who would strangle travelers using handkerchiefs "always of a white or a yellow color, those being the favourite colours of their tutelary deity" (Stevenson 1834, 281). British colonial officers would often begin to refer to these crimes as "thugee" and such groups as "thugs" from the Hindi word *thag*, meaning to cheat or deceive (Wagner 2007).

In a five-page document, Stevenson (1834) describes the composition of the gang ("they admit into their fraternity persons of all castes and persuasions"), their rules and values ("they were sworn to a fair division [of booty], to secrecy, and to inviolable fidelity to each other"), their interaction with the justice system ("there are but few instances of the Phansigars being convicted in a court of justice, although they have been repeatedly apprehended"), and even the motivations for gang involvement ("if we don't *p'hansigar*, how are we to live?").

Stevenson's manuscript is the first academic description of gangs found in Pyrooz and Mitchell's (2015) systematic review of gang literature, which this chapter seeks to extend. Even then, we can see through Stevenson's description of many of the themes and questions modern gang scholars have grappled with. In this chapter, I examine how gang research has evolved over time by analyzing its scholarly publication record. Rather than conduct a narrative review of the literature, I follow Pyrooz and Mitchell's lead in conducting as systematic and all-encompassing review of the publication record as possible. The objective is to take a data-driven approach to this review and highlight trends in productivity and focus in gang scholarship. While systematically coding and reviewing every publication of the history of gang research would provide a more complete overview, it would be incredibly complex and labor intensive. Instead, I use natural language processing (NLP) techniques and other data analytic techniques to examine the evolution of gang research from 1834 to 2021.

Pyrooz and Mitchell (2015) show that gang scholarship experienced incredible growth starting in the 1990s. The authors relied on the concept of "little science, big science," introduced by De Solla Price (1963), the father of modern scientometrics, in arguing that we entered the era of "big gang research" in the 1990s. De Solla Price (1963) was himself influenced by an article published a few years before by Weinberg (1961), who referred to the major scientific accomplishments of the twentieth century—space exploration, particle accelerators, nuclear energy, and so on—as "Big Science." While Weinberg does not provide a clear definition of what constitutes "Big Science," he describes it as science that is receiving large-scale support both financially and in the popular discourse. Weinberg's concerns were that "Big Science" would ruin science with a "triple disease—journalitis, moneyitis, administratitis" (162)—by judging the merit of scientific ideas through the popular press or congressional hearings rather than in scientific forums (journalitis); allocating funding and resources to big, popular projects as opposed to smaller, basic science projects (moneyitis); and creating a bloated administrative structure to oversee and direct scientific efforts toward public agendas (administratitis).

De Solla Price (1963) argued that we should not be surprised by the apparent sudden transition from little to big science. In fact, the author argued that it is a fundamental law of science that scientific production should grow exponentially until reaching saturation. De Solla Price (1963) proposed that growth in science should follow a logistic curve, making the era of "Big Science" inevitable but short-lived—a period of transition between little science and what the author optimistically called the period of "New Science": "Saturation seldom implies death but rather that we have the beginning of new and exciting tactics for science, operating with quite new ground rules" (32). As of 2013, Pyrooz and Mitchell (2015) showed that there were many reasons to be optimistic that growth would continue and explored the factors that led the field to an era of big gang research.

Pyrooz and Mitchell (2015) argued that the transition from little to big gang research was facilitated by generalized changes in social sciences and the fields of criminology and criminal justice in particular, such as a larger number of publication outlets and publications per issues, a turn to quantitative research, lower costs of doing research due to innovations in computing, open access to data for secondary analysis, and technologies that facilitate collaborations. The authors end their chapters with optimism for the continued growth of the discipline, primarily due to the internationalization of research on gangs and the inclusion of cross-disciplinary efforts.

An important contribution of Pyrooz and Mitchell's chapter was their survey of key gang researchers to identify key turning points and important periods in the history of gang scholarship. They identified five important periods in the history of gang research: (1) the Classic Era (early twentieth century–1950s), generally establishing the gang as an object of empirical study, most notably through the work of Thrasher's *The Gang* (1927); (2) the Golden Era (1950s–mid-1960s), during which "the study of gangs *was* the study of delinquency" (Pyrooz and Mitchell 2015, 41) with several classic theoretical treatises published, a focus on empirical theory testing, and a blending of theory and practice; (3) the Social Problems Era (1960s–to the present), when scholars began to focus more on the criminal and problematic aspects of gangs and their members, the national scope of the gang problem, and a general shift from sociological to criminological perspectives, which continues to this day; (4) the Empirical Turn (late 1980s–to the present), which was fostered by large-scale efforts to collect longitudinal data on gang members, most notably through the Causes and Correlates of Delinquency studies, and led to an increase in quantitative analyses as well as the development of life-course perspectives; and (5) the International Turn (2000s–to the present), referring to the growth of research outside the United States, in large part due to the Eurogang Program of Research.

The use of surveys for the purpose of mapping the history of gang scholarship and important turning points provides great insights, especially for the earliest periods. This is consistent with De Solla Price's theory: During "little gang research," it is relatively easy to be aware of most of the important ideas, innovations, and perspectives in the field. However, such an approach becomes problematic as the field transitions to "big gang research." An important characteristic of "Big Science" is that it becomes exponentially more difficult to be aware of all research that is being produced in our own field. This could explain why survey respondents identify more turning points and more definite periods with clear signposts in the early days of gang research and fewer turning points and indefinite periods in later periods.

In this chapter, I set out to explore what fueled growth in gang research and examine whether these turning points in the productivity of gang scholars lead to changes in the makeup of gang scholarship. Growth in scientific publications can indicate an increase in interest in the topic, which can be driven by internal or external factors to a discipline. Internally, new discoveries can stimulate growth by opening up new avenues of research, which may cascade into even more new research and even specialization over time. Externally, social changes or discoveries in other fields can drive interest in a given area of research by injecting more resources into the field and increasing the number of scientists willing to dedicate their time to the topic, particularly students choosing to focus on an area for their dissertations.

Growth can also be reflective of changes in the way science is being conducted more generally. For instance, an increase in the number of scientific outlets, changes in the pressure to publish and other norms regarding career advancements (e.g., the value of journal articles versus books), and a shift from solo publications to team science are all factors that could lead to growth in a field, even if the field in question does not appreciatively evolve in its substance or popularity. Therefore, growth or productivity are not inherently good or bad for a discipline and they are not necessarily a gauge of scientific advancement. However, I posit that changes in productivity—especially those with sudden onset leading to sustained levels of productivity—are likely to have root causes that can tell us much about the evolution of a discipline. It is through this lens that I explore the history of gang research in this chapter.

Current Study

With the benefits of eight additional years of gang publications since Pyrooz and Mitchell's analysis, an important goal of this chapter is to investigate whether gang scholarship has indeed continued its trajectory into big gang research. Furthermore, given the difficulties inherent in identifying turning points and providing a complete overview of gang scholarship given the volume of research, I rely on computational tools to identify both turning points in the productivity of gang scholars and to explore the evolving composition of gang research. My goal is to build on the work of Pyrooz and Mitchell (2015) by examining sudden changes in the productivity of gang scholars and examine the composition of research produced between these changes in the hope that it will shed light on the causes for these shifts in productivity.

To identify turning points, I rely on change point detection (CPD) methods. CPD is a technique that identifies abrupt disruptions in time-series where the properties of the series (e.g,. its mean and variance) change. CPD is often used to identify anomalies in the monitoring of medical conditions (e.g., heart rate, electroencephalogram), abrupt climate change, or speech pattern recognition (Aminikhanghahi and Cook 2017). By applying this technique to the volume of yearly gang publications, I can break down the history of gang scholarship in slices of time punctuated by abrupt changes. These change points—which I call turning points—reflect rapid but sustained changes in the publication pattern of gang scholars. The assumption is that these changes are caused by exogenous or endogenous factors that stimulate or decrease the intensity of gang research. This approach also identifies periods in between these turning points of relative stability, either in the mean of a time-series or its variance.

An important point of departure from Pyrooz and Mitchell's (2015) quantitative analysis of growth is that the CPD model is applied on the yearly count of publications, rather than the cumulative count of publications they use to identify a major turning point in the growth of gang scholarship. The authors point to 1993 as the beginning of the transition from "little gang research" to "big gang research" on the basis that it marks the largest year-over-year growth rate in the history of gang research. Furthermore, Pyrooz and Mitchell (2015) argue that there is "little reason to draw attention to the first half of the twentieth century [because] the size of that body of research pales in comparison to what took place in the beginning of the 1990s" (35). While it is clear that the 1990s saw a dramatic change in productivity, 1993 is the end point of this change. A goal of this analysis is to shed light on the conditions that led to the rapid growth in the 1990s (and other periods), which requires the identification of the beginning point of this change. Moreover, other important shifts in productivity may have occurred in the earlier and later periods in the history of gang research that may be masked by the size of the shift in productivity in the 1990s but are nevertheless meaningful.

To shed light on how gang scholarship changes at and between these turning points, I use NLP techniques and topic modeling to explore how the interest and attention of gang scholars shift over time. These techniques allow me to efficiently classify thousands of journal articles into groups of topics within gang research. By doing so, I am able to explore what areas of gang scholarship are most responsible for changes in productivity, how research interests have evolved over time, whether new topics emerge at specific points in time, and generally how gang research diversifies over time.

In the next sections, I describe the methodology used to expand the systematic search of gang studies conducted by Pyrooz and Mitchell, the development of the topic model, and the implementation of the change point detection algorithm.

Methodology

Data Collection and Coding

The main goal of this chapter is to expand the review conducted by Pyrooz and Mitchell (2015), which covered all gang-related research published until 2013. Pyrooz and Mitchell gave me access to the list of documents they identified in their original search, and I replicated their methodology to add to that list any documents published between 2014 and July 2021. Below is an overview of the methodology used for the expanded search; I refer interested readers to Pyrooz and Mitchell for a more detailed description of the methods used for the earliest time periods.

To remain consistent with the previous search, I used the same search strategy and inclusion criteria as Pyrooz and Mitchell (2015). We relied primarily on Google Scholar (GS), looked for the search terms "gang" or "gangs" included as part of the title of the article, and conducted the search by year. Although restricting the search to articles with keywords in the title is an important limitation, this strategy was necessary due to GS limiting the search results returned from a query to 1,000. A query producing results above this threshold would introduce bias due to GS's sorting algorithm, about which little public information is available. For instance, searching GS for documents published in 2021 using gang* or gangs* "anywhere in the article" produces an estimated 106,000 results, whereas limiting the search to "in the title" produces 558 results. However, for studies published before 1993, the setting "anywhere in the article" was used since the number of search results for yearly searches was below the GS result threshold. Pyrooz and Mitchell (2015) also supplemented their search with searches of Web of Knowledge (now Web of Science [WoS]) using the same search criteria described above.

The greatest concern with this approach is that studies that might be relevant to this review might not include the string "gang" as part of the title. I supplemented and updated Pyrooz and Mitchell's initial searches with WoS. Using the same keywords, I used the "topic" setting to refine the results, which directs the search engine to look for keywords in titles, abstracts, author-provided keywords, and KeyWords Plus.[1] Even after the inclusion of these articles and the removal of duplicates, the majority of articles (93.7%) in the final database included the string "gang" in their titles.

Following the work of Pyrooz and Mitchell, I excluded articles that were primarily discussing chain gangs, gang rape, motorcycle gangs, and other organized criminal groups (e.g., the mafia) unless they included a comparative element with gangs that met the Eurogang definition: "any durable, street-oriented youth group whose involvement in illegal activity is part of its group identity" (Weerman et al. 2009, 20). I also excluded conference presentations, book reviews, news articles, and grant proposals from the results, and included all articles published in English or at the very least provided an English translation of the title and abstract of the article.

Each entry was extracted from GS and entered in a Zotero database. Research assistants reviewed each entry to remove duplicates and articles not meeting our search criteria, as well as classifying entries in seven types of documents: (1) scholarly journal articles, which includes articles in peer-reviewed publications; (2) book chapters or encyclopedia entries;

(3) reports (e.g., government reports, white papers); (4) dissertations and theses; (5) trade publications (e.g., specialized magazines and non-peer-reviewed journals of professional associations); (6) books; and (7) others (e.g., unpublished manuscripts, conference papers).

Topic Modeling

To identify subareas in gang research, I used NLP techniques to clean and analyze the titles and abstracts of journal articles. Specifically, I used a technique called topic modeling using the Python package BERTopic (version 0.10.0; Grootendorst 2022). This topic modeling technique is an unsupervised machine learning technique, meaning that the model can extract meaningful categories of documents without requiring any kind of a priori classification of these documents into a set of categories (i.e., training set). This is advantageous from both a practical and analytical perspective. From a practical standpoint, the sheer number of documents would require a considerable amount of time and effort to generate a classification. From an analytical standpoint, using a data-driven approach to identify subareas of gang research avoids potential biases associated with the a priori creation of labels. As we will see later in this chapter, the growth of gang scholarship has been associated with an impressive diversification of subtopics investigated. Given the size and complexity of modern gang research, it would be foolish to expect even the most well-read gang scholar to be able to keep up with the pace of progress in the field.

The goal of topic modeling is to extract a set of coherent topics from documents by examining co-occurrences of certain words or common multi-word expressions (e.g., n-grams) across the entirety of the set of documents. BERTopic is an algorithm that incorporates three stages: (1) document embedding, (2) document clustering, and (3) creation of topic representations. Document embedding creates a numeric representation of documents using a type of neural network architecture called transformers. Transformers are based on pre-trained models and can learn the meaning of text by examining the use of different words in context. As the name suggests, BERTopic relies on a version of the BERT (Bidirectional Encoder Representations from Transformers; Devlin et al. 2018) called SBERT (Sentence BERT; Reimers and Gurevych 2019). Once embedding is complete, the algorithm reduces the dimensionality of the embedding of the documents using UMAP (Uniform Manifold Approximation and Projection) and then does a cluster analysis of the documents using the HDBSCAN algorithm to create clusters of topics. Finally, BERTopic creates representations of topics using a class-based version of the term frequency-inverse document frequency (TF-IDF) metric. C-TF-IDF quantifies the relative importance of any given word within a class of document (in this case, a cluster of documents returned by the first two steps of the algorithm) relative to its frequency in all documents.

Topic modeling, of course, is nothing more than that: a model. In this context, there are many caveats to consider before interpreting the findings of topic models. First, the texts used for the analyses are limited to the title and abstracts of these articles. The main reason for this decision is simple: extracting thousands of pdfs from paywalled publisher websites is a cumbersome task to do manually, and often too complex to accomplish via automation (e.g., web crawlers). Abstracts in peer-reviewed articles are typically publicly accessible, which allowed us to automate their extraction. From an analytical standpoint, while using abstracts limits the amount of information we can leverage about each article, it also has several advantages over using full texts for our analyses. When well-designed, titles and abstracts should be reflective of the main focus of the documents. Full texts, on the other hand, include several sections that may not be useful for the purpose of classification. For instance, literature reviews often cover several topics of prior research that are only tangential to the article's actual focus, which could make it difficult to properly classify documents.

Second, relying on abstracts limits the analysis to articles in some types of scholarly journals (n = 2,722). For instance, articles in law review journals often do not include abstracts, which led me to exclude law review articles altogether (8.2% of articles). Furthermore, many older articles often did not include abstracts, and machine-readable text from these articles was often more difficult to extract as they tend to be published in pdf formats of lower quality. To ensure that my models are not overly biased against older articles, I used optical character recognition wherever possible to transcribe the first few paragraphs of articles without abstracts. Of the 2,498 articles excluding law reviews, abstracts could not be found for 7.5%. Those missing abstracts are disproportionately from older articles: While papers published before 1990 make up 9.5% of all articles, they make up 22.3% of the articles without abstracts. The final number of articles used for the topic model is 2,311.

Third, the model we used assigns articles to a single topic based on a probabilistic model. Some articles may not neatly fit into a single topic, either because they cover several topics or because the topics they cover are unique. We explored other topic modeling strategies such as Latent Dirichlet Allocation models, which assigns multiple topics with a certain probability to each document. The results from these models were difficult to interpret and did not create useful categories, perhaps because such techniques perform better on longer documents. That said, the BERTopic model does not force articles into topic categories if the probability of assignment to any topic is too low or if more than one topic has a high probability of assignment. The initial model could not classify 25.4% of articles. However, upon manual inspection of the assignment probabilities of the model, many of these articles were assigned to one of the two topics with the highest assignment probability (61.1%). After manual assignment, a little under 10% of articles (n = 228) could not be classified in any specific topic.

Change Point Detection

To identify turning points, I used a time-series analysis technique called change point detection (CPD), which is an algorithm that breaks down a time-series into segments whose points have similar statistical properties (i.e., mean and variance). By doing so, I can identify important changes in the time-series and the periods of stability they intersect. I used the binary segmentation algorithm (Edwards and Cavalli-Sforza 1965) implemented in the *changepoint* (version 2.2.3) R package (Killick et al. 2022) to identify important changes in the overall trend in publishing. For this analysis, I focused on the number of documents published yearly between 1920 and 2021 (only 10 articles were published before 1920). I also restricted the algorithms to identify change points separated by at least three or more years to avoid capturing single-year outliers.

Organization of the Analysis and Discussion of Findings

The analysis and discussion of the findings is organized as follows. First, I describe the database of gang scholarship Pyrooz and Mitchell and I have created. Second, I report on the findings of the CPD model and examine growth rates in the cumulative growth of gang scholarship and compare these trends with other trends in the general sciences, and criminology more specifically. Third, I explore the years of entry to gang scholarship of the most productive gang scholars. Fourth, I describe the results of the topic model. Fifth, I combine these different analyses to describe each of the periods identified by the CPD model. It is important to note that the identification of periods of gang scholarship is strictly based on the results of the CPD model, not the topic model. I use the topic model to describe qualitative differences between periods identified by the CPD model. Finally, I discuss the findings and propose some explanations for important shifts in productivity over the history of gang research.

RESULTS

Growth in Gang Scholarship and Identification of Turning Points

The search yielded a total of 6,452 documents published between 1834 and 2021 from 6,149 unique contributors. Of those documents, 42.2% were scholarly journal articles, 15.6% were book chapters or encyclopedia entries, 12.4% were various types of reports, 12.4% were dissertations and theses, 7.6% were articles published in trade publications, and 6.0% were books. The remaining 3.8% was made up mostly of unpublished manuscripts and conference papers.

Figure 9.1 shows the evolution of scholarly publication on gangs over time. The most striking observation are two incredible periods of growth in gang research—the first

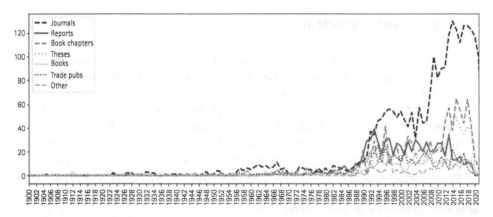

FIGURE 9.1 Gang Publications by Type (1900–2022)

starting in the late 1980s and the second starting in the late 2000s. Although the earliest document found was published 189 years ago, over 90% of all gang scholarship has been produced since 1990, and over 45% was published in the last decade. Pyrooz and Mitchell (2015) identified the 1990s as a key turning point in the study of street gangs. The authors also homed in on the year 1993 as a watershed moment for the field. They also noted a slowing of the growth rate during the 2000s. With an additional eight years to add to their data, we can examine whether this trend continued.

When considering all publications, the CPD analysis revealed four important change points: 1956, 1987, 1991, and 2008 (Figure 9.2). These change points therefore reveal five periods of potential importance in the history of gang research, some of which reflect the periods identified by participants in Pyrooz and Mitchell's (2015) survey of prominent gang scholars.

When looking at the cumulative count of gang publications since 1950, we find that the average growth rate of the gang literature is 6.0% per year, meaning that, on average, the gang literature doubles in size every 11.9 years. Of course, as the results of the CPD analysis suggest, growth is not constant over that period: Between 1988 and 1991 the average growth rate was 10.7%, compared to 4.3% between 1920 and 1956, 5.8% between 1957 and 1987, 9.0% between 1992 and 2008, and 5.2% between 2009 and 2021. Reflecting on the literature up to 2013, Pyrooz and Mitchell (2015) concluded that "gang research has entered into a period of decelerating growth" (35). This study confirms this prediction: Since 2003 the year-over-year growth rate was at its highest in 2013 (6.5%), and averaged about 5.0% between 2014 and 2019, though it has been consistently below 5.0% since 2017. The growth rate plummeted to 2.5% in 2020 but returned to 4.3% in 2021.

A recent study places the average growth of natural and life sciences around 4.10%, with an average growth of 5.08% since the 1950s (Bornmann, Haunschild, and Mutz 2021). Few

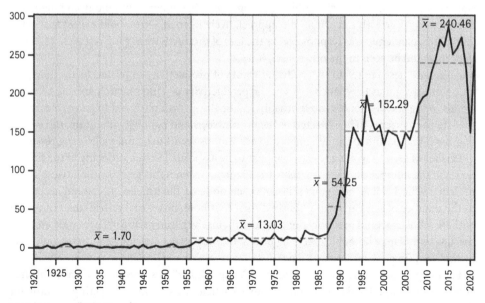

FIGURE 9.2 CPD Results

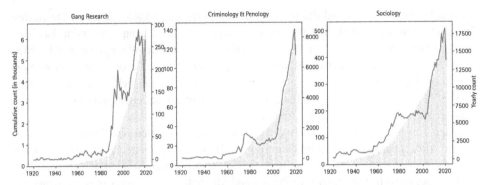

FIGURE 9.3 Comparison of Fields Growth

studies have assessed growth in social sciences specifically, but Larsen and Von Ins (2010) found a growth rate between 2% and 7% since the 1990s, depending on the database used. To compare growth in gang research to similar fields, I extracted search results from WoS for the number of records per year for studies indexed under "Criminology and Penology" and "Sociology" (excluding studies overlapping with criminology and penology). The yearly and cumulative counts of publications for these two disciplines and for gang research are shown in Figure 9.3.

Over the entire period, the rate of growth of gang research is slightly higher than criminology and penology (5.26%) and sociology (5.01%). For sociology, the best years for growth were in the 1920s with double-digit increases between 1923 and 1927, which steadily declined to between 3% and 5% by the 1940s, returned to above 5% in the late 1960s through 1980, and has been hovering between 2% to 4% since. For criminology and penology, the only double-digit growth rates were between 1975 and 1977, and by 1985 growth would remain below 4% until the late 2000s, where it would climb to between 6% and 7% and remain stable to this day. Interestingly, unlike for gang research, neither criminology and penology nor sociology's growth rate would dip appreciatively in 2020. One would expect that if the COVID-19 pandemic was responsible for the loss of productivity in gang research, the same pattern would be seen in the other disciplines.

Although these are relatively crude indicators of productivity in related fields, they provide some insight as to what changes in the productivity of gang research are due to larger trends in the social sciences more broadly. While the growth observed in gang research in the late 2000s seems to be reflected in the criminology and penology literature, the period of growth that occurs in the late 1980s and early 1990s seems to be unique to gang research.

Periods of growth in gang research appear to be associated with a widening of the field in terms of the number of new gang scholars. Figure 9.4 shows this growth using two metrics to define what I call a "new gang scholar." Each node on the timeline is colored according to the number of scholars who published their first book or journal article that year. Most of these scholars would probably not consider themselves "gang scholars," since for 46.1% of the 3,648 scholars who published gang books and/or journal articles, their first would also be their last (in gang research, to date).

For the purposes of Figure 9.4, I define a "gang scholar" as someone who has published at least four gang-related books and/or journal articles (at or above the 95th percentile for the number of publications per author in the database). Furthermore, a "new" gang scholar

THE HISTORY AND EVOLUTION OF GANG SCHOLARSHIP   149

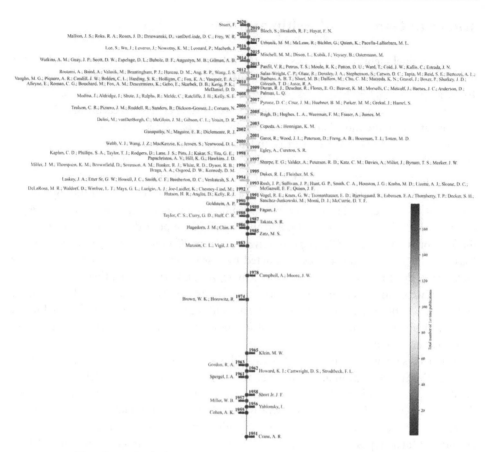

FIGURE 9.4 Timeline of Scholars

simply denotes the year of the first publication in our database (any type of publication).[2] In total, 232 individuals fit this definition. While these individuals represent 3.8% of all contributors to the gang literature, they have collectively contributed 2,080 documents (32.24%), including 1,134 journal articles (41.7%) and 138 books (35.7%).[3]

Prior to 1991, the field had never welcomed more than three "new" scholars in a single year. In each of 1991, 1992, and 1993, 10 gang scholars made their first entry to gang scholarship, surpassing in three years the number of new gang scholars between 1951 and 1990 (26). The 1990s would see a high of 11 new scholars in 1998 and a total of 70 new gang scholars. The 2000s would produce 5.4 new scholars per year (on average), with a low of 2 (2003) and a high of 9 (2009) and a total of 54 new scholars. By far, the two largest cohorts of gang scholars would come in 2010 (17) and 2011 (18).[4] These periods of growth in new gang scholars tend to be consistent with the periods of growth in overall production observed in Figure 9.1.

Such growth in the number of publications and gang scholars is likely to be reflected in the diversification of topics in gang research. Before examining these five periods identified by the CPD model in more depth, I provide an overview of the topic model for journal articles.

Topics in Gang Scholarship and Their Evolution

The topic model identified 43 topics from the titles and abstracts of articles on gangs. The first step in interpreting the results of the model was to create labels for each of the topics. To do so, I relied on two key pieces of information from the model: the keywords returned as topic representations and the assignment probability of articles to each topic. The topic representations of the model are computed using class-based term frequency-inverse document frequency (cTF-IDF) of words and phrases in documents. The cTF-IDF metric indicates how frequent a given word or phrase is used in articles in this topic, compared to its frequency in articles of all topics. In other words, it identifies words that discriminate well between topics. While these keywords can be useful in labeling the topics, it is important to note that cTF-IDF can be misleading, sometimes putting too much weight on words and phrases that are unique to the topic but are poor descriptors. For instance, the keywords for topic 25 (*Police perspectives on the proliferation of gangs*) include "North Carolina" because several studies conducted by researchers based in North Carolina are included in this topic (e.g., Yearwood and Rhyne, 2007). Furthermore, these keywords are often extracted from their meanings and require more context. For instance, both topics 2 and 15 include the keywords "sex" and "sexual," but topic 2 refers to sex and sexual in the context of differences between males and females, whereas topic 15 focuses on risky sex practices and sexual harassment.

To put these keywords in context, I used the assignment probability, which refers to the probability that a given article belongs to any given topic in the model. Many articles (34.8%) are core members of their topics and are assigned the probability 1, which indicates that their titles and abstracts include words and phrases that uniquely link them to other articles in their topic and discriminate among other topics. Therefore, these articles can be considered "archetypes" of each topic, and each were reviewed to create the topic labels. Table 9.1 provides a list of the 44 topics returned by the model, along with the cumulative distribution of each topic over time and a representative article. The representative article in Table 9.1 was chosen based on two criteria: (1) the article's representativeness according to the model (probability = 1), and (2) citations per year. It is important to note that the representative article is not necessarily the most cited article within each topic, but rather the most cited articles with a topic assignment probability of 1. A star next to the reference indicates when the article is both among the most representative and most cited within each topic.

Figure 9.5 shows the distribution of the topics over time between 1920 and 2021 (which coincide with the topics listed in Table 9.1). Most topics follow the overall trends in publishing discussed previously, with a few notable exceptions. A striking observation from Figure 9.5 is the incredible diversification of gang research over the last 30 years in terms of the number of topics.

Turning Points in Gang Research

In the following sections, I discuss each of the five periods identified by the CPD model. For each period, I will explore the level of productivity associated with the period, examine some

Table 9.1 Descriptive Analysis of Topic Groups and Subtopics

Subtopic	Cumulative Distribution (1950-2020)	Representative Study
Gangs in the Central and South American contexts (n=172)	1950–2010	Cruz, J. M. 2010. Central American Maras: From Youth Street Gangs to Transnational Protection Rackets. *Global Crime*.
Gangs in the UK and European contexts (n=124)	1950–2010	McLean, R. 2018. An Evolving Gang Model in Contemporary Scotland. *Deviant Behavior*.
Gangs in the African, South Asian, and Caribbean context (n=84)	1950–2010	Jensen, S. 2010. The Security and Development Nexus in Cape Town: War on Gangs, Counterinsurgency and Citizenship. *Security Dialogue*.
Aboriginal gangs and other gang issues in the Canadian context (n=43)	1950–2010	Grekul, J., and P. LaBoucane-Benson. 2008. Aboriginal Gangs and Their (Dis)Placement: Contextualizing Recruitment, Membership, and Status. *Canadian Journal of Criminology and Criminal Justice*.
Gangs, globalization, and armed groups (n=26)	1950–2010	Hagedorn, J. M. 2005. The Global Impact of Gangs. *Journal of contemporary criminal justice*.

(continued)

Table 9.1 Continued

Subtopic	Cumulative Distribution (1950–2020)	Representative Study
Latin gangs in Spain (n=16)	1950–2020	Palmas, L. Q. 2015. The Policies and Policing of Gangs in Contemporary Spain An Ethnography of a Bureaucratic Field of the State. *Sociologica–Italian Journal of Sociology.*
Peer effects, differential association, and social learning (n=78)	1950–2020	Thornberry, T. P. et al. 1993. The Role of Juvenile Gangs in Facilitating Delinquent Behavior. *Journal of Research in Crime and Delinquency.*
Predictors of offending and violent victimization (n=47)	1950–2020	Taylor, T. J. et al. 2007. Gang Membership as a Risk Factor for Adolescent Violent Victimization. *Journal of Research in Crime and Delinquency.*
Predictors of gang membership (n=42)	1950–2020	Hill, K. G. et al. 1999. Childhood Risk Factors for Adolescent Gang Membership: Results from the Seattle Social Development Project. *Journal of Research in Crime and Delinquency.*
Exposure to violence, perceptions of safety, bullying, and homophobia (n=26)	1950–2020	Ellis, B. H. et al. 2022. A Qualitative Examination of How Somali Young Adults Think about and Understand Violence in Their Communities. *Journal of Interpersonal Violence.*

Topic	Timeline	Reference
Gun carrying, access, and violence (n=17)	1950–2010	Papachristos, A. V. et al. 2012. Why Do Criminals Obey the Law? The Influence of Legitimacy and Social Networks on Active Gun Offenders. *Journal of Criminal Law & Criminology*.
Women and girls in gangs (n=111)	1950–2010	Joe-Laidler, K., and M. Chesney-Lind. 1995. Just Every Mothers Angel: An Analysis of Gender and Ethnic Variations in Youth Gang Membership. *Gender & Society*.
Masculinity and street culture (n=50)	1950–2010	Sandberg, S. 2009. Gangster, Victim or Both? The Interdiscursive Construction of Sameness and Difference in Self-Presentations. *British Journal of Sociology*.
Risky sexual behaviors and intimate partner relationships (n=40)	1950–2010	Palmer, C. T., and C. F. Tilley. 1995. Sexual Access to Females as a Motivation for Joining Gangs—An Evolutionary Approach. *Journal of Sex Research*.
Drug selling and substance use (n=59)	1950–2010	Fagan, J. 1989. The Social Organization of Drug Use and Drug Dealing among Urban Gangs. *Criminology*.
Gang joining, leaving, and embeddedness (n=58)	1950–2010	Pyrooz, D. C. et al. 2014. The Ties That Bind: Desistance from Gangs. *Crime & Delinquency*.

(continued)

Table 9.1 Continued

Subtopic	Cumulative Distribution (1950–2020)	Representative Study
Consequence of gang membership over the life course (n=47)	1950 1960 1970 1980 1990 2000 2010	Melde, C., and F. A. Esbensen. 2011. Gang Membership as a Turning Point in the Life Course. *Criminology*.
Mental health, PTSD, and trauma exposure in gang members (n=27)	1950 1960 1970 1980 1990 2000 2010	Coid, J. W. et al. 2013. Gang Membership, Violence, and Psychiatric Morbidity. *American Journal of Psychiatry*.
Public policy and perceptions of the gang problem (n=47)	1950 1960 1970 1980 1990 2000 2010	Spergel, I. A. 1990. Youth Gangs—Continuity and Change. *Crime and Justice–a Review of Research*.*
Police perspectives on gang migration and the proliferation of gangs (n=35)	1950 1960 1970 1980 1990 2000 2010	Evans, W. P. et al. 1999. Are Rural Gang Members Similar to Their Urban Peers? Implications for Rural Communities. *Youth & Society*.
Gang units, intelligence, and police perceptions of gangs (n=31)	1950 1960 1970 1980 1990 2000 2010	Katz, C. M. 2001. The Establishment of a Police Gang Unit: An Examination of Organizational and Environmental Factors. *Criminology*.

Theme	Timeline	Reference
Focused deterrence and group violence interventions (n=29)	1950–2010	Braga, A. A. et al. 2018. Focused Deterrence Strategies and Crime Control: An Updated Systematic Review and Meta-Analysis of the Empirical Evidence. *Criminology & Public Policy*.
Civil gang injunctions and trust in the police (n=23)	1950–2010	Ridgeway, G. et al. 2019. Effect of Gang Injunctions on Crime: A Study of Los Angeles from 1988–2014. *Journal of Quantitative Criminology*.
Chicano communities, Latino gangs, and marginalization (n=49)	1950–2010	Vigil, J. D. 1988. Group Processes and Street Identity—Adolescent Chicano Gang Members. *Ethos*.
African-American gangs, social change, politics, and community organization (n=45)	1950–2010	Alonso, A. A. 2004. Racialized Identities and the Formation of Black Gangs in Los Angeles. *Urban Geography*.
Asian gangs and organized crime (n=26)	1950–2010	Joe-Laidler, K. 1994. The New Criminal Conspiracy—Asian Gangs and Organized Crime in San Francisco. *Journal of Research in Crime and Delinquency*.
Gangs and the Asian experience (n=20)	1950–2010	Lam, K. D. 2015. Racism, Schooling, and the Streets: A Critical Analysis of Vietnamese American Youth Gang Formation in Southern California. *Journal of Southeast Asian American Education and Advancement*.

(continued)

Table 9.1 Continued

Subtopic	Cumulative Distribution (1950–2020)	Representative Study
Multiple marginality, immigration, race, and ethnicity (n=19)		Freng, A. B., and F. A. Esbensen. 2007. Race and Gang Affiliation: An Examination of Multiple Marginality. *Justice Quarterly*.
Gangs and gang membership in prisons and jails (n=78)		Griffin, M. L., and J. R. Hepburn. 2006. The Effect of Gang Affiliation on Violent Misconduct among Inmates during the Early Years of Confinement *Criminal Justice and Behavior*.
Predictors of recidivism, post-release interventions, and barriers to re-entry (n=31)		Huebner, B. M. et al 2007. Gangs, Guns, and Drugs: Recidivism among Serious, Young Offenders. *Criminology & Public Policy*.
Prison gang organization, governance, and illicit trade (n=20)		Skarbek, D. B. 2011. Governance and Prison Gangs. *American Political Science Review*.
Group life, socialization, and street corner groups (n=79)		Chambliss, W. J. 1973. The Saints and the Roughnecks. *Society*.

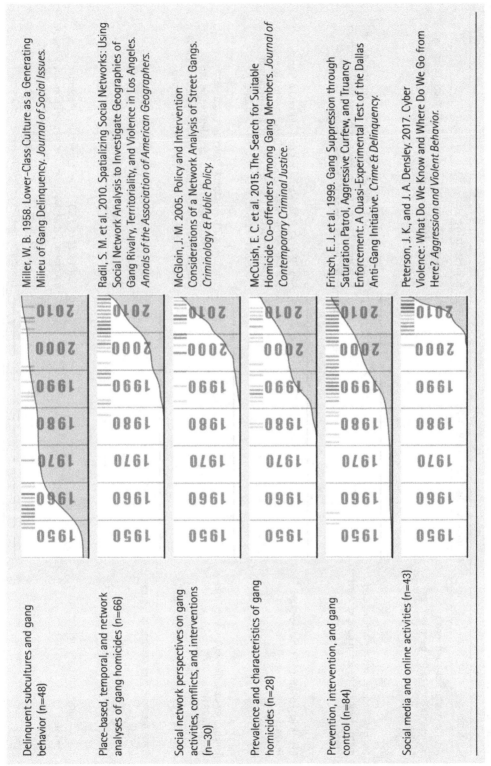

Category	Representative Reference
Delinquent subcultures and gang behavior (n=48)	Miller, W. B. 1958. Lower-Class Culture as a Generating Milieu of Gang Delinquency. *Journal of Social Issues*.
Place-based, temporal, and network analyses of gang homicides (n=66)	Radil, S. M. et al. 2010. Spatializing Social Networks: Using Social Network Analysis to Investigate Geographies of Gang Rivalry, Territoriality, and Violence in Los Angeles. *Annals of the Association of American Geographers*.
Social network perspectives on gang activities, conflicts, and interventions (n=30)	McGloin, J. M. 2005. Policy and Intervention Considerations of a Network Analysis of Street Gangs. *Criminology & Public Policy*.
Prevalence and characteristics of gang homicides (n=28)	McCuish, E. C. et al. 2015. The Search for Suitable Homicide Co-offenders Among Gang Members. *Journal of Contemporary Criminal Justice*.
Prevention, intervention, and gang control (n=84)	Fritsch, E. J. et al. 1999. Gang Suppression through Saturation Patrol, Aggressive Curfew, and Truancy Enforcement: A Quasi-Experimental Test of the Dallas Anti-Gang Initiative. *Crime & Delinquency*.
Social media and online activities (n=43)	Peterson, J. K., and J. A. Densley. 2017. Cyber Violence: What Do We Know and Where Do We Go from Here? *Aggression and Violent Behavior*.

(continued)

Table 9.1 Continued

Subtopic	Cumulative Distribution (1950–2020)	Representative Study
Artistic productions and media representations of the gang problem (n=38)	1950–2010	Esbensen, F. A., and K. E. Tusinski. 2007. Youth Gangs in the Print Media. *Journal of Criminal Justice and Popular Culture*.
Gang definitions, self-definitions, and methodological issues in gang research (n=50)	1950–2010	Wood, J. L., and E. Aleyne. 2010. Street Gang Theory and Research: Where Are We Now and Where Do We Go from Here? *Aggression and Violent Behavior*.
Extremist, terrorist, and hate groups (n=24)	1950–2010	Simi, P. et al. 2016. Narratives of Childhood Adversity and Adolescent Misconduct as Precursors to Violent Extremism: A Life-Course Criminological Approach. *Journal of Research in Crime and Delinquency*.
Emergency care, gunshot injuries, and gangs (n=31)	1950–2010	Morris, E. J. 2012. Respect, Protection, Faith, and Love: Major Care Constructs Identified within the Subculture of Selected Urban African American Adolescent Gang Members. *Journal of Transcultural Nursing*.
Gang presence and violence in schools (n=26)	1950–2010	Thompkins, D. E. 2000. School Violence: Gangs and a Culture of Fear. *Annals of the American Academy of Political and Social Science*.
Fear of gangs and gang-related crime (n=15)	1950–2010	Curtis, J. W. et al. 2014. The Prospects and Problems of Integrating Sketch Maps with Geographic Information Systems to Understand Environmental Perception: A Case Study of Mapping Youth Fear in Los Angeles Gang Neighborhoods. *Environment and Planning B: Planning and Design*.

THE HISTORY AND EVOLUTION OF GANG SCHOLARSHIP 159

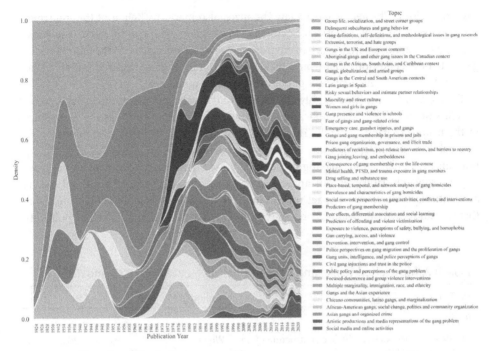

FIGURE 9.5 Density of Topic Groups over Time

of the most cited publications from these periods, and describe the most prevalent topics during each period. I also illustrate the focus of gang scholars using word clouds representative of the period. For each period, a figure will contain two sets of word clouds representing all publications in this era (not restricted to journal articles). The top set of words simply represent the 100 most common words used in abstracts and titles of publications of this era, with the sizes of the words representing their relative frequencies. The bottom set of words represent 100 words that most uniquely represent publications of this era using cTF-IDF. The sizes of the words in this second word cloud represent the relative frequency of the word during this period compared to other periods.

Period 1: 1920–1956

The first period spans from 1920–1956 and somewhat aligns with the era Pyrooz and Mitchell (2015) identified as the "Classic Era," beginning in the early twentieth century and ending in the 1950s. This period is one punctuated by many important historical events (e.g., the Great Depression, World War II, and the beginning of the Cold War) that had dramatic effects on all aspects of life, including the conditions that gave rise to the emergence of gangs in urban areas and structural changes in academia that made the study of gangs possible. Of course, the phenomenon of gangs in the United States predates the 1920s by at least over a century (Adamson 2000; Howell 2015). However, the early decades of the twentieth century were marked by waves of immigration from Europe to northeastern and midwestern US cities, which saw the emergence of white ethnic gangs, which would eventually be replaced by Black gangs as the Great Migration would substantially change the composition of major east coast cities, Chicago in particular. The 1920s also mark the height of the influence of the Chicago School of American Sociology (Martindale 1976; Cavan 1983). The convergence of the rapidly changing urban environment and the emergence of the Chicago School generated the conditions that would fuel the beginnings of gang research but also a large part of the scholarly history throughout the 1950s and 1960s.

Table 9.2 shows the most highly cited books and articles published during this period.[5] Scholars often point to the publication of Thrasher's *The Gang* (1927) as the first signpost in the history of gang research. The influence of Thrasher's work on contemporary gang research is undeniable: *The Gang* has been cited 4,403 times, an average of 46.3 times per year since its publication, making it the third most highly cited document in the history of gang research. However, our analysis shows that Thrasher's classic book did not have a statistically discernable impact on the number of gang publications. Figure 9.1 shows that the number of publications on gangs in the three decades that followed its publication

Table 9.2 Most Cited Books and Articles Published between 1920 and 1956

Rk	Title (Year)	Author(s)	NC	CPY	ATR
Books					
1	Street Corner Society: The Social Structure of an Italian Slum (1943)	Whyte	9,618	120.2	1
2	Delinquent Boys: The Culture of the Gang. (1955)	Cohen	8,022	118.0	2
3	The Gang: A Study of 1,313 Gangs in Chicago (1927)	Thrasher	4,403	45.9	15
4	Teen-Age Gangs (1953)	Kramer and Karr	25	0.4	259
5	Street Gangs in Toronto: A Study of the Forgotten Boy (1945)	Rogers	24	0.3	266
6	The City Boy and His Problems: A Survey of Boy Life in Los Angeles (1926)	Bogardus	25	0.3	269
Articles					
1	Effects of Different Conditions of Acceptance upon Conformity to Group Norms (1956)	Dittes and Kelley	388	5.8	369
2	The Gangster as Tragic Hero (1948)	Warshow	355	4.7	463
3	Gangs of Mexican-American Youth (1943)	Bogardus	96	1.2	1,314
4	The Psychology of Gang Formation and the Treatment of Juvenile Delinquents (1945)	Redl	89	1.1	1,349
5	Gangs and Delinquent Groups in London (1956)	Scott	58	0.9	1,475
6	Some Factors Influencing the Selection of Boys' Chums. (1927)	Furfey	74	0.8	1,522
7	Gang Membership and Juvenile Misconduct (1950)	Wattenberg and Balistrieri	53	0.7	1,549
8	Corner Boys: A Study of Clique Behavior (1941)	Whyte	57	0.7	1,564
9	How to Study the Boys' Gang in the Open (1928)	Thrasher	38	0.4	1,861
10	Outbreak of Gang Destructive Behavior on a Psychiatric Ward (1954)	Boyd et al.	23	0.3	1,905

Note: Rk = Rank in period; NC = Number of citations; CPY = Citations per year; ATR = All-time rank within category (books vs. articles)

remained relatively stable. The delayed impact of *The Gang* can also be seen in the fact that the manuscript was only cited 121 times between 1927 and 1957—an average of four citations a year. This may be due to the timing of the publication, as the Great Depression followed by World War II likely affected academic productivity and therefore citation counts. When considering the number of citations per year the book received, it ranks as the fifteenth most highly cited gang book.

Another notable publication to come out of this era is Whyte's *Street Corner Society* (1943), by far the most highly cited publication in the history of gang research (9,618; 121.7 per year). Interestingly, *Street Corner Society* had a similar impact as *The Gang* when it first came out in 1943. Although now considered a classic of sociology, the first edition garnered little attention in academic circles and sold very few copies until it was reissued in 1955 (Whyte 1993).

While the work of Thrasher and Whyte would eventually have a great influence on gang scholarship and beyond, theirs are the only notable publications of this era that averaged 1.7 publications per year, most of which have remained in relative obscurity. Arguably, a more important milestone of gang research—at least to scholars active at the time—comes at the very end of this period with the publication of Cohen's *Delinquent Boys* (1955). Cohen's book is the second most cited document with 8,022 citations (118 per year) and, unlike its predecessors, *Delinquent Boys* was immediately influential, generating both praise and critiques in academic circles (Cavender 2010). This is reflected in the 305 citations the book received in the first 10 years following its publication. Combined with the reissue of Whyte's *Street Corner Society*, the publication of Cohen's *Delinquent Boys* in 1955 marks an important turning point when it comes to productivity in gang research.

The earliest period of gang research was dominated by the *Group life, socialization, and street corner groups* (40.7%) topic with a handful of studies on *Delinquent subcultures and gang behavior* (11.1%). Figure 9.6 shows that the words "boy," "group," and "behavior" are all a frequently used and are words unique to this period relative to others. Words like "clique," "child," "character," "society," and "warfare" are lower in frequency than other words, but they are far more likely to be used during this period than in other periods. These words likely reflect the concerns of this area related to the formation of cliques in the period between childhood and adulthood, their adjustment to society (see additional words such as "adjustment," "conformity," "acceptance") and their involvement in "gang warfare" (e.g., Bogardus 1943). While crime, violence, and other problems were in the minds of gang scholars at the time, it is clear that much of the research of the time, following Thrasher and the Chicago School, was more interested in describing young boys' natural inclination to form groups, the psychological and personality characteristics of young people in gangs, and the neighborhood and societal conditions associated with street corner groups.

Period 2: 1957–1987

The second era identified covered the 1957–1987 period and encapsulates two periods Pyrooz and Mitchell (2015) called the "Golden Era" and the "Social Problems Era." Although the number of publications during this period pales in comparison to later periods, the "Golden/Social Problems Era" is the most pronounced increase relative to prior periods. While the 1920–1956 era averaged 1.7 publications per year, the period between 1957 and 1987 averaged 13.03 publications per year—a 666% increase over the previous period. This

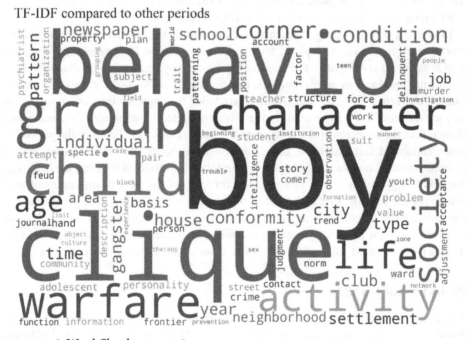

FIGURE 9.6 Word Cloud 1920–1956

era includes the publication of some of the most influential works in gang research (see Table 9.3): Miller's "Lower-Class Culture as a Generating Milieu of Gang Delinquency" (1958), Cloward and Ohlin's *Delinquency and Opportunity* (1960), Yablonsky's *The Violent Gang* (1962), Short and Strodtbeck's *Group Processes and Gang Delinquency* (1965), Suttles' *The Social Order of the Slum* (1968), and Klein's *Street Gangs and Street Workers* (1971).

Although there is no denotable shift in productivity, there are good reasons to identify two qualitatively distinct periods during this era, as Pyrooz and Mitchell do. An important shift occurs in the *focus* of gang scholars from the late 1950s and 1960s to the later work of the 1970s and 1980s. We can see a hint of this evolution in the sequence of classic works listed in the previous paragraphs: Research from the early years of this period focus on theoretical explanations of gang delinquency while later works focus on addressing gang delinquency. While *Group life, socialization, and street corner groups* remain an important topic of interest during this period (14.4%), it is surpassed by *Delinquent subcultures and gang behavior* (23.0%). Many new topics begin to emerge during this period, most notably *Chicano communities, Latino gang, and marginalization (6.5%)* and *Women and girls in gangs* (6.5%).

We also see the emergence of a concern for the problems gangs might pose for society, as studies on *Public policy and perceptions of the gang problem* (4.3%) and *Prevention, intervention, and gang control* (3.6%) make up 7.9% of the research of this era. This is also reflected in the word clouds of articles of this period. With words such as "delinquency" and "problem" (Figure 9.7) being prominent. The continuing quest to explain but also test theoretical propositions about gangs and delinquency are represented by words like "theory," "class," "subculture," "difference," and "observation," but the emergence of community-based and social work approaches to gang delinquency is evident with terms like "worker," "community," "work" (often referring to social work), "staff," "service," and "program." Many of the words also reflect scholars' interest in group processes: "cohesiveness," "leader," "structure," "process" (as in group processes), and an emergent interest in female gang members ("female," "girl").

As we will see, this is only the beginning of gang scholars' concerns with addressing gang delinquency and, in later periods, this concern will be at least partially responsible for increases in production. The turn to what Pyrooz and Mitchell called the "Social Problems Era" was not associated with an increase in production but a qualitative shift in the focus of gang scholars. The 1957–1987 period was one where few new gang scholars emerged (see Figure 9.4), suggesting that this focal shift in gang research was the doing of the same few scholars who developed and tested theories in the 1950s and 1960s but were now redirecting their efforts to solving the problems they observed.

The end of this period will also see the beginning of the diversification of gang scholarship. With the publication of her paper "Honor, Normative Ambiguity and Gang Violence" (Horowitz and Schwartz 1974), Ruth Horowitz was the first female gang scholar to make a lasting impact on gang research. In the years that followed, a quick succession of highly influential women would make their first contributions to gang scholarship: Joan W. Moore (1978), Anne Campbell (1978), and Cheryl Maxson (1983). In 1983, James Diego Vigil—the first non-white gang scholar to make a lasting impact on the field—made his first contribution. It is likely not a coincidence that a slight increase in diversity of the field was associated with an increase in the diversity of the topics studied, most notably in the emergence of the first studies focused on female gangs and members and an increase in the study of Chicano and Mexican-American gangs and communities. Whereas studies between 1920 and 1956 covered nine distinct topics, that number would jump to 22 between 1957 and 1987.

Table 9.3 Most Cited Books and Articles Published between 1957 and 1987

Rk	Title (Year)	Author(s)	NC	CPY	ATR
Books					
1	Delinquency and Opportunity: A Study of Delinquent Gangs (1960)	Cloward and Ohlin	6,748	107.1	3
2	The Social Order of the Slum: Ethnicity and Territory in the Inner City (1968)	Suttles	2,601	47.3	14
3	Group Process and Gang Delinquency (1965)	Short and Strodtbeck	1,382	23.8	28
4	Street Gangs and Street Workers (1971)	Klein	929	17.9	42
5	Homeboys: Gangs, Drugs, and Prison in the Barrios of Los Angeles (1978)	Moore and Garcia	759	16.9	44
6	The Violent Gang (1962)	Yablonsky	953	15.6	49
7	The Girls in the Gang (1984)	Campbell	517	13.3	63
8	Violence by Youth Gangs and Youth Groups as a Crime Problem in major American Cities (1975)	Miller	351	7.3	89
9	The Vice Lords: Warriors of the Streets (1969)	Keiser	294	5.4	111
10	The Gang: A Study in Adolescent Behavior (1958)	Bloch and Niederhoffer	282	4.3	121
Articles					
1	Lower-Class Culture as a Generating Milieu of Gang Delinquency (1958)	Miller	3,272	50.3	1
2	Social Disorganization and Stake in Conformity: Complementary Factors in the Predatory Behavior of Hoodlums (1957)	Toby	565	8.6	199
3	The Saints and the Roughnecks (1973)	Chambliss	405	8.1	218
4	Chicano Youth Gangs and Crime—The Creation of a Moral Panic (1987)	Zatz	254	7.1	277
5	Girls, Guys and Gangs—Changing Social-Context of Female Delinquency (1978)	Giordano	265	5.9	354
6	Self Definition by Rejection—The Case of Gang Girls (1987)	Campbell	191	5.3	412
7	Differences between Gang and Nongang Homicides (1985)	Maxson et al.	201	5.3	416
8	The Etiology of Female Juvenile Delinquency and Gang Membership—A Test of Psychological and Social Structural Explanations (1983)	Bowker and Klein	204	5.1	429
9	Research in Delinquent Subcultures (1958)	Cohen and Short	329	5.1	431
10	Street Gangs Behind Bars (1974)	Jacobs	240	4.9	449

Note: Rk = Rank in period; NC = Number of citations; CPY = Citations per year; ATR = All-time rank within category (books vs. articles)

Word frequency in period

TF-IDF compared to other periods

FIGURE 9.7 Word Cloud 1957–1987

Period 3: 1988-1991

The third period identified is also the shortest and covers the period between 1988 and 1991. The period is characterized by both a sudden shift in the number of publications of the time-series in 1988—from an average of 13.03 per year between 1956–1987 to an average of 54.25 between 1988–1991—and a large within-period increase (109% increase between 1988 and 1991). Although this is not a period identified by Pyrooz and Mitchell (2015), it leads up to the major turning point they identified in 1993, which they attribute to the rise of longitudinal surveys conducted in the late 1980s and 1990s, eventually leading to an ongoing "empirical turn" of gang research. Pyrooz and Mitchell do, however, point out that "between 1988 and 1992, the rate of doubling [in the cumulative growth of gang research] dropped down to five years or less" (35). After nearly 30 years of relatively slow, stable growth, it is undeniable that *something* happens in the late 1980s to spark the production of an impressive amount of gang scholarship during a very short period.

Most studies published during this period were concerned with the control of gangs and gang members: *Gangs and gang membership in prisons and jails* (16.2%) and *Public policy and perceptions of the gang problem* (13.5%) are the two largest topics of this period. Other studies focused on the violence (*Place-based, temporal, and network analyses of gang homicides*) and gang–drug connections (*Drug selling and substance use*) with 8.1% each. However, focusing on peer-reviewed articles may be somewhat missing the point for this period. The 1988–1991 period is the only time where the number of reports (66) surpassed the number of journal articles (51; see Figure 9.1). To put this number in perspective, the database only includes 59 reports published between 1840 and 1987. Reports have the potential to be published far quicker than peer-reviewed publications, which could explain in part the abrupt rather than gradual change in this era.

While this could be seen as a continuation of the Social Problems Era beginning at the end of the 1957–1987 period, Figure 9.8 shows just how different the policy focus of the 1988–1991 period was from the community and social work approaches of the 1970s and 1980s. Table 9.4 shows that while some of the most influential work of this period advanced theoretical understanding of gangs, many focused on the interplay between gangs and drugs (e.g., Klein, Maxson, and Cunningham 1991; Fagan 1989; Skolnick et al. 1990) and gangs' involvement in violence (e.g., Curry and Spergel 1988; Taylor 1990).

Period 4: 1992-2008

After the explosion of research in the previous period, the 1992–2008 period sees the production stabilize at its highest level up to this point in its history. During this period, the yearly average number of publications (152.29) almost tripled the mean production of the previous period (54.25) and was 11.5 times greater than the 1956–1987 period. A notable characteristic of this period is an explosion in the diversity of topics in gang scholarship. By this period, no single topic made up more than 10% of the research published, with *Women and girls in gangs* (7.4%), *Gangs in the Central and South American contexts* (5.8%), *Peer effects, differential association, and social learning* (4.6%), and *Prevention, intervention, and gang control* (4.5%) being the most common topics. Up to this point, the model had only detected 26 different topics over the entirety of the gang literature, with 49.7% of all articles falling under five topics. In this period, 18 new topics emerged (total: 45), and all but two

THE HISTORY AND EVOLUTION OF GANG SCHOLARSHIP 167

Word frequency in period

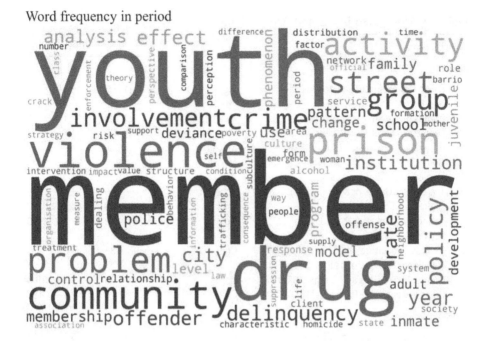

TF-IDF compared to other periods

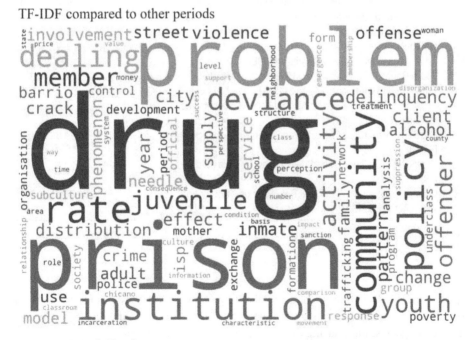

FIGURE 9.8 Word Cloud 1988–1991

Table 9.4 Most Cited Books and Articles Published between 1988 and 1991

Rk	Title (Year)	Author(s)	NC	CPY	ATR
Books					
1	Barrio Gangs: Street Life and Identity in Southern California (1988)	Vigil	1,603	45.8	16
2	Islands in the Street (1991)	Sanchez-Jankowski	1,187	37.1	19
3	People and Folks. Gangs, Crime and the Underclass in a Rustbelt City. (1988)	Hagedorn and Macon	1,100	31.4	21
4	Going Down to the Barrio: Homeboys and Homegirls in Change (1991)	Moore	915	28.6	23
5	The Lobster Gangs of Maine (1988)	Acheson	740	21.1	35
6	Dangerous Society (1990)	Taylor	476	14.4	57
7	Delinquent Gangs: A Psychological Perspective (1991)	Goldstein	228	7.1	90
8	Chinese Subculture and Criminality: Non-traditional Crime Groups in America (1990)	Chin	231	7.0	92
9	Cholas: Latino Girls and Gangs (1988)	Harris	229	6.5	100
10	Chinese Gangs and Extortion (1989)	Chin	70	2.1	166
Articles					
1	The Social Organization of Drug Use and Drug Dealing among Urban Gangs (1989)	Fagan	533	15.7	63
2	Youth Gangs—Continuity and Change (1990)	Spergel	356	10.8	131
3	Gang Homicide, Delinquency, and Community (1988)	Curry and Spergel	371	10.6	136
4	Group Processes and Street Identity—Adolescent Chicano Gang Members (1988)	Vigil	317	9.1	181
5	Youth Gangs and Public Policy (1989)	Huff	223	6.6	315
6	Crack, Street Gangs, and Violence (1991)	Klein et al.	205	6.4	325
7	Acute and Chronic Effects of Alcohol Use on Violence (1988)	Collins and Schlenger	194	5.5	383
8	The Social Structure of Street Drug Dealing (1990)	Skolnick et al.	157	4.8	458
9	Gangs, Neighborhoods, and Public Policy (1991)	Hagedorn	147	4.6	483
10	Constructing Gangs: The Social Definition of Youth Activities (1991)	Decker and Kempf-Leonard	143	4.5	501

Note: Rk = Rank in period; NC = Number of citations; CPY = Citations per year; ATR = All-time rank within category (books vs. articles)

topics contributed less than 5% of the total output of the period. Pyrooz and Mitchell (2015) argued that after 1993, gang research moved from "little" to "big" gang research. The diversification of gang studies during this era reinforces their assessment.

The trend that began in the 1988–1991 period continues with a relatively heavy emphasis on the gang "problem." Figure 9.9 shows an emphasis on the words "drug," "crime," "violence," "problem," and "homicide" in the abstracts and titles of articles published during this era. This is also reflected in the highly cited research from this period, with several articles

Word frequency in period

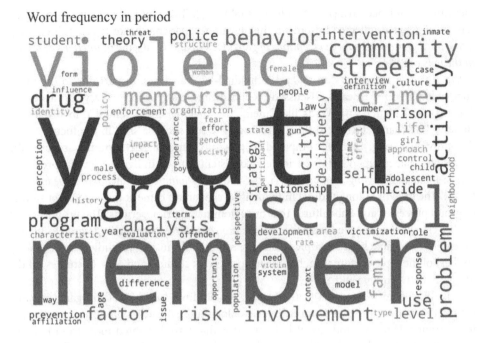

TF-IDF compared to other periods

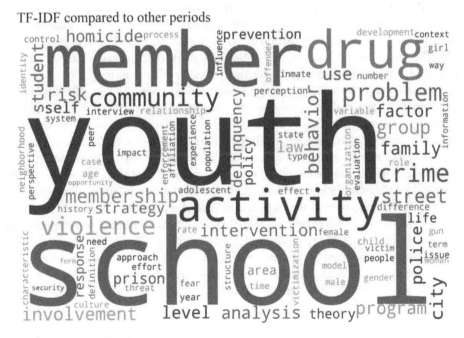

FIGURE 9.9 Word Cloud 1992–2008

focusing on violence, drugs, and policing (Table 9.5). This emphasis on the problematic aspects of gangs is reflected in some of the new topics that emerge for the first time: *Gang units, intelligence, and police perceptions of gangs* (2.6%) and *Civil gang injunctions and trust in the police* (1.1%).

We also begin to see a shift toward individual-level analyses, in part due to the influence of longitudinal research discussed previously and many school surveys in this era in Table 9.5 and Figure 9.9. Words like "member," "membership," "school," "involvement," "family," "risk," and "factor" in the TF-IDF word cloud shows a shift in the focus toward the individual gang member compared to previous periods. Furthermore, some of the new topics that emerged in this period are consistent with an individual-level approach to gangs: *Predictors of gang membership* (1.9%) and *Gang joining, leaving, and embeddedness* (1.0%). The growth of longitudinal individual-level analyses came at the expense of studies of group processes and subcultures that once dominated prior periods: The proportion of studies classified under the *Group life, socialization, and street corner groups* and *Delinquent subcultures and gang behavior* topics made up, respectively, 16.4% (34 studies) and 17.9% (37 studies) of the topics before 1992, but make up 2.8% (25 studies) and 0.7% (6 studies) of the literature between 1992 and 2008.

It is difficult to truly quantify the impact longitudinal surveys had on gang research during this period using topic modeling since longitudinal studies do not fall neatly into topic groups. However, individual-level analyses that have benefited most from longitudinal surveys typically fall in the *Peer effects, differential association, and social learning* (4.6%), *Predictors of offending and violent victimization* (2.1%), *Predictors of gang membership* (1.9%), and *Gang joining, leaving, and embeddedness* (1.0%) categories. Together, these topics make up 9.6% of the literature on gangs during the 1992–2008 period.

Another trend that begins to emerge in this period are topics related to research outside the United States. Among new topics in this period are *Gangs in the Central and South American contexts* (5.8%), *Gangs in the Canadian context* (1.4%), *Gangs, globalization, and armed groups* (0.9%), and *Latin gangs in Spain* (0.7%). When combined with *Gangs in the UK and European contexts* (2.9%) and *Gangs in the African, South Asian, and Caribbean* (1.8%), at least 13.5% of the research published during the 1992–2008 reflects research in the international context, compared to 4.3% for any period before 1992. Such an increase is no coincidence given the formation of the Eurogang program in the late 1990s, an initiative developed by Malcolm Klein to examine the presence of gangs in Europe (Weerman et al. 2009). The first Eurogang workshop was held in Schmitten, Germany, in 1998 and continues to be held regularly. As Weerman et al. (2009) explain, these workshops were instrumental in dispelling media-fueled myths about American street gangs. These workshops led to the realization by many European scholars and practitioners of the commonalities among youth groups they observed across Europe and elsewhere and the reality of street gangs in United States. Workshops soon directly led to publications, methodological manuals, and other resources.

Period 5: 2009–2021

After an almost two-decade plateau in gang research productivity, the 2010s would usher in another period of impressive growth: The average number of publications per year would

Table 9.5 Most Cited Books and Articles Published between 1992 and 2008

Rk	Title (Year)	Author(s)	NC	CPY	ATR
Books					
1	Homegirls: Language and Cultural Practice among Latina Youth Gangs (2008)	Mendoza-Denton	1,014	67.6	4
2	The American Street Gang: Its Nature, Prevalence, and Control (1997)	Klein	1,646	63.3	5
3	Street Gang Patterns and Policies (2006)	Klein and Maxson	1,062	62.5	6
4	Gangs and Delinquency in Developmental Perspective (2003)	Thornberry et al.	1,196	59.8	7
5	Gang Leader for a Day: A Rogue Sociologist Takes to the Streets (2008)	Venkatesh	825	55.0	10
6	Life in the Gang: Family, Friends, and Violence (1996)	Decker and VanWinkle	1,364	50.5	12
7	One of the Guys: Girls, Gangs, and Gender (2001)	Miller	948	43.1	17
8	A World of Gangs: Armed Young Men and Gangsta Culture (2008)	Hagedorn	598	39.9	18
9	The Youth Gang Problem: A Community Approach (1995)	Spergel	963	34.4	20
10	The Gangs of Chicago: An Informal History of the Chicago Underworld (2003)	Asbury	583	29.1	22
Articles					
1	An Economic Analysis of a Drug-Selling Gang's Finances (2000)	Levitt and Venkatesh	955	41.5	3
2	Problem-Oriented Policing, Deterrence, and Youth Violence: An Evaluation of Boston's Operation Ceasefire (2001)	Braga et al.	755	34.3	7
3	The Role of Juvenile Gangs in Facilitating Delinquent Behavior (1993)	Thornberry et al.	993	33.1	8
4	Youth Gangs and Definitional Issues: When Is a Gang a Gang, and Why Does It Matter? (2001)	Esbensen et al.	695	31.6	9
5	Gangs, Drugs, and Delinquency in a Survey of Urban Youth (1993)	Esbensen and Huizinga	812	27.1	12
6	Childhood Risk Factors for Adolescent Gang Membership: Results from the Seattle Social Development Project (1999)	Hill et al.	622	25.9	14
7	Gangstas, Thugs, and Hustlas: Identity and the Code of the Street in Rap Music (2005)	Kubrin	454	25.2	16
8	The Contribution of Gang Membership to Delinquency beyond Delinquent Friends (1998)	Battin-Pearson et al.	586	23.4	21
9	Sweet Mothers and Gangbangers: Managing Crime in a Black Middle-Class Neighborhood (1998)	Pattillo	550	22.0	27
10	Antisocial Behavior and Youth Gang Membership: Selection and Socialization (2004)	Gordon et al.	408	21.5	28

Note: Rk = Rank in period; NC = Number of citations; CPY = Citations per year; ATR = All-time rank within category (books vs. articles) increase by 58% to over 240 per year. The amount of gang publications produced during the 13 years of this period is equivalent to 95.9% of all the research published in the previous 177 years. In addition, there were more journal articles published during this period (1,543) than for the entirety of the history of gang research before 2009 (1,179). Unlike growth observed in the late 1980s and 1990s, growth between this period and the previous period can at least partially be attributed to a generalized growth in the field of criminology in general, and perhaps social sciences more broadly (see Figure 9.3).

Figure 9.1 also shows that the 2009–2021 period saw the rise of a new type of gang publication in the form of book chapters: 54.7% of all book chapters were published during this period. Several specialized handbooks were published during this period, such as *The Handbook of Gangs* (Decker and Pyrooz 2015) and the *Routledge International Handbook of Critical Gang Studies* (Brotherton and Gude, 2021), and more generalized versions such as *The Wiley Handbook of Violence and Aggression* (Sturmey 2017) and *The Routledge International Handbook of Aggression* (Ireland, Birch, and Ireland 2018). Given the incredible diversification of gang research in the previous period, the emergence of outlets that seek to review the state of research in different subareas of gang research is timely.

However, another role edited volumes seem to play during this period is furthering the research agendas of new emerging topics (e.g., *Looking beyond Suppression: Community Strategies to Reduce Gang Violence*, Gebo and Bond 2012) but especially to discuss research in different locales, for instance, *Gangs in the Caribbean: Responses of State and Society* (Harriott, Katz, and Harriott 2015), *Global Perspectives on Youth Gang Behavior, Violence, and Weapons Use* (Harding and Palasinski 2016), *Youth Gangs in International Perspective: Results from the Eurogang Program of Research* (Esbensen and Maxson 2012), *Gang Transitions and Transformations in an International Context* (Esbensen and Maxson 2016), *Youth in Crisis: Gangs, Territoriality and Violence* (Goldson 2011), *Maras: Gang Violence and Security in Central America* (Bruneau, Dammert, and Skinner 2011). This trend is also observed in the topics of journal articles, as the top three individual topics during this period making up over 22.8% of the published articles are *Gangs in the Central and South American context* (9.9%), *Gangs in the UK and European context* (7.5%), and *Gangs in the African, South Asian, and Caribbean context* (5.4%). The interest in Central and South American gangs is also reflected in the list of the most cited books published during this period (Table 9.6). In fact, of the top 10 books published between 2011 and 2019, half of the books focus on gang issues outside the United States.

Another notable trend during this period is the emergence of a new cohort of gang scholars in the early 2010s (see Figure 9.4). In 2010 and 2011 alone, 35 of the most productive gang scholars made their debut—the two largest cohorts observed. This pattern is also reflected in the 444 theses and dissertations published in the 2009–2021 period, which represents nearly 55% of all theses and dissertations ever published.

While the internationalization of gang research began in the later parts of the 1992–2008 period, it was dominated by research on *Gangs in the Central and South American* contexts. In the 2009–2021 period, the proportion of gang research dedicated to that topic continued to grow (+70% from the previous period), but research in other parts of the world showed much larger growth: *Gangs in the African, South Asian, and Caribbean contexts* (+203%) driven in large part by research in South Africa, and *Gangs in the UK and European contexts* (+158%).

Table 9.6 Most Cited Books and Articles Published between 2009 and 2021

Rk	Title (Year)	Author(s)	NC	CPY	ATR
Books					
1	Inside Criminal Networks (2009)	Morselli	793	56.6	8
2	Gangs in America's Communities (2018)	Howell and Griffiths	277	55.4	9
3	The Social Order of the Underworld: How Prison Gangs Govern the American Penal System (2014)	Skarbek	471	52.3	11
4	A Rainbow of Gangs: Street Cultures in the Mega-City (2010)	Vigil	621	47.8	13
5	Space of Detention: The Making of a Transnational Gang Crisis between Los Angeles and San Salvador (2011)	Zilberg	310	25.8	24
6	How Gangs Work: An Ethnography of Youth Violence (2013)	Densley	243	24.3	26
7	Guys, Gangs, and Girlfriend Abuse (2019)	Totten	97	24.2	27
8	Mano Dura the Politics of Gang Control in El Salvador (2017)	Wolf	140	23.3	30
9	Homies and Hermanos: God and Gangs in Central America (2012)	Brenneman II	236	21.5	34
10	The History of Street Gangs in the United States: Their Origins and Transformations (2015)	Howell	164	20.5	37
Articles					
1	Focused Deterrence Strategies and Crime Control: An Updated Systematic Review and Meta-Analysis of the Empirical Evidence (2018)	Braga et al.	230	46.0	2
2	Murder by Structure: Dominance Relations and the Social Structure of Gang Homicide (2009)	Papachristos	570	40.7	4
3	The Effects of Focused Deterrence Strategies on Crime: A Systematic Review and Meta-Analysis of the Empirical Evidence (2012)	Braga and Weisburd	430	39.1	5
4	The Corner and the Crew: The Influence of Geography and Social Networks on Gang Violence (2013)	Papachristos et al.	384	38.4	6
5	Continuity and Change in Gang Membership and Gang Embeddedness (2013)	Pyrooz et al.	285	28.5	10
6	What Do We Know about Gangs and Gang Members and Where Do We Go from Here? (2013)	Decker et al.	273	27.3	11
7	Legitimacy in Criminal Governance: Managing a Drug Empire from Behind Bars (2019)	Lessing and Willis	106	26.5	13
8	Taking Stock of the Relationship between Gang Membership and Offending a Meta-Analysis (2016)	Pyrooz et al.	180	25.7	15
9	Governance and Prison Gangs (2011)	Skarbek	298	24.8	17
10	Internet Banging: New Trends in Social Media, Gang Violence, Masculinity and Hip Hop (2013)	Patton et al.	244	24.4	18

Note: Rk = Rank in period; NC = Number of citations; CPY = Citations per year; ATR = All-time rank within category (books vs articles)

While there are no new topics emerging during the 2009–2021 period, some topics really begin to take off during this time. Unsurprisingly, the topic with the single largest growth in its proportion of the gang literature over the 1992–2008 period is *Social media and online activities* (+1,408%). Analyzing shifts in the proportion of articles devoted to certain topics between these two periods also suggests a change in the perspective of scholars about gang membership. For instance, scholars in the period devoted less attention to the threats gang members posed to communities and institutions, predictors of gang membership, and explanations of the criminogenic effects of gang membership on individual behaviors. In this period, scholars paid proportionally more attention to how gang membership affects the well-being of gang members themselves: *Mental health, PTSD, and trauma exposure in gang members* (+489%) and *Consequences of gang membership over the life course* (+250%). Similarly, scholars began to pay far more attention to the processes and key turning points associated with joining and leaving the gang as well as thinking about gang membership beyond a dichotomous indicator (*Gang joining, leaving, and embeddedness*, +301%) and how trauma and victimization may play a role in gang joining (*Exposure to violence, perceptions of safety, bullying, and homophobia*, +100%).

This period also shows an evolution in some topics that had a long history in gang scholarship. Most notably, research on issues associated with the experiences of gang members in prisons and jails appears to shift during this period. First, while the proportion of research on *Gangs and gang membership in prisons and jails* declined by 22%, research on *Prison gang organization, governance, and illicit trade* increased by 317%. In part, this shift can be attributed to the internationalization of gang research, as many studies about this latter topic take place outside the United States. Prison research also appears to follow a similar trajectory as research on gang membership: less attention to the dichotomous designations of gang membership and predictors of misconduct, and more attention to the processes that make gangs important to the informal social life in prison and challenging to deal with. Furthermore, research on gangs and gang membership in prison have increasingly examined the unique challenges gang membership poses to re-entry and the consequences of gang membership in prison on recidivism (*Predictors of recidivism, post-release interventions, and barriers to re-entry*, +55%).

Among the topics that declined significantly during this period are studies of the role of race, ethnicity, and gender in gangs. Studies on Asian (*Asian gangs and organized crime*, –89%; *Gangs and the Asian experience*, –86%), African-American (*African-American gangs, social change, politics and community organization*, –77%), and Latino (*Chicano communities, Latino gangs, and marginalization*, –61.7%) issues in gangs are among the topics that declined the most compared to the previous period. Research on *Women and girls in gangs* also declined by 61% over the previous period.

Finally, gang scholars have devoted less attention to almost all policy solutions to gangs except one: *Focused deterrence and group violence interventions* (+121%). Prior topics, including law enforcement assessments of the gang problem and other suppression-based strategies besides focused deterrence, were particularly affected by this shift: *Police perspectives on gang migration and the proliferation of gangs* (–77%), *Gang units, intelligence, and police perceptions of gangs* (–74%), and *Public policy and perceptions of the gang problem* (–72%) are among the topics with the largest decrease in this period. *Prevention, intervention, and gang control* (–34%) also declined, though not to the same extent. In part, this shift in policy interests could be explained by a redirection of the focus of scholars on gangs' role in facilitating gun violence in communities (*Gun carrying, access, and violence*, +243%)

away from drug-related crimes (*Drug selling and substance use*, −39%) and gang-related crimes more broadly (*Fear of gangs and gang-related crime*, −59%) and more minor forms of violence in schools (*Gang presence and violence in schools*, −71%).

Figure 9.10 and Table 9.6 show that the 2009–2021 period shed some light on these last trends, suggesting that the field showed an interest in understanding the role gangs play in violence and the evaluation of intervention to reduce gang-related violence. Many of the most highly cited articles from this period either focus on the effectiveness of focused deterrence strategies or social network perspectives on gangs and violence. Words like "youth," "violence," "member," and "group" are by far the most frequent words used in publications, and words like "intervention," "crime," "police," "network," and "relationship" reflect the importance of network research and focused deterrence policing in this period of gang scholarship. The return of "group" as a distinctive keyword during this period is a reflection of the rise of network studies during this time (*Place-based, temporal, and network analyses of gang homicides*, +37%) and the increase in interest toward group-level interventions, but also studies on *Extremist, terrorist, and hate groups* (+47%).

LIMITATIONS

Before discussing the findings of this study, it is important to understand the limitations of the techniques I use to map the history of gang scholarship. First, relying primarily on GS as a database for the identification of gang studies limits the analysis in two important ways. I already discussed the restrictions associated with GS in the methods section. The second important limitation of GS is in the quality of the citation information and citation counts provided by the search engine. Unlike other academic search engines that rely primarily on structured, indexed citation data, data about publications in GS (e.g., author names, title, journal, year of publication) often come from automated processes that extract information from the websites that host the articles and sometimes the reference lists of articles citing them. This process is prone to many types of errors, such as different spellings of the same names, wrong attribution of the date of publication (especially in the era of "online first" and "preprint"), and even in some rare cases the association of authors to papers they were not involved in. The sheer size of the database and the lack of personnel made it impossible to manually clean and correct all the data, though substantial efforts have been made to clean author names and merge different versions of a single name together. This is likely to be an important source of error in some of the figures and tables in this chapter.

Relatedly, the automation of the collection of abstracts for the purpose of topic modeling sometimes generated incomplete abstracts or abstracts with misspellings and led to the inclusion of additional words or phrases outside the abstract that could influence the classification of the article (labels in structured abstracts, copyright information, etc.). The latter issues were corrected to the best of my ability, either by removing certain common words from the topic modeling and word clouds (e.g., findings, discussion, objectives) and by using regular expressions ("regex") to remove unwanted information. While misspellings were corrected as they were found throughout the cleaning and creation of the database, there was no way to identify incomplete abstracts, other than by validating each article manually, which could not be accomplished. Therefore, a source of misclassification of articles into topic categories may be due to incomplete abstracts.

176 GRAVEL

FIGURE 9.10 Word Cloud 2009–2021

There are important caveats associated with the specific topic modeling techniques I used. As described in the methodology section, BERTopic relies on pre-trained sentence transformers, which allows the model to find abstracts that are similar to one another. Sentence transformers are trained using machine learning techniques based on billions of pairs of sentences (or short documents) that have been identified by humans to have degrees of similar meanings. As is the case for many machine learning approaches, the specific steps that lead the model to group two particular abstracts together are difficult to identify. A strength of the BERTopic approach is that it tries to identify keywords that uniquely describe each topic based on the articles the algorithm groups together. However, these keywords are identified through a completely independent process than the one used for the grouping, which sometimes leads to topic representations that are difficult to interpret (I gave a few examples of those difficulties in the methodology section). Ultimately, it can be challenging to make sense of why an article is included under one topic and not another. Furthermore, BERTopic is at its core a cluster analysis technique—an inherently exploratory data reduction technique—and objective assessment of model suitability is extremely challenging, especially given the novelty of the sentence-encoding techniques.

My approach for this chapter has been to limit as much as I could any human intervention in the classification of articles of topics and the labeling of these topics, hoping to reduce the injection of my own biases into the modeling processes, so I have resisted reassigning any articles to a different topic than the one the model assigned it too. The only instances where manual classification was necessary was for articles the model failed to classify, despite a relatively high probability of assignment to one or more topics (see the methodology section for a description of this process). Throughout the process of evaluating the usefulness of the model, I have noticed certain patterns that highlight some peculiarities in the classification of topics.

The model appears to place a lot of weight on named entities (e.g., names of geopolitical entities, nationalities, ethnicities, organizations) for the grouping of articles. On one hand, this ended up being an interesting feature of the model in identifying the internationalization of gang research. On the other hand, since not all research carried out in a specific country is focused on a single topic, it also introduces some noise in the model, making the classification of substantive topics—as opposed to regional topics or other topics based on named entities (e.g., race, ethnicity, gender)—more challenging. In other words, topics that seemed to be anchored around named entities are typically very diverse in their composition, reducing the distance between these topics and other substantive topics, leading to articles either failing to be classified or pulled into topics that may not provide the best classification.

Another limitation of the topic model is the nature of the information included in titles and abstracts. Abstracts tend to include many generic statements that reduce the usefulness of the information for classification purposes. For instance, an abstract may begin with a general statement about the importance of a gang problem in society, yet the article focuses on a very specific or narrow aspect of gang research. It is also common for abstracts to include statements about policy implications of findings that may confuse the classification of articles. As for titles, it is increasingly common for scholars to include a quote or idiom as part of the title followed by a colon and a more descriptive title. Such titles may produce some additional difficulties in classifying articles.

Since articles are classified based on semantic similarity, it is possible that changes in the lexicon used to describe gangs, but also research more broadly, might introduce a temporal element in the classification of articles. Articles published around the same time may have a tendency to be grouped together. A similar process might lead to the grouping of articles based on regional dialects. For instance, the word "Aboriginal" is commonly used to describe Indigenous peoples in Canada and Australia, leading to a few articles of gangs in the Australian context being grouped in a topic on Canadian research (hence the label *Aboriginal gangs and other gang issues in the Canadian context*).

Discussion

After two impressive growth spurts in the late 1980s and late 2000s, gang research appears to have plateaued. Over its history, gang scholarship has not only grown in size but diversified immensely both in terms of the topics covered by scholars and the locales where gangs have been studied. The size of the gang literature is so large and its foci so diverse that being a "gang" scholar nowadays is not as descriptive of one's specialization as it once was. As Pyrooz and Mitchell (2015) point out, keeping up with gang scholarship in the era of "big gang research" is more challenging than ever. Specialization within gang scholarship seems inevitable. In the next sections, I summarize the findings associated with each period and propose some explanations for the changes I have observed and additional observations I have made throughout the process of conducting this review.

Little Gang Research, or the Beginnings and Solidification of the Science of Gangs

The history of gang research begins with an era of early discovery of the gang phenomenon (1920–1956) that included the foundational work of Thrasher and Whyte and ends with the first turning point of gang research: the publication of Cohen's *Delinquent Boys* in 1955. There are many factors that makes this particular publication meaningful in the history of gang scholarship, and it is difficult to pinpoint a single one. Perhaps because it was the first notable attempt to develop a theory of the gang, or perhaps because it drew much criticism for the lack of empirical data supporting the theory (see Short 1968), *Delinquent Boys* galvanized the field. *Delinquent Boys* always has a particular place in the history of sociology because it merged ideas from the original Chicago School of the 1920s and anomie theory, which comes from a key member of the second wave of the Chicago School, Robert K. Merton (Barmaki 2016). Following Cohen's lead, a few dedicated scholars began theorizing and testing hypotheses about the formation of gangs and the group processes that influence individual gang member behaviors (1957–1987). James Short, Walter Miller, Irving Spergel, Malcolm Klein, Richard Cloward, Lloyd Ohlin, and a few others became architects of our theoretical understanding of gangs, but importantly, they were keenly aware of the potential policy implications of their work. In fact, the classic works produced by these scholars often came from their partnerships with community organizations dedicated to address problems associated with gangs and gang membership. It is therefore unsurprising that during the 1957–1987 era, this same group of scholars became invested in these policy implications, studying the impact of social programs and social work (particularly detached workers) on gangs and their members.

Little Gang Research Is Growing Up, or What Happened in 1988?

It is far more difficult to attribute a single cause to the next turning point in 1988. What the results show is that there is a dramatic shift in the content of gang research from the previous periods, with a greater emphasis on drugs, violence, and law enforcement. Of course, this aspect of gang scholarship does not go away in 1992, but it is in stark contrast from earlier periods. Many scholars have discussed the shift toward suppression, but perhaps the most insightful voice on this issue is Malcolm Klein, who started writing *The American Street Gang* (1997) in late 1992 with this transition period fresh in his mind. Klein argued that the shift from community-based and social work approaches of prior decades to suppression were a combination of several co-occurring factors: the failure to demonstrate the effectiveness of previous approaches, the proliferation of gangs, the perception of an increase in the violent character of gangs and the randomness of their targets, the assumed connection between the emergence of crack and gangs, and the succession of increasingly conservative national policies—starting with the "law and order rhetoric of the Nixon campaigns . . . it flowered in the Reagan and Bush eras" (Klein 1997, 151).

I argue that the last point raised by Klein plays an important role in the rapid growth of gang scholarship between 1988 and 1991 and marks the beginning of the large influence of federal funding agencies and the criminal justice system on gang research, most notably the United States Department of Justice's (DOJ) Office of Justice Programs (OJP), particularly its component of the Office of Juvenile Justice and Delinquency Prevention (OJJDP). I argue that their involvement also redirected much of gang research to focus on the most problematic aspects of gangs—crime, drugs, and violence—and led to a focus on law enforcement control strategies. Why did this happen specifically in 1988? The answer is probably that it did not really *happen* that year specifically but had been brewing for a few years. That said, there are interesting coincidences in the policy changes that occurred specifically in 1988.

Gangs were not really on the radar of (national) politicians before the mid- to late 1980s. The Juvenile Justice and Delinquency Prevention Act (JJDPA) of 1974—which is responsible for the creation of the OJJDP—made no mention of gangs until congressional amendments in the 1980 added a subsection to the list of programs for which states can use formula grants funds: "projects designed both to deter involvement in illegal activities and to promote involvement in lawful activities on the part of juvenile gangs and their members" (Juvenile Justice Amendments 1980, 94:2757). In 1984, further amendments to the JJDPA mandated the OJP to make grants designed to develop and implement programs to prevent illegal activities by "gangs whose membership is substantially composed of juveniles" (Continuing Appropriations for Fiscal Year 1985 1984, 98:2114) and to fund studies to prepare recommendations about effective programs to promote "lawful activities on the part of gangs"(Continuing Appropriations for Fiscal Year 1985 1984, 98:2119).

Most importantly, the Anti-Drug Abuse Act of 1988 made numerous references to gangs, mandated the establishment of drug abuse education and prevention programs relating to youth gangs, gave priority for funding to jurisdictions where drug-related crimes were committed by gangs, provided millions of dollars to the Drug Enforcement Administration and law enforcement agencies specifically dedicated to gang-related enforcement, and amended the JJDPA further to include more funding for gang prevention and intervention, as well as statements prioritizing applications for grants and contracts "based on the incidence and severity of crimes committed by gangs . . . in the geographical area" (Anti-Drug Abuse Act of 1988, sec. 4452) of the proposed programs and activities. The act placed youth gangs in the center of the war on drugs:

> there has been a severe, cancer-like growth of youth gangs who abuse, transport, and traffic in illegal drugs . . ., engage in acts of violence, often on a random basis, resulting in death or serious bodily injury to thousands of people, as well as terrorizing tens of thousands of others. Such youth gangs have spread their activities from southern California to more than 50 cities throughout the United States, thereby clearly indicating that the threat posed by these gangs is national in nature, requiring a strong Federal response." (Anti-Drug Abuse Act of 1988, sec. 4803)

I argue that the US federal criminal justice agencies' interest in addressing gang violence and gang involvement in drug trafficking in the late 1980s and 1990s is probably one of the most important turning points in gang research history. Starting in the 1988–1991 period but continuing to this day, a significant proportion of gang research has been motivated by US policy goals of the 1980s and 1990s of controlling gangs, drug trafficking, and gang violence in schools—areas of focus clearly outlined in bills passed by congress in 1984, 1988, and 1992 to first create the OJP and then dictate the allocation of funding by the agencies it oversees, particularly the National Institute of Justice (NIJ), Bureau of Justice Assistance (BJA), and OJJDP (National Research Council 2013). The focus on gangs is evident by the formation of not one but two national centers on gang issues within the OJP: the National Youth Gang Center within the OJJDP in 1995 and the National Gang Center within the BJA in 2003.[6] In addition, Congress created the National Gang Intelligence Center within the Federal Bureau of Investigation in 2005.

Was the attention to gangs in the late 1980s warranted? Absolutely, especially given the record high violence in many urban areas at the time, an outsized proportion of which was believably attributed to gangs. What is more questionable is the insistence—from politicians, the media, and law enforcement—that the drug problem, and in particular the crack epidemic, was a result of highly organized gang activity and that the drug and gang problem were essentially synonymous. As Klein (1997) puts it, "everything we knew about street gangs said, 'Hold on, that doesn't fit'" (17).

At least part of the increase in scholarship during that period could be attributed to scholars attempting to challenge the ideas about the drug-gang connection. Klein et al.'s (1991) study rebutting the assumed connection between crack, street gangs, and violence, and Fagan's (1989) study showing the spurious relationship between drug use, drug selling, gang membership, and violence is emblematic of this movement. Both these studies were funded by the DOJ. However, Klein (1997) states that findings of their study were actively ignored by the federal agency. When faced with the finding that 75% of crack sale incidents did not involve gangs, law enforcement agencies dismissed the findings, and the NIJ declined to publish the findings saying they were out of date: "Balderdash! The institute just didn't like the findings because they didn't fit the institute's belief about gangs and crack" (Klein 1997, 17). The NIJ then rejected a proposal to update the findings.

I argue that placing gangs at the center of the war on drugs and increasing the availability of federal funding associated with gangs created an incentive structure for local governments and law enforcement agencies to look for gangs in their communities and perhaps redefine their jurisdiction's crime problems with gangs in mind. As a result, criminal justice actors became heavily invested in creating gang profiles, risk assessments, and emphasizing the difficulties of policing gangs. Most emblematic of this shift is the emergence of the National Gang Crime Research Center (NGCRC) in 1990 and its official publication the *Journal of Gang Research*, which specifically caters to law enforcement officials and publishes research conducted by law enforcement personnel and academics alike. The *Journal of Gang Research* alone published at least 245 articles in the database between 1992 and 2018, 12.6% of those authored or co-authored by the journal's editor, George Knox, or the NGCRC. The journal also highlights an important aspect to keep in mind about this and future periods of gang scholarship: Productivity does not equate scholarly impact. Despite being the single largest producer of gang scholarship, the *Journal of Gang Research* is not very impactful in academic literature: While the average article in the database has 46.85 citations and 3.20 citations per year, articles in the *Journal of Gang Research* have, on average, 9.98 citations and 0.53 citations per year.

Becoming Big Gang Research, or the Diversification of Gang Scholarship

Gang scholars benefited tremendously from federal investments in gang research, most obviously through new sources of substantial funding. Indirectly, federal investments in addressing gang issues, combined with parallel changes in policing that emphasized data-driven approaches (see Ratcliffe 2016), led to more available data on gangs from law enforcement agencies and other parts of the criminal justice system (e.g., prisons). For instance, the creation of specialized gang units is directly related to investments by the DOJ starting in the late 1980s and 1990s (Katz and Webb 2006). Access to data collected by law enforcement is directly associated with the development of new areas of gang scholarship, such as the emergence of spatial and network approaches in gang research. In addition, more available funding likely meant more resources to train new scholars.

It is difficult to attribute the next two eras of gang research—1992–2008 and 2009–2021—to single, discrete turning points. The reason for such difficulties lies in the fact that, much like Pyrooz and Mitchell observed, the 1990s marked the moment where "little gang research" turns into "big gang research"—when gang research became diversified to the point that many subfields begin to emerge. As these changes were occurring, another important change in the gang literature was being engineered: the rise of the longitudinal survey.

Pyrooz and Mitchell's survey of gang scholars identified the advent of longitudinal surveys in the late 1980s and 1990s as the turning point receiving the largest number of responses. Furthermore, the authors also point out that 1993 saw both the largest year-to-year increase in publications and the publication of four articles from the Rochester Youth Development Study and the Denver Youth Survey, which are among the most highly cited articles in gang scholarship. The 1992–2008 period includes the publications of the first results from the longitudinal studies of the Causes and Correlates of Delinquency Research Program. Funded by the OJJDP, this program supported three large-scale longitudinal studies in Rochester, Pittsburgh, and Denver, which all began data collection in the late 1980s and began generating publications in the early 1990s. The late 1990s and early 2000s would also see the emergence of more longitudinal studies that would make contributions to the gang literature, such as the Seattle Social Development Survey, the Montreal Longitudinal and Experimental Study, and the Gang Resistance Education and Training Evaluation.

However, upon closer inspection of the publication record, these large longitudinal studies play a relatively minor role in the volume of gang research during this period, at least in terms of journal articles. While four studies using data from the Causes and Correlates studies were published in 1993, only three more will be published between 1995 and 2008. The G.R.E.A.T. study—besides the evaluations of the program itself—produced 11 studies between 1998 and 2007. The Seattle Social Development Survey (two) and the Montreal Longitudinal and Experimental Study (four) would produce an additional six studies. In total, these six studies contributed 24 journal articles during this period, or 2.2% of articles produced. Despite their importance to the gang literature, longitudinal surveys are not responsible for the sustained production during this period, at least not directly.

Nevertheless, what is clear is that these few studies were immensely influential on gang scholarship and likely motivated the individual-level focus that sustained production during this period. Studies that came from the Causes and Correlates studies, G.R.E.A.T., and the other studies are among the most highly cited studies in the history of gang research (see Appendix 1), and *Gangs and Delinquency in Developmental Perspective* (Thornberry et al. 2003), which reports on the results of the Rochester Youth Development Survey, ranks seventh in the most cited books (see Appendix 2). These studies provided answers to questions that are easy to take for granted today, but these answers most likely allowed the field of gang research to continue to grow. As I described previously, scholarship in the next period of gang research used data from these longitudinal surveys and others (e.g., the National Longitudinal Survey of Youth, Pathways to Desistance, the National Longitudinal Study of Adolescent to Adult Health) to go far beyond the initial questions the scholars who designed the Causes and Correlates studies had in mind. Thanks in large part to many of these studies and the focus on individual-level factors they inspired, a meta-analysis of the relationship between gang membership and offending was possible (Pyrooz et al. 2016), the first and only published quantitative meta-analysis on an empirical question in gang research outside a handful of meta-analyses of gang programs.

Another important milestone in the history of gang research was the establishment of the Eurogang Program of Research. As I discussed previously, the 1992–2008 periods saw the beginning of the internationalization of gang research, though it is difficult to truly assess this growth from the topic model, since research in other countries may be combined with other substantive topics. Using another NLP technique called named entity recognition (NER), I extracted references to specific countries from titles and abstracts of journal

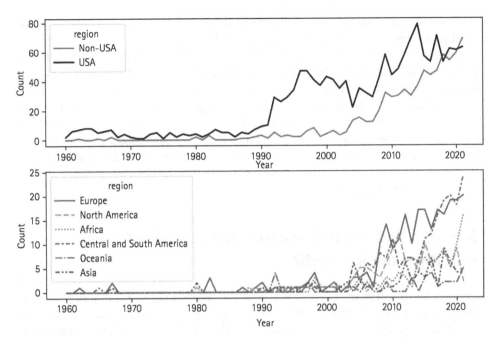

FIGURE 9.11 Gang Research by Region: Comparing US to Non-US Research, 1960–2021

articles. Over the entire history of gang scholarship, I found mentions of 74 different countries, which I classified into regions of the world. Given the domination of American gang research for most of its history, I found that it was common for most gang research conducted outside the United States to name the specific country where the research took place in the abstract and sometimes the title, as it is often a key aspect of the novelty of the work. This also implies that it is generally safe to assume that abstracts that do not mention any specific countries or regions outside the United States are likely referring to US-based research. Figure 9.11 shows in the top panel a comparison of the yearly volume of journal publications in US and in non-US settings, and in the bottom panel it shows the breakdown of non-US research by continent.

Figure 9.11 makes it clear that gang research outside the United States has been growing rapidly since the mid-2000s, so much so that in 2018 it produced more research than US-based research for the first time and would do so again in 2021. While the timing does coincide with the establishment of the Eurogang project, breaking down the output of scholarship by continent shows that the Eurogang project is an important but not the only reason for the internationalization of gang research, especially during the 1992–2008 period. Much of the growth comes from research in Central and South America and in North America, primarily driven by research from Canada, which were not necessarily regions of focus for the Eurogang project. Research in Europe, primarily driven by UK-based scholarship, increases rapidly starting in 2008 and contributes a large proportion of the rise of international research thereafter. The internationalization of research, then, plays a much larger role in the last period I have identified: 2009–2021.

What is unique about the 1992–2008 period is the sudden diversification of topics in gang scholarship. Responding to the policy decisions of the 1980s and 1990s played a big role in this diversification, as did the individual-level focus brought about by the longitudinal studies and the beginning of the internationalization of gang research. The growth of police intelligence apparatus fostered by the federal government's investment in the fight against gangs also provided scholars with much data on gangs, allowing for place-based research and research on the uniqueness of gang-related homicides to flourish and for social network analyses to begin to emerge. The continued involvement of federal agencies, influenced by landmark legislations (e.g., the 1994 crime bill; see Decker, Pyrooz, and Densley 2022) also made evaluations of G.R.E.A.T. programs and the availability of its longitudinal data and the funding of many gang studies possible.

Toward a New Era of Gang Research, or What Comes after Big Gang Research?

Exponential growth in science is simply unsustainable: If gang research would have continued to grow at the rate it did in the 1988–1991 period, we would have had, by the end of 2022, 14,448 articles in gang scholarship—more than double the number of studies found in this analysis. De Solla Price (1963) argues that science does not grow exponentially, but rather follows a logistic curve, where exponential growth quickly meets a saturation point. Natural phenomena following logistic curves rarely have the smooth S-shape we see in textbooks. De Solla Price (1963) argues that exponential curves "seem to relish the idea of being flattened. Before they reach a midpoint, they begin to twist and turn, and, like impish spirits, change their shapes and definitions so as not to be exterminated against that terrible ceiling" (23). Phenomena following a logistic curve typically follow one of two trajectories. If conditions do not allow further growth, the logistic curve will fluctuate violently until it reaches a local minimum or a slow decline toward zero. The other possibility depends on whether the phenomena can evolve to take on a slightly different definition:

> If a slight change of definition of the thing that is being measured can be so allowed as to count a new phenomenon on equal terms with the old, the new logistic curve rises phoenixlike on the ashes of the old (De Solla Price 1963, 25).

This second possibility beautifully explains the trajectory of gang research. Gang scholarship grew exponentially in the 1990s and gradually became something new during the 2000s, until it rose "phoenixlike" in the 2010s, where it has since remained against the ceiling of a second logistic curve. The 1992–2008 period did show evidence of a "slight change of definition" in gang research—from the beginning of the internationalization of gang research to the emergence of several new topics. These changes have allowed gang scholarship to grow one more time and bring in a new generation of gang scholars who have, since then, continued to grow these new topics of gang scholarship, leaving aside some ideas of previous periods.

The 2009–2021 period shows a field adapting to the new world gangs and their members operate in. Studies examining the importance of social media for gang violence (e.g., Stuart 2020; Patton et al. 2019; Leverso and Hsiao 2021), the trauma and PTSD associated with gang membership (e.g., Dierkhising, Sanchez, and Gutierrez 2021; Beresford and Wood 2016; Wood and Dennard 2017), the rise of "alt-right" gangs (Reid and Valasik 2018; 2020), and homosexuality in gangs (Panfil 2020) are all topics have been developed in the last few years. Researchers have also undertaken important work in overlooked and challenging areas of gang scholarship. The process of joining a gang (e.g., Densley 2012; Descormiers and Corrado 2016; Gallupe and Gravel 2018; Pyrooz and Densley 2016), the barriers to re-entry to society associated with gang membership (e.g., Wolff et al. 2020; Pyrooz, Clark et al. 2021), and the role gangs play in facilitating access to firearms (e.g., Roberto, Braga, and Papachristos 2018; Hureau and Braga 2018) are all topics that had not received much attention until recent years. We are also seeing new research in prisons and jails that overcome the challenges of doing interviews with gang members in these settings (e.g., Wood et al. 2014; Pyrooz, Mitchell et al. 2021; Mitchell et al. 2017; Scott and Maxson 2016) and assesses the impact of the common practice of restrictive housing and isolation on gang members (e.g., Pyrooz and Mitchell 2020; Motz, Labrecque, and Smith 2021).

On the policy front, focused deterrence has dominated this most recent period. It is safe to say that at this time, no other policy has received the level of attention and evaluation that focused deterrence has up to this point. Importantly, many evaluations of focused deterrence programs have gone beyond simple assessments of effectiveness and have attempted to unpack the mechanisms that make this type of intervention effective. Just a few years ago, my colleagues and I lamented the lack of attention to the theory of change in gang programs in general (Gravel et al. 2013), and for group-based intervention such as focused deterrence specifically (Gravel and Tita 2015). Scholars studying focused deterrence and group violence interventions have responded to these critiques admirably. Studies have examined the spread of deterrent effects to gangs connected to the targeted gangs (Braga et al. 2019), used social network analysis and simulations to identify the best-positioned "messengers" to spread deterrence in gangs (Wheeler et al. 2019), have compared community-level and gang-level impacts of the program (Roman et al. 2019), and have looked at the role social media plays in mediating the effect of focused deterrence (Hyatt, Densley, and Roman 2021).

One reason for concern is that police programs still dominate policy discussions in gang research, and evaluations of these programs have been based on law enforcement data (Roman, 2021). For instance, focused deterrence policing is widely recognized as the best evidence-based programs we have to deal with gangs, but it is also a program that has received considerable financial support for its evaluation, unlike others that do not involve law enforcement (Roman 2021; Gravel, Valasik, and Reid 2021). This is not new: Even one of the most celebrated gang prevention programs—G.R.E.A.T.—is typically administered by law enforcement officials. When law enforcement agencies are funding gang research, it may not come as much surprise that gang research focuses on the most serious behaviors of gang members and finds policing to be an acceptable solution to deal with these problems (see Van Hellemont and Densley 2021 for a recent discussion).

There are reasons to be hopeful for a change on that front both from the perspective of the funding preferences of federal agencies and the identification of effective programs not involving law enforcement. Recent work on adapting functional family therapy (Thornberry et al. 2018) and multisystemic therapy (Boxer et al. 2017) to gang populations have shown promise, and both evaluations have been funded at least partially by the OJJDP. The injection of public health perspectives in gang research has also generated new and promising ideas to gang programming, such as trauma-informed approaches to reduce gang violence (Jennings-Bey et al. 2015). Even evaluations of re-entry programs that were practically non-existent by the early 2010s (Gravel et al. 2013) have begun to emerge (e.g., Spooner et al. 2017).

Finally, an area that has much promise for the future of gang research and has emerged as a relatively important area of gang scholarship in the 2009–2021 period are studies employing social network analysis. This area is promising because it could provide the tools to build on recent advances, suggesting a move away from the typical dichotomous label of "gang membership" toward a more flexible notion of "gang embeddedness" (Pyrooz, Sweeten, and Piquero 2013). When Decker et al. (2013) reviewed the state of research on group processes in gang scholarship, they held out hope that the increased use of social network analysis would yield new findings, hypotheses, and theories about group processes and the social structure of these groups. Pyrooz and Mitchell (2015) also held out hope that network studies would help gang research return to group-level analyses. Recent advances in network studies have begun to examine intergroup interactions (e.g., Bichler, Norris, and Ibarra 2020; Lewis and Papachristos 2020; Nakamura, Tita, and Krackhardt 2020) and the stability of groups over time (e.g., Ouellet, Bouchard, and Charette 2019). However, most network studies of gang issues are limited by their use of arrest or court records to map the structure of groups and individual networks, which is inherently a flawed enterprise (Faust and Tita 2019). Networks extracted from police data are influenced by changes in organizational focus, staffing, and public policy in ways we simply do not clearly understand (Gravel 2018).

Advancing group-level research on gangs using social network analysis will not happen through data requests or by sitting in front of a computer screen: It will require us to go out in the field and map the social networks of gangs using observational or survey methods. Few scholars have been successful in doing so, but when they have they have produced unique contributions to gang scholarship. such as Roman, Cahill, and Mayes' (2021) multi-wave survey of gang members' personal networks before and after leaving the gang, Descormiers and Morselli's (2011) use of focus groups with gang members to map rivalries and alliances in Montreal, and Grund and Densley's (2012) use of observations and fieldwork to study the role of ethnicity in co-offending among gang members in London. Ethnographers have produced some of most insightful group-level research and network scholars would do well to learn from them and forge collaborations to both gain access to the relevant populations necessary for network surveys, but also provide context for the complex structures that would likely emerge. Furthermore, gang scholars already engage in research in settings such as schools and prisons that provide ideal conditions for the collection of network data (Bouchard 2021).

Conclusion

I began this chapter by discussing the first article about gangs written by Stevenson in 1834, and given my findings it is important to briefly revisit the context in which it was written. Many scholars have argued that the discovery of "thugs" by British colonialists in India was either a complete invention or at least greatly exaggerated (Wagner 2007; Macfie 2008; Gordon 1969; Brown 2001). These exaggerations were often published in academic outlets by explorers documenting the atrocities committed by these criminal groups, often arguing that the problem was far more widespread and growing than previously thought (Brown 2001). Eventually, these pseudoscientific depictions convinced the government to create a department dedicated to the enforcement of newly enacted vague laws targeting these groups. This department commissioned more studies to examine the threat posed by the Phansigar and other similar groups, which legitimized the need for a vicious suppression campaign (Singha 1993; Brown 2001). These studies were uncritically cited by many contemporary scholars who sought to understand crime in India (Macfie 2008), contributing to their legitimacy and the policies and practices they inspired.

Gang scholarship since the 1980s has been heavily influenced by policy preferences of governments who fund our research, as well as the mechanisms of federal funding. As Klein (2007) reminds us, this is nothing new and not limited to government funding: "Gang research has too often been driven by the interests of government and private foundations. The result has been emphases based too often on politics and ideology, at the expense of theory and knowledge building" (xiv). Research and programs of the 1950s, 1960s, and 1970s too were influenced by social reform and liberal ideas of the politicians of the time (Klein 1997). However, the concerns about gangs that motivated politicians in the 1980s and 1990s were almost certainly misguided (see the previously quoted passage from the Anti-Drug Abuse Act of 1988), yet—often with the assistance of gang scholars—they managed to find *some* data or research that fit their narratives and went full steam ahead creating extremely damaging policies.

While gang research has been built by scholars with a strong commitment to producing policy-relevant research, most of them offered policy proposal after being deeply embedded in the communities they studied and proposing (and then testing) theories. An important goal for the latest generation of gang scholars (and the next) will be to confront the role gang scholarship has played in legitimizing policies and practices that have exacerbated and sometimes created the community conditions we have known for a long time fosters gang formation and violence. An important way to improve gang scholarship is to resist the temptation to use whatever data are available or convenient (e.g., police data, official records), get out in the real world, and generate new, rich data on gangs to produce new theories, insights—and *eventually*—innovative policy solutions. This review shows that our field is already starting to go in that direction and is reaping the rewards in the form of stronger policy and program recommendations. If we keep moving in that direction and continue adapting to an ever-changing world that we and the subjects of our studies live in, our field will yet again, in the words of De Solla Price (1963), rise phoenixlike from the ashes of the current period of decelerating growth in gang scholarship.

Appendix 1

Top 100 Most Cited Articles

Rk	Title (Year)	Author(s)	Topic	NC	CPY
1	Lower-Class Culture as a Generating Milieu of Gang Delinquency (1958)	Miller	Delinquent subcultures and gang behavior	3,272	50.3
2	Focused Deterrence Strategies and Crime Control: An Updated Systematic Review and Meta-Analysis of the Empirical Evidence (2018)	Braga et al.	Focused deterrence and group violence interventions	230	46.0
3	An Economic Analysis of a Drug-Selling Gang's Finances (2000)	Levitt and Venkatesh	Drug selling and substance use	955	41.5
4	Murder by Structure: Dominance Relations and the Social Structure of Gang Homicide (2009)	Papachristos	Social network perspectives on gang activities, conflicts, and interventions	570	40.7
5	The Effects of Focused Deterrence Strategies on Crime: A Systematic Review and Meta-Analysis of the Empirical Evidence (2012)	Braga and Weisburd	Focused deterrence and group violence interventions	430	39.1
6	The Corner and the Crew: The Influence of Geography and Social Networks on Gang Violence (2013)	Papachristos et al.	Place-based, temporal, and network analyses of gang homicides	384	38.4
7	Problem-Oriented Policing, Deterrence, and Youth Violence: An Evaluation of Boston's Operation Ceasefire (2001)	Braga et al.	Focused deterrence and group violence interventions	755	34.3
8	The Role of Juvenile Gangs in Facilitating Delinquent Behavior (1993)	Thornberry et al.	Peer effects, differential association, and social learning	993	33.1
9	Youth Gangs and Definitional Issues: When Is a Gang a Gang, and Why Does It Matter? (2001)	Esbensen et al.	No topic	695	31.6
10	Continuity and Change in Gang Membership and Gang Embeddedness (2013)	Pyrooz et al.	Gang joining, leaving, and embeddedness	285	28.5

Rk	Title (Year)	Author(s)	Topic	NC	CPY
11	What Do We Know about Gangs and Gang Members and Where Do We Go from Here? (2013)	Decker et al.	Gang definitions, self-definitions, and methodological issues in gang research	273	27.3
12	Gangs, Drugs, and Delinquency in a Survey of Urban Youth (1993)	Esbensen and Huizinga	Peer effects, differential association, and social learning	812	27.1
13	Legitimacy in Criminal Governance: Managing a Drug Empire from Behind Bars (2019)	Lessing and Willis	Prison gang organization, governance, and illicit trade	106	26.5
14	Childhood Risk Factors for Adolescent Gang Membership: Results from the Seattle Social Development Project (1999)	Hill et al.	Predictors of gang membership	622	25.9
15	Taking Stock of the Relationship between Gang Membership and Offending a Meta-Analysis (2016)	Pyrooz et al.	Predictors of offending and violent victimization	180	25.7
16	Gangstas, Thugs, and Hustlas: Identity and the Code of the Street in Rap Music (2005)	Kubrin	Masculinity and street culture	454	25.2
17	Governance and Prison Gangs (2011)	Skarbek	Prison gang organization, governance, and illicit trade	298	24.8
18	Internet Banging: New Trends in Social Media, Gang Violence, Masculinity and Hip Hop (2013)	Patton et al.	Social media and online activities	244	24.4
19	Why Do Criminals Obey the Law? The Influence of Legitimacy and Social Networks on Active Gun Offenders (2012)	Papachristos et al.	Gun carrying, access, and violence	268	24.4
20	Criminal and Routine Activities in Online Settings: Gangs, Offenders, and the Internet (2015)	Pyrooz et al.	Social media and online activities	190	23.8
21	The Contribution of Gang Membership to Delinquency beyond Delinquent Friends (1998)	Battin-Pearson et al.	Peer effects, differential association, and social learning	586	23.4
22	The Ties That Bind: Desistance from Gangs (2014)	Pyrooz et al.	Gang joining, leaving, and embeddedness	207	23.0

Rk	Title (Year)	Author(s)	Topic	NC	CPY
23	Motives and Methods for Leaving the Gang: Understanding the Process of Gang Desistance (2011)	Pyrooz and Decker	Gang joining, leaving, and embeddedness	275	22.9
24	Gangs, Urban Violence, and Security Interventions in Central America (2009)	Jutersonke et al.	Gangs in the Central and South American contexts	319	22.8
25	'Going Viral' and 'Going Country': The Expressive and Instrumental Activities of Street Gangs on Social Media (2017)	Storrod and Densley	Social media and online activities	136	22.7
26	Cyber Violence: What Do We Know and Where Do We Go from Here? (2017)	Peterson and Densley	Social media and online activities	132	22.0
27	Sweet Mothers and Gangbangers: Managing Crime in a Black Middle-Class Neighborhood (1998)	Pattillo	Place-based, temporal, and network analyses of gang homicides	550	22.0
28	Antisocial Behavior and Youth Gang Membership: Selection and Socialization (2004)	Gordon et al.	Peer effects, differential association, and social learning	408	21.5
29	Street Gang Theory and Research: Where Are We Now and Where Do We Go from Here? (2010)	Wood and Alleyne	Gang definitions, self-definitions, and methodological issues in gang research	277	21.3
30	Bullies, Gangs, Drugs, and School: Understanding the Overlap and the Role of Ethnicity and Urbanicity (2013)	Bradshaw et al.	No topic	208	20.8
31	Gang Membership as a Turning Point in the Life Course (2011)	Melde and Esbensen	Consequence of gang membership over the life course	245	20.4
32	Youth Violence in Boston: Gun Markets, Serious Youth Offenders, and a Use-Reduction Strategy (1996)	Kennedy et al.	Focused deterrence and group violence interventions	539	20.0
33	Gangs and Violence: Disentangling the Impact of Gang Membership on the Level and Nature of Offending (2013)	Melde and Esbensen	Predictors of offending and violent victimization	199	19.9
34	Drug Battles and School Achievement: Evidence from Rio de Janeiro's Favelas (2017)	Monteiro and Rocha	Gangs in the Central and South American contexts	119	19.8

Rk	Title (Year)	Author(s)	Topic	NC	CPY
35	How the Street Gangs Took Central America (2005)	Arana	Gangs in the Central and South American contexts	355	19.7
36	Collective and Normative Features of Gang Violence (1996)	Decker	Social network perspectives on gang activities, conflicts, and interventions	527	19.5
37	Gang Talk and Gang Talkers: A Critique (2008)	Hallsworth and Young	Gangs in the UK and European contexts	290	19.3
38	Social Networks and the Risk of Gunshot Injury (2012)	Papachristos et al.	Gun carrying, access, and violence	211	19.2
39	Moving Risk Factors into Developmental Theories of Gang Membership (2005)	Howell and Egley	Predictors of gang membership	345	19.2
40	Combining Propensity Score Matching and Group-Based Trajectory Analysis in an Observational Study (2007)	Haviland et al.	Predictors of offending and violent victimization	305	19.1
41	Disengagement from Gangs as Role Transitions (2014)	Decker et al.	Gang joining, leaving, and embeddedness	171	19.0
42	Disengaging from Gangs and Desistance from Crime (2013)	Sweeten et al.	Gang joining, leaving, and embeddedness	190	19.0
43	'From Your First Cigarette to Your Last Dyin' Day': The Patterning of Gang Membership in the Life Course (2014)	Pyrooz	Consequence of gang membership over the life course	170	18.9
44	Gang Membership as a Risk Factor for Adolescent Violent Victimization (2007)	Taylor et al.	Predictors of offending and violent victimization	299	18.7
45	Youth Gang Affiliation, Violence, and Criminal Activities: A Review of Motivational, Risk, and Protective Factors (2013)	OBrien et al.	Gang joining, leaving, and embeddedness	186	18.6
46	Gang Membership and Violent Victimization (2004)	Peterson et al.	Predictors of offending and violent victimization	353	18.6
47	Central American Maras: From Youth Street Gangs to Transnational Protection Rackets (2010)	Cruz	Gangs in the Central and South American contexts	239	18.4
48	Slum Wars of the 21st Century: Gangs, Mano Dura and the New Urban Geography of Conflict in Central America (2009)	Rodgers	Gangs in the Central and South American contexts	256	18.3

Rk	Title (Year)	Author(s)	Topic	NC	CPY
49	Working County Lines: Child Criminal Exploitation and Illicit Drug Dealing in Glasgow and Merseyside (2019)	Robinson et al.	Gangs in the UK and European contexts	73	18.2
50	Deterring Gang-Involved Gun Violence: Measuring the Impact of Boston's Operation Ceasefire on Street Gang Behavior (2014)	Braga et al.	Focused deterrence and group violence interventions	162	18.0
51	The Social Organization of Street Gang Activity in an Urban Ghetto (1997)	Venkatesh	African-American gangs, social change, politics, and community organization	466	17.9
52	Living in the Shadow of Death: Gangs, Violence and Social Order in Urban Nicaragua, 19962002 (2006)	Rodgers	Gangs in the Central and South American contexts	304	17.9
53	Gang Involvement: Psychological and Behavioral Characteristics of Gang Members, Peripheral Youth, and Nongang Youth (2010)	Alleyne and Wood	Peer effects, differential association, and social learning	231	17.8
54	The Effect of Gang Affiliation on Violent Misconduct among Inmates during the Early Years of Confinement (2006)	Griffin and Hepburn	Gangs and gang membership in prisons and jails	298	17.5
55	Code of the Tweet: Urban Gang Violence in the Social Media Age (2020)	Stuart	Social media and online activities	52	17.3
56	Youth Gangs, Delinquency and Drug Use: A Test of the Selection, Facilitation, and Enhancement Hypotheses (2005)	Gatti et al.	Peer effects, differential association, and social learning	311	17.3
57	Spatializing Social Networks: Using Social Network Analysis to Investigate Geographies of Gang Rivalry, Territoriality, and Violence in Los Angeles (2010)	Radil et al.	Place-based, temporal, and network analyses of gang homicides	221	17.0
58	Narratives of Childhood Adversity and Adolescent Misconduct as Precursors to Violent Extremism: A Life-Course Criminological Approach (2016)	Simi et al.	Extremist, terrorist, and hate groups	119	17.0

Rk	Title (Year)	Author(s)	Topic	NC	CPY
59	Understanding the Black Box of Gang Organization—Implications for Involvement in Violent Crime, Drug Sales, and Violent Victimization (2008)	Decker et al.	Peer effects, differential association, and social learning	251	16.7
60	'I Got Your Back': An Examination of the Protective Function of Gang Membership in Adolescence (2009)	Melde et al.	Predictors of offending and violent victimization	231	16.5
61	The Contribution of Gang Membership to the Victim-Offender Overlap (2014)	Pyrooz et al.	Predictors of offending and violent victimization	146	16.2
62	Urban Violence and Street Gangs (2003)	Vigil	Chicano communities, Latino gangs, and marginalization	319	15.9
63	The Social Organization of Drug Use and Drug Dealing Among Urban Gangs (1989)	Fagan	Drug selling and substance use	533	15.7
64	It's Gang Life, But Not As We Know It: The Evolution of Gang Business (2014)	Densley	Gangs in the UK and European contexts	141	15.7
65	Gang Membership and Adherence to the 'Code of the Street' (2013)	Matsuda et al.	Peer effects, differential association, and social learning	154	15.4
66	Diffusion in Homicide: Exploring a General Method for Detecting Spatial Diffusion Processes (1999)	Cohen and Tita	Place-based, temporal, and network analyses of gang homicides	367	15.3
67	Reducing Gang Violence Using Focused Deterrence: Evaluating the Cincinnati Initiative to Reduce Violence (CIRV) (2013)	Engel et al.	Focused deterrence and group violence interventions	152	15.2
68	The Influence of Prison Gang Affiliation on Violence and Other Prison Misconduct (2002)	Gaes et al.	Gangs and gang membership in prisons and jails	319	15.2
69	Monoamine Oxidase A Genotype Is Associated with Gang Membership and Weapon Use (2010)	Beaver et al.	Gun carrying, access, and violence	197	15.2
70	Treat a Cop Like They Are God: Exploring the Relevance and Utility of Funds of Gang Knowledge among Latino Male Students (2021)	Huerta and Rios-Aguilar	Chicano communities, Latino gangs, and marginalization	30	15.0

Rk	Title (Year)	Author(s)	Topic	NC	CPY
71	The Company You Keep? The Spillover Effects of Gang Membership on Individual Gunshot Victimization in a Co-offending Network (2015)	Papachristos et al.	Gun carrying, access, and violence	118	14.8
72	Going to Extremes: Social Identity and Communication Processes Associated with Gang Membership (2014)	Goldman et al.	Gang definitions, self-definitions, and methodological issues in gang research	132	14.7
73	Artificial Intelligence and Inclusion: Formerly Gang-Involved Youth as Domain Experts for Analyzing Unstructured Twitter Data (2020)	Frey et al.	Social media and online activities	44	14.7
74	Adverse Childhood Experiences (ACEs) and Gang Involvement among Juvenile Offenders: Assessing the Mediation Effects of Substance Use and Temperament Deficits (2020)	Wolff et al.	Predictors of offending and violent victimization	44	14.7
75	Street Gang Violence in Europe (2006)	Klein et al.	No topic	249	14.6
76	Gang Membership, Violence, and Psychiatric Morbidity (2013)	Coid et al.	Mental health, PTSD, and trauma exposure in gang members	146	14.6
77	Changing the Street Dynamic Evaluating Chicago's Group Violence Reduction Strategy (2015)	Papachristos and Kirk	Focused deterrence and group violence interventions	116	14.5
78	Validating Self-Nomination in Gang Research: Assessing Differences in Gang Embeddedness Across Non-, Current, and Former Gang Members (2014)	Decker et al.	Gang joining, leaving, and embeddedness	129	14.3
79	Just Every Mothers Angel: An Analysis of Gender and Ethnic Variations in Youth Gang Membership (1995)	Joe-Laidler and Chesney-Lind	Women and girls in gangs	400	14.3
80	Hiding Violence to Deal with the State: Criminal Pacts in El Salvador and Medellin (2016)	Cruz and Duran-Martinez	Gangs in the Central and South American contexts	100	14.3

Rk	Title (Year)	Author(s)	Topic	NC	CPY
81	Policy and Intervention Considerations of a Network Analysis of Street Gangs (2005)	McGloin	Social network perspectives on gang activities, conflicts, and interventions	257	14.3
82	Prison Gangs, Norms, and Organizations (2012)	Skarbek	Prison gang organization, governance, and illicit trade	156	14.2
83	Reducing Homicide through a 'Lever-Pulling' Strategy (2006)	McGarrell et al.	Focused deterrence and group violence interventions	237	13.9
84	Delinquency and the Structure of Adolescent Peer Groups (2011)	Kreager et al.	Peer effects, differential association, and social learning	167	13.9
85	The Cascading Effects of Adolescent Gang Involvement across the Life Course (2011)	Krohn et al.	Consequence of gang membership over the life course	167	13.9
86	Gender Differences in Gang Participation, Delinquency, and Substance Use (1993)	Bjerregaard and Smith	Women and girls in gangs	416	13.9
87	The Semiotic Hitchhiker's Guide to Creaky Voice: Circulation and Gendered Hardcore in a Chicana/o Gang Persona (2011)	Mendoza-Denton	Artistic productions and media representations of the gang problem	165	13.8
88	The Ecology of Gang Territorial Boundaries (2012)	Brantingham et al.	Place-based, temporal, and network analyses of gang homicides	150	13.6
89	Mara Salvatrucha: The Most Dangerous Street Gang in the Americas? (2012)	Wolf	Gangs in the Central and South American contexts	150	13.6
90	Imagining the Asian Gang: Ethnicity, Masculinity and Youth after 'the Riots' (2004)	Alexander	Gangs in the UK and European contexts	255	13.4
91	Street Habitus: Gangs, Territorialism and Social Change in Glasgow (2013)	Fraser	Gangs in the UK and European contexts	134	13.4
92	The Global Impact of Gangs (2005)	Hagedorn	Gangs, globalization, and armed groups	240	13.3
93	Youth Gang Membership and Serious Violent Victimization—The Importance of Lifestyles and Routine Activities (2008)	Taylor et al.	Predictors of offending and violent victimization	199	13.3

Rk	Title (Year)	Author(s)	Topic	NC	CPY
94	Cut from the Same Cloth? A Comparative Study of Domestic Extremists and Gang Members in the United States (2018)	Pyrooz et al.	Extremist, terrorist, and hate groups	65	13.0
95	Gang Violence on the Digital Street: Case Study of a South Side Chicago Gang Member's Twitter Communication (2017)	Patton et al.	Social media and online activities	78	13.0
96	From Colors and Guns to Caps and Gowns? The Effects of Gang Membership on Educational Attainment (2014)	Pyrooz	Consequence of gang membership over the life course	116	12.9
97	Counterproductive Punishment: How Prison Gangs Undermine State Authority (2017)	Lessing	No topic	77	12.8
98	An Ecological Study of the Location of Gang 'Set Space' (2005)	Tita et al.	Place-based, temporal, and network analyses of gang homicides	230	12.8
99	Facilitating Violence: A Comparison of Gang-Motivated, and Nongang Youth Homicides (1999)	Rosenfeld et al.	Place-based, temporal, and network analyses of gang homicides	301	12.5
100	Dangerous Associations: Joint Enterprise, Gangs and Racism (2016)	Petrillo	Gangs in the UK and European contexts	87	12.4

Note: Rk = Rank in period; NC = Number of citations; CPY = Citations per year

Appendix 2

Top 50 Most Cited Books

Rk	Title (Year)	Author(s)	NC	CPY
1	Street Corner Society: The Social Structure of an Italian Slum (1943)	Whyte	9,618	120.2
2	Delinquent Boys: The Culture of the Gang (1955)	Cohen	8,022	118.0
3	Delinquency and Opportunity: A Study of Delinquent Gangs (1960)	Cloward and Ohlin	6,748	107.1

Rk	Title (Year)	Author(s)	NC	CPY
4	Homegirls: Language and Cultural Practice among Latina Youth Gangs (2008)	Mendoza-Denton	1,014	67.6
5	The American Street Gang: Its Nature, Prevalence, and Control (1997)	Klein	1,646	63.3
6	Street Gang Patterns and Policies (2006)	Klein and Maxson	1,062	62.5
7	Gangs and Delinquency in Developmental Perspective (2003)	Thornberry et al.	1,196	59.8
8	Inside Criminal Networks (2009)	Morselli	793	56.6
9	Gangs in America's Communities (2018)	Howell and Griffiths	277	55.4
10	Gang Leader for a Day: A Rogue Sociologist Takes to the Streets (2008)	Venkatesh	825	55.0
11	The Social Order of the Underworld: How Prison Gangs Govern the American Penal System (2014)	Skarbek	471	52.3
12	Life in the Gang: Family, Friends, and Violence (1996)	Decker and VanWinkle	1,364	50.5
13	A Rainbow of Gangs: Street Cultures in the Mega-City (2010)	Vigil	621	47.8
14	The Social Order of the Slum: Ethnicity and Territory in the Inner City (1968)	Suttles	2,601	47.3
15	The Gang: A Study of 1,313 Gangs in Chicago (1927)	Thrasher	4,403	45.9
16	Barrio Gangs: Street Life and Identity in Southern California (1988)	Vigil	1,603	45.8
17	One of the Guys: Girls, Gangs, and Gender (2001)	Miller	948	43.1
18	A World of Gangs: Armed Young Men and Gangsta Culture (2008)	Hagedorn	598	39.9
19	Islands in the Street (1991)	Sanchez-Jankowski	1,187	37.1
20	The Youth Gang Problem: A Community Approach (1995)	Spergel	963	34.4
21	People and Folks. Gangs, Crime and the Underclass in a Rustbelt City (1988)	Hagedorn and Macon	1,100	31.4
22	The Gangs of Chicago: An Informal History of the Chicago Underworld (2003)	Asbury	583	29.1
23	Going Down to the Barrio: Homeboys and Homegirls in Change (1991)	Moore	915	28.6
24	Space of Detention: The Making of a Transnational Gang Crisis between Los Angeles and San Salvador (2011)	Zilberg	310	25.8
25	Confronting Gangs: Crime and Community (2003)	Curry and Decker	498	24.9
26	How Gangs Work: An Ethnography of Youth Violence (2013)	Densley	243	24.3

Rk	Title (Year)	Author(s)	NC	CPY
27	Guys, Gangs, and Girlfriend Abuse (2019)	Totten	97	24.2
28	Group Process and Gang Delinquency (1965)	Short and Strodtbeck	1,382	23.8
29	The Almighty Latin King and Queen Nation (2004)	Brotherton and Barrios	446	23.5
30	Mano Dura the Politics of Gang Control in El Salvador (2017)	Wolf	140	23.3
31	The Gang as an American Enterprise (1992)	Padilla	704	22.7
32	Gangs in America III (2002)	Huff	473	22.5
33	Gangs, Politics and Dignity in Cape Town (2008)	Jensen	334	22.3
34	Homies and Hermanos: God and Gangs in Central America (2012)	Brenneman II	236	21.5
35	The Lobster Gangs of Maine (1988)	Acheson	740	21.1
36	Youth, Popular Culture and Moral Panics: Penny Gaffs to Gangsta Rap, 1830–1996 (1999)	Springhall	496	20.7
37	The History of Street Gangs in the United States: Their Origins and Transformations (2015)	Howell	164	20.5
38	Ballad of the Bullet: Gangs, Drill Music, and the Power of Online Infamy (2020)	Stuart	56	18.7
39	An Appeal to Justice: Litigated Reform of Texas Prisons (2010)	Crouch and Marquart	240	18.5
40	Bo-tsotsi: The Youth Gangs of Soweto (2000)	Glaser	419	18.2
41	Who You Claim (2010)	Garot	234	18.0
42	Street Gangs and Street Workers (1971)	Klein	929	17.9
43	Street Casino: Survival in Violent Street Gangs (2014)	Harding	160	17.8
44	Homeboys: Gangs, Drugs, and Prison in the Barrios of Los Angeles (1978)	Moore and Garcia	759	16.9
45	Always Running: La Vida Loca: Gang Days in LA (2005)	Rodriguez	299	16.6
46	The Gang and Beyond: Interpreting Violent Street Worlds (2013)	Hallsworth	165	16.5
47	Gang Life in Two Cities: An Insider's Journey (2013)	Duran	160	16.0
48	Adios Nino: The Gangs of Guatemala City and the Politics of Death (2013)	Levenson	160	16.0
49	The Violent Gang (1962)	Yablonsky	953	15.6
50	Gangs of Russia: From the Streets to the Corridors of Power (2015)	Stephenson	121	15.1

Note: Rk = Rank in period; NC = Number of citations; CPY = Citations per year

Notes

1. KeyWords Plus is based on a proprietary algorithm that generates keywords from "words or phrases that frequently appear in the titles of an article's references, but do not appear in the title of the article itself" (Clarivate 2022).
2. The label "new gang scholar" is used as a convenient shorthand for "scholar who published a number of books and journal articles on gangs included in our database above the 95th percentile of the total number of articles in a given publication year included in the search result for the article." I found it more succinct to use the term "gang scholar" from a writing standpoint, and mean no offense to those who would not choose to self-identify as such.
3. It is entirely possible, nay highly likely, that the year of first publication for some researchers may not be accurate. This can be due to the search strategy missing an earlier article, the citation data retrieved being inaccurate, or errors in the merging of different versions of an author's name across different citation styles.
4. Changing the cutoff from four or more articles (95th percentile) to three or more articles (90th percentile) adds 147 scholars to Figure 9.4, though the conclusions remain similar: no more than three new scholars in any given year prior to 1990, a notable increase in 1991 (13), 1992 (15), and 1993 (14), and 2010 and 2011 are also by far the largest cohorts. The most notable difference is in 2002, where 17 new scholars would be included using the 90th percentile, compared to 3 using the 95th percentile. However, at least 8 of these 14 additional scholars would be included because they are part of large research teams who have published three articles on a single project. The cutoff of four or more articles reaches a good balance between inclusion of the majority of scholars who have dedicated significant portions of their time to the study of gangs and those who have contributed to the gang literature because of overlap in their main areas of interest. The approach is not perfect: Some scholars barely miss the cutoff and probably would be included if this review were completed in the next year or two (e.g., Ellen Van Damme, Adrian Huerta, Elke Van Hellemont, Sally Atkinson-Sheppard), and some are included that probably would themselves agree that they do not fit the label (e.g., Alex Piquero).
5. Citation counts for this table and all subsequent tables were collected from Google Scholar as of May 2022. Books or articles with less than 10 citations were removed from those tables.
6. The two centers merged in 2009.

References

Adamson, Christopher. 2000. "Defensive Localism in White and Black: A Comparative History of European-American and African-American Youth Gangs." *Ethnic and Racial Studies* 23 (2): 272–298. https://doi.org/10.1080/014198700329051.

Aminikhanghahi, Samaneh, and Diane J. Cook. 2017. "A Survey of Methods for Time Series Change Point Detection." *Knowledge and Information Systems* 51 (2): 339–367. https://doi.org/10.1007/s10115-016-0987-z.

Anti-Drug Abuse Act of 1988. 1988. *Stat.* Vol. 102.

Barmaki, Reza. 2016. "On the Origin of the Concept of 'Deviant Subculture' in Criminology: W. I. Thomas and the Chicago School of Sociology." *Deviant Behavior* 37 (7): 795–810. https://doi.org/10.1080/01639625.2016.1145023.

Beresford, Hayley, and Jane L. Wood. 2016. "Patients or Perpetrators? The Effects of Trauma Exposure on Gang Members' Mental Health: A Review of the Literature." *Journal of Criminological Research Policy and Practice* 2 (2): 148–159. https://doi.org/10.1108/jcrpp-05-2015-0015.

Bichler, Gisela, Alexis Norris, and Citlalik Ibarra. 2020. "Evolving Patterns of Aggression: Investigating the Structure of Gang Violence during the Era of Civil Gang Injunctions." *Social Sciences* 9 (11): 203. https://doi.org/10.3390/socsci9110203.

Bogardus, Emory S. 1943. "Gangs of Mexican-American Youth." *Sociology and Social Research* 28 (1): 55–66.

Bornmann, Lutz, Robin Haunschild, and Rüdiger Mutz. 2021. "Growth Rates of Modern Science: A Latent Piecewise Growth Curve Approach to Model Publication Numbers from Established and New Literature Databases." *Humanities and Social Sciences Communications* 8 (1): 224. https://doi.org/10.1057/s41599-021-00903-w.

Bouchard, Martin. 2021. "Social Networks and Gangs: Moving Research Forward with Low-Cost Data Collection Opportunities in School and Prison Settings." *Journal of Aggression Conflict and Peace Research* 13 (2/3): 110–124. https://doi.org/10.1108/jacpr-12-2020-0563.

Boxer, Paul, Meagan Docherty, Michael Ostermann, Joanna Kubik, and Bonita Veysey. 2017. "Effectiveness of Multisystemic Therapy for Gang-Involved Youth Offenders: One Year Follow-up Analysis of Recidivism Outcomes." *Children and Youth Services Review* 73 (February): 107–112. https://doi.org/10.1016/j.childyouth.2016.12.008.

Braga, Anthony A., Greg Zimmerman, Lisa Barao, Chelsea Farrell, Rod K. Brunson, and Andrew V. Papachristos. 2019. "Street Gangs, Gun Violence, and Focused Deterrence: Comparing Place-Based and Group-Based Evaluation Methods to Estimate Direct and Spillover Deterrent Effects." *Journal of Research in Crime and Delinquency* 56 (4): 524–562. https://doi.org/10.1177/0022427818821716.

Brown, Mark. 2001. "Race, Science and the Construction of Native Criminality in Colonial India." *Theoretical Criminology* 5 (3): 345–368. https://doi.org/10.1177/1362480601005003003.

Bruneau, Thomas C., Lucía Dammert, and Elizabeth Skinner, eds. 2011. *Maras: Gang Violence and Security in Central America*. Austin: University of Texas Press.

Cavan, Ruth Shonle. 1983. "The Chicago School of Sociology, 1918–1933." *Urban Life* 11 (4): 407–420. https://doi.org/10.1177/0098303983011004003.

Cavender, Gray. 2010. "Cohen, Albert K.: Delinquent Boys." In *Encyclopedia of Criminological Theory*, edited by Francis Cullen and Pamela Wilcox. Thousand Oaks, CA: Sage Publications. https://doi.org/10.4135/9781412959193.n50.

Clarivate. 2022. KeyWords Plus generation, creation, and changes. June 9. Accessed August 4, 2023, https://support.clarivate.com/ScientificandAcademicResearch/s/article/KeyWords-Plus-generation-creation-and-changes?language=en_US.

Cloward, Richard A., and Lloyd E. Ohlin. 1960. *Delinquency and Opportunity: A Study of Delinquent Gangs*. New York: Routledge.

Cohen, Albert K. 1955. *Delinquent Boys: The Culture of the Gang*. Glencoe, IL: The Free Press.

Continuing Appropriations for Fiscal Year 1985. 1984. *Stat.* Vol. 98.

Curry, G. David, and Irving A. Spergel. 1988. "Gang Homicide, Delinquency, and Community." *Criminology* 26 (3): 381–406. https://doi.org/10.1111/j.1745-9125.1988.tb00847.x.

Decker, Scott H, Chris Melde, and David C Pyrooz. 2013. "What Do We Know about Gangs and Gang Members and Where Do We Go from Here?" *Justice Quarterly* 30 (3): 369–402.

Decker, Scott H., and David C. Pyrooz, eds. 2015. *The Handbook of Gangs*. Hoboken, NJ: John Wiley & Sons, Inc. https://doi.org/10.1002/9781118726822.

Decker, Scott H., David C. Pyrooz, and James A. Densley. 2022. *On Gangs*. Philadelphia, PA: Temple University Press.

Densley, James A. 2012. "Street Gang Recruitment: Signaling, Screening, and Selection." *Social Problems* 59 (3): 301–321. https://doi.org/10.1525/sp.2012.59.3.301.

Descormiers, Karine, and Raymond R. Corrado. 2016. "The Right to Belong: Individual Motives and Youth Gang Initiation Rites." *Deviant Behavior* 37 (11): 1341–1359. https://doi.org/10.1080/01639625.2016.1177390.

Descormiers, Karine, and Carlo Morselli. 2011. "Alliances, Conflicts, and Contradictions in Montreal's Street Gang Landscape." *International Criminal Justice Review* 21 (3): 297–314. https://doi.org/10.1177/1057567711418501.

De Solla Price, Derek J. 1963. *Little Science, Big Science*. New York: Columbia University Press. https://doi.org/10.7312/pric91844.

Devlin, Jacob, Ming-Wei Chang, Kenton Lee, and Kristina Toutanova. 2018. "BERT: Pre-Training of Deep Bidirectional Transformers for Language Understanding." https://doi.org/10.48550/ARXIV.1810.04805.

Dierkhising, Carly B., Jose A. Sanchez, and Luis Gutierrez. 2021. "'It Changed My Life': Traumatic Loss, Behavioral Health, and Turning Points Among Gang-Involved and Justice-Involved Youth." *Journal of Interpersonal Violence* 36 (17–18): 8027–8049. https://doi.org/10.1177/0886260519847779.

Edwards, A. W. F., and L. L. Cavalli-Sforza. 1965. "A Method for Cluster Analysis." *Biometrics* 21 (2): 362. https://doi.org/10.2307/2528096.

Esbensen, Finn-Aage, and Cheryl Lee Maxson. 2012. *Youth Gangs in International Perspective: Results from the Eurogang Program of Research*. New York: Springer.

Esbensen, Finn-Aage, and Cheryl L. Maxson, eds. 2016. *Gang Transitions and Transformations in an International Context*. Cham: Springer. https://doi.org/10.1007/978-3-319-29602-9.

Fagan, Jeffrey. 1989. "The Social Organization of Drug Use and Drug Dealing among Urban Gangs." *Criminology* 27 (4): 633–670. https://doi.org/10.1111/j.1745-9125.1989.tb01049.x.

Faust, Katherine, and George E. Tita. 2019. "Social Networks and Crime: Pitfalls and Promises for Advancing the Field." *Annual Review of Criminology* 2 (1): 99–122. https://doi.org/10.1146/annurev-criminol-011518-024701.

Gallupe, Owen, and Jason Gravel. 2018. "Social Network Position of Gang Members in Schools: Implications for Recruitment and Gang Prevention." *Justice Quarterly* 35 (3): 505–525. https://doi.org/10.1080/07418825.2017.1323114.

Gebo, Erika, and Brenda J. Bond, eds. 2012. *Looking beyond Suppression: Community Strategies to Reduce Gang Violence*. Lanham, MD: Lexington Books.

Goldson, Barry. 2011. *Youth in Crisis? 'Gangs', Territoriality and Violence*. New York: Routledge. http://site.ebrary.com/id/10452691.

Gordon, Stewart N. 1969. "Scarf and Sword: Thugs, Marauders, and State-Formation in 18th Century Malwa." *The Indian Economic and Social Review* 6 (4): 403–429.

Gravel, Jason. 2018. "On the Use of Police Records for Social Network Analysis." Ph.D Dissertation, University of California, Irvine. http://www.proquest.com/docview/2099592804/abstract/E82FBC53F01A475CPQ/1.

Gravel, Jason, Martin Bouchard, Karine Descormiers, Jennifer S. Wong, and Carlo Morselli. 2013. "Keeping Promises: A Systematic Review and a New Classification of Gang Control Strategies." *Journal of Criminal Justice* 41 (4): 228–242. https://doi.org/10.1016/j.jcrimjus.2013.05.005.

Gravel, Jason, and George E. Tita. 2015. "With Great Methods Come Great Responsibilities: Social Network Analysis in the Implementation and Evaluation of Gang Programs." *Criminology & Public Policy* 14 (3): 559–572. https://doi.org/10.1111/1745-9133.12147.

Gravel, Jason, Matthew Valasik, and Shannon E. Reid. 2021. "Guest Editorial." *Journal of Aggression, Conflict and Peace Research* 13 (2/3): 73–82. https://doi.org/10.1108/JACPR-07-2021-605.

Grootendorst, Maarten. 2022. "BERTopic: Neural Topic Modeling with a Class-Based TF-IDF Procedure." https://doi.org/10.48550/ARXIV.2203.05794.

Grund, Thomas U., and James A. Densley. 2012. "Ethnic Heterogeneity in the Activity and Structure of a Black Street Gang." *European Journal of Criminology* 9 (4): 388–406. https://doi.org/10.1177/1477370812447738.

Harding, Simon, and Marek Palasinski, eds. 2016. *Global Perspectives on Youth Gang Behavior, Violence, and Weapon Use*. Hershey, PA: Information Science Reference.

Harriott, Anthony, Charles M. Katz, and Anthony Harriott, eds. 2015. *Gangs in the Caribbean: Responses of State and Society*. Kingston, Jamaica: University of the West Indies Press.

Horowitz, Ruth, and Gary Schwartz. 1974. "Honor, Normative Ambiguity and Gang Violence." *American Sociological Review* 39 (2): 238–251. https://doi.org/10.2307/2094235.

Howell, James C. 2015. *The History of Street Gangs in the United States: Their Origins and Transformations*. Lanham, MD: Lexington Books.

Hureau, David M., and Anthony A. Braga. 2018. "The Trade in Tools: The Market for Illicit Guns in High-Risk Networks." *Criminology* 56 (3): 510–545. https://doi.org/10.1111/1745-9125.12187.

Hyatt, Jordan M., James A. Densley, and Caterina G. Roman. 2021. "Social Media and the Variable Impact of Violence Reduction Interventions: Re-Examining Focused Deterrence in Philadelphia." *Social Sciences* 10 (5): 147. https://doi.org/10.3390/socsci10050147.

Ireland, Jane L., Philip Birch, and Carol A. Ireland. 2018. *The Routledge International Handbook of Human Aggression: Current Issues and Perspectives*. New York: Routledge.

Jennings-Bey, Timothy, Sandra D. Lane, Robert A. Rubinstein, Dessa Bergen-Cico, Arnett Haygood-El, Helen Hudson, Shaundel Sanchez, and Frank L. Fowler. 2015. "The Trauma Response Team: A Community Intervention for Gang Violence." *Journal of Urban Health* 92 (5): 947–954. https://doi.org/10.1007/s11524-015-9978-8.

Juvenile Justice Amendments. 1980. *Stat*. Vol. 94.

Katz, Charles M., and Vincent J. Webb. 2006. *Policing Gangs in America*. Cambridge Studies in Criminology. Cambridge, UK: Cambridge University Press.

Killick, Rebecca, Kaylea Haynes, Idris Eckley, Paul Fearnhead, and Jamie Lee. 2022. "Changepoint: Methods for Changepoint Detection." https://cran.r-project.org/web/packages/changepoint/changepoint.pdf.

Klein, Malcolm W. 1971. *Street Gangs and Street Workers*. Englewood Cliffs, NJ: Prentice-Hall.

Klein, Malcolm W. 1997. *The American Street Gang: Its Nature, Prevalence, and Control*. New York: Oxford University Press.

Klein, Malcolm W. 2007. *Chasing after Street Gangs: A Forty-Year Journey*. Upper Saddle River, NJ: Pearson Prentice Hall.

Klein, Malcolm W, Cheryl L. Maxson, and Lea C. Cunningham. 1991. "'Crack', Street Gangs, and Violence." *Criminology* 29 (4): 623–650. https://doi.org/10.1111/j.1745-9125.1991.tb01082.x.

Larsen, Peder Olesen, and Markus von Ins. 2010. "The Rate of Growth in Scientific Publication and the Decline in Coverage Provided by Science Citation Index." *Scientometrics* 84 (3): 575–603. https://doi.org/10.1007/s11192-010-0202-z.

Leverso, John, and Yuan Hsiao. 2021. "Gangbangin on the (Face) Book: Understanding Online Interactions of Chicago Latina/o Gangs." *Journal of Research in Crime and Delinquency* 58 (3): 239–268. https://doi.org/10.1177/0022427820952124.

Lewis, Kevin, and Andrew V. Papachristos. 2020. "Rules of the Game: Exponential Random Graph Models of a Gang Homicide Network." *Social Forces* 98 (4): 1829–1858. https://doi.org/10.1093/sf/soz106.

Macfie, Alexander Lyon. 2008. "*Thuggee*: An Orientalist Construction?" *Rethinking History* 12 (3): 383–397. https://doi.org/10.1080/13642520802193262.

Marsh, P., and Campbell, A. 1978. "Youth Gangs of New York and Chicago Go into Business." *New Society*. 46 (836): 67–69.

Martindale, Don. 1976. "American Sociology before World War II." *Annual Review of Sociology* 2: 122–143. https://www.jstor.org/stable/2946089.

Maxson, C. L., and Klein, M. W. 1983. "Gangs: Why We Couldn't Stay Away." In *Evaluating Juvenile Justice*, edited by James R. Kluegel, 149–155. Thousand Oaks, CA: Sage Publications.

Miller, Walter B. 1958. "Lower-Class Culture as a Generating Milieu of Gang Delinquency." *Journal of Social Issues* 14 (3): 5–19. https://doi.org/10.1111/j.1540-4560.1958.tb01413.x.

Mitchell, Meghan M., Chantal Fahmy, David C. Pyrooz, and Scott H. Decker. 2017. "Criminal Crews, Codes, and Contexts: Differences and Similarities across the Code of the Street, Convict Code, Street Gangs, and Prison Gangs." *Deviant Behavior* 38 (10): 1197–1222. https://doi.org/10.1080/01639625.2016.1246028.

Motz, Ryan T., Ryan M. Labrecque, and Paula Smith. 2021. "Gang Affiliation, Restrictive Housing, and Institutional Misconduct: Does Disciplinary Segregation Suppress or Intensify Gang Member Rule Violations?" *Journal of Crime & Justice* 44 (1): 49–65. https://doi.org/10.1080/0735648x.2020.1772095.

Moore, J. W. 1978. *Homeboys: Gangs, Drugs, and Prison in the Barrios of Los Angeles*. Temple University Press.

Nakamura, Kiminori, George E. Tita, and David Krackhardt. 2020. "Violence in the 'Balance': A Structural Analysis of How Rivals, Allies, and Third-Parties Shape Inter-Gang Violence." *Global Crime* 21 (1): 3–27. https://doi.org/10.1080/17440572.2019.1627879.

National Research Council. 2013. *Reforming Juvenile Justice: A Developmental Approach*. Washington, DC: National Academies Press. https://doi.org/10.17226/14685.

Ouellet, Marie, Martin Bouchard, and Yanick Charette. 2019. "One Gang Dies, Another Gains? The Network Dynamics of Criminal Group Persistence." *Criminology* 57 (1): 5–33. https://doi.org/10.1111/1745-9125.12194.

Panfil, Vanessa R. 2020. "'I Was a Homo Thug, Now I'm Just Homo': Gay Gang Members' Desistance and Persistence." *Criminology* 58 (2): 255–279. https://doi.org/10.1111/1745-9125.12240.

Patton, Desmond U., David C. Pyrooz, Scott H. Decker, William R. Frey, and Patrick Leonard. 2019. "When Twitter Fingers Turn to Trigger Fingers: A Qualitative Study of Social Media-Related Gang Violence." *International Journal of Bullying Prevention* 1 (3): 205–217. https://doi.org/10.1007/s42380-019-00014-w.

Pyrooz, David C., Kendra J. Clark, Jennifer J. Tostlebe, Scott H. Decker, and Erin Orrick. 2021. "Gang Affiliation and Prisoner Reentry: Discrete-Time Variation in Recidivism by Current, Former, and Non-Gang Status." *Journal of Research in Crime and Delinquency* 58 (2): 192–234. https://doi.org/10.1177/0022427820949895.

Pyrooz, David C., and James A. Densley. 2016. "Selection into Street Gangs: Signaling Theory, Gang Membership, and Criminal Offending." *Journal of Research in Crime and Delinquency* 53 (4): 447–481. https://doi.org/10.1177/0022427815619462.

Pyrooz, David C., and Meghan M. Mitchell. 2015. "Little Gang Research, Big Gang Research." In *The Handbook of Gangs*, edited by Scott H. Decker and David C. Pyrooz, 28–58. Hoboken, NJ: John Wiley & Sons, Inc. https://doi.org/10.1002/9781118726822.ch3.

Pyrooz, David C., and Meghan M. Mitchell. 2020. "The Use of Restrictive Housing on Gang and Non-Gang Affiliated Inmates in US Prisons: Findings from a National Survey of Correctional Agencies." *Justice Quarterly* 37 (4): 590–615. https://doi.org/10.1080/07418 825.2019.1574019.

Pyrooz, David C., Meghan M. Mitchell, Richard K. Moule, and Scott H. Decker. 2021. "Look Who's Talking: The Snitching Paradox in a Representative Sample of Prisoners." *British Journal of Criminology* 61 (4): 1145–1167. https://doi.org/10.1093/bjc/azaa103.

Pyrooz, David C., Gary Sweeten, and Alex R. Piquero. 2013. "Continuity and Change in Gang Membership and Gang Embeddedness." *Journal of Research in Crime and Delinquency* 50 (2): 239–271. https://doi.org/10.1177/0022427811434830.

Pyrooz, David C., Jillian J. Turanovic, Scott H. Decker, and Jun Wu. 2016. "Taking Stock of the Relationship between Gang Membership and Offending: A Meta-Analysis." *Criminal Justice and Behavior* 43 (3): 365–397. https://doi.org/10.1177/0093854815605528.

Ratcliffe, Jerry H. 2016. *Intelligence-Led Policing*. New York: Routledge. https://doi.org/10.4324/9781315717579.

Reid, Shannon E., and Matthew A. Valasik. 2018. "Ctrl plus ALT-RIGHT: Reinterpreting Our Knowledge of White Supremacy Groups through the Lens of Street Gangs." *Journal of Youth Studies* 21 (10): 1305–1325. https://doi.org/10.1080/13676261.2018.1467003.

Reid, S. E., and M. Valasik. 2020. *Alt-Right Gangs: A Hazy Shade of White*. Oakland: University of California Press.

Reimers, Nils, and Iryna Gurevych. 2019. "Sentence-BERT: Sentence Embeddings Using Siamese BERT-Networks." https://doi.org/10.48550/ARXIV.1908.10084.

Roberto, Elizabeth, Anthony A. Braga, and Andrew V. Papachristos. 2018. "Closer to Guns: The Role of Street Gangs in Facilitating Access to Illegal Firearms." *Journal of Urban Health-Bulletin of the New York Academy of Medicine* 95 (3): 372–382. https://doi.org/10.1007/s11 524-018-0259-1.

Roman, Caterina G. 2021. "An Evaluator's Reflections and Lessons Learned about Gang Intervention Strategies: An Agenda for Research." *Journal of Aggression, Conflict and Peace Research* 13 (2/3): 148–167. https://doi.org/10.1108/JACPR-02-2021-0576.

Roman, Caterina G., Meagan Cahill, and Lauren R. Mayes. 2021. "Changes in Personal Social Networks across Individuals Leaving Their Street Gang: Just What Are Youth Leaving Behind?" *Social Sciences* 10 (2): 39. https://doi.org/10.3390/socsci10020039.

Roman, Caterina G., Nathan W. Link, Jordan M. Hyatt, Avinash Bhati, and Megan Forney. 2019. "Assessing the Gang-Level and Community-Level Effects of the Philadelphia Focused Deterrence Strategy." *Journal of Experimental Criminology* 15 (4): 499–527. https://doi.org/10.1007/s11292-018-9333-7.

Scott, Daniel W., and Cheryl L. Maxson. 2016. "Gang Organization and Violence in Youth Correctional Facilities." *Journal of Criminological Research Policy and Practice* 2 (2): 81–94. https://doi.org/10.1108/jcrpp-03-2015-0004.

Short, J. 1968. *Gang Delinquency and Delinquent Subcultures*. New York: Harper & Row.

Short, James F., and Fred L. Strodtbeck. 1965. *Group Process and Gang Delinquency*. Chicaco, IL: University of Chicago Press.

Singha, Radhika. 1993. "'Providential' Circumstances: The Thuggee Campaign of the 1830s and Legal Innovation." *Modern Asian Studies* 27 (1): 83–146.

Skolnick, Jerome H, Theodore Correl, Elizabeth Navarro, and Roger Rabb. 1990. "The Social Structure of Street Drug Dealing." *American Journal of Police* 9: 1.

Spooner, Kallee, David C. Pyrooz, Vincent J. Webb, and Kathleen A. Fox. 2017. "Recidivism among Juveniles in a Multi-Component Gang Reentry Program: Findings from a Program Evaluation in Harris County, Texas." *Journal of Experimental Criminology* 13 (2): 275–285. https://doi.org/10.1007/s11292-017-9288-0.

Stevenson, James Arthur Robert. 1834. "Some Account of the P'hansigárs, or Gang-Robbers, and of the Shúdgarshids, or Tribe of Jugglers." *Journal of the Royal Asiatic Society* 1 (2): 280–284. https://doi.org/10.1017/S0035869X00142443.

Stuart, Forrest L. 2020. "Code of the Tweet: Urban Gang Violence in the Social Media Age." *Social Problems* 67 (2): 191–207. https://doi.org/10.1093/socpro/spz010.

Sturmey, Peter, ed. 2017. *The Wiley Handbook of Violence and Aggression*. Chichester, UK: John Wiley & Sons.

Suttles, Gerald D. 1968. *The Social Order of the Slum: Ethnicity and Territory in the Inner City*. Chicago, IL: University of Chicago Press.

Taylor, Carl S. 1990. *Dangerous Society*. East Lansing, MI: Michigan State University Press.

Thornberry, Terence P., Brook Kearley, Denise C. Gottfredson, Molly P. Slothower, Deanna N. Devlin, and Jamie J. Fader. 2018. "Reducing Crime among Youth at Risk for Gang Involvement: A Randomized Trial." *Criminology & Public Policy* 17 (4): 953–989. https://doi.org/10.1111/1745-9133.12395.

Thornberry, Terence P., Marvin D. Krohn, Alan J. Lizotte, Carolyn A. Smith, and Kimberly Tobin. 2003. *Gangs and Delinquency in Developmental Perspective*. Cambridge, YK: Cambridge University Press.

Thrasher, Frederic Milton. 1927. *The Gang: A Study of 1,313 Gangs in Chicago*. Chicago, IL: University of Chicago Press.

Van Hellemont, Elke, and James Densley. 2021. "If Crime Is Not the Problem, Crime Fighting Is No Solution: Policing Gang Violence in the Age of Abolition." *Journal of Aggression, Conflict and Peace Research* 13 (2/3): 136–147. https://doi.org/10.1108/JACPR-12-2020-0561.

Vigil, J. D. 1983. "Chicano Gangs: One Response to Mexican Urban Adaptation in the Los Angeles Area." *Urban Anthropology* 12 (1): 45–75.

Wagner, Kim A. 2007. *Thuggee: Banditry and the British in Early Nineteenth-Century India*. Basingstoke, UK: Palgrave Macmillan.

Weerman, Frank M., Cheryl L. Maxson, Finn-Aage Esbensen, Judith A. Aldridge, Juanjo Medina, and Frank Van Gemert. 2009. "Eurogang Program Manual: Background, Development, and Use of the Eurogang Instruments in Multi-Site, Multi-Method Comparative Research." https://www.umsl.edu/ccj/old/Eurogang/EurogangManual.pdf.

Weinberg, Alvin M. 1961. "Impact of Large-Scale Science on the United States: Big Science Is Here to Stay, but We Have yet to Make the Hard Financial and Educational Choices It Imposes." *Science* 134 (3473): 161–164. https://doi.org/10.1126/science.134.3473.161.

Wheeler, Andrew P., Sarah J. McLean, Kelly J. Becker, and Robert E. Worden. 2019. "Choosing Representatives to Deliver the Message in a Group Violence Intervention." *Justice Evaluation Journal* 2 (2): 93–117. https://doi.org/10.1080/24751979.2019.1630661.

Whyte, William Foote. 1943. *Street Corner Society: The Social Structure of an Italian Slum*. Chicago, IL: University of Chicago Press.

Whyte, William Foote. 1993. "Revisiting Street Corner Society." *Sociological Forum* 8 (2): 285–298. https://doi.org/10.1007/BF01115494.

Wolff, Kevin T., Michael T. Baglivio, Katherine E. Limoncelli, and Matt Delisi. 2020. "Pathways to Recidivism: Do Behavioral Disorders Explain the Gang-Recidivism Relationship during Reentry?" *Criminal Justice and Behavior* 47 (7): 867–885. https://doi.org/10.1177/0093854820915631.

Wood, Jane L., Emma Alleyne, Katarina Mozova, and Mark James. 2014. "Predicting Involvement in Prison Gang Activity: Street Gang Membership, Social and Psychological Factors." *Law and Human Behavior* 38 (3): 203–211. https://doi.org/10.1037/lhb0000053.

Wood, Jane L., and S. Dennard. 2017. "Gang Membership: Links to Violence Exposure, Paranoia, PTSD, Anxiety, and Forced Control of Behavior in Prison." *Psychiatry-Interpersonal and Biological Processes* 80 (1): 30–41. https://doi.org/10.1080/00332747.2016.1199185.

Yablonsky, Lewis. 1962. *The Violent Gang*. New York: Macmillan.

Yearwood, D. L., and Rhyne, A. 2007. "Hispanic/Latin Gangs: A Comparative Analysis of Nationally Affiliated and Local Gangs." *Journal of Gang Research* 14 (2). 1–18.

CHAPTER 10

FUNDING GANG RESEARCH TO ADVANCE POLICY AND PRACTICE

PHELAN A. WYRICK, BARBARA TATEM KELLEY,
AND MARY POULIN CARLTON

THIS chapter examines the critical role of funders in supporting gang research. It presents key issues, lessons learned, and examples drawn from over three decades of experience in the OJP, the primary grant-making agency within the US Department of Justice. Over this period, the OJP has provided financial support for research projects directly and indirectly focused on gangs and strategies to reduce gang violence. Funders, including the OJP, do far more than simply provide financial support for research salaries, equipment, and travel costs. To varying degrees, but in many possible ways, funders may shape the design and the course of the research itself. The pre-award and post-award decisions that funders make can influence the direction, quality, and likelihood of success for any scientific work.

ABOUT THE OFFICE OF JUSTICE PROGRAMS

The OJP provides federal leadership, grants, training, technical assistance, and other resources to improve the nation's capacity to prevent and reduce crime, assist victims, and enhance the rule of law by strengthening the criminal and juvenile justice systems. Its six program offices provide support to US states, territories, localities, and tribes to advance justice and crime-fighting efforts, fund victim service programs, help communities manage sex offenders, address the needs of youth in the system and children in danger, and provide vital research and data (Office of Justice Programs, 2022). The OJP comprises the Bureau of Justice Assistance (BJA); Bureau of Justice Statistics (BJS); National Institute of Justice (NIJ); Office of Juvenile Justice and Delinquency Prevention (OJJDP); Office for Victims of Crime; and Office of Sex Offender Sentencing, Monitoring, Apprehending, Registering, and Tracking. Through legislation and statutes, Congress authorizes programs and sets priorities for the OJP and its six program offices. Congress provides annual appropriations to fund these programs and priorities. The OJP provides support and guidance to thousands of state, local, territorial, and tribal justice agencies and their partners, but no part of the Department of Justice directs or dictates the actions of these state, local, territorial, or tribal agencies.

Historically, the NIJ and OJJDP have administered the vast majority of OJP's gang research, although some notable projects have also been supported by the BJA, BJS, and the DOJ's Office of Community Oriented Policing Services, which is situated outside of the OJP. This chapter will focus on the gang research contributions of the NIJ and OJJDP. For most of their history, these two agencies acted independently, but in a complementary and sometimes cooperative fashion to support gang research. In 2018, the OJP instituted an organizational change that transitioned all OJJDP research functions to the NIJ, thereby concentrating the primary responsibility for all of the DOJ's gang research within the NIJ.

The OJP, NIJ, and OJJDP operate under statutorily defined missions that focus on, inter alia, preventing and reducing delinquency, crime, violence, and victimization, and improving the functioning of the juvenile and criminal justice systems. The scientific aspects of these missions include supporting research, evaluation, statistics, and technology to advance these same purposes. Political appointees lead these executive branch agencies and set priorities within these missions that advance or align with those of the presidential administration. To be sure, priorities related to gangs have shifted from one administration to another. However, it has remained the case that the OJP takes an applied approach to supporting research intended to improve public safety and engages the topic of gangs with primary interest in how these groups facilitate crime, violence, and victimization among individuals and within communities. In this regard, the vast majority of the OJP's gang research fits squarely within what Pyrooz and Mitchell (2015) labeled the "Empirical Turn" in the history of gang research.

Reasons to Fund Gang Research

For funders, governmental or otherwise, applying resources to study one question or issue may involve a trade-off in which a different issue does not get similar attention. Under these circumstances, investing in gang research may be a difficult decision. In the United States there is nothing inherently illegal about being a member of a gang. Affiliation or membership in a gang is a right of association protected by the Constitution. So why fund gang research? Why is it not sufficient to simply invest in research on crime and violence? The answers to these questions may have changed over time, but a clear case for funding further gang research can be based on what we now know about communities where gangs persist and the impact of gangs on communities, the justice system, and the individuals who engage in the gang lifestyle.

Individuals who are involved with gangs commit more violence and other crime than those without any gang involvement, and gang-involved individuals are responsible for a disproportionate amount of violent crime in the communities in which they exist (Thornberry et. al. 2003; Pyrooz et al. 2016). Gangs tend to accumulate in communities of color that are most deprived of resources and opportunities, marginalized, and subjected to discriminatory policies and practices (Vigil 2020). These are often communities that are overpoliced and underserved. The gangs themselves are symptoms of these conditions, even as the crimes that gang-involved individuals commit, particularly violent crimes, contribute to the decline of these communities by expanding victimization and trauma and reducing public safety. These impacts, in turn, have the effect of decreasing the likelihood of business investment and economic activity in the community (Irvin-Erickson et al. 2016).

Gangs endure and persist in communities from one generation to the next, with gang involvement starting most frequently during early adolescence (Pyrooz and Sweeten 2015). Gang involvement is a function of "pushes"—forces that drive individuals toward gangs—and "pulls"—forces that attract individuals to gangs. Researchers studying these pushes and pulls find that many young people gravitate toward gangs as a means of coping with or attempting to master the difficult, unsafe, and unhealthy circumstances in their communities and families (Decker and Van Winkle 1996).

We know that gangs do not simply attract individuals who are more likely to be violent or commit crime. The group dynamics within the gang—including the norms, beliefs, and group activities—increase the likelihood that individuals will commit serious crime and violence during gang membership (Short and Strodtbeck 1965; Decker, Melde, and Pyrooz 2013). The facilitation effect refers to the increase in offending that is directly related to an individual's affiliation with the gang (Thornberry, Huizinga, and Loeber 2004) and also applies to the increased risk of becoming a victim of violence during gang involvement (Pyrooz, Moule, and Decker 2014).

The facilitation effect also provides some hope that when individuals break their gang affiliation, the likelihood of committing crime and violence will decrease significantly, and their likelihood of violent victimization will likewise decrease. However, this is offset to some degree by life-course research findings that show that those formerly involved in gangs, even for a short period, continue to experience ongoing negative impacts from this gang involvement that may degrade the quality of their family life, job prospects, and more (Thornberry et al. 2003).

In short, gangs are not just groups of individuals who happen to commit offenses. They are enduring and evolving networks that employ a complex assortment of social dynamics to fuel violence and other offending behavior starting in early adolescence and extending into adulthood. Gangs are an inherent risk to communities, and they have a far-reaching toll on individuals, families, and institutions, including increased burdens on the justice system and public health resources.

To the question of why to fund gang research, the answer includes our need to better understand research questions such as the following:

- What are the community and societal conditions that give rise to gangs and are most related to their persistence over time? How can we overcome those conditions and create more healthy communities?
- How can we develop and implement the most effective practices or programs to prevent young people from joining gangs, entice individuals who are gang affiliated to depart the gang lifestyle, enforce the law in a way that holds individuals involved with gangs accountable for their crimes, and provide rehabilitative supports to allow those who have been incarcerated to successfully return to their communities without re-engaging in gang activity?
- What steps can we take to disrupt the intergenerational transmission of gang activity?

- What steps can we take to be most effective in helping those who are formerly gang involved to lead healthy, fulfilling, and productive lives?

In highlighting the importance of investing in gang research, it is equally important to sound a note of caution. Early in the history of national-level gang research, Walter Miller (1975) warned of the "persisting tendency to exaggerate the seriousness of gang activity, and to represent the 'gang of today' as more violent than at any time of the past" (76). The same note of caution applies today. Care must be taken to avoid attaching negative and dehumanizing labels to individuals who commit crimes or participate in gangs. It is critical that research, as well as policy and practice, support the humanity and social development of youth confronted with gang involvement. To do this, we must recognize that gangs have been used to stoke fears and justify oppressive policies and practices. For example, the erroneous predictions of the mid-1990s envisioned an onslaught of super-predators lacking empathy and perpetrating escalating violence in the United States (Perrone and Chesney-Lind 1997; Pizarro, Chermak, and Gruenewald 2007). The super-predator myth contributed to the ill-informed, widespread sense of moral panic and severely punitive changes in juvenile and criminal justice policies and practices. Among the most likely targets to be labeled as super-predators were youth involved in street gangs.

Attention needs to be paid to how individuals are identified as gang members and what criteria are used before labeling a youth as gang involved. High-risk youth, and those involved in gangs, merit full consideration for opportunities that will advance positive social development and productive lives. Many of these same individuals were victims of violence long before they were perpetrators (Quinn et al. 2017). It is imperative in all research, policy, prevention, intervention, and violence suppression efforts that we recognize the humanity of youth confronted with gang involvement and embrace the ultimate goals of advancing positive life-course development of these individuals while also achieving public safety.

Setting Gang Research Priorities

As noted above, research priorities at the OJP are set within the context of statutorily defined missions, administration priorities, and the availability of appropriated funding. Beyond those forces, decisions regarding what gang research to prioritize are driven by three key questions: What do we know? What are the gaps in knowledge? What are the expressed interests of key stakeholders? To answer these three questions the OJP examines existing literature and consults with practitioners and researchers to identify the needs and priorities of those working to address problems associated with gangs and gang violence. The NIJ has embraced the Listen, Learn, Inform Model (National Institute of Justice, 2022a). This begins with listening to key stakeholders to identify the needs of the field; the NIJ then learns about ways to meet those needs by funding research, development, and evaluation projects; and this allows the NIJ to inform the field to strengthen science and advance justice.

A few examples demonstrate the role of stakeholders in helping set research priorities.

The 1992 Congressional reauthorization of the Juvenile Justice and Delinquency Prevention Act (JJDP Act) directed the OJJDP to establish two new discretionary grant programs, Gang-Free Schools and Communities and Community-Based Gang Intervention, to prevent and control youth gang activity. Appropriations accompanying this legislation could be used to fund research on juvenile gangs and the effectiveness of juvenile gang programs. In response to this, the OJJDP consulted with a variety of stakeholders to develop a plan to provide national leadership on gang-related program development, research, statistics, evaluation, training, technical assistance, and information dissemination (Kelley 1994). This plan produced the OJJDP's Comprehensive Response to America's Youth Gang Problem, an initiative that included, among other elements, the implementation and testing of the Comprehensive Gang Model, the establishment of the National Youth Gang Center, and the launch of the National Youth Gang Survey. This work set the stage for much of what the OJJDP would emphasize in the rest of the 1990s and the early 2000s.

In 2006, the DOJ developed the Comprehensive Anti-Gang Initiative (CAGI) in response to concerns about gang violence, particularly gang-related gun homicides. CAGI was an extension of the department's Project Safe Neighborhoods (PSN) program, and like PSN, CAGI was structured around a strong leadership role for US attorneys to coordinate strategies and resources within their districts. Funds were provided to local communities to assist in their efforts to prevent, deter, and control gang crime (US Department of Justice, 2006). In 2007, the NIJ provided funding to Michigan State University to conduct a process and outcome evaluation of the CAGI program (McGarrell et al. 2013). The evaluation found a statistically significant 11.9% reduction in gun homicide rates the year after the CAGI strategy was implemented across the target sites; however, the CAGI strategy proved to be a fleeting priority of the DOJ.

In 2020, the NIJ convened a group of researchers and practitioners for a meeting to inform the development of evidence-based programs, policies, and practices to address problems associated with gangs and gang violence, as well as advise the NIJ on the use of robust research and evaluation methods to address problems associated with gangs and gang violence. Participants were selected based on their knowledge and background to address the meeting goals. All researchers had expertise in studying various topics related to gangs as well as other relevant areas, including program evaluation, youth violence, researcher–practitioner partnerships, policing, and criminal networks. Practitioners' backgrounds included experience with gang prevention and intervention program design and implementation, prior gang membership, community organizing, and law enforcement. Discussions at the meeting centered on three themes: the state of knowledge on addressing gang and gang violence problems, identifying and addressing hurdles to using robust research and evaluation methods, and identifying priorities to advance knowledge. The NIJ published a report on this meeting, which is currently being used to inform the NIJ's gang research priorities (Carlton 2021).

Administering Gang Research

It is beyond the scope of this chapter to examine all the policy frameworks and business processes that influence the funding and administration of gang research projects. In addition to the fundamental responsibility to ensure proper financial and legal oversight, it is worth noting several of the key administrative elements that may have particular bearing on gang research. These include policies that establish principles of scientific independence and integrity, protect research participants, and make use of external peer reviewers in the selection of applications for funding. There are three important aspects of administering gang research—the decisions that funders make about framing funding opportunities, making funding decisions, and disseminating research findings—that have major implications for the types of gang research projects that receive funding and the utility of the findings from these studies.

Framing Funding Opportunities

One of the most consequential decisions that funders make prior to announcing any funding opportunity is related to how specific they will be in framing the funding opportunity. This chapter uses the OJP's chosen term "solicitation" to refer to public notices of grant funding availability and defines three categories of solicitations based on their levels of specificity. The OJP does not use these category labels; they reflect the authors' analysis of the approaches the OJP has used to fund gang research (see Table 10.1).

The first category is "open" solicitations. Open solicitations set broad parameters for research funding and do not identify gangs or call out gangs in any way as a priority. For example, the NIJ has received and funded applications for research focused on gang topics in response to solicitations that do not mention gangs but address topics like firearms violence, school safety, corrections, policing, and domestic terrorism. In submitting a gang research application to an open solicitation, applicants are under an increased burden to provide a clear justification for why their proposed gang-focused research project will meet the purposes of the original solicitation. Funders must decide whether the applicant has made a sufficiently strong case to justify a study that may only address a subpopulation or portion of the original topic of interest.

Open solicitations have advantages for both funders and applicants. Open solicitations tend to be very broad. Funders may only go as far as to identify general areas of interest related to public safety, justice systems, crime prevention, or public health. Open solicitations may also specify priority topics or research questions, but they often leave considerable discretion in the hands of the applicants. This discretion provides opportunities for applicants to propose research projects that will build knowledge related to gangs in ways that are also integrated into broader research portfolios. For funders, open solicitations do not require much gang-specific knowledge during the development stage. However, this can become a detriment when the time comes for assessing the proposal and making award decisions. If gangs were not anticipated as an area of emphasis, the initial pool of reviewers may not be well equipped to assess the quality of a gang research application. Funders can reduce these risks by anticipating needs for, and preparing to enlist, if necessary, individuals with gang expertise to assist in the review process.

The second category is "identified" solicitations. Identified research solicitations designate gangs as a substantive focus, but they do not further limit funding to specific projects or types of research. Identified solicitations may include the word "gang" in the title, or they may identify gangs as a substantive area of interest within the body of the document. They are intended to attract top researchers in the field who specialize in studying gangs, as well as other researchers who may not specialize in gang research but wish to put a proposal forward to extend their work in this area. Funders often develop identified solicitations with an understanding of the state of gang research and may even specify some priority gang-related topics or research questions deemed to be particularly important or timely.

Table 10.1 Gang Research Solicitation Categories, Titles, and Awards: 2010–2021

Category[1]	Fiscal Year	Agency[2]	Solicitation Title[3] and Link	Grant Recipient(s)	Project Title(s)	Award Amount(s)
Open	2010	NIJ	Research on International Organized Crime https://nij.ojp.gov/sites/g/files/xyckuh171/files/media/document/NIJ-2010-2621.pdf	The University of California	It Came from the North: Estimating the Production of Synthetic Drugs in Quebec, Canada	$367,845
Open	2010	NIJ	Information Technologies: Improved Delivery of Information to the Officer at the Scene https://nij.ojp.gov/sites/g/files/xyckuh171/files/media/document/NIJ-2010-2409.pdf	Redlands Police Department	Developing an iPhone-Based Crime Mapping Application to Assist Law Enforcement Officers with Understanding Spatial and Temporal Crime Patterns	$473,161
Open	2010	OJJDP	National Evaluation of the Community-Based Violence Prevention Program https://ojjdp.ojp.gov/sites/g/files/xyckuh176/files/media/document/OJJDP-2010-2721.PDF	CUNY John Jay College of Criminal Justice	Community-Based Violence Prevention National Evaluation	$1,074,992
Open	2011	NIJ	PhD Graduate Research Fellowship Program https://nij.ojp.gov/sites/g/files/xyckuh171/files/media/document/NIJ-2011-2821.pdf	Arizona State University	The Long-Term Consequences of Gang Membership	$25,000
Open	2012	NIJ	Research and Evaluation on Trafficking in Persons https://nij.ojp.gov/sites/g/files/xyckuh171/files/media/document/NIJ-2012-3096.pdf	University of San Diego	Sex Trafficking and Gangs in the San Diego/Tijuana Border Region Area	$398,824

(continued)

Table 10.1 Continued

Category[1]	Fiscal Year	Agency[2]	Solicitation Title[3] and Link	Grant Recipient(s)	Project Title(s)	Award Amount(s)
Open	2012	OJJDP	Community-Based Violence Prevention Field-Initiated Research and Evaluation Program https://ojjdp.ojp.gov/sites/g/files/xyckuh176/files/media/document/OJJDP-2012-3300.PDF	Baylor College of Medicine City of San Jose	Environmental and Personal Factors in Community-Based Juvenile Offender Intervention A Comprehensive Retrospective and Prospective Evaluation of the City of San Jose's Mayor's Gang Prevention Task Force	$500,000 $499,712
— Open	2013	NIJ	Graduate Research Fellowship Program https://nij.ojp.gov/sites/g/files/xyckuh171/files/media/document/NIJ-2013-3374.pdf	University of Massachusetts Amherst Princeton University	Social Networks and Organized Crime Trajectories of Job Search and Wellbeing among Reentering Individuals	$24,990 $25,000
Open	2013	NIJ	Building and Enhancing Criminal Justice Researcher Practitioner Partnerships https://nij.ojp.gov/sites/g/files/xyckuh171/files/media/document/NIJ-2013-3468.pdf	Temple University	Measuring Success in Focused Deterrence	$298,264
Open	2014	NIJ	Research and Evaluation on Firearms and Violence https://www.ojp.gov/sites/g/files/xyckuh241/files/media/document/sl001085.pdf	University of Chicago	Underground Gun Markets in Chicago	$459,849
Open	2014	NIJ	Developing Knowledge about What Works to Make Schools Safe https://www.ojp.gov/sites/g/files/xyckuh171/files/media/document/NIJ-2014-3878.pdf	Board of Education City of Chicago	Chicago Public Schools' Connect and Redirect to Respect (CRR) Program	$2,197,178

Open	2014	NIJ	Graduate Research Fellowship Program in the Social and Behavioral Sciences https://nij.ojp.gov/sites/g/files/xyckuh171/files/media/document/NIJ-2014-3739.pdf	SUNY, University of Albany	Life Fast, Die Young: Anticipated Early Death and Adolescent Violence and Gang Involvement	$25,869
Open	2015	NIJ	Social Science Research on Implementation, Dissemination, and Translation https://nij.ojp.gov/sites/g/files/xyckuh171/files/media/document/NIJ-2015-4027.pdf	Suffolk University	Comprehensive Gang Model Evaluation: Integrating Research into Practice	$286,740
Open	2015	NIJ	Data Resources Program: Funding for Analysis of Existing Data https://nij.ojp.gov/sites/g/files/xyckuh171/files/media/document/NIJ-2015-3974.pdf	Institute for Intergovernmental Research	An Examination of the Link between Gang Involvement and Victimization among Youth in Residential Placement	$40,000
Open	2017	NIJ	W.E.B. Du Bois Program of Research on Race and Crime https://nij.ojp.gov/sites/g/files/xyckuh171/files/media/document/NIJ-2017-12000.pdf	Multnomah County	Disrupting the Pathways to Gang Violence for Youth of Color	$468,740
Open	2017	NIJ	Graduate Research Fellowship in the Social and Behavioral Sciences https://nij.ojp.gov/sites/g/files/xyckuh171/files/media/document/NIJ-2017-10720.pdf	Temple University	Quantifying Gang Locations: A Systematic Test of Validity Using a Partial Test of Messick's Unified Perspective	$31,998
Open	2018	NIJ	Graduate Research Fellowship in Science, Technology, Engineering, and Mathematics https://nij.ojp.gov/sites/g/files/xyckuh171/files/media/document/NIJ-2018-13638.pdf	University of California, Los Angeles	Large-Scale Deep Point Process Models for Crime Forecasting	$149,999

(continued)

Table 10.1 Continued

Category[1]	Fiscal Year	Agency[2]	Solicitation Title[3] and Link	Grant Recipient(s)	Project Title(s)	Award Amount(s)
Open	2019	NIJ	Research and Evaluation on Domestic Terrorism Prevention https://nij.ojp.gov/sites/g/files/xyckuh171/files/media/document/NIJ-2019-15303.pdf	Harvard College	Applying a Development Evaluation Approach to Address Community Safety and Health Challenges of Reintegration Programs in the USA	$1,114,933
Open	2019	NIJ	Graduate Research Fellowship in the Social and Behavioral Sciences https://nij.ojp.gov/sites/g/files/xyckuh171/files/media/document/NIJ-2019-15466.pdf	Temple University	Adverse Childhood Experiences and Adolescent Gang Membership: Utilizing Latent Class Analysis to Understand the Relationship	$50,000
Open	2020	NIJ	Research into Immigration and Crime https://nij.ojp.gov/sites/g/files/xyckuh171/files/media/document/NIJ-2020-17310.pdf	California State University, Fullerton	Assessing the Relationship between Immigration Status, Crime, Gang Affiliation, and Victimization	$462,165
Open	2021	NIJ	Longitudinal Research on Delinquency and Crime https://nij.ojp.gov/funding/o-nij-2021-45005.pdf	Michigan State University	Long-Term Follow-Up of the National Evaluation of Gang Resistance Education and Training Project	$1,055,202
Identified	2010	NIJ	Evaluation of Programs to Reduce Gang Membership, Crime, and Violence https://www.ojp.gov/sites/g/files/xyckuh241/files/media/document/sl000903.pdf	No gang research projects funded	n/a	$0
Identified	2011	NIJ	Research and Evaluation in Crime Control and Prevention https://www.ojp.gov/sites/g/files/xyckuh241/files/media/document/sl000963.pdf	University of Missouri, St. Louis	A Multi-Method, Multi-Site Study of Gang Desistance	$501,337

Identified	2011	OJJDP	Gang Field Initiated Research and Evaluation Programs https://ojjdp.ojp.gov/sites/g/files/xyckuh176/files/media/document/OJJDP-2011-2964.PDF	RAND Corporation	Gangs, Social Networks and Geography: Understanding the Factors of Gang Desistance	$991,171
				Arizona State University	Understanding the Long-Term Consequences of Gang Membership: Desistance, Amplification, and Impacts on Post-Adolescent Outcomes	$124,606
				National Council on Crime and Delinquency	Girls and Gangs. Improving Our Understanding and Ability to Respond	$375,000
				Fund for the City of New York/Center for Court Innovation	A Multi-Site Study of Tribal Youth Gang Activity: Dynamics, Networks, and Tribal Community Initiatives	$898,714
Identified	2011	OJJDP	Field-Initiated Research and Evaluation Program https://ojjdp.ojp.gov/sites/g/files/xyckuh176/files/media/document/OJJDP-2011-2897.PDF	Rutgers, the State University	Evaluation of Intervention Services for Gang-Involved Youth	$372,570
Identified	2012	NIJ	Research on Domestic Radicalization https://nij.ojp.gov/sites/g/files/xyckuh171/files/media/document/NIJ-2012-3163.pdf	Children's Hospital Corporation	Understanding Pathways to and away from Violent Radicalization among Resettled Somali Refugees	$593,894
Identified	2013	NIJ	Research and Evaluation on Transnational Issues: Trafficking in Persons, Organized Crime, and Violent Extremism https://nij.ojp.gov/sites/g/files/xyckuh171/files/media/document/NIJ-2013-3457.pdf	American University	Assessing the Transnational Criminal Capacity of MS-13 in the US and El Salvador	$671,615

(continued)

Table 10.1 Continued

Category[1]	Fiscal Year	Agency[2]	Solicitation Title[3] and Link	Grant Recipient(s)	Project Title(s)	Award Amount(s)
Identified	2013	OJJDP	Community-Based Violence Prevention Field-Initiated Research and Evaluation Program https://ojjdp.ojp.gov/sites/g/files/xyckuh176/files/media/document/OJJDP-2013-3579.PDF	No gang research projects funded	n/a	$0
Identified	2014	NIJ	Research on Gangs and Gang Violence https://www.ojp.gov/sites/g/files/xyckuh171/files/media/document/NIJ-2014-3747.pdf	University of Maryland	Reducing Gang Violence: A Randomized Trial of Functional Family Therapy	$472,906
				Arizona State University	Gangs on the Street, Gangs in Prison: Their Mature, Interrelationship, Control, and Re-Entry	$840,807
Identified	2014	NIJ	Research and Evaluation on Domestic Radicalization to Violent Extremism https://www.ojp.gov/sites/g/files/xyckuh171/files/media/document/NIJ-2014-3751.pdf	Children's Hospital Corporation	Gang Affiliation and Radicalization to Violent Extremism within Somali American Communities	$331,241
				University of Maryland	A Comparative Study of Violent Extremism and Gangs	$639,736
Identified	2015	NIJ	Comprehensive School Safety Initiative https://www.ojp.gov/sites/g/files/xyckuh241/files/media/document/sl001161.pdf	No gang research projects funded	n/a	$0
Identified	2016	NIJ	Comprehensive School Safety Initiative https://nij.ojp.gov/sites/g/files/xyckuh171/files/media/document/NIJ-2016-9093.pdf	SRI International	Project SECURE: Keeping Kids Safe in San Francisco Unified School District	$4,641,134
				City of New York	A Randomized Controlled Trial of Participatory Peace Circles in New York City Schools	$4,181,239

Identified	2017	NIJ	Investigator-Initiated Research and Evaluation on Firearms Violence https://nij.ojp.gov/sites/g/files/xyckuh171/files/media/document/NIJ-2017-11146.pdf	No gang research projects funded	n/a	$0
Identified	2017	OJJDP	Field-Initiated Research and Evaluation Program https://ojjdp.ojp.gov/sites/g/files/xyckuh176/files/media/document/OJJDP-2017-10960.PDF	No gang research projects funded	n/a	$0
Identified	2018	NIJ	Research and Evaluation on Gangs and Gang Violence https://nij.ojp.gov/sites/g/files/xyckuh171/files/media/document/NIJ-2018-13941.pdf	University of Colorado	Leaving Gangs and Desisting from Crime Using a Multidisciplinary Team Approach: A Randomized Control Trial Evaluation of the Gang Reduction Initiative of Denver	$600,797
				University of Maryland	Reducing Gang Violence: A Long-Term Follow-Up of a Randomized Trial of Functional Family Therapy	$770,657
Identified	2018	OJJDP	Juvenile Reentry Research and Evaluation Program https://ojjdp.ojp.gov/sites/g/files/xyckuh176/files/media/document/OJJDP-2018-13708.PDF	No gang research projects funded	n/a	$0
Identified	2019	NIJ	Research and Evaluation on Gangs and Gang Violence https://nij.ojp.gov/sites/g/files/xyckuh171/files/media/document/NIJ-2019-15270.pdf	National Council on Crime and Delinquency	Research and Evaluation on Gangs and Gang Violence: Female Desistance from Gangs	$650,000
				University of California, Los Angeles	A Randomized Controlled Trial of the Scenarios and Solutions Gang Prevention Program	$550,610

(continued)

Table 10.1 Continued

Category[1]	Fiscal Year	Agency[2]	Solicitation Title[3] and Link	Grant Recipient(s)	Project Title(s)	Award Amount(s)
Identified	2020	NIJ	Investigator-Initiated Research and Evaluation on Firearm Violence https://nij.ojp.gov/sites/g/files/xyckuh171/files/media/document/NIJ-2020-17327.pdf	Texas A&M International University	Gun Wars and Community Terrorization: Investigating Longitudinal Gang Violence in New Jersey from a Networked Perspective	$435,020
Specified	2014	OJJDP	National Gang Center https://ojjdp.ojp.gov/sites/g/files/xyckuh176/files/media/document/OJJDP-2014-3925.PDF	Institute for Intergovernmental Research	National Gang Center	$1,500,000
Specified	2018	OJJDP	Initiative to Develop a Research-Based Practice Guide to Prevent and Reduce Youth Violence in Communities https://ojjdp.ojp.gov/sites/g/files/xyckuh176/files/media/document/OJJDP-2018-13554.PDF	The Urban Institute	Research-Based Practice Guide to Address Gang Violence	$749,956
Specified	2020	NIJ	National Youth Gang Survey https://nij.ojp.gov/sites/g/files/xyckuh171/files/media/document/NIJ-2020-18233.pdf	The RAND Corporation	National Youth Gang Survey	$996,640

[1] Open solicitations do not identify gangs as a topic of interest, but resulted in funding of at least one gang research project. Identified solicitations identify gangs as a topic of interest in the title or text of the solicitation. Specified solicitations identify gangs as a topic of interest and further limit funding to specific categories of research, or even specific studies.

[2] Funding agencies are the National Institute of Justice (NIJ) or the Office of Juvenile Justice and Delinquency Prevention (OJJDP).

[3] In cases where the official solicitation titles included the name of the funding agency or the fiscal year, this information was removed from the titles in this table.

By the time that an identified solicitation is released, the funder has already considered the relative importance of gangs and made a commitment to supporting gang research. This allows potential applicants to focus less on justifying the relevance of gangs and permits them to focus more on the contributions that a given proposal will make to advancing the body of knowledge on gangs. Identified solicitations may provide the greatest opportunities to extend or replicate previous gang research. At various points, OJP agencies have released solicitations for field-initiated research on gangs, which exemplify the identified solicitation model and maximize the potential for drawing on the creativity and ingenuity of the gang research community.

Though identified solicitations signal the interest of the funding agency to support research on gangs, they do not necessarily represent a commitment to do so. In multiple years, OJP agencies released identified solicitations that did not result in awards for gang research projects. This may be a reflection of the quality of gang research applications submitted to the funding agency, or the relative quality of those applications compared to non-gang research applications that could be funded with the same money. Some identified solicitations list gang research as one of multiple priority areas, which may signal that the available grant resources for that solicitation may or may not be applied to any given priority area.

The third category is "specified" solicitations. Specified solicitations identify gangs as the topic of interest and go further to limit funding to specific categories of research, or even specific studies. In these cases, the funder has highly defined and limited goals and objectives. Applicants can work within the parameters defined by the specified solicitation, which may allow for some flexibility, but applicants are not at liberty to propose their own novel ideas or studies outside of the defined boundaries of the solicitation. For example, a funder might release a specified solicitation that is only open to supporting an evaluation of a specific gang violence reduction program. The OJJDP took this approach in the 1990s and early 2000s with evaluations of the Gang-Free Schools Program and the Gang Reduction Program. The NIJ took a similar approach to a different type of study in 2020, when it released a solicitation to carry out a National Youth Gang Survey (National Institute of Justice, 2020).

Funders should carefully consider the strengths and limitations of these approaches to designing solicitations. Just as different research methods are more or less suited to answer different research questions, each of these solicitation categories is more or less suited to different purposes established by the funder.

Making Funding Decisions

The Department of Justice has adopted a scientific and research integrity policy that establishes and protects standards of research validity, reliability, accuracy, objectivity, and integrity (US Department of Justice, 2013). This policy protects against political or otherwise improper interference in the scientific process of presentation of results. The policy also confirms that the NIJ director has final authority over the awards made by the institute. And while the NIJ director is a political appointee, that individual serves for the primary purpose of leading the scientific mission of the institute. The OJP is also committed to enforcing standards of protection and privacy for research participants (National Institute of Justice, 2022b). These policies are extremely important to gang research because gangs can become a politically charged issue, and gang researchers must manage sensitive situations and information in the course of their work. For the research enterprise to move forward, research participants must understand that they are properly protected and that the information they share will remain confidential.

The OJP supports gang research through competitive awards that are typically open to a variety of eligible non-foreign applicants, including units of state, local, and tribal governments; institutions of higher learning; and non-profit organizations. With a large number of universities and non-governmental research organizations across the United States, the OJP is able to generate a high level of competition for gang research funding opportunities, which is central to the OJP's efforts to maximize the quality of incoming applications and subsequently funded projects. OJP agencies are committed to using structured peer review processes to inform the selection of applications to receive awards. These peer reviews typically involve three to four outside technical and practitioner experts who carry out independent reviews on all applications and then engage in a collaborative discussion about a subset of the most viable applications. The OJJDP and NIJ have frequently enlisted the highly valuable contributions of external gang researchers and practitioners with gang expertise from law enforcement, social services, and community-based organizations. The written notes, comments, and scores from these reviews are combined with input from internal OJP personnel to inform final award decisions.

Disseminating Gang Research

Funders have a responsibility to ensure that the research they support is published and disseminated so that it may contribute to scientific knowledge and benefit practitioners and policymakers. The OJP, NIJ, and OJJDP encourage research grantees to publish their findings in academic journals and practitioner-focused outlets, but the agencies have also developed several important mechanisms for disseminating the research they sponsor. The most specialized outlet is the National Gang Center (National Gang Center 2022b), which the OJJDP established in the 1990s and has been producing and curating a library of gang research and other practical gang-related resources ever since. With OJJDP funding, the National Gang Center also supported a series of periodic National Youth Gang Symposia, which provided opportunities to disseminate gang research in a conference setting directed at practitioners. The National Criminal Justice Reference Services is a more general resource that serves as the primary archive for research reports funded by the NIJ and OJJDP (National Criminal Justice Reference Service 2022). CrimeSolutions is a website that translates the findings from rigorous program evaluations and meta-analyses into accessible profiles of evidence-based programs and practices (CrimeSolutions 2022). Many of the gang programs discussed in this chapter are profiled in CrimeSolutions as promising or effective programs or practices. The OJP supports the National Archive of Criminal Justice Data where funded gang-related data collections are deposited, curated, and released for secondary analysis by additional researchers (National Archive of Criminal Justice Data 2022). In this way the utility and impact of these data collections are maximized through expansion, extension, and replication of the original analysis. The NIJ and OJJDP also highlight selected research findings with agency-specific publications such as the *NIJ Journal*, OJJDP bulletins, and other reports.

The OJJDP's Program of Gang Research

Part D of the 1992 JJDP Act authorized funding and set priorities for gang programs and research. It also explicitly extended the authority of the OJJDP beyond legal definitions of "juvenile" to include those less than 22 years of age. This act set the stage for the OJJDP's extensive program of gang research, which was defined to a large degree by its investments in collecting national statistics on youth gangs, its support for longitudinal research on causes and correlates of delinquency, and its research and development of multi-strategy, community-based programs to reduce gang activity and violence. Each of these three lines of research will be described in more detail below.

In addition to these major ongoing research activities, the OJJDP produced research on a wide range of related topics to better understand and develop findings to improve responses to the nation's youth gang problem. These included studies on female gangs (Moore and Hagedorn 2001), youth gang drug trafficking (Howell and Gleason 1999); youth gangs in Indian Country (Major et al. 2004), Vietnamese gang involvement (Wyrick 2000), hybrid and other modern gangs (Starbuck, Howell, and Lindquist 2001), youth gang homicides (Curry, Maxson, and Howell 2001), preventing adolescent gang involvement (Esbensen 2000), youth gangs in schools (Howell and Lynch 2000), gang migration (Maxson 1998), the youth gangs, drugs, and violence connection (Howell and Decker 1999), and more.

National Statistics on Gangs

Gangs have had a presence throughout US history (Howell 2015; Thrasher 1927). For most of these years, gangs were viewed as wayward boys engaging in relatively low-level delinquent and criminal activities, which were of local concern for some jurisdictions, but did not rise to a national concern. In the late 1960s and early 1970s, youth gangs were given varying levels of attention by several federal-level commissions that examined national issues related to criminal justice, law enforcement, and violence (Commission on Law Enforcement and Justice 1967; National Commission on the Causes and Prevention of Violence 1969; National Advisory Commission on Criminal Justice Standards and Goals 1973). As described by Walter Miller (1975), all three of these national commissions conveyed a similar message that gangs should not become a major object of concern, gang violence was not viewed as a major crime problem, and the primary method for addressing gangs should be through provision of services by community-based agencies. However, this benign view of gangs was not shared by all. Following the publication of these commission reports, the OJJDP provided funding for Miller (1975) to carry out the first-of-its-kind national-level survey on youth gangs and groups. This study produced a very different conclusion. Based on systematic interviews with over 150 respondents across the nation, Miller concluded that gang violence was more lethal than in prior periods, it was affecting more people, and gang crime showed little prospect of abating.

Irving Spergel and David Curry (1993) surveyed gang problems across 85 cities. This was followed by Curry's NIJ-sponsored National Assessment of Law Enforcement Anti-Gang Information Resources (Curry et al. 1992). This latter assessment expanded the sample of jurisdictions surveyed to include the 79 largest cities (with minimum populations of approximately 200,000) and an additional 78 cities with populations under 200,000. Curry found major increases in law enforcement reports of gang problems in cities of all sizes, as compared to previous prevalence estimates dating back to Miller's (1975) pilot study.

The OJJDP soon came to appreciate the need to establish a recurring statistical data collection from law enforcement that would (1) be built on a sound, representative sampling frame to generate valid national estimates of gangs, gang members, and gang-related crime; (2) increase our understanding of the comparability of definitions of gang-related terms across jurisdictions; (3) provide the basis for trend analysis of emergence of gangs in additional jurisdictions; (4) detect fluctuation across time of gang-related problems within jurisdictions; and (5) gather law enforcement's perspective on promising community responses to the gang problem. A key provision under the OJJDP's 1994 Comprehensive Strategy to Address America's Gang Problem (Kelley 1994) was to establish the National Youth Gang Center and include among its key tasks the design and launch of the National Youth Gang Survey (NYGS), which was administered annually from 1996 until 2012 (see **Chapter 11** in this text).

The NYGS was based on a nationally representative sample of more than 2,500 law enforcement agencies serving larger cities, suburban counties, smaller cities, and rural counties. As of the last year of this annual survey administration in 2012, there were an estimated 30,700 gangs with approximately 850,000 gang members in the United States. The total number of gang-related homicides reported by respondents in the NYGS sample averaged nearly 2,000 annually from 2007 to 2012, which accounted for approximately 13% of the FBI's annual estimates of homicides nationwide (National Gang Center 2022a). Through this purposeful survey effort, the OJJDP advanced annual national estimates, which over the years captured key indicators of the emergence of gang activities across the nation, permeating both suburban and rural areas. Knowledge gleaned from this survey research helped funding agencies better target resources at those jurisdictions most in need of gang prevention, intervention, and suppression efforts.

Currently, the NIJ is supporting the redesign and relaunch of the NYGS with an emphasis on drawing a nationally representative sample of law enforcement agencies; increasing the comparability of key gang-related terms; assessing contemporary gang-related issues; gathering information on current law enforcement gang responses; understanding the diversity of gang organization, membership, and criminal involvement; enhancing the utility of findings and feedback to the responding agencies; and deriving and disseminating policy and practice implications to the field. Systematically collecting and analyzing national statistics on gangs is considered a key priority for federal funding support.

Longitudinal Research

The OJJDP launched the Program of Research on the Causes and Correlates of Delinquency in 1986, which included three longitudinal samples of high-risk inner-city youth in Denver, Rochester, and Pittsburgh (Thornberry et al. 2004). In both the Rochester Youth Development Study led by Terence Thornberry and the Denver Youth Survey led by David Huizinga, the investigators first determined there was a sufficient gang presence in those two emerging gang cities to merit incorporation of gang measures. This allowed for longitudinal examination of self-reported delinquency prior to, during, and after gang membership. While those youth who chose to join gangs generally reported some involvement in delinquency prior to gang membership, during active gang membership youth reported higher rates of violent offenses than either before they joined or after they left the gang. Gang members who made up only one-third of the Rochester sample accounted for 86% of serious delinquent acts, 69% of violent delinquent acts, and 70% of drug sales (Browning, Thornberry, and Porter, 1999). These findings suggest that gang norms and group dynamics facilitate delinquent and violent behavior.

Longitudinal research provides an entry for examining when and why in the life course a youth is recruited to join a gang, choses to become actively engaged in a gang, participates in gang-related crime, and then desists from such criminal involvement. Researchers have identified both risk and protective factors for gang involvement and examined more closely what youth find attractive about gangs, in terms of satisfying basic needs for peer affiliation, support, and recognition. One promising finding from life-course examinations of gang involvement is that most youth enter and then desist from criminal gang involvement in a relatively short period of time—approximately 1-2 years (Thornberry et al. 2004). Longitudinal investigations of gang enrollment and desistance both justify and inform the development of age-appropriate strategies to prevent gang enrollment targeting at-risk children and youth, and intervention strategies for gang-involved youth that minimize the duration of their active participation in gang-related crime. These findings suggest paths for communities to effectively prevent the onset of gang involvement and also hasten youth desistance from gang-related crime, which will improve public safety at lower social and financial costs than relying exclusively on law enforcement and gang suppression efforts.

The Comprehensive Gang Model

Throughout the 1990s and into the early 2000s, the OJJDP led an extended and ambitious program of research and development to design, implement, and evaluate community-based, multi-strategy approaches for reducing gang activity and violence. With OJJDP support, Irving Spergel and David Curry conducted the first comprehensive, national assessment of organized agency and community group responses to gang problems through the late 1980s. This effort extended to 45 cities and 6 institutional sites. The study included interviews of former gang members, a client evaluation of youth gang services, and a survey of diverse knowledgeable representatives of the various components of the justice system, schools, and youth, community, and church organizations. The final report from this project, titled *Youth Gangs Problem and Response* (Spergel 1991) was a seminal contribution that set forth five central strategies that would continue to influence and define gang responses for decades to come: (1) community organization/mobilization; (2) social intervention/youth outreach, street work; (3) opportunities provision; (4) gang suppression; and (5) organizational change and development.

The OJJDP packaged these five strategies into the Comprehensive Communitywide Approach to Gang Prevention, Intervention, and Suppression. This came to be known as the Comprehensive Gang Model. Spergel accessed OJP formula funds, which flowed through the State of Illinois, to implement and evaluate the initial version of the Comprehensive Gang Model in the Little Village area of Chicago. The OJJDP came to view the Little Village project as a pilot for what would become a series of demonstration initiatives starting in the mid-1990s to fund, replicate, and evaluate the Comprehensive Gang Model in jurisdictions across the country. This started in 1995 with a five-site demonstration (Burch and Chemers 1997; Howell 2000), and the OJJDP continued to support and refine this model based on iterative cycles of action evaluation through the 1998 Rural Gang Initiative and the 2000 Gang-Free Schools and Communities Initiative.

In 2003, the OJJDP launched the Gang Reduction Program (GRP), which was a modified version of the Comprehensive Gang Model. The GRP is an example of how changing governmental leadership may impact the course of research and development activities. With new administration leadership at the OJJDP in the early 2000s, there remained a strong interest in addressing gangs and developing community-based anti-gang strategies; however, there was also a strong interest in breaking with the past and developing new approaches.

The GRP drew on violence prevention concepts borrowed from the public health field with the intention of producing a more direct and accessible model for aligning anti-gang strategies with community populations. With practitioner audiences in mind, this approach distilled the anti-gang strategies down to primary prevention, secondary prevention, gang intervention, and targeted enforcement (Wyrick 2006). The GRP de-emphasized the strategies of community organization/mobilization and organizational change and development. But it retained the emphasis on social intervention and opportunities provision (under the heading of "gang intervention") and suppression (under the heading of "targeted enforcement"). The GRP added new emphasis on primary and secondary prevention, which received little attention under the Comprehensive Gang Model. These modifications were informed by the emerging findings from OJJDP-funded longitudinal studies that identified risk factors for gang membership at the individual, family, school, peer group, and community levels. The growing understanding of the role of risk factors allowed for the articulation of a strategic, risk-based response to gangs (Wyrick and Howell 2004) that was incorporated into the GRP approach.

The adaptation of the Comprehensive Gang Model continued when the DOJ embraced the GRP as an aspect of the department's PSN program. In what became the Comprehensive Anti-Gang Initiative (CAGI) in 2006, the GRP model was linked to the PSN model, which featured strong leadership from US attorneys working in coordination with local officials to enhance federal prosecutions of gang-involved individuals.

In the years that followed the GRP and CAGI, the OJJDP continued to support gang research and development, but the profile and priority of this work waned considerably. The designated funding and authorization that appeared in the 1992 JJDP Act under Part D, "Gang-Free Schools and Communities: Community-Based Gang Intervention," had been removed in the 2002 reauthorization of the JJDP Act. New leadership brought new priorities, and the period of multisite demonstration evaluations came to an end.

Through these multisite demonstration initiatives, many lessons were learned that led to further innovations. One of these early lessons was that gang activity varied in important ways from one jurisdiction to another. The OJJDP observed that communities involved in demonstration projects often did not have accurate information about the gang activity that was occurring in their jurisdictions. Instead of drawing on local data or knowledge from individuals with lived experiences close to the gangs, planners often drew their information from stereotypes or impressions generated by the media and the entertainment industry.

This would often contribute to inaccurate problem diagnoses, which could lead to improper and inefficient responses.

The OJJDP encouraged cities participating in Comprehensive Gang Model demonstrations to carry out data-driven assessments of their local gang problems. The first set of demonstration sites were reluctant to do so and delayed assessments until long after program implementation had already begun. When they eventually completed local gang problem assessments, they found that it was necessary to revise elements in their program designs. In the late 1990s, the OJJDP produced the first *Guide to Assessing Your Community's Youth Gang Problem*, which has been updated since (Office of Juvenile Justice and Delinquency Prevention, 2009). Later funded sites in OJJDP demonstration initiatives were required to carry out the problem assessment as part of the program development process prior to program implementation. Baseline and ongoing assessment of the community's gang-related problems is critical to strategically develop prevention, intervention, and suppression strategies that effectively move the needle in terms of achieving measurable objectives. Recognizing the variety of gangs across localities, this local assessment process provides community practitioners with the necessary understanding of how gangs operate in their own community.

Another major lesson learned across all these demonstration initiatives was that the actual implementation of any of the OJJDP-sponsored approaches varied considerably from one location to the next. Evaluations found that the various models could be effective, but a wide range of local factors, history, resources, and decisions could make the difference between a locality that saw positive results and another locality that experienced few measurable benefits. The word "model" itself became somewhat problematic with the rise of the evidence-based movement in the 2000s and the expectation that a "model" could be reproduced with fidelity from one location to another with similar results. It is more accurate to think of the OJJDP Comprehensive Gang Model as a framework that can help guide local communities in their thinking and planning for how to understand gang activity, what strategies to put in place and how to implement them, what partners to engage, and what organizational structures (e.g., steering committee, operational teams) are needed to manage and sustain the efforts.

The NIJ's Program of Gang Research

Since the late 1980s, the NIJ has supported research and evaluation with a focus on filling gaps in our knowledge about gangs and gang violence and has made major contributions to our understanding of promising and effective gang violence prevention, intervention, and enforcement strategies. The early goals of the NIJ's gang research agenda were to (1) define and explain gangs and their activities, (2) determine what programs successfully combat gang violence and why they work, and (3) establish model approaches to preventing and suppressing gang violence. With the OJJDP's focus on youth gangs, risk factors, and the Comprehensive Gang Model, the NIJ was able to focus on a wide range of other topics of interest to practitioners and policymakers. In working to define and explain gangs, the NIJ sponsored research on gang offending, gang structures, gang migration from larger cities to smaller ones, and connections between street gangs and organized crime groups.

The NIJ also supported a variety of studies examining justice system responses to gangs, including police, prosecution, probation, and correctional responses and strategies (e.g., Klein, Maxson, and Gordon 1987).

There is a longstanding interest at the NIJ to invest in rigorous evaluation of anti-gang efforts. This includes wanting to know what is effective and why it is effective (or ineffective). In 2002, the NIJ released a seminal book titled *Responding to Gangs: Evaluation and Research*, edited by former NIJ scientist Winifred "Winnie" Reed and Scott Decker. Decker's first chapter in this book expressed great concern about how little was known about anti-gang intervention efforts: "The lack of even basic knowledge about the impact of interventions on gangs should be a clarion call to researchers, practitioners, and policymakers" (Reed and Scott 2002, 19). It appears this call was well-heeded, because a recent review of NIJ gang research from fiscal years 2012 to 2019 identified nine NIJ-funded program evaluations, including six randomized controlled trials (Carlton 2021). The NIJ's efforts to evaluate and identify effective approaches for reducing gang violence have included studies of programs specifically designed to address gangs and others that were focused primarily on violence reduction but are highly applicable to gangs.

In the latter half of the 1990s, the NIJ funded the evaluation of the G.R.E.A.T. program, a school-based gang-prevention training curriculum delivered by police officers to sixth and seventh grade students. This rigorous evaluation found no differences between youth who participated in the G.R.E.A.T. program and those that did not in terms of future gang membership and involvement in delinquent behavior (Esbensen et al. 2002). To the credit of the program developers, they worked closely with the NIJ-funded evaluator, Dr. Finn Esbensen, to update and revise the program curriculum with an approach informed by educational and prevention research and theory. NIJ provided Esbensen and his colleagues with funding to carry out a second evaluation of the new G.R.E.A.T. program curriculum. This study featured an experimental, multisite, longitudinal panel design across seven cities and produced more convincing results in terms of improved odds of resisting gang involvement and other positive outcomes (Esbensen et al. 2013).

The NIJ and OJJDP both contributed funding to the development and testing of another important program specifically focused on gang-involved individuals. The development and positive outcomes of the Functional Family Therapy-Gang (FFT-G) program has been hailed as a breakthrough in gang prevention and intervention programming (Howell 2018). OJJDP funding supported Terrence Thornberry and Denise Gottfredson as they worked to identify and develop an existing evidence-based delinquency prevention program into a viable gang-focused intervention. Researchers selected the well-established Functional Family Therapy (FFT) program, which had previously demonstrated its efficacy in the reduction of delinquency and substance abuse in a general delinquency population. They worked with program developers to modify FFT into FFT-G. Then the researchers turned to the NIJ to support a randomized controlled trial to determine whether the new FFT-G program reduced gang involvement and whether positive outcomes could be sustained over time. The results were very encouraging, with those at high risk of gang involvement showing significant improvements in recidivism measures including arrests, charges, and adjudications up to 18 months post program participation (Gottfredson et al. 2018). The NIJ is currently supporting an extension of this study that will provide longer-term follow-ups with participants in the original study to examine outcomes up to five years post program participation (Carlton 2020). Additional analysis will focus on whether the FFT-G program results in reduced gang involvement, and whether reductions in violent offending, drug abuse, drug sales, and negative attitudes and behavior will be sustained.

The NIJ's early support for the development and evaluation of the Boston Ceasefire model (National Institute of Justice 2001) laid the groundwork for focused-deterrence models and group violence intervention models, in which individuals involved in high-rates of violence are presented with incentives and consequences to deter them from future violence. These focused-deterrence strategies were frequently integrated into the DOJ's PSN program, which emphasizes complementary federal prosecution and the leadership of US attorneys to help foster coordinated, multi-strategy violence reduction efforts in targeted areas. PSN has been embraced by the DOJ as a primary violence reduction strategy since the early 2000s, in part because of the promising results from the NIJ-funded national evaluation, which found that as the level of PSN intervention increased, a greater decrease in crime occurred (McGarrell et al. 2009).

Cure Violence is a different kind of violence intervention program, with roots in a public health approach to preventing the spread of disease. A key aspect of the Cure Violence program is the use of credible messengers from the local community to engage with those most at risk for perpetrating violence. The NIJ-funded evaluation of this model (formerly known as CeaseFire-Chicago) produced mixed findings that included statistically significant reductions in shootings, killings, and retaliatory homicides in some, but not all, of the seven targeted neighborhoods (Skogan et al. 2009). This was one of the first studies to demonstrate that a community-based intervention strategy, in the absence of a coordinated enforcement approach, could have promising results in reducing serious violence.

Conclusion

Funders play an essential role in advancing gangs research and developing evidence-based programs and practices to reduce gang activity and violence. As the primary grant-making component of the US Department of Justice, the OJP carries out this work primarily through the leadership of the NIJ and OJJDP. For more than three decades, these agencies have demonstrated that the role of a funder extends far beyond the provision of financial support. The ability to write checks is essential, but not sufficient. Funders can help establish a vision and set direction for the field; they can help define challenges and priorities; they can convene disparate and multidisciplinary experts to forge solutions; they can illuminate and demystify complex issues; and they can share this information widely in accessible formats.

As a governmental funding agency, the OJP has experienced many leadership changes over this period, and Congress has modified authorities and appropriations. Crime levels in the United States have experienced a dramatic decline in recent decades. Yet the nation continues to confront the challenges created by gangs, and a recent spike in homicides is prompting a renewed search for solutions. This search for solutions will not have to rely on anecdotes, guesses, or assumptions. The extant and growing body of research made possible through the support of the OJP, OJJDP, and NIJ provides the knowledge base to inform promising and effective solutions, even as it also sets the stage for further inquiry to take us well beyond what we have learned already. In response to violent crime challenges, the

DOJ has articulated a comprehensive federal response that re-emphasizes its commitment to an updated version of PSN (US Department of Justice 2021), while the administration has prioritized investments in community violence intervention (CVI) strategies (White House 2021). Neither of these initiatives is framed in terms of gangs or gang violence. However, they are built on a knowledge base that is derived from many investments in gang research. For example, CVI strategies benefit from the many research and demonstration projects funded by the OJJDP and NIJ to advance gang intervention strategies and the use of outreach workers and violence interrupters.

This chapter highlights the activities, functions, and lessons learned from US governmental funding agencies. Non-governmental funders, and funders outside of the United States, may find benefit in considering the example that the OJP, OJJDP, and NIJ provide. Our collective understanding of gangs and methods for countering them will grow with further well-conceived and strategic investments in gang research. The findings from this research provide the evidence base to inform policies and practices that save lives and create safer communities for all.

Opinions or points of view expressed in this chapter are those of the authors and do not necessarily reflect the official position or policies of the US Department of Justice, the Office of Justice Programs (OJP), the National Institute of Justice (NIJ), or the Office of Juvenile Justice and Delinquency Prevention (OJJDP).

Acknowledgments

The authors would like to acknowledge the following individuals who made many essential contributions to gang research at the OJP, NIJ, and OJJDP as federal personnel and as outside contributors: James "Buddy" Howell, Winifred "Winnie" Reed, Jim Burch, Lois Mock, Betty Chemers, John Moore, Irving Spergel, Walter Miller, Candice Kane, Malcolm Klein, Terry Thornberry, Scott Decker, and Finn Esbensen.

References

Browning, Katherine, Terrence P. Thornberry, and Pamela K. Porter. 1999. *OJJDP Fact Sheet. Highlights of Findings from the Rochester Youth Development Study*. Washington, DC: US Department of Justice, Office of Justice Programs, Office of Juvenile Justice and Delinquency Prevention.

Burch, James H., and Betty M. Chemers. 1997. *OJJDP Fact Sheet. A Comprehensive Response to America's Youth Gang Problem*. Washington, DC: US Department of Justice, Office of Justice Programs, Office of Juvenile Justice and Delinquency Prevention.

Carlton, Mary Poulin. 2020. "Functional Family Therapy—Gangs: Adapting an Evidence-Based Program to Reduce Gang Involvement." *National Institute of Justice Journal* 282: 59–63.

Carlton, Mary Poulin. 2021. *Advancing Knowledge to Reduce Gangs and Gang Violence: Perspectives from Researchers and Practitioners*. Washington, DC: US Department of Justice, Office of Justice Programs, National Institute of Justice.

CrimeSolutions. 2022. "CrimeSolutions." Accessed on March 5. https://crimesolutions.ojp.gov/.

Commission on Law Enforcement and Justice. 1967. *The Challenge of Crime in a Free Society*. Washington, DC: US Government Printing Office.

Curry, G. David, Robert J. Fox, Richard A. Ball, and Darryl Stone. 1992. *National Assessment of Law Enforcement Anti-Gang Information Resources*. Washington, DC: US Department of Justice, Office of Justice Programs, National Institute of Justice.

Curry, G. David, Cheryl L. Maxson, and James C. Howell. 2001. 2004. *OJJDP Juvenile Justice Fact Sheet. Youth Gang Homicides in the 1990's*. Washington, DC: US Department of Justice, Office of Justice Programs, Office of Juvenile Justice and Delinquency Prevention.

Decker, Scott H., and Barrik Van Winkle. 1996. *Life in the gang: Family, friends, and violence*. Cambridge, UK: Cambridge University Press.

Decker, Scott H., Chris Melde, and David C. Pyrooz. 2013. "What Do We Know about Gangs and Gang Members and Where Do We Go from Here?" *Justice Quarterly* 30 (3): 369–402.

Esbensen, Finn-Aage. 2000. *OJJDP Juvenile Justice Bulletin. Preventing Adolescent Gang Involvement*. Washington, DC: US Department of Justice, Office of Justice Programs, Office of Juvenile Justice and Delinquency Prevention.

Esbensen, Finn-Aage, Adrienne Freng, Terrance J. Taylor, Dana Peterson, and D. Wayne Osgood. 2002. "National Evaluation of the Gang Resistance Education and Training (G.R.E.A.T.) Program." In *Responding to Gangs: Research and Evaluation*, edited by Winifred L. Reed and Scott H. Decker, 139–167. Washington, DC: US Department of Justice, Office of Justice Programs, National Institute of Justice.

Esbensen, Finn-Aage, Wayne Osgood, Dana Peterson, Terrance J. Taylor, Dena Carson, Adrienne Freng, and Kristy Matsuda. 2013. *Process and Outcome Evaluation of the G.R.E.A.T. Program*. Washington, DC: US Department of Justice, Office of Justice Programs, National Institute of Justice. Accessed March 6, 2022. https://www.ojp.gov/pdffiles1/nij/grants/244346.pdf.

Gottfredson, Denise C., Terence P. Thornberry, Molly Slothower, Deanna Devlin, Brook Kearley, and Jamie J. Fader. *Reducing Gang Violence: A Randomized Trial of Functional Family Therapy*. Washington, DC: US Department of Justice, Office of Justice Programs, National Institute of Justice. 2018. Accessed March 6, 2022. https://www.ojp.gov/pdffiles1/nij/grants/251754.pdf.

Howell, James C. 2000. *Youth Gang Programs and Strategies*. Washington, DC: US Department of Justice, Office of Justice Programs, Office of Juvenile Justice and Delinquency Prevention.

Howell, James C. 2015. *The History of Street Gangs in the United States: Their Origins and Transformations*. Lanham, MD: Lexington Books.

Howell, James C. 2018. "What Works with Gangs: A Breakthrough." *Criminology & Public Policy* 17 (4): 991–999.

Howell, James C., and Scott H. Decker. 1999. *OJJDP Juvenile Justice Bulletin. Youth Gang, Drugs, and Violence Connection*. Washington, DC: US Department of Justice, Office of Justice Programs, Office of Juvenile Justice and Delinquency Prevention.

Howell, James C., and Debra K. Gleason. 1999. *OJJDP Juvenile Justice Bulletin. Youth Gang Drug Trafficking*. Washington, DC: US Department of Justice, Office of Justice Programs, Office of Juvenile Justice and Delinquency Prevention.

Howell, James C., and James P. Lynch. 2000. *OJJDP Juvenile Justice Bulletin. Youth Gangs in Schools*. Washington, DC: US Department of Justice, Office of Justice Programs, Office of Juvenile Justice and Delinquency Prevention.

Irvin-Erickson, Yasemin, Bing Bai, Annie Gurvis, and Edward Mohr. 2016. *The Effect of Gun Violence on Local Economies: Gun Violence, Business, and Employment Trends in Minneapolis*, Oakland, CA: The Urban Institute.

Kelley, Barbara Tatem. 1994. *Comprehensive Strategy to Address America's Gang Problem*. Washington, DC: U.S. Department of Justice, Office of Justice Programs, Office of Juvenile Justice and Delinquency Prevention.

Klein, Malcom W., Cheryl L. Maxson, and Margaret A. Gordon. 1987. *Police Response to Street Gang Violence: Improving the Investigative Process*. Washington, DC: US Department of Justice, Office of Justice Programs, National Institute of Justice. Accessed June 26, 2022. https://www.ojp.gov/pdffiles1/Digitization/107463NCJRS.pdf.

Major, Aline K., Arlen Egley, Jr., James C. Howell, Barbara Mendenhall, and Troy Armstrong. 2004. *OJJDP Juvenile Justice Bulletin. Youth Gangs in Indian Country*. Washington, DC: US Department of Justice, Office of Justice Programs, Office of Juvenile Justice and Delinquency Prevention.

Maxson, Cheryl M. 1998. *OJJDP Juvenile Justice Bulletin. Gang Members on the Move*. Washington, DC: US Department of Justice, Office of Justice Programs, Office of Juvenile Justice and Delinquency Prevention.

McGarrell, Edmund F., Natalie Kroovand Hipple, Nicholas Corsaro, Timothy S. Bynum, Heather Perez, Carol A. Zimmermann, and Melissa Garmo. 2009. *Project Safe Neighborhoods— A National Program to Reduce Gun Crime: Final Project Report*. Washington, DC: US Department of Justice, Office of Justice Programs, National Institute of Justice. Accessed March 6, 2022. https://www.ojp.gov/pdffiles1/nij/grants/226686.pdf.

McGarrell, Edmund F., Nicholas Corsaro, Chris Melde, Natalie Hipple, Jennifer Cobbina, Timothy Bynum, and Heather Perez. 2013. *An Assessment of the Comprehensive Anti-Gang Initiative: Final Project Report*. Washington, DC: U.S. Department of Justice. Office of Justice Programs, National Institute of Justice. Accessed March 6, 2022. https://www.ojp.gov/pdffiles1/nij/grants/240757.pdf.

Miller, Walter B. 1975. *Violence by Youth Gangs and Youth Groups as a Crime Problem in Major American Cities*. Washington, DC: US Department of Justice, Office of Justice Programs, Office of Juvenile Justice and Delinquency Prevention.

Moore, Joan, and John Hagedorn. 2001. *OJJDP Juvenile Justice Bulletin. Female Gangs: A Focus on Research*. Washington, DC: US Department of Justice, Office of Juvenile Justice and Delinquency Prevention.

National Advisory Commission on Criminal Justice Standards and Goals. 1973. *Report on Community Crime Prevention*. Washington, DC: National Advisory Commission on Criminal Justice Standards and Goals.

National Archive of Criminal Justice Data. 2022. "National Archive of Criminal Justice Data." Accessed on March 5. https://www.icpsr.umich.edu/web/pages/NACJD/index.html.

National Criminal Justice Reference Service. 2022. "About NCJRS." Accessed on March 5. https://www.ojp.gov/ncjrs/new-ojp-resources.

National Commission on the Causes and Prevention of Violence. 1969. *Final Report*. Washington, DC: US Government Printing Office.

National Gang Center. 2022a. "National Youth Gang Survey Analysis: Measuring the Extent of Gang Problems." Accessed on March 5. https://nationalgangcenter.ojp.gov/survey-analysis/measuring-the-extent-of-gang-problems.

National Gang Center. 2022b. "Who We Are." Accessed on March 5. https://nationalgangcenter.ojp.gov/.

National Institute of Justice. 2001. *Reducing Gun Violence: The Boston Gun Project's Operation Ceasefire*. Washington, DC: US Department of Justice, Office of Justice Programs, National Institute of Justice.

National Institute of Justice. 2020. *National Youth Gang Survey, Fiscal Year 2020*. Washington, DC: US Department of Justice, Office of Justice Programs, National Institute of Justice. Accessed March 6, 2022. https://nij.ojp.gov/sites/g/files/xyckuh171/files/media/document/NIJ-2020-18233.pdf.

National Institute of Justice. 2022a. "About the National Institute of Justice." Accessed on March 5. https://nij.ojp.gov/about-nij.

National Institute of Justice. 2022b. "Human Subjects and Privacy Protection." Accessed on March 5. https://nij.ojp.gov/funding/human-subjects-and-privacy-protection.

Office of Juvenile Justice and Delinquency Prevention. 2009. *OJJDP Comprehensive Gang Model: A Guide to Assessing Your Community's Youth Gang Problem*. Washington, DC: US Department of Justice, Office of Justice Programs, Office of Juvenile Justice and Delinquency Prevention.

Office of Juvenile Justice and Delinquency Prevention. 2022. *OJJDP FY 2011 Gang Field Initiated Research and Evaluation Programs*. Washington, DC: U.S. Department of Justice, Office of Justice Programs. Accessed March 6. https://www.ojjdp.ojp.gov/sites/g/files/xyckuh176/files/media/document/OJJDP-2011-2964.PDF.

Perrone, Paul A., and Meda Chesney-Lind. 1997. "Representations of Gangs and Delinquency: Wild in the Streets?" *Social Justice* 24 (4): 96–116.

Pizarro, Jesenia M., Steven M. Chermak, and Jeffrey A. Gruenewald. 2007. "Juvenile 'Super-Predators' in the News: A Comparison of Adult and Juvenile Homicides." *Journal of Criminal Justice and Popular Culture* 14 (1): 84–111.

Pyrooz, David C., and Meghan M. Mitchell. 2015. "Little Gang Research, Big Gang Research." In *The Handbook of Gangs*, edited by Scott H. Decker and David C. Pyrooz, 28–58. Hoboken, NJ: John Wiley & Sons, Inc.

Pyrooz, David C., and Gary Sweeten. 2015. "Gang Membership between Ages 5 and 17 Years in the United States." *Journal of Adolescent Health* 56 (4): 414–419.

Pyrooz, David C., Richard K. Moule Jr., and Scott H. Decker. 2014. "The Contribution of Gang Membership to the Victim-Offender Overlap." *Journal of Research in Crime and Delinquency* 51 (3): 315–348.

Pyrooz, David C., Jillian J. Turanovic, Scott H. Decker, and Jun Wu. 2016. "Taking Stock of the Relationship between Gang Membership and Offending: A Meta-Analysis." *Criminal Justice & Behavior* 43 (3): 365–397.

Quinn, Katherine, Maria L. Pacella, Julia Dickson-Gomez, and Liesl A. Nydegger. 2017. "Childhood Adversity and the Continued Exposure to Trauma and Violence among Adolescent Gang Members." *American Journal of Community Psychology* 59 (1–2): 36–49.

Reed, Winifred L., and Scott H. Decker, eds. 2002. *Responding to Gangs: Evaluation and Research*. Washington, DC: US Department of Justice, Office of Justice Programs, National Institute of Justice.

Short, James F., and Fred L. Strodtbeck. 1965. *Group Process and Gang Delinquency*. Chicago, IL: University of Chicago Press.

Skogan, Wesley G., Susan M. Hartnett, Natalie Bump, and Jill Dubois. *Evaluation of CeaseFire-Chicago*. Washington, DC: US Department of Justice, Office of Justice Programs, National Institute of Justice. 2009. Accessed March 6, 2022. https://www.ojp.gov/pdffiles1/nij/grants/227181.pdf.

Spergel, Irving A. 1991. *Youth Gangs: Problem and Response*. Washington, DC: US Department of Justice, Office of Justice Programs, Office of Juvenile Justice and Delinquency Prevention.

Spergel, Irving A., and G. David Curry. 1993. "The National Youth Gang Survey: A Research and Development Process." In *The Gang Intervention Handbook*, edited by A. Goldstein and C. R. Huff, 359–400. Champaign, IL: Research Press.

Starbuck, David., James C. Howell, and Donna J. Lindquist. 2001. *OJJDP Juvenile Justice Bulletin. Hybrid and Other Modern Gangs*. Washington, DC: US Department of Justice, Office of Justice Programs, Office of Juvenile Justice and Delinquency Prevention.

Thornberry, Terence P., Marvin D. Krohn, Alan J. Lizotte, Carolyn A. Smith, and Kimberly Tobin. 2003. *Gangs and Delinquency in Developmental Perspective*. Cambridge, UK: Cambridge University Press.

Thornberry, Terrence P., David Huizinga, and Rolf Loeber. 2004. "The Causes and Correlates Studies: Findings and Policy Implications." *Juvenile Justice: Journal of the Office of Juvenile Justice and Delinquency Prevention* 9 (1) (September): 3–19.

Thrasher, Frederic M. 1927. *The Gang: A Study of 1,313 Gangs in Chicago*. Chicago, IL: University of Chicago Press.

US Department of Justice. 2006. "Attorney General Alberto R. Gonzales Highlights Achievements under Project Safe Neighborhoods and New Initiatives on Combatting Gang Violence." Accessed on March 5, 2022. https://www.ojp.gov/sites/g/files/xyckuh241/files/archives/pressreleases/2006/OJP06262.htm.

US Department of Justice. 2013. "U.S. Department of Justice Scientific and Research Integrity Policy." Accessed on March 5, 2022. https://www.justice.gov/sites/default/files/open/legacy/2013/07/29/doj-scientific-integrity-policy.pdf.

US Department of Justice. 2021. "Attorney General Merrick B. Garland Announces New Effort to Reduce Violent Crime." Accessed on March 6, 2022. https://www.justice.gov/opa/pr/attorney-general-merrick-b-garland-announces-new-effort-reduce-violent-crime.

White House. 2021. "Fact Sheet: More Details on the Biden-Harris Administration's Investments in Community Violence Interventions." Accessed on March 6, 2022. https://www.whitehouse.gov/briefing-room/statements-releases/2021/04/07/fact-sheet-more-details-on-the-biden-harris-administrations-investments-in-community-violence-interventions/.

Vigil, James Diego. 2020. *Multiple Marginality and Gangs: Through a Prism Darkly*. Lanham, MD: Lexington Books.

Wyrick, Phelan A. 2000. *OJJDP Fact Sheet. Vietnamese Youth Gang Involvement*. Washington, DC: US Department of Justice, Office of Justice Programs, Office of Juvenile Justice and Delinquency Prevention.

Wyrick, Phelan A. 2006. "Gang Prevention: How to Make the 'Front End' of Your Anti-Gang Effort Work." *United States Attorneys' Bulletin*, 54 (3) (May): 52–60.

Wyrick, Phelan A., and James C. Howell. 2004. "Strategic Risk-Based Responses to Youth Gangs." *Juvenile Justice* 9 (1) (September): 20–29.

CHAPTER 11

THE NATIONAL YOUTH GANG SURVEY
Past, Present, and Future

MEAGAN CAHILL, JAMES C. HOWELL, AND
ARLEN EGLEY, JR.

ONE of the key problems facing gang research and policymaking is the lack of broad statistics on gangs and their characteristics—who is in gangs, how organized are they, what crimes do they commit, and where are they located? This information is critical for decision making on what interventions are needed, where, and targeting what individuals and is used by policymakers, researchers, law enforcement, and service providers to guide their work. From 1996 to 2012, the National Youth Gang Survey (NYGS), funded by the Office of Juvenile Justice and Delinquency Prevention in the US Department of Justice, was conducted annually. However, at the time of this writing, the survey had not been fielded for a decade. Other sources of information on gang-related violence and deaths, like the Centers for Disease Control and Preventions's National Violent Death Reporting System and National Survey of Children's Exposure to Violence (NatSCEV), or self-reported youth gang involvement provided by the National Longitudinal Survey of Youth (NLSY), provide some insight into gang activity and membership. But the NYGS was the only nationwide source of estimates on the size and nature of gangs in the United States (McDaniel, Logan, and Schneiderman 2014). In that sense, the survey was invaluable.

In some ways, the survey can be considered a blunt instrument for studying gangs—one of its main uses has been to identify the number of jurisdictions with gangs, providing trends over time and space (Maxson 2011). Yet the survey results have also provided insight into the number of gang members in the United States, the types of gangs in different areas, and a sense of law enforcement's relative concern about gang violence in their jurisdictions over time. Researchers have also demonstrated its utility for studies on patterns of gang involvement in metropolitan and non-metropolitan areas (Wells and Weisheit 2001) and on racial and ethnic heterogeneity among gangs (Pyrooz, Fox, and Decker 2010), among other topics.

The NYGS is cited extensively by gang researchers—however, it is most widely cited as background to gang and policing studies to set the context for work in a specific study area and involving specific types of gangs or gang members. As such, the NYGS estimates play an important role in putting local studies in the context of larger patterns. However, as Katz et al.'s (2012) assessment of the 2005–2009 NYGS results noted, the data have rarely been used to support rigorous research (for notable exceptions, see Pyrooz 2012 and Wells and Weisheit 2001). Yet it has high potential to be used more widely, contribute valuable information to decision makers, and provide a template for state-level police data collection efforts, making more standard data on gangs even more readily available (Katz et al. 2012). The existing NYGS data (covering the 1996–2012 period) could be used to support more extensive historical research on gangs, but because it had not been fielded for a decade at the time of this writing, it is not as useful for informing current policymaking around gangs.

In 2020, the National Institute of Justice, in the US Department of Justice, committed funding to revive the NYGS. This presents a prime opportunity to review the history of the NYGS and its contributions to the field over the past two decades and to look to the future of the survey, including its ability to contribute to discussions about how gangs are defined, consider how the survey is administered, revisit what questions are included, and identify how it can best be used to support rigorous research moving forward. This chapter first presents a history of the survey, its origins and evolution over the 17 years it was fielded, and its eventual discontinuation. The chapter then reviews the survey's contributions to knowledge about gangs and to the field of gang research. Finally, plans for the revived NYGS are discussed.

History of the NYGS

Precursors of the NYGS

The development of national-scope youth gang surveys began in the mid-1970s (see Curry and Decker 2003, 17–30), with Walter Miller's (1975) pioneering major city gang surveys. Miller's initial survey was conducted in 1975 via interviews with experts in 12 large US cities and was subsequently expanded—still using interview methods—to 26 metropolitan areas (Miller 1982). The work revealed the widespread presence of gangs—contradicting media accounts that after the 1960s gangs had seemingly disappeared from the nation's landscape. Miller (1982) estimated that during the late 1970s, there were about 2,300 gangs with 98,000 members located in approximately 300 US cities and towns. He also calculated the relative proportion of police arrests in the largest gang problem cities, estimating that 42% of all arrests of male youth for serious and violent crimes and about 23% of all homicide arrests were gang members. Because of the pervasiveness and seriousness of gang crime, Miller (1976; 1990) recommended a new federal initiative to systematically gather nationwide information on youth gangs. After his seminal survey, Miller continued to compile a list of localities with gang problems and reported in the early 2000s that the number of cities experiencing youth gang problems had increased nearly tenfold between the 1970s and the late 1990s (Miller 2001).

Miller's baseline was the first national survey of youth gangs, and it would eventually prompt the federal government to survey all large cities and suburban counties and representative samples of small cities and towns and rural counties, thus yielding generalizable findings. Miller suggested that "using the data and methods of this study to obtain detailed, long-term information on gang locality numbers and trends will enable future researchers to determine with considerable precision the character and magnitude of future developments and to provide reliable answers to the critical question—'Is the gang situation getting better or worse?'" (Miller 2001, vi).

The next major gang survey was conducted in the early 1980s by Needle and Stapleton (1983). Their work also used interviews to assess law enforcement responses to youth gangs in 60 cities; 27 of them reported gang problems. The survey revealed that, in dealing with youth gangs, the majority of police departments operated without written policies and procedures and relied on personnel with no formal training in gang intervention techniques. The study's findings identified numerous opportunities to improve police responses to youth gangs. Although limited in scope, Needle and Stapleton's study established the need for law enforcement training and technical assistance in dealing with youth gangs.

Further efforts into the 1980s saw research that broadened the scope of youth gang surveys, beginning with the only national assessment of organized community agency and police efforts to combat gangs (Spergel 1995; Spergel and Curry 1993; 1990). As part of this landmark study, the authors identified 45 cities and 6 institutional sites classified as having "chronic" or "emerging" gang problems; the authors interviewed 254 respondents in those sites. Gang programs and strategies were also examined in detail in these cities. This comprehensive study is best known for the foundation it laid for the most sustained federal gang program, the Comprehensive Gang Prevention, Intervention, and Suppression framework (Spergel 1995; Spergel and Curry 1993; 1990) that a number of communities continue to implement.

Interest in macro-level data collection efforts on gangs began to gain momentum among gang researchers in the late 1980s and early 1990s. In 1992, Maxson and Klein conducted an independent survey on gang member migration (sometimes referred to as the University of Southern California study or the Maxson–Klein gang migration study) using surveys mailed to law enforcement respondents. The survey provided a proof of concept for a nationwide data collection effort on gangs (Maxson 2011). The survey asked about the history of gangs in the respondents' cities and provided solid evidence of the expansion and proliferation of gangs throughout US cities since 1960 (Klein 1995; Maxson 2011). The survey sample included all cities with a population of more than 100,000 and approximately 900 cities and towns that "serve as likely environments for street gangs or gang migration" (Maxson 1998, 5); about 1,000 cities responded to the survey. A major conclusion of the study was that "gang member migration, although widespread, should not be viewed as the major culprit in the nationwide proliferation of gangs" (Maxson 1998, 8).

A 1992 survey of law enforcement agencies (Curry, Ball, and Fox 1994) provided the first national estimates of gangs—at just under 5,000 (4,881) in the United States—and the approximate number of gang members at just under 250,000. In a comparison with prior surveys, Curry's survey showed sharp increases in the number of cities reporting gang problems, prompting researchers to conduct an extended survey in 1993 (Curry, Ball, and Decker 1996a; 1996b). This survey included the 79 largest city police departments from the 1992 survey plus all US cities ranging in population from 150,000 to 200,000, and a random sample of 284 municipalities ranging in population from 25,000 to 200,000. This survey produced conservative estimates of approximately 8,625 gangs and 378,807 gang members.

Three main gang survey developments led to federal support from the Office of Juvenile Justice and Delinquency Prevention (OJJDP) for the annual national youth gang surveys of law enforcement that are reported in this chapter. Although its recommendations were initially rejected, Miller's (1990) work later stimulated support for a sustained federal youth gang program of research, program development, and survey research. Spergel and Curry's (1993) national assessment of gang problems and responses to them increased federal interest in better understanding the problems that youth gangs presented and possible solutions. Lastly, the success of Curry's two surveys and the quality of the gang information they produced increased federal officials' confidence in the value of information on youth gangs that could be obtained in surveys of law enforcement agencies.

With growing recognition in the United States that gangs were creating problems in cities large and small, the OJJDP funded the establishment of the National Youth Gang Center (NYGC) in 1995. The center was intended to address the fact that "there was no single source of uniform data that could be used to compare changes and trends over time" (Moore 1997), and one of its main charges was to conduct a national survey to estimate the size and scope of youth gangs in the United States. A second center, the National Gang Center, was established in 2003 with a focus on law enforcement training to respond to street gang crime. In 2009, the two centers were merged into a single National Gang Center, in recognition of the fact that gang issues can span youth and adult populations and that law enforcement responses to criminal behavior from both types of gangs are needed (National Gang Center 2022b).

The NYGC conducted its first survey of law enforcement about gangs in their jurisdictions in 1995, strategically including jurisdictions from previous similar surveys, including the Maxson–Klein gang migration study and Miller's 1980 survey (Moore 1997). Ultimately, the survey was sent to more than 4,000 police and sheriff's departments and received responses from 3,440 agencies. The survey produced higher estimates of gangs and gang members than recent prior surveys had reported (Moore 1997), providing support for continued assessment of gang issues.

Starting in 1996, the NYGS was conducted to provide more consistent data across years—this is the year considered as the official start of the NYGS because it was designed to be statistically representative, unlike prior gang surveys, including the 1995 NYGS. The NYGC conducted all annual NYGSs, led by two authors of this chapter, Howell and Egley. The NYGS was the first study in any country that surveyed a nationally representative sample of respondents annually regarding the prevalence of gang activity. From 1996 to 2012, data were obtained for the NYGS from a sample of more than 2,500 local law enforcement agencies across the United States, covering rural, suburban, and urban jurisdictions.

Police records served as the primary law enforcement sources used in responding to the NYGS. While law enforcement records suffer from some limitations in estimating the number of gangs and gang members (discussed in more detail below), one of the main reasons for their use is that there are no other real data sources that are viable for creating accurate and reliable national-level estimates. Two decades before the NYGS began, Miller identified the main reason for this—which will be to the chagrin of gang researchers in the 2020s who continue to lament this fact, 40 years later:

> Probably the most significant obstacle to obtaining reliable information is the fact... that there does not exist, anywhere in the United States, one single agency which takes as a continuing

responsibility the collection of information based on explicit and uniformly applied data collection categories which would permit comparability from city to city and between different periods of time. (Miller 1975, 3).

Other early gang surveys followed suit, relying on data from law enforcement, even the ethnographer Malcolm Klein. The Maxson–Klein gang migration survey collected data from a variety of sources outside of law enforcement but ultimately decided "it would seem that law enforcement is the best available source of information on national patterns of gang migration" (Maxson 1998, 6). Still, Maxson warned readers to be aware of caveats when using such data. The creation of the NYGC addressed the issue of having a single agency responsible for collecting data on gangs, but the NYGS necessarily had to rely on data from localities—and the only source of jurisdiction-wide gang information has been law enforcement agencies. The NYGS doesn't address Miller's call for uniform data collection categories, but nonetheless provides a relatively strong basis for comparison across geographies and time.

Each survey included core questions that were asked each year. Core questions gathered information on gang presence within jurisdictions; the number of gangs and gang members; incidents of gang-related homicide; and the responding agency's assessment of whether the jurisdiction's gang problem was worsening, remaining the same, or improving.

The survey's core questions also ask law enforcement about their criteria for defining gangs. The survey is unique in part because it does not define "gang" for agencies—it allows agencies to submit data based on their own definition. According to the National Gang Center (2012), for the purpose of the survey "gangs" were defined as "a group of youths or young adults in your jurisdiction that you or other responsible persons in your agency or community are willing to identify as a 'gang.'" To rule out gangs not typically considered youth gangs, respondents were asked to exclude motorcycle gangs, prison gangs, hate or ideology groups, or adult gangs (National Gang Center 2012).

The instrument also included questions about law enforcement agencies' organizational capacity for gathering and reporting gang intelligence, and their implementation of existing programs and strategies. Recurrent (non-annual) questions focused on the demographic characteristics of gangs and gang members (gender, age, race/ethnicity); the types and amount of crime that gang members engaged in; and new and emerging trends related to gangs, gang membership, and gang crime. Throughout the original implementation of the NYGS, the average response rate was 84%—remarkable considering relatively low response rates achieved for most national-level law enforcement surveys in the 2020s (e.g., the National Incident-Based Reporting System). Many of the same agencies were continuously surveyed in that time span, allowing longitudinal analysis within and across jurisdictions and adding reliability to the findings. Annual survey data also allowed an examination of the scope and seriousness of gang activity nationwide and cross-sectional analyses of gang characteristics.

Defining Gangs

Across academia, defining gangs remains an actively debated issue. The issue's importance, however, goes beyond academia and mere knowledge accumulation. Settling on a uniform definition of a gang and gang membership has implications not only for researchers, but also for policymakers and practitioners seeking to prevent and reduce gang involvement and the attendant violence. An earlier section of this volume discusses gang definitions, so a full explication of the topic is not necessary here. However, it is worth discussing the role the NYGS plays in understanding how law enforcement identifies gangs, gang activity, and gang membership.

The NYGS contains data that help summarize the criteria used in practice by law enforcement agencies to identify gangs and can contribute to the discussion around gang definitions. In the NYGS, a group of the "greats" in gang research—Curry, Howell, Klein, Maxson, and Miller—voted on the definition of gangs that would be used in the survey: "a group of youths or young adults in your jurisdiction whose involvement in illegal activities over months or years marks them in their own view and in the view of the community and police as different from other youthful groups" (Curry 2015). Over time, the definition was refined and simplified, and by 2012 respondents were asked to consider gangs "a group of youths or young adults in your jurisdiction that you or other responsible persons in your agency or community are willing to identify as a gang" (National Gang Center 2012). From the start, the NYGS used a broad definition that allowed a great deal of latitude to police agencies to apply their own criteria in summarizing and reporting their data. An analysis of gang definitions used by respondents in the NYGS illustrates, however, a great deal of consistency across jurisdictions. NYGS respondents were asked in 2002 and 2011 what criteria they used to define or identify gangs, ranking six potential identifiers. The data were reported by four different types of agencies: larger cities, suburban counties, smaller cities, and rural counties. The identifiers, in decreasing order of importance for all agencies in the 2011 survey, were groups of youths who (1) commit crimes together, (2) have a name, (3) display common colors or symbols, (4) hang out together, (5) claim turf or territory, and (6) have a leader(s) (National Gang Center 2022a). The top two criteria were also ranked as the most important for defining gangs among respondents in larger cities, suburban counties, and rural areas. Agencies in smaller cities, however, ranked "hangs out together" as their second most important criteria (National Gang Center 2022a).

Law enforcement agencies in larger cities were slightly more likely than agencies in other types of jurisdictions to report that having a gang name was a key criterion for defining gangs. Displaying colors or symbols and claiming turf or territory were more important in cities and suburban areas, whereas having a leader and hanging together were more important in smaller cities and rural areas. Even so, these variations are extremely small; in general, law enforcement in all types of jurisdictions applied substantively similar criteria for defining youth gangs, and committing crimes together and having a name were considered virtually universal criteria (National Gang Center 2022a). The prior work to summarize gang definitions has been vital to understanding how NYGS data may differ from other sources of data on gangs and gang membership, such as the NLSY, and understanding the law enforcement perspective on youth gangs in particular.

Quality of NYGS Data

Although there were early concerns over the validity and reliability of police data for measuring the number of gangs, gang members, and gang crimes (Hagedorn 1990), research has demonstrated the capacity of law enforcement agencies to accurately reflect the degree of gang threat within their jurisdictions with the benefit of gang intelligence information (Katz, Webb, and Schaefer 2000) and police arrest records on gang members (Curry 2000). Pyrooz, Decker, and Owens (2020) examined correspondence between self-reported gang membership and prison administrative data on gangs and gang membership, finding a relatively high degree of similarity across multiple testing methods. Their work further demonstrated the legitimacy of using criminal justice administrative records for estimating gang membership.

Further, independent evaluations provided support for the quality of NYGS data across its core national estimates. In 2010, Decker and Pyrooz examined gang homicide statistics in the nation's 100 largest cities from three national data sources—Uniform Crime Reports, Supplementary Homicide Reports, and the NYGS (Decker and Pyrooz 2010, 359). The authors concluded that their "results provide strong support for the use of NYGS measures of gang homicide" as nationally representative data.

With the last NYGS being conducted over a decade ago, however, it is difficult to determine just how up to date the results from the survey currently are. In 2012, Katz and colleagues examined NYGS data from 2005–2009 on various points, including missing data analysis, test-retest reliability, internal consistency reliability, and interobserver reliability. The authors found that 30% of participating jurisdictions with populations over 200,000 had missing data (Katz et al. 2012). The analysis also found that larger cities typically reported having more gang problems than smaller cities, and that larger cities also had more missing data than smaller jurisdictions (Katz et al. 2012). A last key finding was that regions in the south and Midwest were missing more data than other regions, which implies that the size of the community and the region of the country play a part in whether an agency is likely to have missing data (Katz et al. 2012).

Their conclusions, however, suggested that the NYGS data on gangs and gang members were "fairly robust," and data on gang homicides in larger urban areas exhibited a "high degree of reliability," further recommending that they are of sufficient quality "to be used by policy makers and academics alike" (Katz et al. 2012, 121). Their results were further emphasized by Curry, Decker, and Pyrooz (2014) who concluded that "NYGS statistics are held up as the most consistent and systematic of national surveys regarding gang problems" (14).

Outside of law enforcement, no agency or organization that is commonly found in cities, towns, and counties nationwide is likely to have extensive knowledge of nearly all gangs in their jurisdiction.

Undercounting Youth Gang Members?

While researchers have largely demonstrated the validity and reliability of past NYGS datasets, one additional point is worth noting: The survey asks about youth and young adult gang members only, asking respondents to exclude "exclusively adult gangs." The survey also specifies that "juvenile" and "youth" do not mean the same thing; NYGS respondents can count young adults—those over age 18 but no older than about 24—as youth gang members. In some years, respondents were asked to estimate the number of gang members in different age ranges or to estimate the number of adult (over 18 years old) gang members in their jurisdiction, but in most years the data were simply provided on "youth and young adult" gangs and gang members with no differentiation between juveniles and adults. This approach may result in conservative estimates of *youth* gang members reported in the NYGS, because law enforcement agencies are likely to have less data, and less reliable data, on youth gang members.

Case in point: In the 2011 NYGS, 12% of responding agencies reported excluding juveniles from their gang intelligence databases (Egley and Howell 2013). From a policy perspective this makes sense—misidentifying a juvenile as a gang member in an official record could be very damaging to the youth. But unless agencies are systematically and reliably tracking their youth gang members in another way, they are likely to rely on their own estimates of youth gang members, introducing the potential for biased data.

The potential undercounting of youth gang members in law enforcement data is borne out in Pyrooz and Sweeten's (2015) study of youth gang membership, which used data from the 1997 National Longitudinal Survey of Youth (NLSY97). That survey was representative of youth born between 1980 and 1984. Since the initial survey, 14 rounds of interviews with participants have been conducted; Pyrooz and Sweeten's study is focused on the first nine rounds, the only ones in which gang questions were asked. The researchers estimated that 1,059,000 youth gang members lived in the United States in 2010, with 401,000 members joining gangs annually and 378,000 members leaving annually. Thus, the prevalence of youth gang membership is 2%—higher than most researchers previously believed (Pyrooz and Sweeten 2015). The NLSY estimate is approximately three times higher than the membership identified by the NYGS for the same time period.

Pyrooz and Sweeten (2015) suggest that undercounting youth gang members stems from law enforcement's focus on crime. Police are likely more aware of older, more violent, and more crime-involved gang members than of younger, newer members. The youngest gangs and gang members may not yet be actively involved in criminal activity. In addition, many of the criminal acts of young gang members are not yet carried out in concert and in the streets. "Commits crimes together" is ranked the most important criterion for defining gangs among national samples of law enforcement—in large cities, suburban counties, small cities, towns, villages, and in rural counties (Howell, Egley, and Gleason 2002). Among NLSY respondents, the level of self-reported gang involvement grew over time, and older respondents began to more closely resemble the levels of gang involvement reflected in law enforcement records, such as reported in the NYGS. Surveys like the NLSY also have limitations but provide a solid complement to the NYGS data and researcher efforts to identify the extent of youth gang membership in the United States.

What Has the NYGS Taught Us about Gangs in the United States?

Data from the 1995 NYGS showed that few large cities and no states were completely gang free at the time (Kapinos 1998). The data also indicate that the northeast region had smaller gangs (i.e., the most gangs with 1-9 members), while the west region had the greatest number of large gangs—those with 30 or more members (Kapinos 1998)—setting the stage for subsequent findings that region and city population both play roles in a jurisdiction's gang characteristics.

Overall, nearly one-third of cities, towns, and rural counties in the United States reported gang problems via the NYGS in 2011 (Egley and Howell 2013). The number and size of gang memberships vary directly with the population of gang problem areas. Rural counties and small cities, towns, and villages (with populations of 50,000 or fewer) typically reported three or fewer gangs with fewer than 30 total members. In the second category, larger cities (with populations greater than 50,000) typically reported about 10 gangs with about 150 total members. Cities with populations between 100,000 and 250,000 typically reported about 20 gangs and about 400 total members. Cities with populations greater than 250,000 typically reported more than 30 gangs and more than 1,000 total members (Egley 2005). Across these population groups, localities that reported a persistent gang problem also tended to have far more gangs and gang members. For example, in Egley, O'Donnell, and Howell's (2009) NYGS analysis, respondents who consistently reported gang problems from 2002 to 2008 estimated 15 gangs and 250 members. In contrast, the respondents who inconsistently reported gang problems over the same period averaged only six gangs and 74 members.

The most recent results from the 2012 NYGS showed that there were an estimated 30,700 gangs throughout 3,100 jurisdictions in the United States with gang problems (Egley, Howell, and Harris 2014). The number of gangs compared to 2011 increased, but the number of jurisdictions reporting any gangs decreased (Egley et al. 2014). In 2012, gang homicides appeared to have increased 20% from 2011, but this finding may have been due more to complete reporting in 2012 (Egley et al. 2014).

Ages of Gang Members

The ages of typical street gang members are asked in alternate years to provide information on the ages of members of all gangs in their respective jurisdictions. Law enforcement representatives said that one-third of gang members were age 18 and older in 2011 (National Gang Center 2012). However, as Howell, Moore, and Egley (2002) assert, to some extent the observed increasing proportion of adults could reflect the parallel increase in gang intelligence systems. Absent regular purging of these databases—which Barrows and Huff (2009) contend is seldom done—young gang members age in the database with the passage of time. While respondents are asked to name the sources of their data (records, estimates based on personal knowledge, or both), the survey does not capture what percentage of respondents draw specifically from a gang intelligence database, so the extent to which aging of gang members in intelligence databases is a problem is not known.

Race/Ethnicity of Gang Members

According to the 2011 NYGS, 46% of gang members nationwide were Hispanic or Latino, 35% were African-American/Black, slightly more than 12% were white, and 7% were of other races and ethnicities (National Gang Center 2022a). These figures are significantly different than the proportions of racial/ethnic groups that self-report gang membership in student surveys and law enforcement surveys (Pyrooz and Sweeten 2015). Compared to the NLSY, the largest differences are for white youth, where the NYGS indicates drastically fewer white gang members and greater numbers of Hispanic or Latino gang members and Black gang members than the NLSY (Pyrooz and Sweeten 2015). The fact that law enforcement reports far more minority gang members is cause for further investigation, especially given that racial disparities have been found in law enforcement data on other topics, like traffic stops and stop-question-frisk strategies. Discrepancies in gang data may stem from, for example, greater police presence in minority neighborhoods that makes minority youth more visible to law enforcement, or implicit biases that can lead law enforcement to more readily label minority youths as gang members or groups of minorities as gangs. Police may be less likely to draw those conclusions when assessing white youths. On the other hand, the NYGS data may accurately reflect that minority youth are more involved in gangs that are known to law enforcement. These are important considerations that a new NYGS can provide further insight into.

Gender of Gang Members

Law enforcement agencies consistently report a far greater percentage of male gang members than female gang members. A typical finding from law enforcement surveys is about 10% female membership, but this estimation is an acknowledged undercount. Two factors appear to account for most of this discrepancy. First, law enforcement officers mainly observe older gang members (girls drop out earlier than boys), and second, a smaller proportion of female gang members are actively involved in violent activity, particularly firearm possession and use. From a public safety perspective, the most important consideration is the accuracy of law enforcement classification of gang-related violence.

Use of NYGS Data

Despite evidence for the quality of the NYGS data, the survey never quite met its potential with researchers or with federal policymakers. Despite its wide citing as a source of contextual information, few examples exist of researchers conducting analyses with the dataset. An early effort to take advantage of the NYGS data was Wells and Weisheit's (2001) comparison of gangs in metropolitan and non-metropolitan areas, which analyzed 1996–1998 NYGS data. Not surprisingly, fewer non-metropolitan areas reported having gangs than did metropolitan areas. However, nearly 30% of non-metropolitan areas reported the presence of gangs, significantly more than was expected at the time. The analysis showed that a county's social and demographic characteristics were more relevant to the presence and characteristics of gangs than were economic indicators or isolation (Wells and Weisheit 2001). Further, the authors found only modest support for the notion that gangs diffuse from urban to rural areas—despite the prevailing wisdom at the time that diffusion was responsible for increasing rural gangs. The work highlighted the need to pay more attention to growing gang levels in small cities and rural areas—a trend that was assumed by experts but made explicit by the NYGS data. The Wells and Weisheit study suggested that small and rural areas faced different types of gangs and gang challenges. The findings naturally called for different approaches to gangs in those areas. The work also supported the role of social and economic factors in determining the presence or absence of gangs in an area.

The practical utility of NYGS findings was also never realized by the federal government. While there is no clear explanation as to why the NYGS data were not readily used by the federal government, the most likely answers are politics and visibility. Changing federal personnel at all levels brings changes in priorities and interests while discarding institutional knowledge about what data are available on different topics. NYGS findings could have easily been used to pinpoint cities for gang interventions and greatly reduced gang homicides by better targeting resources to locations that needed it most. An NYGS trajectory analysis clearly demonstrated that gang activity—in terms of size of gang membership and the occurrence of gang violence—remained concentrated in the most populated areas in the United States (Egley, Howell, and Major 2004; 2006; Howell and Egley 2005). A subsequent analysis focused only on jurisdictions with populations greater than 50,000 (Howell et al. 2011). The analysis identified five city trajectories related to trends in gang activity, including gang homicides. Several conclusions can be drawn from that analysis.

First, for over two-thirds of the cities with populations of 50,000 or more, prevalence rates of gang activity had remained unchanged for the prior decade and a half. By comparison, this observed consistency was rare in smaller localities (Howell and Egley 2005), where gang activity was more transitory and the associated violence less serious over time.

Second, the remaining one-third of the large cities exhibited widely varying trends. Some agencies experienced substantial declines or the complete desistence of gang activity, while others have exhibited rather extraordinary increases since the turn of the century. Second, almost eight out of ten cities with populations greater than 100,000 regularly reported gang homicides.

Third, a remarkable degree of consistency in the rate of gang-related homicides across trajectory groups was observed. None of the cities found in these trajectory groups displayed a pattern of declining gang homicides. In the two largest trajectory groups (T2 and T4), which contained 70% of all the cities, between 20% and 40% of all homicides annually were gang related.

The trajectory analysis clearly identified cities in the United States that struggled to contain and reduce their gang issues. The federal government could have targeted these cities for assistance with gang homicide prevention and reduction. While the federal government supports the collection of data on gang membership and violence over time, it has then demonstrated reluctance to use those same data to inform its own practice. To be sure, numerous factors go into federal funding and assistance decisions. However, the federal government can lead the way in demonstrating the utility of the NYGS by making more explicit and consistent use of its ready insights.

Discontinuation of the NYGS

According to National Gang Center staff and those who worked on the NYGS in 2012, the OJJDP offered no clear explanation or rationale for its discontinuation after the 2012 survey. Topics of federal interest change over time, and it appears that the appetite for gang surveys waned while interest in other topics became more pressing. Results from the last few NYGS datasets indicated that gang activity had leveled off, and gangs were no longer proliferating at concerningly fast rates. Thus, it was no longer the same pressing issue that demanded federal attention or funding as it had been in prior years. The issue with halting data collection when things improve, however, is similar to what Miller complained about in 1975: Gang activity increases and decreases in waves. If the country stops collecting data on gangs because their numbers have stabilized or are decreasing, as they were in the late 1960s, law enforcement will be caught by surprise again when another upswing starts. The lack of data continuity compromises the ability of researchers and practitioners to understand how gang activity is changing and how the profile of gangs and gang members is changing. Without this vital information, we cannot offer the best approaches to addressing gang violence.

Since the NYGS's discontinuation after the 2012 survey, however, no alternative data sources have emerged. Authors providing background on the size of the gang problem in the United States still consistently cite the 2012 NYGS results despite its age, as we lack any more up-to-date statistics on the issue (e.g., Whaling and Sharkey 2020). After it was last conducted in 2012, the best sources for researchers have been data collected from individual jurisdictions that typically study specific aspects of gangs, for example, reassessments of Boston's Operation Ceasefire on gang behavior (Braga, Hureau, and Papachristos 2014), gang involvement among justice-involved youth in multiple cities (e.g., Boxer et al. 2015; Pyrooz, Sweeten, and Piquero 2013), gang social networks in Chicago (Papachristos, Hureau, and Braga 2013); and intergang violence in Long Beach, California (Nakamura, Tita, and Krackhardt 2020).

As Howell (2019) argues, these types of single and multicity gang studies over the past two to three decades have moved public policy to better understand risk factors for joining gangs, gang member behavior and crime, and importantly how to address gang problems. He makes the argument, however, that not all cities' gang problems are the same, and one-size-fits-all solutions will not work everywhere (Howell 2019). These studies, though, typically produce small and unique datasets that are often not made publicly available. Moreover, the measures collected in these types of studies are often not generalizable, making it hard to identify comprehensive findings across many sites.

Following on that approach, a decade ago Pyrooz, Fox, and Decker (2010) decried the lack of macro-level gang research and contributed a study that used data from the 2002–2006 NYGS datasets, Census data, and Law Enforcement Management and Administrative Statistics data from the BJS to conduct a study of racial and ethnic heterogeneity and gangs. The analysis uncovered the importance of the role of social and economic variables relative to criminal justice system characteristics in explaining the existence of gangs across large cities. The work demonstrated the utility of the NYGS data and the potential uses of the data for informing policymaking. Since the findings show that social and economic variables can help explain gang membership, it may also contribute to recommendations for law enforcement to improve approaches to reducing gang problems (Pyrooz et al. 2010).

Reviving the NYGS

Limited national-level data on the current extent or characteristics of the gang problem in the United States exist, and the last NYGS was conducted in 2012—over a decade ago at the time of writing. There is a pressing need to continue quantifying the gang problem across the United States. When the National Institute of Justice (NIJ) decided to relaunch the NYGS, it was already past time to provide the country with data on gangs to support better decision making in addressing gang problems. The NIJ selected the RAND Corporation and the Police Executive Research Forum to field an updated NYGS; the new NYGS was underway at the time of writing, led by one author of this chapter, Meagan Cahill. The new NYGS aims to follow in the footsteps of the National Gang Center, which conducted extensive prior work in developing and fielding all prior waves of the survey. The most important part of the pre-survey work is getting input from current experts on gangs, including both researchers and practitioners. Just as the leading gang researchers voted on the NYGS's first definition of gangs (Curry 2005), so too will the new NYGS bring together the leaders in gang research and practice of the early 2020s. These experts will contribute knowledge about challenges such as gang definition issues, new topics that should be introduced to the survey, and how to get the most accurate data from law enforcement agencies. A successful modern NYGS will provide useful and timely information on the magnitude of youth gang activity in the United States and law enforcement's response to that activity—information that is vital for researchers, practitioners, policymakers, and others. The data will contribute practical suggestions for programmatic improvements at various jurisdictional levels to improve responses to gangs.

The review of the NYGS's history revealed that existing NYGS data have been historically underutilized, except in a few research studies. A focus of the new NYGS is to improve awareness and understanding of the data and increase its use beyond simple citations of the number of gangs and gang members in the United States. Developing a survey instrument that is both consistent enough with prior surveys to allow longitudinal comparisons over time, but that also incorporates updated perspectives on gangs and key characteristics of interest to the field is key to ensuring such expanded use of the data to support a range of research and policymaking functions that address gang issues.

Updating the NYGS Instrument

The instrumentation task is the highest priority for the new NYGS. Core questions will be maintained in the new NYGS, including standard questions about the presence or absence of gang activity, the number of gangs and gang members, the number of homicides involving gangs, and the assessment of the gang problem from the previous year—whether issues worsened or improved. As with the National Gang Center's work in developing and revising the NYGS, a variety of academic and practitioner gang experts will provide input to the new NYGS survey instrument, ensuring that the most pressing gang issues are included and that the burden of survey response is reduced to ensure that law enforcement agencies respond and fully complete the survey. Because the last NYGS was fielded in 2012, the revived survey needs to take into account the significant changes related to gang membership and gang interventions that have emerged since then. The new NYGS will include questions that assess what types of new gang-related issues police agencies may be facing, the extent of those problems, and the law enforcement response.

Revisiting Gang Definitions

The 2012 NYGS defined youth gangs for respondents as "a group of youths or young adults in your jurisdiction that you or other responsible persons in your agency or community are willing to identify or classify as a gang." Previously, users were explicitly instructed to exclude information on "motorcycle gangs, hate or ideology groups, prison gangs, or other exclusively adult gangs." While maintaining some similarity to prior surveys for comparability, the new NYGS will consider other gang definitions or incorporate more nuanced questions into the survey to provide insight on definitional issues—particularly hate or ideology groups, which have become a growing issue in many cities in the 2020s.

Earlier in this chapter we highlighted the consistency across agencies in their gang definitions. The new NYGS will provide an opportunity to investigate how those definitions have changed over time. For example, with the growth in the use of social messaging apps to sell drugs (Moyle et al. 2019), gangs are moving toward "digital street corners" for sales, potentially making street-level sales less important. In this scenario, is claiming turf still an important characteristic of gangs? Is it important to identify common colors or symbols, or are other signals more readily expressed online better for indicating membership in a group? The new NYGS will contribute to conversations on this topic and other gang-related issues that have emerged since 2012.

Also related to definitional issues is the exclusion of hate groups. The appeal of the far-right violent extremism ideology has grown over the last decade, with corresponding hate groups notably increasing their membership in recent years (Southern Poverty Law Center 2020). The online reach of the extremist groups is vast (Berger 2018). White nationalists in the United States, particularly neo-Nazis, have been far more active on Twitter than jihadist groups; between 2012 and 2016, accounts created by major white nationalists increased their followers by 600% (Berger 2016). These trends, along with the recent extremist events in the United States, such as the El Paso mass shooting in August 2019 (Andone et al. 2019), point to a far-right extremist threat as an urgent societal issue. The ties between far-right (or alt-right, or white supremacist) groups to gangs has been noted in the literature (Valasik and Reid 2022). Concerns about collecting data on these groups from law enforcement sources should be noted; because these groups are experiencing recent growth, and because they have not been included in traditional gang definitions, it is likely that law enforcement data on these groups are limited. The new NYGS is an opportunity to gather information on the spread of hate groups throughout the country. Any new questions on these types of groups will be accompanied by questions on how law enforcement have been tracking and collecting data on them.

Gang Activity as Measured by Law Enforcement

The main reason that the NYGS relies on reports from local law enforcement agencies, despite the documented issues with those numbers (see Barrows and Huff 2009), is that there is no clear alternative source for gang data that provides national coverage. One potential emerging data source may be street outreach workers, who have become increasingly professionalized with the growth of violence interruption programs. These workers could offer the breadth and depth of knowledge desired about gangs. However, interventions that employ street outreach workers are more common in larger cities than smaller ones, and the workers have little incentive to share their knowledge with a national-level survey effort. Thus, they are likely an insufficient alternative to law enforcement data. Despite the drawbacks of relying on police to identify youth gang members, then, we lack other viable sources of data. Prior NYGS data have not been without criticism for its reliance on law enforcement reports, and researchers who argue that gang databases are important also argue that such databases need significant improvement in reliability and validity (Densley and

Pyrooz 2020). Improvement is specifically needed in data collection consistency, how gangs and gang members are identified, and how individuals can be removed from the dataset.

Data collection from law enforcement agencies also creates the need to be particularly sensitive to the identification criteria or gang definitions used, because their focus is on suppression and enforcement, not prevention or early identification of gang members followed by intervention. This can contribute to undercounting of youth gang members in particular, because youth gang members tend to be less criminally involved. It is possible that some of the youth have marginal or fringe gang status (what police agencies might call "associates") and are not current core members of street gangs—or that they do not meet academic definitions of gangs but are simply a group of youths committing crimes together. But if they are involved in group-related violent activities even a few times in a short period, should they be considered gang members? More importantly, are they counted by law enforcement as gang members (Kennedy 2009)?

Another significant challenge to the new NYGS effort is assessing whether responding agencies are still collecting data on gang activity in their jurisdictions that allows them to estimate gangs and gang membership. When the NYGS ended in 2012, gang activity had seemed to stabilize; did law enforcement agencies pull back from collecting gang data at that point? Criticisms of local and state gang intelligence databases got louder in the mid-2010s and may have also contributed to a reduction in the quality and quantity of gang data collected by law enforcement since 2012 (Densley and Pyrooz 2020).

In 2016, for example, an audit of California's CalGang database identified numerous issues with oversight of the data and criteria for adding individuals to the database (California State Auditor 2016). Since then, the state has worked to revise how it governs the database and restricted how individuals are added to the database. In 2017, the Portland Police Bureau (Oregon) decided to purge gang identifications from its datasets and stop recording gang designations (Portland City Auditor 2018). A 2018 audit identified other gang-data-related issues that should be addressed by the bureau to improve its data governance and its accountability with the community. An investigation into the Chicago Police Department's gang database by the city's inspector general called the database "extensive and deeply flawed, with poor quality controls" (City of Chicago 2021). The Chicago investigation yielded criticisms similar to those leveled at the California and Portland databases. A follow-up investigation in 2021 found that the Chicago Police Department continued to rely on the flawed data despite promising to upgrade and update their system (City of Chicago 2021).

While these reforms of gang databases are needed in many cities, as Pyrooz and Densley point out "the opposite of bad data is not no data, but good data" (Pyrooz and Densley 2018). The response for the new NYGS to these significant but addressable problems will be to collect metadata on the responding agencies' records, criteria for how gangs and gang members are identified, and information on how gang data are kept, reviewed, and updated—suggestions made by Katz et al. (2012) in their assessment of NYGS reliability. This information will help to fully capture the limitations and caveats of the final dataset. Better understanding how law enforcement define, identify, and treat gangs will improve both understanding how best to use the NYGS data and the relevancy of gang research to police policy and practice.

Current Trends in Gang Membership and Gang Interventions

While a full review of trends in gang issues in the last decade is beyond the scope of this chapter, we highlight three important trends that were not covered in any prior NYGS but have emerged as topics that will be considered in the new NYGS: retaliation as a driver of gang violence, and two interventions: focused-deterrence approaches and public health interventions—both of which were well established by 2012 yet relatively limited in terms of the number of jurisdictions using the approaches and therefore not common enough to be included in the NYGS.

Drivers of Gang Violence

The National Gang Center estimates that 2,000 homicides each year are gang related—between 20% and 50% of all homicides in major US cities (Egley and Howell 2012). In 2008, over 90% of gang-related homicides involved firearms (Cooper and Smith 2011). The high rates of gang-involved firearm violence highlight the role of gangs as amplifiers of violence in the areas in which they are present. Papachristos et al. (2013) identify retaliation as one mechanism through which this amplification takes place. In neighborhoods where social norms support retaliation and violence, youth are significantly more likely to report violent delinquency (e.g., physical assault, threatening others). Reciprocity and retaliation foster violence as a means to right a perceived wrong, punish disrespect, and signal a gang's willingness to respond to threats (Papachristos et al. 2013). Mutual retaliation often causes violence that is continuously perpetuated in a vicious cycle. The 2012 NYGS instrument asked respondents to identify factors that significantly influenced gang crime in their jurisdiction; retaliation was not included. This is a key area where the new NYGS can contribute a more nuanced understanding of drivers of gang violence in different jurisdictions.

Group Violence Interventions

The group violence intervention (GVI) model, developed under the terms "pulling levers" or "focused deterrence," was first implemented in Boston in the 1990s. This well-known early implementation of the model was known as Operation Ceasefire and was designed to reduce street-based group violence and homicide (Braga et al. 2001). In the late 2010s, focused-deterrence approaches were being used extensively throughout the country to address gang and gun violence, conduct drug market interventions, and target high-risk individuals to reduce their criminality and their chances of being killed (Braga, Weisburd, and Turchan 2019; Braga and Weisburd 2012). The GVI model was well known but not extensively implemented when the original NYGS was fielded, so it was not included in any of the annual surveys. Given how widely GVI approaches are now used, the new NYGS will incorporate questions to determine how many agencies are using this type of approach to address gangs, how it is being implemented, and how well they feel it has worked to reduce gang violence. Moreover, agencies implementing focused deterrence will necessarily have collected the most information on the most violent groups and their members, potentially skewing their reporting toward older and more criminally involved individuals.

The Public Health Model

The public health model, also called the Cure Violence model, of street outreach was initially implemented in Chicago (Slutkin, Ransford, and Decker 2015) as Operation CeaseFire. Cure Violence builds on the idea of retaliation as a driver of gun violence, aiming to stop the spread of violence to individuals and communities by interrupting it. The model also stops it among those who have already been "infected" or participated in the violence. Violence interrupters (VIs) play the role of mediators. Most VIs are often ex-gang members, with networks and contacts within local gang(s) (Skogan et al. 2008). This approach has been incorporated into a number of gang responses across the United States, including in Los Angeles' Gang Reduction and Youth Development initiative (Cahill et al. 2015).

As with GVI approaches, Cure Violence was also well known but largely limited to implementation in Chicago while the original NYGS was being fielded. The new NYGS will also incorporate questions on Cure Violence to address the extent of its use and perspectives on its effectiveness to address gang issues. Because Cure Violence approaches are especially aimed at retaliatory violence, questions about this approach in the new NYGS will complement questions about new drivers of gang violence, like retaliation.

Discussion

There is widespread consensus among law enforcement officers, citizens, and researchers that the presence of gangs in the community is associated with the heightened commission of crimes, particularly violent crimes. In addition to the offending behavior during gang involvement, negative long-term life consequences can continue long after individuals leave the gang. The original NYGS offered important information to policymakers, researchers, practitioners, but it did not realize its full potential and was cited mainly as context or background information for studies of individual cities. Notably, the federal government did not use the NYGS to help it target assistance to those jurisdictions struggling the most with gang activity. The practice community, which includes law enforcement agencies and gang intervention organizations among others, is an important target audience for the NYGS and one that has also not historically called upon the NYGS for guidance on how to best address gang issues.

Updating the NYGS instrument to reflect changes in the field since it was last fielded a decade ago is an important change. An updated NYGS can provide the field with a current understanding of risk factors for joining gangs, gang member behavior, and importantly how to address gang problems. Even more important is increasing the extent to which the NYGS is used for policymaking, informing practice, and rigorous research. The new NYGS will be widely disseminated to ensure broad awareness of the resource. Once the first round of the new NYGS dataset is available, providing example analyses and guides on how to properly use the data, including how to employ weights and interpret the data and what types of analyses and conclusions the data can and cannot support will go a long way to increasing its use. This type of high-quality macro-level dataset can provide new insights into gangs across the United States and advance policymaking and interventions to reduce the influence of gangs.

References

Andone, D., E. Levenson, N. Chavez, and A. Vera. 2019. "The El Paso Shooter Faces the Death Penalty in a 'Domestic Terrorism' Case." *CNN*, August 4.

Barrows, Julie, and C. Ronald Huff. 2009. "Gangs and Public Policy: Constructing and Deconstructing Gang Databases." *Criminology & Public Policy* 8 (4): 675–703.

Berger, J. M. 2016. *Nazis vs. ISIS on Twitter: A Comparative Study of White Nationalist and ISIS Online Social Media Networks*. Washington, DC: George Washington University Program on Extremism.

Berger, J. M. 2018. "The Alt-Right Twitter Census: Defining and Describing the Audience for Alt-Right Content on Twitter." VOX-Pol Network of Excellence, October 15.

Boxer, Paul, Bonita Veysey, Michael Ostermann, and Joanna Kubik. 2015. "Measuring Gang Involvement in a Justice-Referred Sample of Youth in Treatment." *Youth Violence and Juvenile Justice* 13 (1): 41–59.

Braga, Anthony A., David M. Hureau, and Andrew V. Papachristos. 2014. "Deterring Gang-Involved Gun Violence: Measuring the Impact of Boston's Operation Ceasefire on Street Gang Behavior." *Journal of Quantitative Criminology* 30 (1): 113–139.

Braga, Anthony A., David M. Kennedy, Elin J. Waring, and Anne Morrison Piehl. 2001. "Problem-Oriented Policing, Deterrence, and Youth Violence: An Evaluation of Boston's Operation Ceasefire." *Journal of Research in Crime and Delinquency* 38 (3): 195–225.

Braga, Anthony A., and David L. Weisburd. 2012. "The Effects of Focused Deterrence Strategies on Crime: A Systematic Review and Meta-Analysis of the Empirical Evidence." *Journal of Research in Crime and Delinquency* 49 (3): 323–358.

Braga, Anthony A., David Weisburd, and Brandon Turchan. 2019. "Focused Deterrence Strategies Effects on Crime: A Systematic Review." *Campbell Systematic Reviews* 15 (3): e1051.

Cahill, Meagan, Jesse Jannetta, Emily Tiry, Samantha Lowry, Miriam Becker-Cohen, Ellen Paddock, Maria Serakos, Loraine Park, and Karen Hennigan. 2015. "Evaluation of the Los Angeles Gang Reduction and Youth Development Program." Washington, DC: Urban Institute. https://www.urban.org/sites/default/files/publication/77956/2000622-Evaluation-of-the-Los-Angeles-Gang-Reduction-and-Youth-Development-Program-Year-4-Evaluation-Report.pdf.

California State Auditor. 2016. "The CalGang Criminal Intelligence System." https://www.auditor.ca.gov/pdfs/reports/2015-130.pdf.

City of Chicago. 2021. "Follow-Up Inquiry on the Chicago Police Department's 'Gang Database.'" City of Chicago Office of Inspector General. https://igchicago.org/wp-content/uploads/2021/03/OIG-Follow-Up-Inquiry-on-the-Chicago-Police-Departments-Gang-Database.pdf.

Cooper, A., and E. Smith. 2011. "Homicide Trends in the United States, 1980–2008." https://www.bjs.gov/index.cfm?ty=pbdetail&iid=2221.

Curry, G. David. 2000. "Self-Reported Gang Involvement and Officially Recorded Delinquency." *Criminology* 38 (4): 1253–1274.

Curry, G. David. 2015. "The Logic of Defining Gangs Revisited." In *The Handbook of Gangs*, edited by Scott H. Decker and David Pyrooz, 28–58. Chichester, UK: John Wiley & Sons.

Curry, G. David, Richard A. Ball, and Scott H. Decker. 1996a. "Estimating the National Scope of Gang Crime from Law Enforcement Data." In *Gangs in America*, edited by C. Ronald Huff, 21–36. Thousand Oaks, CA: Sage.

Curry, G. David, Richard A. Ball, and Scott H. Decker. 1996b. "Update on Gang Crime and Law Enforcement Recordkeeping: Report of the 1994 NIJ Extended National Assessment Survey of Law Enforcement Anti-Gang Information Resources." Washington, DC: US Department of Justice.

Curry, G. David, Richard A. Ball, and Robert J. Fox. 1994. "Gang Crime and Law Enforcement Recordkeeping." Washington, DC: US Department of Justice, National Institute of Justice.

Curry, G. David, and Scott H. Decker. 2003. *Confronting Gangs: Crime and Community*. 2nd ed. Los Angeles, CA: Roxbury.

Curry, G. David, Scott Decker, and David Pyrooz. 2014. *Confronting Gangs: Crime and Community*. 3rd ed. New York: Oxford University Press.

Decker, Scott, and David Pyrooz. 2010. "On the Validity and Reliability of Gang Homicide: A Comparison of Disparate Sources." *Homicide Studies* 14 (4): 359–376.

Densley, James, and David Pyrooz. 2020. "The Matrix in Context: Taking Stock of Police Gang Databases in London and Beyond." *Youth Justice* 20 (1–2): 11–30.

Egley, Arlen. 2005. "Highlights of the 2002–2003 National Youth Gang Surveys." Washington, DC: Office of Juvenile Justice and Delinquency Prevention.

Egley, Arlen, and James C. Howell. 2012. "Highlights of the 2010 National Youth Gang Survey." Washington, DC: Office of Juvenile Justice and Delinquency Prevention. www.nationalgangcenter.gov/Survey-Analysis/.

Egley, Arlen, and James C. Howell. 2013. "Highlights of the 2011 National Youth Gang Survey." Washington, DC: Office of Juvenile Justice and Delinquency Prevention.

Egley, Arlen, James C. Howell, and Meena Harris. 2014. "Highlights of the 2012 National Youth Gang Survey." Washington, DC: Office of Juvenile Justice and Delinquency Prevention. https://ojjdp.ojp.gov/sites/g/files/xyckuh176/files/pubs/248025.pdf.

Egley, Arlen, James C. Howell, and Aline Major. 2004. "Recent Patterns of Gang Problems in the United States: Results from the 1996–2002 National Youth Gang Survey." In *American Youth Gangs at the Millennium*, edited by F.-A. Esbensen, S. G. Tibbetts, and L. Gaines, 90–108. Long Grove, IL: Waveland Press.

Egley, Arlen, James C. Howell, and Aline Major. 2006. "National Youth Gang Survey 1999–2001." Washington, DC: Office of Juvenile Justice and Delinquency Prevention.

Egley, Arlen, C. E. O'Donnell, and James C. Howell. 2009. "Over a Decade of National Youth Gang Survey Research: What Have We Learned?" In *Annual Meeting of American Society of Criminology*. Philadelphia, PA.

Hagedorn, John. 1990. "Back in the Field Again: Gang Research in the Nineties." In *Gangs in America*, edited by C. Ronald Huff, 240–259. Thousand Oaks, CA: Sage.

Howell, James C. 2019. "Youth Gangs: Nationwide Impacts of Research on Public Policy." *American Journal of Criminal Justice* 44 (4): 628–644.

Howell, James C., and Arlen Egley. 2005. "Gangs in Small Towns and Rural Counties." *NYGC Bulletin* 1: 1–6. https://www.ncjrs.gov/App/Publications/abstract.aspx?ID=235196.

Howell, James C., Arlen Egley, and D. K. Gleason. 2002. "Modern Day Youth Gangs." *Juvenile Justice Bulletin, Youth Gang Series*, 2002.

Howell, James C., Arlen Egley, George Tita, and Elizabeth Griffiths. 2011. "U.S. Gang Problem Trends and Seriousness,1996–2009." *National Gang Center Bulletin* 6 (May): 1–23.

Howell, James C., John P. Moore, and Arlen Egley. 2002. "The Changing Boundaries of Youth Gangs." In *Gangs in America*, 3rd ed., edited by C. Ronald Huff, 3–18. Thousand Oaks, CA: Sage.

Kapinos, T. S. 1998. "Youth Gang Survey: Violence on the Rise?" *Alternatives to Incarceration* 4 (1): viii–xi.

Katz, Charles M., Andrew M. Fox, Chester L. Britt, and Phillip Stevenson. 2012. "Understanding Police Gang Data at the Aggregate Level: An Examination of the Reliability of National Youth Gang Survey Data." *Justice Research and Policy* 14 (2): 103–128.

Katz, Charles M., Vincent J. Webb, and David R. Schaefer. 2000. "The Validity of Police Gang Intelligence Lists: Examining Differences in Delinquency between Documented Gang Members and Nondocumented Delinquent Youth." *Police Quarterly* 3 (4): 413–437.

Kennedy, David M. 2009. "Policy Essay: Gangs and Public Policy: Constructing and Deconstructing Gang Databases." *Criminology & Public Policy* 8 (4): 711–716.

Klein, Malcolm W. 1995. *The American Street Gang: Its Nature, Prevalence, and Control.* New York: Oxford University Press.

Maxson, Cheryl. 1998. "Gang Members on the Move. Juvenile Justice Bulletin, Youth Gang Series." Washington, DC: US Department of Justice, Office of Juvenile Justice and Delinquency Prevention.

Maxson, Cheryl. 2011. "Street Gangs." In *Crime and Public Policy*, edited by James Q. Wilson and Joan Petersilia, 158–182. New York: Oxford University Press.

McDaniel, Dawn D., J. E. Logan, and Janet U. Schneiderman. 2014. "Supporting Gang Violence Prevention Efforts: A Public Health Approach for Nurses." *Online Journal of Issues in Nursing* 19 (1): 1–16.

Miller, Walter B. 1975. "Violence by Youth Gangs and Youth Groups as a Crime Problem in Major American Cities." Washington, DC: US Department of Justice, Office of Juvenile Justice and Delinquency Prevention.

Miller, Walter B. 1976. "New Federal Initiatives Re: Serious Collective Youth Crime." Hearings before the Subcommittee to Investigate Juvenile Delinquency of the Committee on the Judiciary. United States Senate, 95th Congress, 2nd Session.

Miller, Walter B. 1982. "Crime by Youth Gangs and Groups in the United States." Washington, DC: US Department of Justice, Office of Juvenile Justice and Delinquency Prevention.

Miller, Walter B. 1990. "Why the United States Has Failed to Solve Its Youth Gang Problem." In *Gangs in America*, edited by C. Ronald Huff, 263–287. Newbury Park, CA: Sage.

Miller, Walter B. 2001. "The Growth of Youth Gang Problems in the United States: 1970–1998." Washington, DC: US Department of Justice, Office of Juvenile Justice and Delinquency Prevention.

Moore, John P. 1997. "Highlights of the 1995 National Youth Gang Survey." Washington, DC: U.S. Department of Justice, Office of Juvenile Justice and Delinquency Prevention.

Moyle, Leah, Andrew Childs, Ross Coomber, and Monica J. Barratt. 2019. "#Drugsforsale: An Exploration of the Use of Social Media and Encrypted Messaging Apps to Supply and Access Drugs." *International Journal of Drug Policy* 63 (January): 101–110.

Nakamura, Kiminori, George Tita, and David Krackhardt. 2020. "Violence in the 'Balance': A Structural Analysis of How Rivals, Allies, and Third-Parties Shape Inter-Gang Violence." *Global Crime* 21 (1): 3–27.

National Gang Center. 2012. "National Youth Gang Survey Analysis." https://nationalgangcenter.ojp.gov/survey-analysis.

National Gang Center. 2022a. "National Youth Gang Survey Analysis." Accessed February 15. http://www.nationalgangcenter.gov/Survey-Analysis.

National Gang Center. 2022b. "History of the National Gang Center." Accessed August 23. https://nationalgangcenter.ojp.gov/#history-of-the-national-gang-center.

Needle, Jerome, and William Vaughn Stapleton. 1983. "Police Handling of Youth Gangs." Washington, DC: Office of Juvenile Justice and Delinquency Prevention.

Papachristos, Andrew V., David M. Hureau, and Anthony A. Braga. 2013. "The Corner and the Crew: The Influence of Geography and Social Networks on Gang Violence." *American Sociological Review* 78 (3): 417–447.

Portland City Auditor. 2018. "Gang Crime Investigations: Lack of Accountability and Transparency Reduced the Community's Trust in Police." Portland City Auditor, Audit Services Division. https://www.portlandoregon.gov/auditservices/article/677594.

Pyrooz, David. 2012. "Structural Covariates of Gang Homicide in Large U.S. Cities." *Journal of Research in Crime and Delinquency* 49 (4): 489–518.

Pyrooz, David, Scott Decker, and Emily Owens. 2020. "Do Prison Administrative and Survey Data Sources Tell the Same Story? A Multitrait, Multimethod Examination with Application to Gangs." *Crime & Delinquency* 66 (5): 627–662. https://journals.sagepub.com/doi/abs/10.1177/0011128719879017.

Pyrooz, David, and James Densley. 2018. "Is Gang Activity on the Rise? A Movement to Abolish Gang Databases Makes It Hard to Tell." *The Conversation*, July 5. https://theconversation.com/is-gang-activity-on-the-rise-a-movement-to-abolish-gang-databases-makes-it-hard-to-tell-99252.

Pyrooz, David, Andrew Fox, and Scott Decker. 2010. "Racial and Ethnic Heterogeneity, Economic Disadvantage, and Gangs: A Macro-Level Study of Gang Membership in Urban America." *Justice Quarterly* 27 (6): 867–892.

Pyrooz, David, and Gary Sweeten. 2015. "Gang Membership between Ages 5 and 17 Years in the United States." *Journal of Adolescent Health* 56 (4): 414–419.

Pyrooz, David, Gary Sweeten, and Alex Piquero. 2013. "Continuity and Change in Gang Membership and Gang Embeddedness." *Journal of Research in Crime and Delinquency* 50 (2): 239–271.

Skogan, W. G., S. M. Hartnett, N. Bump, and J. Dubois. 2008. *Evaluation of CeaseFire-Chicago*. Chicago, IL: Northwestern University.

Slutkin, Gary, Charles Ransford, and R. Brent Decker. 2015. "Cure Violence: Treating Violence as a Contagious Disease." In *Envisioning Criminology*, edited by Michael D. Rice and Stephen K. Maltz, 43–56. Cham: Springer.

Southern Poverty Law Center. 2020. "The Year in Hate and Extremism: 2019." https://www.splcenter.org/sites/default/files/yih_2020_final.pdf.

Spergel, Irving A. 1995. *The Youth Gang Problem*. New York: Oxford University Press.

Spergel, Irving A., and G. David Curry. 1990. "Strategies and Perceived Agency Effectiveness in Dealing with the Youth Gang Problem." In *Gangs in America*, edited by C. Ronald Huff, 288–309. Newbury Park, CA: Sage.

Spergel, Irving A., and G. David Curry. 1993. "The National Youth Gang Survey: A Research and Development Process." In *The Gang Intervention Handbook*, edited by Arnold Goldstein and C. Ronald Huff, 359–400. Champaign, IL: Research Press.

Valasik, Matthew, and Shannon E. Reid. 2022. "Alt-Right Gangs and White Power Youth Groups." Oxford Bibliographies Online: Criminology. Accessed August 5, 2023. https://www.oxfordbibliographies.com/display/document/obo-9780195396607/obo-9780195396607-0243.xml.

Wells, L. Edward, and Ralph A. Weisheit. 2001. "Gang Problems in Nonmetropolitan Areas: A Longitudinal Assessment." *Justice Quarterly* 18 (4): 792–823.

Whaling, K. M., and J. Sharkey. 2020. "Differences in Prevalence Rates of Hopelessness and Suicidal Ideation Among Adolescents by Gang Membership and Latinx Identity." *Child and Adolescent Social Work Journal*. 37 (5): 557–569.

CHAPTER 12

HISTORICAL GANG RESEARCH METHODS
An Overview

MITCHEL P. ROTH

THIS chapter offers various ways researchers can use historical data to supplement whatever types of research strategies they employ. What follows is an explanation of what constitutes historical research and where this documentation can be found. Readers will better understand the differences between primary and secondary research sources and how to access these sources. The value and deficiencies of important source material found in newspapers and oral interviews are explained, as are comparative research methodologies. Examples are offered to chronicle the evolution of historical research from the works of Thrasher and Asbury beginning in the 1920s to the present, warts and all.

As early as 1967, the sociologist Dale G. Hardman observed that most social scientists "would agree that there seems to be no 'best' theory or research method." He recognized over a half century ago that completely leaving "certain research methodologies out of scholarship can ... discredit certain findings" (Hardman 1967, 5). It is not so easy to describe the historical research process. However, when historians elucidate how they conduct their research it usually hinges on several steps, beginning, of course, with selecting a subject and then looking at secondary sources, conducting what social scientists refer to as a literature review. This will also involve collecting source material and primary data (Witkowski and Jones 2007, 148).

Historical resources comprise either primary or secondary data. Secondary sources include literature written after the period being studied, "such as books and articles written at a later date" (Belk 2007, 148). Primary data should be understood as information and evidence compiled during the actual historical period being studied. Primary resources come in a variety of incarnations, not all of them textual. These resources can include images and artifacts from the period. However, written primary resources in the historical process are most common. These can include looking through public records, including legal documents, governmental records, and other institutional records. In addition, period articles, letters in newspapers, magazines, and scholarly journals can sometimes be regarded as primary sources (Belk 2007, 148).

Like all sources, as we shall see with oral history and newspapers, some of the aforementioned have their limitations. Often antiquated written materials can be hard to read and are at times ambiguous. These "should never be taken at face value" (Belk 2007, 148). Primary resources, like other sources, have their limitations, and the researcher needs to be on "guard against overgeneralization from written sources and be alert for possible biases, even hard demographic data can be untrustworthy . . . social statistics are no more absolute facts than newspaper reports, private letter or published biographies—all represent either from individual standpoints or aggregated, the social perception of facts" (Belk 2007, 148).

What Is Historical Research?

Sociologists, criminologists, and other social scientists have dominated modern gang research for decades. Their research methodologies have been the gold standard for academic research, considered more or less "scientific" compared to methods used by historians. Testing specific hypotheses runs counter to historical research methods, which some social scientist regard as "less scientific" and hence inapplicable to the research process. Or as one campus committee member once wrote on my application for a research grant, "this might be history, but it is not research." There has been a longstanding bias against historical research in the social sciences to the point where it is almost heretical to employ this type of research in many criminal justice and criminology graduate programs. It was not always this way.

Rather than testing hypotheses, the historical researcher usually is guided by "broad open-ended questions in lieu of hypotheses" (Bayens and Roberson, 2010, 165) in which there are no easy answers. By relegating historical methods and data to the sidelines, "we often have no other window into the past." Indeed, if we "reject historical data for broad explorations of this issue, we are cutting off an important source of information" for better understanding gangs at all levels (Ferdinand 1984, 10–11).

Historical research involves the use of historical narratives and data to analyze and develop conclusions regarding the latent meaning of past events. The historical method of research applies to all fields of study, and both quantitative and qualitative variables can be used in the collection of historical information. Historical research generally focuses not only on events that have occurred but why they occurred. History allows us to understand the values, experiences, and social forces that have shaped our culture and institutions. Historical research depends on data that have been observed and reported by others.

The historian assembles their notes and sources like any other scholarly researcher, working toward an understanding of the topic at hand—a process that has been reduced to a truly "scientific" methodology. These data often include documents and original manuscripts that are the raw data of historical research.

There are a variety of places to obtain historical information. Primary firsthand accounts are the most sought after documents/data. These can include archival records, government documents, diaries, and oral histories. Often the only way to find this information is through literally hundreds of hours of looking through fading, often illegible manuscripts. And then of course there is the bane of all researchers—microfilm and microfiche.

Secondary sources include newspapers, documents, records, first-person accounts, and other materials prepared by someone other than those who participated in the original events. Secondary research materials vastly outnumber primary resources, and they vary widely—for example, some either lack notes or bibliographies (Haskins 1974). There are countless articles and books, many in narrative form. This should not exclude them from being considered as historical sources. There are many excellent scholarly and journalistic histories of gangs covering countries from Asia to the United States (Galeotti 2018; English 2009; Stephenson 2015; Grann 2004).

While the quality of secondary materials varies widely, it is worth looking at compilation books, such as historical readers or encyclopedias. For example, the historian Wiley B. Sanders spent decades gathering documents related to juvenile delinquency to write *Juvenile Offenders for a Thousand Years: Selected Readings from Anglo-Saxon Times to 1900* (1970). He scoured special collections in England and the United States looking for "data on juvenile delinquency" that had been "long forgotten," including material on teenage gangs in 1791 Philadelphia (Sanders 1970, 325). Likewise, trying to pin down the origins of the Gypsy Jokers of Washington state prison fame, one recent encyclopedia traces its origins to San Francisco in 1956 before opening chapters in the Pacific Northwest (Hayes 2011, 93).

Historical Research on Gangs

Historians have identified gang behavior in most parts of the world for hundreds of years. Of course, definitional disputes still flare up when identifying "gang" behavior, but this is beyond the scope of this chapter. One criminologist observed that the conflict of the Montagues and Capulets in Shakespeare's 1597 work *Romeo and Juliet* (see also *West Side Story*) could be interpreted as a version of the gang experience (Fraser 2017). Others suggest that the criminal activities of outlaws in the American west and elsewhere would also meet some of the criteria used to identify gangs today (Fraser 2017, 46).

One source that typically appears in books and articles on the birth of historical gang research is the work of Fredric Milton Thrasher. Originally published in 1927 as *The Gang: A Study of 1,313 Gangs in Chicago*, this work was an outgrowth of his dissertation. According to gang researcher George W. Knox, no known copies of it exist. Knox asserted in 2000 that this book was "the one single book that started the field of 'gangology'" (Thrasher 2000).

Sixty years ago Lewis Yablonsky noted the ubiquity of Thrasher's work in academic circles. In 1962 he perused 10 of the most widely used current college textbooks on criminology and found that Thrasher's work was "the basis for its discussion of gangs" (Yablonsky 1962, 121). Thrasher remains the foundation for modern historical research on gangs.

However, from a historical perspective, Thrasher's survey of gangs was "too comprehensive," including too many variations of gang subcultures. Moreover, there are many questions about his research methods that remain unanswered. Besides lacking analysis, "we do not even know how he collected his material, how he chose his informants, or how representative they were" (Bennett 1987, 161). Nonetheless, James F. Short has suggested that "the nature of the gang, in terms of etiology and typology, ongoing process, and behavioral consequences still is unfinished business, but in Thrasher a significant beginning was made" (Bennett 1987, 160–161). Following on the heels of Thrasher, the work of Herbert Asbury, beginning in 1927, can be found in any historical discussion of early American gangs. Open any textbook on gangs and readers can be guaranteed to find historical "research" featuring journalistic works by Herbert Asbury. Beginning with *The Gangs of New York: An Informal History of the Underworld* (1927) and carrying through to *The French Quarter: An Informal History of the New Orleans Underworld* (1936) and *Gem of the Prairie: An Informal History of the Chicago Underworld* (1940), Asbury evoked the earliest gangs in American history with great narrative skills. These books are a joy to read but come up short as historical sources on gangs, mainly because there are no footnotes or attributions. Each of his books offers bibliographies and claim to have used files of various magazines and newspapers, police and court records, and reports from crime commissions. These are supplemented with interviews with contemporary police officers and politicians. Unfortunately, it is a fool's errand to find most of the sources cited by Asbury. Through no fault of his, historical researchers will often find that newspapers, police and court records, and related sources have either been thrown away or destroyed. In many cases they have been tossed away like detritus, to make room for computers and more storage. As a result, historians have often been more dependent on written reminiscences and memoirs.

Doing History Using a Comparative Approach

The criminologist Alistair Fraser has found that a comparative historical approach can be used to observe how gangs change over time, arguing for the importance of "understanding gangs in both a historical and comparative context" (Fraser 2017, 62, 63). He uses this approach to compare youth gangs in four cities (Glasgow, Chicago, Hong Kong, and Shanghai), using what he describes as micro and macro levels of gang histories in each city. He asserts he does this "to emphasize the large scale diversities in meanings associated with such groups across diverse contexts (Fraser, 2017, p. 63)." The historian Clive Emsley, likewise, suggests that it is the "historian's craft" to "examine a topic over a period of time of much greater length than other researchers so as to assess the content of change over time" (Emsley 2007, 122).

Another example of using the comparative method can be found in the work of Sanchez-Jankowski, who used three American cities with long histories of gang activity and diverse ethnic groups—Boston, Los Angeles, and New York (1991, p. 6). Similarly, Tapia uses oral histories and newspaper archives to compare the closely linked cities of El Paso and Juarez. This allows him to make a "broad overview" of the history of the century-old Chicano gang experience in the United States (Tapia 2019).

This author used a comparative approach to study the development of prison gangs around the world (Roth 2020). This book, *Power on the Inside: A Global History of Prison Gangs*, was probably the first to examine the prison gang phenomenon throughout the world from a historical perspective. What was most startling to this researcher was the fact that prison gang subcultures developed in a variety of incarnations on every continent except for Antarctica. Most previous historical research on prison gangs was based on the "thesis of American exceptionalism" (Roth 2020, 10). However, several researchers have convincingly suggested that this notion "rests more on ignorance of possible comparisons than on a comprehensive examination of comparable phenomena elsewhere" (Hazlehurst and Hazlehurst 1998, 7).

Sources for Historical Research on Gangs

Perhaps the lack of historical research methods reflects preferred modern criminal justice and criminology research methodologies, which all but relegate historical sources to the sidelines. However, today's graduate students and academics would be surprised to learn that it wasn't that long ago that major criminology and criminal justice journals were open to scholarship based on historical research. But it seems that the very terms "history" and "historical research" have become anathema to editors of leading journals, who expect quantitative and qualitative methods. Moreover, it is deemed almost heretical to pursue anything but statistical research in criminal justice and criminology graduate programs. As far back as 1984, the Swiss criminologist Martin Killias noted that before 1970 there was an "absence of any serious interest in historical data among continental criminologists" and "traditional European criminology . . . had no real use of historical and/or comparative research" (Killias 1984).

The word "data" can be best understood as information, evidence, statistics, and facts. However, ask most graduate students (and many faculty) in the social sciences what "data" consists of and in most cases they will construe data and data collection in terms of statistics or numbers. This is perhaps half right, but according to most definitions of the word "data," the term should refer to "facts and statistics collected for reference or analysis." The point being made here is that both facts and non-statistical information are as invaluable to the research process as statistical evidence.

Sources for historical gang research come in numerous forms, including newspaper archives, police records, public and classified intelligence reports from local and federal agencies, the federal government's Freedom of Information Act (FOIA), insights and information from other works, and interviews (Tapia 2019, 5).

Newspaper Archives

As the author Luc Sante (Lucy Sante since 2021) researched her seminal work, *Low Life* (1992b) she kept an eye out for "flavor and incident, anecdote and eyewitness." As she explored aging microfilms and crumbling newspapers she reached an epiphany on such sources, commenting that she "did not suspect that nineteenth century journalism could be so wanting in concrete details of time, place, circumstance, and visual appearance." Moreover, "the vagueness of much newspaper writing, especially in the police-blotter category, makes the average gazette of the 1800s read like a succession of blind items" (Sante 1992b, 363). Sante applied her now skeptical eye to the iconic Herbert Asbury book, *Gangs of New York* (1927). She found that many of Asbury's assertions were derived from the *Police Gazette* of the day. Nonetheless, Sante found the book "a compelling if somewhat ragtag of a book, cobbled from legend, memory, police records, the self-aggrandizement of aging crooks, popular journalism, and solid historical research" (Sante 1992a, 363).

There are a number of stories and historical topics that could not be written without the use of newspapers (Asbury 2003). Quite often, historical newspaper stories offer much greater details than modern-day papers and can lead to other sources as well (Duran

2018; Diamond 2018). However, there are inherent problems in their usage. Researchers relying on newspapers will often be faced with "sloppy journalism" and the "problem of sensationalism" (Asbury 2003). If a researcher, for example, just uses headlines to direct their investigation, gang nomenclature can lead to missteps. For example, if one was researching newspaper archives online one might find the headline "8 Ex-Convicts Hunted in Kidnapping of Boy" (*Brooklyn Times Union*, April 6, 1928). One sentence suggests that the hunted convicts "were members of a prison gang." However, further reading indicates they were not part of a "prison gang" in the conventional sense, but in the parlance of the day, they were working as a crew or "gang" under the direction of a supervisor at Folsom Prison. Thus, in many accounts prior to the 1950s, the term "prison gang" was used as shorthand for prisoner work crews. So this would misrepresent the notion of a traditional prison gang. Newspapers should not be the end all or be all of research. But they can function as a starting point or a source for further verification when other records are unavailable or suspect.

No matter which country or time period, newspaper researchers should be cognizant of the changing nomenclature over time. For example, anyone studying the gangs of Great Britain between 1870 and 1900 would find that gang members in Manchester were known as "scuttlers," in Liverpool as "cornermen," "sloggers" in Birmingham (later on as "peaky blinders"), and so forth. Material from newspapers have informed the research on gangs in Great Britain, especially in the Victorian era (Gooderson 2010, 11; Davies 2014).

One barrier to using newspaper sources is that not all are digitized or available. The United States has abundant newspaper resources online for researchers, including www.newspaperarchive.com. Great Britain offers a newspaper site for a variety of nineteenth-century papers (www.britishnewspaperarchive.co.uk). These can be valuable for looking for first mentions of gangs in England. For example, on January 22, 1850, the *Morning Chronicle* published an oral history indicating there were juvenile gangs in this era. The description would be familiar to anyone investigating gangs today. One interviewee in this article describes casual gangs "in large bodies of twenty or thirty, with sticks hidden down the legs of their trousers, and with these they rob and beat those who do not belong to their gang. The gang will often consist of 100 lads, all under twenty, one fourth of whom regularly come together in a body" (Bennett 1987, 57).

Without historical research methods, scholars and students alike are left with an understanding of gang-related research that is often inaccurate or just downright wrong. One of the best examples can be found in the historian Humbert S. Nelli's tome *The Business of Crime* (Nelli 1981). Until its publication, the notion that some type of bloody Castellamarese War between the old-world Sicilian godfathers led to the Americanization and formation of modern Italian-American crime families. Even today there are books that parrot this theory. Nelli observed that "successful and self-perpetuating institutions, both private and public, develop a history [such as criminal gangs], often laced with fiction, of how they became great and important" (179). This is especially true in the consideration of "America's crime syndicates."

As the old saw goes, on September 10–11, 1931, the younger generation of street hoodlums led by Charles "Lucky" Luciano overthrew the "Mustache Petes," or old school dons. On this day Luciano ordered the assassination of Salvatore Maranzano and the elimination of his allies and friends all over the country. Within a time frame of perhaps two days, September 10 and 11, this plot went down with breathtaking efficiency. Depending on who was chronicling this event, the number of victims ranged widely, usually in the dozens (Turkus and Feder 1951, 73; Cressey 1969, 43; Talese 1971, 192).

For future scholars, none of these claims were ever verified. In the *Valachi Papers* (Maas 1986) and many other books, readers are treated to the fact that "on the day Maranzano died, some forty Cosa Nostra leaders allied with him were slain across the country" (111). Nelli and others have verified that "available evidence indicates that not ninety, or forty, or twenty, or even five murders were carried out across the U.S. in conjunction with, or as a consequence of, Maranzano's death" (Nelli 1981, 182). Nelli's findings would not have been possible without his historical research methods using newspapers as a major source.

Nelli's research method could be used by other researchers seeking to pin down similar claims about the historical origins of other American organized crime groups and gangs. In this case, he painstakingly perused all of the New York City newspapers for this period. He only came up with three murders on September 10 that might have been linked to the purported purge of the old-world bosses (Nelli 1981, 183). Naturally, there were gangs in other major cities at this time connected to the machinations of the New York City gangsters. Nelli went a step further with his research by making a further examination of newspapers issued during September, October, and November 1931 in 12 cities.[1] He came up with only one murder that "might have been linked" to this purported carnage and the murder of Maranzano (Nelli 183). Ultimately, Nelli put to rest the notion that a bloodbath occurred in the New York City area at the time of Maranzano's murder. Nelli concluded that "the facts do not support" the theory of a "nationwide purge" (Nelli 1981, 182).

Newspapers have played an important role in the search for America's first prison gang. The long-held belief that the Gypsy Jokers, in 1950, were the first has been an accepted fiction by gang researchers since 1985. Much of the research on gangs stems from a west coast–centric approach that was heavily reliant on information coming out of California and Washington State. Newspaper research debunks the belief that the Gypsy Jokers were the first prison gang, created in 1950 in Washington State (Camp and Camp 1985). What is probably most troubling from a research perspective is that there has been virtually no discussion over this unsubstantiated "fact." Since 1985, the Washington State saga has become the starting point for criminologists, sociologists, penologists, and others studying prison gangs. Looking at the sources used by gang researchers, particularly those that write textbooks, it is clear that historians had not chimed in on this claim. Perhaps it is the lack of historical research methodologies that has allowed this questionable claim to stand for almost 40 years.

However, a study of prison history suggests that the east coast, with its many prisons and diverse inmate populations in the years before 1950, might hold the answer. There are numerous examples of gang culture imported into prisons in the 1930s. For example, the *New York Times* featured an article on February 21, 1936, titled "'Big Shot' Gambling Charged in Prison," which suggested that "moneyed prisoners had controlled the institution in the 1910–1935 period."

Newspaper search engines available on the internet are valuable tools for researching, or at least looking for the country's first prison gang. There is enough evidence in the *New York Times* alone to support the fact that there were prison gangs active in New York in the late 1920s and early 1930s, long before the phenomenon was identified on the west coast (see, for example, *New York Times*, January 25, 1934).

Oral History

Not all historians are of one mind when it comes to using oral history as a research source. In fact, some have dismissed it as "little more than the collection of sentimental memories from old people. Clearly some interviewee remarks are self-serving to always get the better of opponents" (Ritchie 1995, 92). Oral historians often encounter informant nostalgia; they "remember the past as better than it was lived and thus [the interviewer] needs to press for more candid and critical responses" (Witkowski and Jones 2007, 72).

However, oral history has become a well-established research tool for gang researchers over the past several decades. "Oral history interviews" are a form of primary data, usually assembled "years after events occurred" (Witkowski and Jones 2007, 72). Of course, with such a time lapse, it would lead the researcher to question the veracity of certain memories. This goes for the past and the present. Sanchez-Jankowski points to the lack of nineteenth-century oral history related to western outlaw gangs, due to an absence of cooperation and accessibility. He recognized that "outlaws had little reason to cooperate with researchers," and considering the "lifestyles" of western outlaws it was "too dangerous a field to study" (Sanchez-Jankowski 1991, 2).

Early historical research on gangs was based on oral history. Some scholars credit the Victorian English journalist Henry Mayhew (1812–1887) with inventing the term "oral history" a century before the term was coined (Bennett 1987, 11). Others trace its introduction into the lexicon to 1863 and into public usage in the 1930s (Bennett 1987, 283). The sociologist James Bennett claims that Mayhew was one of the earliest and most "successful exponents of the technique of collecting first hand material by direct interviews and observations." Indeed, the noted Chicago oral historian Studs Turkel said that if he had "a model, it's Mayhew" (Bennett 1987, 11).

In an era before the existence of technology to record the words of the interviewee, the recording of oral history was at the mercy of the interviewer. Few criminally inclined gang members have left their voices for future researchers. Henry Mayhew is considered "a pioneer" in the study of criminal offenders and "should give us a running start for understanding oral histories of delinquents" (Bennett 1987, 16). Sadly, his nineteenth-century oral histories can only take the modern researcher so far, since he leaves out specific commentary related to "juvenile gangs" (Bennett 1987, 57).

In the 1990s gang researchers increasingly turned to field research. Scott Decker and Barrik Van Winkle let "a single premise" guide their research, deciding that "the best information about gangs and gang activity would come from gang members contacted directly in the field" (Decker and Van Winkle 1996, 27). Indeed, using field work to study gangs, beginning with Thrasher in 1927, is "one of the oldest traditions in criminology" (Decker and Van Winkle 1996).

More recently, gang researchers such as Mike Tapia have used the oral interviews of El Paso residents stored in library special collections. These offer valuable historical and sociological details "about barrio life in bygone eras" (Tapia 2019, 5). Tapia's valuable research on the gangs of the southwest borderlands has been informed by both interviews and newspaper accounts, as well as police records, public and classified intelligence, and insights from other researchers.

There are a number of memoirs and reminiscences written by former inmates and gang members chronicling historical periods of various prison gangs in wide-ranging settings, including South Africa, New Zealand, Thailand, and elsewhere (Dlamini 1984; Newbold 1982; Isaac and Haami 2007). One of these authors has gone on to a scholarly career as a criminologist. These works are excellent supplements to traditional historical research sources.

Dictionaries

One of the best ways to start research on a specific gang-related topic is to peruse a variety of dictionaries. The first use of a particular term will sometimes free it from its murky origins and put the researcher on the chronological path to enlightenment. For example, the apparent earliest use of the term "gang" dates back, according to the *Oxford English Dictionary*, to perhaps the tenth century. It meant an "action or mode of going or moving" or "action or an act of traveling." Over time it would refer to a "collective movement such as a band of travelers or company of workmen," in other words a "collective noun for a group of men" used as a verb "to go" (Fraser 2017, 47). Similarly, the origins of the Yakuza, Japan's best-known gangsters, have long been a subject of debate. More often than not, they have been traced back to the 1600s and the samurai. However, modern historians assert it is more likely that they emerged sometime toward the end of the 1700s, and like the origins of the word "gang" above, the Yakuza seem to be the product of a traveling tradition, in this case *traveling* peddlers, or *tekiya* (Hill 2003).

When it comes to researching the argot and culture of Russian prison gangs, one of the most important sources is a dictionary of the Russian prison camps (Baldaev, n.d.). Dictionaries can challenge or debunk long-held assumptions. Perhaps the best example is the origin of the word "mafia." Long shrouded in its mythic origins in the 700-year-old tale of the Sicilian Vespers, the term "mafia" cannot be found in an Italian dictionary until the 1860s, leading one to discount the notion that it was used centuries earlier, although its concepts regarding honor and respect were already hardwired in western Sicilian culture much earlier (Fentress 2000). These are just a few examples of how consulting dictionaries for word origins can play a role in historical research through the use of secondary sources.

John Hagedorn is a believer in historical research. In his coverage of the transformation of the Vice Lords, he was able to throw light on where the name comes from. The gang actually started out as a group of friends who took the name "vice lords." However, it's almost counterintuitive how this name evolved. Home to the Chicago Outfit since Prohibition, it controlled much of the city's criminal enterprises and were said to be "the lords of all vice." In "the midst of the civil rights movement, rising levels of black pride and the growing influence of black people in Chicago, gang leaders decided to change course" (Hagedorn 2008, 136).

Other Sources

As noted earlier in this chapter, some of the best early history regarding gangs can be found in the journalistic accounts of Herbert Asbury. Journalists have chronicled the history of most major cities. These can be valuable tools for researchers. For example, in their examination of the early gangs of St. Louis, two criminologists (Decker and Van Winkle 1996) found helpful material in the book *A Tour of St. Louis: Or, the Inside Life of a Great City*, written by the journalists Joseph A. Dacus and James W. Buel (1878).

This author emphasizes the importance of searching stacks at libraries, since they are organized by subject matter. Students and researchers are encouraged to open each book in the section on gangs and organized crime and review its footnotes, the index, and bibliographic sources. A burgeoning scholar can quickly separate the wheat from the chaff. If a book does not contain any notes on sources, the student would be wasting their time by looking any further in the book. But it is worthwhile to scan stacks at your campus library. While on the subject of libraries, one would be remiss not to investigate what kind of primary sources it might contain in its archives or special collections, including unpublished manuscripts and archival material.

In his quest to chronicle the gangs of the world, John Hagedorn attests to the importance of historical research, writing "the scholar in me has found a way to make use of some rusty academic tools and I have become something of a historian" (Hagedorn 2008, 120). While he does devote a chapter to historical research, which very few books on gangs do, he doesn't quite explain why he thinks he became "something of a historian." Nonetheless, his work on the early Vice Lords gang in Chicago is eye opening. He not only made use of newspapers and books, but also used the *1922 Race Relations Report*, which details gangs and their activities during the seminal 1919 race riots. As mentioned earlier, by using sources such as government documents a researcher can get a clearer impression and different vantage point on how a gang undergoes transformation over time.

Hagedorn observed that "his Chicago students were unaware of the accomplishments of the Conservative Vice Lords (CVL)" in the Lawndale area. His historical research exemplified the fact that gangs do not develop in a vacuum, as he traced the emergence of the more criminally inclined Vice Lords of today to what he describes as "prosocial organizations" and a "social athletic club" in the 1960s. This allows Hagedorn to make an important observation: "that a future other than drugs, violence and the streets is possible and in *their own hands*" (Hagedorn 2008, 136).

Conclusion

The cultural historian Mike Davis has voiced his displeasure at the absence of historical research in gang studies. In his foreword to John Hagedorn's *A World of Gangs* (2008), he challenges social scientists to cast a wider net in their research strategies, writing somewhat hyperbolically that gangs "are as ancient as the hills of Rome and as American as the spoils system (if not apple pie) . . . Yet it has been the smug mission of modern American criminology and allied social science fields to reduce complex realities and largely unexplored histories to simplistic pathologies" (Hagedorn 2008, xii). This is a bold statement but has a ring of truth to it. The lack of historical research has led to countless dissertations, books, and articles pushing the notion that gangs are of recent vintage, when history is mentioned at all. Yet any historian worth their salt would peruse each of these publications looking for historical sources in the bibliography before vouching for its academic reliability. Chances are all they would find would be the works of Herbert Asbury and Frederic Milton Thrasher. As a longtime professor of criminology, this author has found a startling quantity of ahistorical information in many of these works, when there are any historical mentions at all. This chapter does not discount the great and important work by modern gang researchers but argues for a more inclusive research strategy when appropriate, one that would include less conventional sources of information—oral history, newspapers, memoirs, dictionaries, archival materials, and so forth. The field of gang studies can only benefit from this outreach.

Note

1. These were Boston, Philadelphia, Pittsburgh, Baltimore, New Orleans, Cleveland, Detroit, Chicago, Kansas City, Denver, Los Angeles, and San Francisco.

References

Asbury, Herbert. 1927. *The Gangs of New York*. New York: Alfred Knopf.
Asbury, Herbert. 1936. *The French Quarter: An Informal History of the New Orleans Underworld*. Garden City, NY: Garden City Publishing.
Asbury, Herbert. 1940. *The Gangs of Chicago: An Informal History of the Chicago Underworld*. New York: Alfred Knopf.
Asbury, Herbert. 2003. *The Gangs of Chicago: An Informal History of the Chicago Underworld*. London: Arrow Books. Originally titled *Gem of the Prairie: An Informal History of the Chicago Underworld* in 1940 by Knopf. Garden City Publishing.
Baldaev, Dantsik Sergeyevic. n.d. "Dictionary: Prison Camp, *Blatnoi*." In *Speech and Graphic Portraits of Soviet Prison*, translated by Vladimir Kuz'mich Belko and Igor Mikhailovich Isupov.
Bayens, Gerald, and Cliff Roberson. 2010. *Criminal Justice Research Methods: Theory and Practice*. Boca Raton, FL: CRC Press.
Bennett, James. 1987. *Oral History and Delinquency: The Rhetoric of Criminology*. Chicago, IL: University of Chicago Press.
Camp, G. M., and G. C. Camp. 1985. *Prison Gangs: Their Extent, Nature, and Impact on Prisons*. South Salem, NY: Criminal Justice Institute.
Cressey, Donald R. 1969. *Theft of a Nation: The Structure and Operations of Organized Crime in America*. New York: Harper and Row.
Dacus, J. A., and James W. Buel. 1878. *A Tour of St. Louis: Or, the Inside Life of a Great City*. St. Louis: Western Publishing Company.
Davies, Andrew. 2014. *City of Gangs: Glasgow and the Rise of the British Gangster*. London: Hodder and Stoughton.
Decker, Scott H., and Barrik Van Winkle. 1996. *Life in the Gang: Family, Friends, and Violence*. Cambridge, UK: Cambridge University Press.
Diamond, Andrew J. 2018. *Mean Streets: Chicago Youths and the Everyday Struggle for Empowerment in the Multiracial City, 1908–1969*. Vol. 27. Berkeley: University of California Press.
Dlamini, Moses. 1984. *Hell-hole, Robben Island*. Nottingham, UK: Spokesman Books.

Duran, Robert J. 2018. *The Gang Paradox: Inequalities and Miracles on the US-Mexico Border.* New York: Columbia University Press.

Emsley, Clive. 2007. "Historical Perspectives on Crime." In *Handbook of Criminology*, edited by M. Maguire, R. Morgan, and R. Reiner, 4th ed., 122–138. Oxford: Oxford University Press. Cited in Fraser, p. 49.

English, T. J. 2009. *Born to Kill: The Rise and Fall of America's Bloodiest Asian Gang.* New York: William Morrow.

Ferdinand, Theodore N. 1984. "Some Problems of Interpretation in Historical Studies." Unpublished paper, October 7. Northeastern University.

Fraser, Alistair. 2017. *Gangs & Crime: Critical Alternatives.* Los Angeles, CA: Sage.

Galeotti, Mark. 2018. *The Vory: Super Mafia.* New Haven, CT: Yale University Press.

Gooderson, Philip. 2010. *The Gangs of Birmingham: From the Sloggers to the Peaky Blinders.* Preston, UK: Milo Books.

Grann, David. 2004. "The Brand: How the Aryan Brotherhood Became the Most Murderous Prison Gang in America." *New Yorker*, February 16: 157–171.

Hagedorn, John M. 2008. *A World of Gangs: Armed Young Men and Gangsta Culture.* Minneapolis: University of Minnesota Press.

Hardman, D. G. 1967. "Historical Perspectives of Gang Research." *Journal of Research in Crime and Delinquency* 4 (1): 5–27.

Haskins, James. 1974. *Street Gangs: Yesterday and Today.* New York: Hastings House.

Hayes, Bill. 2011. *The One Percenter Encyclopedia: The World of Outlaw Motorcycle Clubs from Abyss Ghosts to Zombie Zombies Elite.* Minneapolis, MN: Motorbooks.

Hazlehurst, Kayleen, and Cameron Hazlehurst. 1998. *Gangs and Youth Subcultures: International Explorations.* Piscataway, NJ: Transaction Publishers.

Hill, Peter. 2003. *The Japanese Mafia: Yakuza, Law, and the State.* Oxford, UK: Oxford University Press.

Isaac, Tuhoe, and Bradford Haami. 2007. *True Red: The Life of an Ex-Mongrel Mob Gang Leader.* Self-published.

Killias, Martin. 1984. "On the Use of History in Criminal Justice: Historical or Historicistic Criminology." Unpublished paper presented at the ASC Annual Conference, November 8. Cincinnati, Ohio.

Maas, Peter. 1986. *The Valachi Papers.* New York: Pocket Books.

Nelli, Humbert S. 1981. *The Business of Crime: Italians and Syndicate Crime in the United States.* Chicago, IL: University of Chicago Press.

Newbold, Greg. 1982. *The Big Huey: An Inmate's Candid Account of Five Years inside New Zealand's Prisons.* New York: Harper Collins.

Ritchie, Donald A. 1995. *Doing Oral History.* New York: Twayne Publishing.

Roth, Mitchel P. 2020. *Power on the Inside: A Global History of Prison Gangs.* London: Reaktion Books.

Sanchez-Jankowski, Martin. 1991. *Islands in the Street: Gangs and American Urban Society,* Berkeley: University of California Press.

Sanders, Wiley B., ed. 1970. *Juvenile Offenders for a Thousand Years: Selected Readings from Anglo-Saxon Times to 1900.* Chapel Hill: University of North Carolina Press.

Sante, Luc. 1992a. *Evidence.* New York: Farrar, Straus and Giroux.

Sante, Luc. 1992b. *Low Life: Lures and Snares of Old New York.* New York: Vintage Books.

Stephenson, Svetlana. 2015. *Gangs of Russia: From the Streets to the Corridors of Power.* Ithaca, NY: Cornell University Press.

Talese, Gay. 1971. *Honor Thy Father*. New York: Fawcett World Library.

Tapia, M. 2019. *Gangs of the El Paso-Juarez Borderland: A History*. Albuquerque: University of New Mexico Press.

Thrasher, Frederic M. (1927) 2000. *The Gang: A Study of 1,313 Gangs in Chicago*. Chicago, IL: University of Chicago Press. Reprint, Chicago IL: New Chicago School Press.

Turkus, Burton B., and Sid Feder. 1951. *Murder, Inc.: The Story of 'The Syndicate.'* New York: Farrar, Strauss and Young.

Witkowski, Terence H., and D. G. Brian Jones. 2007. "Qualitative Historical Research in Marketing." In *Handbook of Qualitative Research Methods in Marketing*, edited by Russell W. Belk. Cheltenham, UK: Edward Elgar.

Yablonsky, Lewis. 1962. *The Violent Gang*. New York: Macmillan.

CHAPTER 13

CRITICAL APPROACHES TO GANGS

TILMAN SCHWARZE AND ALISTAIR FRASER

IN recent years, critical approaches to gangs have developed increasing momentum. A loose, evolving movement of scholars working in the traditions of urban ethnography, critical criminology, and cultural criminology, this emerging field approaches the gang phenomenon as an arena of social, cultural, and political contestation, intimately bound up with questions of power and inequality (Brotherton 2015; Fraser 2017; Brotherton and Gude 2021; Brotherton and Kontos 2003). In doing so, this research "seeks to move beyond a narrow focus on gangs and crime towards recognition of the multiple forms that gangs can take, their change over time, and incorporate both the harmful and supportive roles that gang identification can play in both individual lives and community context" (Fraser 2017, 17).

This chapter discusses innovations to the study of gangs introduced by critical scholars drawing on examples across geographical spaces from both the Global North and South. The first section provides a brief history of critical approaches to gang research. In the second, we focus on the role of politics in studying the gang phenomenon. Critical gang scholars view gangs as the product of specific historical contexts that are shaped by socioeconomic, cultural, and political currents over time (Brotherton 2015; Aspholm 2020). For these scholars, locating gangs within the context of global inequality (Smith 2010; Venkatesh and Kassimir 2007), racial injustice, and community development are crucial for understanding how gangs emerge and exist (Hagedorn 1998, 2006; Moore 1991; Mendoza-Denton 2008).

Finally, this chapter discusses how critical approaches to gangs have scrutinized racialized representations of gangs and how particularly young people of color are often mislabeled as "gang members." Here, we focus on the criminalizing effects of these labeling practices and the racism that underpins media and policy discourses on the gang phenomenon. We conclude by pointing to some limitations of current critical approaches and how these might be addressed in the future.

CRITICAL APPROACHES TO GANGS: A BRIEF HISTORY

In this section, we briefly sketch out some historical trajectories important to the development of critical approaches to the study of gangs.

The history of gang research is often located within the sphere of the Chicago School of Sociology, specifically Frederic Thrasher's pathbreaking text *The Gang* (1927). But the approach to urban scholarship that has evolved into critical gang studies perhaps shares more of a genealogical connection with the social critiques of Jane Addams, who was ostracized by the Chicago School (Deegan 1988; Hayward 2016), or W.E.B. DuBois and his detailed urban ethnography of racialized poverty in Philadelphia (Morris 2017). While Thrasher's study demonstrated a marked openness to diverse forms of gang association, its pages held neither a theoretical account of the political, economic, or structural causes of gang identification nor an activist manifesto for resistance or reform—central components of critical gang research.

Though the 1950s and 1960s saw a marked sociological attentiveness to youthful deviance (Cohen 1955; Matza 1964), Coughlin and Venkatesh (2003) argue that this period also saw stronger links develop between sociology and social policy research, which resulted in a criminalizing approach to gangs: "The inner-city, minority youth gang . . . the principal empirical object, and the gang was viewed primarily as a social problem" (42). Social policy research shifted the focus toward the violent and delinquent aspects of gangs where gangs were primarily perceived as a social problem "riddled with deficits" (Brotherton 2015, 39) and as a "social threat that requires intervention from enforcement and judicial institutions" (Coughlin and Venkatesh 2003, 53).

Instead of viewing gangs as a social problem, critical approaches to gangs tend to follow constructivist traditions in critical criminology that interrogate the powerful interests implicated in practices of labeling and criminalization (Box 1983; Taylor, Walton, and Young 1983), or lineages drawn by cultural criminologists with the Birmingham Centre for Contemporary Cultural Studies (Hall et al. 1978). Critical approaches do not try to dismiss the fact that gangs are involved in violence and harm, but seek to situate this within the context of the systemic violence that is invariably behind it. Gangs, as John Hagedorn (2008) notes, are "alienated youth socialized by the street or the prison, not conventional institutions."

Rather than a "continual reproduction of stereotypical, cardboard-type, folk images" of gangs (Wacquant 1997, 348), critical gang scholars have demonstrated the significance of gangs as a site of belonging, surrogate family, and collective identity (Padilla 1992; DiChiara and Chabot 2003; Venkatesh and Levitt 2000; Venkatesh 2003; Garot 2010; Conquergood 1994a; Jankowski 1991; McDonald 2003; see also Murer and Schwarze 2020). Critical approaches to gangs, therefore, argue for a more empathic and appreciative way of looking at the gang phenomenon (Brotherton 2015) where gang researchers are open to the heterogeneity, complexity, and fluidity of gang identities and dynamics (Hazen and Rodgers 2014) while bracketing these experiences from their external construction (Hall et al. 1978).

Methodologically, critical approaches tend to prioritize interpretivist methodologies designed to capture and decipher the complexities, subjectivities, and fluidities of gang dynamics, identities, and performances to arrive, following Max Weber, at better levels of *verstehen* of the gang phenomenon (Brotherton 2008; Fraser 2017). Drawing from traditions of urban ethnography, critical gang studies seek to generate thick descriptions of gangs' lived everyday experiences, often through situated ethnographic research that is attentive to localized and different patterns, dynamics, histories, and structures of geographical spaces.

By shifting focus from the empiricist methodologies that often characterize criminological research on deviance and social control (Young 2011), critical gang research argues against the tendency to study gangs within a self-referential framework. The result of this "gang talk" (Katz and Jackson-Jacobs 2004) is that gang research remains in a closed loop of research production that reproduces the hegemonic (Gramsci 1971) conceptualizations of gangs as deviant and delinquent, while "wider complexities of life in multiple deprived areas are overlooked" (Hallsworth and Young 2008, 186). In response, critical gang studies urge gang researchers to show openness toward interdisciplinary approaches to the study of gangs and to draw on sociological, anthropological, geographical, and cultural scholarship in deciphering the interconnectedness of gangs, space, culture, and the political economy across spaces in the Global South and Global North (Hazen and Rodgers 2014; Hagedorn 2008).

For example, Mendoza-Denton's (2008) work draws on linguistics in deciphering the role of language in the formation of gang identities. For her, "language becomes the loudspeaker through which emergent political consciousness can be broadcast" (105), with the use of specific language and pronunciations of words determining local belongingness to different gangs. Dennis Rodgers' (2017) anthropological work on gangs in Nicaragua embeds the evolution of gangs within specific national, political, and historical circumstances, namely the shifting politics and local drug markets of a post-conflict society.

These studies suggest that the gang phenomenon needs to be understood from local and context-specific circumstances (Fraser and Hagedorn 2016; Hagedorn 2009) and that research on gangs needs to embrace other perspectives and research approaches outside the hegemonic Western frameworks that continue to dominate large parts of criminological research (Franko Aas 2012). In this respect, critical gang scholars have argued in favor of scrutinizing the legacy of colonialism in thinking about the gang phenomenon (Brotherton 2015; Winton 2014). Fraser, Laidler, and Leung (2021), for example, detail how the evolution of Hong Kong's triad gangs has been influenced by the colonial legacy of British territorial and political administration and how triad gangs have developed into political actors involved in Hong Kong's local politics at various points in time in the history of the city. Engagements with colonialism's role in shaping gang dynamics foreground how critical gang studies are more open toward global perspectives that challenge the hegemony of US and European-based research, building on and embracing southern theory in understanding the gang phenomenon outside of the Global North (Carrington, Hogg, and Sozzo 2016).

Because of its interdisciplinary research approach, critical gang studies encourage theoretical and methodological innovation and engagement outside the field of criminology. Critical gang studies are open to collaborative and co-productive methods where participants are positioned as having expert knowledge. Here, the researcher listens and learns from gang members as experts in the production of knowledge, rather than imposing predefined and prejudicial assumptions about life in a gang. Such interdisciplinarity in theory and methods allows for a radical openness to alternative framings of gangs.

For example, Conquergood's (1994a, 1994b, 1997) ethnographic work on gangs in Chicago is inspired by performance theory and has foregrounded how gang identities are created through bodily and cultural performances in urban spaces through, for example, graffiti or the dress codes of gang members. Openness toward other theories and research traditions allowed Conquergood "to see gangs as social and cultural agents who function both as subjects and as objects in their own theater of operations as well as in the gaze of the researcher" (Afary and Brotherton 2021, 675). Critical approaches to gangs, therefore, urge criminologists to embrace theories outside criminology to find innovative ways of studying the gang phenomenon and to avoid a predetermined criminological framework.

Feminist perspectives in criminology and gang research have similarly criticized the narrowness of studying gangs purely through the lens of crime, deviance, and social control, arguing in favor of research that recognizes the methodological and theoretical complexities of gender (Miller 2001; Batchelor 2009; Hagedorn 1998). For example, discussions of sexuality are becoming increasingly integrated into gang research (Panfil 2014), making connections between queer criminology and gang research. In line with recent developments within critical gang studies to understand the effects of globalization on gang dynamics (Fraser and Van Hellemont 2020; Winton 2014; Hagedorn 2007; Van Hellemont and Densley 2019), feminist approaches to gangs have focused on global, comparative, and transnational approaches, exploring local, national, and international differences in the relationship between gangs and gender (see **Chapter 14**).

David Brotherton, for example, has comparatively studied the glocalized politics of young women involved in the Almighty Latin King and Queen Nation (ALKQN) in New York, Quito, and Barcelona (Brotherton and Salazar-Atias 2003; Brotherton 2007; Brotherton and Barrios 2004). His research foregrounds how gang identification was mobilized to "symbolically subvert and/or invert their marginalized sociocultural status" (Brotherton and Salazar-Atias 2003, 186), with young women in particular "looking for excitement, opportunity, responsibility, and status" (188). He concludes that:

> the ALKQN functioned for these women as the only grassroots movement that was sufficiently indigenous that it could be trusted by the most marginalized of urban females; could or would address their multiple needs at critical junctures in their life course; and offered the opportunities for emotional, spiritual, social, and political growth that few other organizations have dared to imagine. (Brotherton and Salazar-Atias 2003 205–206)

Another focus of feminist perspectives in critical gang studies has been the complex relationship between gangs and masculinities (Mullins 2007; see **Chapter 19**). Feminist approaches have urged criminological research to not assume that men's experiences constitute the entirety of the empirical foundation of gangs. Instead, they point to the complex relationship between the performative nature of masculinity within gangs and its relationship to broader structures of class, gender, and patriarchy (Baird 2011).

In this respect, critical feminist approaches have emphasized the intersections that exist between gangs and masculinities and how gang identification also comprises a form of compensatory masculinity. Bourgois (1995), for example, shows in his ethnographic study of street-level crack cocaine dealing in New York that structural obstacles to traditional "breadwinner" models of masculinity are important in the creation of a violent street masculinity, which serves as a form of symbolic compensation. Similarly, Connell (2005) argues that "youth gang violence of inner-city streets is a striking example of the assertion of marginalized masculinities against other men, continuous with the assertion of masculinity in sexual violence against women" (83). For Maher (1997), however, accounts of street culture that stress this compensatory function are problematic insofar as they fail to adequately recognize the complexities and consequences of masculine street culture for young women.

Thus, critical gang studies argue for a renewed critical engagement with the methodological and theoretical frameworks that allow gangs to be interpreted within their specific sociospatial environments (see **Chapter 8**) while being attentive to the power structures shaping society and urban social spaces under neoliberal capitalism, globalization (Hagedorn 2007), and the destructive forces of sexism and racism. The following section discusses these power dynamics and the role of politics and political economy for gang research in more detail.

Gangs and Politics

Thrasher (1927) famously defined the gang as "an interstitial group originally formed spontaneously and then integrated through conflict.... The result of this collective behavior is the development of tradition, unreflective internal structure, esprit de corps, solidarity, morale, group awareness, and attachment to a local territory" (46). With its focus on understanding ecological and community-specific sociocultural forces and how gangs can be found in areas that are "interstitial" within the social ecology of the city, Thrasher's work managed to avoid "fixation[s] with violence, alcohol, drugs or various realms of deviance" (Brotherton 2015, 30) in defining gangs. In the tradition of Thrasher's humanistic definition of the gang and his focus on the social ecology of cities, critical approaches have studied the inherent connectivity between gangs and their sociospatial environments (Fraser 2015; Sánchez-Jankowski 2008; Venkatesh 2008; Hagedorn 1998; Vigil 1988; Moore 1978).

Building on the tradition of the Chicago School to study gangs via ethnographic research in situ of their urban environment, scholars have advanced gang research by also studying the structures and processes of multiple deprivations, marginalities, and inequalities (Fraser 2015; Hagedorn and Rauch 2007; Vigil 2002), racism (Hagedorn 2006), state strategies of social control and punishment (Rios 2011; Wolf 2017; Jütersonke, Muggah, and Rodgers 2009), and the forces of a neoliberal and capitalist global economy (Fraser and Van Hellemont 2020; Hagedorn 2005, 2007; Winton 2014). For these scholars, the gang phenomenon cannot be detached from broader socioeconomic and political forces, which shape power dynamics in society and the social production of urban space. As stated by Fraser (2015), "too often, gangs are understood and explained at the level of the individual, with structural and cultural factors relegated" (38). Since gangs are "inherently urban in nature" (Jones and Rodgers 2015, 214), political and economic processes shaping city development need to be scrutinized by gang researchers as well.

In the context of post-industrial and rustbelt cities in the United States and the United Kingdom, "capitalism has transformed the opportunity structures in poor neighborhoods where gangs have always been found. Many of the generic-labor jobs—factory work which requires little skill or education—have moved away from inner cities" (Hagedorn 2001, 43). Approaches to gangs building on these traditions seek to excavate the role of urban development in the stratification of urban space, specifically the ways that housing policy and urban exclusion confine and contain deprived, marginalized, and racially segregated members of society (Sassen 1991, 2007; Wacquant 2008; Moore 1978). By scrutinizing how uneven geographical development (Smith 2010), processes of deterritorialization and reterritorialization (Brenner 1999; Swyngedouw 2004), and state-led interventions such as public housing transformation (Aspholm 2020; Venkatesh 2000) influence gangs, critical gang studies foreground the role of politics and urban exclusion.

The significance of geography and politics to the study of gangs is particularly highlighted by Zilberg (2011). In contrast to the political pronouncements of former President Trump on so-called "migrant gangs" at the border, Zilberg notes that US deportation policies have resulted in the spread of gang identities from Los Angeles to Central American countries where gangs have adopted cultural codes and affiliations from Los Angeles gangs (Levenson 2013; Brotherton and Barrios 2011). These deportations have resulted in a transnational migration flow where localized gang identities spread across countries and where, in the context of migration, gangs have become "suitable targets for externalization" (Volkan 2009, 8) and scapegoats "onto which popular fears can be projected" (Fraser and Van Hellemont 2020, 9). Writing on Mara gangs in Guatemala City, Levenson (2013) argues that gang violence is the result of historical currents of political violence, war, and trauma that have shaped Guatemalan society for decades. Thus, for Levenson:

> the notion that the gangs and their violence are apolitical . . . is a misleading conceptualization. While it is descriptively accurate that neither the Maras nor their violence falls within the realm of what one sociologist defines as political violence, . . . the Maras have come out of a political crucible, and politicians have found political uses for them that range from no doubt paying them to disrupt rallies for rival candidates to using images of them to garner support for right-wing candidates. The politically generated depoliticization of youth is in itself a historical watershed that has changed Guatemalan urban politics. (Levenson 2013, 8)

Another example of the role of politics in shaping gang dynamics is offered by Aspholm (2020) in his study of how Black gangs on Chicago's South Side have transformed from highly structured and hierarchical organizations into more loosely organized cliques with no clear leadership. Aspholm argues that, among other things, the transformation of public housing in Chicago, which started in the early 2000s by demolishing most of the city's large public housing "projects," has resulted in urban migration processes where gangs formerly organized around public housing units were displaced to other neighborhood, which, in turn, fundamentally altered established gang dynamics and structures (Schwarze forthcoming; Hagedorn 1998). Jensen (2008, 2014) similarly explores the role of urban transformation in his study of how gangs in Cape Town, South Africa, emerged as a result of their forced relocation from their home neighborhoods in central Cape Town to the Cape Flats, an area of townships established during the apartheid era. Jensen shows how gangs not only emerged as a response to these urbanization processes but also how they have become tools for the government to justify and allow certain state interventions (e.g., the war on drugs) in those communities associated with gang activities. As Lindegaard (2018) argues, the structural violence of the apartheid regime has imprinted a distinct, racialized, and spatialized urban geography on the city that is quite distinct.

Dennis Rodgers (2004, 2009, 2012) chronicles in his analysis of violence and gangs in Nicaragua that spatial segregation in cities through the proliferation of gated communities, closed condominiums, and neglect of public spaces has contributed to increasing levels of urban violence. In these new spatial governance arrangements, the state plays a crucial role in maintaining sociospatial differentiation and segregation:

> New forms of urban governance that involve regular police patrolling in rich areas of the city and on the new roads, on the one hand, and unpredictably and violently patrolling slums and poor neighborhoods on the other ... precipitate localized conditions of terror and symbolically demonstrate the arbitrary power of the elite-captured state. (Rodgers 2009, 965)

These forms of "infrastructural violence" (Rodgers 2012) through state spatial interventions seek to contain gang violence by spatially isolating it in poor neighborhoods, which, in turn, has resulted in the concomitant intensification of violence in these areas through changing gang structures and dynamics. Rodgers points to the political nature of gang violence, which cannot be viewed as a "natural" phenomenon but rather needs to be understood as the outcome of broader sociostructural, political, and economic forces in city-building efforts.

These examples foreground how critical approaches position the role of politics at the center of the gang phenomenon. In particular, they emphasize the interconnectedness of state spatial interventions into the urban built environment of cities and how these interventions, in turn, impact local gang dynamics. In doing so, critical gang studies have shifted the analytical focus away from traditional understandings of what gang spaces are toward more critical conceptualizations that acknowledge the intrinsic political quality and nature of urban space (Lefebvre 1991; Elden 2007). Instead of understanding space purely through the notion of "turf"—an understanding that reduces gang spaces to fixed territorialities for economic reproduction and control (see Spergel 1995; Valasik and Tita 2018)—critical gang studies have argued that urban space needs to be conceptualized as a relational social product (Fraser 2015; Schwarze 2021b) that is constantly produced and reproduced through socioeconomic and political processes and structures. Space is not a static container onto which social relations are simply projected, but rather a relational social product produced by the political, social, and economic forces that shape society. Thus, by viewing space as relational, gang dynamics and violence are studied as outcomes of broader sociospatial transformations within the political economy of cities instead of viewing them purely as outcomes of individual pathologies of gang members.

Finally, the role of politics in shaping local gang dynamics has also been studied from the perspective of the gangs as quasi-political actors and how they respond to state spatial strategies of segregation, gentrification, and securitization of urban spaces. In their ethnographic study of the Almighty Latin King and Queen Nation in New York, Brotherton and Barrios (2004), for example, argue that the ALKQN comprises a street organization that formed in response to the historical forces of precarity, exclusion, and spatial violence. For the authors, a "street organization" denotes:

> [a] group formed largely by youth and adults of a marginalized social class which aims to provide its members with a resistance identity, an opportunity to be individually and collectively empowered, a voice to speak back to and challenge the dominant culture, a refuge from the stresses and strains of barrio or ghetto life and a spiritual enclave within which its own sacred rituals can be generated and practiced. (Brotherton 2004, 272)

The ALKQN provides its members with various and complex belief systems, rituals, and symbolic universes (Brotherton 2014; Barrios 2003), which allow them to develop a collective resistance identity against the spatial violence shaping their urban communities, at both local and transnational levels (Brotherton 2008). For Barrios (2003), the ALKQN is first and foremost a site for collective resistance to systems of domination where spiritual practices among members "extend, perpetuate, and reinforce their coherence" and where "spirituality is very concrete and functions almost like a form of self-organized theory for the poor and marginalized" (Barrios 2003, 119, 126). By foregrounding the role of resistance identities as part of life in a gang, critical approaches argue that cultural practices and performances are important ways for gang members to deal with the everyday pressures and struggles associated with multiple deprived and marginalized communities. In this understanding, the gang performs a political function for members to collectively resist the structural violence of their urban environments.

Gangs, Race, and Criminalization

In the aftermath of the August 2011 riots that took place across several cities in the United Kingdom, during which young people from Britain's most deprived communities poured into the streets in a moment of violent upheaval, UK media outlets and the political establishment, including Prime Minister David Cameron, quickly concluded that "gangs" were the instigators of these riots. Cameron (2011) stated that "it's time for something else too. A concerted, all-out war on gangs and gang culture. This isn't some side issue. It is a major criminal disease that has infected streets and estates across our country. Stamping out these gangs is a new national priority." After initially claiming that as many as 28% of those arrested in London were gang members, the Metropolitan Police revised this figure downward to 19%, a figure that dropped to 13% countrywide (Lewis et al. 2011, 21). By the time the government's policy document was published in response, the role of gangs in the riots was considerably downplayed.

For Hallsworth and Brotherton (2011), the framing of disorder through the lens of "gangs" is a well-worn stereotype. Warning against such "gang talk," they draw on established work on the construction of urban youth (Hall et al. 1978) as a distraction from the deeper drivers of structural and socioeconomic inequality, consumerism, and advanced marginality (Hall, Winlow, and Ancrum 2008; Hayward 2004; Ferrell, Hayward, and Young 2008). Instead of mislabeling communities affected by the riots as "gang-afflicted areas" and people living in them as "gang affiliated," Hallsworth and Brotherton (2011) identify that these communities are "populated by volatile, alienated young men, many from chaotic backgrounds, whose formative experiences of formal institutions is highly negative" (10) and that the riots need to be contextualized within contemporary neoliberal society "where poverty has literally been criminalized, where welfare means workfare and where the prison has become the institution par excellence for regulating poverty and its symptoms" (16). The framing of youth crime and disorder through the lens of "gangs" represents a common theme in media, policy discourses, and critical gang studies alike (Fraser and Atkinson 2014). This strand of scholarship demonstrates the secondary harms that can be caused by labeling young people as "gang members." In the context of the United Kingdom, Ralphs, Medina, and Aldridge (2009), for example, have argued that:

> being labeled as a gang member or associate created a greater vulnerability to police attention and surveillance. Armed police raids on family homes in search of firearms were common and brought stigma, stress and feelings of violation to the families involved. Young people living in these areas and labelled as "gang associates" were often subjected to police checks and exclusion from community events including carnivals and family fun days. (491)

The attribution of "gang membership" by law enforcement agencies has immediate implications for young people's everyday lives, leaving them vulnerable to discriminatory police practices and social exclusion and stigmatization within their communities. As Ian Hacking (2004) argues:

> The use of these categories often has real effects upon people. Not necessarily direct effects, related to the mere knowledge that the authorities or experts classify you in a certain way. The effect can be indirect, when the classifications are incorporated into the rules of institutions, for example prisons. Few criminals know the elaborate theories and structures of criminological classification. (297)

Processes of labeling and gang categorization have been demonstrated to have serious consequences for individuals. Recent scholarship has powerfully shown, for example, how Black, Asian, and Minority Ethnic (BAME) populations and cultures are criminalized in media and policy discourses as "gang associated" (Williams and Clarke 2018b; Alexander 2008; Fatsis 2019b; Schwarze and Fatsis 2022), with criminalizing consequences. Williams and Clarke (2016), for example, identified that young Black people are much more at risk than white teenagers to be labeled and mistaken as gang members by police forces. Furthermore, Williams and Clarke (2016) point out that due to limitations and imprecisions within academic and policy discourses to clearly define "the gang," prosecutors in court proceedings against alleged gang members rely on common sense, racialized, and stereotypical definitions of the gang that, in turn, make BAME individuals much more likely to end up in police gang databases (Williams and Clarke 2018a).

Beyond individual and personal repercussions, the gang label is also a powerful ideological force in criminalizing and stigmatizing entire communities as "gang afflicted" (Schwarze 2021a) and in generating moral panic (Cohen 1972) about urban places in disadvantaged and marginalized Black communities. The current intense public debates over increasing levels of knife crime in English cities, for example, are fueled and reproduced by hyperbolic and misleading media and policy representations of the relationship between drill music, gangs, and urban violence, which, in turn, leaves particularly Black communities vulnerable to prejudicial and discriminatory policing practices (Fatsis 2019b; Schwarze and Fatsis 2022; Ilan 2020; Lynes, Kelly, and Kelly 2020; Irwin-Rogers and Pinkney 2017).[1] For Fatsis, the criminalization of drill music comprises yet another moment in the long history of criminalizing and stigmatizing Black populations and (sub)cultures in the United Kingdom and elsewhere (Fatsis 2019a, 2021a; Gilroy 1987; Owusu-Bempah 2017). Drill music videos and lyrics frequently feature as evidence in court proceedings against drill artists (Fatsis 2019b; Kubrin and Nielson 2014; Quinn 2018; Nielson and Dennis 2019), which has been criticized by scholars as a testimony to a "culture of control" (Garland 2001), where the violence in drill lyrics is interpreted by police and prosecutors as desired lifestyles instead of a lived reflection of social life in deprived communities (Fatsis 2019b, 1309; Kubrin and Nielson 2014). Such a limited and restricted understanding of drill music, which ignores that this music genre, too, is first and foremost a cultural performance rather than real-life testimonies, is, according to Ilan (2020), street illiterate:

> Interpreting drill music as nothing more than an incitement to violence or online "gang" conflict street-illiterately substitutes stereotypes for deeper understanding. It dismisses the ability of the (particularly black) urban disadvantaged to produce and participate in abstract artistic expression and cultural complexity. (1003)

Scholars like Alexander (2008) point out that such racialized gang "mythmaking" (Pitts 2014) "serves to collectively implicate and criminalize all 'young black boys' and, by extension, the broader 'black community'" (Alexander 2008, 14). Furthermore, it reduces complex and complicated problems like knife crime and youth violence to set-piece arguments about the inherent correlation between Blackness and criminal behavior. Media and policy discourses that view 'young black boys' as more likely to join gangs also homogenize racialized identities, thereby erasing differences between and within African, Caribbean, and Black British populations (Grund and Densley 2012). Critical approaches to gangs, therefore, seek to formulate correctives and counterhegemonic narratives to criminalizing and racist common sense representations of Black and Brown populations as prone to violent and gang-associated behavior.

Conclusion

Youth gangs have become a defining symbol of fear, anxiety, and regulation across a range of global contexts. In many jurisdictions, public fears over youth have been matched by increasingly punitive criminal justice policies targeted at gangs, such as the *mano dura* (iron fist) legislations in Central American contexts (Wolf 2017; Rodgers 2009). Yet, as critical gang scholars have demonstrated, defining gangs and gang membership is inherently problematic, reflecting deep prejudices and bias. It is not coincidental that the individuals most frequently labeled as gang members, and subject to gang-specific policy interventions, are also most often drawn from communities that are already structurally marginalized by the social system—be it by class, ethnicity, or nationality. In this sense, gangs might be considered as an avatar, or totem, for racialized or class-based prejudice and regulatory measures predicated on social control of the perceived "dangerous classes." Amid this complexity, the narrow definition of gangs favored by criminological research concerned mostly with deviance and crime glosses these deeper, systemic, and political issues and forecloses understanding of ways street-based groups can exhibit pro-social traits, conflicting identities, and change over time. In exposing these blind spots and inbuilt prejudices, the intention in this chapter has not been to simply criticize but to build the foundations for a sociology of gangs fit for the twenty-first century—grounded, human, and critical while remaining sensitive to policy, practice, and pragmatism.

We have demonstrated in this chapter that critical gang studies situate gangs in wider societal processes of socioeconomic marginality, punishment, and political processes of spatial exclusion, and that understanding gang identity needs to consider how these processes and structures influence the broader lifeworld of gangs. Further, our overview has shown that interrogating the iatrogenesis of gang labels is crucial for arriving at understandings of the gang phenomenon that do not reproduce stigmatizing and marginalizing conceptualizations of gangs. In this respect, scrutinizing the role of power, politics, and labeling in how gangs are frequently portrayed as violent and criminal in research and policy discourse comprises a central feature and goal of critical gang studies. Such scrutinizing, we have demonstrated, requires new coalitions between scholars from across different geographical contexts and academic backgrounds to break down barriers and stereotypes in researching gangs. Critical gang studies allow an expansive theoretical framework to facilitate global comparative analysis, encouraging studies predicated less on the discovery of similarities but on that of difference, embedding explanations for group offending in "space, time and social setting" (Brotherton 2015, 25).

In considering the future trajectories of critical approaches to gangs, two issues might be addressed. The first, following Becker (1967), is the question of "Whose side are we on?" For Becker, social science research is always also a political endeavor where the researcher should side with those individuals who are at the margins of society, excluded and suppressed by those in a position of power. For gang research, this involves an explicit "siding" with individuals who identify as gang members against police, criminal justice, and those in positions of authority. Certainly, some voices within critical gang scholarship have mounted vocal critiques of those in powerful positions and responsible for the social exclusion of gang-involved individuals. Yet, following Gouldner's (1968) critique of Becker, such a political stance in gang research also gives rise to a counter-argument of bias, resulting in the reduction of the sociologist to that of a "zoo-keeper of deviance." In light of this critique, critical gang researchers might seek to conduct empirical work with lawmakers, policy groups, and journalists to more fully comprehend the competing interests at stake (Wolf 2017).

The second issue is the need for a more established oeuvre and ambitious empirical program for research. Insofar as critical gang studies emerged as correctives and counternarratives to criminological research predominantly concerned with crime, deviance, and social control, the development of its own coherent program for empirical research remained somewhat underdeveloped until recently. Yet the publication of several edited collections and monographs specifically on critical approaches (Brotherton and Gude 2021; Fraser 2017; Brotherton 2015; Brotherton and Kontos 2003), as well as large-scale European Research Council studies, such as the "Gangs, Gangsters, and Ganglands: Towards a Global Comparative Ethnography" (European Commission 2022) have turned critical gang studies into an important research agenda in criminology that cannot be ignored by scholars across the spectrum of criminological thought.

NOTE

1. UK drill music, a subgenre of rap music that originated on Chicago's South Side in the mid-noughties (Stuart 2020), has been portrayed as "the knife crime rap" (*Sunday Times Magazine* 2019), "demonic" (Mararike, Harper, and Gilligan 2018) and "the soundtrack to London's murders" (Knight 2018), made responsible by mainstream media outlets, conservative policy reports, and politicians for the current "knife crime epidemic" (Fatsis 2021b; see also Squires 2009).

REFERENCES

Afary, Kamran, and David C. Brotherton. 2021. "Dwight Conquergood. An Appreciation of His Intellectual Life and Contribution to Critical Gang Studies." In *Routledge International Handbook of Critical Gang Studies*, edited by David C. Brotherton and Rafael Jose Gude, 667–677. Abingdon, UK: Routledge.

Alexander, Claire. 2008. *(Re)Thinking "Gangs."* London: Runnymede.

Aspholm, Roberto R. 2020. *Views from the Streets: The Transformation of Gangs and Violence on Chicago's South Side*. New York: Columbia University Press.

Baird, Adam. 2011. "Negotiating Pathways to Manhood: Rejecting Gangs and Violence in Medellin's Periphery." *Journal of Conflictology* 3 (1): 30–41.

Barrios, Luis. 2003. "The Almighty Latin King and Queen Nation and the Spirituality of Resistance: Agency, Social Cohesion, and Liberating Rituals in the Making of a Street Organization." In *Gangs and Society. Alternative Perspectives*, edited by Louis Kontos, David C. Brotherton, and Luis Barrios, 119–135. New York: Columbia University Press.

Batchelor, Susan. 2009. "Girls, Gangs and Violence: Assessing the Evidence." *Probation Journal* 56 (4): 399–414.

Becker, Howard. 1967. "Whose Side Are We On?" *Social Problems* 14 (3): 239–247.

Bourgois, Philippe. 1995. *In Search of Respect: Selling Crack in El Barrio*. Cambridge, UK: Cambridge University Press.

Box, Steven. 1983. *Power, Crime and Mystification*. Abingdon, UK: Routledge.

Brenner, Neil. 1999. "Globalisation as Reterritorialisation: The Re-Scaling of Urban Governance in the European Union." *Urban Studies* 36 (3): 431–451.

Brotherton, David C. 2004. "What Happened to the Pathological Gang? Notes from a Case Study of the Latin Kings and Queens in New York." In *Cultural Criminology Unleashed*, edited by Jeff Ferrell, Keith Hayward, Wayne Morrision, and Mike Presdee, 263–274. London: Glass House Press.

Brotherton, David C. 2007. "Proceedings from the Transnational Street Gang/Organization Seminar." *Crime Media Culture* 3 (3): 372–381.

Brotherton, David C. 2008. "Beyond Social Reproduction: Bringing Resistance Back in Gang Theory." *Theoretical Criminology* 12 (1): 55–77.

Brotherton, David C. 2014. "Jock Young and the Criminological Imagination as a Life Force." *Crime Media Culture* 10 (3): 227–237.

Brotherton, David C. 2015. *Youth Street Gangs. A Critical Appraisal*. New York: Routledge.

Brotherton, David C., and Luis Barrios. 2004. *The Almighty Latin Kings and Queen Nation*. New York: Columbia University Press.

Brotherton, David C., and Luis Barrios. 2011. *Banished to the Homeland: Dominican Deportees and Their Stories of Exile*. New York: Columbia University Press.

Brotherton, David C., and Rafael Jose Gude, eds. 2021. *Routledge International Handbook of Critical Gang Studies*. Milton Park, UK: Routledge.

Brotherton, David C., and Louis Kontos, eds. 2003. *Gangs and Society. Alternative Perspectives*. New York: Columbia University Press.

Brotherton, David C., and Camila Salazar-Atias. 2003. "Amore De Reina! The Pushes and Pulls of Group Membership among the Latin Queens." In *Gangs and Society. Alternative Perspectives*, edited by Louis Kontos, David C. Brotherton, and Luis Barrios, 183–209. New York: Columbia University Press.

Cameron, David. 2011. "PM's Speech on the Fightback after the Riots." https://www.gov.uk/government/speeches/pms-speech-on-the-fightback-after-the-riots.
Carrington, Kerry, Russell Hogg, and Máximo Sozzo. 2016. "Southern Criminology." *British Journal of Criminology* 56: 1–20.
Cohen, Albert. 1955. *Delinquent Boys: The Culture of the Gang*. Glencoe, IL: Free Press.
Cohen, Stanley. 1972. *Folk Devils and Moral Panic: The Creation of the Mods and Rockers*. London: MacGibbon and Kee.
Connell, Raewyn. 2005. *Masculinities*. Cambridge, UK: Polity Press.
Conquergood, Dwight. 1994a. "For the Nation! How Street Gangs Problematize Patriotism." In *After Postmodernism. Reconstructing Ideology Critique*, edited by Herbert W. Simons and Michael Billig, 200–221. Thousand Oaks, CA: Sage Publications.
Conquergood, Dwight. 1994b. "Homeboys and Hoods: Gang Communication and Cultural Space." In *Group Communication in Context. Studies of Natural Groups*, edited by Lawrence R. Frey, 23–55. Mahwah, NJ: Lawrence Erlbaum.
Conquergood, Dwight. 1997. "Street Literacy." In *Handbook of Research on Teaching Literacy through the Communicative and Visual Arts*, edited by J. Flood, S. B. Heath, and D. Lapp, 354–375. Mahwah, NJ: Lawrence Erlbaum.
Coughlin, Brenda C., and Sudhir Alladi Venkatesh. 2003. "The Urban Street Gange after 1970." *Annual Review of Sociology* 29: 41–64.
Deegan, Mary Jo. 1988. *Jane Addams and the Men of the Chicago School, 1892–1918*. New Brunswick, NJ: Transaction Books.
DiChiara, Albert, and Russell Chabot. 2003. "Gangs and the Contemporary Urban Struggle: An Unappreciated Aspect of Gangs." In *Gangs and Society. Alternative Perspectives*, edited by Louis Kontos, David Brotherton, and Luis Barrios, 77–94. New York: Columbia University Press.
Elden, Stuart. 2007. "There Is a Politics of Space Because Space Is Political: Henri Lefebvre and the Production of Space." *Radical Philosophy Review* 10 (2): 101–116.
European Commission. 2022. "Gangs, Gangsters, and Ganglands: Towards a Global Comparative Ethnography. Accessed January 26. https://cordis.europa.eu/project/id/787935.
Fatsis, Lambros. 2019a. "Grime: Criminal Subculture or Public Counterculture? A Critical Investigation into the Criminalization of Black Musical Subcultures in the UK." *Crime Media Culture* 15 (3): 447–461.
Fatsis, Lambros. 2019b. "Policing the Beats: The Criminalisation of UK Drill and Grime Music by the London Metropolitan Police." *Sociological Review* 67 (6): 1300–1316.
Fatsis, Lambros. 2021a. "Sounds Dangerous: Black Music Subcultures as Victims of State Regulation and Social Control." In *Harm and Disorder in the Urban Space: Social Control, Sense and Sensibility*, edited by Nina Peršak and Anna Di Ronco. Abingdon, UK: Routledge.
Fatsis, Lambros. 2021b. "Stop Blaming Drill for Making People Kill." *The BSC Blog* (blog). October 18. https://thebscblog.wordpress.com/2021/10/18/stop-blaming-drill-for-making-people-kill/.
Ferrell, Jeff, Keith Hayward, and Jock Young. 2008. *Cultural Criminology: An Invitation*. London: Sage.
Franko Aas, Katja. 2012. "'The Earth Is One but the World Is Not': Criminological Theory and Its Geopolitical Divisions." *Theoretical Criminology* 16 (1): 5–20.
Fraser, Alistair. 2015. *Urban Legends: Gang Identity in the Post-Industrial City*. Oxford, UK: Oxford University Press.

Fraser, Alistair. 2017. *Gangs & Crime. Critical Alternatives.* Los Angeles, CA: Sage Publications.
Fraser, Alistair, and Colin Atkinson. 2014. "Making Up Gangs: Looping, Labelling and the New Politics of Intelligence-Led Policing." *Youth Justice* 14 (2): 154–170.
Fraser, Alistair, and John M. Hagedorn. 2016. "Gangs and a Global Sociological Imagination." *Theoretical Criminology* 22 (1): 42–62.
Fraser, Alistair, Karen Laidler, and Helen Leung. 2021. "A Genealogy of Gangs in Hong Kong." In *Routledge International Handbook of Critical Gang Studies*, edited by David C. Brotherton and Rafael Jose Gude, 351–363. Abingdon, UK: Routledge.
Fraser, Alistair, and Elke Van Hellemont. 2020. "Gangs and Globalization." *Oxford Research Encyclopedia of Criminology and Criminal Justice.* Oxford, UK: Oxford University Press.
Garland, David. 2001. *The Culture of Control: Crime and Social Order in Contemporary Society.* Chicago, IL: University of Chicago Press.
Garot, Robert. 2010. *Who You Claim: Performing Gang Identity in School and on the Streets.* New York: New York University Press.
Gilroy, Paul. 1987. "The Myth of Black Criminality." In *Law, Order and the Authoritarian State: Readings in Critical Criminology*, edited by Phil Scraton, 47–56. London: Open University Press.
Gouldner, Alvin W. 1968. "The Sociologist as Partisan: Sociology and the Welfare State." *American Sociologist* 3 (2): 103–116.
Gramsci, Antonio. 1971. *Selections from the Prison Notebooks.* New York: International Publishers.
Grund, Thomas U., and James A. Densley. 2012. "Ethnic Heterogeneity in the Activity and Structure of a Black Street Gang." *European Journal of Criminology* 9 (4): 388–406.
Hacking, Ian. 2004. "Between Michel Foucault and Erving Goffman: Between Discourse in the Abstract and Face-to-Face Interaction." *Economy and Society*, 33 (3): 277–302.
Hagedorn, John M. 1998. *People and Folks: Gangs, Crime and the Underclass in a Rustbelt City.* 2nd ed. Chicago, IL: Lake View Press.
Hagedorn, John M. 2001. "Globalization, Gangs, and Collaborative Research." In *The Eurogang Paradox*, edited by M. Klein, H.-J. Kerner, C. Maxson, and E. Weitekamp, 41–58. Dordrecht: Springer.
Hagedorn, John M. 2005. "The Global Impact of Gangs." *Journal of Contemporary Criminal Justice* 21 (2): 153–169.
Hagedorn, John M. 2006. "Race Not Space: A Revisionist History of Gangs in Chicago." *Journal of African American History* 91 (2): 194–208.
Hagedorn, John M., ed. 2007. *Gangs in the Global City.* Urbana, IL: University of Illinois Press.
Hagedorn, John M. 2008. *A World of Gangs: Armed Young Men and Gangsta Culture.* Minnesota: University of Minnesota Press.
Hagedorn, John M. 2009. *A World of Gangs.* Minnesota: University of Minnesota Press.
Hagedorn, John, and Brigid Rauch. 2007. "Housing, Gangs, and Homicide: What We Can Learn from Chicago." *Urban Affairs Review* 42 (4): 435–456.
Hall, Steve, Charles Critcher, Tony Jefferson, John Clarke, and Brian Roberts. 1978. *Policing the Crisis: Mugging, the State and Law and Order.* London: Macmillan.
Hall, Steve, Simon Winlow, and Craig Ancrum. 2008. *Criminal Identities and Consumer Culture: Crime, Exclusion and the New Culture of Narcissism.* Devon, UK: Willan Publishing.
Hallsworth, Simon, and David C. Brotherton. 2011. *Urban Disorder and Gangs: A Critique and a Warning.* London: Runnymede.

Hallsworth, Simon, and Tara Young. 2008. "Gang Talk and Gang Talkers: A Critique." *Crime Media Culture* 4 (2): 175–195.

Hayward, Keith. 2004. *City Limits: Crime, Consumer Culture and the Urban Experience*. London: Glass House Press.

Hayward, Keith. 2016. "Cultural Criminology: Script Rewrites." *Theoretical Criminology* 20 (3): 297–321.

Hazen, Jennifer M., and Dennis Rodgers, eds. 2014. *Global Gangs. Street Violence across the World*. Minnesota: University of Minnesota Press.

Ilan, Jonathan. 2020. "Digital Street Culture Decoded: Why Criminalizing Drill Music Is Street Illiterate and Counterproductive." *British Journal of Criminology* 60: 994–1013.

Irwin-Rogers, Keir, and Craig Pinkney. 2017. "Social Media as a Catalyst and Trigger for Youth Violence." *Catch22*, January 17. https://www.catch-22.org.uk/resources/social-media-as-a-catalyst-and-trigger-for-youth-violence.

Jankowski, M. S. 1991. *Islands in the Street: Gangs and American Urban Society*. Berkeley: University of California Press.

Jensen, Steffen. 2008. *Gangs, Politics & Dignity in Cape Town*. Oxford and Chicago: James Currey and University of Chicago Press.

Jensen, Steffen. 2014. "Intimate Connections: Gangs and the Political Economy of Urbanization in South Africa." In *Global Gangs: Street Violence across the World*, edited by Jennifer M. Hazen and Dennis Rodgers, 29–48. Minnesota: University of Minnesota Press.

Jones, Gareth A., and Dennis Rodgers. 2015. "Gangs, Gun and the City: Urban Policy in Dangerous Places." In *The City in Urban Poverty*, edited by Charlotte Lemanski and Colin Marx, 205–226. New York: Palgrave MacMillan.

Jütersonke, Oliver, Robert Muggah, and Dennis Rodgers. 2009. "Gangs, Urban Violence, and Security Interventions in Central America." *Security Dialogue* 40 (4–5): 373–397.

Katz, Jack, and C. Jackson-Jacobs. 2004. "The Criminologists' Gang." In *The Blackwell Companion to Criminology*, edited by C. Summer, 91–124. Oxford, UK: Blackwell.

Knight, Sam. 2018. "The Soundtrack to London's Murders." *The New Yorker*, April 20.www.newyorker.com/news/letter-from-the-uk/the-soundtrack-to-londons-murders.

Kubrin, Charis E., and Erik Nielson. 2014. "Rap on Trial." *Race and Justice* 4 (3): 185–211.

Lefebvre, Henri. 1991. *The Production of Space*. Malden, MA: Blackwell Publishing.

Levenson, Deborah T. 2013. *Adios Niño: The Gangs of Guatemala City and the Politics of Death*. Durham, NC: Duke University Press.

Lewis, Paul, Tim Newburn, Matthew Taylor, Catriona Mcgillivray, Aster Greenhill, Harold Frayman, and Rob Proctor. 2011. *Reading the Riots: Investigating England's Summer of Disorder*. London: The Guardian and the London School of Economics and Political Science. http://eprints.lse.ac.uk/46297/.

Lindegarrd, Marie Rosenkrantz. 2018. *Surviving Gangs, Violence and Racism in Cape Town: Ghetto Chameleons*. Abingdon, UK: Routledge.

Lynes, Adam, Craig Kelly, and Emma Kelly. 2020. "Thug Life: Drill Music as Periscope into Urban Violence in the Consumer Age." *British Journal of Criminology* 60: 1201–1219.

Maher, Lisa. 1997. *Sexed Work: Gender, Race, and Resistance in a Brooklyn Drug Market*. Oxford, UK: Clarendon Press.

Mararike, Shingi, Tom Harper, and Andrew Gilligan. 2018. "Drill, the 'Demonic' Music Linked to Rise in Youth Murders." *The Times*, April 8, 2018. https://www.thetimes.co.uk/article/drill-the-demonic-music-linked-to-rise-in-youth-murders-0bkbh3csk.

Matza, David. 1964. *Delinquency and Drift*. New York: John Wiley and Sons.

McDonald, Kevin. 2003. "Marginal Youth, Personal Identity, and the Contemporary Gang: Restructuring the Social World?" In *Gangs and Society. Alternative Perspectives,* edited by Louis Kontos, David Brotherton, and Luis Barrios, 62–74. New York: Columbia University Press.

Mendoza-Denton, Norma. 2008. *Homegirls, Language and Cultural Practice among Latina Youth Gangs.* Malden, MA: Blackwell Publishing.

Miller, Jodi. 2001. *One of the Guys: Girls, Gangs, and Gender.* New York: Oxford University Press.

Moore, Joan W. 1978. *Homeboys: Gangs, Drugs and Prison in the Barrios of Los Angeles.* Philadelphia, PA: Temple University Press.

Moore, Joan W. 1991. *Going Down to the Barrio: Homeboys and Homegirls in Change.* Philadelphia, PA: Temple University Press.

Morris, Aldon. 2017. *The Scholar Denied: W.E.B. Du Bois and the Birth of Modern Sociology.* Berkeley: University of California Press.

Mullins, Christopher W. 2007. *Holding Your Square: Masculinities, Streetlife, and Violence.* Cullompton, UK: Willan.

Murer, Jeffrey Stevenson, and Tilman Schwarze. 2020. "Social Rituals of Pain: The Socio-Symbolic Meaning of Violence in Gang Initiations." *International Journal of Politics, Culture, and Society* 35: 95–110. https://doi.org/10.1007/s10767-020-09392-2.

Nielson, Erik, and Andrea L. Dennis. 2019. *Rap on Trial: Race, Lyrics, and Guilt in America.* New York: New Press.

Owusu-Bempah, Akwasi. 2017. "Race and Policing in Historical Context: Dehumanization and the Policing of Black People in the 21st Century." *Theoretical Criminology* 21 (1): 23–34.

Padilla, Felix M. 1992. *The Gang as an American Enterprise.* New Brunswick, NJ: Rutgers University Press.

Panfil, Vanessa R. 2014. "Gangs, Gang-, and Crime-Involved Men's Experiences with Homophobic Bullying and Harassment in Schools." *Crime and Delinquency* 37 (1): 79–103.

Pitts, John. 2014. "Who Dunnit? Gangs, Joint Enterprise, Bad Character and Duress." *Youth & Policy* 113: 48–59.

Quinn, Eithne. 2018. "Lost in Translation? Rap Music and Racial Bias in the Courtroom." *Policy@Manchester Blogs* (blog). October 4. https://blog.policy.manchester.ac.uk/posts/2018/10/lost-in-translation-rap-music-and-racial-bias-in-the-courtroom/.

Ralphs, Robert, Juanjo Medina, and Judith Aldridge. 2009. "Who Needs Enemies with Friends Like These? The Importance of Place for Young People Living in Known Gang Areas." *Journal of Youth Studies* 12 (5): 483–500.

Rios, Victor M. 2011. *Punished: Policing the Lives of Black and Latino Boys.* New York: New York University Press.

Rodgers, Dennis. 2004. "'Disembedding' the City: Crime, Insecurity and Spatial Organization in Managua, Nicaragua." *Environment and Urbanization* 16 (2): 113–124.

Rodgers, Dennis. 2009. "Slum Wars of the 21st Century: Gangs, Mano Dura and the New Urban Geography of Conflict in Central America." *Development and Change* 40 (5): 949–976.

Rodgers, Dennis. 2012. "Haussmannization in the Tropics: Abject Urbanism and Infrastructural Violence in Nicaragua." *Ethnography* 13 (4): 413–438.

Rodgers, Dennis. 2017. "Of Pandillas, Pirucas, and Pablo Escobar in the Barrio: Historical Change and Continuity in Patterns of Nicaraguan Gang Violence." In *Politics and History of Violence and Crime in Central America,* edited by Sebastian Huhn and Hannes Warnecke-Berger, 65–84. New York: Palgrave MacMillan.

Sánchez-Jankowski, Martín. 2008. *Cracks in the Pavement: Social Change and Resilience in Poor Neighborhoods*. Berkeley: University of California Press.
Sassen, Saskia. 1991. *The Global City: New York, London, Tokyo*. Princeton, NJ: Princeton University Press.
Sassen, Saskia. 2007. "The Global City: One Setting for New Types of Gang Work and Political Culture?" In *Gangs in the Global City*, edited by John Hagedorn, 97–119. Urbana, IL: University of Illinois Press.
Schwarze, Tilman. 2021a. "Discursive Practices of Territorial Stigmatization: How Newspapers Frame Violence and Crime in a Chicago Community." *Urban Geography* 43 (9): 1415–1436. https://doi.org/10.1080/02723638.2021.1913015.
Schwarze, Tilman. 2021b. "Gangs, Space and the State: Bringing Henri Lefebvre's Spatial Theory to Critical Gang Studies." In *Routledge International Handbook of Critical Gang Studies*, by David C. Brotherton and Rafael Jose Gude, 89–107. Abingdon, UK: Routledge.
Schwarze, Tilman. Forthcoming. *Space, Urban Politics, and Everyday Life. Henri Lefebvre and the U.S. City*. Cham: Palgrave MacMillan.
Schwarze, Tilman, and Lambros Fatsis. 2022. "Copping the Blame: The Role of YouTube Videos in the Criminalisation of UK Drill Music." *Popular Music* 41 (4): 463–480.
Smith, Neil. 2010. *Uneven Development: Mature, Capital and the Production of Space*. 3rd ed. London: Verso.
Spergel, Irving A. 1995. *The Youth Gang Problem*. New York: Oxford University Press.
Squires, Peter. 2009. "The Knife Crime 'Epidemic' and British Politics." *British Politics* 4 (1): 127–157.
Stuart, Forrest. 2020. *Ballad of the Bullet: Gangs, Drill Music, and the Power of Online Infamy*. Princeton, NJ: Princeton University Press.
Swyngedouw, Erik. 2004. "Globalisation or 'Glocalisation'? Networks, Territories and Rescaling." *Cambridge Review of International Affairs* 17 (1): 25–48.
Sunday Times Magazine. 2019. "The Knife Crime Rap: Everything You Should Know about Drill Music." May 5.
Taylor, Ian, Paul Walton, and Jock Young. 1983. *Critical Criminology*. New York: Routledge.
Thrasher, Frederick. 1927. *The Gang: A Study of 1,313 Gangs in Chicago*. Chicago, IL: University of Chicago Press.
Valasik, Matthew, and George E. Tita. 2018. "Gangs and Space." In *The Oxford Handbook of Environmental Criminology*, edited by Gerben J. N. Bruinsma and Shane D. Johnson, 839–867. New York: Oxford University Press.
Van Hellemont, Elke, and James A. Densley. 2019. "Gang Glocalization: How the Global Mediascape Creates and Shapes Local Gang Realities." *Crime Media Culture*, 15 (1): 169–189.
Venkatesh, Sudhir Alladi. 2000. *American Project: The Rise and Fall of a Modern Ghetto*. Cambridge, MA: Harvard University Press.
Venkatesh, Sudhir Alladi. 2003. "A Note on Social Theory and the American Street Gang." In *Gangs and Society. Alternative Perspectives*, edited by Louis Kontos, David Brotherton, and Luis Barrios, 3–11. New York: Columbia University Press.
Venkatesh, Sudhir Alladi. 2008. *Gang Leader for a Day: A Rogue Sociologist Crosses the Line*. London: Penguin.
Venkatesh, Sudhir Alladi, and Ronald Kassimir, eds. 2007. *Youth, Globalization and the Law*. Stanford, CT: Stanford University Press.
Venkatesh, Sudhir Alladi, and Steven D. Levitt. 2000. "'Are We a Family or a Business?' History and Disjuncture in the Urban American Street Gang." *Theory and Society* 29: 427–462.

Vigil, James Diego. 1988. *Barrio Gangs: Street Life and Identity in Southern California*. Austin: University of Texas Press.

Vigil, James Diego. 2002. *A Rainbow of Gangs: Street Cultures in the Mega-City*. Austin: University of Texas Press.

Volkan, Vamik D. 2009. "Large Group Identity: 'Us and Them' Polarizations in the International Arena." *Psychoanalysis, Culture & Society* 14 (1): 4–15.

Wacquant, Loïc. 1997. "Three Pernicious Premises in the Study of the American Ghetto." *International Journal of Urban and Regional Research* 21 (2): 341–353.

Wacquant, Loïc. 2008. *Urban Outcasts: A Comparative Sociology of Advanced Marginality*. Cambridge, UK: Polity Press.

Williams, Patrick, and Becky Clarke. 2016. *Dangerous Associations: Joint Enterprise, Gangs and Racism: An Analysis of the Processes of Criminalisation of Black, Asian and Minority Ethnic Individuals*. London: Centre for Crime and Justice Studies.

Williams, Patrick, and Becky Clarke. 2018a. "Contesting the Single Story: Collective Punishment, Myth-Making and Racialised Criminalisation." In *Media, Crime and Racism*, edited by Monish Bhatia, Scott Poynting, and Waqas Tufail, 317–336. Cham, Switzerland: Palgrave MacMillan.

Williams, Patrick, and Becky Clarke. 2018b. "The Black Criminal Other as an Object of Social Control." *Social Sciences* 7 (234): 1–14.

Winton, Ailsa. 2014. "Gangs in Global Perspective." *Environment and Urbanization* 26 (2): 1–16.

Wolf, Sonja. 2017. *Mano Dura: The Politics of Gang Control in El Salvador*. Austin: University of Texas Press.

Young, Jock. 2011. *The Criminological Imagination*. Cambridge and Malden: Polity Press.

Zilberg, Elana. 2011. *Spaces of Detention: The Making of a Transnational Gang Crisis between Los Angeles and San Salvador*. Durham, NC: Duke University Press.

CHAPTER 14

WOMEN IN GANG RESEARCH
An Overview

MARTA-MARIKA URBANIK AND
SANDRA M. BUCERIUS

RESEARCHER–PARTICIPANT relationships are significantly shaped by individuals' identities and contextual processes. One of the most salient factors influencing field access and relations, and thereby also data, is gender (Arendell 1997; Presser 2005). When reading this, many will subconsciously conflate "gender" with "women," assuming that gender is *inherent* to women while being somehow *less relevant* to men. Much academic discourse and writing on researcher–participant relationships—including in gang research—has traditionally co-opted gender as something that applies primarily to researchers who are not cisgender men, with a primary focus on those identifying as women. In those works, it is often assumed that women and female researchers must account for their gender in the research process (see, e.g., Bucerius 2013). In contrast, male researchers reflecting on gaining field access or building rapport often do not reflect—or do not reflect to a similar level—on their gender and gendered dynamics (Baird 2020; McKeganey and Bloor 1991).

Buffered by the growth in feminist work and an increasing acknowledgment of the salience of gender in fieldwork, there has been an explosion of analyses documenting female scholars' fieldwork experiences, particularly with respect to research with male participants and in male-dominated settings. This expansive literature illuminates the process of gaining access (e.g., Easterday et al. 1977; Figenshou 2010; Gurney 1985; Jørgensen and Esholdt 2021; Mills 2004; Mügge 2013; O'Brien 2019; Pante 2014; Pawelz 2018; Poulton 2012; Woodward 2008), fears/experiences of sexualization and sexual harassment (e.g., Congdon 2015; Riley, Shouten, and Cahill 2003; Schmidt 2021), gendered interactions' effects on data and field experiences (e.g., Kaspar and Landolt 2016; Prior and Peled 2021; Yassour-Borochowitz 2012), and the consequences of "doing gender" during fieldwork (e.g., Tarrant 2016). While this literature varies by discipline, country, participant sample, method, and topic of inquiry, findings pertaining to female scholars' gendered experiences are remarkably consistent, demonstrating patriarchy's ubiquitous influence.[1] As such, budding and experienced qualitative researchers can learn a great deal from this methodologically rich and often instructive literature. However, this body of work does not adequately account for the unique process—including the challenges and benefits—of conducting research on gangs or other criminally involved groups as a woman. While all researchers can certainly face risks across diverse field sites, the unique challenges associated with studying criminally involved groups, including gangs, can *compound* such risks.

This chapter provides a comprehensive overview of female researchers in gang research.[2] Three qualifications are in order. First, the research covered in this chapter reflects the state of scholarship and is therefore heavily based on research from the United States, Canada, and Europe. Second, while gender is socially constructed and fluid, existing scholarship does not allow for a systematic review of researcher roles and experiences beyond the male–female binary. As such, we focus our chapter on female researchers, drawing attention to the role gender—and specifically, the ethnographer's gender—plays in dictating how personal biographies and backgrounds shape data collection. Third, while there is robust literature on gangs and criminally involved groups, this chapter only analyzes ethnographic studies. Ethnography is typically characterized by a researcher deeply immersing themself into a community to observe their behavior and interactions up close. There is an intimate relationship between gang studies and ethnography (Decker and Pyrooz 2012, 274), and this focus allows us to highlight gender dynamics in prolonged field research.

We have aimed to be as inclusive and broad as possible. Our review spans several generations, continents, disciplines, research foci, and gang classifications, uncovering a rich and innovative mixture of interview, experiential, and observational data. We have mostly excluded studies solely based on in-depth interviews. Despite our efforts to produce an exhaustive review highlighting the breadth and depth of female ethnographers' contributions and experiences—which are curiously often rendered invisible in scoping literature reviews (c.f. Durán 2018)—this chapter is intended to be illustrative.[3] We hope that by illuminating these works, future examinations of the topic will be less androcentric, acknowledging women's contribution to gang studies.

This chapter is organized into four sections. In the first section, we list and provide brief descriptions of ethnographies conducted by female scholars studying "gangs" and similarly positioned groups to showcase the geographical and disciplinary variance of this body of work. Second, we provide an overview of female ethnographers' contributions to gang research, particularly illuminating several areas where female gang scholars have pushed the field forward, both substantially and methodologically. Third, we provide several observations about the process of doing gang research as a woman, considering how the intersection of other identity markers affects field access, experiences, and data. In the final section, we identify gaps in this literature and provide directions for future research. We maintain that despite great contributions of female ethnographers[4] to gang studies, their research is often blanketly considered "gendered"—sheerly because they are women usually studying men. As such, this work, and examinations of gender within criminology more broadly, remain "tokenized" (see also Miller and Van Damme 2020, 85). This is consistent with the field of urban criminology more broadly, which remains male dominated and often continues to dismiss gendered processes (Miller and Van Damme 2020, 85).

The main findings presented in this chapter are as follows:

- Female researchers have strongly advocated for gang research to consider the roles of girls and women in gangs and criminally involved groups and have shown that gang research conducted by female researchers can reveal themes less likely to be accessed by male researchers.

- Female researchers have been pathbreakers in advancing gender theory and feminist, queer, and applying novel methodologies in gang research, including in conducting comparative gang studies.
- Female researchers face unique benefits and challenges while conducting ethnographic research with gang members, largely due to gendered processes. This includes unique experiences with navigating research access, risks, and researcher roles.
- Future research should consider a more expansive array of research topics and investigations and propel broader researcher diversity.

Female Gang Ethnographies

Gang ethnographies—both historically and contemporarily—tend to be conducted by male researchers (e.g., Brotherton and Barrios 2011; Chin 2000; Contreras 2013; Densley 2013; Durán 2013, 2018; Fontes 2018; Fraser 2015; Garot 2010; Padilla 1992; Rodgers 2007; Roks 2019; Scott 2004; Stuart 2020; Tertilt 2001; Thrasher 1927; Van Gemert and Fleisher 2005; Venkatesh 2008; Ward 2013; Whyte 1943). Gang ethnographies conducted by women are less common, particularly those focusing on predominantly male participants. This likely reflects the general "malestream" of gang scholarship (Fraser 2017, Chapter 6); for decades, criminologists considered gangs to be a uniquely male phenomenon. Perhaps this contributed to the fact that most gang research was carried out by men. When we move beyond this androcentric focus, however, a meticulous review of the literature uncovers female gang ethnographers have made notable contributions to the development of a somewhat geographically diverse scholarly body of ethnographic work on gangs and criminally involved groups. This scholarship is not only disciplinarily diverse (spanning, for example, criminology, sociology, anthropology, women and gender studies, sociolinguistics, and economics), but has also built a foundation of examining how gender interactions can and do shape how we build rapport, experience, interpret, and write about the field and our data.

Indeed, women have conducted several ethnographies that have changed how we think about gangs today. In Table 14.1 we provide a list of female ethnographers who studied gangs and criminally involved groups.

Contributions to the Field

In this section, we outline female gang ethnographers' contributions to scholarship on gangs and criminal groups. We identify four broad areas where female ethnographers have advanced the field, either by problematizing taken-for-granted but empirically unsound assumptions, by proposing and strengthening new investigative analysis, or by strengthening research methodologies. These areas are as follows:

1. Groundbreaking, meaningful empirical attention to and investigation of female gangs and gang members

Table 14.1 Contributions of Female Ethnographers to Gang Research

Author	Year	Noteworthy *Those marked with an * do not use the gang label but have done research with similarly situated groups.*
Joan Moore	1978	• Fieldwork in Los Angeles • Studies the relationship between Chicano gangs, colonialism, and prison
Ruth Horowitz	1983	• Fieldwork on inner-city Chicago's "Chicano" (people of Mexican ancestry) community in the 1970s • Highlighted the community's divergent set of values, showing the juxtaposition of residents striving to achieve the American dream through hard work and education while gang-affiliated residents were fighting for honor in the streets
Anne Campbell	1984	• Comparative study on three different gangs, including a street gang, a biker gang, and a religious-cultural gang • Spent six months with each of these gangs • Foregrounded the role of girls within these groups
Laura Fishman	1995	• Published in 1990s but fieldwork in the 1960s on auxiliary girl gang members in Chicago • First to pay close attention to girls in gangs • Unmasked girls' autonomy
Mary Pattillo-McCoy	1998	• Fieldwork in a middle-class Black neighborhood in Chicago • Illuminated how gang membership provides an alternative opportunity structure and how gang members can provide critical informal social control, including by protecting neighborhood safety
Susan Philipps	1999	• Fieldwork with Chicano and Black gangs in Los Angeles • Examined the role of gang graffiti and its influence on cultural systems • Pointed to the concretization of "gang politics": function of intergang relationships within and across cultural systems formed by gang members
Claire Alexander	2000	• Fieldwork with Bangladeshi men in inner-city London • Urged us to think critically about labeling boys and young men as gang members, stating the label is racially charged and ignites processes of control
Jody Miller	2001	• Comparative ethnography examining the lives of female gang members in Columbus, Ohio, and St. Louis, Missouri • Underscored the importance of contextual factors when trying to understand gangs and their members • Illuminated how the respective cities' historical, social, and economic contexts shaped and affected local gangs • Examined gendered processes and victimization
Elana Zilberg	2011	• Traced the "transnational gang crisis" between the United States and El Salvador • Followed the deportation of Salvadoran immigrant gang members raised in Los Angeles back to El Salvador • Turned the ethnographic gaze to global dynamics and the effect of migration flows on gangs[a]
Susan Philipps	2012	• Fieldwork of Operation Fly Trap—an FBI-led task force—in Los Angeles • Took a uniquely multipronged approach to gang studies • Associated with drug trafficking gangs and law enforcement officials committed to incarcerating them • Documented the trajectory of widespread drug policy failures and their collateral consequences on marginalized communities
Norma Mendoza-Denton	2008	• Fieldwork with female gang members in North California, the "Norteños" and the "Sureños" • Unmasked the symbolic importance of numbers, language, clothing, appearance, music, locality, and geographic affiliation to gang affiliation

Table 14.1 Continued

Author	Year	Noteworthy *Those marked with an * do not use the gang label but have done research with similarly situated groups.*
*Sandra Bucerius	2014	• Fieldwork on male Muslim drug traffickers in Germany, examining the positions of Muslims in Western societies • Provided unprecedented insights into the relationship between immigration, social exclusion, and the informal economy • Attuned us to how social, economic, and political exclusion plays out beyond the United States; interrogated the role of culture and double stigmatization
*Alice Goffman	2014	• Controversial ethnography[b]—traced the lives and hardships of poor, Black men on the run from police in Philadelphia • Unmasked how the broad threat of imprisonment has transformed tenuous social relations, and how precarious legal status affects street dynamics, victimization, and vulnerability
Elke Van Hellemont	2015	• Ethnographically immersed herself with male members of Black, African gangs in Brussels (Belgium) • Examined 170 blogs of alleged gang members to consider how they affect the spread of "gang talk," the virtual world's role in communicating "gang-ness," and the creation of a virtual "gang land"
Marta-Marika Urbanik	2017	• Fieldwork with gang-involved men in Toronto's inner-city • Focused on inner-city shootings and patterns of retaliation among local street gangs during a period of mass neighborhood change • One of the first ethnographic works on gangs in the Canadian context
Vanessa Panfil	2017	• Studied current and former gay gang members in Columbus, Ohio • First to focus on non-heterosexual gang members • Contributed to bringing queer theory into criminology and providing a non-heteronormative gaze on gang members
Ellen Van Damme	2019	• Fieldwork examining the role of women in gangs in urban marginalized communities and detention centers in Central America (Nicaragua, Honduras, El Salvador, and Guatemala) • Uncovered women's critical role within these informal economies and street violence
*Rivka Jaffe	2019	• Fieldwork examining how criminal leaders, or "dons," in Kingston, Jamaica intersect with the state and inner-city residents, often providing order and social welfare • Showed how neoliberal retrenchment combined with a shifting social, political, and economic milieu responsibilized citizens to care for their own security, contributing to a vacuum where criminal leaders moved in to securitize marginalized urban settings
Naomi van Stapele	2020	• Fieldwork with marginalized young men in Mathare/Nairobi (Kenya) labeled as "thugs" and involved in local gangs • Examined the imaginative practices and aspirations of young men residing in "ghettos," deciphering how they navigate living in communities where many men are killed by their mid-20s
Amy Martinez	2022	• Ethnographic study examining the intersections of US settler-colonial ideology and contemporary constructions of race, carcerality, and gang affiliation among Mexican/Chicano boys and men from Santa Barbara, California • Examines gangs beyond sociological and criminological frameworks and is adapting a decolonial framework to highlight the historical continuities of racial domination in the absence of formal colonial rule

[a] See also Brotherton and Barrios 2011; Hazen and Rodgers 2014.
[b] See, for example, Betts (2014) and Lubet (2015).

2. Significant advancements in gender theory, analysis, and comparisons, including via feminist and queer methodologies and analytical approaches
3. Being able to uncover sociological phenomena typically out of the purview of male gang ethnographers, likely due to gendered restraints on the researcher–participant relationship
4. Building upon, bolstering, and internationalizing critical, historically, politically, and socially grounded examinations of gang emergence, labeling, sustenance, and responses
5. Novel methodological advances in wedding traditional urban ethnography with diverse instruments of study and raising expectations for researcher reflexivity

Peer Group, Female Delinquency, and Female Gang Members

Early crime ethnographies were conducted by male researchers and focused on male research groups (e.g., Thrasher 1927; Whyte 1943). Thus, girls' and women's experiences were either overlooked or "their roles were described by male gang members to male researchers and interpreted by male academics" (Campbell 1991, 48).[5] The absence of systematically collected data and the prevalence of gendered stereotypes resulted in much of this early work portraying delinquent girls and women as isolated lone actors or as mentally unwell. While male peer groups were considered central to male delinquency (e.g., Thrasher 1927), these early crime ethnographies minimized/ignored girls and women's peer groups and networks (c.f., Miller 1966; Miller 2011), portraying girls and women as unilaterally absorbed in securing a husband and framed women's delinquency as intimately connected to immorality, as a pathology, and transgression against her family and gender role, particularly of a sexual nature (e.g., Campbell 1991, 43; Fishman 1995, 86–88). To illustrate, Joe and Chesney-Lind (1995) summarized this work as portraying girl gang members as "maladjusted tomboys or sexual chattel, who, in either case, are no more than mere appendages to boy members of the gang" (412).

One of the clearest contributions has been female ethnographers' attention to gendered perspectives of "delinquent peer groups" and gangs. Female gang ethnographers also broke the tradition of examining and writing about girl gang members as appendages to males.[6] Fishman—who produced one of the first ethnographies on girl gangs—(1988, 1995, 85–87) showed gang-involved girls demonstrated elements of autonomy, maintained tight ingroup connections, held their own meetings, had their own forms of building status, protected themselves from unsavory local men, commited traditionally "male crimes" like violence, and invaded rival gang territory (Fishman 1988). Likewise, Campbell (1984) was committed to redressing the existing limitations within the literature where "women appear[ed] at second hand and only through the reports of male speakers" (1)[7] and often as "interesting comparative footnotes to the male gang" (Campbell 1995, 73). Prior to Campbell's work, girls and women in gangs were presented as only occupying one of two roles: sex object or tomboy (Campbell 1984, 31). Campbell (1984) opposed the early scholarship's preoccupation with girls' peripheral roles and female sexuality, especially the disparate focus on gang-involved girls' sexuality, whereas "writers on male gang members provide almost no information on the boys' sexual activity" (28). Her work was pivotal: Campbell demonstrated that contrary to common rhetoric, female gang members could operate as active agents in street gangs and function independently from males (e.g., via their own initiation rituals, commitment expectations, and their own leadership) and did not view themselves as sexual objects for their male counterparts. Further, she highlighted that girls and women similarly found social and emotional support beyond the family, revealing that peer groups also played a critical role for gang-involved girls and women, and that like for (young) men, their experiences were affected by macro-level factors such as class context or micro-level factors such as community context (Campbell 1995, 73).

As evidenced, female ethnographers solidified the true nature of women's *participation* in the gang, not just their presence. They were also at the fore of correcting official police reports, which significantly underestimated girls' and women's involvement in gang membership at the time. The near exclusive focus on male gang members not only impeded empirical knowledge on gang processes and the role of women and girls, but simultaneously perpetuated stereotypes of girls and women as incapable of serious offending. Here, Miller's (2001) exceptional comparative ethnography is of particular importance. Miller's work showed the portrayals of gang-affiliated women and girls that permeated both academic accounts and law enforcement statistics were inaccurate. Rather than relegating gang-involved girls to the margins of the informal and street economy, Miller's work highlighted the important role girls could play for gangs . Bolstering knowledge in this area, Mendoza-Denton (2008) further challenged lingering gendered assumptions about female gang members, particularly around perceptions they were failing at femininity. Mendoza-Denton's deeply reflective work questioned official and academic rhetoric at the time, as her data revealed that, by and large, gang membership for girls and women did not necessarily predict social injury. These strides in empirical knowledge on gangs have been made possible through the immense contributions of female gang ethnographer pioneers.

Gendered Dynamics: Feminist Analysis and Queer Theory

Apart from drawing our attention to and empirically documenting the lived realities of female gang members, female gang ethnographers have significantly bolstered our knowledge of the gendered nature of gang membership. Miller (2001), for example, provided a feminist perspective and interpretation of how the gang-involved girls in her sample "did gender," unmasking the nuances of gendered performances and igniting sociological debate about masculinities and femininities in street culture.[8] Specifically, she acknowledged that gender and its effects on crime is variable (Miller 2001, 10). Further, female ethnographers have paved the way for examining gendered power struggles. To illustrate, Mendoza-Denton's (2008, 149–150) analysis of power, femininity, ethnicity, language, and class provided an intersectional critique about the normative discourses around gang-involved girls, revealing how gang-involved girls subverted the gendered categories they were expected to inhabit.

Her work questioned common perceptions about gang girls being unfeminine, breaking gender norms, and that having girls adhere to heteronormative expectations by making them more "feminine" can "cure" them of their delinquency. Instead, she demonstrated how gang-involved girls resisted white hegemonic expectations and saw themselves as resisting sexism; for example, by performing different types of femininities and desiring egalitarian marriage (Mendoza-Denton 2008, 166–170). Similarly, Bucerius' (2014) ethnography unmasked the gender dynamics and perceptions of young Muslim immigrant men. Bucerius unpacked how hypermasculinity was embedded in a host of decisions made by the young men she studied; for example, by recounting an incident where one of her participants attacked a stranger at a café for sexualizing Bucerius. The participant felt the stranger's objectification was disrespectful to him, as the stranger did not consider the possibility that Bucerius could have been the participant's girlfriend (Bucerius 2018). Other female ethnographers have equally commented on how interactions with them have revealed something about the gendered perceptions and dynamics of their research groups (e.g., Bucerius and Urbanik 2019; Horowitz 1986).

Most recently, Panfil's (2017) examination of LGBTQ2+ issues provided another critical contribution to gang studies and criminology more broadly. Studying gang members belonging to a sexual minority group, Panfil skillfully wedded queer theory with criminology, urging us to pay attention to sexuality and sexual orientation when studying criminally involved groups. Panfil's work instructs us on how to rectify some of previous gang research's analytical faults, specifically by centering and examining the construction, performance, and social relations of the intersectional nature of gender expression, sexuality, and resistance to heteronormativity. This rich feminist and queer focus called into question the gendered processes taken for granted in much of the literature to date, particularly in hypermasculinized environs. Panfil's urge for a broader and more inclusive shift in how we approach gender and sexuality in gang studies was long-awaited and subversive, particularly given the growing recognition that hyperpolicing, police misconduct, incarceration, and other arms of the carceral state not only afflict women and members of LGBTQ2+ communities, but pose unique though often masked harms to these groups (e.g., Bucerius, Haggerty, and Dunford 2021; Greene, Urbanik, and Yankey 2021; Robinson 2020; Van Damme 2021).

Taboo Topics

Female gang scholars have also advanced the field in terms of knowledge on male gang members, documenting that their gender facilitated building rapport—which we discuss in greater depth in the following section—and that they were able to elicit and analyze data on sensitive topics that male researchers may be excluded from (Bucerius 2013; Goffman 2015; Urbanik 2018a, 317–318). These scholars have revealed how these cross-gender dynamics created safe spaces for male participants to express vulnerability, which the presence of a male researcher would have likely stunted. For example, Bucerius (2013, 2015) recounted her participants seeking her help to understand women's sexuality and bodies and her advice on romantic relationships with women. Most strikingly, however, her participants discussed sensitive topics with her, such as their parents' divorces or other family-related concerns, that they generally withheld from the men in their lives. Similarly, Van Hellemont

(2015, 73) documented how her outsider status—including gender difference—facilitated her participants' openness to discuss topics considered indecorous within their community, including marijuana use, being gay, and religion.

Critical Ethnography and Global Focus

Female gang ethnographers have also advanced the field by contributing humanistic perspectives to gang studies. Indeed, female gang ethnographers have bolstered the growing foundation of critical work in this area, further revealing and triangulating the role social and economic exclusion, racialized inequality, and structural and systemic violence play in gang emergence and relations. By drawing our attention to racial, political, social, and economic marginalization, many of these works have added a critical lens to moral panics, critiqued social policies and broader politics that are propelling oppression and more administrative focuses on gangs, and focused on experiences/gang dynamics that depart from the gang–crime nexus (e.g., Alexander 2000; Bucerius 2015; Mendoza-Denton 2008; Urbanik and Roks 2021).[9] These works have also moved into adding to the scholarship, demonstrating the nefarious effects of hyperpolicing and other invasive policing tactics (e.g., gang injunctions, deportations, raids) within marginalized neighborhoods (e.g., Muniz 2014; Urbanik and Greene 2020; Zilberg 2011). These analyses emphasized the role racism, xenophobia, and classism play in the demonization of communities, demonstrating the mechanisms by which gang members "popularly become the savage enemy" (Phillips 1999, 11). For example, Miller (2001) maintained "the gang assists young women and men in coping with their lives in chaotic, violent and economically marginalized communities" (118).

Critically, gang ethnographies conducted by women have also contributed to developing a more global understanding of gangs, providing empirical testament to the fact that political and societal contexts matter in shaping gang dynamics. Alexander's (2000) account of ethnic tensions allowed us to understand the daily struggles of her participants in the UK context. Bucerius' (2014) illustration of how Germany's immigration law and exclusionary education system marginalized the young men in her study provided insights into why drug dealing offered greater opportunities than the formal economy. And Urbanik's description of neighborhood tensions in a post-revitalization context helped us understand why and how Canadian neoliberal policymaking failed and contributed to gang tensions (Urbanik, Thompson, and Bucerius 2017). Likewise, Zilberg's (2011) transnational ethnography of migration flows allowed us to appreciate how the deportation of gang members from the United States affects families and communities in both the United States and El Salvador. Similarly, Van Damme's (2021) work—drawing on insights from three countries in South America—also shifted away from American-focused ethnographic work on gangs.

Methodological Advances

Female gang ethnographers also significantly developed novel and advanced existing research methodologies. Specifically, they have merged traditional ethnographic methods—often exclusively focused on formal/informal interviews and participant observation—with other methodological tools to develop a broader and more holistic understanding of the phenomena under study. For example, Moore et al. (1978) demonstrated the possibility and benefits of ethnographers forging research collaborations with affected community members, such as incorporating the work of Chicano ex-prisoners and gang members who are part of the prison subculture. Likewise, Campbell and Miller's comparative ethnographies not only unmasked critical differences between their participants, but also provided ethnographers with a blueprint for future comparative ethnographic studies. Others (e.g., Miller and Goffman) employed surveys to complement their observations, revealing the strengths of gathering more in-depth demographic data and drawing broader conclusions. Other female ethnographers have chosen to use the advantages of intermittent ethnographic data collection, entering the field multiple times over several years, allowing for clear recognition and "snapshots" of changes in the field period (Urbanik 2017, 189). In response to recognizing the increasing digitization of social life, including gang processes, two contemporary female gang ethnographers pioneered the merging of social media research with old-school shoe-leather ethnography; Van Hellemont (2012) examined gang presentation and performance online via blogs, and Urbanik (2017) documented and compared gang members' in-person activities and dynamics with their online performances. These scholars have pushed the boundaries of ethnographic research methods to keep up with our ever-changing world by developing the appropriate tools[10] to examine the intersection of gangs, social media, and urban violence. Shifting gang scholars' gaze to social media was paramount given the increasing use of social media posts as "evidence" of gang membership and criminal activity content in police gang databases and criminal trials (Howell and Bustamente 2019; Ilan 2020).

Female scholars have also advanced research methods pertaining to deep reflections on experiences in the field and raw reflexivity. While "being reflexive is not a female issue" (Van Damme 2021, 7), the breadth and depth of considerations of reflexivity in crime ethnographies seems to suggest that male crime ethnographers might see it as such. In reviewing this literature, many of these studies expose readers to the truly "messy business" (Bucerius, Haggerty, and Berardi 2021; Maher 1997, 232) of ethnography, presenting highly intimate, raw, and truly vulnerable reflections on the *process* of doing gang research, particularly as women. Female gang ethnographers' fieldwork reflections tend to show that "no ethnographer is a blank notepad . . . the perceptual filters that we bring to fieldwork situations are powerful indeed, and not always conscious" (Mendoza-Denton 2008, 48). For example, demonstrating her commitment to this claim, Mendoza-Denton (2008, 72) was remarkably forthcoming with her own tensions; she described her discomfort following an interaction where she scolded her female participants for how they interacted with a male, drawing attention to how their behavior could have propelled sexualized stereotypes about Latinas. Similarly, Panfil (2017, 249) intimately reflected on her participation in misogynistic and objectifying conversations about women while in the field, expressing her discomfort. Bucerius and Urbanik (2019) echoed these concerns, sharing "we both struggled with the idea that, by not always challenging our participants' stereotypical portrayals of women, and even worse, by consciously feeding into them when distancing *ourselves* from these stereotypical categories and falling into more 'superior' ones, we *legitimized* them and *participated* in their reproduction. And yet, we continued carving out subjectivities as 'superior' women, because of the need we felt to produce data, which not only affected our research decisions but also power relations within the field" (470). As such, it is clear that female ethnographers are honest in their efforts to engage participant reciprocity and build/maintain rapport, sometimes at the expense of their own values.

Female ethnographers have also maintained and infused their work with careful attention to the existence and reproduction of gendered inequality. This reflexivity is stark and undeniably exposes ethnographers—and, we posit, female ethnographers particularly—to criticism and scrutiny. Mendoza-Denton (2008) uncovered the vulnerability that comes with such a degree of reflexivity, proposing that writing about oneself "gives the reader a chance to question you. And yet I am mortified to do it" (44). Mendoza-Denton then went on to contemplate where this discomfort comes from, questioning whether this was due to gendered practices, "where I am embarrassed by drawing attention to myself in performance." Thus, we posit—and female ethnographers have uncovered—the process of *doing, reflecting upon, and writing about* ethnographic research with gang members is—in itself—a gendered experience.

Process of Doing Gang Research as a Woman

In discussing the process of conducting gang research as a woman, we must center its intersectional nature; apart from gender, female researchers' field experiences are influenced by other identity markers interacting with each other. Female ethnographers have consistently demonstrated how their race interacts with their gender and (perceived) class position (e.g., Alexander 2000; Bucerius and Urbanik 2019; Miller 2001; Panfil 2017, 247). Simultaneously, however, "there are so many distinctions above and beyond the supra-categories of race, gender, and class that affect data collection" (Buford May and Pattillo-McCoy 2000, 81), and female gang ethnographers have routinely illustrated how other personal characteristics "were of inescapable significance" to their rapport building and data collection (Alexander 2000, 37), such as age, religion, education level, employment, neighborhood of residence,[11] marital status, and appearance (e.g., Horowitz 1983 6, 10). However, these characteristics do not impact data collection uniformly or unilaterally, as they uniquely interact with the demographics and positioning of our respective participant groups (Horowitz 1986, 410), which vary widely. As such, "fieldwork roles are not matters dictated solely, or even largely by the stance of the fieldworker, but are instead better viewed as interactional matters based on processes of continuing negotiation between the researcher and the researched" (Horowitz 1986, 410). Female ethnographers are particularly cognizant of how they appear or are perceived by their participants and use these insights to inform how they negotiated their identities, modifying this identity negotiation to the field site and participants (e.g., Horowitz 1983, 7; Bucerius 2015). Below, we outline some of these tensions.

Navigating Access and Field Identity

Crime ethnographers often report that questions about gaining and maintaining access and field safety dominate reactions to their research. This includes scholarly interest in rapport building and efforts to gain institutional access (Bucerius 2021) and research ethics/

institutional review board approvals (Bucerius 2021; Van Damme 2019; Urbanik 2018b). The question of access and rapport is likely especially pronounced and suspect for women who spend time hanging out with criminally involved groups, as many "may wonder how a woman could possibly have joined gang members as they loitered on street corners and around park benches and developed relationships that allowed her to gather sufficient and reliable data" (Horowitz 1983, 6). Though some may view women conducting this type of work—particularly alone, with "dangerous" young men—as a liability and something that should be avoided (Bucerius and Urbanik 2019; Van Hellemont 2015, 71),[12] female ethnographers who have successfully completed these projects have almost uniformly shared that their gender enabled their access. While some intending to study gangs opt for a male escort (e.g. Adler 1993; Maher 1997), most female scholars work alone, gaining access via introductions by youth workers (e.g., Alexander and Bucerius), police officers, schools (e.g., Mendoza-Denton), community members (e.g., Goffman), gatekeepers (e.g., Van Damme), or by merely spending time in communities where gang-involved persons live (e.g. Horowitz and Urbanik). Irrespective of the initial mode of contact, female scholars report their participants being intrigued by their presence and have cited males' curiosity about why a woman was interested in their lives as enabling their access, sometimes citing male participants approached them (e.g., Alexander 2000, 37; Urbanik 2017, 108). Others have noted that male participants/gatekeepers, specifically police officers, remarked they were more inclined to participate if the ethnographer was a woman (Van Hellemont 2015, 60).

Apart from their gender, female ethnographers generally tend to be different from their participants and are "acutely visible" within their field sites (Alexander 2000, 37; see also Horowitz 1983, 7). Many posit the distance between them and their participants—most commonly racial/ethnic/religious/class based—aided their data collection and produced richer insights. For example, Bucerius (2013) was able to capture her participants' perceptions of the German majority group, illuminating why they detested German norms and gender roles, and their perceptions of German female sexuality. Bucerius maintained such insights were possible precisely because she belonged to the majority group, and the young men tested their stereotypes about German women against her. Similarly, Mendoza-Denton (2008, 64) reported that a prominent girl gang member exclaimed she was only able to conduct her research as "someone from the outside," external to the neighborhood and not associated with the groups in question. Further, female scholars have noted that because their stark differences as "outsiders" meant participants did not assume the ethnographer and participants had shared understandings, they provided more thorough explanations (e.g., Horowitz 1983, 7; Van Hellemont 2015, 71–73). This demonstrates that "social distances facilitate respondents' recognition of themselves as experts of their social world" (Miller 2001, 32). Irrespective of these advantages, female scholars have pointed out that "merely being a woman [did] not provide smooth access to this social world" (Buford May and Pattillo-McCoy 2000, 81), stating their "relationship with the male gang members never was easy" (Horowitz 1983, 9).

Most female ethnographers report male participants being surprisingly forthright about their experiences (Alexander 2000, 36), including about topics considered taboo to discuss with male researchers, given gendered expectations surrounding masculinity. To illustrate, Urbanik (2018a, 317–318) documented serving as her male participants' "go-to person" for moral support and her participants admitting "they could not be as open with their male counterparts, out of fears of appearing 'soft' and/or 'weak.'" While there is a clear advantage to these cross-gendered field relationships, such as potentially deeper trust and openness to discuss emotionally laden and often private topics, this may also expose female researchers to emotional labor that male colleagues may be shielded from. Horowitz (1986) succinctly attuned us to this, positing that her male participants came to feel threatened by her over time, as she was not easily controlled by them and "knew too much about them as people— their problems, weaknesses, hopes, and fears" (422). Jaffe (2019, 390–391) described being "shaken and numb" after a male participant shared a "gory account" of his violent past, with seemingly little warning and relation to her project. Female gang ethnographers are often vulnerable to "trauma dumping" or confessional monologues by their participants and must navigate these situations carefully.

Multiple female gang ethnographers have shared their challenges in building rapport with typically distrustful groups, particularly with respect to demonstrating they were not undercover law enforcement officials and sometimes having to pass multiple "tests" to prove they were trustworthy (e.g., Bucerius 2015; Horowitz 1983, 8; Van Hellemont 2015, 59). These challenges were compounded by racial differences, as most female gang ethnographers are white women and belong to the dominant racial/ethnic group of their societies (e.g., Bucerius, Goffman, Miller, Panfil, Urbanik, Van Hellemont), while their participants belonged to racial/ethnic minority groups.[13] Some participants recognized and sometimes resisted the power imbalance between themselves and white female researchers (Alexander 2000, 27–29; Panfil 2017, 249–250), while others felt pressured to behave with a certain level of decorum in the researcher's presence, potentially to counteract negative and racist stereotypes of Black men as dangerous to white women (e.g., Bucerius and Urbanik 2019, 466; Panfil 2017, 247–248).

Navigating Risks: Sexual Harassment and Violence

Female gang ethnographers must navigate sexual harassment and violence more often than their male counterparts,[14] as some street-involved men hold negative views of women and victimize them (e.g., Bourgois 2003; Contreras 2013; Miller 2008). Unfortunately, female gang ethnographers have also reported being sexually harassed by (potential) gatekeepers, specifically police officers, attuning us to the realities that patriarchy and sexism are not the exclusive or even stipulated purview of marginalized men. Van Damme (2021) writes "during my fieldwork, I have never been harassed by (former) gang members or people I was working with within gang-controlled neighborhoods" (6) Undeniably, research in this area demonstrates that sexism and misogyny within the field are common and that most female ethnographers must navigate some degree of sexual advances or gendered harassment. In fact, one of the most glaring differences between gang ethnographies conducted by men and those conducted by women is the striking absence of having to navigate unwanted sexual/romantic advances or threats and gendered violence. These experiences range from field interactions with men being "always governed by the rules of heterosexual courtship" (Buford May and Pattillo-McCoy 2000, 70), to uncomfortable questions about their romantic or sexual lives (e.g., Alexander 2000, 37; Bucerius 2015; Bucerius and Urbanik 2021,

11, 14; Panfil 2017, 249), to serious threats such as rape (Bucerius 2013) or actualization of (sexual) violence. Almost every female gang ethnography conducted with male participants with a descriptive methodology section outlines the scholars' efforts to try to hinder and stay safe from these encroachments (e.g., Alexander 2000, 44; Bucerius 2013; Horowitz 1986, 420–422; Van Hellement 2015, 59). For example, Urbanik (2018a) writes: "As a young woman studying a hypermasculine group of men, I was immediately sexualized by my participants. . . . My initial interactions were largely dominated by the men seeing me as a sexual conquest, which I worked to try and overcome" (318).

Given the continued realities of navigating society as a woman, such uncomfortable interactions are unfortunately unsurprising, and most female ethnographers are likely experienced in diffusing these encounters. This is evident in the literature, where female gang ethnographers have documented trying to "politely" dodge such advances, recognizing that they had to be clear in their objections but simultaneously needed to tread carefully to protect rapport. For example, Pattillo-McCoy reported having to "handle occasional flirting in an effective yet unoffensive manner because flirting is part of how young men interact" in some field settings, like the one she studied (Buford May and Pattillo-McCoy 2000, 82). Female ethnographers have thus acknowledged that rejections not cased in niceness may limit access to intergender relationships, observations, and experiences and have adapted accordingly. Further, being single appeared to shape relations or to be a source of participants' fixation. For example, Alexander (2000, 37) described her participants frequently discussing her potential marriage and insisting she should prioritize finding a husband. They also used her marriage status to police her interactions with other community members. Certainly, a careful examination of female scholars' gang ethnographies reveal that unattached women have historically been and continue to be viewed as particularly risqué and in need of intervention or greater surveillance.

While such instances can be uncomfortable and problematic, serious instances of sexual harassment and harm to female gang scholars are rare. Bucerius (2014, 2022) has documented the most egregious instances of participants' sexual and gendered violence against female ethnographers to date. During her fieldwork, several participants threatened to rape her, and another made startling phone calls suggesting he was stalking her at her home. Perhaps most shockingly, another participant locked them in an office space at the youth center where he masturbated in her presence. An engaged reading of these ethnographies reveals that most female ethnographers report suppressing fears and taking risks to bolster data collection.[15] In another example, Horowitz (1983, 8) described being frightened to accompany some gang members to a local tavern, but she privileged the research opportunity over her fear.

Though unmasking and sharing the unfortunate realities of women's fieldwork with male groups is important, such concerns are often rooted in heteronormative assumptions that do not adequately reflect the full reality of fieldwork. For example, Panfil's (2017) pivotal work has highlighted that we need to consider instances where researchers and participants identify as members of LGBTQ2+ communities. As Panfil demonstrated, these identities and their intersections—though often overlooked or taken for granted in much of the existing criminological literature—undoubtedly shift field relations and dynamics. To illustrate, Panfil (2017, 248) expressed that as a gay woman interviewing gay men (though some were bisexual), she did not need to worry too much about sexualized field dynamics and did not have to navigate sexual tension. Relatedly, Panfil suggested her "butchy gender presentation" (248) deterred interactions with her respective participants from progressing into sexual or romantic ones. Clearly then, apart from LGBTQ2+ identification, gender presentations—and (correct or incorrect) assumptions surrounding how they map onto sexual and romantic interests—may also shape cross-gender field interactions. As such, concerns over sexual harassment while in the field should be qualified with acknowledgment of the potential of sexual and gender diversity within the field.

Cross-gender field dynamics are rarely straightforward. To illustrate, while female ethnographers have certainly documented male participants threatening to harm them, they have also reported other male participants portraying themselves or acting as their "protectors" (Alexander 2000, 41; Bucerius 2018, 54; Urbanik 2018a, 319; Van Hellemont 2015, 76). While many female gang ethnographers are certainly exposed to gendered harms and harassment in the field, they may also experience gendered and unique benefits such as protective and chivalrous treatment, which may not be extended to male ethnographers. To illustrate, Van Hellemont (2015, 76, 80) described a participant coming to her aid to remove her from a dangerous situation, and Urbanik (2018a, 319) shared that her participants exclaimed if anyone troubled her in the neighborhood, they would "handle it." We therefore posit that gendered perceptions that place female ethnographers at risk, in some cases, shelter the female ethnographer from other forms of risk. This is most evident in female gang ethnographers' claims that their gender likely insulated them from participants' expectations or pressures they participate in serious criminality. For example, Horowitz (1986, 9) shared that her gender enabled her to not attend gang fights and other illegal activities and attributed her "lady" status to indicating she had her participants' respect and to protecting her from having to hide a gun and decreasing uncomfortable discussions about sexual exploits (417–419). Similarly, police officers direct less attention to women; consequently, female ethnographers may potentially be subjected to fewer legal risks and police attention.

Another uniquely gendered issue relates to the strong emphasis on the ethnographer's appearance, and particularly on assumed/performed "attractiveness" via clothing, hair, and makeup choices, which can affect the research role (Horowitz 1986, 421). Such references typically related to how the ethnographer managed her field presentation and participants' unsolicited comments. Horowitz (1983, 6; 1986, 421), for example, described that dressing "slightly sloppily but not too sloppily" affected how participants interacted with her, and that male and female participants commented on her lack of "styling," which was one technique of being "extremely careful not to develop a sexual identity" (1983, 9). Urbanik described carefully selecting her clothing to present as "desexualized" and to downplay her femininity. Similarly, Mendoza-Denton's (2008, 54–57) female participants frequently discussed and even modified her appearance to make her look "presentable"; Van Hellemont's (2015, 77) male participants prided themselves on allegedly improving her style during her fieldwork (a balance of attractive but not sexy); one of Panfil's (2017, 250–251) male participants inquired to see what she planned to wear to a gay club; and Van Damme (2019, 7) had an NGO gatekeeper instruct her on what not to wear in the field. We cannot elicit whether this attention to appearance is the result of gendered socialization or committees, reviewers, or editors requesting this information or a mix of both. However, the near absence of such considerations in male ethnographies (c.f. Bourgois 2003) is startling by comparison.

Navigating Gendered Categories

Women gang ethnographers also have to navigate the socially and culturally embedded gendered categories their participants prescribe to them (see Horowitz 1986, 411). Female ethnographers enter field sites with established gendered and cultural expectations about women's behavior, which often brand it unacceptable for an "unattached" woman[16] to spend time with men in often "unsavory" settings like street corners, staircases, night clubs, and trap houses. As such, many female ethnographers violate local, cultural, and sometimes broader social expectations and norms, particularly in relation to hanging out, oftentimes alone, with gang-associated men (e.g., Horowitz 1983, 7, 11; Van Hellemont 2015, 72), and at times, participants have had to "justify" the ethnographer's presence to others (Bucerius and Urbanik 2019; Horowitz 1986). In part due to these unwritten norms and to signal the ethnographer's exceptionalism, male participants have often assigned female ethnographers to (allegedly superior) gendered categories. Several female ethnographers described their male participants labeling them as "decent," "respectable," or "a lady," despite their field sites spanning several countries and decades (Alexander 2000, 39, 44; Bucerius and Urbanik 2019; Horowitz 1986, 414–416).

Such categorizations are rooted in misogyny and sexism; the ethnographer is poised to be "better than" other women, thereby "justifying" her presence (and comparatively respectful treatment) in male-dominated settings, which serves to reaffirm patriarchal notions about "acceptable" women (Bucerius and Urbanik 2019; see also Panfil 2017, 248).[17] Perhaps unsurprisingly, female ethnographers have expressed not resisting—or even leaning into—such distinctions to secure data collection, despite how uncomfortable this made them feel (Bucerius and Urbanik 2019). Panfil (2017) characterized this as the "patriarchal bargain"; where female ethnographers become "one of the guys" at the expense of girls and women (249; see also Miller 2001). Apart from debates about the female ethnographer's alleged respectability, female ethnographers describe occupying other highly gendered roles for their participants. For example, Alexander (2000) wrote about forming "pseudo-familial" or "motherly" bonds with her participants, including as "mother substitute, older sister, youth worker, taxi driver, confidante and ally" (44–45). Horowitz (1983, 10) shared that her participants viewed her as a "big sister" and "good friend" or Lois Lane (a reporter, and Superman's girlfriend), and suggested this role may have "transcended gender" (1986, 415–416), though later conceded this may have shifted to "lady reporter."

FUTURE RESEARCH

Despite the immense contributions of the female scholars outlined above, we identify gaps and limitations within the existing literature future research should address. These gaps are double-pronged; they relate to (1) research topics and investigations and (2) researcher positionality.

The first subset of gaps relates to the breadth of topics explored by female gang ethnographers. For instance, we call out a lack of rigorous comparative work around gender, ethnography, and gangs (c.f., e.g., Miller 2001), paying attention to important contextual differences (such as racial, socioeconomic, cultural, and historical factors) between gangs and the localities they operate in.

Comparative work should also include researchers comparing data and field experiences. While some gang ethnographers have compared data in recent years (Urbanik and Roks 2020; Urbanik and Roks 2021), there is a near absence of female gang scholars comparing their field experiences, particularly with respect to gendered processes and research methods (c.f. Bucerius and Urbanik 2019). Notably, "entry into the gang world via different doors will probably yield different perspectives" (Klein 2005, 146). Cross-gender ethnographic comparisons (like Buford May and Pattillo-McCoy's 2000 work) could expose new topics and methodological lessons that we might not otherwise unearth.

The role of women and girls in prison gangs also warrants attention. The absence of evidence of girls/women's involvement in prison gangs suggests that women do not play a (notable) role in prison gangs (see Decker, Pyrooz, and Densley 2022; Pyrooz 2022). Our own qualitative/ethnographic work in prisons finds they actively smuggle drugs into prison and critically facilitate gangs (Urbanik, Bucerius, and Haggerty *In Progress*). Given that silence of the "un- and non-researched" has "wide-reaching implications for the process and progress of discovery" (Alexander 2000, 28), such omissions reproduce stereotypes of women as less criminally sophisticated and render them to the margins of the informal economy.

The paucity of comparative writings limits the field in several ways. First, only via comparative work can we expose nuances related to local contexts and how they may affect research access, field relations, data, experiences, and findings. Gender dynamics, expectations, and roles vary drastically between contexts and can affect research methods and conclusions (see Bucerius and Urbanik 2019). Second, it is difficult to examine female scholars' experiences when their field encounters are presented with varying levels of detail and considerations of positionality. Third, the general absence of this work leaves many female ethnographers to plan, execute, and write up their research in silos. The lack of openly accessible scholarly dialogue leaves budding female ethnographers with limited preparation for fieldwork, which may discourage women from conducting research on gangs and can jeopardize access or safety. The lack of texts on the pragmatics of this type of research (c.f. Bucerius 2021) creates a dearth for training future scholars (Bucerius and Urbanik 2019) and limits the field's progression in terms of thoroughly revealing the gendered processes that shape our body of knowledge on gangs.

Much of what we know about gangs is still derived from research conducted in the United States (see Moore and Stuart 2022; Van Hellemont 2022). However, varying social, political, and economic contexts across the globe foster diverse conditions in which gangs emerge, operate, and dissolve (e.g., Stephenson 2015). There are also vast variations in the historical and cultural processes and significances, symbolic meanings, and methods of resistance that gang-involved persons and groups navigate, which limits the applicability of the US experience elsewhere. Such differences may be particularly pronounced with respect to women and girls' involvement in gangs, as gender oppression, dynamics, and roles vary (see Van Damme 2019). Thus, the field would benefit from international or cross-national ethnographies examining girls and women's roles in gangs.

Similarly, though empirical work examining the intersection of gang life with social media is growing (e.g., Patton, Eschmann, and Butler 2013; Roks 2016; Roks 2019; Stuart

2020), scholars have not yet meaningfully examined how this changing social milieu is affecting gang-affiliated women (c.f. Storrod and Densley 2017). Social media has changed many aspects of social life and has also created a novel setting for criminally involved groups. However, given how social media shape inter-, intra-, and community gang relations on the ground (e.g., Urbanik and Haggerty 2018; Urbanik 2021), the relative absence of work pertaining to how it has affected gang-affiliated women is concerning.

Given "issues of positionality are crucial to the ethnographic enterprise" (Alexander 2004, 136), questions about *who* has traditionally conducted this type of research are paramount. Most of the aforementioned female scholars are white, holding positions of racial and class power. In fact, there is a starling absence of women of color conducting this type of work (c.f. Alexander; Pattillo-McCoy, Amy Martinez).[18] Since data, analyses, and findings are inherently shaped by the ethnographer, and given that most of the participant groups come from racially privileged groups, these "outsider" perspectives likely produce different types of data (or knowledges) than perspectives from ethnographers who can expand our knowledge and contribute to strengthening the field through an "insider" status.[19]

Apart from racial/ethnic proximity, researchers of lower socioeconomic backgrounds or who might share other similarities with their participants (e.g., religion, neighborhood of residence) could provide new perspectives. This includes scholars who have lived experience with oppression and gangs or gang violence. Central to this is the importance of empowering and drawing upon local knowledge and scholars embedded within the communities in question.

In addition, future research should examine whether/how gender non-binary and gender non-conforming scholars experience their participants and navigate field site differently and compare these insights and findings to the literature on gendered processes in the field. It is imperative that scholars pay particular attention to research by and on LGBTQ2+ researchers, gang members, and affiliates, as Panfil (2017) has pioneered. While contributing from a representation standpoint, shared lived experience and particularly the use of queer research methodologies can facilitate recruitment and potentially result in more nuanced interpretations.

Conclusion

Gang ethnographies conducted by women tend to be innovative, empirically rich, and deeply nuanced. They have immensely contributed to the field of gang studies, providing both substantive and methodological advances as well as comparative works and global inquiries. Perhaps most importantly, they have enriched gang research by adding knowledge on issues that male ethnographers can often not tap into. Thus, while we concur that twenty-first-century researchers must "more centrally document and analyze the intersectional nature of gang life" (Moore and Stuart 2022, 315), we suggest that gang scholars—across the gender and sexual spectrum—more thoroughly evaluate the gendered nature of gang membership and the gendered nature of gang ethnography.

Notes

1. Patriarchy is known as a social stratification system in which men dominate women and make use of a variety of social control mechanisms and policies to exert their power over women. This has pushed women into an inferior role in society.
2. There are multiple gang definitions (see Bjerregaard 2002; Brotherton and Barrios 2004; Klein 1971; Thrasher 1927). Scholars, practitioners, community members, and even gang-associated persons disagree on what constitutes a gang, who is a gang member, and the usefulness and ethics of this label (e.g., Decker, Pyrooz, and Densley 2022; Durán 2018; Esbensen, He, and Taylor 2001, 106; Fraser and Hagedorn 2018). Given the term's unsystematic use, its social construction, and geographical differences that complicate gang definitions and comparisons, for this chapter we take a broad and inclusive approach to the categorization. We therefore include works that employ *and* problematize this label, drawing attention to the diverse work in this area.
3. We limit this exploration to works published in English (see Van Hellmont 2022 for critical commentary).
4. We use "female gang ethnographers" not to denote that these scholars require qualification or that they are an appendage to the assumed *default* male gang ethnographer, but instead to highlight that the *process and experience* of this research varies across gender.
5. We are not positing that female ethnographers studying girls and women automatically produces richer or more accurate representations. Indeed, differences between the researcher and participants—including gendered differences—can produce richer insights and potentially even elicit greater responses. To illustrate, male interviewers can sometimes have an easier time interviewing girls and women on some matters (see, for example, Miller 2001, 31–32), while male participants may refuse to discuss certain things with female researchers they label as "ladies" (Horowitz 1986, 417; but see Van Hellemont 2015, 72). Moreover, cross-gender access may be easier than same-gender access, particularly given that male attempts may be considered a challenge whereas perceptions of women as unthreatening may allow women to immerse themselves in the field (see Horowitz 1986, 414, but see Van Damme 2021, 4). To further complicate matters, Van Hellemont (2015, 72) writes about challenges accessing women, and especially her male participants' current/former female partners given perceptions that as a white woman she was "preying on their men." Evidently, gender dynamics and gendered processes occur during cross- and same-gender interactions and are also shaped by race/ethnicity.
6. See Moore and Hagedorn (2001) for a critical review of the early literature.
7. See Campbell (1995, 70–77) for a critique of the early research on female delinquency/gang participation.
8. This is consistent with Maher's (1997) exceptional ethnographic work demonstrating that street involvement can exacerbate girls' and women's exclusion and marginalization.
9. Many of these works fall under critical ethnography (see Brotherton 2020).
10. See also Urbanik and Roks (2020).
11. Urbanik (2017, p.141) documented how neighborhood of residence could serve as a master status and betray contextually important information about an ethnographer and affect field-relations.
12. Van Hellemont (2015, p.71) reported being denied funding at least partially because the project was "unwise" given she was a "young white female."
13. See Durán (2018) for a discussion of this and the insider/outsider role in gang ethnography.

14. While male ethnographers are not immune to such abuse, we focus on women's experiences in this chapter. Concerns over female scholars' safety are sometimes laden with racist stereotypes, with some individuals asking whether our research is too dangerous to be conducted by (white) women (see Jaffe 2019, 388).
15. See Bucerius and Urbanik 2019 for a critical analysis of this commitment.
16. In a non-sexual/romantic/familial capacity.
17. Such distinctions also occur in broader social life and are not unique to the informal economy.
18. For a reflection on the role of ethnographic authority, questions about "native" ethnographers' neutrality, and criticism of how ethnographers write in "race" within their methods sections, see Alexander 2004. See Mendoza-Denton (2008, 53–54, 42–43) for discussions of "native" and "halfie anthropologist" and academics racially stereotyping her as a gang member from the barrio.
19. Such projects should only be undertaken by women of color who have a genuine interest in pursuing these; we should not *expect* this labor from women of color.

REFERENCES

Adler, Patricia A. 1993. *Wheeling and Dealing*. New York: Columbia University Press.
Alexander, Claire. 2000. *The Asian Gang: Ethnicity, Identity, Masculinity*. Oxford, UK: Oxford University Press.
Alexander, Claire. 2004. "Writing Race." In *Researching Race and Racism*, edited by Martin Bulmer and John Solomos, 146–161. New York: Routledge. DOI: 10.4324/9780203643808
Arendell, Terry. 1997. "Reflections on the Researcher-Researched Relationship: A Woman Interviewing Men." *Qualitative Sociology* 20 (3): 341–368.
Baird, A. 2020. "Macho Research: Bravado, Danger, and Ethnographic Safety." London School of Economics (blog). https://blogs.lse.ac.uk/latamcaribbean/2020/02/13/macho-research-bravado-danger-and-ethnographic-safety/.
Betts, Dwayne. 2014. "The Stoop Isn't the Jungle." *Slate*. https://slate.com/news-and-politics/2014/07/alice-goffmans-on-the-run-she-is-wrong-about-black-urban-life.html.
Bjerregaard, Beth. 2002. "Self-Definitions of Gang Membership and Involvement in Delinquent Activities." *Youth & Society* 34 (1): 31–54.
Bourgois, Philippe I. 2003. *In Search of Respect: Selling Crack in El Barrio*. Cambridge University Press.
Brotherton, David. 2020. "Studying the Gang through Critical Ethnography." In *The Oxford Handbook of Ethnographies of Crime and Criminal Justice*, edited by Sandra Bucerius, Keving Haggerty, and Luca Berardi. New York: Oxford University Press.
Brotherton, David C., and Luis Barrios. 2004. *The Almighty Latin Kings and Queen Nation*. New York: Columbia University Press.
Brotherton, David C., and Luis Barrios. 2011. *Banished to the Homeland: Dominican Deportees and Their Stories of Exile*. New York: Columbia University Press.
Bucerius, Sandra. 2013. "Becoming a 'Trusted Outsider': Gender, Ethnicity, and Inequality in Ethnographic Research." *Journal of Contemporary Ethnography* 42 (6): 690–721.
Bucerius, Sandra. 2014. *Unwanted: Muslim Immigrants, Dignity, and Drug Dealing*. New York: Oxford University Press.

Bucerius, Sandra. 2015. "Being Trusted with Inside Knowledge: Ethnographic Research with Male Muslim Drug Dealers." In *Advances in Criminological Theory*, edited by J. Miller and W. Palacios, 135–155. Piscataway, NJ: Transaction Publishers. DOI: 10.4324/9781315127880.

Bucerius, Sandra. 2018. "The Sense and Nonsense of Planning Ahead: The Unanticipated Turns in Ethnographies on Crime and Drug Dealing." In *Using Ethnography in Criminology: Discovery through Fieldwork*, edited by M. Maltz, and S. Rice, 39–55. New York: Springer.

Bucerius, Sandra. 2021. "Pragmatics of Crime Ethnographies." In *The Oxford Handbook of Ethnographies of Crime and Criminal Justice*, edited by Sandra Bucerius, Kevin Haggerty, and Luca Berardi, 60–83. New York: Oxford University Press. DOI: 10.1177/1466138116686803.

Bucerius, Sandra, Kevin D. Haggerty, and David T. Dunford. 2021. "Prison as Temporary Refuge: Amplifying the Voices of Women Detained in Prison." *The British Journal of Criminology*. 61 (2): 519–537.

Bucerius, Sandra, Kevin D Haggerty, and Luca Berardi. 2021. *The Oxford Handbook of Ethnographies on Crime and Criminal Justice*. New York: Oxford University Press.

Bucerius, Sandra, and Marta Urbanik. 2019. "When Crime Is a 'Young Man's Game' and the Ethnographer Is a Woman: Gendered Researcher Experiences in Two Different Contexts." *Journal of Contemporary Ethnography* 48 (4): 451–481.

Buford May, Reuben, A., and Mary Pattillo-McCoy. 2000. "Do You See What I See? Examining a Collaborative Ethnography." *Qualitative Inquiry* 6 (1): 65–87.

Campbell, A. 1984. *The Girls in the Gang*. New York, NY: Basil Blackwell.

Campbell, Anne. 1991. "On the Invisibility of the Female Delinquent Peer Group." *Women & Criminal Justice* 2 (1): 41–62.

Campbell, Anne. 1995. "Female Participation in Gangs." In *The Modern Gang Reader*, edited by Malcolm Ward Klein, Cheryl L Maxson, and Jody Miller. New York: Oxford University Press.

Chin, Ko-lin. 2000. *Chinatown Gangs: Extortion, Enterprise, and Ethnicity*. New York: Oxford University Press.

Congdon, V. 2015. "The 'Lone Female Researcher.'" *Journal of the Anthropological Society of Oxford* 7 (1): 15–24.

Contreras, Randol. 2013. *The Stickup Kids*. Oakland: University of California Press.

Decker, S. H., D. C. Pyrooz, and J. A. Densley. 2022. *On Gangs*. Temple University Press.

Decker, Scott, and David Pyrooz. 2012. "Contemporary Gang Ethnographies." In *Oxford Handbook of Criminological Theory*, edited by Francis T. Cullen, and Pamela Wilcox, 274–293. New York: Oxford University Press.

Decker, Scott H., David C. Pyrooz, and Densley, James A. 2022. *On Gangs*. Philadelphia, PA: Temple University Press.

Densley, James. 2013. *How Gangs Work*. New York: Palgrave Macmillan.

Durán, Robert. 2013. *Gang Life in Two Cities*. New York: Columbia University Press.

Durán, Robert. 2018. "Ethnography and the Study of Gangs." In *Oxford Research Encyclopedia of Criminology*. https://doi.org/10.1093/acrefore/9780190264079.013.420

Easterday, Lois, Diana Papademas, Laura Schorr, and Catherine Valentine. 1977. "The Making of a Female Researcher: Role Problems in Field Work." *Urban Life* 6 (3): 333–348.

Esbensen, Finn-Aage, Ni He, and Terrance Taylor. 2001. "Youth Gangs and Definitional Issues." *Crime & Delinquency* 47 (1): 105–130.

Figenschou, Tine Ustad. 2010. "Young, Female, Western Researcher vs. Senior, Male, Al Jazeera Officials." *Media, Culture & Society* 32 (6): 961–978.

Fishman, L. 1988. "The Vice Queens: An Ethnographic Study of Black Female Gang Behavior." Paper presented at the American Society of Criminology Meetings, Chicago, IL.

Fishman, L. 1995. "The Vice Queens: An Ethnographic Study of Black Female Gang Behavior." In *The Modern Gang* Reader, edited by M. W. Klein, C. L. Maxson, and J. Miller, 83–92. Los Angeles, CA: Roxbury.

Fontes, Anthony W. 2018. *Mortal Doubt*. Oakland: University of California Press.

Fraser, Alistair. 2015. *Urban Legends*. Oxford, UK: Oxford University Press.

Fraser, Alistair. 2017. *Gangs and Crime: Critical Alternatives*. Thousand Oaks, CA: Sage Publications.

Fraser, Alistair, and John M. Hagedorn. 2018. "Gangs and a Global Sociological Imagination." *Theoretical Criminology* 22 (1): 42–62.

Garot, Robert. 2010. *Who You Claim*. New York: New York University Press.

Goffman, Alice. 2015. *On the Run*. London: Picador.

Greene, Carolyn, Marta-Marika Urbanik, and Manzah-Kyentoh Yankey. 2021. "'I'm Wise to the Game': How Inner-City Women Experience and Navigate Police Raids." *Feminist Criminology* 16 (4): 403–423.

Gurney, J. N. 1985. "Not One of the Guys." *Qualitative Sociology* 8: 42–62.

Hazen, Jennifer M., and Dennis Rodgers, eds. 2014. *Global Gangs*. Minneapolis: University of Minnesota Press.

Horowitz, Ruth. 1983. *Honor and the American Dream*. New Brunswick, NJ: Rutgers University Press.

Horowitz, Ruth. 1986. "Remaining an Outsider: Membership as a Threat to Research Rapport." *Urban life* 14 (4): 409–430.

Howell, Babe, and Priscilla, Bustamante. 2019. "Report on the Bronx 120 Mass 'Gang' Prosecution." https://papers.ssrn.com/sol3/papers.cfm?abstract_id=3406106.

Ilan, Jonathan. 2020. "Digital Street Culture Decoded." *British Journal of Criminology* 60 (4): 994–1013.

Jaffe, Rivke. 2019. "Writing around Violence." *Ethnography* 20 (3): 379–396.

Joe, K. A., and M. Chesney-Lind. 1995. "'Just Every Mother's Angel': An Analysis of Gender and Ethnic Variations in Youth Gang Membership." *Gender & Society* 9 (4): 408–431.

Jørgensen, Kathrine Elmose, and Henriette Frees Esholdt. 2021. "'She Is a Woman, She Is an Unbeliever—You Should Not Meet with Her': An Ethnographic Account of Accessing Salafi-Jihadist Environments as Non-Muslim Female Researchers." *Qualitative Criminology* 10 (3): 1–30. DOI: 10.21428/88de04a1.91da5a02.

Kaspar, Heidi, and Sara Landolt. 2016. "Flirting in the Field: Shifting Positionalities and Power Relations in Innocuous Sexualisations of Research Encounters." *Gender, Place & Culture* 23 (1): 107–119.

Klein, Malcolm. 1971. *Street Gangs and Street Workers*. Englewood Cliffs, NJ: Prentice-Hall.

Klein, Malcolm. 2005. "The Value of Comparisons in Street Gang Research." *Journal of Contemporary Criminal Justice* 21 (2): 135–152.

Lubet, Steven. 2015. "Ethics on the Run." *The New Rambler Review*. Accessed May 2015. https://newramblerreview.com/book-reviews/law/ethics-on-the-run.

Maher, Lisa. 1997. *Sexed Work*. New York: Oxford University Press.

McKeganey, Neil, and Michael Bloor. 1991. "Spotting the Invisible Man." *British Journal of Sociology* 42 (2): 195–210.

Mendoza-Denton, Norma, C. Homegirls. 2008. *Language and Cultural Practice among Latina Youth Gangs*. Hoboken, NJ: Wiley-Blackwell.

Mills, Julie. 2004. "'There's a Lot in Those Keys Isn't There?' The Experience of a Female Researcher Researching Rape in a Male Prison." In *Policing in Central and Eastern Europe: Dilemmas of Contemporary Criminal Justice*. Slovenia: University of Maribor.

Miller, W. B. 1966. "Violent Crimes in City Gangs." *The Annals of the American Academy of Political and Social Science*. 364 (1): 96–112.

Miller, Jody. 2001. *One of the Guys*. New York: Oxford University Press.

Miller, Jody. 2008. "Violence against Urban African American Girls: Challenges for Feminist Advocacy. *Journal of Contemporary Criminal Justice* 24 (2): 148–162.

Miller, W. B. 2011. *City Gangs*. Tempe: Arizona State University School of Criminology and Criminal Justice.

Miller, Jody, and Ellen Van Damme. 2020. "On Urban Criminology Encounters: Gender, Race, and Class in Urban Contexts. An Interview with Jody Miller." *Criminological Encounters* 3 (1): 82–91.

Moore, Caylin Louis, and Forrest Stuart. 2022. "Gang Research in the Twenty-First Century." *Annual Review of Criminology* 5: 299–320.

Moore, Joan W., Robert Garcia, and Carlos Garcia. 1978. *Homeboys: Gangs, Drugs, and Prison in the Barrios of Los Angeles*. Philadelphia, PA: Temple University Press.

Moore, Joan W., and John Hagedorn. 2001. *Female Gangs: A Focus on Research*. Washington, DC: US Department of Justice, Office of Justice Programs, Office of Juvenile Justice and Delinquency Prevention.

Mügge, Liza. 2013. "Sexually Harassed by Gatekeepers: Reflections on Fieldwork in Surinam and Turkey." *International Journal of Social Research Methodology* 16 (6): 541–546.

Muniz, Ana. 2014. "Maintaining Racial Boundaries: Criminalization, Neighborhood Context, and the Origins of Gang Injunctions." *Social Problems*. 61 (2): 216–236.

O'Brien, Rachel Ann. 2019. "'Who's That Girl Sitting with the Boys?': Negotiating Researcher Identity in Fieldwork with Adolescent Boys." *Sport, Education and Society* 24 (9): 954– 966.

Padilla, Felix. 1992. *The Gang as an American Enterprise*. New Brunswick, NJ: Rutgers University Press.

Panfil, Vanessa. 2017. *The Gang's All Queer*. New York: New York University Press.

Pante, Ma Bernadeth. 2014. "Female Researchers in a Masculine Space: Managing Discomforts and Negotiating Positionalities." *Philippine Sociological Review* 62: 65–88.

Patton, Desmond U., Eschmann, Robert D., and Dirk A. Butler. 2013. "Internet Banging: New Trends in Social Media, Gang Violence, Masculinity and Hip Hop." *Computers in Human Behavior* 29 (5): A54–A59.

Pawelz, Janina. 2018. "Researching Gangs." *Forum: Qualitative Social Research* 19 (1): 1–24.

Phillips, Susan. 1999. *Wallbangin': Graffiti and Gangs in LA*. Chicago, IL: University of Chicago Press.

Poulton, Emma. 2012. "If You Had Balls, You'd Be One of us!' Doing Gendered Research." *Sociological Research Online* 17 (4): 67–79.

Presser, Lois. 2005. "Negotiating Power and Narrative in Research." *Signs* 30 (4): 2067–2090.

Prior, Ayelet, and Einat Peled. 2021. "Gendered Power Relations in Women-to-Men Interviews on Controversial Sexual Behavior." *International Journal of Social Research Methodology* 25 (3): 277–291. DOI: 10.1080/13645579.2021.1882193.

Pyrooz, D. C. 2022. "The Prison and the Gang." *Crime and Justice* 51 (1): 237–306.

Riley, Sarah, Wendy Schouten, and Sharon Cahill. 2003. "Exploring the Dynamics of Subjectivity and Power between Researcher and Researched." *Forum: Qualitative Social Research* 4 (2). https://doi.org/10.17169/fqs-4.2.713.

Robinson, Brandon Andrew. 2020. "The Lavender Scare in Homonormative Times." *Gender & Society* 34 (2): 210–232.

Rodgers, Dennis. 2007. "Joining the Gang and Becoming a Broder: The Violence of Ethnography in Contemporary Nicaragua." *Bulletin of Latin American Research* 26 (4): 444–461.

Roks, R. A. 2016. "In de h200d. Een eigentijdse etnografie over de inbedding van criminaliteit en identiteit. [In the h200d. A Contemporary Ethnography on the Embeddedness of Crime and Identity]." PhD thesis, Department of Criminology, Erasmus University, The Netherlands.

Roks, Robert A. 2019. "In the 'H200d': Crips and the Intersection between Space and Identity in the Netherlands." *Crime, Media, Culture* 15 (1): 3–23.

Schmidt, Rachel. 2021. "When Fieldwork Ends: Navigating Ongoing Contact with Former Insurgents." *Terrorism and Political Violence* 33 (2): 312–323.

Scott, Greg. 2004. "'It's a Sucker's Outfit': How Urban Gangs Enable and Impede the Reintegration of Ex-Convicts." *Ethnography* 5 (1): 107–140.

Stephenson, Svetlana. 2015. *Gangs of Russia*. Ithaca, NY: Cornell University Press.

Storrod, Michelle L., and James A. Densley. 2017. "'Going Viral' and 'Going Country': The Expressive and Instrumental Activities of Street Gangs on Social Media." *Journal of Youth Studies* 20 (6): 677–696.

Stuart, Forrest. 2020. *Ballad of the Bullet*. Princeton, NJ: Princeton University Press.

Tarrant, Anna. 2016. "'Betweenness' and the Negotiation of Similarity and Difference in the Interview Setting: Reflections on Interviewing Grandfathers ad a Young, Female Researcher." In *Gender Identity and Research Relationships*, edited by Michael Ward, 43–62. Emerald Group Publishing.

Tertilt, Hermann. 2001. "Patterns of Ethnic Violence in a Frankfurt Street Gang." *The Eurogang Paradox*, edited by M. W. Klein et al., 181–193. Springer, Dordrecht.

Thrasher, Frederic. 1927. *The Gang*. Chicago, IL: University of Chicago Press.

Urbanik, Marta-Marika. 2017. "'More People Are Dying': An Ethnographic Analysis of the Effects of Neighbourhood Revitalization on the Lives of Criminally Involved Men." PhD Dissertation, University of Alberta.

Urbanik, Marta-Marika. 2018a. "Shots Fired: Navigating Gun Violence and a University's Intervention While in the Field." In *Doing Ethnography in Criminology*, edited by Stephen Rice and Michael Maltz, 303–323. Springer. https://doi.org/10.1007/978-3-319-96316-7_26.

Urbanik, Marta-Marika. 2018b. "Drawing Boundaries or Drawing Weapons?" *Qualitative Sociology* 41 (4): 497–519.

Urbanik, Marta-Marika. 2021. "'Gangbangers Are Gangbangers, Hustlers Are Hustlers': The Rap Game, Social Media, and Gang Violence in Toronto." In *Routledge International Handbook of Critical Gang Studies*, edited by David Brotherton and Rafael Gude, 582–600. New York: Routledge.

Urbanik, Marta-Marika, and Carolyn Greene. 2020. "'I've Never Been Straight Up Robbed Like That': Resident Perceptions and Experiences of Inner-City Police Raids." *Journal of Qualitative Criminal Justice & Criminology* 9 (1). DOI: 10.21428/88de04a1.6f2a66fb.

Urbanik, Marta-Marika, and Kevin D. Haggerty. 2018. "'#It's Dangerous': The Online World of drug Dealers, Rappers and the Street Code." *British Journal of Criminology* 58 (6): 1343–1360.

Urbanik, Marta-Marika, and Robert A. Roks. 2020. "GangstaLife: Fusing Urban Ethnography with Netnography in Gang Studies." *Qualitative Sociology* 43 (2): 213–233.

Urbanik, Marta-Marika, and Robert A. Roks. 2021. "Making Sense of Murder: The Reality versus the Realness of Gang Homicides in Two Contexts." *Social Sciences* 10 (1): 17. https://doi.org/10.3390/socsci10010017.

Urbanik, Marta-Marika, Sandra M. Bucerius, and Kevin D. Haggerty. In Progress. "Womens' Roles in Sustaining Prison Gangs."

Urbanik, Marta-Marika, Robert Roks, Michelle Lyttle Storrod, and James Densley. 2020. "Ethical and Methodological Issues in Gang Ethnography in the Digital Age." In *Gangs in the Era of Internet and Social Media*, 21–41. New York: Springer.

Urbanik, Marta-Marika, Sara K. Thompson, Sandra M. Bucerius. 2017. "'Before There Was Danger but There Was Rules and Safety in Those Rules': Effects of Neighbourhood Redevelopment on Criminal Structures." *British Journal of Criminology* 57 (2): 422–440.

Van Damme, Ellen. 2019. "When Overt Research Feels Covert." *Journal of Extreme Anthropology* 3 (1): 1–14.

Van Damme, Ellen. 2021. "Corruption, Impunity and Mistrust: Moving beyond Police Gatekeepers for Researching Gangs." *Journal of Aggression, Conflict and Peace Research* 13 (2–3): 125–135. http://dx.doi.org/10.1108/JACPR-01-2021-0572.

Van Germert, Frank, and Mark Fleisher. 2005. *In the Grip of the Group*. Walnut Creek, CA: Altamira.

Van Hellemont, Elke. 2012. "Gangland Online." *European Journal of Crime, Criminal Law, and Criminal Justice* 20: 165–180.

Van Hellemont, Elke. 2015. "The Gang Game: The Myth and Seduction of Gangs." PhD Dissertation, KU Leuven.

Van Hellemont, Elke. 2022. "A Tour of Gang Ethnographies." In *The Oxford Handbook of Ethnographies of Crime and Criminal Justice*, edited by Sandra Bucerius, Kevin Haggerty, and Luca Berardi. New York: Oxford University Press.

Venkatesh, Sudhir. 2008. *A Gang Leader for a Day*. New York: Penguin.

Ward, Thomas. 2013. *Gangsters without Borders*. Oxford, UK: Oxford University Press.

Whyte, William Foote. 1943. *Street Corner Society*. Chicago, IL: University of Chicago Press.

Woodward, Kath. 2008. "Hanging Out and hanging About." *Ethnography* 9 (4): 536–560.

Yassour-Borochowitz, Dalit. 2012. "'Only if She Is Sexy': An Autoethnography of Female Researcher-Male Participants Relations." *Equality, Diversity and Inclusion* 31 (5/6): 402–417.

Zilberg, Elana. 2011. *Spaces of Detention: The Making of a Transnational Gang Crisis between Los Angeles and San Salvador*. Durham, NC: Duke University Press.

CHAPTER 15

INDIGENOUS GANGS AND GANG RESEARCH

ADRIENNE FRENG AND HANNAH ST. CLAIR

GANGS endure in Indigenous[1] communities throughout the Americas and the larger world. However, compared to other racial/ethnic groups, the development of gangs among Native populations is a relatively recent phenomenon, with most communities in the United States and Canada only recognizing issues with these groups after 1990 (Major and Egley 2002). Given the extent to which these communities have been impacted by gangs, the information available remains relatively limited both in scope and by methodology focusing largely on law enforcement data and interviews as well as individual accounts (Henderson, Kunitz, and Levy 1999; Major et al. 2004). Thus, a comprehensive understanding of gangs among this population remains somewhat elusive.

Currently, 574 federally recognized tribes in the United States and 1.67 million Indigenous individuals in Canada (comprising 630 First Nations and 53 Inuit communities, as well as approximately 600,000 Métis) exist (Federally Recognized Indian Tribes and Resources for Native Americans 2022; Government of Canada 2022a). These Native populations share many historical, social, institutional, economic, and political circumstances (Grekul and LaBoucane-Benson 2006; Mowatt and Matz 2014) influencing gang development. However, as outlined by Vigil (2002), the expansion of gangs among various racial/ethnic groups requires that we consider the particular history and culture, as well as the macro-historical and macro-structural forces acting upon specific groups, as street gangs often develop from marginalization in respect to status/place, which is influenced by their unique pasts. Therefore, while the result is the same—street socialization leading to gang membership—the path is unique to that group's history and interaction with society.

Indigenous Peoples, especially in Canada and the United States, have suffered inequities, injustices, racism, discrimination, and institutional isolation due to colonization, broken treaties, displacement, and forced assimilation that ultimately have affected individuals, families, communities, education, employment, and the larger social fabric, creating the optimal situation for the development of gangs (e.g., Beare 2011; Bucerius, Jones, and Haggerty 2021; Dunbar 2017; Preston, Carr-Stewart, and Bruno 2012; Shantz 2010; White 2009). Within this context, "the gang lifestyle appears to offer an [attractive] alternative to lives filled with helplessness and hopelessness" and represents a way to act against the continued exclusion of these communities from mainstream society (Comack et al. 2013; Dunbar 2017; Grekul and LaBoucane-Benson 2008, 67).

Historical Context

Beginning with colonization and the forced removal of Native populations from their traditional lands, policies such as the creation of reservations/reserves, boarding/residential schools, and relocation and termination led to a loss of land, culture, language, values, kinship structures, and established traditional legal systems, ultimately resulting in several social problems continually affecting these communities, including gang membership (Beare 2011; Feldmeier 2011; Grekul and LaBoucane-Benson 2006; Sinclair and Grekul 2012; Totten 2009, 2010). The history of colonization for these groups ultimately began with policies intended to address the "Indian problem" by pushing them from their lands and criminalizing or forbidding cultural practices (Comack et al. 2013). This resulted from broken treaties and the elimination of entire tribes through battles such as Little Big Horn and the Sand Creek massacre (Jaimes 1992). To decrease conflict, but also to acquire valuable lands used by Native populations, the United States passed the Indian Removal Act of 1830, which forcibly removed many Indigenous tribes to areas west of the Mississippi River (Churchill and Morris 1992). The Trail of Tears, in which Native peoples were relocated from states in the south such as Florida, Georgia, Alabama, Tennessee, and North Carolina to Oklahoma, perhaps represents the most well-known enactment of these policies. The lands chosen for this exchange were often isolated and did not allow for the traditional food-gathering ways of these groups. Furthermore, the reserves and reservations were significantly smaller than the previous land masses held by these populations and of course did not hold the same cultural and religious significance as their original lands. This process also disrupted the social networks created by these groups within their traditional communities. Canada saw similar processes and impacts on these groups as they developed the reserve system through the Indian Act of 1876 (Indigenous Foundations 2022).

To further assimilate Indigenous Peoples, both countries enacted policies creating boarding school systems with disastrous effects. The residential school system was based on the philosophy of "kill the Indian, save the man" and that abandoning Native culture and traditional ways, including language, clothing, and customs, was in people's best interest (Richland and Deer 2004; Indigenous Foundations 2022). Children were often forcibly removed from their homes to be placed in these systems. In fact, in Canada, through the Indian Act, attendance at residential schools was mandatory for First Nations children (Indigenous Foundations 2022). These schools primarily ran from the late 1800s until the 1960s. The detrimental impacts of these policies not only on the individuals required to attend these schools but the families of these children and the communities in which these children belonged continue. Tribal communities lost at least one, but in some cases multiple, generations, which severely affected the transmission of customs and traditional languages. Families missed a generation of parenting, while individuals in this system were also often subjected to harsh conditions, including abuse (Richland and Deer 2004; Indigenous Foundations 2022). In recognition of the long-lasting effects of these policies, the Canadian government provided a formal apology in 2008 outlining the legacy of these impacts on today's First Nations communities (Government of Canada 2022b).

The forced removal of children from Indigenous families also occurred due to social welfare policies in both the United States and Canada. In the United States, Native children were often removed from their families and placed in non-Native households. A 1977 report from the Association on American Indian Affairs outlined the full extent of this policy, indicating that one out of every 200 children was not living in their original Indigenous home and this was a "rate 20 times the national average" (Mindell and Gurwitt 1977, in Richland and Deer 2004, 208). Additionally, the vast majority of these homes were non-Native. This ultimately resulted in the Indian Child Welfare Act of 1978, which outlined specific practices for the adoption or foster care of Native children, including priority given for placement with other Native families or Indigenous relatives (Churchill and Morris 1992). Canada enacted similar policies regarding First Nations populations. The involvement of the child welfare system in the "Sixties Scoop," which lasted well into the 1980s, reflected comparable policy to the United States in placing First Nations' children in non-Native homes or residential facilities, in many ways continuing the practices seen with the residential school system (Indigenous Foundations 2022). Also similar to the United States, these policies later resulted in changes to the law, culminating in the creation of the First Nations Child and Family Services program, which allowed for Indian bands to seize control of their child welfare systems (Indigenous Foundations 2022).

Often assimilation policies are associated with the past and seen as an artifact of history. However, in more recent times policies in both the United States and Canada moved toward completely integrating Indigenous individuals into mainstream society by formally terminating tribal status and providing incentives to relocate to large urban centers from the reservations (Churchill and Morris, 1992; Indigenous Foundations 2022). In the United States, these policies included the Termination Act of 1953 and the Relocation Act of 1956. The Termination Act removed tribal status and thus all of the services associated with that status for several tribal nations (Churchill and Morris 1992; Deloria and Lytle 1983). The Relocation Act continued this push for assimilation and the elimination of reservations by providing incentives, such as job opportunities, for tribal members to move to large urban areas (Churchill and Morris 1992). This act also decreased funding for programs on reservations and often required individuals taking advantage of these opportunities to agree not to return to the reservation (Churchill and Morris 1992). In Canada, the White Paper of 1969 outlined similar strategies, which called for the end of the Indian Act and thus Indian status (Indigenous Foundations 2022). It also sought to allow for the conversion of reserve land to private property, "terminate existing treaties," and essentially remove all rights to services of First Nations peoples and provide services resembling those of other Canadian citizens (Indigenous Foundations 2022). Many of these efforts to essentially once again "eliminate" the Native status of individuals in both Canada and the United States were rejected in efforts to recognize the self-determination and rights of these groups.

While the previous paragraphs provide only a cursory review of Indigenous history by focusing on a few of the policies that have impacted Native communities, it offers some context to how these larger issues of social, economic, political, and cultural isolation historically have created structural inequalities that are tied to the numerous issues plaguing Indigenous communities still today. Given that decades and in some cases centuries of historical injustices cannot be erased, these communities continue to bear the consequences of these policies. As an example, reservations in the United States still represent some of the most economically disadvantaged spaces in the country, indicating their exclusion from the mainstream economy and the effects of racialized poverty (Comack et al. 2013). As a result, Indigenous communities continue to experience high unemployment rates, high placements into child welfare systems, poverty, poor housing, high infant mortality rates, poor health outcomes, mental health issues, increased recidivism rates, alcohol and drug abuse, low educational attainment and high dropout rates, limited social bonds and poor social influences, high rates of suicide, overrepresentation in the criminal justice system, and increased rates of violence, including intergenerational violence (e.g., Bell and Lim 2005; Comack et al. 2013; Donnermeyer et al. 2000; Feldmeier 2011; Grekul and LaBoucane-Benson 2006; Henderson et al. 1999; Preston et al. 2012; Pridemore 2004; Sinclair and Grekul 2012; Totten 2009, 2010; Whitbeck et al.2002). It is often proposed that these issues, including gang membership, represent a reflection of and reaction to long-lasting, intergenerational collective and community trauma caused by historical injustices.

Gang Research in Indigenous Communities

Gangs have endured in Indigenous communities for decades, and yet a paucity of information on Native or Aboriginal gangs persists (Dunbar 2017; Grekul and LaBoucane-Benson 2006, 2008; Mowatt and Matz 2014; Preston et al. 2012). The lack of focus on these populations results partially from several challenges brought on by the historical injustices experienced by these groups. Case in point, communities are often reluctant to participate in any non-reciprocal relationship with non-Native individuals (Comack et al. 2013). Research with these populations often requires someone internal to the community who understands the cultural aspects and traditional expectations of sharing information and who has garnered respect (Comack et al. 2013). Moreover, because a large percentage of this population still resides on reserves or reservations, traveling to remote and rural areas is often necessary. On the other hand, researching this population within urban areas also presents some difficulties as Indigenous individuals often represent a much smaller overall percentage of urban populations. Furthermore, there is often a tendency to lump all Native groups together, and yet each tribe or band represents a unique group with its own rich history and culture. Thus, focusing on the larger characterization of "Indigenous" is often a misnomer, and getting an actual representative sample often requires extensive involvement of numerous groups. Finally, given that many tribes/bands are considered sovereign nations in their rights, this often necessitates negotiating with each group separately to conduct research within their communities.

In terms of gang research, the overall gang literature in the United States is more expansive than in Canada but tends to focus specifically on groups such as Black and Hispanic gangs. On the other hand, in Canada, an overwhelming amount of gang research does not exist, but a fair amount of concentration on Aboriginal gangs among the prevailing research does appear (Grekul and LaBoucane-Benson 2006). However, the information remains minimal, impeding our understanding and preventing the development of effective strategies for addressing gangs in these communities (Grekul and LaBoucane-Benson

2006). Recent research, however, does touch on topics of emergence, entry, gang characteristics, gang exit, and policy/programming as it relates to Native gangs.

Scope and Growth of Indigenous Gangs

The emergence of Indigenous gangs is not a new phenomenon; it has been a growing problem in Native communities for decades (Bucerius et al. 2021; Comack et al. 2013; Grekul and LaBoucane-Benson, 2006, 2008; Hautala, Sittner, and Whitbeck 2016; Major et al. 2004; Preston et al. 2012; Theriot and Parker 2007). Names such as Redd Alert, Indian Posse, Alberta Warriors, Native Syndicate, Native Mob, Cree Boys, Native Blood, Manitoba Warriors, Native Posse Native Outlawz, Rez Dwellers, and Shanob Mob indicate ties to various Native communities as well as Indigenous culture (Bucerius et al. 2021; CBC 2022; Comack et al. 2013; Eckholm 2009; Grant and Feimer 2007; Grekul and LaBoucane-Benson 2006; Hailer and Hart 1999; Preston et al. 2012). While it remains unclear exactly where Indigenous gangs originated both in Canada and the United States, some evidence exists that within the United States some of the most powerful groups, such as the Native Mob, may have started in Minnesota (CBS News 2120). In Canada, Winnipeg seems to possess intense Indigenous gang involvement, including one of the original Aboriginal gangs, the Indian Posse (Comack et al. 2013).

Given the relatively trivial amount of data regarding this population, estimates related to gang membership vary widely across time, so adequately outlining the scope of the issue is difficult (Beare 2011; Chalas and Grekul 2017; Dunbar 2017). What does seem apparent, especially by media accounts, is that the abundance of gangs in Native communities has grown over time and is becoming an issue of concern due to the rise in Indigenous gang members as these gangs grow in popularity (Associated Press 1994; Chalas and Grekul 2017; Dunbar 2017; Eckholm 2009; Kelley 1997; Misjack 2009; "Native Mob" 2009). As an example of the existence of gangs in Native communities, in 2002 researchers found that at least 23% of Indian communities in the United States reported youth gang activity (Major and Egley 2002). Surveyed individuals estimated anywhere from 1 to 40 youth gangs in their communities (Major and Egley 2002). Another study showed that around 15% of Native Americans living on reservations or in rural areas represent either gang members or associates (Donnermeyer et al. 2000). However, this research represents the last comprehensive examination of these groups in the United States, severely limiting our knowledge regarding more recent Native gangs.

Several contributors to potential growth in Indigenous gangs could include cultural ties, increases in youth populations, and migration. Ties to cultural components can assist in the recruitment process for some groups by capitalizing on traditional elements (Beare 2011; Bucerius et al. 2021). Thus, in a way gang membership becomes a way to celebrate and engage with their Native heritage. In Canada, concern about continuing growth prevails, as Indigenous groups represent the youngest and fastest-growing population as of 2016, providing a larger cluster from which to recruit gang members (Government of Canada 2022a). Moreover, while much of the research has concentrated on reservation/reserves populations, the path for gang members back and forth from those areas to urban locations seems very fluid (Chalas and Grekul 2017; Comack et al. 2013; Feldmeier 2011; Mowatt and Matz 2014). This migration between urban and rural areas can also contribute to the growth of these gangs, as individuals involved in gangs travel back and forth from the cities to the reserves/reservations, bringing the gang culture with them (Whitbeck et al. 2002). One example of this is the Native Mob, which has influence both in large urban areas such as Minneapolis and more rural tribal communities (Pember 2018). Law enforcement also reports this connection, with the majority feeling outside gangs had influence in developing gangs in their communities (Major et al. 2004). While some evidence of migration of these gangs from larger, urban areas exists, similar to what we see with other gangs, many of the groups still represent homegrown gangs, often resulting from families moving from one community to another bringing the gang lifestyle with them (Donnermeyer et al. 2000; Maxson 1998). Furthermore, those Native communities situated closer to larger urban areas also tend to see more gang involvement and increased levels of gang violence (Robbins and Alexander 1985; but see Hailer 2008). Thus, the influence of urban gangs cannot be ignored, as some influence on the development of gangs among this population seems to exist (Bell and Lim 2005; Hailer and Hart 1999; Joseph and Taylor 2003; Major et al. 2004).

Prisons often represent another source of recruitment. While not unique just to these populations, because of the overinstitutionalization of Indigenous persons individuals often find themselves within the correctional system where they become gang members for protection from others (Beare 2011; Bucerius et al. 2021; Chalas and Grekul 2017; Comack et al. 2013; Grekul and LaBoucane-Benson 2008; Preston et al. 2012). Prison policies in Canada also may have contributed to the growth of prison gangs. When Aboriginal gangs started to grow, policy dictated the concentration of gang members into a few facilities. However, as troubles arose between groups, the distribution of gang members among various institutions occurred, thus extending the reach of these groups (Koch and Scherer 2016). Furthermore, gang members from prison were often released into nearby local communities (Koch and Scherer 2016). This reciprocal relationship ultimately led to the institutionalizing of the relationship between street and prison gangs in Canada (Grekul and LaBoucane-Benson 2008).

Joining Indigenous Gangs

As is true with gangs in general, numerous reasons and risk factors exist for Native gang involvement. In his work in Canada, Totten (2009, 2010) outlines several pathways that Aboriginal youth might take to gang membership. Many of these pathways find themselves embedded within the primary reasons that individuals give for joining gangs or the risk factors associated with gang membership in general (e.g., Esbensen et al. 2010; Hill et al. 1999). The first pathway is violentization and constitutes a response to past victimization, typically within the home. The use of the child welfare system and out-of-home placements characterizes a second pathway that individuals take toward gang membership. Totten (2009, 2010) also refers to several traumas, including brain impairment and mental health, as well as symptoms of fetal alcohol spectrum disorders, as possible risk factors (Preston et al. 2012). Issues related to social exclusion and devaluation, including the loss of cultural identity, indicate another pathway. Finally, Totten (2009, 2010) discusses hypermasculinities and sexualized femininities as the final pathway to gang involvement for Indigenous youth (see also Comack et al. 2013).

Marginalization, especially economic marginalization, can also explain not only how susceptible Indigenous communities are to crime and gangs, but also why so many Native youth lean into Indigenous gangs (Theriot and Parker 2007; Vigil 2002). Some of the poorest counties in the United States include reservation communities, and thus competition regarding limited and valuable resources may foster Indigenous gangs (Buddle 2011; Grant and Feimer 2007; Joseph and Taylor 2003). A plethora of support for social disorganization, characterized largely by a lack of educational and employment opportunities in and around reserves/reservations, exists (Grant and Feimer 2007; Grekul and LaBoucane-Benson 2006; Lilly, Cullen, and Ball 2002; Theriot and Parker 2007). Additionally, economic marginalization often results from educational marginalization. As such, decreased school adjustment or lack of attachment, lack of educational success, and poor attitudes toward school constitute risk factors for gang membership for Aboriginal youth (Dunbar 2017; Feldmeier 2011; Preston et al. 2012). Thus, one of the primary reasons for involvement in gang life, especially for Canadian groups, is money (Bucerius et al. 2021; Chalas and Grekul 2017; Comack et al. 2013; Grekul and LaBoucane-Benson 2006; Preston et al. 2012).

The family aspect embodies another notable characteristic that contributes in several ways to the development of Indigenous gangs. Unstable family situations signify a primary component of gang membership (Grekul and LaBoucane-Benson 2006; White 2009). Historically, Native families were disrupted by governmental policies, such as boarding/residential schools and child welfare policies such as the Sixties Scoop, during which agencies placed high numbers of Indigenous children outside the home (Bucerius et al. 2021; Dunbar 2017; Schantz 2010; Sinclair and Grekul 2012). These strategies separated families, often over the course of multiple generations, and fostered low levels of parental involvement, poor parenting skills, minimal supervision, and dysfunctional families (Feldmeier 2011; Hautala et al. 2016; Preston et al. 2012; Pridemore 2004; Whitbeck et al. 2002). This path influenced family involvement and attachment, creating a situation in which gangs often became substitute families providing structure and support (Amber et al. 2021; Bucerius et al. 2021; Goldsmith and Halsey 2013; Sinclair and Grekul 2012; White 2009). On the other hand, exposure and recruitment to gangs often happens within the family context, and this explains, in part, how Indigenous youth enter gangs (Grekul and LaBoucane-Benson 2006, 2008). Many youths learn gang ideals from their parents, and Indigenous gangs are often intergenerational, with connections to extended families such as cousins, aunts, and uncles (Chalas and Grekul 2017; Comack et al. 2013; Dunbar 2017; Goodwill 2016; Hailer 2008; Mowatt and Matz 2014; Preston et al. 2012; Totten 2009, 2010; White 2009).

Other than the family, arguably the largest predictor of gang involvement among this population is peer gang involvement (Dunbar 2017; Goodwill 2016; Theriot and Parker 2007). Gangs often grow out of homogeneous delinquent peer groups within Native communities (Grekul and LaBoucane-Benson 2006, 2008; Preston et al. 2012). Henderson and colleagues (1999) also point out that drug and alcohol use facilitate the creation of Indigenous gangs, as gang activity mimics peer drinking groups. Protection from other peers points to another reason that youth in Indian country may seek out gang life (Bell and Lim 2005; Chalas and Grekul 2017; Grekul and LaBoucane-Benson 2008). Research shows that Indigenous youth displaced into dysfunctional reservations often bring gang ideals with them, whereas other adolescents buy into their ideals (Hailer and Hart 1999; Joseph and Taylor 2003; Theriot and Parker 2007). Major and colleagues (2004) assert that gang activity among Native American youth displays itself as youthful experimentation and results from a strained environment coupled with popular gang culture and boredom.

Culture is often pointed to as a unique exception to the traditional risk factors for gang membership for Indigenous individuals. As an example, Totten's (2009, 2010) third pathway presents itself in a loss of connection with Indigenous identity and group or tribe (Grekul and LaBoucane-Benson 2006, 2008). This can manifest through cultural conflict, creating an identity crisis—one that the gang can help to combat. Hailer and Hart (1999) found that often Indigenous individuals feel pulled between two cultures—their "traditionalist" version on the reservation and the "dominant" version associated with mainstream society. This often corresponds to a lack of recognition and respect from both cultures, eventually influencing self-esteem. Indigenous gangs often emerge due to the need for Indigenous individuals to feel powerful and less isolated, and as a way for them to gain status and respect, although this is not unique to Native gangs (Chalas and Grekul 2017; Preston et al. 2012; Pridemore 2004). However, evidence also suggests that Native individuals that have thought more about cultural loss are also more likely to become gang members (Feldmeier 2011).

This isolation from culture can also stem from both individual and systematic racism that produces labeling, creating further discrimination and marginalization (Grekul and LaBoucane-Benson 2006, 2008). Racial profiling by law enforcement, for example, triggers continued overinvolvement in the system, further isolating individuals from their traditional communities (Beare 2011; Grekul and LaBoucane-Benson 2008; Koch and Scherer 2016; White 2009). Furthermore, stereotypes created by the media publicizing gangs and violence among Native communities result in negative perceptions of these communities. The cycle endures, becoming difficult to break and could ultimately hamper desistance from the gang (Dunbar 2017; Grekul and LaBoucane-Benson 2008; Koch and Scherer 2016).

The Characteristics of Indigenous Gangs

In general, Indigenous gangs in both the United States and Canada seem to resemble and possess similar characteristics to members of typical street gangs (Bucerius et al. 2021; Dunbar 2017; Goodwill and Giannone 2017; Gordon 2000; Grekul and LaBoucane-Benson 2006; Mowatt and Matz 2014; Totten 2009, 2010). American Native gangs tend to be smaller than typical street gangs and consist primarily of juveniles (Mowatt and Matz 2014). Indigenous gangs are largely inter-ethnic (Grekul and LaBoucane-Benson 2006; Hailer 2008; Major et al. 2004; Totten 2009, 2010). This may be, in part, due to the areas where Indigenous gangs reside. Males between the ages of 11 and 18 years old also tend to make up Native American gangs (Hailer and Hart 1999). However, some research indicates significant percentages of female involvement, which more closely mirrors that of self-report studies on gang membership (Egley, Howell, and Major 2006; Esbensen, Deschenes, and Winfree 1999; Esbensen and Huizinga 1993; Freng et al. 2012; Major and Egley 2002). Furthermore, evidence demonstrates that Canadian gangs share many similarities with the "typical" American gang (Deane, Bracken, and Morrissette 2007; Grekul and LaBoucane-Benson 2006), including having lower levels of education and reporting being economically disadvantaged (Grekul and LaBoucane-Benson 2008).

Group Structure and Processes

It is important to note that gangs do not necessarily exist for delinquency, but gang involvement often corresponds to higher levels of delinquency and criminal behavior (Curry and Spergel 1992). Evidence exists that much like other street gangs, hanging out and partying represent the primary activities of these groups (Henderson et al. 1999; Klein 1995). In terms of criminal activities, while many urban gangs are financially motivated, Native American gangs seem to stray away from economic pursuits and lean toward property crimes, vandalism, and alcohol-related offenses (Hailer and Hart 1999; Joseph and Taylor 2003; Major et al. 2004; Theriot and Parker 2007). In Canada, however, some evidence exists that Aboriginal gangs seem to be more profit driven (Grekul and LaBoucane-Benson 2006; Totten 2009, 2010). Native American gangs often fight for control of the drug trade, as it allows for financial independence (Amber et al. 2021; Bucerius et al. 2021; Chettleburgh 2003). Due to their remoteness, reservations/reserves furnish an ideal place to conduct illegal activities, including drug sales, as law enforcement capacity is often limited, especially given the large land masses involved (Joseph and Taylor 2003; Major et al. 2004; Mowatt and Matz 2014).

In contrast to other gangs, gang violence tends to be somewhat limited, although it seems more characteristic of gangs in larger communities (Hailer 2008; Hailer and Hart 1999; Joseph and Taylor 2003; Major et al. 2004). Indigenous gang members tend to perpetuate violence to achieve a higher status rather than in a fight over turf like most gangs (Major et al. 2004; Starbuck, Howell, and Lindquist 2001; Theriot and Parker 2007). For this reason, firearms tend not to be used (Freng et al. 2012; Joseph and Taylor 2003; Major et al. 2004). Other reasons for violence include revenge, retaliation, and reputation, which then enhance honor, respect, and self-esteem (Totten 2009, 2010). In Canada, Aboriginal gangs tend to engage in more violence than other Canadian gangs (Chettleburgh 2007; Comack et al. 2013; Goodwill 2016; Grekul 2007).

Native gangs tend to be less structured and organized, although this varies from group to group, much like gangs overall (Dunbar 2017; Grant and Feimer 2007; Grekul and LaBoucane-Benson 2006, 2008; Hailer and Hart 1999; Major et al. 2004; Mowatt and Matz 2014; Theriot and Parker 2007; Tobin 2008). While these gangs tend to be fluid, without a significant amount of organization, they do seem to possess some structure in terms of leadership hierarchy, rules, symbols, colors, and territory (Bucerius et al. 2021; Freng et al. 2012; Grekul and LaBoucane-Benson 2006, 2008; Totten 2009, 2010). Interestingly, some gangs restrict membership, including needing sponsorship for entry, making it difficult for non-members to access them (Buddle 2011; Totten 2009, 2010). Violence often marks initiation strategies in Canada, with individuals required to do "minutes" or "missions" (Chalas and Grekul 2017; Totten 2009, 2010).

Exiting Indigenous Gangs

Exiting, on the other hand, consists of an ongoing process related to a multitude of factors, much like what we see with gang members in general (e.g., Carson and Vecchio 2015; Decker and Lauritsen 2002; Pyrooz and Decker 2011). Although recent research provides limited explanations on desistance from Indigenous gangs, one study established 13 categories for why Native individuals leave their gangs or what assists with their departure (Goodwill 2009):

> Working in the legal workforce, accepting support from family or girlfriend, helping others stay out of or move away from gang life, not wanting to go back to jail, accepting responsibility for family, accepting guidance and protection, participating in ceremony, avoiding alcohol, publicly expressing that you are out of the gang, wanting legitimate relationships outside gang life, experiencing a native brotherhood, stopping self from reacting like a gangster, and acknowledging the drawbacks of gang violence. (Goodwill 2009, 151–152)

Additionally, gang-involved Native individuals may desist due to gaining maturity or beginning a religious path (MacRae-Krisa 2013). Noted by MacRae-Krisa (2013) is the assertion that most individuals explain that they have left the gang due to social processes and experiences within the gang. Life-course events, such as wanting to provide for a new child, represent other notable desistance factors (Chalas and Grekul 2017). Leaving the gang represents a process that may require additional "minutes" or getting "stripped" internally to the gang. Externally, previous gang members often face retaliatory attacks as they find their new path (Chalas and Grekul 2017).

Programming

Given the multitude of reasons for Indigenous individuals to join and leave gangs, many approaches to programming have been suggested. Foremost among these include prevention and intervention (Grekul and LaBoucane-Benson 2006, 2008). For both, addressing the reasons that individuals join gangs in the first place, including issues related to employment, education, and family, seem pertinent (Beare 2011; Chalas and Grekul 2017; Feldmeier 2011; Grekul and LaBoucane-Benson 2006, 2008; Preston et al. 2012; Totten 2009, 2010; White 2009). Given that many of the risk factors for joining gangs among Native individuals mirror those among other groups, conventional general gang or delinquency prevention programming aimed at several factors related to gang membership, such as the Gang Resistance Education and Training Program (G.R.E.A.T.), Gang Prevention through Targeted Outreach, and the comprehensive model as originally proposed by Spergel, should be effective (Burch and Kane 1999; Dunbar 2017; Esbensen 2004; Hailer and Hart 1999; Hautala et al. 2016; Major et al. 2004; Spergel et al. 1994; Theriot and Parker 2007; Totten 2009, 2010; Wyrick 2000). Other programs, such as Strengthening Families, directed at conflict resolution, communication skills, and the role of law enforcement have also been shown to decrease drug use and delinquent involvement, both factors associated with gang membership (Grant and Feimer 2007; Major et al. 2004). Other likely effective general strategies include wraparound services, public health visitation models, fetal alcohol spectrum disorder prevention programs, and mentoring (Totten 2009, 2010). Research has also indicated that collaboration and problem-solving partnerships, including restructuring both the juvenile justice and child welfare systems, would address some of the reasons for gang joining (Totten 2009, 2010). Developing and sustaining community capacities while providing adequate and sustained support and resources represents other ways to manage gangs within these communities. Finally, concentrating resources on the highest needs, while also immersing the community in public engagement, identifies some other successful general strategies (Totten 2009, 2010).

On the other hand, many researchers, as well as many tribes, have integrated cultural and traditional practices into their prevention/intervention programs in the hopes of strengthening cultural identity for youth and lowering their risk of participating in crime and gangs (Donnermeyer et al. 2000; Dunbar 2017; Grant and Feimer 2007; Hailer 2008; Mowatt and Matz 2014; Sanchez-Way and Johnson 2000; Sinclair and Grekul 2012; Theriot and Parker 2007). Thus, many identify a need for policy and programming geared specifically toward the unique circumstances of Indigenous individuals (Feldmeier 2011; Donnermeyer et al. 2000; Goodwill and Giannone 2017; Hailer 2008; Grant and Feimer 2007; Hautala et al. 2016; Mowatt and Matz 2014; Pridemore 2004; Theriot and Parker 2007). Often these programs target cultural activities such as language, traditional foods, and traditional customs often provided through a mentoring relationship with an elder (Sanchez-Way and Johnson 2000; Theriot and Parker 2007). One program that specifically focuses on Indigenous populations is the Safe Futures program (Guilmet et al. 1998). This program, developed in the late 1990s, sought to address the alcohol use, violence, and gang problem in Native schools (Guilmet et al. 1998). Community approaches with policies and strategies have shown a fair amount of promise for addressing Native American gangs due to their ability to understand the complexities of Indigenous living (Grekul and LaBoucane-Benson 2006; Major et al. 2004; Shantz, 2010; Theriot and Parker, 2007). These approaches require immense collaboration, though, and may be complex (Major et al. 2004; Theriot and Parker 2007). Furthermore, some research indicates that cultural identity did not differ between gang and non-gang members, and that cultural activity increased gang membership, indicating that cultural elements might not be the solution (Freng et al. 2012; Whitbeck et al. 2002).

In Canada, given the strong connection between street gangs and prison gangs, creating specialized units within prisons that incorporate cultural awareness and traditional spirituality to focus on desistance has been suggested (Chalas and Grekul 2017; Grekul and LaBoucane-Benson 2006, 2008). Other programs that show the realities of gang life, including those that involve ex-gang member mentors, might also provide support for desistance (Chalas and Grekul 2017; Grekul and LaBoucane-Benson 2006, 2008). Another interesting program, Ogijiita Pimatiswin Kinamatwin, involves gang members in employment and skills development but does not require that they desist from gang membership (Deane et al. 2007). Recognizing that it is difficult to remove oneself from social networks, this program instead focuses on assisting gang members from desisting in criminal activity with the hope that this will also result in decreased gang involvement. The program has been extremely successful with no recidivism for gang-related activities (Deane et al. 2007).

While a plethora of policies and strategies for preventing and dealing with gangs exist, there is little evidence of their success when specifically discussing Indigenous gangs (Esbensen 2004; Jackson, Bass, and Sharpe, 2005; Theriot and Parker, 2007). This is especially true when exploring the effectiveness of the specific culturally informed programs developed in many of these communities. Many programs are also conducted in schools or detention and may not reach most individuals (Gottfredson and Gottfredson 2001; Hernandez 2002). Furthermore, the complicated law enforcement system created by multiple jurisdictions on reservations leads to difficulties in policing the gang problem, thus influencing the overall success of such efforts (Joseph and Taylor 2003). Thus, this hastens a call for more extensive evaluation with this population to more effectively eradicate gangs from these communities (Chalas and Grekul 2017; Goodwill and Giannone 2017; Sinclair and Grekul 2012; Theriot and Parker 2007).

Conclusions and Future Directions

As is true for others, Indigenous communities are not immune to the issue of gangs. Gangs, as well as other social problems, have often been linked back to the unique history of these groups, including one marked by inequities, injustices, racism, discrimination, and institutional isolation. As Vigil (2002) argued, it is important to understand these unique histories to provide context to the realities of today. That said, the marginalization experienced by these groups in many ways mirrors other groups, and thus much of the evidence points to similar characteristics and processes as gangs in general with some additional unique qualities present. While evidence indicates a significant impact of these groups on Indigenous populations, a lack of more recent comprehensive examinations prevents us from fully understanding the scope and nature of gangs and thus how to best address these groups for Native communities. If we are to fully understand the impact of gangs on Indigenous populations, more research is needed.

Effective programming represents another area that calls for more extensive research. Given that other social problems, such as drug and alcohol use, characterize more of an issue for these communities than gangs, we might reap more benefits from focusing on these issues. As found in the general gang prevention literature, if we focus on delinquency given the ties with gang membership, decreasing delinquency often has similar impacts on gang membership (Major and Egley 2002). Furthermore, we need to more fully understand the role that culture can play in the prevention of these groups. Some evidence exists that programs should involve cultural elements, and thus calls for culturally specific programming are usually made for addressing gangs in this population (Wyrick 2000). However, the evidence on this is both scant and mixed, further increasing calls for evaluation of culturally informed programming. Future research should focus on the effectiveness of these programs both in terms of decreasing gang membership overall and then specifically for these populations. Without extending our research reach, our knowledge regarding the impact and prevention of gangs among Native individuals will remain inadequate, thus hindering our ability to positively impact Indigenous communities and the people within them.

A lack of recent comprehensive examinations prevents us from fully understanding the scope and nature of gangs and thus how to best address these groups for Native communities. To fully understand the impact of gangs on Indigenous populations, more research is needed.

Note

1. It is valuable to note that no universally accepted or accurate broad labels for the Indigenous Peoples exist, as these often represent social identities forced upon these groups (White 2009). Thus, we have chosen to use the broadest terms possible, including American Indian, Native American or Native, First Nations, Aboriginal, or Indigenous, to represent the collective populations discussed in previous works.

REFERENCES

Amber, Bev, Chantel Jazmyne, Faith Jorgina, and Robert Henry. 2021. *Indigenous Women and Street Gangs: Survivance Narratives*. Edmonton: University of Alberta Press.

Associated Press. 1994. "More Indian Kids Joining Gangs."

Beare, Margaret E. 2011. "Aboriginal Justice Issues—Trying for New Approaches, While Clinging to the Old: Our Shared Experiences." *Australian & New Zealand Journal of Criminology* 44: 291–308.

Bell, James, and Nicole Lim. 2005. "Young Once, Indian Forever: Youth Gangs in Indian Country." *American Indian Quarterly* 29 (3/4): 626–745.

Bucerius, Sandra, Daniel Jones, and Kevin Haggerty. 2021. "Indigenous Gangs in Western Canada." In *Routledge International Handbook of Critical Gang Studies*, edited by David C. Brotherton and Rafael Jose Gude, 284–297. London: Taylor & Francis Group.

Buddle, Kathleen. 2011. "Urban Aboriginal Gangs and Street Sociality in the Canadian West: Places, Performances, and Predicaments of Transition." In *Aboriginal People in Canadian Cities: Transformations and Continuities*, edited by Heather Howard and Craig Proulx, 171–202. Waterloo, ON: Wilfrid Laurier University Press.

Burch, Jim, and Candice Kane. 1999. "Implementing the OJJDP Comprehensive Gang Model." Washington, CD: US Department of Justice, OJJDP Fact Sheet.

Carson, Dena C., and J. Michael Vecchio. 2015. "Leaving the Gang: A Review and Thoughts on Future Research." In *The Wiley Handbook of Gangs*, edited by Scott H. Decker and David C. Pyrooz, 257–275. Chichester, UK: Wiley-Blackwell.

CBC. 2022. "How Gangs Are Recruiting Some Canadian Teens into a Life of Crime." https://www.cbc.ca/cbcdocspov/features/gangs-are-recruiting-some-canadian-teens-into-a-life-of-crime.

CBS News. 2021. "3 Members of 'Native Mob' Gang Sentenced to Prison for Distributing Meth, Assault." September 2. https://www.cbsnews.com/minnesota/news/native-mob-members-sentenced-methamphetamine-assault/.

Chalas, Dawn, and Jana Grekul. 2017. "'I've Had Enough': Exploring Gang Life from the Perspective of (ex) Members in Alberta." *Prison Journal* 97: 364–386.

Chettleburgh, Michael. 2003. "Results of the 2002 Canadian Policy Survey on Youth Gangs." Astwood Strategy Corporation. https://www.publicsafety.gc.ca/lbrr/archives/hv%206439.c2%20r47%202002-eng.pdf.

Chettleburgh, Michael. 2007. *Young Thugs: Inside the Dangerous World of Canadian Street Gangs*. Toronto, ON: HarperCollins Publishers.

Churchill, Ward, and Glenn Morris. 1992. "Key Indian Laws and Cases." In *The State of Native America: Genocide, Colonization, and Resistance*, edited by M. A. Jaimes, 13–22. Boston, MA: South End Press.

Comack, Elizabeth, Lawrence, Larry Morrissette, and Jim Silver. 2013. *Indians Wear Red: Colonialism, Resistance, and Aboriginal Street Gangs*. Winnipeg, MB: Fernwood Publishing.

Curry, David, and Irving A. Spergel. 1992. "Gang Involvement and Delinquency Among Hispanic and African American Adolescent Males." *Journal of Research in Crime and Delinquency* 29 (3): 273–291.

Deane, Lawrence, Denis Bracken, and Larry Morrissette. 2007. "Desistance within an Urban Aboriginal Gang." *Probation Journal* 54 (2): 125–141. https://doi.org/10.1177/0264550507077231.

Decker, Scott H., and Janet Lauritsen. 2002. "Leaving the Gang." In *Gangs in America*, edited by C. Ronald Huff, 51–70. Thousand Oaks, CA: Sage.

Deloria, Vine, and Clifford Lytle. 1983. *American Indians, American Justice*. Austin: University of Texas Press.

Donnermeyer, J. F., R. W. Edwards, E. L. Chavez, and F. Beauvais. 2000. "Involvement of American Indian Youth in Gangs." *Gangs, Drugs & Violence* 28 (1): 3–11.

Dunbar, Laura. 2017. "Youth Gangs in Canada: A Review of Current Topics and Issues." Public Safety Canada. https://www.publicsafety.gc.ca/cnt/rsrcs/pblctns/2017-r001/index-en.aspx.

Eckholm, Erik. 2009. "Gang Violence Grows on an Indian Reservation" *New York Times*, December 14, A14.

Egley, Arlen, Jr., James C. Howell, and Aline K. Major. 2006. *National Youth Gang Survey, 1991–2001*. Washington, DC: OJJDP Report.

Esbensen, Finn-Aage. 2004. "Evaluating G.R.E.A.T.: A School-Based Gang Prevention Program." Washington, DC: US Department of Justice. Office of Justice Programs. National Institute of Justice.

Esbensen, Finn-Aage, Elizabeth Deschenes, and L. Thomas Winfree. 1999. "Differences between Gang Girls and Gang Boys: Results from a Multisite Survey." *Youth and Society* 31: 27–53.

Esbensen, Finn-Aage, David Huizinga. 1993. "Gangs, Drugs, and Delinquency in a Survey of Urban Youth." *Criminology* 31: 565–589.

Esbensen, Finn-Aage, Dana Peterson, Terrance J. Taylor, and Adrienne Freng. 2010. *Youth Violence: Sex and Race Differences in Offending, Victimization, and Gang Membership*. Philadelphia, PA: Temple University Press.

Federally Recognized Indian Tribes and Resources for Native Americans. 2022. https://www.usa.gov/tribes.

Feldmeier, Jenna K. 2011. "Emergence of Indigenous Gangs in the Upper Midwest: An Inquiry into the Lives of Gang-Involved Youth." *University of Minnesota Digital Conservancy*. https://conservancy.umn.edu/handle/11299/113888.

Freng, Adrienne, Taylor Davis, Kristyn McCord, and Aaron Roussell. 2012. "The New American Gang? Gangs in Indian Country." *Journal of Contemporary Criminal Justice* 28 (4): 446–464.

Goldsmith, Andrew, and Mark Halsey. 2013. "Cousins in Crime: Mobility, Place, and Belonging in Indigenous Youth Co-offending." *British Journal of Criminology* 53 (6): 1157–1177.

Goodwill, Alanaise O. 2009. *In and Out of Aboriginal Gang Life: Perspectives of Aboriginal Ex-gang Members*. Vancouver: University of British Columbia. https://open.library.ubc.ca/collections/ubctheses/24/items/1.0053903.

Goodwill, Alanaise. 2016. "A Critical Incident Technique Study of the Facilitation of Gang Entry: Perspectives of Indigenous Men Ex-Gang Member." *Journal of Aggression, Maltreatment, & Trauma* 25 (5): 518–536.

Goodwill, Alanaise, and Zarina Giannone. 2017. "From Research to Practice: Bridging the Gaps for Psychologists Working in Indigenous Communities Affected by Gangs." *Canadian Psychology* 58 (4): 345–353. https://doi.org/10.1037/cap0000091.

Gordon, Robert. 2000. "Criminal Business Organization, Street Gangs, and 'Wanna-Be' Groups: A Vancouver Perspective." *Canadian Journal of Criminology* 42: 39–60.

Gottfredson, Gary D., and Denise C. Gottfredson. 2001. "Gang Problems and Gang Programs in a National Sample of Schools." Washington, DC: US Department of Justice. Office of Justice Programs, Office of Juvenile Justice and Delinquency Prevention.

Government of Canada. 2022a. "Indigenous Peoples and Communities." https://www.rcaanc-cirnac.gc.ca/eng/1100100013785/1529102490303.

Government of Canada. 2022b. "Statement of Apology to Former Students of Indian Residential Schools." https://www.rcaanc-cirnac.gc.ca/eng/1100100015644/1571589171655.

Grant, Christopher M., and Steve Feimer. 2007. "Street Gangs in Indian Country: A Clash of Cultures." *Journal of Gang Research* 14 (4): 27–66.

Grekul, Jana. 2007. "An Investigation into the Formation and Recruitment Processes of Aboriginal Gangs in Western Canada" Public Safety Canada.

Grekul, Jana, and Patti LaBoucane-Benson. 2006. "An Investigation into the Formation and Recruitment Processes of Aboriginal Gangs in Western Canada." In *When You Have Nothing to Live for, You Have Nothing to Die For*. Government of Canada. https://publications.gc.ca/site/eng/9.572162/publication.html.

Grekul, J., and P. LaBoucane-Benson. 2008. "Aboriginal Gangs and Their (Dis)placement: Contextualizing Recruitment, Membership, and Status." *Canadian Journal of Criminology and Criminal Justice* 50(1): 59–82.

Guilmet, George M., David L. Whited, Norm Dorpat, and Cherlyn Pijanowski. 1998. "The Safe Future Initiative at Chief Leshi Schools: A School-Based Tribal Response to Alcohol-Drug Abuse, Violence-Gang Violence, and Crime on an Urban Reservation." *American Indian Culture and Research Journal* 22: 407–440.

Hailer, Julie A. 2008. "American Indian Youth Involvement in Urban Street Gangs: Invisible No More?" PhD Dissertation. University of Arizona.

Hailer, Julia A., and Cynthia Baroody Hart. 1999. "A New Breed of Warrior: The Emergence of American Indian Youth Gangs." *Journal of Gang Research* 7 (1): 23–33.

Hautala, Dane S., Kelly J. Sittner, and Les B. Whitbeck. 2016. "Prospective Childhood Risk Factors for Gang Involvement Among North American Indigenous Adolescents." *Youth Violence and Juvenile Justice* 14 (4): 390–410.

Hill, Karl, James Howell, J. David Hawkins, and Sara Battin-Pearson. 1999. "Childhood Risk Factors for Adolescent Gang Membership: Results from the Seattle Social Development Project." *Journal of Research in Crime and Delinquency*, 36: 300–322.

Henderson, Erik, Stephen J. Kunitz, and Jerrold E. Levy. 1999. "The Origins of Navajo Youth Gangs." *American Indian Culture and Research Journal* 23 (3): 243–264.

Hernandez, Arturo. 2002. "Can Education Play a Role in the Prevention of Youth Gangs in Indian Country? One Tribe's Approach." *ERIC Digest*. https://files.eric.ed.gov/fulltext/ED471717.pdf.

Indigenous Foundations. 2022. "Identity." Accessed July 2. https://indigenousfoundations.arts.ubc.ca/identity/.

Jackson, Mary S., Lessie Bass, and Elizabeth Sharpe. 2005. "Working with Youth Street Gangs and Their Families: Utilizing a Nurturing Model for Social Work Practice." *Journal of Gang Research* 12 (2): 1–17.

Jaimes, M. Annette. 1992. "Introduction: Sand Creek: The Morning After." In *The State of Native America: Genocide, Colonization, and Resistance*, edited by M. Annette Jaimes, 1–12. Boston, MA: South End Press.

Joseph, Janice, and Dorothy Taylor. 2003. "Native-American Youths and Gangs." *Journal of Gang Research* 10 (2): 45–54.

Kelley, Matt. 1997. "Indian Reservations Harries by Youth-Gang Crime Wave." *Los Angeles Times*. https://www.latimes.com/archives/la-xpm-1997-oct-12-me-41947-story.html.

Klein, Malcolm. 1995. *The American Street Gang: Its Nature, Prevalence, and Control.* New York: Oxford University Press.

Koch, Jordan, and Jay Scherer. 2016. "Redd Alert! (De)coding the Media's Production of Aboriginal Gang Violence on a Western Canadian First Nation." *Aboriginal Policy Studies* 6 (1): 34–62. https://doi.org/10.5663/aps.v6i1.25531.

Lilly, J. Robert, Francis T. Cullen, and Richard Ball. 2002. *Criminological Theory: Context and Consequences,* 3rd ed. Thousand Oaks, CA: Sage Publications.

MacRae-Krisa, Leslie. 2013. "Exiting Gangs: Examining Processes and Best Practice within an Alberta Context." *International Journal of Child, Youth, & Family Studies* 4 (1): 5–23. https://doi.org/10.18357/ijcyfs41201311818.

Major, Aline K., and Arlen Egley, Jr. 2002. "2000 Survey of Youth Gangs in Indian Country." *National Youth Gang Center Fact Sheet.* Washington DC: Office of Juvenile Justice and Delinquency Prevention.

Major, Aline K., Arlen Egley, Jr., James C. Howell, Barbara Mendenhall, and Troy Armstrong. 2004. "Youth Gangs in Indian Country." Washington, DC: Office of Juvenile Justice and Delinquency Prevention. Office of Justice Programs. United States Department of Justice.

Maxson, Cheryl. 1998. *Gang Members on the Move.* Washington, DC: OJJDP Juvenile Justice Bulletin.

Misjak, Laura. 2009. "Mexican Gangs Target American Indian Land." *Casper Star Tribune.* http://trib.com/news/state-and-regional/article_a5a67089-2a24-5ddd-a17d-4d1da4a5cfae.html.

Mowatt, Mary A., and Adam K. Matz. 2014. "Native American Involvement in Gangs." *Perspectives* 38 (3): 34–49.

"Native Mob, A Violent American Indian Gang, Is Most Active in Minnesota, North Dakota, South Dakota, Michigan, and Wisconsin." 2009, February 5. http://extendedcare.blogspot.com/2009/02/native-mob-violent-american-indian-gang.html.

Pember, Mary Annette. 2018. "Native Mob: A Scourge in Minnesota Plagues Indian Communities." ICT, September 13. https://ictnews.org/archive/native-mob-a-scourge-in-minnesota-plagues-indian-communities.

Preston, Jane P., Sheila Carr-Stewart, and Charlene Bruno. 2012. "The Growth of Aboriginal Youth Gangs in Canada," *Canadian Journal of Native Studies* 32 (2): 193–207.

Pridemore, William Alex. 2004. "Review of the Literature on Risk and Protective Factors of Offending Among Native Americans." *Journal of Ethnicity in Criminal Justice* 2 (4): 45–63.

Pyrooz, David C., and Scott H. Decker. 2011. "Motives and Methods for Leaving the Gang: Understanding the Process of Gang Desistance." *Journal of Criminal Justice* 39: 417–425.

Richland, Justin, and Sarah Deer. 2004. *Introduction to Tribal Legal Studies.* New York: AltaMira.

Robbins, Susan, and Rudolph Alexander, Jr. 1985. "Indian Delinquency on Urban and Rural Reservations." *Free Inquiry in Creative Sociology,* 13 (2): 179–182.

Sanchez-Way, Ruth, and Sadie Johnson. 2000. "Cultural Practices in American Indian Prevention Programs." *Juvenile Justice* 7 (2): 20–30.

Shantz, Jeff. 2010. "'The Foundation of Our Community': Cultural Restoration, Reclaiming Children and Youth in an Indigenous Community." *Journal of Social Welfare & Family Law* 32 (3): 229–236. https://doi.org/10.1080/09649069.2010.520515.

Sinclair, Raven, and Jana Grekul. 2012. "Aboriginal Youth Gangs in Canada: (De)constructing an Epidemic." *First Peoples Child & Family Review* 7 (1): 8–28. https://doi.org/10.7202/1068862ar.

Spergel, Irving, David Curry, Ron Chance, Candice Kane, Ruth Ross, Alba Alexander, Edwina Simmons, and Sandra Oh. 1994. *Gang Suppression and Intervention: Problem and Response, Research Summary*. Washington, DC: OJJDP Juvenile Justice Bulletin.

Starbuck, David, James C. Howell, and Donna J. Lindquist. 2001. *Hybrid and Other Modern Gangs*. Washington, DC: OJJDP Juvenile Justice Bulletin.

Theriot, Mathew T., and Barbara Parker. 2007. "Native American Youth Gangs: Linking Culture, History, and Theory for Improved Understanding, Prevention and Intervention." *Journal of Ethnicity in Criminal Justice* 5 (4): 83–97.

Tobin, Kimberly. 2008. *Gangs: An Individual and Group Perspective*. Upper Saddle River, NJ: Pearson.

Totten, Mark. 2009. "Aboriginal Youth and Violent Gang Involvement in Canada: Quality Prevention Strategies," *IPC Review* 3: 135–56.

Totten, Mark. 2010. "Preventing Aboriginal Youth Gang Involvement in Canada: A Gendered Approach." Aboriginal Policy Research Consortium International. https://ir.lib.uwo.ca/cgi/viewcontent.cgi?article=1389&context=aprci.

Vigil, James Diego. 2002. *A Rainbow of Gangs: Street Culture in the Mega-City*. Austin: University of Texas Press.

Whitbeck, Les, Dan Hoyt, Xiaojin Chen, and Jerry Stubben. 2002. "Predictors of Gang Involvement among American Indian Adolescents." *Journal of Gang Research* 10 (1): 11–26.

White, Rob. 2009. "Indigenous Youth and Gangs as Family." *Youth Studies Australia* 28 (3): 47–56.

Wyrick, P. 2000. "Understanding and Responding to Youth Gangs in Indian Country." *Juvenile Justice* 7 (2): 1–31.

CHAPTER 16

STUDYING GANGS IN CENTRAL AND SOUTH AMERICA
Reflections on Gender and Researcher Positionality

MARÍA JOSÉ MÉNDEZ AND ELLEN VAN DAMME

IN this chapter, we analyze qualitative studies in Central and South America published since 2010 and demonstrate how their lack of engagement with methodological questions, including the impact that positionality has on research, contributes to gender biases—the marginalization of women's perspectives, the privileging of male researchers, and the reinforcement of gender stereotypes on gangs. Building on the few self-reflexive accounts provided by gang researchers, we argue in favor of more methodological reflections that take positionality—a person's specific social, cultural, and political location in relation to others—and specifically the gendered status of scholars, seriously. Before exploring these gender biases, it is important to acknowledge the crucial work that qualitative gang researchers have done to nuance the study of the gang phenomenon in this region.

Studies on gangs in Central and South America tend to rely on secondary material—from the state, non-governmental organizations (NGOs), and journalistic sources. The lack of firsthand material from gang members themselves has to do with several problems. The first is the moral reluctance to engage with gang members, which grows out of state and societal prejudiced perceptions of gangs. Although the problem of stigmatization also surfaces in gang research elsewhere, nowhere is it more apparent than in Latin America, where it has become institutionalized in anti-gang legislation. Central America's so-called *mano dura* laws, for example, not only criminalize certain groups of young people as alleged gang members but also prohibit NGOs from working on gang prevention or rehabilitation.[1] While organizations like Homeboy Industries in the United States can openly work with (former) gang members (Schockman and Thompson 2021), this is forbidden in Central America, where social workers can and have been prosecuted for their association with gangs.

Second, the security of researchers is an issue. Qualitative research methods can require immersion in the field, as researchers try to capture social reality holistically. As such, these studies involve exposure and vulnerability to many risks. While studying gangs in their context was a possibility in the 1980s and still in the 1990s, this is much more difficult today in a region that accounts for the highest homicide rates in the world (UNODC 2019). The rise of criminal violence in Latin America after the Cold War and the transformation of gangs into more organized criminal groups present more serious risks to the safety of researchers. One example is how while Rodgers (2007) was able to "join a gang" in Nicaragua, nobody has really embedded themselves in a gang recently in Latin America.

The infamous death of filmmaker Christian Poveda, who conducted extensive fieldwork with gangs in El Salvador, for the making of his documentary *La Vida Loca*, is a reminder of the difficulties of qualitative research in the present (Fontes 2018). Despite having earned the trust of the Barrio 18 gang in La Campanera, he was killed by some of its members who believed him to be an informant (Carroll 2011). Poveda was not an academic but undertook similar risks to those faced by scholars who wish to get to know gang members intimately.

Third, there is the challenge of getting access to gang members and gang-controlled territories. Related to the rise of violence and crime in Latin America, the intense repression and incarceration of gang members, for example through *mano dura* policies (Hume 2007; Wolf 2017), has pushed gangs to become more clandestine and secretive, making access to them difficult. This difficulty in access is not unique to research in this region; scholars in the United States and elsewhere also confront this obstacle. Nonetheless, the latter takes on more acute dimensions in Central and South America, where punitive policies have led to "micro-genocidal massacres of youth in poor neighborhoods for the crimes of having tattoos on their body or baggy blue jeans" (Bourgois 2015, 312). Unlike in the United States—where a model of mass incarceration has been adopted to deal with the gang problem—lack of state resources in Latin America to build and sustain prisons, as well as violent state logics, inherited from US-sponsored counterinsurgency during the Cold War, have paved the way for the "social cleansing" of gang youth (Bourgois 2015, 312). This punitive approach used in Latin America has resulted in a heightened suspicion of researchers, which far exceeds the one observed in other settings.

Despite the challenges posed by moral prejudices, insecurity, and restricted access, some scholars have devoted their efforts to conducting qualitative research in Central and South America. This research has foregrounded the perspectives of gang members and challenged moralized stereotypes of them. Still, and even though the region has been affected by gang violence since the late 1990s and early 2000s, this research is scarce. Indeed, while all three countries in northern Central America (El Salvador, Guatemala, and Honduras) are almost equally negatively affected by the Barrio 18 and Mara Salvatrucha (MS-13) gangs, among others (Cruz 2010), sustained academic research is more present in postwar El Salvador (e.g., Martínez D'Aubuisson 2017; Hernández-Anzora 2017) and Guatemala (e.g., Fontes 2018; Saunders-Hastings 2015) than in Honduras. The other two Central American countries, Nicaragua and Costa Rica, are less affected by gangs and have also received less attention from researchers (see Rocha and Rodgers 2008 for Nicaragua). Staying in the northern part of Latin America, Mexico is dealing more with violence and crime related to drug cartels, some of which are linked to collaborations with gangs in Central America (Farah 2012; Gomez 2020). Few researchers have also studied gangs in Belize (Baird 2021; Pitts and Inkpen 2021). Moving on to the Caribbean, some research on gangs has been conducted in Jamaica (Katz, Harriott, and Hedberg 2020), but little is known about gangs in other Caribbean countries (see **Chapter 17**). Finally, in South America, most gang research has been conducted in Colombia (Baird 2018; Botero et al. 2019; Drummond, Dizgun, and Keeling 2019; Krakowski 2021), followed by Brazil (Carvalho and Soares 2016; Johnson 2017; Johnson and Densley 2018; Silveira Rocha and Davis Rodrigues 2020), Ecuador (Brotherton and Gude 2020), and Venezuela (Vandenbogaerde and Van Hellemont 2016; Werlau 2014).

While qualitative studies have made room for gang members' perspectives, contributing more nuanced views on the gang phenomenon, they have not successfully pushed against the gender imbalances that continue to structure the study of gangs across the globe and criminological research more generally (Chesney-Lind 2006). Since the pioneering gang studies conducted in the United States in the twentieth century, qualitative research on gangs has suffered from a strong gender imbalance, focusing overwhelmingly on the experiences of young men, involving mainly male researchers, and often featuring women, if at all, in stereotyped roles of subordination, such as "mere weapon holders, or sex objects" (Panfil and Peterson 2015, 202). Notwithstanding the important interventions by US feminist criminologists, particularly in the 1990s, to rectify gender bias, gang research remains colored by it. This is certainly the case in Central and South America, where very little research is conducted on and by women (Van Damme 2020).

It is worthwhile, nonetheless, to recognize some female scholars studying gangs in the region, as well as some studies focusing on gang-affiliated women. The former include Deborah Levenson (2013) and Katherine Saunders-Hastings (2015) focusing on Guatemala; Lirio Gutiérrez Rivera (2013) on Honduras; Caroline Doyle (2021) on Colombia; Ellen Vandenbogaerde (2016) and Maria Werlau (2014) on Venezuela; Karina Biondi (2016) on Brazil, and Pamela Ruiz (2019) and María José Méndez (2019) on Central America. Only a few studies focus specifically on women, although not always based on empirical data. Those drawing on empirical research include María Lizet Santacruz Giralt and Elin Cecilie Ranum's (2010) work on imprisoned female gang members in El Salvador; Nelly Erandy Reséndiz Rivera's (2017) study of imprisoned female gang members in Guatemala; Carolina Sampó's (2016) research on the role of women in Central American gangs; Ellen Van Damme's (2020) study of women in and around gangs in Honduras; and María José Méndez's (2022) work on imprisoned female gang members in Guatemala, El Salvador, and Honduras.

In the next section, we point to the lack of methodological reflections accompanying qualitative gang studies in Central and South America and take a closer look at their gender bias. Following this, we consider some of the few self-reflexive accounts in which gang scholars explore the impact of their gendered status on research. Crossing the insights derived from these accounts with our personal experiences as female researchers studying gangs in Central America, we argue that gang researchers must critically assess the gendered power relations they navigate in their field sites.

GANG STUDIES IN CENTRAL AND SOUTH AMERICA

When we talk about gangs, we use the Eurogang definition to define and delimit what we consider to be gangs: "A street gang (or troublesome youth group corresponding to a street gang elsewhere) is any durable, street-oriented youth group whose involvement in illegal activity is part of its group identity" (Weerman et al. 2009, 20). In doing so, we do not seek to privilege a static view of gangs that neglects their fluidity or the unstable boundaries of gang membership. Without going into an in-depth discussion of their significant divergences throughout Central and South America, we recognize that the definition of gangs may alter according to their local specificities. For instance, gangs in northern Central America (El Salvador, Guatemala, and Honduras) are unique because of their division between the so-called "maras" and "pandillas," the two biggest gangs: Mara Salvatrucha (MS-13) and Pandilla 18 or Barrio 18. Although both terms are translated equally as "gangs" in English, they have a unique connotation in Central America, whereby the word *mara* is synonymous with Mara Salvatrucha and *pandilla* is used to refer to Barrio 18.

In what follows, we discuss Latin American gang literature from the past decade (starting from 2010). The aim is not to be exhaustive; for a more detailed overview, see Rodgers and Baird (2015). We focus our state-of-the-art analysis on gang-related studies in Latin America, which use primary sources. We are aware that several studies were conducted based on a literature review, such as Applebaum and Mawby's (2018) article on women, gangs, and gang violence in Central America. We do not include this type of work in our discussion. Furthermore, we do not include studies where we were unable to discern methodology; sometimes it is not clear whether an article is based on literature or secondary sources. For instance, Blake's (2017) analysis of the impact that the labeling of MS-13 as a terrorist organization has on Central American asylum seekers does not include a discussion of the methodology, though the use of legal sources makes clear it is a legal analysis. Furthermore, we do not include some of the most recent empirical studies conducted by women as they are under embargo or are not yet published (e.g., Ruiz 2019, Van Damme 2020, Méndez 2022).

In Table 16.1, we critically analyze the methodological discussions of empirical gang studies that are based on interviews, ethnography, and mixed methods. One observation emerging out of this table is that many studies provide little to no information on the exact number of interviews conducted. There is also no consistency in exploring methodological questions concerning the sample, techniques, context of the interview, demographical data of the interviewers and interviewees, ethical reflections, and so on. Although we do not doubt that researchers spent a lot of time in the field and have conducted many interviews, we would argue for more transparency regarding this and other methodological aspects. Furthermore, most studies focus on male gang members, or only include women in the sample as a minority, without any critical examination. The lack of women's perspectives perhaps explains why some studies reproduce stereotypical views of women as "sex objects." A case in point is when Brenneman (2012) writes, "many female gang members provide sex, forced or consensual, for the male membership of the clica" (35). In reducing female gang members to sexually subservient individuals, Brenneman fails to analyze or at least mention in passing the varied roles they play. Finally, regarding gender and positionality, details are often missing on the gender, age, class, and so on of the gang members and how this could have potentially influenced the research process. We use "ND" (no data or missing data) to indicate where these kinds of discussions are missing.

Several of the studies mentioned in Table 16.1 include surveys, which often face security and veracity challenges that are important for researchers to consider. First of all, Cruz and Rosen (2020) recognize the danger of conducting surveys with gang members and how

Table 16.1 Summary of Gang Research in Central and South America

Country	Study	Methodology	Gender & Positionality
Brazil	Wilding (2014)	Qualitative; 74 interviews and 12 workshops with 122 participants; details on age, gender, and how interviewees were approached etc.; details on research site: political, socioeconomic, and geographical background; details on case study: the place, how many favelas were involved, how many people and homes there are in these favelas, how many institutions are present in these favelas, etc.; details on drug gangs: Comando Vermelho, Amigos dos Amigos, and Terceiro Comando	See methodology
Colombia	Baird (2018)	Qualitative; 40 life-history interviews with male gang members; discussion of age and positions in the gang	Focus on male gang members
El Salvador	Amaya and Martínez (2015)	Qualitative; document analysis (academic, journalistic, police intelligence documents), ND; in-depth interviews with (former) gang members of the Barrio 18, ND	ND
	Martínez-Reyes and Navarro-Pérez (2020)	Qualitative; interviews; ND	ND
	Santacruz Giralt (2019)	Qualitative; 16 interviews with incarcerated women, 23–39 years old, lower educated, majority have children and joined the gang at a young age (on average 13 years old); expert interviews, ND	Focus on female gang members
Guatemala	Cruz et al. (2020b)	Qualitative; 105 in-depth interviews with community stakeholders (20 females, 28 males) and former gang members (13 females and 44 males)	Gender imbalance because study was hampered due to COVID-19 outbreak
	Fontes (2018, 2019)	Ethnography; details about how he got access to and gained the trust of gang members; why joining a gang as a researcher was not feasible; why he chose to use the real name of the gang member he interviewed; and how he responded to the recurrent question "What can you give me?" with "Not much... I can tell your story far from these streets where you have seen so many like you die." (320-321)	Disclaimer for the focus on only male gang members
	Saunders-Hastings (2018)	Ethnography; 16 months of fieldwork, interviews; ND	ND
	Reséndiz Rivera (2017)	Qualitative; interviews with female and male gang members in detention centers and gang-controlled neighborhoods; ND	Focus on women, gangs and gang violence

(continued)

Table 16.1 Continued

Country	Study	Methodology	Gender & Positionality
Honduras	Carter (2014)	Qualitative; interviews; ND	ND
Various countries in Central America	Boerman and Knapp (2017)—Northern Central America	Qualitative; 100+ interviews; ND	Focus on gangs and violence against women
	Boerman and Golob (2020)	Qualitative; 200+ semi-structured expert interviews, and 200+ semi-structured interviews with people "who have been subjected to gangs' attempts to coerce them into criminal service and/or exploitative male–female relationships" (2)	ND
	Brenneman (2012)	Qualitative; in-depth interviews with former gang members (59 males, 4 females)	ND
	Cruz (2018); Cruz et al. (2017, 2020a); Cruz and Rosen (2020)—Northern Central America	Mixed methods; detailed descriptions of how many interviews and surveys they conducted, in which detention centers, etc.; discussion of ethical issues regarding the security of respondents and institutional review board (IRB) related matters; discrepancies between seemingly comparable studies: one study did receive IRB approval (Cruz et al. 2020a), the other "was granted IRB exemption... due to the fact that it did not meet the definition of research" (Cruz 2018, 6)	ND
	Farah and Babineau (2017)—El Salvador & Honduras	Qualitative; interviews; ND	ND

to mitigate that: "Given the hyperviolent Salvadoran context, the research team discarded the possibility of conducting survey interviews on the streets or in households as other studies previously have done (Cruz and Portillo 1998; Santacruz and Concha-Eastman 2001). Therefore, to undertake the survey, the research team focused on subjects housed in detention centers or participating in rehabilitation programs" (Cruz and Rosen 2020, 4).

Second, surveys that are not followed up by more in-depth interviews run the risk of receiving socially desirable responses. One of the authors of this chapter participated in a national gang survey in Central America and witnessed how gang-affiliated boys lied when they answered "no" to a question about their personal drug use. A few minutes after the survey completion, they talked openly about their marijuana use with other survey participants. If quantitative surveys are not triangulated with experience-near interviews or observations, ticking boxes can lead to false interpretations. Moreover, socially desirable responses are also influenced by what is deemed culturally acceptable (Kemmelmeier 2016; Kammigan, Enzmann, and Pauwels 2018). In northern Central America, marijuana consumption and dealing are linked to gang membership. Hence, for someone living in a gang-controlled area to state in a survey that they consume marijuana would be to admit that they belong to a gang. The same question is likely answered differently in, for example, Uruguay, where cannabis is legal.

Methodological reflections in surveys are usually limited to discussions on the selection process and questions of anonymity. These discussions should be expanded to include reflections on security and veracity challenges, as well as the impact that the researcher's identity and social context have on data. Although the latter has been relatively absent from gang research in Latin America, several qualitative studies have given attention to questions of positionality. In the next section, we analyze self-reflexivity in gang research, with a focus on gender.

Self-Reflexivity

In contrast to mainstream scholarly traditions that hold on to the figure of the neutral and distant researcher, feminist methodologists have long argued that the scholar's identity enables and inhibits particular kinds of insights, shaping what the researcher can learn and know. Thus, they have encouraged researchers to reflect deeply on how their intersectional and structural locations (socioeconomic, gendered, racialized, cultural, ideological, geopolitical, historical, and institutional) inform every aspect of the investigative process, from decisions about the choice of data and research questions to interactions with study participants and their representation of them (Harding 1987; Mohanty 2003; Ackerly and True 2008).

Self-reflexivity matters for how it discloses the partiality of research, providing readers with a sense of the particular perspective from which findings arise. Being reflexive also matters because it compels researchers to attend to the unexpected ways in which their positionality can lead to the silencing of narratives and subjects who have long been marginalized in knowledge production. Most fundamentally, self-reflexivity invites researchers to think about how the research can be done better and in a more ethical way.

Until recently, there has been a relative paucity of methodological discussions in qualitative studies on gangs in Central and South America. Although often relegated to footnotes or appendices, reflections on the gendered status of the scholar are gaining prominence in the literature. In what follows, we review some of the main topics that gang researchers submit to critical evaluation while invoking insights gleaned from our respective studies on gangs in Central America. It is important to note that the next part explores what it means for researchers to study gangs as man-identifying and woman-identifying heterosexual subjects. In doing so, we do not seek to elevate gender binarism or heterosexuality as the main lenses through which to analyze the impact of gendered status on research. Rather, this focus simply reflects the existing literature on the subject.

Gendered Status

Within the context of heavy state repression, mass incarceration, and transnational punitive measures (Wolf 2017) that characterizes Latin America, gang members tend to heavily distrust researchers and are reluctant to participate in their studies. While North American scholars often must deal with the suspicion that they are members of US law enforcement—whether FBI, CIA, or Interpol (Fontes 2018, 257)—local researchers are sometimes suspected of being part of their country's security apparatus. These misgivings are often compounded by the researcher's gendered status.

Most gang researchers in Latin America argue that the gang phenomenon is shaped by a sexist culture associated with ideals of toughness and power, reluctance to express emotion, denigration of femininity, and dominance over women (Rodgers 2007; Baird 2018). As such, scholars who engage with gangs often navigate a hypermasculine context, where their gendered status has a tremendous impact on their ability to access and establish rapport with research participants. While the researcher's gendered positioning can be advantageous for the latter, it also raises a wide host of empirical and normative issues that scholars must address so as not to reproduce problematic interactions with and representations of gangs.

Studying Gangs as Male Researchers

Given that gang research in Central and South America is still a male-dominated endeavor, much of the gender analysis published in the last decade has revolved around the pros and cons of being a male researcher. One main advantage identified in these discussions concerns the role that masculinity plays in accessing and building rapport with male gang members. To allay any fears about his presence in the community, Adam Baird (2018) writes about leveraging his "male advantage" to connect with gang members in Medellín's urban periphery. He found that incorporating local male banter into his interviews helped overcome dynamics of suspicion. For instance, when asking to record interviews, he would try to break the ice by saying that he could not write and talk at the same time, using the vernacular phrase "*no puedo mamar y silbar a la vez*," "I can't suck and whistle at the same time" (346). Baird attributes the fact that most participants agreed to be interviewed and voice-recorded to his conscious attempt to engage in a homosocial masculine culture, exchanging playful remarks about football, beer, or women. Becoming "one of the boys" not only allowed him to develop rapport but opened the space for discussing "manly" gang activities such as fighting, gun use, participation in violence, and sexual relations.

Anthony Fontes (2018) also writes about how "deep hanging out" enhanced his rapport with male gang members in Guatemala City. Although not explicitly, one can surmise from Fontes' account that engaging with his "maleness" and the world of his research subjects—drinking prison moonshine and playing sports with inmates—helped break the ice with them. The same for Dennis Rodgers (2007), who suggests that Nicaraguan *pandilleros* hung out with him—spending "many nights chatting, drinking, and laughing together" (452)—thanks to his gender and age affinity, as well as his willingness to display bravado.

Notwithstanding the closer rapport that a male-gendered status affords, gang researchers recognize that leveraging male privilege is a double-edged sword. Epistemologically, one of the problems with "bromancing" gang members is that it can shape the data in masculinist ways. By imposing a tone of bravado to conversations, whereby men are supposed to be strong and in control, male bonding can make gang members less willing to make themselves vulnerable and expose their feelings about sensitive areas of their life (Baird 2020, 354). Men's talk, particularly its basis on dynamics of masculine competition, often induces gang members to exaggerate their exploits and overemphasize their risk-taking abilities. This performative dimension brings up important questions about the veracity of data and the problem of "ethnographic seduction." Fontes (2018, 48), for instance, discusses how he was drawn in by the eloquence and bravado of his interlocutors and had to actively gain distance from this seduction.

Another issue, broached within these epistemological discussions, concerns gender bias and the power dynamics that prevent male researchers from accessing women interlocutors. Gang researchers tend to talk only with men, inadvertently reproducing power dynamics whereby women's bodies and perspectives are relegated to the societal peripheries (Wilding 2012, 4). The fact that researchers derive their findings on gangs almost exclusively from men, considering women from the latter's vantage point, if at all, has important empirical and normative implications. As a Honduran female gang member told Ellen (Van Damme 2020), "I think that the story of a male gang member is often heard, but if you sit down and listen to the story of a female gang member you will be amazed because, as women, we experience things differently than men do, we are also treated differently."

During our respective research experiences in Central America, we sat down and listened to female gang members, noticing stark differences between male gang members' depiction of gang-affiliated women and the latter's self-understandings. Male gang members typically circumscribed women's gang membership to historical portrayals of female gang members as "lures, spies, mere weapon holders, or sex objects" (Panfil and Peterson 2015, 202)—women whose roles were structured to serve gang males and were ensured through their victimization and maneuvering. In contrast, female gang members spoke about gaining empowerment through their participation in the logistics and organization of illicit activities. Both representations—of gang-affiliated women as victims or agents—cannot be taken for granted as they are interpretations embedded within dominant cultural discourses. However, the gap between these representations is crucial for interrogating the widespread scholarly and political consensus that women in Central America are only victimized by gangs. Beyond Central America, ignoring women's perspectives in gang research has the detrimental effect of furthering stereotypes about them and re-creating the widespread depiction of gang members as merely hypermasculine violent subjects—an image that politicians often use to justify their use of extreme punitive measures against gangs (Hume and Wilding 2015, 103).

Male gang researchers increasingly include disclaimers that acknowledge the gender bias of their studies and the need to correct this imbalance. According to them, women's absence from their studies owes to their male-gendered status. For instance, in his study of gangs in Guatemala, Kevin O'Neill (2015) writes about how his identity as a young North American man made access to the female relatives of his main informants difficult: "It turned out to be improper to engage any of them individually for any extended amount of time, putting their reputation as well as my personal safety at risk" (202). Fontes also attributes the dearth of conversations with women to the gender dynamics and sexual politics of the prisons where he conducted fieldwork (260). He was hesitant to pursue interviews with the inmates' female companions because he wanted to avoid adding tension to the relationships between gang members and their families. Similarly, in his analysis of a Salvadoran street gang, Thomas Ward (2013) writes about the difficulties of accessing women interlocutors. He stopped interviewing women because male gang members became suspicious of his intentions toward them.

Underpinning these justifications is the assumption that contacting gang-affiliated women might motivate their male relatives to engage in jealous behavior, which can bring harm to both research subjects and researchers. Being careful about how the researcher's proximity to interlocutors affects their relationships with relatives, friends, or neighbors is crucial in qualitative studies, as it may be "a boon to some, but a threat to others" (Fujii 2012, 721). The "male sexual jealousy excuse," however, warrants additional scrutiny as it can evolve dangerously into a given—hardly begging any substantiation—that reproduces power differences and further entrenches the dominant culture of male bravado that both shapes the gang phenomenon and the study of gangs. Ward (2013), for instance, recognizes that his decision to not include women was a choice he made, not an overdetermined decision.

In adopting the "male sexual jealousy" excuse uncritically, researchers also run the risk of reifying a patriarchal cultural world and overestimating the obstacles male possessiveness poses to accessing a more diverse pool of subjects. For instance, Ellen was advised by her male gatekeepers to contact imprisoned male gang leaders for permission to do research with female gang members. However, the day she visited the male prison, she was informed that all the male leaders had just been transferred to a different prison. She headed straight to the female prison and found that she was still able to do research without the male leaders' permission.

The problem of accessing gang-affiliated women is certainly exacerbated when conducting research in violent settings due to heightened concerns about the researcher's and participants' safety, but we would like to suggest that this selection bias can be addressed by revisiting selection criteria. Being deliberate about including women's perspectives in gang research might involve identifying a subject pool of women from the outset. Both O'Neill and Fontes explain that part of the difficulty of accessing women interlocutors has to do with their snowball sampling technique—that is, their reliance on being introduced to new contacts by their trusted interlocutors. What if instead of employing a chain-referral sampling that relies on male gang members to generate female contacts, gang researchers were to deliberately include a sample of women from the beginning of the research? Choosing an anti-snowball sampling technique to speak with women would lessen the "male sexual jealousy" problem that is exacerbated by the researcher's connection to male gang members. Of course, researchers would still need to be conscious of the potential risks that their interaction might bring to those they interview.

Another strategy to avoid selection criteria that marginalize women might also involve collaborating with female scholars. Faced with reluctance on the part of young women to discuss sexual violence by gangs, Baird (2020), for example, learned that he could only gain access to these experiences by collaborating with a female researcher. In trying to challenge the gender imbalance of research, however, scholars should be careful not to narrow down the experiences of women to their sexual victimization, a common trope in gang research. It's not enough to simply include women's experiences; it is necessary to rethink the frameworks within which one includes their stories (Van Damme 2020). Writing about the mothers of armed youth, for instance, Zubillaga, Llorens, and Souto (2015) highlight how understanding the complexities of violence in Caracas's barrios "implies ... understanding other logics of action that are associated with female participation—how women contribute to as well as challenge violence in their daily contexts" (165).

In addition to potentially furthering gender bias and a culture of bravado in gang research, male camaraderie with gang members raises the ethical dilemmas of overrapport and "fake friendship" (Duncombe and Jessop 2002). Qualitative researchers are often encouraged to establish close relations of trust and affinity with their interlocutors to encourage them to open up. However, how close is too close? This "dilemma of proximity" (Fujii 2012, 720) is especially prominent in studies that center the illicit activities of gangs. Is hanging out with gang members while they victimize others morally justifiable? When does male bonding become disingenuous—a "fake friendship"? These are questions that gang researchers are increasingly reflecting on in their works. Fontes (2018, 260), for instance, relates how it became ethically untenable for him to hang out with gang extortionists on the streets as spending time with them could make him an accomplice to their crimes.

Baird (2018, 354) speaks to another important ethical conundrum associated with "faking friendship." Reflecting on the discomfort and guilt he felt when El Mechudo, a male gang member, greeted him like a close friend, Baird confesses to having made some ethically dubious decisions by playing along as El Mechudo's buddy to obtain data from him. While Baird does not state it explicitly, the ethical tensions of creating the illusion of friendship are associated with one key principle of research ethics: the management of consent. Duncombe and Jessop (2002) capture the way an outwardly friendly stance for the instrumental purpose of getting data complicates the principle of obtaining voluntary and informed consent from study participants: "If interviewees are persuaded to participate in the interview by the researcher's show of empathy and the rapport achieved in conversation, how far can they be said to have given their 'informed consent' to make the disclosures that emerge during the interview?" (11). While the dilemma of proximity is not one that can be easily resolved, the ethical conundrums it raises point to the need of not substituting a more open negotiation of the interviewees' consent with the doing of friendly rapport.

The issue of overrapport to which male gang researchers have devoted attention also concerns female gang researchers, perhaps in a more acute way. Before exploring these dilemmas, let us begin with how a woman-gendered status opens but also closes possibilities of engagement with gang members. Here, we would like to turn the critical gaze inwards as woman-identifying researchers to raise further questions about the empirical and normative implications of gendered status for research on gangs.

Studying Gangs as Female Researchers

Being a female gang researcher means experiencing discrepancies in levels of access. Unlike male researchers, who often report feeling relatively comfortable hanging out with male gang members, the same is not true for female researchers. Reflecting on her fieldwork in El Salvador and Haiti, Gaëlle Rivard Piché notes how, while male researchers could meet with gang members later into the evening, she could not do the same because of concerns about her safety (Tempera 2014). Notwithstanding these reported limitations on avenues of engagement, female-gendered status potentially offers other forms of access.

Female researchers often encounter cultural expectations in their field sites based on stereotypical views of women as "weak, naive, unresourceful, and, in some settings, sexually provocative" (Lee 1995, 57). These gender norms, which also include the portrayal of women as more nurturing and empathetic, sometimes facilitate access to gang members and create paths for more intimate conversations. In the context of Central America, the aforementioned depictions of women are widespread and influenced how we and other female researchers were perceived (Saunders-Hastings 2018, 365). As young female graduate student researchers, we noticed how we were both assigned a less threatening image than our male counterparts because we were neither seen as a source of danger nor as a source of resources. Like Zubillaga (2003, 320), in her research in Venezuela, we found that our gendered status mitigated initial suspicion by those affiliated with gangs, probably because, as Zubillaga argues, being a woman allows one to escape the initial dynamic of male rivalry that shapes the self-understandings of gang members and their encounters with male strangers. Moreover, in the case of Central America, where most gang members are young men, women are less likely to be confused for the enemy. Similar to how gang-affiliated women are recruited because they raise less suspicion among the authorities and rival gangs, prevailing gender norms helped with our access to interlocutors.

Beyond being perceived as relatively harmless, we found that our gendered status opened the way for intimate confessions and expressions of self-doubt. In contrast to male gang researchers, who found it difficult to broach sensitive areas in the lives of male gang members, we were instead overwhelmed by their openness to explore them with us. An instance that exemplifies the intimacy of these conversations was when a young male gang member from Honduras asked María, "Do you think homosexuality is wrong?" María was taken aback by the comfort with which her interlocutor asked this question, especially because in suggesting that homosexuality is open for debate, he violated the gang sexist culture of Central America that sees homosexuality as an unforgivable affront that is worthy of violent punishment, including death.

Unlike the dynamics of masculine competition and heterosexist atmospheres that often mediate contact between male gang researchers and male gang members, we found that our encounters were instead shaped by our perceived appearance as nurturing figures willing to listen to our interlocutors' innermost thoughts. This was not a reflection of our deep essence as females, however. Gender is a doing that requires constant engagement in discursive and embodied practices that suggest masculinity or femininity (Butler 1990). Like male researchers who performed gender in masculine ways to create bonds, we established rapport by conforming to the stereotype of women as caring. Although not always consciously, we managed our behavior, self-presentation, and emotions along feminine lines and in ways that encouraged female and male gang members to have an honest discussion with us about matters that could be deemed "feminine" or "weak" by their peers, such as their roles in caregiving. Speaking in a friendly and smooth tone, maintaining encouraging half-smiles and nods, and listening attentively through verbal and non-verbal acknowledgments (such as nodding or adopting verbal empathic gestures like "um humm") without challenging or showing disapproval were some feminist criminology strategies that aided access to our interlocutors' stories (Renzetti 2013). To be sure, these are interview techniques that men have also used to gain access.

It is important to recognize that not only female researchers are assigned a feminine identity by interlocutors or feminine traits that can open paths for engagement. Consider how Puerto Rican crack dealers in East Harlem revealed to Phillipe Bourgois (1995) that, in the beginning, they thought he was gay. One can surmise from his account, that his "effeminacy" lessened their reservations to engage with him. In light of this, one might ask, How necessary is it to consciously engage in macho banter and behavior that reinforces patriarchal culture, if ostensibly feminine traits do not always foreclose possibilities of interaction with male gang members?

Similar to how "male bonding" opened paths of engagement for male researchers, a dynamic of "female bonding" facilitated our interactions with female gang members. Here, our goal is not to appeal to a problematic ideal of female sisterhood that transcends class and racial differences. Female gang members were well aware of these differences, sometimes mentioning how distinct their lives were from our privileged upbringing and backgrounds. Rather, we want to point to how, despite these differences, some female gang members interpreted our meetings as embodied sites of self-disclosure and emotional sharing. When Ellen, for instance, conducted a focus group with three female gang members, they prefaced their confession about the history of intrafamilial violence that triggered their participation in gangs by saying, "*hablar entre mujeres*," "speaking among women." This phrase captures how female gang members felt more comfortable making themselves vulnerable among women than among men because to be taken seriously by the gang they needed to appear tough.

María also found that moments of physical intimacy—such as holding hands and invitations on the part of female gang members to touch scars resulting from injuries—gestured at a type of bonding often unavailable to male researchers given gendered patterns of social touch in Central America, where men are more likely to touch women than vice versa. It is important to note that our "female bonding" experiences, particularly in the prison space, were highly contingent on our status as gang outsiders. On numerous occasions, female gang members told María how they did not feel comfortable sharing their experiences with other women at the prison for fear that it would have repercussions; they often did so by mobilizing tropes of female gossip and envy.

While our status as female researchers opened windows into conversations where both male and female gang members let their guards down, our status was not always advantageous. For the most part, our interlocutors were willing to share their difficult trajectories and stories of victimization. However, the same was not true for their participation in organized violence and illicit economies, as they sometimes avoided these topics or diminished their role in them. One example of how a female gang member downplayed her position in the gang was when, after interviewing her at a prison in El Salvador, María found out she was not necessarily the low-level member she claimed to be. Barrio 18 had designated her as the spokesperson for imprisoned female gang members, according to another female gang member at the same prison. Some male gang members showed a similar hesitation to discuss their personal engagement in criminal activities. For instance, a former MS-13 member from El Salvador whom María interviewed had no problem talking about the gang's illicit economies but presented himself as a bystander and not a participant in the violent actions he described.

Unlike the experience of male gang researchers who faced the problem of overstatement—gang members exaggerating their exploits—we faced the problem of understatement and avoidance. One possible reason why gang members might feel less willing to talk about their participation in illicit activities with female researchers might have to do with the fact that the gendered interaction at play does not pivot around a kind of masculine competition that promotes the disclosure of risky and aggressive behavior. Moreover, regarding specific interactions with male gang members, it is possible that, as Zubillaga (2003) observes in her research in Venezuela, they sought to install a dynamic of seduction, which "juxtaposed the image of the researcher to that of a woman susceptible to be seduced" (322). Another more obvious reason, however, might be that they simply refused to be subjected to inquiries about their illicit actions or share information that could incriminate them.

In addition to encountering evasiveness about illicit activities, an important issue we faced as a result of our gendered status was the dilemma of intimacy. Although male gang researchers also confront the problem of overrapport, the ethical conundrum we encountered was less about the insincerity of interviews or our complicity in criminal activities and more about the danger of turning a research interview into therapy. Guided by feminist research ethics, we adopted an empathic stance that was not judgmental and that strove to establish reciprocal communication. Yet we discovered that the intimate spaces of sharing we worked hard to create brought disclosures of great emotional intensity that were sometimes beyond our ability to handle.

The female gang members that María spoke with often invoked relief as a result of sharing sensitive experiences with her, including experiences of sexual violence that led to their participation in gangs. In one interview, for instance, when María asked a Barrio 18 female gang member from Honduras how she felt after the conversation, she replied, "I feel like a heavy burden lifted off my shoulders." Notwithstanding the sense of self-acknowledgment expressed by some gang members, one that has also been expressed to gang researchers in other settings like the United States (Mitchell et al. 2022), María was concerned when some of her interlocutors wept quietly and wondered if she was adding to their burden in the long run. Shortly after speaking with gang members at the female prison in Honduras, she wrote in her field notes, "Am I just re-opening wounds that are better kept closed?" Her sense of guilt had to do with the fact that by doing rapport in empathic ways, she had invited her interlocutors to reveal more about their lives than perhaps they wished to, all without allowing them to work through these feelings since she was not a psychological counselor. As a result of these interactions, María sought to steer gang members away from sensitive areas that could move the conversation into a quasi-therapeutic interview; she also resolved to pause or stop interviews at indications of affliction.

María's grappling with the ethics of her research points to the need for more trauma-informed methods that in addition to attending to the suffering of research participants pay attention to the distress of researchers themselves. Researchers sometimes experience vicarious traumatization, even posttraumatic stress disorder, which often goes unrecognized or is misunderstood at home institutions. Both Ellen and María underestimated the emotional impact of research. As Markowitz (2019) argues, mental health stigmas, the reluctance of researchers to analyze their feelings amidst the traumas of their interlocutors, and the positivist bent of academia "silences our ability to engage with what we see, hear, do, and feel as we gather information" (1).

When Ellen and María returned to their respective universities in Belgium and the United States, they were sucked into an emotional rollercoaster every time they analyzed and wrote about their field notes, reliving the feelings of distress they experienced when listening to gang members' stories. Aware of how they shared their interlocutor's feelings of distress, albeit in a way that did not compare to how their interlocutors experienced them day in and day out, Ellen and María realized the importance of pondering the emotional complexities of fieldwork.

The emotional complications of research have not only ethical but also epistemological consequences. Saunders-Hastings (2018), for instance, reflects on how the feelings of nostalgia and fear she shared with her informants structured her narrative of gang violence as a story of declining barrio moral codes. In sum, attending to the emotional dimensions of research can lead to more ethical interactions and nuanced accounts of gangs, especially in contexts where researchers experience the dilemma of intimacy.

To return to the problem of seduction mentioned previously, the creation of a space of intimacy can also have the negative effect of leading to seductive maneuvers on the part of male gang members. Elizabeth Velásquez Estrada (Berry et al. 2017) reflects on this issue in her research on gangs in her home country, El Salvador, where months after establishing a good rapport with gang members, one of them told her he wanted a romantic relationship with her. Estrada decided to end her study and writes "the clear implication was that romantic involvement would become a prerequisite for continuing my fieldwork, a cost I was not willing to pay" (543). What Estrada faced was not just an epistemological problem of "ethnographic seduction"—that is, trading one's critical stance as a researcher for an illusion of amiability that detracts from probing our interlocutor's discourses and self-understandings (Robben 1996)—but a problem of patriarchal gender expectations that can put female researchers in danger if they refuse unwelcomed romantic pursuits.

Although neither of us had to deal with unwanted advances by male gang members, we sought to discourage them by sometimes assuming a "professional" distance and wearing more masculine clothes. To give off a "nerdy masculine vibe," Ellen made sure her hair was always tied in a low bun; her standard way of dressing was a white T-shirt, blue jeans and sneakers, and no jewelry. With hopes of avoiding unwanted attention during her fieldwork, María also chose to enact a more masculine style. She cut her hair short and wore loose pants, T-shirts, and sneakers. At some point, in a market in Guatemala, a seller who was facing her back even confused her for a *muchacho* (young guy) and apologized sheepishly when she turned around. Our grappling with gendered power relations in the field by "playing with gender," engaging in various performances that suggest masculinity and femininity, point to how one's gendered status in research is not an inherent characteristic, but one that is constructed and contingent on context.

Reflecting on the impact that one's gendered status has on gang research involves being attentive to one's embeddedness within the researcher–researched relation but also one's complex relationship with gatekeepers. From the beginning of their research project, gang scholars rely heavily on local contacts—including violence prevention specialists, journalists, academics, government officials, human rights defenders, and community and church leaders—who can introduce them to gang members (Van Damme 2021). This is often acknowledged by researchers, but little is written about how the gendered relation between gatekeepers and researchers affects one's access to and interactions with gang members. Regarding access, on numerous occasions Ellen had to reject romantic advances by gatekeepers, including a writer and a government official. In doing so, she lost access to important gang member contacts. Although some female researchers have turned the disadvantage of being common targets of male attention to their benefit by "playing with their sexuality" and using flirting where they deemed it safe (Kaspar and Landolt 2016), Ellen was unwilling to entertain unwanted advances for the benefits of data gathering.

The gendered relation between gatekeepers and scholars also affects interactions with gang members. When Ellen visited a juvenile center with a male gatekeeper, she noticed how the female gang members' assumption that Ellen was his girlfriend fanned the flames of distrust, interfering with her ability to talk to them. Once Ellen dispelled this assumption and took some distance from the male gatekeeper, the teenagers were much more willing to engage with her. Their reservation perhaps had to do with the fact that Ellen's presumed romantic relationship with the male gatekeeper installed an environment of antagonism, where the youth were competing for male attention or connection.

Altogether, the experiences of gang scholars point to how researching gangs involves stepping into and grappling with a complex field of gendered power relations. Being identified as men or women has a tremendous impact on whom scholars can access as research participants and the types of stories conveyed to them. Moreover, these identifications introduce ethical dilemmas of rapport that researchers need to be attentive to. As we have tried to argue, reflecting on one's gendered status can lead to being more intentional about how one tries to access subjects, how one goes about it, and how one assesses the material one can produce. More specifically, it can lead us to a more nuanced approach to the gang phenomenon that resists the pull to order it in a male fashion, marginalizing women's perspectives and reinforcing gender stereotypes.

Conclusion

The shifting power dynamics that both female and male gang scholars must navigate extend well beyond the gendered relations we have discussed so far in this chapter. The advantages and disadvantages that accompany one's gendered status intersect with other important categories of difference, such as race, class, and nationality, as well as the situated nature of one's location (Crenshaw 1989; Burgess-Proctor 2006; Méndez 2018). For instance, gang scholars in Central and South America have pointed to how their outsider position as white Americans and Europeans has been another salient feature in their lived experiences as researchers, sometimes mitigating the initial suspicion associated with their gender status.

Fontes (2018, 259) speaks about how being perceived as a "gringo" encouraged people to share more truthful stories with him because, unlike insiders, he did not have to navigate the class and racial prejudices that make Guatemalans sometimes distrust one another. Echoing Fontes' observation, María found that being assigned a Honduran identity or insider status sometimes created difficulties in access. The privileges of a white foreigner status highlighted by Fontes, however, can also come with language-related challenges. For instance, Ellen encountered some constraints as a native Dutch/Flemish speaker conducting research in Spanish. During the interview transcription process, she experienced difficulties with interpreting certain gang speech varieties. In light of this and the lengthy nature of her more than 65 interviews and focus groups, she chose to hire a Honduran university student to help with transcriptions.

While we do not have space to flesh out the manifold relationships between gender and other categories of difference as they relate to our research, we encourage gang scholars to engage in methodological reflections that take these intersections seriously. This requires treating gender not as an autonomous construct but as collectively shaping, along with other categories of difference, the scholar's outlook on the world. Furthermore, it requires approaching gender as not something one is born with. Gender is shaped throughout our life and highly influenced by the culture within which we grow up and live, and this also applies to the people with whom we engage in the field. To some extent, we have a choice of how to perform gender, although a lot of it is enforced by the local contexts within which we live, move, and conduct research. It is important to be aware of what parts are within our power to adapt, and how this influences how our interlocutors perceive us and the way we conduct research.

Reflecting on one's positionality is of utmost importance in studies of gangs in Latin America. As we have shown, these works lack a critical assessment of how the scholars' identity influences research. Although some studies engage in self-reflexivity, mostly by gang ethnographers, the reflections contained therein tend to be relegated to footnotes or appendices. The dearth of sustained discussions about positionality, specifically regarding gendered status, is just the expression of a general methodology blind spot in the literature. As such, we suggest that, as a bare minimum, the following aspects should be included in gang publications: the sample, methods, who conducted the interviews and under which circumstances (cf. positionality; if a team other than the authors, what is their profile), demographic data of the interviewees, and ethical reflections beyond review board requirements and informed consent.

The purpose of encouraging more methodological reflections among gang scholars is not to promote self-absorbed academic exercises. As we have emphasized in this chapter, self-reflexivity can lead to better and more ethical research. For instance, we have pointed to how it can help us avoid studying gangs as a male issue, from a male perspective, and through a male lens. In this vein, we encourage the following measures to address the gender imbalances that characterize research in the region: not only relying on snowball sampling that starts with male gang members or other male subjects, but actively looking for female contacts, including female scholars and gatekeepers; encouraging more male–female research collaborations; and training in more ethical fieldwork and interview techniques. In sum, we argue that pondering our social positions as gang scholars will prevent us from reinforcing the unjust structures of domination, including patriarchal arrangements, that reproduce the very gangs we study.

Note

1. Decreto núm. 117-2003 por el que se reforma el artículo 332 del Código Penal, contenido en el Decreto núm. 144-83 del 23 de agosto de 1983, *La Gaceta*, August 15, 2003.

References

Ackerly, Brooke, and Jacqui True. 2008. "Reflexivity in Practice: Power and Ethics in Feminist Research on International Relations." *International Studies Review* 10 (4): 693–707.

Amaya, Luis Enrique, and Juan José Martínez. 2015. "Escisión Al Interior De La Pandilla Barrio 18 En El Salvador: Una Mirada Antropológica." *Revista Policía y Seguridad Pública* 5: 149–178. https://doi.org/10.5377/rpsp.v5i1.1987.

Applebaum, Anna, and Briana Mawby. 2018. "Women and 'New Wars' in El Salvador." *Stability: International Journal of Security and Development* 7: 18. https://doi.org/10.5334/sta.641.

Baird, Adam. 2018. "Becoming the 'Baddest': Masculine Trajectories of Gang Violence in Medellín." *Journal of Latin American Studies* 50: 183–210. DOI:10.1017/S0022216X17000761.

Baird, Adam. 2020. "Macho Research: Bravado, Danger, and Ethnographic Safety." *LSE Latin America and Caribbean*, February 13, https://blogs.lse.ac.uk/latamcaribbean/2020/02/13/macho-research-bravado-danger-and-ethnographic-safety/.

Baird, Adam. 2021. "'Man a Kill a Man for Nutin': Gang Transnationalism, Masculinities, and Violence in Belize City." *Men and Masculinities* 24 (3): 411–431. https://doi.org/10.1177/1097184X19872787.

Berry, Maya J., Claudia Chávez Argüelles, Shanya Cordis, Sarah Ihmoud, and Elizabeth Velásquez Estrada. 2017. "Toward a Fugitive Anthropology: Gender, Race, and Violence in the Field." *Cultural Anthropology* 32 (4): 537–565. https://doi.org/10.14506/ca32.4.05.

Biondi, Karina. 2016. *Sharing This Walk: An Ethnography of Prison Life and the PCC in Brazil*. Edited and translated by John F. Collins. Chapel Hill: University of North Carolina Press.

Blake, Jillian. 2017. "MS-13 as a Terrorist Organization: Risks for Central American Asylum Seekers." *Michigan Law Review Online* 39. https://ssrn.com/abstract=3097254.

Boerman, Thomas, and Adam Golob. 2021. "Gangs and Modern-Day Slavery in El Salvador, Honduras and Guatemala: A Non-Traditional Model of Human Trafficking." *Journal of Human Trafficking* 7 (3): 241–257. https://doi.org/10.1080/23322705.2020.1719343.

Boerman, Thomas, and Jennifer Knapp. 2017. "Central American Gang Culture and Violence against Females in El Salvador, Honduras and Guatemala." *Thompson Reuters Immigration Briefings* 17 (3): 3–14.

Botero, Juan D., Weisi Guo, Guillem Mosquera, Alan Wilson, Samuel Johnson, Gicela A. Aguirre-Garcia, and Leonardo A. Pachon. 2019. "Gang Confrontation: The Case of Medellin (Colombia)." *PLoS One* 14 (12): e0225689–e89. https://doi.org/10.1371/journal.pone.0225689.

Bourgois, Phillipe. 1995. *In Search of Respect: Selling Crack in El Barrio*. Cambridge, UK: Cambridge University Press.

Bourgois, Phillipe. 2015. "Insecurity, the War on Drugs, and Crimes of the State: Symbolic Violence in the Americas." In *Violence at the Urban Margins*, edited by Javier Auyero, Philippe Bourgois, and Nancy Scheper-Hughes, 305–318. New York: Oxford University Press.

Brenneman, Robert. 2012. *Homies and Hermanos: God and Gangs in Central America*. New York: Oxford University Press.

Brotherton, David C., and Rafael Gude. 2020. "Social Control and the Gang: Lessons from the Legalization of Street Gangs in Ecuador." *Critical Criminology* 29 (4): 931–955. https://doi.org/10.1007/s10612-020-09505-5.

Burgess-Proctor, Amanda. 2006. "Intersections of Race, Class, Gender, and Crime: Future Directions for Feminist Criminology." *Feminist Criminology* 1: 27–47. https://doi.org/10.1177/1557085105282899.

Butler, Judith. 1990. *Gender Trouble: Feminism and the Subversion of Identity*. New York: Routledge.
Carroll, Rory. 2011. "Killers of Filmmaker Christian Poveda Jailed." *The Guardian* March 11. https://www.theguardian.com/world/2011/mar/11/christian-poveda-murders-jailed.
Carvalho, Leandro S., and Rodrigo R. Soares. 2016. "Living on the Edge: Youth Entry, Career and Exit in Drug-Selling Gangs." *Journal of Economic Behavior & Organization* 121: 77–98.
Carter, Jon Horne. 2014. "Gothic Sovereignty: Gangs and Criminal Community in a Honduran Prison." *South Atlantic Quarterly* 113 (3): 475.
Chesney-Lind, Meda. 2006. "Patriarchy, Crime, and Justice: Feminist Criminology in an Era of Backlash." *Feminist Criminology* 1: 6–26. https://doi.org/10.1177/1557085105282893.
Crenshaw, Kimberle. 1989. "Demarginalizing the Intersection of Race and Sex: A Black Feminist Critique of Antidiscrimination Doctrine, Feminist Theory and Antiracist Politics." *University of Chicago Legal Forum* 1: 139–167.
Cruz, José Miguel. 2010. "Central American Maras: From Youth Street Gangs to Transnational Protection Rackets." *Global Crime* 11 (4): 379–398. doi:10.1080/17440572.2010.519518.
Cruz, José Miguel. 2018. "El Salvador Feasibility Study. Final Report." https://pdf.usaid.gov/pdf_docs/PA00TNK9.pdf.
Cruz, José Miguel, Andi Coombes, Yemile Mizrahi, Yulia Vorobyeva, Manolya Tanyu, Patricia Campie, Josué Sánchez, and Chandler Hill. 2020a. *A Study of Gang Disengagement in Honduras*. Washington, DC: American Institutes for Research & Florida International University. https://lacc.fiu.edu/research/the-new-faces-of-street-gangs-in-central-america/honduras-gang.pdf.
Cruz, José Miguel, and Nelson Portillo. 1998. "Solidaridad y violencia en las pandillas del gran San Salvador. Más allá de la vida loca." San Salvador: UCA Editores.
Cruz, José Miguel, and Jonathan D. Rosen. 2020. "Mara Forever? Factors Associated with Gang Disengagement in El Salvador." *Journal of Criminal Justice* 69: 101705. https://doi.org/10.1016/j.jcrimjus.2020.101705.
Cruz, José Miguel, Jonathan D. Rosen, Luis Enrique Amaya, and Yulia Vorobyeva. 2017. *The New Face of Street Gangs: The Gang Phenomenon in El Salvador*. https://lacc.fiu.edu/research/the-new-face-of-street-gangs_final-report_eng.pdf.
Cruz, José Miguel, Manolya Tanyu, Yulia Vorobyeva, Yemile Mizrahi, Andi Coombes, Josué Sánchez, Chandler Hill, and Patricia Campie. 2020b. *A Study of Gang Disengagement in Guatemala*. American Institutes for Research & Florida International University.
Doyle, Caroline. 2021. "The Criminal Actors Have a Social Base in Their Communities: Gangs and Service Provision in Medellín, Colombia." *Latin American Politics and Society* 63: 27–47. https://doi.org/10.1017/lap.2020.31.
Drummond, Holli, John Dizgun, and David Keeling. 2019. "Cross-Group Investigations: Youth Gangs in Medellin, Colombia." *Youth & Society* 51 (1): 73–100. https://doi.org/10.1177/0044118X16662536.
Duncombe, Jean, and Julie Jessop. 2012. "'Doing Rapport' and the Ethics of 'Faking Friendship.'" In *Ethics in Qualitative Research*, edited by Melanie Mauthner, Julie Jessop, Tina Miller, and Maxine Birch, 108–121. London: Sage Publications.
Farah, Douglas. 2012. "Central American Gangs: Changing Nature and New Partners." *Journal of International Affairs* 66 (1): 53–67.
Farah, Douglas, and Kathryn Babineau. 2017. "The Evolution of MS 13 in El Salvador and Honduras." *Prism: A Journal of the Center for Complex Operations* 7: 58–73.
Fontes, Anthony W. 2018. *Mortal Doubt: Transnational Gangs and Social Order in Guatemala City*. Oakland: University of California Press.

Fontes, Anthony W. 2019. "Portrait of a 'Real' Marero: Fantasy and Falsehood in Stories of Gang Violence." *Ethnography* 20 (3): 320–341.

Fujii, Lee Ann. 2012. "Research Ethics 101: Dilemmas and Responsibilities." *APSC* 45 (4): 717–723. https://doi.org/10.1017/S1049096512000819.

Gomez, Camilo Tamayo. 2020. "Organised Crime Governance in Times of Pandemic: The Impact of COVID-19 on Gangs and Drug Cartels in Colombia and Mexico." *Bulletin of Latin American Research* 39 (1): 12–15. https://doi.org/10.1111/blar.13171.

Gutiérrez Rivera, Lirio. 2013. *Territories of Violence: State, Marginal Youth, and Public Security in Honduras*. New York: Palgrave Macmillan.

Harding, Sandra G. 1987. *Feminism and Methodology: Social Science Issues*. Bloomington: Indiana University Press.

Hernández-Anzora, Marlon. 2017. *¿Hemos perdido el combate contra las maras? Un análisis multidisciplinario del fenómeno de las pandillas en El Salvador*. San Salvador: Fundación Friedrich Ebert.

Hume, Mo. 2007. "Mano Dura: El Salvador Responds to Gangs." *Development in Practice* 17 (6): 739–751. https://doi.org/10.1080/09614520701628121.

Hume, Mo, and Polly Wilding. 2015. "'Es que para ellos el deporte es matar': Rethinking the Scripts of Violent Men in El Salvador and Brazil." In *Violence at the Urban Margins*, edited by Javier Auyero, Philippe Bourgois, and Nancy Scheper-Hughes, 93–111. New York: Oxford University Press.

Johnson, Andrew. 2017. *If I Give My Soul: Faith Behind Bars in Rio de Janeiro*. Oxford, UK: Oxford University Press.

Johnson, Andrew, and James Densley. 2018. "Rio's New Social Order: How Religion Signals Disengagement from Prison Gangs." *Qualitative Sociology* 41 (2): 243–262.

Kammigan, Ilka, Dirk Enzmann, and Lieven J. R. Pauwels. 2018. "Over- and Underreporting of Drug Use: A Cross-National Inquiry of Social Desirability through the Lens of Situational Action Theory." *European Journal on Criminal Policy and Research* 25 (3): 273–296. https://doi.org/10.1007/s10610-018-9397-y.

Kaspar, Heidi, and Sara Landolt. 2016. "Flirting in the Field: Shifting Positionalities and Power Relations in Innocuous Sexualisations of Research Encounters." *Gender, Place and Culture: A Journal of Feminist Geography* 23: 107–119.

Katz, Charles M., Anthony Harriott, and E. C. Hedberg. 2020. "Mediating Violence in Jamaica through a Gang Truce." *International Criminal Justice Review* 32 (2): 129–150. https://doi.org/10.1177/1057567720975631.

Kemmelmeier, Markus. 2016. "Cultural Differences in Survey Responding: Issues and Insights in the Study of Response Biases." *International Journal of Psychology* 51 (6): 439–444. https://doi.org/10.1002/ijop.12386.

Krakowski, Krzysztof. 2021. "Adjustments to Gang Exposure in Early Adolescence." *Journal of Peace Research* 59 (3): 337–352. https://doi.org/10.1177/00223433211017204.

Lee, Raymond M. 1995. *Dangerous Fieldwork*. Thousand Oaks, CA: Sage Publications.

Levenson, Deborah. 2013. *Adiós Niño: The Gangs of Guatemala City and the Politics of Death*. Durham, NC: Duke University Press.

Markowitz, Ariana. 2019. "The Better to Break and Bleed With: Research, Violence, and Trauma." *Geopolitics* 26: 1–24. https://doi.org/10.1080/14650045.2019.1612880.

Martínez d'Aubuisson, Juan José. 2017. *Ver, oír y callar: Un año con la Mara Salvatrucha 13*. Primera edición. Ciudad de México: Surplus Ediciones.

Méndez, María José. 2018. "'The River Told Me': Rethinking Intersectionality from the World of Berta Cáceres." *Capitalism, Nature, Socialism* 29: 7–24.

Méndez, María José. 2019. "The Violence Work of Transnational Gangs in Central America." *Third World Quarterly* 40 (2): 373–388. https://doi.org/10.1080/01436597.2018.1533786.

Méndez, María José. 2022. *Violence as Work: Living and Producing in Central America's Gang Necroeconomies*. Minneapolis: University of Minnesota.

Martínez-Reyes, Alberto, and José-Javier Navarro-Pérez. 2020. "The Effects of the Gang Truce on Salvadoran Communities and Development Agents." *International Social Work* 64 (6): 959–974. https://doi.org/10.1177/0020872820901765.

Mitchell, Meghan M., Kallee McCullough, Jun Wu, David C. Pyrooz, and Scott H. Decker. 2022. "Survey Research with Gang and Non-Gang Members in Prison: Operational Lessons from the LoneStar Project." *Trends in Organized Crime* 25: 378–406. https://doi.org/10.1007/s12117-018-9331-1.

Mohanty, Chandra Talpade. 2003. *Feminism without Borders: Decolonizing Theory, Practicing Solidarity*. Durham, NC: Duke University Press.

O'Neill, Kevin Lewis. 2015. *Secure the Soul: Christian Piety and Gang Prevention in Guatemala*. Oakland: University of California Press.

Panfil, Vanessa R., and Dana Peterson. 2015. "Gender, Sexuality, and Gangs: Re-envisioning Diversity." In *The Handbook of Gangs*, edited by Scott H. Decker and David C Pyrooz, 208–234. Chichester, UK: Wiley.

Pitts, Wayne J., and Christopher S. Inkpen. 2021. "Past and Present Trends in Gun Violence and Gangs and Their Implications in Belize: 2011–2020." In *Guns, Gun Violence and Gun Homicides: Perspectives from the Caribbean, Global South and Beyond*, edited by Wendell C. Wallace, 211–228. Switzerland: Palgrave Macmillan.

Renzetti, Claire M. 2013. *Feminist Criminology*. Abingdon, UK: Routledge.

Reséndiz Rivera, and Nelly Erandy. 2017. "Mujeres, Pandillas y Violencia en Guatemala." *Cuadernos Intercambio sobre Centroamérica y el Caribe* 14: 50–75. https://doi.org/10.15517/c.a..v14i1.28614.

Robben, Antonius C. G. M. 1996. "Ethnographic Seduction, Transference, and Resistance in Dialogues about Terror and Violence in Argentina." *Ethos* 24: 71–106.

Rocha, José Luis, and Dennis Rodgers. 2008. *Gangs of Nicaragua*. Managua. http://eprints.lse.ac.uk/28422/1/Rocha_and_Rodgers_-_Gangs_of_Nicaragua.pdf.

Rodgers, Dennis. 2007. "Joining the Gang and Becoming a Broder: The Violence of Ethnography in Contemporary Nicaragua." *Bulletin of Latin American Research* 26 (4): 444–461. https://doi.org/10.1111/j.1470-9856.2007.00234.x.

Rodgers, Dennis, and Adam Baird. 2015. "Understanding Gangs in Contemporary Latin America." In *The Handbook of Gangs*, edited by Scott H. Decker and David C Pyrooz, 478–502. Chichester, UK: Wiley.

Ruiz, Pamela. 2019. "The Evolution of Mara Salvatrucha 13 and Barrio 18: Violence, Extortion, and Drug Trafficking in the Northern Triangle of Central America" *CUNY Academic Works*. https://academicworks.cuny.edu/gc_etds/3458.

Sampó, Carolina. 2016. "El Rol De Las Mujeres En Las Maras: Una Aproximación a La Violencia Que Sufren E Infringen." *Si Somos Americanos* 16 (2): 127–142. https://doi.org/10.4067/S0719-09482016000200005.

Santacruz Giralt, María, and Alberto Concha-Eastman. 2001. "Barrio adentro. La solidaridad violenta de las pandillas." San Salvador: IUDOP-UCA/OPS-OMS.

Santacruz Giralt, María. 2019. "Mujeres En Pandillas Salvadoreñas y Las Paradojas De Una Agencia Precaria." *Papeles del CEIC, International Journal on Collective Identity Research* 2019, 206: 1–20. https://doi.org/10.1387/pceic.19552.

Santacruz Giralt, María Lizet, and Elin Cecilie Ranum. 2010. "'Seconds in the Air': Women Gang-Members and Their Prisons." San Salvador: University Institute of Public Opinion.

Saunders-Hastings, Katherine E. 2015. *Order and Insecurity Under the Mara: Violence, Coping, and Community in Guatemala City.* New York: Oxford University Press.

Saunders-Hastings, Katherine. 2018. "Red Zone Blues: Violence and Nostalgia in Guatemala City." *Ethnography* 20 (3): 359–378. https://doi.org/10.1177/1466138118795975.

Schockman, H. Eric, and Cody Thompson. 2021. "Workplace Well-Being and Human Flourishing: A Case Model of Homeboy Industries and Reducing Gang Recidivism." In *The Palgrave Handbook of Workplace Well-Being*, edited by Satinder K. Dhiman, 297–317. Cham, Switzerland: Springer.

Silveira Rocha, Rafael Lacerda, and Corinne Davis Rodrigues. 2020. "Membership, Structure and Rivalries of Youth Gangs in Belo Horizonte, Brazil." *Estudios sociológicos (Mexico City, Mexico)* 38 (113): 341–374. https://doi.org/10.24201/ES.2020V38N113.1/19.

Tempera, Jacqueline. 2014. "Gaëlle Rivard Piché: Gangs and Security in Fragile States." *Belfer Center Newsletter*, Fall/Winter. https://www.belfercenter.org/publication/gaelle-rivard-piche-gangs-and-security-fragile-states.

UNODC. 2019. *Global Study on Homicide 2019*. Vienna. https://www.unodc.org/unodc/en/data-and-analysis/global-study-on-homicide.html.

Van Damme, Ellen. 2020. *The Ecology of Violence and Silence: The Position and Role of Women in and around Gangs in Honduras.* Leuven: KU Leuven.

Van Damme, Ellen. 2021. "Corruption, Impunity and Mistrust: Moving Beyond Police Gatekeepers for Researching Gangs." *Journal of Aggression, Conflict and Peace Research* 13 (2/3): 125–135. https://doi.org/10.1108/JACPR-01-2021-0572.

Vandenbogaerde, Ellen, and Elke Van Hellemont. 2016. "Fear and Retaliation: Gang Violence in Brussels and Caracas." In *Gang Transitions and Transformations in an International Context*, edited by Cheryl Maxson, and Finn-Aage Esbensen, 51–63. Switzerland: Springer.

Ward, Thomas W. 2013. *Gangsters without Borders: An Ethnography of a Salvadoran Street Gang.* New York: Oxford University Press.

Weerman, Frank, Cheryl L Maxson, Finn-Aage Esbensen, Judith Aldridge, Juanjo Medina, and Frank Gemert. 2009. *Eurogang Program Manual: Background, Development and Use of the Eurogang Instruments in Multi-Site, Multi-Method Comparative Research.* St. Louis: University of Missouri Press.

Werlau, Maria. 2014. "Venezuela's Criminal Gangs: Warriors of Cultural Revolution." *World Affairs* 177 (2): 90–96.

Wilding, Polly. 2014. "Gendered Meanings and Everyday Experiences of Violence in Urban Brazil." *Gender, Place & Culture* 21 (2): 228–243. https://doi.org/10.1080/0966369X.2013.769430.

Wolf, Sonja. 2017. *Mano Dura: The Politics of Gang Control in El Salvador.* Austin: University of Texas Press.

Zubillaga, Verónica. 2003. "Un testimonio reflexivo sobre la experiencia de construir historias de vida con jóvenes de vida violenta." *Revista Mexicana de Sociología* 65 (2): 305–338.

Zubillaga, Verónica, Manuel Llorens, and John Souto. 2015. "*Chismosas* and *Alcahuetas*: Being the Mother of an *Empistolado* within the Everyday Armed Violence of a Caracas Barrio." In *Violence at the Urban Margins*, edited by Javier Auyero, Philippe Bourgois, and Nancy Scheper-Hughes, 162–188. New York: Oxford University Press.

CHAPTER 17

GANG RESEARCH IN THE CARIBBEAN

EDWARD R. MAGUIRE

THE Caribbean region is a well-known tourist destination due to its beautiful white sand beaches and crystal blue water, as well as its many unique natural, cultural, and historical attractions. At the same time, the region also has a significant violent crime problem, due in part to the presence of criminal gangs.[1] This chapter reviews the current state of scientific knowledge on gangs in the Caribbean. The chapter focuses specifically on the research methods used to understand gangs in the region, including their emergence, their size and scope, the risk and protective factors associated with gang membership and other related behaviors, the association between gangs and crime, and the effectiveness of interventions intended to address these issues. The chapter concludes by discussing how these methods have evolved, major gaps in the scholarly literature, and how researchers can begin to fill those gaps.

A BRIEF HISTORY OF THE CARIBBEAN REGION

The Caribbean region is home to a variety of sovereign nations and dependent territories located in and around the Caribbean Sea. The region consists of 16 sovereign nations, including 13 island nations and three continental or mainland nations. The 13 island nations include Antigua and Barbuda, the Bahamas, Barbados, Cuba, Dominica, Dominican Republic, Grenada, Haiti, Jamaica, St. Kitts and Nevis, St. Lucia, St. Vincent and the Grenadines, and Trinidad and Tobago. The three continental nations include Belize, Guyana, and Suriname. The region is also home to a host of dependent territories associated with four nations, including France (Guadaloupe, Martinique, St. Barthelemy, and St. Martin), the Netherlands (Aruba, the Caribbean Netherlands, Curaçao, and Sint Maarten), the United Kingdom (Anguilla, British Virgin Islands, Cayman Islands, Montserrat, and Turks and Caicos), and the United States (Puerto Rico and the US Virgin Islands).[2] The primary languages spoken in the region, in descending order of usage, are Spanish, Haitian, English, French, and Dutch. In addition, there are numerous "heritage languages, many of which are in various stages of obsolescence" (Ferreira 2012, 131).[3] Many people in the Caribbean also speak localized creole languages that emerged in the sixteenth to eighteenth centuries, often among slaves and indentured servants (Carrington 1999; Higman 2010; Youssef 2002).

The Caribbean region continues to be a product of its tumultuous history of conquest and colonization (Wilson 1993). Understanding this history is important for understanding the social structures, cultures, and conflicts that continue to define the region. On August 3, 1492, Christopher Columbus set out on his first voyage in search of a western route to India. On October 12 that same year, Columbus and his crew made landfall on a Bahamian island where they first encountered the region's native Taíno inhabitants. Columbus planted the Spanish flag and claimed the island for Spain. Over the next dozen years, Columbus made three more journeys to the Caribbean, during which he colonized the entire region for Spain. The Caribbean not only served as "a staging post for the Spanish-American empire" (Higman 2010, 69), it also played a pivotal role as the base of operations for the first "sustained encounters between the New and Old Worlds, heralding the mass movement of people, goods and ideas between two previously unconnected parts of the world" (Hofman et al. 2014, 590). Columbus's epic failure to discover a western route to India remains embedded in the English language today, with the Caribbean region known as the *West Indies* and the native people of the Americas often referred to as *Indians* or *Amerindians*.

Spanish settlers in the Caribbean and elsewhere in the New World operated on the principle that "only by pushing aside, removing, enslaving, or killing" the native peoples they encountered could European colonization succeed (Higman 2010, 64). For instance, in Hispaniola, the island now shared by Haiti and the Dominican Republic, the native Taíno population was reduced "from several million in 1492 to fewer than 25,000 by 1515" (Deagan 1988, 198).[4] The native population of the Caribbean experienced a sudden and rapid depopulation due to multiple factors, including "open slaughter, the extreme labor demands, and the destruction of food resources" as well as exposure to diseases (such as smallpox, influenza, measles, and others) for which the natives had no natural immunity (Higman 2010, 77). The depopulation of the Caribbean resulted in a labor shortage that led the Spanish Crown to begin importing slaves from Africa (Hennessy 1993). The first African slaves arrived in the region around 1500 to provide construction and mining labor for the Spanish. As one historian summarized the situation, "people from one continent forced those from a second continent to produce a narrow range of consumer goods in a third—having first found the third's native population inadequate to their purpose" (Eltis 1993, 1399). By 1620, African slaves comprised almost half the population of Cuba (Higman 2010). The people and the civilizations that existed in the region before Columbus "had been virtually obliterated" (Higman 2010, 97). The massive growth of sugar plantations in the region required an ongoing source of labor. The sugar revolution resulted in the forced migration of slaves from Africa, thereby shifting the balance of the population in the Caribbean from white to black (Eltis 1993; Higman 2010).

Spanish control of the region began to fragment as Spain's naval strength declined and other European countries began to colonize some of the smaller and less fortified islands.

In the 1620s and 1630s, the English colonized Antigua, Barbados, Montserrat, Nevis, and St. Kitts; the French colonized Guadeloupe and Martinique; and the Dutch colonized Aruba, Bonaire, Curaçao, and Tobago. Fierce naval battles took place in the Caribbean Sea as European powers sought to acquire territories claimed by their rivals. Many islands changed hands several times, although the conflicts over territory had largely subsided by 1770, at which point "every piece of Caribbean land was the colonial possession of some European state" (Higman 2010, 109).

By the early 1800s, the Danish, British, and Dutch colonies in the Caribbean chose to stop receiving enslaved people from Africa. The French and Spanish colonies continued to participate in the Atlantic slave trade until the mid-1800s. The decision to stop participating in the Atlantic slave trade was separate from the decision to abolish slavery, with the former occurring earlier than the latter. For instance, Britain stopped receiving enslaved people from Africa in 1808, but did not ban the institution of slavery in its colonies until 1834. By 1886, every government with colonies in the Caribbean had abolished slavery (Higman 2010). At abolition, the vast majority of formerly enslaved people in the Caribbean could not read or write. Plantation owners had sought to limit education "to the teaching of practical agricultural knowledge, attitudes of civil obedience, and acceptance of a social order in which black people were destined to perform manual labour on plantations" (Higman 2010, 185). As former slaves left the plantations, they formed peasant communities, with some ex-slaves acquiring land either individually or collectively through "purchase, rental, or squatting" (Besson 1995, 78). For instance, in Trinidad, many former slaves bought, rented, or squatted on small plots of land in the hills around Port of Spain in communities that would later form the nucleus of the nation's gang and violence problems (Brereton 1996; Dudley 2008).

Due to labor demands in the region, the abolition of slavery was quickly followed by a movement to acquire indentured laborers from India and China. Indentured servants continued to come into the Caribbean until the 1920s (Higman 2010; Tinker 1974). More than a half million indentured Indian laborers were brought to the Caribbean, with more than 70% of them delivered to just two destinations: British Guiana (now Guyana) and Trinidad (Vertovek 1995). Many of the Indian migrants remained in the Caribbean when their term of service was completed, thus Indians now make up about 40% of the population in Guyana and 38% in Trinidad and Tobago. Chinese indentured laborers were also imported into the region. In Cuba alone, nearly 125,000 Chinese laborers were brought in between 1847 and 1874 to work on sugar plantations. One historian classified the Chinese laborers as occupying an "in-between space between black and white, slave and free" (Hu-DeHart 2002, 68). Indeed, for both Indian and Chinese migrants, the indenture system was less oppressive than slavery but more oppressive than outright freedom (Emmer, 1990). Brereton (2008) argues that one of the key sources of oppression in the indenture system was its sanctions. Indentured laborers could be prosecuted and imprisoned for violating the terms of their contracts, although breach of contract was typically treated as a civil matter for other issues. Furthermore, "pass laws" made it a criminal offense for the laborers to be more than two miles away from the plantation during working hours without authorization. Laborers were typically not informed ahead of time about these criminal sanctions, thus these provisions represented a form of "deliberate, institutionalized deception" (Brereton 2008, 108).

Access to education improved in many Caribbean territories toward the end of the nineteenth century, leading to gradual improvements in literacy and social mobility during the early twentieth century (Higman 2010; Lowenthal 1971). Students were taught to read and write in European languages, and "native speakers of African languages became rare in Caribbean populations" (Higman 2010, 242). Creole was looked down upon, with colonial governments favoring European languages as part of a broader perspective that viewed education as a form of social control (Higman 2010, 242). The United States began to play a much larger role in the region, making Puerto Rico a US territory and purchasing the Virgin Islands from Denmark in 1917. The United States also began to exert an increasingly strong cultural influence on the Caribbean through cinema, sports, religion, education, and other institutions (Aho 1987; Bolland 1987; Gunst 1996; Higman 2010).

Afro-Caribbeans also began to develop a greater sense of racial consciousness in the early twentieth century. Marcus Garvey, a Jamaican activist, began to spread influential racial and anti-colonial messaging throughout the region. In 1914, Garvey established the United Negro Improvement Association, an organization dedicated to improving the lives of people of African descent. In 1918, Garvey established a weekly newspaper entitled *Negro World* that focused primarily on racial injustice and labor rights. Garvey inspired a wave of Afrocentric activism throughout the Caribbean motivated by a sense of "racial awakening and pan-African consciousness" (Ewing 2013, 37). Garvey also played an important role in the emergence of the Rastafarian religion in Jamaica in the 1930s. Rastafarians celebrated African heritage and envisioned a repatriation of the region's Afro-Caribbean residents to Ethiopia. One scholar characterized Rastafarianism as "the voice of Africa crying out in the Caribbean" (Forsythe 1980, 62).

Racial issues continued to pervade West Indian society after the abolition of slavery and into the twentieth century. According to one historian, skin color "was a crucial determinant of the West Indian's life chances at least until the postwar era" (Brereton 1989, 92). One distinctive characteristic of the drive for racial equality in the Caribbean during the twentieth century is that it was fused with an anti-colonial spirit and a powerful drive toward self-government (Lowenthal 1971). In the four decades following World War II, many Caribbean colonies achieved independence. However, even post-independence, scholars continued to emphasize the importance of race in the Caribbean. As Lowenthal (1971) noted, "because race, class, and personal identity are all intimately linked, racial awareness suffuses every aspect of West Indian life" (376). The Caribbean region also continued to struggle with poverty. As the region moved away from a primarily agrarian economy, many people migrated from rural areas to larger cities. Impoverished people built makeshift homes in shantytowns using whatever materials they could find (Higman 2010, 305). Many of the homes in these communities had no electricity or running water. These communities have continued to struggle with a litany of endemic social problems, including gangs and violence (Eyre 1972; Gunst 1996; Johnson et al. 2016; Morris and Maguire 2016).

The colonial history of the Caribbean region remains deeply imprinted in the culture, language, geography, and institutions of Caribbean nations and territories today. European colonialism, genocide, slavery, and indentured servitude left an indelible influence on the multiethnic character and culture of modern Caribbean societies (Valtonen 1996). The research shows that these historical and cultural factors also played a key role in shaping a variety of social issues in the region, including the gang problem.

Twentieth-Century Research on Gangs in the Caribbean

Virtually all English-language research on gangs in the Caribbean prior to the year 2000 focused on only two nations: Jamaica and Trinidad and Tobago.[5] Given that these were clearly not the only two nations or territories in the region with evidence of gang-related issues, this is an unfortunate gap in the scientific literature on gangs that I will discuss in more detail at the end of this chapter. Because the vast majority of twentieth-century research on gangs in the Caribbean took place in Jamaica and Trinidad and Tobago, this section focuses on research on gangs and gang-related issues in those two nations.

Jamaica

In Jamaica, early research on gangs emerged from various disciplines, including anthropology (Harrison 1988; Moser and Holland 1997), geography (Eyre 1984), history (Gunst 1996), political science (Lacey 1977; Payne 1983; Wilson 1980), and sociology (Harriott 1996; Headley 1988). Scholars first began exploring criminal gangs in Jamaica, often referred to as "posses," in the 1970s and 1980s. For instance, Lacey (1977) discussed the role of gangs in political violence between the nation's two major political parties, the People's National Party (PNP) and the Jamaica Labour Party (JLP) in the 1960s. Similarly, Wilson (1980) provided a detailed accounting of the emergence of political violence in the mid-1960s when members of both parties "recruited street gangs and brought them into the political process" (5) According to Stone (1979), both political parties had affiliated with "gangs of youths, some on motorcycles, some on foot, and others in motor cars who terrorised opposing activists, controlled political territory and generally acted as a reserve force backing up the non-violent campaign" (38). In a separate section, I will discuss later evidence that traces the emergence of gangs in Jamaica to political dynamics in the 1940s (Williams 2011).

Eyre (1984, 24) provided the first detailed geographic analysis of gang territory and conflict in a Kingston ghetto divided spatially into "two hitherto irreconcilable territories," one allied with the PNP and the other with the JLP. His analysis focused primarily on the border between the two areas, a border that "few individuals—some politicians excepted—would be rash enough to risk crossing" (Eyre 1984, 24). He noted that gang warfare between the two areas is an inherently geographic phenomenon due to territoriality, boundaries between territories, and invasion routes via which members of opposing territories travel to commit acts of violence. His findings suggest that in impoverished developing countries that experience acute levels of deprivation, elections "may generate petty, warring, territorially organized fiefs, supported by patronage and upheld by force and fear" (Eyre 1984, 36).

Harrison (1988) provided the first detailed anthropological analysis of gangs in Jamaica based on fieldwork in Oceanview (a pseudonym), a community of 6,500 people in the Kingston metropolitan area. Oceanview was home to two rival gangs, one affiliated with the PNP and the other with the JLP. Their conflict was not solely based on political affiliation, however. Some of the conflict emerged from competition for criminal markets, including the ganja trade. The gangs also engaged in violent and sometimes deadly conflict over government contracts. Based on her analysis, Harrison (1988) characterized Jamaican gangs as "age-graded networks that provide a basis for association, cooperation, and exchange among ghetto males. They provide a framework for informal economic activities and often embody brokerage channels for obtaining formal wage-work, mostly in the government sector" (265).

Harriott (1996), a sociologist, examined changes in the social organization of crime and criminals in Jamaica since the mid-1970s. He observed that property crime rates decreased, while violent crime rates increased dramatically. He attributed an increase in murder to "income generating activity in the underground economy" (62). The proportion of murders associated with gangs increased, due either indirectly or directly to the defense of turf "in order to establish a monopoly on protection rackets, the local drug market, or to enhance the political leverage of the gang" (62). He further noted that the gangs exercise control over turf for instrumental reasons, not simply as "an expression of some primeval territorial instinct" (62). Harriott explained that criminal groups in Jamaica vary widely in terms of size, hierarchy, specialization, spatial reach, and other organizational characteristics. The most structured groups are those specializing in the drug trade. One of these groups—the well-known Shower Posse—was estimated to have a net worth of approximately US$300 million. Another variable on which the criminal groups vary is their duration. Some of them have been in existence for more than three decades. These tend to be located in "politically homogeneous communities" in which gang leaders work closely with political leaders (67). The variation in the nature and structure of criminal groups in Jamaica raises questions about where these gangs fall on the continuum from less organized criminal street gangs to more organized criminal networks (for a discussion of the distinction between street gangs and organized crime, see Decker and Pyrooz 2014).

Gunst (1996) provided a fascinating account of Jamaican posses based on a rich "street ethnography" (including interviews and participant observations) conducted in Jamaica and the United States. Gunst, a historian, traces the emergence of the posses to the island's history of colonialism and oppression, noting that "every trip I took to the island showed me a present heavy with the burden of the past" (Gunst 1996, xviii). Consistent with earlier scholarship, Gunst draws clear connections between the posses, politics, and violence. By the late 1960s, "the gunmen who worked for the politicians had become the new lords of the streets, politely hailed as 'community leaders,' who could wage war and make peace" (83). A symbiotic relationship developed in which the posses delivered blocs of votes for politicians, who in turn invested in their communities with housing developments, government contracts, and other forms of political patronage.

Moser and Holland (1997) used a qualitative methodology called *participatory urban appraisal* to examine violence in five Jamaican communities (for information on this methodology, see Moser and McIlwaine 1999). In four of the five communities, residents viewed gang violence as the most serious type of violence in their area. Moser and Holland found that in a garrison community in which a gang leader (or don) was firmly in control, residents perceived lower levels of violence. Yet in non-garrison communities that did not have a single gang leader or political leader who exerted firm control over the area, there was more competition for control, and residents perceived more violence. According to Moser and Holland (1997), residents viewed gang violence as "inversely linked to the existence of a 'strong leader' in the community. A powerful don could reduce fractional fighting and maintain cohesiveness" (15).[6] Moser and Holland's detailed qualitative findings are useful for understanding how criminal gangs influence the lives of residents in these Jamaican communities. These findings are also reminiscent of the broader literature on criminal governance, particularly in the developing world (e.g., Feldman and Luna 2022; Lessing 2021).

Trinidad and Tobago

Early research on gangs in Trinidad and Tobago represents a fascinating blend of scholarship from multiple disciplines. To truly understand the emergence of gangs in Trinidad and Tobago, one must understand the complex blend of (at least) three factors: the nation's colonial history, its race relations, and its Carnival culture. Carnival is a pre-Lenten celebration that is held each year on the Monday and Tuesday before Ash Wednesday, usually in February or March. There are many unique traditions associated with Carnival, but one of the principal ones is the Road March, in which participants wear colorful costumes and dance to loud music in parades that wind through the streets of various communities. However, Carnival "is not just a two-day event for the average Trinidadian: It is an all-year-round statement of identity" (Mason 1998, 7). Carnival is deeply embedded in the nation's spirit and culture (Mason 1998; Riggio 1998; Van Koningsbruggen 1997).

The history of Carnival is closely linked with two homegrown styles of music developed by Afro-Trinidadians: Calypso and the steel pan. Calypso is a style of "popular folksong" that emerged among African slaves in Trinidad (Elder 1966, 1). Prior to World War II, when Trinidad was still a British colony, its British rulers did not appreciate the subversive political and social commentary in many of the Calypso songs. As a result, they censored, surveilled, and harassed the Calypso artists relentlessly (Guilbault 2007; Mason 1998). The steel pan, an instrument originally made from used 55-gallon oil drums, was invented in Trinidad in the 1930s. It met the same fate as Calypso. As noted by one observer:

> Calypso and steel pan were quickly associated with each other because they shared similar backgrounds, political affiliations, and performance contexts. Both were connected to Afro-Trinidadans from the most deprived socio-economic areas; both were also targets of, and responses to, the colonial regime. (Mason 1998, 59)

The invention and evolution of the steel pan occurred in impoverished communities inhabited largely by people of African descent (Aho 1987). For the British colonial government, musical forms that sounded African were associated with "the primitive, the barbarous, and the uncivilized" and therefore needed to be tightly controlled (Braithwaite 1954, 90; see also Aho 1987; Gomes 1974).

For the pan artists, playing in a steel band was a form of recreation as well as cultural expression. They "rejected the norms of morality enforced on them in a society that denied them recognition" (Elder 1966, 163). Aho (1987, 32) explains that these young people were often poorly educated and had difficulty finding work. Due to limited opportunities for recognition or success

> they channeled their energies and talents into whatever areas were available to them, in spite of, in some cases, precisely because of, resistance by the ruling colonial government and elites. In the case of steel band music, they were using their own distinctive culture, instruments and music of their own creation, to express themselves and to define an acceptable and comfortable social location for themselves in their own eyes, in the eyes of their peers, and in the eyes of the communities in which their bands were based. (Aho 1987, 32)

The steel band was one of the few options available to impoverished young Black residents for earning status and respect (Aho 1987).

Although the steel bands provided valuable opportunities for young people from disadvantaged communities to express their creative spirit, intergroup tensions between rival steel bands often resulted in violence (Braithwaite 1954).[7] In 1962, the Trinidadian government commissioned a report to investigate the violence. The resulting report concluded that "the members of the steelbands in the Port of Spain area also shared membership in youthful gangs of one kind or another. In fact, historically, the youthful gang in the urban and semi-urban area of Trinidad had tended to be the supporting incubus for the steelband movement" (Elder 1966, 169–170). Trinidadian novelist Earl Lovelace (1998, 54) eloquently captured these linkages between the steelbands and gangs:

> Those were the days when every district around Port of Spain was its own island, and the steelband within its boundaries was its army, providing warriors to uphold its sovereignty. Those were the war days, when every street corner was a garrison; and to be safe, if you came from Belmont, you didn't let night catch you in St. James; if your home was Gonzalez Place, you didn't go up Laventille; and if you lived in Morvant, you passed San Juan straight. (54)

Early research showed clearly that the emergence of gangs in Trinidad and Tobago was associated with the nation's tumultuous colonial history and a variety of endemic social issues, including poverty and race relations.

Mieczkowski (1983, 95) carried out the first ethnography of a gang in Trinidad based on his interactions with a group that he referred to as the *Ras Boys*. He met members of the group in 1972 while working as a sailor who stopped frequently in Trinidad. The Ras Boys lived in an impoverished but cohesive community in the nation's capital in which residents "shared a common history and set of experiences intimately tied into Trinidad's struggle against and liberation from colonialism" (Mieczkowski 1983, 94). The Ras Boys were responsible for organizing the community's annual Carnival celebration and other legitimate social functions. Although engaging in various forms of crime and violence, the Ras Boys also served as informal community leaders who provided security and mediated disputes. According to Mieczkowski, "the legitimate functions blended into the illegitimate ones. Service to the community was in both legitimate and illegitimate domains. They both served and exploited. They had both altruistic and profit-seeking motives" (96). This early finding about the involvement of gangs in both legal and illegal ventures is consistent with research on gangs in Trinidad and Tobago conducted decades later (Figuera 2020; Katz, Maguire, and Choate 2011; Pawelz 2018a, 2018b).

TWENTY-FIRST-CENTURY RESEARCH ON GANGS IN THE CARIBBEAN

Twenty-first-century research on gangs within individual nations and territories in the Caribbean has continued to be dominated by research from Jamaica and Trinidad and Tobago, although research on gangs in Belize and Haiti has begun to accumulate over the past two decades.[8] Over that same period, a rich body of comparative research on gangs in the Caribbean region has also emerged. This section begins by briefly discussing twenty-first-century research on gangs in Jamaica and Trinidad and Tobago, the two nations I examined in the previous section. After that, I briefly describe the emerging research on gangs in Belize and Haiti, followed by comparative research on gangs and related phenomena in the region.

Jamaica

Twenty-first-century research on gangs in Jamaica has continued to rely heavily on qualitative and historical research methods. Qualitative research has produced numerous useful insights about gangs and their origins and effects based on fieldwork with gang leaders, gang members, residents of gang-controlled communities, and other stakeholders (Blake 2013; Charles 2004; Charles and Beckford 2012; Jackson 2016; Lewis, McIntosh, and Perkins 2019). Historical research has also continued to produce key insights about the overlap between gangs, politics, and violence in Jamaica (Clarke 2006; Edmonds 2016; Sives 2002, 2010). Much of the historical scholarship on gangs in Jamaica begins its coverage in the 1960s, particularly around the political violence that took place following the nation's independence from British colonial rule in 1962. However, Williams (2011) traces the emergence of gangs back to the early 1940s when Jamaicans were given the right to vote. Williams argues that "local gangs were created by politicians who used poverty and desperation to build up armies in the slums of west Kingston" (91). The nation's two political parties each used gangs composed of "desperate, poor, and unemployed young men" to protect their supporters while voting or attending rallies (114). They also counted on gangs to mobilize voters during elections. Gangs defended their communities and supported their party using violence if necessary, thus setting in motion decades of "political gangsterism" in Jamaica (114).

In addition, several lines of quantitative research on gangs have emerged in recent years. For example, drawing on school-based surveys, researchers have examined exposure to violence, including gang violence, among Jamaican youth (Bourne and McLymont 2020). Several studies have relied on official crime reports and police data to understand patterns of violence, including gang violence (Lemard and Hemenway 2006; Morris and Graycar 2011; Morris and Maguire 2016). For instance, Morris and Maguire (2016) found that homicide rates in Kingston neighborhoods have a significant positive relationship with voter turnout; a relationship the authors attribute to the association between gangs and partisan politics. Two studies have used quantitative methods to test the effects of gang-related interventions using quasi-experimental or experimental methods. Katz, Harriott, and Hedberg (2020) used a quasi-experimental design to test the effects of a gang truce in Greater August Town, Jamaica. They found that the truce was not effective in reducing violence. Walker et al. (2011, 2021) conducted a randomized controlled trial to test the effects of an early childhood psychosocial intervention on adult mental health and behavioral outcomes. They found that the intervention reduced participants' scores on a composite scale measuring involvement in serious misbehavior[9] at 22 years of age (Walker et al. 2011), but those effects had dissipated by 31 years of age (Walker et al. 2021).

Trinidad and Tobago

Twenty-first-century research on gangs in Trinidad and Tobago has been more active than in any other nation in the Caribbean. Qualitative research on gangs in Trinidad and Tobago has continued to reveal key insights about gangs and their effects. As in Jamaica, several researchers have conducted fieldwork with gang leaders, gang members, residents of gang-controlled communities, and other stakeholders in Trinidad and Tobago (Adams 2012; Adams, Morris, and Maguire 2021; Alexis, 2013; Figuera 2020; Maguire and Gordon 2015; Mahabir 2013; Mendez 2019; Pawelz 2018a, 2018b; Townsend 2009; Wallace 2018). In addition, several lines of quantitative research on gangs have emerged. For example, drawing on the Eurogang "expert survey," researchers have examined the number and size of gangs in Trinidad and Tobago (Katz, Fox, and Gill 2019). Another emerging line of quantitative research on gangs in Trinidad and Tobago uses large-scale surveys of youth to examine the risk and protective factors associated with gang membership and related behaviors (Katz and Fox 2010; Maguire 2013; Maguire and Fishbein 2016; Maguire, Wells, and Katz 2011). Various other types of quantitative analyses have also been useful for understanding gang-related phenomena, including a study of firearm possession among arrestees (Wells, Katz, and Kim 2010), a quasi-experimental evaluation of a gang violence reduction strategy (Maguire, Oakley, and Corsaro 2018), and a study of substances present in the corpses of homicide victims (including gang-related homicides) based on post-mortem toxicology data (Kuhns and Maguire 2012).

Belize

Research on gangs has also begun to accumulate in Belize. Once known as British Honduras, Belize gained its independence from the United Kingdom in 1981. Gang formation in Belize can be traced back to the deportation of Belizean migrants from the United States in the 1980s (Baird 2021; Flores 2018; Warnecke-Berger 2019). Deportees who were associated with the Bloods and the Crips in the United States brought these associations and experiences back with them to Belize. The first wave of Bloods and Crips returned to a nation with a "limited institutional capacity to enforce the rule of law" (Baird 2021, 418). These new gangs quickly formed connections with political parties "that peaked in the run-up to elections" (Baird 2021, 418). Gayle and Mortis (2010) found that some politicians in Belize "have symbiotic links with gangs" (144). Their interviews with gang members found that some gangs form enduring relationships with a single political party, whereas others offer their services to the party in power or the party that is willing to pay them or offer them other favors (Gayle and Mortis 2010).

Gangs in Belize are heavily involved in a variety of criminal offenses, including street-level drug distribution. According to a Belizean gang member interviewed by Gayle and Mortis (2010), "no gang do just one thing. We do several things" (311). One of the activities that Belizean gangs engage in is violence. As gangs in Belize proliferated, they began to splinter, which led to increases in intergang conflict and violence (Baird 2021; Warnecke-Berger 2019). This splintering led to a "dramatic rise in deaths related to beefs—street level disputes, spats, and tit-for-tat killings—between gang rivals" (Baird 2020, 88). Young (2019) concluded that the intersection of gangs and guns has resulted in "an epidemic of violence in Belize City which compromises residents' quality of life, exposes youth and children to trauma, and kills or injures hundreds of people annually" (xi). At the same time, gangs in Belize also help provide a social and economic safety net in marginalized communities. Warnecke-Berger (2019) notes that Belizean gangs provide money "to send children to school or to support families in times of economic hardship" (217). Communities, in turn, help protect gangs by maintaining a code of silence and refusing to cooperate with police. Thus, consistent with findings from other Caribbean nations and territories, gangs have multifaceted roles in the communities in which they are embedded.

Haiti

Research on gangs has also begun to accumulate in Haiti, the poorest and most populous nation in the region. President Jean-Bertrand Aristide fled Haiti and went into exile in 2004. While still in office, Aristide had distributed weapons to youth groups "in exchange for their support" (Becker 2011, 137; also see Beer 2016). The weapons provided by Aristide gave the groups the tools necessary "to commit crimes and dominate neighborhoods" (Becker 2011, 137). Gangs stepped into the vacuum created by the absence of a functioning government in the fragile nation.[10] While Haiti's gangs engage in many types of criminal activity, they also play an important role in politics. As in Jamaica, politicians and other elites in Haiti exploit gangs "as instruments of political warfare, providing them with arms, funding, and protection from arrest" (Dziedzic and Perito 2008, 1).

The roles of gangs fluctuate between the criminal and the political depending on the needs of their patrons. Based on fieldwork with Haitian gangs, Schuberth (2015) found that "during periods of decreasing demand for their violent service by politicians . . . gangs appear to resort to two alternative sources of income: either they increase their collaboration with organised crime groups, or they extract resources from their own communities" (3). Consistent with research evidence from other countries in the region, politicians in Haiti rely most heavily on gangs during election periods. Schuberth (2015) argues that during elections, "gangs are paid to carry out acts of armed violence which advance the political power of their patrons. In between elections, gangs are hired to increase the economic power of their patrons through organised criminal activities" (13). During those times when politicians have less need for them, gangs compensate for the loss of revenue by "extracting resources from their own or neighbouring communities" (16). Consistent with findings from other nations and territories in the region, the relationships between gangs in Haiti and the communities in which they are embedded are ambiguous. Gangs also provide a variety of services for their communities; they fill the void left by an absent or poorly functioning state (Becker 2011; Schuberth 2015).

Gang violence issues in Haiti intensified after the nation was struck by a tragic earthquake in 2010. Residents attribute the increase in violence in part to "the collapse of the state penitentiary and subsequent escape of prisoners," including gang leaders and members who were able to resume their gang activity (Marcelin and Cena 2020, 272). Gang violence issues intensified again in 2021 after Haiti's prime minister, who was alleged to have close ties with criminal gangs, was assassinated in his home on July 7, 2021. The assassination left a power vacuum in Haiti that has resulted in violent clashes between criminal gangs vying for control over territory. Observers argue that the increasing power of Haitian gangs "threatens the country's social fabric and its fragile, anemic economy" (Coto and Arce 2021).

Comparative Research

To our knowledge, the first comparative study of gangs in the Caribbean was Mahabir's (1988) historical analysis of the evolution of gangs in Jamaica and Trinidad and Tobago. Twenty-first-century research on gangs in the Caribbean has built on that early research, using data from multiple nations and territories both within and outside the region. For example, Baird (2020) used qualitative methods to compare gang violence in Port of Spain, Trinidad, and Belize City, Belize. Hill (2013) used qualitative and quantitative data to examine gangs and gang violence in four nations with the highest homicide rates in the Caribbean. Blum and Ireland (2004) and Ohene, Ireland, and Blum (2005) conducted quantitative analyses of survey data from nearly 16,000 youth from eight Caribbean nations to identify the factors associated with health-compromising behaviors, including violence and gang involvement. Similarly, Cheon, Katz, and Freemon (2023) examined survey data from more than 18,000 youth from nine Caribbean nations to identify the factors associated with delinquent behavior, including violence and gang involvement. Katz et al. (2011) used arrestee surveys to compare gang members in Trinidad and Tobago with gang members in the United States. They concluded that "gang members in Trinidad reported substantially more violence than gang members in the United States" (Katz et al. 2011, 243). Pyrooz et al. (2012) used both arrestee surveys and youth surveys to compare gang members in Trinidad and Tobago with gang members in the United States. In short, twenty-first-century research on gangs in the Caribbean has begun to embrace the use of qualitative and quantitative data to conduct informative, comparative analyses of gangs and gang-related violence. This research is useful for understanding the differences and similarities in these phenomena across nations and territories.

DISCUSSION AND CONCLUSION

Gangs and gang violence are highly salient issues in the Caribbean. The region is known to be among the most violent in the world, and research evidence reveals that much of the violence is due to gangs (Katz et al. 2011; UNDP 2012). In a region filled with small-island developing states, government capacity to address these and other serious social issues is often quite limited. Gangs have emerged primarily in communities with deeply entrenched social and economic issues in which young people lack access to social services, high-quality education, and legitimate employment opportunities. Moreover, as shown earlier in this chapter, the emergence of gangs in the Caribbean is also associated with a complex mix of historical, political, and cultural issues. Most of the twentieth-century research on gangs in the Caribbean took place in just two nations: Jamaica and Trinidad and Tobago. These two nations have continued to dominate twenty-first-century research on gangs in the region, but research has also begun to accumulate in Belize and Haiti. Together, the populations of these four nations constitute about 36% of the population of the Caribbean as a whole.

Since these are not the only four nations (or territories) in the Caribbean with serious gang issues (UNDP 2012), expanding the geographic scope of research on gangs in the region is an important next step.

Throughout the Caribbean region, there is evidence of deep connections among gangs, violence, and politics. For example, on May 6, 2013, a politician named Helmin Wiels was shot dead while drinking a beer on a beach in Curaçao. Wiels was the leader of Curaçao's *Pueblo Soberano* party. His murder was orchestrated by the No Limits Soldiers, a criminal gang based in Willemstad, Curaçao. The party that Wiels led had placed first in the 2012 general election and held five of the nation's 21 parliamentary seats (BBC 2013). Gang involvement and interference in politics is consistent with a perspective outlined by Manwaring (2007), who argues that gangs in the region represent a significant threat to state sovereignty. While researchers have documented the ties between gangs, violence, and politics in Jamaica, Trinidad and Tobago, Belize, and Haiti, little is known about these dynamics elsewhere in the Caribbean. Understanding these dynamics, and their influence on the viability and security of Caribbean nations and territories, represents another important avenue for future research.

The methodologies used in research on gangs in the Caribbean have evolved over the past half century or more. Twentieth-century research on gangs and related phenomena was dominated by qualitative and historical research. These studies made important contributions to our understanding of gangs, primarily in Jamaica and Trinidad and Tobago. That research has continued into the twenty-first century, but it has been supplemented with an emerging body of quantitative research that relies on a variety of data sources and methodologies. Much of that emerging research is based on data from school-based youth surveys (Blum and Ireland 2004; Bourne and McLymont 2020; Cheon et al. 2023; Katz and Fox 2010; Maguire 2013; Maguire and Fishbein 2016; Maguire et al. 2011; Ohene et al. 2005). This valuable data source has resulted in numerous insights about topics such as the risk and protective factors associated with gang membership and related phenomena, the degree of youth involvement in gangs, and exposure to gangs and gang-related violence. At the same time, there is some evidence that gang members in the Caribbean may join gangs at an older age than gang members elsewhere, thus youth surveys may exclude a non-trivial segment of gang members (Katz et al. 2011; Rodgers 1999). Arrestee surveys have been used in Trinidad and Tobago and represent an important avenue for continued research on gangs in the Caribbean (Katz et al. 2011). The "gang expert" survey developed by the Eurogang project (Van Gemert 2005) has also been adapted for use in Trinidad and Tobago and represents an especially useful method for capturing information about the number and nature of gangs in a particular area (Katz et al. 2019). Finally, recent research in Jamaica and Trinidad and Tobago has begun to use experimental and quasi-experimental methods to test the effect of interventions intended to reduce gang-related outcomes such as gang membership (Walker et al. 2011, 2021) and gang violence (Katz et al. 2020; Maguire et al. 2018).

A vibrant, multidisciplinary body of research on gangs in the Caribbean has emerged over the past five decades. That research has relied on a variety of different methodologies, including historical, qualitative, and quantitative. Major gaps in this research remain to be filled. One of the most obvious gaps is geographic. The vast majority of the research has taken place in just two nations—Jamaica and Trinidad and Tobago—which together represent only 9.2% of the region's population. A cumulative body of research, primarily qualitative, has recently begun to emerge in Belize and Haiti, which together represent an additional 26.5% of the region's population. Yet there is clear evidence of serious gang activity in many other nations and territories in the region. Learning more about gangs, gang violence, and related phenomena in these locations represents a vital next step.

There are also numerous substantive gaps in the research. Due to space limitations, I will highlight just three of them. First, little is known about the difference between gangs and organized crime in the region, particularly the process through which neighborhood-based street gangs evolve into more structured organized crime syndicates. Second, much remains to be learned about the cumulative effects of exposure to trauma among children and adolescents living in communities with some of the world's highest homicide rates. Finally, perhaps the most serious substantive gap is a lack of high-quality evaluation research on what works to reduce gang involvement and gang-related crime and violence in the region. This lack of research leaves Caribbean governments and non-governmental organizations with an insufficient body of local research evidence on how to address these important issues. Filling these gaps will enable policymakers, practitioners, and scholars to understand Caribbean gangs more deeply and to work together in developing and implementing appropriate and effective solutions.

Notes

1. From 2018 to 2020, 8 of the 16 sovereign Caribbean nations were included at least once among the 10 nations in the world with the highest annual homicide rates. These nations included the Bahamas, Belize, Dominica, Guyana, Jamaica, St. Kitts and Nevis, St. Vincent and the Grenadines, and Trinidad and Tobago. In 2020, Jamaica had the highest homicide rate in the world (44.7 per 100,000 population) (UNODC, 2022).
2. Determining which islands and nations fall within the Caribbean region is not always straightforward. For example, most Caribbean nations are island states located in the Caribbean Sea, but some mainland nations (Belize, Guyana, and Suriname) bordering the Caribbean Sea also identify as falling within the region. CARICOM, which stands for Caribbean Community, is a regional body established in 1973 that currently has 15 member states, including 14 independent nations and one dependent territory (Montserrat). Cuba and the Dominican Republic are island nations in the Caribbean Sea that are not included in the list of member states. Bermuda is an associate member of CARICOM although it is located in the North Atlantic Ocean, not the Caribbean Sea.
3. Heritage languages are the "ancestral, traditional, ethnic, family, home or first language, usually any language first used in the home other than the official dominant language(s)" (Ferreira 2012, 131).
4. The size of the native Taíno population prior to contact with Europeans in 1492 is contested, but the catastrophic demise of the Taínos post-contact is well established (e.g., Stevens-Arroyo 1993).
5. There have been isolated efforts to study gangs in other Caribbean nations and territories, including Cuba (Salas 1979) and Puerto Rico (Ferracuti, Dinitz, and De Brenes 1975). Unfortunately, the only two nations or territories in the region in which a cumulative body of research on gangs had emerged by the year 2000 were Jamaica and Trinidad and Tobago.

6. This observation is consistent with findings from Trinidad and Tobago, where outbreaks of violence have often taken place in communities in which gang leaders whose control over their communities was less firmly established (Maguire et al. 2008; Maguire and Gordon 2015).
7. The association between steel bands and gangs in Trinidad and Tobago is reminiscent of a more general association between distinct forms of subcultural expression and gang emergence and identity. Other examples of such phenomena include "car clubs" and lowrider culture (Holtz 1975; Myerhoff and Myerhoff 1964) and breakdancing and rapping groups (Huff 1989; Roks and Densley 2020).
8. There have been isolated efforts to study gangs in other Caribbean nations and territories during this period, including the Bahamas (Duba and Jencius 2004), Cuba (Galeotti 2006), the Dominican Republic (Bobea 2015), Guyana (Owen and Grigsby 2012), and St. Kitts and Nevis (Joseph 2013).
9. The scale contained six items, five of which tapped into involvement with weapons or violence (fights with weapons, hurt someone with a weapon, carried a gun in past month, threatened someone with a gun, and shot someone with gun), and one measuring gang membership.
10. Researchers who have carried out fieldwork in Haiti draw a distinction between different types of armed groups, including gangs, militias, insurgents, and organized crime networks (Kivland 2020; Kolbe 2013; Schuberth 2015).

References

Adams, Ericka B. 2012. "'We Are Like Prey': How People Negotiate a Violent Community in Trinidad and Tobago." *Race and Justice* 2 (4): 274-303.
Adams, Ericka B., Patrice K. Morris, and Edward R. Maguire. 2021. "The Impact of Gangs on Community Life in Trinidad." *Race and Justice* 11 (4): 543-566.
Aho, William R. 1987. "Steel Band Music in Trinidad and Tobago: The Creation of a People's Music." *Latin American Music Review* 8: 26-58.
Alexis, Simon. 2013. "A Gang Leader through the Eyes of His Mother." In *Gangs in the Caribbean*, edited by Randy Seepersad and Ann Marie Bissessar, 175-194. New Castle upon Tyne, UK: Cambridge Scholars Publishing.
Baird, Adam. 2020. "From Vulnerability to Violence: Gangs and 'Homicide Booms' in Trinidad and Belize." *Urban Crime: An International Journal* 1 (2): 76-97.
Baird, Adam. 2021. "'Man a Kill a Man for Nutin': Gang Transnationalism, Masculinities, and Violence in Belize City." *Men and Masculinities* 24 (3): 411-431.
BBC. 2013. "Curacao Politician Helmin Wiels Shot Dead." May 6. https://www.bbc.com/news/world-latin-america-22424009.
Becker, David C. 2011. "Gangs, Netwar, and 'Community Counterinsurgency' in Haiti." *Prism* 2 (3): 137-154.
Beer, David. 2016. "Haiti: The Gangs of Cité Soleil." *Criminalized Power Structures: The Overlooked Enemies of Peace*, 111-154. National Defense University.
Besson, Jean. 1995. "Land, Kinship, and Community in the Post-Emancipation Caribbean: A Regional View of the Leewards." In *Small Islands, Large Questions: Society, Culture, and Resistance in the Post-Emancipation Caribbean*, edited by Karen F. Olwig, 73-99. New York: Routledge.

Blake, Damion Keith. 2013. "Shadowing the State: Violent Control and the Social Power of Jamaican Garrison Dons." *Journal of Ethnographic & Qualitative Research* 8: 56–75.

Blum, Robert W., and Marjorie Ireland. 2004. "Reducing Risk, Increasing Protective Factors: Findings from the Caribbean Youth Health Survey." *Journal of Adolescent Health* 35 (6): 493–500.

Bobea, Lilian. 2015. "Organized and Disorganized Crime: Gangs, Naciones and Pandillas in the Dominican Republic." In *Gangs in the Caribbean: Responses of State and Society*, edited by Anthony Harriot, and Charles Katz, 69–94. Kingston, Jamaica: University of the West Indies Press.

Bolland, O. Nigel. 1987. "United States Cultural Influences on Belize: Television and Education as 'Vehicles of Import.'" *Caribbean Quarterly*, 33 (3–4): 60–74.

Bourne, Paul Andrew, and Enid McLymont. 2020. "The Social Psychology of Violence on Children in an Urban School in Jamaica." *Insights of Anthropology* 4. 239–267.

Braithwaite, Lloyd, 1954. "The Problem of Cultural Integration in Trinidad." *Social and Economic Studies* 3 (1): 82–96.

Brereton, Bridget. 1989. "Society and Culture in the Caribbean: The British and French West Indies." In *The Modern Caribbean*, edited by Franklin W. Knight, and Colin A. Palmer, 85–110. Chapel Hill: University of North Carolina Press.

Brereton, Bridget. 1996. *An Introduction to the History of Trinidad and Tobago*. Oxford, UK: Heinemann.

Brereton, Bridget. 2008. "The Other Crossing: Asian Migrants in the Caribbean: A Review Essay." *Journal of Caribbean History* 28: 99–128.

Carrington, Lawrence D. 1999. "The Status of Creole in the Caribbean." *Caribbean Quarterly* 45 (2/3): 41–51.

Charles, Christopher A. D. 2004. "Political Identity and Criminal Violence in Jamaica: The Garrison Community of August Town and the 2002 Election." *Social and Economic Studies* 53 (2): 31–73.

Charles, Christopher A. D., and Orville Beckford. 2012. "The Informal Justice System in Garrison Constituencies." *Social and Economic Studies* 61 (2): 51–72.

Cheon, Hyunjung, Charles M. Katz, and Kayla Freemon. 2023. "Validating Social Control, Self-Control, and Social Learning Constructs among a Sample of Youth in Nine English-Speaking Caribbean Nations." *Crime & Delinquency*.

Clarke, Colin. 2006. "Politics, Violence and Drugs in Kingston, Jamaica." *Bulletin of Latin American Research* 25 (3): 420–440.

Coto, Danica, and Alberto Arce. 2021. "Desperate Haitians Suffocate Under Growing Power of Gangs." *AP News*, October 21. https://apnews.com/article/business-caribbean-port-au-prince-haiti-gangs-8793b917718e5f67f27317e765c410aa.

Deagan, Kathleen. 1988. "The Archaeology of the Spanish Contact Period in the Caribbean." *Journal of World Prehistory* 2 (2): 187–233.

Decker, Scott H., and David C. Pyrooz. 2014. "Gangs: Another Form of Organized Crime?" In *Oxford Handbook of Organized Crime*, edited by Letizia Paoli, 270–287. New York: Oxford University Press.

Duba, Jill D., and Marty Jencius. 2004. "The Bahamas." In *Teen Gangs: A Global View*, edited by Maureen P. Duffy and Scott E. Gillig, 27–38. Westport, CT: Greenwood.

Dudley, Shannon. 2008. *Music from Behind the Bridge: Steelband Spirit and Politics in Trinidad and Tobago*. Oxford, UK: Oxford University Press.

Dziedzic, Michael, and Robert M. Perito. 2008. *Haiti: Confronting the Gangs of Port-au-Prince*. Washington, DC: United States Institute of Peace. www.usip.org/publications/haiti-confronting-the-gangs-port-au-prince.

Edmonds, Kevin. 2016. "Guns, Gangs and Garrison Communities in the Politics of Jamaica." *Race & Class* 57 (4): 54–74.

Elder, Jacob D. 1966. *Evolution of the Traditional Calypso of Trinidad and Tobago: A Socio-Historical Analysis of Song-Change*. PhD Dissertation, University of Pennsylvania.

Eltis, David. 1993. "Europeans and the Rise and Fall of African Slavery in the Americas: An Interpretation." *American Historical Review* 98 (5): 1399–1423.

Emmer, P. C. 1990. "Immigration into the Caribbean: The Introduction of Chinese and East Indian Indentured Labourers between 1839 and 1917." *Itinerario* 14: 61–95.

Ewing, Adam. 2013. "Caribbean Labour Politics in the Age of Garvey, 1918–1938." *Race & Class* 55: 23–45.

Eyre, L. Alan. 1972. "The Shantytowns of Montego Bay, Jamaica." *Geographical Review* 62 (3): 394–413.

Eyre, L. Alan. 1984. "Political Violence and Urban Geography in Kingston, Jamaica." *Geographical Review* 74: 24–37.

Feldmann, Andreas E., and Juan Pablo Luna. 2022. "Criminal Governance and the Crisis of Contemporary Latin American States." *Annual Review of Sociology* 48: 441–461.

Ferracuti, Franco, Simon Dinitz, and Esperanza Acosta de Brenes. 1975. *Delinquents and Nondelinquents in the Puerto Rican Slum Culture*. Columbus: Ohio State University Press.

Ferreira, Jo-Anne S. 2012. "Caribbean Languages and Caribbean Linguistics." In *Caribbean Heritage*, edited by Basil A. Reid, 130–147. Mona, Jamaica: University of the West Indies Press.

Figuera, Renée. 2020. "'Doh Go Dey' Crime in Conversations with Gang Members in Trinidad." *Caribbean Quarterly* 66 (2): 258–280.

Flores, Francisca. 2018. "Community Resilience, Health, and Human Security: A Stakeholder-Engaged Case Study on Gang Violence and Its Harmful Effects on Adolescents in Belize." PhD Dissertation, University of Pittsburgh.

Forsythe, Dennis. 1980. "West Indian Culture through the Prism of Rastafarianism." *Caribbean Quarterly*, 26 (4): 62–81.

Galeotti, Mark. 2006. "Forward to the Past: Organized Crime and Cuba's History, Present and Future." *Trends in Organized Crime* 9 (3): 45–60.

Gayle, Herbert, and Nelma Mortis. 2010. *Male Social Participation and Violence in Urban Belize: An Examination of their Experience with Goals, Guns, Gangs, Gender, God, and Governance*. https://issuu.com/7newsbelize/docs/male_social_participation_and_violence_in_urban_be.

Gomes, Albert. 1974. *Through a Maze of Colour*. Port of Spain, Trinidad: Key Caribbean Publications.

Guilbault, Jocelyne. 2007. *Governing Sound: The Cultural Politics of Trinidad's Carnival Musics*. Chicago, IL: University of Chicago Press.

Gunst, Laurie. 1996. *Born Fi' Dead: A Journey through the Jamaican Posse Underworld*. New York: Henry Holt and Company.

Harriott, Anthony. 1996. "The Changing Social Organization of Crime and Criminals in Jamaica." *Caribbean Quarterly* 42 (2/3): 54–71.

Harrison, Faye V. 1988. "The Politics of Social Outlawry in Urban Jamaica." *Urban Anthropology and Studies of Cultural Systems and World Economic Development* 17 (2/3): 259–277.

Headley, Bernard D. 1988. "'War Ina 'Babylon': Dynamics of the Jamaican Informal Drug Economy." *Social Justice* 15 (3/4): 61–86.

Hennessy, Alistair. 1993. "The Nature of the Conquest and the Conquistadors." *Proceedings of the British Academy* 81: 5–36.

Higman, B. W. 2010. *A Concise History of the Caribbean*. New York: Cambridge University Press.

Hill, Sheridon. 2013. "The Rise of Gang Violence in the Caribbean." In *Gangs in the Caribbean*, edited by Randy Seepersad and Ann Marie Bissessar, 36–79. New Castle upon Tyne, UK: Cambridge Scholars Publishing.

Hofman, Corinne, Angus Mol, Menno Hoogland, and Roberto Valcárcel Rojas. 2014. "Stage of Encounters: Migration, Mobility and Interaction in the Pre-Colonial and Early Colonial Caribbean." *World Archaeology* 46 (4): 590–609.

Holtz, Janice-Marie Allard. 1975. "The 'Low-Riders': Portrait of an Urban Youth Subculture." *Youth and Society* 6 (4): 495–508.

Hu-DeHart, Evelyn. 2002. "*Huagong* and *Huashang*: The Chinese as Laborers and Merchants in Latin America and the Caribbean." *Amerasia Journal* 28 (2): 64–91.

Huff, C. Ronald. 1989. "Youth Gangs and Public Policy." *Crime and Delinquency* 35 (4): 524–537.

Jackson, Asheka. 2016. "Gang Risk Factors among Urban Jamaican Youth: A Qualitative Analysis." *International Journal of Criminal Justice Sciences* 11 (2): 132–147.

Johnson, Devon, Edward R. Maguire, Stephanie A. Maass, and Julie Hibdon. 2016. "Systematic Observation of Disorder and other Neighborhood Conditions in a Distressed Caribbean Community." *Journal of Community Psychology* 44 (6): 729–746.

Joseph, Janice. 2013. "Paradise Lost: Gangs and Gang Violence in St. Kitts and Nevis." In *Gangs in the Caribbean*, edited by Randy Seepersad and Ann Marie Bissessar, 114–130. Newcastle upon Tyne, UK: Cambridge Scholars Publishing.

Katz, Charles M., and Andrew M. Fox. 2010. "Risk and Protective Factors Associated with Gang-Involved Youth in Trinidad and Tobago." *Revista Panamericana de Salud Pública* 27 (3): 187–202.

Katz, Charles M., Andrew M. Fox, and Lexi Gill. 2019. "Gangs, Structural Disadvantage, and Homicide in a Caribbean Nation." In *Caribbean Perspectives on Criminology and Criminal Justice, Volume 1*, edited by Wendell C. Wallace, 59–81. Washington, DC: Westphalia Press.

Katz, Charles M., Anthony Harriott, and E. C. Hedberg. 2020. "Mediating Violence in Jamaica through a Gang Truce." *International Criminal Justice Review* 32 (2): 129–150. https://doi.org/10.1177/1057567720975631.

Katz, Charles M., Edward R. Maguire, and David Choate. 2011. "A Cross-National Comparison of Gangs in the United States and Trinidad and Tobago." *International Criminal Justice Review* 21 (3): 243–262.

Kivland, Chelsey L. 2020. *Street Sovereigns: Young Men and the Makeshift State in Urban Haiti*. Ithaca, NY: Cornell University Press.

Kolbe, Athena R. 2013. *Revisiting Haiti's Gangs and Organized Violence*. Rio de Janeiro, Brazil: Humanitarian Action in Situations Other than War.

Kuhns, Joseph B., and Edward R. Maguire. 2012. "Drug and Alcohol Use by Homicide Victims in Trinidad and Tobago, 2001–2007." *Forensic Science, Medicine, and Pathology* 8 (3): 243–251.

Lacey, Terry. 1977. *Violence and Politics in Jamaica, 1960–1970: Internal Security in a Developing Country*. Manchester, UK, Manchester University Press.

Lemard, Glendene, and David Hemenway. 2006. "Violence in Jamaica: An Analysis of Homicides 1998–2002." *Injury Prevention* 12: 15–18.

Lessing, Benjamin. 2021. "Conceptualizing Criminal Governance." *Perspectives on Politics* 19 (3): 854-873.
Lewis, Marjorie, Dianne McIntosh, and Anna Kasafi Perkins. 2019. "Some Girls Are so Vicious that Even the Boys Fear Them: Girls and Gangs in Jamaica." In *Female Child Soldiering, Gender Violence, and Feminist Theologies*, edited by Susan Willhauck, 93-107. Cham, Switzerland: Palgrave Macmillan.
Lovelace, Earl, 1998. *The Dragon Can't Dance*. New York: Persea Books.
Lowenthal, David. 1971. "Post-Emancipation Race Relations: Some Caribbean and American Perspectives." *Journal of Interamerican Studies and World Affairs* 13 (3/4): 367-377.
Maguire, Edward R. 2013. "Exploring Family Risk and Protective Factors for Adolescent Problem Behaviors in the Caribbean." *Maternal and Child Health Journal* 17 (8): 1488-1498.
Maguire, Edward R., and Diana H. Fishbein. 2016. "The Influence of Family Characteristics on Problem Behaviors in a Sample of High-Risk Caribbean Adolescents." *Family Relations* 65 (1): 120-133.
Maguire, Edward R., and C. Jason Gordon. 2015. "Faith-Based Interventions for Reducing Gang Violence in the Caribbean: Reflections from a Professor and a Priest." In *Gangs in the Caribbean: Responses of State and Society*, edited by Anthony Harriott, and Charles Katz, 307-336. Mona, Jamaica: University of the West Indies Press.
Maguire, Edward R., Megan T. Oakley, and Nicholas Corsaro. 2018. *Evaluating Cure Violence in Trinidad and Tobago*. Washington, DC: Inter-American Development Bank.
Maguire, Edward R., William Wells, and Charles M. Katz. 2011. "Measuring Community Risk and Protective Factors for Adolescent Problem Behaviors: Evidence from a Developing Nation." *Journal of Research in Crime and Delinquency* 48 (4): 594-620.
Maguire, Edward R., Julie Willis, Jeffrey B. Snipes, and Megan Gantley. 2008. "Spatial Concentrations of Violence in Trinidad and Tobago." *Caribbean Journal of Criminology and Public Safety* 13 (1/2), 48-92.
Mahabir, Cynthia. 1988. "Crime in the Caribbean: Robbers, Hustlers, and Warriors." *International Journal of the Sociology of Law* 16 (3): 315-338.
Mahabir, Cynthia. 2013. "Allah's Outlaws: The Jamaat al Muslimeen of Trinidad and Tobago." *British Journal of Criminology* 53: 59-73.
Manwaring, Max G. 2007. *A Contemporary Challenge to State Sovereignty: Gangs and Other Illicit Transnational Criminal Organizations in Central America, El Salvador, Mexico, Jamaica, and Brazil*. Strategic Studies Institute, US Army War College.
Marcelin, Louis H., and Toni Cela. 2020. "Justice and Rule of Law Failure in Haiti: A View from the Shanties." *Journal of Community Psychology* 48 (2): 267-282.
Mason, Peter. 1998. *Bacchanal: The Carnival Culture of Trinidad*. Philadelphia, PA: Temple University Press.
Mendez, Melissa. 2019. *Youthmen with Big Man Mentality: An Exploration and Analysis of the Narratives of Young Offenders in Trinidad and Tobago*. PhD Dissertation, Cardiff University.
Mieczkowski, Thomas. 1983. "Syndicated Crime in the Caribbean." In *Career Criminals*, edited by Gordon P. Waldo, 89-102. Beverly Hills, CA: Sage.
Morris, Patrice K., and Adam Graycar. 2011. "Homicide through a Different Lens." *British Journal of Criminology* 51 (5): 823-838.
Morris, Patrice K., and Edward R. Maguire. 2016. "Political Culture, Neighbourhood Structure and Homicide in Urban Jamaica." *British Journal of Criminology* 56 (5): 919-936.
Moser, Caroline, and Jeremy Holland. 1997. *Urban Poverty and Violence in Jamaica*. Washington, DC: World Bank.

Moser, Caroline, and Cathy McIlwaine. 1999. "Participatory Urban Appraisal and Its Application for Research on Violence." *Environment and Urbanization* 11 (2): 203–226. https://doi.org/10.1177/095624789901100217.

Myerhoff, Howard L., and Barbara G. Myerhoff. 1964. "Field Observations of Middle-Class Gangs." *Social Forces* 42 (3): 328–336.

Ohene, Sally-Ann, Marjorie Ireland, and Robert W. Blum. 2005. "The Clustering of Risk Behaviors among Caribbean youth." *Maternal and Child Health Journal* 9: 91–100.

Owen, Taylor, and Alexandre Grigsby. 2012. *In Transit: Gangs and Criminal Networks in Guyana*. Geneva, Switzerland: Small Arms Survey.

Pawelz, Janina. 2018a. "Researching Gangs: How to Reach Hard-to-Reach Populations and Negotiate Tricky Issues in the Field." In *Forum: Qualitative Social Research* 19 (1): 1–24.

Pawelz, Janina. 2018b. "Hobsbawm in Trinidad: Understanding Contemporary Modalities of Urban Violence." *Conflict, Security & Development* 18 (5): 409–432.

Payne, Anthony. 1983. "The Rodney Riots in Jamaica: The Background and Significance of the Events of October 1968." *Race and Politics in the Caribbean* 21 (2): 158–174.

Pyrooz, David C., Andrew M. Fox, Charles M. Katz, and Scott H. Decker. 2012. "Gang Organization, Offending, and Victimization: A Cross-National Analysis." In *Youth Gangs in International Perspective*, edited by Finn-Aage Esbensen, and Cheryl Maxson, 85–105. New York: Springer.

Riggio, Milla C. 1998. "Resistance and Identity: Carnival in Trinidad and Tobago." *TDR* 42 (3): 6–24.

Rodgers, Dennis. 1999. *Youth Gangs and Violence in Latin America and the Caribbean: A Literature Survey*. Washington, DC: World Bank.

Roks, Robert A., and James A. Densley. 2020. "From Breakers to Bikers: The Evolution of the Dutch Crips 'Gang.'" *Deviant Behavior* 41 (4): 525–542.

Salas, Luis. 1979. *Social Control and Deviance in Cuba*. New York: Praeger.

Schuberth, Moritz. 2015. "A Transformation from Political to Criminal Violence? Politics, Organised Crime and the Shifting Functions of Haiti's Urban Armed Groups." *Conflict, Security & Development* 15 (2): 169–196.

Sives, Amanda. 2002. "Changing Patrons, from Politician to Drug Don: Clientelism in Downtown Kingston, Jamaica." *Latin American Perspectives* 29 (5): 66–89. https://doi.org/10.1177/0094582X0202900505.

Sives, Amanda. 2010. *Elections, Violence, and the Democratic Process in Jamaica, 1944–2007*. Kingston, Jamaica: Ian Randle Publishers.

Stevens-Arroyo, Anthony M. 1993. "The Inter-Atlantic Paradigm: The Failure of Spanish Medieval Colonization of the Canary and Caribbean Islands." *Comparative Studies in Society and History* 35 (3): 515–543.

Stone, Carl. 1979. "The 1976 Parliamentary Election in Jamaica." *Caribbean Studies* 19 (1–2): 33–50.

Tinker, Hugh. 1974. *A New System of Slavery: The Export of Indian Labour Overseas, 1830–1920*. Oxford, UK: Oxford University Press.

Townsend, Dorn. 2009. *No Other Life*. Geneva, Switzerland: Small Arms Survey.

UNDP. 2012. *Caribbean Human Development Report 2012: Human Development and Shift to Better Citizen Security*. United Nations Development Program.

UNODC. 2022. "United Nations Homicide Country Data." https://dataunodc.un.org/content/homicide-country-data.

Valtonen, Kathleen. 1996. "Bread and Tea: A Study of the Integration of Low-Income Immigrants from Other Caribbean Territories into Trinidad." *International Migration Review* 30 (4): 995–1019.

Van Gemert, Frank. 2005. "Youth Groups and Gangs in Amsterdam; An Inventory Based on the Eurogang Expert Survey." In *European Street Gangs and Troublesome Youth Groups*, edited by Scott H. Decker, and Frank M. Weerman, 147–168. New York: Routledge.

Van Koningsbruggen, Petrus Hendrikus. 1997. *Trinidad Carnival: A Quest for National Identity*. London: MacMillan Education.

Vertovek, Steven. 1995. "Indian Indentured Migration to the Caribbean." In *The Cambridge Survey of World Migration*, edited by Robin Cohen, 57–62. Cambridge, UK: Cambridge University Press.

Walker, Susan P., Susan M. Chang, Marcos Vera-Hernández, and Sally Grantham-McGregor. 2011. "Early Childhood Stimulation Benefits Adult Competence and Reduces Violent Behavior." *Pediatrics* 127 (5): 849–857.

Walker, Susan P., Susan M. Chang, Amika S. Wright, Rodrigo Pinto, James J. Heckman, and Sally M. Grantham-McGregor. 2021. "Cognitive, Psychosocial, and Behaviour Gains at Age 31 Years from the Jamaica Early Childhood Stimulation Trial." *Journal of Child Psychology and Psychiatry* 63 (6): 626–635.

Wallace, Wendell C. 2018. "Understanding the Evolution of Localized Community-Based Street Gangs in Laventille, Trinidad." *Journal of Gang Research* 26: 1–16.

Warnecke-Berger, Hannes. 2019. "Belize: Transnationalization by Coincidence and the Rise of Violence." In *Politics and Violence in Central America and the Caribbean*, edited by Hannes Warnecke-Berger, 197–232. Cham, Switzerland: Palgrave Macmillan.

Wells, William, Charles M. Katz, and Jeonglim Kim. 2010. "Firearm Possession among Arrestees in Trinidad and Tobago." *Injury Prevention* 16 (5): 337–342.

Williams, Kareen F. 2011. *The Evolution of Political Violence in Jamaica, 1940-1980*. PhD Dissertation, Columbia University.

Wilson, Basil. 1980. *Surplus Labour and Political Violence in Jamaica: The Dialectics of Political Corruption, 1966-1976*. PhD Dissertation, City University of New York.

Wilson, Samuel M. 1993. "The Cultural Mosaic of the Indigenous Caribbean." *Proceedings of the British Academy* 81: 37–66.

Young, Michelle. 2019. *Belize City Community Gang Assessment*. Washington, DC: Inter-American Development Bank. http://dx.doi.org/10.18235/0001860

Youssef, Valerie. 2002. "Issues of Bilingual Education in the Caribbean: The Cases of Haiti, and Trinidad and Tobago." *International Journal of Bilingual Education and Bilingualism* 5 (3): 182–193.

SECTION 3
CORE AND EMERGING ISSUES

CHAPTER 18

WHAT IS GANG CULTURE?
Three Conceptualizations of an Elusive Concept

CAYLIN LOUIS MOORE AND FORREST STUART

IN the field of gang research, it is difficult to find a more ubiquitous yet underdefined term than "gang culture." Since Fredric Thrasher's (1927) pioneering research in *The Gang: A Study of 1,313 Gangs in Chicago*, scholars have forwarded gang culture, or some aspect of gang culture, as an explanation for everything from gang formation and organization (Sánchez-Jankowski 1991; Conquergood 1993) to delinquency (Cohen 1955), violence (Anderson 1999; Garot 2010), and geographic diffusion (Hagedorn 1998). Its use as an ambiguous, yet motivating force has led to fundamental disagreements: What, precisely, have researchers meant when they deployed the phrase "gang culture," and how might contemporary studies reconcile these past conceptions to productive effect?

Toward improving the theoretical, analytical, and methodological precision of ongoing gang scholarship, this chapter contends that researchers have historically adhered to three primary conceptualizations of gang culture (see Table 18.1). Each generates divergent frameworks for understanding what gang culture "is," as well as its causal influence on the attitudes, behaviors, and social organization of gangs and gang-associated individuals (also see Lauger and Horning 2020). The first conceptualization treats culture as the values, norms, and collective attitudes (i.e., something gangs *have*) that guide gang-associated individuals' behavior in more or less deterministic ways (see Thrasher 1927; Miller 1958; Anderson 1999). The second rejects the idea of culture as monolithic values. Instead, it views culture as the repertoires, frames, and schemas (i.e., something gangs *use*) for developing non-deterministic strategies of action to solve the problems and situations in their daily lives (see Swidler 1986; Garot 2010; Rios 2011). The final, and certainly newest, perspective conceptualizes culture as cultural products such as music, slang, clothing styles, and other commodities (i.e., something gangs *create*), often used in the pursuit of economic, social, and reputational gain (see Becker 1982; Bourdieu 1996; Stuart 2020a, 2020b).

The shift from the historical embrace of the culture-as-values perspective to the increasing adoption of the culture-as-toolkit and culture-as-products perspectives is, we contend, a welcome and necessary advance. The latter two approaches move research away from analyses that, by treating gang culture as something intrinsic to gang-associated people or

Table 18.1 Three Conceptions of Gang Culture

Perspective	Definition of Culture	Theoretical Foundations	Illustrative Case Studies
Culture-as-values	Collective attitudes that direct social actors' behaviors; "ends" toward which actors strive	Social disorganization (Shaw and McKay 1942); Subcultural theory of deviance (Cohen 1955); culture of poverty (Lewis 1966)	Vigil (1988); Sánchez-Jankowski (1991); Anderson (1999)
Culture-as-toolkit	Repertoires, scripts, strategies, and practices that social actors draw upon to address everyday needs and problems	Dramaturgical theory (Goffman 1959); culture in action (Swidler 1986); cultural boundaries (Lamont 1992)	Hannerz (1969); Garot (2010); Rios (2011)
Culture-as-products	Material and symbolic items that social actors create, commodify, consume, or disseminate	Art worlds (Becker 1982); field theory (Bourdieu 1996); authenticity (Peterson 1997)	Conquergood (1993); Hagedorn (1998); Stuart (2020a)

to gangs at the group level, pathologize and exoticize gangs. Scholars' uptake of these more instrumental and productive perspectives further provides valuable insights for addressing the harms imposed upon gang-associated individuals—as well as their peers, families, and communities—by punitive state interventions (Stuart, Armenta, and Osborne 2015; Moore and Stuart 2022).

CULTURE-AS-VALUES

The first perspective approaches gang culture as something that gangs and gang-associated individuals *have*. This tradition, which has predominated classical criminology and the study of gangs, understands culture as a set of values—the ends toward which behavior is directed—that arise and are accepted under sets of structural constraints. According to this conceptualization, then, poverty might produce a distinct set of accepted cultural values that differs significantly from "mainstream" middle-class culture. In fact, the "culture of poverty" thesis forwarded by Oscar Lewis (1966) explicitly orders the process, claiming that the socioeconomic marginalization of populations catalyzes the development of a distinct set of behaviors that help individuals cope with unsavory circumstances; over time, this set of behaviors calcifies into shared values that contrast with more socially normative, middle-class values, leading to outcomes such as social disorganization and low educational attainment. According to this perspective, even as structural conditions change, these habituated cultural values can persist. Along similar lines, Senator Daniel Patrick Moynihan (1965) famously argued that the structural conditions produced by slavery and

Jim Crow discrimination had resulted in a "ghetto culture"—a distinct set of values held by urban-dwelling Black Americans. Moynihan's pathologizing report persuaded many that phenomena such as single parenthood were cultural values through which poverty was sustained and increased by people living in poverty. In President Lyndon B. Johnson's War on Poverty era, scholars, legislators, and much of the public saw inner-city street gangs as the concentrated embodiment of the culture of poverty and its wayward values.

Early criminologists adopted the culture-as-values approach as they observed the development of delinquent subcultures when structural barriers prevented the attainment of conventional standards of success. In other words, where youth are otherwise denied opportunities and resources, delinquent subcultures such as gangs afford them status and self-esteem (Cohen 1955). Further, argued Shaw and McKay (1942), social disorganization—namely, when communities cannot exert sufficient social control over the behavior of local youth—facilitates delinquency and feeds into the "pseudo cultures" of gangs, in which conventional social mores against deviant behavior such as drug use and violence are loosened. Thrasher (1927), who initiated the study of gang culture, reported examples of gang values that served to regulate behavior, including that gang affiliates must maintain chivalrous relationships with "ladies and girls" by coming to their defense, avoid group in-fighting, and refrain from snitching. Youth facing structural barriers to middle-class cultural signs of status strive for it through more immediately attainable means, for instance, defending their masculinity through displays of bravado and violence (Cloward and Ohlin 1960; Miller 1958).

Aligning with early criminological thought on cultural values, Miller (1958) outlines six distinct "focal concerns" of lower-class culture—toughness, trouble, autonomy, smartness, excitement, and fate—which he asserts are present among all social classes, but are the most salient in the degree of emotional involvement for the lower classes. Miller theorized that adolescent peer groups, or gangs, serve as incubators for cultural value distinctiveness while gang-associated individuals must more willingly adhere to the focal concerns to maintain belonging and a reputable status within the gang. The theoretical significance of focal concerns has mostly diminished in criminology, as critics, such as Kornhauser (1978), argued that Miller does not adequately distinguish between culture and social structure, the latter having greater implications for delinquent behavior. In Miller's (2011) posthumously published work *City Gangs*, he elaborates more on social structure, finding, for instance, that young gang-associated individuals might value education less, given that the career they would eventually be eligible for in their social context would not necessarily require a high school degree. In the more nuanced focal concerns perspective, strict adherence to focal concern values would clearly lead to illegal behavior, but such behavior does not occur automatically or without evaluation. Moule (2015) maintains that the focal concerns framework is best used as a culture in action perspective, which will be discussed in the next section, to better explain gang-associated behavior as partly a function of social relationships and social contexts.

The culture-as-values approach is perhaps best encapsulated by Elijah Anderson's (1999) concept of the "code of the street." Drawing upon William Julius Wilson's (1987) urban underclass thesis, Anderson (1999) offers an ethnographic account of structural conditions under which oppositional culture arises in the case of a predominantly Black neighborhood in urban Philadelphia. He specifically points to the confluence of poverty, unemployment, deindustrialization, and racial stigma for Black men and how, together, these conditions give rise to a level of alienation that encourages opposition to mainstream middle-class values. Like Cohen (1955), Anderson (1999) argues that disaffected youth seek out those forms of esteem made accessible to them. But he goes further by exploring the idea that social alienation also produces a distinct distrust among inner-city residents in the ability of the legal system to resolve disputes and protect their interests, therefore heightening the risk of engaging in illicit dispute resolution. Thus, the use of aggression and the performance of a street-tough persona are granted value within the oppositional culture (see also Vigil 1988; Sánchez-Jankowski 1991).

The titular code of the street that young men develop and embrace to maintain credible (and protective) reputations for violence is, for Anderson (1999), institutionalized at a neighborhood level. Violence is not merely about individual action, but also an expression of whole communities in which this street code bears influence. Living by the code means never backing down from a fight, never tolerating disrespect of any sort, and never hesitating to demonstrate a propensity for aggression. Anderson (1999) presents the example of 15-year-old Tyree, a Black boy attacked by multiple peers as he ran an errand to the corner store. After the attack, Tyree advises his grandmother not to call the police, demonstrating his distrust of conventional institutions as well as his preference to personally respond to the perceived affront. When Tyree catches one of his attackers walking alone, he unleashes a flurry of punches (Anderson 1999, 188). Through such violent retribution, Tyree regained respect (status attainment) and avoided further confrontation (dispute resolution).

Ruth Horowitz (1983) also applied a culture-as-values framework in her study of a Chicano gang in inner-city Chicago. Horowitz (1983) examines the cultural codes that direct behavior in gang-affiliated youth's lives, beginning with an initial adherence to the American dream, structured around economic success through traditional means. As in similar studies (see Anderson 1999; Cohen 1955; Wilson 1987), when youth are thwarted in their attempts to achieve such goals they begin to privilege an honor-bound set of cultural values governed by notions of manhood and the maintenance of peer respect. For instance, being verbally denigrated in public or failing to intervene when a female relative is disrespected become reasons for others to question one's honor and masculinity. In turn, full readiness for physical violence is prized.

Critics of the culture-as-values perspective express skepticism toward the tight cause-and-effect relationship espoused between values and behavior assumed in this literature (see Lauger and Horning 2020). There is, for instance, scant support for the claim that values are predictive of behavior or that subcultural values differ significantly from mainstream values. Quite the opposite, in fact; ample research finds widespread adoption of mainstream values among impoverished populations (Young 2004; Newman 2009; Edin and Kefalas 2011; Dohan 2003; Hayes 2003; Carter 2005; Waller 2002; Duneier 1992). A number of studies do find that self-reported adherence to the code of the street is associated with offending behavior (Moule and Fox 2021), and street code values moderately correlate with the "convict code" (Mitchell, Pyrooz, and Decker 2021).

Nevertheless, researchers have grown increasingly critical of the view that high-poverty minority neighborhoods distinctively value oppositional masculinity, arguing that codes of violence and toughness have always been central features of American masculinity more broadly (Matsueda, Drakulich, and Kubrin 2006). Scholarship on desistance, which focuses on the processes of disengaging from gang affiliation or gang activity, similarly casts doubt on the notion that gang-associated individuals have drastically different values. In fact, studies reveal that roughly half or more of youth are gang affiliated for less than a year and desist from activity altogether afterward (Carson and Vecchio 2015). A multitude of push and pull factors draw individuals away from gangs; former gang-associated individuals often credit experiences such as the birth of a first child, successfully obtaining gainful employment, and committing to a serious romantic relationship as grounds for desistance (Pyrooz and Decker 2011). By all classifications, childrearing, formal employment, and marriage reflect adherence to purportedly mainstream, middle-class values and markers of success. The important caveat is that the structural barriers that many gang-associated individuals face as poor people of color negatively impact the likelihood of successful expression of these values. Therefore, an improved culture-as-values perspective might instead acknowledge that gang-associated individuals share mainstream values, but they are negated under the contexts in which they are found relatively useless, irrelevant, or unattainable.

The heterogeneity of gangs is another significant challenge to the culture-as-values perspective. There is no uniform gang subculture, and gang researchers have long documented a wide range of values and behaviors. In their typology of subcultural differentiation among delinquent gangs, Cloward and Ohlin (1960) provide classical theoretical underpinnings for understanding the heterogeneity of cultural values in gangs. The first category, the "criminal subculture," is principally based on criminal values, where gang-associated individuals organize to pursue material gain through illicit means. Second, the "conflict subculture" is where gang-associated individuals maintain and seek formidable reputations through force or the threat of force. And third, the "retreatist subculture" describes a gang where associates respond to alienation from conventional family and community roles through drug usage. Therefore, according to Cloward and Ohlin (1960), gangs in their entirety, or lone gang-associated individuals, could adopt different economic, conflict, or substance-use subcultural values at different periods, undermining the notion that gangs hold a unitary set of values.

More recent scholarship on gangs that transgress stereotypical gender and sexual orientation composition further elucidates the heterogeneity of gang values and behaviors. Among Columbus, Ohio, gang affiliates, criminologist Vanessa Panfil (2017) differentiates between the illicit behaviors of gay gang-associated individuals compared to their straight counterparts, finding that gay gang-associated individuals sometimes augment the traditional illicit economic activity by participating in the selling of sexual services (Panfil 2017). Where Panfil decenters masculinity compared to traditional gang research, Jody Miller's (2001) work finds that women perform normative masculinity in gangs. Miller (2001) also demonstrates that the methods by which women are initiated into gangs appear to differ in ways that are patterned by individual gangs' gender composition. Women can be "sexed in" to the gang, where they must undergo sexual acts with male gang-associated individuals as a means of initiation, as opposed to being "jumped in."

In contrast to attributing a broader set of cultural values to gangs, as Cohen's (1955) delinquent subculture argument would suggest, prominent sociological scholarship contends that residents' values are localized to their specific context (Whyte 1943; Suttles 1968). Suttles (1968) finds that as residents of low-income neighborhoods are deemed suspicious by mainstream groups, usually due to their poverty or belonging to low-status minoritized groups, they are pushed to the margins, to the "slum," the "skid row," or contemporarily, "the hood." Marginalization of these groups creates what Suttles (1968) terms a "differential moral isolation," where these residents who are already subject to suspicion of their moral integrity are often pragmatic by falling back on a mix of local and mainstream values available in their social context. Similarly, Whyte's (1943) empirical study of a low-income Italian neighborhood in Boston concludes that gang values and behaviors are patterned by the tension between succeeding in their local context and then being rejected by society at large or succeeding in a manner that society at large recognizes yet is contradicted by their local context. Therefore, instead of a gang's cultural values arising homogeneously from status frustration across different contexts (Cohen 1955), what scholars identify as culture is actually something that emerges heterogeneously in localized contexts.

Contemporary scholars have become hesitant to use the term "culture" concerning gang behavior, as the culture-as-values scholarship has painted a pathological picture of subcultures, especially those predominantly populated by people of color. Stating that a group has fundamentally distinct, *deviant* values is hardly neutral when culture is understood as a set of values that internally direct behavior. If applied to policy, this perspective can produce victim blaming, as was the case when the culture of poverty thesis treated poverty as an outcome of pathological culture (Ryan 1976). It also provides an ideological basis for the implementation of policies to coercively and harmfully control marginalized groups' behaviors and associations (Stuart et al. 2015). Civil gang injunctions, for example, are a type of city-level restraining order on a particular group. Injunctions across the United States treat gang-associated individuals' behavior as a public nuisance requiring regulation, thereby prohibiting alleged gang affiliates from everything from walking with another suspected gang member to "congregating" in groups of two or more, wearing gang-associated attire, or loitering for more than several minutes in a public space (see Maxson, Hennigan, and Sloane 2005; Muñiz 2014). Those targeted by injunctions can even be arrested for merely visiting private residences without prior written permission, riding bicycles, and climbing trees. As Caldwell (2010) points out, along with their serious civil liberties implications, such policies negatively impact community participation, familial engagement, and employment, all of which are ostensibly mainstream behaviors. The culture-as-values approach has failed to animate efficacious gang policy because it establishes a spurious connection between values and behavior. Though gang culture may involve distinct behaviors, these behaviors do not necessarily stem from a distinct set of *values*.

Culture-as-Toolkit

A second major conception treats gang culture as something that gangs *use*. Recent advances in cultural sociology adopt this "culture in action" approach, rooted in Erving Goffman's (1959) dramaturgical metaphor, in which individuals construct the self through adjustment, response, and performance for outside audiences. Cultural sociologists contend that individual behaviors are produced collectively, through iterative, daily social interactions. In this deeply sociological view, culture provides the resources for coordinating social action while embracing the apparent randomness in the ways individuals respond to social stimuli (even the same social stimuli) in agentic ways. In his classic study of an inner-city Washington, DC, neighborhood, anthropologist Ulf Hannerz (1969) was among the first to argue that such "modes of action" provide a more accurate understanding of behaviors in context. As a counter to the then-dominant culture-as-values approach, Hannerz (1969) demonstrated that poor residents draw on modes of action appropriate to both the "mainstream" and their localized "ghetto" culture, performing them differently depending on the context and audience.

Two decades later, sociologist Ann Swidler (1986) expanded on these ideas to propose the toolkit approach, which treats culture as the repertoires and strategies of action individuals and groups use to address everyday needs and dilemmas. Such repertoires and strategies are differentially available depending on social location, context, and other conditional factors. Formulated as such, it is superior to the culture-as-values approach in accounting for the heterogeneity of behavior and the agency of individuals with the ability to select from multiple options for behaving in a particular social interaction or context. For scholars embracing this perspective, it is unsurprising—expected, even—that a gang-associated youth will adopt a particular style of interaction with peers and rivals in the streets but otherwise adopt a strikingly different repertoire when interacting with these same individuals in the school setting (for additional discussion, see Lauger and Horning 2020). In this manner, the culture-as-toolkit approach aligns with a Bourdieusian (Bourdieu 1977, 1987) approach to culture, which highlights the manner in which people in divergent social classes embody a divergent "habitus," possessing different kinds and amounts of "cultural capital" available to accomplish their various goals. Where the culture-as-values approach frames the behaviors of urban youth as evidence of cultural deficits, the culture-as-toolkit perspective might instead understand stigmatized behavior as evidence of a mismatch between an individual's cultural repertoires and the social context in which they are operating.

Victor Rios' work exemplifies the culture-as-toolkit approach to the study of gang-associated youth. Through his in-depth ethnographic study in Oakland, California, Rios (2011) examines how hyper-criminalization, surveillance, and punishment practices impact Black and Brown boys' lives, including their social behaviors. He points to authority figures' "misrecognition" of youths' behaviors in moments when a youth's repertoire misaligns with their social fields. For example, one participant, a Black youth named Ronny, attempts to acquire a job at a local restaurant. Due to his prior interactions with the criminal justice system, Ronny found that being alone with the White woman interviewer felt precarious. Not wanting to be perceived as making a sexual advance, Ronny avoided any physical contact, even shaking the woman's hand after the interview. Where those in the culture-as-values camp might have explained Ronny as holding "different values" or "not being raised correctly," Rios (2011) notes the youth's well-intentioned strategy, as well as other instances in which Ronny behaves differently. Indeed, in other circumstances, with different potentialities, Ronny may have been more gregarious or felt comfortable with a handshake. Ronny did not get the job, leading Rios (2011) to argue that the misrecognition of cultural repertoires frequently inhibits gang-associated and criminalized youth's upward mobility.

Rios (2011) notably moves away from the culture-as-values perspective as he demonstrates the performative nature of gang identity, providing insight into how gang-associated people may engage in culturally appropriate actions that remain disconnected from their personal values. In institutional interactions with authority figures like teachers, "street-oriented" youth may feign gang stereotypes—going "dumb" and getting "hyphy" (a nod to Bay Area hip-hop slang)—as a defiant response to what they perceive as punitive treatment (Rios 2011, 120). One participant Rios (2011) highlights, a young Black man named Darius, responds to a teacher he finds condescending by consciously acting defiant and ignorant when called upon. But in an interaction with law enforcement, he quickly pivots from defiance to a performance of respectability and cordiality, leading to a more satisfactory outcome. The fact that youth can choose and alter their performances from one moment to the next makes plain that culture is not determinist. On the contrary, social actors use culture creatively as they exert agency.

Robert Garot (2010) also illustrates how youth of color use gang culture as a social resource and performance (also see Lauger and Densley 2018). Drawing on ethnographic data collected in a California alternative school, Garot (2010) demonstrates that gang culture is not a monolithic organizational culture bent on crime and violence, but rather a context-based performance. Youth use culture as a resource particularly when they are "banged on," or "hit-up"—that is, confronted with the question, "Where are you from?" Similar to bullying or taunting, this challenge is meant to "punk" or "check" someone, thereby establishing dominance. The culture-as-values perspective might expect youth to uniformly respond violently to such challenges. But as Garot (2010) finds, they do not. For example, when banged on and asked about his gang affiliation while walking through rival Bloods gang territory, a young man affiliated with the Crips gang falsely claimed that he was unaffiliated with any and all gangs. As it turns out, young, gang-affiliated men frequently "rank out," or disassociate from their gang, when challenged in public, thus ensuring safe passage. In sharp contrast to notions of the code of the street, youth use the status-diminishing claim that they are from "nowhere" to distance themselves not only from gangs, but also from masculine status. In such micro-level interactions, gang association does not operate as a master identity; rather, it is but one fluid component of an individual's heterogenous identities and repertoires.

Building explicitly on Bourdieu's theoretical foundations, Fraser (2013) draws from fieldwork alongside youth in Scotland to similarly demonstrate how the embodied interpretive schemas associated with "gang life" represent a cultural adaptation to marginalization (see also Fraser and Hagedorn 2018). Constrained by limited mobility and economic opportunities, impoverished youth develop what Fraser (2013) terms "street habitus"—that is, a deep seated, preconscious connection between self and space. As young people traverse the same constrained paths and routes, they come to ascribe additional meaning to that territory. "Local places and spaces," writes Fraser (2013), "bound up with individual and collective memory, become fused with self-identity, and the family, friendships and relationships that occur there" (974). In turn, that territory becomes inscribed in youths' habitus—the embodied set of durable dispositions through which they engage in daily actions and habitual responses. In this framework, a range of behaviors, including retaliatory violence, are reinterpreted as a social practice in which young people are not merely defending their affiliated peers and economic enterprises, but also their surrounding territory and the meaningful role it holds in their senses of self.

One drawback of the culture-as-toolkit approach is the potential theoretical ambiguity in its underlying conception of culture, and thus its broader explanatory power. By challenging the causal link (assumed by the culture-as-values perspective) between culture and behavior, this perspective ushers in new, potentially unresolved questions, which are now fiercely debated (see Lamont 1992; Vaisey 2009; Martin 2010; Pugh 2013): If culture is indeed something that people "use," why do different people use different aspects of culture when, where, and how they do? What determines the specific cultural tool that an individual uses in one situation but not another? How consciously aware are individuals of the assortment of tools at their disposal, and how much of their selection and use of a tool is subconscious and taken for granted? Is culture primarily implicated in motivation, justification, or both? Applied to gang research, scholars have yet to develop a general theory capable of systematically explaining, much less predicting, why and under what conditions individuals draw from the cultural tools and repertoires derived from their gang affiliation rather than the tools associated with non-gang-related roles and identities. Why, for instance, when facing interpersonal challenges do some individuals engage in violent performances of masculinity yet others quickly elect to "rank out"?

Despite the continued academic debate over these issues, the culture-as-toolkit perspective provides an advantageous framework for researchers and policymakers intent on approaching gangs and gang interventions in more productive, less harmful ways. By moving past pathologizing depictions of fundamentally criminal gang-associated youth, this approach allows scholars to avoid the trap of victim blaming while studying the cultural repertoires spurred by structural conditions and institutional contexts. The understanding that all youth experiment with identity and cultural performances is pivotal, particularly for policy. It urges that we provide youth with the necessary space for evolution and change and underscores the degree to which behaviors need not be read as expressions of personal values. The performances of gang-associated youth are, in other words, demonstrations of the toolkits they have developed to navigate their social environments. It is also critical to consider how repertoires developed by gang-associated youth might serve as strengths in other educational and employment opportunities, allowing scholars and policymakers to move from a "deficit model" to an "asset model." Policies could better shape and support youth by creating what Rios (2011) terms a "youth support complex" as opposed to the more outdated mode represented by the "youth control complex."

CULTURE-AS-PRODUCTS

The culture-as-products perspective provides the freshest, if least systematically theorized, conceptualization of gang culture. In this approach, researchers treat culture as something gangs *produce*, whether it takes the form of fashion, slang, music, or other cultural commodities and symbolic forms of expression (Conquergood 1993; Stuart 2020a; Stuart and Miller 2017). This perspective can be traced to developments in the sociology of culture that, beginning in the late twentieth century, have fundamentally reoriented prevailing theories of art and cultural production. In the 1970s and 1980s, a cadre of American sociologists, led by Howard Becker (1976, 1982) and Richard Peterson (1976, 1997) spearheaded the reconception of creative works not as objects produced and distributed by artists alone, but as the result of collaborative activities and a complex division of labor. These "art worlds," as Becker (1982) famously calls them, include, for instance,

> people who conceive the idea of the work (e.g., composers or playwrights); people who execute it (musicians and actors); people who provide the necessary equipment and materials (e.g., musical instrument makers); and people who make up the audience for the work (playgoers, critics, and so on). (Becker 1976, 703–704)

Across the Atlantic, French sociologist Pierre Bourdieu developed a framework for analyzing competition *between* artists and other cultural producers. In *The Rules of Art*, Bourdieu (1996) theorizes that all producers attempt to outcompete peers and rivals located in their particular "fields" by amassing profitable reputations—what he refers to as the "capital of consecration." The strategies—or "position-takings"—they deploy to accumulate this capital are heavily influenced by the economic and social resources at their disposal (e.g., familial wealth, educational background, and social networks). Although Bourdieu initially articulated this theory to analyze nineteenth-century literature, scholars have successfully applied this framework to explain why certain individuals and companies dominate cultural industries as diverse as print journalism, television broadcasting, and music nightlife (Benson 1999; Hesmondhalgh 2002; Grazian 2003; Stuart 2020a).

Whereas the previous two conceptualizations of culture center primarily on economic and other material conditions that engender the values or practices of "gang culture," this third conceptualization intentionally privileges the seemingly "immaterial" objects that gangs create and distribute, asking how this ephemera emerges from, and institutionalizes, particular social relations. As recent empirical research increasingly demonstrates, this framework provides much-needed avenues for conceiving of gang-associated individuals as agentic and innovative social actors, while offering novel insights into a host of longstanding topics, from the geographic diffusion and transnationalization of gangs, to intragang organization, intergang antagonisms, and gang intervention policies.

Gang researchers have systematically attended to the dynamics of cultural production and consumption since at least the 1990s. In a foundational study of Chicago gangs, Conquergood (1993) emphasized that gangs develop and rely on a range of cultural products as forms of non-verbal communication. By adopting specific clothing brands and colors, hand signs, tattoos, slang, and jewelry, gangs imbue mundane objects with rich meanings and symbolism. Though such products are often inscrutable to outsiders, for insiders they sustain boundaries, ensure bonds, and ultimately assist in the larger task of "transform[ing] marginal, somewhat forbidding urban space into . . . a world of meaning, familiarity, adventure, and affective intensity through ritual, symbol, and dramaturgy" (39). Conquergood offers gang handshakes—rituals of familiarity—as premier examples of this process. Through elaborate gestures of communal fellowship, gang handshakes provide momentary but profound displays of respect and dignity that serve as bulwarks against the "social indignities and status deprivations that the homeboys and other low-income people endure when they venture into mainstream society as busboys, dishwashers, janitors, and common laborers" (43).

The culture-as-products perspective has also advanced research on the cultural transmission and geographical diffusion of gangs, wherein the *same* gang ostensibly appears in multiple cities, embracing similar names, symbols, and styles (for a review, see Moore and Stuart 2022; also Felson 2006; Van Hellemont and Densley 2019; Decker, Van Gemert, and Pyrooz 2009). As research shows, transmission typically occurs when a gang in a given city develops cultural commodities and symbols, which are then disseminated and popularized through popular culture industries, most notably hip-hop music and popular films such as *Colors*, *Boyz in the Hood*, and *Menace II Society*. Indigenously formed gangs in other cities are key consumers of these products and adopt them as their own, despite having no direct contact with their originators. Hagedorn (1998) was among the first to document this process, finding Milwaukee residents who formed gangs with peers and neighbors but adopted the names of notorious Chicago gangs (also see Maxson 1998). Since that time, studies have shown transmission across far greater distances. Factions of the Crips gang—which originated among young Black youth in South Central Los Angeles—are now found in the Netherlands, where economically marginalized Black immigrants from Suriname and Dutch Antilles increasingly emulate American gang symbols and practices (Van Gemert 2001; Roks 2019; Roks and Densley 2020; Urbanik 2021). Over time, such emulation gives rise to new, unique cultural products, which join the global circulation of gang culture that other individuals might emulate in the future.

Given its explicit focus on the relations of cultural production, the sociology of culture is particularly powerful for analyzing the social organization of gangs in the digital age. Today, researchers find that poor urban residents are increasingly turning away from participation in the street-corner drug economy and toward the online attention economy to make ends meet, build street cred, and attain dignity (Stuart 2020a; also see Storrod and Densley 2017; Lauger and Densley 2018). As the means of cultural production continue to democratize, gang-associated youth are more able to sidestep traditional gatekeepers, such as music labels and advertising firms, to generate their own cultural commodities on their own terms. Of course, gang scholarship has long revealed the central role of hip hop, dance, and other musical forms among gangs and gang-associated youth (Hagedorn 2008; Harkness 2014). Yet this focus has undoubtedly intensified with the mass democratization of the means of cultural production and the subsequent proliferation of an internationally celebrated genre of homemade, DIY-style gangsta rap, or "drill music," created by gang-associated youth and passed directly to consumers through social media platforms such as YouTube, Twitter, Instagram, and TikTok (Patton et al. 2013; Johnson and Schell-Busey 2016; Urbanik and Haggerty 2018; Stuart 2020a).

The culture-as-products perspective takes seriously the co-constitutive relationship between gangs' cultural products and their intraorganizational dynamics; changes in the former lead to changes in the latter, and vice versa (Aspholm 2020; Stuart 2020a; Urbanik 2021). In a study of drill music–oriented Chicago gangs, for example, Stuart (2020a) demonstrates that the traditional vertical hierarchy of gang life has evolved into a more concentric (or horizontal) structure tied, in part, to the division of labor associated with digital cultural production. The "drillers," or "rappers," who embody the gang's cultural commodities and reputation seeking hold the center, maintaining extensive social media followings and serving as the face for songs and music videos released by their gangs. Moving outward, the next ring comprises "shooters," who act as drillers' bodyguards and enforcers and make good on social media threats and challenges so that drillers can avoid physical conflicts and criminal legal entanglements. On the periphery is the largest and most heterogeneous group: the "guys"—a sort of residual category who neither create rap songs and videos nor engage in the lion's share of offensive violence (though they may retaliate defensively when rivals intrude on their territory). Some portion of the guys, however, possess special skills, networks, and other resources valuable to the drillers' and shooters' endeavors. These young men may turn their access to recording equipment, firearms, Wi-Fi passwords, or other resources necessary to the gang's cultural production efforts into status that brings them closer to the center of the drill-affiliated gang structure. Research conducted by Urbanik (2021) in Toronto similarly demonstrates the power of digital cultural production to alter gang structures. In the past, Toronto gangs were bifurcated into "hustlers"—those more concerned with economic pursuits than violence—and "gangbangers"—those more heavily involved in intergang rivalries and violence. Today, Urbanik (2021) writes, "the growing expectation that gang members perform and advertise their 'gang-ness' online via rap music and videos has blurred these distinctions, putting increasing pressure on hustlers to participate in gang beefs" (587).

The culture-as-products perspective also encourages novel perspectives and analyses of intergang antagonisms and potential violence. The proliferation of social media and the democratization of the means of cultural production, in particular, have created new venues for gang conflicts that may have previously been confined to face-to-face interactions. Early research on this phenomenon focused on expressive and symbolic dynamics (see Melde and Weerman 2020), conceptualizing social media platforms and online spaces as akin to "virtual graffiti walls," where gang-associated individuals use utterances, images, and other content to promote their gang, threaten rivals, and boast of criminal activity (Moule, Decker, and Pyrooz 2017). This collection of online behaviors—what Patton, Eschmann, and Butler (2013) term "internet banging"—allows gang-associated individuals to demonstrate their adherence to the "code of the street" (Anderson 1999), thereby seeking, earning, and defending street cred through online displays of toughness and aggression (Patton et al. 2017; Lauger and Densley 2018; Lane 2019).

Yet, despite a consensus that digital cultural production creates new spaces and opportunities for antagonisms, to date there exist no systematic data or analyses that definitively determine the causal relationship between such online performances and offline physical violence. This has led to considerable debate. Some researchers adhere to what is sometimes referred to as the "parallelism thesis," which posits that social media create an additional and *duplicate* venue for violent antagonisms, necessarily increasing the frequency and intensity of offline violence as a result (Patton et al. 2013). As Patton et al. (2017) argue, "gang members . . . use Twitter to threaten rival groups (including police), posture, and 'campaign for respect' through the incitement of violence. . . . [T]he same gang violence mechanisms . . . on the urban street unfold online" (1012). "Online identities and behaviors," Pyrooz et al. (2015) similarly contend, "are reflections of offline identities and behaviors, thus one is the analogy of the other" (475). Unfortunately, the parallelism thesis overestimates the causal link between internet behavior and offline violence, which reached historic lows in the same years that gang-associated youth *increased* their use of social media and other online platforms. Drawing primarily on self-report surveys, content analyses of disembodied and decontextualized social media posts, and interviews with people other than the original gang-associated content creators, these studies tend to overlook the ways in which online performances *transform* (rather than merely mirror or amplify) conflicts and alter the dynamics of potential offline violence (Lane 2019; Leverso and Hsiao 2020).

Recognizing these methodological and conceptual limitations, other researchers have sought to conduct direct, real-time, on-the-ground observations alongside the actual producers of online cultural products. Refuting the parallelism thesis, these studies offer strong evidence that online cultural production does not independently exacerbate offline violence and, in some cases, may offer gang-associated individuals and their surrounding communities new avenues for preventing, de-escalating, and avoiding violence (Urbanik and Haggerty 2018; Lane 2019, Stuart 2020a, 2020b; McCuddy and Esbensen 2020; Lane and Stuart 2022). These studies demonstrate that taunts and challenges exchanged online carry significantly different meanings, thereby demanding different responses, than they would in face-to-face interactions. In fact, some gang-associated individuals now engage in online antagonisms as part of innovative and intentional efforts to build violent reputations *without* the necessity of behaving violently offline (Stuart 2020a). Analyzing the three primary strategies by which gang-associated youth challenge others on social media, Stuart (2020b) concludes that, despite much public alarm to the contrary, the majority of challenges and antagonisms remain confined to online spaces. Rather than introducing new risk that is somehow independent of offline conditions, the likelihood that an online challenge leads to offline violence is often a function of the amount and depth of counterevidence necessary to refute that challenge, particularly if that rebuttal brings feuding parties into shared physical space or if the online challenge threatens an individual's existing social ties.

Further challenging the parallelism thesis, Lane and Stuart (2022) demonstrate that the probability that online challenges will lead to offline violence is frequently mitigated by newfound avenues for intervention. As new media scholars have long shown, social media afford a historic level of "communication visibility" (Leonardi 2014; Treem, Leonardi, and Van den Hooff 2020), which allows third parties to not only observe others' relationships, exchanges, and actions, but to exert direct and indirect influence over subsequent relationships, exchanges, and actions. In poor urban communities, this takes the form of friends, families, and community members exploiting communication visibility—specifically, monitoring the social media activity of loved ones—to intercede into violent conflicts, either preventing them from occurring or limiting their reach and intensity once they begin.

The emerging culture-as-products perspective carries notable implications and public policy lessons. First and foremost, by centering research on individuals *as cultural producers* rather than treating their gang membership as a determinative master status, this approach allows researchers to more fully recognize and analyze the multidimensional complexity of gang-associated people (see Rios 2017; Moore and Stuart 2022). Explanations of individuals' actions—including criminal behavior and violence—are enhanced when researchers consider the identities, networks, and strategies they adopt to compete in the field of cultural production. In turn, this approach opens new possibilities for gang, violence, and poverty interventions. Second, much of the public remains hesitant about providing assistance to gang-associated youth; however, particularly in the United States, there is widespread support for assisting cultural producers during difficult economic periods. Among the Roosevelt Administration's 1930s-era New Deal programs, for instance, was Federal Project Number One, which provided unemployed artists, musicians, actors, and writers weekly wages to beautify public space, collect oral histories, produce theatrical performances, and teach community arts classes (Stuart 2020a). More recently, during the COVID-19 pandemic, the federal government and large grant-making foundations established several programs to provide financial assistance to artists and art organizations. The popularity and visibility of these programs suggests that responses to gang-associated individuals might be positively influenced by emphasizing these individuals' membership in cultural production communities. Third, recognizing gang-associated people as artists and creative producers places an increased emphasis on the *performativity* of gang-ness. As emerging research demonstrates, many displays of crime and violence, especially those made online, are exaggerations, even pure fabrications (Stuart 2020a; Urbanik 2021; Moore and Stuart 2022). If, as some research demonstrates, some gang-associated individuals even use online displays of aggression to avoid offline physical violence, then those in academia, the media, and the criminal legal system must reject the assumption that online performances are straightforward indications of individuals' offline identities, behaviors, or propensities.

We anticipate that, for some readers, the culture-as-products approach may appear to suffer from at least one particular drawback: Is it overly narrow in its potential application? Do we lose the ability to analyze empirical phenomena and substantive topics, often central to gang scholarship, because they do not directly involve cultural products? Such issues include illegal drug enterprises, criminal activity, and desistance. At first glance, the culture-as-products approach seems ill equipped to analyze and explain such behaviors. Yet, even though it might not consider these empirical topics "cultural," the foundational insights of Becker' art worlds theory and Bourdieu's fields framework nonetheless provide valuable analytical tools for examining virtually *any* empirical phenomenon. Indeed, the culture-as-products perspective directs much needed attention to the ecological factors—that is, the networks, norms, and institutions—required for any social action to take place when, where, and how it does. Take, for example, the act of carrying out a drive-by shooting. The culture-as-products framework reminds us that completion of such an act of violence requires a number of material and social elements, including a functioning car, a driver, a shooter, intelligence about a target's physical location, and adequate knowledge about surrounding streets and thoroughfares (Stuart 2020a; Sanders 2017). Such an act is also shaped by a range of institutional and contextual factors often overlooked in a conventional analysis. This might include local police policies and practices regarding traffic stops, which shape how would-be assailants understand and amass any necessary elements; the density and size of gang territories, which condition assailants' willingness to risk police contact and expectations of evading capture; and the layout of the physical street grid and sight lines of homes and apartment buildings, which may alter the success and potential lethality of the drive-by shooting attempt.

Conclusion

Over the past century of gang research, the broad usage of the term "gang culture" has come to encompass practically *every* aspect of gang behavior and organization. Unfortunately, the term's lack of conceptual specificity has prevented researchers from fully capturing important variation and identifying causal mechanisms. A close reading of key empirical case studies reveals three dominant conceptions of gang culture implicit in extant analyses. For those scholars adopting a culture-as-values approach, gang culture refers to gang-specific values that animate and propel behavior, often toward oppositional and criminal expressions. For others, culture is best understood as a toolkit, with different repertoires and strategies of action deployed creatively to navigate social interactions. Still others examine gang culture as the products created and distributed by gang-associated individuals as part of their individual and group competition in the various fields of cultural production.

Rather than continue to mobilize the term "gang culture" in unthinking fashion or attempt to reach some consensus definition, we urge that researchers move forward by asking *what*, precisely, we aim to describe and analyze when we use the concept "gang culture" in a given study. This entails more than inserting a few obligatory sentences clarifying the intended use in a published study. It will mean spelling out the intended conceptualization at the earliest stages of study design. Are we conducting survey and interview-based research to document gang-associated individuals' opinions and attitudes, estimating how these diverge from those of other populations? Are we observing interactions and practices within gang organizations to analyze how individuals gain status through performances of commitment and toughness? Are we conducting a comparative content analysis of gang-associated individuals' music, videos, and other social media products as they seek to build online popularity? Each object of analysis lends itself to (perhaps *demands*) a different conception of gang culture.

This call for conceptual precision is not simply academic; it carries real-world implications. Explanations of gang-associated individuals' behaviors—particularly cultural explanations—have long informed law, policy, and public discourse, often in ways that perpetuate harm to long-marginalized populations. Although the culture-as-values perspective is on the decline in academic scholarship, it continues to animate the punitive orientation of law enforcement and policy responses to gangs. For many police, prosecutors, and other state actors, gang-associated individuals are perceived to be so deeply committed to monolithic, oppositional values that few economic, educational, or employment-related resources could meaningfully alter their behaviors (Wacquant 2009; Zilberg 2011; Phillips 2012). Viewing people, rather than systems, as fundamentally "broken," the resulting state responses privilege the exclusion and incapacitation of individuals—exemplified by gang injunctions and gang sentencing enhancements—and the continued siphoning of social safety net resources away from entire communities. This process reifies gang stereotypes, fueling the cycle of surveillance and criminalization.

As we contend, those who wish to disrupt the punitive exclusion of gang-associated individuals and their communities have an ethical responsibility to challenge the values-based conceptions of culture, explicitly supplanting it with frameworks that understand culture as a collection of non-deterministic resources and products deployed by multidimensional, agentic social actors. Rather than treat gang culture as a liability, the move away from the culture-as-values perspective invites scholars to forge an asset-based discourse that highlights the creativity of gang-associated individuals in the face of major structural injustices, perhaps even looking to these stigmatized groups for fresh insights about fairness, resilience, and possibility.

REFERENCES

Anderson, Elijah. 1999. *Code of the Street: Decency, Violence, and the Moral Life of the Inner City*. New York: W.W. Norton & Company.
Aspholm, Roberto. 2020. *View from the Streets: The Transformation of Gangs and Violence on Chicago's South Side*. New York: Columbia University Press.
Becker, H. S. 1982. *Art Worlds*. Berkeley: University of California Press.
Becker, H. S. 1976. "Art Worlds and Social Types." *American Behavioral Scientist* 19 (6): 703–718.
Benson, Rodney. 1999. "Field Theory in Comparative Context: A New Paradigm for Media Studies." *Theory and Society* 28 (3): 463–498.
Bourdieu, Pierre. 1977. *Outline of a Theory of Practice*. Cambridge, UK: Cambridge University Press.

Bourdieu, Pierre. 1987. *Distinction: A Social Critique of the Judgment of Taste*. Cambridge, MA: Harvard University Press.

Bourdieu, Pierre. 1996. *The Rules of Art: Genesis and Structure of the Literary Field*. Stanford, CT: Stanford University Press.

Caldwell, Beth. 2010. "Criminalizing Day-to-Day Life: A Socio-Legal Critique of Gang Injunctions." *American Journal of Criminal Law* 37: 241–290.

Carson, Dena C., and J. Michael Vecchio. 2015. "Leaving the Gang." In *The Handbook of Gangs*, edited by Scott H. Decker, and David C. Pyrooz, 257–275. Chichester, UK: Wiley Blackwell.

Carter, Prudence L. 2005. *Keepin' It Real: School Success beyond Black and White*. New York: Oxford University Press.

Cloward, Richard A., and Lloyd E. Ohlin. 1960. *Delinquency and Opportunity: A Theory of Delinquent Gangs*. Glencoe, IL: Free Press.

Cohen, Albert K. 1955. *Delinquent Boys: The Culture of the Gang*. Glencoe, IL: Free Press.

Conquergood, Lorne D. 1993. *Homeboys and Hoods: Gang Communication and Cultural Space*. Evanston, IL: Northwestern University Center for Urban Affairs and Policy Research.

Decker, Scott H., Frank Van Gemert, and David C. Pyrooz. 2009. "Gangs, Migration, and Crime: The Changing Landscape in Europe and the USA." *Journal of International Migration and Integration* 10 (4): 393–408.

Dohan, Daniel. 2003. *The Price of Poverty: Money, Work, and Culture in the Mexican American Barrio*. Berkeley: University of California Press.

Duneier, Mitchell. 1992. *Slim's Table: Race, Respectability, and Masculinity*. Chicago, IL: University of Chicago Press.

Edin, Kathryn, and Maria Kefalas. 2011. *Promises I Can Keep: Why Poor Women Put Motherhood before Marriage*. Berkeley: University of California Press.

Felson, Marcus. 2006. *Crime and Nature*. Thousand Oaks, CA: Sage Publications.

Fraser, Alistair. 2013. "Street Habitus: Gangs, Territorialism and Social Change in Glasgow." *Journal of Youth Studies* 16 (8): 970–985.

Fraser, Alistair, and John Hagedorn. 2018. "Gangs and a Global Sociological Imagination." *Theoretical Criminology* 22 (1): 42–62.

Garot, Robert. 2010. *Who You Claim: Performing Gang Identity in School and on the Streets*. New York: New York University Press.

Goffman, Erving. 1959. *The Presentation of Self in Everyday Life*. Garden City, NY: Doubleday.

Grazian, David. 2003. *Blue Chicago: The Search for Authenticity in Urban Blues Clubs*. Chicago, IL: University of Chicago Press.

Hagedorn, John. 1998. *People and Folks: Gangs, Crime, and the Underclass in a Rustbelt City*. Chicago, IL: Lake View Press.

Hagedorn, John. 2008. *A World of Gangs: Armed Young Men and Gangsta Culture*. Minneapolis: University of Minnesota Press.

Hannerz, Ulf. 1969. *Soulside: Inquiries into Ghetto Culture and Community*. New York: Columbia University Press.

Harkness, Geoff. 2014. *Chicago Hustle and Flow: Gangs, Gangsta Rap, and Social Class*. Minneapolis: University of Minnesota Press.

Hayes, Sharon. 2003. *Flat Broke with Children: Women in the Age of Welfare Reform*. New York: Oxford University Press.

Hesmondhalgh, David. 2002. *The Cultural Industries*. London: Sage.

Horowitz, Ruth. 1983. *Honor and the American Dream: Culture and Identity in a Chicano Community*. New Brunswick, NJ: Rutgers University Press.

Johnson, Joseph D, and Natalie Schell-Busey. 2016. "Old Message in a New Bottle: Taking Gang Rivalries Online through Rap Battle Music Videos on YouTube." *Journal of Qualitative Criminal Justice & Criminology* 4 (1).

Kornhauser, Ruth Rosner. 1978. *Social Sources of Delinquency: An Appraisal of Analytic Models.* Chicago, IL: University of Chicago Press.

Lamont, Michèle. 1992. *Money, Morals and Manners: The Culture of the French and American Upper-Middle Class.* Chicago, IL: University of Chicago Press.

Lane, Jeff. 2019. *The Digital Street.* New York: Oxford University Press.

Lane, Jeff, and Forrest Stuart. 2022. "How Social Media Help to Mitigate Urban Violence: Communication Visibility and Third-Party Intervention Processes in Digital-Urban Contexts." *Qualitative Sociology* 45: 457–475.

Lauger, Timothy R., and James A. Densely. 2018. "Broadcasting Badness: Violence, Identity, and Performance in the Online Gang Rap Scene." *Justice Quarterly* 35 (5): 816–841.

Lauger, Timothy R., and Brooke Horning. 2020. "Street Culture and Street Gangs." In *Routledge Handbook of Street Culture*, edited by Jeffrey Ian Ross, 422–423. New York: Routledge.

Leonardi, Paul M. 2014. "Social Media, Knowledge Sharing, and Innovation: Toward a Theory of Communication Visibility." *Information Systems Research* 25 (4): 796–816.

Leverso, John, and Yuan Hsiao. "Gangbangin on the (Face) Book: Understanding Online Interactions of Chicago Latina/o Gangs." *Journal of Research in Crime and Delinquency* 58 (3): 239–268.

Lewis, Oscar. 1966. "The Culture of Poverty." *Scientific American* 215 (4): 19–25.

Martin, John Levi. 2010. "Life's a Beach but You're an Ant, and Other Unwelcome News for the Sociology of Culture." *Poetics* 38 (2): 229–244.

Matsueda, Ross L., Kevin Drakulich, and Charis E. Kubrin. 2006. "Race and Neighborhood Codes of Violence." In *The Many Colors of Crime: Inequalities of Race, Ethnicity, and Crime in America*, edited by Ruth D. Peterson, Lauren J. Krivo, and John Hagan, 334–356. New York: New York University Press.

Maxson, Cheryl L. 1998. *Juvenile Justice Bulletin: Gang Members on the Move.* Washington, DC: United States Department of Justice.

Maxson, Cheryl L, Karen M. Hennigan, and David C. Sloane. 2005. "'It's Getting Crazy Out There': Can a Civil Gang Injunction Change a Community?" *Criminology and Public Policy* 4 (3): 577–605.

McCuddy, Timothy, and Finn-Aage Esbensen. 2020. "The Role of Online Communication among Gang and Non-Gang Youth." In *Gangs in the Era of Internet and Social Media*, edited by Chris Melde and Frank Weerman, 81–104. Cham, Switzerland: Springer.

Melde, Chris, and Frank Weerman. 2020. *Gangs in the Era of Internet and Social Media.* Cham, Switzerland: Springer.

Miller, Jody. 2001. *One of the Guys: Girls, Gangs, and Gender.* New York: Oxford University Press.

Miller, Walter B. 1958. "Lower Class Culture as a Generating Milieu of Gang Delinquency." *Journal of Social Issues* 14 (3): 5–19.

Miller, Walter B. 2011. *City Gangs.* Phoenix: Arizona State University, School of Criminology and Criminal Justice.

Mitchell, Megan M., David C. Pyrooz, and Scott H. Decker. 2017. "Criminal Crews, Codes, and Contexts: Differences and Similarities across the Code of the Street, Convict Code, Street Gangs, and Prison Gangs." *Deviant Behavior* 38 (10): 1197–1222.

Moore, Caylin Louis, and Forrest Stuart. 2022. "Gang Research in the Twenty-First Century." *Annual Review of Criminology* 5 (1): 299–320.

Moule, Richard K., Jr. 2015. "The Legacy of Walter B. Miller." In *The Handbook of Gangs*, edited by Scott H. Decker, and David C. Pyrooz, 458–477. Chichester, UK: Wiley- Blackwell.

Moule, Richard K., Jr., Scott H. Decker, and David C. Pyrooz. 2017. "Technology and Conflict: Group Processes and Collective Violence in the Internet Era." *Crime, Law and Social Change* 68: 47–73.

Moule, Richard K., Jr., and Bryanna Fox. 2021. "Belief in the Code of the Street and Individual Involvement in Offending: A Meta-analysis." *Youth Violence and Juvenile Justice* 19 (2): 227–247.

Moynihan, Daniel Patrick. 1965. *The Negro Family: The Case for National Action*. Washington, DC: US Government Printing Office.

Muñiz, Ana. 2014. "Maintaining Racial Boundaries: Criminalization, Neighborhood Context, and the Origins of Gang Injunctions." *Social Problems* 61 (2): 216–236.

Newman, Katherine S. 2009. *No Shame in My Game: The Working Poor in the Inner City*. New York: Vintage.

Panfil, Vanessa R. 2017. *The Gang's All Queer: The Lives of Gay Gang Members*. New York: New York University Press.

Patton, Desmond U., Robert D. Eschmann, and Dirk A. Butler. 2013. "Internet Banging: New Trends in Social Media, Gang Violence, Masculinity and Hip Hop." *Computers in Human Behavior* 29 (5): A54–A59.

Patton, Desmond U., Jeffrey Lane, Patrick Leonard, Jamie Macbeth, and Jocelyn R. Smith Lee. 2017. "Gang Violence on the Digital Street: Case Study of a South Side Chicago Gang Member's Twitter Communication." *New Media & Society* 19 (7): 1000–1018.

Peterson, R. A. 1976. "The Production of Culture: A Prolegomenon." *American Behavioral Scientist* 19: (6): 669–684.

Peterson, R. A. 1997. *Creating Country Music: Fabricating Authenticity*. Chicago, IL: University of Chicago Press.

Phillips, Susan. 2012. *Operation Fly Trap: L.A. Gangs, Drugs, and the Law*. Chicago, IL: University of Chicago Press.

Pugh, Allison J. 2013. "What Good are Interviews for Thinking about Culture? Demystifying Interpretive Analysis." *American Journal of Cultural Sociology* 1 (1): 42–68.

Pyrooz, David C., and Scott H. Decker. 2011. "Motives and Methods for Leaving the Gang: Understanding the Process of Gang Desistance." *Journal of Criminal Justice* 39 (5): 417–425.

Pyrooz, David, Scott Decker, and Richard Moule. 2015. "Criminal and Routine Activities in Online Settings: Gangs, Offenders, and the Internet." *Justice Quarterly* 32 (3): 471–499.

Rios, Victor M. 2011. *Punished: Policing the Lives of Black and Latino Boys*. New York: New York University Press.

Rios, Victor M. 2017. *Human Targets: Schools, Police, and the Criminalization of Latino Youth*. Chicago, IL: University of Chicago Press.

Roks, Robert A. 2019. "In the 'h2ood': Crips and the Intersection between Space and Identity in the Netherlands." *Crime, Media, Culture* 15 (1): 3–23.

Roks, Robert A., and James A. Densley. 2020. "From Breakers to Bikers: The Evolution of the Dutch Crips 'Gang.'" *Deviant Behavior* 41 (4): 525–542.

Ryan, William. 1976. *Blaming the Victim*. New York: Vintage Books.

Sánchez-Jankowski, Martín. 1991. *Islands in the Street: Gangs and American Urban Society*. Berkeley: University of California Press.

Sanders, William. 2017. *Gangbangs and Drive-Bys: Grounded Culture and Juvenile Gang Violence*. New York: Routledge.

Shaw, Clifford Robe, and Henry Donald McKay. 1942. *Juvenile Delinquency and Urban Areas*. Chicago, IL: University of Chicago Press.

Storrod, Michelle L., and James A. Densley. 2017. "'Going Viral' and 'Going Country': The Expressive and Instrumental Activities of Street Gangs on Social Media." *Journal of Youth Studies* 20 (6): 677–696.

Stuart, Forrest. 2020a. *Ballad of the Bullet: Gangs, Drill Music, and the Power of Online Infamy*. Princeton, NJ: Princeton University Press.

Stuart, Forrest. 2020b. "Code of the Tweet: Urban Gang Violence in the Social Media Age." *Social Problems* 67 (2): 191–207.

Stuart, Forrest, Amada Armenta, and Melissa Osborne. 2015. "Legal Control of Marginal Groups." *Annual Review of Law and Social Science* 11 (1): 235–254.

Stuart, Forrest, and Reuben Jonathan Miller. 2017. "The Prisonized Old Head: Intergenerational Socialization and the Fusion of Ghetto and Prison Culture." *Journal of Contemporary Ethnography* 46 (6): 673–698.

Suttles, Gerald D. 1968. *The Social Order of the Slum: Ethnicity and Territory in the Inner City*. Chicago, IL: University of Chicago Press.

Swidler, Ann. 1986. "Culture in Action: Symbols and Strategies." *American Sociological Review* 51 (2): 273–286.

Thrasher, Frederic. 1927. *The Gang: A Study of 1,313 Gangs in Chicago*. Chicago, IL: University of Chicago Press.

Treem, Jeffrey W., Paul M. Leonardi, and Bart Van den Hooff. 2020. "Computer-Mediated Communication in the Age of Communication Visibility." *Journal of Computer-Mediated Communication* 25 (1): 44–59.

Urbanik, Marta-Marika. 2021. "'Gangbangers Are Gangbangers, Hustlers Are Hustlers': The Rap Game, Social Media, and Gang Violence in Toronto." In *Routledge International Handbook of Critical Gang Studies*, edited by David C Brotherton, and Rafael Jose Gude, 582–600. London: Routledge.

Urbanik, Marta-Marika, and Kevin D Haggerty. 2018. "'#It's Dangerous': The Online World of Drug Dealers, Rappers and the Street Code." *British Journal of Criminology* 58 (6): 1343–1360.

Vaisey, Stephen. 2009. "Motivation and Justification: A Dual-Process Model of Culture in Action." *American Journal of Sociology* 114 (6): 1675–1715.

Van Gemert, Frank. 2001. "Crips in Orange: Gangs and Groups in the Netherlands." In *The Eurogang Paradox: Street Gangs and Youth Groups in the U.S. and Europe*, edited by Malcolm W. Klein, Hans-Jürgen Kerner, Cheryl L. Maxson, and Elmar G. M. Weitekamp, 145–152. Dordrecht: Springer.

Van Hellemont, Elke, and Densley, James A. 2019. "Gang Glocalization: How a Global Mediascape Creates and Shapes Local Gang Realities." *Crime, Media, Culture* 15 (1): 169–189.

Vigil, Diego. 1988. *Barrio Gangs: Street Life and Identity in Southern California*. Austin: University of Texas Press.

Wacquant, Loïc. 2009. *Punishing the Poor: The Neoliberal Government of Social Insecurity*. Durham, NC: Duke University Press.

Waller, Maureen R. 2002. *My Baby's Father: Unmarried Parents and Paternal Responsibility*. Ithaca, NY: Cornell University Press.

Whyte, William F. 1943. *Street Corner Society*. Chicago, IL: University of Chicago Press.

Wilson, William J. 1987. *The Truly Disadvantaged: The Inner City, the Underclass, and Public Policy*. Chicago, IL: University of Chicago Press.
Young, Alford A., Jr. 2004. *The Minds of Marginalized Black Men: Making Sense of Mobility, Opportunity, and Life Chances*. Princeton, NJ: Princeton University Press.
Zilberg, Elana. 2011. *The Making of a Transnational Gang Crisis between Los Angeles and San Salvador*. Durham, NC: Duke University Press.

CHAPTER 19

MASCULINITIES AND RESPECT IN THE GROUP CONTEXT OF GANGS

LORINE A. HUGHES AND LISA M. BROIDY

GANGS, gang crime, and violence are male-dominated phenomena. Every major data source, including official records, self-reports, and field observations, confirms this pattern (see Decker et al. 2022). Thus, it seems only natural to wonder what it is about boys and men that contributes to their involvement in the lifestyle—and what it is about girls and women that helps them stay out? Biological differences notwithstanding, gendered socialization and experiences typically are implicated in the literature. Indeed, despite periods of "benign neglect" (Hagedorn 1998, 153), masculine and feminine gender identities, as well as gendered actions and social structures, have emerged as prominent themes in gang theory and research. In this chapter, we review this body of work, focusing on the role attributed to manhood, masculinities, and *machismo* in joining, being active in, and exiting the gang. We also situate these concepts within broader theoretical frameworks focused on street culture and group structure and processes.

DEFINITIONS AND ORIGINS

Masculinity is the expected gender identity of males. It is negotiated continuously in relation to historical, political, social, and personal contexts and interactions influenced by hegemonic norms and values "defined in contradistinction from some model (whether real or imaginary) of femininity" (Connell and Messerschmidt 2005, 848). Early interest in the significance of masculinity in gangs appeared more than a decade before the revolution of gender studies in the 1970s. Describing the lure of the adolescent gang, Herbert Bloch and

Arthur Niederhoffer (1958, 163) drew upon Alfred Adler's ([1910] 1956, 9) psychoanalytic concept of "masculine protest," which encapsulates the practices undertaken by males and females to (over)compensate for feelings of inferiority and reject traditional feminine roles. In addition to providing protection for lower-class boys, they argued, gangs function as social spaces in which to rebel against feelings of anxiety and guilt caused by the adult world and "become a man" by demonstrating loyalty and fighting prowess. Although this thesis failed to generate strong empirical scrutiny and support, results from at least two direct tests confirmed the importance of toughness in gangs and showed that "successful feats of delinquency secured status within the group and augmented feelings of masculinity and independence" (Baittle 1961, 706–707; Reuterman, Love, and Fiedler 1973).

Masculinity themes also were evident in Walter Miller's (1958) pioneering study of gangs in a troubled neighborhood in Boston. Based on his findings, Miller argued that the same-sex peer group, not the family nucleus, is "the most significant relational unit for both sexes in lower class communities" and that masculinity is a key criterion for achieving belonging and status in the street corner group representing "the adolescent variant of this lower class structural form" (14). In *City Gangs*, published posthumously in 2011, Miller presaged later work defining gender as a performative resource, noting that the self-esteem of the gang boys he observed was linked intrinsically to masculine ideals and achievement in masculine spheres of activity, from athletics and occupational arenas to sexual and criminal exploits. While Miller defined gangs as fundamentally male domains, he recognized that girls could be involved in their own autonomous gangs, in mixed-sex gangs, or as male gang auxiliaries oriented around romantic and family ties to male gang members. He also viewed masculinity as central to the experiences of gang girls during the "tomboy phase of adolescence," suggesting that "youthful rehearsal of the male role was related to the fact that it was necessary for adult women in female-based households to perform a range of functions generally" (Miller 2011, 576). Here he linked displays of masculinity among gang-involved girls, including the way they dressed, their demeanor, and their criminal proficiency, to the demands of poverty and single motherhood in violent urban contexts.

Short and Strodtbeck's (1965) large-scale study of Black and white youth in Chicago in the early 1960s provided support for Miller's propositions, finding gang and lower-class boys to evaluate sex-identity images and physical toughness, as well as lower-class and illegitimate images, more favorably than did middle-class boys. Their research also uncovered evidence of masculinity being a crucial part of gang status, which observational data had implicated as a primary cause of gang violence. However, neither Miller, Short and Strodtbeck, nor any of their mostly male contemporaries pursued such gender issues further, and work conducted during the period—including Miller's (1973) analyses of female gangs such as the Molls—soon was chided for portraying women and girls in ways that either neglected or misrepresented their experiences. This critical literature extended Richard Cloward and Lloyd Ohlin's (1960) characterization of Bloch and Niederhoffer's (1958) "adolescent-crisis" theory as contradictory, unclear, and underdeveloped; Miller's "culture-conflict" thesis as logically inconsistent and incomplete; and broader "masculinity identification" perspectives within sociology as failing to specify mechanisms leading from so-called "protest" and "compulsive" masculinities to delinquent behaviors (Parsons [1949] 1954; see also Adler [1910] 1956).

The Second Women's Movement

The second wave of feminism entered criminological consciousness through the work of Freda Adler (1975) and Rita Simon (1975), both of whom argued that increases in crime among girls and women were to be expected as a result of cultural and social shifts associated with the women's movement. Adler believed females would commit more crime and violence because, as opportunities opened up to them in the public sphere, they would become more like men in terms of their attitudes and behaviors. By contrast, Simon believed that, while reductions in the stressors associated with patriarchal conditions would reduce women's violence, expanding labor market opportunities were likely to increase their involvement in financial and white-collar offending. Despite their disagreements and broad focus on female offending in general, these two perspectives helped spark criminological interest in the experiences and behaviors of gang girls in their own right rather than as mere appendages of male gangs and gang members. Adler's work, like Miller's (1958), also foregrounded masculinity as being fundamental to the involvement of girls in gangs and gang crime and violence.

An important line of inquiry emerging from this literature focused on relationships between gang girls themselves (Brown 1977; Quicker 1983). Reviewing the evidence, Anne Campbell (1984)—who was establishing herself as a prominent feminist voice—suggested the possibility of a "sisterhood" outside of Miller's dominant categorization of female gangs based on their relations with male gangs. However, her own research in New York City, along with a handful of later studies, provided strong evidence of gang-involved girls being mistreated not only by gang boys but by other gang girls as well. According to Campbell (1984), behind a veneer of sisterly relations and professed loyalty laid extensive internal divisions and "a cultural dictate of womanhood from which there was no escape" (266). Similarly, Jody Miller's (2001) in-depth study of gang girls in Columbus, Ohio, and St. Louis, Missouri, failed to uncover a sisterhood among her research subjects, who "drew on many of the same cultural frames found in the larger society with regard to negative characterizations of women" (203). Rather than being a source of sisterly solidarity, she argued, gang involvement is viewed more accurately as a means by which girls "bargain with patriarchy" and reap the social benefits of the gang (e.g., protection and status) in exchange for acceptance and support of female marginalization. In other words, the gang girls she observed tended to enact gender in ways that worked to their individual advantage while simultaneously reinforcing patriarchal norms of femininity that contributed to their collective vulnerability and need for protection.

Another line of inquiry attended to the gendered motives and implications of gang girl behaviors. James Messerschmidt (1993), who is best known for drawing criminological attention to the behavioral effects of masculine gender identities, suggested that gang girls, like violent female offenders in general, use violence to construct a kind of "bad girl femininity" that enables them to shield themselves from and transcend patriarchal street realities without compromising their "essential nature" as feminine beings. Studies in Phoenix (Portillos 1999) and the San Francisco Bay Area (Laidler and Hunt 2001; see also Hunt et al. 2000, 2002; Hunt and Joe-Laidler 2001) provided support for this argument, finding gang girls in these cities to negotiate femininity continuously amid "a multitude of contrasting and, at times, conflicting notions of what is respectable in differing social contexts" (Hughes, Botchkovar, and Short 2019, 497). Contradicting this perspective, however, Miller (1998, 2001, 2002) reported that the gang girls she observed were more likely to respond to patriarchal oppression by engaging in "gender crossing" and constructing a masculine identity as "one of the guys" than through situational deviations from some inherent femininity. While this seems to support Adler's masculinization thesis, Miller was careful to note that the girls still "engaged in violence less frequently than the boys and usually at the spur of the moment, they mostly fought other girls and employed less lethal weapons, and they realized that, while their involvement in the male-dominated world of street gangs offered protection against some types of victimizations, it increased their risk of several others" (Hughes et al. 2019, 497). They had, in other words, hardly been liberated (cf. Anderson et al. 2002; Lauderback, Hansen, and Waldorf 1992; Mendoza-Denton 2008; Taylor 1993).

Gender, Masculinities, and Crime

Although feminism was applauded for shedding light on women's issues, which had been neglected throughout much of the history of criminological theory and research, it faced strong criticism for advancing a myopic view of men that blamed their bad behaviors on patriarchy and ignored diversity in masculinities (Messerschmidt 1986, 1993; Miller and Mullins 2006; Mullins 2010; Mullins and Kavish 2020). "To structure a comprehensive feminist theory of gendered crime," Messerschmidt (1993, 62) argued, "we must bring men into this framework." From his perspective, masculinity "is accomplished, it is not something done to men or something settled beforehand. And masculinity is never static, never a finished product" (80). Rather, masculinity—like femininity—is constructed dynamically through situated social actions that reproduce and are reproduced by social structural constraints and possibilities. As they "do gender," men enact cultural scripts based on a hegemonic masculine ideal "defined through work in the paid-labor market, the subordination of women, heterosexism, and the driven and uncontrollable sexuality of men" (82). However, depending on the position they occupy within social structural divisions of labor and power, boys and men have more or less access to jobs, education, and other legitimate means by which to accomplish masculinity. Among those whose race and social class intersect to limit such access and the ability to separate "from all that is feminine" (84), crime and violence are likely to emerge as alternative resources for accomplishing masculinity. For marginalized "lower-working-class, racial-minority" boys, who "have no access to [mental or manual] paid labor" and whose "parents are unable to subsidize their youth culture needs (as are the parents of white, middle-class boys), the youth gang ... takes on a new and significant meaning inasmuch as it is here where resources are available with which to sustain a masculine identity" (102). According to Messerschmidt, the centrality of physical violence is what distinguishes this type of masculinity from masculinities constructed by white middle- and working-class boys.

Messerschmidt's (1993) structured action theory, including subsequent statements and refinements (Messerschmidt 1995, 1997, 2000, 2004; see also Messerschmidt 1986, 2018), has had a notable influence in criminology, gendering the behaviors of boys and men while highlighting situational constructions of multiple masculinities and the significance of intersecting racial and class identities.[1] Indeed, his view of crime as a "masculine-validating resource" (Messerschmidt 1993, 83) has stimulated criminological analyses of "hypermasculinity" (e.g., Rios 2009) and even "subordinated" masculinities apart from "hegemonic masculinity" (Connell 1987), including "protest," "rugged," "toxic," and "vulnerable" (Bartie and Fraser 2017; McLean and Holligan 2018; Sanders 2011; see Connell and Messerschmidt 2005). These analyses clearly show there are "different ways of enacting manhood, different ways of learning to be a man, different conceptions of the self and different ways of using the male body" (Connell 2000, 10).

Although Jody Miller (2002, 2014; see also Lobo de la Tierra 2016) acknowledged the potential explanatory value of viewing crime and violence as "doing gender," her own research suggested existing applications of the concept often were tautological, limited by the tendency to reify gender dualism and normative constructs of masculinity and femininity, and negligent of agency, gender stratification, and intersections between gender and other sources of inequality, such as race and social class. In short, she argued, female gang involvement, crime, and violence still tend to be interpreted simplistically as reflecting a kind of non-normative femininity (Miller 2002, 2014; see also Peterson and Panfil 2017). A related deficiency is the lack of quantitative assessments of the criminogenic influence of masculinities, which is "in part due to the difficulties of quantified operationalization of key concepts" (Mullins 2010, 622; see also Miller and Mullins 2006). This is true even in the gang literature, where masculinity long has been considered a key explanatory construct.

Gangs and Masculinities

The concept of masculinity has been a mainstay of the gang literature, albeit less so in terms of "doing gender" than as a defining feature of delinquent gang subcultures. Walter Miller (1958), who was one of the first to express interest in the salience of masculinity in gang life, disagreed with the prevailing view advanced by Albert Cohen (1955) that gang status and delinquency can be understood as challenging the cultural mainstream. According to Miller (1958), "the cultural system which exerts the most direct influence on behavior is that of the lower class community itself—a long-established, distinctively patterned tradition with an integrity of its own—rather than a so-called 'delinquency subculture' which has arisen through conflict with middle class culture and is oriented to the deliberate violation of middle class norms" (5–6). Within the adolescent male corner group, which he suggested had emerged as a common and influential adaptation to the prevalence of female-headed households in lower-class communities, status and belonging had to be earned by demonstrating qualities, states, and conditions valued in lower-class culture: trouble, toughness, smartness, excitement, fate, and autonomy. Masculinity was described as a key feature of these "focal concerns," particularly toughness, and was "symbolized by a distinctive complex of acts and avoidances (bodily tattooing; absence of sentimentality; nonconcern with 'art,' 'literature,' conceptualization of women as conquest objects, etc.)" (9).

Despite having said little about masculinities and being criticized for advancing a sexist perspective filtered through a middle-class lens,[2] Cohen's (1955) study of gang boys remains important because it identified conditions that appear to be associated with the development of a variety of subcultural adaptations: enduring subordination, proximity of subordinates to one another, and regular interaction concerning shared problems stemming from their subordination (Tittle and Paternoster 2000). This perspective, combined with Miller's ideas about the orientation and focal concerns of the street corner group, provides the framework for masculinity in the gang literature, where it has been conceived as part of an intergenerational street culture oriented toward respect earned through public displays of toughness and violence.

Analyzing archival records from the first half of the twentieth century, Diamond (2009) found considerable evidence of early Chicago gangs being immersed within a broad subculture characterized by strong emphases on manly honor, including displays of toughness, sexual exploits and prowess, access to cars and other symbols of consumer culture, and skillful performances in such leisure activities as ritualistic verbal banter and duels (e.g., "ball busting" and "the dozens"). Regardless of racial and ethnic differences, expressions of masculinity were "not just reflected in the culture of physical combat [gang youth] created on the streets" but also were "on one level or another, at the moral center of the movies they saw, the books and magazines they read, and the sporting culture they were part of—both as spectators and participants" (33–34). Similarly, Schneider's (1999) historical analysis of gang boys in postwar New York, 1940–1975, discovered masculinities at the forefront of everyday life, identity, relationships, and behaviors. Although prominent studies of gangs in Chicago (Short and Strodtbeck 1965) and Los Angeles (Moore 1978, 1991) during this same period did not focus on masculinity per se, they, too, pointed to manliness and respect in relation to toughness and violent behaviors.

Following the women's movement, interest in the salience of masculinities in the gang context proceeded along two trajectories. As described previously, the first was stimulated by Messerschmidt's ideas and subsequent critiques regarding their limited application to female gangs and gang members. The second trajectory continued to delineate a street gang culture in which respect is a top priority and deeply enmeshed with cultural understandings and expressions of masculinity. For example, Ruth Horowitz's (1983) study of the Lions, a Latino male gang in Chicago, revealed the influence of an honor culture that had developed around the establishment and protection of manhood or *machismo* in the streets through violence and sexual potency. At the heart of this culture was "normative ambiguity" stemming from clashes between street realities for young inner-city males and the American dream of achieving success through education, hard work, and conventional family life. Similar subcultural themes were observed among Chicano gangs in Los Angeles, where, as a result of "multiple marginalities," street socialization and *machismo* permeated barrio life and provided alternative means for acquiring and expressing masculine status (Vigil 1988). Finally, masculinity is central to the "badass" street identity described by Katz (1988) as being "disproportionately seductive to males" (81). Conceptualizing street gangs or "street elites" as collective representations of the badass, Katz argued that the kind of masculine toughness they display "is, in part, a matter of failing to perform . . . prophylactic rituals on the moral health of everyday life [e.g., conversational niceties], but it is also a matter of inventing substitutes" (84) devoid of any sign one is "sensitive to others" (87).

By the turn of the century, substantial evidence of a link between manly honor and gang life had accumulated in the United States and elsewhere in the world, such as Africa and the United Kingdom (e.g., Davies 1999; Decker and Van Winkle 1996; Luyt and Foster 1998). The first typology of gang masculinities also had been advanced, distinguishing between the dope-dating "Frat Boy," the "Bossman" in total control of his lady and family, the misogynistic and sexually promiscuous "Stud," and the "Gentleman" who placed women on a pedestal (Hagedorn 1998). Finally, Elijah Anderson's (1999; see also Anderson 1978, 1990, 1994) *Code of the Street* elaborated earlier themes involving subcultural pressures felt by inner-city Black males, including gang members, to be respected *as men*. According to the code of the street thesis, such respect is of paramount importance in urban street cultures rooted in disadvantage and oppression, including racism and discrimination by the police, and featuring normative systems that differ from, if not conflict with, the dominant social order (see also Bourgois 1995; Wilson 1997).

In the first two decades of the new millennium, the gang literature has evidenced continued interest in masculinities among gangs in the United States, Australia, and countries in Asia, Africa, Europe, and South America (Barker 2005; Baird 2012a, 2012b, 2017; Deuchar 2018; Durán 2013; Garot 2010; Heinonen 2011; Jensen 2008; Kersten 2001; McLean and Holligan 2018; Streicher 2011; White 2008; Zubillaga 2009; see also Peterson and Panfil 2014). Much of this literature builds on the work described above, focusing on gang involvement and gang crime and violence as alternative routes to masculine status among marginalized males. Together with sexual conquests and visible symbols of masculinity embedded in clothing, speech and language, tattoos and hairstyles, and other embellishments and accoutrements (e.g., cars and money), publicly displaying aggression and toughness is how boys and young men, including "homo thugs" who identify as gay (Panfil 2017), are said to prove their masculinity when more conventional means are unavailable. Engaging in such behaviors is also depicted as a way for poor and marginalized girls and young women to find acceptance and help ensure their own protection and safety.

Importantly, contemporary contributions extend prior work by documenting the diverse and dynamic nature of masculinities, not only in terms of differences between gang members but also with respect to situational constructions leading to individual change over time and from one social context to the next. For example, in addition to recent observations of queer gang members constructing masculinity in non-heteronormative and stereotypically feminine ways, such as by caring for and treating one another like family (Panfil 2017), Rios and Sarabia (2016) found that the gang-involved Latino youth they observed in California tended to respond to race, class, and gender subordination by enacting "synthesized masculinities" consisting of conventional and compensatory forms (e.g., subordinate, street, working-class, dominant, and hypermasculinity) and "depending heavily on context and the type of interaction (i.e., peer-peer, male-female, youth-authority figure)" (168). Masculinities also have been observed to change over the life course due to maturation, disillusionment with the gang, and "masculinity dilemmas" stemming from exposure to "new dominant practices of masculinity centered on different social institutions like family, work, and religion" (Leverso and Hess 2021, 1206; see also Maloney et al. 2009). Finally, there is growing support for programmatic interventions aimed at reshaping street, barrio, and criminal masculinities into more positive versions involving religion and other conventional pursuits, such as raising a family. In *God's Gang*, for example, Edward Flores (2016) shows how the success of two well-known urban ministries in promoting gang desistance hinged on their ability to redefine masculinity by reshaping street embodiments into more conventional ones (e.g., replacing a shaved head, tattoos, and gang clothing with religious pronouncements and more ordinary attire). Similar results were reported by Ross Deuchar (2018; see also Deuchar and Weide 2019) based on interviews and ethnographic observations of gangs across North America, Europe, and Asia. For young men transitioning out of gang life, he noted, "substitute forms of brotherhood and trust" resulting in "alternative forms of male status" were crucially important (Deuchar 2018, 13). Likewise, the success of a faith-based organization in reducing gang violence in an East London borough appears to have been attributable largely to efforts to induce "reformed masculinity" among individual members (Armstrong and Rosbrook-Thompson 2017).

In sum, the concept of masculinity has appeared regularly throughout the history of the gang literature. Nearly all of this work has been rooted in the subcultural perspective advanced by Cohen and Miller, focusing on masculinities and gangs as defining features of street culture. Although gang membership is not the only resource used by marginalized young men to accomplish masculinity, and although violence is only one of multiple resources for gang members to establish masculinity, street culture respect is earned primarily by demonstrating toughness and heart to an audience of peers both on and off the scene. In the next section, we suggest adding to this framework insights from a group process perspective and interpreting the influence of masculinities in gang life in terms of the street culture emphasis on respect.

Street Culture, Gang Masculinities, and Group Structure and Processes

In *Understanding Street Culture: Poverty, Crime, Youth and Cool*, Jonathan Ilan (2016) argues that street cultures oriented toward respect earned through masculine displays of toughness develop initially among structurally deprived populations and later diffuse to the more well-to-do and relatively unstrained populations via technological advances, population mobility, and urban changes such as gentrification. He applies the concept of "habitus" (Bourdieu 1990) to explain individual differences in interpreting the streets and acquiring street capital for future success in street contexts. Consisting of "dispositions, habits and instincts that form in a person over time" (Ilan 2016, 57), habitus is shaped largely by race, class, gender, and culture, with street culture being almost second nature among excluded populations versus more performative and divorced from crime and violence among the affluent and included.

This formulation stands out from decades of subcultural theory and research not only by identifying the source and spread of street cultures but also by incorporating individual differences in a way that improves upon applications of the concept of "doing gender" that neglect agency and intersections with race, social class, and other sources of inequality. However, it is similar to prior analyses of street culture in that it pays only limited attention to gangs *as groups*. Ilan even goes so far as to argue against "gang discourse," suggesting the word "gang" is "loaded with assumptions and ideological baggage" (77) and less useful for explaining stylistic and expressive variations among gangs and differentiating between gangs and other criminal groups. There are good reasons to abandon the term, which has been notoriously hard to define (see Esbensen and Maxson 2021), but the fact remains that gangs are groups with distinct structures and processes that relate to masculinities and gang crime and violence. In the remainder of this section, we illuminate the salience of group contexts at the nexus of street culture, masculinities, and gang involvement and gang crime and violence.

Although much of the focus of the street culture literature has been on macro- and individual-level variables, such as structural strain and now habitus, we argue that how these background variables play out among gang youth in the streets also depends on proximal group contexts as they relate to behavioral expectations, interactions, situational arrangements, and a sanctioning system of status gains and losses, including the possibility of ridicule, ostracism, and violent victimization (see Short 1998). These contexts involve both group structure and process and have implications for masculinity, which, as indicated above, is a key component of respect in street culture contexts.

Gang structure is important because it sets the stage for enactments of masculinity, influencing the nature and frequency of interactions and situations in which to uphold and advance manly honor. For example, recent studies have highlighted the importance of considering the sex composition of gangs as a way to understand the gendered behavior of gang members. Contrary to "generic" approaches to understanding group gender dynamics, which contend that members of one sex are likely to assimilate to a greater extent in groups with more balanced sex ratios than in those that skew toward the opposite sex (Blau 1977; see also Kanter 1977), quantitative and qualitative findings from these studies consistently reveal the most striking gender differences in sex-balanced gangs (Hunt and Joe-Laidler 2001; Joe-Laidler and Hunt 1997; Miller and Brunson 2000; Peterson, Miller, and Esbensen 2001; Peterson, Carson, and Fowler 2018). Coupled with evidence of token female members in majority-male gangs behaving and being accepted as "one of the guys" (Miller 2001), as opposed to being marginalized, this supports a minority-group hypothesis (see Blalock 1967) suggesting that, as the gender balance of male-dominated gangs approaches parity, male members experience "precarious manhood" (Bosson and Vandello 2011) and double down on performances of masculinity that reinforce their status in the group, such as by behaving aggressively toward female members and overtly sexualizing and marginalizing them. An important consequence of these performances appears to be that, regardless of sex, members of these gangs are at greater risk of delinquent involvement and violent victimization than is true of their counterparts in all-male or all- or majority-female gangs (Peterson and Carson 2012; Peterson et al. 2001, 2018). Thus, the degree of antisocial behaviors in a gang depends partly on the extent to which girls and women participate alongside boys and men, rather than being due solely or even largely to gendered learning or persistent differences between males and females. With more girls in the gang, there appears to be greater adherence to group norms favorable to violence, members may be interacting more frequently and monitoring more closely their own status and the behaviors of others, and the specific configuration of situational variables (e.g., setting, offender–victim relationships, third parties, co-offenders and co-victims, intoxicants, and weapons) likely generates more status threats and opportunities to demonstrate manly honor than in all-male or all-female gangs (see Hughes and Short 2005). In short, the sex composition of gangs influences enactments of street culture masculinity among gang members oriented toward earning and maintaining respect in a gendered group context. To the extent that other aspects of group structure, such as organization and cohesion, produce these same kinds of conditions and situations, they too can be expected to influence violent displays of masculinities.

Even more proximal than gang structure are group processes consisting of ongoing social interactions within and between gangs. Since the pioneering work of Short and Strodtbeck (1965), an extensive body of literature has emerged to show that gang violence is best understood as the outcome of collective and personal quests to be respected among peers in the streets (see Decker and Pyrooz 2021; Decker et al. 2013; McGloin and Collins 2015). As we have noted throughout this chapter, masculinity is an intrinsic part of this respect and is likely to be enacted through violence because expectations for this behavior are embedded in interactions between gang members, particularly those signaling disrespect or otherwise inducing status challenges. These expectations also are likely to be supported by related situational cues, such as the offender–victim relationship, co-offender involvement, and instigating actions taken by onlookers (Hughes and Short 2005). Although similar micro-level processes have been observed among violent offenders more generally (e.g., Collison 1996; Jacobs and Wright 2008; Luckenbill 1977; Mullins 2006), we contend that gang violence is distinct because gangs are groups that not only embed members within networks of institutionalized conflict but also link "valued perceptions of masculinity, such as respect, honor, and righteousness, with an avenue to accomplish them (e.g., violence and aggressive behaviors)" (Leverso and Hess 2021, 1209) and continually reinforce such masculinity through a system of status rewards and punishments of immediate relevance in their everyday lives (Melde and Berg 2021; Matsueda and Lanfear 2021; Short and Strodtbeck 1965). To the extent that gang members demonstrate individual or collective masculinity, such as by retaliating violently when attacked by another gang or by aggressively dominating their female counterparts, they prove themselves worthy of respect and entitled to the "masculine capital" this entails (Baird 2017), including establishment and reinforcement of their reputations as persons to be feared and not to be messed with. By contrast, if gang members fail to demonstrate masculinity when expected, they will "lose face" and increase their vulnerability to future victimization and disrespect. As discussed above, exactly how these processes unfold likely is influenced by the group structure of the gang (Decker and Pyrooz 2021; Lauger 2019, 2020). While sex composition appears to be particularly important, other structural features, such as organizational hierarchy, size, member age range and race/ethnicity, and cohesiveness, also can be expected to shape situational configurations and interactions affecting the nature and scope of masculinity challenges and performances. For example, stronger friendship ties among more cohesive gangs may help limit situations in which individual members feel compelled to prove masculinity through intra-group aggression.

Overall, conceptualizing masculinities in terms of group structure and processes is consistent with decades of evidence showing manhood and *machismo* to be integral to the definition of respect and toughness, bravado, and violence by which marginalized men and women, including gang members, achieve and manage this social status among peers. It also helps overcome limitations associated with earlier approaches to studying and explaining masculinities and crime, including tautology, gender dualism, and neglect of gender stratification and other sources of inequality (see Miller 2002, 2014). If masculinities are a key part of group processes and what it means to be respected, then they necessarily are negotiated through social interactions enacted by males as well as females and shaped by group characteristics (e.g., organization, sex composition, size, cohesion) in addition to more distal processes at the macro and individual levels. As noted by Messerschmidt (1995), because "individuals realize their behavior is accountable to others, they configure and orchestrate their actions in relation to how they might be interpreted by others in the particular social context in which they occur" (172). In the street culture context of gangs, where opportunities to be respected in conventional ways are limited, crime, violence, sexual dominance, and conspicuous consumption are resources for demonstrating manhood. The extent to which members enact masculinity in these ways depends not just on macro and individual influences but also on group processes involving street culture respect, which is imbued with notions of masculinity and contingent on situational arrangements that are themselves a function of different aspects of group structure, such as sex composition. When the group context of gangs is considered, it becomes possible to understand masculinities as something more than individual adherence to gender norms and the result of structural patterns of gender stratification. They also can be seen as performative resources central to social interactions within and between gangs. It is in the context of the gang where gang members invoke specific enactments of masculinity to enhance their sense of respect. In addition, for young men and women in street culture contexts, the gang tends to be where gender intersects with other systems of stratification, such as age, race/ethnicity, social class, and sexuality in ways that determine how and by whom masculinity and femininity are accomplished.

Conclusion and Future Directions

Masculinities feature prominently in the gang literature, both in terms of girls' gang involvement and as a performative resource used by male and female gang members to obtain respect when more conventional means are unavailable. Although each of these two streams of thought has advanced understanding of what draws youth into gangs, helps keep them gang involved, and causes them to engage in gang crime and violence, they have developed along distinct lines and largely have "stalled" in their ability to account for differences in the emphasis on masculinity and its connection to violence within marginalized populations as well as in "attempts to apply the concept of doing gender to explanations of female participation in crime" (Miller 2002, 436).

In this chapter, we suggest a group process perspective as a framework for unifying disparate masculinity literatures within criminology. Here masculinity is conceptualized as a crucially important, albeit not the only, component of street cultures emphasizing respect earned by marginalized men and women through sexual conquests, violence, conspicuous consumption, and other outward appearances and demeanor symbolizing one's possession of street capital. How this street culture unfolds is neither determined by social structure nor the same for all oppressed persons. Rather, it depends to a large degree on interaction processes and other variables that influence the way individuals read the situation in terms of likely status gains and losses associated with various courses of action. For both male and female gang members, this "presentation of self" is made for an audience of gang peers whose positive evaluation they aim to secure. While peers on the scene may encourage street culture behaviors directly as co-offenders/co-victims or as instigating third parties (Hughes and Short 2005), group structure variables, such as cohesiveness, organization, and sex composition, are also likely to influence behavior by feeding into group processes involving respect earned through successful displays of masculinity.

Moving forward, theory and research should attend to the specific group contexts in which displays of masculinity develop and relate to the respect members seek to earn as men or as women in a man's world. Although masculinities appear to manifest in broadly similar ways among excluded populations, it would be helpful to know whether and how definitions and enactments of masculinities differ between gangs, and between gangs and other troublesome groups that vary in terms of structural characteristics, including but not limited to sex composition. Relatedly, for both male and female members, how does gang structure affect masculinity dilemmas and commitment to, or disillusionment with, the gang?

Another important avenue for research involves masculine identities and enactments as potential mediators and moderators of the effects of group structure on collective and individual violence and disengagement and desistance from the gang. If, for example, gangs with certain organizational and relational structures are more violent because they are more likely to emphasize hegemonic masculinities, reward members for demonstrating such masculinity, and place them in situations in which they feel compelled to enact masculinity violently, then it would make sense to consider ways to privilege and provide members of these gangs with conventional means of proving manhood (Flores 2014). Finally, future research should consider the short- and long-term consequences of varying gender identities and enactments of masculinities in gang contexts. How, for example, does the structure of gangs and interactions between members evolve in response to successful and failed efforts to accomplish masculinity? Do they become more or less cohesive and violent? Are more masculine gangs and gang members more resilient and respected?

Much remains to be learned about the nature and salience of masculinities in street cultures evident among gangs and excluded population segments across the globe. While we have emphasized microsocial interactions in the group context of gangs, it is important to recognize the dynamic interplay between masculinities and broader social, political, and economic forces (Patton, Eschmann, and Butler 2013). Thus, as in post-Fordist American society, particularly following the women's movement and widespread access to firearms and automobiles, the rise of mass media, hip hop and rap music, and the internet has profoundly affected masculine identity formation and displays. Unlike any other societal shift, social media platforms provide "a perfect stage for . . . masculine identity to be performed in front of an audience of millions" (Patton et al. 2013, A57). They also offer unprecedented opportunities for the masculine identities of the excluded to diffuse to diverse populations throughout the world. How these masculinities unfold in the lives and behaviors of young men and women is likely to depend on the kinds of impressions they can be expected to leave in the minds of others whose opinions are valued. In the immediate context of gangs, what conventional society is apt to dismiss as "toxic masculinity" or "non-normative femininity" may be for male and female members one of few available ways by which to construct respected individual and collective identities.

Notes

1. As observed by Connell and Messerschmidt (2005), a major criticism of the "masculinity turn" in criminology is that, even when divorced from the Gramscian focus on "structural change involving the mobilization and demobilization of whole classes" (831), the

concept of hegemonic masculinity came to be reified and "associated solely with negative characteristics that depict men as unemotional, independent, non-nurturing, aggressive, and dispassionate—which are seen as the causes of criminal behavior" (840).

2. Drawing on the work of Talcott Parsons, Cohen (1955) argued that, although a boy's delinquency "incontestably confirms, in the eyes of all concerned, his essential masculinity" (140), it reflects an "attempt to cope with a basic anxiety in the area of sex-role identification" and "has the primary function of giving reassurance of one's essential masculinity" only in the middle class. Because the working-class boy "is more likely from the very beginning to have clearly defined for him . . . his sex role and the distinctive patterns of behaviors that go with it and to be systematically rewarded for assuming characteristically masculine behavior," he is "not so likely resort to 'badness' simply as a device to prove to himself and the world that he is really masculine" (165). Rather, motivation for his delinquency stems from the problem of adjustment "in the area of ego-involved status differences in a status system defined by the norms of respectable middle-class society" (168). The fact that delinquency is "symbolic of masculinity" is of secondary importance and increases the appeal of this response to the working-class boy only "because it is consistent with his conception of himself as a male and because there are few other avenues of distinctively masculine achievement open to him which are also instrumental to the solution of his status problems" (168–169).

REFERENCES

Adler, Alfred. (1910) 1956. "Inferiority Feeling and Masculine Protest." In *The Individual Psychology of Alfred Adler: A Systematic Presentation in Selections from His Writings*, edited by Heinz L. Ansbacher and Rowena R. Ansbacher, 45–52. New York: Basic Books.

Adler, Freda. 1975. *Sisters in Crime: The Rise of the New Female Criminal*. New York: McGraw-Hill.

Anderson, Elijah. 1978. *A Place on the Corner: An Ethnography of a Shifting Collection of Black Men*. Chicago, IL: University of Chicago Press.

Anderson, Elijah. 1990. *Streetwise: Streetwise: Race, Class, and Change in an Urban Community*. Chicago, IL: University of Chicago Press.

Anderson, Elijah. 1994. "The Code of the Street." *The Atlantic Monthly* 273 (5): 81–93.

Anderson, Elijah. 1999. *Code of the Street: Decency, Violence, and the Moral Life of the Inner City*. New York: WW Norton & Company.

Anderson, James F., Willie Brooks Jr., Adam Langsam, and Laronistine Dyson. 2002. "The 'New' Female Gang Member: Anomaly or Evolution?" *The Gang Journal* 10: 47–65.

Armstrong, Gary, and James Rosbrook-Thompson. 2017. "'Squashing the Beef': Combating Gang Violence and Reforming Masculinity in East London." *Contemporary Social Science* 12 (3–4): 285–296.

Baird, Adam. 2012a. "The Violent Gang and the Construction of Masculinity amongst Socially Excluded Young Men." *Safer Communities* 11 (4): 179–190.

Baird, Adam. 2012b. "Negotiating Pathways to Manhood: Rejecting Gangs and Violence in Medellín's Periphery." *Journal of Conflictology* 3 (1): 30–41.

Baird, Adam. 2017. "Becoming the 'Baddest': Masculine Trajectories of Gang Violence in Medellín." *Journal of Latin American Studies* 50: 183–210.

Baittle, Brahm. 1961. "Psychiatric Aspects of the Development of a Street Corner Group: An Exploratory Study." *American Journal of Orthopsychiatry* 31: 703–712.

Barker, Gary. 2005. *Dying to be Men: Youth, Masculinity and Social Exclusion.* Abingdon, UK: Routledge.

Bartie, Angela, and Alistair Fraser. 2017. "Speaking to the 'Hard Men': Masculinities, Violence and Youth Gangs in Glasgow, c. 1965–75." In *Nine Centuries of Man: Manhood and Masculinity in Scottish History,* edited by Lynn Abrams and Elizabeth L. Ewan, 258–277. Edinburgh, Scotland: Edinburgh University Press.

Blalock, Hubert M. 1967. *Toward a Theory of Minority-Group Relations.* New York: John Wiley.

Blau, Peter M. 1977. *Inequality and Heterogeneity: A Primitive Theory of Social Structure.* New York: Free Press.

Bloch, Herbert A., and Arthur Niederhoffer. 1958. *The Gang: A Study in Adolescent Behavior.* New York: Philosophical Library.

Bourdieu, Pierre. 1990. *The Logic of Practice.* Stanford, CT: Stanford University Press.

Bourgois, Phillipe. 1995. *In Search of Respect: Selling Crack in El Barrio.* Cambridge, UK: Cambridge University Press.

Bosson, Jennifer K., and Joseph A. Vandello. 2011. "Precarious Manhood and Its Links to Action and Aggression." *Current Directors in Psychological Science* 20 (2): 82–86.

Brown, Waln K. 1977. "Black Female Gangs in Philadelphia." *International Journal of Offender Therapy and Comparative Criminology* 21 (3): 221–228.

Campbell, Anne. 1984. *The Girls in the Gang.* Cambridge, MA: Basil Blackwell.

Cloward, Richard A., and Lloyd E. Ohlin. 1960. *Delinquency and Opportunity: A Theory of Delinquent Gangs.* Glencoe, IL: Free Press.

Cohen, Albert K. 1955. *Delinquent Boys: The Culture of the Gang.* Glencoe, IL: Free Press.

Collison, Mike. 1996. "In Search of the High Life: Drugs, Crime, Masculinities and Consumption." *British Journal of Criminology* 36 (3): 428–444.

Connell, R. W. 1987. *Gender and Power.* Sydney, Australia: Allen and Unwin.

Connell, R. W. 2000. *The Men and the Boys.* Berkeley: University of California Press.

Connell, R. W., and James W. Messerschmidt. 2005. "Hegemonic Masculinity: Rethinking the Concept." *Gender and Society* 19 (6): 829–859.

Davies, Andrew. 1999. "Youth Gangs, Masculinity and Violence in Late Victorian Manchester and Salford." *Journal of Social History* 32 (2): 349–369.

Decker, Scott H., and David C. Pyrooz. 2001. "Levels of Explanation and the Group Process Perspective." In *Social Bridges and Contexts in Criminology and Sociology: Reflections on the Intellectual Legacy of James F. Short, Jr.,* edited by Lorine A. Hughes, and Lisa M. Broidy, 100–118. New York: Routledge.

Decker, Scott, David Pyrooz, and Chris Melde. 2013. "What Do We Know about Gangs and Gang Members and Where Do We Go from Here?" *Justice Quarterly* 30 (3): 369–402.

Decker, Scott H., David C. Pyrooz, and James A. Densley. 2022. *On Gangs.* Philadelphia, PA: Temple University Press.

Decker, Scott H., and Barrick Van Winkle. 1996. *Life in the Gang: Family, Friends, and Violence.* Cambridge, UK: Cambridge University Press.

Deuchar, Ross. 2018. *Gangs and Spirituality: Global Perspectives.* New York: Springer.

Deuchar, Ross, and Robert D. Weide. 2019. "Journeys in Gang Masculinity: Insights from International Case Studies of Interventions." *Deviant Behavior* 40 (7): 851–865.

Diamond, Andrew. 2009. *Mean Streets: Chicago Youths and the Everyday Struggle for Empowerment in the Multiracial City, 1908–1969.* Berkeley: University of California Press.

Durán, Robert J. 2013. *Gang Life in Two Cities: An Insider's Journey.* New York: Columbia University Press.

Esbensen, Finn-Aage, and Cheryl L. Maxson. 2021. "Core Controversies and Debates in the Study of Gangs." In *Social Bridges and Contexts in Criminology and Sociology: Reflections on the Intellectual Legacy of James F. Short, Jr.*, edited by Lorine A. Hughes, and Lisa M. Broidy, 83–99. New York: Routledge.

Flores, Edward O. 2014. *God's Gangs: Barrio Ministry, Masculinity, and Gang Recovery*. New York: New York University Press.

Garot, Robert. 2010. *Who You Claim: Performing Gang Identity in School and on the Streets*. New York: New York University Press.

Heinonen, Paula. 2011. *Youth Gangs and Street Children: Culture, Nurture and Masculinity in Ethiopia*. New York: Berghahn Books.

Horowitz, Ruth. 1983. *Honor and the American Dream: Culture and Identity in a Chicano Community*. New Brunswick, NJ: Rutgers University Press.

Hagedorn, John M. 1998. "Frat Boys, Bossmen, Studs, and Gentlemen: A Typology of Gang Masculinities." In *Masculinities and Violence*, edited by Lee H. Bowker, 152–167. Thousand Oaks, CA: Sage Publications.

Hughes, Lorine A., and James F. Short Jr. 2005. "Disputes Involving Youth Street Gang Members: Micro-social Contexts." *Criminology* 43: 3–76.

Hughes, Lorine A., Ekaterina V. Botchkovar, and James F. Short Jr. 2019. "'Bargaining with Patriarchy' and 'Bad Girl Femininity': Relationships and Behaviors among Chicago Gang Girls, 1959–62." *Social Forces* 98 (2): 493–517.

Hunt, Geoffrey, and Karen Joe-Laidler. 2001. "Situations of Violence in the Lives of Girl Gang Members." *Health Care for Women International* 22 (4): 363–384.

Hunt, Geoffrey, Karen Joe-Laidler, and Kathleen Mackenzie. 2000. "'Chillin', Being Dogged and Getting Buzzed': Alcohol in the Lives of Female Gang Members." *Drugs: Education, Prevention and Policy* 7 (4): 331–353.

Hunt, Geoffrey P., Karen Joe-Laidler, and Kristy Evans. 2002. "The Meaning and Gendered Culture of Getting High: Gang Girls and Drug Use Issues." *Contemporary Drug Problems* 29 (2): 375–415.

Ilan, Jonathan. 2016. *Understanding Street Culture: Poverty, Crime, Youth and Cool*. New York: Palgrave Macmillan.

Jacobs, Bruce A., and Richard Wright. 2008. "Moralistic Street Robbery." *Crime and Delinquency* 54 (4): 511–531.

Jensen, Steffen. 2008. *Gangs, Politics and Dignity in Cape Town*. Oxford, UK: James Currey.

Joe-Laidler, Karen A., and Geoffrey Hunt. 1997. "Violence and Social Organization in Female Gangs." *Social Justice* 24 (4): 148–169.

Kanter, Rosabeth M. 1997. "Some Effects of Proportions on Group Life: Skewed Sex Ratios and Responses to Token Women." *American Journal of Sociology* 82 (5): 965–990.

Katz, Jack. 1988. *Seductions of Crime: Moral and Sensual Attractions in Doing Evil*. New York City: Basic Books.

Kersten, Joachim. 2001. "Groups of Violent Young Males in Germany." In *The Eurogang Paradox*, edited by Malcolm W. Klein, Hans-Jürgen Kerner, Cheryl L. Maxson, and Elmar G. M. Weitekamp, 247–255. Dordrecht: Springer.

Laidler, Karen J., and Geoffrey Hunt. 2001. "Accomplishing Femininity among the Girls in the Gang." *British Journal of Criminology* 41 (4): 656–678.

Lauger, Timothy R. 2019. "Group Processes within Gangs." Criminology and Criminal Justice, Oxford Research Encyclopedias. https://doi.org/10.1093/acrefore/9780190264079.013.438.

Lauger, Timothy R. 2020. "Gangs, Identity, and Cultural Performance." *Sociology Compass* 14 (4): 1–12.

Lauderback, David, Joy Hansen, and Dan Waldorf. 1992. "'Sisters Are Doin' It for Themselves': A Black Female Gang in San Francisco." *The Gang Journal* 1: 57–72.

Leverso, John, and Chris Hess. 2021. "From the Hood to the Home: Masculinity Maturation of Chicago Street Gang Members." *Sociological Perspectives* 64 (6): 1206–1226.

Lobo de la Tierra, Albert. 2016. "Essentializing Manhood in 'the Street': Perilous Masculinity and Popular Criminological Ethnographies." *Feminist Criminology* 11 (4): 375–397.

Luckenbill, David F. 1977. "Criminal Homicide as a Situated Transaction." *Social Problems* 25 (2): 176–186.

Luyt, Russell, and Don Foster. 1998. "Hegemonic Masculine Conceptualization in Gang Culture." *South African Journal of Psychology* 31 (3): 1–12.

Maloney, Molly, Kathleen MacKenzie, Geoffrey Hunt, and Karen Joe-Laidler. 2009. "The Path and Promise of Fatherhood for Gang Members." *British Journal of Criminology* 49 (3): 305–325.

McLean, Robert, and Chris Holligan. 2018. "The Semiotics of the Evolving Gang Masculinity and Glasgow." *Social Sciences* 7 (125): 1–17.

McGloin, Jean M., and Megan E. Collins. 2015. "Micro-Level Processes of the Gang." In *The Handbook of Gangs*, edited by Scott H. Decker, and David C. Pyrooz, 276–293. Chichester, UK: John Wiley and Sons.

Matsueda, Ross L., and Charles C. Lanfear. 2021. "Collective Action, Rational Choice, and Gang Delinquency: Appreciating Short and Strodtbeck ([1965] 1974)." In *Social Bridges and Contexts in Criminology and Sociology: Reflections on the Intellectual Legacy of James F. Short, Jr.*, edited by Lorine A. Hughes, and Lisa M. Broidy, 151–168. New York: Routledge.

Melde, Chris, and Mark T. Berg. 2021. "Status Management and Situational Inducements to Violence." In *Social Bridges and Contexts in Criminology and Sociology: Reflections on the Intellectual Legacy of James F. Short, Jr.*, edited by Lorine A. Hughes, and Lisa M. Broidy, 133–150. New York: Routledge.

Mendoza-Denton, Norma. 2008. *Homegirls: Language and Cultural Practice among Latina Youth Gangs*. Oxford, UK: Wiley-Blackwell.

Messerschmidt, James W. 1986. *Capitalism, Patriarchy, and Crime: Toward a Socialist Feminist Criminology*. Totowa, NJ: Rowman and Littlefield.

Messerschmidt, James W. 1993. *Masculinities and Crime: Critique and Conceptualization of Theory*. Lanham, MD: Rowman and Littlefield.

Messerschmidt, James W. 1995. "From Patriarchy to Gender: Feminist Theory, Criminology and the Challenge of Diversity." In *International Feminist Perspectives in Criminology: Engendering a Discipline*, edited by Nicole Hahn Rafter, and Frances Heidensohn, 167–188. Philadelphia, PA: Open University Press.

Messerschmidt, James W. 1997. *Crime as Structured Action: Gender, Race, Class and Crime in the Making*. Thousand Oaks, CA: Sage Publications.

Messerschmidt, James W. 2000. *Nine Lives: Adolescent Masculinities, the Body, and Violence*. Boulder, CO: Westview Press.

Messerschmidt, James W. 2004. *Flesh and Blood: Adolescent Gender Diversity and Violence*. Lanham, MD: Rowman & Littlefield.

Messerschmidt, James W. 2018. *Masculinities and Crime: A Quarter Century of Theory and Research*. Lanham, MD: Rowman and Littlefield.

Miller, Jody. 1998. "Gender and Victimization Risk among Young Women in Gangs." *Journal of Research in Crime and Delinquency* 35 (4): 429–453.

Miller, Jody. 2001. *One of the Guys: Girls, Gangs, and Gender.* New York: Oxford University Press.
Miller, Jody. 2002. "The Strengths and Limits of 'Doing Gender' for Understanding Street Crime." *Theoretical Criminology* 6 (4): 433–460.
Miller, Jody. 2014. "Doing Crime as Doing Gender? Masculinities, Femininities, and Crime." In *The Oxford Handbook of Gender, Sex, and Crime*, edited by Rosemary Gartner, and Bill McCarthy, 19–39. New York: Oxford University Press.
Miller, Jody, and Rod K. Brunson. 2000. "Gender Dynamics in Youth Gangs: A Comparison of Males' and Females' Accounts." *Justice Quarterly* 17 (3): 419–448.
Miller, Jody, and Christopher W. Mullins. 2006. "The Status of Feminist Theories in Criminology." In *Taking Stock: The Status of Criminological Theories*, edited by Francis T. Cullen, John P. Wright, and Kristie R. Blevins, 217–249. Piscataway, NJ: Transaction Publishers.
Miller, Walter B. 1958. "Lower Class Culture as a Generating Milieu of Gang Delinquency." *Journal of Social Issues* 14 (3): 5–19.
Miller, Walter B. 1973. "The Molls." *Society* 11: 32–35.
Miller, Walter B. 2011. *City Gangs.* Phoenix: Arizona State University, School of Criminology and Criminal Justice.
Moore, Joan W. 1978. *Homeboys: Gangs, Drugs, and Prison in the Barrios of Los Angeles.* Philadelphia, PA: Temple University Press.
Moore, Joan W. 1991. *Going Down to the Barrios: Homeboys and Homegirls in Change.* Philadelphia, PA: Temple University Press.
Mullins, Christopher W. 2006. *Holding Your Square: Masculinities, Streetlife and Violence.* Portland, OR: Willan Publishing.
Mullins, Christopher W. 2010. "Messerschmidt, James W.: Masculinities and Crime." In *Encyclopedia of Criminological Theory*, edited by Francis T. Cullen, and Pamela Wilcox, 620–624. Thousand Oaks, CA: Sage Publications.
Mullins, Christopher W., and Daniel R. Kavish. 2020. "Street Life and Masculinities." In *Routledge Handbook of Street Culture*, edited by Jeffrey I. Ross, 183–193. New York: Routledge.
Panfil, Vanessa R. 2017. *The Gang's All Queer: The Lives of Gay Gang Members.* New York: New York University Press.
Parsons, Talcott. (1949) 1954. *Essays in Sociological Theory.* Glencoe, IL: Free Press.
Patton, Desmond Upton, Robert D. Eschmann, and Dirk A. Butler. 2013. "Internet Banging: New Trends in Social Media, Gang Violence, Masculinity, and Hip Hop." *Computers in Human Behavior* 29: A54–A59.
Peterson, Dana, and Dena C. Carson. 2012. "The Sex Composition of Groups and Youths' Delinquency: A Comparison of Gang and Non-Gang Peer Groups." In *Youth Gangs in International Perspective: Tales from the Eurogang Program of Research*, edited by Finn-Aage Esbensen and Cheryl L. Maxson, 189–210. New York: Springer.
Peterson, Dana, Dena C. Carson, and Eric Fowler. 2018. "What's Sex (Composition) Got to Do with It? The Importance of Sex Composition of Gangs for Female and Male Members' Offending and Victimization." *Justice Quarterly* 35 (6): 941–976.
Peterson, Dana, Jody Miller, and Finn-Aage Esbensen. 2001. "The Impact of Sex Composition on Gangs and Gang Member Delinquency." *Criminology* 39 (2): 411–440.
Peterson, Dana, and Vanessa R. Panfil. 2014. "Street Gangs: The Gendered Experiences of Female and Male Gang Members." In *The Oxford Handbook of Gander, Sex, and Crime*, edited by Rosemary Gartner, and Bill McCarthy, 468–489. Oxford, UK: Oxford University Press.
Peterson, Dana, and Vanessa R. Panfil. 2017. "Toward a Multiracial Feminist Framework for Understanding Females' Gang Involvement." *Journal of Crime and Justice* 40 (3): 337–357.

Portillos, Edwardo L. 1999. "Women, Men and Gangs: The Social Construction of Gender in the Barrio." In *Female Gangs in America: Essays on Girls, Gangs and Gender*, edited by Meda Chesney-Lind, and John M. Hagedorn, 232–244. Chicago, IL: Lake View Press.

Quicker, John C. 1983. *Homegirls: Characterizing Chicana Gangs*. San Pedro, CA: International University Press.

Reuterman, Nicholas A., Mary J. Love, and Fred Fiedler. 1973. "A Partial Evaluation of Bloch and Niederhoffer's Theory of Gang Delinquency." *Criminology* 10 (4): 415–425.

Rios, Victor M. 2009. "The Consequences of the Criminal Justice Pipeline on Black and Latino Masculinity." *Annals of the American Academy of Political and Social Science* 623 (1): 150–162.

Rios, Victor M., and Rachel Sarabia. 2016. "Synthesized Masculinities: The Mechanics of Manhood among Delinquent Boys." In *Exploring Masculinities: Identity, Inequality, Continuity, and Change*, edited by C. J. Pascoe, and Tristan Bridges, 166–177. New York: Oxford University Press.

Sanders, Jolene M. 2011. "Coming of Age: How Adolescent Boys Construct Masculinities via Substance Use, Juvenile Delinquency, and Recreation." *Journal of Ethnicity in Substance Abuse* 10: 48–70.

Schneider, Eric. 1999. *Vampires, Dragons, and Egyptian Kings: Youth Gangs in Postwar New York*. Princeton, NJ: Princeton University Press.

Short, James F. Jr. 1998. "The Level of Explanation Problem Revisited—The American Society of Criminology 1997 Presidential Address." *Criminology* 36: 3–36.

Short, James F. Jr., and Fred L. Strodtbeck. 1965. *Group Process and Gang Delinquency*. Chicago, IL: University of Chicago Press.

Simon, Rita J. 1975. *Women and Crime*. Lexington, MA: Lexington Books.

Streicher, Ruth. 2011. "The Construction of Masculinities and Violence: 'Youth Gangs' in Dili, East Timor." Working Paper No. 2, Freie Universität Berlin. https://www.polsoz.fu-berlin.de/en/polwiss/forschung/international/vorderer-orient/publikation/working_papers/wp_02/WP2_Streicher_FINAL_web.pdf.

Taylor, Carl. 1993. *Girls, Gangs, Women and Drugs*. East Lansing: Michigan State University Press.

Tittle, Charles R., and Raymond Paternoster. 2000. *Social Deviance and Crime: An Organizational and Theoretical Approach*. New York: Oxford University Press.

Vigil, James D. 1988. *Barrio Gangs: Street Life and Identity in Southern California*. Austin: University of Texas Press.

White, Rob. 2008. "Weapons Are for Wimps: The Social Dynamics of Ethnicity and Violence in Australian Gangs." In *Street Gangs, Migration, and Ethnicity*, edited by Frank van Gemert, Dana Peterson, and Inger-Lise Lien, 140–155. Devon, UK: Willan.

Wilson, William J. 1997. *When Work Disappears: The World of the New Urban Poor*. New York: Vintage Books.

Zubillaga, Verónica. 2009. "'Gaining Respect': The Logic of Violence among Young Men in the Barrios of Caracas." In *Youth Violence in Latin America: Gangs and Juvenile Justice in Perspective*, edited by Gareth A. Jones, and Dennis Rodgers, 83–103. New York: Palgrave Macmillan.

CHAPTER 20

BIRDS OF A FEATHER?
Individual Differences and Gang Membership

JENNIFER J. TOSTLEBE AND JOSE ANTONIO SANCHEZ

[V]iolent gangs are essentially a product of the unstable slum; however, this fact alone does not explain why certain boys "join" violent gangs and many others, with the same opportunity, do not. The explanation of this more explicit issue necessitates going beyond the sociocultural influences into the social-psychological condition of the *individual violent-gang member*. (Yablonsky 1962, 236, emphasis in original)

The researcher who *fails to seek the structural differences or who studies but one gang or one gang type* will *publish false generalizations* and mislead his or her colleagues. (Klein and Maxson 2006, 165, emphasis added)

It is well-documented that gang members engage in higher levels of offending and violence than non-gang members (Pyrooz et al. 2016). Researchers have spent the better part of a century trying to explain the causes and consequences of gang joining. To this end, typologizing gang and non-gang members based on individual differences, which are characteristics—generally time stable—an individual possesses that *may* raise their proclivity for gang joining, has become one of the more contentious subjects in criminology. Prominent gang research—like the works cited above—varies widely in terms of whether gang members can be differentiated based on individual characteristics. Some researchers argue that individuals who join gangs are inherently different from those who do not, even when residing within the same neighborhood (e.g., Sanchez-Jankowski 1991). Others disagree and contend the key difference lies within the social environment individuals are embedded within, which creates the driver for gang joining (e.g., Klein 1995; Short and Strodtbeck 1965).

Today, merely posing the question of whether gang members are unique from non-gang members at the individual level is a surefire way to ignite debates, which are often spearheaded with emotion rather than grounded in science. This emotion centers on where the blame for gang membership lies. That is, typologizing gang members at the individual level shifts the blame from structural inequalities and racism that give rise to gangs to the individuals themselves being inherently different. While there may be a scientific basis for rejecting individual-level explanations, critical scholars who oppose this research often fall short in key areas. First, they largely rely on invoking emotion to argue that individual level research "demonizes" or "dehumanizes" gang members and displays a lack of cultural knowledge, while selectively choosing poor examples or misrepresenting the research (Marzo 2020; Swaner 2022; Weide 2022). Second, these scholars rarely attempt to tackle one of the most important questions in gang research focused on structural explanations: Why do *most* people, even in the most disadvantaged of neighborhoods, never join a gang? Finally, critical scholars propose inadequate theoretical frameworks to solve the perceived shortcomings of the gang literature. For example, intersectionality, while growing in popularity, has run into definitional issues, raising questions among scholars about whether it is a theory, a methodology for feminist research, or a method that is only applicable to those with multiple marginalized identities (e.g., Cho, Crenshaw, and McCall 2013).

Despite opposition, we argue that studying gang members at the individual level is beneficial for two reasons. First, it could aid in determining why not everyone joins a gang. Second, the findings of this research could have implications for responses to gangs and gang members. This chapter begins by discussing theoretical frameworks found in criminological research to explain antisocial behavior (and gang joining): state dependence and population heterogeneity. State dependence is the idea that one's previous actions influence future actions, while population heterogeneity argues that the focus should be on stable individual differences. We also discuss Thornberry et al.'s (1993) model of selection, facilitation, and enhancement. Selection argues certain people self-select into gangs, facilitation states that gangs are responsible for an individual's higher rate of offending, and enhancement argues for a combination of both. Next, while systematic reviews of risk and protective factors for gang membership have been done (Higginson et al. 2018; O'Brien et al. 2013; Raby and Jones 2016), we instead provide a review of 11 individual level differences that have been studied in relation to joining gangs. For each individual difference, we (1) define the concept; (2) identify its origins and evolution, including the stability of the factor over the life course; (3) describe its relationship to criminal behaviors; (4) discuss the theoretical mechanisms giving rise to gang membership; and (5) detail empirical evidence for its relationship with gang joining. We conclude this chapter with recommendations for future directions regarding micro-level gang research.

POPULATION HETEROGENEITY, STATE DEPENDENCE, AND GANG INVOLVEMENT

Theories in criminology that seek to explain continuity in criminal behavior have historically fallen into two camps (Nagin and Paternoster 2000). One side, *state dependence*, argues that the future state of an individual (i.e., criminality) is dependent upon their current state. In other words, continuation in crime results from prior criminal behavior eroding conventional ties and strengthening incentives to a criminal lifestyle. While there is nothing inherently criminal about the status of affiliating with a gang, a state dependence argument would say that differences in social settings, structures, and circumstances (e.g., low socioeconomic status and school failure) are the key factors for determining differences in joining a gang.

Alternatively, and critical to this chapter, the *population heterogeneity* perspective states that observed correlations between past and future offending are due to stable differences between individuals in their proclivity to commit crime. In other words, there are individual differences that distinguish those who commit crime from those who do not commit crime. Individual differences are relatively time-stable characteristics present in a person (e.g., self-control). This means outside influences will only incrementally, and without rank-order shifts, fluctuate across people throughout the life course (Nagin and Paternoster 1993). As such, disparities in the likelihood of joining a gang are due to these mostly rank-order and time-stable characteristics that vary between people.

Theoretically, individual differences have generally been applied to criminal behavior. In some instances, they have also been applied to the onset of gang membership. Thornberry et al.'s (1993) seminal piece on the gang–offending link outlines, among others, the selection hypothesis, which contends that individual differences can be found *before* the onset of gang membership. When it comes to the selection hypothesis, individual deficits, such as poor self-control, personality deficits, or conduct disorders, encourage selection into gangs. There is nothing special about gangs; instead, gangs are an assortment of individuals with common pre-existing characteristics that predispose them to "flock together," assuming the opportunity is available (e.g., Gottfredson and Hirschi 1990). They come together because prosocial peer groups often shun youth who exhibit criminal propensities, increasing the likelihood that antisocial youth will end up in the company of each other.

Since Thornberry et al.'s (1993) seminal piece, a large body of research has focused on why people join gangs (e.g., poor parental supervision or personality characteristics), but the mechanisms that explain selection remain mostly understudied largely owing to a tunnel vision on macro-level societal problems. Importantly, Kerig et al. (2013) state, "youth do not experience themselves as the helpless pawns of social forces, nor as the 'dependent variable' affected by these 'independent variables'; rather, they experience themselves as the protagonists of their own life stories" (775–776). As such, it is critical to investigate the mechanisms linking micro-level explanations (e.g., psychopathologies) of gang membership. As the study of gangs was once the study of delinquency (Pyrooz and Mitchell 2015), the current inventory of explanations on risk factors for gang joining center on four major perspectives from general theories of crime (i.e., propensity theory, social bond theory, general strain theory, and social learning theory). There are also a variety of gang-centered perspectives (e.g., integrated theory, multiple marginality, and unified theory) and alternative perspectives from other disciplines that are applied to gangs (i.e., signaling theory). An in-depth discussion of these falls outside the scope of this chapter (for a discussion, see Decker, Pyrooz, and Densley 2022). Suffice it to say, many explanations exist highlighting ongoing questions regarding how people enter gangs and the consequent implications. In this review, we focus on propensity theory, specifically individual differences, which falls under the population heterogeneity perspective, and its relationship to gang membership.

Individual Differences and Gang Membership

To determine the current body of research on individual differences and gang joining, we proceeded in three steps. First, we referenced empirical works on individual differences within the broader criminological research (e.g., Nagin and Paternoster 1993), as well as prior work we were aware of (e.g., Kissner and Pyrooz 2009) to determine a starting array of individual differences linked to gang membership. Second, we conducted a systematic literature review search using Google Scholar and keywords of individual differences (e.g., self-control, psychopathy) identified in step one. Finally, reference lists from identified journal articles were reviewed to ascertain potential studies that were not captured during the Google Scholar search.

Table 20.1 provides an overview of the studies we identified in rank order by the frequency with which the individual differences were used to study gang joining in published works. Before we elaborate theoretically and empirically on these relationships, we reach several observations. First, there are many studies examining individual differences as they relate to gang membership. Indeed, we uncovered 38 studies on this topic, which as a collective is quite substantial. However, within each of the 11 individual differences identified, there is a dearth of research; psychopathy (11) and self-control (8) had the largest inventories of empirical study, with the remaining individual differences are covered by four or fewer studies each. Second, nearly all these studies employed cross-sectional research designs. While individual differences are theoretically rank order and time stable, there is research demonstrating attitudinal and behavioral shifts corresponding with gang joining and leaving. As such, longitudinal research would provide further evidence to reach firm conclusions about selection into gangs. Finally, for most of the individual differences, evidence of a selection mechanism into gangs is mixed, a point we return to after each section.

Low Self-Control

Low self-control is the inability to consider long-term consequences or delay immediate gratification for long-term benefits. Individuals with low self-control exhibit six characteristics that elevate one's predisposition to engage in deviance: impulsivity, short-sightedness, risk seeking, action oriented, volatile tempered, and self-centeredness. Gottfredson and Hirschi (1990) introduced self-control to criminology in their general theory of crime, where they argued that self-control is developed through parental socialization and is rank-order stable after age 10. There is a long record of studies linking self-control to a variety of criminal behaviors. A meta-analysis of 99 empirical studies looked at the relationship between self-control and deviance (Vazsonyi, Mikuška, and Kelley 2017). Findings indicated that self-control is a moderately strong predictor of all types of deviance ($r = 0.53$), with general deviance ($r = 0.56$) and physical violence ($r = 0.46$) having the strongest effect sizes.

From a self-control perspective, individuals who eventually join gangs will demonstrate low self-control before, during, and after gang membership, making the relationship between gang membership and offending spurious. This is decisively clear according to Gottfredson and Hirschi (1990), who stated that "there is no need for theories designed specifically to account for gang crime" (214). Youth with low self-control are "unreliable, untrustworthy, selfish, and thoughtless" and "do not tend to make good friends" (89–90). Because of these qualities, they have trouble forming lasting relationships with prosocial peers and tend to "gravitate to the street," in turn, winding up in the company of

Table 20.1 Summary of Studies on the Gang Membership/Individual Differences Links

PSYCHOPATHY

STUDY	SAMPLE	STUDY DESIGN	FINDING(S)
Ang et al. (2015) Singapore	– Student sample – 1,027 adolescents – 5% gang	Cross-sectional	– No association – Psychopathy was not a significant predictor of self-reported gang membership.
Carson and Ray (2019) Philadelphia and Phoenix, USA	– Offender sample – 1,264 adolescents – 17% gang	Prospective longitudinal	– + Association – Compared with non-gang members, the adult joiner, persister group scored lower on antisocial/lifestyle factors and higher on affective/interpersonal factors.
Chu et al. (2014) Singapore	– Offender sample – 168 adolescent males – 64% gang	Cross-sectional	– No association – The impulsive-irresponsible dimension significantly predicted gang membership. After controlling for covariates that could be endogenous to psychopathy, this difference disappeared.
Dmitrieva et al. (2014) Philadelphia and Phoenix, USA	– Offender sample – 1,170 adolescents – 26% gang; 11% gang leadership over the last 7 pooled-period years	Prospective longitudinal	– + Association – Psychopathy was not predictive of low-level gang membership. The grandiose-manipulative dimension was predictive of gang leadership, which changed from a negative to a positive relationship over age.
Dupéré et al. (2007) Canada (nationally representative sample)	– Community sample – 3,522 adolescents – 6% gang	Prospective longitudinal	– + Association – Adolescents with pre-existing psychopathic tendencies had 1.75 times greater odds of joining a gang than their peers without such tendencies.

(continued)

Table 20.1 Continued

PSYCHOPATHY

STUDY	SAMPLE	STUDY DESIGN	FINDING(S)
Joseph (2022) Philadelphia and Phoenix, USA	– Offender sample – 1,085 adolescents – 22% gang	Cross-sectional	– Mixed association – The interpersonal/affective and socially deviant/lifestyle factors were significantly correlated with gang membership across sexes. Girls with higher scores on the socially deviant/lifestyle factors were 1.3 times more likely to be a gang member. Boys with higher scores on the interpersonal/affective factor were 1.1 times more likely to be a gang member, however, this was marginally significant (p=0.05). When examining the full sample, there was no association between the factors of psychopathy and gang membership.
Joseph and Rembert (2021) Philadelphia and Phoenix, USA	– Offender sample – 948 adolescents – 24% gang	Cross-sectional	– + Association – Psychopathy significantly predicted gang membership in both males and females. Youth with psychopathic characteristics were 1.05 times more likely to be a gang member.
Mallion and Wood (2021) UK (Category C public-sector training prison)	– Offender sample – 73 male adults – 60% gang	Cross-sectional within-participants design	– No association – Callous-unemotional traits could not differentiate between street gang members and non-prisoners.
Thornton et al. (2015) Jefferson Parish, LA; Orange County, CA; Philadelphia, PA	– Offender sample – 1,216 adolescent boys – 5% gang during the past 6 months; 5% gang during life	Cross-sectional	– + Association – Callous-unemotional traits were associated with gang membership.
Valdez et al. (2000) Texas, USA	– Community sample – 75 adolescent boys – 67% gang	Cross-sectional	– + Association – Gang members demonstrated higher levels of overall psychopathy and higher levels on the affective and behavioral psychopathy factors than non-gang members.

Table 20.1 Continued

PSYCHOPATHY			
STUDY	SAMPLE	STUDY DESIGN	FINDING(S)
Vaughn et al. (2009) Missouri, USA	– Offender sample – 267 adolescents – 46% gang	Cross-sectional	– + Association – Secondary psychopaths, characterized by traits within the affective and lifestyle facets, were more likely to join a gang (59.8%) than primary psychopaths, characterized by traits within the interpersonal facet (50.0%) and individuals without psychopathic traits (37.8%).

LOW SELF-CONTROL			
STUDY	SAMPLE	STUDY DESIGN	FINDING(S)
Fox et al. (2013) Florida, USA	– Offender sample – 2,008 adults – 15% gang	Cross-sectional	– + Association – Gang members reported significantly lower self-control compared to non-gang members; variation in gang joining existed across all self-control groups.
Hope (2003) Hope and Damphousse (2002) Fayetteville, AR	– Student sample – 1,139 adolescents	Cross-sectional	– + Association – Both attitudinal and behavioral self-control were significant predictors of current gang membership. – Low self-control was a significant predictor of former and current gang membership.
Kissner and Pyrooz (2009) California, USA	– Offender sample – 200 adults – 17% current and 14% former gang	Cross-sectional	– + Association – Self-control significantly predicted current gang membership, but not former gang membership. Controlling for differential association nullified the relationship.
Lynskey et al. (2000) Eleven cities in the USA	– Student sample – 5,935 adolescents – 12% gang	Cross-sectional	– + Association – Low self-control was a significant predictor of gang centrality; youth who were more deeply involved self-reported lower levels of self-control.

(continued)

Table 20.1 Continued

PSYCHOPATHY

STUDY	SAMPLE	STUDY DESIGN	FINDING(S)
Olate et al. (2015) San Salvador, El Salvador	– Community sample – 184 adolescents and adults – 65% gang	Cross-sectional	– + Association – Compared with non-gang high-risk youth, gang members reported significantly lower levels of self-control.
Pyrooz et al. (2021) Seven cities in the USA	– Student sample – 3,820 adolescents – 13% gang over the five pooled years	Prospective longitudinal	– + Association – Low self-control had a direct positive effect on the likelihood of onset of gang membership at the subsequent wave. However, it was not the only significant factor.
Wu and Pyrooz (2016) Arizona, Massachusetts, New Mexico, and South Carolina, USA	– Student sample – 1,185 adolescents – 26% gang	Prospective longitudinal	– + Association – Compared to those who did not join a gang, future gang joiners showed significantly higher levels of risk seeking, temper, and self-centeredness, as well as lower levels of empathy, four factors related to self-control.

ANTISOCIAL PERSONALITY DISORDER

STUDY	SAMPLE	STUDY DESIGN	FINDING(S)
Coid et al. (2013) UK (representative sample of young men)	– Community sample – 4,664 adult males – 2% gang	Cross-sectional	– + Association – Antisocial personality disorder (ASPD) traits were more prevalent among gang members than non-gang members; 57.4 times greater odds in gang than non-gang non-violent men and 6.5 times greater odds in gang than non-gang violent men.
Egan and Beadman (2011) UK (Category B prison)	– Offender sample – 152 adult males – 38% former; 9% current; 10% intend to join	Cross-sectional	– + Association – ASPD predicted gang involvement.
Mallion and Wood (2021) UK (Category C public-sector training prison)	– Offender sample – 73 adult males – 60% gang	Cross-sectional within-participants design	– + Association – Street gang prisoners scored significantly higher ($p=0.004$) on ASPD traits than non-gang prisoners.
Wood et al. (2017) UK (representative sample of young men)	– Community sample – 1,539 adult males – 15% gang (7% gang members, 8% gang affiliates)	Cross-sectional	– + Association – Gang members had the highest levels of ASPD, followed by gang affiliates, while non-gang violent men maintained the lowest levels.

Table 20.1 Continued

PSYCHOPATHY

STUDY	SAMPLE	STUDY DESIGN	FINDING(S)

BEHAVIORAL DISORDERS: CONDUCT DISORDER AND OPPOSITIONAL DEFIANT DISORDER

STUDY	SAMPLE	STUDY DESIGN	FINDING(S)
Lahey et al. (1999) Pittsburgh, USA	– Student sample – 185 Black adolescent males – 14% gang	Prospective longitudinal	– + Association – A higher prevalence of conduct disorder (CD) behavior at baseline predicted future gang joining. Results showed considerable overlap in the distributions of CD at baseline, indicating variation within groups.
Harris et al. (2013) Texas, USA	– Offender sample – 7,615 adolescents – 11% gang	Retrospective cross-sectional design with an official-report clinical interview	– + Association – Gang membership was associated with 4.05 greater odds of diagnosis of CD. – Gang membership was associated with 1.24 greater odds of diagnosis of oppositional defiant disorder (ODD).
Gomez Auyong et al. (2018) Avon, UK	– Community sample – 7,219 adolescent females – 1% gang	Prospective longitudinal	– No association – ODD was not a predictor of future gang membership among women who admitted to crime commission.
Smith et al. (2019) Avon, UK	– Community sample – 15,445 adolescents – 5% gang	Prospective longitudinal	– No association – ODD was not a predictor of future gang membership.

EMOTIONAL INTELLIGENCE AND EMPATHY

STUDY	SAMPLE	STUDY DESIGN	FINDING(S)
Mallion and Wood (2021) UK (Category C public-sector training prison)	– Offender sample – 73 adults – 60% gang	Cross-sectional	– No association – Compared to non-gang prisoners, street gang prisoners scored lower on emotional intelligence, but this difference was not statistically significant ($p=0.06$).
Lenzi et al. (2015) California, USA	– Student sample – 26,232 adolescents – 8% gang	Cross-sectional	– + Association – High levels of empathy were predictive of a decreased likelihood of gang membership.

(continued)

Table 20.1 Continued

PSYCHOPATHY

STUDY	SAMPLE	STUDY DESIGN	FINDING(S)
Lenzi et al. (2019) California, USA	– Student sample – 11,753 adolescents – 6% gang	Cross-sectional	– + Association – High levels of emotional competence, including empathy, were predictive of a decreased likelihood of gang membership.
Olate et al. (2012) San Salvador, El Salvador	– Community sample – 174 adolescents – 67% gang	Cross-sectional	– + Association – Youth gang members had significantly lower levels of empathy than non-gang member counterparts.
Wu and Pyrooz (2016) Arizona, Massachusetts, New Mexico, and South Carolina, USA	– Student sample – 1,185 adolescents – 26% gang	Prospective longitudinal	– + Association – Respondents who had joined a gang at wave 2 showed significantly ($p<0.05$) lower levels on empathy at wave 1 compared to non-gang youth.

GENETICS

STUDY	SAMPLE	STUDY DESIGN	FINDING(S)
Barnes et al. (2012) USA (nationally representative sample)	– Student sample – 4,534 adolescents (used sibling/cousin pairs) – 17% "ever" gang	Prospective longitudinal design and behavioral genetic modeling	– + Association – Genetic factors accounted for approximately 26% of the variance in gang membership. Non-shared environments accounted for a larger percentage (~74%) of the variance in gang membership.
Beaver et al. (2010) USA (nationally representative sample)	– Student sample – 2,196 adolescents – 4% gang	Prospective longitudinal	– Mixed association – For males, MAOA was a predictor of gang membership; those with low MAOA genotype were 1.94 times more likely to join a gang. For females, MAOA was not a predictor of gang membership.
Connolly and Beaver (2015) USA (nationally representative sample)	– Community sample – 1,304 sibling pairs – 11% "ever" gang	Prospective longitudinal	– + Association – Genetic factors account for 77% of the variance in gang membership.

Table 20.1 Continued

PSYCHOPATHY

STUDY	SAMPLE	STUDY DESIGN	FINDING(S)

LOW SELF-ESTEEM

STUDY	SAMPLE	STUDY DESIGN	FINDING(S)
Dukes et al. (1997) Colorado, USA	– Student sample – 11,023 adolescents – 3.9% wannabes; 4.7% former; 5.4% current gang	Cross-sectional	– + Association – Those who wanted to join gangs had low self-esteem, which increased when they joined. Wannabes had significantly lower self-esteem than non-gang members.
Wang (1994) Florida, USA	– Student sample – 155 adolescents – 32% gang	Cross-sectional	– + Association – Gang members exhibited lower levels of self-esteem than non-gang members.
Watkins and Melde (2016) USA (nationally representative sample)	– Student sample – 11,153 adolescents – 5% gang	Prospective longitudinal	– No Association – Differences in self-esteem between gang and non-gang members were negligible.

MORAL DISENGAGEMENT

STUDY	SAMPLE	STUDY DESIGN	FINDING(S)
Alleyne and Wood (2010) UK	– Student sample – 798 adolescents – 9% peripheral – 7% gang	Cross-sectional	– No Association – Anti-authority attitudes may justify gang involvement better than moral disengagement or it could be that those who join gangs have already set aside their morals.
Frisby-Osman and Wood (2020) UK	– Student sample – 91 adolescents – 35% gang	Cross-sectional between-participants design	– + Association – Gang-involved youth scored significantly higher ($p<0.001$) on moral disengagement than non-gang youth.

INTELLIGENCE

STUDY	SAMPLE(S)	STUDY DESIGN	FINDING(S)
Seals and Stern (2013) – USA (nationally representative sample) – Chicago (city representative sample)	– Community sample – 6,491 adolescents – 14.4% gang – Community sample – 4,937 adolescents – 8% gang	Prospective longitudinal	– Association – Lower measures of cognitive ability significantly predicted gang participation even after accounting for a variety of other characteristics.

Note. Psychopathy section revised from Tostlebe and Pyrooz (2022).

one another. However, it is possible that the association between gang membership and offending is not spurious owing to self-control; many sociological perspectives privilege the role of peers and gangs in the explanation of crime. Furthermore, while Gottfredson and Hirschi viewed self-control as rank-order stable across the life course, recent research suggests there is rank-order *in*stability in self-control (Burt 2020), which may be influenced by environmental influences (Wikström and Treiber 2007) or intra-group processes that alter behaviors, identity, beliefs, and routines (Melde and Esbensen 2011).

Evidence that explores the link between self-control and gang membership leads to unclear conclusions. Research on this association points to a weak relationship between self-control and gang membership; however, this research relies primarily on cross-sectional data, which prevents strong conclusions on the selection hypothesis. One exception is Pyrooz et al. (2021), who used a prospective longitudinal research design over five years and concluded that while low self-control has a significant direct positive effect on the onset of gang membership, self-control was not the singular selection factor contributing to gang joining. Even so, this study provides clarity to the selection hypothesis: "self-control is one, but not the only, source of selection into gangs" (Pyrooz et al. 2021, 243).

Psychopathy

Psychopathy is a personality disorder generally defined by a constellation of interpersonal (e.g., superficial charm), affective (e.g., callous), lifestyle (e.g., thrill seeking), and antisocial (e.g., criminal versatility) characteristics (Cleckley 1941; Hare 2003). Although the concept of psychopathy has been around for over 200 years (Pinel 1806; Prichard 1842) and the term has existed for over 100 years, it was popularized and precisely defined in 1941 by Hervey Cleckley and later elaborated on by Robert Hare (1983, 1996). Currently, psychopathy falls under antisocial personality disorder in the DSM-5. While low self-control is commonly conceived as the quintessential population heterogeneity perspective, "the constellation of features that comprise psychopathy may better measure antisocial propensity" (McCuish, Bouchard, and Beauregard 2021, 694). Indeed, psychopathy combines characteristics of low self-control *and* interpersonal deficits that often provide a vehicle for offending. Furthermore, psychopathy "[is] diffuse and inflexible, begins in adolescence or early adulthood, [and] it is stable over time" (American Psychiatric Association 2013, 645). Researchers report moderate-to-high rank-order stability (ρ = 0.31 to 0.76), as well as individual-level stability from mid-adolescence to early adulthood (e.g., Lynam et al. 2007; Hemphälä et al. 2015). There is a long record of empirical studies linking psychopathy to a wide range of criminal behaviors with an overall meta-analytic effect size between 0.23 and 0.68 (e.g., Geerlings et al. 2020; Fox and DeLisi 2019), akin to self-control, with stronger effect sizes related to violent behavior.

The features of psychopathy and psychopathic traits provide a basis for selection into a gang (Sanchez-Jankowski 1991; Yablonsky 1962; see also, Tostlebe and Pyrooz 2022). Evidence for the selection explanation of gang membership using psychopathy begins akin to low self-control: by acknowledging that people with psychopathic personality traits may have difficulty making and keeping friends due to traits within the interpersonal and affective facets of the personality disorder, "pushing" them to select into delinquent peer groups, like gangs (for a review of push and pull factors, see Densley 2015). The gang also "pulls" those with psychopathic personality characteristics toward it. Indeed, those with "impulsive, selfish, callous, egocentric, and aggressive tendencies can easily blend in with—and may even set the tone for—many of the gang's activities" (Hare 1999, 176). Studies have demonstrated evidence of within-individual change in psychopathy, highlighting developmental malleability in this construct (e.g., Hawes et al. 2018; McCuish and Lussier 2018), particularly between the ages of 16–18 and 32 (Bergstrøm and Farrington 2021), the former describing a common age range for joining a gang (Pyrooz and Sweeten 2015). This body of research raises continued questions about the gang–psychopathy link, including whether psychopathy is a rank-order stable individual difference that can predict who will join gangs.

When it comes to the empirical evidence, Tostlebe and Pyrooz (2022) contend that "the state of the evidence is premature to afford empirical primacy to either [psychopathy as a source or consequence of gang membership]" (324). This conclusion is spurred by the fact that nearly all studies examining the psychopathy–gang membership link employ cross-sectional research designs. Given that there is evidence of within-individual change in psychopathy, there is a need for longitudinal research. Additionally, the evidence of a selection effect is mixed—some research reveals psychopathy is an individual difference that corresponds to gang membership, while other work reveals no association at all.

Antisocial Personality Disorder

Antisocial personality disorder (ASPD) is defined as a pattern of maladaptive behavior characterized by deception and violation of the personal and property rights of others without remorse. ASPD has four diagnostic criteria (American Psychiatric Association 2013):

A. A pervasive pattern of disregard for and violation of the rights of others, occurring since age 15, as indicated by three (or more) of the following:
  1. Failure to conform to social norms with respect to lawful behaviors, as indicated by repeatedly performing acts that are grounds for arrest.
  2. Deceitfulness, as indicated by repeated lying, use of aliases, or conning others for personal profit or pleasure.
  3. Impulsivity or failure to plan ahead.
  4. Irritability and aggressiveness, as indicated by repeated physical fights or assaults.
  5. Reckless disregard for safety of self or others.
  6. Consistent irresponsibility, as indicated by repeated failure to sustain consistent work behavior or honor financial obligations.
  7. Lack of remorse, as indicated by being indifferent to or rationalizing having hurt, mistreated, or stolen from another.
B. The individual is at least age 18 years.
C. There is evidence of conduct disorder with onset before age 15 years.
D. The occurrence of antisocial behavior is not exclusively during the course of schizophrenia or bipolar disorder. (659)

Influential to the diagnostic criteria for ASPD was the work of Lee Robins (1966), who conducted a longitudinal study of 524 adolescents. Robins concluded that "ASPD is a chronic, persistent disorder that seldom remits" (Black 2015, 310). Indeed, research reports high rank-order stability (ρ = 0.58 to 0.65) over a 10 year period, while mean levels of ASPD traits decrease to a moderate degree over time from late adolescence throughout adulthood (Reichborn-Kjennerud et al. 2015; Hopwood et al. 2013). Additionally, case reports and longitudinal studies link a high prevalence of ASPD traits in childhood to antisocial and violent behaviors in adulthood (Wojciechowski 2020; Shepherd, Campbell, and Ogloff 2018).

Given that violent behavior is also common among gang members, it is perhaps unsurprising that ASPD traits are related to gang membership (Raby and Jones 2016). As psychopathy falls under the category of ASPD, the theoretical mechanisms giving rise to gang membership align in large part with those from psychopathy. To be diagnosed with ASPD, individuals must be at least 18 years old. As individuals tend to join gangs around 15 years of age, a formal diagnosis of ASPD is off-the-table until after the selection process has generally occurred. However, early indicators of ASPD can be observed among children (see the discussion on conduct disorder below) and nearly 80% of people with ASPD develop their first symptom by age 11 (Black 2015). There are also indicators that crime-related traumatic events experienced *during* gang membership may increase the risk of developing ASPD (e.g., Wood and Dennard 2017). To establish whether ASPD influences selection into gang membership, longitudinal research is required. While the current inventory of empirical studies on ASPD demonstrates a positive association between ASPD traits and gang membership, all four studies employ cross-sectional research designs, severely restricting our ability to discern selection effects.

Behavioral Disorders: Conduct Disorder (CD) and Oppositional Defiant Disorder (ODD)

Conduct disorder is a behavioral disorder with three diagnostic criteria (American Psychiatric Association 2013):

A. A repetitive and persistent pattern of behavior in which the basic rights of others or major age-appropriate societal norms or rules are violated, as manifested by the presence of at least three of the following 15 criteria in the past 12 months from any of the categories below, with at least one criterion present in the past 6 months:

Aggression to People and Animals

1. Often bullies, threatens, or intimidates others
2. Often initiates physical fights
3. Has used a weapon that can cause serious physical harm to others (e.g., a bat, brick, broken bottle, knife, gun)
4. Has been physically cruel to people
5. Has been physically cruel to animals

6. Has stolen while confronting a victim (e.g., mugging, purse snatching, extortion, armed robbery)
7. Has forced someone into sexual activity

Destruction of Property

8. Has deliberately engaged in fire setting with the intention of causing serious damage
9. Has deliberately destroyed others' property (other than by fire setting)

Deceitfulness or Theft

10. Has broken into someone else's house, building, or car
11. Often lies to obtain goods or favors or to avoid obligations (i.e., "cons" others)
12. Has stolen items of nontrivial value without confronting a victim (e.g., shoplifting, but without breaking and entering; forgery)

Serious Violations of Rules

13. Often stays out at night despite parental prohibitions, beginning before age 13 years
14. Has run away from home overnight at least twice while living in parental or parental surrogate home (or once without returning for a lengthy period)
15. Is often truant from school, beginning before age 13 years

B. The disturbance in behavior causes clinically significant impairment in social, academic, or occupational functioning,

C. If the individual is age 18 years or older, criteria are not met for Antisocial Personality Disorder.

Children and adolescents with CD demonstrate stable and persistent patterns of behavior (Frick and Loney 1999). However, as with psychopathy, recent research has identified possible distinct trajectories of CD traits, with some trajectories demonstrating individual variability and change in problem behavior (both increasing and decreasing) over time (e.g., Frick and Nigg 2012). Individuals who are diagnosed with CD are, by definition, more likely to engage in deviant and criminal behavior than those who do not satisfy the criteria for the disorder. In a thirty-year follow-up of former Norwegian child psychiatric in-patients, Mordre et al. (2011) found that a conduct disorder diagnosis significantly predicted future criminal behavior.

Oppositional defiant disorder (ODD) is a disorder of emotion regulation characterized by irritability, hostility, and vindictive behavior. Specifically, ODD has three diagnostic criteria (American Psychiatric Association 2013):

A. A pattern of angry/irritable mood, argumentative/defiant behavior, or vindictiveness lasting at least 6 months as evidenced by at least four symptoms from any of the following categories, and exhibited during interaction with at least one individual who is not a sibling:

Angry/Irritable Mood

1. Often loses temper
2. Is often touchy or easily annoyed
3. Is often angry and resentful

Argumentative/Defiant Behavior

4. Often argues with authority figures or, for children and adolescents, with adults
5. Often actively defies or refuses to comply with requests from authority figures or with rules
6. Often deliberately annoys others
7. Often blames others for his or her mistakes or misbehavior

Vindictiveness

8. Has been spiteful or vindictive at least twice within the past 6 months

B. The disturbance in behavior is associated with distress in the individual or others in his or her immediate social context (e.g., family, peer group, work colleagues) or it impacts negatively on social, educational, occupational, or other important areas of functioning,

C. The behavior does not occur exclusively during the course of a psychotic, substance use, depressive, or bipolar disorder. Also the criteria are not met for disruptive mood dysregulation disorder.

Typically, ODD has early onset at home and escalates to other contexts, such as school. Studies suggest that ODD is usually present as a precursor to childhood-onset conduct disorder (which is a precursor to psychopathy), but *most* children with ODD do not develop conduct disorder. However, independent of conduct disorder, ODD is a mostly stable disorder. A longitudinal study of preschool children demonstrated stability in ODD over a five-year period, leading the authors to conclude that "[w]hile some young children with ODD 'grow out of it,' a substantial proportion do not" (Lavigne et al. 2001, 1399). Like conduct disorder, ODD is significantly related to antisocial behavior in adolescence and adulthood (Langbehn et al. 1998; Plattner et al. 2009; for an exception see Boduszek et al. 2014).

Both CD and ODD can be diagnosed in childhood, making them relevant to the onset of gang membership during adolescence. As these behavioral disorders are disruptive in nature—characterized by a struggle to respect authority figures and behaviors that are disrespectful or harmful— they may naturally lead adolescents to self-select into gangs. Opposition toward authorities is common within gangs (e.g., Decker and Van Winkle 1996; Vigil 1988), and a lack of guilt and sympathy for others has been indicated as a risk factor for selecting into a gang (Peterson and Morgan 2014).

To our knowledge, only one study, which used a longitudinal research design, has examined the relationship between CD and gang membership. Lahey and colleagues (1999) conducted a six-year longitudinal study of 185 adolescent Black males (reduced sample) and found that conduct disorder traits identified at baseline were associated with an increased risk of joining a gang by subsequent waves. Retrospective cross-sectional studies have demonstrated an association between ODD and gang membership, where gang members had higher rates of ODD diagnosis than non-gang members (e.g., Harris et al. 2013). Only one project on ODD employed a longitudinal research design, concluding that ODD traits measured at age seven were *not* predictive of future gang involvement at age 17 (Smith, Gomez Auyong, and Ferguson 2019; Gomez Auyong, Smith, and Ferguson 2018). All and all, the research is decisively mixed regarding the selection hypothesis for behavioral disorders and gang joining, with some support for CD.

Emotional Intelligence and Empathy

Emotional intelligence refers to the ability to think about one's emotions and use them to aid reasoning and to identify with another's emotional state. Empathy is the ability to understand and share the feelings of another. These are individual characteristics that have been identified as moderately rank-order stable constructs from early childhood to young adulthood (Oh et al. 2020; Parker et al. 2005). Additionally, both have been linked with deviant behavior (e.g., Megreya 2015; Jolliffe and Farrington 2004), in particular violence. This finding is unsurprising, as high levels of emotional intelligence and empathy would constrain people from engaging in harmful criminal activities.

Furthermore, low emotional intelligence and a lack of empathy have been identified—both theoretically and in research—as possible risk factors for gang joining (Mallion and Wood 2018). Drawing from research on the gang–offending link, it seems feasible that low levels of emotional intelligence may be associated with gang membership. This is because gang membership commonly involves acts of interpersonal violence, and the influence of emotions is established as a predictor of violent and aggressive behaviors (García-Sancho, Salguero, and Fernández-Berrocal 2016). "[S]election on propensity toward *violence and aggression is built into the DNA of gangs*" (Wu and Pyrooz 2016, 533), which naturally leads to a description of gang members as lacking in emotional intelligence and empathy. Furthermore, through intra-gang micro-level processes (McGloin and Collins 2015), such as *normative influence*, which is the way gangs establish and enforce commitment to the group, as well as the display of acceptable norms and values, gang members may be socialized to beliefs, norms, and practices that place value on violence while deemphasizing victims and their emotional states.

Research surrounding emotional intelligence and gang membership is sparse. A recent study on 74 prisoners in the United Kingdom concluded that emotional intelligence was lower among street gang prisoners (Mallion and Wood 2021), although results were not statistically significant, the sample was small, and the research design was cross-sectional. A lack of empathy is commonly observed among gang members (e.g., Salas-Wright, Olate, and Vaughn 2013), which has led scholars to examine whether low empathy predicts gang joining. The bulk of work on the gang–empathy link is cross-sectional; although results do indicate differences, with gang members reporting significantly lower levels of empathy than non-gang members. Only one study employed a longitudinal design, finding support for a selection effect between empathy and gang membership. Using a three-wave sample of 2,353 students, Wu and Pyrooz (2016) examined empathy before and during gang membership, finding that those low in empathy were at a greater risk of joining a gang and that their empathy further declined during gang membership.

Genetics

The term "genetics," or how certain traits are passed from parents to offspring as a result of changes in DNA sequence, was coined in 1906 to designate the science of heredity (Gayon 2016). Regarding stability, "the genetic composition of individuals is . . . fixed at contraception" (Knafo and Plomin 2006, 773). However, different genes may be expressed at different developmental periods (Knafo and Plomin 2006), indicating that behavioral changes may occur through shifts in genetic effects at different ages. In criminology, there has been an accelerated amount of research examining genetic influences—as stable individual differences—on antisocial behaviors (e.g., Wright et al. 2008). Most of this research has focused on partitioning the variation in deviance into the proportion caused by genetic influences and the proportion caused by the environment. Studies on genetic influences (i.e., heritability) commonly compare phenotypes within and between families, revealing that genetic factors explain a substantial portion (e.g., 30–90%) of the variance in criminal and analogous behaviors, and little significance is provided to shared environments (e.g., Wright et al. 2008; Beaver et al. 2013).

Behavioral genetic research has also examined gang membership, focusing on general genetic factors, as well as the candidate gene, monoamine oxidase A (MAOA) or the "warrior gene," which is related to increased levels of aggression and violence. The idea is that those with certain genetic coding are more likely to join gangs because they self-select into groups based on shared characteristics (e.g., personality traits and behaviors). Recent research in genetics and psychiatry suggests that friendship dyads appear to have correlated genotypes (i.e., the genetic constitution of a person; e.g., Fowlera, Settles, and Christakis 2011) and variation in the propensity to affiliate with antisocial friendship networks is partially accounted for by genetic factors (Kendler et al. 2007).

Results from studies examining the genetic–gang link suggest that much of the selection process into gangs can be explained by genetic factors. Indeed, analyses of kinship pairs (e.g., twin pairs, full sibling pairs, cousin pairs) point to genetic influences as an explanation for a large amount of variance in gang membership, while the remaining variance was accounted for by non-shared environmental influences (Connolly and Beaver 2015; Barnes, Boutwell, and Fox 2012). Specific polymorphism variants in the MAOA gene (i.e., low MAOA activity alleles) also predicted gang joining (Beaver et al. 2010), however, this result was only found among males and the DNA data were not nationally representative. While genetic research designs suggest that gang affiliation is significantly influenced by genetic factors, only a handful of empirical studies have been devoted to the influence of genetics on selection into gangs, and the range of genetic factors' influence on the variance in gang membership is large (26–77%), invoking questions regarding the precision of this information. Additionally, much of the research on the genetic–gang link is conceptually flawed as it is atheoretical (i.e., it lacks details on how and why genetics matter) and fails to account for household discordances in gang involvement[1] or sturdy *shared* predictors of gang involvement (e.g., parental supervision; Hill et al., 1999). As such, it is premature to reach any sound conclusions on the topic.

Low Self-Esteem

Self-esteem is a person's evaluation of their personal worth, value, or importance (Blascovich and Tomaka 1991). Rosenberg (1979) explained that self-esteem is composed of self-acceptance, self-respect, and self-worth. Self-esteem scholars have generally discussed self-esteem as a stable trait (Harter 1998; Rosenberg 1965), however, the assumption of stability has not gone unquestioned (see Conley 1984). One study found that self-esteem was a relatively stable trait, with its stability becoming more pronounced as one ages (Trzesniewski, Donnellan, and Robins 2003). In other words, self-esteem stability is weakest in childhood but grows stronger in adolescence and early adulthood, which could be influenced by other factors. A meta-analysis of 42 studies between 1990 and 2015 found that self-esteem had a significant negative relationship with delinquency, albeit a small one (Mier and Ladny 2018).

Scholars have argued that low self-esteem could lead to self-selection into gang membership as gangs offer those with low self-esteem a sense of belonging and peer approval (Hirschi 1969; Leary, Schreindorfer, and Haupt 1995). A study concluded that low self-esteem was correlated with gang joining across all ethnoracial categories (Wang 1994). In testing Thornberry et al.'s (1993) model, Dukes et al. (1997, 159) found support for the selection hypothesis—self-esteem predicted gang membership—and concluded that gang members often had low self-worth and identity problems. Finally, Alleyne and Wood (2010) observed that prospective, current, and former gang members had lower self-esteem than people with no gang involvement.

Despite these findings, scholars have often failed to find that self-esteem predicts gang membership (e.g., Thornberry et al. 2003; Watkins and Melde 2016). A shortcoming of most studies on the self-esteem–gang link is that they use a cross-sectional research design. This is only truly problematic when attempting to determine causality and if self-esteem is not rank-order stable. Additionally, most studies (e.g., Dmitrieva et al. 2014) observe the relationship between participants and self-esteem *after* they have joined a gang versus before, which would better indicate whether self-esteem predicts gang joining. At best, self-esteem appears to be correlated with gang joining; however, the evidence is not robust enough to make such claims.

Moral Disengagement

Moral disengagement is a process through which an individual sidelines their moral standards, allowing justification for deviant behavior (Bandura et al. 1996). Bandura et al. (1996) outlined eight interrelated mechanisms—advantageous comparison, attribution of blame, dehumanization, diffusion of responsibility, displacement of responsibility, distorting consequences, euphemistic language, and moral justification—that allow a person to set aside their morality and engage in injurious behavior (367, 374). Although there is some malleability, moral disengagement is generally seen "as a relatively stable cognitive orientation" (Moore 2015, 202) and has been found to be correlated with delinquent behavior (Agnew 1994; Férriz-Romeral et al. 2019).

Moral disengagement may lead to self-selection into gangs. For example, moral disengagement may be conducive to gang joining as gangs foster an environment where violence is encouraged (Alleyne, Fernandes, and Pritchard 2014), and people scoring high on this individual difference may feel at home in their attitudes and behaviors compared to when in conventional society. When entering a gang, individuals with higher levels of moral disengagement may experience positive reinforcement, which could further elevate their already heightened moral disengagement (Bandura et al. 1996; Frisby-Osman and Wood 2020).

Studies on the effects of moral disengagement on gang joining are few and far between. What research has been done, however, found that gang members typically engage in moral disengagement more often than non-gang members. Alleyne and colleagues (2014) highlighted that dehumanizing victims mediated the gang membership to violence relationship. A study of 91 youths (ages 11–18) found that moral disengagement was the second strongest predictor of gang involvement (behind rumination) out of eight potential predictors included in the study (Frisby-Osman and Wood 2020). However, the cross-sectional design restricted the study's ability to untangle whether this link was predictive. In other words, are the people who engage in moral disengagement also those most inclined to join a gang, or is it a spurious effect? An earlier study found no direct effect of moral disengagement on gang involvement after it was mediated by anti-authority attitudes (Alleyne and Wood 2010). Indeed, the authors concluded "since moral disengagement on its own did not have an effect on gang involvement, anti-authority attitudes may serve as a justification for gang membership, perhaps serving as a cognitive strategy to rationalize gang involvement" (22), which is in concordance with a selection hypothesis. The evidence appears to support the selection hypothesis; however, moral disengagement is one of the most understudied individual differences we reviewed.

Intelligence

Intelligence is the ability to acquire and apply knowledge and skills. Lower intelligence quotient (IQ) level, a score from standardized tests designed to assess human intelligence, has been critiqued as simply reflecting middle-class membership rather than innate intelligence (Richardson 2002). Even so, while highly disputed, it is expected that individual differences in intelligence profiles remain relatively stable over the lifespan (Larsen, Hartmann, and Nyborg 2008), which is consistent with a rank-order stable individual difference. Within criminological scholarship, low IQ has been linked to criminogenic outcomes (e.g., Beaver and Wright 2011; although see Ozer and Akbas 2020).

IQ may be a risk factor for gang membership (Spergel 1995). Intelligence is generally very controversial; however, scholars have examined intelligence when looking at selection into gangs and we look to establish its credence. Sociologists have noted gang members tend to have lower levels of cognitive ability compared to non-gang members (e.g., Short and Strodtbeck 1965). A variety of factors play into this relationship. For example, individuals with low IQ may experience a lack of inclusion, integration, motivation, and differential treatment in school, causing them to seek alternative forms of success and socialization, which could be a gang (Cohen 1955). Indeed, between 19–25% of students report gang activity in their public schools, and 10–30% of students self-report gang membership (Clark, Pyrooz, and Randa 2018). Second, low IQ individuals may find safety and socioeconomic advantages in gang activities not provided to them through other avenues (Seals and Stern 2013). Third, gangs are active in the selection process, reading "between the signs" to avoid adverse selection, an evolving process that continues throughout gang membership (Pyrooz and Densley 2016, 460). Through this process, gangs may purposefully select low IQ individuals into the gang, as they may have fewer options outside gang life (Seals and Stern 2013), thus increasing commitment.

When it comes to the evidence, using longitudinal data from the National Longitudinal Survey of Youth and the Project on Human Development in Chicago Neighborhoods, Seals and Stern (2013) concluded that low IQ was a robust predictor of gang participation in both datasets. While research does find support for IQ as a risk factor, we emphasize that this conclusion is based on one empirical study—although longitudinal in design and drawing from two sources of data—and more research is required to make any firm conclusions.

Charting Directions Forward

We conclude this chapter by highlighting key areas that future research on individual differences should address. Specifically, we will discuss three broad areas: empirics, data, and theory. Addressing these areas will be critical for research moving forward on individual propensities and selection into gangs. We also believe it is crucial to acknowledge that many of our recommendations for directions forward are not mutually exclusive, but rather intertwined.

The best tool to have in a controversial debate is sound empirical evidence. There is almost de facto opposition to this line of inquiry, which comes from ideological *not* empirical grounds, and therein lies the problem. We should be free to formulate falsifiable hypotheses, test these hypotheses, and let science guide the argument. Even if critics of studies on individual differences and gang joining are *correct* in their presumption that this research has no merit, why not allow research to solidify their stance so we can continue moving forward in other directions? If critics are *wrong* about the merits of this research, they could be obstructing the development of appropriate and effective theoretical knowledge, as well as practitioner responses to gangs. If the current body of research tells us nothing else, it is that there is some salience to individual differences. Indeed, as stated by Dupéré and colleagues (2007), "when facing the opportunity to join a gang, preexisting configurations of individual traits may greatly increase the likelihood that any given adolescent actually join the gang" (1036). Moreover, some individual differences may be stronger risk factors than others; we found the best evidence for self-control and psychopathy as risk factors for gang joining. Perhaps this is an artifact of the larger body of research dedicated to these individual differences compared to the others identified, but we will only solidify our knowledge on the value of individual differences by examining them further. Rather than engaging in an emotionally charged debate about the relevance of individual differences, we encourage scholars to return to empirical research, which can help drive research, policy, and practice.

Second, better data are needed to parse out which individual differences are most—if at all—relevant for joining a gang. By "better" we mean both in research design and measurement. When it comes to design, longitudinal studies were scarce in our review. This scarcity is likely attributed to the lack of current evidence on these individual differences, as well as the expense and time required to conduct a longitudinal study. Additionally, some individual differences require licensed practitioners to administer the survey questions, further heightening the expense of the study. However, despite these complications, longitudinal designs provide us with prospective and temporally ordered information needed to examine if there are statistically and substantively significant individual differences between those who join gangs and those who do not. Regarding measurement, many of the studies examined in this chapter used a measure of "ever" gang membership. This is problematic, as it combines selection and facilitation effects. Additionally, capturing current membership status (active or former) can provide a more nuanced discussion of variability. We also believe qualitative research could further examine the processes underlying the tripartite model (Tewksbury 2009). Unlike quantitative research, qualitative studies allow for the exploration of meaning and decision making. They can also establish causality, answering the question of why people acted a certain way.

Third, the study of individual differences should be further embedded within developmental and life-course criminological theory. The first aspect of this venture will be considering the interaction between individual differences and social influences. Based on our review of the literature, we find preliminary support for individual-level differences. However, given the lack of causal methodologies, most studies could not establish causality. Based on the research, we find it highly likely that both selection and facilitation mechanisms are interacting across each study included in this chapter, akin to a genetic-environment interaction (GxE). Much research favors Thornberry et al.'s enhancement hypothesis, followed by facilitation, and finally selection. Pyrooz et al. (2021) support this by stating, "[a] meta-analysis (Pyrooz et al. 2016) quantitatively synthesizing [the gang membership and delinquency] relationship found little evidence for pure selection, some evidence for pure facilitation, and *the most evidence for a blended, or enhancement, perspective*" (230, emphasis added). The second part of this venture regards the obvious fact that these risk factors are theorized to be rank-order stable over the life course; empirical research suggests otherwise, at least to some degree. What this means for research in the realm of individual differences is unclear, though there is evidence suggesting the possibility of social-environmental influences compromising their rank-order stability. Furthermore, the instability of individual differences indicates hope for future and current gang members through social influences, such as rehabilitative programming opportunities.

Conclusion

Individual differences have been a topic of inquiry since the early days of criminology (e.g., Lombroso 2006; Quetelet 1984; Wolfgang, Figlio, and Sellin 1972). Regarding gang members, however, the cupboard is relatively bare. We contend that some of the reasons for this have been sociologists' preference to focus on the macro-level of explanation or scholars being reluctant to pursue this line of research out of fear of the potential backlash they may face. The purpose of this chapter was to review what the literature says on individual differences and gang joining with the hope that it would bring empirical evidence back to this important scholarly debate. As discussed in the introduction, there are scholars who dismiss and even antagonize this area of research. These individuals often fall into the trap of trivializing or ignoring the crime and violence committed and experienced by gang members (for a review on gang homicide, see Sanchez, Decker, and Pyrooz 2021).

Jim Short (1998) once argued that we must be "*sensitive* to context. Doing so requires that our inquiries be guided by theoretically informed questions that are contextualized in terms of time and social location" (28). Short highlighted the importance of knowing what level of measurement and observation we are dealing with and that linking macro- and micro-level research may yield the nuances we need to understand human behavior. We concur. While we are not arguing individual differences hold *the* answer, we *do* contend that they are a piece of the puzzle, and we should not ignore them; preliminary research supports this contention.

Note

1. Hashimi, Wakefield, and Apel (2021) demonstrate a statistically significant, but not perfect, sibling influence on gang entry and reentry. There was not a significant sibling influence on gang exit.

References

Agnew, Robert. 1994. "The Techniques of Neutralization and Violence." *Criminology* 32 (4): 555–580.

Alleyne, Emma, Isabel Fernandes, and Elizabeth Pritchard. 2014. "Denying Humanness to Victims: How Gang Members Justify Violent Behavior." *Group Processes and Intergroup Relations* 17 (6): 750–762.

Alleyne, Emma, and Jane Wood. 2010. "Gang Involvement: Psychological and Behavioral Characteristics of Gang Members, Peripheral Youth, and Nongang Youth." *Aggressive Behavior* 36 (6): 423–436.

American Psychiatric Association. 2013. *Diagnostic and Statistical Manual of Mental Disorders*. 5th ed. Washington, DC.

Ang, Rebecca, Vivien Huan, Wei Teng Chan, Siew Ann Cheong, and Jia Ning Leaw. 2015. "The Role of Delinquency, Proactive Aggression, Psychopathy and Behavioral School Engagement in Reported Youth Gang Membership." *Journal of Adolescence* 41: 148–156.

Bandura, Albert, Claudio Barbaranelli, Gian Vittorio Caprara, and Concetta Pastorelli. 1996. "Mechanisms of Moral Disengagement in the Exercise of Moral Agency." *Journal of Personality and Social Psychology* 71 (2): 364.

Barnes, J. C., Brian Boutwell, and Kathleen Fox. 2012. "The Effect of Gang Membership on Victimization: A Behavioral Genetic Explanation." *Youth Violence and Juvenile Justice* 10 (3): 227–244.

Beaver, Kevin, Matt Delisi, Michael Vaughn, and J. C. Barnes. 2010. "Monoamine Oxidase A Genotype Is Associated with Gang Membership and Weapon Use." *Comprehensive Psychiatry* 51 (2): 130–134.

Beaver, Kevin, and John Paul Wright. 2011. "The Association between County-Level IQ and County-Level Crime Rates." *Intelligence* 39 (1): 22–26.

Beaver, Kevin, John Paul Wright, Brian Boutwell, J. C. Barnes, Matt DeLisi, and Michael Vaughn. 2013. "Exploring the Association between the 2-Repeat Allele of the MAOA Gene

Promoter Polymorphism and Psychopathic Personality Traits, Arrests, Incarceration, and Lifetime Antisocial Behavior." *Personality and Individual Differences* 54 (2): 164–168.

Bergstrøm, Henriette, and David Farrington. 2021. "Stability of Psychopathy in a Prospective Longitudinal Study: Results from the Cambridge Study in Delinquent Development." *Behavioral Sciences and the Law* 39 (5): 611–623.

Black, Donald. 2015. "The Natural History of Antisocial Personality Disorder." *Canadian Journal of Psychiatry* 60 (7): 309–314.

Blascovich, Jim, and Joseph Tomaka. 1991. "Measures of Self-Esteem." In *Measures of Personality and Social Psychological Attitudes*, edited by J. P. Robinson, P. R. Shaver, and L. S. Wrightsman, 115–1160. San Diego, CA: Academic Press.

Boduszek, Daniel, Rachel Belsher, Katie Dhingra, and Maria Ioannou. 2014. "Psychosocial Correlates of Recidivism in a Sample of Ex-Prisoners: The Role of Oppositional Defiant Disorder and Conduct Disorder." *Journal of Forensic Psychiatry & Psychology* 25 (1): 61–76.

Burt, Callie. 2020. "Self-Control and Crime: Beyond Gottfredson & Hirschi's Theory." *Annual Review of Criminology* 3 (1): 43–73.

Carson, Dena, and James Ray. 2019. "Do Psychopathic Traits Distinguish Trajectories of Gang Membership?" *Criminal Justice and Behavior* 46 (9): 1337–1355.

Cho, Sumi, Kimberlé Williams Crenshaw, and Leslie McCall. 2013. "Toward a Field of Intersectionality Studies: Theory, Applications, and Praxis." *Signs: Journal of Women in Culture and Society* 38 (4): 785–810.

Chu, Chi Meng, Michael Daffern, Stuart Thomas, Yaming Ang, and Mavis Long. 2014. "Criminal Attitudes and Psychopathic Personality Attributes of Youth Gang Offenders in Singapore." *Psychology, Crime and Law* 20 (3): 284–301.

Clark, Kendra, David Pyrooz, and Ryan Randa. 2018. "School of Hard Knocks: Gangs, Schools, and Education in the United States." In *The Wiley Handbook on Violence in Education: Forms, Factors, and Preventions*, edited by Harvey Shapiro, 203–225. Chichester, UK: John Wiley & Sons Inc.

Cleckley, Hervey. 1941. *The Mask of Sanity: An Attempt to Reinterpret the so-Called Psychopathic Personality*. St. Louis, MO: Mosby Company.

Cohen, Albert K. 1955. *Delinquent Boys: The Culture of the Gang*. Glencoe, IL: Free Press.

Coid, Jeremy, Simone Ullrich, Robert Keers, Paul Bebbington, Bianca DeStavola, Constantinos Kallis, Min Yang, David Reiss, Rachel Jenkins, and Peter Donnelly. 2013. "Gang Membership, Violence, and Psychiatric Morbidity." *American Journal of Psychiatry* 170 (9): 985–993.

Conley, James. 1984. "The Hierarchy of Consistency: A Review and Model of Longitudinal Findings on Adult Individual Differences in Intelligence, Personality and Self-Opinion." *Personality and Individual Differences* 5 (1): 11–25.

Connolly, Eric, and Kevin Beaver. 2015. "Guns, Gangs, and Genes: Evidence of an Underlying Genetic Influence on Gang Involvement and Carrying a Handgun." *Youth Violence and Juvenile Justice* 13 (3): 228–242.

Decker, Scott, David Pyrooz, and James Densley. 2022. *On Gangs*. Philadelphia, PA: Temple University Press.

Decker, Scott, and Barrik Van Winkle. 1996. *Life in the Gang: Family, Friends, and Violence*. Cambridge, UK: Cambridge University Press.

Densley, James. 2015. "Joining the Gang: A Process of Supply and Demand." In *The Handbook of Gangs*, edited by Scott Decker and David Pyrooz, 235–256. Chichester, UK: Wiley-Blackwell.

Dmitrieva, Julia, Lauren Gibson, Laurence Steinberg, Alex Piquero, and Jeffrey Fagan. 2014. "Predictors and Consequences of Gang Membership: Comparing Gang Members, Gang

Leaders, and Non-Gang-Affiliated Adjudicated Youth." *Journal of Research on Adolescence* 24 (2): 220–234.

Dukes, Richard, Ruben Martinez, and Judith Stein. 1997. "Precursors and Consequences of Membership in Youth Gangs." *Youth & Society* 29 (2): 139–165.

Dupéré, Véronique, Éric Lacourse, J. Douglas Willms, Frank Vitaro, and Richard Tremblay. 2007. "Affiliation to Youth Gangs during Adolescence: The Interaction between Childhood Psychopathic Tendencies and Neighborhood Disadvantage." *Journal of Abnormal Child Psychology* 35 (6): 1035–1045.

Egan, Vincent, and Matthew Beadman. 2011. "Personality and Gang Embeddedness." *Personality and Individual Differences* 51 (6): 748–753.

Férriz-Romeral, Laura, Maria Patricia Navas-Sánchez, Jose Antonio Gómez-Fraguela, and Jorge Sobral-Fernández. 2019. "Moral Disengagement and Serious Juvenile Crime: A Meta-Analysis about Its Relationship." *Revista Latinoamericana de Psicología* 51 (3): 162–170.

Fowlera, James, Jaime Settle, and Nicholas Christakis. 2011. "Correlated Genotypes in Friendship Networks." *Proceedings of the National Academy of Sciences of the United States of America* 108 (5): 1993–1997.

Fox, Bryanna, and Matt DeLisi. 2019. "Psychopathic Killers: A Meta-Analytic Review of the Psychopathy-Homicide Nexus." *Aggression and Violent Behavior* 44: 67–79.

Fox, Kathleen, Jeffrey Ward, and Jodi Lane. 2013. "Selection for Some, Facilitation for Others? Self-Control Theory and the Gang-Violence Relationship." *Deviant Behavior* 34 (12): 996–1019.

Frick, Paul, and Bryan Loney. 1999. "Outcomes of Children and Adolescents with Oppositional Defiant Disorder and Conduct Disorder." In *Handbook of Disruptive Behavior Disorders*, edited by Herbert Quay, and Anne Hogan, 507–524. New York: Kluwer Academic/Plenum Publishers.

Frick, Paul, and Joel Nigg. 2012. "Current Issues in the Diagnosis of Attention Deficit Hyperactivity Disorder, Oppositional Defiant Disorder, and Conduct Disorder." *Annual Review of Clinical Psychology* 8: 77–107.

Frisby-Osman, Sarah, and Jane Wood. 2020. "Rethinking How We View Gang Members: An Examination into Affective, Behavioral, and Mental Health Predictors of UK Gang-Involved Youth." *Youth Justice* 20 (1–2): 93–112.

García-Sancho, E., J. Salguero, and P. Fernández-Berrocal. 2016. "Angry Rumination as a Mediator of the Relationship between Ability Emotional Intelligence and Various Types of Aggression." *Personality and Individual Differences* 89: 143–147.

Gayon, Jean. 2016. "From Mendel to Epigenetics: History of Genetics." *Comptes Rendus—Biologies* 339: 225–230.

Geerlings, Yoni, Jessica Asscher, Geert Jan J. M. Stams, and Mark Assink. 2020. "The Association between Psychopathy and Delinquency in Juveniles: A Three-Level Meta-Analysis." *Aggression and Violent Behavior* 50: 101342.

Gomez Auyong, Zenta, Sven Smith, and Christopher Ferguson. 2018. "Girls in Gangs: Exploring Risk in a British Youth Context." *Crime and Delinquency* 64 (13): 1698–1717.

Gottfredson, Michael, and Travis Hirschi. 1990. *A General Theory of Crime*. Stanford, CT: Stanford University Press.

Hare, Robert. 1983. "Diagnosis of Antisocial Personality Disorder in Two Prison Populations." *American Journal of Psychiatry* 140 (7): 887–890.

Hare, Robert. 1996. "Psychopathy: A Clinical Construct Whose Time Has Come." *Criminal Justice and Behavior* 23 (1): 25–54.

Hare, Robert. 1999. *Without Conscience: The Disturbing World of the Psychopaths among Us.* New York: Guilford Press.

Hare, Robert. 2003. "The Hare PCL-R." Toronto, ON: Multi-Health Systems.

Harris, Toi, Sara Elkins, Ashley Butler, Matthew Shelton, Barbara Robles, Stephanie Kwok, Sherri Simpson, et al. 2013. "Youth Gang Members: Psychiatric Disorders and Substance Use." *Laws* 2 (4): 392–400.

Harter, S. 1998. "The Development of Self-Representations." In *Handbook of Child Psychology: Social, Emotional, and Personality Development*, edited by W. Damon, and N. Eisenberg, 553–617. New York: John Wiley & Sons, Inc.

Hashimi, Sadaf, Sara Wakefield, and Robert Apel. 2021. "Sibling Transmission of Gang Involvement." *Journal of Research in Crime and Delinquency* 58 (5): 507–544.

Hawes, Samuel, Amy Byrd, Raul Gonzalez, Caitlin Cavanagh, Jordan Bechtold, Donald Lynam, and Dustin Pardini. 2018. "The Developmental Course of Psychopathic Features: Investigating Stability, Change, and Long-Term Outcomes." *Journal of Research in Personality* 77: 83–89.

Hemphälä, Malin, David Kosson, Johan Westerman, and Sheilagh Hodgins. 2015. "Stability and Predictors of Psychopathic Traits from Mid-Adolescence through Early Adulthood." *Scandinavian Journal of Psychology* 56 (6): 649–658.

Higginson, Angela, Kathryn Benier, Yulia Shenderovich, Laura Bedford, Lorraine Mazerolle, and Joseph Murray. 2018. "Factors Associated with Youth Gang Membership in Low- and Middle-Income Countries: A Systematic Review." *Campbell Systematic Reviews* 14 (1): 1–128.

Hill, Karl, James Howell, J. David Hawkins, and Sara Battin-Pearson. 1999. "Childhood Risk Factors for Adolescent Gang Membership: Results from the Seattle Social Development Project." *Journal of Research in Crime and Delinquency* 36 (3): 300–322.

Hirschi, Travis. 1969. *Causes of Delinquency*. Berkeley: University of California Press.

Hope, Trina. 2003. "Do Families Matter? The Relative Effects of Family Characteristics, Self-Control, and Delinquency on Gang Membership." In *Readings in Juvenile Delinquency and Juvenile Justice*, edited by Thomas Calhoun and Constance Chapple, 168–185.

Hope, Trina, and Kelly Damphousse. 2002. "Applying Self-Control Theory to Gang Membership in a Non-Urban Setting." *Journal of Gang Research* 9 (2): 41–61.

Hopwood, Christopher, Leslie Morey, M. Brent Donnellan, Douglas Samuel, Carlos Grilo, Thomas Mcglashan, M. Tracie Shea, Mary Zanarini, John Gunderson, and Andrew Skodol. 2013. "Ten-Year Rank-Order Stability of Personality Traits and Disorders in a Clinical Sample." *Journal of Personality* 81 (3): 335–344.

Jolliffe, Darrick, and David Farrington. 2004. "Empathy and Offending: A Systematic Review and Meta-Analysis." *Aggression and Violent Behavior* 9 (5): 441–476.

Joseph, Justin, and David Rembert. 2021. "Exploring Psychopathy's Relationship with Youth Gang Membership in Males and Females." *Women and Criminal Justice* 32 (4): 1–19.

Joseph, Justin J. 2022. "Exploring Sex Differences between Dimensions of Psychopathy, Executive Functioning and Youth Gang Membership." *Psychology, Crime & Law* 1–26.

Kendler, Kenneth, Kristen Jacobson, Charles Gardner, Nathan Gillespie, Steven Aggen, and Carol Prescott. 2007. "Creating a Social World: A Developmental Twin Study of Peer-Group Deviance." *Archives of General Psychiatry* 64 (8): 958.

Kerig, Patricia, Cecilia Wainryb, Michelle Sinayobye Twali, and Shannon Chaplo. 2013. "America's Child Soldiers: Toward a Research Agenda for Studying Gang-Involved Youth in the United States." *Journal of Aggression, Maltreatment and Trauma* 22 (7): 773–795.

Kissner, Jason, and David Pyrooz. 2009. "Self-Control, Differential Association, and Gang Membership: A Theoretical and Empirical Extension of the Literature." *Journal of Criminal Justice* 37 (5): 478–487.

Klein, Malcolm. 1995. *The American Street Gang: Its Nature, Prevalence and Control.* New York: Oxford University Press.

Klein, Malcolm, and Cheryl Maxson. 2006. *Street Gang Patterns and Policies.* New York: Oxford University Press.

Knafo, Ariel, and Robert Plomin. 2006. "Prosocial Behavior from Early to Middle Childhood: Genetic and Environmental Influences on Stability and Change." *Developmental Psychology* 42 (5): 771–786.

Lahey, Benjamin, Rachel Gordon, Rolf Loeber, Magda Stouthamer-Loeber, and David Farrington. 1999. "Boys Who Join Gangs: A Prospective Study of Predictors of First Gang Entry." *Journal of Abnormal Child Psychology* 27 (4): 261–276.

Langbehn, Douglas, Remi Cadoret, William Yates, Edward Troughton, and Mark Stewart. 1998. "Distinct Contributions of Conduct and Oppositional Defiant Symptoms to Adult Antisocial Behavior." *Archives of General Psychiatry* 55 (9): 821–829.

Larsen, Lars, Peter Hartmann, and Helmuth Nyborg. 2008. "The Stability of General Intelligence from Early Adulthood to Middle-Age." *Intelligence* 36 (1): 29–34.

Lavigne, John, Colleen Cicchetti, Robert Gibbons, Helen Binns, Lene Larsen, and Crystal Devito. 2001. "Oppositional Defiant Disorder with Onset in Preschool Years: Longitudinal Stability and Pathways to Other Disorders." *Journal of the American Academy of Child and Adolescent Psychiatry* 40 (12): 1393–1400.

Leary, Mark, Lisa Schreindorfer, and Alison Haupt. 1995. "The Role of Low Self-Esteem in Emotional and Behavioral Problems: Why Is Low Self-Esteem Dysfunctional?" *Journal of Social and Clinical Psychology* 14 (3): 297–314.

Lenzi, Michela, Jill Sharkey, Alessio Vieno, Ashley Mayworm, Danielle Dougherty, and Karen Nylund-Gibson. 2015. "Adolescent Gang Involvement: The Role of Individual, Family, Peer, and School Factors in a Multilevel Perspective." *Aggressive Behavior* 41 (4): 386–397.

Lenzi, Michela, Jill Sharkey, Allie Wroblewski, Michael Furlong, and Massimo Santinello. 2019. "Protecting Youth from Gang Membership: Individual and School-Level Emotional Competence." *Journal of Community Psychology* 47 (3): 563–578.

Lombroso, Cesare. 2006. *Criminal Man.* Durham, NC: Duke University Press.

Lynam, Donald, Avshalom Caspi, Terrie Moffitt, Rolf Loeber, and Magda Stouthamer-Loeber. 2007. "Longitudinal Evidence That Psychology Scores in Early Adolescence Predict Adult Psychopathy." *Journal of Abnormal Psychology* 116 (1): 155–165.

Lynskey, Dana Peterson, L. Thomas Winfree, Finn-Aage Esbensen, and Dennis Clason. 2000. "Linking Gender, Minority Group Status, and Family Matters to Self-Control Theory: A Multivariate Analysis of Key Self-Control Concepts in a Youth-Gang Context." *Juvenile And Family Court Journal* 51 (3): 1–19.

Mallion, Jaimee, and Jane Wood. 2018. "Emotional Processes and Gang Membership: A Narrative Review." *Aggression and Violent Behavior* 43: 56–63.

Mallion, Jaimee, and Jane Wood. 2021. "Comparison of Emotional Dispositions between Street Gang and Non-Gang Prisoners." *Journal of Interpersonal Violence* 36 (9–10): 4018–4038.

Marzo, Lea. 2020. "Set Trippin': An Intersectional Examination of Gang Members." *Humanity & Society* 44 (4): 422–448.

McCuish, Evan, Martin Bouchard, and Eric Beauregard. 2021. "A Network-Based Examination of the Longitudinal Association between Psychopathy and Offending Versatility." *Journal of Quantitative Criminology* 37 (3): 693–714.

McCuish, Evan, and Patrick Lussier. 2018. "A Developmental Perspective on the Stability and Change of Psychopathic Personality Traits across the Adolescence–Adulthood Transition." *Criminal Justice and Behavior* 45 (5): 666–692.

McGloin, Jean, and Megan Collins. 2015. "Micro-Level Processes of the Gang." In *The Handbook of Gangs*, edited by Scott Decker, and David Pyrooz, 276–293. Chichester, UK: John Wiley & Sons, Inc.

Megreya, Ahmed. 2015. "Emotional Intelligence and Criminal Behavior." *Journal of Forensic Sciences* 60 (1): 84–88.

Melde, Chris, and Finn-Aage Esbensen. 2011. "Gang Membership as a Turning Point in the Life Course." *Criminology* 49 (2): 513–552.

Mier, Carrie, and Roshni T. Ladny. 2018. "Does Self-Esteem Negatively Impact Crime and Delinquency? A Meta-Analytic Review of 25 Years of Evidence." *Deviant Behavior* 39 (8): 1006–1022.

Moore, Celia. 2015. "Moral Disengagement." *Current Opinion in Psychology* 6: 199–204.

Mordre, Marianne, Berit Groholt, Ellen Kjelsberg, Berit Sandstad, and Anne Margrethe Myhre. 2011. "The Impact of ADHD and Conduct Disorder in Childhood on Adult Delinquency: A 30 Years Follow-up Study Using Official Crime Records." *BMC Psychiatry* 11 (1): 1–10.

Nagin, Daniel., and Ray Paternoster. 2000. "Population Heterogeneity and State Dependence: Future Research." *Journal of Quantitative Criminology* 16 (2): 117–144.

Nagin, Daniel, and Raymond Paternoster. 1993. "Enduring Individual Differences and Rational Choice Theories of Crime." *Law & Society Review* 27 (3): 467–496.

O'Brien, Kate, Michael Daffern, Chi Meng Chu, and Stuart Thomas. 2013. "Youth Gang Affiliation, Violence, and Criminal Activities: A Review of Motivational, Risk, and Protective Factors." *Aggression and Violent Behavior* 18 (4): 417–425.

Oh, Jeewon, William Chopik, Sara Konrath, and Kevin Grimm. 2020. "Longitudinal Changes in Empathy across the Life Span in Six Samples of Human Development." *Social Psychological and Personality Science* 11 (2): 244–253.

Olate, René, Christopher Salas-Wright, and Michael Vaughn. 2012. "Predictors of Violence and Delinquency among High Risk Youth and Youth Gang Members in San Salvador, El Salvador." *International Social Work* 55 (3): 383–401.

Olate, René, Christopher Salas-Wright, Michael Vaughn, and Mansoo Yu. 2015. "Preventing Violence among Gang-Involved and High-Risk Youth in El Salvador: The Role of School Motivation and Self-Control." *Deviant Behavior* 36 (4): 259–275.

Ozer, Mustafa, and Halil Akbas. 2020. "The Predictability of IQ on Delinquency: A Structural Equation Model (SQM)." *International Journal of Criminal Justice Sciences* 15 (2): 283–297.

Parker, James, Donald Saklofske, Laura Wood, Jennifer Eastabrook, and Robyn Taylor. 2005. "Stability and Change in Emotional Intelligence: Exploring the Transition to Young Adulthood." *Journal of Individual Differences* 26 (2): 100–106.

Peterson, Dana, and Kirstin Morgan. 2014. "Sex Differences and the Overlap in Youths' Risk Factors for Onset of Violence and Gang Involvement." *Journal of Crime and Justice* 37 (1): 129–154.

Pinel, Philippe. 1806. *A Treatise on Insanity*. Trans. Sheffield, UK: Cadell and Davies.

Plattner, Belinda, Hans Steiner, Steve The, Helena Kraemer, Susanne Bauer, Jochen Kindler, Max Friedrich, Siegfried Kasper, and Martha Feucht. 2009. "Sex-Specific Predictors of

Criminal Recidivism in a Representative Sample of Incarcerated Youth." *Comprehensive Psychiatry* 50 (5): 400–407.

Prichard, James Cowles. 1842. *On the Different Forms of Insanity in Relation to Jurisprudence.* London: Bailliere.

Pyrooz, David, and James Densley. 2016. "Selection into Street Gangs: Signaling Theory, Gang Membership, and Criminal Offending." *Journal of Research in Crime and Delinquency* 53 (4): 447–481.

Pyrooz, David, Chris Melde, Donna Coffman, and Ryan Meldrum. 2021. "Selection, Stability, and Spuriousness: Testing Gottfredson and Hirschi's Propositions to Reinterpret Street Gangs in Self-Control Perspective." *Criminology* 59 (2): 224–253.

Pyrooz, David, and Meghan Mitchell. 2015. "Little Gang Research, Big Gang Research." In *The Handbook of Gangs*, edited by Scott Decker, and David Pyrooz, 28–58. New York: John Wiley & Sons Inc.

Pyrooz, David, and Gary Sweeten. 2015. "Gang Membership between Ages 5 and 17 Years in the United States." *Journal of Adolescent Health* 56 (4): 414–419.

Pyrooz, David, Jillian Turanovic, Scott Decker, and Jun Wu. 2016. "Taking Stock of the Relationship between Gang Membership and Offending: A Meta-Analysis." *Criminal Justice and Behavior* 43 (3): 365–397.

Quetelet, Adolphe. 1984. *Research on the Propensity for Crime at Different Ages.* Cincinnati, OH: Anderson.

Raby, Carlotta, and Fergal Jones. 2016. "Identifying Risks for Male Street Gang Affiliation: A Systematic Review and Narrative Synthesis." *Journal of Forensic Psychiatry and Psychology* 27 (5): 601–644.

Reichborn-Kjennerud, T., N. Czajkowski, E. Ystrom, R. Orstavik, S. Aggen, K. Tambs, S. Torgersen, et al. 2015. "A Longitudinal Twin Study of Borderline and Antisocial Personality Disorder Traits in Early to Middle Adulthood." *Psychological Medicine* 45 (14): 3121–3131.

Richardson, Ken. 2002. "What IQ Tests Test." *Theory & Psychology* 12 (3): 283–314.

Robins, Lee. 1966. *Deviant Children Grown Up: A Sociological and Psychiatric Study of Sociopathic Personality.* Philadelphia, PA: Williams & Wilkins.

Rosenberg, Morris. 1965. "Rosenberg Self-Esteem Scale (RSE)." *Acceptance and Commitment Therapy. Measures Package* 61 (52): 18.

Rosenberg, Morris. 1979. *Conceiving the Self.* New York: Basic Books.

Salas-Wright, Christopher, René Olate, and Michael Vaughn. 2013. "Assessing Empathy in Salvadoran High-Risk and Gang-Involved Adolescents and Young Adults: A Spanish Validation of the Basic Empathy Scale." *International Journal of Offender Therapy and Comparative Criminology* 57 (11): 1393–1416.

Sanchez-Jankowski, Martin. 1991. *Islands in the Street: Gangs and American Urban Society.* Berkeley: University of California Press.

Sanchez, Jose, Scott Decker, and David Pyrooz. 2021. "Gang Homicide: The Road so Far and a Map for the Future." *Homicide Studies* 26 (1): 68–90.

Seals, Richard, and Liliana Stern. 2013. "Cognitive Ability and the Division of Labor in Urban Ghettos: Evidence from Gang Activity in U.S. Data." *Journal of Socio-Economics* 44: 140–149.

Shepherd, Stephane, Rachel Campbell, and James Ogloff. 2018. "Psychopathy, Antisocial Personality Disorder, and Reconviction in an Australian Sample of Forensic Patients." *International Journal of Offender Therapy and Comparative Criminology* 62 (3): 609–628.

Short, James. 1998. "The Level of Explanation Problem Revisited—The American Society of Criminology 1997 Presidential Address." *Criminology* 36 (1): 3–36.

Short, James, and Fred Strodtbeck. 1965. *Group Process and Gang Delinquency*. Chicago, IL: University of Chicago Press Chicago.

Smith, Sven, Zenta Gomez Auyong, and Chris Ferguson. 2019. "Social Learning, Social Disorganization, and Psychological Risk Factors for Criminal Gangs in a British Youth Context." *Deviant Behavior* 40 (6): 722–731.

Spergel, Irving. 1995. *The Youth Gang Problem: A Community Approach*. New York: Oxford University Press.

Swaner, Rachel. 2022. "'We Can't Get No Nine-to-Five': New York City Gang Membership as a Response to the Structural Violence of Everyday Life." *Critical Criminology* 30 (1): 95–111.

Tewksbury, Richard. 2009. "Qualitative versus Quantitative Methods: Understanding Why Qualitative Methods Are Superior for Criminology and Criminal Justice." *Journal of Theoretical and Philosophical Criminology* 1: 38–58.

Thornberry, Terence, Marvin Krohn, Alan Lizotte, and Deborah Chard-Wierschem. 1993. "The Role of Juvenile Gangs in Facilitating Delinquent Behavior." *Journal of Research in Crime and Delinquency* 30 (1): 55–87.

Thornberry, Terence, Marvin Krohn, Alan Lizotte, Kimberly Tobin, and Carolyn Smith. 2003. *Gangs and Delinquency in Developmental Perspective*. Cambridge, UK: Cambridge University Press.

Thornton, Laura, Paul Frick, Elizabeth Shulman, James Ray, Laurence Steinberg, and Elizabeth Cauffman. 2015. "Callous-Unemotional Traits and Adolescents' Role in Group Crime." *Law and Human Behavior* 39 (4): 368–377.

Tostlebe, Jennifer, and David Pyrooz. 2022. "Are Gang Members Psychopaths?" In *Psychopathy and Criminal Behavior: Current Trends and Challenges*, edited by Paulo Barbosa Marques, Mauro Paulino, and Laura Alho, 311–332. Cambridge, MA: Elsevier.

Trzesniewski, Kali, M. Brent Donnellan, and Richard Robins. 2003. "Stability of Self-Esteem across the Life Span." *Journal of Personality and Social Psychology* 84 (1): 205–220.

Valdez, Avelardo, Charles Kaplan, and Edward Codina. 2000. "Psychopathy among Mexican American Gang Members: A Comparative Study." *International Journal of Offender Therapy and Comparative Criminology* 44 (1): 46–58.

Vaughn, Michael, John Edens, Matthew Howard, and Shannon Toney Smith. 2009. "An Investigation of Primary and Secondary Psychopathy in a Statewide Sample of Incarcerated Youth." *Youth Violence and Juvenile Justice* 7 (3): 172–188.

Vazsonyi, Alexander, Jakub Mikuška, and Erin Kelley. 2017. "It's Time: A Meta-Analysis on the Self-Control–Deviance Link." *Journal of Criminal Justice* 48: 48–63.

Vigil, James Diego. 1988. *Barrio Gangs: Street Life and Identity in Southern California*. Austin: University of Texas Press.

Wang, Alvin. 1994. "Pride and Prejudice in High School Gang Members." *Adolescence* 29 (114): 279.

Watkins, Adam, and Chris Melde. 2016. "Bad Medicine: The Relationship between Gang Membership, Depression, Self-Esteem, and Suicidal Behavior." *Criminal Justice and Behavior* 43 (8): 1107–1126.

Weide, Robert. 2022. "Structural Disorganization: Can Prison Gangs Mitigate Serious Violence in Carceral Institutions?" *Critical Criminology* 30 (1): 113–132.

Wikström, Per Olof, and Kyle Treiber. 2007. "The Role of Self-Control in Crime Causation: Beyond Gottfredson and Hirschi's General Theory of Crime." *European Journal of Criminology* 4 (2): 237–264.

Wojciechowski, Thomas. 2020. "The Salience of Antisocial Personality Disorder for Predicting Substance Use and Violent Behavior: The Moderating Role of Deviant Peers." *Journal of Drug Issues* 50 (1): 35–50.

Wolfgang, Marvin, Robert Figlio, and Thorsten Sellin. 1972. *Delinquency in a Birth Cohort*. Chicago, IL: University of Chicago Press.

Wood, Jane, and Sophie Dennard. 2017. "Gang Membership: Links to Violence Exposure, Paranoia, PTSD, Anxiety, and Forced Control of Behavior in Prison." *Psychiatry* 80 (1): 30–41.

Wood, Jane, Constantinos Kallis, and Jeremy Coid. 2017. "Differentiating Gang Members, Gang Affiliates, and Violent Men on Their Psychiatric Morbidity and Traumatic Experiences." *Psychiatry* 80 (3): 221–235.

Wright, John, Kevin Beaver, Matt DeLisi, and Michael Vaughn. 2008. "Evidence of Negligible Parenting Influences on Self-Control, Delinquent Peers, and Delinquency in a Sample of Twins." *Justice Quarterly* 25 (3): 544–569.

Wu, Jun, and David Pyrooz. 2016. "Uncovering the Pathways between Gang Membership and Violent Victimization." *Journal of Quantitative Criminology* 32 (4): 531–559.

Yablonsky, Lewis. 1962. *The Violent Gang*. New York: Macmillan.

CHAPTER 21

RATIONAL CHOICE, GANG MEMBERSHIP, AND CRIME

Moving Actors and Choice to Center Stage

KYLE J. THOMAS

SCHOLARSHIP on gangs and gang members possesses a rich history in criminology. From the seminal work of Thrasher (1927) and other Chicago School scholars in the early 1900s emphasizing the role of neighborhoods in promoting gang involvement, to the "Golden Era" of gang research assessing how group dynamics facilitate criminal and delinquent tendencies (Cloward and Ohlin 1960; Cohen 1955; Short and Strodtbeck 1965), to modern assessments on societal reactions and the broader social problems they promote (Pyrooz and Mitchell 2015), the study of gangs as a prominent criminological construct has been persistent since the inception of the field. Much of the gang literature has been dominated by sociological perspectives rooted in structural and cultural explanations (Decker, Melde, and Pyrooz 2013). This is, of course, not surprising, as the ties to social structure and the group dynamics that they imply make "gangs" a quintessential sociological risk factor for crime (Warr 2002). Further, discussions on the criminal behavior of gang members tends to attribute such acts not to the self-interested choices of the individual, but rather to some selfless desire of the group. As a result, research into the etiology of gangs and their impact on the behavior of gang members have been dominated by sociological explanations that focus almost exclusively on factors external to the individual—neighborhood conditions, exposure to gang members, and group dynamics (Thornberry et al. 1993).

Put simply, much of the sociological work examining gangs and gang members has largely taken an *externalist* view. As recently detailed by Matsueda and Lanfear (2020), much of the work on gangs has ignored some of the rich elements in Short and Strodtbeck (1965). Short and Strodtbeck offered a classic work detailing gangs and gang membership, and while most of the attention of this work has focused on their discussion of group dynamics, they also offered a rational choice theory of gang membership and gang-related offending. Rational choice models take an *internalist* view and emphasize human agency and the preferences and expectations of the individual actor (Paternoster 2017). Thus, while not ignoring the potential influence of structure and culture on gang-related actions, a rational choice model instead brings individual actors themselves to the center stage of inquiry to consider how the perceptions and preferences of actors impact action choices.

In this chapter, I argue that much can be gained by viewing gangs and gang involvement through the lens of a rational choice perspective and by focusing on the decision calculus of the individual actors themselves. Such a view would provide a sound theoretical model that can explain four processes that dominate the gang literature in the field of criminology: (1) decisions to become gang involved (i.e., non-random selection into gangs); (2) observed "enhancement" effects by which individuals increase their criminal activity after becoming gang involved; (3) situational group (gang) processes that contribute to gang-related activities such as group fights (McGloin and Collins 2015); and (4) decisions to "disengage" from gang involvement. Specifically, each decision can be seen as a function of subjective expected utility, whereby an individual is predicted to choose to become gang involved and engage in crime when the marginal benefits of doing so exceed the marginal risks and costs. This approach recognizes the capacity of human beings to make purposeful, deliberate, and *agentic* choices, and in doing so places the individual actor at the center of their own social world (Paternoster 2017; Thomas, Pogarsky, and Loughran 2022). Further, as I will argue in detail below, the rational choice perspective emphasizing expectations and preferences is compatible with sociological theories stressing structure and culture, and indeed "offers a parsimonious microfoundation for macrosociological concepts and causal mechanisms" (Matsueda 2013, 285).

Rational Choice Theory in Criminology

Rational choice models of behavior are typically rooted in subjective expected utility theory first introduced by Von Neumann and Morgenstern (1947) and later revised by Simon (1986). There are many potential variants of rational choice theories that can differ in important respects. The rational choice model employed here is based on several core assumptions. First, it assumes that human beings possess agency—that is, the capacity to reflect, deliberate, imagine alternatives, and act purposefully (Paternoster 2017; Thomas, O'Neill, and Loughran 2022). This necessarily means that individuals are not compelled to join gangs or commit crime due to forces outside of their control but are active participants in such decisions. Stated differently, the notion of agency is consistent with the interactionist idea that humans are not merely *reactors*, but rather play active roles in their own lives (Blumer 1969). Second, it is assumed that individuals are generally *self-interested* beings that seek to engage in action choices that they believe improve their likelihood of attaining goals and wants. Third, one's evaluation of action choices is consistent with a subjective expected utility model, whereby individuals choose actions that provide them benefits or reduce potential costs and risks. This can be stated in a "weaker" form by asserting simply that individuals are *responsive to incentives*. Fourth, the subjective expected utility of an action is a function of two choice components: *subjective expectations*, which are the anticipated consequences of action, such as likelihood of arrest, and one's *preferences*, which reflect the value or weight individuals place on subjective expectations when making action choices. Fifth, subjective expectations and preferences are malleable and can change over time. As I will detail below, subjective expectations are thought to be formed through a communication process that is influenced by life circumstances, such as one's status as a gang member, and preferences too can shift based on the availability of choice sets. Finally, it is assumed that the proximate cause of behavior is an individual's *choice*—individuals join or leave a gang when *they choose* and offend when *they choose*.

Thus, rational choice models view action choices through a subjective expected utility model, where an individual is expected to engage in a behavior when the expected utility of the action (U) is greater than the anticipated disutility of the action (dU). The factors that go into the U and dU have been the subject of some conversation in the field of criminology, but recent work has generally outlined prominent (dis)incentives associated with crime (Loughran et al. 2016; Matsueda et al. 2006). Generally, the rewards from crime-related decisions involve the potential for material gain, increases in social rewards and status, and intrinsic or personal rewards such as excitement, rush, and thrill. Simply put, when making decisions such as whether to join a gang or engage in criminal activity, individuals consider the potential rewards and benefits they expect to garner from the action (e.g., how friends will react). At the same time, individuals also weigh these rewards when considering how to act, which reflects how much they desire and value the potential benefits. This weighting factor, δ, is the analog of individual *preferences* for monetary, social, or intrinsic gains. Thus, for example, the social reward utility derived from offending is determined both by one's expectations of the anticipated social rewards (*Social Status*), but also by how much they desire social status (δ). Thus, the overall utility derived from the benefits associated with crime can be described as:

$$U(Material) = \delta \, Monetary \; Returns \qquad [1]$$

$$U(SocRew) = \delta \, Social \; Status \qquad [2]$$

$$U(PersRew) = \delta \, Excitement \qquad [3]$$

where the expectations (*Monetary Returns, Social Status,* and *Excitement*) reflect individuals' perceptions of the anticipated benefits, and the associated δ's capture individual preferences for these rewards. Thus, the total utility derived from a crime-related decision can be thought of as the sum of these marginal utilities:

$$Total \; Utility = U(Material) + U(SocRew) + U(PersRew) \qquad [4]$$

The disutilities associated with crime generally come in two forms: the risks associated with an action choice (e.g., likelihood of being arrested, likelihood of experiencing victimization) and the potential social costs that can be incurred by engaging in criminal activity. Thus, we can think of the marginal disutilities associated with crime as:

$$dU(Risk) = \delta \, Risks \qquad [5]$$

$$dU(Costs) = \delta \, Social \; Costs \qquad [6]$$

And the overall disutility from crime as:

$$Total \; Disutility = dU(Risk) + dU(Costs) \qquad [7]$$

As described by Becker (1968) and discussed above, the (dis)utility derived from each choice component for each individual i is a function of two parameters: (1) the *subjective expectations* regarding the rewards, risks, and costs, which are reflected in, for example, individual perceptions of "Social Status," "Risks," and "Social Costs," in equations [2], [5], and [6], respectively, and; (2) individual *preferences* for these inputs (δ), which reflect the weight or value individuals place on the subjective expectations or the marginal (dis)utility derived from changes in the expectations. Importantly, behavioral choices are thought to be *jointly* impacted by expectations and preferences, whereby individuals consider the potential consequences of the action and then weigh these potential consequences to determine their own subjective expected utility. This means that individuals who are generally risk averse may still decide to offend if the expectations of the anticipated risk are sufficiently low, and that some individuals who view the risks associated with gang life as high may still choose to become gang involved if they are sufficiently tolerant of such risks (Thomas et al. 2022).

To be clear, subjective expectations capture individuals' beliefs about the anticipated outcomes of the action—for example, the likelihood of arrest, the degree of social rewards, or the anticipated excitement. Some individuals, for example, may view the likelihood of arrest when offending as low while others view it as relatively high. Similarly, some individuals may believe their friends are likely to reward criminal conduct, while others do not hold such beliefs. All else being equal, rational choice theories predict that those with higher perceptions of arrest risk and lower perceptions of social rewards will be less likely to offend.

Preferences capture how much individuals value and weigh subjective expectations when making choice inputs. For example, some individuals may be risk averse, in that the potential threat of arrest risk weighs heavily on their decision to offend (or not). Others may be risk tolerant, such that they are relatively indifferent to considerations of arrest risk (Thomas et al. 2022). In this way, two individuals can have the same perceptions of arrest risk but act differently depending on their differing preferences for risk. The same logic applies to other expectations of the anticipated consequences of crime—for example, individuals can hold the same expectations about the social rewards associated with crime but may be differentially impacted by the influence of peers and other groups (Giordano et al. 2003; Thomas and McGloin 2013).

Following the seminal description of hedonic calculus offered by Bentham, an individual is predicted to choose to engage in an action when the sum total of the utility from the action is greater than the sum total of the disutility, such that

$$\text{Total Utility} > \text{Total Disutility or,} \quad [8]$$

$$(\delta \text{Monetary Returns} + \delta \text{Social Status} + \delta \text{Excitement}) > (\delta \text{Risks} + \delta \text{Social Costs}) \quad [9]$$

Thomas and Vogel (2019) argued that the model proposed in equation [9] can be translated into a general regression framework. In this model, we can predict the outcome Y for crime c and individual i through the equation:

$$Y_{ic} = \beta_{0i} + \beta_{1i} Monetary_{ic} + \beta_{2i} SocRew_{ic} + \beta_{3i} PersRew_{ic} + \beta_{4i} Risk_{ic} + \beta_{5i} SocCosts_{ic} \quad [10]$$

where the observed variables X (e.g., *Risk, SocRew, SocCosts*) capture the subjective expectations associated with engaging in act Y, and the associated coefficients (β_{ki}) reflect preferences for risks, costs, and rewards and how they are differently weighted. Although the models are expressed in mathematical equations, the main components of the action model are one's perceptions of the anticipated consequences and one's preferences, which indicate that individuals play active roles in their own behaviors—that is, they contemplate the potential consequences of an action, determine the (un)desirability of the potential consequences, and choose a behavioral option that is thought to yield some degree of utility.

Tests of rational choice theories have received considerable empirical attention in recent years. Overall, the research assessing rational choice theories has provided considerable support in a wide range of criminological issues. For example, Matsueda, Kreager, and Huizinga (2006) found that subjective expectations about the risks, costs, and rewards associated with crime were a strong predictor of both violence and theft. Thomas, Loughran, and Hamilton (2020) found that rational choice variables can help explain the types of crimes individuals commit (i.e., the tendency to specialize in offending). Research has also provided evidence that changes in expectations and in preferences can help explain desistance from crime in adulthood (Thomas and Vogel 2019; Thomas et al. 2022). Even further, research has shown that rational choice variables can help explain terrorism (Dugan, LaFree, and Piquero 2005), corporate crime (Paternoster and Simpson 1996) and sexual assault (Bachman, Paternoster, and Ward 1992). Indeed, the literature suggests that rational choice theories are capable of explaining a wide range of crime-related outcomes for a broad range of populations. It is for this reason that Loughran et al. (2016) concluded that "rational choice is as general of a theory as learning, control and strain theories."

Despite the relative growth in rational choice studies in criminology, the application of rational choice to the study of gangs and gang members has been relatively sparse (Matsueda and Lanfear 2020), despite the fact that some have observed that "gang members are rational agents" and that "gangs are rational organizations" (Densley 2013, 3). Some of this may be attributed to the disciplinary ownership of "gangs" in sociology, and sociologists have long been skeptical of choice and agent-based models of crime due in part to the erroneous belief that a recognition of human agency would render prominent sociological risk factors irrelevant (Cullen 2017; see also Sampson 2012). Indeed, much of the early seminal work on gangs came out of the Chicago School, which emphasized neighborhood characteristics and social structure as particularly salient contributors to gang involvement (Thrasher 1927). At the same time, "structural" explanations and choice-based explanations have long been viewed as being at odds with one another under the false idea that the acknowledgment of "choice would render the environment impotent" (Sampson 2012, 374). I argue that a rational choice model is well suited to explain key foci of the gang literature and is a compatible model of action that can link structural characteristics to the behavior and choice of individual actors (Thomas et al. 2022). In doing so, the rational choice model can address some limitations of prominent sociological explanations of gang involvement and crime.

Rational Choice and Gangs

Pyrooz and Mitchell (2015) traced the history of the gang literature in the field of criminology. They separated the literature into three eras. First, the "Classical Era" largely revolved around seminal works by early Chicago School theorists like Thrasher. As Pyrooz and Mitchell noted, this era was dominated by an understanding of how structural—and in particular, neighborhood—characteristics contributed to gangs in lower-class communities (Thrasher 1927). The second era was referred to as the "Golden Era," which was dominated by considerations of social class and subcultures (Cohen 1955; Cloward and Ohlin 1960). In describing this era, Pyrooz and Mitchell discuss Short and Strodtbeck (1965), whose seminal work was rooted in the structural characteristics commonly employed by classic Chicago School theorists. In other words, Short and Strodtbeck (1965) highlight how experiences with socioeconomic disadvantage and exposure to cultural norms conducive to crime can promote gangs and gang membership. At the same time, these authors went beyond the typical urban ecological approach and situated individual actors into the group dynamics of the gang. In this way, Short and Strodtbeck (1965) focused some of the attention on the individual actors themselves and the role they played in their own gang involvement and delinquency.

Matsueda and Lanfear (2020) recently discussed how much of the research on gang members and gangs have largely neglected these important insights from Short and Strodtbeck's (1965) seminal work. Notably, and despite the fact that they offer an array of influential insights, Short and Strodtbeck outline a rational choice model within their framework. They argued that much of the desire to join gangs revolves around a potential reward—social status. In this way, Short and Strodtbeck suggest that the decision to join a gang is a *choice* made by individual actors done in part to garner utility and rewards (or to prevent them from losing social status). Further, the discussions of group dynamics and the role the gang plays in influencing the perceptions of weighing rewards and risks associated with gang-related behavior also invokes rational choice ideas.

Matsueda and Lanfear (2020) also discussed explicitly the implications of Short and Strodtbeck's rational choice model for gangs and outlined the implications for gang membership, aleatory risk, collective behavior, and game theory. I do not wish to regurgitate their excellent discussion on these topics. Rather, the goal of this chapter is to reflect on how broader rational choice perspectives of crime might address limitations to extant theorizing on gangs and offer new puzzles for scholars interested in gangs to explore. Specifically, I wish to detail the implications of embracing a rational choice perspective for understanding gang membership and gang-related offending. I draw on Cornish and Clarke's (1986) distinction between *criminal involvement* and *crime* to describe how rational choice models can account for *gang involvement* and *gang-enhanced crime* (i.e., the "enhancement" hypothesis). Both can be viewed as the result of a "rational" decision made by agentic actors who are responsive to considerations of the subjective beliefs about the risks, costs, and rewards from crime, as well as the preferences associated with such beliefs. Such an emphasis moves us away from theoretical perspectives that seemingly view "gang" related decisions as determined predominately by structural or personality characteristics beyond individual control and instead recognizes that individual actors themselves play an active role in their own lives. Importantly, and as will be detailed below, a rational choice approach to understanding gang involvement and gang-related offending does *not* negate social structural factors (Matsueda 2013; Thomas et al. 2021), as such factors likely play a role in both belief and preference formation (Thomas, Baumer, and Loughran 2022). The main purpose of this chapter is to provide a formal theory of gang involvement and enhancement that can allow for future formal tests of a rational choice model.

Gang Involvement

The decision to become gang involved is a longer-term choice that extends beyond immediate situational concerns (Densley 2015). Rather, the decision to be an active gang member is more enduring, often involving new sets of norms and expectations, as well as a lifestyle change that is, in some ways, partially rooted in crime and violence. Such a decision inevitably carries with it consequences. For example, becoming gang involved is inherently risky (Densley 2015), both in the sense that it can potentially lead to increased law enforcement attention and thus the likelihood of experiencing an arrest or becoming justice involved (Tapia 2011), but also because it can increase one's risk of experiencing violent victimization (Petersen, Taylor, and Esbensen 2004). Further, joining a gang can also incur notable social costs such as disapproval from peers and parents, potential negative consequences to work and school, and perhaps have negative consequences for one's romantic prospects (Johnston 1983; Yiu 2021). Put simply, gang involvement has a number of potential risks and costs that can potentially deter one from deciding to do so.

At the same time, becoming gang involved can also carry with it potential rewards (Densley 2015). The lifestyle that comes with gang involvement—crime, quick money, sexual partners (Anderson 1999)—can be thrilling and exciting, much more so than lifestyles typically associated with middle-class standards (Miller 1958). Even further still, the feeling of being part of a social group with shared identities can provide further intrinsic rewards for individuals. Perhaps most notably, gang involvement can also bring with it improvements in social status for some individuals. Becoming involved in a gang can confer "respect" that is often highly valued in certain communities (Anderson 1999). Indeed, qualitative research assessing gangs in the United States have highlighted how structural disadvantage can promote gang involvement. One common theme in this literature is that, due to restricted choice sets, individuals come to place a premium on alternative goals (e.g., status, respect, and honor) that involvement in gangs can help them achieve (Hagedorn and Macon 1988; Padilla 1992). For example, Durán's (2013) ethnographic work in Denver, Colorado, and Ogden, Utah, stressed that gangs and gang involvement is an adaptation to the structural disadvantages faced by Latinx youth in the American southwest. As a result of such disadvantage, some individuals place greater value on social status and respect, something that is believed to be increased through gang involvement. Leverso and Hess (2021) have argued that gang involvement provides a unique opportunity to accomplish masculinity (gaining honor and respect). A central argument in their work is that structural disadvantages and lack of access to legitimate opportunities for success can make gangs a particularly viable means to achieving masculinity ends. Simply put, a common feature of much of the gang literature is that socioeconomic and structural disadvantages can lead individuals to seek out alternative goals and definitions of success, and that gangs can provide one avenue to achieving these goals and thus can increase the perceptions of the anticipated rewards associated with gang membership.

Beyond these beliefs about the potential consequences of gang involvement, it is likely that individuals also differ in how much they value and weigh these different consequences—that is, the preferences for the risks, costs, and rewards associated with gang involvement likely vary across persons and would also contribute to one's decision to become gang involved. Some individuals may be particularly affected by the risks associated with gang involvement (e.g., worried about being a victim of violence) and thus may be deterred from joining a gang even if they do not view the risks as particularly high (see Thomas et al. 2022). Others may care little about such risks, and thus are tolerant of the potential to experience arrests or becoming a victim of crime. Further, some individuals may be particularly cost averse as it pertains to the potential negative social costs associated with gang involvement, whereas others can be tolerant of such costs (e.g., not care if their parents would be upset if they joined a gang). Even further still, individuals are thought to differ in the extent to which they weigh or value "respect" and social rewards within their community (Thomas and Vogel 2019). Anderson (1999), for example, argued that adolescents from "street" families are particularly concerned about social status and the level of respect they garner. This is all to say that it is not just subjective expectations or beliefs about the potential outcomes associated with gang involvement that influences decisions to join a gang, but also preferences for the risks, costs, and rewards associated with gang involvement.

Drawing on this explication, a rational choice model of gang involvement can be formally expressed (and tested) through the equation:

$$Gang\ Involvement_i = \beta_{0i} + \beta_{1i} Monetary_i + \beta_{2i} Socrew_i + \beta_{3i} PersRew_i + \beta_{4i} Risk_i + \beta_{5i} Soc\ Costs_i \quad [11]$$

As with equation [10], *Monetary*, *SocRew*, and *PersRew* capture one's expectations of the material, social, and intrinsic rewards from becoming gang involved, and their associated coefficients (β_{ki}) reflect individual preferences for these rewards. *Risk* captures the risks associated with gang involvement, while the associated coefficient β_{4i} reflects one's tolerance for risk. *SocCosts* captures the informal social costs and β_{5i} captures one's cost tolerance.

What is important in this explication are the subscripts *i* that denote each of the choice inputs on the right-hand side of the gang involvement equation: suggesting that the decision to become gang involved is a choice made by the individual actor themself. Thus, individuals are not strictly a product of their social environment but formulate their own perceptions and preferences regarding the risks, costs, and rewards associated with gang involvement, and are predicted to choose to join a gang when the *subjective* marginal rewards from gang involvement exceed the subjective marginal risks and marginal costs. In this way, individuals within the same social context (e.g., neighborhood) can formulate unique beliefs on the risks, costs, and rewards of gang involvement and may further differ in important ways in their preferences related to gang involvement. Simply put, involvement in gangs is a *choice made by the individual actor*. This does not mean that structural characteristics are irrelevant for decisions to join a gang. After all, social context necessarily provides (or constrains) opportunities for gang involvement (Moore 2010; Vigil 2007; see also Cloward and Ohlin 1960). But beyond the direct opportunities afforded or limited by context, social structural factors may also impact one's perceptions of the risks, costs, and rewards associated with gang involvement (Thomas et al. 2022).

Social Structure and Decisions to Become Gang Involved

The rational choice model of gang involvement presented in equation [11] suggests that the decision to join a gang is the result of an individual choice—a combination of the individual's subjective expectations deriving from gang involvement and their own preferences associated with such expectations. A common misconception among many criminologists is that the acknowledgment of choice renders environmental factors impotent (Sampson 2012). This, unfortunately, reinforces the idea that economic theories of choice and sociological theories emphasizing structure are incompatible (see Cullen 2017 for a recent example). Becker (1968) is partly responsible for this perceived incompatibility, as he asserted in his seminal rational choice model of offending that an adequate explanation of crime can do away with an emphasis on structure and focus solely on the economist's analysis of choice. Yet subsequent work in the social sciences has highlighted the compatibility of rational choice models with social structural explanations (Coleman 1990; Hechter and Kanazawa 1997). In criminology, McCarthy (2002) and Matsueda (2013) have both argued that rational choice theories are compatible with sociological theories of offending. The central idea being that structural characteristics such as neighborhood disadvantage and exposure to criminal associates influence individual behavior through their impact on perceptions of and preferences for the risks, costs, and rewards associated with crime (Thomas et al. 2022).

Pyrooz, Fox, and Decker (2010) have found evidence that socioeconomic disadvantage is related to gang membership: Individuals residing in economically disadvantaged neighborhoods have an increased risk of becoming gang involved. From a rational choice theory, such structural characteristics influence individual decisions because they impact individual perceptions of and preferences for the risks, costs, and rewards associated with behaviors. Thomas et al. (2022) recently outlined a multilevel rational choice model of offending that can be extended to decisions to become gang involved. For example, individuals residing in neighborhoods characterized by socioeconomic disadvantage may come to hold the belief that the risks associated with gang membership (both legal and nonlegal) are relatively low compared to those from more advantaged areas. Similarly, if gang membership is tolerated to a greater extent in disadvantaged communities or even just a part of life in disadvantaged communities, then informal social costs imposed by community residents may be lower (Sampson and Wilson 1995). Moreover, in severely disadvantaged communities, economic and educational prospects may already be low and are unlikely to be greatly impacted by one's involvement in a gang or the potential consequences associated with gang membership (e.g., arrest). In this way, individuals from neighborhoods characterized by socioeconomic disadvantage may view the potential informal social costs associated with gang membership as lower compared to others. In total, then, there are reasons to suspect that the restraining influences of risks and costs associated with gang membership may be lower in some communities (Thomas et al. 2022).

At the same time, individuals residing in disadvantaged neighborhoods may particularly believe that gang membership brings about certain benefits. For example, classic gang scholarship has highlighted that high levels of disadvantage can give rise to adaptive codes that emphasize the social rewards, status, and respect that can accrue from gang involvement (Anderson 1999; Cloward and Ohlin 1960; Mitchell et al. 2017). Put simply, high levels of socioeconomic disadvantage can contribute to "differential social organization" (Sutherland 1947; see also Matsueda 2006) that can increase the transmission of norms that reward gang involvement. This may be particularly important because it can be *believed* by residents that the acquisition of such social status and respect can protect, in some ways, against violent victimization (Anderson 1999). Further, there are reasons to suspect that individuals from areas characterized by high levels of socioeconomic disadvantage may be socialized to believe that gang involvement incurs other rewards, such as excitement and monetary success (Miller 1958; Stodolska, Berdychevsky, and Shinew 2019).

Beyond the subjective expectations, structural characteristics may also impact the preferences associated with gang involvement. For example, several scholars have noted that experiences with arrest can simply be "part of doing business" in some highly disadvantaged areas (Sullivan 1989). It may further be believed that being gang involved increases one's earnings through illicit activity and thus can lead individuals to be more tolerant of the risks associated with gang involvement. This idea is consistent with the notion of a *criminal reservation wage*, the amount of risk or costs an individual is willing to accept before choosing to engage in an illegal activity (Fagan and Freeman 1999; Nguyen 2020). Simply put, residing in areas with high levels of disadvantage where educational and economic opportunities are limited may lead individuals to be more risk and cost tolerant as it pertains to gang involvement. It may also lead individuals to place greater value on social and intrinsic rewards associated with crime. Anderson (1999), for example, has suggested that an individual's sense of worth is determined by the respect they get from others in their community, suggesting that individuals in disadvantaged neighborhoods place a particular premium on social status. This may be particularly true for gang members, for whom prior research has shown there is a premium on social status (Hughes and Short 2005). Further, others have argued that individuals from disadvantaged communities may have a particularly strong preference for excitements and thrills (Cohen 1955; Miller 1958). Thus, structural disadvantage may not only impact individuals' perceptions of the risks, costs, and rewards associated with gang involvement, but may also shift preferences in a way that make gang membership more likely.

The point is that although rational choice perspectives are often seen as being at odds with sociological theories that emphasize structure, and to even downplay the importance of structure entirely, this need not be the case (McCarthy 2002; Thomas et al. 2022). Rational choice explanations are entirely consistent with perspectives that highlight the influence of structural characteristics on the likelihood of being gang involved. Such perspectives simply suggest that the influence structural factors have on one's decision to join a gang operate (at least primarily) by impacting one's perceptions of and preferences for the risks, costs, and benefits of gang involvement. This leads to important empirical questions concerning the factors that account for the relationship between neighborhood characteristics and gang involvement (which are discussed later in this chapter). In doing so, it leads to testable predictions.

A multilevel rational choice model of gang involvement would predict that individuals from socioeconomically disadvantaged communities are more likely to be gang involved than individuals from less disadvantaged areas (Pyrooz, Fox, and Decker 2010) because they view joining a gang as less risky and costly or more rewarding. Yet, unlike perspectives that focus strictly on structural risk factors for gang involvement, a choice-based model emphasizing agency and preferences can also account for the fact that most individuals from disadvantaged communities do not become gang involved (Maxson 2010). At the same time, individuals from less disadvantaged areas are not predicted to be entirely immune from gang involvement. One limitation of perspectives that focus entirely on structural factors—and ignore the individual actor—is that they often have difficulty explaining gang membership among individuals from middle-class communities. Indeed, research has highlighted that gangs and gang involvement is not uniquely limited to urban areas characterized by disadvantage, but rather distributed across geographic areas and social classes (Curry, Decker, and Egley 2002). This can be accounted for in a rational choice model of gang involvement, which places the emphasis on the individual actor rather than structure itself and thus allows for the possibility that individuals from less disadvantaged areas hold expectations and preferences conducive to gang involvement when the opportunities arise.

Increasing Criminal Activity among Gang Members

One area of inquiry that has received considerable attention is whether joining a gang increases one's criminal activity after joining (Pyrooz et al. 2016). To be sure, few scholars would dispute that there is a strong correlation between gang involvement and offending, but there has been considerable disagreement over the meaning of this relationship. On one hand, the "selection" hypothesis suggests that individuals with proclivities to engage in criminal conduct self-select into delinquent peer groups—including gangs—and that this selection accounts for the correlation between gang involvement and offending (Glueck and Glueck 1950; Gottfredson and Hirschi 1990). On the other hand, the "enhancement" hypothesis suggests that group dynamics present in gangs can increase one's likelihood and rate of engaging in criminal activity. Although the mechanism driving the enhancement of criminal and deviant behavior is unclear (Thornberry et al. 1993), the research findings overall tend to suggest that gang involvement does indeed have a crime-enhancing effect (Pyrooz et al. 2016).

It should be apparent from the above that a rational choice model does argue for an element of selection into gangs—selection that is driven by individuals' perceptions of and preferences for the risks, costs, and rewards associated with gang involvement. Importantly, however, the rational choice model discussed here also allows for gang involvement to enhance criminal and delinquent tendencies and offers tractable mechanisms to explain such enhancement. Specifically, a rational choice model would predict that criminal behavior increases after joining a gang because (1) subjective expectations of the risks, costs, and rewards to crime change; (2) preferences for the risks, costs, and rewards change; or (3) some combination of both.

Thus, we can conceptualize one's perceived utility of engaging in crime prior to gang involvement (PGI) through the equation:

$$Crime_i^{PGI} = \beta_{0i}^{PGI} + \beta_{1I}^{PGI} Monetary_i^{PGI} + \beta_{2i}^{PGI} SocRew_{2i}^{PGI} + \beta_{3i}^{PGI} PersRew_{3i}^{PGI} \\ + \beta_{4I}^{PGI} Risk_{4i}^{PGI} + \beta_{5I}^{PGI} SocCosts_{5i}^{PGI} \quad [12]$$

and their perceived utility of engaging in crime after becoming gang involved through the equation:

$$Crime_i^{GI} = \beta_{0i}^{GI} + \beta_{1I}^{GI} Monetary_i^{GI} + \beta_{2i}^{GI} SocRew_{2i}^{GI} + \beta_{3i}^{GI} PersRew_{3i}^{GI} \\ + \beta_{4I}^{GI} Risk_{4i}^{GI} + \beta_{5I}^{GI} SocCosts_{5i}^{GI} \quad [13]$$

As is evident, the model of offending decisions is identical, structurally, both prior to and after joining a gang. That suggests that the factors that lead to differences in offending can be attributed to the subjective expectations and preferences (see also Thomas and Vogel 2019). There are indeed reasons to predict that individuals may shift perceptions and preferences after joining a gang. Increases in the direct and indirect experiences with offending and arrest may lead individuals to hold lower perceptions of arrest risk (Anwar and Loughran 2011; Wilson, Paternoster, and Loughran 2017) and the potential sloughing off of relationships with prosocial associates can lead to a decrease in the anticipated informal social costs of crime (Petkovsek et al. 2016). Moreover, the enmeshment into a criminal gang can lead one to increase the anticipated social rewards associated with crime, as well as socializing individuals to view crime as more intrinsically rewarding (Bishop et al. 2017).[1] Similarly, the potential shift to a more "criminal" identity likely leads individuals to become more tolerant of the risks and costs of crime and to place greater weight on social and intrinsic rewards (Paternoster and Bushway 2009).

A common criticism of contemporary gang scholarship (and of group influence work more generally) is a lack of attention toward mechanisms that may account for the "facilitation" effect of gangs (Thornberry et al. 1993; see also McGloin and Thomas 2019). As noted above, Short and Strodtbeck (1965) offered up a rational choice model to account for increases in offending, and Matsueda and Lanfear (2020) have similarly suggested that rational choice models offer a micro-level mechanism that may account for how group dynamics influence individual behavior. Moreover, the rational choice models laid out in equations [12] and [13] outline a formal theoretical model to be tested. Choice inputs as a mechanism of the facilitation hypothesis can be examined descriptively by assessing how perceptions of the risks, costs, and rewards from crime change before and after an individual becomes gang involved. Further, an assessment of changes in preferences can be done by comparing the coefficients on the impact of subjective expectations pre-gang involvement and during gang involvement. The idea that choice inputs act as a mechanism that can partially account for gang facilitation effects would be supported to the extent that perceptions (e.g., mean levels) of risks, costs, and rewards change or preferences for the risks, costs, and rewards change.

Another approach could be to decompose the extent to which the increases in offending after becoming involved in a gang are due to changes in expectations or changes in preferences. Thomas and Vogel (2019) took a similar approach when assessing a rational choice model of desistance from crime. They employed a Blinder-Oaxaca decomposition model to assess the extent to which the declines in offending from adolescence to young adulthood were attributed to changes in the perceptions of the risks, costs, and rewards versus changes in unobserved preferences. They found evidence that perceptions changed in a manner that is largely consistent with rational choice predictions—individuals came to view crime as more risky and costly in adulthood and also viewed the social and intrinsic rewards as lower. They also found that preferences largely changed in ways that could account for desistance from crime—individuals became more risk and cost averse and generally placed less weight on the social rewards associated with offending. Indeed, their decomposition model showed that around half of the declines in offending could be accounted for by changing perceptions, with the other half due to changes in unobservable factors (e.g., preferences). A similar modeling strategy could be employed when assessing a rational choice model of gang facilitation and could be against some of the seminal rational choice-based ideas first introduced by Short and Strodtbeck (1965; see also Matsueda and Lanfear 2020).

Situational Influences: Gangs and Collective Behavior

The section above outlined how gang involvement can influence one's overall propensity to engage in criminal conduct (i.e., their criminality). An important distinction in rational choice literature is the difference between criminality (one's propensity to commit crime) and criminal events (the act itself). I noted above that gang involvement may lead to longer-term changes in one's overall expectations on the risks, costs, and rewards associated with crime, as well as perhaps leading to changes in one's preferences associated with crime (e.g., tolerance for risk), which directly corresponds to one's overall criminality. However, there are also reasons to suspect that gangs may provide situational inducements toward offending that, in the moment, make criminal acts more likely. I argue that this occurs largely through situational group dynamics that influence one's *expectations*, and not through one's preferences. This is because preferences are assumed to be at least *relatively stable* across individuals in a given time period. In this way, one's tolerance for risk or preferences for social rewards are thought to be something that individuals carry with them across different contexts (Hoeben and Thomas 2019). Perceptions on the likelihood of arrest and expectations as to how others will respond to criminal activity, on the other hand, are thought to be partially situationally malleable.

Some prior work has explicitly highlighted the group dynamics involved in gang activity, and how such dynamics may impact decisions to engage in group crime (Matsueda and Lanfear 2020; McGloin and Collins 2015). Indeed, this was a key element of the choice-based discussion in Short and Strodtbeck's (1965) seminal work on gang processes and offending. As noted above, Matsueda and Lanfear (2020) provided a detailed and excellent discussion of the implications of Short and Strodtbeck's choice perspective, one that I encourage those interested in choice and gangs to read. As such, my goal is to outline extant research on group dynamics and choice and how these may be extended to better understand gang-related offending *in the situation*.

Several criminologists have invoked choice-based explanations to explain the group nature of crime. Osgood et al. (1996), for example, noted that unstructured socializing with similarly aged peers makes deviance easier to commit (i.e., less risky) and more rewarding (i.e., increases social rewards from crime). Further, Warr's (2002) seminal book on the group nature of crime highlighted several group processes that affect the likelihood of offending. These include normative influences, diffusion of responsibility, anonymity, and opportunity. McGloin and Collins (2015) applied these group processes to explain gang dynamics. Importantly, however, many of these group processes can be thought to influence offending through individual expectations on the anticipated risks, costs, and rewards associated with crime.

Before discussing gangs specifically, it is worthwhile to discuss the research on group processes and offending generally. Much of this work stems from the work of McGloin and her colleagues. McGloin and Rowan (2015) found evidence that individuals are more likely to report a willingness to offend when with others than when they are alone and, further, that this relationship is stronger the larger the group. In a follow-up study, McGloin and Thomas (2016) found evidence that this observed relationship may be accounted for via rational choice inputs—notably, individual perceptions of the risks, costs, and rewards from crime. For example, they hypothesize that as the group size gets larger, individuals view their own individual probability of arrest for an act as lower. Further, their findings suggest that perceptions of moral responsibility for offending are lower when in a group than when alone, which they argue can be explained through diffusion of responsibility. McGloin and Thomas (2016) further found that when offending with a group, individuals tend to feel a stronger identity with said group and that respondents would find that behavior more exciting, which can be thought of as being related to perceptions of the social and intrinsic rewards associated with crime. Simply put, there are strong theoretical and empirical reasons to suspect that group offending, in the situation, shifts perceptions of the anticipated consequences of offending.

There are reasons to expect that these changes in the perceived expectations from crime in the group context may be particularly salient when the group is a gang. First, gangs tend to carry with them stronger senses of ingroup identification that can make group processes and the potential rewards from gang-related offending stronger. In other words, a stronger sense of group identity can make the potential social rewards from crime larger, while at the same time this group attachment can also make collective behavior more exciting (Matsueda 2006). Further, the nature of gangs may lead to further reductions in the formal and informal sanctions that can deter criminal activity in a given situation. To be sure, one central element in Osgood et al.'s (1996) theory of co-offending is that committing crime in a group can lead to reductions in the perceived probability of arrest (i.e., offending with others can make crime easier to commit). This is likely to be particularly true in groups where the members have experience committing crime. Further, because gang members tend to hold attitudes and norms against "snitching," individuals may further believe that committing gang-related offenses is unlikely to result in an arrest (Pyrooz et al. 2021; see also Morris 2010).

At the same time, the situational group processes that can lower moral inhibitions against crime may also be particularly salient when the group is a gang. Extant research indicates that most everyone—even those who offend at relatively high rates—view crime as morally wrong (Agnew 1994; Thomas 2018), but some individuals are able to situationally rationalize crime and bypass these general moral inhibitions (Thomas 2019). As Sykes and Matza (1957) asserted, one technique of neutralization that individuals invoke is an *appeal to higher loyalties*. In this way, gang members may know that crime and violence are morally wrong but are able to rationalize and situationally approve of the behavior when with fellow gang members because they view loyalty to the gang (and protection of fellow gang members) as more important than following the law, thus reducing the informal social control that moral beliefs tend to impose.

McGloin and Collins (2015) offered a number of group processes that may account for gang-related behaviors, including a diffusion of responsibility, enhanced social rewards and excitement, and reductions in perceptions of risk (see also Warr 2002). Rather than increasing one's general criminality, I argue that this is best seen as a *situational group effect*, which fits nicely with the rational choice distinction between criminality and crime (Cornish and Clarke 1986). Put simply, the group processes outlined by McGloin and Collins (2015) can be viewed through a choice-based lens, whereby mechanisms such as diffusion of responsibility, ingroup identification, and collective action more generally impact situational decisions to offend by enhancing perceptions of the social and intrinsic rewards from crime and decreasing one's perceptions of risks and social costs (Matsueda and Lanfear 2020; Short and Strodtbeck 1965). Extant research has provided findings that suggest group processes and collective behavior can impact individual perceptions of the risks, costs, and rewards associated with crime (McGloin and Thomas 2016; see also Matsueda 2006), but such ideas have not been directly applied to gang delinquency, despite the salient role of group processes and choice embedded within the classic work of Short and Strodtbeck (1965; see also Matsueda and Lanfear 2020).

Disengagement from Gangs

A common misconception is the notion that individuals who become gang involved are making a lifetime commitment. In reality, most gang membership is relatively short lived, and most individuals who become gang involved leave the life after some time (Melde and Esbensen 2014; Pyrooz 2014). Further, there seems to be convincing evidence that many individuals leave gangs on their own accord (see Tonks and Stephenson 2019). Indeed, a central issue in the gang literature is understanding how gang membership unfolds over the life course (Pyrooz 2014).

Over the last few decades there have been a number of studies seeking to assess the factors that promote disengagement from gangs. As with other aspects in the gang literature, much of the research on gang disengagement has focused on changes in external life circumstances that are commonly attributed to criminal desistance generally (Laub and Sampson 2003; Pyrooz and Decker 2011). Tonks and Stephenson (2019) recently conducted a systematic review of the gang disengagement literature, and many of the major themes identified by these authors emphasized the role of external events, such as romantic involvement with a significant other (Decker et al. 2014; Munoz 2014), parenthood (O'Neal et al. 2016; Pyrooz, McGloin, and Decker 2017), victimization (Decker and Lauritsen 2002), and "physical removal" such as imprisonment or joining the military (Harris et al. 2011).

As several scholars have highlighted, this emphasis on changing external life circumstances downplays the active role that individuals play in their own disengagement process (Densley 2013). Densley and Pyrooz (2019), for example, note that many gang members experience external "pulls" such as romantic relationships, employment, and parenthood long before they disengage from gang activity. Thus, disengagement from gangs is not an *event* due solely to external factors, but rather a *process* that involves some element of "inner change" (Densley and Pyrooz 2019; see also Sweeten, Pyrooz, and Piquero 2013). Densley and Pyrooz (2019) introduce a signaling theory, whereby active gang members communicate to others (e.g., members of their gang, members of rival gangs) that such an inner change has taken place, and this signaling process thus plays a seminal role in gang disengagement. Importantly, the notion of "inner changes" does not completely negate the influence that potential changes in life circumstances have on gang disengagement (Decker et al. 2014; Pyrooz and Decker 2011) but rather highlights the important role of "conscious intention" (Densley and Pyrooz 2019, 37).

Thus, it is generally suggested that both external life transitions that may shift individuals' perceptions of the consequences of gang involvement and inner changes in one's intentions can contribute to gang disengagement. Yet what is absent is a unified theoretical framework that can parsimoniously account for these multiple contributors in a logically consistent manner. I argue that a rational choice model is well suited to meet this challenge. That individual perceptions of consequences are formed through communication and experiential learning—which can be influenced by life circumstances—is consistent with the rational choice model offered here (McCarthy 2002). Further, signaling theory, which Densley and Pyrooz (2019) draw on, is rooted in economic theory and compatible with choice-based perspectives (Shannon 1948). That is, the inner changes that assist in the gang disengagement process not only lead individuals to communicate such intentions to others, but also lead to changes in one's values and preferences that play seminal roles in choice-based models (Paternoster and Bushway 2009).

A rational choice perspective would view disengagement from a gang as a decision one makes after deliberating the (dis)utility associated with continued gang involvement. That is, individuals may come to view gang life as garnering less utility than it once did or come to believe that risks and costs associated with gang activity are no longer worth the time allocation required. Thus, the decision to leave a gang is the direct converse of the decision to join a gang—a function of one's beliefs about the utility and disutility of staying in and leaving the gang. As with other behavioral and life choices, the decision to desist from gang involvement is thought to be a function of one's expectations and preferences.

The expectations about gang involvement may change if individuals—through direct or vicarious experiences—come to view the risks of being a gang member as high. For example, individuals may get arrested or see several of their companions arrested and the justice system get involved (Hastings, Dunbar, and Bania 2013; Sweeten et al. 2013). They may also have direct or indirect experiences with violent victimization that similarly increases their perceptions of the risks associated with gang involvement. Further, perceptions of the informal social costs associated with continued gang involvement may also change as gang-involved individuals begin to encounter life transitions that are thought to increase one's bonds to society (Sampson and Laub 1993). Pyrooz et al. (2017), for example, have found that parenthood can spur disengagement from gang activity. Several other scholars have argued that romantic relationships/marriage and employment may also play a central role in gang disengagement (Carson and Vecchio 2015; Pyrooz and Decker 2011; see also Tonks and Stephenson 2019). One possible mechanism that can explain the influence of life transitions on gang disengagement is that these new roles highlight to individuals the potential negative consequences and informal social costs that may occur if an individual is arrested, incarcerated, or seriously injured through gang activity (Pyrooz and Decker 2011; see also Laub and Sampson 2003). It is also possible that individuals do not see gang life as socially or intrinsically rewarding like they once did. Even if one is still gang involved, other social networks may change in such a manner that an individual comes to see gang involvement as producing less social rewards than it once did. This could occur simply due to a shared misunderstanding that occurs in adolescence where we believe that crime and crime-related activities (e.g., gang involvement) are socially valued in adolescence, but realize that this belief is false in early adulthood (Matza 1964). Finally, gang life can be less exciting than an individual once thought it was. Crime and other gang-related activities can be exhausting and physically draining, and thus individuals come to see less thrill and fun in such activities.

At the same time, preferences are also believed to change over time. This is particularly salient in the work of Paternoster and Bushway (2009), whose identity theory of desistance is rooted in a rational choice perspective. They argue that some individuals come to adopt a "criminal identity" that leads them to hold preferences conducive to criminal activity (e.g., tolerance for risks and costs and a preference for social and intrinsic rewards). As they come to revisit past failures (crystallization of discontent) and contemplate their prospects for the future (feared self) they may shed the criminal identity and begin to value prosocial institutions and life outcomes. Paternoster and Bushway explicitly argued that changes in identity are reflected to oneself and to others as a change in preferences. Thus, individuals can purposefully shed their gang identity and in turn become less tolerant of the risks and costs associated with gang involvement. They may also come to be less concerned about issues of social status and respect—and thus place less weight on the potential social rewards associated with continued gang involvement—as well as care less about seeking out behaviors and lifestyles that are "exciting" or thrilling. Importantly, and as I will detail further below, the notion of shifting preferences as a function of changing identity necessarily suggests that individuals may choose to "desist" from gang involvement even without experiencing changes in their life circumstances. In other words, individuals need not view gang involvement as being increasingly risky or costly or that the rewards are somehow less and can still choose to disengage from gang involvement.

Importantly, as noted above, this notion of inner changes resulting in changes in preferences is consistent with some prior work examining gang disengagement. Densley and Pyrooz's (2019) signaling theory attributes a non-trivial portion of gang disengagement to the conscious efforts of gang members. And while these authors explicitly state that their proposed signaling theory is not about "internal self-concept and social identity" (37), it is not necessarily *incompatible* with an identity and choice-based explanation. That is, consistent with the explanation of criminal desistance offered by Paternoster and Bushway (2009), individuals may become disillusioned by gang involvement (Harris et al. 2011) in a manner similar to Paternoster and Bushway's crystallization of discontent. Such individuals change their identity toward one that is more prosocial, and as a result shift their preferences in a manner that makes them less tolerant of the risks and costs of gang involvement and less responsive to potential rewards (Thomas and Vogel 2019), while at the same time leading individuals to signal such inner changes to others (Densley and Pyrooz 2019). In sum, a rational choice model is well suited to account for the nuanced influences of external life circumstances and inner changes to oneself in the process of gang disengagement.

Implications of a Rational Choice Model: Moving Agency and Choice to Center Stage

Thus, there are three processes associated with gang involvement at the individual level that have dominated scholarship over the last century: (1) non-random selection into gangs, (2) the enhancement of criminal behavior after joining a gang, and (3) disengagement from gang involvement. Yet even though these dynamic processes all have the *individual* as the theoretical unit of interest, much of the gang literature has proceeded by divorcing the individual agent from these processes. Instead, extant literature on gang membership has tended to focus on structural and cultural factors that lead disadvantaged youth to join gangs (Duran 2013; Katz and Schnebly 2011 Pyrooz et al. 2010; Thrasher 1927), or to focus on individual personality traits that increase the likelihood of gang involvement (Tostlebe and Pyrooz 2022).[2] Such explanations, however, have problems when it comes to explaining the dynamic nature of gang involvement over time. To be sure, structural and cultural explanations have difficulty explaining why few individuals in disadvantaged neighborhoods become gang involved, and they seem ill-equipped to explain why individuals from middle- and upper-class areas sometimes find themselves members of gangs. Further, given limited class mobility and the general stability of personality traits, prominent explanations of gang involvement seem ill-suited to explain disengagement from gangs.

I argue that the limitations of these perspectives stem from the fact that they have downplayed the active role that individual actors play when seeking to explain behaviors, choosing instead to focus their attention on external (structure) and internal (traits) factors that are outside the control of human agents. A rational choice model of gang involvement, like the one offered here, is well suited to explain (1) selection into gangs, (2) why individuals tend to offend at a higher rate after becoming gang involved, and (3) disengagement from gangs. Simply put, it is a general model of human action that is capable of explaining the dynamics of gang membership. It does so by suggesting that these decisions are a joint function of individual perceptions of and preferences for the risks, costs, and rewards associated with gang membership and offending—individuals are predicted to become (and stay) gang involved and increase their offending when the marginal utility of doing those actions exceeds the marginal disutility of those actions. Importantly, the rational choice model offered here does not negate the important influence of structural risk factors for gang involvement and offending. In fact, it stresses that such factors likely play an important role in the decision to become a gang member and one's criminal tendencies, but suggests that such factors matter through the impact they have on individual subjective expectations and preferences (Thomas et al. 2022).

The rational choice perspective offered here recognizes that human beings possess *agency* and are thus not determined or compelled to join a gang based on structural or individual characteristics. Paternoster (2017) recently provided a detailed discussion of human agency and its implications for criminological theory. Human agency is defined as the capacity to reflect, deliberate, imagine alternatives, and act purposefully. It recognizes the ability of human beings to construct their own social lives and reality rather than merely reacting to their social environments (Blumer 1969). This contrasts with the usual positivist approaches to crime (and gangs) that tend to dominate criminological thought (Thomas et al. 2021). These approaches—usually emphasizing the "causal" role of structural factors—tend to frame individuals as reactive products of their own environments. Thus, it is at least implicitly suggested that individuals from disadvantaged communities and who are exposed to certain cultural values are determined to become gang involved, that the pressures exerted by the gang *compel* individuals to commit criminal acts the individuals themselves have no interest in engaging in, and that individuals need to experience structural turning points like marriage and employment to disengage from gang involvement because they are incapable of leaving a gang on their own. Of course, such positivist explanations of gang involvement and crime are consistent with the lofty goal of many criminologists to make the study of crime and human behavior emulative of the physical and natural sciences by specifying theoretical perspectives rooted in "causality," but in doing so they paint a picture of human beings that is decisively not human (Thomas et al. 2021).

The rational choice model offered here is one that begins with the assumption that human beings possess agency (Paternoster 2017)—the ability to deliberate, evaluate consequences, imagine alternative futures, reflect on the past, and simply to *choose*. It is an agent-centered approach that necessarily has implications for many of the processes of interest to gang scholars. Notably, it stresses that many of the key gang processes are a result of individual choice: Individuals *choose* if and when to become gang involved, individuals *choose* if and when to engage in crime, and individuals *choose* if and when to disengage from the gang. As I have stated repeatedly, this does not negate the influence that structure and culture have on such decisions, but it does reject the idea that these factors force or compel individuals to make such decisions. Matza (1969) and Paternoster (2017) have detailed the meaning and implications of human agency for criminology in general. It means individuals are not forced to join criminal peer groups such as gangs and play an active role in selecting their own social networks. This necessarily means that some individuals experiencing high levels of disadvantage commonly used to explain gang involvement can "simply stroll away" and choose not to become gang involved (Matza 1969). Conversely, individuals from less disadvantaged neighborhoods, when given the opportunity, can choose to become gang involved despite the fact they are not facing the structural disadvantages commonly used to explain gang involvement in sociological theories. Such individuals may believe that the risks of gang involvement are relatively high and that they could potentially experience informal social costs for joining a gang, but they still decide to do so if gang involvement is consistent with their preferences for risks, costs, and rewards (e.g., they are risk and cost tolerant or strongly value potential social rewards from gang involvement).

Even further, the notion of agency and the purported seminal role that preferences play in gang-related decisions also suggests that individuals need not experience structural turning points (e.g., marriage, employment) to disengage from gang life. Pyrooz (2014) found that disengagement from gangs typically occurs long before major life transitions such as marriage, children, and stable employment. Thus, although such factors can contribute to gang disengagement (see Pyrooz et al. 2017), they are not *necessary* for desistance from gang life (Densley and Pyrooz 2019). This is difficult to explain from perspectives that emphasize external life transitions as the catalyst for change (e.g., Sampson and Laub 1993), but is consistent with the agentic rational choice model offered here: Individuals can choose to disengage from gangs on their own, perhaps due to changes in one's identity that impacts their preferences (Paternoster and Bushway 2009; Pyrooz 2014). Simply put, individuals play active roles in their own decisions to disengage from gang involvement.

At the same time, and contrary to some concerns of agent-oriented perspectives of choice (Piquero 2022), the perspective offered here does not revert to an untestable internalist view of humans. It instead offers a tractable formal theory that can be tested in relatively straightforward ways. Indeed, several models and predictions of a rational choice theory of gang involvement have been detailed here, and future work seeking to understand gang membership and its influence on behavior should examine the validity of the predictions offered here.

First, future work should assess how well a rational choice model can explain selection into gang involvement by estimating equation [11]. Such a test would require knowledge of individual perceptions on the risks, costs, and rewards associated with gang involvement and to examine the extent to which perceptions and preferences account for variation in the decision to become gang involved.

Second, because the rational choice model offered here is inherently multilevel in nature (see also Coleman 1990; Matsueda 2017), future work should also examine the extent to which choice inputs (i.e., expectations and preferences) are influenced by neighborhood characteristics and structural disadvantage. Thomas et al. (2022) recently found that concentrated disadvantage at the block-group level was associated with lower perceptions of the risks and costs associated with crime and higher perceptions of the social rewards associated with crime. Neighborhood characteristics also influenced preferences in a manner that was consistent with predictions, although the influence of concentrated disadvantage was largely indirect and operated through individual perceptions of the neighborhood. A similar analysis could be conducted as it pertains to the subjective expectations and preferences associated with gang involvement.

Third, future work should assess how rational choice ideas can account for the enhancement of criminal involvement after joining a gang. Rational choice theories would predict that an individual comes to view crime as more rewarding and less risky and costly after becoming gang involved, and may become more tolerant of the risks and costs and to place greater value on the rewards associated with offending. These changes in subjective expectations and preferences should, at least in part, account for the increases in crime that are observed during the state of gang membership (Pyrooz et al. 2016). Finally, more work is needed to assess the processes by which individuals disengage from gang involvement and to assess the role of agency and choice in this process. This can involve qualitative research that takes seriously the view of the individual and the factors they believe influence their own disengagement. It can also involve quantitative work that examines how perceptions of and preferences for the risks, costs, and rewards of gang involvement change and how such changes may promote "desistance" from a gang life.

There are several other interesting puzzles that can be examined from a choice-based perspective. I focused on three issues that make up seminal areas of inquiry in the gang literature—selection into gangs, crime enhancement after joining a gang, and disengagement from gangs—but other outcomes may be of interest that a rational choice model could be well suited to explain, such as the recruitment of gang members (Densley 2012) and the types of crimes certain gangs take part in (Adams and Pizarro 2014; see also Thomas et al. 2020). Further, the focus of this chapter was on traditional, or rather *normative*, rational choice models of behavior. Yet alternative choice models, such as those rooted in behavioral economics, also exist (see Pogarsky, Roche, and Pickett 2018). Thus, future researchers may be interested in how heuristics and biases (Pogarsky, Roche, and Pickett 2017), threats of status loss (Thomas and Nguyen 2020), as well as emotions and fear contribute to gang-related decisions (Barnum and Solomon 2019). Still, it is my view that it is imperative to first examine the strengths and limitations of more traditional normative subjective expected utility models, such as the framework offered here, and how such models can contribute to our understanding of gang involvement, gang disengagement, and crime.

Conclusion

Few concepts have been as influential to the study of crime and delinquency as "the gang" (Pyrooz and Mitchell 2015). Research into gangs and gang membership have contributed key insights into structural influences on crime and how behavior can be shaped by group dynamics. At the same time, scholars have argued that the focus on structure and culture has left some of the more proximate mechanisms influencing gang involvement and crime unclear (Thornberry et al. 1993; see also McGloin and Thomas 2019). More recently, a number of scholars have argued that rational choice perspectives offer an individual-level theory of action that is well suited to link structural and cultural characteristics to individual behavior (Matsueda 2013; McCarthy 2002). Thus, far from being oppositional with sociological theories of structure, rational choice theories are compatible with theories of structure and can even address some of the limitations inherent in some prominent sociological perspectives. Research linking social context to choice has grown over the last several years in the study of crime (Thomas and McGloin 2013; Thomas et al. 2022), but have not yet gained traction as it pertains to the literature on gangs. Such an approach has the potential to more faithfully describe the true nature of humans as agentic, to provide new puzzles for future work to assess, and to advance our understanding of gangs and gang membership.

Notes

1. The perception formation process implied in rational choice theories is similar to the process discussed in Akers' (1990) social learning theory. Indeed, a number of scholars have highlighted some of the parallels between learning and rational choice perspectives (Akers 1990; Matsueda et al. 2006; McCarthy 2002), in that both perspectives argue that perceptions of anticipated outcomes can be learned through communication and experiences, and that such perceptions play a role in influencing behavior. Contrary to Akers' (1990) assertion, however, rational choice is not simply subsumable under social learning theory. Rational choice and social learning are based on fundamentally different assumptions, with one notable difference being that the idea that humans possess agency is central to the choice model offered here while Akers' theory largely paints a *reactive* picture of humans. The assumption of human agency that gets manifestly projected through one's internal values and preferences—a central concept in choice theories—is absent in most learning perspectives. Indeed, while "choice" is arguably present to varying degrees in most theories (see McCarthy 2002), *rational* choice differs in emphasizing the active role individuals play in their own lives and brings choice to "center stage" of the behavioral process (Nagin 2007).
2. This is not to say that prominent perspectives *deny* choice. Rather, most of the perspectives give lip service to choice but are constructed in an epistemologically positivist framework whereby external and internal factors are thought to be *the* cause of gang membership and crime. The rational choice perspective offered here begins with an assumption of human agency, and thus brings choice and the human actor to the center stage of their own social world (Matza 1964; Nagin 2007; Paternoster 2017).

References

Adams, J. J., and J. M. Pizarro. 2014. "Patterns of Specialization and Escalation in the Criminal Careers of Gang and Non-Gang Homicide Offenders." *Criminal Justice and Behavior* 41 (2): 237–255.

Agnew, R. 1994. "The Techniques of Neutralization and Violence." *Criminology* 32 (4): 555–580.

Akers, R. L. 1990. "Rational Choice, Deterrence, and Social Learning Theory in Criminology: The Path Not Taken." *Journal of Criminal Law and Criminology* 81 (3): 653–676.

Anderson, E. 1999. *Code of the Street: Decency, Violence, and the Moral Life of the Inner City.* New York: WW Norton and Company.

Anwar, S., and T. A. Loughran. 2011. "Testing a Bayesian Learning Theory of Deterrence among Serious Juvenile Offenders." *Criminology* 49 (3): 667–698.

Bachman, R., R. Paternoster, and S. Ward. 1992. "The Rationality of Sexual Offending: Testing a Deterrence/Rational Choice Conception of Sexual Assault." *Law and Society Review* 26 (2): 343–372.

Barnum, T. C., and S. J. Solomon. 2019. "Fight or Flight: Integral Emotions and Violent Intentions." *Criminology* 57 (4): 659–686.

Becker, G. S. 1968. "Crime and Punishment: An Economic Approach." In *The Economic Dimensions of Crime*, edited by Nigel Fielding, Alan Clarke, and Robert Witt, 13–68. London: Palgrave Macmillan.

Bishop, A. S., K. G. Hill, A. B. Gilman, J. C. Howell, R. F. Catalano, and J. D. Hawkins. 2017. "Developmental Pathways of Youth Gang Membership: A Structural Test of the Social Development Model." *Journal of Crime and Justice* 40 (3): 275–296.

Blumer, H. 1969. *Symbolic Interactionism: Perspective and Method.* Englewood Cliffs, NJ: Prentice-Hall.

Carson, D. C., and J. M. Vecchio. 2015. "Leaving the Gang." In *The Handbook of Gangs*, edited by Scott Decker and David Pyrooz, 257–275. Chichester, UK: Wiley.

Cloward, Richard A., and Lloyd E. Ohlin. 1960. *Delinquency and Opportunity: A Theory of Delinquent Gangs.* Glencoe, IL: Free Press.

Cohen, Albert K. 1955. *Delinquent Boys: The Culture of the Gang.* Glencoe, IL: Free Press.

Coleman, J. S. 1990. *Foundations of Social Theory.* Cambridge, MA: Harvard University Press.

Cornish, D. B., and R. V. Clarke, eds. 1986. *The Reasoning Criminal: Rational Choice Perspectives on Offending.* New Brunswick, NJ: Transaction Publishers.

Cullen, F. T. 2017. "Choosing Our Criminological Future: Reservations about Human Agency as an Organizing Concept." *Journal of Developmental and Life-Course Criminology* 3 (4): 373–379.

Curry, G. D., S. H. Decker, and A. Egley Jr. 2002. "Gang Involvement and Delinquency in a Middle School Population." *Justice Quarterly* 19 (2): 275–292.

Decker, S., and J. Lauritsen, eds. 2002. *Leaving the Gang.* Thousand Oaks, CA: Sage Publications.

Decker, S. H., C. Melde, and D. C. Pyrooz. 2013. "What Do We Know about Gangs and Gang Members and Where Do We Go from Here?" *Justice Quarterly* 30 (3): 369–402.

Decker, S., D. Pyrooz, and R. Moule. 2014. "Disengagement from Gangs as Role Transitions." *Journal of Research on Adolescence* 24 (2): 268–283.

Densley, J. A. 2012. "Street Gang Recruitment: Signaling, Screening, and Selection." *Social Problems* 59 (3): 301–321.

Densley, J. 2013. *How Gangs Work: An Ethnography of Youth Violence.* New York: Palgrave Macmillan.

Densley, J. 2015. "Joining the Gang: A Process of Supply and Demand." In *The Handbook of Gangs*, edited by Scott H. Decker and David C. Pyrooz, 235–256. Chichester, UK: Wiley-Blackwell.

Densley, J. A., and D. C. Pyrooz. 2019. "A Signaling Perspective on Disengagement from Gangs." *Justice Quarterly* 36: 31–58.

Dugan, L., G. LaFree, and A. R. Piquero. 2005. "Testing a Rational Choice Model of Airline Hijackings." *Criminology* 43 (4): 1031–1065.

Durán, R. 2013. *Gang Life in Two Cities: An Insider's Journey*. New York: Columbia University Press.

Fagan, J., and R. B. Freeman. 1999. "Crime and Work." *Crime and Justice* 25: 225–290.

Gatti, U., R. E. Tremblay, F. Vitaro, and P. McDuff. 2005. "Youth gangs, Delinquency and Drug Use: A Test of the Selection, Facilitation, and Enhancement Hypotheses." *Journal of Child Psychology and Psychiatry* 46 (11): 1178–1190.

Giordano, P. C., S. A. Cernkovich, & D. D. Holland. 2003. "Changes in Friendship Relations Over the Life Course: Implications for Desistance From Crime." *Criminology* 41 (2): 293–328.

Glueck, S., and E. Glueck. 1950. *Unraveling Juvenile Delinquency*. Cambridge, MA: Harvard University Press.

Gottfredson, M. R. And T. Hirschi. 1990. *A General Theory of Crime*. Stanford, CA: Stanford University Press.

Hagedorn, J. M., and P. Macon. 1988. *People and Folks: Gangs, Crime and the Underclass in a Rustbelt City*. Chicago, IL: Lake View Press.

Hastings, R., L. Dunbar, and M. Bania. 2013. *Leaving Criminal Youth Gangs: Exit Strategies and Programs*. Ottawa, ON: Crime Prevention Ottawa.

Hechter, M., and S. Kanazawa. 1997. "Sociological Rational Choice Theory." *Annual Review of Sociology* 23 (1): 191–214.

Hoeben, E. M., & K. J. Thomas. 2019. "Peers and Offender Decision-Making." *Criminology & Public Policy* 18 (4): 759–784.

Hughes, L. A., and J. F. Short. 2005. "Disputes Involving Youth Street Gang Members: Micro-Social Contexts." *Criminology* 43 (1): 43–76.

Johnstone, J. W. 1983. "Recruitment to a Youth Gang." *Youth and Society* 14 (3): 281–300.

Katz, C. M., and S. M. Schnebly. 2011. "Neighborhood Variation in Gang Member Concentrations." *Crime & Delinquency* 57 (3): 377–407. https://doi.org/10.1177/0011128708317065

Laub, J. H. and R. J. Sampson. 2003. *Shared Beginnings, Divergent Lives: Delinquent Boys to Age 70*. Cambridge, MA: Harvard University Press.

Leverso, J., and C. Hess. 2021. "From the Hood to the Home: Masculinity Maturation of Chicago Street Gang Members." *Sociological Perspectives* 64 (6): 1206–1223.

Loughran, T. A., R. Paternoster, A. Chalfin, and T. Wilson. 2016. "Can Rational Choice Be Considered a General Theory of Crime? Evidence from Individual-Level Panel Data." *Criminology* 54 (1): 86–112.

Matsueda, R. L. 2006. "Differential Social Organization, Collective Action, and Crime." *Crime, Law and Social Change* 46 (1): 3–33.

Matsueda, R. L. 2013. "Rational Choice Research in Criminology: A Multi-Level Framework." In *The Handbook of Rational Choice Social Research*, edited by Rafael Wiettek, Rom Snijders, and Victor Nee, 283–321. Berlin, Germany: De Gruyter.

Matsueda, R. L. 2017. "Toward an Analytical Criminology: The Micro–Macro Problem, Causal Mechanisms, and Public Policy." *Criminology* 55 (3): 493–519.

Matsueda, R. L., and C. C. Lanfear. 2020. "Collective Action, Rational Choice, and Gang Delinquency: Appreciating Short and Strodtbeck ([1965] 1974)." In *Social Bridges and Contexts in Criminology and Sociology*, edited by Lorine A. Hughes and Lisa M. Broidy, 151–168. New York: Routledge.

Matsueda, R. L., D. A. Kreager, and D. Huizinga. 2006. "Deterring Delinquents: A Rational Choice Model of Theft and Violence." *American Sociological Review* 71 (1): 95–122.

Matza, D. 1964. *Delinquency and Drift*. New York: Routledge.

Matza, D. 1969. *Becoming Deviant*. New York: Routledge.

Maxson C. 2010. "Street Gangs: How Research Can Inform Policy." In *Public Policies for Crime Control*, edited by J. Q. Wilson and J. Petersilia. New York: Oxford University Press.

McCarthy, B. 2002. "New Economics of Sociological Criminology." *Annual Review of Sociology* 28 (1): 417–442.

McGloin, Jean, and Megan Collins. 2015. "Micro-Level Processes of the Gang." In *The Handbook of Gangs*, edited by Scott Decker, and David Pyrooz, 276–293. Chichester, UK: John Wiley & Sons, Inc.

McGloin, J. M., and Z. R. Rowan. 2015. "A Threshold Model of Collective Crime." *Criminology* 53 (3): 484–512.

McGloin, J. M., and K. J. Thomas. 2019. "Peer Influence and Delinquency." *Annual Review of Criminology* 2: 241–264.

McGloin, J. M., and K. J. Thomas. 2016. "Incentives for Collective Deviance: Group Size and Changes in Perceived Risk, Cost, and Reward." *Criminology* 54 (3): 459–486. https://doi.org/10.1111/1745-9125.12111

Melde, C., and F.-A. Esbensen. 2014. "The Relative Impact of Gang Status Transitions: Identifying the Mechanisms of Change in Delinquency." *Journal of Research in Crime and Delinquency* 51 (3): 349–376. https://doi.org/10.1177/0022427813507059

Miller, W. B. 1958. "Lower Class Culture as a Generating Milieu of Gang Delinquency." *Journal of Social Issues* 14: 5–19.

Mitchell, M. M., C. Fahmy, D. C. Pyrooz, and S. H. Decker. 2017. "Criminal Crews, Codes, and Contexts: Differences and Similarities across the Code of the Street, Convict Code, Street Gangs, and Prison Gangs." *Deviant Behavior* 38 (10): 1197–1222.

Moore, J. 2010. *Going Down to the Barrio: Homeboys and Homegirls in Change*. Philadelphia, PA: Temple University Press.

Morris, E. W. 2010. "'Snitches End Up in Ditches' and other Cautionary Tales." *Journal of Contemporary Criminal Justice* 26 (3): 254–272.

Nagin, D. S. 2007. "Moving Choice to Center Stage in Criminological Research and Theory." *Criminology* 45: 259–272.

Nguyen, H. 2020. "On the Conceptualization of Criminal Capital." *Journal of Research in Crime and Delinquency* 57 (2): 182–216.

O'Neal, E. N., S. Decker, R. K. Moule, and D. C. Pyrooz. 2016. "Girls, Gangs, and Getting Out: Gender Differences and Similarities in Leaving the Gang." *Youth Violence and Juvenile Justice* 14 (1): 43–60. https://doi.org/10.1177/1541204014551426

Padilla, F. M. 1992. *The Gang as an American Enterprise*. New Brunswick, NJ: Rutgers University Press.

Paternoster, R. 2017. "Happenings, Acts, and Actions: Articulating the Meaning and Implications of Human Agency for Criminology." *Journal of Developmental and Life-Course Criminology* 3 (4): 350–372.

Paternoster, R., and S. Bushway. 2009. "Desistance and the 'Feared Self': Toward an Identity Theory of Criminal Desistance." *Journal of Criminal Law and Criminology* 99 (4): 1103–1156.

Paternoster, R., and S. Simpson. 1996. "Sanction Threats and Appeals to Morality: Testing a Rational Choice Model of Corporate Crime." *Law and Society Review* 30 (3): 549–583.

Peterson, D., T. J. Taylor, and F. A. Esbensen. 2004. "Gang Membership and Violent Victimization." *Justice Quarterly* 21 (4): 793–815.

Petkovsek, M. A., B. B. Boutwell, J. C. Barnes, and K. M. Beaver. 2016. "Moffitt's Developmental Taxonomy and Gang Membership: An Alternative Test of the Snares Hypothesis." *Youth Violence and Juvenile Justice* 14 (4): 335–349.

Pogarsky, G., S. P. Roche, and J. T. Pickett. 2017. "Heuristics and Biases, Rational Choice, and Sanction Perceptions." *Criminology* 55 (1): 85–111.

Pogarsky, G., S. P. Roche, and J. T. Pickett. 2018. "Offender Decision-Making in Criminology: Contributions from Behavioral Economics." *Annual Review of Criminology* 1: 379–400.

Pyrooz, D. C. 2014. "'From Your First Cigarette to Your Last Dyin' Day': The Patterning of Gang Membership in the Life-Course." *Journal of Quantitative Criminology* 30 (2): 349–372.

Pyrooz, D. C., and S. H. Decker. 2011. "Motives and Methods for Leaving the Gang: Understanding the Process of Gang Desistance." *Journal of Criminal Justice* 39 (5): 417–425.

Pyrooz, D. C., and M. M. Mitchell. 2015. "Little Gang Research, Big Gang Research." In *The Handbook of Gangs*, edited by Scott Decker and David Pyrooz, 28–58. Chichester, UK: Wiley.

Pyrooz, D. C., A. M. Fox, and S. H. Decker. 2010. "Racial and Ethnic Heterogeneity, Economic Disadvantage, and Gangs: A Macro-Level Study of Gang Membership in Urban America." *Justice Quarterly* 27 (6): 867–892.

Pyrooz, D. C., M. M. Mitchell, R. K. Moule Jr, and S. H. Decker. 2021. "Look Who's Talking: The Snitching Paradox in a Representative Sample of Prisoners." *The British Journal of Criminology* 61 (4): 1145–1167. https://doi.org/10.1093/bjc/azaa103

Pyrooz, D. C., J. M. McGloin, and S. H. Decker. 2017. "Parenthood as a Turning Point in the Life Course for Male and Female Gang Members: A Study of Within-Individual Changes in Gang Membership and Criminal Behavior." *Criminology* 55 (4): 869–899.

Pyrooz, D. C., J. J. Turanovic, S. H. Decker, and J. Wu. 2016. "Taking Stock of the Relationship between Gang Membership and Offending: A Meta-Analysis." *Criminal Justice and Behavior* 43 (3): 365–397.

Sampson, R. J. 2012. *Great American City*. Chicago, IL: University of Chicago Press.

Sampson, R. J., and J. H. Laub. 1993. *Crime in the Making: Pathways and Turning Points through Life*. Cambridge, MA: Harvard University Press.

Sampson, R. J., and W. J. Wilson. 1995. "Toward a Theory of Race, Crime, and Urban Inequality." In *Crime and Inequality*, edited by John Hagan and Ruth Peterson, 37–56. Stanford, CA: Stanford University Press.

Shannon, C. E. 1948. "A Mathematical Theory of Communication." *Bell System Technical Journal* 27 (3): 379–423.

Short, J. F., and F. L. Strodtbeck. 1965. *Group Process and Gang Delinquency*. Chicago, IL: University of Chicago Press.

Simon, H. A. 1986. "Rationality in Psychology and Economics." *Journal of Business* 59: S209–S224.

Stodolska, M., L. Berdychevsky, and K. J. Shinew. 2019. "Gangs and Deviant Leisure." *Leisure Sciences* 41 (4): 278–293.

Sullivan, M. L. 1989. *Getting Paid: Youth Crime and Work in the Inner City*. Ithaca, NY: Cornell University Press.

Sutherland, E. H. 1947. *Principles of Criminology*. New York: Lippincott.
Sweeten, G., D. C. Pyrooz, and A. R. Piquero. 2013. "Disengaging from Gangs and Desistance from Crime." *Justice Quarterly* 30 (3): 469–500.
Sykes, G. M., and D. Matza. 1957. "Techniques of Neutralization: A Theory of Delinquency." *American Sociological Review* 22 (6): 664–670.
Tapia, M. 2011. "US Juvenile Arrests: Gang Membership, Social Class, and Labeling Effects." *Youth and Society* 43 (4): 1407–1432.
Thomas, K. J. 2018. "Revisiting Delinquent Attitudes: Measurement, Dimensionality and Behavioral Effects." *Journal of Quantitative Criminology* 34 (1): 313–341.
Thomas, K. J. 2019. "Rationalizing Delinquency: Understanding the Person-Situation Interaction through Item Response Theory." *Journal of Research in Crime and Delinquency* 56 (1): 3–41.
Thomas, K. J., T. A. Loughran, and B. C. Hamilton. 2020. "Perceived Arrest Risk, Psychic Rewards, and Offense Specialization: A Partial Test of Rational Choice Theory." *Criminology* 58 (3): 485–509.
Thomas, K. J., and H. Nguyen. 2020. "Status Gains versus Status Losses: Loss Aversion and Deviance." *Justice Quarterly* 39 (4): 871–896.
Thomas, K. J., J. O'Neill, and T. A. Loughran. 2022. "Estimating Latent Preferences for Crime: Implications for Rational Choice, Identity, and Desistance Theories." *Justice Quarterly*: 1–31.
Thomas, K. J., G. Pogarsky, and T. A. Loughran. 2021. "Paternoster on Human Agency and Crime: A Rejoinder to Critics on His Behalf." *Journal of Developmental and Life-Course Criminology* 7: 524–542.
Thomas, K. J., and M. Vogel. 2019. "Testing a Rational Choice Model of 'Desistance': Decomposing Changing Expectations and Changing Utilities." *Criminology* 57 (4): 687–714.
Thornberry, T. P., M. D. Krohn, A. J. Lizotte, and D. Chard-Wierschem. 1993. "The Role of Juvenile Gangs in Facilitating Delinquent Behavior." *Journal of Research in Crime and Delinquency* 30 (1): 55–87.
Thrasher, F. M. 1927. *The Gang: A Study of 1,313 Gangs in Chicago*. Chicago, IL: University of Chicago Press.
Tonks, S., and Z. Stephenson. 2019. "Disengagement from Street Gangs: A Systematic Review of the Literature." *Psychiatry, Psychology and Law* 26 (1): 21–49.
Tostlebe, J. J., and D. C. Pyrooz. 2022. "Are Gang Members Psychopaths?" In *Psychopathy and Criminal Behavior*, edited by Paulo Marques, Mauro Paulino, and Laura Alho, 311–331. Cambridge, MA: Academic Press.
Vigil, J. D. 2007. *The Projects: Gang and Non-gang Families in East Los Angeles*. Austin: University of Texas Press.
Von Neumann, J., and Morgenstern, O. 1947. *Theory of Games and Economic Behavior*. 2nd rev. Princeton, NJ: Princeton University Press.
Wilson, T., R. Paternoster, and T. Loughran. 2017. "Direct and Indirect Experiential Effects in an Updating Model of Deterrence: A Research Note." *Journal of Research in Crime and Delinquency* 54 (1): 63–77.
Yiu, H. L. 2021. "Community and School Contexts in Youth Gang Involvement: Combining Social Bonds and Social Organization Perspectives." *Urban Review* 53 (2): 295–317.

CHAPTER 22

PSYCHOPATHOLOGY AS A CAUSE OR CONSEQUENCE OF YOUTH GANG INVOLVEMENT

PATRICIA K. KERIG, LUCYBEL MENDEZ, AVA R. ALEXANDER, AND SUSAN CHEN

EMPIRICAL evidence of the links between adolescent gang involvement and mental health (MH) problems (also termed psychopathology) has emerged consistently, leading scholars to attempt to clarify whether MH problems play the role of either causes or consequences of youth participation in gangs involvement (Beresford and Wood 2016; Macfarlane 2019; Osman and Wood 2018). However, to date, these efforts have been sparse and scattered across diverse fields. To refine our understanding of how psychopathology and youth gang involvement are intertwined and to guide future research, an overview of the available evidence is much needed that incorporates developmental, psychological, criminological, and sociological perspectives (Beresford and Wood 2016; Kerig and Mendez 2022; Wood and Alleyne 2010). To this end, this chapter presents a developmental psychopathology framework for understanding the interrelations of MH problems and youth gang membership. To accomplish this aim, the present chapter provides an overview of the research investigating whether MH problems represent risks for or consequence of gang participation, with an emphasis on recent work published since Osman and Wood's (2018) scoping review. This chapter also describes transdiagnostic factors, which refer to the transcending of traditional diagnostic classifications to uncover the underlying developmental processes that lead to MH problems, gang participation, and the dynamic transactions between the two. Lastly, we discuss directions for future research regarding promising but understudied purported mechanisms that might account for the association between MH problems and youth gang involvement.

Before continuing, some caveats are worth noting regarding terminology and methodology. There is a substantial literature devoted to the study of youth gangs; as such, diverse terms and definitions have been used to operationalize youth gang involvement. However, a widely accepted definition is youth self-nomination as a gang member (Decker et al. 2014; Esbensen et al. 2001). In turn, the term "psychopathology" (i.e., illness of the mind) refers to the entire range of MH problems that might emerge across development, whether or not those fall under the rubric of any specific diagnostic framework. Importantly, psychopathology is an overarching concept that encompasses a wide array of psychological and behavioral problems and is thus distinct from the term "psychopathy," which refers to one particular personality disorder, as is discussed later in this chapter. Additionally, there are currently two competing diagnostic systems used to classify MH problems, the Diagnostic and Statistical Manual of Mental Disorders (DSM) and the International Classification of Diseases (ICD), both of which have undergone repeated and substantial revisions over the past two decades, making it challenging to integrate findings across studies and time periods (Kerig, Mozley, and Mendez 2020). Another methodological issue that complicates our ability to draw firm conclusions from the extant empirical evidence is that the measures used to assess MH problems across studies are various, not always high quality, and often not indexed to the actual diagnostic criteria of any given disorder; instead, most studies use youth self-report scales or brief screening tools that assess symptoms rather than diagnostic status.

Theories of Gang Involvement Implicating MH Problems

Theories within the disciplines of criminology and sociology have provided frameworks for studying the intersection of MH problems and youth gang membership. For example, scholars have adapted Thornberry et al.'s (2003) selection, facilitation, and enhancement hypotheses to frame purported relations between MH problems and youth gang involvement (Macfarlane 2019; Osman and Wood 2018; Wood and Alleyne 2010). Specifically, selection processes may come into play such that youth with pre-existing MH problems may be at increased risk for being recruited or choosing to join a gang; facilitation may occur when, once in a gang, youth develop MH problems; and enhancement processes may take place when youth gang members who are vulnerable, whether by virtue of being at risk for MH problems or due to pre-existing conditions, encounter adversities during gang life that lead to psychopathology. Indeed, in their review of the existing literature, Osman and Wood (2018) indicated that evidence points to this latter process of enhancement whereby "mental illness may increase [youths'] likelihood of joining a gang, but once in a gang, they experience further mental health deterioration" (13). In turn, Macfarlane (2019) interprets the connections between MH problems and youth gang membership within a framework of "pushes" and "pulls." For example, negative "pushes from society and culture" (2), such as community violence, family victimization, social disorganization, and antisocial norms, may result in psychopathology. In turn, existing emotional and behavioral problems, or the stigmatization and marginalization of those with MH disorders, may propel youth toward gang membership. In contrast "pulls from within the gang" (2), such as protection from victimization and the promise of status, identity, and a sense of belonging, may be particularly attractive to vulnerable youth with psychopathology.

These conceptualizations are valuable; however, missing is a framework that integrates adolescent development with psychological, sociological, and criminological perspectives (Beresford and Wood 2016; Wood and Alleyne 2010). The developmental psychopathology framework is well suited for this task (Cicchetti 2010; Kerig, Ludlow, and Wenar 2012). Developmental psychopathology is an integrative framework that helps guide the understanding of the emergence of psychopathology versus resilience, as well as the continuity versus discontinuity of psychopathology over the lifespan (Cicchetti 2016; Cicchetti and Rogosch 2002). In particular, the developmental psychopathology framework proposes that adaptive development requires the successful resolution of stage-salient tasks in successive life epochs to progress on a positive developmental trajectory. For example, key stage-salient tasks include secure attachment in infancy, autonomous selfhood in the toddler years, self regulation and mastery of academic and social contexts in the school-age years, and individuation and identity in adolescence (see Kerig et al. 2012). In turn, youth who do not successfully achieve earlier milestones or who resolve stage-salient tasks in maladaptive ways may deviate from a healthy developmental pathway, and these deviations may have cascading effects that exacerbate psychopathology over time.

Aligning with principles from the developmental psychopathology perspective, and consistent with a life-course approach (e.g., Pyrooz 2014), youth gang involvement may represent a turning point in development that represent a maladaptive strategy to resolve the stage-related tasks of adolescence, including identity, independence, and the formation of mutually autonomous close personal relationships (Becker-Blease and Kerig 2016; Cicchetti 2010; Macfarlane 2019; Thornberry et al. 2003; Vigil 1988; Wood and Alleyne 2010). As suggested by this framework, unresolved childhood stage-salient tasks disrupt biological, social, emotional, psychological, cognitive, and behavioral development in ways that manifest in psychopathology and lead to cascading difficulties in achieving later developmental tasks in adaptive and prosocial ways (Cicchetti and Rogosch 2002). Even when early developmental tasks have been successfully achieved, the extensive biological and psychosocial changes that occur during adolescence can heighten vulnerability to victimization and reactivity to environmental challenges (Kerig 2017). Thus, for adolescents who lack more adaptive ways of meeting these challenges, gang membership may appear to offer an accessible solution for achieving key developmental goals, albeit a path that is likely to exacerbate their difficulties (Kerig and Mendez 2022; Wojceichowski 2021). All told, placing the relations among psychopathology and youth gang involvement within a developmental framework will help clarify how their interrelations emerge over time.

Studies of the Prevalence of MH Problems among Gang-Involved Youth

In recent years, researchers have made efforts to document the extent of MH problems among gang-involved youth (Osman and Wood 2018). As emphasized in Macfarlane's (2019) narrative review, and consistent with research on adults (Coid et al. 2013), gang-involved youth report elevated levels of emotional and behavioral problems across the board. Specifically, cross-sectional studies drawn from diverse samples have found that, in comparison to their peers, youth gang members report a wide range of MH problems, including higher levels of anxiety, depression, paranoia, hallucinations, hostility, paranoia, suicidal ideation, and suicide attempts (e.g., Baćak, DeWitt, and Reid 2021; Roberts and Corcoran, 2005; Harper, Davidson, and Hosek 2008; Harris et al. 2013; Li et al. 2002; Petering 2016; Watkins and Melde 2016). Many studies pinpoint difficulties on the internalizing end of the psychopathology spectrum, particularly anxiety and depression, among youth gang members (Dierkhising, Sánchez, and Gutierrez 2021; Frisby-Osman and Wood 2020; Valdez 2021; Whaling and Sharkey 2020).

Especially marked are the high rates of posttraumatic stress reported by youth gang members (see Kerig and Mendez 2022). For example, in a large-scale (N = 7,615) retrospective file review of clinical interviews conducted in the Harris County, Texas, juvenile probation department, Harris et al. (2013) found that youth who were gang involved were 1.77 times more likely to be deemed to meet the criteria for a diagnosis of posttraumatic stress disorder (PTSD) in comparison to their peers. Similarly, other studies have found that gang involvement is associated with elevated risk for PTSD or posttraumatic stress symptoms (PTSS; Dierkhising et al. 2021; Li et al. 2002; Petering 2016; Valdez 2021) and that these risks are particularly heightened for girls (Kerig et al. 2016). This pattern is consistent with the disproportionate rates of traumatic events youth report experiencing prior to, as a function of, and in the aftermath of gang-related activity (Kerig and Mendez 2022; Madan, Mrug, and Windle 2011), as well as longitudinal research demonstrating that a history of childhood trauma exposure predicts adolescent gang involvement (Kubik, Docherty, and Boxer 2019; Wojciechowski 2020). Moreover, Nydegger et al. (2019) uncovered that exposure to multiple forms of trauma was associated with the highest levels of PTSS among youth gang members, as well as a wide range of other emotional and behavioral problems. In fact, although anxiety, depression, and paranoia constitute clinical disorders in their own right, these symptoms also are features of PTSD (Kerig 2017); thus, it is possible other MH problems may in fact be manifestations of underlying PTSS. Consequently, future research will benefit from investigating MH problems among gang-involved youth from a trauma-informed perspective (Beresford and Wood 2016; Kerig and Mendez 2022). Notably, no studies we identified have applied the new ICD-11 criteria, which include a separate diagnosis of Complex PTSD (CPTSD). CPTSD comprises the standard symptoms of PTSD as well as three additional constellations involving difficulties in affect regulation, self-organization, and interpersonal relationships. Importantly, CPTSD is conceptualized as following in the wake of exposure to prolonged, inescapable interpersonal traumas, such as domestic violence and childhood maltreatment; given that the histories of gang-involved youth often feature just such forms of trauma, CPTSD might be a concept that is relevant to gangs (Kerig and Mendez 2022).

Although much of the research on MH problems has focused on those in the internalizing spectrum, psychopathology also can take externalizing forms, such as disruptive behavior disorders (American Psychiatric Association [APA] 2013). In this vein, research also shows elevated rates of oppositional defiant disorder, conduct disorder (CD), and substance abuse among youth gang members (Frisby-Osman and Wood 2020; McDaniel 2012; Harper et al. 2018). For example, the study of MH screenings cited previously by Harris et al. (2013) found that even more elevated than the rates of PTSD were the differential odds of gang-involved youth meeting DSM-IV criteria for CD (4.05 odds) and substance abuse (2.58 odds).

It may seem an oxymoron to inquire as to whether CD is associated with gang involvement, given that gang activity comprises just the sort of persistent pattern of rule violation that meets the criteria for the CD diagnosis. However, an important reason for doing so is the addition in the DSM-5 (APA 2013) of a specifier for the presence of "limited prosocial emotions," referred to in most of the developmental research as callous-unemotionality (CU). CU, which involves a lack of empathy, remorse, and genuine emotional engagement with others, is a key dimension of the downward extension of the psychopathy construct to youth (Frick et al. 2003). CU is associated with the most severe and intractable forms of youth offending (Frick et al. 2014), and lack of empathy has been cited as a potential risk factor for gang involvement (Mallion and Wood 2018). Indeed, although findings are somewhat mixed (see Tostlebe and Pyrooz 2022 for a review), several studies have found that adolescent gang members exhibit high levels of psychopathy in general (e.g., Dmitrieva et al. 2014) and CU in particular (e.g., Mendez, Mozley, and Kerig 2020), and that these traits predict gang membership independently of other risk factors (e.g., Thornton et al. 2015). Interestingly, Dmitreiva et al. (2014) found that youth who are high in the grandiose-manipulative dimension of psychopathy are disproportionately represented among those who emerge as gang leaders as opposed to followers or hangers-on. Therefore, there may be important distinctions to consider among youth who engage in gang activity for appetitively aggressive reasons (i.e., to dominate or victimize others) versus those who are drawn into gang activity for other motives (e.g., protection from victimization, social mimicry). In this regard, there seems to be wisdom in older classification systems that differentiated a subtype of conduct disordered youth who were "socialized" – that is, those who were inclined toward disruptive behavior due to their socialization within the norms of an antisocial subculture. This group was often observed among gang-joiners who were growing up in underresourced and high-crime communities (Jenkins and Boyer 1968).

MH Problems as Predictors and Precipitants of Gang Involvement

Although empirical evidence confirms that there are high rates of MH problems among gang-involved youth, the causal direction of this association is often unclear, given that most research conducted on this topic has been cross-sectional (Osman and Wood 2018). In a notable exception, Hautala, Sittner, and Whitbeck's (2016) nine-year longitudinal study of Indigenous youth showed that depressive symptoms were prospectively related to gang initiation, membership, and length of involvement. Correspondingly, Watkins and Melde (2016) analyzed data from the National Longitudinal Study of Adolescent to Adult Health and found that, antecedent to joining a gang, youth gang members endorsed higher levels of past-year depressive symptoms, suicidal thoughts, and suicide attempts relative to non-gang-involved peers. Further supporting the proposition that internalizing problems may predispose youth toward gang involvement, a recent longitudinal study using the Pathways to Desistance dataset, which involved 1,354 youth followed over 10 years, found that the subset of youth who met the criteria for a DSM-IV PTSD diagnosis at baseline were at elevated risk (170% greater odds) of following an early and chronic trajectory of gang membership (Wojciechowski 2021).

As noted, a limitation of the existing research is that it has tended to be selective in identifying the forms that psychopathology might take, with most studies focusing on MH problems in the internalizing spectrum. Nevertheless, longitudinal studies also have found that externalizing MH problems, such as attention-deficit and hyperactivity disorder (ADHD), CD, and substance abuse, precede and predict gang involvement (Hautala et al. 2016; Hill, Lui, and Hawkins 2001; Lahey et al. 1999). Further, Dupéré et al. (2007) leveraged the National Longitudinal Survey of Children and Youth dataset and found pre-existing psychopathic traits, characterized by low levels of anxiety and prosociality, predicted youths' likelihood of joining a gang. All told, there is support for the idea that both internalizing and externalizing MH problems may function as precipitants of youth gang activity.

MH Problems as Consequences of Gang Involvement

Results from longitudinal studies also provide evidence for the idea that MH problems increase after youth join a gang (Bjerregaard 2010; Coffman, Melde, and Esbensen 2015; Gilman, Hill, and Hawkins 2014; Gordon et al. 2004). For example, using a longitudinal design and propensity score matching, Gilman et al. (2014) found that adolescent gang involvement predicted adulthood DSM-IV symptoms of substance abuse and dependence. Recent literature corroborates that gang involvement precipitates a wide range of MH problems. For example, in a longitudinal study of 426 sibling pairs from a nationally representative dataset, Connolly and Jackson (2019) found that siblings who became gang affiliated in adolescence were those most likely to report severe anxiety and depression in early adulthood. More recently, using the Pathways to Desistance dataset, Baćak et al. (2021) found that joining a gang in adolescence predicted increased self-reported DSM-IV symptoms of anxiety, depression, hostility, and paranoid ideation in later waves. Regarding trauma, Valdez (2021) offers one of the few studies that ties PTSD among gang members specifically to traumatic experiences that were directly related to their gang activities. On the other hand, it must be noted that Gilman et al. (2014) did not find a significant link between adolescent gang membership and adults' reports of DSM-IV depression or anxiety, and that Rima et al. (2020) also reported null results in their longitudinal study of MH problems following gang involvement (although the latter investigators relied on participants' recall of having been given a psychiatric diagnosis, which may not be an accurate or sensitive measure). Accordingly, additional prospective research will be necessary to reach firmer conclusions regarding MH problems as a result of youth gang membership.

Enhancement, Bidirectional, and Transactional Effects

Although the Watkins and Melde (2016) study cited earlier evinced MH problems as precipitants to gang involvement, another important finding of this study was that, over time, MH symptoms increased following initiation into gang life; specifically, youth who joined gangs subsequently reported elevated depression, a 67% increase in suicidal thoughts, and a 104% increase in suicide attempts. These results suggest that MH problems can be exacerbated by gang activity and support the notion of bidirectional and enhancement effects in the association between gang involvement and psychopathology (Thornberry et al. 2003; Macfarlane 2019). Gang involvement and psychopathology also may have dynamic transactional associations, such that gang involvement and MH problems select for, potentiate, and transform one another. Youth with existing risk factors and MH problems may seek out gangs for protection (Quinn et al. 2017) or because they fulfill a developmental need (Wojciechowski 2021), whereas after youth join gangs, MH problems may worsen and new ones may arise. The underlying causal links that account for these associations, however, remain underresearched. To identify effective intervention points in the cycle of distress that orbits youth gangs, attention must be given to uncovering the mechanisms that promote and maintain the links between MH problems and youth gang involvement, which we turn to later in this chapter.

Transdiagnostic Perspectives

As noted, a major limitation of the research to date is its reliance on psychiatric diagnoses, which are based on the fluctuating definitions presented in successive revisions of each of the two competing major diagnostic manuals. Given that the validity and reliability of this kind of categorical diagnostic compendium (or "book of names," as per Jensen and Hoagwood 1997) has been called into question, researchers increasingly have begun adopting dimensional frameworks for characterizing MH problems (Kotov et al. 2017). For example, the National Institute of Mental Health's Research Domain Criteria (RDoc) initiative calls for abjuring diagnoses in favor of assessing dysfunctions in emotional, cognitive, social, regulatory, and sensorimotor systems that might be disrupted by psychopathology (Sanislow et al. 2020). This call has turned attention to the task of identifying *transdiagnostic* facets of psychopathology—that is, those that transcend traditional diagnostic classification systems and are relevant to a wide range of disorders (Nolen-Hoeksema and Watkins 2011). This new direction for the field is also in keeping with an overarching developmental psychopathology perspective, which searches for the underlying developmental processes that account for various psychopathologies (Conradt, Crowell, and Cicchetti 2021; Kerig et al. 2012).

Within the body of literature on putative transdiagnostic facets, emotion dysregulation has emerged as a prominent feature of many different disorders, whether represented by the overmodulation or undermodulation of emotional arousal (Beauchaine and Cicchetti 2019). Deficits in executive functions, low effortful control, and negative affectivity also are widely implicated across disorders (see Nolen-Hoeksema and Watkins 2011). In addition, the concept of irritability has garnered attention as a transdiagnostic feature of child and adolescent psychopathology (Smith et al. 2019). Given the potential relevance of these constructs to gang activity, it will be exciting to see future research on MH problems among adolescent gang members that adopts a transdiagnostic perspective.

Transdiagnostic Risk Factors

In addition to transdiagnostic facets underlying psychopathologies, there may be transdiagnostic risk factors that link internalizing and externalizing MH problems to gang involvement.

Trauma Exposure

Childhood trauma exposure is a primary transdiagnostic risk factor that may derail development in ways that lead to both MH problems and gang involvement. It is well established that childhood traumatic experiences negatively affect a multitude of developmental domains, including psychological, emotional, cognitive, physiological, and behavioral systems (Becker-Blease and Kerig 2016; Cicchetti 2016; Hoppen and Chalder 2018). Consequently, childhood trauma exposure is a gateway to the emergence of numerous MH problems, including PTSD, depression, anxiety, suicidal ideation, and CD (APA 2013; Kerig 2017; Vasileva and Petermann 2018; see McKay et al. 2021). The links to gang involvement are clearly implicated in the research showing that gang-involved youth are differentially likely to report extensive histories of childhood traumatic events, including neglect, sexual and physical abuse, peer victimization, and witnessing community violence (Augustyn, Ward, and Krohn 2017; Dierkhising et al. 2021; Kerig et al. 2016; see Kerig and Mendez 2022) and the prospective research confirming that trauma exposure functions as a predictive risk factor for chronic youth gang involvement (Kubik et al. 2019; Madan et al. 2011; Wojciechowski 2020).

Intergenerational Transmission

Evidence is strong for a heritable component to many MH problems (Smoller et al. 2019) as well as to a general vulnerability to psychopathology (i.e., p factor; Allegrini et al. 2019), although these effects are tempered by gene–environment interactions and epigenetic processes (Koss and Gunnar 2018). Notably, Connolly and Beaver (2015) used kinship data to estimate that genetic factors account for 77% of the variance in the likelihood of gang membership. A candidate gene implicated in both gang membership and psychopathology, at least among boys and men, is the low-activity monoamine oxidase-A (MAOA) allele, which is associated with aggression and antisocial behavior in general (Eme 2013) and gang involvement and weapon use in particular (Beaver et al. 2010). Moreover, the MAOA short-form allele serves as a potentiator of the effects of early adversity on MH, including both internalizing (Kim-Cohen et al. 2006) and externalizing forms of psychopathology (e.g., Caspi et al. 2002; Fite et al. 2020; Frazzetto et al. 2007; Kim-Cohen et al. 2006; McDermott et al. 2013). Therefore, the MAOA gene may confer a transdiagnostic vulnerability that enhances the risk that early adversity will result in the development of multiple maladaptive outcomes, including gang involvement and MH problems.

It also is notable that for many youth, gang involvement itself is a matter of family legacy (Decker and Curry 2000; Descormiers and Corrado 2016; Pearce and Pitts 2011), which can be accounted for by processes involving social learning and differential association (Hashimi, Wakefield, and Apel 2021; Kissner and Pyrooz 2009). Some youth refer to being "born into the gang" (Quinn et al. 2017, 4) given their many family members with gang ties and the assumption made from an early age that the child will affiliate with the gang accordingly. A fascinating longitudinal study followed children into adolescence and found that fathers' gang membership predicted their sons' involvement, just as having a gang-involved mother substantially increased the likelihood that daughters would join a gang (Augustyn et al. 2017). Here too there was an interaction with trauma: Gang-involved fathers were nine times more likely than other fathers to maltreat their sons, and this trauma history accounted for the intergenerational transmission of father-to-son gang involvement, in keeping with other studies indicating that harsh parenting is connected both to gang involvement (Vuk 2017) and to multiple forms of psychopathology (Wiggins et al. 2015).

Cultural Contextual Factors

Transdiagnostic risk factors that contribute to both MH problems and gang participation also may occur in the cultural context. Cultural forces, including race, ethnicity, acculturation, and values and beliefs within the community and family, may shape developmental trajectories and inform perspectives on what is considered adaptive or maladaptive (Cicchetti and Rogosch 2002; Garcia-Coll et al. 1996; Garcia-Coll, Akerman, and Cicchetti 2000). Accordingly, a large body of research indicates that BIPOC youth and other disadvantaged populations, including immigrant and refugee youth, have disparately high rates of MH problems (Guruge and Butt 2015; Cook et al. 2019). In turn, BIPOC youth are overrepresented among gang members (Merrin, Hong, and Espelage 2015) and cultural risk factors, such as marginalization, a minoritized identity, and racial discrimination, are related to an increased likelihood of youth gang membership (Dinh et al. 2013; Hautala et al. 2016; Knight et al. 2012). Cultural influences also may dictate the expression of MH symptoms (APA 2013) and the avenues deemed acceptable to cope with MH problems. For example, although for some youth seeking treatment may be culturally acceptable, others may be expected to "toughen up" and thus use more indirect, risky, or aggressive ways to address their MH difficulties, which may include gang involvement (Anderson 1999; Cicchetti and Rogosch 2002; Garcia-Coll et al. 2000). In sum, there may be important cultural influences on the links between gang membership and the ways in which youth express and cope with MH problems.

DIRECTIONS FOR FUTURE RESEARCH

In the presence of existing psychopathology, what might be the underlying mechanisms that propel youth toward gang involvement? And following initiation into a gang, what underlying mechanisms increase MH problems in late adolescence and young adulthood? In this next section of the chapter, we go beyond the extant research to highlight promising prospects for future research focused on identifying the underlying developmental processes that might serve as risk factors, protective mechanisms, and targets for intervention.

Mechanisms Underlying Links between MH Problems and Later Gang Involvement

Pre-existing PTSD and Its Sequelae

Posttraumatic symptoms of intrusions and hypervigilance may elicit intense feelings of danger, increase threat perception, and activate the need for protection and social support among adolescents (APA 2013; Decker et al. 2014; Kerig 2017; Quinn et al. 2017). In turn, to meet these needs and increase their sense of security, youth may take defensive measures, including joining a gang for protection (Decker et al. 2014).

Another specific manifestation of PTSD, emotional numbing, might serve as a maladaptive desensitization strategy to quell the overwhelming distress resulting from trauma exposure (Kennedy and Ceballo 2016; Kerig and Becker 2010). Research has established that posttraumatic emotional numbing is linked to risky, antisocial, and aggressive behaviors (Allwood, Bell, and Horan 2011; Lansford et al. 2006) and may generalize over time into a callous interpersonal stance. For example, Kerig, Bennett, and Becker (2012) found that emotional numbing accounted for the association between trauma exposure and CU in a sample of justice-involved youth, some of whom were gang involved. It is notable that, in contrast to the high-CU youth described earlier, a secondary subtype has been identified that is conceptualized as arriving at a callous presentation not through a deficit in the capacity to experience empathy (termed primary CU) but through emotional disengagement in the aftermath of trauma (termed secondary, or acquired, CU; Karpman 1941; Kerig and Becker 2010; Porter 1996; see Craig, Goulter, and Moretti 2021 for a review). Although much of this research has identified the secondary subtype through assessing the presence of trait anxiety, the original theory and more recent research evidence point toward trauma exposure and PTSS as the key differentiating factors (Bennett and Kerig 2014). Whereas there is available research indicating that CU accounts for the association between trauma exposure and youth gang involvement (Mendez et al. 2020), we are not aware of existing research on the secondary subtype in the context of gangs. However, it is interesting to posit that traumatized youth with secondary CU might be drawn to gang activity as a way to bolster a "tough façade," and yet these youth might be particularly vulnerable to the negative MH effects of exposure to gang-related violence and victimization.

Futurelessness, a sense that one's lifespan is limited, may also stem from trauma exposure and resulting PTSD (APA 2013; Kerig 2017; Kerig and Becker 2010) and is associated with youth engagement in violent and antisocial behavior (Craig 2019; Piquero 2016). When viewed through a trauma lens, futurelessness may be a manifestation of posttraumatic reckless/self-destructive behavior, or risk-seeking (Kerig 2019), which may serve as an attempt to achieve mastery over what is terrifying and uncontrollable as well as congruence between one's inner and outer experience. From an evolutionary perspective, futurelessness promotes the adoption of a fast life strategy focused on quickly acquiring status, resources, and access to sexual partners by whatever means necessary, including aggression, antisocial behavior, and social dominance (Ellis and Del Giudice 2019; Simmons et al. 2019). For adolescents living in disadvantaged communities, gang membership may seem to provide the most swift and accessible avenue to achieving these goals. Suggestively, some evidence confirms that there are elevated levels of futurelessness among gang-involved youth relative to their peers (Li et al. 2002; Whaling and Sharkey 2020). Indeed, the risk of mortality by homicide is three times greater for young Black males who are gang involved when compared to demographically matched peers, and thus the basis for a sense of foreshortened future is profoundly real (Pyrooz et al. 2020).

Insecure Attachment

Early experiences with abusive, insensitive, or neglectful caregivers may lead youth to develop a number of forms of psychopathology, underlying which are insecure internal working models of self and other that are driven by anxiety and preoccupation, avoidance and dismissiveness, or failure to develop a coherent strategy for maintaining close personal relationships (Fearon et al. 2016). Consistent with Bowlby's (1944) observations of "44 juvenile thieves," a large body of research confirms that insecure attachment in childhood is a predictor of adolescent involvement in antisocial behavior (see Kerig and Becker 2010), with particularly strong effects for the disorganized attachment style (Fearon et al. 2010). Although we have not uncovered any published research on gang involvement specifically, we speculate that for youth with anxious attachment styles, particularly those who seek closeness to others but expect and fear rejection, the intensity of loyalties and mutual affiliation offered by gangs might be attractive by virtue of seeming to promise to fulfill unmet attachment needs (Kerig and Mendez 2022). Indeed, De Vito (2020) offers some qualitative observations in support of the hypothesis that gangs might serve as alternative attachment figures for disaffected youth.

Social Deficits and Peer Rejection

Children with behavioral and emotional problems often demonstrate poor interpersonal skills and, along with the larger stigma attached to MH problems and non-normative behavior, are vulnerable to peer rejection, neglect, and victimization (see Kerig et al. 2012). In turn, longitudinal research shows that social skills deficits and peer rejection in childhood are powerful predictors of adolescent gang involvement (Dishion, Nelson, Yasui 2005). A consequence of this stigma and marginalization may be the weakening of prosocial support and bonds, resulting in alienation from mainstream peer groups (Kerig and Becker 2010; Lacourse et al. 2003; Macfarlane 2019; Wood and Alleyne 2010). Rejection and failure in the social realm are particularly impactful during the adolescent years, when social belongingness and mastery are important stage-salient goals. For youth facing these challenges, gangs may offer a haven, with gang membership functioning as a way to garner acceptance, belonging, and peer support (Kerig et al. 2012; Vigil 1988; Wood 2014). Indeed, in qualitative interviews, many youth attribute their gang entry to alienation and social exclusion (Stretesky and Pogrebin 2007) and describe the positive attributes of gang life as involving a sense of belonging and social status (Goldman, Giles, and Hogg 2014). Youth who feel alienated from prosocial peers also may be attracted to gang life because it offers a "cool" cachet via promoting an identity and value system that are counter to the mainstream— in other words, by turning passive into active they can experience themselves as rejecting rather than being rejected. From the perspective of youth, then, knowing "who is rejecting whom" seems critical given that attempts to promote prosocial attitudes and "appropriate" interpersonal skills may be met with little interest by gang-involved youth who are invested in maintaining an "alternative" identity and countercultural value system.

Deficits in Self and Identity Development

Self and identity development are critical stage-salient issues of adolescence, so it is noteworthy that many forms of youth psychopathology are associated with deficits in the self-system, ranging from low perceived competence in depression, to difficulties in self-organization in Complex PTSD, to brittle narcissism in conduct disorder, to an unstable sense of self in nascent borderline personality (see Kerig et al. 2012). Gangs may offer youth who are struggling with self-development a pre-established identity to adopt (Wojceichowski 2021; Van Ngo et al. 2017) and, for boys in particular, this is an embellished one replete with symbols of power, fearsomeness, and hyper-masculinity (Stretesky and Pogrebin 2007). Stigma and marginalization also may engender self-alienation such that adolescents with MH problems are intolerant of the discrepancy between their perceived and ideal selves (Lacourse et al. 2003; Lauger 2020). Gang involvement thus may provide an opportunity to cultivate and present an idealized alternative persona, one that is dominant, invulnerable, and integrally connected to a select and valued group, thereby counteracting the effects of denigration at the hands of the self or others (Lauger 2020; Vigil 1988). Further, minoritized youth who are not well acculturated also are at risk for gang membership (Krohn et al. 2011), and thus social exclusion due to cultural differences may lead youth to embrace a gang identity.

On the other hand, identity development also may play a crucial role in disengagement from gangs, when youth come to realize that gang life imposes barriers to achieving developmental goals, such as starting a family or securing employment, and to actualizing a desired future self (Kelly and Ward 2020; Panfil 2020). For example, some LGBTQ+ youth report that coming to terms with their sexuality led to their desistance from gang activity in that their newfound identity was incompatible with the gang ethos (Panfil 2020). It is interesting to speculate that the popularity of tattoo removal programs among former gang members may be not only instrumental for reducing stigma from others but also may represent a concrete manifestation of the emergence of a self-concept that is incongruent with gang membership (Boyle 2011; Densley and Pyrooz 2019; Poljac and Burke 2008).

Legal Cynicism

Negative perceptions of the legal system may represent an additional mechanism that links childhood trauma and PTSD to gang involvement. Youth who experience negative interactions with legal socialization agents, and who consequently develop beliefs that the legal system is illegitimate and that laws are not binding (i.e., legal cynicism), are more likely to engage in rule violations and lawbreaking behaviors (Cavanaugh, Fine, and Cauffman 2020; Fagan and Tyler 2005; Reisig, Wolfe, and Holtfreter 2011). The risk of developing legal cynicism may be particularly high for youth who experience betrayal trauma (Gobin and Freyd 2014), which refers to victimization experienced at the hands of those who should have provided protection (such as caregivers) or maltreatment that has gone unaddressed by systems intended to provide redress (such as police or child welfare agents).

These failures in the social contract may contribute to the development of contemptuous and even vengeful attitudes toward legal authorities (Ford et al. 2006; Kerig and Becker 2010). Research confirms that adolescents who have experienced childhood maltreatment endorse lowered perceptions of police legitimacy (Kolivoski et al. 2016; Penner, Shaffer, and Viljoen 2017) and, furthermore, that youth's own negative experiences with legal actors (e.g., being stopped by police due to racial profiling, being treated disrespectfully or abusively) contribute to legal cynicism (Cavanagh et al. 2020) and overall negative perceptions of law enforcement (Novich and Hunt 2017, 2018).

Once established, these negative attitudes may open the door to adolescent gang involvement; accordingly, legal cynicism and negative legal legitimacy beliefs have been found to be elevated among some youth gang members (Papachristos, Meares, and Fagan 2012; Pauwels and Hardyns 2016). Youth who have been victimized without redress, and who consequently have lost faith in the legal system's fairness and ability to protect them, may seek out alternative sources of justice and security in the context of gangs. Furthermore, beliefs that laws are unjust and need not be followed may allow youth to rationalize their own offending behavior, rendering gang-related violence and antisocial activities less abhorrent (Nivette et al. 2015). However, it should be noted that, whereas gang members may reject broader societal norms, gangs typically employ their own complex structure of rules and codes (Matsuda et al. 2013; Ruble and Turner 2000). Thus, whereas low perceptions of police legitimacy might encourage some youth with MH problems to join gangs, broader aspects of legal cynicism, which reflect an aversion to rules and laws in general, may make other youth loath to participate in the hierarchical authority and rigid structure of gang life.

Mechanisms Underlying Links between Gang Involvement and Later MH Problems

Ongoing Trauma and Posttraumatic Symptoms

Once gang involved, rather than achieving a respite from trauma, youth frequently are exposed to ongoing victimization and witnessing of violence against others (Barnes, Boutwell, and Fox 2012; Melde, Taylor, and Esbensen 2009; Peterson, Taylor, and Esbensen 2004; Valdez 2021). For example, data drawn from the National Longitudinal Study of Adolescent Health study show that, after accounting for prior victimization, youth who identified as gang members endorsed the highest levels of current *and* subsequent victimization (DeLisi et al. 2009). This ongoing retraumatization is likely to worsen existing psychological, emotional, cognitive, physiological, and behavioral problems, and the cascading deterioration of these systems may help explain the predictive link between gang involvement and MH problems in later adolescence and young adulthood (e.g., Gilman et al. 2014).

Recurrent victimization and trauma exposure may worsen posttraumatic hypervigilance in particular (APA 2013). Indeed, in Quinn et al.'s (2017) qualitative study, gang-involved adolescents described escalating patterns of fear of revictimization, hypervigilant behavior, and a desire for safety and protection, leading to further isolation from prosocial influences and entrenchment into the gang. Elevated posttraumatic hypervigilance also may increase the use of risky self-defensive tendencies (e.g., carrying weapons; Huff 1998; Rich 2009). In turn, weapon carrying is likely to amplify the risk for additional traumatic violent encounters (Klein and Maxson 2010) and ensuing MH difficulties, particularly resurging PTSD (Rich 2009).

Perpetration Trauma, Moral Injury, and Moral Disengagement

As a counterpart to victimization, gang-involved youth may perceive their own involvement in perpetrating violence toward others as a traumatic experience, a phenomenon termed "perpetration trauma" (MacNair 2002). Having to integrate into their sense of self their capacity to inflict harm and make morally compromising decisions can disrupt youths' moral development, which may lead to the emergence or continuity of psychopathology (Kerig et al. 2013; Wainryb 2011). Consistent with this idea, gang-involved youth report perpetration trauma with higher frequency than their non-gang-involved peers (Naldrett and Wood 2020), and many youth gang members recount their acts of commission of violence against others as constituting some of their most traumatic experiences (Kerig et al. 2016). Further, Kerig and colleagues (2016) found that perpetration trauma helped to account for the link between gang involvement and PTSS, suggesting that perpetration as well as victimization may contribute to gang-related MH problems.

Perpetration trauma is only one facet of a larger construct, moral injury (MI), which refers to the damaging effects of perpetrating, witnessing, allowing, or learning about actions that violate one's own deeply held beliefs or moral codes (Litz et al. 2009; Litz and Kerig 2019). Largely studied in military contexts, MI has been found to have unique associations beyond PTSD with negative outcomes, including depression, suicidality, and aggression (see Griffin et al. 2019). Moreover, the construct recently has been extended downward to youth (Kidwell and Kerig 2021), including youth in the juvenile justice system (Chaplo, Kerig, and Wainryb 2019). Although we have not identified any research to date that has empirically studied MI among adolescent gang members, the concept has been implicated in recent thinking on the topic (Kerig et al. 2013; Kerig and Mendez 2022) and may play an important, unexamined role in the ongoing MH problems incumbent on gang involvement. In fact, moral injury may account for the fact that many former gang members report that their inability to continue tolerating the violence played a key role in their decision to desist from gang activity, and yet they remain haunted and disturbed by those experiences long after leaving the gang (Carson and Vecchio 2015; Decker et al. 2014; Dierkhising et al. 2021).

Alternatively, some gang-involved youth faced with the moral dilemma of justifying perpetration against others may engage in moral disengagement strategies, particularly victim dehumanization, to quell their distress (Bandura et al. 1996; Bandura 1999; Kerig et al. 2013; Wilkinson and Carr 2008). Over time, however, moral disengagement is associated with exacerbating MH problems, including externalizing symptoms and antisocial behavior (Hyde, Shaw, and Moilanen 2010). Researchers have found that gang members display higher levels of moral disengagement relative to their peers (Alleyne, Fernandes, and Pritchard 2014; Frisby-Osman and Wood 2020; Niebieszczanski et al. 2015), so this may be a promising construct for further research on the association between gang involvement and MH problems.

Ongoing Stigma

Even after desistance from gang membership, past members continue to experience fear of repercussions and retaliation, as well as stigma related to their gang involvement (Dierkhising and Kerig 2018; Lee and Bubolz 2020). As former gang members have described, society often continues to perceive them as a part of the gang (Pyrooz and Decker 2011). This is particularly true if they have remaining social ties to active gang members and visible identifiers of their gang participation, such as scars and tattoos (Pyrooz 2014). Consistent with these propositions, participants in Quinn et al.'s (2017) qualitative study indicated that they "always carried the gang member label," which increased their fear of hostility and violent victimization (9). This state of constant fearfulness, continued victimization, and marginalization may contribute to further MH problems, particularly PTSD and anxiety (Quinn et al. 2017; Roman, Decker, and Pyrooz 2017).

Unresolved Grief

A striking observation made by Saltzman et al. (2001) in their work with inner-city youth, some of whom were gang involved, was the marked contrast between their desensitized attitudes toward their own victimization and their openly expressed distress about the many losses of loved ones for whom they continued to grieve. Gang-involved youth are at particularly heightened risk of losing friends and family members to violence; for example, in a sample of justice-involved youth, Dierkhising et al. (2021) found that 82.8% of gang-involved participants had experienced at least one traumatic loss; moreover, this loss was commonly reported as their most distressing traumatic experience. Prolonged grief disorder currently has only recently been included in the newest edition of the DSM, but a growing body of research supports its standing as a bona fide MH problem (Kaplow et al. 2012). Unresolved grief, particularly when the decedent was a fellow gang member, may embed youth even more deeply into gang life and fuel retributive behaviors that incur the risk of further violence and trauma; as Moore (2010) describes, youth may become "frozen in gang values because of traumatic incidents" (125), particularly those involving grief.

Incorporating Developmental Psychopathology into Interventions for Gang-Involved Youth

Effective evidence-based interventions have been developed for most of the adolescent MH problems described in this chapter (see Prinstein et al. 2019), including CU, despite its reputation for intractability (e.g., Ribeiro da Silva et al. 2021). However, less attention has been paid to addressing the underlying developmental processes linking youth MH problems to gang involvement, which might strengthen and sharpen those treatments. Moreover, traditional methods of MH service provision are unlikely to effectively address the complex intersection of MH problems and youth gang involvement. Gang-involved youth in need of MH care are likely to face many barriers common to those from disadvantaged communities, including lack of accessible and affordable services, discomfort with traditional MH settings, and fears about mandatory reporting (Platell, Cook, and Martin

2017; Valdez 2021), as well as scarcity of culturally responsive services (see Kawaii-Bogue, Williams, and MacNear 2017). Moreover, youth with histories of gang involvement often encounter a lack of relevant expertise (Dierkhising and Kerig 2018) and even discrimination from treatment providers due to their highly stigmatized identities (Barrows and Huff 2009; Lee and Bubolz 2020). Further, MH care for youth gang members may not be recognized as a priority despite their high level of need, especially for those whose difficulties are masked by emotional numbing and adherence to the "code of the street" (Anderson 1999; Rich and Grey 2005), which lends them the outward appearance of psychopathic callousness rather than emotional distress (Bailey et al. 2014; Kerig et al. 2012).

To date, promising steps have been taken to enhance the early identification and treatment engagement of gang-involved youth at risk for developing MH problems, particularly those related to posttraumatic stress (e.g., Kerig and Alexander 2014; Stolbach and Reese 2020). Yet another potential path not yet taken would involve broadening trauma-focused therapies for gang-involved youth to address MH symptoms stemming from perpetration as well as victimization. A starting point for these interventions could be programs designed for the treatment and reintegration of child soldiers, given that these two groups share common experiences (Garbarino, Governale, and Nesi 2020; Kerig et al. 2013).

Alternatively, innovations in comprehensive community MH care systems could allow for earlier and more accessible interventions for gang-involved youth in need. Community-based participatory research (Bogart and Uyeda 2009) provides one possible framework for the development of collaborative, community-led treatments and intervention plans. Implementation science researchers also have demonstrated successes using ecological approaches, in which MH care is integrated into existing community settings while also involving key community members throughout all stages of intervention development and implementation (Atkins et al. 2016). These frameworks offer opportunities to work collaboratively with gang-dominated communities that have been villainized as "criminogenic," to assess current needs and address gaps, and to create viable solutions that empower community stakeholders and youth themselves.

Conclusion

This chapter presented a developmental psychopathology framework as an integrative approach to understanding the intertwined connections among MH problems and youth gang involvement over the course of adolescent development. The evidence and ideas discussed in this chapter serve as a call to action for researchers, clinicians, and policymakers to re-evaluate the issue of gang involvement through an integrative developmental psychopathology lens that emphasizes MH needs. Although MH concerns sometimes receive brief media attention following mass shootings by disturbed lone assailants, these issues are rarely raised in relation to gang violence. However, empirical evidence increasingly suggests that MH is relevant to the discussion of youth gang involvement. Additional high-quality longitudinal research, particularly studies using updated conceptualizations of psychopathology, such as the transdiagnostic perspective, will be valuable for untangling the relations among MH problems, trauma exposure, and gang involvement. Longitudinal research investigating dynamic transactional relations among these constructs over time will be particularly important. Ultimately, further community-based and culturally informed efforts are needed to pave the way for effective, trauma-informed approaches to working with youth from underserved populations at risk for MH problems and gang participation.

REFERENCES

Allegrini, Andrea G., Rosa Cheesman, Kaili Rimfeld, Saskia Selzam, Jean-Baptiste Pingault, Thalia C. Eley, and Robert Plomin. 2020. "The p Factor: Genetic Analyses Support a General Dimension of Psychopathology in Childhood and Adolescence." *Journal of Child Psychology and Psychiatry* 61 (1): 30–39. https://doi.org/10.1111/jcpp.13113.

Alleyne, Emma, Isabel Fernandes, and Elizabeth Pritchard. 2014. "Denying Humanness to Victims: How Gang Members Justify Violent Behavior." *Group Processes and Intergroup Relations* 17 (6): 750–762. https://doi.org/10.1177/1368430214536064.

Allwood, Maureen A., Debora J. Bell, and Jacqueline Horan. 2011. "Posttrauma Numbing of Fear, Detachment, and Arousal Predict Delinquent Behaviors in Early Adolescence." *Journal of Clinical Child & Adolescent Psychology* 40 (5): 659–667. https://doi.org/10.1080/15374416.2011.597081.

American Psychiatric Association. 2013. *Diagnostic and Statistical Manual of Mental Disorders: DSM-5*. Washington, DC: American Psychiatric Association.

Anderson, Elijah. 1999. *Code of the Street: Decency, Violence, and the Moral Life of the Inner City*. New York: WW Norton & Company.

Atkins, Marc S., Dana Rusch, Tara G. Mehta, and Davielle Lakind. 2016. "Future Directions for Dissemination and Implementation Science: Aligning Ecological Theory and Public Health to Close the Research to Practice Gap." *Journal of Clinical Child and Adolescent Psychology* 45 (2): 215–226. https://doi.org/10.1080/15374416.2015.1050724.

Augustyn, Megan B., Jeffrey T. Ward, and Marvin D. Krohn. 2017. "Exploring Intergenerational Continuity in Gang Membership." *Journal of Crime and Justice* 40 (3): 252–274. https://doi.org/10.4324/9781351027106-2.

Baćak, Valerio, Samuel E. DeWitt, and Shannon E. Reid. 2021. "Gang Membership and Mental Health During the Transition to Adulthood." *Journal of Quantitative Criminology* 38: 567–596. https://doi.org/10.1007/s10940-021-09502-z.

Bailey, Caroline E., Caitlin Smith, Stanley J. Huey Jr., Dawn D. McDaniel, and Kalina Babeva. 2014. "Unrecognized Posttraumatic Stress Disorder as a Treatment Barrier for a Gang-Involved Juvenile Offender." *Journal of Aggression, Maltreatment and Trauma* 23 (2): 199–214. https://doi.org/10.1080/10926771.2014.872748.

Bandura, Albert. 1999. "Moral Disengagement in the Perpetration of Inhumanities." *Personality and Social Psychology Review* 3(3): 193–209.

Bandura, Albert, Claudio Barbaranelli, Gian Vittorio Caprara, and Concetta Pastorelli. 1996. "Mechanisms of Moral Disengagement in the Exercise of Moral Agency." *Journal of Personality and Social Psychology* 71 (2): 364. https://doi.org/10.1037/0022-3514.71.2.364.

Bandura, Albert. 2014. "Moral Disengagement in the Perpetration of Inhumanities." In *Perspectives on Evil and Violence*:193–209. Psychology Press.

Barnes, J. C., Brian B. Boutwell, and Kathleen A. Fox. 2012. "The Effect of Gang Membership on Victimization: A Behavioral Genetic Explanation." *Youth Violence and Juvenile Justice* 10 (3): 227–244. https://doi.org/10.1177/1541204011429948.

Barrows, Julie, and C. Ronald Huff. 2009. "Gangs and Public Policy: Constructing and Deconstructing Gang Databases." *Criminology & Public Policy* 8 (4): 675–703. https://doi.org/10.1111/j.1745-9133.2009.00585.x.

Beauchaine, Theodore P., and Dante Cicchetti. 2019. "Emotion Dysregulation and Emerging Psychopathology: A Transdiagnostic, Transdisciplinary Perspective." *Development and Psychopathology* 31 (3): 799–804. DOI:10.1017/S0954579419000671.

Beaver, Kevin M., Matt DeLisi, Michael G. Vaughn, and J. C. Barnes. 2010. "Monoamine Oxidase A Genotype Is Associated with Gang Membership and Weapon Use." *Comprehensive Psychiatry* 51 (2): 130–134. https://doi.org/10.1016/j.comppsych.2009.03.010.

Becker-Blease, Kathryn, and Patricia K. Kerig. 2016. *Child Maltreatment: A Developmental Psychopathology Approach*. Washington, DC: American Psychological Association.

Bennett, Dianna C., and Patricia K. Kerig. 2014. "Investigating the Construct of Trauma-Related Acquired Callousness among Delinquent Youth: Differences in Emotion Processing." *Journal of Traumatic Stress* 27 (4): 415–422. https://doi.org/10.1002/jts.21931.

Beresford, Hayley, and Jane L. Wood. 2016. "Patients or Perpetrators? The Effects of Trauma Exposure on Gang Members' Mental Health: A Review of the Literature." *Journal of Criminological Research, Policy and Practice* 2 (2): 148–159. https://doi.org/10.1108/JCRPP-05-2015-0015.

Bjerregaard, Beth. 2010. "Gang Membership and Drug Involvement: Untangling the Complex Relationship." *Crime and Delinquency* 56 (1): 3–34. https://doi.org/10.1177/0011128707307217.

Bogart, Laura M., and Kimberly Uyeda. 2009. "Community-Based Participatory Research: Partnering with Communities for Effective and Sustainable Behavioral Health Interventions." *Health Psychology* 28 (4): 391–393. https://doi.org/10.1037/a0016387.

Bowlby, John. 1944. "Forty-Four Juvenile Thieves: Their Characters and Home-Life (II)." *International Journal of Psycho-Analysis* 25: 107–128.

Boyle, Greg. 2011. *Tattoos on the Heart: The Power of Boundless Compassion*. New York: Simon and Schuster.

Carson, Dena C., and J. Michael Vecchio. 2015. "Leaving the Gang." In *The Handbook of Gangs*, edited by Scott Decker and David Pyrooz, 257–275. Chichester, UK: John Wiley & Sons.

Caspi, Avshalom, Joseph McClay, Terrie E. Moffitt, Jonathan Mill, Judy Martin, Ian W. Craig, Alan Taylor, and Richie Poulton. 2002. "Role of Genotype in the Cycle of Violence in Maltreated Children." *Science* 297 (5582): 851–854. https://doi.org/10.1126/science.1072290.

Cavanagh, Caitlin, Adam Fine, and Elizabeth Cauffman. 2020. "How Do Adolescents Develop Legal Cynicism? A Test of Legal Socialization Mechanisms among Youth Involved in the Justice System." *Justice Quarterly* 39 (3): 478–496. https://doi.org/10.1080/07418825.2020.1801805.

Chaplo, Shannon D., Patricia K. Kerig, and Cecilia Wainryb. 2019. "Development and Validation of the Moral Injury Scales for Youth." *Journal of Traumatic Stress* 32 (3): 448–458. https://doi.org/10.1002/jts.22408.

Cicchetti, Dante. 2010. *Developmental Psychopathology*. Hoboken, NJ: John Wiley & Sons, Inc.

Cicchetti, Dante. 2016. "Socioemotional, Personality, and Biological Development: Illustrations from a Multilevel Developmental Psychopathology Perspective on Child Maltreatment." *Annual Review of Psychology* 67 (1): 187–211. DOI:10.1146/annurev-psych-122414-033259.

Cicchetti, Dante, and Fred A. Rogosch. 2002. "A Developmental Psychopathology Perspective on Adolescence." *Journal of Consulting and Clinical Psychology* 70 (1): 6–20. https://doi.org/10.1037/0022-006X.70.1.6.

Coffman, Donna L., Chris Melde, and Finn-Aage Esbensen. 2015. "Gang Membership and Substance Use: Guilt as a Gendered Causal Pathway." *Journal of Experimental Criminology* 11 (1): 71–95. https://doi.org/10.1007/s11292-014-9220-9.

Coid, Jeremy W., Simone Ullrich, Robert Keers, Paul Bebbington, Bianca L. DeStavola, Constantinos Kallis, Min Yang, David Reiss, Rachel Jenkins, and Peter Donnelly. 2013. "Gang Membership, Violence, and Psychiatric Morbidity." *American Journal of Psychiatry* 170 (9): 985–993. DOI:10.1176/appi.ajp.2013.12091188.

Connolly, Eric J., and Dylan B. Jackson. 2019. "Adolescent Gang Membership and Adverse Behavioral, Mental Health, and Physical Health Outcomes in Young Adulthood: A Within-Family Analysis." *Criminal Justice and Behavior* 46 (11): 1566–1586. https://doi.org/10.1177/0093854819871076.

Connolly, Eric J., and Kevin M. Beaver. 2015. "Guns, Gangs, and Genes: Evidence of an Underlying Genetic Influence on Gang Involvement and Carrying a Handgun." *Youth Violence and Juvenile Justice* 13 (3): 228–242. https://doi.org/10.1177/1541204014539522.

Conradt, Elisabeth, Sheila E. Crowell, and Dante Cicchetti. 2021. "Using Development and Psychopathology Principles to Inform the Research Domain Criteria (RDoC) Framework." *Development and Psychopathology* 33 (5): 1521–1525. DOI:10.1017/S0954579421000985.

Cook, Benjamin Lê, Sherry Shu-Yeu Hou, Su Yeon Lee-Tauler, Ana Maria Progovac, Frank Samson, and Maria Jose Sanchez. 2019. "A Review of Mental Health and Mental Health Care Disparities Research: 2011–2014." *Medical Care Research and Review* 76 (6): 683–710.

Craig, Jessica M. 2019. "The Potential Mediating Impact of Future Orientation on the ACE-Crime Relationship." *Youth Violence and Juvenile Justice* 17 (2): 111–128. https://doi.org/10.1177/1541204018756470.

Craig, Stephanie G., Natalie Goulter, and Marlene M. Moretti. 2021. "A Systematic Review of Primary and Secondary Callous-Unemotional Traits and Psychopathy Variants in youth." Clinical *Child and Family Psychology Review* 24 (1): 65–91. https://doi.org/10.1007/s10567-020-00329-x.

De Vito, Katherine. 2020. "Seeking a Secure Base: Gangs as Attachment Figures." *Qualitative Social Work* 19 (4): 754–769. https://doi.org/10.1177/1473325019852659.

Decker, Scott H., and G. David Curry. 2000. "Addressing Key Features of Gang Membership: Measuring the Involvement of Young Members." *Journal of Criminal Justice* 28 (6): 473–482. https://doi.org/10.1016/s0047-2352(00)00063-5.

Decker, Scott H., David C. Pyrooz, Gary Sweeten, and Richard K. Moule. 2014. "Validating Self-Nomination in Gang Research: Assessing Differences in Gang Embeddedness Across Non-, Current, and Former Gang Members." *Journal of Quantitative Criminology* 30 (4): 577–598. https://doi.org/10.1007/s10940-014-9215-8.

DeLisi, Matt, J. C. Barnes, Kevin M. Beaver, and Chris L. Gibson. 2009. "Delinquent Gangs and Adolescent Victimization Revisited: A Propensity Score Matching Approach." *Criminal Justice and Behavior* 36 (8): 808–823. https://doi.org/10.1177/0093854809337703.

Densley, James A., and David C. Pyrooz. 2019. "A Signaling Perspective on Disengagement from Gangs." *Justice Quarterly* 36 (1): 31–58. https://doi.org/10.1080/07418825.2017.1357743.

Descormiers, Karine, and Raymond R. Corrado. 2016. "The Right to Belong: Individual Motives and Youth Gang Initiation Rites." *Deviant Behavior* 37 (11): 1341–1359. https://doi.org/10.1080/01639625.2016.1177390.

Dierkhising, Carly B., and Patricia K. Kerig. 2018. "Pilot Evaluation of a University-based Training in Trauma-informed Services for Gang Intervention Workers." *Journal of Aggression, Maltreatment & Trauma* 27 (3): 291–308. https://doi.org/10.1080/10926771.2017.1382634.

Dierkhising, Carly B., José A. Sánchez, and Luis Gutierrez. 2021. "'It Changed My Life': Traumatic Loss, Behavioral Health, and Turning Points Among Gang-Involved and Justice-Involved Youth." *Journal of Interpersonal Violence* 36 (17-18): 8027–8049. https://doi.org/10.1177/0886260519847779.

Dinh, Khanh T., Traci L. Weinstein, Jenn-Yun Tein, and Mark W. Roosa. 2013. "A Mediation Model of the Relationship of Cultural Variables to Internalizing and Externalizing Problem Behavior Among Cambodian American Youth." *Asian American Journal of Psychology* 4 (3): 176–184. https://doi.org/10.1037/a0030165.

Dishion, Thomas J., Sarah E. Nelson, and Miwa Yasui. 2005. "Predicting Early Adolescent Gang Involvement from Middle School Adaptation." *Journal of Clinical Child and Adolescent Psychology* 34 (1): 62–73. https://doi.org/10.1207/s15374424jccp3401_6.

Dmitrieva, Julia, Lauren Gibson, Laurence Steinberg, Alex Piquero, and Jeffrey Fagan. 2014. "Predictors and Consequences of Gang Membership: Comparing Gang Members, Gang Leaders, and Non-Gang-Affiliated Adjudicated Youth." *Journal of Research on Adolescence* 24 (2): 220–234. DOI:10.1111/jora.12111.

Dupéré, Véronique, Éric Lacourse, J. Douglas Willms, Frank Vitaro, and Richard E. Tremblay. 2007. "Affiliation to Youth Gangs during Adolescence: The Interaction between Childhood Psychopathic Tendencies and Neighborhood Disadvantage." *Journal of Abnormal Child Psychology* 35 (6): 1035–1045. https://doi.org/10.1007/s10802-007-9153-0.

Ellis, Bruce J., and Marco Del Giudice. 2019. "Developmental Adaptation to Stress: An Evolutionary Perspective." *Annual Review of Psychology* 70 (1): 111–139. https://doi.org/10.1146/annurev-psych-122216-011732.

Eme, Robert. 2013. "MAOA and Male Antisocial Behavior: A Review." *Aggression and Violent Behavior* 18 (3): 395–398. https://doi.org/10.1016/j.avb.2013.02.001.

Esbensen, Finn-Aage, L., Thomas Winfree, Ni He, and Terrance J. Taylor. 2001. "Youth Gangs and Definitional Issues: When Is a Gang a Gang, and Why Does It Matter?" *Crime & Delinquency* 47 (1): 105–130. DOI:10.1177/0011128701047001005.

Fagan, Jeffrey, and Tom R. Tyler. 2005. "Legal Socialization of Children and Adolescents." *Social Justice Research* 18 (3): 217–241. https://doi.org/10.1007/s11211-005-6823-3.

Fearon, R. Pasco, Marian J. Bakermans-Kranenburg, Marinus H. Van IJzendoorn, Anne-Marie Lapsley, and Glenn I. Roisman. 2010. "The Significance of Insecure Attachment and Disorganization in the Development of Children's Externalizing Behavior: A Meta-Analytic Study." *Child Development* 81 (2): 435–456. https://doi.org/10.1111/j.1467-8624.2009.01405.x.

Fearon, R. M. Pasco, Ashley M. Groh, Marian J. Bakermans-Kranenburg, Marinus H. van IJzendoorn, and Glenn I. Roisman. 2016. "Attachment and Developmental Psychopathology." In *Developmental Psychopathology*, edited by Dante Cicchetti, 1–60. Hoboken, NJ: Wiley. https://doi:10.1002/9781119125556.devpsy108.

Fite, Paula J., Shaquanna Brown, Waheeda A. Hossain, Ann Manzardo, Merlin G. Butler, and Marco Bortolato. 2020. "Sex-Dimorphic Interactions of MAOA Genotype and Child Maltreatment Predispose College Students to Polysubstance Use." *Frontiers in Genetics* 10: 1–10. https://doi.org/10.3389/fgene.2019.01314.

Ford, Julian D., John Chapman, Judge Michael Mack, and Geraldine Pearson. 2006. "Pathways from Traumatic Child Victimization to Delinquency: Implications for Juvenile and Permanency Court Proceedings and Decisions." *Juvenile and Family Court Journal* 57 (1): 13–26. https://doi.org/10.1176/appi.psychotherapy.2006.60.4.335.

Frazzetto, Giovanni, Giorgio Di Lorenzo, Valeria Carola, Luca Proietti, Ewa Sokolowska, Alberto Siracusano, Cornelius Gross, and Alfonso Troisi. 2007. "Early Trauma and

Increased Risk for Physical Aggression during Adulthood: The Moderating Role of MAOA Genotype." *PloS One* 2 (5): 1–6. https://doi.org/10.1371/journal.pone.0000486.

Frick, Paul J., Amy H. Cornell, Christopher T. Barry, S. Doug Bodin, and Heather E. Dane. 2003. "Callous-Unemotional Traits and Conduct Problems in the Prediction of Conduct Problem Severity, Aggression, and Self-Report of Delinquency." *Journal of Abnormal Child Psychology* 31 (4): 457–470. DOI:10.1023/A:1023899703866.

Frick, Paul J., James V. Ray, Laura C. Thornton, and Rachel E. Kahn. 2014. "Annual Research Review: A Developmental Psychopathology Approach to Understanding Callous-Unemotional Traits in Children and Adolescents with Serious Conduct Problems." *Journal of Child Psychology and Psychiatry* 55 (6): 532–548. DOI:10.1111/jcpp.12152.

Frisby-Osman, Sarah, and Jane L. Wood. 2020. "Rethinking How We View Gang Members: An Examination into Affective, Behavioral, and Mental Health Predictors of UK Gang-involved Youth." *Youth Justice* 20 (1-2): 93–112. https://doi.org/10.1177/1473225419893779.

Garbarino, James, Amy Governale, and Danielle Nesi. 2020. "Vulnerable Children: Protection and Social Reintegration of Child Soldiers and Youth Members of Gangs." *Child Abuse and Neglect* 110: 1–9. https://doi.org/10.1016/j.chiabu.2020.104415.

Garcia-Coll, Cynthia, Anna Akerman, and Dante Cicchetti. 2000. "Cultural Influences on Developmental Processes and Outcomes: Implications for the Study of Development and Psychopathology." *Development and Psychopathology* 12 (3): 333–356. https://doi.org/10.1017/s0954579400003059.

Garcia-Coll, Cynthia, Keith Crnic, Gontran Lamberty, Barbara Hanna Wasik, Renee Jenkins, Heidie Vazquez Garcia, and Harriet Pipes McAdoo. 1996. "An Integrative Model for the Study of Developmental Competencies in Minority Children." *Child Development* 67 (5): 1891–1914. DOI:10.1111/j.1467-8624.1996.tb01834.x.

Gilman, Amanda B., Karl G. Hill, and J. David Hawkins. 2014. "Long-Term Consequences of Adolescent Gang Membership for Adult Functioning." *American Journal of Public Health* 104 (5): 938–945. DOI:10.2105/AJPH.2013.301821.

Gobin, Robyn L., and Jennifer J. Freyd. 2014. "The Impact of Betrayal Trauma on the Tendency to Trust." *Psychological Trauma: Theory, Research, Practice, and Policy* 6 (5): 505–511. https://doi.org/10.1037/a0032452.

Goldman, Liran, Howard Giles, and Michael A. Hogg. 2014. "Going to Extremes: Social Identity and Communication Processes Associated with Gang Membership." *Group Processes & Intergroup Relations* 17 (6): 813–832. https://doi.org/10.1177%2F1368430214524289.

Gordon, Rachel A., Benjamin B. Lahey, Eriko Kawai, Rolf Loeber, Magda Stouthamer-Loeber, and David P. Farrington. 2004. "Antisocial Behavior and Youth Gang Membership: Selection and Socialization." *Criminology* 42 (1): 55–88. https://doi.org/10.1111/j.1745-9125.2004.tb00513.x.

Griffin, Brandon J., Natalie Purcell, Kristine Burkman, Brett T. Litz, Craig J. Bryan, Martha Schmitz, Claudia Villierme, Jessica Walsh, and Shira Maguen. 2019. "Moral Injury: An Integrative Review." *Journal of Traumatic Stress* 32 (3): 350–362. https://doi.org/10.1002/jts.22362.

Guruge, Sepali, and Hissan Butt. 2015. "A Scoping Review of Mental Health Issues and Concerns among Immigrant and Refugee Youth in Canada: Looking Back, Moving Forward." *Canadian Journal of Public Health* 106 (2): e72–e78. https://doi.org/10.17269/cjph.106.4588.

Harper, Gary W., Jonathan Davidson, and Sybil G. Hosek. 2008. "Influence of Gang Membership on Negative Affect, Substance Use, and Antisocial Behavior Among

Homeless African American Male Youth." *American Journal of Men's Health* 2 (3): 229–243. DOI:10.1177/1557988307312555.

Harris, Toi Blakley, Sara Elkins, Ashley Butler, Matthew Shelton, Barbara Robles, Stephanie Kwok, Sherri Simpson et al. 2013. "Youth Gang Members: Psychiatric Disorders and Substance Use." *Laws* 2 (4): 392–400. https://doi.org/10.3390/laws2040392.

Hashimi, Sadaf, Sara Wakefield, and Robert Apel. 2021. "Sibling Transmission of Gang Involvement." *Journal of Research in Crime and Delinquency* 58 (5): 507–544. https://doi.org/10.1177/0022427820986592.

Hautala, Dane S., Kelley J. Sittner, and Les B. Whitbeck. 2016. "Prospective Childhood Risk Factors for Gang Involvement among North American Indigenous Adolescents." *Youth Violence and Juvenile Justice* 14 (4): 390–410. https://doi.org/10.1177/1541204015585173.

Hill, Karl G., Christina Lui, and J. David Hawkins. 2001. *Early Precursors of Gang Membership: A Study of Seattle Youth.* US Department of Justice, Office of Justice Programs, Office of Juvenile Justice and Delinquency Prevention.

Hoppen, Thole Hilko, and Trudie Chalder. 2018. "Childhood Adversity as a Transdiagnostic Risk Factor for Affective Disorders in Adulthood: A Systematic Review Focusing on Biopsychosocial Moderating and Mediating Variables." *Clinical Psychology Review* 65: 81–151. http://dx.doi.org/10.1016/j.cpr.2018.08.002.

Huff, C. R. 1998. *Comparing the Criminal Behavior of Youth Gangs and At-Risk Youths.* US Department of Justice, Office of Justice Programs, National Institute of Justice.

Hyde, Luke W., Daniel S. Shaw, and Kristin L. Moilanen. 2010. "Developmental Precursors of Moral Disengagement and the Role of Moral Disengagement in the Development of Antisocial Behavior." *Journal Of Abnormal Child Psychology* 38 (2): 197–209.

Jenkins, Richard L., and Andrew Boyer. 1968. "Types of Delinquent Behavior and Background Factors." *International Journal of Social Psychiatry* 14 (1): 65–76. DOI:10.1177/002076406801400108.

Jensen, Peter S., and Kimberly Hoagwood. 1997. "The Book of Names: DSM-IV in Context." *Development and Psychopathology* 9 (2): 231–249. DQI:10.1017/s0954579497002034.

Kaplow, Julie B., Christopher M. Layne, Robert S. Pynoos, Judith A. Cohen, and Alicia Lieberman. 2012. "DSM-V Diagnostic Criteria for Bereavement-Related Disorders in Children and Adolescents: Developmental Considerations." *Psychiatry: Interpersonal & Biological Processes* 75 (3): 243–266. https://doi.org/10.1521/psyc.2012.75.3.243.

Karpman, Ben. 1941. "On the Need of Separating Psychopathy into Two Distinct Clinical Types: The Symptomatic and the Idiopathic." *Journal of Criminal Psychopathology* 3: 112–137.

Kawaii-Bogue, Babe, Norissa J. Williams, and Kameron MacNear. 2017. "Mental Health Care Access and Treatment Utilization in African American Communities: An Integrative Care Framework." *Best Practices in Mental Health* 13 (2): 11–29.

Kelly, Jane F., and Catherine L. Ward. 2020. "Narratives of Gang Disengagement Among Former Gang Members in South Africa." *Criminal Justice and Behavior* 47 (11): 1509–1528. https://doi.org/10.1177/0093854820949603.

Kennedy, Traci M., and Rosario Ceballo. 2016. "Emotionally Numb: Desensitization to Community Violence Exposure among Urban Youth." *Developmental Psychology* 52 (5): 778–789. https://doi.org/10.1037/dev0000112.

Kerig, P. K. 2017. *Posttraumatic Stress Disorder in Childhood and Adolescence: A Developmental Psychopathology Perspective.* New York: Momentum Press.

Kerig, Patricia K. 2019. "Linking Childhood Trauma Exposure to Adolescent Justice Involvement: The Concept of Posttraumatic Risk-Seeking." *Clinical Psychology: Science and Practice* 26 (3): e12280. https://doi.org/10.1037/h0101756.

Kerig, Patricia K., and James F. Alexander. 2014. "Family Matters: Integrating Trauma Treatment into Functional Family Therapy for Traumatized Delinquent Youth." *Journal of Child and Adolescent Trauma* 5 (3): 205–223. https://doi.org/10.1080/19361521.2012.697103.

Kerig, Patricia K., and Stephen P. Becker. 2010. "From Internalizing to Externalizing: Theoretical Models of the Processes Linking PTSD to Juvenile Delinquency." In *Posttraumatic Stress Disorder (PTSD): Causes, Symptoms and Treatment*, edited by Sylvia J. Egan, 1–46. Hauppauge, NY: Nova Science Publishers.

Kerig, Patricia K., Diana C. Bennett, and Stephen P. Becker. 2012. "'Nothing Really Matters': Emotional Numbing as a Link between Trauma Exposure and Callousness in Delinquent Youth." *Journal of Traumatic Stress*, 25 (3): 272–279. DOI:10.1002/jts.21700.

Kerig, Patricia K., Shannon D. Chaplo, Dianna C. Bennett, and Crosby A. Modrowski. 2016. "'Harm as Harm': Gang Membership, Perpetration Trauma, and Posttraumatic Stress Symptoms among Youth in the Juvenile Justice System." *Criminal Justice and Behavior* 43 (5): 635–652. https://doi.org/10.1177/0093854815607307.

Kerig, Patricia K., Amanda Ludlow, and Charles Wenar. 2012. *Developmental Psychopathology: From Infancy through Adolescence*, 6th edition. New York: McGraw-Hill.

Kerig, Patricia K. and Lucybel Mendez. 2022. "The Role of Trauma in the Developmental Trajectories of Gang-Involved Youth." In *Psychology of Gang Involvement*, edited by Jane Wood, Jaimee Mallion, and Sarah Frisby-Osman. New York: Routledge.

Kerig, Patricia K., Michaela M. Mozley, and Lucybel Mendez. 2020. "Forensic Assessment of PTSD Via DSM-5 Versus ICD-11 Criteria: Implications for Current Practice and Future Research." *Psychological Injury and Law* 13 (4): 383–411. DOI:10.1007/s12207-020-09397-4.

Kerig, Patricia K., Cecilia Wainryb, Michelle Sinayobye Twali, and Shannon D. Chaplo. 2013. "America's Child Soldiers: Toward a Research Agenda for Studying Gang-Involved Youth in the United States." *Journal of Aggression, Maltreatment & Trauma* 22 (7): 773–795. https://doi.org/10.1080/10926771.2013.813883.

Kidwell, Mallory C., and Patricia K. Kerig. 2021. "To Trust Is to Survive: Toward a Developmental Model of Moral Injury." *Journal of Child and Adolescent Trauma* 16: 459–475. https://doi.org/10.1007/s40653-021-00399-1.

Kim-Cohen, Julia, Avshalom Caspi, Alan Taylor, Brenda Williams, Rhiannon Newcombe, Ian W. Craig, and Terrie E. Moffitt. 2006. "MAOA, Maltreatment, and Gene-Environment Interaction Predicting Children's Mental Health: New Evidence and a Meta-Analysis." *Molecular Psychiatry* 11 (10): 903–913. https://doi.org/10.1038/sj.mp.4001851.

Kissner, J., and D. C. Pyrooz. 2009. "Self-Control, Differential Association, and Gang Membership: A Theoretical and Empirical Extension of the Literature." *Journal of Criminal Justice* 37 (5): 478–487. https://doi.org/10.1016/j.jcrimjus.2009.07.008.

Klein, Malcolm W., and Cheryl L. Maxson. 2010. *Street Gang Patterns and Policies*. Oxford, UK: Oxford University Press.

Knight, George P., Sandra H. Losoya, Young Il Cho, Laurie Chassin, Joanna Lee Williams, and Sonia Cota-Robles. 2012. "Ethnic Identity and Offending Trajectories among Mexican American Juvenile Offenders: Gang Membership and Psychosocial Maturity." *Journal of Research on Adolescence* 22 (4): 782–796. https://doi.org/10.1111/j.1532-7795.2012.00819.x.

Kolivoski, Karen M., Jeffrey J. Shook, Heath C. Johnson, Sara Goodkind, Rachel Fusco, Matt DeLisi, and Michael G. Vaughn. 2016. "Applying Legal Socialization to the Child Welfare System: Do Youths' Perceptions of Caseworkers Matter?" *Child and Youth Care Forum*, 45 (1): 65–83. http://dx.doi.org/10.1007/s10566-015-9317-y.

Koss, Kalsea J., and Megan R. Gunnar. 2018. "Annual Research Review: Early Adversity, the Hypothalamic–Pituitary–Adrenocortical Axis, and Child Psychopathology." *Journal of Child Psychology and Psychiatry* 59 (4): 327–346. https://doi.org/10.1111/jcpp.12784.

Kotov, Roman, Robert F. Krueger, David Watson, Thomas M. Achenbach, Robert R. Althoff, R. Michael Bagby, Timothy A. Brown et al. 2017. "The Hierarchical Taxonomy of Psychopathology (HiTOP): A Dimensional Alternative to Traditional Nosologies." *Journal of Abnormal Psychology* 126 (4): 454–477. https://doi.org/10.1037/abn0000258.

Krohn, Marvin D., Jeffrey T. Ward, Terence P. Thornberry, Alan J. Lizotte, and Rebekah Chu. 2011. "The Cascading Effects of Adolescent Gang Involvement across the Life Course." *Criminology* 49 (4): 991–1028. https://doi.org/10.1111/j.1745-9125.2011.00250.x.

Kubik, Joanna, Meagan Docherty, and Paul Boxer. 2019. "The Impact of Childhood Maltreatment on Adolescent Gang Involvement." *Child Abuse & Neglect* 96: 104096. DOI:10.1016/j.chiabu.2019.104096.

Lacourse, Eric, Daniel Nagin, Richard E. Tremblay, Frank Vitaro, and Michel Claes. 2003. "Developmental Trajectories of Boys' Delinquent Group Membership and Facilitation of Violent Behaviors during Adolescence." *Development and Psychopathology* 15 (1): 183–197. https://doi.org/10.1017/s0954579403000105.

Lahey, Benjamin B., Rachel A. Gordon, Rolf Loeber, Magda Stouthamer-Loeber, and David P. Farrington. 1999. "Boys Who Join Gangs: A Prospective Study of Predictors of First Gang Entry." *Journal of Abnormal Child Psychology* 27 (94): 261–276. https://doi.org/10.1023/B:JACP.0000039775.83318.57.

Lansford, Jennifer E., Patrick S. Malone, Kristopher I. Stevens, Kenneth A. Dodge, John E. Bates, and Gregory S. Pettit. 2006. "Developmental Trajectories of Externalizing and Internalizing Behaviors: Factors Underlying Resilience in Physically Abused Children." *Development and Psychopathology* 18 (1): 35–55. https://doi.org/10.1017/s0954579406060032.

Lauger, Timothy R. 2020. "Gangs, Identity, and Cultural Performance." *Sociology Compass* 14 (4): e12772. https://doi.org/10.1111/soc4.12772.

Lee, Sou, and Bryan F. Bubolz. 2020. "The Gang Member Stands Out: Stigma as a Residual Consequence of Gang Involvement." *Criminal Justice Review* 45 (1): 64–83. https://doi.org/10.1177/0734016819867385.

Li, Xiaoming, Bonita Stanton, Robert Pack, Carole Harris, Lesley Cottrell, and James Burns. 2002. "Risk and Protective Factors Associated with Gang Involvement Among Urban African American Adolescents." *Youth & Society* 34 (2): 172–194. https://doi.org/10.1177/004411802237862.

Litz, Brett T., and Patricia K. Kerig. 2019. "Introduction to the Special Issue on Moral Injury: Conceptual Challenges, Methodological Issues, and Clinical Applications." *Journal of Traumatic Stress* 32 (3): 341–349. https://doi.org/10.1002/jts.22405.

Litz, Brett T., Nathan Stein, Eileen Delaney, Leslie Lebowitz, William P. Nash, Caroline Silva, and Shira Maguen. 2009. "Moral Injury and Moral Repair in War Veterans: A Preliminary Model and Intervention Strategy." *Clinical Psychology Review* 29 (8): 695–706. https://doi.org/10.1016/j.cpr.2009.07.003.

Macfarlane, Alastair. 2019. "Gangs and Adolescent Mental Health: A Narrative Review." *Journal of Child & Adolescent Trauma* 12 (3): 411–420. https://doi.org/10.1007/s40653-018-0231-y.

MacNair, Rachel. 2002. *Perpetration-Induced Traumatic Stress: The Psychological Consequences of Killing*. Westport, CT: Greenwood Publishing Group.

Madan, Anjana, Sylvie Mrug, and Michael Windle. 2011. "Brief Report: Do Delinquency and Community Violence Exposure Explain Internalizing Problems in Early Adolescent Gang

Members?" *Journal of Adolescence* 34 (5): 1093–1096. https://doi.org/10.1016/j.adolescence.2010.06.003.

Mallion, Jaimee S., and Jane L. Wood. 2018. "Emotional Processes and Gang Membership: A Narrative Review." *Aggression and Violent Behavior* 43: 56–63. https://doi.org/10.1016/j.avb.2018.10.001.

Matsuda, Kristy N., Chris Melde, Terrance J. Taylor, Adrienne Freng, and Finn-Aage Esbensen. 2013. "Gang Membership and Adherence to the 'Code of the Street.'" *Justice Quarterly* 30 (3): 440–468. https://doi.org/10.1080/07418825.2012.684432.

McDaniel, Dawn Delfin. 2012. "Risk and Protective Factors Associated with Gang Affiliation among High-Risk Youth: A Public Health Approach." *Injury Prevention* 18 (4): 253–258. https://doi.org/10.1136/injuryprev-2011-040083.

McDermott, Rose, Chris Dawes, Elizabeth Prom-Wormley, Lindon Eaves, and Peter K. Hatemi. 2013. "MAOA and Aggression: A Gene-Environment Interaction in Two Populations." *Journal of Conflict Resolution* 57 (6): 1043–1064. https://doi.org/10.1177/0022002712457746.

McKay, Michael T., Mary Cannon, Derek Chambers, Ronán M. Conroy, Helen Coughlan, Philip Dodd, Colm Healy, Laurie O'Donnell, and Mary C. Clarke. 2021. "Childhood Trauma and Adult Mental Disorder: A Systematic Review and Meta-Analysis of Longitudinal Cohort Studies." *Acta Psychiatrica Scandinavica* 143 (3): 189–205. DOI:10.1111/acps.13268.

Melde, Chris, Terrance J. Taylor, and Finn-Aage Esbensen. 2009. "'I Got Your Back': An Examination of the Protective Function of Gang Membership in Adolescence." *Criminology* 47 (2): 565–594. https://doi.org/10.1111/j.1745-9125.2009.00148.x.

Mendez, Lucybel, Michaela M. Mozley, and Patricia K. Kerig. 2020. "Associations among Trauma Exposure, Callous-Unemotionality, Race or Ethnicity, and Gang Involvement in Justice-Involved Youth." *Criminal Justice and Behavior* 47 (4): 457–469. https://doi.org/10.1177/0093854819897940.

Merrin, Gabriel J., Jun Sung Hong, and Dorothy L. Espelage. 2015. "Are the Risk and Protective Factors Similar for Gang-Involved, Pressured-to-Join, and Non-Gang-Involved Youth? A Social-Ecological Analysis." *American Journal of Orthopsychiatry* 85 (6): 522–535. https://doi.org/10.1037/ort0000094.

Moore, Joan. 2010. *Going Down to the Barrio: Homeboys and Homegirls in Change*. Philadelphia, PA: Temple University Press.

Naldrett, Georgia A., and Jane L. Wood. 2020. "Gang Involvement, Mental Health Difficulties and Exposure to Violence in 11-16-Year-Old School Students." *Adolescent Psychiatry* 10 (4): 244–255. https://doi.org/10.2174/2210676610999201229141153.

Niebieszczanski, Rebecca, Leigh Harkins, Sian Judson, Kenny Smith, and Louise Dixon. 2015. "The Role of Moral Disengagement in Street Gang Offending." *Psychology, Crime and Law* 21 (6): 589–605. https://doi.org/10.1080/1068316X.2015.1008476.

Nivette, Amy E., Manuel Eisner, Tina Malti, and Denis Ribeaud. 2015. "The Social and Developmental Antecedents of 'Legal Cynicism.'" *Journal of Research in Crime and Delinquency* 52 (2): 270–298. https://doi.org/10.1177/0022427814557038.

Nolen-Hoeksema, Susan, and Edward R. Watkins. 2011. "A Heuristic for Developing Transdiagnostic Models of Psychopathology: Explaining Multifinality and Divergent Trajectories." *Perspectives on Psychological Science* 6 (6): 589–609. https://doi.org/10.1177/1745691611419672.

Novich, Madeleine, and Geoffrey Hunt. 2017. "'Get Off Me': Perceptions of Disrespectful Police Behaviour among Ethnic Minority Youth Gang Members." *Drugs: Education, Prevention and Policy* 24 (3): 248–255. https://doi.org/10.1080/09687637.2016.1239697.

Novich, Madeleine, and Geoffrey Hunt. 2018. "Trust in Police Motivations during Involuntary Encounters: An Examination of Young Gang Members of Colour." *Race and Justice* 8 (1): 51–70. https://doi.org/10.1080/09687637.2016.1239697.

Nydegger, Liesl A., Katherine Quinn, Jennifer L. Walsh, Maria L. Pacella-LaBarbara, and Julia Dickson-Gomez. 2019. "Polytraumatization, Mental Health, and Delinquency among Adolescent Gang Members." *Journal of Traumatic Stress* 32 (6): 890–898. https://doi.org/10.1002/jts.22473.

Osman, Sarah, and Jane Wood. 2018. "Gang Membership, Mental Illness, and Negative Emotionality: A Systematic Review of the Literature." *International Journal of Forensic Mental Health* 17 (3): 223–246. http://dx.doi.org.ezproxy.lib.utah.edu/10.1080/14999013.2018.1468366.

Panfil, Vanessa R. 2020. "'I Was a Homo Thug, Now I'm Just Homo': Gay Gang Members' Desistance and Persistence." *Criminology* 58 (2): 255–279. https://doi.org/10.1111/1745-9125.12240.

Papachristos, Andrew V., Tracey L. Meares, and Jeffrey Fagan. 2012. "Why Do Criminals Obey the Law? The Influence of Legitimacy and Social Networks on Active Gun Offenders." *Journal of Criminal Law and Criminology* 102: 397–404. DOI:0091-4169/12/10202-0397.

Pauwels, Lieven Jr., and Wim Hardyns. 2016. "Micro-Place Conditions and Social, Personal, and Situational Control Mechanisms: Testing an Integrated Theory of Gang Membership in Belgium." In *Gang Transitions and Transformations in an International Context*, edited by Cheryl L. Maxson and Finn-Aage Esbenson, 65–94. Cham, Switzerland: Springer.

Pearce, Jenny J., and John Pitts. 2011. *Youth Gangs, Sexual Violence and Sexual Exploitation: A Scoping Exercise for the Office of the Children's Commissioner for England*. Bedfordshire, UK: University of Bedfordshire. https://uobrep.openrepository.com/bitstream/handle/10547/315158/OCC_Uni-of-Beds-Literature-Review_FINAL.pdf?sequence=1.

Penner, Erika K., Catherine S. Shaffer, and Jodi L. Viljoen. 2017. "Questioning Fairness: The Relationship of Mental Health and Psychopathic Characteristics with Young Offenders' Perceptions of Procedural Justice and Legitimacy." *Criminal Behaviour and Mental Health* 27 (4): 354–370. https://doi.org/10.1002/cbm.2004.

Petering, Robin. 2016. "Sexual Risk, Substance Use, Mental Health, and Trauma Experiences of Gang-involved Homeless Youth." *Journal of Adolescence* 48 (1): 73–81. DOI:10.1016/j.adolescence.2016.01.009.

Peterson, Dana, Terrance J. Taylor, and Finn-Aage Esbensen. 2004. "Gang Membership and Violent Victimization." *Justice Quarterly* 21 (4): 793–815. https://doi.org/10.1080/07418820400095991.

Piquero, Alex R. 2016. "'Take My License n' All That Jive, I Can't See... 35': Little Hope for the Future Encourages Offending Over Time." *Justice Quarterly* 33 (1): 73–99. https://doi.org/10.1080/07418825.2014.896396.

Platell, Monique, Angus Cook, and Karen Martin. 2019. "Barriers to Mental Health Care for Disadvantaged Adolescents: Perspectives of Service Providers." *Advances in Mental Health* 15 (2): 198–210. https://doi.org/10.1080/18387357.2017.1317216.

Poljac, Bakir, and Tod Burke. 2008. "Erasing the Past: Tattoo-Removal Programs for Former Gang Members." *FBI Law Enforcement Bulletin* 77: 13–18. https://doi.org/10.1037/e511472010-005.

Porter, Stephen. 1996. "Without Conscience or without Active Conscience? The Etiology of Psychopathy Revisited." *Aggression and Violent Behavior* 1 (2): 179–189. https://doi.org/10.1016/1359-1789(95)00010-0.

Prinstein, Mitchell J., Eric A. Youngstrom, Eric J. Mash, and Russell A. Barkley. 2019. *Treatment of Disorders in Childhood and Adolescence*. New York: Guilford.

Pyrooz, David C. 2014. "'From Your First Cigarette to Your Last Dyin' Day': The Patterning of Gang Membership in the Life-Course." *Journal of Quantitative Criminology* 30 (2): 349–372. https://doi.org/10.1007/s10940-013-9206-1.

Pyrooz, David C., and Scott H. Decker. 2011. "Motives and Methods for Leaving the Gang: Understanding the Process of Gang Desistance." *Journal of Criminal Justice* 39 (5): 417–425. https://doi.org/10.1016/j.jcrimjus.2011.07.001.

Pyrooz, David C., Ryan K. Masters, Jennifer J. Tostlebe, and Richard G. Rogers. 2020. "Exceptional Mortality Risk among Police-Identified Young Black Male Gang Members." *Preventive Medicine* 141: 106269. https://doi.org/10.1016/j.ypmed.2020.106269.

Quinn, Katherine, Maria L. Pacella, Julia Dickson-Gomez, and Liesl A. Nydegger. 2017. "Childhood Adversity and the Continued Exposure to Trauma and Violence among Adolescent Gang Members." *American Journal of Community Psychology* 59 (1–2): 36–49. https://doi.org/10.1002/ajcp.12123.

Reisig, Michael D., Scott E. Wolfe, and Kristy Holtfreter. 2011. "Legal Cynicism, Legitimacy, and Criminal Offending: The Nonconfounding Effect of Low Self-Control." *Criminal Justice and Behavior* 38 (12): 1265–1279. https://doi.org/10.1177/0093854811424707.

Ribeiro da Silva, Diana, Daniel Rijo, Nélio Brazão, Marlene Paulo, Rita Miguel, Paula Castilho, Paula Vagos, Paul Gilbert, and Randall T. Salekin. 2021. "The Efficacy of the Psychopathy.COMP Program in Reducing Psychopathic Traits: A Controlled Trial with Male Detained Youth." *Journal of Consulting and Clinical Psychology* 89 (6): 499–513. https://doi.org/10.1037/ccp0000659.

Rich, John A. 2009. *Wrong Place, Wrong Time: Trauma and Violence in the Lives of Young Black Men*. Baltimore, MD: Johns Hopkins University Press.

Rich, John A., and Courtney M. Grey. 2005. "Pathways to Recurrent Trauma among Young Black Men: Traumatic Stress, Substance Use, and the 'Code of the Street.'" *American Journal of Public Health* 95 (5): 816–824. https://doi.org/10.2105/AJPH.2004.044560.

Rima, Dzhansarayeva, Malikova Sholpan, Atakhanova Gulzagira, Bisenova Meruert, and Kevin M. Beaver. 2020. "Exploring the Potential Association Between Gang Membership and Health Outcomes in a Longitudinal Sample of Youth and Young Adults." *Journal of Criminal Justice* 66: 101629. https://doi.org/10.1016/j.jcrimjus.2019.101629.

Roberts, Albert R., and Kevin Corcoran. 2005. "Adolescents Growing Up in Stressful Environments, Dual Diagnosis, and Sources of Success." *Brief Treatment and Crisis Intervention* 5 (1): 1–8. DOI:https://doi.org/10.1093/brief-treatment/mhi009.

Roman, Caterina G., Scott H. Decker, and David C. Pyrooz. 2017. "Leveraging the Pushes and Pulls of Gang Disengagement to Improve Gang Intervention: Findings from Three Multi-Site Studies and a Review of Relevant Gang Programs." *Journal of Crime and Justice* 40 (3): 316–336. https://doi.org/10.1080/0735648x.2017.1345096.

Ruble, Nikki M., and William L. Turner. 2000. "A Systemic Analysis of the Dynamics and Organization of Urban Street Gangs." *American Journal of Family Therapy* 28 (2): 117–132. https://doi.org/10.1080/019261800261707.

Saltzman, William R., Robert S. Pynoos, Christopher M. Layne, Alan M. Steinberg, and Eugene Aisenberg. 2001. "Trauma-and Grief-Focused Intervention for Adolescents Exposed to Community Violence: Results of a School-Based Screening and Group Treatment Protocol." *Group Dynamics: Theory, Research, and Practice* 5 (4): 291–303. https://doi.org/10.1037/1089-2699.5.4.291.

Sanislow, Charles A., Sarah E. Morris, Jennifer Pacheco, and Bruce N. Cuthbert. 2020. "The National Institute of Mental Health Research Domain Criteria." In *New Oxford Textbook of Psychiatry*, edited by John R. Geddes, Nancy C. Andreasen and Guy M. Goodwin, 62–72. Oxford, UK: Oxford University Press. DOI:10.1093/med/9780198713005.003.0008.

Simmons, C., Z. Rowan, A. Knowles, L. Steinberg, P. J. Frick, and E. Cauffman. 2019. "A Life History Approach to Understanding Juvenile Offending and Aggression." *Aggression and Violent Behavior*. https://doi.org/https://doi.org/10.1016/j.avb.2019.07.012

Smith, Justin D., Lauren Wakschlag, Sheila Krogh-Jespersen, John T. Walkup, Melvin N. Wilson, Thomas J. Dishion, and Daniel S. Shaw. 2019. "Dysregulated Irritability as a Window on Young Children's Psychiatric Risk: Transdiagnostic Effects Via the Family Check-Up." *Development and Psychopathology* 31 (5): 1887–1899. https://doi.org/10.1017/s0954579419000816.

Smoller, Jordan W., Ole A. Andreassen, Howard J. Edenberg, Stephen V. Faraone, Stephen J. Glatt, and Kenneth S. Kendler. 2019. "Psychiatric Genetics and the Structure of Psychopathology." *Molecular Psychiatry* 24 (3): 409–420. https://doi.org/10.1038/s41380-017-0010-4.

Stolbach, Bradley C., and Carol Reese. 2020. "Healing Hurt People—Chicago: Supporting Trauma Recovery in Patients Injured by Violence." In *Violence, Trauma, and Trauma Surgery*, edited by Mark Sigler and Selwin O. Rogers Jr., 237–248. New York: Springer.

Stretesky, Paul B., and Mark R. Pogrebin. 2007. "Gang-Related Gun Violence: Socialization, Identity, and Self." *Journal of Contemporary Ethnography* 3 (1): 85–114. https://doi.org/10.1177%2F0891241606287416.

Thornberry, Terence P., Marvin D. Krohn, Alan J. Lizotte, Carolyn A. Smith, and Kimberly Tobin. 2003. *Gangs and Delinquency in Developmental Perspective*. Cambridge, UK: Cambridge University Press. doi:10.1017/cbo9780511499517.

Thornton, Laura C., Paul J. Frick, Elizabeth P. Shulman, James V. Ray, Laurence Steinberg, and Elizabeth Cauffman. 2015. "Callous-Unemotional Traits and Adolescents' Role in Group Crime." *Law and Human Behavior* 39 (4): 368. https://doi.org/10.1037/lhb0000124.

Tostlebe, Jennifer J., and David C. Pyrooz. 2022. "Are Gang Members Psychopaths?" In *Psychopathy and Criminal Behavior*, edited by Paulo B. Marques, Mauro Paulino and Laura Alho, 311–331. New York: Academic Press.

Valdez, Christine. 2021. "Posttraumatic Distress and Treatment Barriers among Former Gang Members: Implications for Improving Access to Traumatic Stress Resources in Marginalized Populations." *Journal of Traumatic Stress* 34 (2): 309–321. https://doi.org/10.1002/jts.22651.

Van Ngo, Hieu, Avery Calhoun, Catherine Worthington, Tim Pyrch, and David Este. 2017. "The Unravelling of Identities and Belonging: Criminal Gang Involvement of Youth from Immigrant Families." *Journal of International Migration and Integration* 18 (1): 63–84. https://doi.org/10.1007/s12134-015-0466-5.

Vasileva, Mira, and Franz Petermann. 2018. "Attachment, Development, and Mental Health in Abused and Neglected Preschool Children in Foster Care: A Meta-Analysis." *Trauma, Violence, & Abuse* 19 (4): 443–458. https://doi.org/10.1177/1524838016669503.

Vigil, James Diego. 1988. "Group Processes and Street Identity: Adolescent Chicano Gang Members." *Ethos* 16 (4): 421–445. https://doi.org/10.1525/eth.1988.16.4.02a00040.

Vuk, Mateja. 2017. "Parenting Styles and Gang Membership: Mediating Factors." *Deviant Behavior* 38 (4): 406–425. https://doi.org/10.1080/01639625.2016.1197011.

Wainryb, Cecilia. 2011. "'And So They Ordered Me to Kill a Person': Conceptualizing the Impacts of Child Soldiering on the Development of Moral Agency." *Human Development* 54 (5): 273–300. http://dx.doi.org/10.1159/000331482.

Watkins, Adam M., and Chris Melde. 2016. "Bad Medicine: The Relationship Between Gang Membership, Depression, Self-Esteem, and Suicidal Behavior." *Criminal Justice and Behavior* 43 (8): 1107–1126. https://doi.org/10.1177/0093854816631797.

Whaling, Kelly M., and Jill Sharkey. 2020. "Differences in Prevalence Rates of Hopelessness and Suicidal Ideation among Adolescents by Gang Membership and Latinx Identity." *Child and Adolescent Social Work Journal* 37 (5): 557–569. https://doi.org/10.1007/s10560-019-00644-5.

Wiggins, J. L., C. Mitchell, L. W. Hyde, and C. S. Monk. 2015. "Identifying Early Pathways of Risk and Resilience: The Codevelopment of Internalizing and Externalizing Symptoms and the Role of Harsh Parenting." *Development and Psychopathology* 27 (4pt1): 1295–1312. https://doi.org/doi:10.1017/S0954579414001412

Wilkinson, Deanna L., and Patrick J. Carr. 2008. "Violent Youths' Responses to High Levels of Exposure to Community Violence: What Violent Events Reveal about Youth Violence." *Journal of Community Psychology* 36 (8): 1026–1051. https://doi.org/10.1002/jcop.20278.

Wojciechowski, Thomas W. 2020. "PTSD as a Risk Factor for the Development of Violence among Juvenile Offenders: A Group-Based Trajectory Modeling Approach." *Journal of Interpersonal Violence* 35 (13-14): 2511–2535. DOI:10.1177/0886260517704231.

Wojciechowski, Thomas. 2021. "PTSD as a Risk Factor for Chronic Gang Membership During Adolescence and Early Adulthood: A Group-Based Trajectory Modeling Approach." *Crime & Delinquency* 67 (10): 1536–1560. DOI:10.1177/0011128720944890.

Wood, Jane L. 2014. "Understanding Gang Membership: The Significance of Group Processes." *Group Processes & Intergroup Relations* 17 (6): 710–729. https://doi.org/10.1177/1368430214550344.

Wood, Jane, and Emma Alleyne. 2010. "Street Gang Theory and Research: Where Are We Now and Where Do We Go from Here?" *Aggression and Violent Behavior* 15 (2): 100–111. DOI:10.1016/j.avb.2009.08.005.

CHAPTER 23

THE EMERGING FRONTIER
Gangs in Developing Countries

HERBERT C. COVEY

GANGS have drawn an increasing amount of attention over recent decades, with most of the gang research focused on the United States. However, according to Pyrooz and Mitchell (2015), in the early 1990s there was an "international turn" as research expanded to other regions of the world, especially Europe. The rapid growth of gang research has not occurred to the same extent for developing countries. Developing countries are those with lower levels of economic and industrial development that result in social, economic, political, and environmental challenges that impede the quality of life. Information about gangs in many developing countries continues to be sparse (Chu et al. 2012). However, some recent gang anthologies include chapters on gangs in developing countries (see Brotherton and Gude 2021; Hazen and Rodgers 2014).

Currently, knowledge about gangs in developing countries is a patchwork quilt of information, and no total estimate of the number of gangs and gang members in the developing world exists. Furthermore, longitudinal studies of gangs in developing countries, similar to developed countries, are rare. The absence of studies on gangs in developing countries can be partially attributed to factors such as the brief duration of street gangs (although some become institutionalized), transitory memberships, political barriers, secrecy, fear, civil unrest, and public tolerance of street gangs (for comparable factors limiting prison gang research, see Fong and Buentello 1991). Some communities see gangs as a natural and embedded feature of society. Gangs in developing countries can be overlooked because of overriding issues, such as religious extremism, civil wars, ineffective government, political struggles, and greater concern over organized crime. In developing countries, financial support for gang research is a low priority compared to other competing interests, such as providing basic education, health, and law enforcement. The lack of funding for gang research is common, even in developed countries. For example, even in the United States funding for gang research and programs has been modest. One funding source, the National Institute of Justice, awarded slightly above $19 million from 2000–2020 for 27 gang-related research or evaluation projects (National Institute of Justice 2021). These figures represent approximately 0.4% of the 6,879 projects and 0.53% of the total $3.56 billion funding awarded over this 20-year timespan.

In addition, female involvement in gangs in developing countries remains a neglected topic (Moore 2007; Van Damme 2019; Van Damme and Carballo 2020). Females may be more involved in gangs than once thought. One study on gangs in the Caribbean found that 17–24% of males and 11–16% of females reported gang participation (Ohene, Ireland, and Blum 2005). The absence of research on female participation in gangs can be attributed to barriers found in developing countries. For example, Van Damme (2019) found female gang members in Honduras were less visible, subject to male gatekeeping and oversight, victims of domestic violence, and subject to a higher code of silence than males. In addition, Van Damme and Carballo (2020) found Honduran and El Salvadoran media downplayed females in gangs. This underscores the need for more research on female gang participation in developing countries.

Do Gangs Exist in Developing Countries?

To begin, there is debate about how to define a developing country. There is no consensus on how to define or classify a country as developed or developing. Terminology and definitions of "developed," "transitional," "least developed," "lower income," and "developing" countries frequently change. Countries generally align along a continuum based on gross domestic product, living standards, and other quality-of-life indicators. The International Monetary Fund and United Nations' World Economic Situation and Prospects data identify between 142 and 152 countries as having developing economies (International Monetary Fund 2018; United Nations 2014). With a few exceptions, most of these countries are located primarily in Africa, South America, and Asia, excluding China and India, with many countries located on or below the Tropic of Cancer.

Prior gang researchers have focused on specific developing countries or regions, such as Central America, Papua New Guinea, Brazil, and South Africa. For instance, beginning in the late 1990s, interest in South African gangs swelled and resulted in several studies (see Glaser 1998, 2000; Houston and Prinsloo 1998; Kynoch 1999; Mooney 1998; Pinnock and Douglas-Hamilton 1997). Recently, Central American gangs have drawn considerable research attention due to violence and drug trafficking, although some authorities observe that information remains limited and inconsistent (Rodgers and Baird 2015).

Researchers have conducted comparative studies relying on data from international databases, such as Gatti, Haymoz, and Schadee's (2011) study that compared data from 30 countries to assess whether gang (deviant youth group) membership led to increased antisocial behaviors such as crime. Higginson et al. (2018) performed a major review of gang membership in nine countries. Pyrooz et al. (2016) carried out a cross-national meta-analysis that pulled together numerous gang studies. A few governmental or quasi-governmental studies have been prepared, such as regional research by the Organization of American States. However, most contemporary international studies of gangs have been case studies within local or national boundaries (see Covey 2021; Hazen and Rodgers 2014).

This chapter contends that gang research in developing countries remains limited, and favorable conditions for gang emergence in some developing countries are increasing. This will result in a greater need to expand such research. Gang researchers have identified factors that promote gang emergence in developed countries; this chapter encourages an assessment of the applicability of these existing factors to gangs in developing countries. Cultural and historical antecedents in developing countries, such as colonization, imperialism, and civil wars, differ from developed countries where most gang research has been conducted. Undoubtedly, some current concepts and approaches are directly applicable to understanding gangs in developing countries, but others may require modification. Studies of gangs in developing countries in Africa and Central America illustrate how macro-level factors, such as civil wars, colonization, and globalization, promote the emergence of gangs.

Developing Countries' Characteristics Conducive to Gangs

Many of the macro-level factors (correlates) conducive to gang formation, operations, and institutionalization are present and will expand in developing countries. For example, research has found gangs are typically located in urban settings and are composed of impoverished, marginalized groups that are disenfranchised from mainstream society (see Howell and Griffiths 2018; Vigil 2016). Research has found impoverished groups lacking opportunities and living in ungoverned settings have a greater risk of gang involvement.

Drawing on previous studies, researchers have chosen varying combinations of macro-level factors to describe the conditions promoting gang emergence (see Franzese, Covey, and Menard 2016; Vigil 2016). Howell and Griffiths (2018) identified factors that influence gang emergence, such as poverty, social disorganization, discrimination, migration, colonization, unemployment, and strained ethnic relations. They added that historical events, such as civil wars, could have major impacts on crime and gang formation (Isla and Míguez 2011; Levenson 2013). Other factors could be added, such as economic abandonment (Sassen 2007), government corruption, percentage of at-risk youth in the population (Fischer 1975), globalization (Hagedorn 2007, 2008), economic inequality (Swift 2011; Venkatesh and Kassimir 2007), rapid urbanization (Rus and Vigil 2007), expansion of informal economies (Hagedorn 2008), inadequate public services, ineffective law enforcement, and marginalization (Vigil 2016). These macro-level factors converge differently in countries to generate breakdowns of social, economic, and government order. Gangs are responsive to existing macro-level factors (conditions) and either adapt to, contribute to, develop alternatives to, or oppose whatever order exists.

These same macro-level factors play out at the community, small group, and individual levels. Some of the individual risk factors at the micro level for gang membership include being young (age of onset), having prior criminal involvement, having delinquent peers, family involvement in gangs, illicit drug use, and absence of academic success (for a summary, see Franzese et al. 2016; Howell and Griffiths 2018). Chances for the presence of gangs and gang members are greater when multiple risk factors are present at the macro and micro levels.

Population Growth

Demographic changes are occurring in developing countries that create more favorable contexts for gang formation and operations. Populations are currently declining in some developed countries but are dramatically increasing in many developing countries. The world's population is expected to increase by almost 2 billion by mid-century, and most of that growth will take place in less developed regions. Over the coming three decades, Africa is projected to grow by more than 1.1 billion people and Asia by about 650 million. In comparison, Europe's population is projected to decrease by 37 million over this same time period (Chamie 2020).

According to Population Reference Bureau (2020) estimates, Africa is the region with the highest fertility and projected population growth. Although fertility rates vary across the continent, the total fertility rate for the region is 4.4 and is as high as 5.8 in middle Africa. From 2020 to 2050 the population is expected to nearly double, from roughly 1.3 to 2.6 billion. In 2020, Africa had a high population growth rate of about 2.54% per year (Worldometer 2021). The current population of Africa is close to 1.4 billion people with the median age being 19.7 years—thus, it has a high proportion of young people. Specifically, 41% of its population are aged below 15 years. As research has consistently shown, the ages of onset for participation in gangs is typically during adolescence or early adulthood. Thus, the proportion of individuals at risk of gang participation is higher in Africa and will increase in the immediate decades. While most youth do not join gangs, the risk pool will increase, and consequently the number of gang members in some developing countries will increase. The impacts of drought, struggling economies, famine, income inequality, poverty, civil wars, and other social calamities have negatively touched many Africans and left numerous youths on their own to raise themselves. A history of colonialism, imperialism, and racism have also had an impact.

Regarding population growth in the Americas, the Population Reference Bureau (2020) projects declines in fertility rates and modest population growth in much of the Western hemisphere. The bureau projects total population growth of 17% from 2020 to 2050, ranging from 1 billion to 1.2 billion. Population increases will be highest in Central America at 21%, compared to 7% for the Caribbean. Much of this growth will be individuals less than 15 years of age (28%). Some of the highest increases in population will be in Guatemala (53%), Nicaragua (29%), Honduras (28%), and Mexico (16%). This is important, because gangs have a major presence in these countries.

The world's most populous region is Asia. Population Reference Bureau (2020) population projections estimate an increase of 15% from 2020 to 2050. Again, projections vary from country to country, with East Asia declining (−3%) and Western Asia increasing (38%). Of particular interest are the population projections showing increases in Syria (71%), Iraq (62%), and Yemen (61%). All three countries have had violent and ongoing civil wars with mass migrations of refugees.

Inequitable Distribution of Wealth

Regarding the distribution of world wealth, developing countries are comparatively disadvantaged. While income equality among countries has improved, much of the change is due to the economic development of China and India. Nevertheless, wealth gaps among countries remain considerable (United Nations 2020a). A United Nations (2020b, 22) report noted the average incomes of European Union and North America countries were respectively 11 and 16 times higher than developing sub-Saharan Africa. Economic inequality within countries, which drives quality of life, has increased. Currently, 71% of the world's population live in countries where individual inequality has increased (United Nations 2020a). Economic inequality has been linked to gangs and gang membership (see Swift 2011; Venkatesh and Kassimir 2007).

Civil Conflicts

History has shown that civil wars have created fertile grounds for gangs to thrive due to the increased access to firearms, social disorder, and the incapacity of government to respond. Following civil conflicts, research suggests that gangs and gang violence are typically more pronounced, as illustrated by some Central and South American countries. Scholars have documented postwar escalations of gangs in Central and South American countries (Kerr 2019), such as the civil wars in the Northern Triangle (El Salvador, Honduras, and Guatemala). According to Baird (2019), these civil wars created ideal conditions for violent gangs. In South America, gangs have borrowed or imitated political rebel organizations' political movements, such as the Shining Path in Peru, FARC, and M-19 in Colombia (Isla and Míguez 2011). Rodgers and Muggah (2009) describe how this pattern manifested for the *pandillas* (street gangs) in Central America. Other researchers have documented examples of this pattern in countries including Colombia (Kerr 2019), El Salvador (Cruz 2014), Guatemala (Kurtenbach 2008; Levenson 2013), and Haiti (Kolbe 2013).

The same pattern holds true in other developing countries, such as Angola, where following the revolution some children turned to the streets and gangs (Cole and Chipaca 2014), and South Africa, where the elimination of apartheid bolstered gangs (Standing 2005). Following civil wars, gang expansion occurred in Nepal, Tajikistan, Bosnia, and between Hutus and Tutsi in Rwanda. Whether history will repeat itself following civil conflicts in other regions of the world remains to be seen.

Armed Groups

Related to civil conflicts and wars in developing countries is the involvement of children and youth in armed groups (Dowdney 2005). With armed conflicts, violence becomes institutionalized and viewed by postwar survivors as a natural feature of life. In developing countries, militaries, religious extremists, cartels, and armed groups recruit, enlist, and coerce children and youth into combat roles. At least seven African countries officially use children in their militaries. This is important because many of the risk factors for gang involvement are present with former child and youth soldiers. When they exit their combat roles, they return to their respective communities desensitized to violence, traumatized, sexually abused, and trained in the use of weapons. These previous child warriors become excellent recruits for armed forces, violent groups, and gangs. Lessons learned from international research on child soldiers, such as their exposure to trauma, ease of manipulation, and ethnic pride, are important factors to gang research (Kerig et al. 2013). While combat experience does not always result in future gang involvement, it enhances the odds.

Migration and Immigration

Other demographic trends impact the presence of gangs in developing countries, such as population migration and immigration. Immigration has increased in recent years, with about 272 million people, or about 3.5% of the world's population, living in countries different from their birth country (Edmond 2020). In addition, the forced displacement of populations due to factors such as civil war, drought, or political persecution hit a new high of 82.4 million at the end of 2020 (United Nations Refugee Agency 2020). Future international migration flows will likely continue despite barriers, border patrols, and native population resistance.

Gang researchers have long noted that the movement of populations can impact gang emergence. For example, Decker, Van Gemert, and Pyrooz (2009) reviewed the role immigration has played in American and European gang formation. They observed that immigration in Europe has occurred for a variety of reasons, including colonization, historical imperialism, economic improvement, civil conflict, and demands for labor. In Europe, the immigration of people created fertile ground for the formation of native and immigrant street gangs. In all the countries that have street gangs, the ethnic backgrounds—or more specifically, minority group status—of subgroups has played an important role in the establishment of street gangs. Some studies have also found that rates of gang involvement for immigrants and native-born youth are similar (see Van Gemert, Peterson, and Lien 2008). For example, in England, Germany, and the Netherlands, reaction to immigrants fueled the development of various racist and hate gangs that targeted immigrant groups (e.g., Pitts 2007). In response to marginalization and native attacks, Weitekamp, Reich, and Kerner (2005) reported on immigrant Pakistani, Turkish, Algerian, and Russian-German gangs attacking native French, Norwegian, and German youth. If it has not already, this pattern may emerge in developing countries, such as in Asia and the Middle East.

Climate change, especially prolonged drought and rising sea levels in regions of the world, could result in accelerated migration of populations. It is not difficult to envision how climate change will indirectly impact migration to urban areas, increase economic hardship, and impact populations in ways conducive to native and immigrant gang formation.

Rapid Urbanization

Currently, over half the world's population lives in urban settings, which is expected to rise to 70% by 2050 (Chamie 2020). Many developing countries are experiencing rapid migration of rural populations to cities, such as in Cairo, Nairobi, and Mexico City. Cities and rapid urban growth do not cause gangs, but these trends are correlated with their presence. While there are a few exceptions, research has found that gangs are almost exclusively the product of urban or near-urban settings. Urban settings in developing countries are often ungoverned or ungovernable. Ungoverned spaces and absence of infrastructure in developing countries create ideal circumstances for gang formation and expansion. Hazen (2011) observed the following:

> Gangs tend to operate in areas that are under-governed. In these situations, the determining factor is not an absence of government, or that government services are not available, but that both are inadequate. While this provides opportunities for gangs to take advantage of this gap in state control, the causal arrow points both ways; under-governed areas also contribute to the creation of gangs as a result of the insecurity there. Gangs and gang violence can also contribute to the ineffectiveness of government services, such as health and education. Kinnes (2014) found this to be the case in South Africa, where gangs and gang violence unintentionally disrupted school and health clinic operations. (381)

In Africa, approximately 43% of the population live in urban settings (United Nations 2018). The rate of urbanization in Africa is unprecedented, and many countries have inadequate infrastructures to support this rapid urban growth. The slums of African cities offer few opportunities for residents other than home-based businesses and local markets, where earnings are at best meager. Faced with poor prospects, a portion of African youth turn to street gangs or informal groups for survival. For example, Kinnes (2014) concluded what other studies have found, that gangs and involvement in drug sales help young people sustain their livelihoods. To some youth, gangs augment or have become substitutes for family by performing functions that normally would be available from families. For example, gangs have provided shelter for homeless and abandoned urban youth. De Benitez (2007) described a typical African gang pattern:

> Street gang hierarchies both protect and inflict violence. Intimidation is the order of the day. Younger children are at the mercy of violent behavior, risking losing earnings and possessions to older, bigger boys. As they grow, they in turn socialize new children into street-based hierarchies and rules enforced by violence. (38)

The extent to which this pattern occurs is unknown, but studies from other developing countries provide similar descriptions of gang growth in urban areas. As the trend for urbanization in developing countries in Asia, Africa, and the Americas continues, it is safe to surmise that cities will increasingly be conducive to gangs and criminal groups.

Impact on Economies

In addition to demographic changes occurring in the developing world, there are other reasons why researchers should pay more attention to gangs in developing countries. Among them is the negative economic impact of gangs on developing economies. Research has found that the presence of gangs and violence in neighborhoods has negative impacts on formal economic development (Scherer 2020). Gang and organized crime group-controlled neighborhoods do not fare as well as similar gang-free neighborhoods. For example, regarding macroeconomics in El Salvador, Melnikov, Schmidt-Padilla, and

Sviatschi (2020) noted, "results suggest that organized crime appears to have had statistically and economically significant effects on economic development" (20). Gangs may impact local economies in developing countries by discouraging investment and infrastructure development.

One way gangs may influence developing economies is through the drug trade. Discussions regarding gangs in the developing world generally include references to the illegal drug trade. For example, researchers often identify drug trafficking in Asia, Africa, the Caribbean, and Central and South Americas as having important gang involvement. For example, the Caribbean is well known for the production and distribution of cocaine, marijuana, and pharmaceuticals. Decker and Chapman (2008) noted the Caribbean is "an important area for understanding drug smuggling because of its proximity to source and destination countries as well as its long history as a site for smuggling illegal goods and for piracy" (55). There is also agreement that Central American *mara* (a Latino term to describe a form of gang originating in the United States) and *pandilla* gangs have become increasingly involved in the drug trade (Rodgers and Baird 2015). Prison gangs also can be involved in the drug trade. Gundur's (2020) research on the prison gang, Barrio Azteca, found it was involved in wholesale drug distribution outside prison walls. Barrio Azteca provided protection services for cartels and was involved in proxy wars and distributed drugs. World demand for illicit drugs shows no signs of waning; thus it is important to continue to study the roles gangs in developing countries play in drug sales and distribution.

Politicization and Radicalization

There are other subjects that warrant research attention, such as the nature and extent of the politicization and radicalization of gangs in developing countries. On one hand, there seems to be little evidence that gangs are heavily involved in political causes (Decker and Pyrooz 2011). Typically, gangs operate outside of politics and do not have a robust government presence. Gangs do not seek to overthrow governments, but instead use them to their advantage (Hazen 2011). As Winton (2014) observed, "gangs are, after all, generally concerned more with survival than with political change" (409). However, there is evidence that when gangs are participants and integrated into the mainstream society, such as in Ecuador, they can be instrumental in making prosocial change (Brotherton and Gude 2020).

Nevertheless, some researchers propose that gangs are increasingly becoming radicalized and politicized. Gangs have been enlisted in political causes in developing countries, similar to their involvement in American politics (for a recent American example, see Reid and Valasik 2020). Gangs have been very active in political parties and corruption in Haiti, Hong Kong, Jamaica, Nepal, and African countries. Gang involvement in Jamaican politics, such as the Jamaican Labor Party and others, has been well documented (Black 2004; Clarke 2006; Edmonds 2016; Murphy 2010). In Haiti, opposing parties have enlisted gangs for decades to support or oppose those with political power. In Nepal, after the Maoist insurgency, political parties began to identify gangs as a better means to defend armed and semi-armed Maoist cadres (Kumar 2018). Klausen (2019) coined the term "gangster jihadism" to describe the connection between the criminal underworld and Islamic extremists. Klausen proposed that criminal groups, including gangs, are good recruitment grounds for extremist religious groups, and some European street gangs have become radicalized. She suggested that Islamic extremist groups view gang members as ideal recruits because they are prone to violence and are easy to engage. Given the divergent views of radicalization and politicization, the subject warrants further study.

Globalization

The globalization of gang culture has been noted by multiple researchers (Hagedorn 2007, 2008; Hazen and Rodgers 2014; Van Gemert, Roks, and Drogt 2016; Van Hellemont and Densley 2019). It should be noted that gangs were documented in many countries and cultures before the concept of globalization surfaced. Gang culture and practices are easily spread throughout the world. Mass media depictions of gangs can be influential in shaping local gang myths and identities (Van Hellemont and Densley 2019). There is increased transnational interconnectivity that extends beyond neighborhoods and communities to the global stage (Winton 2014). This globalization (global capitalism) has had a negative impact on marginalized groups in both developed and developing countries, as jobs and wealth are redistributed (for one discussion of the role of gangs on economic development, see Melnikov et al. 2020).

Globalization has expanded the need for public services and infrastructure in developing countries, which often do not have the capacity to meet increasing demands for housing, law enforcement, transportation, health care, and education. Socioeconomic marginalized groups are often excluded from wealth, public services, and opportunities. Consequently, some individuals turn to the streets, underground economies, drug sales, and gangs to make money. Gangs have become sources of income, socialization, identity, employment, educators, protectors, service providers, and in the end they have become embedded in some communities.

Some scholars credit globalization and the expansion of transnational crime networks for the spread of gangs in developed and developing countries. However, globalization and transnational crime are not the sole explanations for the expansion of gangs (Dammert 2017; Rodgers and Baird 2015). Globalization does not always imply transnational networks of criminally involved gang members (for a discussion, see Papachristos 2005).

An illustration of this is *mara* gangs, which some scholars characterize as being transnational. Rodgers and Baird's (2015) review of gangs in developing Latin America countries concluded *mara* gangs are at their core locally oriented. Other references to local orientation are abundant in the gang literature (Rodgers and Jensen 2009). For example, Rus and Vigil (2007) observed that gangs in southern Mexico were local actors in drug sales, territories, and conflicts, in terms of respect and membership. This is true even for the confederations of gangs, such as MS-13. Drug distribution networks are transnational, but this matters little to street gangs. Sassen (2007) observed, "because the network is global does not mean that it all has to happen at the global level" (111). It is safe to conclude that street gangs are a product of both global and local factors, and globalization will continue to influence the nature of gangs throughout the developing world. How this globalization plays out in developing countries will be important.

Social Media and the Internet

In a similar vein, as the internet and social media have grown, gangs and gang members have increasingly relied on new technologies to further their objectives. Studies have found that gangs "use social media to promote gang affiliation and interests" (Fernández-Planells et al. 2020). Scholars have noted that the internet and social media are now places where gang life prospers (Irwin-Rogers, Densley, and Pinkney 2018; McCuddy and Esbensen 2020; Pyrooz and Moule 2019). Reliance on internet platforms is already underway in developing countries, as gangs have used the internet to commit fraud in Nigeria (Jegede, Oyesomi, and Olorunyomi 2016) and Egypt (Ganesani 2017). In Sierra Leone, gang members have started posting photographs of themselves on websites (Abdullah 2020).

Social media and the internet have reduced the effect of geographical marginalization (Fernández-Planells et al. 2020). Individuals, groups, gangs, and gang members can reach well beyond their neighborhood and not solely rely on personal contacts (McCuddy and Esbensen 2020). As Lauger and Densley (2018) observed, street corners often associated with gang activity have been supplemented by the virtual world. With the rise of social media and the internet, classic concepts associated with gangs are evolving. Besides face-to-face relationships, traditional elements used to characterize gangs require reconceptualization, such as the importance of defending geographical territory, peer relations, having organizational structures, and group cohesiveness.

However, developing countries generally have less access to technology and communications and less advanced information systems. While there is emerging discussion about the role the internet and social media play regarding gangs, there remain regions in the developing world where such technology is not available. Rosner, Ritchie, and Ortiz-Ospina (2015) estimate that 50% of the world's population lacks access to the internet. The United Nations (2021a) estimated 3.7 billion people, mostly living in developing countries, remain offline. A key question will be how the expansion of social media and the internet will affect gang emergence and operations in developing countries, where many people lack access to electricity and the internet.

APPLICABILITY OF EXISTING GANG LITERATURE TO DEVELOPING COUNTRIES

Existing gang approaches and concepts may or may not be applicable to, or need modification for, understanding gangs in developing countries. Some insights on gangs seem to have near-universal applicability, such as gangs being primarily located in urban and impoverished areas. However, there remain important questions regarding how well existing ideas and research approaches to the study of gangs apply to developing countries. The historical and cultural contexts of developed countries differ from developing countries. Vigil's (2002, 2008) research has demonstrated the importance of historical and cultural factors in gang formation. The United States, Europe, and other developed countries experienced colonization, immigration, migration, imperialism, and economic development differently than developing countries. How gangs in developing countries evolve over time in terms of motivation, developmental stages, membership, structure, and group dynamics may differ from developed countries.

Besides historical and cultural differences, there are challenges in studying gangs in developing countries. Klein (2011) noted there are definitional, measurement, policy, operational, theoretical, and other issues inherent to international and comparative gang research. These challenges may be amplified by the historical and cultural diversity of developing countries. This diversity plays out in a number of ways, starting with the definition of what is a "gang." Gang experts have long debated how to best define gangs. While existing definitions are applicable to some gangs in developing countries, these definitions may require modification due to local variations on how gangs or gang-like groups operate. In developing countries, groups, whether gangs or not, can be referred to as criminal, street, paramilitary, vigilante, terrorist, drug, poaching, pirate, break boys, militias, smuggling, tribal, ethnic, conflict, football, or human trafficking gangs. It is unclear if some of these referenced groups are gangs or other types of groups. For example, in Benin, the Seychelles, and Guinea, researchers describe "pirate gangs." In Zambia and Bhutan, references are made to "poaching gangs." In Burundi Africa, tribal-based youth groups or gangs conflict over inequalities among Tutsi, Hutu, and TWA tribes. In Argentina and Croatia, descriptions of soccer (football) gangs, similar to the body of literature regarding European hooligans, have drawn attention of the media and academics (Paradiso 2016; Perasović and Mustapić 2018; Tregoures 2017). Côte d'Ivore (Ivory Coast) locals refer to gang members as "microbes." In Namibia gang members are called "Taranoas," which means "watch me carefully," and in Senegal they are "Bboys." Iraq and Lebanon have religious Islamic faction gangs that carry out crimes against Shiite or Sunni populations. In Pakistan, there is evidence that groups or gangs serve as fundraisers for the Taliban. It is unclear if some of these referenced groups are gangs or other forms of groups. The applicability of primarily American or European definitions of gangs and approaches to the study of gangs needs to be assessed. Historical and current contexts and cultures matter when viewing gangs in developing countries in ways that may differ from the developed world. Comparative gang researchers need to factor in local and regional variations in their research instruments (Rodríguez, Pérez Santiago, and Birkbeck 2015).

Gangs and the Drug Trade

The connection between gangs with the use and distribution of illegal drugs has served as a focal point for international gang research. Some scholars have concluded that gangs have been key players in the sales and distribution of illicit drugs (see Clarke 2006; Dammert 2017). They surmise that gangs are so involved in the drug trade that they have formed elaborate organizational structures that operate in sizable regions, as in the case of Central America. In Central America, a limited number of gangs have become transnational organizations. Other researchers disagree and observe that gangs typically are not sophisticated or organized, and apart from local drug sales are not deeply involved in drug trafficking in some regions (Government Accounting Office 2010; United Nations Office on Drugs and Crime 2007). They conclude that gangs are more involved in social use and local sales rather than large-scale drug trafficking activities. For instance, a Government Accounting Office report (2010) stated that for Central America, individual gangs and gang members might work with drug trafficking organizations for personal gain, but there was no evidence of high-level, organized cooperation between gangs and drug trafficking organizations. In the same vein, a United Nations Office on Drugs and Crime report (2007) identified reasons why the relationship between *mara* gangs and drug trafficking is unclear, including the low use of cocaine among local citizens. The report noted that in 2004, of the 12,000 people arrested for drug trafficking in the United States, less than 1% of those arrested were Central Americans. The report concluded this was strikingly low in a context of tens of thousands of *mara* gang members with Central American ties living in the United States.

There is no question of gang involvement in drug use and trade, but the nature of this involvement in developing countries is not fully documented. Gang researchers seem to agree that illicit drug sales, especially of cocaine, heroin, marijuana, and methamphetamine, provides a way for gang members to make money and for gangs to expand. There is also agreement that the more involved gangs are in drug sales, the more their operations and processes are shaped by this involvement. However, information about the drug trade in Central America and other developing regions does not provide a complete picture of gang involvement in the drug trade.

Migration, Immigration, and Gangs

International and comparative gang researchers have focused on the roles of migration and immigration in gang formation and expansion. Themes of intolerance, colonization, discrimination, deportation, nationalism, and marginalization surface in much of the migration and immigration gang literature in developed countries. Decker et al. (2009) viewed immigration, culture, and ethnicity as important elements in understanding the changing landscape of gangs in the United States and Europe. From their perspective, gangs acquire local characteristics, and immigration, culture, and ethnicity matter in terms of mistrust, fear, and misunderstandings in areas where immigrants are arriving. Peterson, Lien, and Van Gemert (2008) noted migration in Europe was related to gang formation in multiple ways, including cultural traditions tended to isolate some ethnic groups, which in turn fueled distrust; migrant groups were easy to identify and thus discriminate against; host populations often reacted to immigrants; and immigration could spread gang culture.

Political evacuees often face prejudice and discrimination when they find refuge in new regions or areas. Cultural differences in socioeconomic background, religion, and ethnicity work to separate immigrant youth from mainstream host societies (see Choo 2007). Wars displace populations and in doing so can worsen marginalization, a potential factor in gang formation. For example, since 2011, over 6.6 million Syrians have been forced to flee their homes and 6.7 million are displaced within the country (United Nations 2021b). How the world responds to the exiled Syrians and similar marginalized groups from Yemen, Myanmar, South Sudan, Central America, and other countries might follow previous gang patterns witnessed in the developed world. How immigration patterns operate in developing countries where large political refugee camps and sizable populations seeking asylum or better lives exist is an important question.

Closing Thoughts

This review justifies a growing need for gang research because of changing world demographics and limited information about gangs in developing countries. Many of the factors conducive to gang formation and prevalence in developing countries will strengthen in the future. Without systematic research on gangs in these countries, the default may be to go to the media and the internet for information. With this information comes a risk that both sources will fuel misconceptions about gangs. The time is ripe for gang researchers to develop a coordinated effort, similar to the Eurogang Program of Research (see Maxson and Esbensen 2016; Melde and Weerman 2020) and the Transgang Project (see Feixa et al. 2019) to discuss what is known, what is unknown, and to share approaches to studying gangs in developing countries. For example, the Transgang initiative views gangs not as security problems but as adaptive mediation agents in their communities (Feixa et al. 2019). The Transgang Project focuses on mediation between, among, and within groups (gangs) and the social environment. It strives to build theory recognizing cultural diversity, migration patterns, and shared or unique features of gangs and transnational street youth.

This review also encourages discussion and assessment of the applicability of existing gang concepts and approaches to gangs in developing countries, beginning with the definition of what is a gang and what range of groups should be considered gangs. Given the wide variety of cultures, ethnicities, and contexts in the developing world, the definition of a gang needs to be at the forefront of the discussion. Other concepts, such as gang involvement in the drug trade, the role of host cultures, migration of populations, marginalization, and gang evolutionary stages need to be assessed for applicability to developing countries. There is much to be investigated in the frontier of gangs in developing countries.

References

Abdullah, Ibrahim. 2020. "Marginal Youths or Outlaws? Youth Street Gangs, Globalisation, and Violence in Contemporary Sierra Leone." *Africa Development* 45 (3): 33–52.

Baird, Adam. 2019. "'Man a Kill a Man for Nutin': Gang Transnationalism, Masculinities, and Violence in Belize City." *Men and Masculinities* 24 (3): 411–431. https://journals.sagepub.com/doi/abs/10.1177/1097184X19872787?journalCode=jmma.

Black, Lorna. 2004. "Jamaica." In *Teen Gangs: A Global View*, edited by Maureen P. Duffey, and Scott E. Gillig, 121–136. Westport, CT: Greenwood Press.

Brotherton, David C., and Rafael Gude. 2020. "Social Control and the Gang: Lessons from the Legalization of Street Gangs in Ecuador." *Critical Criminology* 2020: 1–25. DOI:https://doi.org/10.1007/s10612-020-09505-5.

Brotherton, David C., and Rafael Jose Gude, eds. 2021. *Routledge International Handbook of Critical Gang Studies*. London: Routledge.

Chamie, Joseph. 2020."World Population: 2020 Overview." *South Asia Journal*. http://southasiajournal.net/world-population-2020-overview/.

Choo, Kyung-Seok. 2007. *Gangs and Immigrant Youth*. New York: LFB Scholarly Publishing.

Chu, Chi Meng, Michael Daffern, Stuart Thomas, and Jia Ying Lim. 2012. "Violence Risk and Gang Affiliation in Youth Offenders: A Recidivism Study." *Psychology, Crime and Law* 18 (3): 299–315. https://doi.org/10.1080/1068316X.2010.481626.

Clarke, Colin. 2006. "Politics, Violence and Drugs in Kingston, Jamaica." *Bulletin of Latin American Research* 25 (3): 420–440.

Cole, Bankole, and Adelino Chipaca. 2014. "Juvenile Delinquency in Angola." *Criminology and Criminal Justice* 14 (1): 61–76. DOI:10.1177/1748895813503465.

Covey, Herbert C. 2021. *Street Gangs Throughout the World*, 3rd ed. Springfield, IL: Charles Thomas.

Cruz, José Miguel. 2014. "Maras and the Politics of Violence in El Salvador." In *Global Gangs: Street Violence Across the World*, edited by Jennifer M. Hazen and Dennis Rodgers, 123–143. Minneapolis: University of Minnesota.

Dammert, Lucía. 2017. "Gang Violence in Latin America." In *The Wiley Handbook of Violence and Aggression*, edited by Peter Sturmey, 102. Hoboken, NJ: John Wiley and Sons.

De Benitez, Sarah Thomas. 2007. *State of the World's Street Children: Violence*. London: Consortium for Street Children.

Decker, Scott H., and Margaret Townsend Chapman. 2008. *Drug Smugglers on Drug Smuggling: Lessons from the Inside*. Philadelphia, PA: Temple University Press.

Decker, Scott H., and David C. Pyrooz. 2011. "Gangs, Terrorism, and Radicalization." *Journal of Strategic Security* 4 (4): 151–166.

Decker, Scott H., Frank Van Gemert, and David C. Pyrooz. 2009. "Gangs, Migration, and Crime: The Changing Landscape in Europe and the USA." *Journal of International Migration and Integration* 10 (4): 393–408.

Dowdney, Luke. 2005. *Neither War nor Peace: International Comparisons of Children and Youth in Organized Violence*. SER/IANSA/Viva Rio. https://resourcecentre.savethechildren.net/node/5014/pdf/5014.pdf.

Edmond, Charlotte. 2020. "Global Migration, by the Numbers: Who Migrates, Where They Go and Why." World Economic Forum. https://www.weforum.org/agenda/2020/01/iom-global-migration-report-international-migrants-2020/.

Edmonds, Kevin. 2016. "Guns, Gangs and Garrison Communities in the Politics of Jamaica." *Race & Class* 57 (4): 54–74.

Feixa, Carles, José Sanchez Garcia, Eduard Ballesté, Ana Belén Cano, Maria-Jose Masanet, Margot Mecca, and Maria Oliver. 2019. *The (Trans) Gang: Notes and Queries on Youth Street Group Research*. Barcelona, Spain: Universitat Pompeu Fabra & European Research Council. https://repositori.upf.edu/handle/10230/42215.

Fernández-Planells, Ariadna, José Sánchez-García, María Oliver, and Carles Feixa. 2020. "Researching Transnational Gangs as Agents of Mediation in the Digital Era." In *Gangs in the Era of Internet and Social Media*, edited by Chris Melde, and Frank Weerman, 43–60. Cham, Switzerland: Springer.

Fischer, Claude S. 1975. "Toward a Subcultural Theory of Urbanism." *American Journal of Sociology* 80 (6): 1319–1341.

Fong, Robert S., and Salvador Buentello. 1991. "Detection of Prison Gang Development: An Empirical Assessment." *Federal Probation* 55 (1): 66–69.

Franzese, Robert J., Herbert C. Covey, and Scott Menard. 2016. *Youth Gangs*, 4th ed. Springfield, IL: Charles C. Thomas.

Ganesani, A. 2017. "Youth, the New Organized Fraud Crime in Internet and the Economy Issues." *Colecccion Jorge Alvarez Illeras* 4 (2): 58–65.

Gatti, Uberto, Sandrine Haymoz, and Hans M. A. Schadee. 2011. "Deviant Youth Groups in 30 Countries: Results from the Second International Self-Report Delinquency Study." *International Criminal Justice Review* 21 (3): 208–224.

Glaser, Clive. 1998. "Swines, Hazels and the Dirty Dozen: Masculinity, Territoriality, and the Youth Gangs of Soweto, 1960-1976." *Journal of Southern African Studies* 24 (4): 719–736.

Glaser, Clive. 2000. *Bo-Tsotsi: The Youth Gangs of Soweto, 1935-1976*. Portsmouth, NH: Henneman.

Government Accounting Office. 2010. *Combating Gangs: Federal Agencies Have Implemented a Central American Gang Strategy, but Could Strengthen Oversight and Measurement of Efforts*. Washington, DC: United States Government Accountability Office.

Gundur, R. V. 2020. "Negotiating Violence and Protection in Prison and on the Outside: The Organizational Evolution of the Transnational Prison Gang Barrio Azteca." *International Criminal Justice Review* 30 (1): 30–60.

Hagedorn, John M., ed. 2007. *Gangs in the Global City: Alternatives to Traditional Criminology*. Urbana: University of Illinois.

Hagedorn, John. 2008. *A World of Gangs: Armed Young Men and Gangsta Culture*. Minneapolis: University of Minnesota Press.

Hazen, Jennifer M. 2011. "Understanding Gangs as Armed Groups." *International Review of the Red Cross* 98 (878): 369–386.

Hazen, Jennifer M., and Dennis Rodgers, eds. 2014. *Global Gangs: Street Violence Across the World*. Minneapolis: University of Minnesota Press.

Higginson, Angela, Kathryn Benier, Yulia Shenderovich, Laura Bedford, Lorraine Mazerolle, and Joseph Murry. 2018. "Factors Associated with Young Gang Membership in Low- and Middle-Income Countries: A Systematic Review." *Campbell Systematic Reviews* 10 (1): 1–67.

Houston, James G., and Johan Prinsloo. 1998. "Prison Gangs in South Africa: A Comparative Analysis." *Journal of Gang Research* 5: 41–52.

Howell, James C., and Elizabeth A. Griffiths. 2018. *Gangs in America's Communities*, 3rd ed. Thousand Oaks, CA: Sage.

International Monetary Fund. 2018. *World Economic Outlook*. https://www.imf.org/en/Publications/WEO/Issues/2018/09/24/world-economic-outlook-october-2018.

Irwin-Rogers, Keir, James Densley, and Craig Pinkney. 2018. "Gang Violence and Social Media." In *The Routledge International Handbook of Human Aggression*, edited by Jane Ireland, Carol A. Ireland, and Philip Birch, 400–410. London: Routledge.

Isla, Alejandro, and Daniel Pedro Míguez. 2011. "Formations of Violence in Post-Dictatorial Contexts: Logics of Confrontation between the Police and the Young Urban Poor in Contemporary Argentina." *International Journal of Conflict and Violence* 5 (2): 240–260.

Jegede, Ajibade Ebenezer, Kehinde O. Oyesomi, and Bankole Robert Olorunyomi. 2016. "Youth Crime and the Organized Attributes of Cyber Fraud in the Modern Technological Age: A Thematic Review." *International Journal of Social Sciences and Humanities Reviews* 6 (1): 153–164.

Kerig, Patricia K., Cecilia Wainryb, Michelle Sinayobye, and Shannon D. Chaplo. 2013. "America's Child Soldiers: Toward a Research Agenda for Studying Gang-Involved Youth in the United States." *Journal of Aggression, Maltreatment & Trauma* 22 (7): 773–795.

Kerr, Katie. 2019. "Assessing Gang Risks in Post War Environments: The Case of Columbia." *International Journal of Stability and Development* 9 (1): 5. https://www.stabilityjournal.org/article/10.5334/sta.720/.

Kinnes, Irvin. 2014. "Gangs, Drugs, and Policing the Cape Flats." *Acta Criminologica: Southern African Journal of Criminology* 2: 14–26.

Klausen, Jytte. 2019. "ISIS and the Rise of Gangster Jihadism." *BrandisNOW*. https://www.brandeis.edu/now/2019/april/gangs-jihadism-klausen.html.

Klein, Malcolm W. 2011. "Who Can You Believe? Complexities of International Street Gang Research." *International Criminal Justice Review* 2 (3): 197–207.

Kolbe, Athena R. 2013. "Revisiting Haiti's Gangs and Organized Violence." HASOW Discussion Paper (5). Rio de Janeiro, Brazil.

Kumar, Dipesh K. C. 2018. "Increasing Status of Criminal Gangs in Post-Conflict Nepal: The Case of Kathmandu Valley." *Kathmandu School of Law Review* 6 (2): 65–78.

Kurtenbach, Sabine. 2008. *Youth Violence as a Scapegoat: Youth in Post-War Guatemala*. Duisburg, Germany: Duisburg Essen University. https://doi.org/10.2139/ssrn.2143125.

Kynoch, Gary. 1999. "From the Ninevites to the Hard Livings Gang: Township Gangsters and Urban Violence in Twentieth-Century South Africa." *African Studies* 58 (1): 55–85.

Lauger, Timothy R., and James A. Densley. 2018. "Broadcasting Badness: Violence, Identity, and Performance in the Online Gang Rap Scene." *Justice Quarterly* 35 (5): 816–841.

Levenson, Deborah. 2013. *Adiós Niño: The Gangs of Guatemala City and the Politics of Death*. Durham, NC: Duke University Press.

Maxson, Cheryl L. and Finn-Aage Esbensen. eds. 2016. *Gang Transitions and Transformations in an International Context 2016 Edition*. Cham, Switzerland: Springer.

McCuddy, Timothy, and Finn-Aage Esbensen. 2020. "The Role of Online Communication among Gang and Non-Gang Youth." In *Gangs in the Era of Internet and Social Media*, edited by Chris Melde, and Frank Weerman, 80–104. Cham, Switzerland: Springer.

Melde, Chris, and Frank Weerman, eds. 2020. *Gangs in the Era of Internet and Social Media*. Cham, Switzerland: Springer.

Melnikov, Nikita, Carlos Schmidt-Padilla, and Maria Micaela Sviatschi. 2020. "Gangs, Labor Mobility and Development." NBER Working Paper 27832. DOI:10.3386/w27832.

Mooney, Katie. 1998. "Ducktails, Flick-Knives and Pugnacity: Subcultural and Hegemonic Masculinities in South Africa, 1948–1960." *Journal of Southern African Studies* 24 (4): 162–166.

Moore, Joan W. 2007. "Female Gangs: Gender and Globalization." In *Gangs in the Global City: Alternatives to Traditional Criminology*, edited by John M. Hagedorn, 187–203. Urbana: University of Illinois.

Murphy, Dan. 2010. "Jamaica Attacks: A Legacy of Ties between Politicians and Gangs." *Christian Science Monitor*. https://www.csmonitor.com/World/Americas/2010/0525/Jamaica-attacks-a-legacy-of-ties-between-politicians-and-gangs.

National Institute of Justice. 2021. Awards: Listing of Funding Projects—Gangs. https://nij.ojp.gov/funding/awards/list?field_award_status_value=All&state=All&topic=All&field_fiscal_year_value=&combine_awards=Gangs&awardee=&city=&sort_by=field_fiscal_year_value&sort_order=DESC.

Ohene Sally-Ann, Marjorie Ireland, and Robert Blum. 2005. "The Clustering of Risk Behaviors among Caribbean Youth." *Maternal Child Health Journal* 9 (1): 91–100.

Papachristos, Andrew V. 2005. "Gang World." *Foreign Policy* 147: 48–55.

Paradiso, Eugenio. 2016. "Football, Clientelism and Corruption in Argentina: An Anthropological Inquiry." *Soccer & Society* 17 (4): 480–495.

Perasović, Benjamin, and Marko Mustapić. 2018. "Carnival Supporters, Hooligans, and the 'Against Modern Football' Movement: Life within the Ultras Subculture in the Croatian Context." *Sport and Society* 21 (6): 960–976.

Peterson, Dana, Inger-Lise Lien, and Frank van Gemert. 2008. "Concluding Remarks: The Role of Migration and Ethnicity in Street Gang Formation, Involvement and Response." In *Street Gangs, Migration and Ethnicity*, edited by Frank van Gemert, Dana Peterson, and Inger-Lise Lien, 255–272. Abingdon, UK: Willan.

Pinnock, Don, and Dudu Douglas-Hamilton. 1997. *Gangs, Rituals, and Rites of Passage*. Cape Town, SA: African Sun Press.

Pitts, John. 2007. "Young and Safe in Lambeth, the Deliberations of the Lambeth Executive Commission on Children, Young People and Violent Crime." http://www.downloads.lambethcpcg.org.uk/YandS%20in%20Lambeth%200804.pdf.

Population Reference Bureau. 2020. World Population Data Sheets. https://interactives.prb.org/2020-wpds/.

Pyrooz, David C., and Meghan M. Mitchell. 2015. "Little Gang and Big Gang Research." In *The Handbook of Gangs*, edited by Scott H. Decker, and David C. Pyrooz, 28–58. Chichester, UK: Wiley.

Pyrooz, David C., and Richard K. Moule Jr. 2019. "Gangs and Social Media." In *Oxford Research Encyclopedia of Criminology and Criminal Justice*. Oxford, UK: Oxford University Press. https://doi.org/10.1093/acrefore/9780190264079.013.439.

Pyrooz, David C., Jillian J. Turanovic, Scott H. Decker, and Jun Wu. 2016. "Taking Stock of the Relationship between Gang Membership and Offending: A Meta-Analysis." *Criminal Justice and Behavior* 43 (3): 365–397.

Reid, Shannon E., and Matthew Valasik. 2020. *Alt-Right Gangs: Hazy Shade of White*. Berkeley: University of California Press.

Rodgers, Dennis, and Adam Baird. 2015. "Understanding Gangs in Contemporary Latin America." In *The Handbook of Gangs*, edited by Scott H. Decker and David C. Pyrooz, 478–502. Chichester, UK: Wiley-Blackwell.

Rodgers, Dennis, and Steffen Jensen. 2009. "Revolutionaries, Barbarians, or War Machines? Gangs in Nicaragua and South Africa." *Socialist Register 2009: Violence Today* 45: 220–238.

Rodgers, Dennis, and Robert Muggah. 2009. "Gangs as Non-State Armed Groups: The Central American Case." *Contemporary Security Policy* 30 (2): 301–317.

Rodríguez, Juan A., Nellie Pérez Santiago, and Christopher H. Birkbeck. 2015. "Surveys as Cultural Artefacts: Applying the International Self-Report Delinquency Study to Latin American Adolescents." *European Journal of Criminology* 12 (4): 420–436.

Rosner, Max, Hannah Ritchie, and Esteban Ortiz-Ospina. 2015. "Internet." *Our World in Data*. https://ourworldindata.org/internet.

Rus, Jan, and James Diego Vigil. 2007. "Rapid Urbanization and Migrant Indigenous Youth in San Cristobal, Chiapas, Mexico." In *Gangs in the Global City: Alternatives to Traditional Criminology*, edited by John M. Hagedorn, 152–184. Urbana: University of Illinois.

Sassen, Saskia. 2007. "The Global City: One Setting for New Types of Gang Work and Political Culture?" In *Gangs in the Global City: Alternatives to Traditional Criminology*, edited by John M. Hagedorn, 97–119. Urbana: University of Illinois.

Scherer, Lauri. 2020. "Gang Culture and Economic Development: Evidence from El Salvador." *The Digest* 12. https://www.nber.org/digest-202012/gang-culture-and-economic-development-evidence-el-salvador.

Standing, Andre. 2005. *The Threat of Gangs and Anti-Gangs Policy: Policy Discussion Paper*. Pretoria, SA: Institute for Security Studies. https://issafrica.s3.amazonaws.com/site/uploads/PAPER116.PDF.

Swift, Richard. 2011. *Gangs*. Toronto, ON: Groundwood Books.

Tregoures, Loïc. 2017. "Beyond the Pattern: Corruption, Hooligans, and Football Governance in Croatia." In *Football and Supporter Activism in Europe*, edited by Borja Garcia and Jinming Zheng, 167–186. Cham, Switzerland: Palgrave Macmillan.

United Nations. 2014. "Annex—Country Classification." World Economic Situation and Prospects (WESP). https://www.un.org/en/development/desa/policy/wesp/wesp_current/2014wesp_country_classification.pdf.

United Nations. 2018. "The Speed of Urbanization around the World." *Population Facts* (2018/1). New York, NY: Department of Economic and Social Affairs, Population Division.

United Nations. 2020a. *Inequality: Bridging the Divide*. https://www.un.org/en/un75/inequality-bridging-divide.

United Nations. 2020b. *World Social Report: Inequality in a Rapidly Changing World*. New York: Department of Economic and Social Affairs.

United Nations. 2021a. "With Almost Half of World's Population Still Offline, Digital Divide Risks Becoming 'New Face of Inequality,' Deputy Secretary General Warns General Assembly." New York: United Nations.

United Nations. 2021b. *Syria Refugee Crisis—Globally, in Europe and in Cyprus*. United Nations Refugee Agency. https://www.unhcr.org/cy/2021/03/18/syria-refugee-crisis-globally-in-europe-and-in-cyprus-meet-some-syrian-refugees-in-cyprus/.

United Nations Office on Drugs and Crime. 2007. *Crime and Development in Central America*. New York: United Nations Office on Drugs and Crime.

United Nations Refugee Agency. 2020. *Global Trends Forced Displacement 2020*. https://www.unhcr.org/flagship-reports/globaltrends/.

Van Damme, Ellen. 2019. "When Overt Research Feels Covert: Researching Women and Gangs in a Context of Silence and Fear." *Journal of Extreme Anthropology* 3 (1): 121–134. https://journals.uio.no/JEA/article/view/6696/5996.

Van Damme, Ellen, and Willian Carballo. 2020. "Women and Gangs in the Digital Media: A Distorted Image?" In *Gangs in the Era of Internet and Social Media*, edited by Chris Melde and Frank Weerman, 61–79. Cham, Switzerland: Springer.

Van Gemert, Frank, Dana Peterson, and Inger-Lise Lien, eds. 2008. *Street Gangs, Migration and Ethnicity*. Devon, UK: Willan.

Van Gemert, Frank, Robert A. Roks, and Marijke Drogt, 2016. "Dutch Crips Run Dry in Liquid Society." In *Gang Transitions and Transformations in an International Context*, edited by Finn-Aage Esbensen and Cheryl L. Maxson, 157–172. Cham, Switzerland: Springer.

Van Hellemont, Elke, and James A. Densley. 2019. "Gang Glocalization: How the Global Mediascape Creates and Shapes Local Gang Realities." *Crime Media Culture* 15 (1): 169–189.

Venkatesh, Sudhir Alladi, and Ronald Kassimir, eds. 2007. *Youth, Globalization, and the Law*. Stanford, CA: Stanford University Press.

Vigil, James Diego. 2002. *Rainbow of Gangs: Street Cultures in the Mega-City*. Austin: University of Texas Press.

Vigil, James Diego. 2008. "Mexican Migrants in Gangs: A Second-Generation History." In *Street Gangs, Migration and Ethnicity*, edited by Frank van Gemert, Dana Peterson and Inger-Lise Lien, 49–62. Devon, UK: Willan.

Vigil, James Diego. 2016. "Multiple Marginality: A Comparative Framework for Understanding Gangs." In *Methods That Matter: Integrating Mixed Methods for More Effective Social Science Research*, edited by M. Cameron Hay, 284–305. Chicago, IL: University of Chicago Press.

Weitekamp, Elmar G. M., Kerstin Reich, and Hans-Jürgen Kerner. 2005. "Why Do Young Male Russians of German Descent (Aussiedlers) Tend to Join or Form Gangs Where Violence Plays a Major Role?" In *European Street Gangs and Troublesome Youth Groups: Findings from the Eurogang Research Program,* edited by Scott H. Decker and Frank M. Weerman, 103–136. Walnut Creek, CA: AltaMira.

Winton, Alisa. 2014. "Gangs in Global Perspective." *Environment and Urbanization,* 26 (2): 401–416.

Worldometer. 2021. Population of Africa. https://www.worldometers.info/world-population/africa-population/.

CHAPTER 24

GANG ECOLOGICAL DIVERSITY IN THE HOLLENBECK AREA OF LOS ANGELES, 1978–2012

P. JEFFREY BRANTINGHAM AND MATTHEW VALASIK

CRIMINAL street gangs are flexible social forms (Ayling 2011; Densley 2013; Valasik and Phillips 2017). There is considerable evidence that individuals find few barriers to joining gangs (Pyrooz and Sweeten 2015), seamlessly "code switch" between gang and non-gang social roles while active (Patillo-McCoy 1999; Bolden 2020), and readily desist from gang life when it suits them (Esbensen and Osgood 1999). With individuals coming and going, it stands to reason that gangs as group-scale entities are seen to coalesce and fragment over time, and ultimately disappear (Aspholm 2020; Stuart 2020).

Paradoxically perhaps, gangs are also durable social forms (Brantingham, Valasik, and Tita 2019; Klein and Maxson 2006). Gangs adopt unique names and distinctive "signs or symbols," which collectively mark group identity (Bolden 2018; Lopez-Aguado and Walker 2021). The markers of gang identity are often associated with well-defined geographic territories (Brantingham et al. 2012) or key activity nodes (Tita and Ridgeway 2007), giving them permanence that transcends the involvement of individual members (Valasik and Tita 2018). Individual crimes, or periods of violence, can also be potent markers connected to a specific gang, time, and place (Bichler, Norris, and Ibarra 2020). In the short term, such markers can rally the community for or against the gang as a group (e.g., "anti-violence marches") (Montejano 2010; Spergel and Grossman 1997; Torres-Harding et al. 2018; Zatz and Portillos 2000). Over the long term, such events may create recurrent behavioral patterns that support gang persistence (e.g., crime anniversaries, "hood days") (Aspholm and Mattaini 2017; Horowitz 1987).

Conflict within and between gangs may contribute to either the stability or instability of gangs (Valasik et al. 2018). Conflict within gangs most likely contributes to (or is a symptom of) weak internal organization (Decker and Curry 2002; Papachristos and Kirk 2015; Randle and Bichler 2017). Such gangs may easily fragment if violence happens to remove a key player from the street (see Aspholm 2020; Vargas 2014). Violent attacks from without may also be serious enough to fragment a gang, but it may also make gangs more resilient if their raison d'être is to offer protection (Hughes 2013; McGloin and Collins 2015). Or violence may make existing gangs more attractive for those looking to join for protection (Gravel et al. 2018), strengthening large gangs while weakening small ones. Similar logic applies if the principal utility of gangs is in the "reputational economy" (Cloward and Ohlin 1960; Descormiers and Morselli 2011). Forming a new gang may offer a shorter path to the top of a local reputational hierarchy than joining an existing gang (Densley 2014), a process that encourages more gangs to form. The reputational heights in large existing gangs may be greater, however, which encourages the persistence of fewer large gangs (Felson 2006; Van Gemert 2001).

The tension between group stability and instability raises several important questions about gang diversity over time. While the actual mechanisms are certainly complex and worthy of investigation (see Gravel et al. 2018; Brantingham et al. 2012; Brantingham et al. 2019), we also believe it is important to establish some baseline empirical evidence that goes beyond the anecdotal. Here we examine the diversity of gang cliques in an area of Los Angeles over a 35-year period (1978–2012) (see also Barton et al. 2020; Brantingham et al. 2019; Valasik and Phillips 2017). Specifically, using detailed data on homicides, we record the names of gangs participating in a homicide (as suspect or victim). We then count the number of unique gang names—the clique richness—present each year. We track the temporal evolution of clique richness and seek to understand how richness is related to homicide trends. We offer several conceptual observations for the observed patterns, but do not seek to test any specific model of gang diversity.

Defining Gangs and Gang Crime

An enduring artifact of street gang scholarship is the inability for researchers, criminal justice actors, and policymakers to agree on a common definition of what constitutes a street gang, who is a gang member, or when a crime should be designated a gang-related event (Curry 2015). Many definitions offered over the years share a few elements in common, such as the centrality of youth (Sheldon 1898, 428; Puffer 1912; Klein 1971), group-level structure (Klein and Crawford 1967), territoriality (Thrasher 1927), and often the importance of group-marking symbols and some form of membership requirement (Hughes, Schaible, and Kephart 2022). The problems surrounding the use of crime and delinquency measures as defining characteristics of gangs are well known. Miller (1992), for example, regarded gangs as "a self-formed association of peers, bound together by mutual interests, with identifiable leadership, well-developed lines of authority, and other organizational features who act in concert to achieve a specific purpose or purposes, which generally include the conduct of illegal activity and control over a particular territory, facility, or type of enterprise" (21; see also Klein 1971, 13). Criminal code and policy definitions hinge on this connection between gangs and crime and delinquency. The California state law, for example, defines a gang as "any organization, association or group of 3 or more persons whether formal or informal, which (1) has continuity of purpose, (2) seeks a group identity, and (3) has members who individually or collectively engage in or have engaged in a pattern of criminal activity" (Section 186.22(f) of the California Penal Code). Katz and Jackson-Jacobs (2004), by contrast, point out that to include crime and delinquency as part of the definition of gangs is circular: A group of youth that engages in crime is classed as a gang, and yet we turn around and are surprised that gangs commit so much crime (see also Curry 2015). Despite these concerns, crime and delinquency remain central to how gangs are defined, studied, and policed.

Astutely, Papachristos (2005) notes that this definitional ambiguity has little value to law enforcement officers, victims of gang-related violence, or gang members themselves. Individuals involved in street gangs are uninterested in the legal definitions or scholarly semantics that determine if their group is labeled a street gang. Papachristos (2005), adapting Everett C. Hughes (1948) definition of an ethnic group, argues that street gangs do not exist because of an observable or measurable variation differentiating them from other groups. Instead, street gangs exist because those individuals who are part of the group and those who are not part of the group act, socialize, feel, and believe that the group is a gang. That is, "gangs take their meaning instead from their function and from the consequences of their actions" (Papachristos 2005, 644). Street gangs are thus dynamic, adapting and evolving, and amorphous as a group's boundaries shift with the fluid movement of members joining and leaving the group (Ayling 2011; Densley 2013; Klein and Crawford 1967). We hew closely to this perspective in what follows.

The challenges with defining gangs extends to the definition of gang-related crimes. There is little question that gang crime exists. Rather, the debate has centered on the criteria necessary to identify whether a given crime is gang related or not (Esbensen et al. 2001; Klein and Maxson 2006). A gang-affiliated crime is one where the suspects or victims are known gang associates. A gang-motivated crime is tied to gang activity that directly or indirectly supports the goals of the gang (e.g., territoriality, retaliation, recruitment) (Rosenfeld, Bray, and Egley 1999). Traditionally, the Los Angeles Police Department (LAPD) has been positioned as an example of the gang-affiliated approach to labeling gang-related crime (Klein and Maxson 2006), while the Chicago Police Department has been positioned as an example of the gang-motivated approach (Howell and Griffiths 2018).

It is also important from a methodological standpoint to highlight that gang-affiliated and gang-motivated definitions can result in different subsamples of crime. Gang-motivated crimes often represent a smaller subsample of all crimes where those crimes are committed by people who just happen to be gang members, but the crimes are not motivated by the goals of the gang (e.g., domestic violence; Papachristos 2009). However, gang-affiliated crimes might also represent a smaller subsample of all crimes in situations where crimes have all the hallmarks of gang-motivated violence but suspects or victims are lacking or uncooperative (e.g., drive-by shootings). In practice, police likely rely on the detailed circumstances surrounding individual crimes to determine if they are gang related or not, displaying far more flexibility than this simple distinction between gang-affiliated and gang-motivated approaches allows (Brantingham, Yuan, and Herz 2020). In any case, both the gang-affiliated and gang-motivated definitions are able to statistically differentiate gang-related from non-gang-related crimes with few other substantive differences between member- and motive-based approaches (Klein and Maxson 2006).

Recognizing Unique Gangs in Gang-Related Crimes

An important distinction in our analysis below is whether a reported crime is associated with a named gang. Given the range of criteria used in labeling gang-related crimes, it is possible for some crime to be deemed gang related but simultaneously provide insufficient information to identify which specific gangs might be involved. A drive-by shooting, for example, is a hallmark of gang violence and is usually sufficient to label the crime as gang related. Yet the gang responsible for the shooting and the gang targeted may not be known unless witnesses are willing to come forward (Pyrooz, Wolfe, and Spohn 2011). A different drive-by shooting, however, may have involved the perpetrators calling out the name of their gang just prior to the shooting, while the victim may be from a known gang because they were willing to self-identify. In general, we recognize that there are three unique patterns by which gang-related crimes may be associated with named gangs: (1) the suspect and victim gangs are known; (2) the suspect gang is known, but the victim gang is not; or (3) the suspect gang is not known, but the victim gang is. In addition, we recognize that the suspect and victim gangs associated with an individual crime may be the same or different. If the suspect and victim are from the same gang this is *intra-gang* violence; if they are from different gangs this is *intergang* violence.

As discussed above, defining gangs is a challenging task. Naming conventions for gangs are equally complicated (Pyrooz and Decker 2019). For instance, law enforcement may develop their own set of rules for naming gangs separate from life on the street (Scott 2020). Following Papachristos (2005), we assume that gangs have the freedom to adopt names that are socially relevant to them and that law enforcement reports mostly follow what they hear. At times the social relevance of a gang name is relatively easy to spot. Geographic landmarks such as street or neighborhood names feature in a chosen name (Valasik and Tita 2018). For example, several distinct "Fruit Town" gangs in Los Angeles claim territories encompassing streets with the names of fruit trees. In other instances, names may derive from events or places of historical, cultural, or social significance that are opaque, or at least not obvious to outsiders (Rymes 1996). For example, White Fence, a gang in the Boyle Heights neighborhood of east Los Angeles, with roots stretching back well before 1940 (Ranker 1957), reportedly derives its name from a "white fence" that surrounded the La Purisima Church. The church is still located in White Fence territory today, but the eponymous fence is long gone. Gang names also sometimes hint at hierarchical relationships. It is not uncommon for gangs to be organized by age, with an older age cohort using one name and one or more younger age cohorts using the same name but appended to mark the segments of the "next generation" (Rymes 1996).

Less obvious are the relationships among gangs that share similar names but are clearly competitors rather than hierarchically related. Names such as Crips, Bloods, Mara Salvatrucha (MS-13), and Mexican Mafia, among others, are used repeatedly by gangs in the same area, but with modifiers to distinguish themselves from one another. In Los Angeles, for example, there may be 8–10 different *sets* that use the name East Coast Crips, but distinguish themselves (and claim specific territory) by appending a street number. East Coast Crips are but a few of the hundreds of *sets* in Los Angeles that use Crips in their name. While it is tempting to group gangs that share common name elements together into some type of multiscale or segmentary social order, it is not clear when (or even if) this is warranted. For example, one might seek to group the 118 East Coast Crips with the 68 East Coast Crips (and the other similarly named sets) into a higher-order group called East Coast Crips, group the East Coast Crips with other higher-order groups such as Gangster Crips (which includes at least 15 uniquely named sets) to form a grouping called Crips, and then do the same thing for various Bloods, MS-13, Mexican Mafia, and so on. Yet gangs with similar names seem as likely to be enemies as allies (Decker 1996; Randle and Bichler 2017). We side step these issues in what follows by assuming that each uniquely named gang represents a socially distinct entity at the time the name was recorded.

Clique Diversity

One way in which to measure the scope and scale of the gang problem is to consider the diversity of gangs present in a city. It is commonplace in ecological studies to think of the diversity of life in a place as somehow reflecting the "ecological health" or "resiliency" of that place. More ecological variety equates to greater ecological health. In the case of crime, the opposite assumption has been suggested (Brantingham 2016). The greater the variety of crime types found in a place, the more complex and severe the problems faced by that place. It seems plausible that a similar situation holds for gang diversity. To wit, the greater the number of unique gangs found in a particular place, the more challenging the gang problem is likely to be. While there is much to be debated about this conjecture, a first critical step is simply to document patterns of gang diversity. This is the task of the remainder of this chapter.

What do we mean by "gang diversity"? To avoid confusion stemming from questions of group size and scale implied by the terms "gang" and "set," we will use the term "clique" to refer to any uniquely named gang that appears in the empirical record (Papachristos 2006). Gang studies consider a clique to be an aggregation of members that form a cohesive subgroup where all individuals are strongly connected to each other and participate in a variety of activities on a regular basis. We take gang names at face value and treat even slight variations as representing uniquely named cliques. For example, if three different crimes recorded victims affiliated with (crime 1) the 118 East Coast Crips, (crime 2) the East Coast Crips, and (crime 3) the Crips, these would be considered three unique cliques. We assume that names are used to signify social distinctions that were important to the situation of that specific crime such that *socially* the gang involved in the first crime was different than the one involved in the second and the one involved in the third. A similar argument was made about crime event diversity where, for example, a robbery + car theft is an ecologically distinct "crime type" from a robbery or car theft that occurs alone (Brantingham 2016). The approach may overestimate true gang diversity, but we judge it to be preferrable to clumsy systematics that risk getting the relevant social relationships all wrong (see De Queiroz 1988). It is important to note that we rely on clique names as identified by police in association with homicides. We consider police officers, particularly anti-gang units, as one type of subject matter expert that is well practiced in identifying and recording evidence associated with criminal events (see Katz, Webb, and Shaefer 2000). More is said on this issue in the discussion that follows.

Gang diversity is then simply a count of the number of uniquely named cliques recognized in a bounded area over a particular interval of time. In the ecological literature, this type of diversity is often referred to as (species) richness and is distinguished from (species) evenness, which takes into account both the number of unique entities (species) and the proportion of individuals (or biomass) within those entities. As discussed in more detail below, we only consider cliques that are known through the homicides in which they are involved. This approach is similar to that taken by Papachristos (2009) in his work on gang homicide networks. Other data sources, such as territory maps (Brantingham et al. 2019) or field interview cards (Valasik, Reid, and Phillips 2016) may record a different number of unique gangs (typically more). However, not all of these gangs may be involved in the most serious crimes, and static sources of information such as territory maps may not reflect the dynamic reality of gangs on the ground (e.g., gangs coming into and out of existence). It is well known that ecological diversity increases with the size of the area sampled (Magurran 2004), and a similar phenomenon has been documented with crime diversity (Brantingham 2016; Lentz 2018). Here we focus on a single area and do not examine how clique diversity changes with changing area size.

Data and Analytical Approach

The present research examines patterns in gang clique diversity over time in the LAPD Hollenbeck policing division. Hollenbeck is located on the eastern edge of the City of Los Angeles (Figure 24.1). In the 2010 census, Hollenbeck had a resident population of approximately 187,000 people living in a 15.2-square-mile area. At the time, a quarter of the residents were living below the poverty line (25.2%) and about a third were living in owner-occupied residences (30.5%). The majority population is Hispanic (84.1%), with most individuals tracing their ancestry to Mexico.

Hollenbeck's gangs have a long and well-documented history stretching back more than 70 years (Ranker 1957). Some of the gangs first documented back in the 1940s are present today using the same names. This image of stability is mixed with other evidence of considerable change in gang numbers and territorial coverage (see Figure 24.1). For example, of 14 distinct gang territories recognized in Hollenbeck in 1978, at least one territory was no longer recognized in 2014. In addition, the total number of recognized gang territories had grown to 31 in 2014.

Here we examine gang cliques identified in connection with homicides occurring in Hollenbeck between 1978–2012 (Valasik et al. 2017; see Figure 24.2). A total of 1,425 homicides occurred in Hollenbeck over this period. Homicides in Hollenbeck first peaked in the late 1970s, with 61 total occurring in 1979. Incidents then declined through the bulk of the 1980s, reaching a minimum of 27 in 1982. Homicides rose sharply in the early 1990s, peaking in 1992 with 93 in total (a 52% increase over the prior peak in 1979). Homicides

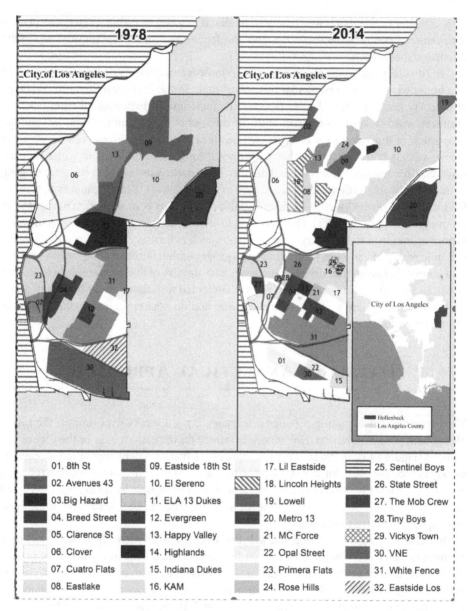

FIGURE 24.1 Map of LAPD's Hollenbeck Policing Division with Named Gang Territories Recorded in 1978 and 2014

then generally declined through the late 1990s and 2010s. Our primary interest is in gang-related homicides. We therefore drop non-gang homicides from further consideration. In Los Angeles, as noted above, the usual assumption is that gang-related designation of a homicide follows from the victim or suspect being gang affiliated in some way. Notably, Hollenbeck homicides were majority non-gang prior to 1988. In each year after 1988, homicides were majority gang related.

GANG ECOLOGICAL DIVERSITY: HOLLENBECK, LA 525

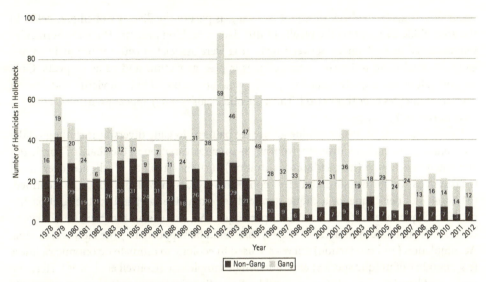

FIGURE 24.2 Homicides in Hollenbeck, 1978–2012

Gang-related homicide files were reviewed to identify the names of gang cliques connected to the crime (see also Valasik et al. 2017). Clique names were recorded as reported by LAPD investigators. We did not attempt to infer clique names from contextual information (e.g., location of the crime in a known gang territory). We recorded clique names associated with victims and suspects separately. We recorded the clique as "unknown" if the homicide was deemed gang related by the LAPD but there was no specific gang affiliation contained in the file. If both suspect and victim gang are unknown, the homicide is dropped from further analysis. Clique names were then scrubbed to correct spelling errors and other minor sources of misalignment (e.g., translation *Calle Ocho* versus 8th St.; abbreviation 8th St. versus 8th Street). We then assume that any difference between names after scrubbing represents a unique clique (e.g., Avenues 43 versus Avenues). The number of unique cliques is then tabulated by year, providing a measure of clique diversity or richness over time. We include all gangs active in the area, even if their nominal territory is outside of Hollenbeck. For example, one homicide in Hollenbeck involved a clique going by the name Pasadena Latin Kings, pointing to an area outside Hollenbeck. Nevertheless, because the crime itself

Table 24.1 Descriptive Statistics

Number of homicides 1978–2012	1,425
Number of gang-related homicides	638
Number of homicides with named victim clique	524
Number of homicides with named suspect clique	489
Number of uniquely named victim cliques	79
Number of uniquely named suspect cliques	78
Number of uniquely named cliques	105

occurred within Hollenbeck we count this gang as part of the diversity of cliques *active* in the area. Table 24.1 reports the results of this data scrubbing process. The 1,425 homicides that occurred in Hollenbeck between 1978–2012 were associated with 105 uniquely named gangs. A total of 79 uniquely named cliques appear as victims and 78 as suspects. Only around half of all uniquely named cliques ($n = 52$) are recorded in both victim and suspect roles in homicides over this period. Thus, the other half ($n = 53$) appear exclusively either as victims ($n = 27$) or suspects ($n = 26$).

Using these data we now examine a series of patterns in gang diversity, including (1) the temporal trends in clique diversity from 1978–2012; (2) variation in the share of homicides attributed to cliques (homicide concentration); (3) the stability of cliques over time, measured as the maximum number of consecutive years in which a clique is identified; (4) homicides per clique, or a clique standardized homicide rate; and (5) the relationship between clique diversity and homicides per clique. We also use an accumulation curve to estimate the maximum number of cliques that could be supported by the Hollenbeck area. Accumulation (and rarefaction) curves are used in ecology to estimate taxonomic richness (e.g., number of unique species) as a function of sample size (Colwell et al. 2012). Here the number of homicides constrains observable clique diversity in a way similar to how sample size constrains observed species diversity in an ecological field study.

Gang Diversity Patterns

We first establish some general boundary conditions for gang diversity. Given the $N = 638$ gang-related homicides that occurred in Hollenbeck between 1978–2012, the maximum possible number of unique cliques is $2 \times N = 1,276$. This maximum diversity estimate would hold if every homicide had a unique clique represented as the victim and a unique clique as the suspect, and we assume that homicides never involve three or more unique cliques. The minimum possible diversity would be one unique clique, which would hold if one clique were present over the entire time period and all homicides were internal to that clique. Though extreme, these boundary conditions provide guidance on the magnitude of the observed clique diversity. For example, the observed number of uniquely named cliques ($N = 105$) in the dataset is just 8.2% of the maximum theoretically possible.

Temporal Trends

Figure 24.3 shows the number of uniquely named cliques involved in gang-related homicides per year in Hollenbeck. Ten unique cliques were recognized in 1978. This number declined through the early 1980s, reaching a minimum of three active cliques in 1982. The number of unique cliques rose sharply starting in 1985 and peaked in 1992 at 34. The number of unique cliques declined approximately linearly since then. Following the peak in 1992, a minimum of nine active cliques were observed in 2008 and again in 2010. The trend in gang diversity follows closely the broader trend for homicides in Hollenbeck (Figure 24.2), a point to which we return below.

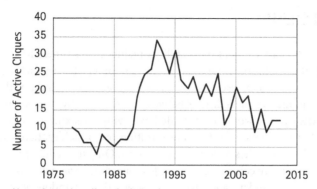

Note: An active clique is defined as a named group with one or more homicides recorded in that year.

FIGURE 24.3 Number of Active Cliques per Year, 1978–2012

Homicide Concentration

Figure 24.4 shows a rank-abundance curve, or Whittaker plot, of the number of homicides connected to each uniquely named clique, sorted in descending rank order. The most active clique (Locke Street), combining roles as both suspect and victim, was connected to 86 homicides over the 35-year period from 1978–2012. This one clique was involved in 8.5% of all homicides with at least one named clique. The first 11 cliques (10.5% of all named cliques) were connected to 50.1% of all homicides as either suspect or victim. Thirty-six cliques (34% of all named cliques) were each involved in just one homicide over the 35-year period. The pattern is indicative of the "concentration of homicide" among just a handful of cliques. A few cliques are connected to the majority of homicides, but most of the diversity in gang homicides is attributable to "singleton" gangs that appeared just once.

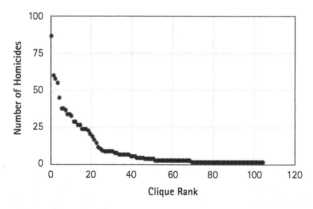

FIGURE 24.4 Number of Homicides Connected to each Named Clique, 1978–2012 (ranked in descending order)

Ecological Stability

Figure 24.5 provides two views of the stability of cliques over time. The first (part (a)) is a variant of a Whittaker plot showing the maximum number of years that a given clique was *continuously active*, sorted in descending rank order. For example, a clique that was involved in one or more homicides in each year between 1986–1990 (five years) and then again in 1993 and 1994 (two years) would be recorded as having a maximum of five years continuously active. As was the case for the concentration of homicides, here we see that just a few cliques have long stretches of continuous activity. Only four cliques display stretches of activity lasting 10 or more consecutive years. Just one clique was active over 15 consecutive years, representing just under half of the total observational window of 35 years. Sixty-five of the 105 uniquely identified cliques (61.9%) were continuously active for only single year at a time.

Part (b) of Figure 24.5 considers the relationship between the maximum number of years continuously active against the total years active. It is possible that some cliques were intensely active only over a short period of time, and then were not active again, while others were intermittently active over long stretches of time. The observed relationship between the maximum number of years continuously active and the total number of active years is wedge-shaped (e.g., Knight et al. 2014). A gang that is active in only one year of the 35 total years can only be continuously active for just one year. By contrast, a gang that is active for 10 years out of the 35 total can be active in consecutive years anywhere between 10 and 1 year in a single stretch. If active for 10 consecutive years, then there are no breaks in the appearance of the clique from its "first historical appearance" to its "last historical appearance" (Stephen 1998). If consecutively active for only one year at a time, then there can be one or more years between each time that a clique appears in the historical record. We see both patterns in Hollenbeck. In general, cliques that are active for more years in total also have longer stretches of time where they are continuously active. For example, one of the cliques tied for the most number of years active (28) was also the clique with the most number of years continuously active (15). However, this pattern is not universally true. For example, the three cliques that were tied for being active for a total of 10 years were continuously active at most for 3, 4, and 7 years in any one stretch.

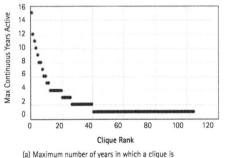
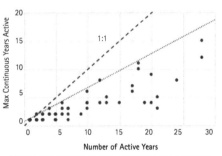

(a) Maximum number of years in which a clique is involved in a homicide

(b) Relationship between maximum number of years continuously active and the number of active years

FIGURE 24.5 Stability of Cliques over Time

Homicides per Clique

While individual cliques may be unstable (i.e., prone to extinction), Figure 24.6 (a) suggests that the central tendency of the relationship between the number of cliques and number of homicides is relatively stable over time. The number of homicides per clique per year fluctuates between 1 and 2.92 with a mean of 1.7 (sd = 0.41). Interestingly, the number of homicides per clique peaks in 1994, two years after the peak in total homicides in Hollenbeck (see Figure 24.2). Figure 24.6 (b) plots the number of homicides per clique against the total number of cliques active per year. This latter visualization reveals that more cliques are generally associated with more homicides per clique ($t = 4.18$, $p < 0.001$, Adjusted R-squared = 0.326). For example, there were 63.8% more homicides per clique with 34 unique cliques on the ground in 1992 compared with the four cliques in 1982.

Estimating Maximum Gang Diversity

We now turn to one final question that can be addressed with the data presented here. While inspection of gang names sometimes makes it feel like every street block has a different resident gang, the substantive question is, How many unique gangs can an urban environment actually support? Clearly, it is many fewer than the total street segments in an area.

Figure 24.7 shows the number of unique cliques against the number of gang-related homicides recognized in each year. The data follow a regular pattern reminiscent of species accumulation curves (Flather 1996; Ugland, Gray, and Ellingsen 2003). Specifically, because we observe gangs through the homicides they are involved in, it is necessarily the case that the number of homicides in any given year places an upper limit on the number of unique gangs we can recognize in that year. For example, a year with only one gang-related homicide at most could reveal two unique gangs (i.e., one as suspect and the other as victim). A year with 10 gang-related homicides could produce observations of up to 20 unique gangs (i.e., each homicide has a unique gang as suspect and another unique gang as victim). Over many years with different numbers of homicides, we get a different sampling window in the diversity of gangs. If we assume that the diversity is stationary in time—which is not

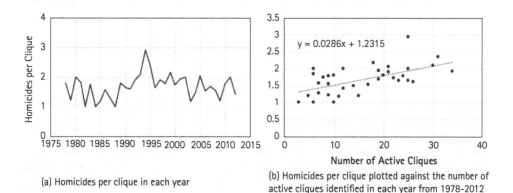

(a) Homicides per clique in each year

(b) Homicides per clique plotted against the number of active cliques identified in each year from 1978–2012

FIGURE 24.6 Stability of Number of Cliques and Number of Homicides over Time

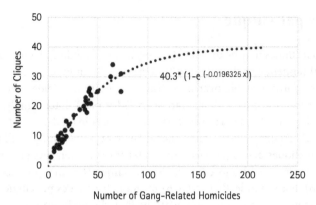

FIGURE 24.7 Number of Unique Cliques against the Number of Gang-Related Homicides in Hollenbeck, 1978–2012

necessarily true—we can fit an accumulation curve to the observed data and estimate the number of gangs that we would expect to see given a sufficiently large number of homicides to sample them all. We fit a negative exponential distribution of the form $y = a(1-e^{-bx})$, where y is the number of unique cliques and x is the number of homicides (Adjusted R-squared = 0.985). The parameter a gives the asymptotic number of unique gangs consistent with the data (Flather 1996), which in this case is 40.3 ± 4.2 gangs (95% CI = 31.8–48.9 gangs) (t = 9.6, p < 0.001). The observed maximum number of unique cliques at any one time was 34, observed in 1992, which is 84.3% of the expected maximum based on the accumulation curve, but is within the 95% confidence interval for the estimate. Hollenbeck is near full saturation for unique gangs. However, this number is well below the theoretical maximum that could exist given the amount of violent crime.

A follow-on observation concerns the number of homicides that would be needed to potentially observe the asymptotic number of unique gangs. In this case, Hollenbeck would need to experience at least 250 gang-related homicides in a single year to fully sample the 40 cliques predicted at saturation. This would be equivalent to Hollenbeck *alone* exhibiting nearly as many homicides (both gang and non-gang) as occurred city wide (n = 295) in 2012.

Discussion

In this chapter we have tried to shed light on empirical patterns in gang clique diversity over time. Our approach relied on identifying uniquely named cliques connected to gang-related homicides that occurred in the Hollenbeck area of Los Angeles between 1978–2012. The data may suggest that clique diversity fluctuated over time, rising in the late 1980s to a peak in 1992 and then falling gradually over the next 20 years. Not surprisingly, the pattern tracks the overall homicide trend, but with one important distinction (Figure 24.8). Homicides in Hollenbeck peaked first in the early 1980s, dropped through the middle 1980s, and peaked

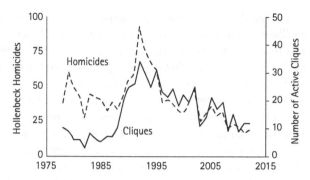

FIGURE 24.8 Homicide Counts in Hollenbeck (dashed line) and the Number of Unique Gang Cliques (solid line), 1978–2012

again in the early 1990s before falling steadily to historically low levels by 2012. The number of homicides in 1992 was 44% higher than the number in 1988. The number of unique gang cliques was also low through the mid-1980s, but the late 1980s saw a massive surge. The number of cliques in 1992 was 240% higher than the number in 1988. This dramatic rise demands an explanation. Several possibilities are immediately obvious.

If we assume the observed pattern reflects real changes in clique diversity, then the first possibility points to a connection between street gangs and open-air drug dealing (Rengert 1996; Taniguchi, Ratcliffe, and Taylor 2011). The appearance of crack cocaine in the mid-1980s may have created entrepreneurial opportunities for gang organizations to thrive (Hagedorn 1994). Even if loosely organized, gangs may provide some corporate structure for controlling local drug markets. However, Klein, Maxson, and Cunningham (1991) argue that this was not the case in Los Angeles. Rather, gang-affiliated individuals increased their participation in drug market activity at about the same rate as non-gang individuals. A variant of the above argument would tie the rise of drug-related violence in the late 1980s to a greater reliance on gangs as a source of protection. This explanation relies *not* on street gangs as drug-dealing organizations, but rather that gangs offer protection via the threat (or actual use) of force to their members. Gang members may independently deal drugs but take the protection offered by their gangs as a beneficial by-product. Alternatively, it is possible that the reputational economy took on a new level of importance in the late 1980s (Cloward and Ohlin 1960; Descormiers and Morselli 2011). While established gangs may have offered a sure route to establish street credibility (Van Gemert 2001), perhaps forming a new gang started to be seen as a faster route to the top (Densley 2014).

We also must consider the possibility that the observed gang diversity pattern is an artifact of some other non-causal process. For example, prior to the late 1980s, law enforcement agencies may have been less aware of criminal street gangs and therefore were less likely to look for gang connections in the homicides they investigated. Some change in perception in the late 1980s, perhaps related to the war on drugs, led law enforcement to suddenly recognize cliques that were always there. If this were the case, clique diversity may have always comprised a fixed fraction of the number of homicides, as emerged to be the case after the 1992 peak. This diversity was simply not recognized until the late 1980s. This possibility seems less plausible given that the LAPD developed specialized gang units (CRASH) in the late 1970s (see Valasik and Brantingham, **Chapter 40** in this volume). Their ability to collect gang intelligence should have been well-developed long before the apparent rise in gang diversity in the late 1980s. In addition, it is hard to reconcile how the increase in gang diversity could arise as just an artifact of investigations given the simultaneous rise in workloads over that same period. Homicides in Hollenbeck peaked in 1992, which meant that clique diversity peaked at a point when detectives were carrying more cases than at any time before or since. One might expect clique diversity to be *lower* as workload increased because of the effort involved in trying to connect gang names to each crime. A variant of the above explanation might hold that gang cliques are a law enforcement fiction that asserted itself only in the late 1980s. That is, there are very few, if any, real gangs. Law enforcement invented the idea of gangs perhaps in response to increasing workload or to engage in punitive labeling of individuals as gang members as part of a broader pattern of repression (Katz, Maguire, and Roncek 2002). It is possible that different subject matter experts, such as civilian gang intervention workers, viewing these homicides might identify a different collection of uniquely named gang cliques. However, both the documented intervention work and numerous ethnographic accounts of gangs and gang members over the years suggest that punitive labeling cannot be the whole story (e.g., Mendoza-Denton 2014; Sanchez-Jankowski 1991; Venkatesh 1997; Stuart 2020).

The pattern observed in Figure 24.8 is consistent with the low prevalence of gang-related homicides noted by Rosenfeld et al. (1999) in St. Louis between 1985–1995. This leads us to suspect that the observed number of cliques is not an artifact of law enforcement behavior. Rather, it may reflect a true explosion of gang diversity at the time perhaps related to a sort of "cultural awakening" of gangs spawned by popular representations in media (Decker, Pyrooz, and Densley 2022). From around 1987 onwards, the number of unique gang cliques almost perfectly tracks the number of homicides in Hollenbeck. However, we also must be aware of how the data constrain our ability to measure clique diversity. Since we can only document gangs through homicides, when homicides are rare clique diversity will appear to be low, but when homicides are common clique diversity *may* appear to be higher. The extreme case would be that gang diversity is constant and only appears to shift due to differences in homicide sample sizes. We used this assumption to estimate the maximum number of gangs that Hollenbeck could support, which we take to be about 40 unique gangs. However, this view of the data is not entirely satisfying since it fails to recognize the substantial turnover in unique gangs over time. Specifically, while the maximum observed number of unique gangs present on the landscape in any one year was 34 (in 1992), the total number of unique gangs recognized over the 35-year period was 105. Thus, most gangs are either quiescent most of the time, or most did not survive for very long. The gang accumulation curve presented in Figure 24.7 provides no indication that the asymptotic number of gangs in the environment is anywhere near 105, so the ephemeral nature of most gangs must be closer to the truth (Klein and Maxson 2006).

Having outlined some of the limitations in our analysis, we want to conclude with some empirical observations that may be important for gang prevention and intervention work. First, homicides are clearly concentrated among some cliques more than others. The most active clique over the 35-year period in Hollenbeck was connected to 8.5% of all gang-related homicides where at least one gang was known. The top 10.5% of active cliques ($n = 11$) were responsible for 50.2% of all gang-related homicides. The top 20% of active cliques ($n = 21$) were responsible for 73.5% of all gang-related homicides. By contrast, the 36 cliques that were observed only once in the 35-year period (34.3% of all active cliques) were connected to just 3.5% of all gang-related homicides. These results are similar to evidence for the concentration of crime among offenders. For example, Spelman and Eck (1989) found that 10% of known offenders were responsible for around 55% of crime. Clarke and Eck (2005) go on to suggest that 20% of offenders are responsible for 80% of the crime. In a recent meta-analysis of 27 studies, Martinez et al. (2017) found similar results that are consistent across different ages, genders, and jurisdictions. We suggest that a similar principle may hold for gang cliques and homicide. However, we do need to be aware that our measure of concentration, which aligns with the so-called *frequency* approach by Martinez et al. (2017), could also be a product of fluctuations in naming conventions, either by the gangs themselves or police. Gangs may seek to distinguish themselves at some times more than others, so a single gang at one point in time may "appear" to be two cliques at another point in time, even though there is no functional difference in how those gangs (and their individuals) behave. Similarly, changing priorities of police departments (e.g., anti-gang units, civil gang injunctions, civilian gang prevention programs) may lead police to sometimes use a finer-grained reification of gangs than at others. Our assumption has been, however, that specific names were recorded because they were salient at that time.

Second, most cliques are active for a very short period of time (for alt-right gangs, see Reid and Valasik 2020). This should not be a surprise as a short lifespan is a characteristic of both species (Marshall 2017) and companies (Daepp et al. 2015). It is widely recognized that a majority of terrorist groups do not survive their first year (Phillips 2019). One is tempted to suggest that a short "lifespan" of criminal groups should be law-like in its regularity (e.g., Felson 2006). Beyond this general pattern, however, we also see that different cliques are either continuously or intermittently active. While it is difficult to provide any concrete determination on what happened at the street level, we should consider the possibility that intermittently active cliques go through periods where there is strong collective action and periods when there is weak (or even non-existent) group organization (Petersen, Osmundsen, and Tooby 2021; Zefferman and Mathew 2015; Decker and Curry 2002). In effect, cliques may come into and out of existence with both ease and regularity. This would parallel, at a higher scale, what is observed for individuals moving into and out of gang social roles with ease.

Third, in spite of the variation in the number and stability of cliques over time, the number of homicides per clique on the whole remains *relatively* stable. It varies between a minimum of around one and three homicides per clique per year over the 35-year period. There are at least two possible explanations for this observed pattern. First, it might reflect a form of "resource partitioning" driven by increased competition (Roughgarden 1976). Broadly, group formation with active territorial defense is a common mechanism for reducing competition overall (see Brantingham et al. 2012). It is possible that the growth in drug markets in the late 1980s created conditions that encouraged greater partitioning of space into regions controlled by ever smaller cliques. Since crack cocaine can be dealt one "hit" at a time (Blumstein, Rivara, and Rosenfeld 2000), the market of users can be carved up into very fine spatial segments where competitive effects can be approximately balanced across cliques (see also Taniguchi et al. 2011). The general stability in homicides per clique over time masks more subtle variations, however. There is a positive relationship between clique diversity (i.e., number of unique cliques) and homicides per clique. In general, the addition of 10 new cliques to the system is worth about 0.3 more homicides per clique per year. In the end, clique diversity is not just an abstract proxy of ecological health, it has real consequences in terms of homicides.

There are several obvious next steps in the study of gang diversity in Los Angeles and elsewhere. Extending the temporal coverage of the sample to include the past 10 years, from 2012–2022, might reveal how gang diversity changed alongside more recent swings in violent crime. Homicides in Los Angeles hit their lowest point in more than 50 years in 2013 ($n = 248$). Homicides rose steadily thereafter, reaching a peak nearly 60% higher in 2021 ($n = 396$). How gang diversity changed in relation to these shifts in violence will be important to evaluate. Extending the geographic coverage would also be welcome. Hollenbeck is home exclusively to Latino gangs. Establishing whether the general patterns in gang diversity over time observed in Hollenbeck also hold in other areas of Los Angeles (and other cities), with different racial-ethnic, socioeconomic, and built environments, will be necessary for generalized model building. It is conceivable that gang diversity adheres to a set of discernable ecological assembly rules common across all communities (Diamond 1975). If true, then we would expect the number of uniquely named gangs to be regulated by intra- and intergang competition across all settings (Brantingham et al. 2012; Brantingham et al. 2019). Alternatively, it is possible that gang diversity is driven by stochastic processes (Connor and Simberloff 1979). In this case, competition would play little or no role, while randomness in the rate at which uniquely named gangs appear and disappear would serve as an explanatory model (see Hubbell 2001; Brantingham 2016). More work is needed to evaluate these two extreme approaches.

Finally, we put forward at the start of this chapter a bold conjecture that gang diversity somehow reflects the "health" or "function" of the community (Schulze and Mooney 2012). Our conjecture parallels thinking in conservation ecology, which posits that each unique species supplies an essential ecosystem service and that removal of those species (i.e., loss of biodiversity) harms the ecosystem. Here we posit that each unique gang performs some ecosystem service, and that changes in gang diversity over time (and space) may variously harm or help the community ecosystem. Framing the community role of gangs in terms of formal ecology may be unexpected, but the idea that gangs perform some type of community function should not be (Sanchez-Jankowski 1991; Decker et al. 2022). We must be careful, however, in seeking to identify exactly what the function (or functions) might be. The positive correlation between the number of unique gang cliques and the number of homicides per clique suggests that more gangs have a negative community impact. Whether this also entails degraded community function is an open question. As in community ecology (e.g., Genung, Fox, and Winfree 2020), intuitions about the relationship between gang diversity and community function may be hard to establish in fact. More work will be needed to map out these potential ecological functions and trace their relationships to individual and group-level processes.

Acknowledgements

This research was supported in part by NSF grants ATD-2027277 and SCC-2125319 and ARO MURI grant W911NF1810208.

REFERENCES

Aspholm, Roberto. 2020. *Views from the Streets: The Transformation of Gangs and Violence on Chicago's South Side*. New York: Columbia University Press.

Aspholm, Roberto R., and Mark A. Mattaini. 2017. "Youth Activism as Violence Prevention." In *The Wiley Handbook of Violence and Aggression*, edited by Peter Sturmey, 1–12. Chichester, UK: Wiley.

Ayling, Julie. 2011. "Gang Change and Evolutionary Theory." *Crime, Law and Social Change* 56 (1): 1–26.

Barton, Michael S., Matthew A. Valasik, Elizabeth Brault, and George Tita. 2020. "'Gentefication' in the Barrio: Examining the Relationship between Gentrification and Homicide in East Los Angeles." *Crime & Delinquency* 66 (13–14): 1888–1913.

Bichler, Gisela, Alexis Norris, and Citlalik Ibarra. 2020. "Evolving Patterns of Aggression: Investigating the Structure of Gang Violence during the Era of Civil Gang Injunctions." *Social Sciences* 9 (11): 203.

Blumstein, Alfred, Frederick P. Rivara, and Richard Rosenfeld. 2000. "The Rise and Decline of Homicide—and Why." *Annual Review of Public Health* 21 (1): 505–541.

Bolden, Christian L. 2018. "Gang Organization and Gang Types." In *Oxford Research Encyclopedia of Criminology and Criminal Justice*. Oxford, UK: Oxford University Press.

Bolden, Christian L. 2020. *Out of the Red*. New Brunswick, NJ: Rutgers University Press.

Brantingham, P. Jeffrey. 2016. "Crime Diversity." *Criminology* 54: 553–586.

Brantingham, P. Jeffrey, George E. Tita, Martin B. Short, and Shannon E. Reid. 2012. "The Ecology of Gang Territorial Boundaries." *Criminology* 50 (3): 851–885.

Brantingham, P. Jeffrey, Matthew Valasik, and George E. Tita. 2019. "Competitive Dominance, Gang Size and the Directionality of Gang Violence." *Crime Science* 8 (1): 7.

Brantingham, P. Jeffrey, Baichuan Yuan, and Denise Herz. 2020. "Is Gang Violent Crime More Contagious than Non-Gang Violent Crime?" *Journal of Quantitative Criminology* 37: 953–977.

Clarke, Ronald V. G., and John E. Eck. 2005. *Crime Analysis for Problem Solvers in 60 Small Steps*. US Department of Justice, Office of Community Oriented Policing Services.

Cloward, Richard A., and Lloyd Ohlin. 1960. *Delinquency and Opportunity: A Theory of Delinquent Gangs*. New York: Free Press.

Colwell, Robert K., Anne Chao, Nicholas J. Gotelli, Shang-Yi Lin, Chang Xuan Mao, Robin L. Chazdon, and John T. Longino. 2012. "Models and Estimators Linking Individual-Based and Sample-Based Rarefaction, Extrapolation and Comparison of Assemblages." *Journal of Plant Ecology* 5 (1): 3–21.

Connor, Edward F., and Daniel Simberloff. 1979. "The Assembly of Species Communities: Chance or Competition?" *Ecology* 60 (6): 1132–1140.

Curry, G. David. 2015. "The Logic of Defining Gangs Revisited." In *The Handbook of Gangs*, edited by Scott H. Decker and David Pyrooz, 7–27. Chichester, UK: John Wiley & Sons.

Daepp, Madeleine I. G., Marcus J. Hamilton, Geoffrey B. West, and Luís M. A. Bettencourt. 2015. "The Mortality of Companies." *Journal of the Royal Society Interface* 12 (106): 20150120.

De Queiroz, Kevin. 1988. "Systematics and the Darwinian Revolution." *Philosophy of Science* 55 (2): 238–259.

Decker, Scott H. 1996. "Collective and Normative Features of Gang Violence." *Justice Quarterly* 13: 243–264.

Decker, Scott H., and G. David Curry. 2002. "Gangs, Gang Homicides, and Gang Loyalty: Organized Crimes or Disorganized Criminals." *Journal of Criminal Justice* 30 (4): 343–352.

Decker, Scott H., David Pyrooz, and James Densley. 2022. *On Gangs*. Philadelphia, PA: Temple University Press.

Densley, James. 2013. *How Gangs Work*. New York: Palgrave Macmillan.

Densley, James A. 2014. "It's Gang Life, but Not as We Know It: The Evolution of Gang Business." *Crime & Delinquency* 60 (4): 517–546.

Descormiers, Karine, and Carlo Morselli. 2011. "Alliances, Conflicts, and Contradictions in Montreal's Street Gang Landscape." *International Criminal Justice Review* 21 (3): 297–314.

Diamond, Jared M. 1975. "Assembly of Species Communities." In *Ecology and Evolution of Communities*, edited by Martin L. Cody, Robert H. MacArthur and Jared M. Diamond. Cambridge, MA: Harvard University Press.

Esbensen, Finn-Aage, and D. Wane Osgood. 1999. "Gang Resistance Education and Training (Great): Results from the National Evaluation." *Journal of Research in Crime and Delinquency* 36 (2): 194–225.

Esbensen, Finn-Aage, L. Thomas Winfree, Ni He, and Terrance J. Taylor. 2001. "Youth Gangs and Definitional Issues: When Is a Gang a Gang, and Why Does It Matter?" *Crime & Delinquency* 47 (1): 105–130.

Felson, Marcus. 2006. *Crime and Nature*. Thousand Oaks, CA: Sage.

Flather, Curtis. 1996. "Fitting Species-Accumulation Functions and Assessing Regional Land Use Impacts on Avian Diversity." *Journal of Biogeography* 23 (2): 155–168.

Genung, Mark A., Jeremy Fox, and Rachael Winfree. 2020. "Species Loss Drives Ecosystem Function in Experiments, but in Nature the Importance of Species Loss Depends on Dominance." *Global Ecology and Biogeography* 29 (9): 1531–1541.

Gravel, Jason, Blake Allison, Jenny West-Fagan, Michael McBride, and George E. Tita. 2018. "Birds of a Feather Fight Together: Status-Enhancing Violence, Social Distance and the Emergence of Homogenous Gangs." *Journal of Quantitative Criminology* 34 (1): 189–219.

Hagedorn, John M. 1994. "Neighborhoods, Markets, and Gang Drug Organization." *Journal of Research in Crime and Delinquency* 31 (3): 264.

Horowitz, Ruth. 1987. "Community Tolerance of Gang Violence." *Social Problems* 34 (5): 437–450.

Howell, James C., and Elizabeth Griffiths. 2018. *Gangs in America's Communities*. Thousand Oaks, CA: Sage Publications.

Hubbell, Stephen P. 2001. *The Unified Neutral Theory of Biodiversity and Biogeography*. Princeton, NJ: Princeton University Press.

Hughes, Everett C. 1948. "The Study of Ethnic Relations." *Dalhousie Review* 27 (4): 477–485.

Hughes, Lorine A. 2013. "Group Cohesiveness, Gang Member Prestige, and Delinquency and Violence in Chicago, 1959–1962." *Criminology* 51 (4): 795–832.

Hughes, Lorine A., Lonnie M. Schaible, and Timothy Kephart. 2022. "Gang Graffiti, Group Process, and Gang Violence." *Journal of Quantitative Criminology* 38 (2): 365–384.

Katz, Jack, and Curtis Jackson-Jacobs. 2004. "The Criminologists' Gang." In *The Blackwell Companion to Criminology*, edited by Colin Sumner, 91–124. Chichester, UK: Wiley-Blackwell.

Katz, Charles M., Edward R. Maguire, and Dennis W. Roncek. 2002. "The Creation of Specialized Police Gang Units: A Macro-Level Analysis of Contingency, Social Threat and Resource Dependency Explanations." *Policing: An International Journal of Police Strategies & Management* 25 (3): 472–506.Katz, C. M., V. J. Webb, and D. R. Schaefer. 2000. "The Validity of Police Gang Intelligence Lists: Examining Differences in Delinquency between

Documented Gang Members and Nondocumented Delinquent Youth." *Police Quarterly* 3 (4): 413–437. https://doi.org/10.1177/109861110000300404.

Klein, M. W. 1971. *Street Gangs and Street Workers*. Englewood Cliffs, NJ: Prentice Hall.

Klein, Malcolm W., and Lois Y. Crawford. 1967. "Groups, Gangs, and Cohesiveness." *Journal of Research in Crime and Delinquency* 4 (1): 63–75.

Klein, Malcolm W., and Cheryl L. Maxson. 2006. *Street Gang Patterns and Policies*. Oxford, UK: Oxford University Press.

Klein, Malcolm W., Cheryl L. Maxson, and Lea C. Cunningham. 1991. "'Crack,' Street Gangs, and Violence." *Criminology* 29 (4): 623–650.

Knight, Rodney R., Jennifer C. Murphy, William J. Wolfe, Charles F. Saylor, and Amy K. Wales. 2014. "Ecological Limit Functions Relating Fish Community Response to Hydrologic Departures of the Ecological Flow Regime in the Tennessee River Basin, United States." *Ecohydrology* 7 (5): 1262–1280.

Lentz, Theodore S. 2018. "Crime Diversity: Reexamining Crime Richness Across Spatial Scales." *Journal of Contemporary Criminal Justice* 34 (3): 312–335.

Lopez-Aguado, Patrick, and Michael Lawrence Walker. 2021. " I Don't Bang: I'm Just a Blood': Situating Gang Identities in Their Proper Place." *Theoretical Criminology* 25 (1): 107–126.

Magurran, Anne E. 2004. *Measuring Biological Diversity*. Oxford, UK: Blackwell.

Marshall, Charles R. 2017. "Five Palaeobiological Laws Needed to Understand the Evolution of the Living Biota." *Nature Ecology & Evolution* 1 (6): 0165.

Martinez, Natalie N., YongJei Lee, John E. Eck, and SooHyun O. 2017. "Ravenous Wolves Revisited: a Systematic Review of Offending Concentration." *Crime Science* 6 (1): 10.

McGloin, Jean M., and Megan E. Collins. 2015. "Micro-Level Processes of the Gang." In *The Handbook of Gangs*, edited by Scott H. Decker and David Pyrooz, 276–293. Chichester, UK: John Wiley & Sons.

Mendoza-Denton, Norma. 2014. *Homegirls: Language and Cultural Practice among Latina Youth Gangs*. Hoboken, NJ: John Wiley & Sons.

Miller, Walter Benson. 1992. *Crime by Youth Gangs and Groups in the United States*. US Department of Justice, Office of Justice Programs.

Montejano, David. 2010. *Quixote's Soldiers: A Local History of the Chicano Movement, 1966–1981*. Austin: University of Texas Press.

Papachristos, Andrew V. 2005. "Interpreting Inkblots: Deciphering and Doing Something about Modern Street Gangs." *Criminology & Public Policy* 4: 643.

Papachristos, Andrew V. 2006. "Social Network Analysis and Gang Research: Theory and Methods." *Studying Youth Gangs*: 99–116.

Papachristos, Andrew V. 2009. "Murder by Structure: Dominance Relations and the Social Structure of Gang Homicide." *American Journal of Sociology* 115 (1): 74–128.

Papachristos, Andrew V., and David S. Kirk. 2015. "Changing the Street Dynamic." *Criminology & Public Policy* 14 (3): 525–558.

Patillo-McCoy, Mary. 1999. *Black Picket Fences: Privilege and Peril among the Black Middle Class*. Chicago, IL: University of Chicago Press.

Petersen, Michael Bang, Mathias Osmundsen, and John Tooby. 2021. "The Evolutionary Psychology of Conflict and the Functions of Falsehood." In *The Politics of Truth in Polarized America*, edited by D. C. Barker and E. Suhay, 131–151. New York: Oxford University Press.

Phillips, Brian J. 2019. "Do 90 Percent of Terrorist Groups Last Less than a Year? Updating the Conventional Wisdom." *Terrorism and Political Violence* 31 (6): 1255–1265.

Puffer, Joseph Adams. 1912. *The Boy and His Gang*. Vol. 10. Boston, MA: Houghton.

Pyrooz, David C., and Scott H. Decker. 2019. *Competing for Control: Gangs and the Social Order of Prisons*. Cambridge, UK: Cambridge University Press.

Pyrooz, David C., and Gary Sweeten. 2015. "Gang Membership between Ages 5 and 17 Years in the United States." *Journal of Adolescent Health* 56 (4): 414–419.

Pyrooz, David C., Scott E. Wolfe, and Cassia Spohn. 2011. "Gang-Related Homicide Charging Decisions: The Implementation of a Specialized Prosecution Unit in Los Angeles." *Criminal Justice Policy Review* 22 (1): 3–26.

Randle, Jasmin, and Gisela Bichler. 2017. "Uncovering the Social Pecking Order in Gang Violence." In *Crime Prevention in the 21st Century: Insightful Approaches for Crime Prevention Initiatives*, edited by Benoit LeClerc and Ernesto U. Savona, 165–186. Cham, Switzerland: Springer.

Ranker, Jesse Elwood. 1957. *A Study of Juvenile Gangs in the Hollenbeck Area of East Los Angeles*. Los Angeles: University of Southern California.

Reid, Shannon E., and Matthew Valasik. 2020. *Alt-Right Gangs*. Berkeley: University of California Press.

Rengert, George F. 1996. *The Geography of Illegal Drugs*. Boulder, CO: Westview Press.

Rosenfeld, Richard, Timothy M. Bray, and Arlen Egley. 1999. "Facilitating Violence: A Comparison of Gang-Motivated, Gang-Affiliated, and Nongang Youth Homicides." *Journal of Quantitative Criminology* 15 (4): 495–516.

Roughgarden, Jonathan. 1976. "Resource Partitioning among Competing Species—A Coevolutionary Approach." *Theoretical population biology* 9 (3): 388–424.

Rymes, Betsy. 1996. "Naming as Social Practice: The Case of Little Creeper from Diamond Street." *Language in Society* 25 (2): 237–260.

Sanchez-Jankowski, Martin S. 1991. *Islands in the Street: Gangs and American Urban Society*. Berkeley: University of California Press.

Schulze, Ernst-Detlef, and Harold A. Mooney. 2012. *Biodiversity and Ecosystem Function*. New York: Springer Science & Business Media.

Scott, Daniel. 2020. "Regional Differences in Gang Member Identification Methods among Law Enforcement Jurisdictions in the United States." *Policing: An International Journal* 43 (5): 723–740.

Sheldon, Henry D. 1898. "The Institutional Activities of American Children." *American Journal of Psychology* 9 (4): 425–448.

Spelman, William, and John E. Eck. 1989. *Sitting Ducks, Ravenous Wolves and Helping Hands: New Approaches to Urban Policing*. Austin: Lyndon B. Johnson School of Public Affairs, University of Texas.

Spergel, Irving A., and Susan F. Grossman. 1997. "The Little Village Project: A Community Approach to the Gang Problem." *Social Work* 42 (5): 456–470.

Stephen, L. Walsh. 1998. "Fossil Datum and Paleobiological Event Terms, Paleontostratigraphy, Chronostratigraphy, and the Definition of Land Mammal 'Age' Boundaries." *Journal of Vertebrate Paleontology* 18 (1): 150–179.

Stuart, Forrest. 2020. *Ballad of the Bullet*. Princeton, NJ: Princeton University Press.

Taniguchi, Travis A., Jerry H. Ratcliffe, and Ralph B. Taylor. 2011. "Gang Set Space, Drug Markets, and Crime around Drug Corners in Camden." *Journal of Research in Crime and Delinquency* 48 (3): 327–363.

Thrasher, Frederic M. 1927. *The Gang: A Study of 1,313 Gangs in Chicago*. Chicago, IL: University of Chicago Press.

Tita, George, and Greg Ridgeway. 2007. "The Impact of Gang Formation on Local Patterns of Crime." *Journal of Research in Crime and Delinquency* 44: 208–237.

Torres-Harding, Susan, Ashley Baber, Julie Hilvers, Nakisha Hobbs, and Michael Maly. 2018. "Children as Agents of Social and Community Change: Enhancing Youth Empowerment through Participation in a School-Based Social Activism Project." *Education, Citizenship and Social Justice* 13 (1): 3–18.

Ugland, Karl I., John S. Gray, and Kari E. Ellingsen. 2003. "The Species-Accumulation Curve and Estimation of Species Richness." *Journal of Animal Ecology* 72 (5): 888–897.

Valasik, Matthew, Michael S. Barton, Shannon E. Reid, and George E. Tita. 2017. "Barriocide: Investigating the Temporal and Spatial Influence of Neighborhood Structural Characteristics on Gang and Non-Gang Homicides in East Los Angeles." *Homicide Studies* 21 (4): 287–311.

Valasik, Matthew, and Matthew Phillips. 2017. "Understanding Modern Terror and Insurgency through the Lens of Street Gangs: ISIS as a Case Study." *Journal of Criminological Research, Policy and Practice* 3 (3): 192–207.

Valasik, Matthew, Shannon E. Reid, and Matthew D. Phillips. 2016. "CRASH and Burn: Abatement of a Specialised Gang Unit." *Journal of Criminological Research, Policy and Practice* 2 (2): 95–106.

Valasik, Matthew, Shannon E. Reid, Jenny S. West, and Jason Gravel. 2018. "Group Process and Gang Delinquency Intervention: Gang Activity Regulation and the Group Nature of Gang Violence." In *The Routledge International Handbook of Human Aggression*, edited by Jane Ireland, Philip Birch, and Carol Ireland, 411–423. New York: Routledge.

Valasik, Matthew, and George Tita. 2018. "Gangs and Space." *The Oxford Handbook of Environmental Criminology*, edited by Gerben Bruinsma and Shane Johnson, 839–867. Oxford, UK: Oxford University Press.

Van Gemert, Frank. 2001. "Crips in Orange: Gangs and Groups in the Netherlands." In *The Eurogang Paradox*, edited by Malcolm Klein, Hans-Jürgen Kerner, Cheryl Maxson, and Elmar Weitekamp, 145–152. Cham, Switzerland: Springer.

Vargas, Robert. 2014. "Criminal Group Embeddedness and the Adverse Effects of Arresting a Gang's Leader: A Comparative Case Study." *Criminology* 52 (2): 143–168.

Venkatesh, Subir A. 1997. "The Social Organization of Street Gang Activity in an Urban Ghetto." *American Journal of Sociology* 103: 82–111.

Zatz, Marjorie S., and Edwardo L. Portillos. 2000. "Voices from the Barrio: Chicano/a Gangs, Families, and Communities." *Criminology* 38 (2): 369–402.

Zefferman, Matthew R., and Sarah Mathew. 2015. "An Evolutionary Theory of Large-Scale Human Warfare: Group-Structured Cultural Selection." *Evolutionary Anthropology: Issues, News, and Reviews* 24 (2): 50–61.

SECTION 4

GANGS IN INSTITUTIONAL CONTEXT

CHAPTER 25

STORMING THE CAPITAL
The Place of Street Capital and Social Capital within Gangs

SIMON HARDING AND ROSS DEUCHAR

THIS chapter reviews the essential internal dynamics of urban street gangs by focusing on what drives the internal economy within them—namely, forms of capital: social, economic, cultural, and the new theorization of "street" capital. We draw on these theoretical insights to explicate how we can use them to gain a deeper understanding of what may motivate the forms of gang-involved crime and violence we are increasingly becoming more aware of in our urban communities, with a particular focus on the United Kingdom.

First, we provide an overview of the multifaceted perspectives on social capital theory and how it has been drawn on to explore and understand what may lead the most disadvantaged and vulnerable young men to seek out a sense of social support and status through street gang membership. Second, we study the theory of "street capital" and how its accumulation can help gang members climb the hierarchical ladder within the street gang. Third, we draw on these theories to consider how police and wider public services may draw on the principles underpinning them to enrich their ability to address gang-related criminality by emphasizing an evidence-based, public health approach to crime prevention.

SOCIAL CAPITAL: PRINCIPLES AND PERSPECTIVES

Bourdieu (1983) argued that "capital" can present itself in three fundamental guises: as *economic capital*, which is convertible into money; as *cultural capital*, which may be "institutionalized in the form of educational qualifications"; and finally as *social capital* (Richardson 1986, 16). Theoretical perspectives on the latter have been around since the early twentieth century, and credit for originally coining the term is generally attributed to Lyda J. Hanifan, a school administrator. Hanifan (1916) believed social capital comprised "those tangible substances [that] count for most in the daily lives of people: namely goodwill, fellowship, sympathy and social intercourse among the individuals and families who make up a social unit" (130). Following Hanifan's analysis, social capital as a concept lay dormant for several decades but was then subsequently reinvented by urban scholars and social theorists from the 1950s onward (Woolcock 2010). To this day, it is still largely viewed as an "essentially contested concept" (Woolcock 2010, 470; see also Baron, Field, and Schuller 2000; Catts 2007), with many differing views about what social capital actually means and just as many critiques of these views (Catts 2007; Deuchar 2009).

Essentially, scholarly insights on social capital have fallen into two traditions. First, the European tradition, which has been significantly influenced by the work of Pierre Bourdieu (1972, 1983); and second, the American tradition, stemming from work by James Coleman (1990) and Robert Putnam (2000).

The European Tradition

Bourdieu initiated his work on social capital in the 1970s (Bourdieu 1972) but produced an extended discussion of the concept in his 1983 paper, "The Forms of Capital" (Bourdieu 1983; see also, Woolcock 2010). Bourdieu defined social capital as a resource "made up of social obligations ('connections') which is convertible, in certain conditions, into economic capital" that could be accrued by individuals (Bourdieu 1983, cited in Terrion and Hogrebe 2007, 404). He believed that the structural features of the social world are organized by *fields*; in each social field a game is in play, where agents accumulate and maximize interrelated forms of cultural, symbolic, and social capital (Bourdieu 1990).

Field (2003), among others, has argued that Bourdieu's views on social capital are individualistic, with social connections defined as a means of cultivating individual superiority and personal economic gain. Others have argued that the development, or "banking of social capital as personal assets" (Pinkerton and Dolan 2007, 222), can enable individuals to access durable forms of support, thus playing a role in the development of general "well-being" (Bassani 2007, 17). As such, individuals rich in social capital may be able to maximize their levels of self-esteem, self-efficacy, emotional stability, and confidence (for a discussion, see Deuchar 2009). In the context of street gangs, these perspectives suggest that the social connections that emerge within the context of the gang may enhance personal reputations, provide increased protection for individuals, and facilitate access to power, status, and financial gain (through, for instance, the accumulation of "street capital," which we elaborate on later in the chapter; Harding 2014).

The American Tradition

Although Bourdieu believed that social capital can be accrued by individuals, many others (particularly within the context of the American tradition) take the alternative stance that social capital has at its heart the need for networking to facilitate community-based action and collective well-being (Coleman 1990; Field 2003). Coleman (1988) argued that social capital "inheres in the structure of relations between actors and among actors" (98). He focused strongly on the family's role in facilitating such a social structure through providing advice, emotional support, and reciprocity (Pinkerton and Dolan 2007). Coleman (1988) identified three forms of social capital: "obligations and expectations," which depend on the trustworthiness of the social environment; "information-flow capability of the social structure"; and "norms accompanied by sanctions" (119). A property shared by most forms of social capital that differentiates it from other forms of capital, he argued, was its "public good aspect: the actor or actors who generate social capital ordinarily capture only a small part of its benefits" (119).

Thus, while many other forms of capital such as financial, human, cultural, and physical contribute to personal well-being, *social* capital should be considered crucial because of its focus on social connectedness (Bassani 2007; Terrion and Hogrebe 2007). As alluded to earlier, Bassani (2007) highlights the common belief that as social capital increases so too does personal welfare since healthy social relationships can lead to better psychological, social, and physical health.

Putnam (2000) focused on the distinction between three basic forms of social capital: bonding, bridging, and linking. *Bonding* social capital, he argued, tends to reinforce exclusive identities, maintain homogeneity, mobilize solidarity, and is characterized by dense, multifunctional ties, localized trust, and unity (Putnam 2000; Western et al. 2005). *Bridging* social capital tends to be characterized by weak ties and thin levels of trust but broadens identities and brings together people across diverse social divisions. The third dimension, *linking* social capital, is simply a particular type of bridging that enables people to forge alliances with authoritative organizations and individuals in positions of power (Woolcock 2010; Western et al. 2005; Terrion and Hogrebe 2007).

The common argument is that people need to move from *bonding* to *bridging* networks, where they transcend their immediate social circumstances to equip themselves for broader social inclusion (Putnam 2000). However, Leonard and Onyx (2004) argue that it is useful to combine the effects of bonding and bridging, and that deprived or isolated communities may not need to shift from bonding to bridging to get ahead. Instead, it is useful for members of such communities to have closely bonded groups, but also to create loose ties with other groups in the same community (Deuchar 2009).

Accordingly, the concept of social capital is generally viewed as having networking at its heart (Wright, Cullen, and Miller 2001; Deuchar 2009; Bouchard, Wang, and Beauregard 2012; Nguyen and Bouchard 2013). Many believe that such socialization and networking are essential for building healthy relationships and for stimulating a sense of collective well-being in communities. The family is seen as an important source of stimulating these social connections. Supporters of Putnam's (2000) views emphasize the move from bonding to bridging social capital as being the only means of achieving wider social goals. However, others highlight the benefits of combining bridging and bonding and draw attention to the positive function of having closely bonded groups within communities, particularly deprived communities. Conversely, some argue that building intense ingroup ties inhibits the development of prosocial networks and may lead people to disassociate themselves from outside groups.

The Dark Side of Social Capital

It is important to consider how social capital operates and presents within the functions of the urban street gang. Putnam (2000) might refer to this as the "dark side of social capital" (350), while Field (2003) would term this, "perverse social capital" (94). Drawing on Putnam's metaphor of the bowling club, he acknowledges that just as bowling club members retain obligations to their club, street gang members will retain obligations to the gang or "hood." Here, bonding social capital instills trust and helps "mobilize solidarity." Putnam notes that "sectarianism" is also a form of social capital but one where the anti-social element predominates. Putnam is the first to acknowledge that strong "in-group loyalty (bonding social capital) may create strong out-group antagonism" (Putnam 2000, 23).

Likewise, Coleman's (1990) view of social capital as generating collective cooperation finds support from Fligstein and McAdam (2015), who document similar dynamics within corporate organizations. This concept of collective action and coalition is also identifiable within street gangs. Street gangs create opportunities for individuals to hasten their sluggish upward social trajectory through collective action and bonding. This dynamic is further scaffolded by the active intensity and durability of the street gang network. Within the gang, the dense durable network that operates at its core becomes the critical component, operating as it does as the principal route for establishing connections that are then used to build personal status.

In the sections that follow, we apply social capital theory to gang research. Key insights from both the European and American traditions associated with social capital theory have relevance to gang research since involvement in street gangs can and does facilitate capital accumulation. We blend European and American theoretical perspectives to highlight this point and advance a deeper understanding of the connections between social capital, gang violence, and organized crime.

Applying Social Capital to Gangs

As we have outlined above, a key argument is that social capital theory has at its heart people's need for networking and creating social connections as a means of facilitating collective agency (Coleman 1990; Putnam 2000; Field 2003; Applied Educational Research Scheme 2004; Leonard and Onyx 2004). Further, social structures determine the success of this resulting agency (Bourdieu 1983, 1984). As McCarthy and Hagan (1995) highlight, "embeddedness in networks of deviant associations provides access to tutelage relationships that facilitate the acquisition of criminal skills and attitudes" (63). McCarthy and Hagan (1995) conceptualize the latter assets as "criminal capital," which ultimately leads to the cooperative pursuit of illegal activity (Coleman 1990; McCarthy, Hagan, and Cohen 1998).

Drawing on previous work by Ruston (2002), the Applied Educational Research Scheme (2004), and Leonard and Onyx (2004), Deuchar (2009) brings attention to the specific indicators of social capital, which include civic participation, control, and self-efficacy; social interaction, socialization networks, and support; and trust, reciprocity, and social cohesion. However, some have argued that it is essential to ensure that the indicators of social capital are valid within the context of interest; for example, we need to take into account the disadvantage that young people living in socially deprived communities experience, the subcultural capital they may generate, and how this may impact on the social connections they make (Thornton 1996; Catts 2007).

Previous research by the second author of this chapter has illustrated how interconnecting and cumulative forms of social deprivation combined with adverse childhood experiences (ACEs) may leave some young people experiencing a distinct lack of positive, supportive social structures around them and even in some cases experiencing trauma (Deuchar 2009, 2013; Deuchar, McLean, and Holligan 2022). ACEs commonly refer to 10 specific abuse, neglect, and household dysfunction exposures, including physical and emotional neglect, domestic violence, household substance abuse, parental separation, and having family members with an incarceration history (Centers for Disease Control and Prevention 2004). Intense feelings of marginalization and powerlessness may emerge among those suffering from multiple ACEs and living against the backdrop of social deprivation. The general lack of opportunity to accrue the type of social capital that enhances psychological well-being may lead to a sense of helplessness, with little self-esteem and self-efficacy. Subsequently, this may lead to the presence of compensatory forms of social capital arising from gang culture (Deuchar 2009). Told in his own words, the case study of 28-year-old Alan (below, reproduced from Deuchar et al. 2022) illustrates the multiple forms of marginality that can lead some young men in Glasgow to initially engage in street gang membership and violence and subsequently experience a transitional journey from expressive to gang-related organized crime (McLean et al. 2019).

Case Study: Alan's Transition from Street Gang to Organized Crime

I was brought up with my mum and my sister in the family home [in Glasgow]. My father was serving life for murder, and he went inside when my mother was six and a half months pregnant so I never met him, he wasnae there, wasn't a figure in the family home . . . my mother was heroin addicted . . . a lot of violence in my family home. Domestic stuff, stepfathers and stuff to my sisters, my mother, and myself and obviously with the prevalence of heroin addiction in the family home, overdoses happening regularly so . . . chaotic really, from birth . . . from seven years of age, I was finding my mother overdosed behind the door convulsing. I actually knew what do in that situation—she had taught me that. But she had also taught me the code of silence, 'you don't tell anyone anything, what goes on in this house stays in this house. And if it does go anywhere else, you will suffer violence.'

When I was going to school I became aggressive, disruptive, violent. Because that was how I had been taught you deal with situations . . . obviously at that time [my housing scheme] was synonymous with territorialism . . . there were seven gangs in that area. I wouldn't have seen it as a gang at that time, I would have seen it as a group of individuals who accepted me. I actually felt safe when I was with them, because I was 9 or 10, and they were 16/17. I felt like—I suppose you could say I was always searchin' for a father figure in some shape or form. And that came with the gang figures. . . . At 14, I horrifically injured another gang member and that's what I was secured for—I went into secure care. I spent two years in there and then got secured again . . . I went from secure to Polmont [Young Offenders' Institution] because of the nature of the crime . . . [After my release] I wore it like a badge of honour . . . I had arrived and I had my own young team below us.

I never committed a crime in sobriety so it was always motivated through alcohol or drugs, always. Valium and alcohol were my mixture . . . I was movin' on to higher, stronger drugs and the stuff I was gettin' involved with was the distribution of drugs. When I was 18, I was approached by a crime family in Glasgow to do running for them. That came off the back of

the reputation I had carved out in the gang . . . I was approached off a member of this family and basically said, 'why are you runnin' about killing each other over nothin', when you could be dain' it for paper?' I said 'that makes sense,' and he gave me a mobile phone and said 'when this rings, go . . .when the mobile rang, I had to go to a destination, pick whatever it was up and was to take it to the other destination. So that's what I done all around the east end of Glasgow . . . I recruited members who were in a gang with me, they were distributin' drugs for me, I was distributin' for the other ones so it was a chain, man. And see the person at the top, they're the ones that are winning, see the ones at our level, we're the ones goin' to the jail, we're the ones that are goin' to get murdered, we're the ones doin' all the dirty work and at the center of this there's a wee boy who just wants his dad in all of this and sufferin' huge amounts of adversity . . .
Three years ago [at age 25], I was seriously assaulted. There was a certain quantity of drugs that were stolen from another family . . . just a group who were distributin' drugs, and a sim card. And the sim card came in contact with myself, and I took the sim card—the sim card was worth more than the drugs were because it was one of these sim cards that you put into a mobile phone and you had a run, because you had addicts constantly phoning it. So you were able to feed their habit and make lots of money. But little did I know that this sim card belonged to a very serious individual within Glasgow. And they told me, I got a phone call that night sayin' to me 'we want the sim card back, no' bothered about the drugs. We want the sim card back.' I told them to fuck off, because I've drugs in my system, I've got a family behind me, I feel like I'm invincible . . . I came home one night and there's a car parked right outside my door . . . a black Audi . . . walks into my path and four guys get out of the car and they stab me nine times . . . my son witnessed all that, seven years of age. I nearly died . . .
(Reproduced from Deuchar et al. 2022, 68–69)

Alan's story illustrates the links between ACEs and trauma and subsequent involvement in gang membership and recreational violence (Deuchar 2009; Fraser 2015; Deuchar et al. 2022). An absent father in combination with domestic violence and drug addiction within the family home and the sense of powerlessness from having no network to offer him emotional encouragement led Alan to seek out an alternative sense of social support and status through street gang membership. As a child, the streets of his housing scheme offered Alan opportunities to become submerged in social bonding with young men in their late teenage years who were immersed in territorial gang violence.

The ingroup identity (Putnam 2000; Leonard and Onyx 2004) became a vehicle for masculine identity expression for Alan, particularly because of his experience of father absence (Deuchar 2018; Deuchar et al. 2022). The street gang provided an alternative, compensating effect in the building of bonding social capital that was missing in Alan's family life and out of reach because of feelings of social marginalization and exclusion (Bassani 2007). However, these intense ingroup ties were complemented by the presence of territorial factionalism, with gang violence directed toward outside groups from other housing schemes (Deuchar 2009).

Building a reputation for violence was an essential expectation within the street gang context, and Alan quickly achieved this. This, combined with his rich knowledge of local street culture, his subsequent enhanced status emerging as a result of spending time in prison, and the right type of networking skills, enabled Alan to transition from being a local member of a young street gang to forming his own young crime gang, which was linked to an organized crime group (Densley, Deuchar, and Harding 2020; McLean 2019;

McLean et al. 2019; Deuchar et al. 2022). The imperative for publicly performing masculinity and defending physical turf in Alan's case gradually became replaced by more business orientations and the creation of entrepreneurial forms of social capital (McLean et al. 2019; Deuchar et al. 2022).

However, Alan's involvement in drug-related organized crime and the compensating forms of dense, multifunctional ties, obligations, and expectations also induced criminal norms that were ultimately accompanied by sanctions (Coleman 1988; Putnam 2000). It was this dark side of social capital that led to tragic violent consequences as Alan ultimately became a victim of gang-related retaliation, an incident that was witnessed by his son. The social capital that had emerged when Alan made the initial step into street gang culture had, somewhere along the line, developed into what could be described as "street capital," ultimately with traumatic consequences. It is to this concept of "street capital" that we now turn.

Street Capital

Street capital is the set of street skills, street knowledge, artifacts, and objects that retain intrinsic value within the economy of street culture (i.e., in social settings of poverty and deprivation where street socialization is normalized and deemed advantageous). As Harding (2014) demonstrates, the accumulation of these items act in concert with other factors to create, then sustain, formidable street reputations that, if they are nurtured, can potentially elevate one's position within the gang. Elevated hierarchal positions can bring the benefits of reducing vulnerability and risk while increasing proximity to information, power, and money.

Street capital theory (Sandberg and Pederson 2011; Harding 2014) is a highly practical concept that retains expansive explanatory utility in gang scholarship. It is instantly recognizable by practitioners working with underprivileged youth in urban street gangs, youth offending teams, and social housing environments, yet it is conceptually complex in its origin and theoretical construction. Below we examine how the concept of street capital dives deeper into the dark side of social capital while melding with social field theory (Bourdieu and Waquant 1992; Swartz 1997; Fligstein and McAdam 2015), concepts of habitus (Bourdieu 1977, 1984), and street code (Anderson 1999).

Social Field Theory

For Bourdieu (1977, 1993), modern society is best understood as a series of overlapping and interrelated social "fields," each relatively autonomous and ordered by its own principles, values, and rules. Social fields, such as education, organized religion, and politics, are locations where "social actors build relationships and act to produce, reproduce and transform their social domain" (Harding 2014, 45). This active network of relations occurs between those in different positions within the field:

> These positions are objectively defined, in their existence and in the determination they impose upon their occupants, agents, or institutions, by their present and potential (situs) in the structure of the distribution of species of power (or capital) whose possession commands

access to the specific profits that are at stake in the field, as well as by their objective relation to other positions. (Bourdieu and Wacquant 1992, 97)

Each field operates its own various versions of power, or capital, which then constructs "social space." The actors within this social space are then defined by their relative position of power within this social space (Bourdieu and Wacquant 1992, 229–230). Thus, a social field can be conceived of as a terrain of action where collective actors strive to advance (Bourdieu and Wacquant 1992). This is sometimes applied by corporate and organizational theorists to the corporate world of "sectors" (Scott and Meyer 1983; Fligstein and McAdam 2015) as "strategic action fields." The overarching aim of actors within a social field is to move beyond their initial allocation of resources (capital, education, parental background) to advance to "distinction" (Bourdieu 1984, 166).

Thus, in any social field, be it in the corporate world, the arts, politics, or even in an urban street gang, the dynamic interaction of relationships between actors is geared competitively toward the same goal or outcome: winning. The challenge for each actor is to learn, understand, and employ the rules of the game to achieve "distinction." Once they reach the top position, they can then set the rules for their own advantage. Martin (2003) establishes the social field as "fields of organized striving" where actors jostle for position and an elevated hierarchal position (20).

Each social field, be that academia, the Catholic church, the police service, or the urban street gang operates its own internal logic, which dominates behaviors and perceptions within the field. Outside of that field, this logic evaporates and has little meaning (e.g., the police ranking system or an academic grading system). The logic helps to generate the operative rules within that field but also provides reasoning for being involved in the specific field. Bourdieu believes that actors within a social field are engaged in constant conflict and struggle toward an agreed upon goal. To achieve this goal, they must employ different forms of strategic action while simultaneously abiding by the rules of their social field, which are bounded by class, power, and "the habitus."

Because social fields operate with internalized power structures, hierarchies, rules, and codes of behavior, it is possible to conceptualize the urban street gang as one form of social field. This social field has relational boundaries with other members of the community, law enforcement, wider society, and rival peer groups. As such it operates its own logic and rules of how to succeed—to rise within the gang hierarchy above one's peers using different forms of strategic action that are deemed suitable and credible within this social field. In the street gang, such strategic action might include violence or it might rely on skill, proven experience, or even charm.

Before looking at how strategic action is employed within an urban street gang, it is useful to examine the concept of habitus, which according to Bourdieu is an internalized learning and reproduction of social behaviors patterned from early social interactions with peers.

Habitus

Habitus is the embodied product of social and historical conditions that have been internalized both mentally and physically into ways of thinking, acting, and being—a form of unspoken mental muscle memory from cumulative factors such as background, upbringing, education, and parental and social influences arising from historical and social conditions. Bourdieu (1990) described it "as a system of durable transposable dispositions" (53–54) that operate subconsciously to govern actions, practice, and behaviors. In short, "early socialization of social conditions have been internalized into a series of mental and bodily dispositions that then govern our actions. Habitus leads actors to assess what actions are possible, or not possible, within their social conditions, or field" (Harding 2014, 47).

Building on past experience, personal provenance, history, tradition, learned behaviors, and ways of being, habitus operates as an internalized blueprint for action. This permits actors to use this blueprint to become "strategic improvisers" (Swartz 1997, 10) whilw at the same time establishing what is a credible course of action. This is sometimes described as having "a feel for the game" and a finely honed sense of what is coming next. Habitus then operates within the actor—both limiting their potential actions and also enabling them. It is a portable disposition that actors carry within them as it guides their actions.

How Street Capital Works

Within the above definitions, an urban street gang can be viewed as a social field in its own right, or as an identifiable arena of struggle (Bourdieu and Wacquant 1992). In areas of multiple deprivations, residents struggle competitively for scarce resources: power, money, advancement, and respect. Achieving distinction within such a community will bring greater opportunities to access these scarce resources and then enjoy them. To achieve success or "distinction," actors within social fields must develop and employ strategies of advancement, both individually and collectively, to improve their position in the social hierarchy. However, they are, as always, bounded by the rules of their social field and their habitus. As each social field is structured with its own hierarchy, actors must find ways to elevate themselves above their peers. Within a social field that is also a deprived community or impoverished neighborhood, the rules of the game might permit forms of illegal behavior, or enterprise, as appropriate strategic actions (Anderson 1999; Miller 1958), like receiving or buying stolen goods. Within the social field of an urban street gang, violence is an acceptable form of strategic action and its skilled usage and deployment will elevate an actor above his peers (Densley 2012b). If physical violence is employed as a strategic action, one identifiable goal or outcome is the creation of a feared reputation and status, even if this is notoriety. In certain neighborhoods or communities, this provides an advantage above other peers and will, over time, elevate an individual to a position where they are avoided if not feared by others.

All social fields have hierarchies, governing rules, and codes of behavior, recognized (if not wholly accepted) by those in the social field. In religion, academia, or the corporate world, formal measurements exist to interpret the volume of capital one has accumulated (e.g., academic qualifications, or the officer rank within the police service). However, such accolades are meaningless within the social field of the street gang. Within the street gang, the form of knowledge that is lauded, validated, and highly prized is street knowledge and street skill, for example, knowing how to exit an estate/project during a police raid; knowing how to sell stolen goods, and to whom; knowing how to access drugs or an illegal firearm; knowing where to stab someone on the body; knowing how to grow cannabis and evade detection. Such street knowledge becomes the essential capital operating within gangs—"street capital" (Harding 2014). While "knowing" generates street capital, "doing" crystallizes it. Its fleeting temporal nature begets an imperative to earn it, keep it, and guard it—lest it vanishes. In turn, this simple economic dynamic instills hypervigilance on gang members who guard their fluctuating account of street capital. If it diminishes, they fall prey to others seeking to advance their street capital. Over time, elevated street capital can be converted to hard cash.

This form of capital has little logical value outside the social field of a street gang, but it operates highly effectively within the gang social field, with some elements also valued in the social field of the wider community or neighborhood as a generator of economic capital. In the social field of the urban street gang, street capital then operates as the premium capital and underpins the de facto economy of the gang. It can be allocated to others as a form of respect and reputational enhancement; it can be won quickly by evading the police or successfully beating down a rival—or lost quickly when disrespected or losing a fight. It can be acquired through personal experience or by close association with anyone with a fearsome reputation for violence. Within the gang social field, it circulates widely, sustaining all actors who carefully monitor their own stock and that of others; its accumulation acts as an arc of provenance, a measurement of belonging, and a scalable account of habitus and a demonstration of gang embeddedness.

Senior gang members can generate street capital when sharing "war stories" with their youngers or when teaching them how to roll a joint or cut drugs. Junior gang members will acquire street capital by employing such techniques effectively or for profit, or when backing up their friends in a fight. Street capital is, however, capricious. Once acquired it must be maintained. It cannot be permitted to be lost or to dwindle. Diminished street capital, or the perception of it dwindling, will leave an actor open to accusations they are "falling" or "have lost it" or that they have become "moist" (weak) or not committed to the street gang and its rules and values. Such perceptions render an individual highly vulnerable. International research has illustrated this to be the case in both American and wider European contexts beyond the UK (Deuchar 2018).

Street capital, therefore, operates with an imperative for constant accumulation and vigilant monitoring of one's own personal account of street capital. All "actors," or in this case gang members, must remain hypervigilant for any disrespect or slight fall in status that might leave them susceptible to ridicule or imply they are untrustworthy. Thus, gossip can be damaging as it acts to diminish or devalue street capital. Any slight perception of disrespect is met with violence as only a violent reaction will restore the balance of street capital. Forms of ultra-violence, such as throwing acid or attacking someone with a pit bull dog, will generate excess quantities of street capital. If violent retribution is carefully planned or executed in front of other gang members or in plain sight of "civils" (civilians), then street capital will rocket, allowing such actions to be venerated and entered into gang mythology.

Examples of Street Capital

The imperative to manufacture, maximize, then monitor personal accounts of street capital leads gang members to strategize continually to improve their hierarchical position within the gang (see Densley 2012a). Younger gang members will do this by employing expressive strategic actions to generate street capital. This might include doing ride-outs into rival territory or by patrolling their "turf" to "defend" their territory from rival incursions (Densley 2013). Older gang members might engage in more instrumental forms of street capital accumulation by employing strategies of drug dealing (Harding 2020) or street robbery (Harding et al. 2019; McLean and Densley 2022).

Lately, street gang members might operate actively on social media or they might seek to write, perform, and produce drill music (Densley 2020; Lauger and Densley 2018; Storrod and Densley 2017; Stuart 2020). In this subgenre of hip hop/grime, street gangs rap about their gang versus rival gangs, often using forms of expression that reflect their lived experience, which can be relentlessly violent and aggressive. Drill music is then performed, filmed, then posted on social media for wider viewing and comment. Often such videos are considered provocative, and some can generate violence through retaliation and perceived disrespect.

The performance of drill music acts as a form of social bonding while permitting key individuals to elevate their status and generate street capital. When such performances are posted on social media, further street capital is generated. Drill videos also generate additional street capital as performative illustrations of gang loyalty and gang commitment (see Densley 2020). Active discussion on social media will ensure street capital is then conferred on the street gang from those far beyond the immediate gang turf. In this way, social media becomes a new performative space for gang activity (e.g., Lauger and Densley 2018; Stuart 2020).

Utility of Street Capital Theory within Gang Scholarship

Within gang scholarship, street capital theory (Sandberg and Pederson 2011; Harding 2014) is quickly developing an explanatory utility that often frustrates or evades other theories. It permits insight and explanation to be offered for new phenomena such as moped crime or acid attacks occurring in London while easily embracing longer-term positional changes and behaviors arising within street gangs. Moreover, it offers an explanatory utility of the street gang social field that transcends regional interpretations as the concept can be universally applied in street gangs from the United Kingdom to the United States. Presently in UK street gangs, one prominent new development is the alarming rise in drug supply networks operating from metropolitan centers out to rural, provincial, or seaside locations—known as "county lines" (McLean, Robinson and Densley 2020). According to the National Crime Agency (2019), approximately 2,000 such drug lines operate across the UK in this way, with an allegedly limitless stream of youngsters ready to "jump on" a line to make money dealing drugs in such locations (Harding 2020).

Street capital theory has sufficient explanatory utility to address both drill music and UK "county lines" as opportunities for strategic action to generate street capital. For many gang-affiliated young people, the visible and credible nature of the street capital generated by performing drill music or working on county lines is now such that both actions are perceived as the most viable route to demonstrate street "authenticity" (see Lauger 2012) within the social field of the street gang. In a social media environment that elevates fakery, or makes it harder to distinguish fakery, to be seen as "genuine" is a peerless evocation of street capital.

Conclusion

In this chapter, we have established that the emergence of social capital and street capital theory is a useful and credible means of enriching our understanding of the internal mechanics of the urban street gang. By revealing internal dynamics and the motivations driving hierarchical advancement, it offers a useful grammar through which to understand the imperatives for hypervigilance to monitor disrespect, the performance of group violence played out in a public domain, and inventive forms of ultra-violence now so characteristic of twenty-first-century gangbanging.

As we have outlined, social capital is generally viewed as having reciprocity and networking at its heart. As Ouellet et al. (2018) highlight, the survival of a street gang over time is often dependent on not only its internal social cohesion but also its embeddedness in the wider gang structure. Those suffering intense marginalization, ACEs, and trauma may come to value the intense ingroup identity associated with urban street gangs, and the violence that acts as a vehicle for building masculine identity may in some cases develop into the emergence of "street capital." The latter is strongly associated with the dark side of social capital, whereby skills and knowledge emerge that hold intrinsic value within street economies. Such street skills and knowledge bring opportunities for acquiring the otherwise scarce commodity of capital. The street gang offers the prime location for the acquisition of this street capital, creating a unique gang "social field" where peers jostle and compete for elevated positions. Strategies of advancement help gang members climb the gang hierarchical ladder to ultimately achieve "distinction." According to street capital theory, these advancement strategies include the imperative to gain, build, and demonstrate street skill and knowledge as premium capital. Constant replenishment of street capital not only drives internal gang members' motivations but also acts as a temporal prophylactic against potential vulnerability and victimhood.

These theories added new depth to gang scholarship, providing helpful insights into how gang members survive and thrive by generating, trading, and maintaining levels of status and distinction (Harding 2014; Deuchar et al. 2022). If they are astute enough, the compensatory forms of social capital that young men acquire within the gang will yield the acquisition of street capital and—ultimately—the distinction they seek. It is this strong drive toward achieving distinction that often drives their participation in forms of ultra-violence and criminality. Drawing on these insights, social capital and street capital theory contribute to policy and practice frameworks for early intervention but also for determining gang embeddedness, gang behaviors, and in preventing escalating forms of criminality that go with them.

Drawing on a UK perspective, by all accounts the years before and after the global pandemic were a watershed period for serious violence and organized crime in several parts of England and Wales (Densley et al. 2020; Deuchar et al. 2022). A perfect storm of austerity, Brexit, and economic stagnation brought a reduction in accessible opportunities for young people—making the street gang more attractive for those mired in poverty and marginality. Correspondingly, following a decade of declines, homicide rates and reported instances of knife/gun crime had begun to rise again in 2014 and in 2018/19 reached their highest point for over a decade, with reported increases across all police force areas in England and Wales (HM Government 2018). Additionally, these increases were accompanied by a shift toward younger victims/perpetrators and an increase in more extreme forms of violence and criminality, including (as we have discussed in this chapter) acid attacks (Grasso 2017), child criminal exploitation through "county lines" (Robinson, McLean, and Densley 2019; Harding 2020), moped crime (Shaw 2017), as well as the rapidly increasing presence of drill rap music celebrating violent crime on the social media sites of gang members (Densley 2020; Irwin-Rogers, Densley, and Pinkney 2018; Pinkney and Robinson-Edwards 2018). In Scotland, there have also been increasing reports of urban gang violence after many years of decline, and evidence that a skeletal form of the county lines practice, known to dominate areas in and around London and other large English cities, is also present (Densley, McLean, and Brick 2023; Holligan, McLean, and McHugh 2020; Deuchar et al. 2022).

A deeper understanding of the motivations for the resurgence in gang violence as well as the emergence of these more extreme forms of violent and economic crimes could help to enrich the emergence of an evidence-based, public health policing approach to reduce these issues (Deuchar 2013; Deuchar et al. 2022). In simple terms, a "public health" approach involves developing insights into the deep-rooted causes of violence and criminality, drawing on smart use of data and working across organizational boundaries (Catch 22, 2019). The approach was set out by the World Health Organization (WHO), a specialized agency of the United Nations responsible for promoting international health and well-being, in 2002 in its *World Report on Violence and Health* (Conaglen and Gallimore 2014). It was pioneered by the Scottish Violence Reduction Unit from 2005 onward and subsequently became embedded within HM Government's (2018) *Serious Violence Strategy*, published in April 2018, which argued that "tackling serious violence is not a law enforcement issue alone [but] requires a multiple strand approach involving a range of partners across different sectors" (9).

One important public health approach to conceptualizing risk factors for violence and criminality is the "highly influential" adverse childhood experiences (ACEs) study, which was undertaken in partnership with the Centers for Disease Prevention and Control in the United States (Batchelor, Armstrong, and MacLellan 2019, 14). Wolff et al. (2020) draw attention to the fact that many of the risk factors identified in previous gang research are related to ACEs, although not always described using that terminology (see also Deuchar et al. 2022). The public health approach emphasizes the importance of "implementing interventions that address ... social determinants" such as ACEs (Williams et al. 2014, 689), drawing on multi-agency collaboration (Deuchar et al. 2022).

As gang scholars, we believe that law enforcement and social care agencies would be well advised to draw on the concepts of social capital and street capital to gain a richer understanding of what lies behind gang performativity among disadvantaged young men and, in particular, what motivates their participation in crime and violence. By linking these conceptual insights to the research evidence around ACEs and trauma, public health approaches and initiatives could become more enriched through adopting a focus on addressing root causes and providing disadvantaged, gang-involved young men with alternative ways of acquiring "distinction" (Harding 2014; Deuchar 2018). It is hoped that this chapter may go some way toward stimulating this depth of insight among policymakers, service managers, and providers in the United Kingdom and beyond.

References

Anderson, Elijah. 1999. *The Code of the Street*. New York: WW Norton.

Applied Educational Research Scheme (AERS). 2004. *Social Capital Project Task Group Report on Project 1: Defining and Measuring Social Capital*. Edingurgh, UK: University of Stirling.

Baron, Stephen, John Field, and Tom Schuller, eds. 2000. *Social Capital: Critical Perspectives*. Oxford, UK: Oxford University Press.

Bassani, Cheryllynn. 2007. "Five Dimensions of Social Capital as They Pertain to Youth Studies." *Journal of Youth Studies* 10 (1): 17–34.

Batchelor, Susan, Sarah Armstrong, and Donna MacLellan. 2019. *Taking Stock of Violence in Scotland*. Glasgow: SCCJR.

Bouchard, Martin, Wei Wang, and Eric Beauregard. 2012. "Social Capital, Opportunity, and School-Based Victimization." *Violence and Victims* 27 (5): 656–673.

Bourdieu, Pierre. 1972. *Esquisse d'une Theorie de la Pratique. Precedee de Trois tudes d'ethnologie Kabyle*. Geneve: Droz.

Bourdieu, Pierre. 1977. *Outline of a Theory of Practice*. Cambridge: Cambridge University Press.

Bourdieu, Pierre. 1983. "The Forms of Capital." In *Soziale Ungleichheiten (Soziale Welt, Sonderheft 2)*, edited by Kreckel Reinhard. Goettingen: Otto Schartz and Co.

Bourdieu, Pierre. 1984. *Distinction: A Social Critique of the Judgement of Taste*, translated by Richard Nice. Cambridge, MA: Harvard University Press.

Bourdieu, Pierre. 1990. *The Logic of Practice*. Stanford, CA: Stanford University Press.

Bourdieu, Pierre. 2018. "The Forms of Capital." *The Sociology of Economic Life*: 78–92. Routledge.

Bourdieu, Pierre, and Loic J. D. Wacquant. 1992. *An Invitation to Reflexive Sociology*. Chicago, IL: University of Chicago Press.

Catch 22. 2019. *Tackling Crime Together: A Public Health Approach*. London: Catch 22.

Catts, Ralph. 2007. "Quantitative Indicators of Social Capital Measurement." In *Social Capital, Lifelong Learning and the Management of Place*, edited by M. Osborne, K. Sankey and B. Wilson, 31–44. London: Routledge.

Centers for Disease Control and Prevention. 2004. *Injury Prevention and Control: Adverse Childhood Experiences (ACE) Study*. https://www.cdc.gov/violenceprevention/aces/index.html.

Conaglen, Phillip, and Annette Gallimore. 2014. *Violence Prevention: A Public Health Priority*. Glasgow: ScotPHN.

Coleman, James S. 1988. "Social Capital and the Creation of Human Capital." *American Journal of Sociology* 94: S95–S120.

Coleman, James S. 1990. *The Foundations of Social Theory*. Cambridge, MA: Harvard University Press.

Densley, James A. 2012a. "The Organisation of London's Street Gangs." *Global Crime* 13 (1): 42–64.

Densley, James A. 2012b. "Street Gang Recruitment: Signaling, Screening, and Selection." *Social Problems* 59 (3): 301–321.

Densley, James A. 2013. *How Gangs Work: An Ethnography of Youth Violence*. New York: Palgrave Macmillan.

Densley, James A. 2020. "Collective Violence Online: When Street Gangs Use Social Media." In *The Handbook of Collective Violence: Current Developments and Understanding*, edited by Carol A. Ireland, Michael Lewis, Anthony Lopez, and Jane L. Ireland, 305–316. London: Routledge.

Densley, James, Robert McLean, and Carlton Brick. 2023. *Contesting County Lines: Case Studies in Drug Crime and Deviant Entrepreneurship.* Bristol: Bristol University Press.

Densley, James A., Ross Deuchar, and Simon Harding. 2020. "Introduction to the Special Issue on Gangs and Serious Youth Violence in the UK." *Youth Justice,* 20 (1-2): 3-10.

Deuchar, Ross. 2009. *Gangs, Social Capital and Marginalised Youth.* Stoke on Trent, UK: Trentham.

Deuchar, Ross. 2013. *Policing Youth Violence: Transatlantic Connections,* London: IOE Press.

Deuchar, Ross. 2018. *Gangs and Spirituality: Global Perspectives.* Cham, Switzerland: Palgrave MacMillan.

Deuchar, Ross, Robert McLean, and Chris Holligan. 2022. *Gangs, Drugs and Youth Adversity; Continuity and Change.* Bristol, UK: Bristol University Press.

Field, John. 2003. *Social Capital.* New York: Routledge.

Fligstein, Neil, and Doug McAdam. 2015. *A Theory Fields.* Oxford, UK: Oxford University Press.

Fraser, A. 2015. *Urban Legends.* Oxford, UK: Oxford University Press.

Grasso, Stéphane. 2017. "Acid Attacks Leave More than Physical Scars—and They're on the Rise in Britain." *CBC News.* https://www.cbc.ca/news/world/uk-acid-attacks-spread-beyond-gangs-1.4207502.

Harding, Simon. 2014. *The Street Casino: Survival in Violent Street Gangs.* Bristol, UK: Policy Press.

Harding, Simon. 2020. *County Lines: Exploitation and Drug Dealing amongst Urban Street Gangs.* Bristol, UK: Bristol University Press.

Harding, Simon, Ross Deuchar, James Densley, and Robert McLean. 2019. "A Typology of Street Robbery and Gang Organization: Insights from Qualitative Research in Scotland." *British Journal of Criminology,* 59 (4): 879-897.

Hanifan, L. J. 1916. "The Rural School Community Center." *Annals of the American Academy of Political and Social Science* 67 (1): 130-138.

HM Government. 2018. *Serious Violence Strategy.* https://www.gov.uk/government/publications/serious-violence-strategy.

Holligan, Chris, Robert McLean, and Richard McHugh. 2020. "Exploring County Lines: Criminal Drug Distribution Practices in Scotland." *Youth Justice,* 20 (1-2): 50-63.

Irwin-Rogers, Keir, James A. Densley, and Craig Pinkney. 2018. "Gang Violence and Social Media." In *The Routledge International Handbook of Human Aggression,* edited by Jane L. Ireland, Phillip Birch, and Carol A. Ireland, 400-410. New York: Routledge.

Lauger, Timothy R. 2012. *Real Gangstas: Legitimacy, Reputation, and Violence in the Intergang Environment.* New Brunswick, NJ: Rutgers University Press.

Lauger, Timothy R., and James A. Densley. 2018. "Broadcasting Badness: Violence, Identity, and Performance in the Online Gang Rap Scene." *Justice Quarterly* 35 (5): 816-841.

Leonard, Rosemary, and Jenny Onyx. 2004. *Social Capital and Community Building: Spinning Straw into Gold.* London: Janus Publishing Company.

Martin, John L. 2003. "What Is Field Theory?" *American Journal of Sociology* 109 (1): 1-49.

Meyer, John, and W. Richard Scott. 1983. *Organizational Environments: Ritual and Rationality.* London: Sage.

McCarthy, Bill, and John Hagan. 1995. "Getting into Street Crime: The Structure and Process of Criminal Embeddedness." *Social Science Research* 24 (1): 63-95.

McCarthy, Bill, John Hagan, and Lawrence E. Cohen. 1998. "Uncertainty, Cooperation, and Crime: Understanding the Decision to Co-Offend." *Social forces* 77 (1): 155-184.

McLean, Robert. 2019. *Gangs, Drugs and (Dis)Organised Crime*. Bristol, UK: Bristol University Press.

McLean, Robert, and James A Densley. 2022. *Robbery in the Illegal Drugs Trade: Violence and Vengeance*. Bristol, UK: Bristol University Press.

McLean, Robert, Ross Deuchar, Simon Harding, and James A. Densley. 2019. "Putting the 'Street' in Gang: Place and Space in the Organisation of Scotland's Drug Selling Gangs." *British Journal of Criminology* 59 (2): 396–415.

McLean, Robert, Grace Robinson, and James A. Densley. 2020. *County Lines: Criminal Networks and Evolving Drug Markets in Britain*. Cham, Switzerland: Springer.

Miller, Walter B. 1958. "Lower Class Culture as a Generating Milieu of Gang Delinquency." *Journal of Social Issues* 14 (3): 5–19.

National Crime Agency. 2019. *National Intelligence Assessment. County Lines, Drug Supply, Vulnerability and Harm*. London: Author.

Nguyen, Holly, and Martin Bouchard. 2013. "Need, Connections, or Competence? Criminal Achievement among Adolescent Offenders." *Justice Quarterly* 30 (1): 44–83.

Ouellet, Marie, Martin Bouchard, and Yanick Charette. 2018. "One Gang Dies, Another Gains? The Network Dynamics of Criminal Group Persistence." *Criminology* 57 (1): 5–33.

Pinkerton, John, and Pat Dolan. 2007. "Family Support, Social Capital, Resilience and Adolescent Coping." *Child and Family Social Work* 12: 219–228.

Pinkney, Craig, and Shona Robinson-Edwards. 2018. "Gangs, Music and the Mediatisation of Crime: Expressions, Violations and Validations." *Safer Communities* 17 (2): 103–118Putnam, Robert. 2000. *Bowling Alone: The Collapse and Revival of American Community*. New York: Simon and Schuster.

Richardson, John. 1986. *Handbook of Theory and Research for the Sociology of Education*. Westport, CT: Greenwood.

Robinson, Grace, Robert McLean, and James Densley. 2019. "Working County Lines: Child Criminal Exploitation and Illicit Drug Dealing in Glasgow and Merseyside." *International Journal of Offender Therapy and Comparative Criminology* 63 (5): 694–711.

Ruston, Dave. 2002. *Social Capital: Matrix of Surveys*. London: Office of National Statistics, Social Analysis and Reporting Division.

Sandberg, Sveinung, and Willy Pederson. 2011. *Street Capital: Black Cannabis Dealers in a White Welfare State*. Bristol, UK: Policy Press.

Scott, J. and Meyer, J. 1983. "The Organisation of Societal Sectors." In J. Meyer and W.R. Scott (eds) *Organizational Environments: Ritual and Nationality*, 129–153. Beverly Hills, CA: Sage Publications.

Shaw, Danny. 2017. "The Moped and Scooter Crime Wave That Has Swept London." *BBC News*. https://www.bbc.co.uk/news/uk-40731485.

Storrod, Michelle L., and James A. Densley. 2017. "'Going Viral' and 'Going Country': The Expressive and Instrumental Activities of Street Gangs on Social Media." *Journal of Youth Studies* 20 (6): 677–696.

Stuart, Forrest. 2020. *Ballad of the Bullet: Gangs, Drill Music, and the Power of Online Infamy*. Princeton, NJ: Princeton University Press.

Swartz. David. 1997. *Culture and Power: The Sociology of Pierre Bourdieu*. Chicago, IL: University of Chicago Press.

Terrion, Jenepher. L., and Anna Hogrebe. 2007. "A Canadian Experience with an Intervention Programme for Vulnerable Families: Lessons for German Social Work and Policy." *European Journal of Social Work*, 10 (3): 401–416.

Thornton, Sarah. 1996. *Club Cultures: Music, Media, and Subcultural Capital.* Cambridge, UK: Polity.

Western, John, Robert Stimson, Scott Baum, and Yolanda Van Gellecum. 2005. "Measuring Community Strength and Social Capital." *Regional Studies* 39 (8): 1095–1109.

Williams, Damien, J. Dorothy Currie, Will Linden, and Peter D. Donelly. 2014. "Addressing Gang Related Violence in Glasgow: A Preliminary Pragmatic Quasi-Experimental Evaluation of the Community Initiative to Reduce Violence (CIRV)." *Aggression and Violent Behavior* 19 (6): 686–691.

Wolff, Kevin. T., Michael T. Baglivio, Hannah J. Klein, Alex R. Piquero, Matt DeLisi, and James C. (Buddy) Howell. 2020. "Adverse Childhood Experiences (ACEs) and Gang Involvement among Juvenile Offenders: Assessing the Mediation Effects of Substance Use and Temperament Deficits." *Youth Violence and Juvenile Justice* 18 (1): 24–53.

Woolcock, Michael. 2010. "The Rise and Routinization of Social Capital, 1988–2008." *Annual Review of Political Science* 13: 469–487.

Wright, John Paul, Francis T. Cullen, and Jeremy T. Miller. 2001. "Family Social Capital and Delinquent Involvement." *Journal of Criminal Justice* 29 (1): 1–9.

CHAPTER 26

ON GANGS AND FAMILY
Primary, Secondary, and Surrogate Family

GABRIEL T CESAR, D'ANDRE WALKER, AND TIFFANY FERNANDEZ

FAMILY plays important and multifaceted roles in the gang, but research rarely explores the link directly (Decker, Pyrooz, and Densley 2022, 256). When family is considered in the context of gangs it is commonly presented as a risk factor for gang involvement tied to the failure of neoliberal political and economic structures to support families via employment, education, and social services. This approach has allowed for the consideration of structural factors in the lives of gang-involved youth, particularly those from inner-city and other marginalized urban and suburban contexts. Roughly summarized, the traditional "family as risk factor" model of gang membership suggests that youth from troubled or marginalized families are pushed toward gangs to fill needs unmet by the family unit such as supportive networks, camaraderie, and protection. The downside to this model is that the gang then further marginalizes and endangers members instead of helping them. Still, gang membership may provide moral, if not functional, support (Melde, Taylor, and Esbensen 2009).

The failure to examine more directly the links between gang membership and family is an important oversight, because over and above the risks associated with coming from a troubled family of origin, gang membership represents an additional risk factor for youth development that can have negative repercussions across the life course. Youth in gangs are at increased risk for violent and sexual victimization, arrest, prosecution, and incarceration (Walker and Cesar 2020). Gang membership also strains school performance, employment prospects, relationships, and parenthood (Moule, Decker, and Pyrooz 2013; Augustyn, Thornberry, and Krohn 2014). As gang-involved youth become adults and start their own families, the risk factors and negative consequences associated with gang membership can be transmitted intergenerationally (Young, Fitgibbon, and Silverstone 2014, 180; Keels 2022). "Family" is not just the place a gang member comes from. "Family" is also where they are headed.[1] In other words, gang membership has important temporal and familial implications.

Gang membership is highly temporal because certain life stages are more prone to joining, persisting, and leaving (or retracting from) gangs. Joining during adolescence and leaving (to some extent) during early or mid-adulthood are common pathways into and away from gangs. The life-course perspective in criminology addresses this temporality by focusing on trajectories (e.g., being born into a troubled home), transitions (i.e., maturation and role change), and turning points (transitions that alter trajectories). At the same time, gang membership is familial in the sense that the gang often fills gaps left by troubled homes of origin and colors members' transitions from childhood to parenthood. Attachment theory seeks to identify how children are taught to connect with and rely on (i.e., attach to) their parents, and how those "attachment styles" influence interactions with others later in life. In this framework, consistent discipline and support lead to healthy attachment styles and relationships, while inconsistent or neglectful parenting lead to unhealthy attachment styles and relationships.

Generations of gang research has demonstrated that socioeconomically marginalized or otherwise troubled primary families (i.e., families of origin) tend to push youth toward gangs. More recent research suggests that later in life, secondary families (i.e., created families) tend to pull young adults away from gangs (Leverso and Hess 2021; Pyrooz, McGloin, and Decker 2017). How the gang functions as a replacement source of attachment (e.g., surrogate family) remains a largely overlooked area of inquiry (Vigil 1988). While gangs are often characterized as a negative source of attachment, both gangs and families could have both negative and positive effects on youth development. Having no support network at all may be more destructive than the risk that comes with gang membership, particularly in hypermasculine or violent social contexts. In this chapter we push the discussion of gangs and families forward by integrating the life-course perspective of gang involvement with attachment theory to generate a more functional, inclusive framework through which to analyze family and gang membership as linked group processes.

The Family, the Gang, and Attachment Theory

Family as Institution

In his foundational work on gangs, Scott Decker framed gang members within four social institutions: schools, the criminal processing system, the employment market, and community groups (Decker and Van Winkle 1996). That work also suggested family as an important social institution relevant to gangs and gang members, a framework that still resonates with the next generation of gang scholars (Decker et al. 2022). The inclusion of family alongside those other four institutions allows for an analysis of gang members through what social workers refer to as a "person-in-environment perspective" or ecological framework that considers the whole environment in which gang members are born and develop (Pardeck 1988). The ecological approach has several implications for contemporary gang research. In addition to integrating the cumulative effects of institutions, the ecological approach allows for the consideration of other factors such as adverse childhood experiences (ACEs), direct and indirect trauma, and healthy family development (Keels 2022; Wolff et al. 2020).

Young et al. (2014) note that consideration of family as central to the process of gang membership dates to the seminal work of Thrasher (1927) almost a century ago. Still, even in situations where youth are at high risk of delinquency, the prospect of gang membership is not universal or guaranteed (see Thornberry et al. 2018). Young et al.'s (2014) literature review therefore suggests "that the evidence that connects the family to 'gang' membership is far from conclusive" and therefore "argues that the aetiology of gang membership cannot simply be reduced to poor home environments or 'broken' families'" (171). Decker and Van Winkle's (1996) inclusion of the institution of family in an ecological framework for understanding gangs and gang members therefore proves prescient. Gang membership does not happen in a vacuum, nor at one distinct moment. Gang membership is a social process, involving the interaction of ever-evolving individuals and institutions *over time*. In other words, gang membership is best considered as a life-course trajectory.

The Gang as Turning Point (and Trajectory)

The life-course perspective is useful in understanding the gang for two key reasons. First, beyond the many risk factors that lead to the initiation of gang membership, involvement with gangs is associated with subsequent risk factors that extend across the life course (Krohn et al. 2011; Moule et al. 2013). These risk factors include heightened risk of violent and drug-related offending (Pyrooz et al. 2016) as well as incarceration for such crimes, even relative to similarly charged but non-gang-affiliated peers (Walker and Cesar 2020). Life in the gang is also associated with a heightened risk for violent victimization (Taylor et al. 2007) and importantly child maltreatment as parents (Augustyn et al. 2014). Initiation of gang membership is associated with marked increases in criminality, even after transitioning out and rejoining (Augustyn and McGloin 2021). In life-course terms, joining a gang constitutes a negatively valenced turning point (Melde and Esbensen 2011) or "snare" for future negative outcomes (Moffitt and Caspi 2001; Pyrooz 2014).

Second, gang membership and the associated outcomes are strongly age graded. The most common age for joining gangs is the early to mid-teens (Densley 2015), while a much smaller proportion join as adults (Pyrooz 2014). Over time, the turning points and transitions that come with continued gang membership develop into a trajectory characterized by increased risk for violent victimization and traumatic loss (Dierkhising, Sánchez, and Gutierrez 2021) and reduced social capital (Moule et al. 2013). At the same time, members grow older, differentially mature, and their perceptions of the gang, the family, and their roles in those and other institutions evolve over time (Decker, Pyrooz, and Moule 2014; Leverso and Matsueda 2019). Given the ecological contexts that contribute to gang membership and the development of humans over time, it makes sense for contemporary gang researchers to look beyond traditional frameworks that position the gang simply as a monolithic risk factor (Brotherton and Kontos 2022). Attachment theory offers a nuanced opportunity to do just that.

The Gang as Source of Attachment

Despite a general lack of research that directly examines the link between family and the gang, the idea that individuals join gangs to offset the lack of support they receive at home is an enduring theme in gang research (Vigil 1988; Deuchar 2018). In other words, kids from troubled families are more likely to use gangs as a "surrogate" family (Ruble and Turner 2000). Sharkey et al. (2011) attribute this process to the "protective influences" of gangs. Specifically, that literature review identified five basic categories of basic human needs identified by gang members in previous research: physiological, safety, love, esteem, and self-actualization (Sharkey et al. 2011, 49). The authors then used criminological theories to explain how gangs could fulfill those if conventional sources failed to do so. Their work suggests that gangs can provide for physiological and safety needs through collectivity, particularly for youth experiencing familial abuse or neglect. Similarly, the collective nature and group process of gang membership provides opportunities for love and belonging, esteem and status, and self-actualization and independence.

Ruble and Turner (2000) argued that the role of the gang should be analyzed through a lens that emphasizes gangs as differentially organized systems, much like family systems. Like families, some gangs are relatively organized, while most are far less so (Decker and Pyrooz 2015). Additionally, joining a gang reduces self-reported fear of victimization, even as objective risk for violence increases (Melde et al. 2009). This suggests that the gang offers at least a subjective sense of safety, regardless of whether they can produce objective structure and protection. Such emotional support may seem inconsequential to an outsider, but to a youth from an abusive, neglectful, or under-resourced family, providing emotional support could be quite effective at fostering loyalty and attachment. Ruble and Turner (2000) note that "many gang members report that they are willing to die or kill for their gangs, expressing their ultimate love and loyalty to their gang family" (120). Professions of loyalty like this are hard to rectify with the image of the gang as a harmful and dangerous risk factor.[2]

It is possible that such professions stem not just from an indoctrinated mythology of gang life, but out of an enduring sense of attachment to a group that they perceive to have provided them with key human needs not supplied by their families of origin. Attachment theory is therefore useful as a theoretical framework to analyze the complex relationship between the family and the gang. Attachment theory focuses on the relationships between a child and their primary caregivers, starting at birth, and then branching out to other individuals, groups, and institutions (Bowlby 1988). In this framework, attachment styles can take three primary forms: secure, insecure, and disorganized.[3] *Secure attachment styles* form when caregivers effectively and consistently provide a safe environment where the child can experience their own world independently, secure in the knowledge that their caregiver is present in case they are needed. Secure attachment styles foster lifelong skills and perceptions that help facilitate connection with others who can support, protect, and nourish a person mentally, emotionally, and physically.

Insecure attachment styles form when the primary caregivers provide inconsistent or ineffective support to a child. In this scenario, the child comes to understand that seeking support or assistance is often (or always) met with rejection, refusal, or inability to help. In contrast to secure attachment styles, insecurely attached people are more likely to internalize their challenges and shy away from help-seeking or community-building behaviors. This approach places them at risk of isolation, ineffectiveness, and failure across life-course domains.

Disorganized attachment styles are characterized by primary caregivers who are overtly abusive or neglectful. In contrast to insecure attachment style, which leads to internalizing behaviors, disorganized attachment style leads to externalizing behaviors (Murphy et al. 2014). Insecure and disorganized styles can be improved through therapeutic programming, but the nature of those styles complicates the process, making people reluctant to trust supporters or clinicians, or even oppositional to treatment or attempts at improvement (Levy et al. 2011).

De Vito (2020) used attachment theory to guide an analysis of the impact of family on the decision to join (and later exit) a gang. The study analyzed semi-structured interviews with 14 former street gang members between the ages of 19 and 56. Four prominent themes were identified: *lack of family consistency, gang as replacement family, "no other option,"* and *making the decision to disengage*. In terms of family consistency, De Vito (2020) noted that every participant reported a "lack of secure, consistent primary care givers/attachment figures during childhood" (759). Respondents discussed having parents who had died, were incarcerated, suffered from substance abuse, or were simply overworked and under-resourced as a single parent. In such cases, even the basic physiological needs discussed by Sharkey et al. (2011) may go partially or completely unmet, along with the emotional needs such as love, belonging, and self-actualization. Families characterized by these deficits may intentionally or unintentionally push children to find ways to meet those needs outside the home.

The second theme identified by De Vito (2020), "gang as replacement family," refers to the consequences of an inconsistent attachment figure. Almost every respondent expressed that they considered their gang to be their family, which is a common feature of gang research. Respondents expressed that their fellow gang members provided "protection, unity, and love to one another" (761). The brotherhood, sisterhood, and unity discussed here were born of shared trauma and loss associated with gang violence, as well as trauma and loss associated with growing up in an unloving or under-resourced home. Another origin for the idea of the gang as replacement family was that the gang provided a sense of belonging and validation. Love and affection, esteem from peers and elders, and the ability to self-actualize through self-expression and agency are key components of youth development. The family is not the only possible resource to facilitate those needs. School, church, or community groups may fill the gap, assuming they are available.

The problem is that those institutions are often struggling or failing right alongside the family in troubled or marginalized communities. This is reflected in the third theme from De Vito's (2020) interviews, where respondents discussed having no other options. These narratives were fatalistic and attributed their decision to join a gang as preordained by fate or destiny for people from backgrounds like theirs. Respondents had a similarly fatalistic view of their prospects after joining the gang, which led to De Vito's (2020) fourth theme "death, jail, or a turnaround" (764). Respondents characterized the most likely outcomes of their lives as involving either being killed, being incarcerated, or disengagement from the gang and desistance from crime. Consistent with previous research, respondents attributed their decisions to exit the gang to the prospect of negative consequences such as the death of a friend, incarceration, or feeling abandoned by the gang (Decker and Lauritsen 2002). How these forces of attachment interact over the life course is less well understood.

Family and Gangs across the Life Course: Joining, Participating, and Exiting

In gang research, "the family" historically refers to families of origin. This approach gave way to research findings that at first seem self-contradictory. For instance, Young et al.

(2014) found that "families play a minimal role in young people's desistance from gang involvement; rather the decision to leave is principally taken by the gang members themselves." However, in the next sentence, they include "threats against families, witnessing violence against family members, [and] starting a new relationship or having children among the influences that might prompt gang exit" (182). This suggests that the role of "family" changes over the life course. In the section that follows, we first provide a brief review of research that outlines how troubled and marginalized families push young people toward gangs in the absence of institutional support. We then discuss the most recent research on how gang members navigate tension between the gang and family concerns as they participate with the gang, and perhaps contemplate moving away from the gang and toward created families of their own.

Family and Joining the Gang

In his book *Crime and Nature*, Marcus Felson (2006) suggested that the defining characteristic of gangs, which delineates gangs from other groups, is grounded in the "dangerous local areas" that gangs tend to inhabit. Felson posited that the "gang promises [members] a specific solution to their security problem" (306). Felson himself admits that he was taken to task for such a bold claim by another well-known criminologist, Malcom Klein (see 321, footnote 9). Klein noted that Felson's assertion overplays the intimidation provided by gangs and underplayed the social and personal reasons young people join gangs. Both perspectives make sense. Felson focuses on tangible intimidation activities and "nastiness" to protect from incursion from other gangs to provide physical, geographic "security." In addition to physical security, however, *emotional* security requires young people to feel a durable sense of safety, love, esteem, and self-actualization (Sharkey et al. 2011; De Vito 2021). In this way gangs may be attractive to people who have insecure, disorganized, or no attachments at all.

Research exploring the link between family and gang membership can be roughly divided into two groups: risk factor and protective factor oriented. Family conflict (along with sexual abuse) has long been viewed as a key risk factor that differentiates girls who join gangs from girls who resist gangs (De La Rue and Espelage 2014). Family conflict also shapes boys' pathways to gang membership. For instance, in a survival model analysis of 1,354 "serious juvenile offenders" over seven years, hostile family relations and having a father who had been arrested was found to increase the risk of boys and girls joining gangs (Merrin et al. 2020). Path analysis of 371 parent–child dyads found gang membership was intergenerationally transmittable between both mothers and daughters and fathers and sons (dependent on paternal contact; Augustyn, Ward, and Krohn 2017). Another recent study of the National Longitudinal Survey of Youth data found having siblings in gangs increases risk for joining gangs within both male–male and female–female sibling dyads (Hashimi, Wakefield, and Apel 2021).

Trauma exposure and other ACEs also increase risk for gang membership and other negative outcomes over the life course (Wolff et al. 2020). Childhood trauma is important to understanding gang membership because social and emotional skills develop primarily out of familial relationships and experiences and color interactions with others over time (De Vito 2020). To that end, research on the intergenerational transmission of gang membership has found that parenting practices mediate the relationship between parent gang membership and child gang membership. Maltreatment, inconsistent discipline, and lack of "affective ties" (i.e., attachment) are associated with heightened risk for gang membership (Augustyn et al. 2017, 259–260). In other words, familial context and attachment patterns go a long way in shaping the eventuality of gang membership. The goal then should be to identify ways to promote secure attachments between parents, caregivers, and children, particularly in marginalized and under-resourced families.

However, research on protective factors to gang membership pales in comparison to the body of work on risk factors. The orientation of criminology toward negative outcomes such as offending, victimization, and incarceration has translated to a preference in the literature for research exploring risks. Direct study of protective factors is relatively rare (Bishop et al. 2017). Importantly, family problems and child maltreatment are well-established risk factors for gang involvement and other forms of juvenile group violence, including recruitment as a child soldier (Garbarino, Governale, and Nesi 2020). Building resources that support families and foster secure attachments could therefore help reduce youth violence substantially and even globally. De Vito (2021) characterizes protective factors as the "opposite" of risk factors, but more research specifically aimed at identifying protective factors is needed (Welsh and Farrington 2007). The most recent studies on protective factors that we could find for this chapter (written in 2022) were published in 2017 and 2018.

In contrast to research that seeks to identify causes and correlates that predict gang membership, protective factor research is concerned with remedies to that well-documented process. A century of gang research has established a stable set of risk factors: troubled families in marginalized neighborhoods in under-resourced cities. Protective factor research aims to identify factors that confound those forces. For instance, one survey of over 26,000 California youth found that higher levels of empathy and family support reduces risk of gang involvement (Lenzi et al. 2015). Based on those findings, the authors argue for comprehensive programming that addresses individual, family, and community-level risk and protective factors such as multisystemic therapy and other "wrap-around" services (Boxer 2011). Findings like these resonate with the ecological or "person-in environment" perspective (Pardeck 1988) and underscore the importance of considering the role of the family and the gang in research, and the prevention and management of gangs and gang membership in practice.

Building on their previous work, Lenzi et al. (2018) found that higher levels of "emotional competence" were associated with reduced levels of self-reported gang membership in another sample of over 12,000 teenage students in California. Their one-paragraph discussion of the implications of their research is limited to suggesting that schools could support the development of emotional competence in students as a means of working toward gang prevention efforts (Lenzi et al. 2018, 574). Similarly, Bishop et al. (2017) used a social development model to analyze youth and gangs in Seattle, Washington. They argued for the continuation of the Gang Resistance Education and Training (G.R.E.A.T.) program and suggested that opportunities for social development should be fostered for family and friend groups, schools, and neighborhood activities (290). However, emotional competency (like empathy) is a product of prosocial attachment styles, which develop primarily out of secure attachment in parental and other close relationships (Bowlby 1988; De Vito 2021).

Like school- and community-based gang prevention and mitigation programming, family-based programming faces several challenges. Family members of youth at risk of gang membership may be reluctant to cooperate with the legal system. Parents may be in denial of their child's gang involvement, or they may perceive a potential for stigmatization or blame as a parent of a gang member (Aldridge et al. 2011). Marginalized families may also be unable to meet the time and resource requirements of family-based services, or they may be reluctant to expose themselves to scrutiny and surveillance by the state (Lee 2016). Shute (2013) suggested gang programs should be "public health oriented" and not "criminal justice oriented" and should focus on behavioral patterns (e.g., crime) not social status (e.g., gang membership). Shute offers multisystemic therapy (MST) and functional family therapy (FFT) as promising in preventing gang membership. While gang membership may reduce completion rates for MST (Boxer 2011), early research suggests FFT may be more applicable to gangs (Thornberry et al. 2018).

FFT therapists commonly encounter gang members and youth at risk for membership because one key source of referrals is the juvenile justice system, but FFT does not have a gang-specific component. To address that issue Thornberry et al. (2018) helped design, implement, and preliminarily evaluate a revised version of FFT that retained all core attributes but added additional content that directly addressed street gang involvement (FFT-G). Their randomized controlled trial of 129 families in Philadelphia found that both high-risk and low-risk families completed the program at the same rate. They also found that FFT-G was effective at reducing recidivism, but the low prevalence of gang membership (even in their sample of justice-involved youth) prevented statistical analysis between groups to assess the effectiveness of FFT-G to prevent gang membership. This is an important area for future gang research, because if the risk factors associated with gang involvement (including insecure/disordered attachment) are not rectified within the family of origin, youth may seek to address their needs via gang membership.

Family and Life in the Gang

Gang research reflects a traditional focus on risk factors associated with joining a gang (i.e., gangs as a dependent variable) and risk factors associated with gang membership (i.e., gangs as an independent variable). There is therefore a running assumption in criminology that the gang is purely negative and destructive. This perspective is supported empirically in generations of mainstream, quantitative gang research that explores victimization, offending, and incarceration rates of gang members. However, that perspective fails to account for benefits (perceived or demonstrable) that gang members may receive from the gang. On the other hand, critical criminologists and ethnographers have illustrated cognitive and functional benefits of the gang, stemming from identities developed in "resistance" or rebellion (Aspholm 2020; Brotherton 2015; Hagedorn 2008). Incorporating attachment theory as a framework could allow for further consideration of potential protective factors of gangs, such as emotional safety, belonging and acceptance, and self-actualization.

In other words, attachment theory helps to humanize gang members within the environments they are born into and grow up in. Understanding gang members in their ecological context can be aided greatly by personal experience with those communities. For instance, Marzo (2020) conducted a docent ethnography with Bloods in the San Diego neighborhood she grew up in. Interviews took place in parked cars and on walkabouts and car rides throughout the neighborhood. Her insider status as a member of the community benefited her study in two important ways. First, because she was a product of the same ecological background, she conceptualized her subjects as people navigating social spheres and not simply "violent criminals who are dangerous to society" (442). Second, her insider status allowed her access to current gang members and helped her establish rapport during interviews. Marzo (2020) identified three takeaways important to the study of family, the gang, and attachment. Those include trauma-bonding, gendered processes, and evolving identities.

Marzo (2020) took an intersectional, race-critical approach to her data collection and analysis. Her research centered the Black experience, with a particular eye for gendered effects. She found evidence for what she refers to as "Black extraordinary adolescent trauma" (434). Marzo argues that the normalization of extreme violence in marginalized Black communities (from historical lynchings to contemporary police killings) helps foster a sense of solidarity and deep-seated attachment and loyalty to the gang. Inter- and intra-gang violence also contributes to the process of bonding to the gang through shared trauma (Murer and Schwarze 2020). News of these violent events are regularly discussed and disseminated on social media, expanding the scope of shared trauma and future violence (Patton et al. 2019). This suggests that while the gang may not serve traditional family functions such as encouraging school attendance or discouraging violence and delinquency, gang membership in the here and now can provide a sense of belonging, opportunities for self-actualization, and sources for attachment.

Regarding gendered effects during gang membership, Marzo (2020) found that for the Black girls and women in her study, gang membership was "familial in nature and encouraged by family members" (437). Marzo's female respondents reported being grandfathered-in to the gang or granted honorary affiliation because they were from families that included several established and respected gang members. They discussed having a sense of pride that included both familial and gang allegiances, whereby through gang membership, whole families achieve a level of fearful respect, and therefore protection. Similarly, Gutierrez-Adams, Rios, and Case (2020) found that the deeply embedded female gang members she studied were able to mobilize power from their gang for protection and revenge for abuse, as well as a revenue source to sustain themselves and their families. However, in both studies, perceptions of the gang as a central concern gave way to considerations of their created family (e.g., their children) over time (Maldonado-Fabela 2022).

Similar findings have been reported for men and boys. The examination of fatherhood and masculinity experiences of gang members was pioneered in large part by James Diego Vigil (1982, 1988, 2007). Vigil's work identified masculinity as a cause for gang membership and reshaping perceptions of masculinity as a means of facilitating gang exit. Regarding the former, Leverso and Hess (2021) identified a masculinity dilemma, whereby youth from families at risk for gang membership have drastically restricted access to opportunities to develop and perform healthy masculinity. In such cases, the gang serves as a valuable resource in the development of masculinity, although not necessarily prosocial forms of masculinity. Some of Leverso and Hess' 29 respondents credited the gang with teaching them how to be "better" men by demonstrating loyalty, love, respect, and giving them something to believe in and stand for. Others saw the gang as an example of how *not* to be a good man and developed a sense of masculinity that opposed gang-based value systems they saw as rooted in violence and conflict (De Vito 2020).

The third theme identified by Marzo (2020) was evolving and bifurcated gang identities. Her respondents reported practicing a distinction between "gang members" and "gang bangers" (440). The Bloods in her study described the gang as a source of pride and identity, even if they were not actively serving the gang or committing crimes (i.e., gang banging). That transition allowed them to develop other identities, including student, parent, and mentor without having to renounce their background, their friends, or their sense of self. Research has identified parenthood as an important turning point in gang membership that pushes gang members away from actively gang banging (a set of behaviors) and toward inactive gang membership (a modified social standing) and eventually to *former* gang member status (Leverso and Hess 2021; Pyrooz et al. 2017). Current gang members also describe parenthood as a "joyous" event that inspires self-improvement and a desire to be an involved and prosocial parent, even as they must learn parenting techniques from peers and siblings (Acevedo-Polakovich et al. 2019).

In sum, a large body of research identifies family problems as an important factor in the process of joining the gang, as well as the dire consequences associated with membership. A small but growing body of human-centered gang research is beginning to identify some of the intangible benefits gang members may receive during and after their tenure (e.g., Panfil 2020). That body of work suggests that in addition to the legal pressures, violence, and trauma associated with gang life, maturation changes perceptions of crime, victimization, family, and the gang itself. At the beginning of gang careers, "family" commonly refers to the family of origin of a youth (e.g., mother, father, and siblings). Later in gang careers, "family" tends to shift in meaning to refer to the "created" family of an adult (e.g., spouse, significant other, or children).[4] These processes are associated with cognitive transformations as people mature individually, but social processes and relationships with others also shape the pathways out of crime, delinquency, and gangs (Copp et al. 2020).

Family and Exiting the Gang

Research on the process of desisting from gang membership has expanded greatly in the 20 years since Decker and Lauritsen (2002) identified a gap in the literature compared to research on the process of joining the gang. Most recently, gang research has explored the role of spirituality (e.g., Deuchar 2020; Decker and Pyrooz 2020) and masculinity (Deuchar 2018; Deuchar and Weide 2019; Panfil 2020) in the desistance and disengagement process. As with other areas of gang research, family represents an ever-present running theme. For instance, both Deuchar (2020) and Decker and Pyrooz (2020) discuss the overlapping effects of spirituality and perceptions of family whereby aging gang members develop deeper understandings of themselves in a spiritual context and start to see themselves as providers for a created family, as opposed to recipients in their family of origin. Similarly, Deuchar's (2018) and Panfil's (2020) work exploring the contours of masculinity finds fatherhood to be a central component of the shift away from gangs and crime and toward family (Leverso and Hess 2021).

There is also evidence that suggests motherhood and created families also pull female members away from gang membership. In one study of over 600 gang members in the National Longitudinal Study of Youth, Pyrooz et al. (2017) found that gang identities and offending rates fade rapidly after girls and women become mothers. Results regarding fathers were less pronounced and dependent on residing with their children. Motherhood plays a central role in gang desistance in qualitative studies as well. For instance, Kolb, Palys, and Green (2019) conducted interviews with 24 self-identified Chicana ex-gang members who were participating in a well-established gang intervention program in Los Angeles. Like Marzo's (2020) work with Black males in San Diego, the Chicanas discussed retaining a gang identity, even if they had stopped "banging" or "doing gang" (Kolb et al. 2019, 4). Nevertheless, they came to value their role as mothers and responsibility to family as key factors in their desistance.

Regardless of how gang members may shift cognitively away from the gang and toward family, structural barriers persist across the life course for both members and ex-members. Maldonado-Fabela's (2021, 2022) photo elicitation work with current and former Chicana gang members found that mothers (*jefas*) who are or were involved with gangs were legally and socially criminalized in ways that made effective motherhood more challenging. Her respondents discussed still being wary of state surveillance and intervention, either from the criminal or child welfare system. That perspective made them suspicious of and reluctant to request or accept assistance from governmental and non-governmental agencies. Like non-gang members, gang members and former members have hopes, dreams, and goals (Panfil 2022). Exploring the life-course experiences from their own perspective should be a priority for gang researchers. Understanding their needs, strengths, and deficits can help design more effective prevention and intervention efforts (Sharkey et al. 2021, 70).

Directions for Future Research: Attachment, Masculinity, and Trauma

This review of recent research suggests three important areas for future research regarding the family and the gang. Attachment theory, trauma-informed practices, and masculinity in the development of gangs and gang members have all been initially addressed in recent years. All three have important and largely unexplored roles in the development of gangs, gang members, and gang careers. All three play a part in joining, participating in, and perhaps leaving the gang or desisting from crime. For instance, attachment to family can represent both a risk and a protective factor regarding gang membership, depending on the status of the family. Gangs can provide attachments when family attachments fail, but how that relationship might function is not well understood. Future research on gangs and family could benefit from considering gang membership as a source of attachment (for better or worse) over the life course with an eye toward how gang membership might fill gaps left by absent, neglectful, abusive, or under-resourced/marginalized families of origin (De Vito 2020).

The role of trauma in the process of joining, continuing in, and exiting a gang has also begun to receive some attention in gang research (Gaston, Shamserad, and Huebner 2021). In addition to the negative effects of gang membership, experiencing trauma through witnessing violence increase the likelihood of violent offending (Boxer et al. 2022). At the same time, gang membership "approximately double[s] youth's exposure to community violence, both direct and witnessed" (Dierkhising et al. 2021, 8041). Ongoing posttraumatic stress disorder associated with gang membership can extend across the life course (Wojciechowski 2021), and left unresolved the trauma of gang membership, violence, and victimization can lead to intergenerational transmission of trauma that extends across generations (Keels 2022). Future research on gangs and family would do well to consider trauma-informed approaches to understanding gang members and their motivations. Analyzing gang membership in the context of both positive and negative attachments over the life course is one step in that direction.

Masculinity is another small but growing area of research that involves both gang membership and family. This work has so far centered on gang members' evolving perceptions of manhood and the process of desisting from crime or gang membership or "masculinity maturation" (Leverso and Hess 2021). But in addition to the natural growth and development that comes with age and experience, purposefully offering opportunities for modified modes of masculine "embodiment" such as "family man" or "man of god" can help generate new universes of positive masculinity (Flores 2016). Researchers have also begun to explore the process of (re)shaping masculinity from toxic to prosocial forms without emasculation (Deuchar and Weide 2019). That body of work suggests that spirituality, yoga and meditation, weightlifting, and martial arts can help foster new perceptions of what it means to be a good man, father, son, and spouse (Deuchar 2018, 2020). Future research could bolster evidence-based practices for gang interventions with systematic evaluations of such efforts.

Conclusion

Taken together, this synthesis of the life-course perspective and attachment theory also suggests two takeaways regarding the family and the gang. First, as an institution, the family is central to the development of gangs, gang members, and gang career trajectories. Being from a troubled or marginalized family pushes kids toward gangs to fill gaps left by their parents and kin networks. Time in the gang is associated with challenges as a parent later in life. At the same time, evolving familial ties and responsibilities are regularly discussed by gang members as a force that tends to pull them away from the gang. Second, joining a gang is a life-altering event that has important repercussions not just legally and socially, but also regarding attachment styles and bonding patterns. Having insecure or disorganized attachment styles makes it more difficult (and less likely) to develop secure bonds with other institutions that may help such as school, church, or community groups. The gang may then serve as a surrogate family of last resort. That surrogacy should be a primary concern for both researchers and practitioners.

Notes

1. We recognize that everyone does not get married or have children, and that all families do not fit traditional "nuclear" forms—for instance, stepfamilies organize as "blended families" (Kumar 2017), and LGBTQ+ folks often develop "families of choice" after being

rejected by their family of origin (Allen and Lavender-Scott 2020). Our main point in making the distinction between families of origin and the families that develop around us as we age is that growing up is generally characterized by moving away from parents and siblings and toward a created group of intimate supporters over time. And like stepchildren and LGBTQ+ folks, kids who end up gang members often face restricted choices in that process.

2. In one sense, the literal, immediate willingness of gang members to "kill and die for the gang" remains another overlooked facet of gang research for ethical reasons. However, the risks of gang membership are widely known. If members were not, on some level at least, willing to die and kill (e.g., on a sliding scale from "willing in the abstract sense" to "literally homicidal/suicidal at any time/place"), there would be no gang violence. In other words, gang researchers who perceive all such statements as purely performative are wrong, at least in some cases.

3. Levy and colleagues (2011) refer to these as secure, preoccupied, and dismissing attachment styles for clinical purposes. They add a fourth style that is only applied in conjunction with one of the first three, which they refer to as "unresolved for trauma or loss" (195).

4. In the seminal words of Frederic Thrasher (1927), "the gang which once supplanted the home, now succumbs to it" (242).

REFERENCES

Acevedo-Polakovich, I. D., V. A. Kassab, K. S. Boress, M. L. Barnett, M. M. Grzybowski, S. Stout, et al. 2019. "Fatherhood among Gang-Involved US Latino Youth: Qualitative Inquiry into Key Stakeholders' Perspectives." *Journal of Latinx Psychology* 7 (2): 137–153.

Allen, K. R., and E. S. Lavender-Stott 2020. "The Families of LGBTQ Older Adults: Theoretical Approaches to Creative Family Connections in the Context of Marginalization, Social-Historical Change, and Resilience." *Journal of Family Theory & Review* 12 (2), 200–219.

Aldridge, J., J. Shute, R. Ralphs, and J. Medina. 2011. "Blame the Parents? Challenges for Parent-Focused Programmes for Families of Gang-Involved Young People." *Children & Society* 25 (5): 371–381.

Aspholm, R. 2020. *Views from The Streets: The Transformation of Gangs and Violence on Chicago's South Side*. New York: Columbia University Press.

Augustyn, M. B., and J. M. McGloin. 2021. "Reconsidering the 'Gang Effect' in the Face of Intermittency: Do First-And Second-Time Gang Membership Both Matter?" *Criminology* 59 (3): 419–453.

Augustyn, M. B., T. P. Thornberry, and M. D. Krohn. 2014. "Gang Membership and Pathways to Maladaptive Parenting." *Journal of Research on Adolescence* 24 (2): 252–267.

Augustyn, M. B., J. T. Ward, and M. D. Krohn. 2017. "Exploring Intergenerational Continuity in Gang Membership." *Journal of Crime and Justice* 40 (3): 252–274.

Bishop, A. S., K. G. Hill, A. B. Gilman, J. C. Howell, R. F. Catalano, and J. D. Hawkins. 2017. "Developmental Pathways of Youth Gang Membership: A Structural Test of the Social Development Model." *Journal of Crime and Justice* 40 (3): 275–296.

Bowlby, J. 1988. *A Secure Base: Parent-Child Attachment and Healthy Human Development*. New York: Basic Books.

Boxer, P. 2011. "Negative Peer Involvement in Multisystemic Therapy for the Treatment of Youth Problem Behavior: Exploring Outcome and Process Variables in 'Real-World' Practice." *Journal of Clinical Child & Adolescent Psychology* 40 (6): 848–854.

Boxer, P., J. F. Duron, A. Williams-Butler, P. Mattson, and K. Algrim. 2022. "Trauma and Gang Affiliation Increase Likelihood of Committing Assault among Juveniles Admitted to Secure Custody." *Journal of Clinical Child & Adolescent Psychology* 52 (4): 570–577.

Brotherton, D. 2015. *Youth Street Gangs: A Critical Appraisal*. New York: Routledge.

Brotherton, D. C., and L. Kontos. 2022. "Introduction: Special Issue Vol. 30 #1—'Critical Gang Studies'." *Critical Criminology* 30: 3–12.

Copp, J. E., P. C. Giordano, M. A. Longmore, and W. D. Manning. 2020. "Desistance from Crime during the Transition to Adulthood: The Influence of Parents, Peers, and Shifts in Identity." *Journal of Research in Crime and Delinquency* 57 (3): 294–332.

De La Rue, L., and D. L. Espelage. 2014. "Family and Abuse Characteristics of Gang-Involved, Pressured-to-Join, and Non–Gang-Involved Girls." *Psychology of Violence* 4 (3): 253–265. https://doi.org/10.1037/a0035492

Decker, Scott, and B. Van Winkle. 1996. *Life in the Gang: Family, Friends and Violence*. Cambridge, UK: Cambridge University Press.

Decker, S. H., and Lauritsen. 2002. "Leaving the Gang." In *Gangs in America III*, edited by Ronald Huff, 51–67. Thousand Oaks, CA: Sage.

Decker, S. H., and D. C. Pyrooz. 2015. "Street Gangs, Terrorists, Drug Smugglers, and Organized Crime." In *The Handbook of Gangs*, edited by S. H. Decker and D. C. Pyrooz, 294–308. Chichester, UK: John Wiley & Sons.

Decker, S. H., and D. C. Pyrooz. 2020. "The Role of Religion and Spirituality in Disengagement from Gangs." In *Gangs in the Era of Internet and Social Media*, edited by C. Melde and F. Weerman, 225–249. Cham, Switzerland: Springer.

Decker, S. H., D. C. Pyrooz, and J. A. Densley. 2022. *On Gangs*. Philadelphia, PA: Temple University Press.

Decker, S. H., D. C. Pyrooz, and R. K. Moule Jr. 2014. "Disengagement from Gangs as Role Transitions." *Journal of Research on Adolescence* 24 (2): 268–283.

Densley, J. A. 2015. "Joining the Gang: A Process of Supply and Demand." In *The Handbook of Gangs*, edited by S. H. Decker and D. C. Pyrooz, 235–256. Chichester, UK: John Wiley & Sons.

Deuchar, R. 2018. *Gangs and Spirituality: Global Perspectives*. Cham, Switzerland: Springer.

Deuchar, R. 2020. "'I Get More in Contact with My Soul': Gang Disengagement, Desistance and the Role of Spirituality." *Youth Justice* 20 (1-2): 113–127.

Deuchar, R., and R. D. Weide. 2019. "Journeys in Gang Masculinity: Insights from International Case Studies of Interventions." *Deviant Behavior* 40 (7): 851–865.

De Vito, K. 2020. "Seeking a Secure Base: Gangs as Attachment Figures." *Qualitative Social Work* 19 (4): 754–769.

De Vito, K. 2021. *Gang Prevention in Schools: Creating a Secure Base and Safe Haven*. New York: Springer Nature.

Dierkhising, C. B., J. A. Sánchez, and L. Gutierrez. 2021. "'It Changed My Life': Traumatic Loss, Behavioral Health, and Turning Points among Gang-Involved and Justice-Involved Youth." *Journal of Interpersonal Violence* 36 (17-18): 8027–8049.

Felson, M. 2006. *Crime and Nature*. Thousand Oaks, CA: Sage Publications.

Flores, E. O. 2016. '"Grow Your Hair Out': Chicano Gang Masculinity and Embodiment in Recovery." *Social Problems* 63 (4): 590–604.

Garbarino, J., A. Governale, and D. Nesi. 2020. "Vulnerable Children: Protection and Social Reintegration of Child Soldiers and Youth Members of Gangs." *Child Abuse & Neglect* 110: 104415.

Gaston, S., F. Shamserad, and B. M. Huebner. 2021. "'Every Thought and Dream a Nightmare': Violence and Trauma among Formerly Imprisoned Gang Members." *Criminal Justice and Behavior* 49 (10): 1418–1436.

Gutierrez-Adams, E., D. Rios, and K. A. Case. 2020. "Female Gang Members Negotiating Privilege, Power, and Oppression within Family and Gang Life." *Women & Therapy* 43 (3-4): 287–308.

Hagedorn, J. 2008. *A World of Gangs: Armed Young Men and Gangsta Culture*. Minneapolis: University of Minnesota Press.

Hashimi, S., S. Wakefield, and R. Apel. 2021. "Sibling Transmission of Gang Involvement." *Journal of Research in Crime and Delinquency* 58 (5): 507–544.

Keels, M. 2022. "Developmental & Ecological Perspective on the Intergenerational Transmission of Trauma & Violence." *Daedalus* 151 (1): 67–83.

Kolb, A. F., T. Palys, and A. Green. 2019. "When You're Out, You're Not Really Out: Exiting Strategies among Gang-Affiliated Chicanas." *Journal of Public and Professional Sociology* 11 (2): 4.

Krohn, M. D., J. T. Ward, T. P. Thornberry, A. J. Lizotte, and R. Chu. 2011. "The Cascading Effects of Adolescent Gang Involvement across the Life Course." *Criminology* 49 (4): 991–1028.

Kumar, K. 2017. "The Blended Family Life Cycle." *Journal of Divorce & Remarriage* 58 (2): 110–125.

Lee, T. 2016. *Catching a Case: Inequality and Fear in New York City's Child Welfare System*. New Brunswick, NJ: Rutgers University Press.

Lenzi, M., J. Sharkey, A. Vieno, A. Mayworm, D. Dougherty, and K. Nylund-Gibson. 2015. "Adolescent Gang Involvement: The Role of Individual, Family, Peer, and School Factors in a Multilevel Perspective." *Aggressive Behavior* 41 (4): 386–397.

Lenzi, M., J. D. Sharkey, A. Wroblewski, M. J. Furlong, and M. Santinello. 2018. "Protecting Youth from Gang Membership: Individual and School-Level Emotional Competence." *Journal of Community Psychology* 47 (3): 563–578.

Leverso, J., & C. Hess. 2021. "From the Hood to the Home: Masculinity Maturation of Chicago Street Gang Members." *Sociological Perspectives* 64 (6): 1206–1223.

Leverso, J., & R. L. Matsueda. 2019. "Gang Organization and Gang Identity: An Investigation of Enduring Gang Membership." *Journal of Quantitative Criminology* 35 (4): 797–829.

Levy, K. N., W. D. Ellison, L. N. Scott, and S. L. Bernecker. 2011. "Attachment Style." *Journal of Clinical Psychology* 67 (2): 193–203.

Maldonado-Fabela, K. L. 2021. "'They Treat Us Like Criminals in Front of Our KIDS': Gang-Affiliated Chicanas and Trails of Violence in the Barrio." In *Routledge International Handbook of Critical Gang Studies*, edited by D. Brotherton and R. J. Gude, 518–536. New York: Routledge.

Maldonado-Fabela, K. L. 2022. "'In and Out of Crisis': Life Course Criminalization for Jefas in the Barrio." *Critical Criminology* 30: 133–157.

Marzo, L. 2020. "'Set Trippin': An Intersectional Examination of Gang Members." *Humanity & Society* 44 (4): 422–448.

Melde, C., and F. A. Esbensen. 2011. "Gang Membership as a Turning Point in the Life Course." *Criminology* 49 (2): 513–552.

Melde, C., T. J. Taylor, and F. A. Esbensen. 2009. "'I Got Your Back': An Examination of the Protective Function of Gang Membership in Adolescence." *Criminology* 47 (2): 565–594.

Merrin, G. J., J. P. Davis, K. M. Ingram, and D. L. Espelage. 2020. "Examining Social-Ecological Correlates of Youth Gang Entry among Serious Juvenile Offenders: A Survival Analysis." *American Journal of Orthopsychiatry* 90 (5): 623.

Moffitt, T. E., and A. Caspi. 2001. "Childhood Predictors Differentiate Life-Course Persistent and Adolescence-Limited Antisocial Pathways among Males and Females." *Developmental Psychopathology* 13 (2): 355–375.

Moule, R. K., S. H. Decker, and D. C. Pyrooz. 2013. "Social Capital, the Life-Course, and Gangs." In *Handbook of Life-Course Criminology*, edited by Chris Gibson and Marvin Krohn, 143–158. New York: Springer.

Murer, J. S., and T. Schwarze. 2020. "Social Rituals of Pain: The Socio-Symbolic Meaning of Violence in Gang Initiations." *International Journal of Politics, Culture, and Society* 35: 95–110.

Murphy, A., M. Steele, S. R. Dube, J. Bate, K. Bonuck, P. Meissner, H. Goldman, and H. Steele. 2014. "Adverse Childhood Experiences (ACEs) Questionnaire and Adult Attachment Interview (AAI): Implications for Parent Child Relationships." *Child Abuse & Neglect* 38 (2): 224–233.

Pardeck, J. T. 1988. "An Ecological Approach for Social Work Practice." *Journal of Sociology & Social Welfare* 15: 133.

Panfil, V. R. 2020. "'I Was a Homo Thug, Now I'm Just Homo': Gay Gang Members' Desistance and Persistence." *Criminology* 58 (2): 255–279.

Panfil, V. R. 2022. "'Ask Me about My Goals!' Challenging Pervasive Assumptions of Gang Members' Fatalism by Exploring Gay Gang Members' Goals." *Critical Criminology* 30 (1): 71–93.

Patton, D. U., D. Pyrooz, S. Decker, W. R. Frey, and P. Leonard. 2019. "When Twitter Fingers Turn to Trigger Fingers: A Qualitative Study of Social Media-Related Gang Violence." *International Journal of Bullying Prevention* 1 (3): 205–217.

Pyrooz, D. C. 2014. "'From Your First Cigarette to Your Last Dyin' Day': The Patterning of Gang Membership in the Life-Course." *Journal of Quantitative Criminology* 30 (2): 349–372.

Pyrooz, D. C., J. M. McGloin, and S. H. Decker. 2017. "Parenthood as a Turning Point in the Life Course for Male and Female Gang Members: A Study of Within-Individual Changes in Gang Membership and Criminal Behavior." *Criminology* 55 (4): 869–899.

Pyrooz, D. C., J. J. Turanovic, S. H. Decker, and J. Wu. 2016. "Taking Stock of the Relationship between Gang Membership and Offending: A Meta-Analysis." *Criminal Justice and Behavior* 43 (3): 365–397.

Ruble, N. M., and W. L. Turner. 2000. "A Systemic Analysis of the Dynamics and Organization of Urban Street Gangs." *American Journal of Family Therapy* 28 (2): 117–132.

Sharkey, J. D., Z. Shekhtmeyster, L. Chavez-Lopez, E. Norris, and L. Sass. 2011. "The Protective Influence of Gangs: Can Schools Compensate?" *Aggression and Violent Behavior* 16 (1): 45–54.

Shute. 2013. "Family Support as a Gang Reduction Measure." *Children & Society* 27 (1): 48–59.

Taylor, T. J., D. Peterson, F. A. Esbensen, and A. Freng. 2007. "Gang Membership as a Risk Factor for Adolescent Violent Victimization." *Journal of Research in Crime and Delinquency* 44 (4): 351–380.

Thornberry, T. P., B. Kearley, D. C. Gottfredson, M. P. Slothower, D. N. Devlin, and J. Fader. 2018. "Reducing Crime among Youth at Risk for Gang Involvement: A Randomized Trial." *Criminology & Public Policy* 17 (4): 953–989.

Thrasher, F. M. 1927. *The Gang: A Study of 1,313 Gangs in Chicago*. Chicago, IL: University of Chicago Press.

Vigil, J. D. 1982. "Human Revitalization: The Six Tasks of Victory Outreach." *Drew (The) Gateway* 52 (3): 49–59.

Vigil, J. D. 1988. *Barrio Gangs: Street Life and Identity in Southern California*. Austin: University of Texas Press.

Vigil, J. D. 2007. *The Projects: Gang and Non-Gang Families in East Los Angeles*. Austin: University of Texas Press.

Walker, D. A., and G. T. Cesar. 2020. "Examining the 'Gang Penalty' in the Juvenile Justice System: A Focal Concerns Perspective." *Youth Violence and Juvenile Justice* 18 (4): 315–336.

Welsh, B. C., and D. P. Farrington. 2007. "Saving Children from a Life of Crime: Toward a National Strategy for Early Prevention." *Victims and Offenders* 2 (1): 1–20.

Wojciechowski, T. 2021. "PTSD as a Risk Factor for Chronic Gang Membership during Adolescence and Early Adulthood: A Group-Based Trajectory Modeling Approach." *Crime & Delinquency* 67 (10): 1536–1560.

Wolff, K. T., M. T. Baglivio, H. J. Klein, A. R. Piquero, M. DeLisi, and J. C. Howell. 2020. "Adverse Childhood Experiences (ACEs) and Gang Involvement among Juvenile Offenders: Assessing the Mediation Effects of Substance Use and Temperament Deficits." *Youth Violence and Juvenile Justice* 18 (1): 24–53.

Young, T., W. Fitzgibbon, and D. Silverstone. 2014. "A Question of Family? Youth and Gangs." *Youth Justice* 14 (2): 171–185.

CHAPTER 27

LINKING EDUCATION AND CRIMINOLOGY RESEARCH TO UNDERSTAND THE SCHOOLING EXPERIENCES OF GANG YOUTH AND ADULTS

ADRIAN H. HUERTA

EVERY day, primary and secondary schools across the country, (un)knowingly, welcome gang-associated youth onto their local campuses. As gang youth make their way to these schools, many must be vigilant to avoid rival gang territories and victimization (Estrada et al. 2018). These daily occurrences contribute to the high rates of posttraumatic stress disorder that gang youth experience, which are often double the rates compared to their non-gang peers (Estrada et al. 2017). Conservative estimates signal that over 1 million children self-reported gang involvement across the United States (Pyrooz and Sweeten 2015). Schools are a central space in local communities but also for gang activities, including recruitment, battling for territory, graffiti, and confrontations with rivals (Carson and Esbensen 2019; Huerta and Rios-Aguilar 2021; Rios 2011; Vigil 1999). However, schools are also places for the (mis)treatment of gang youth, often guided by educators' belief that these gang-involved children have fully committed to a life of crime, deviance, and eventual incarceration (Brotherton 1996; Huerta et al. 2020; Rios 2011, 2017; Vigil 1988, 1999). Many times, school leaders are in denial that gangs are present at their schools (Brotherton 1996; Huerta 2016; Huff and Trump 1996; Vigil 1999). School leaders' inactions and disbelief of gang presence contribute to school personnel being ill-equipped to best engage, support, and guide youth away from further gang involvement (Brotherton 1996; Huff and Trump 1996; Vigil 1999).

At times, educators default to negative attitudes and behaviors such as exhibiting lower expectations for gang-associated students (Brotherton 1996; Huerta 2016), isolating gang youth away from non-gang peers (Brotherton 1996; Huerta 2022; Malagón 2010; Rios 2017; Vigil 1999), or overdisciplining gang youth through suspensions or expulsions (Brotherton 1996; Huerta 2016; Rios 2011; Vigil 1999). Many educators are unaware that youth gang involvement is, on average, less than 12 to 18 months (Pyrooz and Sweeten 2015), and the peak gang membership is during middle school (Estrada et al. 2016; Pyrooz and Sweeten 2015). Collectively, the lack of training, empathy, and misguided school-based practices contribute to why only 50% of gang youth graduate from US high schools (Pyrooz 2014; Vigil 1999). Many educators do not realize that youth join gangs due to fractured relationships within their homes, communities, and schools (Curry and Spergel 1992; Krohn et al. 2011; Rios 2011; Ventura Miller, Barnes, and Hartley 2011; Vigil 1999). As commented by James Diego Vigil (2003), "the streets [remain] the arena for what is learned and expected by others to gain recognition and approval" (230), which signals that gangs can be much more influential than local school educators (Merrin, Hong, and Espelage 2015).

This chapter explores the complicated relationship between adolescent gang membership and educational pathways through an examination of school life course during primary, secondary, and postsecondary education, a needed perspective that will pay attention to factors associated with educational persistence and attrition. This chapter will also embed quotes from former gang members who succeeded in postsecondary education by earning bachelor's and graduate degrees to illustrate these important points about how individual gang members experience and overcome mistreatment throughout the educational pipeline. It is important to stress the significance of reframing the educational experiences for gang-associated youth. Gang membership is treated as an individual act of defiance and cultural resistance instead of being understood as a societal structural problem that requires an ecological investment of resources and culturally aligned support systems (Curry and Spergel 1992; Rios 2011; Vigil 1988, 2003).

Lastly, this chapter encourages educators, mental health professionals, and criminologists to recalibrate how they study and interact with gang-associated youth and adults, as the current practices only serve to dehumanize, isolate, and criminalize individuals within schools and limit opportunities to transition out of the gang. Reframing our cultural knowledge of gangs is needed to understand and support gang-associated youth without further criminalizing them. Gang-associated youth seek peers who can validate and supplement the missing positive influences in their lives. For example, a gang may act as a surrogate family by providing protection, emotional support, clothing, food, and other resources to supplement what is missing from many homes (Conchas and Vigil 2012; Krohn et al. 2011). Prior to engaging the literature on the school life course, this chapter will review the literature on the school-to-prison pipeline to understand how structural conditions contribute to the educational derailment of gang-associated youth. It will follow with a review of the available empirical scholarship on the educational experiences of gang-associated youth in primary, secondary, and postsecondary education to highlight key moments of success and micro-decisions by school personnel directly involved with gang youth. Lastly, recommendations will be provided for educators throughout the educational pipeline, and suggestions for researchers of gang-associated populations.

SCHOOLING CONTEXT

Schools are important environments that play a critical role in the lives of students and families, such as helping children learn how to socialize with peers and educators (Lareau 2011; Lareau and McNamara Horvat 1999) to later stages where they support students to prepare for the college admissions process (Huerta et al. 2018; McDonough 1997; Perna et al. 2008). Another side of schooling is that it often reinforces social class behaviors that embed stratification practices that permit high-income youth to negotiate with educators to maximize individual attention and academic benefits (Calarco 2018; Lareau and McNamara Horvat 1999). In contrast, low-income youth are isolated or unable to match their high-income peers' persistence in fostering strong personal and scholastic relationships (Calarco 2018). Depending on the school culture and location, educators engage in practices that contribute to the social marginalization of children influenced by race, ethnicity, gender, resources, socioeconomic status, and zip code (Howard 2014; Kozol 2012; Nguyen et al. 2019; Noguera, Hurtado, and Fergus 2013; Oakes 2005; Saenz and Ponjuan 2009). For some youth, educators mistreat them due to the unfounded belief that "those kids" will engage in inherent criminal activities that lead to students' premature departure from their schools (Dizon, Enoch-Stevens, and Huerta 2022; Noguera 2003; Rios 2017; Willis 1977).

Understanding how schools' function is important to know *how* and *why* some youth engage with gangs as a potential replacement for relationships within educators and schools (Conchas and Vigil 2010; Vigil 1999, 2003). When youth are identified or perceived as gang members, the negative social reactions and academic restrictions contribute to the *adultification* of these youths within schools, often framed through a racialized and gendered lens (Conchas and Vigil 2012; Brotherton 1996; Rios 2011, 2017). The phenomenon of adultification is especially salient for Black and Latino/x children, who represent nearly half of all adolescent gang members (Ferguson 2000; Noguera 2003; Rios 2011) and are overrepresented in disciplinary infractions in school districts nationwide (Shollenberger 2015).

It is important to become familiar with the school-to-prison pipeline to recognize the cultural shift from traditional learning environments to now educational institutions that support the integration of criminal legal practices (Bahena et al. 2012; Carter et al. 2017AU; Dizon et al. 2022; Hirschfield 2008; Huerta, Calderone, and McDonough 2017; Noguera 2003; Shedd 2015). Across the United States, researchers and youth advocates coined the term "school-to-prison pipeline" to help illuminate the presence of criminal legal practices to control youth behavior, such as the use of hyper-surveillance (Annamma 2017; Rios 2011; Shedd 2015), excessive suspensions and expulsions for minor behavioral infractions (Kennedy-Lewis and Murphy 2016; Musto 2019), the tracking and sorting of youth away from educational opportunities (Flores-Gonzalez 2005; Oakes 2005), and involuntary transfers to alternative learning environments (Brown 2007, 2012; Huerta 2022; Huerta and Hernandez 2021; Vigil 1999).

The school-to-prison pipeline originates from the harsh reality that disproportionate rates of children of color, low-income youth, youth with special needs, and boys were being groomed for lasting interactions with the juvenile or adult legal system through criminal citations, arrests, and other formal connections to law enforcement (Annamma 2017; Gregory, Skiba, and Mediratta 2017; Lopez 2003; Skiba et al. 2002). Even the use of the term "school-to-prison pipeline" is thought provoking for many educators as they struggle to believe that schools would intentionally harm youth through practices that could negatively impact the lives of students (Laura 2014). However, national data clearly show who and why youth are removed from schools across the country. Nearly 2.8 million students experienced at least one suspension, and 120,000 students received expulsion in public schools over the 2013–2014 academic year (Huerta et al. 2022; Novak and Fagan 2022; Office for

Civil Rights 2018). To highlight the severity of this national phenomenon, youth in elementary school have been suspended or expelled for insubordination, such as talking back to teachers or fighting on school property (Ferguson 2000).

The immediate connection between the school-to-prison pipeline and gang membership is captured by recent work by Widdowson, Garduno, and Fisher (2021), as they found that youth who are suspended multiple times are 282% more likely to join a gang than youth who were not suspended. School suspension and expulsion numbers become even direr once a racial and equity lens is applied to reveal stark differences based on race, ethnicity, and gender (Gregory et al. 2017; Nguyen et al. 2019; Shollenberger 2015). Shollenberger (2015) found that by the time they reach middle school, Black and Latino/x boys would already experience at least one school suspension (50% and 49%, respectively). Involuntarily or self-initiated transfer to new schools is a serious concern for youth, as youth who change schools more than four times have a 53% increase in joining a gang (Estrada et al. 2017). In other research, when non-gang-affiliated youth feel connected to educators, they can develop mutual trust and exchange valued forms of social and cultural capital to prepare for life after high school (Stanton-Salazar 1997, 2001, 2011). When Merrin et al. (2015) found that when middle and high school students "feel" connected to adults and perceive equitable treatment from educators at school, students are less likely to join a gang.

However, gang youth who change schools multiple times do not have the opportunity to forge strong or trusting relationships with educators, resulting in students being less likely to receive valued information on preparing for the future (Huerta 2016, 2022; Huerta et al. 2020). To provide further context for the gradual integration of carceral practices within schools, it is important to understand the context of policy decisions related to public fear of school violence and school shootings.

School-to-Prison Pipeline

Due to the fear of increased incidents of gun and physical violence in schools across the United States, the Clinton Administration spearheaded the Gun Free Schools Act of 1994 as an effort to prevent further cases of drugs, violence, and weapons in local schools and contributed to the development of zero-tolerance policies. This federal law helped introduce a gradual acceptance of practices that reinforced and normalized the power of the school-to-prison pipeline elements in the name of safety across primary and secondary schools in the United States (Casella 2003; Dizon et al. 2022; Mendoza et al., 2020; Mittleman 2018). Schools were required to report youth who brought weapons to campus to the legal system (Mendoza et al. 2020). In many school districts, zero-tolerance policies require automatic and predetermined consequences, such as mandated removals through in- and out-of-school suspensions, expulsions, and transfers to alternative learning environments for students who violated school rules and social norms (Bell 2021; Mendoza et al. 2020). As Bell (2021) noted, Michigan legislators mandated state standards for school suspensions and expulsions that resulted in Black youth being unfairly impacted by district discipline policies.

The unintended consequences of zero-tolerance policies contributed to more students of color, low-income students, and boys being labeled as problems or misdiagnosed with cognitive behavioral issues within classrooms and schools (Ferguson 2000; Mendoza et al. 2020; Noguera 2003). Although low-income boys of color engaged in similar childish misbehavior as their white and Asian peers, boys of color received harsher punishment and treatment than their peers (Ferguson 2000; Howard 2014; Huerta et al. 2017; Musto 2019). Law enforcement and educators espoused the gradual normalization of zero-tolerance practices as a reliable method to prevent further youth violence, drugs, weapons, and other possible violations of school safety rules (Casella 2003; Losen 2014; Mendoza et al. 2020). Unfortunately, there is vast evidence highlighting the negative impact of the school-to-prison pipeline practices related to increased adolescent arrests and citations for minor school-based infractions such as wearing hats during school hours (Lopez 2003; Losen 2014) or children wiggling "too much" in classrooms (Ferguson 2000). Mittleman (2018) comments that once youth are "marked" as disciplinary problems in schools, educators are eager to further punish and are less tolerant of misbehavior from those students (Ferguson 2000). Mittleman continues and finds that youth who experience school suspensions are more than twice as likely to be arrested (195). Mittleman cautions that labeling youth as troublemakers can have lifelong consequences for youth that will follow that student beyond primary and secondary school into adulthood. To reinforce this point about the misuse of school discipline policies, Shollenberger (2015) found that for boys who are Black, Latino/x, and white and experienced at least one out-of-school suspension, only one in three will earn a college degree. Like Mittleman's (2018) research, Huerta et al. (2017) found that Latino middle and high school boys who were suspended and expelled were discouraged from requesting college information from educators as students knew they had been labeled troublemakers.

Other instances of the welcomed practices that emphasize the school-to-prison pipeline are directly related to perceptions of youth gang involvement, where school leaders insist on involuntarily transferring youth from traditional schools to alternative learning environments (Huerta 2022; Malagón 2010; Rios 2017; Vigil 1999). The troubling situation of alternative schools is the low quality of education and limited curriculum that underprepare youth for postsecondary education (Huerta 2022; Huerta and Hernandez 2021; Huerta et al. 2020). Over 40% of school districts across the United States offer some type of alternative learning environment for students who have been removed or transferred from a traditional middle or secondary school (Verdugo and Glenn 2006). As found by Lehr and Lange (2003), alternative schools often do not have the fiscal resources; learning facilities such as dedicated library spaces, science labs, foreign languages, or physical education areas; or college-going culture to prepare their students for life after secondary school (Huerta 2016, 2022; Huerta and Hernandez 2021). Between 600,000 to 750,000 youth are enrolled in an alternative school setting, and only two-thirds of students in these types of schools will graduate (Carver, Lewis, and Tice 2010; DePaoli et al. 2016; Vogell and Fresques 2017).

Returning to the school-to-prison pipeline, the actors that negatively impact youth through efforts within the school-to-prison pipeline include not only teachers, counselors, and administration, but also school resource officers who play an active and yet subjective role in inequitably applying school rules and local ordinances on school discipline matters (Kupchik and Bracy 2009; Lopez 2003). For example, research found the active presence of Texas school resource officers in local high schools contributed to lower graduation rates, decreased college application submissions, and increased citations and arrests for Black and Latino/x high school students (Weisburst 2019). Shedd (2015) found that Black and Latino/

x youth had mixed reactions to the increased presence of school resource officers in their local schools. Some youth felt the need for school resource officers to protect them from peers and community members who engage in deviant activities. Yet other youth feared the increased carceral practices embedded within schools that would strip them of traditional school experiences. With the unfortunate increases in shootings across US schools, schools and district leaders continue to wrestle with the appropriate balance of school safety and criminality infused into classrooms.

Collectively, schools have absorbed cultural practices from the criminal legal system that aim to center social control and punishment over student-centered growth with students who require differentiated support and attention from educators (Brotherton 1996; Hirschfield 2008; Rios 2017; Shedd 2015). Unfortunately, most public schools nationwide are not adequately funded to meet the increased social, academic, and mental health needs of their students (Ewing 2018; Martínez and Vasquez Heilig 2022). Since the adoption of the term "school-to-prison pipeline," scholars have argued that the school-to-prison pipeline does not accurately capture the amorphous practices and impacts on students and have suggested the "school-to-prison nexus" (Annamma 2017; Wald and Losen 2003). The school-to-prison nexus exposes how parents and students gradually accept the reality that metal detectors, closed circuit security systems, police substations in local schools, drug-sniffing dogs, and pepper spray are used as practices to stop verbal or physical conflicts (Brotherton 1996; Hirschfield 2008; Shedd 2015). The inclusion of police officers in and near schools to create *safety* parameters to *protect* youth from violence signals the acceptance of a "culture of incarceration" (Annamma 2017; Brotherton 1996, 100; Rios 2017). Shedd (2015) stresses that for many students and families, the concern for school safety, on and off school grounds, overshadows individual liberties, which may contribute to school resource officers having a stronger presence in local schools to prevent potential shootings and gang violence.

With the context of the school-to-prison nexus in the background, youth and teenagers' step into local schools wearing a figurative scarlet letter by their confirmed or perceived gang association that signals they are social outcasts that require public punishment and formal removal. The acceptance of established carceral practices and policies seek to punish and control youth without attending to the conditions that contributed to gang membership. In the following section, a review of literature on primary school settings will highlight that gang membership can begin as early as elementary school for some youth and how schools respond to gang membership.

Primary School

> I don't remember doing any kind of schoolwork in the fifth grade, in the fourth grade, or in the sixth grade . . . By the eighth or ninth [grade], I [was] carrying a weapon [for protection from rival gangs]. Also, I had no association with school.

In the opening quote, Joseph, a former gang member who later earned a bachelor's degree, shares his childhood experiences being involved in a gang from the age of 8 or 9 years old. His earliest childhood memories were shaped by vivid memories of his father's heinous acts of domestic violence and verbal abuse against Joseph, his mother, and his older siblings. Joseph saw gang membership as a natural step since his older siblings were active members of a notorious gang in the western region of the United States. They inspired him to become gang involved in elementary school (Hashimi, Wakefield, and Apel, 2021; Merrin et al. 2015). From a young age, Joseph, like many children involved in gangs, did not trust school teachers and personnel as he felt shame and discomfort talking about the regular abuse he experienced in his home, which made him angry and frustrated at school (Durán 2013). Joseph's distrust of educators could have been elevated by his frequent absences and distractions from a tumultuous household where safety and comfort were unstable. However, Joseph's educators may have focused on his lack of school attendance, his fighting with peers, and inconsistent classroom engagement. There is a continuous thread of school personnel from elementary to high school in a state of denial that gangs exist in their schools or that youth as young as fourth grade could be involved in a gang (Huff and Trump 1996). Educators' intentional rejection of gangs in the local school and community contributes to what Hagedorn (2017) calls a disregard of cultural history and dehumanizing tactics that negatively impact gang-associated youth from the local communities.

Children as young as elementary age are keenly aware of the presence and existence of gangs in their local schools and communities (Monti 1993; Vigil 1988). Depending on the salience of gangs within a community, some youth feel comfortable exploring the idea of being a gang member in the future (Monti 1993). Some youth may see gang leaders and gang members as role models or community leaders due to their strong influence in the neighborhood, as many demand respect and cause fear because of their reputations (Vigil 1988). As youth persist in school, so does the salience of gang involvement and temptation to join a neighborhood gang, especially for youth who feel marginalized and disrespected by educators and see gang membership as the venue for identity validation and support systems (Conchas and Vigil 2012; Estrada et al. 2017; Katz 1996; Krohn et al. 2011; Merrin et al. 2015; Vigil 2003, 2019). Depending on the configuration and organization of the gang, some gangs can provide a multitude of opportunities to refine one's identity within the group and school community (Garot 2007). Thornberry et al. (2003) found in a longitudinal mixed-methods study that some young people are motivated to join a gang for respect, fighting, and opportunities to have fun with peers, but these findings were differentiated by race and ethnicity.

In their quantitative study of four middle schools, Curry and Spergel (1992) found that Black and Latino youth, sixth to eighth graders, join gangs for different reasons. For Latino youth, educational frustration was one of the leading contributors to why they joined gangs, whereas for Black youth, consistent exposure to gangs in their local community is a driving force for individual involvement. Decades later, Merrin et al. (2015) found similar results where middle and high school youth with gang-involved family members are more likely to join gangs than peers with no familial connections to gangs. Gilman et al. (2014) found that if students live with a gang member, family or not, they are eight times more likely to join a gang. If students have gang-involved siblings, it increases the likelihood of gang involvement for younger family members (Hashimi et al. 2021). When students experience educational frustration through subtle snubs or their awareness that schools are unwilling to provide the needed resources or support systems to help them feel connected to schools, they lose faith in schooling and educators (Curry and Spergel 1992, Merrin et al., 2015; Vigil 1988, 1999, 2003; Huerta 2016, 2022; Huerta et al. 2020). Collectively, scholars stress that interventional models must meet the unique cultural, racial, ethnic, and social needs of children in various communities to prevent gang involvement (Curry and Spergel 1992; Merrin et al. 2015).

The thread of gang-associated youth feeling disconnected from their schools is an ongoing problem for educators. In a statewide study of gang membership and violence, Estrada et al. (2013) found that 9.5% of California seventh grade students, or 13,503 of the 149,703 students who completed the self-reported survey, shared their gang involvement. They discovered that gang-associated youth were negatively associated with school protective behaviors and attitudes. For middle school students, gang involved or not, there is tension during this critical juncture as they are exploring relationships with peers and educators and working to envision their future (Martinez 2018; Martinez and Castellanos 2018). Youth are searching for validation from educators and crave respect for their individuality (Martinez 2018). Gang-associated middle school students feel like outsiders in their classrooms, as school personnel overdiscipline them and disrespect their gang identities (Curry and Spergel 1992; Huerta 2016; Huerta and Rios-Aguilar 2021).

In primary and secondary schools, there are vast gender and racial differences, as the teacher workforce is overrepresented by white women who create environments that do not align with the needs of boys, specifically boys of color (Howard 2014; Musto 2019; Saenz and Ponjuan 2009). In comparison, youth gang membership is overrepresented among boys and young men (Estrada et al. 2016; Merrin et al. 2015; Pyrooz and Sweeten 2015; Tapia 2011). This overrepresentation creates the perfect storm of gendered and racialized conflict between gang youth and white women (Calabrese and Barton 1995) and may help shed light on the wide disparities in school discipline and feelings of educational frustration for gang-associated children. Although not explicitly focused on gang-associated youth, sociologists and education scholars identified a gender equity gap between boys and men and have documented the long-term trends of educational underperformance and achievement captured through lower high school completion rates, decreased enrollment in higher education, and uneven degree attainment between men and women (Buchmann 2009; Huerta et al. 2018; Zarate and Gallimore 2005). This national phenomenon is notable for contextualizing the gendered schooling experiences for boys and young men in US schools to highlight how educational systems continue to fail this student population.

As schools fail gang-associated students, school leaders partner with local gang units to take proactive steps to foster relationships with youth (Huff and Trump 1996). Ironically, gang units work to forge meaningful relationships with students to create safer school environments, leading to decreased gang involvement for middle and high school students (Huff and Trump 1996). The acceptance of external agents such as gang unit officers or military recruiters is welcomed on primary and secondary school campuses to build relationships with youth, since educators are limited with their time and cannot build meaningful connections to learn about the lives of students (Ayers 2006; Hill 2012; Huerta 2015). However, as mentioned in the previous section, the active presence of school resource officers has the unintended consequence of students of color being victims of unnecessary citations and arrests while in school (Weisburst 2019). The structural conditions that hinder strong relationships from being forged between educators and students in primary school is only exacerbated in secondary schools as student enrollment and socioemotional needs increase, but resources and staffing do not meet equitable levels (Knight, Hassairi, and Martinez 2022; Martinez and Vasquez Heilig 2022).

The challenges that gang-associated youth experience in primary school do not end as they transition into secondary school but seem to intensify as the stakes increase for students. Secondary schools are spaces for youth to solidify their identities and prepare for future pathways into adulthood. However, DeLuca, Clampet-Lundquist, and Edin (2016) found that for youth of color, school practices and policies do not adequately support them into careers or higher education, as many educators and school leaders are comfortable *pushing out* the "troubled" students from school entirely before earning a high school diploma (Luna and Revilla 2013; Noguera 2003). The following section will review the relationship between educators and students and different intervention models to support gang youth.

Secondary School

Well, I always *liked* school . . . [but] I didn't have time to learn. I didn't have time because . . . my gang became my priority. And when I was [in high] school . . . there was *always* something. I always had to worry about [whether a rival gang member] was going to come up to me [to fight] or when was the next fight because [the gangs] were always fighting in [high] school. At school it was always a fight. So now as I get older, I understand why so many [gang members] dropped out [of high school] because it's [the constant worry about gang violence] in your head. Someone's messing with your head and when's the next fight or are you going to be shot when you get out of school? Just so many [external] things that didn't allow me to focus on school at that time.

In the above quote, Jaime, a Latino man who earned a graduate degree in education and was gang active for more than 15 years, shared how he enjoyed high school but was pulled away from his focus on school due to gang activity. Much of the empirical scholarship on gang youth and education centers on secondary school settings (Durán 2013; Flores-Gonzalez 2005; Rios 2011, 2017; Vigil 1999). The saliency of gang violence and victimization in secondary schools is central for education and criminology scholars. Many have documented how schools have become battlegrounds for gang youth to cement their commitment and identity as gang members (Bradshaw et al. 2013; Carson and Esbensen 2019; Garot 2007; Patton and Roth 2016; Peterson, Taylor, and Esbensen 2004; Vigil 1999). For example, Huerta and Rios-Aguilar (2021) highlight how gang-associated youth are aware that they cannot allow others to "punk" them into submission, which means youth must maintain an elevated awareness of potential fights with peers.

As noted by Jaime, although he enjoyed school and graduated with his high school class, he was unable to concentrate on his academics to the level of his abilities. This instance may help explain why so many gang-associated youth experience quick academic declines in their performance (Pyrooz 2014). Pyrooz (2014) found that gang youth were a quarter year behind their non-gang peers in academics. However, as previously noted, schools also withhold academic and enrichment opportunities from gang youth (Durán 2013; Flores-Gonzalez, 2005; Huerta 2016). So, students' hypervigilance in school focused on gang activities combined with school personnel withholding assignments creates the perfect storm of educational frustration (Merrin et al. 2015). As gang youth attempt to engage in school-based activities, educators actively work to "chill" students from being active participants in the classroom (Huerta 2016). When gang-associated students were persistent in requesting support and clarification with assignments, Huerta (2016) observed teachers yelling at students and telling them they would end up in jail in the future and threatened school suspension for being disrespectful. Thus, the culmination of these schooling experiences sheds more light on why gang youth are three times more likely to earn a GED than non-gang youth (Pyrooz 2014).

Gang Youth and Relationships with Educators

Many gang-associated children are involved with gangs for less than two years (Estrada et al. 2016; Pyrooz and Sweeten 2015). However, the long-term consequences of gang involvement may follow former gang members into adulthood through perpetual interactions with the legal system, unstable employment, and other social conditions that contribute to poverty (Gilman, Hill, and Hawkins 2014). Many gang-associated youth do subscribe to the long-term benefits of educational credentials, including earning a GED or high school diploma and pursuing some form of higher education to earn certificates and college degrees (Curry and Spergel 1992; Huerta 2015, 2016; Tellez and Estep 1997; Van Dommelen-Gonzalez et al. 2015), but school personnel intentionally tend to withhold college admissions information from this group of students (Huerta et al. 2020). Tellez and Estep (1997) found that many gang-associated high school youth feel excluded and ignored by their high school teachers. These gang-associated students were hyperaware of the inattention from teachers and either decided to rebel or submit to being disengaged in future classroom activities (Durán 2013). Not all studies of gang youth and educators result in dysfunction. Gass and Laughter's (2015) study of seven Black high school boys focused on how one school could work to positively engage and try to change the life trajectory of these gang-associated students. These educators focused on reconstructing students' identities and being future oriented to nurture a positive relationship between students and educators. The more common experiences for gang youth are highlighted in the following quote by Jaime, who left high school in the ninth grade and did not return to complete his GED for almost 10 years:

> And then I got called to the office, and one of the counselors . . . told me, 'I need you to bring me a bill from where you live, like a utility bill, because I think you don't live in the district.' I said, 'Yes, I do. I live here and here.' She said, 'Well, I need you to bring it. And I need you to bring it by tomorrow.' So, the next day comes, and I forget . . . because I'm everywhere [with my gang] except at home. And I forget and she calls me and she's like, 'You got that bill?' I said, 'No, I don't. I forgot. But you know what? I'll bring it tomorrow, I promise.' She said, 'No, don't bother.' She's like, 'You can't be in the school anymore.' And I remember begging. I said, 'Come on, I'll bring it. Just give me a chance.' And she's like, 'No, anyways, you're going to die anyways. Die or end up in jail.' And I believed her. I said, 'You know what? You're right.' And she said, 'Stop wasting my time.' And I remember just leaving her office and I was sad when I left. Again, I felt like I failed my mom. I said, 'you're right' and I just left . . . I felt really embarrassed. And so, I left [my high school], and I never went back.

Jaime's quote aligns with much of the gang research in secondary schools, where educators actively work to discourage students from persisting due to their gang status. Unknown to Jaime's educators, his older sister was raising him, and they frequently experienced food and housing insecurity. The driving influence for Jaime to join a gang was because he was being victimized by a local gang and he feared for his life (Rios 2011). As found by Rios (2011) and many others (Thornberry et al. 2003; Vigil 1988), some youth join gangs to avoid bullying and for protection that cannot be provided by school personnel. Although youth are seeking some type of protection from gangs threatening violence, the harsh reality is that victimization increases as new gang members become targets for police, community members, and school personnel (Rios 2011). Some educators may argue that if gang youth simply switched schools, they could create a new identity away from gang life. Carson et al. (2017) found when gang youth switch schools, it results in increased academic performance. The separation from their previous school may be tied to distancing themselves from negative peer networks, which may promote misbehavior and academic disengagement (Carson et al. 2017). In divergent findings, Huerta (2015) found that when Latino youth switched schools, they debated whether to join a gang as a new support system and protection from possible bullies.

The impact of support systems cannot be understated for gang youth, as mentors or trusting adults can positively influence youth to consider new opportunities and identities (Gass and Laughter 2015). Not focused on gang youth, sociologist of education Roberta Espinoza (2011) focused on "pivotal moments" between educators and high school youth. This concept highlights how adults can facilitate transformative moments that empower youth to see new possibilities to change their life trajectories, such as enrolling in higher education.

School and Community-Based Interventions for Gang Youth

Daniel, who was a gang member for five years and became a teenage father, worked at a diner to support his young family. Over time, Daniel forged a relationship with an elderly couple who grew affectionate toward him and would encourage Daniel to do more with his life. Daniel recalls one moment when the older couple told him, "You're smarter than this, you should go back to [college], . . . you can be an electrician because [you] can fix things . . . and have a good career and a good life." Eventually, Daniel enrolled and completed a medical technician program with support from the diner patrons. Daniel later would grow his confidence and interest in medicine, enroll in a local community college, earn his associate degree in science, and then transfer to a four-year university with the ultimate goal of becoming a medical doctor. Recently, he completed his medical residency program and started his career at a research university as a clinical physician.

Pivotal moments can positively change the life trajectories of gang-associated youth and others (Espinoza 2011). School and community-based interventions are critical opportunities available for gang-associated youth through a combination of either mentoring or peer-based support systems (Behr, Marston, and Nelson 2014; Carson et al. 2017; Carson and Esbensen 2019), which can result in youth sharing their goals for a better future and regretting their gang membership (Carson et al. 2017; Carson and Esbensen 2019). Often outside entities provide interventions for gang-associated youth to learn specific life skills or gain access to peer or adult mentors, who can provide advice and support on how to leave gangs (Esbensen et al. 2011; Peterson and Esbensen 2004). Depending on school or district leadership, schools can act as gatekeepers on whether they welcome third-party providers on K–12 campuses to help gang youth learn the short and long-term ramifications of gang membership (Esbensen et al. 2011; Peterson and Esbensen 2004). As mentioned, when youth join gangs, they are not keenly aware of the negative pitfalls of gang membership to their grades, quality of life, peer relationships, or safety (Carson et al. 2017; Carson and Esbensen 2019; Conchas and Vigil 2012; Rios 2011; Pyrooz 2014). So schools have a unique opportunity to positively engage and support gang-involved youth through the involvement of external local, state, or federal interventions that can foster positive relationships with students (Esbensen et al. 2011).

Behr et al. (2014) created an intervention for at-risk Latino high school boys in Colorado. The intervention served youth who were currently or formerly gang associated, experienced truancy, were previously incarcerated, lived in poverty, or had unstable relationships with parental figures. Youth who participated in summer programs decreased their gang involvement by 30% by the third year of the program. What was unique about this program was not simply providing holistic resources for individual students but also training program staff on becoming culturally sensitive and affirming participants to enhance trusting relationships. At the end of the program, youth felt empowered to plan for their future careers and college aspirations, increased academic performance in high school, and decreased truancy rates. A limitation of this program is that it can only serve a few dozen students throughout the program. However, gang involvement in Colorado and beyond may require a more comprehensive approach that tackles multiple levels of schooling, primary and secondary, and community centers to holistically support youth. In the following example, federally funded programs are important to reach a larger volume of youth across the country.

The Gang Resistance Education and Training (G.R.E.A.T.) program has had mixed results with various stakeholders (Peterson and Esbensen 2004). Student participants who completed the G.R.E.A.T. program were less likely to join a gang by 54% (Esbensen et al. 2011). In an evaluation of the G.R.E.A.T. program, parents of middle school students shared that it did not dramatically decrease gang involvement for their children but helped youth change their attitudes toward the police. Educators who participated in the evaluation shared mixed results, as many were unfamiliar with the benefits and outcomes of the G.R.E.A.T. program (Esbensen et al. 2011). This highlights the structural challenges of school staffing and their ability to support and engage in school-based interventions to help youth, shaping the impact on youth and families. Additional benefits of these programs are that youth can gain exposure to positive role models that can facilitate discussions on future opportunities. Gang youth hold high aspirations to achieve middle-class markers such as a home, children, marriage, and stable careers (Calabrese and Noboa 1995), though they are unsure how to navigate social boundaries to achieve those dreams (Huerta 2022). Similarly, Rios (2017) found that gang-associated Latino teenagers were willing to change their gang lifestyle for employment with livable wages and the chance to earn respect.

Collectively, when gang intervention programs are designed correctly, funded properly, and have staff who can develop meaningful relationships with youth, it can lead to positive results for gang youth. As noted by Behr et al. (2014), youth who participated in the multiyear intervention were more likely to develop goals to complete a GED and aspire to pursue higher education. As found by Pyrooz (2014), gang youth who earn a GED are twice as likely to enroll in postsecondary education. The following section reviews the preparation and transition into postsecondary education for former gang members.

Postsecondary School

The academic literature has underexplored the transition into higher education for gang-associated youth and adults. In the available scholarship, scholars have found that gang-associated youth do express hopes to transition out of the gang and prepare for stable careers that require a two- or four-year degree, certificate, or credential (Huerta 2016; Huerta et al. 2020; Panfil 2022; Van Dommelen-Gonzalez et al. 2015). Van Dommelen-Gonzalez et al. (2015) found that almost 90% of gang-associated youth study participants aspired to attend a trade school, vocational school, or become a college graduate (328). Unfortunately, 47% of the gang youth saw paying for higher education as the primary barrier, as they were unsure how to pay for their college expenses, including tuition, books, and related fees. This type of postsecondary education information is often referred to as "college knowledge" and is mainly shared by college counselors in secondary schools (Huerta 2022; Huerta et al. 2018, 2020; McDonough 1997; Perna et al. 2008). Surprisingly, Van Dommelen-Gonzalez et al. (2015) found that the gang youth in their study have friends who are enrolled in higher education. Outside of the gang literature, peers who are enrolled in college can serve as role models or cultural brokers on how to prepare for college, as noted by Tierney and Venegas (2006), who found that high school peers can act as college facilitators. These role models help peers prepare for higher education and may be better sources of support for youth who are marginalized. Returning to Van Dommelen-Gonzalez et al. (2015), they found that gang youth saw their motivation as a potential barrier to being successful in higher education. This finding is similar to Huerta et al.'s (2020) finding that youth were apprehensive about pursuing higher education as many had long histories of being mistreated in K–12 that framed their experiences as "less than" their peers in academic abilities that impinged their confidence (Huerta 2016). Although peers or loved ones can attempt to motivate gang youth to move forward and leave their gang to enroll in higher education (cite), the process can be a long and drawn-out experience for gang members, as highlighted in the quote by Tomás in the next section.

The role of peers is especially acute for gang youth, who may have a strained relationship with secondary school educators. The uncomfortable relationship between gang youth and school personnel related to college preparation is captured through Huerta et al.'s (2020) ethnographic study of one alternative secondary school and found that secondary school counselors intentionally withheld college materials and information from gang youth. Although the youth expressed a desire to pursue a two- or four-year degree or certificate, the school did not believe they were "college material." Gang youth not only need information, but also the scaffolding and motivation to persist to enroll in higher education, as the process is complicated. Klasik (2012) calls the process to prepare for and apply to higher education as the "college application gauntlet," as multiple and synchronized steps are needed to enroll in higher education. Pyrooz (2014), one of the first to study the educational trajectory of gang youth, found that only 5% of gang members earn a college degree. However, the individual and structural barriers for gang youth highlighted in this section help to illuminate the in and out of school experiences that create unsurmountable hurdles to success.

Once former gang members enroll in higher education, it does not mean they can easily break social ties with their peers and the gang (Pyrooz and Decker 2011). In the following quote, Tomás shares the tension he experienced trying to step away from gang life but being easily persuaded to engage in criminal activities again with his gang peers:

> Well, I did four years in the [armed services]. Then I got out, then I came home . . . And the homies were still looking for me and the homies were still like, "Let's do this, let's do that," so I was like, not an active like super heavily invested [in engaging in criminal behaviors with my gang], well kind of active and what happened was I ended up going to [community college] just to try to stay away from the hood. Because I knew it was gonna lead to something that I didn't really want. But I was still like not persuaded, but the homies would still come around . . . So sometimes, depending on the mood, sometimes I would go and do stuff.

The transition into higher education is not always a smooth process for former gang members as they negotiate an identity shift, current or past relationships with their gang, and enter a new and unfamiliar organizational environment (Garcia et al. 2017). Garcia et al. (2017) found that former gang members enrolled in community college experience a type of social stigma from their peers and college faculty due to their style of dress, tattoos, and physical demeanor. This caused former gang members to question their social acceptance and whether to continue with their higher education pursuits. Additionally, community college personnel threatened to call the police on former gang members if they raised their voices or were physically "menacing" in college offices. However, many scholars have focused on desistence and the challenges of breaking away from gang life and criminal activities (Flores and Hondagneu-Sotelo 2013; Moloney et al. 2009; Sampson and Laub 1993), and most recently, the role of higher education as a turning point to mitigate criminal activity for adults (Garcia et al., 2017; Walters 2018). The depth of literature has not fully explored the multiple support systems needed for former gang members to persist and complete a college degree. In the following quote, Daniel, a former gang member who went on to graduate from medical school, shared how an elderly couple and gentleman who were patrons at a diner where Daniel worked offered to pay for his gas money. The gas money was for Daniel to enroll in a vocational college about an hour away from his rural town. Daniel recalls the interaction:

> If you go back to school . . . I will pay you your gas money . . . if you go to college or want to do something with your life. I'll pay your gas money, pay some tuition . . . So, I enrolled at this [for-profit college] program . . . and that [older man] really stuck to his word and he would give me gas money [for the 45-minute commute to another city], so I can drive to and from school and so that's what I did.

Daniel used the moment to change the direction of his life and his young family. Daniel stepped away from gang life toward the end of high school as a teenage father and wanted to provide stability to his child and wife. He completed an 18-month program that allowed him to work in health care and support his family. Years later, he enrolled in a community college, intending to transfer to a four-year university to prepare for medical school (which he later graduated from).

The empirical scholarship has not fully documented the pathways to higher education for current and former gang members. Thus, more qualitative and quantitative research is needed to confirm the nuances, relationships, and other factors that have helped to guide individuals from gang life to college graduates. As highlighted in this section, multiple barriers exist in secondary schools and postsecondary education that contribute to low college degree attainment rates. As captured in the quotes, former gang members experience pressure from their peers to continue to engage in criminal activities, but also moments of support from strangers who want them to improve their lives and pursue positive opportunities.

Conclusion

The path into gang membership for youth is influenced by multiple factors (see **Chapter 22** and **Chapter 26** in this text). But the role of the school-to-prison nexus is often downplayed in organizational efforts to remove and criminalize students who are identified or perceived to be gang members. Although gang membership for many youths is a quick process in their lives, the social stigma is difficult to shed as teachers, counselors, and other school personnel actively collaborate to withhold opportunities and suspend or expel students from school. Schools have a unique opportunity to partner with local non-profits and mental health professionals to better support young people's mental health needs. As noted by Huerta and Rios-Aguilar (2021), school personnel should recognize their professional limitations and abilities in how to engage and support gang youth. It would be best not to isolate or alienate children who they believe are gang members but instead to display empathy and concern for why a young person has joined a gang. Teachers and counselors should work with school staff members to locate community-based organizations that provide violence prevention and mental health support to the students but also the family. A driving reason for gang membership is feeling marginalized, so positive and consistent affirmations are welcomed to ensure the student feels seen and supported at school.

References

Annamma, Subini Ancy. 2017. *The Pedagogy of Pathologization: Dis/abled Girls of Color in the School-Prison Nexus*. New York: Routledge.

Ayers, William. 2006. "Hearts and Minds: Military Recruitment and the High School Battlefield." *Phi Delta Kappan* 87 (8): 594–599.

Bahena, Sofía, North Cooc, Rachel Currie-Rubin, Paul Kuttner, and Monica Ng, eds. 2012. *Disrupting the School-To-Prison Pipeline*. Cambridge, MA: Harvard Education Press.

Behr, Michelle, Christine Marston, and Kyle Anne Nelson. 2014. "A Bridge to Graduation for At-Risk Latino Males: A Case Study." *Journal of Education for Students Placed at Risk* 19 (3–4): 215–228.

Bell, Charles. 2021. *Suspended: Punishment, Violence, and the Failure of School Safety*. Baltimore, MD: John Hopkins University Press.

Bradshaw, Catherine P., Tracy Evian Waasdorp, Asha Goldweber, and Sarah Lindstrom Johnson. 2013. "Bullies, Gangs, Drugs, and School: Understanding the Overlap and the Role of Ethnicity and Urbanicity." *Journal of Youth and Adolescence* 42 (2): 220–234.

Brotherton, David C. 1996. "The Contradictions of Suppression: Notes from a Study of Approaches to Gangs in Three Public High Schools." *The Urban Review* 28 (2): 95–117.

Brown, Tara M. 2007. "Lost and Turned Out: Academic, Social, and Emotional Experiences of Students Excluded from School." *Urban Education* 42 (5): 432–455.

Brown, Tara M. 2012. "The Effects of Educational Policy and Local Context on Special Education Students' Experiences of School Removal and Transition." *Educational Policy* 26 (6): 813–844.

Buchmann, Claudia. 2009. "Gender Inequalities in the Transition to College." *Teachers College Record* 111 (1): 2320–2346.

Calabrese, Raymond L., and Angela M. Barton. 1995. "Mexican-American Male Students and Anglo Female Teachers: Victims of the Policies of Assimilation." *High School Journal* 78 (3): 115–123.

Calabrese, Raymond L., and Julio Noboa. 1995. "The Choice for Gang Membership by Mexican-American Adolescents." *High School Journal:* 226–235.

Calarco, Jessica McCrory. 2018. *Negotiating Opportunities: How the Middle Class Secures Advantages in School.* Oxford, UK: Oxford University Press.

Carson, Dena, and Finn-Aage Esbensen. 2019. "Gangs in Schools: Exploring the Experiences of Gang-Involved Youth." *Youth Violence and Juvenile Justice* 17 (1): 3–32.

Carson, Dena, Melde, Chris, Wiley, Stephanie, and Esbensen, Finn-Aage. 2017. *School Transitions as Turning Point for Gang Status.* Washington, DC: US Department of Justice, National Institute of Justice.

Carter, P. L., R. Skiba, M. I. Arredondo, and M. Pollock. 2017. "You Can't Fix What You Don't Look At: Acknowledging Race in Addressing Racial Discipline Disparities." *Urban Education* 52 (2): 207–235.

Carver, Priscilla Rouse, Laurie Lewis, and Peter Tice. 2010. "Alternative Schools and Programs for Public School Students at Risk of Educational Failure: 2007–08. First Look. NCES 2010-026." National Center for Education Statistics.

Casella, Ronnie. 2003. "Punishing Dangerousness through Preventive Detention: Illustrating the Institutional Link between School and Prison." *New Directions for Youth Development* 2003 (99): 55–70.

Conchas, Gilberto Q., and James Diego Vigil. 2010. "Multiple Marginality and Urban Education: Community and School Socialization among Low-Income Mexican-Descent Youth." *Journal of Education for Students Placed at Risk* 15 (1–2): 51–65.

Conchas, Gilbert Q., and James Diego Vigil. 2012. *Streetsmart Schoolsmart: Urban Poverty and the Education of Adolescent Boys.* Dulles, VA: Teachers College Press.

Curry, G. David, and Irving A. Spergel. 1992. "Gang Involvement and Delinquency among Hispanic and African American Adolescent Males." *Journal of Research in Crime and Delinquency* 29 (3): 273–291.

DeLuca, Stefanie, Susan Clampet-Lundquist, and Kathryn Edin. 2016. *Coming of Age in the Other America.* New York: Russell Sage Foundation.

DePaoli, Jennifer L., Robert Balfanz, John Bridgeland, M. Atwell, and E. S. Ingram. 2016. "Building a Grad Nation: Progress and Challenge in Raising High School Graduation Rates." US Department of Education.

Dizon, Jude Paul Matias, Taylor Enoch-Stevens, and Adrian H. Huerta. 2022. "Carcerality and Education: Toward a Relational Theory of Risk in Educational Institutions." *American Behavioral Scientist* 66 (1): 1319–1341.

Durán, Robert. 2013. *Gang Life in Two Cities: An Insider's Journey.* New York: Columbia University Press.

Esbensen, Finn-Aage, Dana Peterson, Terrance J. Taylor, Adrienne Freng, D. Wayne Osgood, Dena C. Carson, and Kristy N. Matsuda. 2011. "Evaluation and Evolution of the Gang Resistance Education and Training (G.R.E.A.T.) Program." *Journal of School Violence* 10 (1): 53–70.

Estrada, Joey Nunez, Tamika Gilreath, Ron Avi Astor, and Remi Benbenishty. 2013. "Gang Membership of California Middle School Students: Behaviors and Attitudes as Mediators of School Violence." *Health Education Research* 28 (4): 626–639.

Estrada, Joey Nuñez, Tamika D. Gilreath, Ron Avi Astor, and Rami Benbenishty. 2016. "A Statewide Study of Gang Membership in California Secondary Schools." *Youth and Society* 48 (5): 720–736.

Estrada, Joey Nuñez, Adrian H. Huerta, Edwin Hernandez, R. Hernandez, and S. Kim. 2018. "Socio-Ecological Risk and Protective Factors for Youth Gang Involvement." In *The Wiley Handbook of Violence in Education: Forms, Factors, and Prevention*, edited by Harvey Shapiro, 185–202. Chichester, UK: Wiley.

Estrada, Joey Nuñez, Tamika D. Gilreath, Cathia Y. Sanchez, and Ron Avi Astor. 2017. "Associations between School Violence, Military Connection, and Gang Membership in California Secondary Schools." *American Journal of Orthopsychiatry* 87 (4): 443–451.

Espinoza, Roberta. 2011. *Pivotal Moments: How Educators Can Put All Students on the Path to College*. Cambridge, MA: Harvard Education Press.

Ewing, Eve L. 2018. *Ghosts in the Schoolyard: Racism and School Closings on Chicago's South Side*. Chicago, IL: University of Chicago Press.

Ferguson, Ann Arnett. 2020. *Bad Boys: Public Schools in the Making of Black Masculinity*. University of Michigan Press.

Flores-Gonzalez, Nilda. 2005. "Popularity Versus Respect: School Structure, Peer Groups and Latino Academic Achievement." *International Journal of Qualitative Studies in Education* 18 (5): 625–642.

Flores, Edward Orozco, and Pierrette Hondagneu-Sotelo. 2013. "Chicano Gang Members in Recovery: The Public Talk of Negotiating Chicano Masculinities." *Social Problems* 60 (4): 476–490.

Garot, Robert. 2007. "'Where You From!' Gang Identity as Performance." *Journal of Contemporary Ethnography* 36 (1): 50–84.

Gass, Kayla M., and Judson C. Laughter. 2015. "'Can I Make Any Difference?' Gang Affiliation, the School-to-Prison Pipeline, and Implications for Teachers." *Journal of Negro Education* 84 (3): 333–347.

Gilman, Amanda B., Karl G. Hill, and J. David Hawkins. 2014. "Long-Term Consequences of Adolescent Gang Membership for Adult Functioning." *American Journal of Public Health* 104 (5): 938–945.

Gilman, Amanda B., Karl G. Hill, J. David Hawkins, James C. Howell, and Rick Kosterman. 2014. "The Developmental Dynamics of Joining a Gang in Adolescence: Patterns and Predictors of Gang Membership." *Journal of Research on Adolescence* 24 (2): 204–219.

Giraldo, Luis Gustavo, Adrian H. Huerta, and Daniel Solórzano. 2017. "From incarceration to community college." In *Funds of Knowledge in Higher Education: Honoring Students' Cultural Experiences and Resources as Strengths*.

Gregory, Anne, Russell J. Skiba, and Kavitha Mediratta. 2017. "Eliminating Disparities in School Discipline: A Framework for Intervention." *Review of Research in Education* 41 (1): 253–278.

Hagedorn, John M. 2017. "Gangs, Schools, and Social Change: An Institutional Analysis." *Annals of the American Academy of Political and Social Science* 673 (1): 190–208.

Hashimi, Sadaf, Sara Wakefield, and Robert Apel. 2021. "Sibling Transmission of Gang Involvement." *Journal of Research in Crime and Delinquency* 58 (5): 507–544.

Hill, L. D. 2012. "Environmental Threats to College Counseling Strategies in Urban High Schools: Implications for Student Preparation for College Transitions. *The Urban Review*, 44, 36–59.

Hirschfield, Paul J. 2008. "Preparing for Prison? The Criminalization of School Discipline in the USA." *Theoretical Criminology* 12 (1): 79–101.

Howard, Tyrone C. 2014. *Black Male (d): Peril and Promise in the Education of African American Males*. Dulles, VA: Teachers College Press.

Huerta, Adrian H. 2015. "'I Didn't Want My Life to Be Like That': Gangs, College, or the Military for Latino Male High School Students." *Journal of Latino/Latin American Studies* 7 (2): 119–132.

Huerta, Adrian H. 2016. *Gangs and College Knowledge: An Examination of Latino Male Students Attending an Alternative School*. Los Angeles: University of California.

Huerta, Adrian H. 2022. "Accessing Possible Selves with Limited College Knowledge: Case Studies of Latino Boys in Two Urban Continuation Schools." *American Behavioral Scientist* 66 (10): 1342–1367.

Huerta, A. H., and Hernandez, E. 2021. "Capturing the Complexity of Alternative Schools: Narratives of Latino Males in an Overlooked Educational Space." *The Urban Review*, 1–24.

Huerta, Adrian H., Shannon M. Calderone, and Patricia M. McDonough. 2017. "School Discipline Policies that Result in Unintended Consequences for Latino Male Students' College Aspirations." In *Educational Policy Goes to School*, edited by Gilberto Conchas, Michael Gottfried, Briana Hinga, and Leticia Oseguera, 157–172. New York: Routledge.

Huerta, Adrian H., Edgar F. Lopez, Maritza E. Salazar, Gabriela Torres, and Miranda Muñoz. 2022. "Bridging Criminal Justice Scholarship into the Field of Higher Education: Implications for Research, Practice, and Policy." In *Higher Education: Handbook of Theory and Research*, edited by L. W. Perna, 1–42. Cham, Switzerland: Springer.

Huerta, Adrian H., Patricia M. McDonough, and Walter R. Allen. 2018. "'You Can Go to College': Employing a Developmental Perspective to Examine How Young Men of Color Construct a College-Going Identity." *The Urban Review* 50 (5): 713–734.

Huerta, Adrian H., Patricia M. McDonough, Kristan M. Venegas, and Walter R. Allen. "College is...: Focusing on the college knowledge of gang-associated Latino young men." *Urban Education* (2020): 0042085920934854.

Huerta, Adrian H., and Cecilia Rios-Aguilar. 2021. "Treat a Cop Like They Are God: Exploring the Relevance and Utility of Funds of Gang Knowledge among Latino Male Students." *Urban Education* 56 (8): 1239–1268.

Huff, C. Ronald, and Kenneth S. Trump. 1996. "Youth Violence and Gangs: School Safety Initiatives in Urban and Suburban School Districts." *Education and Urban Society* 28 (4): 492–503.

Katz, Susan Roberta. 1996. "Where the Streets Cross the Classroom: A Study of Latino Students' Perspectives on Cultural Identity in City Schools and Neighborhood Gangs." *Bilingual Research Journal* 20 (3–4): 603–631.

Kennedy-Lewis, Brianna L., and Amy S. Murphy. 2016. "Listening to 'Frequent Flyers': What Persistently Disciplined Students Have to Say about Being Labeled as 'Bad.'" *Teachers College Record* 118 (1): 1–40.

Klasik, Daniel. 2012. "The College Application Gauntlet: A Systematic Analysis of the Steps to Four-Year College Enrollment." *Research in Higher Education* 53 (5): 506–549.

Knight, David S., Nail Hassairi, and David G. Martinez. 2022. "Segregation and School Funding Disparities in California: Contemporary Trends 50 Years after Serrano." *BYU Education and Law Journal* (1): 6.

Krohn, Marvin D., Nicole M. Schmidt, Alan J. Lizotte, and Julie M. Baldwin. 2011. "The Impact of Multiple Marginality on Gang Membership and Delinquent Behavior for Hispanic, African American, and White Male Adolescents." *Journal of Contemporary Criminal Justice* 27 (1): 18–42.

Kozol, Jonathan. 2012. *Savage Inequalities: Children in America's Schools*. New York: Broadway Books.

Kupchik, Aaron, and Nicole L. Bracy. 2009. "To Protect, Serve, and Mentor?" In *Schools Under Surveillance: Cultures of Control in Public Education*, edited by Torin Monahan and Rodolfo Torres, 21. New Brunswick, NJ: Rutgers University Press.

Lareau, Annette. 2011. *Unequal Childhoods*. Berkeley: University of California Press.

Lareau, Annette, and Erin McNamara Horvat. 1999. "Moments of Social Inclusion and Exclusion Race, Class, and Cultural Capital in Family-School Relationships." *Sociology of Education* 72 (1): 37–53.

Laura, Crystal T. 2014. *Being Bad: My Baby Brother and the School-to-Prison Pipeline*. Dulles, VA: Teachers College Press.

Lehr, Camilla, and Cheryl Lange. 2003. "Alternative Schools Serving Students With and Without Disabilities: What Are the Current Issues and Challenges?" *Preventing School Failure: Alternative Education for Children and Youth* 47 (2): 59–65.

Lopez, Nancy. 2003. *Hopeful Girls, Troubled Boys: Race and Gender Disparity in Urban Education*. New York: Routledge.

Losen, Daniel J, ed. 2014. *Closing the School Discipline Gap: Equitable Remedies for Excessive Exclusion*. Dulles, VA: Teachers College Press.

Luna, Nora, and Anita Tijerina Revilla. 2013. "Understanding Latina/o School Pushout: Experiences of Students who Left School before Graduating." *Journal of Latinos and Education* 12 (1): 22–37.

Malagón, M. C. 2010. "All the Losers Go There: Challenging the Deficit Educational Discourse of Chicano Racialized Masculinity in a Continuation High School." *Educational Foundations* 24, 59–76.

Martínez, David G., and Julian Vasquez Heilig. 2022. "An Opportunity to Learn: Engaging in the Praxis of School Finance Policy and Civil Rights." *Minnesota Journal of Law and Inequality* 40 (2): 311–334.

Martinez Jr., Eligio. 2018. "The Education of Escobar Cruz: Sports, Identity and Masculinity in Middle School." *Middle Grades Review* 4 (3): article 3.

Martinez, Eligio, and Michelle Castellanos. 2018. "Catching Them Early: An Examination of Chicano/Latino Middle School Boys' Early Career Aspirations." *The Urban Review* 50 (3): 378–401.

McDonough, P. M. 1997. *Choosing Colleges: How Social Class and Schools Structure Opportunity*. Albany, NY: State University of New York Press.

Mendoza, M., J. J. Blake, M. P. Marchbanks, and K. Ragan. 2020. "Race, Gender, and Disability and the Risk for Juvenile Justice Contact." *The Journal of Special Education* 53(4): 226–235. https://doi.org/10.1177/0022466919845113

Merrin, Gabriel J., Jun Sung Hong, and Dorothy L. Espelage. 2015. "Are the Risk and Protective Factors Similar for Gang-Involved, Pressured-to-Join, and Non-Gang-Involved Youth? A Social-Ecological Analysis." *American Journal of Orthopsychiatry* 85 (6): 522.

Mittleman, J. 2018. "A Downward Spiral? Childhood Suspension and the Path to Juvenile Arrest." *Sociology of Education* 91 (3): 183–204. https://doi.org/10.1177/0038040718784603.

Moloney, Molly, Kathleen MacKenzie, Geoffrey Hunt, and Karen Joe-Laidler. 2009. "The Path and Promise of Fatherhood for Gang Members." *British Journal of Criminology* 49 (3): 305–325.

Monti, Daniel J. 1993. "The Culture of Gangs in the Culture of the School." *Qualitative Sociology* 16 (4): 383–404.

Musto, Michela. 2019. "Brilliant or Bad? The Gendered Social Construction of Exceptionalism in Early Adolescence." *American Sociological Review* 84 (3): 369–393.

Nguyen, Bach Mai Dolly, Pedro Noguera, Nathan Adkins, and Robert T. Teranishi. 2019. "Ethnic Discipline Gap: Unseen Dimensions of Racial Disproportionality in School Discipline." *American Educational Research Journal* 56 (5): 1973–2003.

Noguera, Pedro A. 2003. "Schools, Prisons, and Social Implications of Punishment: Rethinking Disciplinary Practices." *Theory into Practice* 42 (4): 341–350.

Noguera, Pedro, Aída Hurtado, and Edward Fergus, eds. 2013. *Invisible No More: Understanding the Disenfranchisement of Latino Men And Boys*. Routledge.

Novak, Abigail, and Fagan, Abigail. 2022. "The conditioning Effects of Positive Experience on the ACEs-Offending Relationship in Adolescence." *Child Abuse and Neglect* 134: 105915.

Oakes, Jeannie. 2005. *Keeping Track: How Schools Structure Inequality*. New Haven, CT: Yale University Press.

Panfil, Vanessa R. 2022. "'Ask Me about My Goals!' Challenging Pervasive Assumptions of Gang Members' Fatalism by Exploring Gay Gang Members' Goals." *Critical Criminology* 30 (1): 71–93.

Patton, Desmond U., and Benjamin J. Roth. 2016. "Good Kids with Ties to 'Deviant' Peers: Network Strategies Used by African American and Latino Young Men in Violent Neighborhoods." *Children and Youth Services Review* 66: 123–130.

Perna, Laura W., Heather T. Rowan-Kenyon, Scott Loring Thomas, Angela Bell, Robert Anderson, and Chunyan Li. 2008. "The Role of College Counseling in Shaping College Opportunity: Variations across High Schools." *Review of Higher Education* 31 (2): 131–159.

Peterson, Dana, and Finn-Aage Esbensen. 2004. "The Outlook is GREAT: What Educators Say about School-Based Prevention and the Gang Resistance Education and Training (G.R.E.A.T.) Program." *Evaluation Review* 28 (3): 218–245.

Peterson, D., T. J. Taylor, and F. A. Esbensen. 2004. "Gang Membership and Violence Victimization." *Justice Quarterly* 21: 793–815.

Pyrooz, David C. 2014. "From Colors and Guns to Caps and Gowns? The Effects of Gang Membership on Educational Attainment." *Journal of Research in Crime and Delinquency* 51 (1): 56–87.

Pyrooz, David C., and Gary Sweeten. 2015. "Gang Membership between Ages 5 and 17 Years in the United States." *Journal of Adolescent Health* 56 (4): 414–419.

Pyrooz, David C., and Scott Decker. 2011. "Motives and Methods for Leaving the Gang: Understanding the Process of Gang Desistance." *Journal of Criminal Justice* 39 (5): 417–425. https://doi.org/10.1016/j.jcrimjus.2011.07.001.

Rios, Victor M. 2011. *Punished: Policing the Lives of Black and Latino Boys*. New York: New York University Press.

Rios, Victor M. 2017. *Human Targets: Schools, Police, and the Criminalization of Latino Youth.* Chicago, IL: University of Chicago Press.

Saenz, Victor B., and Luis Ponjuan. 2009. "The Vanishing Latino Male in Higher Education." *Journal of Hispanic Higher Education* 8 (1): 54–89.

Sampson, Robert J., and John H. Laub. 1993. *Crime in the Making: Pathways and Turning Points through Life.* Cambridge, MA: Harvard University Press.

Shollenberger, Tracey L. 2015. "Racial Disparities in School Suspension and Subsequent Outcomes." In *Closing the School Discipline Gap: Equitable Remedies for Excessive Exclusion* 31.

Shedd, Carla. 2015. *Unequal City: Race, Schools, and Perceptions of Injustice.* New York: Russell Sage Foundation.

Skiba, Russell J., Robert S. Michael, Abra Carroll Nardo, and Reece L. Peterson. 2002. "The Color of Discipline: Sources of Racial and Gender Disproportionality in School Punishment." *The Urban Review* 34 (4): 317–342.

Stanton-Salazar, Ricardo. 1997. "A Social Capital Framework for Understanding the Socialization of Racial Minority Children and Youths." *Harvard Educational Review* 67 (1): 1–41.

Stanton-Salazar, Ricardo D. 2001. *Manufacturing Hope and Despair: The School and Kin Support Networks of US-Mexican Youth.* Dulles, VA: Teachers College Press.

Stanton-Salazar, Ricardo D. 2011. "A Social Capital Framework for the Study of Institutional Agents and Their Role in the Empowerment of Low-Status Students and Youth." *Youth and Society* 43 (3): 1066–1109.

Tapia, Mike. 2011. "US Juvenile Arrests: Gang Membership, Social Class, and Labeling Effects." *Youth and Society* 43 (4): 1407–1432.

Tellez, Kip, and Michelle Estep. 1997. "Latino Youth Gangs and the Meaning of School." *High School Journal* 81 (2): 69–81.

Thornberry, Terence P., Marvin D. Krohn, Alan J. Lizotte, Carolyn A. Smith, and Kimberly Tobin. 2003. *Gangs and Delinquency in Developmental Perspective.* Cambridge, UK: Cambridge University Press.

Tierney, William G., and Kristan M. Venegas. 2006. "Fictive Kin and Social Capital: The Role of Peer Groups in Applying and Paying for College." *American Behavioral Scientist* 49 (12): 1687–1702.

U.S. Department of Education, Office for Civil Rights, Civil Rights Data Collection, "2013-14 Discipline Estimations by Discipline Type." (This table was prepared January 2018.) https://nces.ed.gov/programs/digest/d17/tables/dt17_233.27.asp?referer=raceindicators

Van Dommelen-Gonzalez, Evan, Julianna Deardorff, Denise Heard, and Alexandra Minnis. 2015. "Homies with Aspirations and Positive Peer Network Ties: Associations with Reduced Frequent Substance Use among Gang-Affiliated Latino Youth." *Journal of Urban Health* 92 (2): 322-337.

Ventura Miller, H., J. C. Barnes, and R. D. Hartley. 2011. "Reconsidering Hispanic Gang Membership and Acculturation in a Multivariate Context." *Crime & Delinquency* 57 (3): 331–355. https://doi.org/10.1177/0011128709348460.

Verdugo, Richard R., and Beverly C. Glenn. 2006. "Race and Alternative Schools." Paper presented at the Annual Meeting of the Conference Alternatives to Expulsion, Suspension, and Dropping Out of School, Orlando, FL. https://www.ncjrs.gov/App/Publications/abstract.aspx.

Vigil, James Diego. 1988. *Barrio Gangs: Street Life and Identity in Southern California.* Austin: University of Texas Press.

Vigil, James Diego. 1999. "Streets and Schools: How Educators Can Help Chicano Marginalized Gang Youth." *Harvard Educational Review* 69 (3): 270–289.

Vigil, James Diego. 2003. "Urban Violence and Street Gangs." *Annual Review of Anthropology* 32: 225–242.

Vigil, James Diego. 2019. "Street Gangs: A Multiple Marginality Perspective." In *Oxford Research Encyclopedia of Criminology and Criminal Justice.* Oxford, UK: Oxford University Press.

Vogell, Heather, and Hannah Fresques. 2017. "Alternative Education: Using Charter Schools to Hide Dropouts and Game the System." *ProPublica*, February 21. https://www.propublica.org/article/alternative-education-using-charter-schools-hide-dropouts-and-game-system.

Wald, Johanna, and Daniel J. Losen. 2003. "Defining and Redirecting a School-to-Prison Pipeline." *New Directions for Youth Development* 2003 (99): 9–15.

Walters, Glenn D. 2018. "College as a Turning Point: Crime Deceleration as a Function of College Attendance and Improved Cognitive Control." *Emerging Adulthood* 6 (5): 336–346.

Weisburst, Emily K. 2019. "Patrolling Public Schools: The Impact of Funding for School Police on Student Discipline and Long-Term Education Outcomes." *Journal of Policy Analysis and Management* 38 (2): 338–365.

Widdowson, Alex O., L. Sergio Garduno, and Benjamin W. Fisher. 2021. "The School-to-Gang Pipeline: Examining the Impact of School Suspension on Joining a Gang for the First Time." *Crime and Delinquency* 67 (6–7): 997–1021.

Willis, Paul. 1977. *Learning to Labor.* New York: Columbia University Press.

Zarate, Maria Estela, and Ronald Gallimore. 2005. "Gender Differences in Factors Leading to College Enrollment: A Longitudinal Analysis of Latina and Latino Students." *Harvard Educational Review* 75 (4): 383–408.

CHAPTER 28

RELIGION AND GANGS
An Introduction to the Isolated and Integrated Affiliation Models

TIMOTHY R. LAUGER AND HALEIGH KUBINIEC

In 2007 or 2008, while I (Lauger) engaged in field research with gang members in Indianapolis, I had a brief conversation with Shawn, a central participant in my study, about the intersection of religion and gang membership. He attended church semi-regularly with a mentor, so I asked him if his participation in church conflicted with his life as a gang member. He simply responded "no," and we never talked about it again. It was a passing question, produced by a momentary curiosity, not pertinent to the direction of the study. Now, with multiple studies published on the role of religion and gang disengagement (Berger et al. 2017; Brenneman 2012; Decker and Pyrooz 2020; Deuchar 2018; Flores 2014; Flores and Hondagneu-Sotelo 2013; Johnson 2017; Johnson and Densley 2018; Vasquez, Marquardt, and Gomez 2003), coupled with my personal interest in the sociology of religion, Shawn's response to that question seems worthy of attention. Part of our motivation for this chapter stems from a recognition that gang members are complicated people defined by more than their propensity for criminal behavior. The prospect of religious gang members adds another layer of complexity to understanding gangs that has not been well developed in the literature, and it further departs from gang stereotypes. Still, explaining criminal behavior remains an important endeavor, and religiosity may help explain variations in gang member behavior.

The potential intersection of gang membership and religiosity also produces questions about both the degree to which gang members integrate into non-gang social systems and the impact it has on their identities, cultural sensibilities, and behaviors. An initial read into the literature suggests that gang and religious life are oppositional, maybe even incompatible. Integration (or embeddedness) into gang networks is associated with higher levels of criminal activity, violence, and victimization while also making efforts to leave gang life more challenging (Papachristos, Braga, and Hureau 2012; Papachristos, Wildman, and Roberto 2015; Pyrooz, Sweeten, and Piquero 2013). Gang members struggle to fit into social settings like work or school that have different behavioral expectations and rely on social control systems ill equipped to manage gang members (Decker and Van Winkle 1996; Fleisher 1998; Vigil 2020). Integration into religious communities and acceptance of religious ideas, by contrast, shapes the lives of adherents and reduces many forms of deviant or criminal behavior (Adamczyk, Freilich, and Kim 2017). Yet gang and religious affiliations may overlap, which produces a rich and untapped area of inquiry to examine potential tensions in gang members' roles, cultures, and personal relationships.

This chapter further develops Lauger and Rivera's (2022) isolated and integrated affiliation models to explore how gang membership may intersect with religion to influence behavior. The *isolated affiliation model* posits that gang members will be exposed to religion, but the tension between the gang and religious life is so strong that members will not embrace religious beliefs or interact closely with religious groups/institutions. When gang members do embrace religion, it creates a conflict that forces individuals to choose either gang or religious life. Choosing religion is a step toward gang disengagement and significant reductions in criminal behavior. The *integrated affiliation model* posits that some gang members will engage with religious groups or institutions and embrace religious beliefs even when gang ideals and religious beliefs contradict each other. Yet it also recognizes that some gangs may be openly religious or include elements of religion, like rituals or symbols, as part of their collective identity. The influence of religion on gang member behavior under the integrated affiliation model is uncertain, and this chapter concludes by exploring possible ways religion may impact criminal behavior.

Isolated Affiliation

The isolated affiliation model assumes that street gangs represent a delinquent subculture that opposes central precepts of conventional culture, especially the orthodox teachings of many religious traditions. Gang life creates pressures to abandon or reject cultural norms and values found in other settings, and gang members are unable to or not interested in reconciling oppositional cultural systems. Some seminal theoretical expressions of culture stress a contrast between gang and conventional culture. For example, Cohen's (1955) classic work emphasizes how low-status youth cannot compete with their middle-class counterparts for social status, so they construct delinquent subcultures through collective action, which produces a unique set of attitudes, beliefs, norms, and values that contradict conventional society. Gang subcultures are non-utilitarian, malicious, negativistic, hedonistic, resistant to external pressures, and starkly oppose the virtues embodied by religious systems (Downes, Rock, and McLaughlin 2016). These values allow low-status youth to compete well in an alternative system and achieve a status that is inaccessible to their middle-class counterparts. Miller (1958) also highlights a set of focal concerns (values) found in "lower-class" culture that shape gang life and differ from those concerns common to middle-class society. Lower-class youth emulate the values found in their cultural milieu, which are communicated by influential community members. Gang members gain a sense of belonging and can pursue status in a group that, for example, focuses on the importance of toughness, especially as an indication of masculinity. Opposing cultures that intersect create conflict, highlighting the impossibility of satisfying both systems and, thus, compelling an individual to choose one over the other. The gang member will either reject the conventional social system, be rejected by that system, or embrace it and leave gang life.

Gang members do struggle to maintain connections with some traditional institutions that reinforce behavioral expectations inconsistent with gang life. They are, for example, less likely than non-gang peers to complete school and remain employed. Compared to non-gang youth who, on average, complete 13.6 years of schooling, gang members average only 11.5 years of education and exhibit a 50% graduation rate (Pyrooz 2014). Youth gang members in Boston and San Salvador display relatively high rates of dropping out of school (52.55% and 58.5%, respectively) and even higher rates of unemployment (62.9% and 69.2%) (Olate, Salas-Wright, and Vaughn 2011). Qualitative studies reinforce these findings by noting that gang members are minimally involved in conventional institutions or face substantial challenges when they do participate (e.g., Bolden 2020; Decker and Van Winkle 1996; Fleisher 1998; Garot 2010). According to Vigil (2020), gang members experience cultural conflict in schools. They embrace anti-authority attitudes learned on the street that conflict with an authoritarian mindset adopted by school authorities attempting to control students' behaviors.

Price (2014) similarly argues that the allure of gang life (e.g., money, relationships, and independence) is more appealing than school performance, but gang members also describe being rejected by institutions. They were not allowed to return to school due to gang involvement, or they had acquired too many absences as a result of court dates and being incarcerated. Other scholars have noted how reactionary policies in schools further isolate struggling students, especially those involved with street life, and push them out of formal educational settings (Rios 2017; Vigil 2020). Connections to traditional institutions are especially strained when individuals become increasingly embedded in the gang. When a gang member's social energy is primarily devoted to the maintenance of their gang connections, gang life will both limit their ability to build or maintain connections elsewhere and restrict participation in alternative social outlets like education, employment, and religion (Pyrooz, Sweeten, and Piquero 2013).

There is good reason to suggest that natural tensions exist between gangs and religious institutions, and that embracing religious beliefs and participating in religious settings is difficult to reconcile with gang life. Research generally finds an inverse relationship between religiosity and criminal behavior, as religious beliefs, participation in religious activities, and connections with co-religionists reduce participation in deviant acts and criminal conduct (Adamczyk et al. 2017; Baier and Wright 2001). These findings also hold for populations most at risk for gang membership. Church attendance for youth residing in impoverished inner-city areas reduces the likelihood of participation in drug use and drug sales (Johnson et al. 2000). Religion both socializes adherents to norms opposed to criminal behavior and provides social control that inhibits the opportunity and motivation to engage in crime (Adamczyk et al. 2017; Baier and Wright 2001). Gang members, by contrast, are more likely to engage in crime relative to non-gang members, and active gang membership represents the peak of criminal involvement (Pyrooz et al. 2016). Gang life facilitates or enhances the criminal behavior of members, as group processes socialize gang members to norms that advocate participation in criminal activity (e.g., Lauger 2019). Social processes in gangs and religious institutions represent competing forces that influence behavior, particularly criminal behavior, in opposite directions.

Many gang members are still exposed to religious ideas even when the two social systems appear oppositional (Offutt 2020). Disenfranchised urban neighborhoods are home to an abundance of both gangs and religious institutions (Katz and Schnebly 2011, Laudariji and Livezey 2000). Scholars have noted, for example, that the Black church is an influential social organization within urban communities that produces both bonding and bridging ties central to social life and social action (Patillo-McCoy 1999; Sampson 2012). They also variably engage with street life. Some churches proselytize the "unsaved" and "broken" individuals who participate in street activities while also meeting their practical needs and intervening in their conflicts. Others protect young people in their congregations from the "evils" of street life by isolating them from the streets and advocating strong bonding ties within the congregation (McRoberts 2003).

Churches also provide gang members with a safe space to resolve conflicts, and pastors try to mentor gang members, mediate disputes, and facilitate communications between police and the community to increase the effectiveness of violence reduction initiatives (Brunson et al. 2015; Lane 2019; McRoberts 2003). Regardless of the specific approach churches take to engage elements of street life, they all establish boundaries between those who are "saved" and those who are "lost," which provides a clear message making religious and alternative lifestyles, like gang life, incompatible (McRoberts 2003). Some gang members also come from religious families or attend private schools with strict, religiously based rules. Gang members seem to rebel against the religious traditions of their guardians, implying a division between gang and religious affiliations (Bolden 2020; Horowitz 1983; Offutt 2020; Patillo-McCoy 1999; Ward 2013). For example, Patillo-McCoy (1999) tells the story of "Spider," who grew up in a religious home, read his Bible (albeit sporadically), and respects local religious orders but rebelled by engaging in crime, violence, and gang life. The degree to which exposure to religion or religious others influences personal religiosity and subsequent behavior among gang members is not clear, but most accounts treat religion and gang membership as mutually exclusive.

The beliefs and social support systems of religious groups do seem to contrast those found in street gangs, and embracing religion is a significant factor in leaving gang life both in and outside of prison (Berger et al. 2017; Decker and Pyrooz 2020; Flores and Hondagneu-Sotelo 2013). Religious systems often advocate strict rules to discourage "immoral" behavior while some gangs encourage hedonistic lifestyles (Brenneman 2012; Flores 2014). When male gang members embrace or encounter religious systems, they are exposed to conceptions of masculinity that contrast the hypermasculine ideals and roles of gang life (Deuchar 2018; Flores 2014). Religious groups offer social support to deal with stressful life events and the shame of past behavior (Bolden 2020; Brenneman 2012; Johnson 2017). Former gang members can find a new source for status in the redemption narratives they tell to other religious people who highly value dramatic conversion stories (Vasquez et al. 2003). Johnson and Densley (2018) described Brazilian gang members who became religious converts in prison, performing behaviors during church rituals that reaffirmed a new identity and "signaling" their commitment to religion and disengagement from gang life (see also Densley 2013; Rosen and Cruz 2019). Similar processes also appear to occur outside of prison, as gang members consider becoming religious a legitimate reason for leaving the gang (Ward 2013). These examples position religious and gang affiliation as conflicting while demonstrating that embracing religion signals a departure from gang life, crime, and violence (Johnson and Densley 2018).

Integrated Affiliation

As discussed above, the isolated affiliation model assumes that gang life is incompatible with religious life and that gang members cannot reconcile the difference between these competing social systems. Both assumptions merit further attention, requiring an examination of religious beliefs, the degree to which gang members embrace or discuss religious ideas, and the capacity of gang members to manage both systems. The integrated affiliation model, by contrast, predicts that religious and gang affiliations can overlap. Religion may be integrated into the collective life of the gang so that members do not experience conflict between personal beliefs and gang life when they are with other gang members. Tensions may exist, however, when interacting with religious non-gang members or participating in religious institutions. If religious ideas are not an expressed part of gang life, members may still be religious and experience a degree of conflict between their religious and gang identities. How they negotiate this tension merits attention and may influence behavior, perhaps impacting criminal activity.

Collective Identity Integration: Theology in Gang Life

The integrated affiliation model allows for religious ideas to be present in and even central to the corporate life of the gang. To fully understand the role of religion in collective gang life, researchers should examine both the salience of religious ideas within the group and the type of religious ideas espoused by the group. The salience of religious ideas can range from non-existent to being a central feature of the group's collective identity, evidenced by frequent and public use of religious imagery, ideas, and customs. Clarifying the type of religious beliefs found in gangs is important, because theology has consequences and can influence behavior. Although religious beliefs often reduce deviant and criminal behavior (Adamczyk et al. 2017), some collectivities accept religious ideas that are inconsistent with orthodoxy and can fuel deviant behavior. For example, some hate groups, including those considered "alt-right gangs," embrace an unorthodox version of Christianity (Christian Identity) that elevates the white race as being God's chosen people while claiming that other races are subhuman and evil (Dobratz 2001; Reid, Valasik, and Bagavathi 2018). Religion within gang life may or may not reflect orthodox beliefs, and any theology espoused in gang life, even if informal and not agreed upon, potentially influences collective and individual behavior.

We anticipate that if religious ideas are openly expressed in gang life, their centrality to the gang's collective identity will vary between gangs. Religion can be part of a gang's collective identity to the point that the gang acknowledges "we as a group are religious," and religious practices are a normal and expected part of gang life. The overtly religious gang is likely uncommon but not unheard of. Under the leadership of Jeff Fort, a faction of the Blackstone Rangers transformed into the El Rukins, the group overtly followed elements of Islamic teaching and customs to the point that it became a central part of their collective identity (Moore and Williams 2011). The degree to which the El Rukins' religious beliefs overpowered or combined with both criminality and political ideals is unclear, even after

Fort went to prison for conspiring with Libyan terrorists. Brotherton and Barrios (2004) note how King Tone of the Latin Kings experienced a religious conversion and subsequently used aspects of Christianity as a foundation to alter the group's orientation toward a social movement that sought to improve both the lives of members and their political standing in the community. Barrios (2007) further argues that "Kingism/Queenism" is rooted in a spirituality of liberation, a theology that deviates from orthodox Christianity's beliefs about Jesus and personal salvation in favor of ideas about freeing people from oppression and social injustice. These religious ideas are central to the collective identity of Latin Kings/Queens.

Gangs can also mimic religious practices, like prayers, and use them to establish or reinforce collective identity and group cohesion, but the connection to actual religious beliefs and theology is unclear or questionable. Chicago's Black Disciples incorporate a prayer that uses religious imagery, "God put the stars in the sky, and with the reflections they shine," but it mostly focuses on reinforcing unity in the gang under the leadership of "King David" or David Barksdale (Knox 2004, 110). They also created 10 commandments that were devoid of religious ideas. The Latin King's manifesto describes the group or nation as a "religion which gives us faith in ourselves" and promises that serving the nation will lead one to find Yahweh (God) (Hagedorn 2015, 74; see also Brotherton and Barrios 2004). The Vice Lords include theological statements in its constitution, stating how Allah is a singular force who shares himself with human beings and gives us difficulties to overcome (Knox and Papachristos 2002). Religious imagery is important, as the power of religious or religious-like practices reinforces social cohesion and a belief in the ideals of gang life, but the extent to which members embrace religious ideas and how they impact behavior is unknown.

Religious ideas may also be interwoven into gang traditions or activities even if it does not overtly align with group identity. Hagedorn (2015) describes how a Puerto Rican gang in Chicago prepared for retaliatory violence by reciting both the Lord's Prayer, an orthodox practice of the Catholic Church, along with an official prayer of the gang. Religious culture in the Puerto Rican community was so widespread and expected that gang members did not think their participation in gang wars contradicted religious life. This lack of conflict does not mean, however, that religious ideas, aside from the formality of a rote prayer, are influential in shaping the gang's identity or member behavior. Youth can perform religious practices and even identify as being religious without internalizing their faith (Smith and Denton 2009). Researchers should, therefore, examine both internal and external signs of religious commitment of gang members to determine the extent to which they embrace and apply religious ideas. Collective religious practices, like prayer, may be meaningful to members or it may be a taken-for-granted tradition borrowed from their broader culture.

Personal Identity Integration

Many gangs likely do not express theological ideas or model religious-like customs, but some of their members may still be connected to orthodox religious groups and express personal religious beliefs. They accept a personal theology that is not expressed in the gang. Personal religiosity is a well-developed concept that involves participation in religious groups/communities, evidence of personal religious practices (e.g., prayer or reading scripture), and adherence to personal religious beliefs (e.g., Rivera and Lauger, 2021). Researchers must develop robust measures of religiosity among gang members because people are inclined to report being religious even without exhibiting any commitment to religion. Personal religiosity, which is inversely associated with deviance (Adamczyk et al. 2017), should also not be confused with the concept of spirituality. Religiosity involves "church-centered beliefs" and practices, which include a connection to religious traditions and institutions typically through participation in religious social settings. Spirituality involves a subjective orientation that focuses on personal experience with the sacred, which can deviate from orthodoxy (e.g., mysticism) and be detached from participation in organized religious life (Jang and Franzen 2013). Although the two concepts overlap, people who define themselves as spiritual but not religious are more prone to engage in deviant behavior in part because they are disconnected from the social constraints and socializing influence of religious communities (Jang and Franzen 2013; Seto 2021). Religiosity, by contrast, includes both commitment to personal beliefs and a connection to co-religionists and religious institutions.

Religious systems involve deeply personal beliefs that produce bonds between people who have different affiliations outside of their religious group. Religious individuals are drawn to each other (McPherson, Smith-Lovin, and Cook 2001), but they also participate in groups (e.g., at work, school, or for recreation) that are not expressly religious (Pescosolido and Rubin 2000; Simmel 1955). Participation in multiple groups produces an infinite set of potential combinations of affiliations, which form a person's sense of self (Simmel 1955). Many of these affiliations are compatible with religion but may sometimes also be in opposition, creating an important opportunity for scholars to examine how individuals negotiate conflicting roles (Ammerman 2003). For example, Pitts (2010a and 2010b) examines how some Black gay men attend primarily Black churches that espouse conservative theology in opposition to homosexuality. These men selectively apply religious values to their sexual identity as a way to adapt and challenge the teacher's knowledge, personal morality, and motivation to neutralize anti-gay messages. Religion may intersect with competing social systems and beliefs more prominently during adolescence, when gang membership is most common, as youth are still subject to the social patterns and belief systems of their family (Smith and Denton 2009). Most adolescents interact with different social groups and encounter different belief systems. It is a time of life marked by ambivalence, confusion, and experimentation (Erikson 1959; Vigil 2020).

There is evidence that some gang members embrace roles, identities, orientations, and behaviors that overtly conflict with gang culture. Panfil (2017) demonstrates how some gay gang members function within a gang culture that emphasizes hypermasculine, heteronormative ideals while denigrating homosexual preferences. Yet some gay men perform gang roles that deviate from their personal preferences so they fit in with the gang and do not become a target of aggression. Sexual orientation is not perfectly analogous to either gang or religious affiliation, but the tension experienced by gay gang members or gay men in conservative churches reveals much about how competing social groups can influence identity, social roles, and behavior. There is also some evidence that gang membership and personal religiosity overlap to create similar tensions. Gangs and religion are both so embedded in El Salvador they become entangled in the lives of community members. Gang members come from religious families, attend church with varying degrees of regularity, and sometimes become religious converts but remain committed to gang life (Offutt 2020). Lauger and Rivera (2022) find that gang members in a national sample of youth are less likely than peers to be religious, but many still participate in religious settings and internalize religious beliefs even when the behavioral outcomes of both systems conflict. How these intersecting affiliations influence gang members' identities, social roles, and behavior is largely unknown.

Panfil's (2017) study highlights how gang members can have multifaceted social lives so that their orchestrated behavior around other gang members does not align with other components of their identity. One way to account for this is to use a multidimensional conception of personal identity that explains the existence and negotiation of role conflict. Identity theory is particularly helpful, as it argues personal identity consists of social roles that are structured into a salience hierarchy (Stryker 1980). Social roles derive from personal interactions, so one's understanding of their role (father, gang member, student, etc.) is developed over time by interacting with people who see that person in that role. Such roles are then performed in social settings according to an audience's expectations. For example, my (Lauger) role as a father has developed over time through routine interactions with my children, wife, and other close contacts who see me as a father and talk with me about fatherhood. My students have not influenced my role as a father just as my children have not influenced my role as a professor. I also do not perform the father role when interacting with students or the professor role when interacting with my children. Similarly, a gang member's conception of their gang role is developed over time through interactions with individuals in and around the gang. Yet they may also interact with people outside of gang life and develop social roles unique to those relationships. The multiplicity of roles that develop through a host of interactions can be extensive, and gang members may embrace many roles that are different from their role as a gang member. They then generally perform these roles according to audience expectations (Goffman 1959).

Social roles are structured into a salience hierarchy that determines the extent to which a role is activated across multiple social settings (Stryker 1980). Roles often do not conflict, as people can navigate different situations by activating different roles without experiencing problems. I do not experience much conflict between my roles as Dad and professor/scholar. Role conflicts can arise, however, when issues emerge like contrasting behavioral expectations or conflicts with time management. Such tensions force individuals to negotiate roles in ways that highlight the salience of one role over another within their identity structure.

For example, my role as father is more salient than my role as scholar/professor because when time management conflicts occur, I often choose to engage in "dad activities" like coaching sports teams rather than spending that time writing, researching, or preparing for classes. Many gang members likely experience similar conflicts in their social roles and therefore have to navigate role performances across different social settings and groups. Social roles that are relatively disconnected from gang networks involve a different set of social expectations found in gang or street life. Interactions with parents, especially parents who are not connected to street life nor privy to their child's street activities, require non-gang role performances. Employed gang members likely have to embrace a different social role when working. Yet roles at work or in one's family may conflict with gang life (e.g., time management or behavioral expectations), which forces the gang member to choose one role over the other and undermine their employability, relationships with loved ones, or status as a gang member. This may be especially true with their participation in religious communities, as behavioral expectations between gang and religious life likely differ. Role salience is influenced by embeddedness, and we anticipate that the structure of one's social network and relative connectedness to other gang members will influence the degree to which an individual performs both gang and religious roles across different types of situations. Religious gang members who are deeply embedded within the gang or have broad and strong ties with other gang members are more likely than peripheral gang members to perform their gang member role across many types of situations.

Both gang and religious affiliations can be part of a person's identity through the development and performance of social roles that are influenced by one's immediate social context (Lauger 2020; Stryker and Serpe 1982; Wimberley 1989). "Gang member" is a social role employed in select situations (Garot 2007, 2010), and commitment to that role varies within the gang (Vigil 1988). Some scholars have noted how an individual's conception of the gang role coupled with their commitment to that role influences criminal behavior, especially violence (Bubolz and Lee 2019; Hennigan and Spanovic 2012; Stretesky and Progrebin 2007). Religious identities are similarly situated within a person's sense of self and can be activated dependent on context. Given the likelihood of competing expectations between gangs and many forms of religion, we anticipate that religious gang members experience role conflict and adopt strategies to navigate that conflict. Although religion can transform gang members, causing them to turn away from their gang roles and gang-related behaviors, it may also coexist alongside gang membership as a unique social role within a person's identity. Religious gang members may "do gang" when around gang members and then perform the role of a religious person when around other religious people. The methods used by gang members to navigate dimensions of their multifaceted social lives are not clear at this point and are a topic worthy of further research.

Adjusting or updating conceptions of culture can also lead to new insights into how gang members may navigate gang and religious life. Some traditional theories, like Cohen's (1955) classic work, describe gang culture as being in opposition to and removed from "conventional" culture, but more recent expressions of gang culture suggest members are exposed to and embrace multiple competing cultural systems (Lauger and Horning 2020). For example, Horowitz and Schwartz (1974) argue that gang members embrace conventional culture in addition to an honor-based system that emphasizes the importance of protecting masculinity through aggressive behavior (see also Horowitz 1983). In most circumstances, gang members do not value or pursue violence but may activate aspects of gang culture that encourage a violent response when someone challenges their masculinity. In these moments, gang members experience normative ambiguity or a conflict between cultural systems that they must navigate to resolve an affront to their masculinity.

Harding's (2010) work on cultural heterogeneity within violence-prone Boston neighborhoods similarly illustrates how some adolescents are exposed to, understand, embrace, and use contrasting cultural ideas in their daily lives. They understand and embrace both street-oriented conceptions of sexual behavior in which the pursuit of sex involves a gendered competition between sexes, and more traditional, sometimes religion-based, forms of sexuality that emphasize the importance of romance and long-term commitment. Youth in these communities are culturally ambivalent and communicate a mixture of ideas about sex. Given these examples, one can reasonably expect that gang members can embrace elements of both gang and religious culture even when they seem to oppose each other.

Cultural sociologists have generally moved away from thinking about culture as a coherent set of values, instead emphasizing that it consists of schematic structures used to interpret information and plan strategies of action (DiMaggio 1997; Harding 2010). Culture shapes how individuals understand situations and allows them to anticipate the consequences of their perceived behavioral options (Corsaro 1992; Harding 2010). One's ability to competently navigate a social encounter is contingent on their ability to both interpret that moment accurately and behave accordingly. Swidler (1986) uses the metaphor of a toolkit to describe how people understand and use diverse cultural ideas to navigate complex social interactions across different settings (see also Hannerz 1969). Some people have diverse toolkits, which allow them to competently engage different people across a range of settings. Others are more limited and struggle to understand the meaning of social encounters or the consequences of their behavior beyond select social environments. Regarding gang members and religiosity, the issue is not how gang members reconcile competing values systems, but whether they have the toolkit to function in both settings. A religious gang member, especially one who routinely participates in both social settings, should be able to interpret the meaning of interactions in both settings and then strategize their behavior according to anticipated outcomes.

Gangs, Religion, and Criminal Behavior

We have presented two models to explain how religion may intersect with gang life. The isolated affiliation model posits a simple relationship between gang membership, religion, and criminal behavior. Religion and gang membership conflict so that religious adherence will prevent individuals from becoming gang members or cause gang members to leave gang life. Gang members, in turn, will also reject religious ideas. The relationship between gang membership and criminal behavior is positively associated while the relationship between religiosity and criminal behavior is inversely related (e.g., Adamczyk et al. 2017; Pyrooz et al. 2016). A movement away from gang membership toward religion will, therefore, lead to significant reductions in criminal behavior, which is evidenced by the growing body of research on the role of religion in gang desistance, while a movement toward gang membership and away from religion will lead to significant increases in criminal behavior.

The integrated affiliation model posits a more complex relationship between gang membership and religion, as it accounts for variations in the centrality of religion to the gang's collective identity, the degree to which an individual gang member embraces religious ideas, and the nature of those religious ideas. It also recognizes that gang members can simultaneously embrace elements of gang and religious life, performing those roles differently in different settings or demonstrating the capacity to navigate both gang and religious cultural settings. The following section examines some of the possible ways that personal religiosity may intersect with gang membership to influence criminal behavior. We first examine scenarios in which gangs embrace elements of religion into their collective identity, and then examine possible relationships between religious gang members and criminal behavior when gangs do not corporately embrace religion. Our intent is to develop questions and areas of inquiry to guide future research.

Collective Identity, Gang Membership, Religious Beliefs, and Crime

The centrality of religion to a gang's collective identity will determine how members experience or negotiate tensions between gang and religious life. This prediction is based on an abundance of literature that argues social processes construct gang culture and identity while also socializing individuals to gang life and influencing their behavior (e.g., Lauger 2019). Gangs that are openly religious will likely shape a member's understanding of both gang member and religious person, combining social roles into the single construct of "religious gang member." Earlier in this chapter, we noted that religious salience in gangs will vary, so gangs with a religious collective identity represent one extreme while irreligious gangs represent the other extreme. The closer a gang is to the "religious gang" extreme the less problematic religiosity is for the active gang member, as identity work within the gang constructs the idea of a "religious gang member" for the gang member. This type of identity work is worth examining and likely involves open conversations between active gang members about the meaning of religion to the gang and for gang members. In irreligious gangs, however, religious gang members must engage in identity work independent of social processes within the gang.

The influence of religion on criminal behavior is then contingent on how the gang combines or reconciles the idea of religion with criminal behavior. Collective identities are fluid, as social processes in group life continuously construct ideas that define the group and can simultaneously focus on multiple ideas (Melucci 1995; Snow 2001). Activities in group life both define and reinforce the central characteristics of the group. Many scholars argue that criminal behavior is a central, even defining, element of a gang's identity (e.g., Klein and Maxson 2010). The inclusion of religion into gang life presents interesting questions about how the group navigates and reconciles any differences that arise. Will a gang's emphasis on criminal behavior envelop its religious elements so that any contradiction between the two is either ignored (religion is selectively applied) or used to justify criminal endeavors? The role of religion in gangs may parallel how right-wing hate groups use it to fuel deviance (Dobratz 2001). Will religious ideas change the meaning of criminal behavior, perhaps combining social and political activism with religiosity to resist injustice or pursue justice through illicit means? The El Rukins exhibited an evolving mixture of religious commitment, strict behavioral regulations, political activism, and participation in serious criminal behavior over multiple decades (Moore and Williams 2011), but they may be an exceptional case. Will religious beliefs mute criminal propensities, perhaps, for example, encouraging members to find alternative ways to deal with conflicts? Any of these possibilities are reasonable and worthy of study.

Gangs that fall somewhere in the middle of the two extremes potentially offer a wealth of insight into how openly stated ideas about religion become infused with gang life or gang activities to influence members even if religion is not a defining part of gang life. Although some scholars have noted the presence of religious ideas in gangs (e.g., Hagedorn 2015), the significance of religion has received little attention. Group processes in these gangs will likely not construct the "religious gang member" identity for members. Relative to irreligious gangs, however, identity work accompanying being a religious gang member is less problematic when religious ideas or practices are discussed or modeled but not central to group life. Researchers should examine the experiences of religious gang members in both types of groups to identify differences that may influence behavior. Corporately, the discussion of religious ideas or use of religious practices may contribute to group solidarity and group behavior even when tangential to group life. Examples like Hagedorn's (2015) description of a Puerto Rican gang reciting the Lord's Prayer before a gang war are worth exploring. Does the cultural practice of reciting a religious prayer enhance the sense of group solidarity beyond what is produced by intergroup conflict? Does the prayer help justify a member's participation in violence, somehow making violence righteous, or creating the belief that God is on their side? Is it merely a taken-for-granted activity that has little impact on gang members or group life? At present, we do not know the answers to these questions, but such questions may lead to insights into how religious ideas, symbols, and practices within gangs intersect with group processes to influence individual and collective behavior.

The religious belief system expressed in a gang, or the theology of gang life, is also important to examine, and variations exist across religious belief systems that can influence behavior. For example, members of Christian denominations differ in their conceptions of God, tendencies for fatalistic mindsets, and attitudes about behaviors like abortion, premarital sex, and marijuana use (Bolzendahl and Brooks 2005; Noffke and McFadden 2001; Ulmer et al. 2012). Gang scholars who have focused on the role of religion in desistance have carefully attended to how theological traditions influence group processes and cultural ideas that shape gang members (Brenneman 2012; Flores 2014; Johnson 2017). Brenneman (2012) notably examines how Pentecostal theology emphasizes spiritual renewal (rebirth) within the context of an ongoing struggle between good and evil as the solution to the local gang problem. Adherence to religious ideas is often revealed in strict pious behavior and through emotional conversion experiences that are routinely reinforced during corporate worship. Problematic behavior (sin) may be an indication of reverting to a previous lifestyle, thereby undermining salvation, which creates strong social pressure to both follow behavioral guidelines and monitor fellow believers' behavior (see also Flores 2014; Johnson 2017). The theological framework contributing to desistance involves a radical shift in thinking, but it reflects just one strand of Christianity that differs from other traditions like Catholicism or Reformed theology (Brenneman 2012; Flores 2014). The influence of different religions or religious denominations on active gang members is largely unknown and merits further examination.

Irreligious Gangs, Personal Religiosity, and Crime

Many gangs likely have little to no connection to religious beliefs or practices, and religious gang members are then part of multiple social systems that may have different beliefs or behavioral expectations. Assuming that most gang members are exposed to orthodox religious ideas, their experience in both systems would lead to contradictory demands and different behavioral expectations. Given that most research on religion and crime indicates personal religiosity reduces deviance/criminal behavior (Adamczyk et al. 2017), one can reasonably propose that personal religiosity will reduce the criminal behavior of gang members. Moreover, research on religion and deviance generally supports the antiaesthetic hypothesis, which argues religion reduces participation in forms of deviance that are more commonly accepted in society (e.g., binge drinking, marijuana use, and sexual behavior) but it has less of an impact on behaviors, like violence, that receive disapproval from secular society (e.g., Miller and Vuolo 2018). Because violence is more accepted or encouraged in street gangs than in other secular settings, the protective effect of religion on violence may be greater for gang members than for non-gang peers.

We anticipate that religiosity will protect gang members against criminal behavior, but it may have the opposite effect. Some qualitative studies find that religiosity among street offenders (not gang members) contributes to criminal behavior. Topalli, Brezina, and Bernhardt (2012) examined the prevalence and effect of religious beliefs among 48 active street offenders in Atlanta. Almost all offenders in the study expressed religious beliefs, and some used those beliefs to rationalize criminal behavior and neutralize non-criminal norms. For example, they claimed to be punishing bad people for Jesus or said they can commit crimes without consequence because Jesus will forgive them. Street ideology was more salient to street offenders than their religious beliefs, which changed to better align with the ideals of street life. Other qualitative studies of street offenders, even when they do not focus on religion, have encountered religious ideas embedded in data that seem to rationalize participation in crime (e.g., Jacobs and Wright 1999, 158). The ideas expressed by street offenders either do not align with orthodox religious teachings or are distortions/misapplications of those teachings. Theology matters, and researchers should explore not only if gang members are religious but also how they understand and apply religious ideas.

Research on the effect of religion on criminal behavior among gang members is lacking, but two studies provide some insight into the nature of this relationship. Salas-Wright, Olate, and Vaughn (2013) examine the relationship of both spirituality and religious coping (i.e., the tendency to trust God during hard times) on delinquency among a sample of gang members and high-risk adolescents in El Salvador. Their findings indicate that spirituality is a protective factor against carrying a weapon, property destruction, and public disturbances, whereas religious coping is negatively associated with only theft. They suggest that religious coping reflects momentary reliance on faith during crises, but spirituality captures a higher degree of commitment over time and, therefore, has a stronger protective effect against delinquency. Lauger and Rivera (2022) use Add Health data to examine the relationship between personal religiosity, gang membership, and serious violence. They find that personal religiosity, which is measured by the salience of religious beliefs, participation in private religious activities, and involvement in religious group activities, is inversely related to the prevalence but not the frequency of violence among gang members. More religious gang members exhibit a 39% reduction in their odds of ever having committed a serious act of violence, but the frequency of their participation in violence is not significantly different.

The second finding is perplexing and merits further attention. If future research confirms that religiosity reduces the prevalence but not the frequency of violence among gang members, scholars must further explore how religious beliefs intersect with gang life. Lauger and Rivera (2022) speculate that such findings may indicate variability in how religious gang members navigate competing roles. Some gang members experience ambivalence between gang and religious life. Their role as a religious person is salient enough to decrease the likelihood that they will ever engage in serious violence. They may activate their religious identity to opt-out of violence, or their time spent in religious settings may reduce both exposure to violence and opportunities to engage in violence. They may also have a more diverse cultural toolkit that allows them to navigate contentious situations without escalating to the point of violence. The religious identities of other gang members may not be salient enough to counter group processes that facilitate violence. Once the religious gang member demonstrates a willingness and ability to engage in violence, the gang identity may be more salient than the religious identity, and the person will participate in as much violence as non-religious gang peers. These possibilities are, however, merely speculation and require more attention.

Conclusion

The intersection of gangs and religion is an area of research that can provide insight into the extent to which gang members engage non-gang social systems and the effect they have on gang member behavior. This chapter examined the isolated affiliation and integrated affiliation models (Lauger and Rivera 2022), which predict different relationships between gangs and religion, with the intent to facilitate interest and future research. The isolated affiliation model predicts that although gang members are exposed to religion, the two social systems conflict, and gang members are not likely to seriously embrace religion. When gang members do become religious, it leads them to desist from gang life and criminal behavior. The integrated affiliation model predicts that gang members can simultaneously embrace religion and gang life, even when the two systems conflict. Some gangs may incorporate religious ideas or practices into group life, which allows members to adopt an identity of "religious gang member" that does not conflict with gang life. Most gangs, however, are irreligious, but some members in these gangs may still report being religious. Religious gang members in irreligious gangs likely navigate competing social systems in ways that influence participation in criminal behavior. The influence of religion on active gang members is largely unknown and merits further attention. This area of research may also lead to insights into how gang members experience and navigate diverse cultures, social settings, and social roles, which may provide a more thorough depiction of gangs while also explaining variations in criminal behavior within and across gangs.

Yet there is an absence of data that adequately measures both religiosity and gang membership within the same dataset. My (Lauger) recent study on gangs and religiosity (Lauger and Rivera 2022) relied on Add Health data that included a strong measurement of religiosity across multiple waves, but the dataset lacked strong and consistent gang variables across waves. Our analysis was, therefore, limited in that it could not assess the effect of religiosity over time, and it only included individuals who reported being initiated into a gang "over the last 12 months." This was the best dataset we could find, as many datasets include strong measures of religiosity and no measures of gang membership or vice versa, which indicates a need to include both in a single dataset. Although self-nomination is a robust method of measuring gang membership (Decker et al. 2014), measuring religiosity is more complicated and requires accounting for religious salience (expressed belief/importance of religion), religious participation (e.g., church attendance), and engagement in private religious practices (e.g., reading scripture or praying) (see Rivera and Lauger 2021). Including measurements for these three dimensions of religious life into a longitudinal dataset that also includes robust gang measures may yield substantial findings about how religiosity intersects with gang membership and behavior over time.

The potential intersection of gang membership and religiosity may also create tensions that researchers can best observe through qualitative methods. This chapter introduced ideas about role conflict that may occur when the social roles of "gang member" and "religious person" coexist within a person's identity. Qualitative research can examine the degree to which tensions exist between gang membership and religious life and how individuals negotiate such tensions. Do gang members adapt religious theology to gang or street life, or does religious theology alter gang members' conception of their gang role? It can also allow researchers to observe role salience, or the probability that a given role will be activated in a situation. How do gang members act in a religious setting or in another environment that is distinct from the gang? Do they, as Garot (2007) suggests, perform as a gang member in select settings, like when being "hit up," or does their gang role transfer to other settings that lack a direct need to identify gang affiliation? Qualitative research can also examine if religious ideas directly influence gang member behavior, perhaps reducing participation in criminal activity, and it can identify the possible mechanisms that alter behavior. There is much to be learned about gang life by examining how it intersects with religion.

REFERENCES

Adamczyk, Amy, Joshua D. Freilich, and Chunrye Kim. 2017. "Religion and Crime: A Systematic Review and Assessment of Next Steps." *Sociology of Religion* 78: 192–232.

Ammerman, Nancy T. 2003. "Religious Identities and Religious Institutions." In *Handbook of the Sociology of Religion*, edited by Michelle Dillion, 207–224. New York: Cambridge University Press.

Berger, Rony, Hisham Abu-Raiya, Yotam Heineberg, and Philip Zimbardo. 2017. "The Process of Desistance among Core Ex-Gang Members." *American Journal of Orthopsychiatry* 87: 487–502.

Baier, Colin J., and Bradley R. E. Wright. 2001. "'If You Love Me, Keep My Commandments': A Meta-Analysis of the Effect of Religion on Crime." *Journal of Research in Crime and Delinquency* 38: 2–21.

Bolden, Christian L. 2020. *Out of the Red*. New Brunswick, NJ: Rutgers University Press.

Bolzendahl Catherine, and Clem Brooks. 2005. "Polarization, Secularization, or Differences as Usual? Denominational Cleavage in the U.S. Social Attitudes Since the 1970s." *Sociological Quarterly* 46: 47–78.

Barrios, Luis. 2007. "Gangs and Spirituality of Liberation." In *Gangs in the Global City: Alternatives to Traditional Criminology*, edited by John M. Hagedorn, 225–247. Chicago, IL: University of Illinois Press.

Brenneman, Robert. 2012. *Homies and Hermanos*. New York: Oxford University Press.

Brotherton, David C., and Luis Barrios. 2004. *The Almighty Latin King and Queen Nation*. New York: Columbia University Press.

Brunson, Rod K., Anthony A. Braga, David M. Hureau, and Kashea Pegram. 2015. "We Trust You, but Not That Much: Examining Police–Black Clergy Partnerships to Reduce Youth Violence." *Justice Quarterly* 32: 1006–1036.

Bubolz, Brian F., and Sou Lee. 2019. "Putting in Work: The Application of Identity Theory to Gang Violence and Commitment." *Deviant Behavior* 40: 690–702.

Cohen, Albert K. 1955. *Delinquent Boys*. New York: Free Press.

Corsaro, William A. 1992. "Interpretive Reproduction in Children's Peer Cultures." *Social Psychological Quarterly* 55: 160–177.

Decker Scott H., and Pyrooz David C. 2020. "The Role of Religion and Spirituality in Disengagement from Gangs." In *Gangs in the Era of Internet and Social Media*, edited by Chris Melde and Frank M. Weerman, 225–249. Cham, Switzerland: Springer.

Decker, Scott. H., David C. Pyrooz, Gary Sweeten, and Richard K. Moule, Jr. 2014. "Validating Self-Nomination in Gang Research: Assessing Differences in Gang Embeddedness across Non-, Current, and Former Gang Members." *Journal of Quantitative Criminology* 30: 577–598.

Decker, Scott H., and Barrik Van Winkle. 1996. *Life in the Gang*. Cambridge, UK: Cambridge University Press.

Densley, James A. 2013. *How Gangs Work*. Basingstoke, UK: Palgrave Macmillian

Deuchar, Ross. 2018. *Gangs and Spirituality*. Basingstoke, UK: Palgrave Macmillan.

DiMaggio, Paul. 1997. "Culture and Cognition." *Annual Review of Sociology* 23: 263–287.

Dobratz, Betty A. 2001. "The Role of Religion in the Collective Identity of the White Racialist Movement." *Journal for the Scientific Study of Religion* 40: 287–302.

Downes, David, Paul Rock, and Gene McLaughlin. 2016. *Understanding Deviance: A Guide to the Sociology of Crime and Rule-Breaking*, 7th ed. New York: Oxford University Press.

Erikson, E. 1959. *Identity and the Life Cycle*. Madison, CT: International Universities Press.

Fleisher, Mark S. 1998. *Dead End Kids*. Madison: University of Wisconsin Press.

Flores, Edward O. 2014. *God's Gangs*. New York: New York University Press.

Flores, Edward O., and Pierrette Hondagneu-Sotelo. 2013. "Chicano Gang Members in Recovery: The Public Talk of Negotiating Chicano Masculinities." *Social Problems*, 60: 476–490.

Garot, Robert. 2007. "'Where You From!': Gang Identity as Performance." *Journal of Contemporary Ethnography* 36: 50–84.

Garot, Robert. 2010. *Who You Claim*. New York: New York University Press.

Goffman, E. 1959. *The Presentation of Self in Everyday Life*. New York: Anchor Books.

Hannerz, Ulf. 1969. *Soulside*. New York: Columbia University Press.

Hagedorn, John M. 2015. *The Insane Chicago Way*. Chicago, IL: University of Chicago Press.

Harding, David J. 2010. *Living the Drama*. Chicago, IL: University of Chicago Press.

Hennigan, Karen, and Marija Spanovic. 2012. "Gang Dynamics through the Lens of Social Identity Theory." In *Youth Gangs in International Perspective*, edited by Finn-Aage Esbensen and Cheryl L. Maxson, 127–149. New York: Springer.

Horowitz, Ruth. 1983. *Honor and the American Dream*. New Brunswick, NJ: Rutgers University Press.

Horowitz, Ruth, and Gary Schwartz. 1974. "Honor, Normative Ambiguity and Gang Violence." *American Sociological Review* 39: 238–251.

Jacobs, Bruce A., and Richard Wright. 1999. "Stick-Up: Street Culture, and Offender Motivation." *Criminology* 37: 149–174.

Jang, Sung Joon, and Aaron B. Franzen 2013. "Is Being 'Spiritual' Enough without Being Religious? A Study of Violent and Property Crimes among Emerging Adults." *Criminology* 51: 595–627.

Johnson, Andrew. 2017. *If I Give My Soul*. New York: Oxford University Press.

Johnson, Andrew, and James Densley. 2018. "Rio's New Social Order: How Religion Signals Disengagement from Prison Gangs." *Qualitative Sociology* 41: 243–262.

Johnson, Byron R., David B. Larson, Spencer De Li, and Sung Joon Jang. 2000. "Escaping from the Crime of Inner Cities: Church Attendance and Religious Salience among Disadvantaged Youth." *Justice Quarterly* 17: 377–391.

Katz, Charles M., and Stephen M. Schnebly. 2011. "Neighborhood Variation in Gang Member Concentrations." *Crime and Delinquency* 57: 377–407.

Klein, Malcolm W., and Cheryl Maxson. 2010. *Street Gang Patterns and Policy*. Oxford, UK: Oxford University Press.
Knox, George W. 2004. "Gang Profile: The Black Disciples." In *Gang Profiles: An Anthology*, edited by George W. Knox and Curtis Robinson, 97–116. Peotone, IL: New Chicago School Press.
Knox, George W., and Andrew V. Papachristos. 2002. *The Vice Lords: A Gang Profile Analysis*. Peotone, IL: New Chicago School Press.
Lane, Jeffrey. 2019. *The Digital Street*. New York: Oxford University Press.
Laudariji, Isaac B., and Lowell W. Livezey. 2000. "The Churches and the Poor in a 'Ghetto Underclass' Neighborhood." In *Public Religion and Urban Transformation*, edited by Lowell W. Liezey, 83–106. New York: New York University Press.
Lauger, Timothy R. 2019. "Group Processes within Gangs." *Oxford Research Encyclopedia of Criminology*. Oxford, UK: Oxford University Press. https://doi.org/10.1093/acrefore/9780190264079.013.438.
Lauger, Timothy R. 2020. "Gangs, Identity, and Cultural Performance." *Sociology Compass* 14 (4): e12772.
Lauger, Timothy R., and Brooke Horning. 2020. "Street Gangs and Street Culture." In *Routledge Handbook of Street Culture*, edited by Jeffrey Ian Ross, 238–248. New York: Routledge.
Lauger, Timothy R., and Craig J. Rivera. 2022. "Banging While Believing: Gangs, Religiosity, and Violence." *Social Problems*: spac027. https://doi.org/10.1093/socpro/spac027.
Melucci, Alberto. 1995. "The Process of Collective Identity." In *Social Movements and Culture*, edited by Hank Johnson and Bert Klandermans, 41–63. Minneapolis: University of Minnesota Press.
McPherson, Miller, Lynn Smith-Lovin, and James M. Cook. 2001. "Birds of a Feather: Homophily in Social Networks." *Annual Review of Sociology* 27: 415–444.
McRoberts, Omar M. 2003. *Streets of Glory*. Chicago, IL: University of Chicago Press.
Miller, Walter B. 1958. "Lower Class Culture as a Generating Milieu of Gang Delinquency." *Journal of Social Issues* 14: 5–19.
Miller, Ty, and Milke Vuolo. 2018. "Examining the Antiascetic Hypothesis through Social Control Theory: Delinquency, Religion, and Reciprocation across the Early Life Course." *Crime and Delinquency* 64: 148–1488.
Moore, Natalie Y., and Lance Williams. 2011. *The Almighty Black P. Stone Nation*. Chicago, IL: Lawrence Hill Books.
Noffke, Jaqueline L., and Susan H. McFadden. 2001. "Denominational and Age Comparisons of God Concepts." *Journal for the Scientific Study of Religion* 40: 747–756.
Offutt, Stephen. 2020. "Entangled: Evangelicals and Gangs in El Salvador." *Social Forces* 99: 424–445.
Olate, Rene, Christopher Salas-Wright, and Michael G. Vaughn. 2011. "A Cross-National Comparison of Externalizing Behaviors among High-Risk Youth and Youth Gang Members in Metropolitan Boston, Massachusetts, and San Salvador, El Salvador." *Victims & Offenders* 6: 356–369.
Papachristos, Andrew V., Anthony A. Braga, and David M. Hureau. 2012. "Social Networks and the Risk of Gunshot Injury." *Journal of Urban Health; Bulletin of the New York Academy of Medicine* 89: 992–1003.
Papachristos, Andrew V., Christopher C. Wildman, and Elizabeth Roberto. 2015. "Tragic, but Not Random: The Social Contagion of Nonfatal Gunshot Injuries." *Social Sciences & Medicine* 125: 139–150.

Panfil, Vanessa. 2017. *The Gang's All Queer*. New York: New York University Press.

Patillo-McCoy, Mary. 1999. *Black Picket Fences*. Chicago, IL: University of Chicago Press.

Pescosolido Bernice A., and Beth A. Rubin, 2000. "The Web of Group Affiliations Revisited: Social Life, Postmodernism, and Sociology." *American Sociological Review* 65: 52–76.

Pitts, Richard N. 2010a. "'Killing the Messenger': Religious Black Gay Men's Neutralization of Anti-Gay Religious Messages." *Journal for the Social Scientific Study of Religion* 49: 56–72.

Pitts, Richard N. 2010b. "'Looking for My Jonathan': Gay Black Men's Management of Religious and Sexual Identity Conflicts." *Journal of Homosexuality* 57: 39–53.

Price, Charles E. 2014. "'I Ain't in It to Win It': Why the Educational System Does Not Compare to the Allure of Gang Life." Doctoral Dissertation, North Carolina State University.

Pyrooz, David C. 2014. "From Colors and Guns to Caps and Gowns? The Effects of Gang Membership on Educational Attainment." *Journal of Research in Crime and Delinquency* 51: 56–87.

Pyrooz, David C., Gary Sweeten, and Alex R. Piquero. 2013. "Continuity and Change in Gang Membership and Gang Embeddedness." *Journal of Research in Crime and Delinquency* 50: 239–271.

Pyrooz, David C., Jillian J. Turanovic, Scott H. Decker, and Jun Wu. 2016. "Taking Stock of the Relationship between Gang Membership and Offending: A Meta-Analysis." *Criminal Justice and Behavior* 43: 365–397.

Reid, Shannon E., Matthew Valasik, and Arunkamar Bagavathi. 2018. "Examining the Physical Manifestation of Alt-Right Gangs: From Online Trolling to Street Fighting." In *Gangs in the Era of Internet and Social Media*, edited by Chris Melde and Frank Weerman, 105–134. Cham, Switzerland: Springer.

Rios, Victor. 2017. *Human Targets: Schools, Police, and the Criminalization of Latino Youth*. Chicago, IL: University of Chicago Press.

Rivera, Craig, and Timothy Lauger. 2021. "The Protective Effect of Religious Group Membership, Service Attendance, and Scripture Reading on Binge Drinking among College Students." *Pastoral Psychology* 70: 125–140.

Rosen, Jonathan D., and José Miguel Cruz. 2019. "Rethinking the Mechanisms of Gang Desistance in a Developing Country." *Deviant Behavior* 40: 1493–1507.

Salas-Wright, Christopher P., Rene R. Olate, and Michael G. Vaughn. 2013. "The Protective Effects of Religious Coping and Spirituality on Delinquency: Results among High-risk and Gang-Involved Salvadoran Youth." *Criminal Justice and Behavior* 40: 988–1008.

Sampson. Robert J. 2012. *Great American City*. Chicago, IL: University of Chicago Press.

Seto, Christopher H. 2021. "Understanding the Spiritual but Not Religious." *Sociology of Religion* 82: 156–178.

Simmel, Georg. 1955. *Conflict & the Web of Group Affiliations*. New York: The Free Press.

Smith, Christian, and Melina Lindquist Denton. 2009. *Soul Searching*. New York: Oxford University Press.

Snow, David. 2001. "Collective Identity and Expressive Forms." In *International Encyclopedia of the Social and Behavioral Sciences*, edited by Neil J. Smelser and Paul B. Baltes, 2213–2219. New York: Elsevier Science.

Stretesky, Paul B., and Mark R. Pogrebin. 2007. "Gang-Related Gun Violence: Socialization, Identity, and Self." *Journal of Contemporary Ethnography* 36: 85–114.

Stryker, Sheldon. 1980. *Symbolic Interactionism*. Menlo Park, CA: Benjamin/Cummings.

Stryker, Sheldon, and Richard T. Serpe. 1982. "Commitment, Identity Salience, and Role Behavior: Theory and Research Example." In *Personality, Roles, and Social Behavior*, edited by William Ickes and Eric S. Knowles, 199–218. New York: Springer-Verlag.

Swidler, Ann. 1986. "Culture in Action: Symbols and Strategies." *American Sociological Review* 51: 273–286.

Topalli, Volkan, Timothy Brezina, and Mindy Bernhardt. 2012. "With God on My Side: The Paradoxical Relationship between Religious Belief and Criminality among Hardcore Street Offenders." *Theoretical Criminology* 17: 49–69.

Ulmer, Jeffrey T., Scott A. Desmond, Sung Joon Jang, and Byron R. Johnson. 2012. "Religious Involvement and Dynamics of Marijuana Use: Initiation, Persistence, and Desistance." *Deviant Behavior* 33: 448–468.

Vasquez, Manuel, Marie Friedmann Marquardt, and Ileana Gomez. 2003. "Saving Souls Transnationally: Pentecostalism and Youth Gangs in El Salvador and the United States." In *Globalizing the Sacred*, edited by Manuel Vasquez and Marie Friedmann Marquardt, 119–144. New Brunswick, NJ: Rutgers University Press.

Vigil, James D. 1988. *Barrio Gangs*. Austin: University of Texas Press.

Vigil, James D. 2020. *Multiple Marginality and Gangs*. Lanham, MD: Lexington Books.

Ward, T.W. 2013. *Gangsters without Borders*. New York: Oxford University Press.

Wimberley, Dale W. 1989. "Religion and Role Identity: A Structural Symbolic Interactionist Conceptualization of Religiosity." *Sociological Quarterly* 30: 125–142.

CHAPTER 29

RE-EXAMINING THE LITERATURE ON SOCIAL MEDIA AND GANGS
Critical Race Theory as a Path for New Opportunities

CAITLIN ELSAESSER AND DESMOND PATTON

ONLINE spaces and social media shape all dimensions of young people's lives—including individual behaviors, norms related to communication and appearance, friendships, and romantic relationships. With 89% of teens reporting they are online "almost constantly" or "several times a day," and 95% of teens reporting access to a smartphone (Pew Research Center 2018), no dimension of youth culture is untouched by social media, including experiences of conflict, aggression, and violence. Cyberbullying is one form of online interpersonal aggression that has appropriately received a massive amount of attention in the scholarly literature, with thousands of studies documenting this phenomenon among samples of mostly white and Asian youth for over 30 years (Elsaesser et al. 2017).

Only more recently have scholars turned their attention to the role of social media aggression in communities impacted by high rates of gun violence, communities that disproportionately include Black and Latinx populations, reflecting decades of policies that disinvested in communities of color. In the last 10 years, scholars with expertise in gangs and community violence started to document the ways that social media is used by gang-labeled individuals (Lane 2016; Moule, Decker, and Pyrooz 2017; Patton et al. 2014). This body of work has documented important and understudied trends in how features of social media platforms shape experiences of gang activity, including the community violence that causes so much loss of human life.

Concurrently, the emphasis on the role of social media in shaping gang-related conflict provides an incomplete picture of the factors at play in gang violence. A focus on individual-level behaviors and group processes on social media, while documenting real phenomena, obscures the root causes that create the conditions for community violence—in other words, policies and practices that have created concentrated poverty in Black and Latinx communities, including racially motivated drug laws (Alexander and West 2012; Muhammad 2019), redlining (Krivo, Peterson, and Kuhl 2009), and the concentration of public housing in communities of color (Griffiths and Tita 2009). As researchers, we have the power to define the relevant terms related to the phenomena we observe. Framing research on "problem behaviors" of gang-labeled individuals, including social media conflict—particularly without pointing to the broader context of oppression—can have unintended consequences of implying structural conditions are immutable and placing the responsibility to address violence and delinquency on those experiencing racial and economic oppression. This framing also misses important opportunities for changing these conditions.

With deep investment in addressing the root conditions that produce community violence, in this chapter we draw on a critical race framework to re-examine the literature on the intersection of social media and gang-related activities, including violence. We start by making the case for the importance of a critical race perspective. We then turn to the existing literature, with the goal not of comprehensively summarizing the literature, but rather integrating insights from critical race theory and our reflections related to the work. We end with recommendations for future research. We hope that by integrating a critical race perspective into this body of literature, we contribute to the movement to end the senseless loss of life that stems from economic and racial oppression.

Why Are We Taking a Critical Race Approach to This Research?

The rise of the Black Lives Matter movement has led to amplified calls to examine how research might reproduce oppression. Leading scholars across multiple fields—including those who study community violence (Nation et al. 2021), the criminal justice system (Goddard and Myers 2017), and the child welfare system (Feely and Bosk 2021)—have called on researchers to focus on the structural conditions that create the conditions for health inequities. Critical race theory is a useful framework that can support researchers in centering anti-racism to both understand and determine future directions for the literature on social media, gang activity, and community violence.

Critical race theory (CRT) emerged from legal scholarship in the post-civil rights period (Delgado and Stefancic 2013; Williams 1991). CRT focuses on expanding our understanding of what racism is and dismantling systems of white supremacy through the argument that "race and racism are central, endemic, permanent and a fundamental part of defining and explaining how US society functions" (Yosso 2005). Further, CRT underscores the epistemological perspective that no research is neutral, and no researcher is objective (Yosso 2005). Rather, knowledge is multiply determined and always situated in individual experience. This chapter draws on several key tenets of CRT to inform our understanding of the past and future for scholarship examining social media, gang activity, and community violence.

One tenet of CRT underscores that race is not natural or biological, but rather a socially constructed category primarily used to justify the oppression of groups of people based on their supposed inferiority (Delgado and Stefancic 2013). In this line of thinking, CRT theorists underscore the importance of identifying policies and structures that shape the daily experiences of minoritized groups. We draw on this tenet of CRT to highlight the importance of policies that reinforce racial oppression as a vital context for interpreting experiences on social media for gang-labeled youth. Specifically, in line with the neoliberal movement that emphasized individual responsibility and disinvested in the American social safety net, the last 50 years have seen policies that have systematically created conditions of concentrated poverty in predominantly Black neighborhoods. The targeting of these policies in Black neighborhoods has been referred to as a form of structural violence—in other words, a power system, comprised of ideologies, institutions, and policies, leveraged to privilege one group over another (Farmer 2004; Ho 2007). CRT suggests that this policy context is vital to consider when understanding individual-level behaviors among Black and Brown youth living in disinvested communities.

An additional tenet of CRT we draw on is the importance of storytelling, in line with CRT's foundational stance that knowledge is multiply determined and situated in the individual experience (Solórzano and Yosso 2002). CRT underscores that individuals who have experienced oppression hold unique insight into the nature of that oppression (Solórzano and Yosso 2002). Counter-stories by definition create a counternarrative, which is needed to expand the field by moving beyond current limiting paradigms. In the present chapter, we therefore highlight the importance of centering the perspectives of gang-labeled individuals.[1]

A final feature of CRT we draw on is the notion of intersectionality, a concept introduced to CRT by Kimberle Crenshaw (1990). This perspective underscores that no individual can be defined by membership in a single identity group. Rather, various dimensions of social and political identities—race, sex, class, sexual orientation, for example—create different modes of oppression or empowerment. In this chapter, we integrate this understanding by naming the diversity of the experiences of gang-labeled individuals on social media.

STATE OF THE LITERATURE: SOCIAL MEDIA AND GANG-LABELED INDIVIDUALS

We now turn to some major contributions to and debates in the literature related to the intersection of social media and gang-labeled individuals. Here we intend to bring insights from critical race theory to the major threads in the literature. We start by reviewing the key areas of focus in the scholarship on social media use and gang-labeled individuals, including the debate about the causal role of social media and gun violence. Throughout, we attend to implications for addressing racism, highlighting examples of research that integrate critical race theory, social media, and gang-labeled individuals. Finally, we end with recommendations for practice and future research.

Social Media and Criminal Activity

Social media and other emerging technologies have changed how individuals communicate and interact with one another. Black youth ages 13–17 are the most likely out of any teen group to have access to a smartphone, with 85% of them having access to one versus 71% of white and Hispanic youth (Pew Research Center 2018). However, most research focused on social media conflict has centered on white youth (Elsaesser et al. 2017), and research focused on gang-labeled youth—where Black youth are overrepresented due to structural marginalization—has been slow to recognize the widespread use of social media. In the last decade, scholars in this burgeoning area of research have primarily focused on identifying criminal activities online, including activities that may demonstrate a more definitive relationship between social media and gang violence.

In one early line of research in the field, Pyrooz, Decker, and Moule (2015) identified online behaviors common among individuals who identify as gang involved. In a study of 585 current and former gang-involved individuals in five US cities who had been involved in the criminal justice system, researchers found that gang-involved youth and young adults spend similar amounts of time online and engage in many of the same behaviors as non-gang-involved individuals, including sharing music and connecting with friends (Pyrooz et al. 2015). Conversely, some gang-involved individuals differ regarding participation in online crime and deviance. For example, 45% of the sample from the Pyrooz et al. study engaged in drug sales or the sale of stolen items online.

Another line of research has specifically focused on the role of social media and firearm violence. Growth in social media usage and the formation of the "digital street" has created a new context for the contagion of firearm violence (Lane 2016). Burgeoning research has documented that young people post messages online from street corners, schools, apartment complexes, and other neighborhood spaces embedded in a local ecology of violence (Lane 2016; Patton, Eschmann, and Butler 2013; Stevens et al. 2017). These messages can be violent and mimic gang-related behaviors like bragging about fighting, taunting rival gangs, coordinating illegal activities, distributing videos of beatings, distributing illegal substances, or making light of recent homicides (Patton et al. 2013). In an analysis of 78 rap videos posted by gang members in Buffalo, New York, violence was the dominant theme of the videos (Lauger and Densley 2018).

At times, the content in a social media post reproduces aggressive behavior like direct and indirect threats toward rival groups, taunting rival gangs in text and video, coordinating illegal activities, distributing videos of fights, using or distributing illegal substances, or making light of recent homicides (Patton et al. 2013). Coined as internet or cyber banging, research has documented cases where this online behavior has been followed by offline firearm violence (Patton et al. 2013).

Internet banging differs from cyberbullying, defined by the threat of offline violence and a mutual engagement in conflict, with both parties involved in aggressive communication. While there is a lack of large-scale studies documenting the prevalence of internet banging, qualitative work suggests it is a common challenge for adolescents living in marginalized neighborhoods. Interviews with 60 youth from marginalized neighborhoods revealed that online conflicts spill over into future social interactions, resulting in physical altercations—including fistfights and gun violence (Stevens et al. 2017), a finding confirmed in another study with a similar population (Elsaesser et al. 2021).

Global Context: Social Media and Criminal Activity

A growing number of scholars outside the US context have examined the relationship between social media and gang violence over the last decade (Fernández-Planells, Orduña-Malea, and Feixa Pàmpols 2021). Much of the research has been concentrated in Europe (Roks, Leukfeldt, and Densley 2021; Sandberg and Ugelvik 2017; Storrod and Densley 2017; Van Hellemont 2012), some of which has been derived from the longstanding Eurogang network, with critically important work surfacing from Canada (Urbanik and Haggerty 2018) and the Caribbean (Pawelz and Elvers 2018). The conversations globally are similar in scope, focus, and methodological approach. There tends to be a predominant focus on the extent to which social media shapes criminality among individuals who self-identify as gang involved.

One thread that has become a theme in European research is exploring why gang-involved individuals post criminal behavior online. Sandberg and Ugelvik (2017) examined why Norwegian offenders post criminal behavior. These scholars found that the democratization of technology and the ubiquity of access to technology paved the way for a humiliation culture that centered on posting amateur porn and what they refer to as a "snapshot" or "got you culture" where the aim is to film extraordinary acts in public. Other scholars suggest this unintended use of social media is based in performance and a celebration of gang culture. These scholars have advanced the idea that gangs have capitalized on advances in technology to share gang culture and display bravado and toughness beyond the neighborhood (Densley 2013; Pawelz and Elvers 2018; Roks et al. 2021; Van Hellemont 2012). However, there is still considerable debate concerning whether or not gang social media engagement is focused on individual identity presentation or the goals of the wider group (Whittaker, Densley, and Moser 2020).

Global scholars have also drawn attention to the use of social media for drug sales, facilitating and navigating violence, and coping with trauma related to gang violence. Urbanik and Haggerty (2018) have noted how technology has reconfigured the business of gang life, transforming not only how gangs access capital but the extent to which this new form of e-commerce incites neighborhood beefs and policing (see also Storrod and Densley 2017). These scholars continue to advance the field by describing a social media–based behavior of engaging in risky, performance-based actions online to confront perceived and real danger, a phenomenon they call "edge work." Following this further, Roks et al. (2021) unpack the connections between the possibility of criminality online with the circumstances, opportunities, and context of the physical world, which they call "hybridization."

A critical element of the blending of online behavior and the physical world is a focus on music, particularly rap and drill music. Scholars from Trinidad and Tobago underscore the idea that music generally serves the psychological and social needs of young people (Pawelz and Elvers 2018). However, in a qualitative, case-based analysis of social media engagement among gang-involved youth, Pawelz and Elvers (2018) find that the posting of music online may also be associated with the glorification of gang life and amplify threatening behavior among rival groups. However, Pawelz and Elvers (2018) depart from other gang scholars by also describing how gang-involved youth use social media for collective mourning and bonding.

Methodologically, the global space is mixed methods and interdisciplinary (Urbanik et al. 2020). The research generally falls into three camps: (1) in-depth qualitative work leveraging interviews and focus groups; (2) interpretative work using social media artifacts like YouTube videos or images from Instagram; and (3) content analyses, social network analyses, or computational analyses (e.g., machine learning and computer vision) of gang behavior online. Collectively, research from global cities confirms that the issue of social media–related gang violence is a growing challenge that merits considerable attention at the local, state, national, and global levels. Omitted from the global conversation are deeper analyses and investigations around race-based conclusions, gender differences, the use of language to describe online behaviors (e.g., gang member versus gang-involved individual), and a predominant focus on criminality as opposed to well-being, mental health, and social support online.

Debate around the Causal Role of Social Media and Gun Violence

Whether social media conflict is causally linked to offline violence, including firearm violence, is an area of scholarly debate (Moore and Stuart 2022). One area of scholarship has underscored the role of social media features that intensify peer conflict. Drawing on a decade of studies, Nesi, Choukas-Bradley, and Prinstein's (2018a, 2018b) transformational framework posits that social media amplifies the experiences and demands of peer experiences. Communications happens at a higher speed, with a higher volume of content, and on a public scale through the presence of social media followers/friends (Nesi et al. 2018a, 2018b). Behaviors online are moreover reinforced through metrics that deliver quantifiable, immediate peer responses, such as viewing photos with more "likes"—a quantifiable mode of validation on social media (Sherman et al. 2016).

In line with Nesi et al.'s (2018a, 2018b) transformational framework, a body of evidence suggests that social media offers novel opportunities for conflict for gang-labeled youth. A study using digital trace web data scraped from public Facebook found that Facebook allowed gang members to interact in online spaces with other faraway gangs (Leverso and Hsiao 2021). As it relates to social media conflict and violence, the design of social media platforms like X (formerly known as Twitter) and Facebook can allow conflict to escalate quickly to threats due to social media's hypervisibility, connectivity, and the lack of evidence-based digital mechanisms to allow adequate processing of loss. When conflict occurs on social media, it is witnessed by an active, engaged audience, experienced at any time (Marwick and boyd 2014).

Some evidence suggests that threatening social media posts among gang-labeled individuals are associated with offline violence. One study explored group-level social media usage data to understand correlations with gun violence; the authors found that the extent of social media activity and who is engaging in the activity were associated with the average rate of gang-attributable shootings (Hyatt, Densley, and Roman 2021). In another study drawing on focus groups with 41 adolescents from neighborhoods with high rates of violence, youth shared their perception that social media platforms like Twitter and Facebook allow conflict to escalate quickly because of social media platforms' hypervisibility and connectivity (Elsaesser et al. 2021). Specifically, teens pointed to comments as a space that allows an engaged Facebook audience to participate, reinforcing and amplifying the original conflict as it unfolds. Live streaming was another feature youth mentioned that can quickly bring in a larger audience and, through the presence of video, allowed Facebook friends to watch a conflict unfold in real time. Critically, the proximity of teens' social networks in this study allowed for online conflicts to become offline fights. As Stevens et al. (2017) underscores, conflict is now ever-present through computers or smartphones.

In contrast, another line of research suggests that social media activity is not associated with offline violence. A study drawing on two years of ethnographic fieldwork on Chicago's South Side examined three strategies by which gang-labeled Black youth challenged rivals on social media (Stuart 2020a). Stuart (2020a) found that whether an online challenge led to offline violence predominantly reflected whether the targeted individual could refute an online challenge, made more difficult if the online threat targeted an individual's social ties. However, Stuart (2020a) underscores that most observed online conflicts remained confined to the online space and did not result in violence during the two-year data collection period.

Another important area of scholarship has documented that social media can provide a space to de-escalate and avoid violence. The social ethnography *Ballad of the Bullet* documented that some gang-labeled individuals participated in online hostilities as part of an inventive and deliberate effort to create violent reputations without needing to engage in offline violence (Stuart 2020b). Another study relying on focus group data with marginalized youth found that youth wielded a sophisticated set of strategies to prevent social media conflict from escalating, including deleting comments, avoiding known instigators online, and reaching out to friends for help (Elsaesser et al. 2020). Concurrently, youth emphasized significant challenges to disengaging from social media conflict; the public nature of social media conflict and persistence of content made it exceptionally difficult to drop, given the importance of maintaining their reputation.

The debate regarding whether social media conflict and threats are causally linked to offline violence is unresolved. The studies reviewed above—both those that suggest an association between online threats and offline violence and those that found none—are based on qualitative and correlational evidence that does not meet the standards of causal inference. To demonstrate a causal link would require complex, longitudinal data that captures both online and offline experiences made all the more difficult given that youth report that in some instances an online threat does not result in violence until months later (Elsaesser et al. 2021).

While it remains an open question whether social media plays a causal role in amplifying conflict to offline violence, scholarship that makes this connection has the potential to justify what Daniel Trottier calls "social media policing" (2012). Police and other state agencies have used threatening content posted by gang-labeled youth to justify further criminalization. The use of social media by law enforcement agencies is now nearly universal (Kim, Oglesby-Neal, and Mohr 2017). Police officers or other agents of the state use social media for criminal investigations via manual searches on social media profiles or information requests from a social media platform. More extreme, officers can install software on individual devices and analyze captured social media data (Trottier and Fuchs 2015). Under these circumstances, causal thinking reinforces a narrative that justifies profiling and preemptive policing (Trottier 2012).

Further, drawing on critical race theory, we suggest that accumulating evidence to make a causal link between social media activity and violence misses a more important question. A focus on individual-level behaviors shifts attention away from the structural and systematic inequalities that shape daily life for gang-labeled youth and are a root cause of violence, erroneously implying that solutions are primarily at the individual level and that structural conditions are immutable. A systematic review of research on gangs and social media found that most research has focused on deviant and criminal online activities among gang members, as well as attempts to link social media use with offline violence in communities (Fernández-Planells et al. 2021). In other words, most research has focused on individual-level behaviors of gang-labeled youth (e.g., social media behaviors, delinquent activities, aggression, threats).

This focus on modifiable individual-level behaviors (aggression, lawbreaking) while ignoring the drivers of these behaviors can produce what Clear (2010) has called a "slavery to the present," with an implication that the structural conditions cannot be changed and that individuals in marginalized communities are responsible themselves for change. An alternative story underscores the ways that inequitable systems provide youth with fewer opportunities and explicitly names the structural barriers that have shaped these limited opportunities. This is an important area for future research in the field.

Documenting Meaning-Making and Grief on Social Media

In addition to underscoring the importance of attending to structural causes of violence and delinquency, critical race theory underscores the importance of documenting the full spectrum of lived experiences of gang-labeled youth, centering their perspectives. Although some gang-labeled youth use social media to discuss crime in their community, these experiences provide only a partial picture of their lives. Like non-gang-involved individuals, gang-labeled youth turn to social media to communicate their lived experiences, for entertainment, and to communicate with friends. For gang-labeled youth and youth living in communities with high rates of gang violence, their lived experience often includes significant trauma.

A group of studies is concerned with how individuals develop identities connected with gang culture. These online behaviors may consist of mourning the loss of a fallen member, promoting a gang lifestyle, and recruiting new members—although there is less support for this idea. For example, Morselli and Décary-Hétu (2013) note that online behaviors observed by gang-labeled youth may relate to individual expressions of identity as opposed to a broader connection to gang identity. The idea that gangs use social media to recruit appears to be more myth than fact, however; the convening factor of social media affords a new location and neighborhood for individuals who may self-label as gang involved (Morselli and Décary-Hétu 2013).

Research has also documented that some youth, at times those who are involved with gangs, turn to social media to post about their everyday experiences, frequently expressing grief when friends or family members are shot and killed. Some scholars have documented gang-labeled individuals' use of music to bond socially and mourn collectively (Pawelz and

Elvers 2018). Patton et al. (2018) argue that grief and other painful emotions over loss often precede aggression expressed on social media from youth who may be gang involved, a finding further explored and confirmed in other studies (Stuart, Riley, and Pourreza 2020).

Importance of Including Intersectional Identities

As intersectional scholars underscore, experiences are shaped by multiple identities, including but not limited to gender, socioeconomic status, and sexuality (Collins 2000; Crenshaw 1990). Scholarship examining gang-labeled youth and social media has predominantly focused on the experiences of boys and young men. Yet as documented by scholars in the broader gang literature, the experiences of boys and young men do not stand in for the experiences of girls and young women. For example, specific to violence, the meaning and proximal motivations for entering into offline conflict varies by gender and sexuality (Cobbina, Like, and Miller 2016; Jones 2009).

Experiences on social media among gang-labeled youth may be gendered as well, but notably absent is the inclusion of gang-labeled girls and young women's experiences on social media from their own perspectives (Patton et al. 2020). Reviews of the literature that focus on cyberviolence more broadly (Peterson and Densley 2017) suggest that women's experiences of cyberviolence may differ from men's. For example, one study documenting cyberbullying and victimization found that girls made up 69% of victims (Ybarra, Mitchell, and Korchmaros 2011). Adolescent girls use social media more intensively (Pew Research Center 2018) and invest significant time in managing friendships online (Brandes and Levin 2014). Other work suggests that social media may be a space where girls and young women feel increased safety and liberation behind the protection of a screen (Lane 2016). There is a need to understand experiences of social media conflict through the voices of girls and young women of color who are living in marginalized neighborhoods.

Finally, the age of gang-labeled individuals likely influences their experiences with social media. The social media environment is particularly challenging to navigate for adolescents, who are in a developmental period of heightened vulnerability to risk taking, where youth are highly sensitive to the possible rewards of a risky choice (Steinberg 2008, 2014). Further, given that the development of self-regulation does not reach maturity until early adulthood, adolescents face greater obstacles to exercising self-control (Steinberg 2004). Finally, adolescents are highly sensitive to the influence of peers, particularly during conditions of emotional arousal (Steinberg 2004). As gang-labeled youth exit adolescence, they may use social media less and in different ways. We need more scholarship centering the unique perspectives of gang-labeled young women and LGBTQ+-identified individuals themselves—as well as considering different developmental stages—on how individuals manage and make meaning of social media experiences.

IMPLICATIONS FOR PRACTICE AND POLICY

We consider implications for practice and policy by returning to our frame of viewing gang-labeled individuals' social media experiences through the lens of critical race theory. As we noted above, the field's dominant paradigm has focused on illegal activities and aggressive content on social media among gang-labeled individuals. While perhaps unintended, one implication of this focus is that these individual-level behaviors themselves are public health problems. However, a critical race paradigm posits that these individual and group-level behaviors, while describing real experiences, conceal the root causes stemming from race-based policies that create the conditions for illegal activities and violence.

Historians and policy researchers have documented decades of intentional policies and practices that have created concentrated poverty in Black and Latinx communities, including drug laws written to harshly criminalize minority drug use (Alexander and West 2012; Muhammad 2019), housing laws that deny minority communities access to mortgages (Krivo et al. 2009), and the deliberate concentration of public housing in communities of color (Griffiths and Tita 2009). When our attention shifts to these historical and policy initiatives that created the conditions for concentrated poverty, the importance of policy and practice approaches that seek healing and restitution for those affected by structural inequities as well as address the dismantling of the structural causes themselves becomes clear.

We review here practice and policy implications, the approach to handling illegal and aggressive content on social media, and finally root causes. Throughout, we focus on minimizing harm to gang-labeled youth as well as approaches that address root causes. As a whole, we recommend that the field differentiate practices and policies that address root causes and those focused on healing from harm.

Addressing Social Media Threats and Other Illegal Online Activities via Data Monitoring

There is a range of approaches to handling threats and other illegal behaviors online. One increasingly used approach draws on data science. Data mining uses computer algorithms to process large quantities of publicly available data from social media platforms to identify individuals vulnerable to violence (Bushman et al. 2016; Han, Kamber, and Pei 2011). Social media monitoring companies advertise their ability to monitor social media activity around the clock and flag posts interpreted as dangerous (Sutton 2016). Contracts with such companies have increased, including with some of the largest US cities (Leibowitz 2018). Another approach to addressing threats and illegal behaviors online is criminalization. Anti-cyberbullying laws have become widespread; 44 states now have laws that criminalize cyberbullying or electronic harassment (Hinduja and Patchin 2018). Many schools have adopted zero-tolerance policies for handling cyberbullying and threats online, with no room for dialogue or discussion (Shariff 2009).

Aligned with the critical race framework, and as social workers who have spent much of our careers working with minoritized adolescents, we have concerns with both data monitoring and criminalizing the behaviors of gang-labeled individuals online. As we review above, in the US context, the behaviors of Black and other minority youth are disproportionately criminalized. Further, adolescence and early adulthood is a developmental period where risk taking is common; the features of the social media environment, with the presence of a peer audience, can increase pressure to engage in illegal activities. Further, there is little evidence that data monitoring companies are effective in detecting social media posts concerning specific schools, possibly because only a fraction of social media users share their geographic location and inherent difficulties in interpreting online posts (Leibowitz 2018). Given these issues, we see approaches that emphasize monitoring and punishment of online activities of minoritized youth as having real danger to be wielded as a tool to oppress Black and other minority youth.

Mining social media data for identifying gang behavior is fraught with enumerable challenges when the analysis is left up to artificial intelligence. When analyzing social media data from gang-labeled youth, algorithms, usually developed by researchers with little experience working with gang-labeled youth, cannot accurately interpret offline context, which may lead to dangerous assumptions about those youth that erode their humanity and reduce them to racially charged pathological narratives of criminality. To confront these challenges, the SAFElab at Columbia University pioneered the inclusion of gang-labeled youth as domain experts in the translation of social media comments for the creation of community-informed algorithmic development (Frey et al. 2020). One area in which gang-labeled youth has been critical is in deciphering social media content labeled grief versus aggression. Patton et al. (2018) found that expressions of grief on Twitter tended to precede expressions of aggression.

We further underscore the importance of moving beyond individual-level interpretations of social media behaviors toward a focus on the "digital street," a term developed by communication scholar Jeffrey Lane (2016). The digital street provides contextual information through connections and orientations from a network of people (Gordon and de Souza e Silva 2011). Lane notes that a focus on networked interactions may be top-down as social media companies geocode demographic data that is sold to advertisers (Wilken 2014), and then bottom-up as when the user uses their smartphone to manage the uncertainty they encounter as they navigate safety in their communities (Sutko and de Souza e Silva 2011) or identify their connection to a physical place (Liao and Humphreys 2013). Based on his fieldwork in Harlem, Lane (2016) finds that street life is characterized by its flow online. In Harlem, teens' use of social media affords new ways to manage ongoing safety issues between crews and cliques in neighborhoods.

This contextual approach is also one used by outreach workers who work closely with gang-labeled youth. In a study based on in-depth interviews with Chicago-based violence outreach workers, workers first assess the context and culture of written and media-based content on social media to determine the threat level and appropriate crisis response (Patton et al. 2016). For example, participants described developing tools for de-escalating online conflicts that included using humor and compassion to have deeper, meaningful conversations with youth both online and offline (Patton et al. 2016). However, outreach workers remarked that the most important tool for quelling online beef rested in the rapport the outreach worker built with the youth offline. Social media was a vehicle by which an assault could be made or emotion expressed, but it never replaced the outreach workers' need to sustain robust, supportive mentoring relationships with young people.

In line with a critical race approach, we see great promise in restorative justice approaches to address online threats and illegal behaviors. Restorative justice approaches to harm can vary but emanate from several core principles: recognize the harm done, explore alternative approaches to interrupt harm that do not rely on the state, draw on creative strategies generated and sustained from the impacted community, and transform not only the individual experience but the root causes of violence (Brown 2017). The cumulative effect of these strategies is to offer students, teachers, and administrators the possibility of a dignified response to misbehavior and a way to make amends and repair the harm caused (Amstutz and Mullet 2005). Circle processes such as peace-making circles or talking circles are popular forms of restorative approaches. Specific to social media threats, scholars have explored the possibility of virtual peace rooms to "virtualize" aspects of the restorative justice process and empower coordinators with the advantages of connectivity and persistence of social media platforms (Das, Macbeth, and Elsaesser 2019). A recommendation that stems from our research is for schools and other institutions to channel funds and resources toward restorative approaches to address illegal activity online.

Social Media Regulation

An area with clear policy implications is the regulation of social media platforms. While there is still debate in the literature as to whether social media amplifies and creates new threats implicated in gang violence, or simply mirrors offline spaces, advocates across fields that study violence—for example, terrorism, extremism, and cyberbullying—have underscored the role of social media design in amplifying violent discourse. The deadly insurrection at the US Capitol in January 2021 exposed the power of social media to influence real-world behavior and incite violence, and there is a growing consensus across both US political parties that the technology companies profiting from social media apps need to be more tightly regulated.

For most social media companies, the business model is built around user attention as its product. Companies rely on a sophisticated set of tools to maximize user attention, which can amplify viral content regardless of the subject matter, including sometimes violent and incendiary content. One promising path for researchers is to advocate for humane design in multiple areas. Researchers can support policies that advocate for the protection of minors in social media use, such as social media design that prevents and combats screen addiction. For example, the Kids Act, introduced in the Senate in 2020, would prohibit social media platforms that children use to implement platform features that prompt certain types of content, including content that amplifies violence (Markey 2020). In additional areas of influence, scholars can work with health authorities to draft tech guidelines that center healthy child development, and also broadly disseminate their work to increase awareness around the challenges of social media design for child health.

Addressing Root Causes

Of all approaches to addressing the challenges associated with gang-labeled youth's criminalized threats on social media, a central focus must be on the root causes of these individual-level experiences. While social media amplifies the intensity of conflict among gang-labeled youth, the possibility that these experiences will spill over into offline violence is largely shaped by youth's experiences navigating neighborhoods that, despite residents' enduring resilience, have experienced decades of structural violence. Policies that create the conditions of concentrated poverty are a root cause of community violence, and among the most promising approaches to change these conditions is working in partnership with those who have lived experience in these neighborhoods. Participatory action research with gang-labeled individuals focuses on supporting youth capacity to engage in political action that addresses the root causes of violence (Ginwright and James 2002). Policies that address the conditions of concentrated poverty in neighborhoods and provide reparations for the decades of systemic disinvestment in communities of color are particularly promising approaches.

Throughout, researchers need to work in partnership with community stakeholders and gang-associated youth themselves to develop and implement strategies. As critical race theory suggests, those with direct lived experience with oppression have the clearest insight into what is needed in their community and the strategies that are most likely to be effective. While leading violence prevention researchers have called on engaging youth and community voices in violence prevention (Ozer 2017), only a few studies have involved youth and stakeholders in the development of their programs, and these programs have focused on offline contexts (Leff et al. 2010; Snider et al. 2010; Zimmerman et al. 2011). Working in partnership with youth and community stakeholders, researchers can draw on their expertise in research and access to resources and power to effect change.

Conclusion: Integrating Critical Race Theory into Social Media Research

As researchers in this area, we cannot in good conscience continue to document experiences of violence and criminal incarceration involving gang-labeled youth without also contributing to solutions to the root causes of oppression. The study of social media and violence is far less important than the study and fixing of root causes such as structural inequality. Upstream corrections will solve downstream problems, from gangs to violence and other illegal activities. Critical race theory provides an opportune guide for research on social media and gang-labeled youth. Honoring the work already being pioneered integrating CRT perspectives in this topic, we highlight here some exciting research opportunities to contribute to solutions to dismantle the structural challenges that gang-labeled individuals face.

When choosing to document risk behaviors among gang-labeled youth, we join other researchers' calls to always point to the structural conditions as the root cause that creates the conditions for risk involvement (Boyd et al. 2020). And we are excited by the work of researchers who are shifting attention away from individual-level risk behaviors to document structural challenges, where true solutions lie (Nation et al. 2021; Wendel et al. 2021).

There remains a predominant focus on social media as a tool for identifying gang-labeled individuals or predicting violence. We suggest scholars turn away from the predictive nature of social media toward leveraging social media for resistance, healing, and joy. Radical healing, particularly for communities of color, is imperative during a time when injustice and oppression are being exploited for digital content (French et al. 2020). French et al. (2020) define radical healing as "being able to... exist in both spaces of resisting oppression and moving toward freedom" (24). Social media provides an important space for resistance to racial microaggressions (Eschmann 2020). Further, Black joy is often underlooked as a tool for activism, and we want to further research joy as resistance to oppression. By focusing on radical healing and joy-based resources on social media, scholars may identify new opportunities to study gang culture and prevention that may inform the development of new and innovative tools that prioritize the *needs* of gang-labeled communities and offer healing resources to promote community health and well-being.

Finally, we see great promise in research that draws on the wisdom of those with lived experiences of gang-labeled individuals. Participatory action research offers a valuable set of strategies to leverage researchers' expertise with those who have direct experience of oppression and who will have invaluable insight into systems of oppression. Research identity inevitably influences how we see the world, conceptualize problems, and see solutions (Muhammad et al. 2015). Researchers working in collaborative teams that deliberately seek out a wide range of intersectional identities—particularly those with direct lived experience with issues affecting gang-labeled individuals—and encourage open dialogue regarding the role of identity and its impact on the research process will have great potential to come up with innovative solutions.

What if, as a field, researchers took all the energy focused on risk behaviors and applied it to addressing the conditions, systems, and structures that allow violence and other risk behaviors to occur? The possibility for change would be powerful.

Note

1. How to define who is a gang member has been a topic of significant debate. We choose to use the term "gang-labeled" youth in this chapter. In line with critical race theory, this approach recognizes that gang membership has often had its significance less in a substantive meaning about the activities of the group, but rather as a label from the state and other authorities.

References

Alexander, Michelle, and Cornel West. 2012. *The New Jim Crow: Mass Incarceration in the Age of Colorblindness*. New York: The New Press.

Amstutz, Lorraine Stutzman, and Judy H. Mullet. 2005. *The Little Book of Restorative Discipline for Schools: Teaching Responsibility; Creating Caring Climates*. Intercourse, PA: Good Books.

Boyd, Rhea W., Edwin G. Lindo, Lachelle D. Weeks, and Monica R. McLemore. 2020. "On Racism: A New Standard for Publishing on Racial Health Inequities." *Health Affairs Blog*. https://www.healthaffairs.org/content/forefront/racism-new-standard-publishing-racial-health-inequities.

Brandes, Sigal Barak, and David Levin. 2014. "Like My Status." *Feminist Media Studies* 14 (5): 743–758. https://doi.org/10.1080/14680777.2013.833533.

Brown, Adrienne Maree. 2017. *Emergent Strategy: Shaping Change, Changing Worlds*. Chico, CA: AK Press.

Bushman, Brad J., Katherine Newman, Sandra L. Calvert, Geraldine Downey, Mark Dredze, Michael Gottfredson, Nina G. Jablonski, et al. 2016. "Youth Violence: What We Know and What We Need to Know." *American Psychologist* 71 (1): 17–39. https://doi.org/10.1037/a0039687.

Clear, T. 2010. "Policy and Evidence: The Challenge to the American Society of Criminology: 2009 Presidential Address to the American Society of Criminology." *Criminology* 48 (1): 1–25.

Cobbina, Jennifer E., Toya Z. Like, and Jody Miller. 2016. "Gender-Specific Conflicts among Urban African-American Youth: The Roles of Situational Context and Issues of Contention." *Deviant Behavior* 37 (9): 1032–1051. https://doi.org/10.1080/01639625.2016.1167437.

Collins, Patricia Hill. 2000. "Gender, Black Feminism, and Black Political Economy." *Annals of the American Academy of Political and Social Science* 568 (1): 41–53. https://doi.org/10.1177/000271620056800105.

Crenshaw, Kimberle. 1990. "Mapping the Margins: Intersectionality, Identity Politics, and Violence against Women of Color." *Stanford Law Review* 43: 1241.

Das, Aditi, Jamie Macbeth, and Caitlin Elsaesser. 2019. "Online School Conflicts: Expanding the Scope of Restorative Practices with a Virtual Peace Room." *Contemporary Justice Review* 22 (4): 351–370. https://doi.org/10.1080/10282580.2019.1672047.

Delgado, Richard, and Jean Stefancic. 2013. *Critical Race Theory: The Cutting Edge*, 3rd ed. Philadelphia, PA: Temple University Press. https://scholarship.law.ua.edu/fac_books/14.

Densley, James A. 2013. *How Gangs Work: An Ethnography of Youth Violence*. New York: Palgrave Macmillan.

Elsaesser, Caitlin, Desmond Patton, Allyson Kelley, Jacqueline Santiago, and Ayesha Clarke. 2020. "Avoiding Fights on Social Media: Strategies Youth Leverage to Navigate Conflict in a Digital Era." *Journal of Community Psychology* 49 (3): 806–821.

Elsaesser, Caitlin, Desmond Upton Patton, Emily Weinstein, Jacquelyn Santiago, Ayesha Clarke, and Rob Eschmann. 2021. "Small Becomes Big, Fast: Adolescent Perceptions of How Social Media Features Escalate Online Conflict to Offline Violence." *Children and Youth Services Review* 122 (March): 105898. https://doi.org/10.1016/j.childyouth.2020.105898.

Elsaesser, Caitlin, Beth Russell, Christine McCauley Ohannessian, and Desmond Patton. 2017. "Parenting in a Digital Age: A Review of Parents' Role in Preventing Adolescent Cyberbullying." *Aggression and Violent Behavior* 35 (July): 62–72. https://doi.org/10.1016/j.avb.2017.06.004.

Eschmann, Rob. 2020. "Unmasking Racism: Students of Color and Expressions of Racism in Online Spaces." *Social Problems* 67 (3): 418–436. https://doi.org/10.1093/socpro/spz026.

Farmer, Paul. 2004. "An Anthropology of Structural Violence." *Current Anthropology* 45 (3): 305–325.

Feely, Megan, and Emily Adlin Bosk. 2021. "That Which Is Essential Has Been Made Invisible: The Need to Bring a Structural Risk Perspective to Reduce Racial Disproportionality in Child Welfare." *Race and Social Problems* 13 (1): 49–62. https://doi.org/10.1007/s12552-021-09313-8.

Fernández-Planells, Ariadna, Enrique Orduña-Malea, and Carles Feixa Pàmpols. 2021. "Gangs and Social Media: A Systematic Literature Review and an Identification of Future Challenges, Risks and Recommendations." *New Media & Society* 23 (7): 2099–2124. https://doi.org/10.1177/1461444821994490.

French, Bryana H., Jioni A. Lewis, Della V. Mosley, Hector Y. Adames, Nayeli Y. Chavez-Dueñas, Grace A. Chen, and Helen A. Neville. 2020. "Toward a Psychological Framework of Radical Healing in Communities of Color." *The Counseling Psychologist* 48 (1): 14–46. https://doi.org/10.1177/0011000019843506.

Frey, William R., Desmond U. Patton, Michael B. Gaskell, and Kyle A. McGregor. 2020. "Artificial Intelligence and Inclusion: Formerly Gang-Involved Youth as Domain Experts for Analyzing Unstructured Twitter Data." *Social Science Computer Review* 38 (1): 42–56. https://doi.org/10.1177/0894439318788314.

Ginwright, Shawn, and Taj James. 2002. "From Assets to Agents of Change: Social Justice, Organizing, and Youth Development." *New Directions for Youth Development* 2002 (96): 27–46.

Goddard, Tim, and Randolph R Myers. 2017. "Against Evidence-Based Oppression: Marginalized Youth and the Politics of Risk-Based Assessment and Intervention." *Theoretical Criminology* 21 (2): 151–167. https://doi.org/10.1177/1362480616645172.

Gordon, Eric, and Adriana de Souza e Silva. 2011. *Net Locality: Why Location Matters in a Networked World*. Chichester, UK: Wiley-Blackwell.

Griffiths, Elizabeth, and George Tita. 2009. "Homicide in and Around Public Housing: Is Public Housing a Hotbed, a Magnet, or a Generator of Violence for the Surrounding Community?" *Social Problems* 56 (3): 474–493. https://doi.org/10.1525/sp.2009.56.3.474.

Han, Jiawei, Micheline Kamber, and Jian Pei. 2011. *Data Mining: Concepts and Techniques (The Morgan Kaufmann Series in Data Management Systems)*. 3rd ed. Burlington, VT: Morgan Kaufmann.

Hinduja, Sameer, and Justin W. Patchin. 2018. "State Bullying and Cyberbullying Laws." Cyberbullying Research Center. https://cyberbullying.org/Bullying-and-Cyberbullying-Laws.pdf.

Ho, Kathleen. 2007. "Structural Violence as a Human Rights Violation." *Essex Human Rights Review* 4 (2): 1–17.

Hyatt, Jordan M., James A. Densley, and Caterina G. Roman. 2021. "Social Media and the Variable Impact of Violence Reduction Interventions: Re-Examining Focused Deterrence in Philadelphia." *Social Sciences* 10 (5): 147. https://doi.org/10.3390/socsci10050147.

Jones, Nikki. 2009. *Between Good and Ghetto: African American Girls and Inner-City Violence*. New Brunswick, NJ: Rutgers University Press.

Kim, KiDeuk, Ashlin Oglesby-Neal, and Edward Mohr. 2017. "2016 Law Enforcement Use of Social Media Survey." March 3. Urban Institute. https://www.urban.org/research/publication/2016-law-enforcement-use-social-media-survey.

Krivo, Lauren J., Ruth D. Peterson, and Danielle C. Kuhl. 2009. "Segregation, Racial Structure, and Neighborhood Violent Crime." *American Journal of Sociology* 114 (6): 1765–1802. https://doi.org/10.1086/597285.

Lane, Jeffrey. 2016. "The Digital Street: An Ethnographic Study of Networked Street Life in Harlem." *American Behavioral Scientist* 60 (1): 43–58. https://doi.org/10.1177/0002764215601711.

Lauger, Timothy R., and James A. Densley. 2018. "Broadcasting Badness: Violence, Identity, and Performance in the Online Gang Rap Scene." *Justice Quarterly* 35 (5): 816–841. https://doi.org/10.1080/07418825.2017.1341542.

Leff, Stephen S., Duane E. Thomas, Nicole A. Vaughn, Nicole A. Thomas, Julie Paquette MacEvoy, Melanie A. Freedman, Saburah Abdul-Kabir, et al. 2010. "Using Community-Based Participatory Research to Develop the PARTNERS Youth Violence Prevention Program." *Progress in Community Health Partnerships: Research, Education, and Action* 4 (3): 207–216. https://doi.org/10.1353/cpr.2010.0005.

Leibowitz, Aaron. 2018. "Could Monitoring Students on Social Media Stop the Next School Shooting?" *New York Times*, September 7. https://www.nytimes.com/2018/09/06/us/social-media-monitoring-school-shootings.html.

Leverso, John, and Yuan Hsiao. 2021. "Gangbangin on the [Face]Book: Understanding Online Interactions of Chicago Latina/o Gangs." *Journal of Research in Crime and Delinquency* 58 (3): 239–268. https://doi.org/10.1177/0022427820952124.

Liao, Tony Chung Li, and Lee Humphreys. 2013. "Using Mobile Augmented Reality to Tactically Re-Encounter, Re-Create, and Re-Appropriate Public Spaces." *AoIR Selected Papers of Internet Research*, October. https://journals.uic.edu/ojs/index.php/spir/article/view/9093.

Markey, Edward J. 2020. *Kids Internet Design and Safety Act or the KIDS Act*. https://www.congress.gov/bill/116th-congress/senate-bill/3411.

Marwick, Alice, and Danah boyd. 2014. "'It's Just Drama': Teen Perspectives on Conflict and Aggression in a Networked Era." *Journal of Youth Studies* 17 (9): 1187–1204. https://doi.org/10.1080/13676261.2014.901493.

Moore, Caylin Louis, and Forrest Stuart. 2022. "Gang Research in the Twenty-First Century." *Annual Review of Criminology* 5 (1). https://doi.org/10.1146/annurev-criminol-030920-094656.

Morselli, Carlo, and David Décary-Hétu. 2013. "Crime Facilitation Purposes of Social Networking Sites: A Review and Analysis of the 'Cyberbanging' Phenomenon." *Small Wars & Insurgencies* 24 (1): 152–170. https://doi.org/10.1080/09592318.2013.740232.

Moule, Richard K., Scott H. Decker, and David C. Pyrooz. 2017. "Technology and Conflict: Group Processes and Collective Violence in the Internet Era." *Crime, Law and Social Change* 68 (1–2): 47–73. https://doi.org/10.1007/s10611-016-9661-3.

Muhammad, Khalil Gibran. 2019. *The Condemnation of Blackness: Race, Crime, and the Making of Modern Urban America, With a New Preface*. Cambridge, UK: Harvard University Press.

Muhammad, Michael, Nina Wallerstein, Andrew L. Sussman, Magdalena Avila, Lorenda Belone, and Bonnie Duran. 2015. "Reflections on Researcher Identity and Power: The Impact of Positionality on Community Based Participatory Research (CBPR) Processes and Outcomes." *Critical Sociology* 41 (7–8): 1045–1063. https://doi.org/10.1177/0896920513516025.

Nation, Maury, Derek A. Chapman, Torey Edmonds, Franklin N. Cosey-Gay, Trinidad Jackson, Khiya J. Marshall, Deborah Gorman-Smith, Terri Sullivan, and Aimée-Rika T. Trudeau. 2021. "Social and Structural Determinants of Health and Youth Violence: Shifting the Paradigm of Youth Violence Prevention." *American Journal of Public Health* 111 (S1): S28–S31. https://doi.org/10.2105/AJPH.2021.306234.

Nesi, Jacqueline, Sophia Choukas-Bradley, and Mitchell J. Prinstein. 2018a. "Transformation of Adolescent Peer Relations in the Social Media Context: Part 1—A Theoretical Framework and Application to Dyadic Peer Relationships." *Clinical Child and Family Psychology Review* 21 (3): 267–294. https://doi.org/10.1007/s10567-018-0261-x.

Nesi, Jacqueline, Sophia Choukas-Bradley, and Mitchell J. Prinstein. 2018b. "Transformation of Adolescent Peer Relations in the Social Media Context: Part 2—Application to Peer Group Processes and Future Directions for Research." *Clinical Child and Family Psychology Review* 21 (3): 295–319. https://doi.org/10.1007/s10567-018-0262-9.

Ozer, Emily J. 2017. "Youth-Led Participatory Action Research: Overview and Potential for Enhancing Adolescent Development." *Child Development Perspectives* 11 (3): 173–177. https://doi.org/10.1111/cdep.12228.

Patton, Desmond Upton, Robert D. Eschmann, and Dirk A. Butler. 2013. "Internet Banging: New Trends in Social Media, Gang Violence, Masculinity and Hip Hop." *Computers in Human Behavior* 29 (5): A54–A59.

Patton, Desmond Upton, Robert D. Eschmann, Caitlin Elsaesser, and Eddie Bocanegra. 2016. "Sticks, Stones and Facebook Accounts: What Violence Outreach Workers Know about Social Media and Urban-Based Gang Violence in Chicago." *Computers in Human Behavior* 65 (December): 591–600. https://doi.org/10.1016/j.chb.2016.05.052.

Patton, Desmond Upton, Jun Sung Hong, Megan Ranney, Sadiq Patel, Caitlin Kelley, Rob Eschmann, and Tyreasa Washington. 2014. "Social Media as a Vector for Youth Violence: A Review of the Literature." *Computers in Human Behavior* 35: 548–553.

Patton, Desmond Upton, Owen Rambow, Jonathan Auerbach, Kevin Li, and William Frey. 2018. "Expressions of Loss Predict Aggressive Comments on Twitter among Gang-Involved Youth in Chicago." *NPJ Digital Medicine* 1 (1): 1–2. https://doi.org/10.1038/s41746-018-0020-x.

Patton, Desmond Upton, Robin Stevens, Jocelyn R. Smith Lee, Grace-Cecile Eya, and William Frey. 2020. "You Set Me Up: Gendered Perceptions of Twitter Communication among Black Chicago Youth." *Social Media + Society* 6 (2). https://doi.org/10.1177/2056305120913877.

Pawelz, Janina, and Paul Elvers. 2018. "The Digital Hood of Urban Violence: Exploring Functionalities of Social Media and Music among Gangs." *Journal of Contemporary Criminal Justice* 34 (4): 442–459. https://doi.org/10.1177/1043986218787735.

Peterson, Jillian, and James Densley. 2017. "Cyber Violence: What Do We Know and Where Do We Go from Here?" *Aggression and Violent Behavior* 34 (May): 193–200. https://doi.org/10.1016/j.avb.2017.01.012.

Pew Research Center. 2018. "Teens, Social Media & Technology 2018." Pew Research Center for Internet and Technology. https://www.pewresearch.org/internet/2018/05/31/teens-social-media-technology-2018/.

Pyrooz, David C., Scott H. Decker, and Richard K. Moule. 2015. "Criminal and Routine Activities in Online Settings: Gangs, Offenders, and the Internet." *Justice Quarterly* 32 (3): 471–499. https://doi.org/10.1080/07418825.2013.778326.

Roks, Robert A., E. Rutger Leukfeldt, and James A. Densley. 2021. "The Hybridization of Street Offending in the Netherlands." *British Journal of Criminology* 61 (4): 926–945. https://doi.org/10.1093/bjc/azaa091.

Sandberg, Sveinung, and Thomas Ugelvik. 2017. "Why Do Offenders Tape Their Crimes? Crime and Punishment in the Age of the Selfie." *British Journal of Criminology* 57 (5): 1023–1040. https://doi.org/10.1093/bjc/azw056.

Shariff, Shaheen. 2009. *Confronting Cyber-Bullying: What Schools Need to Know to Control Misconduct and Avoid Legal Consequences*. Cambridge, UK: Cambridge University Press. https://eduq.info/xmlui/handle/11515/18309.

Sherman, Lauren E., Ashley A. Payton, Leanna M. Hernandez, Patricia M. Greenfield, and Mirella Dapretto. 2016. "The Power of the Like in Adolescence: Effects of Peer Influence on Neural and Behavioral Responses to Social Media." *Psychological Science* 27 (7): 1027–1035. https://doi.org/10.1177/0956797616645673.

Snider, Carolyn E., Maritt Kirst, Shakira Abubakar, Farah Ahmad, and Avery B. Nathens. 2010. "Community-Based Participatory Research: Development of an Emergency Department-Based Youth Violence Intervention Using Concept Mapping." *Academic Emergency Medicine* 17 (8): 877–885. https://doi.org/10.1111/j.1553-2712.2010.00810.x.

Solórzano, Daniel G., and Tara J. Yosso. 2002. "Critical Race Methodology: Counter-Storytelling as an Analytical Framework for Education Research." *Qualitative Inquiry* 8 (1): 23–44. https://doi.org/10.1177/107780040200800103.

Steinberg, Laurence. 2004. "Risk Taking in Adolescence: What Changes, and Why?" *Annals of the New York Academy of Sciences* 1021 (1): 51–58. https://doi.org/10.1196/annals.1308.005.

Steinberg, Laurence. 2008. "A Social Neuroscience Perspective on Adolescent Risk-Taking." *Developmental Review* 28 (1): 78–106. https://doi.org/10.1016/j.dr.2007.08.002.

Steinberg, Laurence. 2014. *Age of Opportunity: Lessons from the New Science of Adolescence*. New York: Eamon Dolan/Mariner Books.

Stevens, Robin, Stacia Gilliard-Matthews, Jamie Dunaev, Marcus K. Woods, and Bridgette M. Brawner. 2017. "The Digital Hood: Social Media Use among Youth in Disadvantaged Neighborhoods." *New Media & Society* 19 (6): 950–967. https://doi.org/10.1177/1461444815625941.

Storrod, Michelle L., and James A. Densley. 2017. "'Going Viral' and 'Going Country': The Expressive and Instrumental Activities of Street Gangs on Social Media." *Journal of Youth Studies* 20 (6): 677–696. https://doi.org/10.1080/13676261.2016.1260694.

Stuart, Forrest. 2020a. "Code of the Tweet: Urban Gang Violence in the Social Media Age." *Social Problems* 67 (2): 191–207. https://doi.org/10.1093/socpro/spz010.

Stuart, Forrest. 2020b. *Ballad of the Bullet: Gangs, Drill Music, and the Power of Online Infamy. Ballad of the Bullet*. Princeton, NJ: Princeton University Press. https://doi.org/10.1515/9780691200088.

Stuart, Forrest, Alicia Riley, and Hossein Pourreza. 2020. "A Human-Machine Partnered Approach for Identifying Social Media Signals of Elevated Traumatic Grief in Chicago Gang Territories." *PLoS One* 15 (7): e0236625. https://doi.org/10.1371/journal.pone.0236625.

Sutko, Daniel M., and Adriana de Souza e Silva. 2011. "Location-Aware Mobile Media and Urban Sociability." *New Media & Society* 13 (5): 807–823. https://doi.org/10.1177/1461444810385202.

Sutton, Halley. 2016. "Assess Social Media Threats to Keep Your Students and Campus Safe." *Campus Security Report* 13 (6): 1–6. https://doi.org/10.1002/casr.30198.

Trottier, Daniel. 2012. "Policing Social Media." *Canadian Review of Sociology/Revue Canadienne de Sociologie* 49 (4): 411–425. https://doi.org/10.1111/j.1755-618X.2012.01302.x.

Trottier, Daniel, and Christian Fuchs, eds. 2015. *Social Media, Politics and the State: Protests, Revolutions, Riots, Crime and Policing in the Age of Facebook, Twitter and YouTube*. New York: Routledge.

Urbanik, Marta-Marika, and Kevin D. Haggerty. 2018. "'#It's Dangerous': The Online World of Drug Dealers, Rappers and the Street Code." *British Journal of Criminology* 58 (6): 1343–1360. https://doi.org/10.1093/bjc/azx083.

Urbanik, Marta-Marika, Robby Roks, Michelle Lyttle Storrod, and James Densley. 2020. "Ethical and Methodological Issues in Gang Ethnography in the Digital Age: Lessons from Four Studies in an Emerging Field." In *Gangs in the Era of Internet and Social Media*, edited by Chris Melde and Frank Weerman, 21–41. Cham, Switzerland: Springer.

Van Hellemont, Elke. 2012. "Gangland Online: Performing the Real Imaginary World of Gangstas and Ghettos in Brussels." *European Journal of Crime, Criminal Law and Criminal Justice* 20: 165.

Wendel, Monica L., Maury Nation, Monique Williams, Trinidad Jackson, Gaberiel Jones, Marlena Debreaux, and Nicole Ford. 2021. "The Structural Violence of White Supremacy: Addressing Root Causes to Prevent Youth Violence." *Archives of Psychiatric Nursing* 35 (1): 127–128. https://doi.org/10.1016/j.apnu.2020.10.017.

Whittaker, Andrew, James Densley, and Karin S. Moser. 2020. "No Two Gangs Are Alike: The Digital Divide in Street Gangs' Differential Adaptations to Social Media." *Computers in Human Behavior* 110 (September): 106403. https://doi.org/10.1016/j.chb.2020.106403.

Wilken, Rowan. 2014. "Places Nearby: Facebook as a Location-Based Social Media Platform." *New Media & Society* 16 (7): 1087–1103. https://doi.org/10.1177/1461444814543997.

Williams, Patricia J. 1991. *The Alchemy of Race and Rights*. Cambridge, UK: Harvard University Press.

Ybarra, Michele L., Kimberly J. Mitchell, and Josephine D. Korchmaros. 2011. "National Trends in Exposure to and Experiences of Violence on the Internet among Children." *Pediatrics* 128 (6): e1376–e1386. https://doi.org/10.1542/peds.2011-0118.

Yosso, Tara J. 2005. "Whose Culture Has Capital? A Critical Race Theory Discussion of Community Cultural Wealth." *Race Ethnicity and Education* 8 (1): 69–91. https://doi.org/10.1080/1361332052000341006.

Zimmerman, Marc A., Sarah E. Stewart, Susan Morrel-Samuels, Susan Franzen, and Thomas M. Reischl. 2011. "Youth Empowerment Solutions for Peaceful Communities: Combining Theory and Practice in a Community-Level Violence Prevention Curriculum." *Health Promotion Practice* 12 (3): 425–439. https://doi.org/10.1177/1524839909357316.

CHAPTER 30

COMPARATIVE APPROACHES TO THE STUDY OF PRISON GANGS AND PRISON ORDER

DAVID SKARBEK AND KAITLYN WOLTZ

IN *Prison Truth*, Jesse Vasquez, former editor of the *San Quentin News*, described how after being transferred to San Quentin from another prison he felt "gang and race pressures almost disappear" (Drummond 2020, 108). That difference was even greater in the prison's newsroom: it "turned out to be a place where the old, deadly racial barriers did not exist and where he could free himself from the prejudices and defense mechanisms he had been forced to adopt during the seventeen years he was confined to California'[s] prison gladiator schools" (112). The prison gangs in the California Department of Corrections and Rehabilitation (CDCR) system that contribute to what Drummond describes as a "gladiator school" exist in many prisons in the United States and around the world.

There are several competing explanations for why prison gangs exist: deprivation theory, importation theory, group structure theories, and governance theory. The deprivation theory suggests that the "pains of imprisonment" lead people to develop new identities, adopt new social roles, and structure their lives around the deprivations of prison life (Sykes 1958). One implication of this theory suggests that prison gangs will arise primarily in prisons where incarcerated people lack resources. However, that is not always the case. For example, prisoners in England suffer many of the same deprivations as American prisoners do, but they do not form gangs like those found in California and Texas, and those same prison systems existed for many years with no prison gangs (Skarbek 2020a, 106–132). Likewise, captives at the Andersonville prisoner of war camp in Georgia did not have access to housing, a workable sewage system, or rations with sufficient nutritional value, but no organized prisoner groups or gangs emerged (Skarbek 2020a, 68, 73–78). Deprivation—a feature of nearly all prisons—cannot alone explain where gangs operate.

The importation theory argues that incarcerated people bring their culture into the prison with them, suggesting that prison gangs begin because street gangs import their operations into prisons when their members are arrested (Jacobs 1977; Pyrooz, Gartner, and Smith 2017, 294). The historical evidence in the United States, however, does not support this as a generalizable explanation for the emergence of US prison gangs. In the 1980s, the

Texas prison system saw a growth in the number of prisons gangs, but all of the gangs that existed were started in prison. Moreover, 52% of US prisoners with gang affiliations were not in a gang before being admitted to prison (Winterdyk and Ruddell 2010, 733).[1] In fact, prison gangs sometimes emerged in places that lacked a serious street gang presence, such as Washington, Utah, and Iowa (Skarbek 2014, 63).[2] The cases of California and Illinois are consistent with the importation theory because each state has a long history of street gangs and experienced an early emergence of prison gangs. However, in California, prison gangs did not begin until the late 1950s and 1960s while street gangs had existed since the 1920s. If importation theory is correct that the presence of street gangs drives the presence of prison gangs in that state, we would expect prison gangs to appear coincidentally with, or at least shortly after, the appearance of street gangs. Instead, there is a 20- to 50-year lag between the presence of street gangs in a state and the presence of prison gangs, suggesting that importation theory cannot universally explain the emergence of prison gangs. Clearly, culture and street gang activity affect what happens in prisons, but it does not seem to play a decisive role in explaining variation in prison gang activity.

Group structure theories suggest that prison gangs evolve out of groups that form to meet prisoners' demands for a social support network and that the variation in prisoners' demands explains the variation observed among prison gangs (see especially Buentello, Fong, and Vogel 1991; Thrasher 1927; Cloward and Ohlin 1960; Fagan 1989; Spergel 1964; Taylor 1990; Decker and Curry 2002; Klein and Maxson 2006; Spindler and Bouchard 2011; Valdez 2003). They argue that some groups, initially formed for self-protection, become predatory when they begin restricting who can join, disrupting daily prison life, engaging in violence, and participating in the contraband trade. Eventually, the group evolves into a full-fledged prison gang. While compelling, this explanation is relatively silent on why prisoners' demands for this support change over time.[3] Related to this, Trammell (2011, 314) suggests that prisoners' adherence to hypermasculinity explains their desire for dominating others. However, without explaining why (or whether) hypermasculinity varies across places of punishment, it cannot explain why so many prisons have no gangs. It does not offer a generalizable explanation that can predict or explain the substantial variation in gang activity across jails and prisons through time.

The governance theory of prison gangs relies less on mechanistic or cultural explanations of prison gangs and instead argues that prison gangs arise to meet prisoners' demand for extralegal governance (Skarbek 2010, 2014, 2020a). Specifically, gangs arise to meet prisoners' demand for protection and access to contraband that officials either cannot or will not provide. For example, correctional officers cannot always meet prisoner demand for safety because of (1) limited resources that restrict their ability to be present always and everywhere in the prison, (2) shirking of duties by individual officers, and (3) officer inexperience. To meet prisoners' demand for governance, prison gangs form and create rules to govern the social and economic life of the prison.

Contemporary and historical evidence supports the governance theory. In cases like Bolivia's San Pedro Prison, officials provide nearly no resources, offer incompetent or negligible administration of prison operations, and provide little to no governance over economic and social affairs (Skarbek 2010).[4] In turn, prisoner groups play a major role in governing the prison. Likewise, prison gangs are rare in England where prison populations are smaller than in the United States and reputation mechanisms, like those that enforce the convict code, can operate effectively (Crewe 2009, 247–366).[5] Moreover, in the United

States, prison gangs are likely most prevalent in California, Texas, and Illinois (Gaston and Huebner 2015, 328). This fact fits with the theory that large prison populations undermine reputation-based governance mechanisms, meaning that prisoners must rely on more formal, extralegal governance institutions.

In trying to explain prison gang behavior, group process theories suggest that either (1) individuals inclined toward violence, racism, and drug smuggling select into prison gangs (selection model), (2) the presence of prison gangs influences the environment and consequently individuals' behavior (facilitation model), or (3) some combination of the two (enhancement model) (Pyrooz and Decker 2019, 43-44). The facilitation and enhancement models of group process theories suggest that the presence of prison gangs provides opportunities for violence; influences the responsibilities and group cohesion of prisoners, as well as the norms and values that prisoners hold; and creates external threats as gangs rely on violence and threats of escalation in their daily operations.[6]

Carlson (2001) argues, along the lines of the selection model, that prisoners form gangs to indulge their preference for racism. However, he does not provide a theory of preference formation to explain this preference among gang members. Prison gang members are also perceived as being inherently more violent (California Department of Corrections and Rehabilitation 2012; Beard 2013). However, if the presence of people with a preference for violence was driving the rise of prison gangs, prison gangs should have formed much earlier in the history of prisons when there was a larger proportion of people incarcerated for violent crime. Additionally, only 25% of prison gang members participate in gang-related violence (Fong, Vogel, and Buentello 1992).

There are numerous and varied theories to explain variation in prison gang activity. Many of these theories, however, generate predictions that historical evidence disconfirms. For this reason, they do not provide a sufficient, general explanation for the emergence of prison gangs. Adjudicating between these many theories and potential research strategies requires identifying the most useful combinations of concepts, theories, and types of evidence for studying prison gangs and other forms of prison order. In the remainder of this chapter, we discuss the ability of different methodologies to answer active research questions like those generated by the work detailed above: (1) Why do prison gangs form? (2) What explains the presence of prison gangs in some prisons? (3) What explains the variation in prison gang characteristics? (4) What explains the variation in prison gang activity? We then present the governance theory of prison gangs (Skarbek 2011, 2014) and prison order (Skarbek 2016, 2020a) as models of theories with falsifiable implications that explain (rather than describe) the emergence of prison gangs and the variation in prison social order around the world.

What Are the Most Useful Concepts, Theories, and Evidence for Studying Prison Gangs?

We argue that the study of prison gangs benefits tremendously from a "causes of effects" approach, where one attempts to maximize within-case explanatory power. Questions of why prison gangs form, what functions they serve, and who joins prison gangs and why require identifying causal mechanisms and evaluating comparative institutional structures. Institutions, in this context, are understood to be "the rules of the game in a society or ... the humanly devised constraints that shape human interaction" (North 1990, 3). They provide the information and incentives that drive individuals' behavior, including group formation. Institutions can vary significantly in form and strength, "ranging from legal to extralegal, formal to informal, centralized to decentralized, flexible to rigid, permanent to temporary, and fragile to robust to antifragile" (Skarbek 2020b, 410). They consist of many overlapping rules.[7] For this reason, adequately describing these institutions requires a multifaceted and multidimensional discussion that quantitative measures cannot adequately represent (Skarbek 2020b, 410; Ostrom 1990, 2005).

Criminologists who examine these questions have correctly focused on concepts like "culture," "norms," and "deviance." When evaluating these concepts, many of the earliest and most important classic studies of prison gangs rely on qualitative and ethnographic evidence (Sykes 1958; Davidson 1974; Irwin 1980). More recently, scholars have focused more on the use of quantitative evidence (Gaes et al. 2002; Pyrooz and Decker 2019). In terms of concepts, "simple" concepts are relatively easy to reduce to quantitative measures that do not leave out important aspects and characteristics (Coppedge 1999). An example of this would be the population of prisoners at a particular facility, where some number can accurately and effectively measure how many people are housed there. However, some concepts—like culture, institutions, or norms—are more multidimensional and multifaceted, such that it is difficult to reduce their description to simple quantitative measures without leaving out important characteristics and meaning. For example, the concepts of "deviance" or "culture" are so multidimensional and multifaceted that they are more difficult to describe by one or a few simple quantitative measures.

With the push toward increased quantitative measurement and statistical analysis, some criminologists and sociologists have sought to better quantify deviance and culture without losing meaning in aggregation and abstraction. For instance, Sweeten (2012) documents the myriad ways criminologists have sought to quantitatively measure offending. These include dichotomous and frequency scales among others. Despite these advancements, we argue that the meaning captured in qualitative evidence like interviews and ethnography cannot be fully maintained in quantified abstractions of the data (Mohr et al. 2020, 159). The offending measures that Sweeten (2012) examines rank offenses rather than examine the meaning of deviancy that guides how different offenses are ranked by communities. When researchers use such simple quantitative measures as proxies for cultural meanings, they treat those cultures as homogenous and unchanging. However, all cultures are heterogenous and have competing beliefs (Storr 2002, 4). Identifying and representing the competing beliefs that exist within cultures requires ethnography, archival research, and in-depth case analysis (Storr 2002, 7, 81).

Interpreting concepts and data requires theories, which also vary in how thin or thick they are. Thin theories tend to be relatively parsimonious and have clear comparative static predictions that are (potentially) subject to empirical confirmation or falsification. Economists and many political scientists tend to favor these approaches (Lessing 2017). They provide a clear test to explain phenomena. By contrast, anthropologists and sociologists often prefer thick theories that study social forces and cultural analysis but tend not to be parsimonious or have clear comparative static predictions. Many of the classic

Table 30.1 Combinations of Theories, Concepts, and Evidence

	Rich, qualitative evidence	Simple, quantitative evidence
Thin theory	Analytical narrative	Standard economic analysis • Constrained optimization • Statistical significance
Thick theory	Traditional anthropological, sociological, area studies, political science work, etc. • Social forces and cultural analysis • Case study and ethnography	Statistical sociology, political science, and criminology • "Kitchen sink" statistical analysis, which throws everything in the right side of the equation in search of explaining the left side

Based on Boettke (2000, 378).

studies of prison life use thick theories (see Sykes 1958, for an example). They provide rich descriptions of different phenomena but do not really explain why those phenomena exist in the spaces that they do.

Some combinations of concepts, theories, and evidence are highly compatible and generate new knowledge (Table 30.1 represents different combinations). For example, economic approaches to prison social order tend to use thin, parsimonious theories to explain simple concepts with quantitative evidence (Costa and Kahn 2007; Bayer, Hjalmarsson, and Pozen 2009). Because the concepts are thin, quantitative evidence can measure what is most important about them. Since the theories have clear predictions, it makes sense to use a rigorous statistical test. Similarly, anthropological approaches tend to focus on concepts like "culture," "anomie," and "meaning" that are not easily measured with quantitative data. Likewise, their focus is often on rich descriptions and interpretations of local relationships, rather than offering theories based on comparative static predictions (Geertz 1973). The rich qualitative and ethnographic evidence collected in such studies allows scholars to more fully describe and understand the underlying theories and concepts. Because these theories are not as focused on falsification, statistical tests with quantitative data are less relevant in generating knowledge. Pairing thin theory with rich, qualitative data (as with methods like the analytic narrative) provides clear static predictions with data rich in meaning with which to test those predictions (Skarbek and Skarbek 2022).

Some combinations of theories, concepts, and evidence are less productive. For example, some scholars use simple quantitative measures to describe thick concepts. While these vary in their effectiveness, important aspects of thick concepts are lost in doing so (Storr 2002, 4; Mohr et al. 2020, 159). Moreover, many existing theories lack clear comparative static predictions. As such, new knowledge generation or model testing by statistical analysis does not offset the sacrifice in fidelity to concepts from using (overly) simple quantitative measures. This limitation characterizes some recent work in criminology. As Gerben Bruinsma described in his 2016 address to the European Society of Criminology, work in criminology consists of "a mixture of hundreds of perspectives, definitions, ideas, sketches, multiple factors, theories, and single hypotheses that are partly true and partly untrue, and none are completely true or untrue" (Bruinsma 2016, 659). We argue that, in order to draw clear conclusions about causal mechanisms and adjudicate between institutional structures, scholars need thin parsimonious theories that generate clear, empirically testable predictions that they test using rich, qualitative evidence when examining things like "norms," "culture," or "institutions" and reserve quantitative evidence for simple topics like population demographics. Analytical narratives and other methods like comparative case studies and process tracing (among others) that combine thin theory with rich, qualitative data in this way are best situated to identifying causal mechanisms (Boettke 2000). In the next section, we provide an overview of what prison gangs are and who joins them before turning to the governance theory of prison gangs.

What Are Prison Gangs and Who Joins Them?

We define a prison gang as "a prisoner organization that operates within a prison system, that has a corporate entity, exists into perpetuity, and whose membership is restrictive, mutually exclusive, and often requires a lifetime commitment" (Skarbek 2014, 8–9).[8] Here, perpetuity does not mean that gangs exist forever, but like the financial instrument of the same name, that there is no fixed end date. Likewise, "corporate" does not mean that they have a business-like or "M-form" structure, but that the identity of the group is distinct from the specific individuals currently within it. Prison gangs are not strictly distinct from street gangs. Instead, whether a gang is a street or prison gang depends on its "context of influence" (Pyrooz and Decker 2019, 19). Some gangs may only have influence on the street or only in prison, while others have influence in both contexts (Pyrooz and Decker 2019, 108; Skarbek 2010, 706; 2014). Gangs will use that dual influence as a means by which to control members' behavior (Skarbek 2010, 709). Some prison gangs exert control over street gangs. For instance, the Mexican Mafia extorts payments from drug-dealing street gangs (Skarbek 2014, 133–138).

The organization of prison gangs varies. Some develop highly organized internal structures and "exert higher levels of control and discipline over their members" (Pyrooz and Decker 2019, 18; see also Skarbek 2010; 2011, 704; 2014, 109–128), while others operate informally according to social networks and allegiances that form around identity or background (Phillips 2012, 63; Maitra 2020, 129). Prison gangs also vary in size. For example, one study found that gangs in Texas had anywhere from 150 members (Black Widows) to 46,667 members (Vice Lords) (Pyrooz and Decker 2019, 114). English gangs tend to be much smaller, ranging from 5 to over 15 members (Maitra 2020, 141). Gang members tend to affiliate along racial and ethnic lines (Skarbek 2014, 77–87; Pyrooz and Decker 2019, 17).

Prison gangs have existed since the 1930s, with the first prison gang being documented by the warden of Sing Sing Prison in New York in 1931 (Roth 2020, 8). Since then, they have grown in number and size. Prison gang members constitute approximately 15% of the US prison population (Pyrooz and Decker 2019, 13). Prison gangs operate in many states, including Arizona (Arizona Criminal Justice Commission 2016; Roth 2020, 273, 275), California (Skarbek 2014; Roth 2020, 231), Florida (Office of the Attorney General 2011), Georgia (Roth 2020, 270), Illinois (Roth 2020, 231), Indiana (Roth 2020, 270), Maryland (Maryland Coordination and Analysis Center 2013; Department of Legislative Services 2009; Roth 2020, 271; Skarbek 2011, 712), Michigan (Roth 2020, 229), Minnesota (Roth 2020, 270), Mississippi (Roth 2020, 267), Nebraska (Krienert and Fleisher 2001), Nevada

(Roth 202, 270; Shelden 1991), New Jersey (Roth 202, 270; New Jersey State Police 2017, 2011; Commission of Investigation 2009), New York (Roth 2020, 227; Skarbek 2011, 712), North Carolina (North Carolina Criminal Justice Analysis Center 2008), South Carolina (South Carolina Department of Public Safety et al. 2012), Texas (Ralph et al. 1996; Rufino et al. 2012; Pyrooz and Decker 2019), Washington (Roth 2020, 231), and Wisconsin (Roth 2020, 270; Wisconsin Department of Justice 2008). Prison gangs have likewise been documented in prison systems around the world, including Honduras (Roth 2020, 322–325), Guatemala (Roth 2020, 325–331), Mexico (Roth 2020, 331–337), Puerto Rico (Roth 2020, 337–339), Brazil (Johnson and Densley 2018; Roth 2020, 286–303; Butler et al. 2018), Venezuela (Roth 2020, 303–309), Ecuador (Roth 2020, 285–286), El Salvador (Roth 2020, 311–321), Bolivia (Roth 2020, 284–285), Canada (Ruddell and Gottschall 2011; Scott and Ruddell 2011), the Philippines (Jones, Narag, and Morales 2015; Roth 2020, 152–168), India (Roth 2020, 169–178), Thailand (Roth 2020, 178–185), Singapore (Roth 2020, 185–193), Kyrgyzstand (Butler et al. 2018), Northern Ireland (Butler et al. 2018), the Republic of Ireland (Roth 2020, 219–221), Russia (Roth 2020, 52–76; Varese 2001) Australia (Roth 2020, 118–130), New Zealand (Roth 2020, 130–145), Sweden (Roth 2020, 195–198), Italy (Roth 2020, 28–51), South Africa (Roth 2020, 77–117), Indonesia (Roth 2020, 147–152) and to a lesser degree in England (Maitra 2020; Phillips 2012; Liebling, Arnold, and Straub 2011).

The demographics of prison gang members differ from the general population. They tend to be younger than non-gang members (Krienert and Fleisher 2001; Pyrooz and Decker 2019, 81) and Latino (Pyrooz and Decker 2019, 81). They also tend to have worse employment histories (Krienert and Fleisher 2001; Varano, Huebner, and Bynum 2011; Rufino et al. 2012), work fewer hours and earn less income (Krienert and Fleisher 2001), and are less likely to be employed at the time of their arrest (Shelden 1991). They tend to be less educated than other prisoners (Pyrooz and Decker 2019, 81). Gang members are also less likely to be military veterans, have a lower level of self-control, come from neighborhoods with less informal social control and more gangs, be more stressed, be more embedded in gang networks, be more likely to adhere to the code of the street and the convict code, and view correctional officers' actions as illegitimate or unfair (Pyrooz and Decker 2019, 82–83). Gang members also tend to be younger when they are first arrested (Pyrooz and Decker 2019; Krienert and Fleisher 2001), have been arrested more times and with a greater frequency (Pyrooz and Decker 2019; Krienert and Fleisher 2001; Ralph et al. 1996; Shelden 1991), and are more likely to be convicted for a violent offense (Ralph et al. 1996; Krienert and Fleisher 2001). Gang members are also more likely to have experienced victimization prior to their incarceration (Krienert and Fleisher 2001; Rufino et al. 2012) and tend to commit more misconduct before and during their incarceration than non-gang members (Varano et al. 2011; Rufino et al. 2012).

The Governance Theory of Prison Gangs

The governance theory of prison social order is based on a rational choice institutional framework. Rational choice institutionalism starts from a position of methodological individualism where the individual constitutes the unit of analysis, and group or organizational behavior can be explained using the incentives that individuals within the group face. The governance theory of prison gangs argues that prison gangs maintain the prison social order, often using violence or the threat of violence to exert social control (Skarbek 2014, 2020a). Prison gangs provide governance through property rights protection and facilitate trade in the prison. They arise when prison officials do not provide sufficient governance and more informal systems (like the convict code) cannot succeed. This will most often be in prisons with large, heterogenous populations (Skarbek 2010, 714; 2012, 97).

In California, when the number of prisoners began dramatically increasing in the 1960s, the convict code was no longer an effective way to maintain order in prison (Skarbek 2012, 102). The convict code consisted of informal norms about appropriate behavior among prisoners. Under the convict code, prisoners quickly learned those norms through interactions with those who had more incarceration experience (Skarbek 2014, 37).[9] The large influx of people included many first-time prisoners, who undermined the code. Reputation mechanisms that prisoners previously used to enforce the code no longer worked within the larger prison population; there were too many prisoners for a person's reputation to be known by most others. Gangs emerged amid this failure of norms as a source of social control.

Prison gangs constitute a "community responsibility system," wherein all members of a community are responsible for the actions and obligations of any other member (Greif 2004, 2006). This system equates the individual's reputation with that of the group. This is important in a large prison population setting where the reputation of an individual prisoner is difficult to learn. It is easier for a prisoner to learn a group's reputation than each person's reputation.

For a community responsibility system to work, each group must establish a way to verify each member's affiliation and monitor their own members. To verify members' affiliation, prison gangs rely on signals that are difficult for non-members to imitate, such as a person's race or prominent tattoos (Skarbek 2014, 77; see also Gambetta 2009). Because a person's race/ethnicity is difficult to alter, it provides a relatively easy way to identify gang membership. Tattoos can be imitated, so gang members often assault or kill non-members who adopt their tattoos. Gangs have also established mechanisms for assessing and monitoring the behavior of potential members. Gang leaders often establish information channels throughout the gang hierarchy, between prison facilities, and between the prison and neighborhoods. These mechanisms for enforcing membership and monitoring members allow gangs to establish and enforce rules that facilitate social order (Skarbek 2014 87–90).

Gang leaders in California often work to learn quickly about a new prisoner's past. To do so, they access new prisoners' official records by requiring that new admittances show leaders their official paperwork (Skarbek 2014, 87). Failing to do so is considered a sign of being untrustworthy (Skarbek 2014, 88). Shot callers may distribute a questionnaire to new prisoners or have notes smuggled between prisons to learn what a transferred prisoner's reputation was at their previous facility (Skarbek 2014, 88). When necessary, gang members rely on people outside the prison to access someone's criminal record on the internet. Sometimes, the correctional officers tell gang members if new prisoners are child molesters (Skarbek 2014, 88). Leaders also sometimes keep a list of enemies that shot callers check new admittances' names against.

Not all incarcerated people are members of prison gangs (Pyrooz and Decker 2019, 58). In California, non-members are expected to primarily associate with others in their racial or ethnic group, which the prison gangs in that racial group govern. These prisoners must obey the rules gang leaders establish despite being non-members (Skarbek 2014, 78). In this way, gang members police the behavior of both non-members and members. Non-members typically have the responsibility to defend anyone of their same racial group in violent conflict situations between a prisoner of their race and one of another (Skarbek 2014, 79).

Prison gangs often resolve conflicts between prisoners. Shot callers will resolve prisoners' disputes over drug deals, debts, or theft (Skarbek 2014, 83). Gang members are often also responsible for each other's behavior. For this reason, they have an incentive to monitor each other and maintain the gang's reputation. Shot callers may either force prisoners who threaten the group's reputation to apologize or punish them (Skarbek 2014, 84). Punishments range from having the offending person run laps around the prison yard to violent assaults (Colwell 2009, 449). One member of a gang explained that the punishments are "usually just something so [the other side] see it . . . They see it and know we have unity. We show everybody we go down together and this guy got disciplined" (Colwell 2009, 449). Punishments serve as visible signals to other gangs that gang leaders are enforcing the gang rules (Colwell 2009).

Shot callers often do not arbitrarily enforce their desired rules in a prison. Prison gangs sometimes have formal, written rules of conduct that their members are required to follow (Skarbek 2014, 90). These rules dictate what violence is allowed and when and where it can happen. Gangs dictate how prisoners behave and interact with each other and correctional staff, and who can access what resources in the prison. Likewise, each gang often controls a portion of the common property in the prison (bathrooms, basketball courts, benches, etc.). Gang leaders establish rules for who can use that resource and how. Members primarily use violence to enforce these claims. Through fights, gangs claim new territory and punish violators.

Gangs keep the peace to minimize the disruption of their contraband trade (Skarbek 2010, 713; 2014, 95). One prisoner describes how the community responsibility system allows the contraband trade to continue to operate effectively as follows:

> We don't want a lockdown, we don't want a riot so I've had to beat down my own guys to control the bigger picture. If one of my guys is messing up, then we either offer him up to the other guys or we take him down ourselves. Like I had a guy that ran up a big drug debt, he owed money to the woods [peckerwood skin-head gang] and I had to turn him over to them. They took him to a cell and really beat the shit out of him. We had to do it. If not, then everyone fights, which is bad for business and bad for us. (Trammell 2009, 763–764)

Without an effective way to resolve disputes with minimal violence, persistent lockdowns would make it impossible for gangs to operate their contraband trade. One former prisoner described how lockdowns disrupt gangs' trade: "If I'm locked down, then I'm not working. You can make some serious bank in prison and shot-callers hate it when you're in lockdown" (Trammell 2009, 760). To maintain this trade, gangs often work together to maintain order and peace in the prison (Skarbek 2010, 2014, 87). When a gang fails to punish their own members, other gang leaders must authorize their own members' use of violence and provide a covert place for the violence to avoid a lockdown (Skarbek 2014, 87).

Prison Governance around the World

As predicted by the governance theory, prison gangs have arisen in prisons around the world in places where official governance fails to meet prisoners' demand for protection. In many of these instances, prison gangs enforce rules and provide protection to prisoners. They also often control the contraband trade in the prison. To be clear, we are not suggesting that these are benevolent actors. Likewise, gangs clearly use violence and the threat of violence in capricious and unjust ways. The puzzle in our mind is that given that they are not benevolent actors, why do gangs sometimes provide governance? We argue these gangs arise in situations where prison officials do not provide adequate personal and property protection or resources and the prison population is large and heterogenous (Skarbek 2020a, 2016). In the Philippines (Jones and Narag 2014; Roth 2020, 156, 160, 162, 167), India (Roth 2020, 169), and Brazil (Roth 2020, 286), prison gangs have arisen to fill the governance void left by prison officials. They provide personal and property protection from prisoners as well as greater access to resources (Roth 2020, 14, 171, 292). To a far lesser extent, prison gangs are forming in English prisons. Historically, informal social networks and norms have served as the system of unofficial governance in English prisons over existing street gang relationships because of the small populations that are housed close to their home neighborhoods (Skarbek 2020, 121–125; Roth 2020, 206; Phillips 2012, 63). As the prison population has grown and prison officials have not been able to provide as effective personal protection for prisoners, groups that are somewhat more like prison gangs are beginning to form (Maitra 2020, 128, 135).

Not every prison system has prison gangs. Whether prison governance institutions are primarily provided by correctional staff (legal governance) or by prisoners (extralegal governance) depends on the degree to which official governance institutions meet the demands of prisoners (Skarbek 2020a, 10–11). The quality of extralegal governance institutions within each regime depends on the physical constraints of the prison and the characteristics of the prison population (Skarbek 2020a, 12–18). Large, heterogeneous prison populations tend to develop more centralized extralegal governance institutions to supplement the legal governance institutions maintained by correctional officials (Skarbek 2020a, 13). Prison gangs are only one example of formal extralegal governance institutions; other centralized extralegal governance systems exist. Small, homogenous prison populations, in contrast, develop more informal and decentralized extralegal governance institutions to supplement the legal governance institutions maintained by correctional officials (Skarbek 2020a, 13). The convict code is an example of informal legal governance institutions.

In many Latin American prisons, officials provide little governance, few resources, and poor-quality administration. In Brazilian jails, for example, prison governance is provided by a co-governance regime (Darke 2018). Prisoners cooperate with officials through prisoner associations to maintain prison order.[10] In contrast, San Pedro prison in Bolivia is an example of an extreme self-governance regime. Prisoners create, maintain, and enforce all governance institutions inside the prison. Prison officials rarely enter the prison. Instead, guards remain outside and regulate who enters and exits the prison. The main governance institutions in San Pedro are those provided by housing associations inside the prison, and the enforcement of those institutions usually does not extend beyond the prison neighborhood that the housing association controls (Skarbek 2010).

Prisoners will not always provide governance structures to fill the void left by prison officials. For example, at the Andersonville prison camp in Georgia, neither prison officials nor prisoners maintained any governance institutions despite military officials' failure to provide adequate resources or protection (Skarbek 2020a, 62–86). The lack of resources coupled with prisoners being prevented from trading with outsiders or accessing outside resources resulted in extreme resource deprivation among prisoners and guards. There were often rumors that the captives would be released soon in prisoner exchanges. The combination of the lack of official governance, lack of resources and outside exchange opportunities, and perceived short time horizon resulted in a lack of prisoner-generated governance institutions (Skarbek 2020a, 62–86).

Norwegian officials, in contrast, provide high levels of governance, resources, and administration (Ugelvik 2014). Because of this high level of legal governance and Norway's prison population being relatively small, prisoners have developed decentralized governance norms that rely on reputation mechanisms to enforce them. The population is small enough that prisoners can adequately monitor each other, and ostracism is a meaningful punishment (Ugelvik 2014, 107). For this reason, prison governance in Norway constitutes an official governance regime (Skarbek 2020a, 44–61).

Women's prisons in California stand in stark contrast to men's prisons. Incarcerated women have historically relied on decentralized governance mechanisms and continue to do so today (Owen 1998; Kruttschnitt and Gartner 2005). The small size of women's prison populations and the limited number of prisons allow women to rely on reputation as an enforcement mechanism (Skarbek 2020a, 89–105). As a result, they rely on a code of social norms, much like the convict code (Skarbek 2020a, 95–98). This code outlines norms and prohibited behaviors. Experienced prisoners teach newly incarcerated women the code and how to survive in prison. Prisoners also often form families to provide mutual support, resource sharing, and enforce the accepted social norms.

The Gay and Transgender unit at the Los Angeles County Jail has a small population like the California's women's prisons and has strong pre-prison social ties like people incarcerated in English prisons (Dolovich 2011). In addition to these two characteristics, the population has a relatively low social distance in that they are all gay or transgender prisoners, many of whom share lived experiences and worldviews. Correctional officers in this unit also provide a high level of official governance. They are particularly cognizant of the fact that prisoners from the general population often target gay and transgender prisoners. The small population and the high recidivism rate of the prison population in this unit also contribute to the high quality of legal governance that officials provide. The two main officials who govern that unit know individual prisoners well. For this reason, prisoners in the unit have limited extralegal governance institutions. There is no clear established set of social norms, but prisoners will assert some social pressure to enforce adherence to norms of gender presentation (Dolovich 2011, 45, 222).

Across these cases—prisons in Brazil, Bolivia, Norway, England, and the United States—we observe several governance mechanisms operating to provide governance for incarcerated people: a trustee system, prisoner associations and committees, prison officials, prison gangs, fictive kinships, postcode affiliations, norms, the convict code, and the House Mouse (Skarbek 2020a, 156). In short, there is no single or universal form of prisoner governance. Rather, there is a tremendous diversity of institutional outcomes that can emerge in places of incarceration.

THE CASE OF TEXAS: COMPETING FOR CONTROL

One of the most important works on prison gangs in recent years is David Pyrooz and Scott Decker's 2019 book *Competing for Control: Gangs and the Social Order of Prisons*. They survey prisoners (both gang members and non-gang members) incarcerated in the Texas Department of Corrections system. Of particular relevance, they focus on gangs' control of prison rules, prison order, and the contraband trade (Pyrooz and Decker 2019, 128). In the process, they propose, in part, to test a version of the governance theory using statistical analysis of aggregated, quantitative survey data. As one of the most detailed and comprehensive studies on the topic, it is worth examining how their findings relate to the governance theory. Interestingly, they reach divergent conclusions depending on whether they examine the survey evidence or the open-ended interview evidence.

To measure prison gangs' power over prison rules, they asked prisoners on the survey whether it is most important to follow the rules set by prison staff, prison gangs, or non-gang-affiliated prisoners. They also asked if prisoners were more fearful of retribution from prison staff, prison gangs, or non-gang-affiliated prisoners for not following the rules (129). They conclude from the survey data that "gangs are not recognized as highly powerful in the creation and enforcement of rules" (137). However, the data show that prisoners do not see *any* single group—prison gangs, prison staff, or prisoners—as wielding substantially more influence than others do in the prison, and it appears that gangs are seen as having as much power as prison staff.

To measure prison gangs' influence over the prison order, they asked prisoners to what degree they agreed with statements about the effect of gangs' presence on the prison order: "(1) prisons would be much more violent without gangs; (2) gangs help maintain order in prisons; (3) gangs are better at fixing problems than the prison staff; (4) if there are problems between gangs, the whole prison suffers the consequences; (5) prison staff need to talk to gangs before making any major changes; (6) gangs make you feel safer in prison; and (7) if you have a problem, you would trust gangs to resolve it and not the prison staff" (129). Overall, they conclude that prisoners do not recognize prison gangs as highly influential in "the maintenance of order. Even gang members describe the role of prison gangs in the social order of the prison as somewhat weak" (137). Many prisoners believed that "prisons would be safer without gangs, that gangs make them feel less safe in prison, they prefer prison staff to resolve problems rather than gangs, and that nongang inmates do not have a harder time in prison than gang inmates" (132).

However, at the same time, the qualitative evidence leads them to conclude that "many of the rules had a formal character and specifically identified gangs as their locus of origin as well as enforcement" (144). Likewise, many of the other findings from the qualitative evidence confirm the empirical implications of the governance theory. For example, prisoners explained that prisoners' rules centered on race (144). During violent conflicts, each prisoner is expected to side with other prisoners of his race. As one prisoner reported, "jump in on your side of a race riot is the main one [rule]" (144). Prisoners attest that different groups claim and control different areas of the prison. They also emphasized that prisoners' rules in general overlap considerably with gang rules. Staff rules are regarded as secondary to gang rules—especially by gang members. Pyrooz and Decker explain: "we commonly heard from inmates that the prison rules and prison staff took a secondary status compared to gang rules, particularly among gang members" (144). Most often, prisoners report that norms regarding daily life include "don't snitch," "keep to your own race," and "respect yourself and others." While the authors say that "these are not the rules of governance," these are precisely the sorts of governance rules discussed in earlier work (Skarbek 2014). Other norms forbid cooperating with the correctional officers and deliberately provoking violence (Pyrooz and Decker 2019, 145).

Finally, to measure prison gangs' control of contraband in prison and how much gang members benefit from the contraband trade in prison, they asked prisoners the degree to which they agreed with a statement that prison gangs must approve the sale of drugs, cellphones, and other contraband. They also asked to what degree "gangs get a cut of all profits from goods that are sold in prison" (129). From the survey, they conclude that prisoners do not view gangs as controlling "the sale of contraband by non-gang members" (137). However, the interview evidence again tells a different story. Based on the interviews, they report that "put simply, the respondents who provided qualitative data told us that gangs in prison control the sales and profits from contraband sold in prison" (145). As in the California case, prison violence was kept at "a low ebb" when contraband was being trafficked. The "consistent response" was that new entrants into gang-controlled contraband would be met with "swift, certain, and severe punishment" (145). As one prisoner explains, "if you're not in the gang, you're not going to sell nothing" (145).

More generally, prisoner governance institutions do not preclude the existence of official governance institutions. Instead, these governance structures can exist simultaneously. In fact, the scope and quality of official governance institutions will determine the scope and quality of prisoner governance institutions (Skarbek 2016). In prison systems like Texas, where official governance structures are extensive and of high quality, prisoner governance institutions will be less formalized and operate in more specific contexts. We would not expect the all-encompassing system of prisoner-based governance present in places like San Pedro to exist in Texas prisons, where prison officials provide extensive governance institutions. Similarly, we would not expect prisoner governance in Texas to only consist of informal norms enforced through social ostracization like in Nordic prisons. The prison population is too large and heterogenous for informal norms to provide effective governance.

Concluding Discussion

The research on prison gangs—and prison governance and social order more generally—that we survey here stimulates many compelling questions that remain to be answered. First, we argue that existing theories that attempt to explain variation in prison gang activity need revision. Of those theories discussed above, many of them lack clear empirical implications that would allow one to falsify or confirm each theory with evidence. Moreover, it is unclear which existing theories are compatible.

A second open area of inquiry is why the governance and resources that prison officials provide vary so tremendously across time and place. It seems likely that a large range of factors affect how politicians, bureaucrats, and prison staff influence the quality of official governance in prisons. Recent work on Western Europe, for example, argues that the adoption of "tough on crime" policies depends on public opinion, political systems, the nature of a country's political parties, and the presence of other government entities to explain the embrace of more punitive measures (Wenzelburger 2020).[11] In Nordic countries, we hear both government officials, citizens, and incarcerated people echoing the cultural belief that the role of prisons is to rehabilitate rather than to punish or deprive, suggesting that culture matters. By contrast, people across Latin America tend to be far more punitive. Finally, the degree of economic development and the nature of the political system more generally (more democratic or authoritarian) will influence what life in prison looks like. Studying the political causes of prison social order from a comparative perspective is fertile ground that provides new questions to be answered.

Moving from the macro level to the micro level, prisoner voice may serve as an effective tool for changing legal governance institutions in ways that will not worsen prison conditions. For example, prison journalists have intimate knowledge of the extralegal governance institutions that exist in a prison and can provide feedback on how proposed policy changes will interact with those prevailing institutions. The *San Quentin News* has already provided such feedback to CDCR officials regarding a proposal to integrate cellmates along the margin of race. The paper amplified prisoners' concerns that forced integration could leave them vulnerable to attack by prisoners from their cellmate's race if they have a disagreement (Drummond 2020, 75; Brydon 2008, 3; Hubbard 2008, 1). Because of this feedback, the policy was never implemented (Drummond 2020, 75). In this way, prison journalism can mitigate the principal–agent problem in state criminal justice systems, influencing policy changes on the margin to ensure that policies achieve outcomes closer to their intended purpose (Woltz 2022).

A third area that is broadly open is on assessing the desirability or effectiveness of different prison governance regimes, including ones where prison gangs are active. There are several challenges in doing so. First, one must identify the best way to measure prison performance. Logan (1993) has suggested several margins on which a prison's effectiveness could be evaluated: security, safety, order, care, activity, justice, and management. DiIulio (1987) previously suggested that prisons be evaluated according to their order, amenity, and service. More recently, and in our opinion more promising, is the Measuring the Quality of Prison Life survey that is emerging as a valuable way of judging the "moral performance" of prisons based on how prisoners perceive the level of respect, humanity, fairness, order, and safety in a facility (Liebling, Hulley, and Crewe 2011). Collecting survey data like this across a large and diverse number of different prison systems—and especially over time within a given system—would generate new knowledge about how the legal and extralegal sources of governance affect prison performance.[12]

A related research design challenge for assessing prison governance performance across regimes is to (1) identify the relevant counterfactual case for comparison and (2) identify the direction of causality. For example, we might observe a cross sectional, positive correlation between gang membership and exposure to violence. This could be because joining a gang increases a person's exposure to violence, but it might also be that there is a selection effect where violent people are more likely to join gangs. If so, it might be that gang members would be involved in *even more* violence if they were not in gangs. Longitudinal data are needed to better understand the relationship between gang membership and exposure to violence in prison.

Even if longitudinal data show a positive relationship between prison gang membership and exposure to violence, this relationship could still potentially be plagued with a number of confounding variables. For example, Skarbek (2014) argues that gangs formed in California because of booming prison populations, meaning that changes to the demographics of the population might confound the relationship between gang membership and exposure to violence. This raises the question of what the appropriate comparison group is. That is, in a situation of booming prison populations, gang membership might increase exposure to violence compared to a time when there are both smaller prison populations and no gangs. However, that does not tell us whether exposure to violence is higher or lower than it would be in large prison populations without gangs. Better theory and evidence are needed to unravel these types of complex social relationships.

These and a wide range of other interesting questions about prison gangs and prison governance more generally are open for investigation. More scholars than perhaps ever before are studying prison social order around the world and from more disciplinary backgrounds and with more varied methodological tools and approaches. We have much learning still to do.

Notes

1. While these data rely on prison officials' ability to correctly identify which prisoners are gang members, it is the best data available for most US prisons. Reassuringly, the 2014 LoneStar Project, which relied primarily on self-reported membership, found that about half of Texas prisoners were prison gang members (Pyrooz and Decker 2019, 63).
2. For a study more supportive of the importation approach, see Pyrooz et al. 2017.
3. Ayling (2011) and Densley (2014) suggest that conflict may be a catalyst for these changes for street gangs.
4. Brazil's prisons provide another example where prison gangs (and other prisoner groups) make up for the absence of officially provided protection and resources (Johnson and Densley 2018; Johnson 2017).
5. In more recent research, Maitra (2020, 129) found that prison gangs are more prevalent in English prisons than previously found. These gangs exist as "loosely structured, yet informally delineated" organizations, so are quite different from the examples found in California and Brazil.
6. For work investigating these models, see Thornberry et al. (1993, 2003) and McGloin and Collins (2015). Qualitative work on these models includes Decker and Van Winkle (1996), Klein and Crawford (1967), Short and Strodtbeck (1965), and Vigil (1988).
7. See Ostrom 2005 for a discussion of how institutions (e.g., property rights) require a set of overlapping rules.
8. This definition builds on Lyman (1989, 48). It allows for gang activity that extends beyond the prison walls. Prison gangs are durable organizations, some having operated for several decades, and serve to organize the drug trade in prisons, among other functions. They often require lifelong, exclusive membership of members (Skarbek 2014, 113–114). Multiple memberships would introduce confusion about territory claims and place

members under sets of conflicting rules. Additionally, if members could switch between gangs, it would reduce the gang's ability to use and rely on individual members. An exception to this is Brazilian prison gangs that allow members to switch their membership (Roth 2020, 293).

9. Prisoners were sorted into the prison social hierarchy according to their adherence to the code (Irwin 1980, 12; Sykes 1958). They would use violence to signal their adherence to the code; for example, a prisoner could assault someone convicted of child molestation to signal to others that they are not associated with that individual and establish their place in the social hierarchy. They would also use violence, as well as ostracism, to enforce the code. If someone violated an accepted norm, other prisoners would use varying levels of violence to punish them. At the lowest level, prisoners would slap, punch, or beat an offender as punishment. At the highest level, prisoners would slash an offender's face so that they would have a scar to communicate their bad standing in the hierarchy. If an offense was egregious enough, the offender might even be killed to prevent further norm violations (Skarbek 2014, 28–30). Gambetta (2009, 82) suggests that young offenders also use violence to signal their willingness to fight if threatened and to develop their "violence capital." Within a large prison population, that violence capital is less effective because individual prisoners are less likely to know another individual's reputation and willingness to fight.

10. These prison associations include gangs and religious organizations that serve to structure prisoners' daily lives and reduce violence in the prisons (Johnson and Densley 2018, 248, 255; Johnson 2017).

11. Enns (2014) documents a similar dynamic in the US where incarceration rates increase in response to public punitiveness. Pfaff (2017) also identifies public support and lobbying for prison growth as factors driving the growth of the prison population.

12. See Peirce (2019) for an example of modifying the Measuring the Quality of Prison Life for prisons with little official capacity.

References

Arizona Criminal Justice Commission. 2016. "2014 Arizona Gang Threat Assessment." https://www.jrsa.org/pubs/sac-digest/vol-24/az-2014GTA_Final.pdf.

Ayling, Julie. 2011. "Gang Change and Evolutionary Theory." *Crime, Law and Social Change* 56 (1): 1–26. https://doi.org/10.1007/s10611-011-9301-x.

Bayer, Patrick, Randi Hjalmarsson, and David Pozen. 2009. "Building Criminal Capital Behind Bars: Peer Effects in Juvenile Corrections." *The Quarterly Journal of Economics* 124 (1): 105–147. https://www.jstor.org/stable/40506225.

Beard, Jeffrey. 2013. "Hunger Strike in California Prisons Is a Gang Power Play." *Los Angeles Times*, August 6. https://www.latimes.com/opinion/la-xpm-2013-aug-06-la-oe-beard-prison-hunger-strike-20130806-story.html.

Boettke, Peter. 2000. "Review of *Analytical Narrative* by Robert Bates, Avner Greif, Margaret Levi, Jean Laurent Rosenthal, and Barry Weingast." *Constitutional Political Economy* 11: 377–379.

Bruinsma, Gerben. 2016. "Proliferation of Crime Causation Theories in an Era of Fragmentation: Reflections on the Current State of Criminological Theory." *European Journal of Criminology* 13 (6): 659–676.

Brydon, Kenneth R. 2008. "The SQ Problem of Integration." *San Quentin News*, August 27. https://storage.googleapis.com/sqn-archives/PDF/SQN_Edition_2_August_2008_web.pdf.

Buentello, Salvador, Robert S. Fong, and Ronald E. Vogel. 1991. "Prison Gang Development: A Theoretical Model." *Prison Journal* 71 (1): 3–14. https://dx.doi.org/10.1177/003288559107100202.

Butler, Michelle, Favin Slade, and Camila Nunes Dias. 2022. "Self-Governing Prisons: Prison Gangs in an International Perspective." *Trends in Organized Crime* 25: 1–16.

California Department of Corrections and Rehabilitation. 2012. "Security Threat Group Prevention, Identification and Management Strategy." March 1.

Carlson, Peter M. 2001. "Prison Interventions Evolving Strategies to Control Security Threat Groups." *Corrections Management Quarterly* 5 (1): 10–22.

Cloward, Richard A., and Lloyd E. Ohlin. 1960. *Delinquency and Opportunity: A Theory of Delinquent Gangs*. Glencoe, IL: Free Press.

Colwell, Brian. 2009. *The Prisoner Society: Power, Adaptation, and Social Life in an English Prison*. Oxford, UK: Oxford University Press.

Commission of Investigation. 2009. "Gangland Behind Bars: How and Why Organized Criminal Street Gangs Thrive in New Jersey's Prisons . . . And What Can Be Done About It." State of New Jersey. https://www.state.nj.us/sci/pdf/Gangs%20SCI%20Report%20Full.pdf.

Coppedge, Michael. 1999. "Thickening Thin Concepts and Theories: Combining Large N and Small in Comparative Politics." *Comparative Politics* 31 (4): 465–476.

Costa, Dora L., and Matthew E. Kahn. 2007. "Surviving Andersonville: The Benefits of Social Networks in POW Camps." *American Economic Review* 97 (4): 1467–1487. https://pubs-aea web-org.ccl.idm.oclc.org/doi/pdfplus/10.1257/aer.97.4.1467.

Crewe, Ben. 2009. *The Prisoner Society: Power, Adaptation, and Social Life in an English Prison*. Oxford, UK: Oxford University Press.

Darke, Sacha. 2018. *Conviviality and Survival: Co-Producing Brazilian Prison Order*. Cham, Switzerland: Palgrave Macmillan.

Davidson, R. Theodore. 1974. *Chicano Prisoners: The Key to San Quentin*. New York: Holt, Rinehart and Winston.

Decker, Scott H., and G. David Curry. 2002. "Gangs, Gang Homicides, and Gang Loyalty: Organized Crimes or Disorganized Criminals." *Journal of Criminal Justice* 30 (4): 343–352. https://doi.org/10.1016/S0047-2352(02)00134-4.

Decker, Scott H., and Barrik Van Winkle. 1994. "'Slinging Dope': The Role of Gangs and Gang Members in Drug Sales." *Justice Quarterly* 11 (4): 583–604. https://heinonline.org/HOL/P?h=hein.journals/jquart11&i=593.

Densley, James A. 2014. "It's Gang Life, but Not as We Know It: The Evolution of Gang Business." *Crime & Delinquency* 60 (4): 517–546. https://doi.org/10.1177/0011128712437912.

Department of Legislative Services. 2009. "Criminal Gangs in Maryland." http://dls.maryl and.gov/pubs/prod/CourtCrimCivil/Gangs.pdf.

DiIulio, John J. 1987. *Governing Prisons: A Comparative Study of Correctional Management*. New York: Free Press.

Dolovich, Sharon. 2011. "Strategic Segregation in the Modern Prison." *American Criminal Law Review*, 48 (1): 11 –22. https://heinonline.org/HOL/P?h=hein.journals/amcrimlr48&i=3.

Drummond, William J. 2020. *Prison Truth: The Story of the San Quentin News*. Oakland: University of California Press. https://doi.org/10.1525/9780520970526.

Enns, Peter. 2014. "The Publics Increasing Punitiveness and Its Influence on Mass Incarceration in the United States." *American Journal of Political Science* 58 (4): 857–872.

Fagan. Jeffrey. 1989. "The Social Organization of Drug Use and Drug Dealing among Urban Gangs." *Criminology* 27 (4): 633–670. https://doi.org/10.1111/j.1745-9125.1989.tb01049.x.

Fong, Robert S., Ronald E. Vogel, and Salvardor Buentello. 1992. "Prison Gang Dynamics: A Look Inside the Texas Department of Corrections." In *Corrections: Dilemmas and Directions*, edited by Peter J. Benekos and Alida V. Merlo, 57–77. Cincinnati, OH: Anderson.

Gaes, Gerald. G., Susan Wallace, Evan Gilman, Jody Klein-Saffran, and Sharon Suppa. 2002. "The Influence of Prison Gang Affiliation on Violence and Other Prison Misconduct." *Prison Journal* 82 (3): 359–385. https://doi-org.ccl.idm.oclc.org/10.1177%2F00328855020 8200304.

Gambetta, Diego. 2009. *Codes of the Underworld: How Criminals Communicate*. Princeton, NJ: Princeton University Press.

Gaston, Shytierra, and Beth M. Huebner. 2015. "Gangs in Correctional Institutions." In *The Handbook of Gangs*, edited by Scott H. Decker and David Pyrooz, 328–344. Chichester, UK: Wiley Blackwell.

Geertz, Clifford. 1973. *The Interpretation of Cultures*. New York: Basic Books.

Greif, Avner. 2004. "Impersonal Exchange without Impartial Law: The Community Responsibility System." *Chicago Journal of International Law* 5: 109–138.

Greif, Avner. 2006. *Institutions and the Path to the Modern Economy: Lessons from Medieval Trade*. Cambridge, UK: Cambridge University Press.

Hubbard, Suzan L. 2008. "Integrating Prison Cells." *San Quentin News*, June 18. https://storage.googleapis.com/sqn-archives/PDF/SQN_Edition_1_June_2008_web.pdf.

Irwin, John. 1980. *Prisons in Turmoil*. Boston, MA: Little, Brown, & Co.

Jacobs, James B. 1977. *Stateville: The Penitentiary in Mass Society*. Chicago, IL: University of Chicago Press.

Johnson, Andrew. 2017. *If I Give My Soul: Faith Behind Bars in Rio de Janeiro*. New York: Oxford University Press.

Johnson, Andrew, and James Densley. 2018. "Rio's New Social Order: How Religion Signals Disengagement from Prison Gangs." *Qualitive Sociology* 41 (2): 243–262.

Jones, Clarke R., and Raymund E. Narag. 2014. "Why Prison Gangs Aren't All Bad." *CNN* December 11. https://edition.cnn.com.

Jones, Clarke R., Raymund E. Narag, and Resurrecion S. Morales. 2015. "Philippine Prison Gangs: Control or Chaos?" *Regnet Working Paper* 71. Regulatory Institutions Network.

Klein, Malcolm W., and Lois Y. Crawford. 1967. "Groups, Gangs, and Cohesiveness." *Journal of Research in Crime and Delinquency* 4 (1): 63–75. https://heinonline.org/HOL/P?h=hein.journals/jrcd4&i=63.

Klein, Malcolm W., and Cheryl L. Maxson. 2006. *Street Gang Patterns and Policies*. New York: Oxford University Press.

Krienert, Jessie L., and Mark S. Fleisher. 2001. "Gang Membership as a Proxy for Social Deficiencies: A Study of Nebraska Inmates." *Corrections Management Quarterly* 5 (1) (Winter): 47–58.

Kruttschnitt, Candace, and Rosemary Gartner. 2005. *Marking Time in the Golden State: Women's Imprisonment in California*. New York: Cambridge University Press.

Lessing, Benjamin. 2017. "Counterproductive Punishment: How Prison Gangs Undermine State Authority." *Rationality and Society* 29 (3): 257–297.

Liebling, Alison, Helen Arnold, and Christina Straub. 2011. *An Exploration of Staff-Prisoner Relationships at HMP Whitemoor: 12 Years On*. Revised Final Report. Ministry of Justice, National Offender Management Service. Cambridge Institute of Criminology Prisons

Research Centre. https://assets.publishing.service.gov.uk/government/uploads/system/uploads/attachment_data/file/217381/staff-prisoner-relations-whitemoor.pdf.

Liebling, Alison, Susie Hulley, and Ben Crewe. 2011. "Conceptualising and Measuring the Quality of Prison Life." In *The Sage Handbook of Criminological Research Methods*, edited by David Gadd, Susanne Karstedt, and Steven F. Messner, 358–372. Thousand Oaks, CA: Sage Publications. https://dx.doi.org/10.4135/9781446268285.

Logan, Charles H. 1993. *Criminal Justice Performance Measures for Prisons*. US Department of Justice, Office of Justice Programs, Bureau of Justice Statistics.

Maitra, Dev Rup. 2020. "'If You're Down with a Gang Inside, You Can Lead a Nice Life': Prison Gangs in the Age of Austerity." *Youth Justice* 20 (1-2): 128–145. https://doi.org/10.1177/1473225420907974.

Maryland Coordination and Analysis Center. 2013. "Maryland Gang Threat Assessment." https://www.mcac.maryland.gov/resources/2013%20Public%20Gang%20Threat%20Assessment.pdf.

McGloin, Jean M., and Megan E. Collins. 2015. "Micro-Level Processes of the Gang." In *The Handbook of Gangs*, edited by Scott H. Decker and David C. Pyrooz, 276–293. Chichester, UK: Wiley-Blackwell. DOI: 10.1002/9781118726822.ch15.

Mohr, John W., Christopher A. Bail, Margaret Frye, Jennifer C. Lena, Omar Lizardo, Terence E. McDonnell, Ann Mische, Iddo Tavory, and Frederick F. Wherry. 2020. *Measuring Culture*. New York: Columbia University Press.

New Jersey State Police. 2011. "Gangs in New Jersey: Municipal Law Enforcement Response to the 2010 NJSP Gang Survey." New Jersey Department of Law and Public Safety. https://www.state.nj.us/lps/njsp/info/pdf/gangs_in_nj_2010.pdf.

New Jersey State Police. 2017. "Statewide Gang Assessment." https://nj.gov/njsp/information/pdf/2017_NJSP_Gang_Survey.pdf.

North, Douglass C. 1990. *Institutions, Institutional Change, and Economic Performance*. New York: Cambridge University Press.

North Carolina Criminal Justice Analysis Center. 2008. "Gangs in North Carolina: A Summary of the Law Enforcement Survey." Governor's Crime Commission. https://files.nc.gov/ncdps/documents/files/GangSystemStatssummer08.pdf.

Office of the Attorney General. 2011. "Florida Gang Reduction Strategy 2011 Annual Report: Building a Strategy to Reduce Gangs in Florida." https://trustedpartner.azureedge.net/docs/library/ChoosePeaceStopViolence2014/Understand/Gang_Report_2011_WebFinal.pdf.

Ostrom, Elinor. 1990. *Governing the Commons: The Evolution of Institutions for Collective Action*. Cambridge, UK: Cambridge University Press.

Ostrom, Elinor. 2005. *Understanding Institutional Diversity*. Princeton, NJ: Princeton University Press.

Owen, Barbara. A. 1998. *In the Mix: Struggle and Survival in a Women's Prison*. Albany, NY: State University of New York Press.

Peirce, J. 2019. *Prisoners' Perceptions of Humane Treatment in the Dominican Republic's Prison Reform Process*. Unpublished manuscript, John Jay College.

Pfaff, John. 2017. *Locked In: The True Causes of Mass Incarceration and How to Achieve Real Reform*. New York: Basic Books.

Phillips, Coretta. 2012. "'It Ain't Nothing Like America with the Bloods and the Crips': Gang Narratives inside Two English Prisons." *Punishment & Society* 14 (1): 51–68.

Pyrooz, David C., and Scott H. Decker. 2019. *Competing for Control: Gangs and the Social Order of Prisons*. Cambridge, UK: Cambridge University Press.

Pyrooz, David C., Nancy Gartner, and Molly Smith. 2017. "Consequences of Incarceration for Gang Membership: A Longitudinal Study of Serious Offenders in Philadelphia and Phoenix." *Criminology* 55 (2): 273–306.

Ralph, Paige H., Robert J. Hunter, James W. Marquart, Steven J. Cuvelier, and Dorothy Merianos. 1996. "Exploring the Differences between Gang and Non-Gang Prisoners." In *Gangs in America*, 2nd ed, edited by C. Ronald Huff, 123–136. Thousand Oaks, CA: Sage.

Roth, Mitchel P. 2020. *Power on the Inside: A Global History of Prison Gangs*. London: Reaktion Books.

Ruddell, Rick, and Shannon Gottschall. 2011. "Are All Gangs Equal Security Risks? An Investigation of Gang Types and Prison Misconduct." *American Journal of Criminal Justice* 36 (3): 265–279. DOI:10.1007/s12103-011-9108-4.

Rufino, Katrina A., Kathleen A. Fox, and Glen A. Kercher. 2012. "Gang Membership and Crime Victimization among Prison Inmates." *American Journal of Criminal Justice* 37 (3): 321–337. https://doi.org/10.1007/s12103-011-9134-2.

Scott, Terri-Lynne, and Rick Ruddell. 2011. "Canadian Female Gang Inmates: Risk, Needs, and the Potential for Prison Rehabilitation." *Journal of Offender Rehabilitation* 50 (6): 305–326. https://doi-org.ccl.idm.oclc.org/10.1080/10509674.2011.583717.

Shelden, Randall G. 1991. "A Comparison of Gang Members and Non-Gang Members in a Prison Setting." *Prison Journal* 71 (2): 50–60.

Short, James F., and Fred L. Strodtbeck. 1965. *Group Process and Gang Delinquency*. Chicago, IL: University of Chicago Press.

Skarbek, David. 2010. "Self-Governance in San Pedro Prison." *The Independent Review* 14 (4): 569–585.

Skarbek, David. 2011. "Governance and Prison Gangs." *American Political Science Review* 105 (4): 702–716. https://www.jstor.org/stable/23275348.

Skarbek, David. 2012. "Prison Gangs, Norms, and Organizations." *Journal of Economic Behavior and Organization* 82 (1): 96–109. https://doi.org/10.1016/j.jebo.2012.01.002.

Skarbek, David. 2014. *The Social Order of the Underworld: How Prison Gangs Govern the American Penal System*. New York: Oxford University Press.

Skarbek, David. 2016. "Covenants without the Sword? Comparing Prison Self-Governance Globally." *American Political Science Review* 110 (4): 845–862. DOI:10.1017/S0003055416000563.

Skarbek, David. 2020a. *The Puzzle of the Prison Order: Why Life Behind Bars Varies around the World*. New York: Oxford University Press.

Skarbek, David. 2020b. "Qualitative Research Methods for Institutional Analysis." *Journal of Institutional Economics* 16: 409–422.

Skarbek, David, and Emily Skarbek. 2022. "Analytical Narratives in Political Economy." *History of Political Economy*: 10620913.

South Carolina Department of Public Safety, Office of Justice Programs, and Statistical Analysis Center. 2012. "Gangs and Crime in South Carolina: How Much, How Bad?" https://dc.statelibrary.sc.gov/bitstream/handle/10827/9347/DPS_Gangs_and_Crime_in_SC_2010.pdf?sequence=1&isAllowed=y.

Spergel, Irving A. 1964. *Racketville, Slumtown, Haulbug*. Chicago, IL: University of Chicago Press.

Spindler, Andrea, and Martin Bouchard. 2011. "Structure or Behavior? Revisiting Gang Typologies." *International Criminal Justice Review* 21 (3): 263–282. https://heinonline.org/HOL/P?h=hein.journals/intcrm21&i=263.

Storr, Virgil Henry. 2002. *Understanding the Culture of Markets*. Routledge Foundations of the Market Economy. Oxon, UK: Routledge.

Sweeten, Gary. 2012. "Scaling Criminal Offending." *Journal of Quantitative Criminology* 28 (3): 533–557.

Sykes, Gresham. M. 1958. *The Society of Captives*. Princeton, NJ: Princeton University Press.

Taylor, Carl S. 1990. *Dangerous Society*. East Lansing: Michigan State University Press.

Thornberry, Terence P., Marvin D. Krohn, Alan J. Lizotte, and Deborah Chard-Wierschem. 1993. "The Role of Juvenile Gangs in Facilitating Delinquent Behavior." *Journal of Research in Crime and Delinquency* 30 (1): 55–87. https://heinonline.org/HOL/P?h=hein.journals/jrcd30&i=53.

Thornberry, Terence P., Marvin D. Krohn, Alan J. Lizotte, Carolyn A. Smith, and Kimberly Tobin. 2003. *Gangs and Delinquency in Developmental Perspective*. New York: Cambridge University Press.

Thrasher, Frederic M. 1927. *The Gang: A Study of 1,313 Gangs in Chicago*. Chicago, IL: University of Chicago Press.

Trammell, Rebecca. 2009. "Values, Rules, and Keeping the Peace: How Men Describe Order and the Inmate Code in California Prisons." *Deviant Behavior* 30 (8): 746–771.

Trammell, Rebecca. 2011. "Symbolic Violence and Prison Wives: Gender Roles and Protective Pairings in Men's Prisons." *Prison Journal* 91 (3): 305–324.

Ugelvik, Thomas. 2014. *Power and Resistance in Prison: Doing Time, Doing Freedom*. Cham, Switzerland: Springer.

Valdez, Avelardo. 2003. "Toward a Typology of Contemporary Mexican American Youth Gangs." In *Gangs and Society: Alternative Perspectives*, edited by Louis Kontos, David C. Brotherton and Luis Barrios, 12–40. New York: Columbia University Press.

Varano, Sean P., Beth M. Huebner, and Timothy S. Bynum. 2011. "Correlates and Consequences of Pre-Incarceration Youthful Felons." *Journal of Criminal Justice* 39 (1): 30–38. https://doi.org/10.1016/j.jcrimjus.2010.10.001.

Varese, Federico. 2001. *The Russian Mafia: Private Protection in a New Market Economy*. New York: Oxford University Press.

Vigil, J. Diego. 1988. *Barrio Gangs: Street Life and Identity in Southern California*. Austin: University of Texas Press.

Wenzelburger, Georg. 2020. *The Partisan Politics of Law and Order*. New York: Oxford University Press.

Winterdyk, John, and Rick Ruddell. 2010. "Managing Prison Gangs: Results from a Survey of U.S. Prison Systems." *Journal of Criminal Justice* 38: 730–736.

Wisconsin Department of Justice. 2008. "Northeast Wisconsin Gang Assessment." https://www.doj.state.wi.us/sites/default/files/2008-news/northeast-wi-gang-assessment-20081110.pdf.

Woltz, Kaitlyn. 2022. "The Role of Prisoner Voice in Criminal Justice Reform." *GMU Working paper in Economics No. 20-50*. http://dx.doi.org/10.2139/ssrn.3748768.

CHAPTER 31

TRANSNATIONAL GANGS?
Understanding Migration and Gangs

JOSÉ MIGUEL CRUZ AND JONATHAN D. ROSEN

For many observers, Mara Salvatrucha, also known as MS-13, is the quintessential case of a gang born and forged out of immigration (Dudley 2020; Arana 2005; Barak, León, and Maguire 2020). The notorious Central American street gang was formed out of Salvadoran immigrants who moved to southern California in the early 1980s (Ward 2013; Vigil 2002). According to many authors, it expanded across the region due to the deportation and voluntary return of Central American migrants to their countries of origin and the subsequent migration of Central American gang members to other countries (Jütersonke, Muggah, and Rodgers 2009; Kalsi 2018; Covey 2010).

The link between immigration and gangs, however, is a complex one. Several observers often construe it as one of the most critical factors in the expansion of the gang phenomenon in any society (Bankston 1998; Adamson 1998; Weerman and Decker 2005). The first accounts of gang emergence and expansion in the United States are tied to the immigrant waves of impoverished Europeans arriving in New York in the nineteenth century (Asbury 1928; Sante 2016). Yet the contours and the character of the relationship between gangs and immigration have changed as societies grew and their communities transformed with every wave of immigrants (Spergel 1995). Today, immigration—along with ethnicity, culture, and marginalization—is not only a crucial variable to understanding the domestic proliferation of gangs but also to appreciate the expansion of these groups in the sending countries, namely in the communities where migration originates. The spread of MS-13 in Central America, the Trinitarios in the Caribbean, the Latin Kings in Spain, and the Crips in Belize and the Netherlands speak to the necessity for assessing the role of human movement across borders and cities to understand current gangs (Feixa and Sánchez-García 2019; Roks and Densley 2020; Baird 2021a).

Several authors have underscored the increasingly global character of gangs (Hagedorn 2005, 2008; Winton 2014). Globalization seems to be a catalyst for the rise of transnational gangs (Fraser and Van Hellemont 2020; Rodgers and Hazen 2014). However, as Papachristos (2005) contends, gangs are not global because they are transnational—there are no gangs that have such a large presence—but rather, migration and the spread of information technology have made them hypermobile. Social media has contributed to spreading global gang narratives that shape local gang dynamics (Van Hellemont and Densley 2019).

This chapter explores the role of migration in the current phenomenon of the so-called transnational gang. We understand transnational gangs as street-oriented groups, mainly composed of youth, who share a particular common identity across regions and national borders that allows them to build a sense of global community with a basic understanding of symbols and rituals (Santamaría Balmaceda 2007; Winton 2012). Instead of conceiving the relationship between immigration and transnational gangs as a one-event phenomenon, in which gangs emerge from waves of hopeless immigrants arriving in wealthy but segregated communities (Klein 1995), this chapter focuses on how migration operates in circular and representational ways in shaping transnational gangs. Migration not only transplants new street actors into new communities. More importantly, migration contributes to spreading group identities and street cultures. However, these group tags are recycled in communities where migration is experienced as events of uprooting and dislodgment. They are also reinterpreted where migration is experienced as expatriation and not as an arrival. The transnational character of some gangs means that their identities and symbols were created elsewhere, but they are re-signified locally.

This chapter highlights the prominence of human mobility across borders in the rise and global expansion of gangs. However, despite interpretations that see transnational gangs as simply the result of gang members' international relocation, the following pages pay special attention to the circular implications of immigration; how it helps to explain gangs not only in developed countries but also in developing—and sending—countries.

The chapter is divided into four sections. First, it reviews the reports about the historical role of immigration in the emergence of gangs, especially in the United States. Then it discusses the use of the term "transnational gang" in the literature while proposing a definition. Third, the chapter addresses the different theories seeking to explain the rise and development of transnational gangs. Before concluding, we also discuss the relationship between migration, globalization, and territoriality. This exercise expands our conceptualization of transnational gangs. The chapter pays special attention to Central American gangs, considered the prototypical transnational groups.

The Historical Role of Migration

The emergence and development of street gangs in the United States and Europe cannot be disassociated from immigration. In the United States, the appearance of youth gangs is closely linked to immigrant waves (Howell 2015; Covey 2010). Adamson (1998) traces the first manifestations of street gangs in America to the 1820s, following the surge of European immigration after the War of 1812. However, Curry, Decker, and Pyrooz (2003) identify four distinct periods of gang activity in the United States, which were, in part, associated with increased immigration: the 1890s, 1920s, 1960s, and 1990s. These periods also mark the geographical shifts of gang activities following the main immigrant destinations (Howell 2015). The early periods of gang activity were concentrated in the northeast of the United States due to the flow of northern European immigrants. As new waves of immigrants pushed toward the Midwest in the first half of the twentieth century, gang activity became prevalent in Chicago, which prompted the first systematic study of street gangs by Thrasher (1927). The Great Migration, the massive movement of southern Black Americans to other regions of the country, coupled with increased immigration of Mexicans to the Midwest and the southwest, contributed to the emergence of Chicago and Los Angeles as hotbeds for gang activity since the second half of the twentieth century (Vigil 2002; Hagedorn 2006; Howell 2015). By the early 1990s, the arrival of immigrants and political refugees from Asia, Central America, and other regions of the world had contributed to turning southern California into ground zero of the gang phenomenon in the United States (Howell and Griffiths 2015, Klein 1995).

In Europe, the scholarship on street gangs is more recent, and the study of the links between them and immigration is more uneven (Klein, Weerman, and Thornberry 2006; Klein et al. 2000; Weerman and Decker 2005). Decker, Van Gemert, and Pyrooz (2009) describe how immigration in Europe after World War II brought many nationalities together due to the combined effects of the imperialist and colonialist pasts, economic development, and refugee protection. They contributed to the growth of minority populations raised in contexts favorable to youth gangs. While there is plenty of evidence about the role of immigration in the European gang phenomenon (Weerman and Decker 2005; Van Gemert, Peterson, and Lien 2008; Sela-Shayovitz 2012), the prevalence of gangs varies from country to country (Klein et al. 2006; Weerman and Esbensen 2005). The influence that immigration factors played in the emergence and dynamics of street gangs also depends on the country (Klein et al. 2006; Van Gemert 2012; Hagedorn 2001). For instance, using self-report surveys of middle school students in 19 European countries, Haymoz, Maxson, and Killias (2013) found a link between gang membership and migrant conditions only in Estonia, Germany, and Sweden.

The literature on street gangs in other parts of the world had generally been devoid of links with migration (Palasinski et al. 2016; Higginson and Benier 2015). Apart from Central America (Rodgers and Baird 2015; Reisman 2006; Cruz 2013), most of the research work on gangs in Latin American countries does not refer to immigration processes as key to understanding the proliferation of youth gangs (Dowdney 2005; Rodgers and Baird 2015; Imbusch, Misse, and Carrion 2011). Instead, explanations of the emergence and development of gangs revolve around systemic marginalization, spatial segregation, deficiencies in local governance, lack of economic opportunities, and the establishment of criminal economies, among other factors (Glebbeek and Koonings 2016; Jones and Rodgers 2009; Zaluar 2000; Arias 2014). Similar themes predominate in the literature from other regions of the world, with particular attention given to issues of urbanization, rapid social change, industrialization, and economic transformations (Matusitz and Repass 2009; Zhang 2014; Salagaev and Safin 2014).

While the discussion about the role of immigration and mobility in the gang phenomenon has been a salient topic in the scholarship of the developed world (Peterson, Lien, and Van Gemert 2008; Decker et al. 2009), in many countries of the developing world the issue of immigration does not seem to generate the same attention or the same intensity. This difference in how immigration is addressed when analyzing gangs has to do with the nature of the variables associated with socioeconomic marginalization and cultural segregation. In developed countries, such as the United States, the United Kingdom, Germany, or the Netherlands, the position in the socioeconomic structure and the opportunities available to individuals are often shaped by the condition of immigration and by the way immigrant communities relate to the larger society (Krohn et al. 2011; Sela-Shayovitz 2012; Vigil 1988, 2002; Decker et al. 2009; Sánchez-Jankowski 2003). In contrast, in some developing nations, where immigration to the country is low and social identities do not seem to revolve around nationalities, the theoretical discussions involving immigration are nearly non-existent (Covey 2010; Zaluar 2000; Rodríguez et al. 2017).[1]

However, the rise of transnational gangs has called this apparent difference into question. It has compelled gang scholars working in developing countries to examine the effects of migration (Cruz 2013; Cerbino Arturi 2009; Mateo 2011; Ambrosius 2021). Furthermore, it has pushed scholarship to consider the diverse ways in which migration shapes gangs around the world. What we call "transnational gangs" are groups wielding identities initially forged in other latitudes (Winton 2014; Rodgers and Hazen 2014; Feixa et al. 2012; Hagedorn 2005). Street gangs initially formed and grown in the marginalized *barrios* and slums of wealthy Western societies are now present and strengthened in countries where immigration is practically non-existent and where there are no immigrant communities. Yet it is impossible to understand these gangs and their transnationality without considering the role of migration.

TRANSNATIONAL GANGS

This section articulates our working conceptualization of transnational gangs and then offers a brief account of the recent use of the term. Despite the growing use of the term "transnational gangs," there has been little discussion about the definition and meaning of the expression. Even the definition of what a gang is raises some debate (Feixa and Sánchez-García 2019; Brotherton 2008; Klein et al. 2000). We conceptualize transnational gangs as street-oriented groups that share a particular common identity across regions and national borders. This identity, which revolves around common symbols and rituals, operates as a catalyst for a sense of a regional or global community and facilitates local group dynamics. Hence, rather than referring to a group of people that traverse different countries, transnational gangs refer to groups that share identities, allowing the standardization of symbols and the flow of information across borders. What makes a gang transnational is not the presence of itinerant members but the adoption of identities that are recognized globally. Such recognition provides a sense of community, helping some migrant youth to find belonging and meaning in different and confusing cultural environments.

The first systematic use of the expression "transnational gang" was associated with the Barrio 18 (18th Street) and Mara Salvatrucha (MS-13) gangs (Rogers 2003; Johnson and Muhlhausen 2005). According to Howell (2015), Barrio 18 originally appeared in the streets of Chicago but developed and became better known in Los Angeles (Franco 2008). Mara Salvatrucha was formed by children of Salvadoran refugees living in Los Angeles (Vigil 2002; Ward 2013). These gang identities later appeared in the northern countries of Central America: El Salvador, Honduras, and Guatemala, along with others that faded over time, such as White Fence, Hoyo Maravilla, and Mirada Locos (Cruz 2010; Levenson 2013). Thus, the use of "transnational gang" remains strongly associated with Mara Salvatrucha and Barrio 18, and, in many cases, it is used as a synonym for them (Méndez 2019; Fontes 2018).

In its initial uses, the "transnational gang" expression referred to the noticeable international characteristic of these groups, which were composed of Latinos. It referred to the fact that their presence crossed several national and political boundaries (Rogers 2003). The first articles addressing the issue of transnational gangs also presented them with a strong inclination to operate as active criminal networks in the international arena (Sullivan 2006; Franco 2008). These interpretations aligned with a perspective that saw migration as part of the gangs' deliberate attempt to expand and increase their criminal operations internationally, in some cases as part of terrorist networks (Sullivan and Bunker 2002). In some sense, these interpretations viewed the presence of the same gang in different countries as tantamount to its power and reach. Following the repercussions of the September 11, 2001, terrorist attacks and the singular case of the Chicago-based El Rukn street gang, some debates about the nature of transnational gangs in the early 2000s were whether they could evolve into terrorist networks (Sullivan and Bunker 2002; Papachristos 2005). The early writings qualifying the Central American gangs as transnational organizations portrayed them as "urban warriors" or "urban insurgency" and a threat to national security in the Americas (Sullivan 2006; Manwaring 2006). In addition, some media stories reporting contacts between MS-13 and Al-Qaeda bolstered such views (Rogers 2007; Wolf 2012).

Later works have highlighted aspects of cultural transmission as the defining elements of transnational gangs (Cruz 2013; Hagedorn 2008; Santamaría Balmaceda 2007). These works ask about the extent to which the transnationality of certain groups is related to the global cultural flows and the degree to which the digital age and globalization facilitate the transfer of certain street identities rather than the actual human migratory processes (Hagedorn 2001, 2005; Pyrooz and Moule 2019; Feixa, Leccardi, and Nilan 2016). These debates mirror the discussion about the role of migration and human mobility in the emergence and proliferation of gangs across the United States (Maxson 1998; Decker, Melde, and Pyrooz 2013; Decker and Curry 2000).

In recent years, European scholars working around the Transgang Project have been tackling the definitional issue of transnational gangs, with a particular emphasis on European groups (Feixa and Sánchez-García 2019). This group emphasizes the global character of the spaces inhabited by gangs and youth groups, in which media, technology, neoliberal models, and politics converge. Transnational gangs serve as agents of mediation at the local level, providing identities and resources to relate to different actors and institutions (Feixa and Sánchez-García 2019; Fernández-Planells et al. 2020). Hence, the transnational character is given by their ability to provide virtual—and physical—environments where cultural identities "generate processes of adaptation but also of resistance to oppression" (Feixa and Sánchez-García 2019, 17). The authors working on this perspective recognize the centrality of migration in discussing transnational gangs. Still, they underscore the inter- and multicultural character of the youth groups inhabiting the metropolis and urban spaces and their interconnectedness through global forces (Feixa et al. 2016).

Migration and Transnational Gangs

Moore and Stuart (2022) identify three general perspectives when explaining the emergence of transnational gangs. One view, advanced by most reports on Central American gangs, places the responsibility on the migration flows between the United States and the countries from which migration originates (USAID 2006; Farah 2012; Arana 2005; Franco 2008). Often referring to Central America, they argue that gangs become transnational because of the heavy circular flow of migrants between sending and receiving countries. In some cases, migration policies play a role in stimulating immigration to new areas or deporting individuals to their home countries, creating a revolving door that ends up forming and strengthening gang cliques wherever they land (Johnson and Muhlhausen 2005).

The second perspective highlights the role of the transmission of cultural assets in the formation and spread of transnational gangs. The most vigorous exponent of this theoretical framework is John Hagedorn (2005, 2008), for whom the globalization of cultural identities through popular culture, especially music and cinema, has contributed to the transnational character of several youth groups around the world (Fraser and Van Hellemont 2020). Some authors have also emphasized the role of information technology in this process of transnationalization (Roks and Densley 2020; Fernández-Planells et al. 2020; Pyrooz and Moule 2019). Others have underscored the use of transnational gang identities as forms of collective resistance and social recognition in marginalized communities (Brotherton 2008; Baird 2021b; Moore 2007).

The third view on the relationship between gangs and migration takes the two previous perspectives and argues that transnational gangs arise as a product of the combined effect of migration and the cultural influences—norms and values—that migrants bring with them (Cruz 2013; Papachristos 2005; Feixa 2021). According to some proponents of this perspective, the global identities of street culture are used and reinterpreted to deal with the distressing experiences of immigration, mobility, and forced repatriation (Winton 2012, 2014; Fontes 2019; O'Neill 2015).

Perspectives to understand transnational gangs and their relationship with migration processes are shaped by the characteristics of the objects of study. Research on Central American gangs has dominated most literature on transnational gangs. Given the notoriously violent character of these groups in some communities, much of its initial research focused on security and policy (Arana 2005; Wolf 2012; Bruneau, Dammert, and Skinner 2011). However, research in other regions, such as South America and Europe, has focused more on the cultural aspects that have allowed local groups to adopt extraneous gang identities (Cerbino Arturi 2009; Brotherton 2008; Roks and Densley 2020; Sullivan 2008).

A more detailed examination of the theoretical perspectives about the role of immigration can provide some missing elements to complete our understanding of transnational gangs. The theories explaining the relationship between immigration and transnational gangs generally follow the debate about the immigration–crime connection. There are generally four perspectives when explaining the link between immigration and crime: (1) the importation model, (2) the strain perspective, (3) the cultural model, and (4) the bias viewpoint (Wortley 2009).

In the importation model, several researchers view migration as the essential vehicle for gang expansion and the development of gang activities in new territories and countries. This importation perspective is frequent among the articles attempting to explain the diffusion of gangs within the United States. It has also been commonplace in the initial writings about Central American gangs (Sullivan and Bunker 2002; Rogers 2003; Johnson and Muhlhausen 2005). In the importation model debate, it is possible to identify two types of interpretations related to the gangs' motivations to migrate. In the first interpretation, the authors view a deliberate attempt by gangs to use migration flows to evade law enforcement, expand the gang, or increase the range of their illicit activities and markets (Sullivan 2008; Manwaring 2006). These views are more frequently found in journalistic and law enforcement reports than in academic research (Federal Bureau of Investigation 2008). Gang members decide to migrate, or leaders encourage their gang subordinates to do so as part of their organizational strategies. In the second interpretation, gang members first find themselves subjected to the forces of migration and deportation. Youth migrate as part of family relocation or are deported back to their countries, but then they take advantage of their status by integrating and strengthening the existing criminal networks (Mateo 2011; Cruz 2010; USAID 2006; Kalsi 2018).

The experience of relocating to other countries is usually upsetting, especially among impoverished immigrants, refugees, and asylum seekers (Vigil 1988; Feixa et al. 2012; Klein 1995). In the strain model, some studies highlight how experiences of segregation and marginalization, as well as social and political barriers, push some immigrants to gang membership, facilitating the emergence of gangs that reclaim identities typically associated with their immigrant condition (Van Gemert et al. 2008; Rodgers and Baird 2015). According to this view, transnational gangs arise not so much from the migration experience itself but from the social circumstances in the destination communities that push immigrants to adopt transnational identities. Such experiences have been documented in different places, whether in Spain, Guatemala, Israel, or Belize (Feixa 2021; Fontes 2019; Sela-Shayovitz 2012; Baird 2021a). Identities are thus used for their own survival as a group. These analyses are usually found in research explaining why migrants returning to their home countries, whether as voluntary returnees or deportees, end up swelling the ranks of local gangs with transnational identities. Conditions of economic inequality, social marginalization, and political exclusion are not exclusive to immigrants arriving in new lands. As several studies on the Central American cases show, they are also present to migrants who forcibly return to their home countries (O'Neill 2015; Gutiérrez Rivera 2018; Levenson 2013, Jütersonke et al. 2009).

Like the strain model, the cultural-conflict perspective emphasizes the conflicts deriving from the cultural shock that migrants experience when they arrive in a country with a different culture. However, this view focuses on the cultural tensions that develop when immigrant groups settle in new communities (Feixa and Sánchez-García 2019; Decker et al. 2009). Particular cultural practices put immigrant groups in conflict with the prevailing social norms and laws (Feixa and Romaní 2014). In the case of transnational gangs, those conflicts drive immigrant youths to band together, using their cultural assets to navigate and make sense of the confusing societal norms of the receiving communities. Studies of the original emergence of Central American gangs in southern California discuss this notion (Ward 2013; Vigil 2002) to explain the rise of gangs in the American metropolis. However, research on Central American transnational gangs has highlighted how returned immigrants, who grew up in the United States and were raised as Americans, also had cultural conflicts with the norms prevailing in their home countries (Santamaría Balmaceda 2007; Dudley 2020; Cruz 2014). For instance, a study conducted by Dingeman-Cerda (2017) found that Salvadoran deportees who grew up in the United States before being forcibly returned to El Salvador were more stigmatized and faced more social difficulties than other deportees who had been raised in their home country. As a result, returned immigrants and deportees end up making use of the norms, practices, and identities acquired in other countries. With them, they form groups that would help them navigate and face a culture they no longer recognize as their own.

Finally, in studying transnational gangs, the biased perspective can be better understood as a policy transfer model. This view underscores the role of policies and policy dissemination in the emergence of transnational gangs. According to this view, it is crucial to consider the immigration policies that led to the forced repatriation of thousands of immigrants living in the United States. However, in contrast to the importation perspectives, which focus on the actual movement of people to explain gang proliferation, this model emphasizes the role policies have on the spread of transnational gangs. Accordingly, it is possible to identify at least two approaches in considering how policies impact the dissemination of gangs and gang cultures. First, policies that essentially criminalize immigration have the unintended consequence of increasing the displacement and deportation of immigrants, contributing to the international spread of gangs (Barak et al. 2020; Temple 2011). The surveillance and overpolicing of immigrant youth in the penal system mean that gang-related youth are not only deported to their countries of origin, they are also processed and detained in a penal system that facilitates contact with more seasoned gang members, reinforcing gang identities and criminal practices (Müller 2015; Zilberg 2011; Sánchez-Jankowski 2003; Ambrosius 2021). When immigrants are finally deported or forced to return to their countries, they have all but consolidated their commitment to gang life.

A second view that highlights the role of policies contends that gangs become transnational while interacting with the dissemination of certain models of crime deterrence. These policies and criminal justice approaches contribute to the criminalization of immigrants. More importantly, they propagate law enforcement practices that deal with gangs in the same way across different countries. Furthermore, the growth of the American law enforcement apparatus to tackle international organized crime and terrorism has meant the global expansion of bureaucracies dedicated to policing, persecuting, and capturing suspects and criminals abroad (McGuire and Coutin 2013). In other words, transnational gangs develop in parallel with transnational law enforcement apparatuses that foster the same problems that contributed to the emergence of gangs in the American metropolis. This approach refers to the globalization of law enforcement practices through "zero-tolerance policing strategies . . . [which] reproduce transnational flows and formations" (Zilberg 2004, 777). According to this interpretation, the transnationalization of gangs comes not only as a result of the transference of identities and gang practices across different cultures—sometimes facilitated by deportation and immigration policies—but also as a result of the diffusion of the moral panic and its operationalization through traveling crime deterrence approaches (Osuna 2020; Brotherton and Gude 2021). Gangs become transnational largely because they are conceived as such, viewed as global threats that need to be confronted by an equally global agenda of crime control and punishment apparatus (Gutiérrez Rivera 2018; Müller 2015; Zilberg 2011). This agenda has contributed to building an internationally coherent suppression ideology under the war on drugs and national security banners. As a result, the law enforcement apparatus ends up providing legitimacy to gangs' claims of marginalization and social segregation, whether in an American city or a Latin American community, reinforcing the usefulness of adopting gang-imported identities and symbols.

Migration, Globalization, and Territoriality

The rise of transnational gangs has underlined the centrality of globalization in the study of gangs (Fraser and Van Hellemont 2020; Hagedorn 2001). At the same time, it has questioned the importance of territoriality that the classic studies have placed on the phenomenon (Decker et al. 2013; Klein et al. 2006; Thrasher 1927; Moore, Vigil, and Garcia 1983). Since several contemporary gangs exist and operate on multiple sites as well as in online networks (Pyrooz and Moule 2019; Feixa and Sánchez-García 2019), the subject of territory does not seem to be as crucial for the study of transnational groups as it is for neighborhood groups. For example, Lopez-Aguado and Walker (2021) have argued that as a social geographic area increases, identities become more diffuse and less territorial, yielding more flexibility to what it means to be a member of a particular gang. Similarly, observing the Central American gangs, Winton (2012) and Cruz (2014) found that the defense of the physical neighborhood is more symbolic than real as the vindication of group identities has become more important in the dynamics of gang violence and their activities.

However, an examination of the different transnational phenomena shows that territoriality is still essential to understanding the impact of migration on creating transnational identities. Indeed, the technological advancements in communications, particularly around the internet and social media, have facilitated the diffusion of gang practices and identities. Yet transnational gang cultures flourish in those places where migrants have given communities symbols and meanings that can be understood and repackaged by local peers, even if the latter have never traveled outside their country. This has been the case with the archetypal transnational gangs that originated in the Americas (i.e., MS-13, the 18th Street Gang, the Crips, and the Latin Kings). Even the groups that have appeared in European cities (e.g., Amsterdam, Barcelona, and Milan), and who have brandished transnational identities and connections, were enabled by a sense of community provided by immigrants (Feixa and Sánchez-García 2019; Roks and Densley 2020).

The latter is at the heart of the definitional discussion of transnational gangs. What makes a transnational street gang *transnational* is the sense of being part of a larger community, bound by global identities but reinterpreted locally by some members' experiences of migration and translocation (Baird 2021a; O'Neill 2015; Cruz 2013). The mere use of a gang's name in different localities does not make it transnational. Press reports show several cases of transitory copycat groups that never managed to consolidate and persist as a gang. Hence, what makes MS-13 a transnational gang is not the fact that some youth groups have attempted to use the name to generate respect among their peers and instill fear among their rivals (Dudley 2020; Arana 2005). Instead, it is the sense of being part of the same community anchored by the movement of individuals. Identity plays a key role in this process, but as Lopez-Aguado and Walker (2021) contend, identities become more fluid as the social geographic area occupied by the gang increases. Fluidity allows those identities to respond to the local demands and preserve the sense of extended community. That migrant-built awareness of being part of a larger community enables a gang originally formed in Los Angeles to develop in Central American countries and spread back to the US east coast (Covey 2010; Howell 2015; Dudley 2020). Yet the way MS-13 gang members behave in Los Angeles and how they apply their norms is somewhat different from how gang members operate in San Salvador or Fairfax County, Virginia. The shared identity allows recognition amid high mobility and relocation. In some rare cases, it also allows some attempts of group coordination across borders, like the MS-13, which has struggled to coordinate activities between their groups in El Salvador and the US east coast (Dudley 2020; Farah 2012).

Yet the sense of community through migration is what assists gangs in expanding transnationally. This is what enabled the Almighty Latin King and Queen Nation to spread from Chicago to Spain. In the process, this gang, which was formed by Puerto Rican immigrants, bounced back to Puerto Rico and then to New York, where Ecuadorians picked it up and transmitted it to their home country when deported (Brotherton and Gude 2021; Cerbino

Arturi 2009). Finally, Ecuadorian migrants repackaged it and took it to Barcelona, where its manifestation resembled a typical street youth group more than an American gang (Feixa et al. 2012).

Conclusion

This chapter has shown the importance of migration in the emergence and development of transnational gangs. It underscores how immigration has played a critical role in the emergence and development of youth street gangs across time and space. The recent rise of transnational gangs—youth groups that share a set of identities, norms, and practice frameworks across borders—has prompted us to explore the complex circular role of migration. In doing so, the chapter has examined the different theoretical perspectives that attempt to explain the transnational phenomenon, with a particular focus on the Central American groups considered transnational.

Most traditional literature on immigration and gangs has focused on the one-way perspective of immigrants joining gangs. Globalization, social media, and the circular flows of migration changed the dynamics and have forced us to consider the rebound effects of human mobility. This chapter has pointed out how migration has also played a role in the sending communities where transnational gangs have settled. Gangs also proliferate in emigrant communities by the circular effects of mobility and communications. It reveals how the forces of globalization have facilitated those effects by universalizing identities and practices that, nevertheless, need to be reinterpreted and adapted based on local conditions. These dynamics explain why some gangs became transnational while others did not. They also elucidate the varied nature of such transnationalism. While the gangs operating in El Salvador and Honduras evolved to become organized crime enterprises, the Latin Kings in Ecuador and Barcelona resemble youth clubs and associations. Migration alone sets the initial conditions for transnationalism, but it does not fully anticipate its scope. In studying transnational gangs, we must go back to the local group and the barrio to understand how local forces—social structures, opportunities, and policies—provide meaning to migration and globalization.

Note

1. For instance, most of the articles contained in the global comparative volume about gangs by Hazen and Rodgers (2014) do not address issues of migration as crucial variables in understanding local gangs.

References

Adamson, Christopher. 1998. "Tribute, Turf, Honor and the American Street Gang: Patterns of Continuity and Change Since 1820." *Theoretical Criminology* 2 (1): 57–84. DOI: 10.1177/1362480698002001003.

Ambrosius, Christian. 2021. "Deportations and the Transnational Roots of Gang Violence in Central America." *World Development* 140: 105373. https://doi.org/10.1016/j.worlddev.2020.105373.

Arana, Ana. 2005. "How the Street Gangs Took Central America." *Foreign Affairs* 84: 98–110.

Arias, Enrique D. 2014. "Gang Politics in Rio de Janeiro, Brazil." In *Global Gangs: Street Violence across the World*, edited by Jennifer Hazen and Dennis Rodgers, 237–254. Minneapolis: University of Minnesota Press.

Asbury, Herbert. 1928. *The Gangs of New York: An Informal History of the Underworld*. New York: Knopf.

Baird, Adam. 2021a. "The Fourth Corner of the Triangle. Gang Transnationalism, Fragmentation and Evolution in Belize City." In *Routledge International Handbook of Critical Gang Studies*, edited by David C. Brotherton and Rafael Jose Gude, 386–398. Oxford, UK: Routledge.

Baird, Adam. 2021b. "'Man a Kill a Man for Nutin': Gang Transnationalism, Masculinities, and Violence in Belize City." *Men and Masculinities* 24 (3): 411–431. DOI: 10.1177/1097184x19872787.

Bankston, Carl L. 1998. "Youth Gangs and the New Second Generation: A Review Essay." *Aggression and Violent Behavior* 3 (1): 35–45. https://doi.org/10.1016/S1359-1789(97)00010-4.

Barak, Maya P., Kenneth Sebastian León, and Edward R. Maguire. 2020. "Conceptual and Empirical Obstacles in Defining MS-13." *Criminology & Public Policy* 19 (2): 563–589. https://doi.org/10.1111/1745-9133.12493.

Brotherton, David C. 2008. "Beyond Social Reproduction: Bringing Resistance Back in Gang Theory." *Theoretical Criminology* 12 (1): 55–77. DOI: 10.1177/1362480607085794.

Brotherton, David C., and Rafael Gude. 2021. "Social Control and the Gang: Lessons from the Legalization of Street Gangs in Ecuador." *Critical Criminology* 29 (December): 931–955. https://doi.org/10.1007/s10612-020-09505-5.

Bruneau, Thomas, Lucía Dammert, and Elizabeth Skinner. 2011. *Maras. Gang Violence and Security in Central America*. Austin: University of Texas Press.

Cerbino Arturi, Mauro. 2009. "La Nación Imaginada de los Latin Kings, Mimetismo, Colonialidad y Transnacionalismo." PhD Dissertation, Universitat Rovira i Virgili.

Covey, Herbert C. 2010. *Street Gangs Throughout the World*. 2nd ed. Springfield, IL: Charles C. Thomas Publisher.

Cruz, José Miguel. 2010. "Central American Maras: From Youth Gangs to Transnational Protection Rackets." *Global Crime* 11 (4): 379–398.

Cruz, José Miguel. 2013. "Beyond Social Remittances. Migration and Transnational Gangs in Central America." In *How Migrants Impact Their Homelands*, edited by Susan Eckstein and Adil Najam, 213–233. Durham, NC: Duke University Press.

Cruz, José Miguel. 2014. "Maras and the Politics of Violence in El Salvador." In *Global Gangs Street Violence across the World*, edited by Jennifer Hazen and Dennis Rodgers, 123–143. Minneapolis: University of Minnesota Press.

Curry, G. David, Scott H. Decker, and David C. Pyrooz. 2003. *Confronting Gangs: Crime and Community*. Los Angeles, CA: Roxbury Publishing Company.

Decker, Scott H., and G. David Curry. 2000. "Addressing Key Features of Gang Membership." *Journal of Criminal Justice* 28 (6): 473–482. http://dx.doi.org/10.1016/S0047-2352(00)00063-5.

Decker, Scott H., Chris Melde, and David C. Pyrooz. 2013. "What Do We Know about Gangs and Gang Members and Where Do We Go from Here?" *Justice Quarterly* 30 (3): 369–402. DOI: 10.1080/07418825.2012.732101.

Decker, Scott H., Frank van Gemert, and David C. Pyrooz. 2009. "Gangs, Migration, and Crime: The Changing Landscape in Europe and the USA." *Journal of International Migration and Integration / Revue de l'integration et de la Migration Internationale* 10 (4): 393–1408. DOI: 10.1007/s12134-009-0109-9.

Dingeman-Cerda, Katie. 2017. "Segmented Re/Integration: Divergent Post-Deportation Trajectories in El Salvador." *Social Problems* 65 (1): 116–134.

Dowdney, Luke. 2005. *Neither War nor Peace. International Comparisons of Children and Youth in Organised Armed Violence*. Rio de Janeiro, Brazil: Viveiros de Castro Editora.

Dudley, Steven. 2020. *MS-13: The Making of America's Most Notorious Gang*. New York: Harlequin.

Farah, Douglas. 2012. "Central American Gangs: Changing Nature and New Partners." *Journal of International Affairs* 66 (1): 53–67.

Federal Bureau of Investigation. 2008. "The MS-13 Threat." In *A National Assessment*, edited by Department of Justice. Washington, DC: FBI.

Feixa, Carles. 2021. "Transnationalism and Postnational Identities: The Three Lives of a Latin King." In *Routledge International Handbook of Critical Gang Studies*, edited by David Brotherton and Rafael Gude, 298–315. Oxford, UK: Routledge.

Feixa, Carles, Noemí Canelles, Laura Porzio, and Carolina Recio. 2012. "Latin Kings in Barcelona." In *Street Gangs, Migration and Ethnicity*, edited by Frank Van Gemert, Dana Peterson and Inger-Lise Lien, 63–78. Oxford, UK: Routledge.

Feixa, Carles, Carmen Leccardi, and Pam Nilan. 2016. "Introduction: Chronotopes of Youth." In *Youth, Space and Time: Agoras and Chronotopes in the Global City*, edited by Carles Feixa, Carmen Leccardi and Pam Nilan, 1–16. Leiden: Brill.

Feixa, Carles, and Oriol Romaní. 2014. "From Local Gangs to Global Tribes: The Latin Kings and Queens Nation in Catalonia." In *Youth Cultures in the Age of Global Media*, edited by David Buckingham, Sara Bragg and Mary Jane Kehily, 88–103. London: Palgrave Macmillan.

Feixa, Carles, and José Sánchez-García. 2019. *The (Trans) Gang: Notes and Queries on Youth Street Group Research*. Barcelona: Universitat Pompeu Fabra & European Research Council.

Fernández-Planells, Ariadna, José Sánchez-García, María Oliver, and Carles Feixa. 2020. "Researching Transnational Gangs as Agents of Mediation in the Digital Era." In *Gangs in the Era of Internet and Social Media*, edited by Chris Melde and Frank Weerman, 43–59. Cham, Switzerland: Springer International Publishing.

Fontes, Anthony W. 2018. *Mortal Doubt: Transnational Gangs and Social Order in Guatemala City*. Berkeley: University of California Press.

Fontes, Anthony Wayne. 2019. "Portrait of a 'Real' Marero: Fantasy and falsehood in Stories of Gang Violence." *Ethnography* 20 (3): 320–341. DOI: 10.1177/1466138118805123.

Franco, Celinda. 2008. "The MS-13 and 18th Street Gangs: Emerging Transnational Gang Threats?" In *CRS Report for Congress*. Washington, DC: Congressional Research Service.

Fraser, Alistair, and Elke Van Hellemont. 2020. "Gangs and Globalization." In *Oxford Research Encyclopedia of Criminology and Criminal Justice*, edited by Henry N. Pontell. Oxford, UK: Oxford University Press.

Glebbeek, Marie-Louise, and Kees Koonings. 2016. "Between Morro and Asfalto: Violence, Insecurity and Socio-Spatial Segregation in Latin American Cities." *Habitat International* 54 (1): 3–9. http://dx.doi.org/10.1016/j.habitatint.2015.08.012.

Gutiérrez Rivera, Lirio. 2018. "Transnational and Local Entanglements in the 'Cycle of Violence' of Central American Migration." *Global Crime* 19 (3-4): 192–210. DOI: 10.1080/17440572.2018.1477600.

Hagedorn, John M. 2001. "Globalization, Gangs, and Collaborative Research." In *The Eurogang Paradox*, edited by Malcolm Klein, Hans-Jürgen Kerner, Cheryl Maxson and Elmar Weitekamp, 41–58. Dordrecht: Springer.
Hagedorn, John M. 2005. "The Global Impact of Gangs." *Journal of Contemporary Criminal Justice* 21 (2): 153–169. DOI: 10.1177/1043986204273390.
Hagedorn, John M. 2006. "Race Not Space: A Revisionist History of Gangs in Chicago." *Journal of African American History* 91 (2): 194–208.
Hagedorn, John. 2008. *A World of Gangs: Armed Young Men and Gangsta Culture*. Minneapolis: University of Minnesota.
Haymoz, Sandrine, Cheryl Maxson, and Martin Killias. 2013. "Street Gang Participation in Europe: A Comparison of Correlates." *European Journal of Criminology* 11 (6): 659–681. DOI: 10.1177/1477370813511385.
Hazen, Jennifer M., and Dennis Rodgers. 2014. *Global Gangs. Street Violence across the World*. Minneapolis: University of Minnesota Press.
Higginson, Angela, and Kathryn Benier. 2015. "Gangs in African, Asian, and Australian Settings." In *The Handbook of Gangs*, edited by Scott H. Decker and David C. Pyrooz, 538–557. New York: Wiley-Blackwell.
Howell, James C. 2015. *The History of Street Gangs in the United States: Their Origins and Transformations*. Lanham, MD: Lexington Books.
Howell, James C., and Elizabeth Griffiths. 2015. *Gangs in America's Communities*. Thousand Oaks, CA: Sage Publications.
Imbusch, Peter, Michel Misse, and Fernando Carrion. 2011. "Violence Research in Latin America. A Literature Review." *International Journal of Conflict and Violence* 5 (1): 87–154.
Johnson, Stephen, and David B. Muhlhausen. 2005. "North American Transnational Youth Gangs: Breaking the Chain of Violence." *Trends in Organized Crime* 9 (1): 38–54. DOI: 10.1007/s12117-005-1003-2.
Jones, Gareth, and Dennis Rodgers, eds. 2009. *Youth Violence in Latin America. Gangs and Juvenile Justice in Perspective, Studies of the Americas*. New York: Palgrave Macmillan.
Jütersonke, Oliver, Robert Muggah, and Dennis Rodgers. 2009. "Gangs, Urban Violence, and Security Interventions in Central America." *Security Dialogue* 40 (4–5): 373–397.
Kalsi, Priti. 2018. "The Impact of U.S. Deportation of Criminals on Gang Development and Education in El Salvador." *Journal of Development Economics* 135: 433–448. https://doi.org/10.1016/j.jdeveco.2018.08.010.
Klein, Malcolm W. 1995. *The American Gang*. New York: Oxford University Press.
Klein, Malcolm, Hans-Jürgen Kerner, Cheryl Maxson, and Elmar Weitekamp. 2000. *The Eurogang Paradox: Street Gangs and Youth Groups in the US and Europe*: Cham, Switzerland: Springer Science & Business Media.
Klein, Malcolm W., Frank M. Weerman, and Terence P. Thornberry. 2006. "Street Gang Violence in Europe." *European Journal of Criminology* 3 (4): 413–437.
Krohn, Marvin D., Nicole M. Schmidt, Alan J. Lizotte, and Julie M. Baldwin. 2011. "The Impact of Multiple Marginality on Gang Membership and Delinquent Behavior for Hispanic, African American, and White Male Adolescents." *Journal of Contemporary Criminal Justice* 27 (1): 18–42. DOI: 10.1177/1043986211402183.
Levenson, Deborah T. 2013. *Adiós Niño: The Gangs of Guatemala City and the Politics of Death*. Durham, NC: Duke University Press.

Lopez-Aguado, Patrick, and Michael Lawrence Walker. 2021. "'I Don't Bang: I'm Just a Blood': Situating Gang Identities in Their Proper Place." *Theoretical Criminology* 25 (1): 107–126. DOI: 10.1177/1362480619854152.

Manwaring, Max G. 2006. "Gangs and Coups D'Streets in the New World Disorder: Protean Insurgents in Post-Modern War." *Global Crime* 7: 505–543.

Mateo, Joanna. 2011. "Street Gangs of Honduras." In *Maras: Gang Violence and Security in Central America*, edited by Thomas Bruneau, Lucía Dammert and Elizabeth Skinner, 87–103. Austin: University of Texas Press.

Matusitz, J., and M. Repass. 2009. "Gangs in Nigeria: An Updated Examination." *Crime Law and Social Change* 52 (5): 495–511. DOI: 10.1007/s10611-009-9208-y.

Maxson, Cheryl L. 1998. "Gang Members on the Move." *Juvenile Justice Bulletin*. Washington, DC: U.S. Department of Justice.

McGuire, Connie, and Susan Bibler Coutin. 2013. "Transnational Alienage and Foreignness: Deportees and Foreign Service Officers in Central America." *Identities* 20 (6): 689–704. DOI: 10.1080/1070289X.2013.829773.

Méndez, María José. 2019. "The Violence Work of Transnational Gangs in Central America." *Third World Quarterly* 40 (2): 373–388. DOI: 10.1080/01436597.2018.1533786.

Moore, Caylin Louis, and Forrest Stuart. 2022. "Gang Research in the Twenty-First Century." *Annual Review of Criminology* 5 (1): 299–320. DOI: 10.1146/annurev-criminol-030920-094656.

Moore, Joan W. 2007. "Female Gangs: Gender and Globalization." In *Gangs in the Global City. Alternatives to Traditional Criminology*, edited by John M. Hagedorn, 187–203. Chicago, IL: University of Illinois Press.

Moore, Joan, Diego Vigil, and Robert Garcia. 1983. "Residence and Territoriality in Chicano Gangs." *Social Problems* 31 (2): 182–194.

Müller, Markus-Michael. 2015. "Punitive Entanglements: The 'War on Gangs' and the Making of a Transnational Penal Apparatus in the Americas." *Geopolitics* 20 (3): 696–727. DOI: 10.1080/14650045.2015.1036416.

O'Neill, Kevin Lewis. 2015. *Secure the Soul: Christian Piety and Gang Prevention in Guatemala*. Oakland: University of California Press.

Osuna, Steven. 2020. "Transnational Moral Panic: Neoliberalism and the Spectre of MS-13." *Race & Class* 61 (4): 3–28.

Palasinski, Marek, Lening Zhang, Sukdeo Ingale, and Claire Hanlon. 2016. "Gangs in Asia: China and India." *Asian Social Science* 12 (8): 141–145.

Papachristos, Andrew V. 2005. "Gang World." *Foreign Policy* 147: 48–55.

Peterson, Dana, Inger-Lise Lien, and Frank van Gemert. 2008. "Concluding Remarks: The Roles of Migration and Ethnicity in Street Gang Formation, Involvement and Response." In *Street Gangs, Migration and Ethnicity*, edited by Frank van Gemert, Dana Peterson and Inger-Lise Lien, 255–272. Portland, OR: Willan Publishing.

Pyrooz, David C., and Richard K. Moule Jr. 2019. "Gangs and Social Media." In *Oxford Research Encyclopedia of Criminology*. Oxford, UK: Oxford University Press.

Reisman, Lainie. 2006. "Breaking the Vicious Cycle: Responding to Central American Youth Gang Violence." *SAIS Review of International Affairs* 26 (2): 147.

Rodgers, Dennis, and Adam Baird. 2015. "Understanding Gangs in Contemporary Latin America." In *Handbook of Gangs and Gang Responses*, edited by Scott H. Decker and David C. Pyrooz, 479–502. New York: Wiley.

Rodgers, Dennis, and Jennifer Hazen. 2014. "Introduction: Gangs in Global Perspective." In *Global Gangs. Street Violence across the World*, edited by Jennifer Hazen and Dennis Rodgers, 1–25. Minneapolis: University of Minnesota Press.

Rodríguez, Juan Antonio, Neelie Pérez Santiago, Christopher H. Birkbeck, Freddy Crespo, and Solbey Morillo. 2017. "Internationalizing the Study of Gang Membership: Validation Issues from Latin America." *British Journal of Criminology* 57 (5): 1165–1184.

Rogers, Joseph. 2003. "Confronting Transnational Gangs in the Americas." *Journal of Gang Research* 10 (2): 33–44.

Rogers, Joseph. 2007. "Gangs and Terrorists in the Americas: An Unlikely Nexus." *Journal of Gang Research* 14 (2): 19.

Roks, Robert A., and James A. Densley. 2020. "From Breakers to Bikers: The Evolution of the Dutch Crips 'Gang.'" *Deviant Behavior* 41 (4): 525–542.

Salagaev, Alexander L., and Rustem R. Safin. 2014. "Capitalizing on Change: Gangs, Ideology, and the Transition to a Liberal Economy in the Russian Federation." In *Global Gangs: Street Violence across the World*, edited by Jennifer Hazen and Dennis Rodgers, 65–84. Minneapolis: University of Minnesota Press.

Sánchez-Jankowski, Martín. 2003. "Gangs and Social Change." *Theoretical Criminology* 7 (2): 191–216.

Santamaría Balmaceda, Gema. 2007. "Maras y Pandillas: Límites de su Trasnacionalidad." *Revista Mexicana de Política Exterior* 81 (October): 101–123.

Sante, Luc. 2016. *Low Life: Lures and Snares of Old New York*. New York: Farrar, Straus and Giroux.

Sela-Shayovitz, Revital. 2012. "The Impact of Globalization, Migration, and Social Group Processes on Neo-Nazi Youth Gangs." In *Youth Gangs in International Perspective*, edited by Finn-Aage Esbensen and Cheryl Maxson, 211–223. New York: Springer.

Spergel, Irving A. 1995. *The Youth Gang Problem. A Community Approach*. New York: Oxford University Press.

Sullivan, John P. 2006. "Maras Morphing: Revisiting Third Generation Gangs." *Global Crime* 7 (3–4): 487–504.

Sullivan, John P. 2008. "Transnational Gangs: The Impact of Third Generation Gangs in Central America." *Air & Space Power Journal* 2: 2–10.

Sullivan, John P., and Robert J. Bunker. 2002. "Drug Cartels, Street Gangs, and Warlords." *Small Wars & Insurgencies* 13 (2): 40–53.

Temple, Jonah M. 2011. "The Merry-Go-Round of Youth Gangs: The Failure of the US Immigration Removal Policy and the False Outsourcing of Crime." *Boston College Third World Law Journal* 31: 193.

Thrasher, Frederick. 1927. *The Gang: A Study of 1,313 Gangs in Chicago*. Chicago, IL: University of Chicago Press.

USAID. 2006. *Central America and Mexico Gang Assessment*. Washington, DC: USAID Bureau for Latin American and Caribbean Affairs.

Van Gemert, Frank. 2012. "Five Decades of Defining Gangs in The Netherlands: The Eurogang Paradox in Practice." In *Youth Gangs in International Perspective*, edited by Finn-Aage Esbensen and Cheryl Maxson, 69–83. New York: Springer.

Van Gemert, Frank, Dana Peterson, and Inger-Lise Lien. 2008. *Street Gangs, Migration and Ethnicity*. Portland, OR: Willan Publishing.

Van Hellemont, Elke, and James A. Densley. 2019. "Gang Glocalization: How the Global Mediascape Creates and Shapes Local Gang Realities." *Crime, Media, Culture* 15 (1): 169–189. DOI: 10.1177/1741659018760107.

Vigil, James Diego. 1988. *Barrio Gangs: Street Life and Identity in Southern California*. Austin: University of Texas Press.

Vigil, James Diego. 2002. *A Rainbow of Gangs. Street Culture in the Mega-City*. Austin: University of Texas Press.

Ward, Thomas W. 2013. *Gangsters without Borders: An Ethnography of a Salvadoran Street Gang*. Oxford, UK: Oxford University Press.

Weerman, Frank M., and Scott H. Decker. 2005. "European Street Gangs and Troublesome Youth Groups: Findings from the Eurogang Research Program." In *European Street Gangs and Troublesome Youth Groups*, edited by Scott H. Decker and Frank M. Weerman, 287–309. Oxford, UK: Altamira Press.

Weerman, Frank M., and Finn-Aage Esbensen. 2005. "A Cross-National Comparison of Youth Gangs: The United States and the Netherlands." In *European Street Gangs and Troublesome Youth Groups*, edited by Scott H. Decker and Frank M. Weerman, 219–255. Oxford, UK: Altamira Press.

Winton, Ailsa. 2012. "Analysing the Geographies of the 'Transnational' Gangs of Central America: the Changing Spaces of Violence." *Investigaciones Geográficas* 79: 136–149.

Winton, Ailsa. 2014. "Gangs in Global Perspective." *Environment and Urbanization* 26 (2): 401–416.

Wolf, Sonja. 2012. "Mara Salvatrucha: The Most Dangerous Street Gang in the Americas?" *Latin American Politics and Society* 54 (1): 65–99.

Wortley, Scot. 2009. "Introduction. The Immigration-Crime Connection: Competing Theoretical Perspectives." *Journal of International Migration and Integration / Revue de l'integration et de la Migration Internationale* 10 (4): 349. DOI: 10.1007/s12134-009-0117-9.

Zaluar, Alba. 2000. "Perverse Integration: Drug Trafficking and Youth in the 'Favelas' of Rio de Janeiro." *Journal of International Affairs* 53 (2): 653–671.

Zhang, L. 2014. "Of Marginality and 'Little Emperors': The Changing Reality of Chinese Youth Gangs." In *Global Gangs: Street Violence across the World*, edited by Jennifer Hazen and Dennis Rodgers, 85–103. Minneapolis: University of Minnesota Press.

Zilberg, Elana. 2004. "Fools Banished from the Kingdom: Remapping Geographies of Violence between the Americas (Los Angeles and San Salvador)." *American Quarterly* 56: 759–779.

Zilberg, Elana. 2011. *Space of Detention: The Making of a Transnational Gang Crisis between Los Angeles and San Salvador*. Durham, NC: Duke University Press.

SECTION 5

LEGACIES OF SECOND-GENERATION RESEARCHERS

CHAPTER 32

THE LEGACY OF SCOTT H. DECKER

DAVID C. PYROOZ AND RICHARD K. MOULE JR.

GROWING concerns about juvenile delinquency in the 1950s and the rising crime rates of the 1960s served as strong catalysts for the study of American street gangs (Short and Hughes 2006). Indeed, during this time the study of gangs in cities like Chicago *was* the study of crime and delinquency (Laub 2004; Pyrooz and Mitchell 2015). Gangs would largely recede from the eyes and imperatives of policymakers and the public (and researchers) in the 1970s, only to re-emerge in the 1980s. By this time, gangs appeared not only in the traditional cities of New York, Chicago, and Boston, but also in new cities, like Columbus, Denver, Milwaukee, and, most importantly, St. Louis (see Spergel and Curry 1993). These "emerging gang" cities would serve as the research sites for many "second generation" gang researchers, such as Finn Esbensen, Ron Huff, Jody Miller, John Hagedorn, and, the subject of the current chapter, Scott H. Decker.

Born in 1950 and raised in the suburbs of Chicago, a city well-known for its rich history of gangs, organized crime, and political intrigue (e.g., Thrasher 1927), as well as the race riots of 1967 and the 1968 Democratic National Convention riot (Kerner Commission 1968), Scott would dive deeper into the study of crime as an undergraduate student at DePauw University. Located roughly 200 miles south of Chicago, and a short drive west of Indianapolis, it was here where he was first exposed to several criminological, sociological, and political theories (e.g., Quinney 1970). During the winter term of the 1970–1971 school year, with the assistance of Dr. Paul Thomas, Scott was provided full access to the Indiana Boys School, living onsite and interacting with the young men incarcerated there. The lessons learned while doing research in a correctional setting, including the importance of cultivating trust and credibility with institutional stakeholders and research subjects and the importance of listening to research subjects, continued to be valuable throughout Scott's career. He would go on to attend graduate school at Florida State University, where his dissertation compared data from the Uniform Crime Report and the early National Crime Victimization Survey (Decker 1977).[1]

Graduating from Florida State in 1976, Scott would spend one year at Indiana University-Purdue University Fort Wayne before transitioning to the University of Missouri-St. Louis (UMSL), which is where he would spend the bulk of his career. At UMSL, Scott served as chair of the Department of Criminology and Criminal Justice for 15 years and oversaw the development of the PhD program, one of the very best in the United States. His early work at UMSL was focused primarily on deterrence, but in the mid-1980s he would begin his research on gangs and other active offender populations. After 29 years at UMSL, he left to serve as the director of the School of Criminology and Criminal Justice at Arizona State University (ASU). He would continue his research on gangs during this time, before retiring from ASU as an emeritus foundation professor in 2018.[2] Over the course of four decades, St. Louis and Phoenix would serve as the "home fields" for much of Scott's research, including his research on gangs.

The current chapter situates Scott's "gang career" within the context of the life course, weaving together both the micro- and macro-level factors shaping his research agenda. The life-course perspective is fitting, because while we can make sense of his career, neatly packaging together ideas and projects, it certainly did not unfold in a tightly coordinated and rationally sequenced manner. There may be a clear intellectual lineage connecting his earliest deterrence research to gang research, but Scott was nimble, perceptive, and (in a good way) opportunistic, allowing him to explore new frontiers that would often fail but sometimes flourish. Therefore, we organize our discussion of Scott's career around "getting in" (i.e., onset), "staying in" (i.e., continuity), and "getting out of" (i.e., desistance) gang research. We identify five core themes of his legacy: (1) generating rich, data-driven descriptions of gangs, (2) elaborationg on the group process perspective, (3) establishing gang disengagement as a field of study, (4) employing diversity in research design yielding authority in appraisal, and (5) maintaining a longstanding practice of translating research to policy and practice. The timeline of Scott's research is depicted in Figure 32.1. We supplement our discussion of Scott's research and career with quotes from an interview conducted with him in July 2022, a writeup for DePauw University's alumni association, and his career reflections interview with José Sanchez and Jennifer Tostlebe for *The Criminology Academy* podcast.[3]

Getting in: An Emerging Gang City and Gang Research Career

Why study gangs? Polsby's (1993) centennial address to the University of Chicago, titled "Where do you get your ideas?," raises a question that is as relevant to graduate students as it is to senior scholars like Scott. The oft-quoted statement from Popper (1968) is that there is no "logical method of having new ideas" (32) as scholars draw on many inspirations—from biography to skepticism to available funding to hot topics—to turn ideas into action. It is one thing to be among the educated public who reads about a topic. It is something much different to think about ideas, formulate questions, and execute a research design that contributes to the understanding of a social problem. The former merely requires taking an interest in a subject; the latter requires creativity, grit, and perseverance.

Like other emerging gang cities, St. Louis had undergone substantial demographic and economic shifts prior to the 1980s. The outmigration of middle-class families to the suburbs surrounding the city coincided with the loss of industrial manufacturing jobs. Decker and Van Winkle (1996, 32–33) noted that by the early 1990s, St. Louis had the third highest homicide and robbery rates and the second highest assault rates in the nation. Such

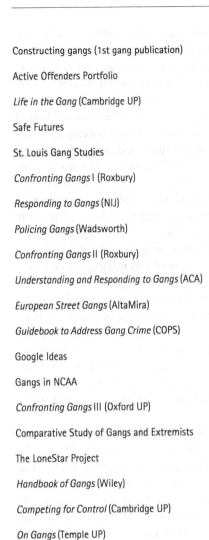
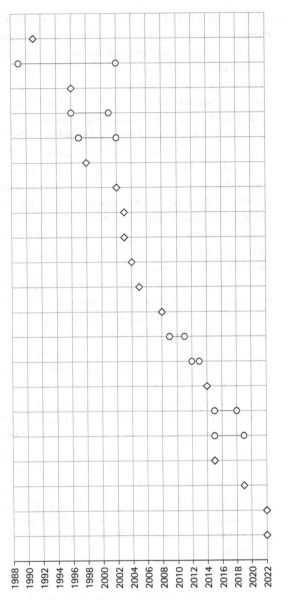

FIGURE 32.1 Timeline of Major Scholarly Works and Research Projects on Gangs

Note: Diamonds refer to the year of scholarly works and connected circles refer to the start and end years of research projects. UP refers to University Press.

circumstances lend themselves not only to the development of street gangs, but also catalyze interest in and concern about the presence of gangs among local stakeholders.

As Scott explained to us, a confluence of circumstances would spur his interest in gangs. Group behavior and group processes, topics that had long been of personal interest to Scott, were closely tied to street gangs. Personal concerns also shaped this interest. Scott noted that the presence of gangs in the city in which he lived (St. Louis), and the perceived impact of these groups on schools and neighborhoods, was troubling. No less troubling, in Scott's view, were the reactions of local stakeholders to the issue of gangs. He described how, seemingly overnight, the characterization of gangs by school officials went from "Oh no, we don't have gangs" to "everyone's a gang member," consistent with observations in other cities (Huff 1989). Law enforcement leadership, on the other hand, was deeply skeptical about the presence of gangs in the city, distinguishing the groups in St. Louis from the "real" gangs of Los Angeles. As a result, policies and responses to gangs, ranging from magnetometers at school entrances to armed guards surrounding buildings, were being called for without a clear understanding of the problem. These circumstances would all influence Scott's early involvement in gang research.

Local stakeholders would eventually come around on the issue of gangs, and the need to better understand this issue, as was the case when there was a change in police chiefs for the city. Many of these stakeholders served as gatekeepers for various institutions in the city (public education, law enforcement). Scott was working with many of them in various capacities, such as serving on the Mayor's Task Force on Gangs and Drugs and St. Louis Public Schools' Anti-Drug, Anti-Gang Task Force. These relationships would provide part of the impetus for Scott's research into gangs, but would not fully address the logistics of locating, interviewing, and surveying gang members.

The other catalyst for Scott's work on gangs, part of his portfolio of research on active offenders, was his fortuitous connection with "Street Daddy," Dietrich Lester Smith. An undergraduate student at UMSL in the mid-1980s, Dietrich was extensively involved in criminal activity until he was shot and paralyzed in a retaliatory shooting (Decker and Smith 2015). Dietrich's connections, and his credibility on the street, provided access to a sizable offending population. With buy-in from local stakeholders, access to a network of offenders through Dietrich, and collaborators such as Dave Curry and Richard Wright, Scott's research on active offenders, including gangs and gang members, would begin shortly thereafter.

STAYING IN: CORE CONTRIBUTIONS TO THE STUDY OF GANGS

Scott's research on gangs has persisted across three decades—a remarkable duration that stands apart from all but a handful of contributors to the gang literature. In his career, he has covered topics ranging from the definition and measurement of gangs and gang membership to issues of gang violence and responses to gangs. As we detail in the following section, we see five core areas where Scott has made substantial contributions to the study of gangs.

"Telling It Like It Is": Describing Gangs and Gang Life

The first of Scott's core contributions involves his in-depth description of gangs, gang members, and gang behavior. This has manifested in two ways. First, Scott has consistently sought to focus on the perspective of gang members directly (Decker and Van Winkle 1996). Of course, many classic and contemporary gang ethnographies offer rich discussions of gang life (e.g., Klein 1971; Miller 2011; Short and Strodtbeck 1965), but Scott's work has always placed the perspectives, beliefs, and actions of these individuals at the forefront. This has been a consistent theme throughout his career, beginning with *Life in the Gang* and continuing through the Google Ideas and LoneStar projects. This consistency reflects his conviction that to best understand gangs and their members, researchers must engage these individuals directly in the contexts in which they reside. As the preface to *Life in the Gang* makes clear:

> It is our belief that attempts to understand gangs and gang members are enhanced by this approach [intense fieldwork and interviews with gang members, meant to directly examine their perspectives] and that programs designed to prevent gang membership or enable gang members to remove themselves from the gang can learn from such a study. (Decker and Van Winkle 1996, ix)

This consideration encompasses a variety of contexts, including the street, correctional facilities, and schools (e.g., Curry, Decker, and Egley 2002; Decker and Van Winkle 1996; Pyrooz and Decker 2019).

The second way in which Scott's descriptive work has moved gang research forward has been his push to repeatedly establish *the denominator* when seeking to understand gang-related phenomena. How many gang members are there? What are they doing? How pervasive is a particular gang behavior? How do organizations respond to gangs? This focus on descriptive research has its roots in Scott's experiences as an undergraduate, particularly the influence of Quinney's (1970) *The Social Reality of Crime*. It was further reinforced in graduate school by his mentor, Charles Wellford. Scott's earliest gang work, with Kimberly Kempf-Leonard (1991), for example, examined whether and to what extent stakeholders (law enforcement, juvenile detainees) differentially evaluated gang-related scenarios (more on this below). With Dave Curry, Scott examined stakeholder perspectives on how to deal with gangs (Decker and Curry 2000b) and how gang and non-gang homicides differed (Decker and Curry 2002). In each of these instances (and many others), Scott's work has served as an important baseline for understanding issues of prevalence and problem identification within the context of gangs.

Related to his description of gang life is Scott's continued engagement in comparative research throughout his career. These comparisons include the experiences of individuals in and across gangs (e.g., Decker and Van Winkle 1996; Pyrooz and Decker 2019), and differences between gangs within and across cities and communities (e.g., Decker, Bynum, and Weisel 1998). Much of this research highlights the commonalities shared among gang members, regardless of location or particular gang affiliation. For example, much like Klein (1971) and Thrasher (1927), Scott consistently observed the power of external threats to unify gangs and foment violence (Decker 1996). Similarly, this research documented how most gangs were only nominally organized—the idea of the "super gang" was a myth. For example, Scott's comparative work between gangs in Chicago and San Diego challenged claims about street gangs moving into the realm of organized crime. Specifically, he showed that dimensions of gang organization were inconsistent across groups and cities and that only one gang (the Gangster Disciples, in Chicago) appeared to be moving into activities consistent with organized crime groups (e.g., owning legitimate businesses, engaging in political activities).

Scott's comparative works extend further across a variety of antisocial groups, ranging from street and prison gangs (Fleisher and Decker 2001; Pyrooz and Decker 2019) to extremist and terrorist organizations (Decker and Pyrooz 2015) and organized crime groups (Decker and Pyrooz 2013). For example, Scott's research has provided compelling evidence about the nature of gang life in total institutions, the factors shaping the growth of prison and street gangs, and the overlap between the two (Pyrooz and Decker 2019). His comparisons of gangs and extremist groups similarly demonstrate how key dimensions of group life, including identity, behavior, and group processes, transcend antisocial organizations. More generally, it highlights how the "siloing" of research on various antisocial groups hinders strong science and sound policies. Concerning the study of terror and extremist groups specifically, Decker and Pyrooz (2015, 109) noted that it was necessary to better incorporate the themes consistently highlighted by gang research, including the characteristics of individuals, groups, and their behavior into this literature. Doing so would help facilitate more effective strategies to intervene in the activities of these groups.

Jared Cohen, the head of Google Ideas, called Scott in 2009 and asked him to lead a study on gangs, internet use, and disengagement from gangs. At the time, articles on gangs and social media use either discounted the role of the internet (Papachristos 2005) or contained alarming news media and law enforcement accounts of gangs using the web. With support from Google ($25,000, which Scott matched with ASU foundation funds), he led a mixed-method, five-site study (Cleveland, Fresno, Los Angeles, Phoenix, and St. Louis) to interview the people purported to be engaging in antisocial online activities: gang members and similarly situated non-gang members (Decker and Pyrooz 2011; Moule, Pyrooz, and Decker 2013; Pyrooz, Decker, and Moule 2015). These studies addressed the descriptive questions near-and-dear to Scott: How common is internet and social media use among gang and non-gang members? In what ways does use converge or diverge for gang and non-gang members? Is the gang enhancement effect for offending reproduced online? Answers to these questions formed the basis for a literature that has expanded to now include narrative and systematic reviews (e.g., Fernandez-Planells et al. 2021; Pyrooz and Moule 2019).

Overall, these descriptive and comparative approaches to gangs have validated the generality of group phenomena, including group processes, the relevance of variability of gang organization for behavior (more on these topics next), and gang conflict. At the same time, these approaches also challenged conventional wisdom about the level of organization among gangs and the (dis)similarities across antisocial groups.

"Hangin' and Bangin'": Gangs, Group Processes, and Collective Behavior

Much of what gang members do involves simply hanging out with friends and fellow gang members. At the same time, gang members also commonly offend together. Scott has made lasting contributions to gang research in the area of group processes—one of the oldest topics in the study of gangs, and one closely associated with "hanging and banging." As Thrasher (1927) noted, external threats from rival gangs and law enforcement are the catalysts for gangs to come together. Short and Strodtbeck (1963) similarly documented the relevance of status threats and violence for (re)establishing dominance within gang hierarchies. Scott's research has elaborated on several dimensions of group processes, including the cycle of gang violence, the dynamics within the group, and the organizational structure of gangs.

Conflict is at the core of gang dynamics, whether it is occurring among members of the same gang or between members of different gangs. Based on his fieldwork (Decker 1996; Decker and Van Winkle 1996) and theories of collective and contagious behavior (Loftin 1986), Scott argued that gang norms undergird this violence and are the primary catalyst for retaliatory violence. This cycle of violence, consistent with observations by early gang researchers, has its origins in perceived threats to the group and escalates based on the occurrence of "mobilizing events." Such events precipitate intergroup conflict and possible retaliation. Subsequent work by Moule, Decker, and Pyrooz (2017) argued the cycle of violence is a consequence of the dispositional characteristics of gang members, the organizational structure of groups, and contextual characteristics. Further, Scott acknowledged that these cycles are not constant; rather, they ebb and flow depending on circumstances, including interventions by third parties, thus paving the way for social network analyses identifying how violence cascades across place and time (Brantingham, Yuan, and Herz 2021; Gravel et al. 2023). Importantly, Scott's work on the cycle of gang violence has also provided the basis for the development of intervention strategies among law enforcement and social service providers (see Decker 2008).

Just as group processes contribute to behavior between gangs, they also shape behavioral dynamics within gangs. Scott's description of group processes includes elements of shared identities and experiences, which are central to gangs. For example, Scott situated the rituals associated with joining gangs—"beat-ins" and missions, among them—within these group processes. Such rituals provide a normative foundation for the group, helping socialize individuals into the gang, enhance group solidarity, and highlight the relevance of violence to the group (Decker 1996). These rituals were also argued to serve an instrumental purpose, allowing prospective members to demonstrate they have "what it takes" to be in the gang, a foundation for theoretical advances in the application of signaling theory to gangs (Densley 2012). On the back end of the gang career, Scott has demonstrated how these same group processes can be a double-edged sword for individuals (see the next section).

Related to gang group processes is the organization of the gang. This involves not only the crystalizing of bonds between members but also the structure of the group itself. Scott's work has served to bridge gaps between the competing accounts of the features of gangs. Decker and Van Winkle (1994) addressed diverging accounts of the role of gangs in the distribution of drugs, particularly whether gangs operated as organized distributors or their members as freelance dealers. In turn, this established a foundation for the use of "ideal types" of gangs as maintaining instrumental-rational and informal-diffuse features, which Scott and others elaborated on in a series of works. With Tim Bynum and Deborah Weisel, Scott found that the "most organized" gangs identified by law enforcement in Chicago and San Diego were far less instrumental and rational than commonly believed (Decker et al. 1998).

In *Life in the Gang* (Decker and Van Winkle 1996), Scott emphasized the dimensions of gang organization, including the presence of leaders, meetings, rules and punishments, recruitment strategies, and profit reinvestment. More recently, using the Google Ideas data (Moule, Pyrooz, and Decker 2014), it was shown that these characteristics not only vary across groups but also that these measures of organization predict group-level behavior. Similarly, data from the Arizona Arrestee Drug Use Monitoring survey revealed that even smaller increases in organization were positively associated with higher levels of victimization among members (Decker, Katz, and Webb 2008).[4]

"I Ain't Killing My Mother": Disengagement from Gangs as a Field of Study

Scott's foray into disengagement from gangs was not unlike his pursuit of many other areas of study. When interviewing gang members for *Life in the Gang*, the repeated apocryphal claim of having to murder one's own mother to leave the group prompted closer scrutiny. Other researchers had offered passing commentary on life after the gang (Thrasher 1927), how and why people leave (Vigil, 1988), durability among central and peripheral members (Horowitz 1983), "defecting" from prison gangs (Fong and Vogel 1995), and changes in the volume of offending after leaving (Thornberry et al. 1993). Yet Chapter 9 with Barrik Van Winkle (Decker and Van Winkle 1996) in *Life in the Gang*, titled "There's Only Two Ways to Leave the Gang, Die or Move," and his chapter with Janet Lauritsen (Decker and Lauritsen 1996) in the second edition of Ron Huff's *Gangs in America*, "Breaking the bonds of membership: Leaving the Gang," constituted the first standalone coverage of the topic in the literature.

Scott played a lead role in establishing disengagement from gangs as a field of inquiry. His earliest work was descriptive. Can people leave gangs? If so, why and how? As he has done throughout his career, he leveraged the deeds and words of the people with lived experience to launch this field of study. His work with Van Winkle and Lauritsen was based on interviews with 99 active and 24 former gang members, revealing several critical findings. First, people leave gangs, doing so on their own accord and without killing their mother, contrary to gang mythology. Second, just like there were pushes and pulls for joining gangs, the reversal was true for leaving. Third, many of the turning points identified in the fledgling field of developmental and life-course criminology—marriage, military service, and work—were largely unavailable to the modal (teenage) gang member. Fourth, violence was a double-edged sword; it was cohesion-building, but also cohesion-breaking. Finally, leaving the gang is a process, not an event; residual emotional and social ties are impactful and must be unwound.

The next stage of Scott's contributions involved greater theoretical and empirical sophistication. After transitioning to ASU, Scott collaborated with doctoral students—including the authors of this chapter—on two lines of inquiry. First, in the Arizona Arrestee Drug Abuse Monitoring Program survey instrument (led by Chuck Katz) were questions concerning former gang membership. The juvenile detention sample included 156 current and 83 former gang members, resulting in the elaboration and extension of Scott's earlier observations: (1) the push/pull framework had applicability to disengagement, most gang members left without ritual violence or ceremony, and methods and motives interacted, such that hostile exits were more common if factors internal to the gang (pushes) motivated leaving (Pyrooz and Decker 2011); and (2) the residual ties to the gang were consequential because emotional and social connections were tied to violent victimization risk (Pyrooz, Decker, and Webb 2014). These works, both of which framed disengagement from gangs in developmental and life-course perspectives, demonstrated the merit and generality of Scott's observations in St. Louis.

The second line of extended inquiry was both theoretical and empirical, prompted by the Google Ideas study. The generality of disengagement was going to be put to the test yet again by comparing gang processes to other groups (e.g., organized crime, political extremists, religious cults). This resulted in the application of Helen Ebaugh's, a former nun and student of Robert Merton, role exit theory to disengagement from gangs (Decker, Pyrooz, and Moule 2014). The work illustrated qualitatively that gang disengagement was a process that unfolds across four stages (first doubts, anticipatory socialization, turning points, and post-exit validation) and quantitatively that gang embeddedness mattered more than years after leaving the gang for being targeted by rival gangs or acting upon disrespect or attacks on the former gang. The article also called for correcting terminology: the use of "disengagement" rather than "desistance." This distinction reflected a conceptual break from the criminal desistance literature emphasizing states rather than events, and has since been embraced by the field.

Disengagement from gangs is now an established area of inquiry in the field. The irony, of course, is that there now appears to be more interest in leaving than joining gangs, a stark contrast to the situation even a decade ago. Scott's recent book with Pyrooz and Densley, *On Gangs* (Decker, Pyrooz, and Densley 2022), includes a table with 42 scholarly works through 2020 on the subject of gang disengagement (and many more already since then). This literature continues to grow in theoretical and empirical breadth and depth, making inroads to policy and practice. Scholars have replicated the role exit model (e.g., Berger et al. 2017) and overlaid it with signaling theory (Densley and Pyrooz 2019), pushed for alternative conceptualizations of disengagement using masculinity and governance frameworks (Cruz and Rosen 2022; Leverso and Hess 2021), extended the research to leaving gangs in prison (Johnson and Densley 2018; Pyrooz and Decker 2019), and in a sign of intellectual maturity, aimed to link this research to predominant gang intervention models (Roman, Decker, and Pyrooz 2017). It should be no surprise that Scott coauthored the latter translational work, yet another of his core contributions to which we now turn.

"Turf, Ego, and Dollars": Advancing Evidence-Based Policy and Practice

Academic careers can take many scholarly forms. Criminology and criminal justice are not simply buzzwords but reflect cohesive interests in the etiology of offending and responses to offending, respectively. Even briefly reviewing the records of prominent members of leading associations—such as past presidents, fellows, and award winners of the American Society of Criminology and Academy of Criminal Justice Sciences—indicates a degree of concentration in the purposes of their scholarship. Some scholars devote their entire careers to understanding the sources of offending among people and communities, while others focus on research and evaluation of criminal justice policy and practice. Others pivot mid-career from etiology to response, oftentimes putting their ideas to the test. Scott has bucked this trend for over 35 years, as reflected in Figure 32.1. Perhaps the most telling example is the temporal overlap between the St. Louis Gang Studies and Safe Futures projects, both of which he led with his long-time collaborator, colleague, and friend Dave Curry. Scott's impact on gang policy and practice is extensive, reflected in translational criminology, collaboration with agencies and organizations, and process and impact evaluations of gang responses.[5]

Scott was practicing "translational criminology" long before John Laub (2011) coined the term. Some of these efforts reflected more traditional routes of translating scientific discovery to those who shape policy or practice, such as delivering keynote addresses to national audiences like the American Prosecutors Association, Police Executive Research Forum, Boys and Girls Club, President's Task Force on 21st Century Policing, and the White House Conference on Gangs, among dozens of local, regional, and international presentations to non-academic groups. Other examples are less common in the academy, but no less important, such as serving on commissions and panels, or providing training and technical assistance, like the St. Louis Public Schools Anti-Drugs and Gangs Task Force and the St. Louis Mayor's Task Force on Gangs and Drugs. When we asked Scott to identify what he believed was his most impactful publication on gangs, he did not list *Life in the Gang* or any other refereed article or book, but instead *Strategies to Address Gang Crime: A Guidebook for Law Enforcement* (2008), which he wrote for the Office of Community-Oriented Policing Services. While being in conversation with peers was important to Scott, the ability to influence policy and practice on gangs is found in conversation with the people for whom such books are *used*. These activities may not constitute breakthroughs in discovery, but they certainly represent important breakdowns of the walls between research, policy, and practice.

There is a branch of the academy that believes any researcher's collaboration with government institutions is inherently problematic. Scott is not among this group. Instead of sitting on the sidelines lobbing critiques, he leveraged relationships to create good policy and programmatic responses in a city that truly needed them. Perhaps most emblematic of his relationships with agency partners was the development of the St. Louis Homicide Project in collaboration with Rick Rosenfeld. This project, which emerged out of Scott's appointment to the St. Louis Mayor's Crime Commission, resulted in data, reports, policy recommendations, and refereed articles, including research on gang homicide (Decker and Curry 2002; Miller and Decker 2001); it also served as the foundation for interagency collaboration and cooperation.

In the 1990s, he brokered meetings between the mayor, police chief, state prosecutor, US attorney, and juvenile court judge, something that had never been done in St. Louis. Indeed, these agencies had not previously worked together to solve common problems. The regular meetings Scott arranged resulted in long-term collaborations, including the formation of a gun review team at the US Attorney's Office. Many criminologists could acquire agency data and use it to produce a report and publish peer-reviewed articles for years to come. Scott's method, however, was neither fleeting nor exploitative; he formed long-term relationships with agencies built on trust and, as he has documented, created a feedback loop from theory to policy and back again. He took the time to explain the research findings, working to get agencies and organizations to understand that the "offenders" they encounter and serve are victims and that victimization is consequential for subsequent involvement in crime. Anyone who has spent time in their career working with agencies understands that this is not an easy thing to do. What is so impressive about Scott is that he has done this consistently at multiple layers of government his entire career.

Scott has been involved in numerous evaluations, but few have been as revealing as Safe Futures St. Louis (Curry and Decker 2002). This was supposed to be the "intervention of all interventions." It was one of six sites with concurrent evaluations in each location. It was comprehensive, integrating social intervention, opportunity provisions, and suppression. It was collaborative, with 15 agencies in St. Louis coming together to address gang violence. It had major financial investment, with over $7 million allocated to the program. It was funded over a sustained period, five years to also include a planning year. It was scientifically grounded and federally supported, with the adoption of Irving Spergel's Comprehensive Gang Model by the Office of Juvenile Justice and Delinquency Prevention. And it did not work, as Scott and Dave painfully learned. Some aspects of the program went right, such as common definitions of gangs and the identification of gang-involved youth, but the remainder offered multiple lessons in implementation failure around turf, ego, and dollars. The disturbing conclusion Scott and Dave reached about implementation failure was that "resolving turf issues may be more difficult for rational organizations than it is for loosely structured gangs." Seeking to change the behavior of organizations was as important as seeking to change the behavior of their clientele. More narrowly focused gang interventions, with fewer service providers and service constituencies, were perhaps more likely to behave and operate rationally, and thus achieve their goals.

Much of these behind-the-scenes activities do not end up on curriculum vitae, are not recognized as traditional metrics of academic success, nor are they rewarded in annual reviews. But it is for these very efforts—partly based on gang research, but in many other areas, too— Scott received the prestigious August Vollmer Award from the American Society of Criminology in 2022, which recognized his scholarship and professional activities that "have made outstanding contributions to justice" and "treatment or prevention of criminal or delinquent behavior." Just like Scott's career has reflected a deep and varied interest in both criminology and criminal justice, so too do his commitments to allow the research questions to drive the design and method of research. The result is a career like few others in the field—of gangs specifically and criminology generally—that reflects an appreciation of data and evidence gleaned from such a wide range of sources to paint a complete picture of gangs.

"Why Not Go Both Ways?" Diversity in Design, Authority in Appraisal

There are many views of gangs. Some offer highly rationalized accounts, describing gangs as revolutionaries or conspiratorial bureaucracies. Others see gangs through a lens of reification, socially constructed by elites or loose groupings of people with individual deficits. Yet another view is of gangs as informal and diffuse social collectives. The vantage point from which people encounter gangs seems highly contoured by the methodologies used to understand and respond to them, among other things (e.g., discipline, background). Most researchers are trained in qualitative or quantitative methods. It is not uncommon for researchers who study gangs to deploy the same methodology throughout their career, using data gathered from surveys using probability sampling or in-depth interviews using snowball sampling. What is so striking about Scott's career is that his research on gangs regularly "went both ways" long before Maruna (2010) called for mixed-methods scholarship. Scott has studied many different populations, used creative ways to generate data, and assessed the reliability and validity of many types of gang data. We believe this afforded him the ability to offer a more complete assessment of gangs, one that is strongly rooted in evidence.

Scott's entry into the gang literature foreshadowed the value he placed on using diverse methodologies. He and Kimberly Kempf-Leonard's (1991) "Constructing Gangs" contained what we believe is the first use of vignettes in gang literature. Scott's observations from serving on the St. Louis Public Schools Anti-Drugs and Gangs Task Force were (1) there was little consensus about gangs from members of the task force, including schoolteachers, juvenile court representatives, and law enforcement; and (2) missing from the task force were the voices of the people involved in or affected by gangs—that is, the youth of St. Louis. Scott and Kimberly leveraged ties to political scientists to construct vignettes and access via the task force to generate a sample to ultimately "understand the basis for the vision of gangs held by members" of the task force and gang and non-gang juvenile detainees. Gang and non-gang juveniles found gang activity to be more impactful to everyday life than the police in the juvenile division or task force participant samples. While juveniles learned about gang activity from their friends, neighborhoods, or firsthand experience, the police and task force relied more on news media and their jobs. The vignettes also revealed large differences in interpreting five hypothetical scenarios as gang related. The main story to emerge from this research was that direct knowledge of gangs was most likely to come from the people who have experiences with gangs, and that formulating responses to gangs must include these voices.

If the people closest to gangs best reflect the reality of gangs, it is no surprise that *Life in the Gang* relied on a sample of active and former gang members. Scott's Active Offenders Portfolio extended beyond gangs to include armed robbers, burglars, and drug traffickers. The research designs of these projects were as creative as his gang research, as Scott and Richard Wright took the burglars on "walk-abouts" (Wright and Decker 1994) and the robbers on "ride-alongs" (Wright and Decker 1997). Scott's gang work also engaged a wide range of populations and institutions. The LoneStar Project consisted of a disproportionate random sample of prisoners in Texas, half of whom were classified as gang affiliates (Pyrooz and Decker 2019). Anecdotes about crime and gangs in collegiate sports led to surveying athletic directors and police chiefs from universities taking part in basketball or football Bowl Championship Series games and interviews with student athletes at two universities (Rojek et al. 2013).[6] Part of the St. Louis Gang Studies portfolio included interviewing middle school students attending schools in various proximities to gang homicide concentrations (Curry et al. 2002; Decker and Curry 2000a). And then there is his research with prisoners (e.g., Decker et al. 1998), arrestees (e.g., Decker et al. 2008), and probationers and parolees (Decker and Pyrooz 2011). There are many dimensions to gangs, and Scott's approach to research ensured that as many of these dimensions as possible were represented.

A final aspect of research design deserving of recognition is Scott's commitment to assessing the reliability and validity of data. If someone builds a career analyzing diverse sources of data, it is incumbent on the researcher to evaluate the properties of such data, but it is rare for researchers to turn the tools of science on themselves to ask hard questions about whether data should be trusted. Scott has routinely tested the veracity of the data on which his conclusions are based. With Vince Webb and Chuck Katz, he used Arizona Arrestee Drug Abuse Monitoring Program data to assess the validity of self-reports by gang and non-gang members (Webb, Katz, and Decker 2006). Drug use captured in urinalysis was used as the criterion, revealing that current and former gang members were no less (or more) likely to disclose drug use than non-gang members. Using multi-trait, multi-method matrices (Rosenfeld and Decker 1993, 1999), Scott compared FBI and National Youth Gang Survey data on gangs and total homicides and associated correlates, finding measurement properties that supported the use of the data (Decker and Pyrooz 2010). Another example of validity testing compared self-reports and official records among prisoners in the LoneStar Project (Pyrooz, Decker, and Owens 2020), finding 82% correspondence in gang affiliation and 86% correspondence in the gang with which people affiliated, which was better than episodic measures (e.g., misconduct) but worse than more durable measures (e.g., race). These studies are important assessments of the quality of data that are prominently used in gang research.

The diversity in research designs deployed by Scott is striking, standing in sharp contrast to the careers of most academic researchers. In Scott's career, the dog has always wagged the tail, never the tail wagging the dog. The research question dictated the research design. This has allowed Scott to contemplate the meanings, impacts, and responses to gangs using a diversity of populations and perspectives. It has also allowed him to reach more authoritative accounts and conclusions about gangs in his appraisals of the literature (Decker, Melde, and Pyrooz 2013; Curry, Decker, and Pyrooz 2014; Decker, Pyrooz, and Densley 2022). And this has allowed Scott to offer a more complete assessment of gangs moored to data and evidence rather than rhetoric and speculation. This, we believe, is a lasting legacy of Scott's, deserving appreciation.

Getting Out: A Legacy of Impact

"What part of the word *retirement* includes writing more books?" This question was posed to Scott and shared in the acknowledgment section of his newest book, *On Gangs* (2022, xii, emphasis in original). When we spoke about writing this chapter, Scott insisted there were no loose ends to tie up or burning questions to address. There are a few more articles on gangs to be published, but those are linked to longstanding commitments. The gradual transition out of the academy and into new ventures—and the teeter-tottering that comes with it—is certainly fitting, as his "disengagement" from gang research bears a strong resemblance to the very processes he helped to uncover about disengagement from gangs.

The five core legacies for gang research outlined in this chapter are impressive. But we would be remiss if we did not acknowledge that Scott had an equally impressive career outside of gang research. Only about half of the 21,000 citations associated with Scott's research concern gangs. Here are some examples: the Active Offenders Portfolio included work on armed robbers, burglars, and drug smugglers (Decker and Chapman 2008; Wright and Decker 1994, 1997); his research on the acquisition and use of firearms by offenders, which also includes an unwritten book (Decker, Pennell, and Caldwell 1997); policing and immigration (Provine et al. 2016) and racial disparities in policing (Rojek, Rosenfeld, and Decker 2012); and prisoner re-entry (Decker et al. 2015). What makes this even more impressive is that Scott was a department chair/school director for 24 years. He led the Department of Criminology and Criminal Justice at the UMSL from a bachelor's to master's to doctoral-granting department, which was ranked number four when he left for ASU in 2006. He led ASU's transition from a Department of Criminal Justice to a School of Criminology and Criminal Justice, including the launch of the doctoral program, which was ranked number two when he retired from the university in 2018. Anyone familiar with administrative work in academia will know these are remarkable feats; doubly so while maintaining such a productive research agenda.

Scott insists that his continued contributions to gang (and non-gang) research are reflective of his co-authors. In one sense, he is right. At UMSL, he hired and worked with a veritable "who's who" of criminologists, including Carol Kohfeld, Richard Wright, Dave Curry, Bob Bursik, Jody Miller, Rick Rosenfeld, Janet Lauritsen, Kimberly Kempf-Leonard, and Finn Esbensen. His list of colleagues and collaborators from ASU is similarly impressive: Chuck Katz, Xia Wang, Mike White, Gary Sweeten, Jacob Young, Kate Fox, Cassia Spohn, Eric Hedberg, David Schaefer, Nancy Rodriguez, and Vince Webb. These collaborations also extend to individuals in fields adjacent to criminology, like Heidi Ellis and Marie Provine. When Scott tells the story of collaborating with people in different disciplines, different subfields in criminology and criminal justice, and different ranks in the field, it would lead to such a conclusion—his collaborators made him better, and we believe him.

But in another sense, he too easily discounts his role. Scott was able to recognize and take advantage of a number of opportunities that presented themselves. After all, he sought out those interdisciplinary connections to which most individuals only pay lip service; identified areas of overlap that could produce impactful collaborations; and secured funding that would provide research assistantships for students and positions for coordinators, managers, and street outreach workers. And perhaps most importantly, Scott had a knack for identifying emerging issues, finding a way to effectively frame them, generating evidence to understand them, and establishing pillars upon which others could enhance and expand.

The authors of this chapter are but two of the dozens of students with whom he has worked, and who benefited greatly from the experience of doing so. Scott's history of mentorship is admirable. It often involved providing opportunities for students to "get a seat at the table" and take on additional research responsibilities over time. For those who met the challenge, Scott would continue to provide new opportunities. At every step of the way, he would consistently provide speedy, decisive feedback on ideas and writing.[7] He has chaired a dozen dissertations and served on an order of magnitude greater number of student thesis and dissertation committees. Indeed, there is a much larger cadre of students and junior faculty Scott has mentored, extending well beyond people at ASU and UMSL. Among his research output, mentoring, training, collaboration, and program development, it is safe to say that there are portions of Scott's legacy that are yet to be told.

Notes

1. Scott's dissertation was chaired by Charles Wellford. In communications with Scott, he indicated that although he had an opportunity to work directly under Wellford on the Des Moines Replication project, he chose not to. At that time at Florida State University, few students had graduated from the PhD program, and not unlike graduate students in most programs, Scott was focused on graduating (personal communication, September 2, 2022).
2. Scott may have retired from academia, but not from research, as he has been the chief scientist at CNA Corporation since 2019.
3. https://thecriminologyacademy.com/episode-9-decker/.
4. Notably, Scott had developed the gang addendum for the Drug Use Forecasting (DUF) program, the predecessor to the ADAM program.
5. When Scott left UMSL to go to ASU in 2006, St. Louis's paper of record, the *Post-Dispatch*, ran a 1,000-word article lamenting his departure from the community. In the article the police chief referred to Scott as an "institution," and the former US attorney was quoted as saying "I think it's a very big loss."
6. The findings from this research were featured in a *Sports Illustrated* article in which Scott was quoted: https://vault.si.com/vault/2011/12/05/straight-outta-compton
7. One common recommendation for paper writing would be a reference to a song by Archie Bell and The Drells: "Tighten up." And with the advent of YouTube, emails would arrive with the URL: https://www.youtube.com/watch?v=FV6olDJQRjs. And when projects would ramp up, he would remind us of the chocolate-wrapping scene from *I Love Lucy*: https://www.youtube.com/watch?v=WmAwcMNxGqM.

References

Berger, Rony, Hisham Abu-Raiya, Yotam Heineberg, and Philip Zimbardo. 2017. "The Process of Desistance among Core Ex-Gang Members." *American Journal of Orthopsychiatry* 87 (4): 487.

Brantingham, P. Jeffrey, Baichuan Yuan, and Denise Herz. 2021. "Is Gang Violent Crime More Contagious than Non-Gang Violent Crime?" *Journal of Quantitative Criminology* 37 (4): 953–977.

Cruz, José Miguel, and Jonathan D. Rosen. 2022. "Leaving the Pervasive Barrio: Gang Disengagement under Criminal Governance." *Social Problems*, February, spac001. https://doi.org/10.1093/socpro/spac001.

Curry, G. David, and Scott H. Decker. 2002. "Safe Futures in St. Louis." St. Louis: University of Missouri-St. Louis, Department of Criminology and Criminal Justice.

Curry, G. David, Scott H. Decker, and Arlen Egley. 2002. "Gang Involvement and Delinquency in a Middle School Population." *Justice Quarterly* 19 (2): 275–292. https://doi.org/10.1080/07418820200095241.

Curry, G. David, Scott H. Decker, and David C. Pyrooz. 2014. *Confronting Gangs: Crime and Community*. 3rd ed. New York: Oxford University Press.

Decker, Scott H. 1977. "Official Crime Rates and Victim Surveys: An Empirical Comparison." *Journal of Criminal Justice* 5 (1): 47–54.

Decker, Scott H. 1996. "Collective and Normative Features of Gang Violence." *Justice Quarterly* 13 (2): 243–264. https://doi.org/10.1080/07418829600092931.
Decker, Scott. 2008. *Strategies to Addreess Gang Crime: A Guidebook for Local Law Enforcement*. Washington, DC: Office of Community-Oriented Policing Services, US Department of Justice.
Decker, Scott H., Tim Bynum, and Deborah Weisel. 1998. "A Tale of Two Cities: Gangs as Organized Crime Groups." *Justice Quarterly* 15 (3): 395–425.
Decker, Scott H., and Margaret Chapman. 2008. *Drug Smugglers on Drug Smuggling*. Philadelphia, PA: Temple University Press.
Decker, Scott H., and G. David Curry. 2000a. "Addressing Key Features of Gang Membership: Measuring the Involvement of Young Members." *Journal of Criminal Justice* 28 (6): 473–482.
Decker, Scott H., and G. David Curry. 2000b. "Responding to Gangs: Comparing Gang Member, Police, and Task Force Perspectives." *Journal of Criminal Justice* 28 (2): 129–137. https://doi.org/10.1016/S0047-2352(99)00037-9.
Decker, Scott H., and G. David Curry. 2002. "Gangs, Gang Homicides, and Gang Loyalty: Organized Crimes or Disorganized Criminals." *Journal of Criminal Justice* 30 (4): 343–352.
Decker, Scott H., Charles M. Katz, and Vincent J. Webb. 2008. "Understanding the Black Box of Gang Organization: Implications for Involvement in Violent Crime, Drug Sales, and Violent Victimization." *Crime & Delinquency* 54 (1): 153–172.
Decker, Scott H., and Kimberly Kempf-Leonard. 1991. "Constructing Gangs: The Social Definition of Youth Activities." *Criminal Justice Policy Review* 5 (4): 271–291.
Decker, Scott H., and Janet L. Lauritsen. 1996. "Breaking the Bonds of Membership: Leaving the Gang." In *Gangs in America*, edited by C. Ronald Huff. 2: 103–122. Newbury Park, CA: Sage.
Decker, Scott H., Chris Melde, and David C. Pyrooz. 2013. "What Do We Know about Gangs and Gang Members and Where Do We Go from Here?" *Justice Quarterly* 30 (3): 369–402. https://doi.org/10.1080/07418825.2012.732101.
Decker, Scott H., Natalie Ortiz, Cassia Spohn, and Eric Hedberg. 2015. "Criminal Stigma, Race, and Ethnicity: The Consequences of Imprisonment for Employment." *Journal of Criminal Justice* 43 (2): 108–121. https://doi.org/10.1016/j.jcrimjus.2015.02.002.
Decker, Scott H., Susan Pennell, and Ami Caldwell. 1997. "Illegal Firearms: Access and Use by Arrestees." Washington, DC: US Department of Justice, Office of Justice Programs, National Institute of Justice.
Decker, Scott H., and David C. Pyrooz. 2010. "On the Validity and Reliability of Gang Homicide: A Comparison of Disparate Sources." *Homicide Studies* 14 (4): 359–376. https://doi.org/10.1177/1088767910385400.
Decker, Scott H., and David C. Pyrooz. 2011. "Leaving the Gang: Logging off and Moving On." Council on Foreign Relations. https://www.cfr.org/sites/default/files/pdf/2011/11/SAVE_paper_Decker_Pyrooz.pdf.
Decker, Scott H., and David C. Pyrooz. 2013. "Gangs: Another Form of Organized Crime?" In *Handbook of Organized Crime*, edited by Letizia Paoli, 270–287. New York: Oxford University Press.
Decker, Scott H., and David C. Pyrooz. 2015. "'I'm Down for a Jihad': How 100 Years of Gang Research Can Inform the Study of Terrorism, Radicalization and Extremism." *Perspectives on Terrorism* 9: 104–112.

Decker, Scott H., David C. Pyrooz, and James A. Densley. 2022. *On Gangs*. Philadelphia, PA: Temple University Press.

Decker, Scott H., David C. Pyrooz, and Richard K. Jr Moule. 2014. "Disengagement from Gangs as Role Transitions." *Journal of Research on Adolescence* 24 (2): 268–283.

Decker, Scott H., and Dietrich Lester Smith. 2015. "A Conversation with Street Daddy: Pulling Back the Curtain on 20 Years of Ethnography." In *Envisioning Criminology: Researchers on Research as a Process*, edited by Michael D. Maltz and Steven K. Rice, 9–25. New York: Springer.

Decker, Scott H., and Barrik Van Winkle. 1994. "'Slinging Dope': The Role of Gangs and Gang Members in Drug Sales." *Justice Quarterly* 11 (4): 583–604. https://doi.org/10.1080/07418829400092441.

Decker, Scott H., and Barrik Van Winkle. 1996. *Life in the Gang: Family, Friends, and Violence*. Cambridge, UK: Cambridge University Press.

Densley, James A. 2012. "Street Gang Recruitment: Signaling, Screening, and Selection." *Social Problems* 59 (3): 301–321. https://doi.org/10.1525/sp.2012.59.3.301.

Densley, James A., and David C. Pyrooz. 2019. "A Signaling Perspective on Disengagement from Gangs." *Justice Quarterly* 36 (1): 31–58. https://doi.org/10.1080/07418825.2017.1357743.

Fernández-Planells, Ariadna, José Sánchez-García, María Oliver, and Carles Feixa. 2020. "Researching Transnational Gangs as Agents of Mediation in the Digital Era." In *Gangs in the Era of Internet and Social Media*, edited by Chris Melde and Frank Weerman, 43–59. Cham, Switzerland: Springer International Publishing.

Fleisher, Mark S., and Scott H. Decker. 2001. "An Overview of the Challenge of Prison Gangs." *Corrections Management Quarterly* 5 (1): 1–11.

Fong, Robert S., and Ronald E. Vogel. 1995. "Blood-in, Blood-out: The Rationale behind Defecting from Prison Gangs." *Journal of Gang Research* 2 (4): 45–51.

Gravel, Jason, Matthew Valasik, Joris Mulder, Roger Leenders, Carter Butts, P. Jeffrey Brantingham, and George E. Tita. 202e. "Rivalries, Reputation, Retaliation, and Repetition: Testing Plausible Mechanisms for the Contagion of Violence between Street Gangs Using Relational Model Events." *Network Science* 11 (2): 324–350.

Horowitz, Ruth. 1983. *Honor and the American Dream*. New Brunswick, NJ: Rutgers University Press.

Huff, C. Ronald. 1989. "Youth Gangs and Public Policy." *Crime & Delinquency* 35 (4): 524–537. https://doi.org/10.1177/0011128789035004001.

Johnson, Andrew, and James Densley. 2018. "Rio's New Social Order: How Religion Signals Disengagement from Prison Gangs." *Qualitative Sociology* 41 (2): 243–262. https://doi.org/10.1007/s11133-018-9379-x.

Kerner Commission. 1968. *Kerner Commission Report on the Causes, Events, and Aftermaths of the Civil Disorders of 1967*. Washington, DC: National Advisory Commission on Civil Disorders in the United States.

Klein, Malcolm W. 1971. *Street Gangs and Street Workers*. Englewood Cliffs, NJ: Prentice-Hall.

Laub, John H. 2004. "The Life Course of Criminology in the United States: The American Society of Criminology 2003 Presidential Address." *Criminology* 42 (1): 1–26.

Laub, John H. 2011. "Strengthening NIJ: Mission, Science and Process." *NIJ Journal* 268: 16–21.

Leverso, John, and Chris Hess. 2021. "From the Hood to the Home: Masculinity Maturation of Chicago Street Gang Members." *Sociological Perspectives* 64 (6): 1206–1223. https://doi.org/10.1177/07311214211040844.

Loftin, Colin. 1986. "Assaultive Violence as a Contagious Social Process." *Bulletin of the New York Academy of Medicine* 62 (5): 550.

Maruna, Shadd. 2010. "Mixed Method Research in Criminology: Why Not Go Both Ways?" In *Handbook of Quantitative Criminology*, edited by Alex R. Piquero and David Weisburd, 123–140. New York: Springer. https://doi.org/10.1007/978-0-387-77650-7_7.

Miller, Jody, and Scott H. Decker. 2001. "Young Women and Gang Violence: Gender, Street Offending, and Violent Victimization in Gangs." *Justice Quarterly* 18 (1): 115–140. https://doi.org/10.1080/07418820100094841.

Miller, Walter B. 2011. *City Gangs*. Phoenix: Arizona State University, School of Criminology and Criminal Justice. http://gangresearch.asu.edu/walter_miller_library/walter-b.-miller-book.

Moule, Richard K. Jr., Scott H. Decker, and David C. Pyrooz. 2017. "Technology and Conflict: Group Processes and Collective Violence in the Internet Era." *Crime, Law and Social Change* 68 (1–2): 47–73. https://doi.org/10.1007/s10611-016-9661-3.

Moule, R. K. Jr., D. C. Pyrooz, and S. H. Decker. 2013. "From 'What the F#@% is a Facebook?' to 'Who Doesn't Use Facebook?': The Role of Criminal Lifestyles in the Adoption and Use of the Internet." *Social Science Research* 42 (6): 1411–1421.

Moule, Richard K. Jr., David C. Pyrooz, and Scott H. Decker. 2014. "Internet Adoption and Online Behaviour among American Street Gangs: Integrating Gangs and Organizational Theory." *British Journal of Criminology* 54 (6): 1186–1206. https://doi.org/10.1093/bjc/azu050.

Papachristos, Andrew V. 2005. "Gang World." *Foreign Policy* 147: 48–55.

Polsby, Nelson W. 1993. "Where Do You Get Your Ideas?" *PS: Political Science and Politics* 26 (1): 83–87. https://doi.org/10.2307/419513.

Popper, K. R. 1968. "Epistemology without a Knowing Subject." In *Studies in Logic and the Foundations of Mathematics*, edited by B. Van Rootselaar and J. F. Staal. 52: 333–373. New York: Elsevier. https://doi.org/10.1016/S0049-237X(08)71204-7.

Provine, Doris Marie, Monica W. Varsanyi, Paul G. Lewis, and Scott H. Decker. 2016. *Policing Immigrants: Local Law Enforcement on the Front Lines*. Chicago, IL: University of Chicago Press.

Pyrooz, David C., and Richard K. Moule Jr. 2019. "Gangs and Social Media." In *Oxford Research Encyclopedia of Criminology*. Oxford, UK: Oxford University Press.

Pyrooz, David C., and Scott H. Decker. 2011. "Motives and Methods for Leaving the Gang: Understanding the Process of Gang Desistance." *Journal of Criminal Justice* 39 (5): 417–425. https://doi.org/10.1016/j.jcrimjus.2011.07.001.

Pyrooz, David C., and Scott H. Decker. 2019. *Competing for Control: Gangs and the Social Order of Prisons*. Cambridge, UK: Cambridge University Press. https://doi.org/10.1017/9781108653473.

Pyrooz, David C., Scott H. Decker, and Emily Owens. 2020. "Do Prison Administrative and Survey Data Sources Tell the Same Story? A Multi-Trait, Multi-Method Examination with Application to Gangs." *Crime & Delinquency* 66 (5): 627–662. https://doi.org/https//:10.13140/RG.2.2.18751.36005.

Pyrooz, David C., Scott H. Decker, and Richard K. Moule. 2015. "Criminal and Routine Activities in Online Settings: Gangs, Offenders, and the Internet." *Justice Quarterly* 32 (3): 471–499.

Pyrooz, David C., Scott H. Decker, and Vincent J. Webb. 2014. "The Ties That Bind: Desistance from Gangs." *Crime & Delinquency* 60 (4): 491–516. https://doi.org/10.1177/0011128710372191.

Pyrooz, David C., and Meghan M. Mitchell. 2015. "Little Gang Research, Big Gang Research." In *The Handbook of Gangs*, edited by Scott H. Decker and David C. Pyrooz, 28–58. Chichester, UK: Wiley-Blackwell.

Quinney, Richard. 1970. *The Social Reality of Crime*. Piscataway, NJ: Transaction Publishers.

Rojek, Jeff, Scott H. Decker, Geoffrey P. Alpert, and J. Andrew Hansen. 2013. "Is the Quarterback a 'Crip'? The Presence of Gangs in Collegiate Athletics Programs." *Criminal Justice Review* 38 (4): 452–472.

Rojek, Jeff, Richard Rosenfeld, and Scott Decker. 2012. "Policing Race: The Racial Stratification of Searches in Police Traffic Stops." *Criminology* 50 (4): 993–1024.

Roman, Caterina G., Scott H. Decker, and David C. Pyrooz. 2017. "Leveraging the Pushes and Pulls of Gang Disengagement to Improve Gang Intervention: Findings from Three Multi-Site Studies and a Review of Relevant Gang Programs." *Journal of Crime and Justice* 40 (3): 316–336.

Rosenfeld, Richard, and Scott Decker. 1993. "Discrepant Values, Correlated Measures: Cross-City and Longitudinal Comparisons of Self-Reports and Urine Tests of Cocaine Use among Arrestees." *Journal of Criminal Justice* 21 (3): 223–230.

Rosenfeld, Richard, and Scott H. Decker. 1999. "Are Arrest Statistics a Valid Measure of Illicit Drug Use? The Relationship between Criminal Justice and Public Health Indicators of Cocaine, Heroin, and Marijuana Use." *Justice Quarterly* 16 (3): 685–699.

Short, James F., and Lorine A. Hughes. 2006. "Moving Gang Research Forward." In *Studying Youth Gangs*, edited by James F. Short Jr. and Lorine A. Hughes, 225–238. Lanham, MD: Rowman Altamira.

Short, James F., and Fred L. Strodtbeck. 1963. "The Response of Gang Leaders to Status Threats: An Observation on Group Process and Delinquent Behavior." *American Journal of Sociology* 68 (5): 571–579.

Short, James F., and Fred L. Strodtbeck. 1965. *Group Process and Gang Delinquency*. Chicago, IL: University of Chicago Press.

Spergel, Irving A., and G. David Curry. 1993. "The National Youth Gang Survey: A Research and Development Process." In *The Gang Intervention Handbook*, edited by Arnold P. Goldstein and C. Ronald Huff, 359–400. Champaign, IL: Research Press.

Thornberry, Terence P., Marvin D. Krohn, Alan J. Lizotte, and Deborah Chard-Wierschem. 1993. "The Role of Juvenile Gangs in Facilitating Delinquent Behavior." *Journal of Research in Crime and Delinquency* 30 (1): 55–87. https://doi.org/10.1177/0022427893030001005.

Thrasher, Frederic M. 1927. *The Gang: A Study of 1,313 Gangs in Chicago*. Chicago, IL: University of Chicago Press.

Vigil, James Diego. 1988. *Barrio Gangs: Street Life and Identity in Southern California*. Austin: University of Texas Press.

Webb, Vincent J., Charles M. Katz, and Scott H. Decker. 2006. "Assessing the Validity of Self-Reports by Gang Members: Results from the Arrestee Drug Abuse Monitoring Program." *Crime & Delinquency* 52 (2): 232–252.

Wright, Richard T., and Scott H. Decker. 1994. *Burglars on the Job: Streetlife and Residential Break-Ins*. Boston, MA: Northeastern University Press.

Wright, Richard T., and Scott H. Decker. 1997. *Armed Robbers in Action: Stickups and Street Culture*. Boston, MA: Northeastern University Press.

CHAPTER 33

THE LEGACY OF FINN-AAGE ESBENSEN

DENA C. CARSON, ADRIENNE FRENG, CHRIS MELDE, AND DANA PETERSON

This chapter presents the story of a Danish boy who "came over on the boat" and how he influenced criminological thought, transformed school-based survey research, shaped youth gang and violence prevention practice, and altered how we think about youth gang involvement. Finn-Aage[1] Esbensen is known for many contributions across the field of criminology, both in US and European contexts. He is also known for his personable and down-to-earth nature. He is the quintessential guy you want to get a beer with (and he'll probably even pay!). These are traits that have made him a wonderful mentor, to the authors of this chapter and many others, a fantastic and reliable colleague, and helped him build successful partnerships with academics and practitioners across the globe. While the scope of his influence is broad, in this chapter we highlight Finn's impact on gang research both methodologically and substantively. We begin by discussing his contributions to gang prevention, particularly the Gang Resistance Education and Training (G.R.E.A.T.) program, followed by his impact on understanding gangs in an international perspective, then we move to his specific contributions to the understanding of gangs, and end with the lasting impact of his mentorship and collaborations.

Finn was born in Denmark and remains a Danish citizen to this day. His family migrated via boat to Canada in 1957 and immigrated to northeastern Massachusetts in 1962, where he completed his adolescent education. He earned a bachelor of arts in German and Sociology from Tufts University in 1973 and followed up with a master's degree in sociology. He continued his education and earned his PhD in sociology from the University of Colorado in 1982. While this might seem like a relatively direct path, several twists and turns appeared along the way, including meeting and marrying his wife Dana (D1[2]) and celebrating the birth of two children, Thor and Heidi. Finn worked as a research assistant/associate on several interesting projects during graduate school that initiated his research training and represent his unconventional approach to life and research, including participant observations in a Pittsfield, Massachusetts, jail and primary data collection on the National Youth Survey.

After earning his PhD, Finn joined the faculty at Western Carolina University in Cullowhee, North Carolina, in 1982 before returning to the University of Colorado as a research associate at the Institute of Behavioral Science in 1987. In 1992, he joined the faculty of the University of Nebraska–Omaha (UNO). It was during this time that he received funding from the National Institute of Justice for the first multisite, multicomponent evaluation of the Gang Resistance Education and Training program (G.R.E.A.T. I). Finn joined the faculty of the University of Missouri-St. Louis (UMSL) in 2001 as the E. Desmond Lee Professor of Youth Crime and Violence, an endowed faculty position, where he received funding from the National Institute of Justice for the second evaluation of G.R.E.A.T. (G.R.E.A.T. II), as well as for an evaluation of the Teens, Crime, and Community Works (Community Works) program. Furthermore, his work with the Eurogang Program of Research transcended his time at both UNO and UMSL. Finn began his retirement in 2019 at his small ranch in rural Oregon, although he is still active in research, consulting, collaborating, and mentoring in the areas of gang and school-based research, as well as participating in professional conferences and workshops.

Contributions from Large-Scale Projects

Throughout the 1990s and early 2000s, the survey research conducted by Finn and his colleagues helped to build much of the broad-based understanding we have of gangs and gang members, as well as to dispel a lot of myths that permeate both popular culture and academic circles surrounding these groups and people. At the beginning of Finn's career, large-scale quantitative gang research was still relatively rare, as many studies consisted of ethnographies or work with police units (i.e., Cohen 1955; Hagedorn 1988; Miller 1958; Moore 1978; Short and Strodtbeck 1965; Thrasher 1927; Vigil 1988). Longitudinal survey research projects, such as the Denver Youth Survey, were becoming more common, however. These projects changed the trajectory of gang research by allowing for a more generalizable understanding of gang involvement. Through research by Finn and his colleagues, as well as others who were at the forefront of this research, this expansion of gang research was driven by a desire to move beyond the focus on singular groups to examine the topic from a national perspective. Furthermore, it allowed for comparisons between gang and non-gang members, providing a novel outlook from a quantitative, longitudinal perspective. This new framework also allowed for studying gang membership in a developmental perspective, an innovation that has had substantial long-term impact on the field. Furthermore, Finn consistently incorporated a multitude of theoretical, behavioral, and attitudinal measures into his surveys, allowing researchers to answer a variety of questions beyond just testing the overall fidelity and effectiveness of the programs he was evaluating. Thus, Finn's early work with the Denver Youth Survey and in his later research, including the G.R.E.A.T. and Community Works evaluations, demonstrated that community- and school-based survey research can contribute greatly to our understanding of the causes and consequences of gangs and gang membership, juvenile delinquency, and youth violence. We trace some of these innovations Finn played a large part in pioneering below.

Denver Youth Survey: The Origins of the Quantitative Examination of Gang Members

The Denver Youth Survey (DYS) was one of the three studies (along with the Pittsburgh Youth Study and the Rochester Youth Development Study) initiated in the 1980s through the Program of Research on the Causes and Correlates of Delinquency funded by the Office of Juvenile Justice and Delinquency Prevention. These funding lines were intended to build a multisite longitudinal and developmental understanding of delinquency during a time when most of the research was cross-sectional and often relied on a single site. To accomplish this, funded research teams were asked to make use of similar sampling strategies to tap "high-risk" populations, as well as make use of common measures. Together these projects, as well as others, ushered in an era of quantitative criminology and remain important to our understanding of the developmental pathways into crime and delinquency (i.e., Browning et al. 1999; Thornberry, Huizinga, and Loeber 2004).[3] Originally, gang membership was not included as a common measure in the Causes and Correlates projects. However, eventually conversation began regarding developing and including common measures about gang membership and activities that allowed Finn (and others) to focus on this topic (Pyrooz and Mitchell 2015). As the DYS developed, Finn became increasingly involved, honing his research skills in survey construction, measurement, data collection, and project management that would serve him well later in his career as he developed his own extensive research projects.

Finn's work on the DYS contributed something much broader to the field of gang research: He helped demonstrate the validity of self-report surveys to study gang members. As noted by Pyrooz and Mitchell (2015), Finn's collaboration with David Huizinga and others would lead not only to the most highly cited work of his career (Esbensen and Huizinga 1993), but two of the most cited gang articles ever (Esbensen and Huizinga 1993; Esbensen, Huizinga, and Weiher 1993). In fact, Esbensen and Huizinga (1993) was so impactful that it has been cited over 800 times and reprinted in multiple juvenile delinquency and gang readers over the years, most recently in 2009, indicating the long-lasting impact of these works. In these articles, they examined (1) the prevalence and demographic composition of gang members in Denver; (2) the degree to which gang members were involved in illegal activities relative to other youth in their sample, as well as how gang and non-gang members differed in other characteristics and activities; and (3) the temporal relationship between criminal offending and gang membership. Finn would later expand on these contributions in his work on the G.R.E.A.T. evaluations. Finn's early collaborations with criminologists such as David Huizinga, Frank Dunford, Del Elliott, and Malcolm Klein also provided the basis for his own extensive mentoring of young scholars and his collaborative approach to research, which was integral throughout his career and even into his retirement.

The G.R.E.A.T.Est Story Ever Told: Contributions to Gang Prevention

One of Finn's most significant contributions to gang research and practice is his work evaluating the G.R.E.A.T. program.[4] While the outcomes of these assessments have certainly improved our knowledge on "what works" for gang prevention, the impact of this research goes well beyond evaluating programmatic outcomes. The G.R.E.A.T. evaluations produced three sets of data drawn from geographically and demographically diverse samples of youth in the United States. Numerous scholars and students have analyzed these datasets resulting in approximately 131 peer-reviewed publications, 27 master's theses and dissertations, as well as 90 pieces of academic scholarship (e.g., book chapters, presentations, and reports).[5] Notably, scholars who worked on the G.R.E.A.T. evaluations account for 58% of these publications, some of which represent some of the most cited gang research articles (Pyrooz and Mitchell 2015). The vast amount of work coming from these datasets is unsurprising given Finn's process for evaluating prevention programs, which has entailed identifying the underlying logic of the program to tie the intended change mechanisms to criminological and social theories of behavior. This process has consistently led to the development and use of surveys that address not only the evaluation goals (e.g., "Does the G.R.E.A.T. program prevent youths from joining gangs?") but can answer a vast number of theoretically informed research questions in the areas of gangs and youth violence, among others.

G.R.E.A.T. I

The G.R.E.A.T. program was originally developed by Phoenix-area law enforcement in 1991 as a response to local gang problems and was eventually implemented in multiple US cities through federal funds provided by the Bureau of Alcohol, Tobacco, and Firearms. The original curriculum consisted of eight lessons with the goal of reducing delinquency, violence, and gang membership (Esbensen et al. 2011; Esbensen 2015). Upon receiving funding from the National Institute of Justice (NIJ), Finn began the first multisite, multicomponent evaluation of G.R.E.A.T., conducted from 1995 to 1999. The outcome evaluation consisted of both an 11-city cross-sectional survey of about 6,000 eighth grade students and a separate longitudinal panel study of over 2,000 youth in six cities. While the cross-sectional study provided initial indications of G.R.E.A.T. program effects, the longitudinal study was more rigorous and consisted of a pre- and post-test survey and four annual follow-ups.

Importantly, the research design contained not only the more traditional outcome element, but also something much more unique to criminological research—a process evaluation. The integration of the process evaluation reflects Finn's innovative and thorough approach to the research enterprise. Many evaluations, then and still today, neglect to examine whether programs are implemented as intended. Without this knowledge, it is difficult to ascertain the true impact of a program or policy, as changes—or lack thereof—could be a result of poor program implementation rather than attributable to the program itself. The process portion of the evaluation consisted of observations of trainings that law enforcement officers received to become certified to teach the G.R.E.A.T. program, observations of delivery of the G.R.E.A.T. program in the classroom, and surveys with key stakeholders (school personnel, law enforcement, and parents) to document how these key personnel understood the main program elements.

Overall, the results of this first evaluation were not favorable, with G.R.E.A.T. having minimal impact on its goals to prevent youth crime and gang involvement and only lagged effects on a small number of attitudinal characteristics (e.g., lower risk-seeking tendencies, more positive perceptions about law enforcement, and more negative views about gangs) (Esbensen, Osgood, et al. 2001; Esbensen 2015). Finn and his colleagues worked to disseminate these results to academic audiences and, importantly, also to practitioners and key stakeholders for the G.R.E.A.T. program. As expected, those heavily involved and supportive of the G.R.E.A.T. program were disappointed by these results. Finn took the time to meet with these key stakeholders, sometimes individually, to talk through the findings and provide guidance on how to move forward.

Often, when evaluation results are less than positive, common responses are to ignore the results or discontinue the program. However, in this case, the lack of programmatic effects from the initial G.R.E.A.T. evaluation resulted in a relatively rare event in the prevention world—a call to improve the curriculum to better address the spoken and unspoken goals of the G.R.E.A.T. program.[6] To begin this curriculum review and reconstruction following the results of the evaluation, Finn convened a group of experts in a variety of areas, including gangs, adolescent development, and school-based prevention, as well as those involved specifically with the program to provide their valued insights and experiences (for more information on the program revision, see Esbensen et al. 2002; Esbensen et al. 2011; Esbensen 2015). The outcome of this group's series of meetings was an outline for how the curriculum should be revised based on evidence-based instructional content and pedagogy, as well as a higher dosage (i.e., more lessons and student contact hours), which were believed to more adequately address the primary goals of the G.R.E.A.T. program. NIJ then convened a separate group of experts similar to those listed above as well as curriculum writers from Blueprints for Healthy Youth Development and Life Skills Training, which resulted in the development of the revised G.R.E.A.T. curriculum (G.R.E.A.T. II). As this "new" program was implemented throughout the United States, Finn remarked to his G.R.E.A.T. I evaluation colleagues, "Now some poor suckers are going to have to evaluate it."

G.R.E.A.T. II.

Who would be the "poor suckers" that would evaluate the revised curriculum? When NIJ released the call for proposals, Finn asked his colleagues "What do you say we throw our hat in the ring?" Finn, with colleagues Dana Peterson, Terrance J. Taylor, and D. Wayne Osgood as co-investigators, submitted a successful proposal to evaluate the revised curriculum of G.R.E.A.T. beginning in 2006. The G.R.E.A.T. II research design was similar to the G.R.E.A.T. I evaluation in that it included both process and outcome components, but Finn took advantage of the unique opportunity to reflect on the prior evaluation experience and improve various aspects of the design to produce higher-quality data, increase confidence in the knowledge obtained, and influence future research with young people. As with G.R.E.A.T. I, the evaluation team conducted systematic structured observations of numerous G.R.E.A.T. officer trainings and classroom delivery of G.R.E.A.T. lessons, as well as observations of classrooms in the same schools and grade levels that did not receive the program. In fact, a total of 500 classroom observations were completed by the research team, which allowed for an understanding of program fidelity at both the classroom and officer level. The outcome evaluation was an experimental design that included random assignment of classrooms to receive the G.R.E.A.T. program or serve as controls. The design also included pre- and post-test surveys of 3,820 students, as well as four annual follow-ups with students in 31 schools in seven cities.

The overall evaluation design for G.R.E.A.T. II was significantly more methodologically rigorous than that of G.R.E.A.T. I, as there were several efforts made by Finn and his team to improve the quality of data based on lessons learned from G.R.E.A.T. I. (e.g., improved active parental consent and response rates, full random assignment). Furthermore, these techniques influenced school-based research going forward. First and foremost, Finn and the evaluation team employed several strategies to improve the active parental consent rate for the sample (see Esbensen et al. 2008). These approaches resulted in a 78% active consent rate (compared with 57% in G.R.E.A.T. I), meaning greater representation of the students in the study schools. Second, Finn dedicated time and resources to improving this process by scheduling multiple visits to each city to attain retention/response rates to ensure representative data. The Wave 6 response rate for G.R.E.A.T. II was 72% compared with 67% in G.R.E.A.T. I. These retention numbers are impressive given the highly mobile nature of the G.R.E.A.T. sample; by Wave 4, for example, two years after the pre-test, students were surveyed in more than 200 schools. The first author remembers calling Finn from Nashville at the end of data collection and he was ecstatic that she surveyed six students in one day because it increased our response rate by one percentage point. This demonstrates how important it was to Finn to ensure that the data collected were truly representative of the students and schools from which they were drawn. Finn, even late into his career when most established researchers would take more of an administrative role, traveled on data collection trips, conducted classroom observations, and administered surveys to students, a testament not only to his commitment to quality data, but also a reflection of his values: he is never "above" putting in hard work to conduct high-quality research.

The results of the evaluation one year post-treatment indicated that the revised G.R.E.A.T. program was effective at reducing gang membership, as youth in the treatment group were 39.2% less likely to report gang membership, and also produced improvement on a number of attitudinal factors (Esbensen et al. 2012). Even more convincing, G.R.E.A.T. II demonstrated the ability to reduce gang membership by 24% four years post-program (Esbensen et al. 2013). There was also a sustained improvement in several attitudinal measures, including more positive attitudes toward police. That said, the effect sizes were relatively small and the results did not show a program effect on delinquency or violence (one of the central program goals) (Esbensen 2015; Esbensen et al. 2013).

Finn and his team's rigorous efforts studying the G.R.E.A.T. program have significantly impacted our knowledge of school-based gang prevention, giving practitioners at least one evidence-based program that targets youth gang involvement. G.R.E.A.T. is currently rated as promising on NIJ's Crime Solutions website (crimesolutions.gov). Furthermore, the revision and re-evaluation of the program represents an important lesson for researcher–practitioner partnerships: In the face of null results from scientifically sound evaluations containing both process and outcome evaluation components, all is not lost. By working together, researchers and practitioners can create a more effective product that ultimately can have significant results for communities.

Following G.R.E.A.T. II, Finn leveraged the high-quality data collected to attain additional NIJ funding to study disengagement from gangs. The Multi-Site, Multi-Method Study of Gang Desistance employed both a quantitative analysis of the G.R.E.A.T. II data and qualitative follow-up interviews with youth who reported gang involvement during the G.R.E.A.T. II survey. True to his commitment to developing young scholars, Finn used the funding to provide the first author an opportunity to act as project director. That does not mean that he was hands off, as Finn also made efforts to visit the neighborhoods of the interviewees. This included traveling to both the Nashville and the Dallas/Fort Worth sites in one day, as well as racing to leave Philadelphia to beat a snowstorm. These data have gone far to improve our understanding of several aspects of gang disengagement, including valid measurement, young people's motivations and methods of leaving, as well as how these motivations and processes vary, such as by race/ethnicity or gender (Carson 2018;

Carson, Peterson, and Esbensen 2013; Carson and Esbensen 2016; Melde and Esbensen 2014; Vecchio 2014; Vecchio and Carson 2022).

Community Works: A Lesson in Being a Good Steward of Resources

On the heels of the G.R.E.A.T. I evaluation, Finn was offered and accepted the E. Desmond Lee Endowed Professor of Youth Crime and Violence position at the University of Missouri-St. Louis (UMSL). Not long after, the NIJ released a call for proposals to evaluate a middle school-based victimization prevention program that used legal professionals such as lawyers, probation officers, and police as teachers or facilitators in the classroom. Known as Teens, Crime, and the Community: Community Works (Community Works), this 31-lesson curriculum had a different instructional design than the somewhat "canned" G.R.E.A.T. I curriculum. That is, there was a set of eight required "core" lessons that made up the foundation of the curriculum, as well as a series of 23 topical lessons that could be delivered as needed. Similar to Finn's work with the G.R.E.A.T. evaluations, he proposed to conduct both an outcome and process evaluation of the curriculum as delivered in schools. Owing in part to his proof of concept with such a robust evaluation of the G.R.E.A.T. I curriculum, Finn was awarded $1.6 million to evaluate Community Works.

The evaluation started simply enough with Finn's research staff, including one of the co-authors of this chapter, Chris Melde, calling each and every school-based site where the Community Works program was advertised as being implemented. The team soon discovered that what was supposed to be a roster of active Community Works sites was in fact a roster of all sites that had ever been *trained* to deliver the curriculum. Many sites never implemented the program after receiving training, while other sites listed as active had not implemented the program in years. As an example, Chris called an "active" site only to be informed that the contact person and instructor had died a number of years previous to the phone call. While ultimately 14 schools across nine cities in four states were located and agreed to be part of a quasi-experimental process and outcome evaluation, the challenges associated with finding sites that delivered the curriculum served as a warning of what was to come.

Consistent with Finn's dedication to rigorous process evaluations to document how programs are implemented versus how they are meant to be delivered, the research team triangulated their observational methods by observing instructor trainings and delivery of program content in treatment classrooms and conducting interviews and surveys with key stakeholders and instructors. As is documented in Melde, Esbensen, and Tusinski (2006), these observations demonstrated a large degree of variability in program delivery across sites and relative to the standards laid out in the curriculum. Specifically, out of the 110 classroom observations of program delivery conducted during the first year of the evaluation, only 18 (16%) class sessions were delivered in the manner described in the curriculum. Some schools and classrooms skipped entire lessons or delivered small parts of a lesson while skipping valuable content. Two issues were discovered during this part of the study: (1) the curriculum was not created with the school in mind as a delivery setting, and (2) there was not clear messaging from program trainers or in the curriculum itself that reinforced the need for adherence to program fidelity. Most importantly, what became evident was that there was no way to tie back any outcome evaluation results to a "program" under study.

Finn was left with a dilemma. He could continue with an outcome evaluation that may result in statistically meaningful differences between control and treatment classrooms for which he would have no reasonable explanation (i.e., there was no systematic treatment across schools). Or he could cancel the outcome evaluation due to program implementation failure. This choice was no small matter for the research team either, for whom five waves of panel data collected over four years from over 1,500 youth could serve as the basis for years if not a decade of research. It was also significant for the program under evaluation, for which their continued funding for program delivery could be in jeopardy due to what the evaluation had uncovered. The lives of multiple stakeholders would be impacted by Finn's decision on how to move forward. Those who know Finn, however, know he is not one to squander resources unnecessarily, even when those resources are not his own.

Posed with this dilemma, Finn contacted NIJ to discuss the preliminary findings associated with the implementation failure and offered a solution. Instead of canceling the project altogether, Finn suggested NIJ transition the time and resources devoted to the outcome evaluation to that of a program review. Using lessons learned from the G.R.E.A.T. I curriculum review and revision, Finn convened a program and curriculum review committee composed of leading experts in the fields of criminology and prevention science, as well as key stakeholders from the Community Works program, including instructors, trainers, and members of the National Crime Prevention Council, which was responsible for the program. Together, this group of scientists, agency personnel, and instructors produced a program and curriculum review that would serve as a guidepost to the National Crime Prevention Council to reorient the program should they choose to do so. This process also served as a lesson to those involved in this project. To be a good steward of resources entrusted to you by funding agencies, in this instance NIJ and the American taxpayer, you have to make difficult choices that are in the best interest of the funder, even if it negatively impacts one's own career. In this instance, it would have been easy to continue with the outcome evaluation that would have produced five waves of panel survey data that had a 72% active consent rate from a diverse body of students from across the United States. Both Finn's and many other researchers' careers could have been enhanced by such a valuable data resource, but the costs associated with such a data collection effort would have been in vain, as there would be no reasonable explanation for any "treatment effects" uncovered. In this instance, as in so many others, Finn proved to be a good steward with the resources entrusted to him.

EUROGANG: CONTRIBUTIONS TO INTERNATIONAL GANG RESEARCH

Throughout most of the twentieth century, street gangs were, by and large, considered an American phenomenon. Discussions of gangs and gang violence in other parts of the world, especially in the European context, were met with skepticism and the common refrain that "we don't have gangs like they do in America." Bolstered by the burgeoning markets for movies (e.g., *Colors*, *Boyz N the Hood*) and rap music (e.g., Tupac, Ice Cube) featuring stereotypical American gangs like the Bloods and Crips in Los Angeles in the late 1980s and early 1990s, the signs and symbols of American street gangs made their way around the globe, raising the concern that street gangs were not isolated to the United States but were also common in major urban centers throughout Europe (Klein et al. 2001).

Originally led by the efforts of Dr. Malcolm "Mac" Klein, a group of American and European scholars began to meet on a near yearly basis to explore the idea of conducting international comparative work on street gangs. The first Eurogang workshop was held in Schmitten, Germany, in 1998 and was attended by a number of leading gang scholars in the world, including Finn. Over the coming years, a steering committee was formed and the group began developing research instruments, consensus definitions of a street gang and gang membership, and a website devoted to sharing these products and information on the Eurogang Program of Research. Throughout this time, Finn emerged as a leading voice of Eurogang. Finn hosted the Eurogang website at UMSL for over 15 years, helped to develop and pilot Eurogang's youth self-report survey instrument that operationalized the consensus definition of gang membership, and co-authored the first publication to conduct a systematic comparison of youth gang membership in the United States and the Netherlands using the Eurogang survey instrument (Esbensen and Weerman 2005).

Finn played a leading role in the developmental stages of the Eurogang Program of Research, when the working group established an identity, created a working model for international comparative gang research, and created tools to guide researchers in documenting gangs and their members across the globe; and he maintained a leadership role as the group transitioned to producing volumes of research on the presence, causes, and correlates of gangs and gang membership globally. Finn, with his long-time colleague and friend Cheryl Maxson, co-edited two volumes (Esbensen and Maxson 2012; Maxson and Esbensen 2016) stemming from research presented at Eurogang workshops. He also helped to usher in and mentor a new generation of Eurogang scholars and steering committee members, as the group's membership naturally turned over.

Finn played a large part in not only the logistics of workshop development but also in funding these near annual events (thanks, in part, to the E. Desmond Lee Endowment Fund), for which the costs of lodging and meals for all attendees are routinely covered. Finn's willingness to make such opportunities available and affordable for young scholars (i.e., PhD students and junior faculty, in the United States and abroad) has resulted in a new generation of gang scholars who have interacted with and learned from some of the most accomplished researchers in this field. This was facilitated through Eurogang's focus on close, intimate workshops that allow for in-depth discussions throughout the formal activities during the day, and the informal interactions over dinner and drinks that follow the long days of work. It is in these moments that Finn's character and dedication to the field shines, as he maintains a staunch focus on the scientific rigor of these meetings, but also recognizes the importance of the informal camaraderie building and socialization of the after-hours interactions of the group. In what has become a slogan of Finn and the Eurogang Program, Finn is known for reminding everyone who attends a workshop, "If you are going to hoot with the owls, then you need to soar with the eagles." That is, while the nights at Eurogang workshops are full of fun and laughs, the days are for hard work—and everyone needs to be wide awake to engage in lively scientific discussions on the state of gangs and research in an international context.

As we write this chapter, the 20th Workshop of the Eurogang Program of Research will be held in the summer of 2022, and again will be sponsored in large part through funds secured by Finn. Even though Finn is retired, he remains dedicated to the advancement of international research on youth, gangs, and gang violence. He remains one of only two scholars (the other being Cheryl Maxson) who has attended every Eurogang workshop to date, a testament to the dedication he has to understanding and preventing the deleterious impacts associated with gang membership in the United States and beyond and to supporting and training the next generations of scholars.

Contributions to Gang Research

"If It Walks Like A Duck": Contributions to Measuring Gang Membership

It is clear to anyone who either knows Finn or has read his work that he is committed to valid measurement. He has dedicated a good portion of his career (beginning with his dissertation, which examined interviewer effects on self-reported delinquency) to better understanding how to systematically identify gang members in self-report surveys, and demonstrating why attention to quality measurement matters for the conclusions we draw from research (Esbensen, Winfree, et al. 2001). Finn has consistently argued in his work that uniform measurement of gang membership across academics and practitioners across the globe is essential to the understanding of gangs and gang behavior. Accordingly, for comparative and triangulation purposes, Finn has regularly included multiple measures of gang membership and gang characteristics in survey instruments for G.R.E.A.T. I, G.R.E.A.T. II, and Community Works, adding considerably to the field's knowledge on gang and member definitions and why or when they matter. The results of his work in this area, comparing multiple definitions of gang membership, indicate that the largest differences in attitudes and behaviors appear between those who were never gang involved and those who report prior gang involvement. Finn's research was one of the first to demonstrate that simple self-nomination (e.g., are you now in a gang?) is not only parsimonious, but also a valid measurement of gang membership for both academics and practitioners. This has significantly changed how we identify gang members both in and outside of academia (Esbensen, Winfree, et al. 2001).

While self-nomination is a valid measure in the US context, the term "gang" does not always translate in a similar way across the globe, and in fact can be politically or ethically objectionable in some countries. The Eurogang project, within which Finn was heavily embedded (see the section on Finn's international work), developed a definition that included characteristics of groups that could be used to measure gangs or gang-like groups across countries. The Eurogang definition states that "a street gang (or troublesome youth group corresponding to a street gang elsewhere) is any durable, street-oriented youth group whose involvement in illegal activity is part of its group identity" (Weerman et al. 2009,

20). To examine the validity of this measure, as well as compare it to self-nomination, Finn included the seven Eurogang definition questions from the Eurogang Youth Survey in the G.R.E.A.T. II and Community Works survey instruments. This allowed for multiple studies to make direct comparisons between the Eurogang measurement of gang membership and self-nomination measures (Matsuda, Esbensen, and Carson 2012), as well as for the replication of research using the Eurogang definition (Peterson and Carson 2012; Melde, Esbensen, and Carson 2016). These latter studies showed that findings from studies using the self-nomination measure, such as the importance of group composition in influencing members' behaviors (Peterson, Miller, and Esbensen 2001), held up using the Eurogang definition, demonstrating the robustness and utility of the Eurogang measure for youth gang research, for example, in ensuring the study of "like" groups even in situations where the term "gang" may not translate properly or may not be explicitly applied or adopted.

Gang Myths: Contributions to the Broad Understanding of Gangs and Their Members

Another of Finn's exceptional contributions to understanding gangs and their members is his commitment to producing research that is disseminated and easily understood by academics, practitioners, and policymakers alike. Finn and his colleagues' survey-based research on gangs has busted many myths around gang membership. First, a belief often perpetuated by the media is that gang membership is the purview of minority males located in marginalized urban contexts. The work by Finn and others found that gang membership is experienced by both males and females (Esbensen and Huizinga 1993; Deschenes and Esbensen 1999; Esbensen and Deschenes 1998; Esbensen, Deschenes, and Winfree 1999), and by youth of all racial and ethnic backgrounds (Esbensen and Huizinga 1993; Esbensen and Winfree 1998; Esbensen and Peterson Lynskey 2001). Furthermore, this research highlights the facts that gangs do not exist just in large urban areas and that gangs and gang members reflect their communities in terms of their racial/ethnic composition. Other research sought to more fully understand the relationship between race/ethnicity and gang affiliation and found that while gang members tend to be marginalized in different capacities, multiple marginalization remains a stronger explanation for minority gang members (Freng and Esbensen 2007). Additionally, gangs vary in their composition, and this group context matters for the experiences of their members; for example, the ratio of males to females in gangs creates particular gender dynamics that result in differing levels of delinquent involvement among young women and men within and across different group types (Peterson et al. 2001). Furthermore, the media often presents gang membership as a lifetime commitment. Finn's earliest work with David Huizinga (Esbensen and Huizinga 1993), along with work by Thornberry et al. (1993), helped to dispel this belief, offering evidence that most youth stayed in a gang for only about one to two years. This finding has now been supported across several longitudinal datasets, including both G.R.E.A.T. I and G.R.E.A.T. II, as well as the Gang Desistance Study.

Another common belief about gangs and gang members perpetuated by the media is that they are primarily focused on violent and drug-dealing behaviors. While this myth has been famously challenged by Malcolm Klein (1995), who stated "it's a boring life; the only thing that is equally boring is being a researcher watching gang members" (11), Finn's work has also contributed to our understanding of the activities of gang members. While finding that gangs and their members do participate in more delinquent and violent behavior, his work extended previously established conversations (such as by qualitative gang researchers) about the types of activities that gang members partake in by establishing that gang members participate in a variety of both criminal and non-criminal behaviors (Esbensen and Huizinga 1993; Esbensen et al. 1993; Esbensen and Winfree 1998).

Mentorship and Collaborations: Contributions to Future Generations of Scholarship

The central thread throughout Finn's entire career has been his dedication to colleagues and mentorship. Finn's contribution to research is evident, but his numerous publications and presentations in collaboration with students and colleagues tells another story. It is the story of a remarkable person who brings out the best in those around him—students, junior faculty, and colleagues. While it is difficult to express the extent of Finn's mentorship, his guidance was and remains crucial to the success of many. For one of the co-authors, Adrienne Freng, Finn provided the opportunity to develop as a scholar by hiring her to work on the national evaluation of the G.R.E.A.T. program after she had lost three advisers during her graduate career. Another co-author, Dana Peterson, began working on G.R.E.A.T. I as a master's student under Tom Winfree at New Mexico State University and was recruited by Finn to UNO for a PhD and to take on a central role on the evaluation that set the stage for a career she could never have imagined for herself. Through these positions, Finn successfully melded research and mentoring by providing opportunities to acquire the methodological and writing skills necessary for a career in academia. This resulted from the collaborative environment created by Finn, including those working on the project but also other professionals in the field. This interaction with professionals, as well as practitioners, was exemplified in the program review for G.R.E.A.T. I in which he included students in the process of communication with practitioners and reviewing and revising the curriculum. These are just a few examples of the support that Finn has extended selflessly over the years to others. There are many others who have benefited from working or interacting with Finn over the years—both directly and indirectly, as is seen, for example, in his vast co-author network (see Figure 33.1).

Finn is one of those people that make you wonder how he gets everything done and does it so well. He is always available, willing to help, and his advice is invaluable. He pushes his colleagues to excel, while also providing the tools with which to succeed. Finn also believes that the education and research enterprise occurs outside the university walls. As such, over the years, he involved numerous students in all aspects of his many research projects to provide a "hands on" experience in the field.[7] However, this was not without the recognition that one must model the behaviors that make one successful for others to follow. He led by example through actively engaging in data collection trips, conducting G.R.E.A.T. officer training and classroom observations, as well as administering student surveys. He

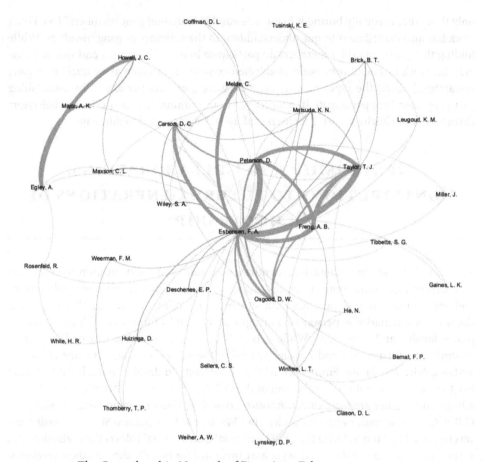

FIGURE 33.1 The Co-authorship Network of Finn-Aage Esbensen

was never "above" getting his "hands dirty" or putting in the hard work to ensure that his mentees learned the skills they would need to succeed.

Being mentored by Finn is certainly not "all work and no play." Throughout his career, Finn has funded travel for countless graduate students to attend professional conferences and workshops across the United States and Europe, which has helped break down hierarchical barriers between graduate students and faculty and provided invaluable training and networking opportunities for students. He has also organized study-abroad trips through which students were able to learn firsthand about criminal justice systems in Europe. In addition, Finn is famous for his more informal mentoring moments, which present themselves during a run or walk and then over a beer or a shot of Akvavit (a traditional Danish spirit). Those who have spent much of their career with Finn come to know him as a mentor, a boss, a colleague, and above all else, a friend.

Finn's commitment to collaborations extends beyond his colleagues to reaching practitioners and policymakers. Throughout the duration of G.R.E.A.T. I and II, he and his team worked closely with stakeholders to create technical reports that presented aggregate information from the collected data on several key issues, including reports to the schools on students' behavioral and risk outcomes, as well as the views of school personnel and law enforcement. Perhaps most importantly, Finn has worked diligently to make cutting-edge research on youth violence and gangs accessible to practitioners working on the frontlines with youth, asserting that "it's important to bring the research and the knowledge to people who can perhaps most benefit, and that's the folks who are actually working with the kids" (Esbensen 2019). For instance, Finn served for years on the advisory board for the Boys and Girls Clubs of America (BGCA). In this role, he translated the latest academic research to shape BGCA's approaches to gang prevention, intervention, and re-entry; guided them toward scientific evaluations of their efforts; and helped plan their annual conference and semi-annual National Youth Gang Symposia co-sponsored by OJJPD (both attended largely by practitioners), as well as presented papers on panels and conducted workshops at these events.

Finn continued this tradition on a larger scale at UMSL with the E. Desmond Lee Collaborative Vision–sponsored annual Youth Violence Prevention Conference. This single-day conference targeted practitioners in the St. Louis area who came to learn about the latest research surrounding youth violence. The university also offered continuing education credits to those practitioners who attended, which usually numbered approximately 200 a year. Through 18 years of the conference, Finn brought in some of the most famous names in violence research, including Robert Crutchfield, Darnell Hawkins, Denise Gottfredson, Andrew Papachristos, and Nancy Rodriguez. Additionally, Finn often invited practitioners as speakers working on the frontlines of America's biggest cities such as Candice Kane who was, at the time, chief operating officer of the Chicago Project on Violence Prevention (now Cure Violence).

Conclusion

In closing, we hope that this chapter has given readers a glimpse at the size and scope of the contributions Finn has made throughout his career. Overall, his collective body of work illustrates Finn's commitment to producing rigorous work that (1) has a large impact on knowledge and (2) is helpful to practitioners, as well as academics. While we focused on his research in the areas of gang prevention, measurement, and comparative research, his work has spanned the much broader areas of youth violence, school safety, and evaluation methodology. There is no doubt that there are many more stories and anecdotes that could be told by other long-time friends and colleagues. One thing is evident: Finn's contributions to gang research are vast, but they are small in comparison to his impact on his mentees, colleagues, and all those important to him. So as Finn is famous for saying—onward and upward!

Acknowledgments

The authors thank Finn-Aage Esbensen, David Huizinga, and Jason Gravel for their contributions to this chapter.

Notes

1. Pronounced Finn-"oo-weh," or you can simply call him Finn.
2. Finn's wife shares a first name with one of the authors, Dana Peterson. To avoid confusion, Finn's wife was often referred to as D1 and Dana Peterson as D2, nicknames that have stuck to this day.
3. The emphasis on quantitative gang research has continued beyond this funding stream with the Seattle Social Development Project, National Longitudinal Survey of Youth, Pathways to Desistance, and the National Longitudinal Survey of Adolescent to Adult Health, all including self-report measures of gang involvement (see Pyrooz and Mitchell 2015 for more detail on this topic).
4. This G.R.E.A.T.est story and Finn's significant contributions may not have occurred if not for Finn's daily newspaper-reading habit. As described by Finn in a November 14, 2019, interview for the Oral History of Criminology Project (OHCP), Finn had submitted a couple of unsuccessful grant proposals in his first couple years at UNO and had not yet been a principal investigator on a grant, but "one day in spring of '94, I was reading the local paper and there was a picture of a cop in a classroom and it said the cop was teaching 'G.R.E.A.T.' ... I read it [the article] and (thought) 'Well this is fortuitous': Dave Huizinga and I had just published two articles on gangs ... and here's the local police department experimenting with a new program; maybe they'd like a local evaluation done" (Esbensen 2019). Finn contacted the local police department, which was interested, and also reached out to the National Institute of Justice to see if there was any money for a small supplemental grant—only to discover that they were drafting an RFP for a national evaluation of the G.R.E.A.T. program. The rest is history.
5. These numbers were drawn from the ICPSR website in May 2022 and are, therefore, dependent on the information recorded by ICPSR. Readers should be aware that there may be inaccuracies in this information, especially with regard to the "other academic scholarship" category.
6. In his OHCP interview, Finn described that when he relayed to the G.R.E.A.T. National Policy Board at a meeting in Salt Lake City that the evaluation found no program effect, "John Magaw, the director of ATF and head of the G.R.E.A.T. program, just sort of put his hands down and said, 'Well if it's not working, what do we do to fix it?'" That meeting led to a five-year process of program overhaul, and Finn reflected that not only was it rewarding to have had that impact, it was a good illustration that "evaluators can work collaboratively with the program people" (Esbensen, 2019). Of course, these relationships take time to cultivate: "In starting up the project, there was some ambivalence, I think, on the part of the G.R.E.A.T. folks, because they were federal law enforcement agencies and local law enforcement agencies and here they are working with this long-haired hippy dude from Nebraska."
7. Finn explains: "My orientation toward mentoring is to treat grad students and young scholars the same way I was treated and that is 'this is what we need to do, get it done, and if we need to talk about it, we'll talk about it' ... Take it and run, make it yours. That's what I've always tried to do with grad students, not treat them as students, but treat them as colleagues. And by doing that, I think there's also the advantage they really buy into the project as opposed to just working on the project; it becomes their project, and I think that really enhances the quality of the product as well as the quality of the experience" (Esbensen 2019).

References

Browning, Katharine, David Huizinga, Rolf Loeber, and Terence P. Thornberry. 1999. *Causes and Correlates of Delinquency Program*. Washington, DC: U.S. Department of Justice, Office of Juvenile Justice and Delinquency Prevention.

Carson, Dena C. 2018. "Examining Racial and Ethnic Variations in Reasons for Leaving a Youth Gang." *Journal of Developmental and Life-Course Criminology* 4: 449–472. https://doi.org/10.1007/s40865-018-0091-z.

Carson, Dena C., and Finn-Aage Esbensen. 2016. "Motivations for Leaving: A Qualitative Comparison of Leaving Processes across Gang Definition." In *Gang Transitions and Transformations in an International Context*, edited by Cheryl L. Maxson and Finn-Aage Esbensen, 139–155. New York: Springer.

Carson, Dena C., Dana Peterson, and Finn-Aage Esbensen. 2013. "Youth Gang Desistance: An Examination of the Effect of Different Operational Definitions of Desistance on the Motivations, Methods, and Consequences Associated with Leaving the Gang." *Criminal Justice Review* 38: 510–534. https://doi.org/10.1177/0734016813511634.

Cohen, Albert K. 1955. *Delinquent Boys: The Culture of the Gang*. Glencoe, IL: The Free Press.

Deschenes, Elizabeth P., and Finn-Aage Esbensen. 1999. "Violence and Gangs: Gender Differences in Perceptions and Behavior." *Journal of Quantitative Criminology* 15: 63–96. https://doi.org/10.1023/A:1007552105190.

Esbensen, Finn-Aage. 2015. "The Gang Resistance Education and Training (G.R.E.A.T.) Program: An Evaluator's Perspective." In *The Handbook of Gangs*, edited by Scott H. Decker and David C. Pyrooz, 369–391. Chichester, UK: Wiley.

Esbensen, Finn-Aage. 2019. "Interview with Finn-Aage Esbensen." Interview by Dana Peterson. November 14. Video. https://www.criminologystories.com/.

Esbensen, Finn-Aage, and Elizabeth P. Deschenes. 1998. "A Mulitsite Examination of Youth Gang Membership: Does Gender Matter?" *Criminology* 36: 799–828. https://doi.org/10.1111/j.1745-9125.1998.tb01266.x.

Esbensen, Finn-Aage, Elizabeth P. Deschenes, and L. Thomas Winfree Jr. 1999. "Differences between Gang Girls and Gang Boys: Results from a Multi-Site Study." *Youth & Society* 31: 27–53. https://doi.org/10.1177/0044118X99031001002.

Esbensen, Finn-Aage, Adrienne Freng, Terrance J. Taylor, Dana Peterson, and D. Wayne Osgood. 2002. "Putting Research into Practice: The National Evaluation of the Gang Resistance Education and Training (G.R.E.A.T.) Program." In *Responding to Gangs: Evaluation and Research*, edited by Winifred L. Reed and Scott H. Decker, 139–167. Washington, DC: U.S. Department of Justice, National Institute of Justice.

Esbensen, Finn-Aage, and David Huizinga. 1993. "Gangs, Drugs, and Delinquency in a Survey of Urban Youth." *Criminology* 31: 565–589. https://doi.org/10.1111/j.1745-9125.1993.tb01142.x.

Esbensen, Finn-Aage, David Huizinga, and Anne W. Weiher. 1993. "Gang and Non-Gang Youth: Differences in Explanatory Factors." *Journal of Contemporary Criminal Justice* 9: 94–116. https://doi.org/10.1177/104398629300900203.

Esbensen, Finn-Aage, and Cheryl Maxson. 2012. *Youth Gangs in International Perspective: Results from the Eurogang Program of Research*. New York: Springer.

Esbensen, Finn-Aage, Chris Melde, Terrance J. Taylor, and Dana Peterson. 2008. "Active Parental Consent in School-Based Research: How Much Is Enough and How Do We Get It?" *Evaluation Review* 32: 335–362. https://doi.org/10.1177/0193841X08315175.

Esbensen, Finn-Aage, D. Wayne Osgood, Dana Peterson, Terrance J. Taylor, and Dena C. Carson. 2013. "Short- and Long-Term Outcome Results from a Multisite Evaluation of The G.R.E.A.T. Program." *Criminology & Public Policy* 12: 375–411. https://doi.org/10.1111/1745-9133.12048.

Esbensen, Finn-Aage, D. Wayne Osgood, Terrance J. Taylor, Dana Peterson, and Adrienne Freng. 2001. "How Great is G.R.E.A.T.? Results From a Quasi-Experimental Design." *Criminology & Public Policy* 1: 87–118. https://doi.org/10.1111/j.1745-9133.2001.tb00078.x.

Esbensen, Finn-Aage, Dana Peterson, Terrance J. Taylor, Adrienne Freng, D. Wayne Osgood, Dena C. Carson, and Kristy N. Matsuda. 2011. "Evaluation and Evolution of the Gang Resistance Education and Training (G.R.E.A.T.) Program." *Journal of School Violence* 10: 53–70. https://doi.org/10.1080/15388220.2010.519374.

Esbensen, Finn-Aage, Dana Peterson, Terrance J. Taylor, and D. Wayne Osgood. 2012. "Results from a Multi-Site Evaluation of the G.R.E.A.T. Program." *Justice Quarterly* 29: 125–151. https://doi.org/10.1080/07418825.2011.585995.

Esbensen, Finn-Aage, and Dana Peterson Lynskey, 2001. "Young Gang Members in a School Survey." In *The Eurogang Paradox: Street Gangs and Youth Groups in the U.S. and Europe*, edited by Malcolm W. Klein, Hanz-Jurgen Kerner, Cheryl L. Maxson and Elmar G.M. Weitekamp, 93–114. Dordrecht, The Netherlands: Kluwer Academic Publishers.

Esbensen, Finn-Aage, and Frank M. Weerman. 2005. "Youth Gangs and Troublesome Youth Groups in the United States and the Netherlands: A Cross-National Comparison." *European Journal of Criminology* 2: 5–37.

Esbensen, Finn-Aage, and L. Thomas Winfree Jr. 1998. "Race and Gender Differences between Gang and Nongang Youths: Results from a Multisite Survey." *Justice Quarterly* 15: 505–526. https://doi.org/10.1080/07418829800093861.

Esbensen, Finn-Aage, L. Thomas Winfree Jr., Ni He, and Terrance J. Taylor. 2001. "Youth Gangs and Definitional Issues: When Is a Gang a Gang and Why Does It Matter?" *Crime & Delinquency* 47: 105–130. https://doi.org/doi.org/10.1177/0011128701047001005.

Freng, Adrienne, and Finn-Aage Esbensen. 2007. "Race and Gang Affiliation: An Examination of Multiple Marginality." *Justice Quarterly* 24: 600–628. https://doi.org/10.1080/07418820701717136.

Hagedorn, John M. 1988. *People and Folks: Gangs, Crime, and the Underclass in a Rustbelt City*. Chicago, IL: Lakeview Press.

Klein, Malcolm W. 1995. *The American Gang*. New York: Oxford University Press.

Klein, Malcolm, Hanz-Jurgen Kerner, Cheryl L. Maxson, and Elmar G.M. Weitekamp, eds. 2001. In *The Eurogang Paradox: Street Gangs and Youth Groups in the U.S. and Europe*. Dordecht, the Netherlands: Kluwer.

Matsuda, Kristy N., Finn-Aage Esbensen, and Dena C. Carson. 2012. "Putting the 'Gang' in 'Eurogang' Characteristics of Delinquent Youth Groups by Definitional Approaches." In *Youth Gangs in International Perspective: Results from the Eurogang Program of Research*, edited by Finn-Aage Esbensen and Cheryl L. Maxson, 17–34. New York: Springer.

Maxson, Cheryl L., and Finn-Aage Esbensen, eds. 2016. *Gang Transitions and Transformations in an International Context*. New York: Springer.

Melde, Chris, and Finn-Aage Esbensen. 2014. "The Relative Impact of Gang Status Transitions: Identifying the Mechanisms of Change in Delinquency." *Journal of Research in Crime and Delinquency* 51: 349–376. https://doi.org/10.1177/0022427813507059.

Melde, Chris, Finn-Aage Esbensen, and Dena C. Carson. 2016. "Gang Membership and Involvement in Violence among U.S. Adolescents: A Test of Construct Validity." In *Gang Transitions and Transformations in an International Context*, edited by Cheryl L. Maxson and Finn-Aage Esbensen, 33–50. New York: Springer.

Melde, Chris, Finn-Aage Esbensen, and Karen Tusinski. 2006. "Addressing Program Fidelity Using Onsite Observations and Program Provider Descriptions of Program Delivery." *Evaluation Review* 30 (6): 714–740. https://doi.org/10.1177/0193841X06293412.

Miller, Walter B. 1958. "Lower Class Culture as a Generating Milieu of Gang Delinquency." *Journal of Social Issues* 14: 5–19.

Moore, Joan W. 1978. *Homeboys: Gangs, Drugs, and Prison in Barrios of Los Angeles.* Philadelphia, PA: Temple University Press.

Peterson, Dana, and Dena C. Carson. 2012. "The Sex Composition of Groups and Youths' Delinquency: A Comparison of Gang and Nongang Peer Groups." In *Youth Gangs in International Perspective: Results from the Eurogang Program of Research*, edited by Finn-Aage Esbensen and Cheryl Maxson, 189–210. New York: Springer.

Peterson, Dana, Jody Miller, and Finn-Aage Esbensen. 2001. "The Impact of Sex Composition on Gangs and Gang Member Delinquency." *Criminology* 39: 411–440. https://doi.org/10.1111/j.1745-9125.2001.tb00928.x.

Pyrooz, David C., and Meghan M. Mitchell. 2015. "Little Gang Research, Big Gang Research." In *The Handbook of Gangs*, edited by Scott H. Decker and David C. Pyrooz, 28–58. Chichester, UK: John Wiley & Sons, Inc.

Short, James F., and Fred L. Strodtbeck. 1965. *Group Processes and Gang Delinquency.* Chicago, IL: University of Chicago Press.

Thornberry, Terence P., David Huizinga, and Rolf Loeber. 2004. "The Causes and Correlates Studies: Findings and Policy Implications." *Juvenile Justice* 9: 3–19.

Thornberry, Terence P., Marvin D. Krohn, Alan J. Lizotte, and D. Chad-Wiersham. 1993. "The Role of Juvenile Gangs in Facilitating Delinquent Behavior." *Journal of Research in Crime and Delinquency* 30: 55–87. https://doi.org/10.1177/0022427893030001005.

Thrasher, Frederick M. 1927. *The Gang: A Study of 1,313 Groups in Chicago.* Chicago, IL: University of Chicago Press.

Vecchio, J. Michael. 2014. "The Role of Violence within and across Self-Identified Gang Youth." PhD Dissertation, University of Missouri-St. Louis.

Vecchio, J. Michael, and Dena C. Carson. (2022). "Understanding the Role of Violence and Conflict in the Stages of Gang Membership." *Youth Violence and Juvenile Justice* 21 (1): 27–43.

Vigil, James Diego. 1988. *Barrio Gangs: Street Life and Identity in Southern California.* Austin: University of Texas Press.

Weerman, Frank M., Cheryl Maxson, Finn-Aage Esbensen, Judith Aldridge, Juanjo Medina, and Frank van Gemert. 2009. *Eurogang Program Manual: Background, Development, and Use of the Eurogang Instruments in Multi-Site, Multi-Method Comparative Research.* St. Louis: University of Missouri.

CHAPTER 34

THE LEGACY OF JOHN M. HAGEDORN

ROBERTO R. ASPHOLM

"You should read this book," my then-girlfriend told me back during our years as undergraduate students. "I think you'd really like it." The book in question was *People and Folks: Gangs, Crime and the Underclass in a Rustbelt City*, which she was reading for a criminology course on street gangs. Given many of my friendships and experiences, as well as my pursuit of a career in social work, she sensed that I would find the book's humane portrayal of young men discarded and denigrated by society to be insightful and resonant. She was right. I tore through the book in a few short days, despite my own full-time course load and part-time job. After marking it up with underlining and comments in the margins, my now-wife demanded that I buy her a new copy; I happily obliged. So began my odyssey into the remarkable work of John M. Hagedorn.

John was a relative latecomer to the academy, completing his bachelor's degree at age 37 and beginning his first faculty job at age 49. In fact, he published *People and Folks*, his first book and a watershed moment in gang research, in 1988, just as he was beginning coursework in his doctoral program. The early decades of John's adulthood, explored in the early sections of this chapter, however, are no mere digression from his academic career. Rather, those formative experiences shaped the substance and trajectory of his career, and an appreciation of those exploits is essential to making sense of John's singular contributions to the field of gang research. Moreover, because those experiences meant that his academic career started in his middle age, they make those contributions all the more extraordinary.

Indeed, while John's impact on gang scholarship has been singular in the sense of its distinction, it has been anything but singular in the sense of its scope. In revisiting John's oeuvre in preparing this chapter and attempting to organize his contributions into coherent themes, it struck me that most scholars would likely consider making a single notable impression in their field to be the mark of a successful and meaningful career; by my count, John has made at least *five* such impressions. The raw numbers, while impressive—five books authored (one with a second edition), two books edited or coedited, some three dozen journal articles and book chapters published, a dozen major reports written, thousands of citations of his work in the scholarship of others—only hint at his impact. The breadth of his scholarly output and influence are without clear parallel in the field of gang research.

A major factor in the range and brilliance of John's work has been his ever-evolving and ever-expanding defiance of disciplinary orthodoxies. While most gang researchers are content to operate within the relatively narrow confines of conventional criminology, occasionally incorporating ideas from related disciplines, John's career has been defined by a steady march away from criminological provincialism and traditionalist doctrines. "Theory isn't something you believe in—that's religion!" he tells me. "Theory is something you use to understand social problems."[1] John credits his mentor in the academy, Joan W. Moore, for instilling in him the lesson that "if the facts don't fit the theory, change the theory," a dictum clearly embedded in his own slogan, "research, not stereotypes." A commitment to these values has meant that John's scholarship has explored not only traditional domains of gang research like neighborhood dynamics, collective violence, and the underground economy, but also much broader matters of racial and gender dynamics, political economy, urban history, globalization, social movements, organized crime, police and political corruption, courtroom processes, and social psychology. In short, his research has followed where the facts have led him—and the facts have led him to empirical and theoretical places that few criminologists have dared to venture.

This critical, inductive approach will be apparent to anyone familiar with John's work and to any reader of the pages that follow. After two sections describing his upbringing, early decades of adulthood, and transition into academia, the remainder of this chapter will examine John's various contributions to gang research in thematic and roughly chronological order, before concluding with some major takeaways to be gleaned from his remarkable career.

The Making of an Organizer

John Martin Hagedorn was born on July 30, 1947, in Milwaukee, Wisconsin. His great-grandparents had fled Germany in the 1870s, as Prussian chancellor Otto von Bismarck was ramping up a series of imperial wars. They made their way to the United States and settled in a German-American farming community in northern Wisconsin. John's grandparents, in turn, all migrated south to Milwaukee as young adults seeking work in the city's booming factories, and his parents, George Hagedorn and Ferne Koeppen, were born, raised, and married in the "Cream City." When John was four, George's job with the Hansen Glove Corporation was relocated to Clintonville, a town of 4,600 residents located 130 miles north of Milwaukee, and the Hagedorns followed suit. John grew up in Clintonville, though his family, staunch Democrats aligned with Milwaukee's socialist-dominated city government, were not particularly popular in the county adjacent to Joseph McCarthy's hometown; they returned to Milwaukee nearly every weekend to visit extended family. John's paternal grandfather maintained the family residence on Palmer Street, in what had become the heart of Milwaukee's north side ghetto, and John regularly played with Black kids in the neighborhood growing up. When he graduated high school in 1965, John returned to Milwaukee full time to attend the University of Wisconsin–Milwaukee (UWM).

In his most recent book, John describes himself during his time at UWM as "just another sixties college student, being slowly drawn into the culture and practice of protest" (Hagedorn 2022, 47). His early experiences with Black playmates and the pull of the civil rights movement led John to participate in a series of marches on Milwaukee's white south side in 1967 in support of a municipal open-housing ordinance. "I just thought that Black people should be able to live anywhere they want," he says. "That just made sense to me." The first night of marching ended in a violent attack by a white mob of 13,000 near Kosciusko Park; the second night ended in the peaceable arrests of John and scores of other protesters early in their march. On the third night, Milwaukee police launched a pre-march assault that left John and many of his fellow protesters beaten, bloodied, and arrested. Indeed, John endured two separate beatings by police that night, from which he suffered a cracked skull and a broken hand—though he points out that a Black compatriot with whom he shared a police paddy wagon ride suffered an even more vicious pounding.

John identifies this experience as the most profound turning point in his life. He dropped out of school in the spring and began working full time for the Milwaukee Organizing Committee, a radical grassroots organization involved in the antiwar and civil rights movements. In the summer of 1968, he signed a public statement pledging to resist the Vietnam War draft and, along with the Milwaukee Fourteen, planned and carried out the public destruction of 10,000 Selective Service records in protest of the war.[2] He was indicted on two felony counts of federal conspiracy charges to which he eventually pled guilty and was, rather miraculously, sentenced to probation.[3]

John spent the next half decade working on various organizing projects with the Milwaukee Resistance and the National Welfare Rights Organization. In 1974, he left Milwaukee for Boston, where he spent five years as a labor and community organizer in a city roiling from a shrinking industrial economy, middle-class suburbanization, and the fallout engendered by the racist reaction of many white Bostonians to a court-ordered school desegregation plan. John returned to Milwaukee in 1979 and continued his labor and community organizing in the context of an increasingly fractured leftist landscape. "I was never really happy with the ideological politics of the movement," John tells me. "So when I came back here, there were all these competing little groups, and everybody had their own ideology. And everybody wanted to do their own thing." Through conversations with these groups, John succeeded in mitigating factional rivalries and establishing the Workers Center, a centralized apparatus for local organizing efforts around issues related to labor, education, and police brutality. "You've got all these views, but there's work to be done here," he says, describing his thinking and approach to organizing at the time. "Let's figure out our differences in the course of the work. It probably doesn't mean anything, in the course of the work. And mostly it didn't."

But conditions in Milwaukee, like many cities across the country, were rapidly deteriorating, as the city's once-vibrant manufacturing sector was being decimated by economic restructuring. Joblessness among Black and Latino youth was skyrocketing, and crime and violence were becoming major issues. In 1981, John took a job as an organizer with the Sherman Park Neighborhood Association, a racially transitioning area on Milwaukee's west side. Residents were concerned with increasing levels of crime in the community, and John started working with young people in the area and getting a sense of the landscape among the local street gangs. A couple years later, the Social Development Commission, a major local anti-poverty organization, secured funding from the state for a youth gang diversion program and hired John as the director. He spent the next few years working closely with Milwaukee's street gangs, building relationships with gang leaders, and mediating disputes on the streets. "I only hired former gang members," John says. "But the thing I did when I hired somebody is that the criterion was you couldn't work for me unless you were willing to work with the rival gang." The move "rankled feathers" with the community agency establishment, who had expected to fill those jobs with their hand-picked people. John, however, was unperturbed. It was not the first time he had rankled feathers, and it would not be the last.

THE MAKING OF A SCHOLAR

A major turning point came when John met Joan Moore, a professor of sociology and director of the former Urban Research Center at UWM, at a forum on gangs and crime organized by the City of Milwaukee in 1984. He had returned to UWM that year to finish his bachelor's degree in the school's community education program, which gave him credit for his organizing experience. Moore had spent more than a decade leading collaborative community research projects with Chicano gangs in the *barrios* of Los Angeles and encouraged John to initiate a formal study of what was happening in Milwaukee. They wrote a grant proposal to the Milwaukee Foundation and were awarded a small sum of $15,000 to carry out interviews with the city's gang leaders. John finished his bachelor's degree, ended his work with the Social Development Commission, enrolled in a master's program, and threw himself into the research. After completing the interviews, John wrote a draft of what would become *People and Folks* for his master's thesis. The paper was rejected by the criminology department for being "not quantitative enough," and he transferred to the sociology program under Moore's aegis, completing his master's degree in 1987.

The following year, at the behest of his friend Howard Fuller, John took a job with the Milwaukee County Department of Health and Human Services (DHHS). Fuller had just been hired as the director of DHHS by the new county executive, who John says wanted to "do something to make a name for himself." In turn, Fuller approached John and, appealing to his rabble-rousing instincts, made him an offer he could not refuse: "John, can you come in and shake it up?" While he planned to take his work with gangs to DHHS, John was convinced by trusted advisers that the child welfare department was in more urgent need of reform. He obliged, and his work in child welfare revealed a range of systemic failures, most notably a bureaucracy in which social workers spent their time in courtrooms and provided almost no actual services to families, and a constellation of public and private service providers located entirely outside of the communities they were charged with serving.

Meanwhile, John enrolled in the urban studies doctoral program at UWM. He wrote his dissertation on his experiences trying to reform the county's child welfare services, which became the basis of his second book, *Forsaking Our Children: Bureaucracy and Reform in the Child Welfare System* (Hagedorn 1995). John's recommendations for reforming the system included decentralizing the frontline work and moving it into the neighborhoods, forming neighborhood councils to create accountability to communities, and changing purchase-of-service policies to prioritize contracting with Black and Latino agencies that were based in those neighborhoods. By 1991, however, his job was eliminated. He was not surprised: "I had earned the hatred of the entire bureaucracy. There was nothing Howard could do about it."

That same year, he and Moore wrote and were awarded the first of two major grants from the National Institute on Drug Abuse (NIDA) to study patterns of drug dealing and drug use among Milwaukee gangs. These projects threw him back into his gang work in the afternoons and evenings, and he wrote his dissertation in the mornings. He completed his doctorate in 1993 and kept working on the NIDA projects. As the second grant was nearing its end in 1996, the Justice Department asked him to apply for a grant to explore gun trafficking. John was wary. His NIDA research had focused on framing drug dealing and drug abuse in economic and public health terms; the Justice Department, however, was interested in using research to inform the investigation and prosecution of gang members. "So I looked at that, and I said, well, why am I doing this work, you know?" John recalls. "I'm not doing this stuff to help people get arrested. Research, to me, is not intended to smooth the way for punitive bureaucracies."

He weighed his options with his partner, Mary, and they decided they didn't want to leave Milwaukee. A faculty job opened up in the criminology department at the University of Illinois at Chicago that would allow him to commute from Milwaukee. He applied, was offered the position, and accepted it. Dr. Hagedorn was going to the academy.

Before turning to his work in Chicago, however, the two sections that follow explore John's Milwaukee research in detail.

Gangs and Drugs in the Post-Industrial City

As described earlier in this chapter, John was an accomplished scholar at the outset of his doctoral studies in 1988. With a coauthor credit to Perry Macon, a founder and leader of the Milwaukee Vice Lords, John published *People and Folks: Gangs, Crime and the Underclass in a Rustbelt City* that same year (Hagedorn 1988).[4] With a handful of notable exceptions, including Ruth Horowitz's (1983) *Honor and the American Dream: Culture and Identity in a Chicano Community*, Malcolm W. Klein's (1971) *Street Gangs and Street Workers*, and Joan W. Moore's (1978) *Homeboys: Gangs, Drugs, and Prisons in the Barrios of Los Angeles*, research on street gangs had largely disappeared in the 1970s and 1980s after an intensive period of inquiry during the postwar decades. *People and Folks*, along with James Diego Vigil's (1988) *Barrio Gangs: Street Life and Identity in Southern California*, proved the opening salvo in a stunning resurgence of gang scholarship over the ensuing three-plus decades.

People and Folks documented the collapse of Milwaukee's industrial economy and the impact that collapse had on Latino and, especially, Black young men. The book was the first comprehensive study to situate gang dynamics within the context of post-1960s urban deindustrialization and drew heavily on University of Chicago sociologist William Julius Wilson's research on economic restructuring and concentrated poverty in Black inner-city communities.[5] The shift in Milwaukee's street gangs from rudimentary adolescent peer groups to more durable social formations, Hagedorn argued, had to be understood against the backdrop of skyrocketing joblessness and poverty in the city's dispossessed Black neighborhoods. The gang research of the interwar and postwar decades, insightful as it was, could not adequately speak to the dire circumstances taking shape in America's post-industrial urban core. Eminent social theorist Mike Davis (2008), in his foreword to one of John's later books, lauds *People and Folks* as "an essential guide to clear thinking about street culture and the wages of injustice" and rightly credits the book with "found[ing] what might be called 'critical gang studies'" (xv).

In the acknowledgements in *People and Folks*, Hagedorn (1988) writes that "it is the common hope of our respondents and the authors that this book might lead to changes in how gangs are viewed and what must be done" (xvi). Some three-and-a-half decades later, John is blunter with me about his early intentions, which he characterizes as "an unsuccessful tactic to get the government to produce more jobs," with *People and Folks* being an attempt to "advance my activism via research." The book also set out to challenge the then-popular narrative that gangs from Chicago had migrated to Milwaukee to "colonize" the city and establish new branches there, an updated "alien conspiracy" theory for the post-industrial Midwest. Though the symbols and lore of their Chicago counterparts certainly influenced collective identities and cultural expressions within Milwaukee's street gangs, John's research revealed that these groups had developed of their own accord. Their genesis and evolution owed to the prevailing conditions in Milwaukee's poor and working-class neighborhoods, not to whatever was happening on the streets of Chicago.

The first edition of *People and Folks* was written in the mid-1980s, just before Milwaukee's crack-cocaine trade exploded. While the book documented the early forays of the city's street gangs into the drug trade, in 1988 those efforts remained rather sporadic and unorganized. Through the NIDA studies, however, John continued to examine the evolution of the drug economy among Milwaukee gangs in the ensuing decade, documenting how jobless gang members turned to drug trafficking in staggering numbers and how gang organization and surging levels of gun violence were increasingly shaped by these economic enterprises (Hagedorn 1991, 1994a, 1994b, 1997). He was also witnessing and experiencing these developments firsthand: Perry Macon, his friend and *People and Folks* coauthor, spent most of the decade following the book's publication in prison on drug charges. John's research in Milwaukee culminated in 1998 with the concurrent publication of the second edition of *People and Folks* (Hagedorn 1998d), which explored the rise in drug trafficking and use among the city's gangs, his report on *The Business of Drug Dealing in Milwaukee* for the Wisconsin Policy Research Institute (Hagedorn 1998a), and his articles "Cocaine, Kicks, and Strain: Patterns of Substance Use in Milwaukee Gangs" (Hagedorn, Torres, and Giglio 1998) and "Gang Violence in the Postindustrial Era" (Hagedorn 1998c).

Frederick M. Thrasher's (1927) seminal interwar study, *The Gang: A Study of 1,313 Gangs in Chicago*, is considered the definitive work on street gangs in the industrial city; John's sweeping series of books and articles based on his research in Milwaukee should likewise be considered the definitive work on street gangs in the post-industrial city.[6] Indeed, John's insistence that street gangs must be understood not only within the context of their neighborhoods but also within the broader context of evolving sociohistorical and political-economic forces is perhaps the single most significant contribution of John's early work to the field of gang research. Another hallmark of his research that took shape during this period, however, may also have a reasonable claim to that distinction.

AGAINST ESSENTIALISM: VARIATION AMONG GANGS AND GANG MEMBERS

While much of John's research with Milwaukee gangs explored the differences between those groups and their forebears of the interwar and postwar periods—that is, variation according to sociohistorical circumstance—this research also explored variation among contemporaneous gangs and, especially, among their members. In his pioneering study, Thrasher (1927) had proclaimed that "no two gangs are just alike" (5). John's work in Milwaukee offered both a contemporary reminder of this dictum as well as an extension of its insight about gangs as collectives to gang members as individuals. These arguments cut strongly against the grain of public discourse during the late 1980s and 1990s, when crude stereotypes of gang members as amoral and irredeemable monsters were reaching a fever pitch and fueling both welfare state retrenchment and the carceral buildup.

John explored these variations primarily in a series of articles and book chapters published between 1994 and 1998. The first and most influential of these was "Homeboys, Dope Fiends, Legits, and New Jacks," which proffered the titular taxonomy of male adult gang members based on constellations of key characteristics, including orientation toward and participation in the conventional and underground economies, violent incidents, substance use, intimate relationships, and life aspirations (Hagedorn 1994a). This typology challenged both popular conceptions of gang members as ontologically committed to violence and criminality as well as more varied but similarly oversimplistic labels of members as "hardcore," "fringe," "wannabes," and the like. In fact, the research revealed that only the "new jacks," who made up less than a quarter of the 90 gang members in the study, approximated conventional stereotypes of gang members in their persistent pursuit of drug dealing as a career and relatively cavalier views regarding the use of violence. Crucially, the study was carried out with current and former gang leaders and other "hardcore" members—in other words, precisely those one might expect to be most committed to a "criminal subculture." John and his community researchers also found that many gang members "moved over time between categories, some had characteristics of more than one category, and others straddled the boundaries" (Hagedorn 1994a, 206). Gang members, in other words, were much more than one thing—and perhaps not all that different from anyone else.[7]

John also applied this lesson in expanding his research with female gang members, challenging the criminological presumption that street gangs are an exclusively (or near-exclusively) male phenomenon. The second NIDA grant that he and Moore secured in 1995 was for a study entitled the Homegirl Project, which focused on Milwaukee's female gang members. The fruits of this research included a chapter that Moore and Hagedorn (1998) published together on "What Happens to Girls in the Gang?" which offered a comparative perspective on female gang members based on Moore's longstanding research in Los Angeles and their joint research in Milwaukee. As with their male counterparts, they found tremendous variation among female gang members on a wide range of experiences and dispositions, exploding one-dimensional stereotypes of girls and young women in gangs as merely exploited sexual objects or hopelessly confused tomboys. "Fighting Female: The Social Construction of Female Gangs," a chapter that John coauthored with his partner, Mary L. Devitt, both expounded on these insights and extended them to the study of gangs as collectives, challenging the social science practice of defining female gangs in terms of their relationships to male gangs: While the latter are routinely classified based on a range of group characteristics and collective behaviors, Hagedorn and Devitt sardonically quip that "female gangs, however, are apparently best defined by whether or not they are tied to a male gang" (Hagedorn and Devitt 1999, 264). "Fighting Female" is also notable as a cornerstone chapter in the book *Female Gangs in America: Essays on Girls, Gangs and Gender* that John coedited with Meda Chesney-Lind, the only published edited volume on female gangs (Chesney-Lind and Hagedorn 1999). John's research with Milwaukee's female gang members was also prominently incorporated into the second edition of *People and Folks*, and he and Moore coauthored a widely cited Justice Department report on female gangs in 2001 (Moore and Hagedorn 2001).

The findings from these studies and the lessons gleaned from the collaborative method in which they were carried out had important and interrelated methodological, theoretical, and public policy implications. John explored the nexus of these issues in his 1996 article "The Emperor's New Clothes: Theory and Method in Gang Field Research" (Hagedorn 1996), in particular, how problematic research methods lead to distorted empirical findings and social theory that are wielded in support of draconian policing and criminal justice policies.[8] While rhetoric from law enforcement and elected officials, media imagery, and gang research were converging in their portrayal of street gangs as hyperviolent drug cartels and their members as callous super-predators, John's own research demonstrated that, in spite of the remarkable explosion of the crack-cocaine economy, the vast majority of gang members retained a rather conventional moral compass and remained committed to the pursuit of conventional employment.[9] Indeed, he pointed out, in a context of near-ubiquitous joblessness, even dealing drugs might be interpreted not as a rejection of conventional values but as an internalization of the values of hard work and success within a severely constricted opportunity structure (see, especially, Hagedorn 1994a, 1997).

The first edition of *People and Folks* had followed Wilson's (1987) work in emphasizing the rise of the urban "underclass" as a sui generis socioeconomic formation characterized by intensifying economic dislocation, racial segregation, and "social isolation," particularly among the Black urban poor. The implication of this view was that members of the underclass were qualitatively distinct from the rest of society. John's subsequent research in Milwaukee led him to reject this position—gang members were not really different from the rest of "us." Following his critical appraisal of interwar and postwar gang theory for the post-industrial era in the first edition of *People and Folks*, this represented the next step in John's questioning of popular orthodoxies. It would not be his last.

Gangs, Race, and History in the Global City

The NIDA projects ended in 1997, and John had taken a faculty job at the University of Illinois at Chicago the preceding year. While his relationships with his gang partners in Milwaukee continued, the locus of his research moved down I-94 to the Windy City. Nonetheless, he was aware that his path-breaking work in Milwaukee would not be easily replicated in Chicago. "You've got to look at the specifics: I lived in Milwaukee and commuted to Chicago," he tells me. "The notion that I could get involved with a neighborhood like you were doing and being into it, that was far-fetched. But what I could do is be a historian." While John's work undoubtedly took a more intentional historical turn in Chicago, this modest assessment in no way captures the dynamic trajectory of his scholarly output over the last two-plus decades.

The first major body of work from John's research in Chicago emerged out of two simultaneous pursuits: deepening historical analysis and broadening political-economic analysis. The first of these was sparked by his work with Bobby Gore and other Vice Lords leaders to document the remarkable transformation of the Conservative Vice Lords during the late 1960s and early 1970s from among the city's most infamous street gangs to a successful prosocial community organization. John learned that Chicago Mayor Richard J. Daley, the former president of the Hamburgs, a notoriously racist Irish gang, had declared "war on gangs" in 1969 and had Gore, the most progressive gang leader in the city, railroaded for murder. How could gang involvement lead to the halls of municipal power for Daley and his Hamburg friends and to prison and death for Gore and his Vice Lords comrades? The history of Chicago's street gangs, organized crime, political machines, and patterns of immigrant and migrant settlement suggested that the main difference shaping these divergent trajectories—and the trajectories of the city's ethnic and racial groups more generally—was race: The Hamburgs were white, and the Vice Lords were Black. "Was the struggle inside the Vice Lords settled?" John asks. "No. But Daley settled it by jailing Bobby. Then there was no opposition to going full-scale into the drug trade." John explored these dynamics in his article "Race Not Space: A Revisionist History of Gangs in Chicago," which issued a direct challenge to the Chicago School of Sociology's emphasis on neighborhood ecology as the defining variable shaping patterns of crime and violence and quality of life in urban communities (Hagedorn 2006).[10]

At the same time, the scope of John's work was quickly spreading from the ghettos of the Midwestern rustbelt to the slums of the developing world. As early as 2001, his work was beginning to grapple with issues of gangs, violence, and inequality on a global scale, and he was traveling and making connections via courses, conferences, and research initiatives the world over—Belfast, Pretoria, Oslo, London, Rio de Janeiro, Frankfurt, Mombasa, Copenhagen, Glasgow.[11] Yet it was his participation in the 10-nation study *Neither War nor Peace: International Comparisons of Children and Youth in Organised Armed Violence* that most decisively pushed him in the direction of globalization (Hagedorn 2005b).

Indeed, urban deindustrialization in the United States—the effects of which John had documented so brilliantly in his Milwaukee research—did not occur in a vacuum: Many of the jobs that disappeared from US cities eventually re-emerged, in severely impoverished forms, in the developing world, spurring unprecedented urbanization and slum proliferation. Similarly, the near-wholesale demolition of public housing in Chicago—which John found to be a key variable in understanding gang organization and patterns of violence—was best understood against the broader re-emergence of cities as essential nodes of global capitalism and related efforts to render those cities safe for business via displacement and redevelopment projects (Hagedorn and Rauch 2007). John's widely cited 2005 article "The Global Impact of Gangs" effectively summarizes the sweeping scope of his analytic lens, which included the ways in which global urbanization creates conditions for gang emergence; how the retreat of the state engendered by neoliberalism and the attendant expansion of the underground economy create openings for armed non-state actors to contest for power; how identities become sources of resistance to dehumanization among the dispossessed; and how gangs often become embedded, or institutionalized, in communities confronting these dynamics (Hagedorn, 2005a).

John's research on the nexuses of gangs, race, and globalization produced a number of additional publications, including *Gangs in the Global City: Alternatives to Traditional Criminology* (Hagedorn 2007), a volume that he edited and to which he contributed an introduction and two chapters (see also Fraser and Hagedorn 2018; Hagedorn 2015a). This research program culminated in his 2008 tour de force, *A World of Gangs: Armed Young Men and Gangsta Culture*, arguably his most forceful critique of conventional criminology and an expansive articulation of an empirical and theoretical alternative. Where criminologists presumed US-style street gangs were a sui generis phenomenon, John pointed out that they were but one variation in a much broader constellation of groups of armed young men throughout the world; where they obsessed over creating a universal definition for street gangs, he argued that gangs embodied a range of divergent purposes and pursuits that often evolved with changing historical circumstances; where they ignored tectonic changes in the global social order and reified political economy, he called for interrogation of how these dynamics shaped social and economic dislocation and outlaw groups like street gangs; where they ignored matters of racism and identity, he brought them back into the center of the analysis.

The proliferation of prisons, the underground drug economy, and defensible spaces in urban slums, John argued, were creating institutionalized gangs in dispossessed urban districts the world over, particularly those inhabited by denigrated racial and ethnic groups. Globalization and the concomitant retreat of the state had rendered these sacrifice zones expendable and their residents redundant. Gangs in the twenty-first century could not be understood outside of this context—nor outside of the additional contexts to which John would soon turn his analysis.

Gangs, Organized Crime, Corruption, and Social Institutions

John's dive into Chicago's history had familiarized him with the intricacies of the city's street gangs and ethnic communities, the Democratic political machine, and the Outfit, Chicago's mafia organization. Though *A World of Gangs* made the persuasive case that distinctions between armed groups operating outside the law—street gangs, prison gangs, cartels, ethnic militias, and the like—were not always neat, John's oeuvre had consistently demonstrated that, despite much media hype and bluster from public officials to the contrary, US street gangs and organized crime were largely distinct phenomena. A chance exchange with a former student and subsequent interviews with "Sal Martino," an Outfit functionary, however, illuminated new dimensions of Chicago's storied history of gangs and organized crime that changed John's perspective. "Most gang kids have always been desperate youth, and most of their gangs are indeed 'disorganized crime.' But not all," he writes in the introduction to *The In$ane Chicago Way: The Daring Plan by Chicago Gangs* *to Create a Spanish Mafia*. "This [book] is a history of the puppeteers, not the puppets" (Hagedorn 2015b, 8).

The In$ane Chicago Way recounts the history of Spanish Growth and Development (SGD), a coalition of Latino gangs whose leaders attempted and failed to form a Commission-style syndicate to organize crime and regulate violence during the 1990s. With Black and Latino gangs controlling neighborhood-level drug dealing and other criminal endeavors throughout much of Chicago, the Outfit discreetly encouraged the development of SGD, aiming to claim a piece of the action. They did this through Martino and the C-Note$, an Outfit "minor league" team for whom Martino served as adviser, one of the few remaining predominantly white gangs in the city and a member of the SGD coalition. Hagedorn documents the involvement of the Outfit, the C-Note$, and various Latino gangs in assorted forms of political and police corruption and describes the workings of this corruption within those public institutions. Police corruption both made the criminal ventures of these groups possible—"Without the cops, none of this stuff could happen," one Outfit blueblood tells Hagedorn—and undermined the delicate alliances within SGD via robberies, rip-offs, betrayals, and romantic entanglements. Gang leaders were ultimately unable to overcome conflicting interests, factionalism, and escalating street wars, and the confederation collapsed.

John was especially well situated to make sense of this history. Aside from his then–three decades of community work, legal consultation, and collaborative research with street gangs, he had also spent years working in and studying the Milwaukee County Department of Health and Human Services and was the lead author of a 2013 report on corruption within the Chicago Police Department (Hagedorn et al. 2013). He was able to apply his understanding of institutional dynamics and dysfunction to make sense of the workings and ultimate demise of SGD. Of equal importance, he convincingly argued that researchers must recognize that the institutions of social control with which gangs interact—in this case, law enforcement and elected officials—are as capable of fueling problems of crime and violence as they are of mitigating them.

In his subsequent article on "Gangs, Schools, and Social Change: An Institutional Analysis," (Hagedorn 2017) John brought this same analytic lens to bear on the interplay between street gangs and public schools. Recounting some 35 years of involvement with gangs and public schools, he describes the disastrous effects of various educational policies—misguided integration efforts, mass school closures, charterization—on gang members and other marginalized Black youth, who are then blamed and demonized for the ensuing failures of those policies. This, he notes, is indicative of a broader dynamic in which street gangs are not only affected by neighborhood conditions but also "by extraneighborhood institutional processes, for example, correctional, housing, and policing policies, and the racist segregation practices of city hall" (Hagedorn 2017, 196). The common scholarly presumption that gangs exist and operate in a vacuum of neighborhoods or, even more myopically, a vacuum of group processes, John demonstrates, is completely upended when examining these phenomena in concrete time and space.

Turning from police, politicians, and schools, the final chapter of John's career saw him set his analytic sights on another institution of social control, the courts, to explore how stereotypes about gang members compromise the administration of justice—and what this says about and has to do with all of us.

"THEM" AND "US": FIGHTING GANG STEREOTYPES

Among the hallmarks of John's research has been its spirited and empirically grounded challenges to stereotypes about street gangs and the official narratives so commonly built upon those misconceptions—a commitment distilled in his motto, "research, not stereotypes." Indeed, *People and Folks*, his very first published work, was written in large part to combat the myths that Chicago gangs were invading and colonizing Milwaukee and other Midwestern cities and that these groups were primarily a crime problem and law enforcement issue. The ensuing decades produced no shortage of stereotypes and false narratives to counter, and John responded ably, as the foregoing sections describe. His 2014 book chapter "America's 'War on Gangs': Response to a Real Threat or a Moral Panic?" offers an overview of how media sensationalism, law-and-order rhetoric, and punitive public policy have converged over the last half century to socially construct gang members as a racialized urban menace (Hagedorn and Chesney-Lind 2014). Indeed, John had seen these dynamics up close firsthand: Beyond his decades of frontline community work, collaborative research, and scholarship with gang members, he had also served as an expert witness in 83 court cases involving actual or alleged gang members, stretching from 1995 through and beyond his retirement from the University of Illinois at Chicago in 2018. And there is perhaps no place where stereotypes of gang members as wanton super-predators are more fervently proselytized and their pernicious ramifications more acutely experienced than in criminal courtrooms where real or alleged gang members are standing trial for murder (Hayat 2019; Howell 2019). "It was a natural step from combating the law enforcement frame academically to combating it in the courtroom," John explains. "From theory to practice."

In 2012, he coauthored a law review article on "Breaking the Frame: Responding to Gang Stereotyping" that drew on much of his expert witness experience (Hagedorn and MacLean 2012). The article provides an overview and an in-depth case study of how gang stereotypes play out in court, the social-psychological processes that shape jurors' perceptions, and strategies that defense attorneys and expert witnesses might employ to combat these stereotypes and perceptions. In particular, John and his coauthor argue that, in addition to presenting jurors with discrepant information based on empirical research and a frame within which they might assemble that information, "it is also important for the defense to explicitly present expert testimony on the nature of stereotyping itself." New facts may not be enough to break jurors' existing stereotypical frames of gang members, and new frames may be rejected out of hand, particularly in high-stress settings like murder trials and death penalty sentencings, without a deeper rationale for why those existing frames may be inaccurate. In other words, "the public's misconceptions of gangs should be one of the subject matters of the trial" (Hagedorn and MacLean 2012, 1041).[12]

John explores these and other lessons from his quarter century of expert witness experience at much greater length in his most recent book, *Gangs on Trial: Challenging Stereotypes and Demonization in the Courts* (Hagedorn 2022). The book weaves together compelling stories of court cases, sociological and psychological analysis, and autobiographical vignettes from John's own life that deepen major analytic themes. Given deeply entrenched societal stereotypes, he argues that the defendants he has worked with typically have three strikes against them: They are Black or Latino, real or alleged gang members, and stand accused of a violent crime. Combined with the widespread presumption that police and prosecutors are "the good guys," challenging what is an often-reflexive tendency toward defendant demonization can be a Herculean task.[13] Complicating matters further, John makes clear that the majority of defendants he has worked with and writes about are, indeed, guilty of the crimes they were charged with. Yet, as he ably demonstrates, these commonly held stereotypes, inflamed by the dehumanizing language and often-baseless claims of prosecutors and their "expert" witnesses, mean that verdicts and sentences are rarely decided on the merits of the evidence, but instead on the power of stereotypes. In his foreword to *Gangs on Trial*, Craig Haney (2022), a leading expert on legal defense in capital cases, writes that it is this "overarching 'crime master narrative' that our society has learned to employ and on which prosecutors invariably rely—that evil deeds are the simple products of evil choices made by evil people . . . that Hagedorn's work so skillfully challenges and thoughtfully rebuts" (x).

As John makes clear in *Gangs on Trial*, a defendant identified as a gang member may or may not be an actual gang member. If they are, they may be one of several different general types of gang member, very few of whom have abandoned conventional morality or aspirations. They likewise may or may not have committed the alleged crime for which they are being charged. If they did, they may or may not have done so for reasons that have anything to do with gang dynamics. Stereotypes about street gangs and gang members short-circuit a careful consideration of the facts of a case and mischaracterize defendants as part of a monstrous "them" that is fundamentally different from the rest of "us." This, John convincingly argues, constitutes a grave miscarriage of justice, one that provides ideological justification for our society's policies of mass incarceration.

And this has a lot more to do with "us" than it does with "them."

Conclusion

In light of his sweeping and penetrating oeuvre, how might we best make sense of John's extraordinary contributions to gang research—and, in some respects, to social science more broadly?

Perhaps more than any other single quality, John's work is most notable as a model for grounded, critical, inductive research. It has been his unwavering commitment to this approach that allowed him to produce a canon with a thematic scope unrivaled in the field. But what this also necessitated was a true openness to questioning and revising his own empirical findings and conclusions. Indeed, within a half-dozen years of publishing *People and Folks*, John had rejected the undercurrents of that book's underclass framing, arguing that gang members were not adherents to a distinct subculture, but human beings like anyone else, doing their best to survive under desperate circumstances. In the preface to the second edition of *People and Folks*, moreover, John urges readers not to "mistake the passion of my arguments for hubris. Like all social science 'truths,' my conclusions must be seen as tentative, not universal, as dynamic, not static, and as firmly rooted in a specific time and place" (Hagedorn 1998d, xvi). He continued to follow his own counsel: A decade later, he wrote that his idea for *A World of Gangs* "began with my dissatisfaction with the way social sciences, including my own earlier book, *People and Folks*, had framed gangs" (Hagedorn 2008, xix). In the introduction to *The Insane Chicago Way*, moreover, John writes that "this book complicates my mission" to dispel stereotypes and humanize gang members, "but does not change it" (Hagedorn 2015b, 10). These reflections were no mere lip service, as each major phase of John's career was marked by the emergence of new findings that deepened, complicated, and often even contradicted what he had previously found.

John's approach to research requires a radical form of honesty and a commitment to values rarely found in academia—or outside of it. It requires the capacity to interrogate and make sense of new information with an open mind and a critical spirit. It requires subjecting one's own work to the same thoroughgoing critiques to which one subjects the work of others (see, especially, Hagedorn 1996). It also requires a fearlessness in confronting difficult questions and inconvenient truths that challenge our assumptions and what we think we know about the world. His most recent book documents in affecting detail how these qualities have likewise shaped and reshaped his broader personal development over the course of his life (Hagedorn 2022). This unflinching commitment to values and approach to research is what I consider to be the greatest legacy of John M. Hagedorn and what, among the very many things, I continue to most admire about him.

John expressed skepticism when I approached him about writing this chapter on his legacy in the field, telling me, "Handbooks like these are not always scientifically neutral, and I'm wary of the possibility that this may privilege the law enforcement perspective I have spent my career fighting against." I shared his reservations, and we took some time to think about how to proceed. "In a way, the two great trends in gang research are the criminalizing and humanizing tendencies," he continued, pointing out that these tendencies largely parallel the discordance between deductive and inductive research methodologies. "It isn't easy to label kids essentially criminals if you start from observing who they really are in their home habitats. You find complexity and humanity."

In the end, I convinced him that there might be no better testament to his legacy than to document it in precisely this forum, as a standing challenge to gang scholars and readers alike to take seriously the complex humanity that gang members share with the broader human community. And to take seriously the singular example of exploring and making sense of those complexities that John has set for us all.

Notes

1. All quotes in this chapter not attributed to a published work are taken from interviews and personal correspondence between John and myself.
2. John situates his draft resistance in his familial lineage, noting that "both families fled Bismarck's draft, so when I was a draft resister, I always said I'm no different than our families; they didn't want to fight for Bismarck, and I didn't want to fight for Lyndon Johnson." John also recalled his father George, a decorated World War II bombardier who passed away in 1965, recounting the horrors of war to him as a child: "He would talk about the 'precision bombing'—there was no such thing, it just was mass murder . . . He would tell me these terrible stories about the reality of war, even though this was the 'grand crusade.'" John continues: "I'm sure that had an impact on me, looking at a war that was an illegitimate war of conquest. I'll be damned if I'm going to go fight in that!"

3. He credits this lenience to the raucous trial of the Chicago Eight. John's attorney had successfully petitioned the Eastern District of Wisconsin for a change of venue due to polarizing pretrial publicity in the Milwaukee area, and his case was transferred to the Northern District of Illinois. John explains what ensued: "They were out to get me because they knew what I did. But the file hadn't been transferred yet. So we go down to Chicago during the Chicago Eight trial. Down the hall, they're dragging people out, and they're screaming, and the place is completely bananas. We sit down with the US attorney looking at it, and so my attorney is sitting there, and I'm here with my jean jacket and my buttons on and my sunglasses. And Harry, my lawyer, says 'This is a political trial. We're bringing in people from around the country. We're going to make this as loud as the one down the hall.' And the US attorney says, 'Um, will he take probation?'... And they didn't have the file to look at it and [see] wait a minute, I was the planner! So that's how I walked out with probation."
4. Such coauthorship followed the template Joan Moore established in her work with *barrio* gangs in Los Angeles, as her first book listed four gang members and community researchers as coauthors (Moore 1978).
5. This was particularly true of Wilson's (1987) widely read *The Truly Disadvantaged*, published the year before *People and Folks*. Wilson reciprocated, providing a blurb for *People and Folks*, calling it "the most insightful book ever written on inner-city gangs."
6. It is worth noting that, unlike the interwar period when Thrasher carried out his research, John was not the only scholar studying gangs and situating them within the postindustrial urban context of the late twentieth century. Nonetheless, his research was the first, the most consistent and comprehensive, and the most focused on street gangs. For similar studies published in the years following *People and Folks*, see Sullivan (1989), Moore (1991), and Bourgois (1995).
7. John found similar variation in exploring male gang members' conceptions of masculinity, from which he constructed a similar taxonomy (Hagedorn 1998b).
8. For an earlier interrogation of methodology and theory in gang research, see Hagedorn (1990).
9. On such rhetoric from public officials, see Brotherton and Barrios (2004), Conquergood (1996), and Zatz (1987). On media stereotypes of gangs and Black and Latino urban youth during this period, see Bogert and Hancock (2020), Esbensen and Tusinski (2007), and Moore (1991). For examples of gang research promoting similar ideas, see Decker (1996), Fleisher (1995), Sánchez-Jankowski (1991), and Taylor (1990).
10. In addition to the various publications that emerged from this research, this collaborative effort led to a traveling museum exhibit curated by the Jane Addams Hull-House Museum that is currently housed at the Institute for Nonviolence Chicago and available online at https://cvlwebsite.wixsite.com/report.
11. For his earliest work on gangs within the context of globalization, see Hagedorn (2001a, 2001b). For a catalogue of the endeavors that shaped this part of his research, see Hagedorn (2008, xxxii).
12. This insight echoes an admonition of gang researchers that John made 15 years prior: "Today's gang researchers must more seriously examine how their methods have influenced their findings and report it to us" (Hagedorn 1996, 119).
13. Having repeated this process scores of times, John frames this work in Sisyphean terms, both in the text and on the book's cover.

References

Bogert, Carroll, and Lynnell Hancock. 2020. "Superpredator: The Media Myth That Demonized a Generation of Black Youth." Marshall Project. https://www.themarshallproject.org/2020/11/20/superpredator-the-media-myth-that-demonized-a-generation-of-black-youth.

Bourgois, Philippe. 1995. *In Search of Respect: Selling Crack in El Barrio*. Cambridge, UK: Cambridge University Press.

Brotherton, David C., and Luis Barrios. 2004. *The Almighty Latin King and Queen Nation: Street Politics and the Transformation of a New York City Gang*. New York, NY: Columbia University Press.

Chesney-Lind, Meda, and John M. Hagedorn, eds. 1999. *Female Gangs in America: Essays on Girls, Gangs and Gender*. Chicago, IL: Lake View Press.

Conquergood, Dwight. 1996. "The Power of Symbols." In *One City*, 11–17. Chicago, IL: Chicago Council on Urban Affairs.

Davis, Mike. 2008. "Foreword: Reading John Hagedorn." In *A World of Gangs: Armed Young Men and Gangsta Culture*, John M. Hagedorn, xi–xvii. Minneapolis: University of Minnesota Press.

Decker, Scott H. 1996. "Collective and Normative Features of Gang Violence." *Justice Quarterly* 13 (2): 243–264.

Esbensen, Finn-Aage, and Karin E. Tusinski. 2007. "Youth Gangs in the Print Media." *Journal of Criminal Justice and Popular Culture* 14 (1): 21–38.

Fleisher, Mark S. 1995. *Beggars and Thieves: Lives of Urban Street Criminals*. Madison: University of Wisconsin Press.

Fraser, Alistair, and John M. Hagedorn. 2018. "Gangs and a Global Sociological Imagination." *Theoretical Criminology* 22 (1): 42–62.

Hagedorn, John M. 1988. *People and Folks: Gangs, Crime and the Underclass in a Rustbelt City*. Chicago, IL: Lake View Press.

Hagedorn, John M. 1990. "Back in the Field Again: Gang Research in the Nineties." In *Gangs in America*, edited by C. Ronald Huff, 240–259. Newbury Park, CA: Sage.

Hagedorn, John M. 1991. "Gangs, Neighborhoods, and Public Policy." *Social Problems* 38 (4): 529–542.

Hagedorn, John M. 1994a. "Homeboys, Dope Fiends, Legits, and New Jacks." *Criminology* 32 (2): 197–219.

Hagedorn, John M. 1994b. "Neighborhoods, Markets, and Gang Drug Organization." *Journal of Research in Crime and Delinquency* 31 (3): 264–294.

Hagedorn, John M. 1995. *Forsaking Our Children: Bureaucracy and Reform in the Child Welfare System*. Chicago, IL: Lake View Press.

Hagedorn, John M. 1996. "The Emperor's New Clothes: Theory and Method in Gang Research." *Free Inquiry for Creative Sociology* 24 (2): 111–122.

Hagedorn, John M. 1997. "Homeboys, New Jacks, and Anomie." *Journal of African American Men* 3 (1): 7–28.

Hagedorn, John M. 1998a. *The Business of Drug Dealing in Milwaukee*. Thiensville, WI: Wisconsin Policy Research Institute.

Hagedorn, John M. 1998b. "Frat Boys, Bossmen, Studs, and Gentlemen: A Typology of Gang Masculinities." In *Masculinities and Violence*, edited by Lee H. Bowker, 152–167. Thousand Oaks, CA: Sage.

Hagedorn, John M. 1998c. "Gang Violence in the Postindustrial Era." *Crime and Justice* 24: 365–419.

Hagedorn, John M. 1998d. *People and Folks: Gangs, Crime and the Underclass in a Rustbelt City*. 2nd ed. Chicago, IL: Lake View Press.

Hagedorn, John M. 2001a. "Gangs and the Informal Economy." In *Gangs in America*, 3rd ed., edited by C. Ronald Huff, 101–120. Thousand Oaks, CA: Sage.

Hagedorn, John M. 2001b. "Globalization, Gangs, and Collaborative Research." In *The Eurogang Paradox: Street Gangs and Youth Groups in the U.S. and Europe*, edited by Malcolm W. Klein, Hans-Jürgen Kerner, Cheryl L. Maxson and Elmar G. M. Weitekamp, 41–58. Dordrecht, The Netherlands: Kluwer.

Hagedorn, John M. 2005a. "The Global Impact of Gangs." *Journal of Contemporary Criminal Justice* 21 (2): 153–169.

Hagedorn, John M. 2005b. "Institutionalized Gangs and Violence in Chicago." In *Neither War nor Peace: International Comparisons of Children and Youth in Organised Armed Violence*, edited by Luke Dowdney, 312–330. Rio de Janeiro, Brazil: 7Letras.

Hagedorn, John M. 2006. "Race Not Space: A Revisionist History of Gangs in Chicago." *Journal of African American History* 91 (2): 194–208.

Hagedorn, John M, ed. 2007. *Gangs in the Global City: Alternatives to Traditional Criminology*. Champaign: University of Illinois Press.

Hagedorn, John M. 2008. *A World of Gangs: Armed Young Men and Gangsta Culture*. Minneapolis: University of Minnesota Press.

Hagedorn, John M. 2015a. "Chicago, I Do Mind Dying." In *Oxford Textbook of Violence Prevention: Epidemiology, Evidence, and Policy*, edited by Peter D. Donnelly and Catherine L. Ward, 219–224. Oxford, UK: Oxford University Press.

Hagedorn, John M. 2015b. *The Insane Chicago Way: The Daring Plan by Chicago Gangs to Create a Spanish Mafia*. Chicago, IL: University of Chicago Press.

Hagedorn, John M. 2017. "Gangs, Schools, and Social Change: An Institutional Analysis." *Annals of the American Academy of Political and Social Science* 673 (1): 190–208.

Hagedorn, John M. 2022. *Gangs on Trial: Challenging Stereotypes and Demonization in the Courts*. Philadelphia, PA: Temple University Press.

Hagedorn, John M., and Meda Chesney-Lind. 2014. "America's 'War on Gangs': Response to a Real Threat or a Moral Panic?" In *Criminal Justice Policy*, edited by Stacy L. Mallicoat and Christine L. Gardiner, 175–190. Thousand Oaks, CA: Sage.

Hagedorn, John M., and Mary L. Devitt. 1999. "Fighting Female: The Social Construction of Female Gangs." In *Female Gangs in America: Essays on Girls, Gangs and Gender*, edited by Meda Chesney-Lind and John M. Hagedorn, 256–276. Chicago, IL: Lake View Press.

Hagedorn, John M., Bart Kmiecik, Dick Simpson, Thomas J. Gradel, Melissa Mouritsen Zmuda, and David Sterrett. 2013. *Crime, Corruption, and Cover-ups in the Chicago Police Department* (Anti-Corruption Report Number 7). Chicago: Department of Political Science, University of Illinois at Chicago.

Hagedorn, John M., and Bradley A. MacLean. 2012. "Breaking the Frame: Responding to Gang Stereotyping in Capital Cases." *University of Memphis Law Review* 42: 1027–1060.

Hagedorn, John M., and Brigid Rauch. 2007. "Housing, Gangs, and Homicide: What We Can Learn from Chicago." *Urban Affairs Review* 42 (2): 435–456.

Hagedorn, John M., Jose Torres, and Greg Giglio. 1998. "Cocaine, Kicks, and Strain: Patterns of Substance Use in Milwaukee Gangs." *Contemporary Drug Problems* 25 (1): 113–145.

Haney, Craig. 2022. "Foreword." In *Gangs on Trial: Challenging Stereotypes and Demonization in the Courts*, edited by John M. Hagedorn, ix–xiii, Philadelphia, PA: Temple University Press.

Hayat, Fareed Nassor. 2019. "Preserving Due Process: Applying Monell Bifurcation to State Gang Cases." *University of Cincinnati Law Review* 88 (1): 129–168.

Howell, K. Babe. 2019. "Prosecutorial Misconduct: Mass Gang Indictments and Inflammatory Statements." *Dickinson Law Review* 123: 691–712.

Horowitz, Ruth. 1983. *Honor and the American Dream: Culture and Identity in a Chicano Community*. New Brunswick, NJ: Rutgers University Press.

Klein, Malcolm W. 1971. *Street Gangs and Street Workers*. Englewood Cliffs, NJ: Prentice-Hall.

Moore, Joan W. 1978. *Homeboys: Gangs, Drugs, and Prisons in the Barrios of Los Angeles*. Philadelphia, PA: Temple University Press.

Moore, Joan W. 1991. *Going Down to the Barrio: Homeboys and Homegirls in Change*. Philadelphia, PA: Temple University Press.

Moore, Joan W., and John M. Hagedorn. 1998. "What Happens to Girls in the Gang?" In *Gangs in America*, 2nd ed., edited by C. Ronald Huff, 205–218. Thousand Oaks, CA: Sage.

Moore, Joan W., and John M. Hagedorn. 2001. *Female Gangs: A Focus on Research* (NCJ 186159). Washington, DC: US Department of Justice.

Sánchez-Jankowski, Martín. 1991. *Islands in the Street: Gangs and American Urban Society*. Berkeley: University of California Press.

Sullivan, Mercer L. 1989. *"Getting Paid": Youth Crime and Work in the Inner City*. Ithaca, NY: Cornell University Press.

Taylor, Carl. 1990. *Dangerous Society*. East Lansing: Michigan State University Press.

Thrasher, Frederic M. 1927. *The Gang: A Study of 1,313 Gangs in Chicago*. Chicago, IL: University of Chicago Press.

Vigil, James Diego. 1988. *Barrio Gangs: Street Life and Identity in Southern California*. Austin: University of Texas Press.

Wilson, William Julius. 1987. *The Truly Disadvantaged: The Inner City, the Underclass, and Public Policy*. Chicago, IL: University of Chicago Press.

Zatz, Marjorie S. 1987. "Chicano Youth Gangs and Crime: The Creation of a Moral Panic." *Contemporary Crises* 11 (2): 129–158.

CHAPTER 35

THE LEGACY OF CHERYL L. MAXSON

SHANNON E. REID

It seems premature to discuss the legacy of Dr. Cheryl Maxson's work and mentorship since she continues to be a guiding force for the individuals who have worked with her and research collaboratives like Eurogang, which she cofounded and helped build. To acknowledge the impact of Cheryl on the field is to not only consider her work itself, but her impact as one of the key women working in mainstream criminology in general, and gang research in particular, over the past 40 years. Cheryl is rightfully considered one of the pioneering gang scholars, whose work, both nationally and internationally, continues to influence and impact future generations of researchers and policymakers. While today we can look around classrooms and conferences and see women better represented in the field, it was people like Cheryl who helped pave the way. In parallel to her research acumen, one must also consider her role in influencing the growth of public criminology, pushing for more applied research and public policy input in research; these achievements should not be understated, especially her impact on southern California's policy and practice.

To fully appreciate the legacy of Cheryl Maxson, this chapter is aimed at providing both an overview of her sometimes non-traditional pathway through academia and her influence on the field and her students. Hers is a unique trajectory: moving from *Rolling Stone* magazine to academia to her now retired (but still active) place as a giant in the field of criminology. While discussing her work, I took the opportunity to interview Cheryl during the 2021 annual meeting of the American Society of Criminology to ask her what she hopes the future holds for the students and researchers who carry on her legacy, and for gang research as a whole. The goals of this paper are not only to highlight the invaluable contributions of Cheryl to the field of criminology and gang research, but also to inspire and guide future pathways as gang research and public criminology move forward and evolve.

From Rolling Stone to Research Leader

Cheryl's research acumen is well established in the many articles, books, and reports she has written over her illustrious career. While this chapter could outline every book and article she has written and edited, the goal of this is not to highlight her impressive CV, but rather to focus on several key areas of gang and youth research where her influence is strongest and the long-lasting impact she has made on the field. To do this, this article discusses how Cheryl found herself in the center of southern California's evolving gang scene during one of the key periods of gang and youth violence. It also explores how her combined interests in quantitative research, theory, and policy helped shape a career that spans decades and has seen several shifts in policy and practice around gangs and gang members. Cheryl's influence on the field can be seen through her perseverance as one of the pioneering female gang scholars, her drive for research to influence policy and practice, and her enduring stamp on the organizations she helped create and the students she mentored.

Looking at the trajectory of Cheryl's career, one sees an interesting pathway from growing up in a small desert town near the Mexico border to starting her studies in Los Angeles at Occidental College. To hear her describe it, moving to the big city of Los Angeles during this unique time period allowed her interest in urban issues to flourish. Cheryl began her academic career in 1974 with a bachelor of arts from Occidental College. Her interest in street gangs began when she took a juvenile delinquency class and the professor introduced her to the work of seminal gang scholar Malcolm (Mac) Klein. After Cheryl graduated, she moved to San Francisco and was working for *Rolling Stone* magazine until Mac reached out to have her join him as a research assistant on a project interviewing youth in the Los Angeles area. This partnership would help build foundational research for gang scholars, both nationally and internationally. She then went on to get a master of arts in 1978 and a PhD in 1983, both from the University of Southern California (USC) in sociology. Her dissertation focused on the development of the large omnibus juvenile justice bill, and as she came close to graduation Mac pulled her in to help write a National Institute of Justice grant to evaluate a large gang program in Los Angeles. After graduating with her PhD, Cheryl held a range of different active academic positions. In 1983, she was appointed as a research assistant professor at USC and then promoted to research associate professor in 1994. From 1993 to 2000 Cheryl served as director of the Center for Research on Crime and Social Control as part of the Social Science Research Institute at USC. During this period, she was highly active in grant writing and research on gangs, youth violence, and policing. In 2000, she joined the faculty at the University of California Irvine as an assistant professor and was promoted to associate professor in 2003. In 2014 Cheryl was promoted to full professor and took on the role of chair in the Department of Criminology, Law, and Society.

When talking to Cheryl, she will often cite the role of Mac Klein in pulling her into the world of gang research and offering her the first opportunities at USC to interview gang-involved youth (even though he thought she was a nun based on a résumé mistake). The role Mac played in her career trajectory influenced Cheryl's approach to mentoring others. One of the most important pieces to any discussion of Cheryl and her work is her support of other students and scholars. Through her academic role as a professor at the University of California Irvine and her role as a founding steering committee member of the Eurogang network, one can see how her mentoring has helped students and researchers grow and flourish. Her willingness to work and publish with students and provide research opportunities (including allowing me and others to add dissertation questions to her larger Division of Juvenile Justice study) has helped build research portfolios and impact research trajectories.

During these years, Cheryl was an active member of the field of criminology. She was elected executive counselor of the American Society of Criminology (ASC) from 1999–2002, vice president from 2009–2011, and an ASC fellow in 2015. Cheryl is also a fellow of the Western Society of Criminology (2003), where she was elected president in 1995. She received the Joseph Lohman Award for outstanding service to the Western Society of Criminology in 1999 and the Paul Tappan Award for outstanding contributions to the field of criminology in 2009. Cheryl is a fellow of the Southern California Studies Center at the University of Southern California. Her work has also had a continued international component. Cheryl was a visiting scholar at the University of Tubingen, Germany, in 2008 and at the International Institute for the Sociology of Law in Spain in 2012. These different roles highlight her investment in international scholarship and mentorship.

Patterns and Policies of Gangs and Gang Members

Cheryl's scholarship on gangs has encompassed a broad range of critical topics for understanding gangs and gang processes. In collaboration with Mac Klein, she has produced seminal works on gang structure (Klein and Maxson 2010), gang homicide (Maxson, Gordon, and Klein 1985), and gang migration (Maxson, Woods, and Klein 1996) that shed light on the variation in gangs and how the stereotypical gang depicted in the media was only one part of a larger gang scene. One of her first gang intervention evaluations was focused on a program adapted from a Philadelphia program that had ex-gang members, law enforcement, and street workers respond to rumors, where Cheryl helped them develop the necessary evaluation tools while working on research on gang and non-gang homicides. Cheryl has also discussed how her work in this area has been motivated by a desire to make sure that discussions about gangs, from law enforcement and policymakers, are grounded in the reality of the situation (such as true differences between gang and non-gang homicides and how law enforcement is applying these definitions). Much of her work on gang migration comes from noticing how the discussion and panic around this idea of well-organized gangs purposefully moving into areas with less experienced law enforcement to set up drug markets and gang cliques did not align with her knowledge about gangs. This disconnect sparked a research agenda focusing on understanding gang migration and proliferation within the United States. Her work helped to dispel misperceptions about the nexus of gangs, drugs, and violence empirically. Her work has provided critical empirical research on gang patterning and structure across places and uncovered how police departments are responding to local gang issues, thus providing police and policymakers with the information necessary to target their gang efforts more effectively.

Cheryl does not always get the credit she deserves for her critical role in these projects—there is no question her analyses made the research possible and her role in the development and execution of these projects cannot be understated. For 15 years, she was constantly writing grants and reports building our knowledge base before joining the faculty at the University of California Irvine. These studies have been critical for developing the foundation of gang research and were the first to systematically investigate the patterns of gang structure, growth, migration, and proliferation of gangs throughout the country. Cheryl's body of work underscores the importance of being focused on the intersection of theory and policy. She is uniquely situated in her training and research areas to be able to speak to both areas in a way that few others are capable of.

THE CRIMINOLOGY OF SOUTHERN CALIFORNIA

To read Cheryl's work is to see the evolution of criminology in the Los Angeles area. The history of drugs, gangs, and corrections in California goes back to her early work in the mid-1980s, when gangs and youth violence exploded. To hear Cheryl discuss how she ended up in the Los Angeles area during this critical time, she often cites the opportunities provided to her by the highly active research faculty at USC. Cheryl talks about how the faculty was heavily involved in the research on deviance, including a National Institute of Health grant that allowed her to be exposed to the top researchers in the country who would come give talks. I would be bold enough to state that Cheryl often downplays her skills to credit those who helped train her and brought her on to grants. However, the way she was sought out to be a part of these large grants speaks highly of her abilities and the additive value she brought to these projects. One of her key additions to this field is the integration of her quantitative skills into the traditionally qualitative field of gang research. While much of this early work was centered on the Los Angeles area where she was based (and gangs were highly active), she was often part of large multisite studies. When Cheryl discusses this period, she will highlight how her location provided the access necessary to begin addressing the broad range of questions about gangs and gang members that had not been quantitatively studied. Her work helped shift the discussion of gangs and gang members away from being purely descriptive to trying to understand what we could say about gangs and gang members generally. This shift is critical for the development of policy aimed at reducing gang violence and gang membership and making law enforcement efforts more efficient.

One example of her ability to integrate policy, practice, theory, and evaluation research can be seen in her evaluation of gang injunctions. While gang injunctions were a popular law enforcement tool in southern California, her work explores theoretically why said intervention should or should not work, and empirically the actual effect of the policy. Her work in southern California has covered not only the changes in gangs and youth delinquency during this critical time, but also how policy needs to reflect the realities of the problem and be theoretically grounded and thoughtfully evaluated. Anyone interested in the evolution of gangs, drugs, and policing in the Los Angeles area should look to her work to better understand this history. Her work can be used as a blueprint for public criminology, especially in large urban areas like Los Angeles.

Her work spans beyond street gangs alone and includes youth violence more broadly (see Maxson and Matsuda 2012); the juvenile justice system (Barnet et al. 2017; Scott and Maxson 2016; Reid and Maxson 2016; Maxson 2012); communities and crime (Maxson, Hennigan, and Sloane 2003; Maxson 1997; and program evaluation (Hennigan et al. 2015, 2013; Maxson 2011. While the citations listed are just a small sample of Cheryl's publications, they highlight her range of research. Her book with Mac Klein, *Responding to Troubled Youth* (Maxson and Klein 1997), is the culmination of work on status offenders and the laws around these offenders that had come out of a grant on the multisite evaluation of the deinstitutionalization of status offenders. This book underscores the intersection of policy, practice, and theory that Cheryl centers her work on. Her research on gang injunctions in southern California is one of the first to examine the impact of civil gang injunctions on crime, disorder, and public perception (Maxson, Hennigan, and Sloane 2003, 2005). This project highlights her focus on evaluating the actual impact of policies that are being widely adopted despite there being little theoretical support for an intervention.

For scholars of gang research, *Street Gang Patterns and Policies* (Klein and Maxson 2010), the many iterations of *The Modern Gang Reader* (Maxson et al. 2014), and *Gang Transitions and Transformations in an International Context* (Maxson and Esbensen 2016) are staples in the classroom and on the shelves of researchers. Cheryl has stated before that *Street Gang Pattern and Policies* is where she sees her largest legacy in the field. This book is a seminal examination of the different gangs and major gang-control programs across the nation. This book is not only an urban analysis of the problem but underscores how street gangs are also a suburban and rural concern. This book discusses gang proliferation, migration, and crime patterns across a range of locations. It also reviews the known risk factors that lead to youth forming and joining gangs. The book also takes on one of Cheryl's key goals of gang research, which is dispelling the longstanding assumptions that the public, the media, and law enforcement have about street gangs. While future research has built on the foundation of *Street Gang Patterns and Policies*, this book should be a cornerstone for any gang researcher's work.

Each of these volumes is essential reading for those interested in understanding gangs in the United States and abroad. These books and edited collections cover a range of foundational topics and, in the case of the edited collections, provide research from both newer and more established gang scholars working from a range of perspectives. For many researchers and students, these volumes provide a central location for key gang studies. This allows people to be exposed to a variety of researchers and perspectives within a well-organized and curated volume. They also feature international gang scholars, thus providing them with a platform to have their work be more accessible and the field to be less dominated by US voices. These books highlight the shifts and evolution in gang research, including providing more research on understudied groups and areas. As the field continues to grow and evolve, the effort Cheryl has put into curating key studies and voices has benefited students and researchers and allows us all to build on the strong foundation of work she has helped establish.

Cheryl's work with the Eurogang network has further provided a range of US and international scholars a platform to engage in and disseminate research from a broad array of topics and methodologies. The Eurogang project came about after Mac Klein noticed that youth groups in Europe had several similarities to gangs in the United States. He commented that one of the hindrances to studying gangs, or troublesome youth groups, in Europe was the misconception of what gangs in the United States looked like because of the stereotypes that were being portrayed. To combat this phenomenon, a group of US and international scholars began meeting to work toward a more unified gang research agenda. The Eurogang project has been and continues to be the driving force in the development of new and cutting-edge gang research. One of the key goals of the Eurogang project is the creation of the Eurogang gang definition of a street gang that has been adopted in hundreds of studies across the Americas, Europe, and Africa. While the Eurogang project has been written about extensively, Cheryl has played a critical role as one of the few original and ongoing members of the steering committee. As this group continues, Cheryl remains a strong and guiding voice as gang research moves forward and tackles new issues, such as the evolving online presence of gangs, changing police expectations, and shifting funding sources.

An Interview with Cheryl Maxson

Since Cheryl continues to be a powerful presence in the field of criminology, through her work with Eurogang and her ongoing engagement with colleagues, the opportunity to interview her and share her knowledge with a broader audience is quite an honor. For this interview, I focused my questions on the future.[1]

On the Future of Gang Research

> SR: So now that you've retired and can look back, how have you seen the field change over the course of your career, good and bad?
>
> CHERYL: We went from knowing very little about a lot of things to knowing a bit more. We accumulated knowledge and then we got to a certain point when things stalled out.... [Previously] there wasn't all that much [data], you had to kind of go with what you could, the best you could come up with, and certainly with the advent of the longitudinal studies, that changed the bar.... [But] how much more do we really understand? I mean, how much more do we really understand about getting at gang dynamics and gang processes? We understand a little bit more about some little differences across space and time, because of the accumulation of all the different studies. But that's stalled out a bit, too. Meta-analyses have helped, but not as much as I would have liked....
>
> SR: So what do you think as gang researchers we are missing? What have we still not learned after all these years, almost a 100 years of gang research, what gaps do we still need to fill?
>
> CHERYL: I would say the variability in group-level processes across time and space is an area that needs growth. If we really think that there are these fundamental dynamics that go on, we need to have the research to show this. There is very little empirical research that really gets at what these processes are at the group level. To be able to tie group-level data to individual-level data in place and time. It's kind of grandiose.
>
> SR: But shouldn't the questions be grandiose? And I feel like now [that] we've covered basic descriptors [and] have a handle on risk factors and even though we keep seeing these studies... how do we get at those group-level dynamics?
>
> CHERYL: And in a way that can be generalized with enough quantitative data that you can kind of try and get into similarities and differences.
>
> SR: Yeah. And I think, interventions and policies.

CHERYL: We really don't know how unique some of these groups are. We do talk about gangs, crime, being on a local level, but there are so many broad patterns that there's got to be something else going on. And to really understand how that really relates to age and the kind of changing cultural dynamics of what it means to be a 14 year old in this time. Obviously, it's not the same cultural landscape as it was 20 years ago. A lot of our theoretical knowledge, as well as our empirical knowledge, really comes from a time when, well, being a 14 year old was kind of different.

SR: I mean, being a 14 year old was different for me than it is for a 14 year old now.

CHERYL: And that matters empirically, in terms of the formation of relationships and the developmental turning points as youth cycle into maturation. How does that affect their criminal activity, their peer relationships, their peer networks, and so on? These are all important questions to try and answer.

SR: I'm taking notes and working on my next research agenda as we're talking here. Currently it seems like there is a kind of back and forth, like, do you think people care about gangs the way they used to?

CHERYL: At the societal level, the interest has always been on violence and provoked by violence. Maybe part of it was the novelty of it. I did my first study in the early 1980s and you know that in Los Angeles this was a period of a shift between a trough and a slow increase in gang homicides, but also it was tied into the professionalization of gang response on law enforcement. And so there were a lot of dynamics there that were happening, and there was kind of an increase in the interest on the part of the politicians and the public. And Ron [Huff] wrote a lot about the response to that seminal event and the moral panic. When you couple that with the development of these increasing emergent cities, and no one really knowing what it was, and how much of it there was, and all of that, it also attracted a lot of scholars. So one wonders now, how much of it is the decrease in violence, or just kind of the feeling of it no longer being as much of a pressing policy issue, and maybe more of a lack of interest on the part of academics. And maybe people not getting trained in the same way. And maybe it's the result of the stagnation of the field. That's just more my read, but then that's an old person looking back.

SR: As a researcher, trying to continue this work forward, there is a sense that funding agencies care less about this research unless it's a topic like gangs and ISIS, or a side effect of particular politics like funding around MS-13. But for youth in these communities, this is still a really serious issue and the funding isn't there.

CHERYL: Absolutely. Of course, the funding priorities have always been cyclical. Think back to the crack distribution and there was a time where you could get anything funded. So, I don't know how that really fits with just a natural cycle of things. I can't help but think that part of it is intellectual. . . . I mean, what questions would engage a young scholar now? Certainly, there are a lot of them out there. But, you'd really want to have the good, deep questions. And then the other part of it—what's stalled out to me is the policy part. The programmatic part. Where's the innovation and experimentation and programming and evaluation?

On Mentoring

SR: So what would you want to pass on to the next generation of advisers and dissertation chairs?

CHERYL: I think as a carryover from my training experience, [I would tell people] to read or have a healthy respect for what people have done before. It's really frustrating to hear the same things 20 years later, and that can only come from not really reading the literature. So, I understand that there's a lot of pressure and that's what this sad emphasis on publication quantity leads you to. Just recycling the same citations. And I see a lot of that. But anyway, I would say read more deeply and think more deeply about the question of, so what? And to the extent that it's possible in career development, to let that be an influence on you. You really want to think a little bit more about what's [going on] behind: What is this telling me then about the processes or what is new about this? So this really led me to think about some of the more theoretical work, and, honestly, in my day, there was so little good descriptive data, that there was so much just in terms of the layout of the land [that we didn't know], that we needed to gather, and maybe now's the time for just trying to get more descriptive data and we can think about what it all means later on. I'm not seeing a lot of good theoretical explanations [coming out]. And even the [international] comparative thing. I was thinking the other day about how the work that Sandrine [Haymoz][2] and I did using the ISRD [International Self-Report Delinquency] data. Trying to make sense of differences between countries [where] there was nothing behind that. Just nothing.

On the Legacy and Future of Eurogang

SR: What do you think the legacy of Eurogang has been on the field?

CHERYL: So first and foremost, there is much more agreement on definitions. Good, bad, or indifferent, this has helped bring consistency to gang research. And I'm not averse to the discussion about making changes to the definition. There's a lot of value to at least thinking about that, depending on what the purpose of that [definitional change] is. For example, the digital/online issue; I think it's important to have those discussions because at the time when we were constructing what "street-oriented" means, the internet was new, there was no social media, and there was no need to understand how that might translate into a digital world. So, that could really help. Just clarifying what street-oriented means and how it's important to get to the dynamics, the theoretical part.

The communication between scholars has been really important. And that's been just a long-term development in terms of really fostering relationships among scholars. The sad thing is that we were never able to pull off a true multi-method, multisite international study. The ISRD was like a tiny baby step that way, but it fell apart. Being able to do comparative research across countries would have helped. And I'm thinking back about comparative projects within the US, how good of a job have we really done explaining why there might be differences between Philadelphia and one of the other G.R.E.A.T. sites? We've never really done a good job explaining site differences and why that might be.

SR: So moving Eurogang forward, are you still pushing for that? Comparative [work]?

CHERYL: Yeah, I mean, that would really [be valuable] at any point in the Eurogang's developmental cycle. I think having one of those big research projects that was really centered on Eurogang principles and fed by the Eurogang design would be invaluable. We had hoped that there would be a study that could be done, you know, with multiple sites and variation across different methods and having them be comparable. I would love to see some consistency in methods across studies and across place.... I've always been a super believer in methods—I love design, development, and implementation of research. And that's just what I've always really liked about being in our field, and [I've] always thought it's incredibly important to pay close attention to all that stuff.... I think that it could have been a whole different situation if we'd been able to do a research project where these large projects that we were proposing at the very beginning could have come to fruition.

SR: Why do you think they didn't come to fruition?

CHERYL: I think the US agencies were willing to fund research in the United States, but they weren't willing to fund international research, certainly not on an order like this. I think that even though there was a growing awareness of gang issues cropping up in Europe, there was a lot of resistance to doing that kind of work, of doing comparable studies across different places. [The perception was that] each country is so unique, and the European Union was just kind of beginning to develop some of these research funds. And then we got one review that talked about not having any reputable scholars [SR: Ouch]. Really? Like Hans Kerner? Mac Klein? So it was probably a number of different things. And we could have tried harder and more often. We really needed strong European leadership in that pursuit because I think there has always been a concern from some of us about having the US [researchers] dominate the group.

SR: That makes sense. The US, we tend to take over and dominate a little bit.

CHERYL: Yeah, because we know exactly what's right and the way we should go about doing it [*sarcastically said*]. In the early years, there were some really fun times trying to kind of pull together the ideas for the proposals.

On Her Legacy

SR: Alright, my last question, and it's a deep one.

CHERYL: [Laughing] So who was my favorite student?

SR: I'm not gonna ask that in case it's not me.

SR: For those of us who have been your students, we have had the honor of working with you, but now that you've retired, people aren't going to get that opportunity to work with you. Similar to the way I never got to work with Mac but know a lot about him through you. So my question is: What would you want your legacy to be? Like, write your own . . .

CHERYL: Like my obit?

SR: Not yet! Like what would you want people to think about? Like, here's what Cheryl would have said, here's what she wants you to remember. Or to take into consideration. Like, what are your words of advice to pass on?

CHERYL: That's an interesting question.

SR: That's why I saved it for last. As I was thinking about how you talk about Mac, and the impact that he had on your life, it made me curious to hear what your thoughts are on what you felt like your stamp was.

CHERYL: I think the work speaks for itself. In the context of the time in which it was done, as I was saying, it was in a landscape where this was pretty clearly a burgeoning issue, which we still don't really know, well, why. So, there was really a lot to be done and I had tremendous advantages of not only great people to work with where I was, and a lot of different kinds of colleagues coming from different fields, and great funding resources. And so, I was really able to do some of these projects, integrating different kinds of methods that probably made for rich research, than I was ever able to take advantage of. I guess my caution to people is the list of papers that didn't get written is a mile long. I think the part of my not being in a traditional academic career meant that I was always writing research proposals, which I love doing, that cost in terms of once the project was done, not being able to pull out as much from the data, so there's always a lot of unused data. And I always felt like that was a hardship for me. I felt bad about that. That's not advice. But just be aware of what your limits are and where your values are. Because, in some sense, it's like I was always on to the next project. I'm always thinking that I would get back to that other dataset. And so, that was one of the advantages I learned early working with students. It was really wonderful on a project to be able to parcel out different areas that were yours and your data and then [have] people to varying degrees develop them or not. And so that's really the way I like to work.

FINAL THOUGHTS

This chapter aimed to highlight Cheryl Maxson's many accomplishments and accolades, while also giving people an opportunity to get insights from Cheryl herself. Cheryl's legacy will be marked by her role as one of the first women to be heavily involved in the gang research field, her instrumental role in creating and maintaining the Eurogang project, and her many contributions to the field of criminology. Throughout her career, Cheryl pushed for research with policy and practice implications, she considered how different data sources and methods can be used to create comparative research, and she asked the difficult questions to get at the underlying dynamics of gangs. Her research will continue to be a touchstone for gang researchers and those interested in integrating research into policy.

However, it would not be a complete discussion of the legacy of Cheryl Maxson without some comments about what it is like to have Cheryl as a mentor. Her heavy participation (and success) in grant writing provided a large number of opportunities for students to be mentored by her through these grant activities. For example, due to her expertise on youth violence and gangs, California's Division of Juvenile Justice (within California's Department of Justice and Rehabilitation) she was called upon to evaluate gangs and violence within these correctional settings. Through this project, she put together a research team of PhD students that worked with her step by step to develop the survey and sampling design, go into the facilities to do the interviews, and then analyze the data. For some students, this opportunity turned into dissertations and articles, and for others it was a unique mentoring opportunity that many students never get to participate in. During this period, our research team suffered loss, saw the addition of a kid, added new members, and watched us move into academic careers. Throughout it all, Cheryl supported, advised, encouraged, and pushed us to excel. As many of us moved into our academic positions, Cheryl continued to be a guiding force in our lives.

Someone to bounce research ideas by, question your life choices, and have a beer with. We all know that eventually Cheryl will actually stop working and we will all feel that loss. Her presence is one of strength, support, and laughter while holding us all accountable to be the best researchers we can be. So to all of those reading this discussion about Cheryl's legacy, take the time to read her work and the work of her contemporaries, contemplate the big questions, and create something interesting.

Notes

1. Questions and answers have been edited for clarity.
2. Haymoz, Maxson, and Killias (2014).

References

Barnert, Elizabeth S., Laura S. Abrams, Cheryl Maxson, Lauren Gase, Patricia Soung, Paul Carroll, and Eraka Bath. 2017. "Setting a Minimum Age for Juvenile Justice Jurisdiction in California." *International Journal of Prisoner Health* 13 (1): 49–56.

Haymoz, Sandrine, Cheryl Maxson, and Martin Killias. 2014. "Street Gang Participation in Europe: A Comparison of Correlates." *European Journal of Criminology* 11 (6): 659–681.

Hennigan, Karen M., Kathy A. Kolnick, Flor Vindel, and Cheryl L. Maxson. 2015. "Targeting Youth at Risk for Gang Involvement: Validation of a Gang Risk Assessment to Support Individualized Secondary Prevention." *Children and Youth Services Review* 56: 86–96.

Hennigan, Karen M., Cheryl L. Maxson, David C. Sloane, Kathy A. Kolnick, and Flor Vindel. 2013. "Identifying High-Risk Youth for Secondary Gang Prevention." *Journal of Crime and Justice* 37 (1): 104–128.

Klein, Malcolm W., and Cheryl L. Maxson. 2010. *Street Gang Patterns and Policies*. Oxford, UK: Oxford University Press.

Maxson, C. L. 1997. *Gang Members on the Move*. US Department of Justice, Office of Justice Programs, Office of Juvenile Justice and Delinquency Prevention.

Maxson, C. L. 2011. "Street Gangs." In *Crime and Public Policy*, edited by J. Q. Wilson & J. Petersilia, 158–182. New York, NY: Oxford University Press.

Maxson, Cheryl L. 2012. "Betwixt and Between Street and Prison Gangs: Defining Gangs and Structures in Youth Correctional Facilities." In *Youth Gangs in International Perspective*, edited by Finn-Aage Esbensen and Cheryl Maxson, 107–124. New York: Springer.

Maxson, Cheryl L., and F. A. Esbensen. 2016. *Gang Transitions and Transformations in an International Context*. New York: Springer.

Maxson, Cheryl L., Margaret A. Gordon, and Malcolm W. Klein. 1985. "Differences between Gang and Nongang Homicides." *Criminology* 23 (2): 209–222.

Maxson, Cheryl L., Karen Hennigan, and David C. Sloane. 2003. "For the Sake of the Neighborhood? Civil Gang Injunction as a Gang Intervention Tool in Southern California." In *Policing Yough Gangs and Violence*, edited by Scott H. Decker, 239–266. Belmont, CA: Wadsworth.

Maxson, Cheryl L., Karen M. Hennigan, and David C. Sloane. 2005. "'It's Getting Crazy Out There': Can a Civil Gang Injunction Change a Community?" *Criminology & Public Policy* 4 (3): 577–605.

Maxson, Cheryl Lee, and Malcolm W. Klein. 1997. *Responding to Troubled Youth*. Oxford, UK: Oxford University Press.

Maxson, Cheryl L., Arlen Egley, Jody Miller, and Malcolm W. Klein. 2014. *The Modern Gang Reader*. New York: Oxford University Press.

Maxson, Cheryl L., and Karen M. Matsuda. 2012. "Gang Delinquency." In *The Handbook of Juvenile Crime and Juvenile Justice*, edited by B. Feld and D. Bishop. New York: Oxford University Press.

Maxson, Cheryl L., Kristi J. Woods, and Malcolm W. Klein. 1996. "Street Gang Migration: How Big a Threat." Washington, DC: US Department of Justice, Office of Juvenile Justice and Delinquency Prevention.

Reid, Shannon E., and Cheryl L. Maxson. 2016. "Gang Youth and Friendship Networks in California Correctional Facilities: Examining Friendship Structure and Composition for Incarcerated Gang and Non-Gang Youth." In *Gang Transitions and Transformations in an International Context*, edited by C. L. Maxson and F.-A. Esbensen, 95–114. Cham, Switzerland: Springer.

Scott, Daniel Walter, and Cheryl Lee Maxson. 2016. "Gang Organization and Violence in Youth Correctional Facilities." *Journal of Criminological Research, Policy and Practice* 2 (2): 81–94.

CHAPTER 36

THE LEGACY OF JOAN W. MOORE

JAMES DIEGO VIGIL

> Our lives, and those of our children, are largely spent in conventional institutionalized settings—home, work, school, formal organizations. The street world is one that we pass through without paying very much attention. (Moore 2002, x)

The above quote summarizes the animating truth of Joan W. Moore's legacy. When one passes through a place, one is on the way to somewhere else. The place of transit is never a destination in and of itself. Joan raised the value of the "place" of her subjects. She was never about collecting data on predetermined terms, as quickly as possible, to return to the ivory tower. Instead, she chose to collaborate with her subjects in the process of research, setting her operation firmly in their "place," spending time and focus there, showing a willingness to let their input change the trajectory of the research. As to Joan's choice of subjects, she is one of the first and few women to concentrate her research on gangs and she is one of only a few social scientists to spend decades researching distinct neighborhoods (Hagedorn 2010).

Joan not only collected and organized data that follow basic social science theory and methods, such as government records, summaries of reports, and basic statistics. Most importantly, she brought innovative approaches to her research. She initiated community studies, using in-depth observations along with interviews of each neighborhood's subjects. This personal touch has led to many detailed insights and hypotheses that have greatly enriched both gang research and urban studies.

When I met Joan in the late 1970s, I had already read some of her work. I was struck by her groundbreaking, immersive, personal approach to research and by her divergent thinking. It is natural for humans to conform to the approaches of those who have come before them. But divergent thinkers are those that create the big leaps in our world; in technology, for instance, the disruptors have given us smartphones, blockchain, artificial intelligence, the cloud, and mRNA technology, to name a few examples. The social sciences are no different; they also have disrupters. Being a disruptor brings risks, but it also brings possibilities of great leaps in strategies and insights. I am only one of many who have benefited from Joan's character, her process, and her work.

Early on in our relationship, when I became a fan of her work, Joan answered my unsolicited inquiries and generously gave me honest input on my projects. Over time, my wife, Polly, and I became friends with Joan and her husband, Burt, and we enjoyed many special times together. Whenever I began a new research project, article, or book, I discussed it with Joan. She generously gave me so much time over the years that I have often (half-jokingly) said that she was like a security blanket to me.

But unlike a security blanket, she wasn't always comfort and fluff. No wallflower, she was not afraid to speak up in an era when most of her academic colleagues were male. She was truthful, sometimes painfully so, and that invigorated me and strengthened my resolve to improve. As one of her students recalled, "She told me I wasn't the best student she ever had, but that I was the hardest-working student she had ever had" (Durán 2020). This student, Robert Durán, a former gang member, was motivated and pushed on to become a professor and author of two important ethnographic books on gangs, *The Gang Paradox* (Durán 2018) and *Gang Life in Two Cities* (Durán 2013). Joan's honest support and feedback deserve much credit for the quality of research generated by those blessed to be her students and colleagues.

Career Background

Joan received both her MA (in 1953) as well as her PhD (in 1959) from the University of Chicago. Her "Chicago School" training, under the best social science thinkers and researchers of that time, gave her both the preparation and insight that shaped her ecological, community-based approach and investigations into urban issues, especially the street gangs in Los Angeles.

One of the most influential sociologists of the Chicago School, Robert Ezra Park (1864–1944), was inspired by Charles Darwin to acknowledge that scarcity in an environment leads to "competition, segregation, and accommodation" and that these reactions occur not only in the plant and non-human animal worlds but also in the world of the human species (Hardyns and Pauwels 2017). Although this was a rich and formative part of Joan's academic growth, this period was not without personal challenges.

Joan recounted to me several times how, during her time in Chicago, she felt left out by a mostly male group of students and researchers. After classes, the only woman among the students gathering in the hallways, she almost always had to jump around to find an open spot. She also felt this isolation when she attended professional conferences, even though she eventually became president of the Social Problems organization at the university.

Joan's marginalization as one of the first women in her field also affected her professionally, even years after she left the University of Chicago. Having earned a reputation as a formidable, established researcher, she gained tenure at the University of California, Riverside. Shortly thereafter, Joan received a large grant to continue her work. After continuing for some time at Riverside, the University of Southern California (USC) took notice of her scholarship and wooed her over to its sociology department, promising her tenure.

She never received tenure.

In a contentious and personal way, she was rejected. One of the male faculty members told me that "the other professors always commented on how Joan would show up at research meetings with 'her pistoleros.'" So much for respecting the value of community research, which Joan championed. At that time, most of the USC sociologists focused on objective data from reports, census records, and interviews with caretakers.

Joan studied under one of Park's students, Everett Hughes, who taught courses on field research and sent her, along with other white students, into the south side of Chicago so that they could witness how poor Black people lived. Hughes' methods courses and Joan's experiences in Chicago would come to play a large role in how she approached her future research in Los Angeles (Hagedorn 2010).

METHODOLOGICAL INNOVATIONS AND SEMINAL WORKS

To properly place Joan's work within the literature and to realize its impact, it's vital to share background information regarding previous approaches to gang research. Various gang theories were established about 95 years ago, beginning with the classic works of Thrasher (1927) and Asbury (1927). Following these seminal works, researchers have largely emphasized a single causal factor in the etiology of gangs.

Some examples include Sutherland (1947), whose research seeks to clarify that subcultural reference groups bring similarly unattached youth together. Cohen (1955) maintains that lower-class boys experience a "reaction-formation" and become oppositional when middle-class values are unattainable. Bloch and Niederhoffer (1958) argue that the process of becoming a man drives lower-class youth to create initiation rituals to form a gang member. Miller (1958) contends that gangs and gang members are an expression of lower-class culture. Yablonsky (1959) suggests that gangs are a near-group and sociopathic. Cloward and Ohlin (1960) seek to show how economic inequality leads to strain when the means to widely valued goals are out of reach for lower-class populations. Finally, for this time period, Hirschi (1969) adds important elements to gang causation by showing how breakdowns in social control are a central cause. The above researchers and their theories provide context to Joan's methods, associations, and her place as a notable contributor to gang literature.

After leaving Chicago, Joan began work at the University of California, Los Angeles as coauthor of the first large-scale study of Mexican-Americans in the United States (Grebler, Moore, and Guzman 1970; Telles and Ortiz 2008). In line with the Chicago School approach, Joan began to seek involvement within the local communities she was studying. Gaining a connection with the Community Concern Corporation, which worked with pintos (released prisoners who were often also addicts), Joan began to examine the local street issues, gathering and seeking relationships within the environment of the drug scene, the dynamics of the gang, and gender issues. She welcomed questions and input from her subjects, using a collaborative strategy that was unique for its time.

In practice, this research technique enabled her to witness how gender attachments, especially in female gang members, unfold under poverty and a life of disenfranchisement. As Freud noted, home attachments and domestic life are shaped by "love and labor," and when these human needs are met and routinized, life's activities are smoother and humans feel hope for the future. Individuals and families that reach these goals struggle, but they often manage to achieve some stability in facing adverse situations and conditions. In the absence or reduction of these attachments, Joan discovered the intense damage that gang involvement brings to females, who are observed by society as doubly deviant due to their unconventional expression of womanhood as well as their gang membership.

Joan's interest in issues reflecting the Mexican-American experience continued as she moved on to the University of California, Riverside. Here, she immersed herself further. During this time, perhaps because of the contacts made during her collaborations with pintos, she became more active in the Los Angeles community. She was invited to participate in an ex-pinto (ex-felon) and ex-tecato (ex-addict) organization, the Chicano Pinto Research Project (CPRP). The CPRP was founded to assist these marginalized individuals and to help them find out why, in one member's words, "we're so screwed up." This organization's name was later changed to the League of United Citizens to Help Addicts. The name change was part of a quest to reach a broader audience to attract more funding and grants to Community Systems Research Incorporated (CSRI), which Moore founded. Because there were so many gaps in the literature, especially among Chicanos, CSRI added some important data and interpretations to extremely neglected areas. Issues related to the secondary labor market drove the attention of economists and sociologists of the time, but most of them failed to apply explanations to the Chicano population.

During Joan's time with CSRI, the organization's research placed the gangs as members within a complex community that contained multiple factors. Most earlier researchers had assessed gangs in isolation from the broader society; the presence of a gang was often explained in a way that was akin to a floating, island-like phenomenon, disconnected from society and generated by single, often malignant factors. CSRI undertook comprehensive investigations in three barrio gang neighborhoods (San Fernando, White Fence, and El Hoyo Maravilla; all three communities date from the 1940s). Research was conducted collaboratively. Participants, researchers, and community leaders, as well as residents of the community, were encouraged to speak up and contribute their insights. The acceptance of complexity in gang theory contributed to efforts to include diverse participants in the research, which resulted in nuanced, multifactor theories. These theories, it was inferred, would contribute to policies that would be more effective at addressing the complexity and diversity surrounding the needs of gang communities.

CSRI's approach uncovered much unexplored ground and contributed greatly to the trajectory of later studies. Personal problems began to emerge in the context of where gang members lived and worked. Social and cultural signs and symbols exhibited significance in relation to beliefs and behaviors. The experience of racism, amid decades of separation and isolation from mainstream culture, appeared to take center stage in gang experiences. Poverty, exclusion, discrimination, and cultural imperialism, present against the backdrop of the barrio, revealed why gang members were produced and found mostly in minority communities. Similar pathways to assimilation and integration were common. Cultural outlooks and group processes were examined in favor of background and historical processes.

Paying special attention to females in gangs, CSRI laid the groundwork for developments in research that would yield insights on drug use and abuse in female gang members. Theory-testing or theory-driven research was de-emphasized, and historical vignettes and depth were highlighted. Joan played an important role in this fresh approach, which generated novel paths to uncovering the complex sources of gang dynamics and barrio life.

In fact, the collaborative methodology developed in the CPRP represents a substantial degree of continuity with the community fieldwork tradition, especially as that tradition appeared in the Chicago School. Chicanos from the barrio, as a result of the collaboration necessary in this tradition, began to see that they could play a role in helping their community; they began to see themselves as agents of change. The roots of community collaboration must be credited to the Chicago School, which mandated that major consideration be given to the point of view of communities and the people under study.

Joan's research continued to reflect her interest in the study of females in gangs. Her first book on gangs, *Homeboys: Gangs, Drugs, and Prison in the Barrios of Los Angeles* (Moore 1978), which is considered a classic in the field, pays tribute to her training at the University of Chicago by its exceptional collaborative approach, along with its quest to go deep into the "place" of "pintos" and gangs and—once again—its inclusion of female gang members. Joan acknowledges that the book drew inspiration from her earlier research with CSRI when she writes that *Homeboys* is

> ... as much—or more—a study of the pintos as it is a study of the gangs. The ex-offenders who collaborated with me, yes, they were gang members; life-long gang members and the way the gang functioned for them—in and out of prison throughout their lives—was the major part of the story we wanted to tell. (Moore, introductory remarks, Chicago, March 11, 2016)

Homeboys was well received and awarded several prizes in recognition, given that the work was from the community and conducted by community members; many gang members who read the book remarked that it covered the most revealing elements of barrio life, highlighting key gang dynamics stemming from family, school, and home experiences.

Joan described it as a research collaboration between the academic world and Chicano ex-convicts and gang members. She writes of their hopes that knowledge gained through the book would help Mexican-American communities throughout Los Angeles. Despite understandable suspicions about researchers' motives, Joan discovered that gang members were beginning to develop the conviction that laws could be changed—for the better of Chicano pintos—through the truths discovered via collaborative research. This conviction opened the door for Joan's research that would illuminate the pinto viewpoint. In the introduction to *Homeboys*, Joan writes of her hope that the book will help support more collaboration between academics and minorities. Despite the sensationalistic exploitation found in the coverage of Chicano gangs during the late 1970s and thereafter, Joan, thanks to the participation of the Chicano community, uncovered both the historical as well as the contemporary perspective.

A few years after *Homeboys* was published, Joan conducted a major study of women and heroin with Alberto Mata from the University of Oklahoma (Moore and Mata 1981). This research took a random sample approach that included males as well as females. Over the decades (since the 1940s; there were over 10 cliques studied, including males and females) there had been a noted increase in drug use (mostly marijuana and upper and downer pills, but also the more deadly and debilitating heroin use and abuse) that took its toll in the early years. Aside from shedding light on this phenomenon, one of the major facts Joan discovered was that—within gangs—females are generally not only poorly regarded by males; they are devalued and mistreated, irrespective of what male gang members say about them to researchers. For example, male gang members often described their female counterparts as "good homegirls" (Moore and Mata 1981). In contrast, female members reported incidents of negative treatment from males.

Joan's goal was to treat and handle females more humanly and accurately, so she gave female gang members extraordinary consideration during the research for this study. She sparked the interest of subsequent gang researchers, who began to place a higher value on discussions regarding females. This discussion would surely have occurred eventually, but Joan accelerated its arrival. Since research on females had previously been absent, Joan began to consider what other depths of information were yet to be discovered. She continued to widen her focus.

Joan's next book, *Going Down to the Barrio: Homeboys and Homegirls in Change* (Moore 1991) describes two neighborhoods in East Los Angeles, the inhabitants of these neighborhoods, and the effects of the related moral panics. These effects included 83 gang suppression bills in the California legislature, the allowance of random stop-and-searches, and the suspension of plea bargains for gang members. Both barrios (El Hoyo Maravilla and White Fence) are small pieces in the study of Los Angeles, but it must be noted that surrounding areas housed the largest single concentration of Mexican-Americans in the country—a sort of Chicano capital, unmatched anywhere except perhaps in certain areas of Texas.

Joan's book is exceptional in that, in addition to the rich information gained from her collaborative approach and long-term follow-up, she examines the responses of lawmakers, law enforcement, the media, and society at large in relationship to the moral panics connected to gangs. She examines, measures, and contrasts these responses with her research and examination of vital economic and social changes occurring within the two barrios that were the focus of her research.

Joan's research revealed that "maturing out" happened, but unfortunately it sometimes took too long, if it happened at all. Years of gang experience prepared members for their "future," which was prison. Preparing for the future meant that barrio youth had to weather the consequences of drug abuse and gang violence through adolescence and adult years, only to eventually find themselves doing long terms in detention. Firmly tied to heroin and drug addiction, prison also led to a refinement and deepening of gang culture and strengthened its ties with its members. Entering the underworld of street gangs and persisting for a time in that environment often led to developing traits consistent with prison culture and involvement with the Mexican Mafia.

After writing *Going Down to the Barrio*, Joan's attention turned to the Chicano Movement, then underway in Los Angeles as well as other Mexican-American neighborhoods found throughout the nation. She was drawn to this unique moment in history:

> That was a time and place and culture that was glaringly special. For Chicanos, self-awareness, political activism, cultural nationalism—all were at a high. It was an exciting period for all of us, but one of real change for Chicanos. (Moore, introductory remarks, March, 11, 2016).

Joan and I, in later years, had many conversations about the ideological goals of the Chicano Movement, as well as the efforts of its leaders and protagonists. She listened and asked questions about the movement and, especially, about the involvement of my brother and me.

My brother and I primarily focused on challenging and changing the limited educational opportunities for Chicanos. My brother, Richard E. Vigil, aka "Mangas Coloradas" (channeling a famous Apache chieftain), was one of the LA Thirteen, who were arrested for plotting the East Los Angeles high school walkouts (aka "blowouts") in March 1968. The following year I was arrested on April 24, 1969, for disrupting the Nuevas Vistas conference, during then-governor Ronald Reagan's speech. Both of these affairs attracted heavy media attention and, obviously, a strong presence of law enforcement in all forms, openly and undercover. Our stance and arrest struck a major chord with the resident Chicano population. Joan was invigorated by this period of activism and, speaking for myself, I was grateful for a researcher of her caliber recognizing the magnitude of the moment.

Joan and her community researchers and colleagues supported the goals and objectives of these actions. She became close to the designated Chicano Movement lawyer, Oscar Z. Acosta, and was very proud of a poster given to her by Acosta when he ran for sheriff of Los Angeles County. Colored by these connections and influence, Joanand her team became even more energized in their research within the Chicano community.

I fear there will be no future for gang members without a focus on the conditions that contribute to the absence of mobility, the absence of jobs, and the absent maturation out of the gang. A collaborative approach, which partners with the affected community, renders the best opportunities to discover a path forward for marginalized gang members. Firmly basing investigation within the community is crucial for understanding and clarifying all the dynamics present.

Legacy

Joan's books *Homeboys* and *Going Down to the Barrio* are celebrated as original contributions for their inclusion of female voices, collaboration with subjects, and the incorporation of longitudinal studies. Amazingly, Joan's work underscores the reliance of gang members on their respective groups to influence and shape the present and future for them. The first answer to the question of deviance is that the gang has an inherent tendency toward an increase in deviance. Each clique forms while its predecessor is actively visible on the streets. It forms, generally, with the sense that it can match or outdo its predecessor. The norms of conduct and the myths and legends of its predecessor clique also become part of the gang's general culture (Cohen 1955; Moore 1991, 45).

Joan's work has influenced the careers of countless scholars. There are many, besides myself, who have set their course and measured their progress based on Joan's approach. One example, John Hagedorn, Professor Emeritus at the University of Illinois, Chicago, was a graduate student mentored by Joan, and he describes how her work "stands out as a model of how to use social science to humanize the gang member, while pulling no punches on the ugly side of gang life" (Hagedorn 2010). Hagedorn, the author of multiple books and studies on gangs, including *People and Folks: Gangs, Crime and the Underclass in a Rustbelt City*, reflects the same appreciation throughout his research that Joan shows for her relationships with her subjects. Although not as directly involved with Joan as myself and Hagedorn, other scholars directed their investigations along similar community and people lines: Lalo Valdez, David Brotherton, Robert Durán, Randol Contreras, Roberto Aspholm, as well as several up-and-coming writers like Robert Weide, Jorge David Mancillas, and Michael Tapia, who wrote the book *Gangs of the El Paso-Juárez Borderland: A History* (Tapia 2019).

Joan also advanced ideas that helped clarify why the maturation process was delayed among a given population, leading to a prolonged gestation period of immobility and a consequent lack of involvement in the labor market. Younger gang members recognized this prolonged gestation period by referring to older members as "dinosaurs." Further, she documented how "labor and love" drive a person to work and find a mate and home. It is a normal developmental phase for humans. Objective research before Joan's time sidestepped the significance of the seeming absence of this drive among gang members. Without the driving connection between labor and love, there was little to no mobility, which resulted in no jobs and no maturing out.

There are distinct features of research that I value and credit to Joan. She conducted research in the community with members of the community, including resident gang members. She interviewed and interacted with parents, friends, and community members at different times and places. "Being there" enabled her and later researchers to "see and hear" and "listen and ask" about events and episodes that are spontaneous and cyclical, expected and random. Longitudinal and impromptu events can provide rationales and explanations otherwise missed in one or two community visits or interviews. Finally, trust and rapport are more easily gained and established when "the studied" feel they are participants and included in the research.

This method and rationale do not ensure that the research information gained is sufficient to the extent that a questionnaire or public records' have no value. However, a prolonged stay with a person at different times and places makes for a deeper and broader template in which to fathom human behavior and a way to confirm what a researcher may have heard and interpreted from one interaction.

Conclusion

The social sciences, no matter the degree of rigor, depend on hindsight as well as an examination of the present. What happened within a community to effect change? What norms have changed recently? How can one measure the past of a community against the present? Joan Moore's contribution was to broaden and deepen the excavation within the communities she studied. Her approach rendered rich, valuable, enduring information, as well as an approach that led the way for researchers who followed in her steps. Her strong and all-encompassing Chicago School approach emphasized community studies. This goal fits into the enduring strategy of conducting research in situ. Although her earliest work had relied on traditional, basic research of archival records, public reports, and government records, she ended her career talking and thinking with the people of the streets as they acted out and explained why-where-when-how the streets were so important to them. Her work and publications remain for the benefit of all and, consequently, fellow researchers see "the street" and its members in a new light. We recognize the importance of "being there."

References

Asbury, Herbert. 1927. *The Gangs of New York: An Informal History of the Underworld.* New York: Vintage.
Bloch, Herbert A., and Arthur Niederhoffer. 1958. *The Gang: A Study in Adolescent Behavior.* Westport, CT: Greenwood.

Cloward, Richard A., and Lloyd E. Ohlin. 1960. *Delinquency and Opportunity: A Theory of Delinquent Gangs*. Glencoe, IL: Free Press.

Cohen, Albert K. 1955. *Delinquent Boys: The Culture of the Gang*. New York: Free Press.

Durán, Robert. 2013. *Gang Life in Two Cities: An Insiders Journey*. New York: Columbia University Press.

Durán Robert. 2018. *The Gang Paradox: Inequalities and Miracles on the US-Mexico Border*. New York: Columbia University Press.

Durán, Robert. 2020. "Honoring Joan Moore through Her Students." YouTube. August 11. https://www.youtube.com/watch?v=fSSuhuv0OLs.

Grebler, Leo, Joan W. Moore, and Ralph C. Guzman. 1970. *The Mexican-American People*. New York: Free Press.

Hagedorn, John. 2010. "Moore, Joan W.: Homeboys and Homegirls in the Barrio." In *Encyclopedia of Criminological Theory*, edited by Francis T. Cullen and Pamela Wilcox, 651–654. Thousand Oaks, CA: Sage. https://dx.doi.org/10.4135/9781412959193.n181

Hardyns, Wim, and Lieven J. R. Pauwels. 2017. "The Chicago School and Criminology." In *The Handbook of the History and Philosophy of Criminology*, edited by Ruth Ann Tripplett, 123–139. Chichester, UK: Wiley.

Hirschi, Travis. 1969. *Causes of Delinquency*. Berkeley: University of California Press.

Miller, Walter B. 1958. "Lower Class Culture as a Generating Milieu of Gang Delinquency." *Journal of Social Issues* 14: 5–19.

Moore, Joan W. 1978. *Homeboys: Gangs, Drugs, and Prison in the Barrios of Los Angeles*. Philadelphia, PA: Temple University Press.

Moore, Joan W. 1991. *Going Down to the Barrio: Homeboys and Homegirls in Change*. Philadelphia, PA: Temple University Press.

Moore, Joan W. 2002. Foreword. In *Vigil's Rainbow of Gangs*, edited by J. Diego. Austin: University of Texas Press.

Moore, Joan W., and Alberto Mata. 1981. *Women and Heroin in Chicano Communities*. Austin: University of Texas Press.

Sutherland, Edwin H. 1947. *Principles of Criminology*, 4th ed. Philadelphia, PA: J. B. Lippincott.

Tapia, Mike. 2019. *Gangs of the El Paso-Juárez Borderland: A History*. Albuquerque: University of New Mexico Press.

Telles, Edward E., and Vilma Ortiz. 2008. *Generations of Exclusion: Mexican-Americans, Assimilation, and Race*. New York: Russell Sage Foundation.

Thrasher, Frederic M. 1927. *The Gang: A Study of 1,313 Gangs in Chicago*. Chicago, IL: University of Chicago Press.

Yablonsky, Lewis. 1959. "The Delinquent Gang as a Near-Group." *Social Problems* 7 (2): 108–117. https://doi.org/10.2307/799161.

CHAPTER 37

THE LEGACY OF JAMES DIEGO VIGIL

MIKE TAPIA AND E. MARK MORENO

THE first author of this chapter (Mike) will not soon forget when in the spring of 2019 he had the honor of joining a discussion panel at the University of Texas at El Paso that included James Diego Vigil, the unequivocal godfather of Chicana/o gang studies. In that talk, Diego diagrammed the latest and most refined version of his multiple marginalization theoretical model, showcasing its multilevel conceptualization consisting of both micro- and macro-level features (Vigil 2020). Developing this framework is Diego's crowning achievement and one of his most impactful contributions to the field, becoming a widely tested model in the literature (e.g., Johnson and Mendlein 2022; Krohn et al. 2011; Quinn, Walsh, and Dickson-Gomez 2019). By the time he reintroduced this model in his second major book in 2002, Diego was already the pre-eminent Chicano gang scholar, with a prolific early career, culminating in his first masterpiece, *Barrio Gangs*, in 1988. That work demonstrated Diego's prowess for conducting avant-garde fieldwork with Chicano gangs in Los Angeles, revealing an authenticity that included the terminology, worldview, and realities of the study population with a level of detail not seen in gang studies to that point. This is also where he first briefly introduced the multiple marginality framework, laying out the history and current landscape of LA's Chicana/o gangs in the process.

Weide (2021) noted that Diego's work has inspired the next generation of Chicana/o gang scholars, which would include the current authors. Given Weide's thorough account of Diego's life and scholarly chronology, we have taken this opportunity to build on that foundation with an exploration of topics pertaining to the history and current state of Chicana/o gang research, in light of Diego's career, and partially through his own lens. Many of the topics we address have been of interest to Diego throughout the years, at times subtly interlaced into his work, and at times done more explicitly. We had the good fortune of consulting with Diego for this chapter to get his firsthand take on some of the topics we address. As his work did much to help establish Chicana/o gang research as a distinct genre, we begin with its early history and a definition, adding what the term "Chicana/o gang research" means to us as Chicano scholars.

What Is Chicana/o Gang Research?

By all appearances, urban street-corner groups of Mexican-American youth were first briefly depicted in the published delinquency literature by Thrasher (1927), as relayed to him by a colleague working in El Paso, Texas, in 1925. This was followed by thorough descriptions of the *pachuco* subculture in works by Bogardus (1943) and Griffith (1948), and then more elaborately by Coltharp (1965). In fact, a large variety of authors have written about Chicana/o deviant street subcultures, their stylistic attributes, and related aspects in the sociological, humanities, arts, and cultural studies literature for decades (e.g. García 1994; McWilliams 1948; Ornstein 1983). But the research that we consider most germane to the issues handled in this chapter perhaps started with Davidson's (1974) book on Chicano prisoners and Joan Moore's (1978) work on the legendary Chicano Pinto project.[1] Since then, the published studies distinctly focused on Chicana/o gangs constitute a considerable corpus of work, and Chicana/o gang research arguably became its own genre in the broader subfield of gang studies at least a few decades ago. As is evidenced in this chapter, Diego Vigil's career has done much to propel its development, perhaps more than any other scholar, and thus, he is *its padrino*.[2]

To be sure, Chicana/o gang research is the study of delinquent and criminal subculture formations among the Mexican-American population of the United States. By this point in its chronology, it has seemingly developed a certain set of unspoken parameters and characteristics observed by those who venture into this area of study. As a distinct form of social justice research, some of its most important features are activist in nature. Weide's legacy piece on Diego made clear that the genre's *padrino* had emerged as a hardcore Chicana/o civil and educational rights activist before becoming a bona fide academic (Weide 2021). This is also true of his forbearers, such as Robert J. Durán while a student at Weber State University, Victor Rios during high school and college in California, and one generation earlier, Lalo Valdez as a college student in Wisconsin, to name a few.

Whereas social science writing and research tends to be a political act in some manner, influenced by the writers' pre-existing orientation to the subject matter (Shermer 2016), the genre of Chicana/o gang studies is a poignant example. In short, it often has a *causa* or ideological impetus in educating other scholars, and in some cases a more public readership about the structural causes and cultural nuances of Chicana/o gangs in the United States (e.g. Rodriguez 1993). This has partly served to demystify these somewhat hidden or taboo social spheres in a struggle against dominant narratives about "those kind of people" belonging to gangs. And perhaps for embodying these social justice ideals, it is typically daring in both substance and its methodological approach, as was Diego's groundbreaking book, *Barrio Gangs* (Vigil 1988a).

For Diego, the existence of racial-ethnic minority gangs represents a structural and psychological adaptation to poverty, systematic bias, and the marginalization of certain segments of youth from mainstream institutions. A number of protégés have since adopted that perspective, elaborating the premise to apply to particular research questions and scenarios in LA and other US locations (Martinez 2016; Durán 2018; Moreno 2006; Rios 2017; Tapia 2020; Weide 2022). In this view, street and prison gangs might also be seen as a form of resistance to social injustices against the racial-ethnic minority communities from which they disproportionately emerge. If so, those in this field know far less about whether that might operate on an aggregate level, or if only certain types of gang members politicize their gang-related activities and behaviors, a topic we return to at various points in this chapter.

SOCIAL CLASS BACKGROUND AND CLOSING THE GAP ON ACCESS

Since southern California-based Mexican and Chicana/o scholars such as Alfredo Mirandé and Diego began writing on gangs in the early 1980s, the most important work on these largely underclass segments of *la raza*[3] in different US locales, but mainly in the southwestern region, seems to have been done by Chicana/os themselves. It is worth noting that much of the work on Chicago and smaller Midwestern rustbelt cities provides an exception (e.g., Hagedorn 2015; Spergel 1990) in capturing the strong Puerto Rican influence on those Latino gang subcultures generally, but especially in north Chicago. In the southwestern Chicana/o case, high-quality field research is often enabled by the social class backgrounds of Chicana/o scholars because entry to some of the harder-to-reach iterations of these subcultures is not as difficult for them as it is for most outsiders.[4] Moreover, most of the cultural insights elucidated in work done by Chicana/o scholars on gangs assume a higher degree of authenticity for reasons Diego himself noted. This pertains to gang members' normative family and friendship ties within the wider layers of social class and ethnicity. That is, among the general US Chicana/o population (as with other historically oppressed racial-ethnic groups), there exists a considerable degree of familiarity with street deviance among broader (i.e., non-gang) segments of the poor and working-class population. This also likely extends to a sizable proportion of Chicana/o academics, providing them access to gang members by virtue of their common ethnic group's marginalized position in the social stratum and the personal upbringing of each within that context. This is part of what made Diego's work so unique at the time of his first such publications, as his family's working-class background created far less social distance between him and the Chicana/o gang population than most academics of that era experienced.

Thus, perhaps for issues related to the lower socioeconomic position of Chicana/os within the larger US strata, social scientists with such backgrounds are often suited for field research on gangs. Many who have conducted it at some point, and some for the better part of their careers, have often done it in the most up-close and personal way possible, via insider ethnography or direct observation. Diego is easily one of if not the most prominent pioneer in this regard, carefully depicting many of that world's anthro-socio nuances in exquisite detail. We thus were immensely fortunate to have drawn on his expertise to inform our own musings in this chapter. Next, we offer several thoughts on how some features of his biography seem to have charted the course of his personal scholarship and, in turn, that of the larger research genre in general.

Diego's Roots and *Chicanisma/o* across the Social Stratum

One of the things that distinguishes Diego's academic career from that of most other Chicana/o gang scholars is that his first major anthropological study was not about gangs per se, but about the struggle of Chicana/os as a general population against racist, classist, and hegemonic forces historically (Vigil 1980). As noted above, this orientation now seems to be a feature of nearly all Chicana/o gang research. It has become clear over time that most Chicana/o gang scholars possess a sense of duty to write in advocacy of *la causa*.[5] It is no coincidence that the nucleus of Diego's own work derived from the Chicana/o Movement, of which he was both participant and witness.

The street gang experience and the Chicana/o Movement seemed to have fused in Diego's life experience, as he was involved in both at a particular time of rising social awareness. "All of that stuff was planted in my head real young: the violence, the gangs, the *pachuco* tattoo (on my hand)," he told us. Born and educated in LA, his political awakening further oriented Diego toward his future unique approach in gang studies and in his post-college job as a schoolteacher. Diego was present during protests at the Nuevas Vistas educational conference of 1969 in Los Angeles, where then-governor Ronald Reagan spoke. This event led to the "Biltmore Six" case, in which Chicano activists faced questionable charges in relation to fires that broke out at the hotel. A larger group of supporters and activists that included Diego, known among themselves as the "Biltmore 14"—were also arrested for "disturbing a public assembly" and "disturbing the peace," he recalled, during a demonstration outside the building (Ehrenreich 2012).

Diego's youthful experiences surrounded by gang life and his adult experience taking lumps for social justice causes became some of the building blocks for his hands-on approach to conducting gang research. It did not emanate from a narrow definition of criminality, but rather from a more complex understanding of how the communities in which gang members were embedded generated the groups he studied. Consequently, his work imparts on future scholars, who are so positioned, the need to shed more light on the social forces that oppress the most marginalized classes of people in the Chicana/o socioeconomic stratum (i.e., gang members). The depth, diversity, and reach of Diego's scholarship is made clear in highlighting select aspects in its evolution, from the streets, to the Biltmore, and finally toward academia.

Diego's earliest and constant work on the educational experiences and acculturation of urban Chicana/os is telling of his own consciousness of the sociopolitical plight of this US ethnic group (Vigil 1999). He is surely one of the few living gang researchers still in possession of his original Brown Beret headwear for example. This group was considered the most radical and militant faction of the Chicana/o Movement. Diego's work eventually demonstrated that gangs are a direct byproduct of the structure and fabric of normative community and family spaces. In fact, his notable multiple marginalization model demonstrated how gang formation and its many typologies are conditioned by numerous aspects of low-income communities, borne of them in combination with the superstructure that envelops them. This orientation eventually evolved into one of his most significant theory-building contributions to the contemporary scholarship on gangs. While Weide

(2021) offers an excellent description of the perspective, we note that it has had broad utility, even in the mainstream gang research. For example, both Freng and Esbensen (2007) and Krohn et al. (2011) conducted rigorous quantitative tests of the perspective using cross-racial survey data, finding robust support for the framework among youth gangs. Johnson and Mendlein (2022) found support for it outside of the United States, testing its merits cross-culturally in an international scope.

A piece stemming from Diego's *Barrio Gangs* book was called "Gang Processes and Street Identity," wherein he depicted the street gang as a socializing mechanism and emphasized how the negative aspects of gang life were seized on by media of the 1980s (Vigil 1988b). This led to distortions, such as the conflation of inner-city Chicano boy subculture with the hardcore criminal lifestyle of the pinto segment of Chicano communities by police and by the non-Chicana/o public (Freng and Esbensen 2007).[6] Even middle- and upper-middle-class Chicana/os who are distant enough from working- and lower-class segments are subject to adopting purely negative views of Chicana/o gangs based on these stereotypes. That a great many of them continue to join the ranks of police forces, even in the midst of the current crisis with the institution's legitimacy (e.g., Todak 2017, and other developments since the George Floyd murder and trial in Minneapolis) is direct evidence of the continued stronghold of colonization on Chicana/os at large.

As Valdez (2003) observed, vast segments of the "traditional" Mexican-American population are also subject to the biases of the mainstream against Chicana/o street types and gang members. Given Valdez's own closeness with Joan Moore as her mentee, this typology was likely influenced by Vigil and Moore's (1987) four family types in Chicana/o barrios. One of these was the *cholo* underclass, a deeply embedded gang member, although Valdez called this type "non-traditional." Moreover, while rebellious Chicana/o youth that are not members of the underclass ("conventional, uncontrolled" per Vigil and Moore) might experiment with the gang lifestyle, it is often short lived.

As Marjorie Zatz (1987) noted about Chicana/o gangs decades ago, exaggerated public attention to their existence and activities perceived as problematic is the stuff of moral panics. It tends to enable overt police action against such a "public enemy" with carte blanche licensure to disrupt, dismantle, and destroy social groups considered threats to public safety (Rios 2017). The theoretical integration that Diego's work employed not only highlighted the control aspects of social disorganization, but complemented Zatz's insights. It borrowed from conflict theory to show how structural and cultural forces create pockets of concentrated disadvantage and violence—the very conditions that criminalize and villainize poor populations.

As an example of Diego's range as a scholar, some of his work more objectively focuses on methods and conceptual approaches in gang research. Such self-discipline allowed him to effectively demonstrate the application of lofty structural frameworks to understand and explain the culturally rich and layered barrio gang phenomenon in traditional academic terms. For example, in 1990 Diego published a piece with John Long (Vigil and Long 1990) that extolled the virtues of conducting grounded anthropological research on Chicano gangs using ethnographic methods. In "Emic and Etic Perspectives on Gang Culture," they laid this out in a comparatively obscure chapter in an edited collection of gang essays. This piece began as purely methodological in nature, and then shifted to demonstrate how to connect insights from direct observation to larger sociological theoretical concepts. It is an example of the generalist tendencies Diego exhibited, making his work more relevant to gang studies at large (Freng and Esbensen 2007; Tita, Cohen, and Enberg 2005). In fact, his contemporary work on the ethnic diversity of gangs in LA, fittingly titled *A Rainbow of Gangs* (Vigil 2010) won him a number of awards and underscored how many of the same mechanisms are at play in gang formation and activity across racial and ethnic groups in that "megacity." In some of his recent works, Diego has also co-written exclusively about the Black gang experience in LA (Brown, Vigil, and Taylor 2012).

Overlap across the Gang and Academic Stratum

Given the social justice orientation of issues in Chicana/o gang research shared by Diego and many of those influenced by his work, we wonder about the relevance of *la causa* to the gang population itself. While Diego's impact on the trajectory of gang studies and its future scholars is clear, the extent to which the people and communities he studied share similar ideological motivations from their position in the stratum is less clear. In this section we address whether influential Chicana/o gang members in particular share the types of awareness and orientation toward the power arrangements and social processes in which they are embedded that gang scholars do. While it may be obvious to gang scholars that the *existence* of Chicana/o gangs resulted from decades or centuries of endemic racism and classism, the level of awareness of these factors among gang members themselves and whether it matters to them is quite another question.

We dare to ponder about the extent to which Chicano gang members, and perhaps most relevantly their leaders, are cognizant of issues of systemic discrimination against *la raza* and if it becomes an impetus to action for them. In doing so, we address the supposed roles of two distinct types of actors in the Chicana/o social sphere—the gang leader with a class sensibility and the academic with the same trait—in combating social injustices against their shared ingroup. Unlike research done on the grassroots political movements of Black and Puerto Rican gang members, such as the work of Dawley (1992), Brotherton and Barrios (2004), and Hagedorn (2015), to our knowledge there are few comparable works in the Chicana/o case. David Montejano (2010) provides a rare exception for Texas in a book length project.

The issue above is important to highlight in that despite Diego's Chicana/o activist background, his research, and its implied concern with the advancement of this ethnic group, there remains a notable knowledge gap on the gang-*movimiento* nexus in the larger genre of Chicana/o studies. Diego briefly addresses the topic in the final chapter of *The Projects* (Vigil 2007), wherein he describes a period in the 1960s when "demonstrations, boycotts, walkouts, and other acts of civil disobedience became new ways for gang members to demonstrate an antisocial attitude" (179). He goes on to tell about a short-lived effort by former gang members to seek barrio betterment by reverse-patrolling the police to document their brutality against *raza* and conduct its own abatement of drug using and dealing in South Central LA. When that effort ended in tragedy, it fizzled and became just another footnote in the slim nexus between Chicana/o gangs and the Chicana/o civil rights movement (a.k.a. *el movimiento*).

Clearly, gang scholars and influential gang members are two distinct, highly capable actors within a diverse class structure in the Chicana/o population, but who are arguably engaged in related battles, despite operating in radically different spheres. Moreover, although the battleground for deeply embedded gang members more often has real-time, physically tangible, and even deadly features associated with their spaces and movements in the struggle against systematic oppression—conscious or not—they may not consider it an ideological battle in the way the gang researcher does. This is a viewpoint shared by Diego when asked about the topic during our writing of this chapter. We think this is an interesting question for Chicana/o studies at large in terms of understanding whether, how, and why each type of actor winds up in their respective but related battle—again, one ideological, and one practical from within their respective "worlds." And yet, adding complexity to this question is that some seem to have broken those otherwise defining strata dividing gangs and academics, evidenced by the higher-profile gang member-turned-scholar in the field, such as Robert Durán and Victor Rios.

Diego, on the other hand, came of age before the sharp demarcation of gang *member* versus non-member became so salient among the lower- and working-class youth population of LA where he grew up, standing in contrast to the 1990s when the next generation of scholars came of age. Here, we are reminded of the apparent influence of early community scholars like Frank Tannenbaum (1938) on Diego's work, which demonstrated that gangs are enmeshed in the fabric of the communities from which they originate. The types of neighborhoods that produced scholars like Durán, Rios, and Vigil likely resemble each other in certain structural characteristics, with each of these scholars being embedded in street-life contexts to varying degrees as youth.

Given Diego's own fieldwork experiences with influential Chicano gang leaders, one of our objectives was to think more deeply about the meaning of their indoctrination into *Chicanismo* and address this issue with Diego directly. Gang leaders relay a certain form of spiritualism and honor virtues to their members, rooted, in part, in the imagery and sentiment emblematic of the Chicana/o Movement era of the early 1970s. For example, Chicano prison gangs throughout the southwest use the mythology and symbolism of Aztec warriors in their artwork and trademark tattoos to denote membership (prohibited for use by non-members). They also employ pieces of Aztec Nahuatl language to code their communication among the membership and non-incarcerated associates (Kolb 2021; Morill 2008; Morales and Santana 2014; Valdez and Enriquez 2011). Often overlooked by Chicana/o gang scholars, these are some of the chosen tools used in conducting the central business of the gang. As they are considered an illegal enterprise both in and out of prison in terms of the repressive state apparatus' efforts to dismantle "organized crime" groups with local Security Threat Group designations and federal Racketeer Influenced and Corrupt Organization (RICO) statutes, these gangs' forms of communication are highly coded and encrypted, often with ancient terminology and symbolism.

This suggests that the Chicano gangs of the highest order have a keen awareness of history, pride, and struggle related to their ethnic group. At the level of repression that they face in institutional and public spaces, the struggle against hegemonic forces is profound in the gang context. It follows that, as an oppressed group in prison and on the streets, the intelligent and capable individuals at the helm of such organizations are also more generally aware of the "normative" struggles of their ethnic group against these forces. Unlike gang researchers, however, it is by no means a chief concern for them, perhaps viewing it as a luxury compared to their imminent reality of daily struggle versus those of the economic or political type in the "free world," which scholars are paid to theorize and write about.[7] This too was a point on which Diego could agree in our discussions with him about this chapter: "You can't get total buy-in from most of these guys on issues of their own self-betterment, let alone political questions for *la raza* at large, as their lives are complicated by many [more immediate] concerns that typically plague the underclass."[8]

Normally, the immediate concerns of the active Chicano gang leadership are in navigating the treacherous waters of street and prison gang politics, instilling a fierce sense of loyalty within the groups they lead, and demonstrating sheer ferocity in plying their trade. We thus wonder about the extent to which these types have considered themselves as modern, frontline warriors against the white dominant establishment, whether on the streets facing the threat of police harassment and brutality or in the oppressive confines of the penitentiary. If this orientation is shared by some or most serious gang members themselves (e.g., prison gang leaders and many of their deeply indoctrinated members), how might this affect the thinking on questions of ethnocentric unity and conflict in the underclass segments where gangs thrive? Finally, given their deviant and outlaw status, their position in the social stratum, and the implications for repressive forces to monitor and control them, the point may be somewhat moot. That is, could gang members, as such, be effective in a political or social unity movement if they decided to engage in these practices? Given they are, by definition, incapacitated, perhaps these issues would be most salient in a prisoner re-entry and reintegration context.[9]

Diego's Influence on the Next Generation of Gang Scholars

Diego's legacy of activism and scholarship made widespread and significant impacts on the field in addition to the careers and future contributions of many of his students and younger colleagues. He continues to make himself available to a host of gang scholars via dedicated mentorship. Not only is his work widely cited and acclaimed, but those who were lucky enough to come under his tutelage have had illustrious careers in the subfield of gang studies and broader fields of sociology and anthropology. His most notable, direct progeny in this regard is probably Victor Rios, a former gang member from Oakland, whose work has received major awards and who is now the most recognized gang scholar of his generation. Rios publicly credits Diego's influence, fully using multiple marginality concepts and other ethnographic methods he learned from Diego's work and through his mentorship.

Another notable gang scholar who has been influenced by Diego and his work is Robert Durán, whose own work best exemplifies the activist-social justice tradition that we described in prior sections. Both Durán and Diego share a connection to Joan Moore, who served on Durán's dissertation committee and who clearly helped to shape his approach to conducting fieldwork. Weide (2021) notes how Durán and Diego also share the style of contextualizing the historical circumstances of their field research sites.

He also states that Durán's work represents an extension or "evolution" of Diego's multiple marginality framework in that it goes even further in delineating systemic oppression against Chicana/os.

Of course, Robert Weide, the LA native and fast-rising critical gang studies scholar who recently penned an excellent legacy chapter on Diego Vigil (Weide 2021), has benefited directly from a personal friendship and collegiality with *El Padrino*. As with the other notable of Diego's mentees, his influence is markedly evident in Weide's reflexive style of fieldwork, his street-oriented positionality, and his historical orientation to gang studies. Above all, the influence of Diego's multiple marginality perspective on the analyses featured in both Weide's dissertation (on which Diego was a committee member) and in his resulting book, *Divide and Conquer: Race, Gangs, and Conflict* (Weide 2022), is clear.

While the career trajectories and scholarly contributions of those who have enjoyed Diego's direct mentorship are easily lauded, a testament to his reach is also evidenced by his influence on others who did not have such personal access. For example, how have the current authors benefitted from Diego's work in guiding their own gang studies? In terms of inspiration and gaining a general orientation to conducting Chicana/o gang research, this has occurred in too many ways to count. But more specifically, Moreno (2006) applied Diego's multiple marginalization concept to the rural Yakima Valley in Washington State. The southwestern urban region's "cholo" style influenced street culture there, at first through the spread of cultural pride such as in *Low Rider* magazine, which was founded in San Jose in 1976 and distributed widely across the west coast. Later gang migrants brought in the opposing Norteño and Sureño ideologies, which influenced a generation of marginalized youth to become violent toward each other beginning in the early 1990s.

When Moreno conducted his study, such gangs of the California brand existed in Yakima for more than 10 years, and this particular subculture was already present in the local communities. Diego's framework fit the conditions of that region as well as his native southern California, which is a thousand miles away and far more urbanized. "There is an internal reasoning to the Chicano gang subculture," Diego observed, "and because of its sense of camaraderie it is able to attract and socialize many youths."[10] Multiple marginalization, in fact, is an application useful for gangs universally, despite geography and specific local conditions. For example, Moreno's ongoing work on gang history in San Jose bears out similar conditions in terms of local dynamics, with gang migration through the 1990s that built upon historic forms of multiple marginalization in neighborhoods and in schools, including factors such as de facto segregation.

Diego's work was instrumental to Tapia's (2017) history of San Antonio barrio gangs, which had a heavy emphasis on the layout of physical spaces, barrio gang territory (both psychological and actual), and its *desarrollo* over time in the midst of city growth. The ability of barrio traditions and boundaries to withstand rapid urban infrastructural developments and its changing of the landscape was a central theme there, as were the dynamics of barrio social networks across generations. These themes are directly influenced by the work that Diego conducted with his peer-mentor, the late Joan Moore, in a piece from the pioneering Chicano Pinto project. In 1983, they and Robert Garcia published "Residence and Territoriality in Chicano Gangs" in the journal *Social Problems* (Moore, Vigil, and Garcia 1983). It addressed these issues of set and psychological space and the dynamics of longstanding barrios in terms of fictive kin, actual residential location and mobility, and changing rules for membership based on the gang's reputation, its geographic boundaries, and homophily.

THE CURRENT STATE OF THE GENRE

We have emphasized that Vigil's work did much to establish Chicana/o gang studies as its own genre. However, today there exists a cloud of irony over the current and future state of Chicana/o gang studies. Unlike many mainstream criminological research topics, or even mainstream gang topics, the genre never became stagnant. But it is questionable whether strictly Chicana/o *street gangs* still exist as a distinct, identifiable social group or delinquent subculture in the same way when the likes of Davidson, Moore, and Vigil introduced that social world to the field. Thus, aside from studying specific contexts, mainly tied to the ongoing carceral state, we are unsure about whether today's gang researchers can legitimately study Chicana/o gangs per se, at the group level, outside of prison walls. Perhaps the only recent evidence to contest the claim comes from documentary films containing interviews and observations of Chicano gang assemblies in places like El Paso, Texas, and Albuquerque, New Mexico (Blazquez 2021). Yet, because these videotaped interactions tend to require some setting up of the interview and observation arrangements (i.e., they are not spontaneous, naturally occurring events), it does not go very far in proving that gangs still exist in their purest form in Mexican-American barrios. If they do exist, certainly they are not nearly as abundant as they once were, nor do they exist in the same form, organizationally (Gundur 2018, 2019; Tapia 2017, 2020).

For reasons that are surely complex and perhaps impossible to fully pin down, there has been a recent decline of the classic archetypal phenomenon that *Chicana/o* gang research has portrayed in print for nearly a century. To begin, the quintessential group-oriented activities of US street gangs are now scarce in public settings, even urban ones. That is, for Chicana/os, the turf-claiming, hand-sign-flashing, color-coded, membership-driven loyalty to the "klika" with all of its rules, regulations, and organizational features appears to be disappearing from the barrio landscape. Even the traditional structure of Chicano prison gangs has changed in ways that make its organizational parameters and integrity ambiguous (Pyrooz and Decker 2019). There is also new evidence from Texas that gang involvement diminishes drastically upon leaving prison (Pyrooz 2022).

Chicana/o street gangs continue to have a presence on social media, but in the physical world they have morphed in ways that make them far less recognizable as gangs per se (Blazquez 2021). For example, in Texas and New Mexico, most Chicana/o gang-affiliated persons roughly in the 18–35 age range are part of street-to-prison hybrid federations now purposely organized loosely under the "Tango" label and generally grouped by major cities (Tapia 2017). As part of this change, underclass youth that might have belonged to longstanding enemy street gangs now ally to combat the oppressive and exploitative practices of the traditional Chicano prison gangs. The latter are also rapidly declining in their organizational integrity in the prison setting and forming new, non-traditional alliances with otherwise dissimilar groups outside of prison walls.

Given high levels of racial-ethnic mixture in modern, normative urban settings but particularly in underclass neighborhoods, delinquent and criminal groupings (typically now smaller, ephemeral crews with no name, symbol, etc.), have become more racially and ethnically mixed, seemingly foreshadowed by Diego's *Rainbow of Gangs* and further confirmed in his book *The Projects*. In the Texas Tango and New Mexico "Tango-like" contexts discussed above, these groups began to accept non-Chicano members into their ranks. At first this was done to achieve a "power in numbers" objective, but now it is simply a rational adaptation to growing racial-ethnic heterogeneity in mate selection and fertility patterns in the larger society (Jones, Marks, and Rios-Vargas 2021). Viewed in this way, the study of the most intense forms of criminal and delinquent subcultures, beyond prison walls, among Mexican-Americans per se has quite possibly become an obsolete specialty among social scientists. Scholars of this persuasion may now be relegated to study either barrio history or cross international borders to find and explore the more archetypal formations that US Chicana/o scholars once depicted in such elaborate detail.

Still, some, perhaps including Diego, would argue that any modern manifestations of Chicana/o gang formations, although shifting and morphing, multiracial in composition, and devoid of clear organizational parameters or geographic boundaries, are still worth analyzing under the rubric of the genre. That is, whatever remnants there are in modern organized crime syndicates involving Chicana/os, their modus operandi, their supposed links to Mexican drug cartels, dealings with other poorly defined groups, and so on is worth exploring in ways that Diego did in *Rainbow of Gangs* (Vigil 2010). However, to do so today might unearth evidence of truces, interracial and interethnic unity, and aversions to the types of reckless and hyperviolent behaviors these subcultures once embodied. In that sense, desistance is perhaps what is currently salient in terms of modern Chicana/o gangs or rather former gang members, even in the prison setting (see Pyrooz and Decker's 2019 work on gang disengagement in prison). In this way, the practices of modern would-be gangs, or those underclass subjects of the millennial generation, seem more practical than those of past generations, conjuring up notions of an evolved form of rationality among modern Chicana/o gang members. Some of this appears to be a deterrent effect, driven in part by vigilant police suppression by specialized gang and street crime tactical units, while some is driven by internet/social media effects and the demographic trends described above.

In terms of possible future courses of work on Chicana/o gangs, it is worth noting that both Moreno (2006) and Tapia (2014) discovered the reproduction of archetypal Chicana/o gangs in non-traditional Latino destinations where these delinquent formations had only a nascent history. Although it has been at least 10 years since each conducted this fieldwork, it is possible that the phenomenon they documented is still occurring in the non-traditional destinations where newly assimilating Mexican immigrants continue to settle. However, given our assessment of the current state of street gang formation in the United States, we would be surprised to find certain marginalized segments of youth in those communities replicating the classic elements of Chicana/o gang subculture. To test this hypothesis in places such as Georgia, North Carolina, Ohio, Tennessee, and other non-traditional receiving places with large influxes of Mexican immigrants would require a unique profile of a bilingual social scientist familiar enough with Mexican national or *paisa* subculture to navigate those worlds. As of this writing, there are seemingly not many U.S.-based scholars with that unique mix of substantive interests and ethnographic skill sets—although there may be such individuals in the scholarly pipeline.

Illusions of Ethnic Gang Unity?

In various parts of his 2007 book titled *The Projects* Diego describes having sought out the assistance of Father Greg Boyle, the now iconic spiritual and practical leader of the Homeboy Industries movement, a remarkably successful program to help improve the lives of former gang members and prison inmates from Los Angeles. At its core, an underlying philosophy of the program is peace—that is, an anti-conflict, anti-violence, self-betterment and unification movement across barrio and racial loyalty. This is important to any discussion of Diego's impact on the field because, although his collaboration with Father Boyle was in part based on the practical objective of gaining the trust of the residents of the Pico Gardens housing project he studied in east LA, it undoubtedly also represents coming "full circle" in an academic career that started out with barrio unity and peace in mind. In fact, Diego wrote about the process and function of establishing peace treaties between gangs in his book on the Pico Gardens housing project in east LA (Vigil 2007).

To date, any amount of recognition of a history of oppression or sentiments of *carnalismo* (brotherhood) outside of one's particular gang shared by any racial-ethnic street or prison gang population was never enough to unify gangs of the same race or ethnicity in the United States. We thus wish to use this opportunity to briefly explore notions of Chicana/o gang member unity and division in light of Vigil's life's work and its underlying philosophy. A conceptual page taken from the colonization model that some Chicana/o gang scholars use in their analyses that might be useful here is the "divide and conquer" premise. It appears that this is accurate in that Chicana/o gang members, like many underclass populations, have long bought into the larger American cultural principle valuing rugged individualism, albeit in a black market street crime context. The harsh reality is that for decades Chicana/os have killed, maimed, cheated, disrespected, belittled, and betrayed each other in the gang context for many reasons, but chief among them is competition in the drug market and control of associated turf. In thinking about the issue historically, this modern (post-1980s) form of intra-ethnic conflict in the urban setting was perhaps more intense than any other comparable context for intra-ethnic Mexican-American conflict, given the abundance and lethality of modern weaponry.

Gangs are undoubtedly embroiled in violence. Yet broad assumptions about acceptance and encouragement of that behavior at all times and in all circumstances overlook more nuanced understandings of who gang members are and what values they collectively promote. The history of gang-related violence in Texas, for example, demonstrates that there are both internal and external factors contributing to shifts in violence and the ways in which gangs decide to embrace or discourage those actions (Tapia 2023). They have also been known to sign peace treaties among themselves and suppress drug-trade violence with street-tax enforcement (Morales and Santana 2014). As noted by Useem and Clayton (2009), the limiting of violent action among gangs is driven more by an immediate functional concern rather than by ideology.

In the history of intra-ethnic gang relations among well-established Chicano and Latino gangs, there is the episodic emergence of truces and peace treaties between some of the more formidable, well-organized groups (e.g., Vigil 2007). Some of these have been short lived, serving an immediate political or economic purpose in prison, on the streets, or both, and some have been long lasting. Indeed, gang organization can have paradoxical effects in this regard. For example, although it might as well be relegated to urban lore given how drive-by shootings proliferated even after the following event took place, the Mexican Mafia in California was said to have established an "edict" prohibiting the use of drive-by shootings by southern California Chicano gangs in 1992 (Valdez and Enriquez 2011; Vigil 2007). Nonetheless, it is widely accepted by both veteran gang officers across the southwest and gang observers of any ilk that Chicano prison gangs across the region followed suit in outlawing drive-by shootings.

While Diego's explorations of Chicana/o gang subculture in the 1980s and 1990s and the multiple marginality thesis had something of an empathetic tone, portions of his later findings became slightly more cynical with regard to the (d)evolution of the Chicana/o gang subculture. For example, in Chapter 3 of *The Projects* (Vigil 2007), he states that modern gangs had become a bastardized version of those of prior generations, citing a decline in honor values since the 1950s and 1960s and becoming a purely destructive force by the 1990s. He attributed these developments to the growing availability of guns and drugs in the barrio.

Similarly, Stoll wrote about Salvadoran *mareros* once possessing a class consciousness—and a Robin Hood mentality (Stoll 2017). But by the late 1990s, their subculture had degraded to war-bent factionalism and territorialism, control for drug markets, and rampant drug addiction. Stoll goes on to write about Central American gangs (MS-13) in LA, stating "they seemed more interested in fighting against other gangs than fighting the police" (6). Thus, the short-sighted concerns that most gang members experience on a daily basis is a point that even Diego himself acquiesces to after decades of knowing and conducting research on them. Given the apparent subjugation of gang leaders and members by the American ideology of individualism and materialism, it appears from the issues entertained in this chapter that for most of their history, and perhaps now permanently, US Chicano gangs have gone the way of the Central American gangs in LA, now each in a state of arrested development.

Conclusion

Diego Vigil's academic career has been nothing short of inspiring and remarkable, mainly in terms of his contributions to the discipline of Chicana/o studies. In that vein, he specialized in and helped to pioneer the subfield of Chicana/o gang studies in particular. While the genre's current status and future appears to be in a state of flux, the anthropological and sociological insights exhibited in Diego's work are valuable lessons frozen in time and written "for the ages," capturing a distinct urban ethnic underclass subculture's structure, causes, and nuances in ways that few have been able to do since. In this chapter, we sought to examine select aspects of Vigil's life and work in relation to the larger genre's ethos, history, and future. We found that the notion of *Chicanisma/o* as a radical, grassroots activist identity geared toward the betterment of a marginalized and systematically oppressed ethnic group in the United States had much to do with the development of a world-class scholar. This type of background, or at least a sympathetic and honorific orientation to it among the generation of Chicana/o gang scholars to come after Diego, is seemingly a common intellectual thread shared by this class of scholars generally. We are proud to be considered part of that tradition, honored that we were asked to write about such an important figure in it, and hope that readers have taken away a better understanding of the *Padrino*'s place as a pioneer and giant in the Chicana/o gang studies genre.

Notes

1. If we consider James Diego Vigil the "Padrino" of Chicano gang research, then Joan Moore is the obvious "Madrina" of this genre. A true pioneer in this subfield, her work preceded Diego's by several years. As such, she mentored and collaborated with Diego in his early career via the funded Chicano Pinto project. A legacy chapter on Joan Moore's life and career contributions to gang studies, written by Mancillas and Weide (2021), details the comradery and working relationship Diego and Joan shared. A tribute piece to her life's work also appears in the current volume, written by Diego himself.
2. In Chicana/o prison gang subculture, a prospective member must be "sponsored" or sanctioned and ushered into the gang by a *padrino*—a trusted, respected and "made" member of the gang, typically an elder who is vouching for the value of the recruit as a worthy member. This individual also provides the new recruit with the knowledge needed to navigate the gang's rules, structure, and politics. The more conventional usage of the term *padrino* in Mexican and Chicana/o culture refers to one's "Godfather" as in a Catholic baptism, wedding, or religious confirmation.
3. This is the most common term used by non-anglicized Mexican-Americans across various strata, but mainly among the working class. It was adopted by 1960s grassroots political movements, namely in Texas, and by many Chicana/o academics to signal to others their political or social justice orientation. It translates literally as "the race" but more accurately as "the *gente*" or "the people."
4. Although there are many important exceptions, including John Hagedorn, Ruth Horowitz, Joan Moore, Bill Sanders, and Robert Weide.
5. "Viva la Causa" was a slogan adopted by Cesar Chavez, Dolores Huerta, and others during formal organization of the United Farm Workers Association at a convention in Fresno, California, in 1962. This labor movement's iconic symbol, the "farmworker eagle," became a symbol of solidarity for young people who identified as Chicana or Chicano and who sported the slogan and emblem on propaganda that was sewn, drawn, or pinned to their clothing, or printed on banners and flags in public demonstrations during the late 1960s and early 1970s. Ironically, the California Norteños, one of the most significant Chicano gang affiliations across the nation, adopted the United Farm Workers eagle as one of their emblems—although many younger adherents may not understand the history of the symbol or the farmworkers' historic struggle. There is an earlier tradition of Norteño gang members and the ensuing Nuestra Familia prison gang adopting symbolism and terminology of the Chicano Movement era, hence the Nuestra Raza (Raza XIV) label for gang members who identified with northern California as a home base. (That faction later became the Northern Structure, as it is now known).
6. See Victor Rios' (2017) work on Chicano gangs for a contemporary elaboration of these concepts.
7. Montejano (2010), however, provides an important exception, where former hardcore gang youth became politicized either in prison or on the streets of San Antonio and south

Texas during the height of the Chicana/o movement, at times even taking up arms for social justice causes in radical fashion in lieu of sustained serious gang involvement.
8. James Diego Vigil, interview, April 4, 2022.
9. An example is the contemporary sect of the national and century-old League of United Latin-American Citizens (LULAC) once called "All of Us or None," now Big Homies United or Formerly Incarcerated Citizens Progressive Movement, composed mainly of gang-involved former prisoners. https://opencorporates.com/companies/us_tx/0801673 492. Perhaps the most poignant example of a successful former gang member and prisoner movement or formal organization is Homeboy Industries, led by its founder, Father Greg Boyle. Based in LA, it has grown into a multimillion-dollar organization with an extensive national and global network.
10. Vigil, quoted in Moreno (2006, 137).

References

Ben Ehrenreich, "Never Stop Fighting," *Los Angeles Magazine*, March 1, 2012, https://www.lamag.com/longform/never-stop-fighting-11/

Blazquez, Frank. 2021. "Nasty Boy Gang 13: Fabens, Texas, El Paso County." YouTube. October 28. Spade Lake Productions. https://www.youtube.com/watch?v=IoIuAFsfrfo&t=11s.

Bogardus, Emory S. 1943. "Gangs of Mexican-American Youth." *Sociology and Social Research* 28 (1): 55–66.

Brotherton, David, and Luis Barrios. 2024. *The Almighty Latin King and Queen Nation: Street Politics and the Transformation of a New York City Gang*. New York: Columbia University Press.

Brown, Gregory C., James D. Vigil, and Eric R. Taylor. 2012. "The Ghettoization of Blacks in Los Angeles: The Emergence of Street Gangs." *Journal of African American Studies* 16 (2): 209–225. DOI:10.1007/s12111-012-9212-7.

Coltharp, Lurline. 1965. "The Tongue of the Tirilones: A Linguistic Study of a Criminal Argot." *Western Folklore* 26 (4): 276. DOI:10.2307/1499333.

Davidson, R. T. 1983. *Chicano Prisoners: The Key to San Quentin*. New York: Holt, Rinehart, and Winston.

Dawley, David. 1992. *A Nation of Lords: The Autobiography of the Vice Lords*. 2nd ed. Long Grove, IL: Waveland Press.

Durán, Robert J. 2018. *The Gang Paradox: Inequalities and Miracles on the U.S.-Mexico Border*. New York: Columbia University Press.

Freng, Adrienne, and Finn-Aage Esbensen. 2007. "Race and Gang Affiliation: An Examination of Multiple Marginality." *Justice Quarterly* 24 (4): 600–628. DOI:10.1080/07418820701717136.

García, Mario T. 1994. *Memories of Chicano History: The Life and Narrative of Bert Corona*. Oakland: University of California Press.

Griffith, Beatrice. 1948. "American Me." *American Sociological Review* 14 (3): 438. DOI:10.2307/2086901.

Gundur, R. V. 2018. "The Changing Social Organization of Prison Protection Markets." *Trends in Organized Crime* 25: 1–19. DOI:10.1007/s12117-018-9332-0.

Gundur, R. V. 2019. "Negotiating Violence and Protection in Prison and on the Outside: The Organizational Evolution of the Transnational Prison Gang Barrio Azteca." *International Criminal Justice Review* 30 (1): 30–60. DOI:10.1177/1057567719836466.

Hagedorn, John. 2015. *The Insane Chicago Way: The Daring Plan by Chicago Gangs to Create a Spanish Mafia*. Chicago: University of Chicago Press.

Johnson, Nichole J., and Alyssa Mendlein. 2022. "Quantifying Marginality across the Globe: Vigil's Multiple Marginality in Predicting Gang Involvement." *International Criminal Justice Review* 32 (2): 151–177.

Jones, N., R. Marks, and M. Rios-Vargas. "Improved Race and Ethnicity Measures Reveal U.S. Population Is Much More Multiracial." United States Census Bureau. https://www.census.gov/library/stories/2021/08/improved-race-ethnicity-measures-reveal-united-states-population-much-more-multiracial.html.

Kolb, Joseph. 2021. *Blood Ties: How a Texas Prison Gang Became a Cartel Proxy*. Fort Worth: Texas Christian University Press.

Krohn, Marvin D., Nichole Schmidt, M. Alan Lizotte, and Julie Marie Baldwin. 2011. "The Impact of Multiple Marginality on Gang Membership and Delinquent Behavior." *Journal of Contemporary Criminal Justice* 27 (1): 18–42.

Mancillas, Jorge D., and Robert D. Weide. 2021. "The Legacy of Joan Moore." In *Routledge International Handbook of Critical Gang Studies*, edited by David Brotherton and Rafael Gude, 678–690. New York: Routledge.

Martinez, Cid. 2016. *The Neighborhood Has Its Own Rules: Latinos and African Americans in South Los Angeles*. New York: New York University Press.

McWilliams, Carey. 1948. *North from Mexico: The Spanish-Speaking People of the United States*. New York: Greenwood.

Montejano, David. 2010. *Quixote's Soldiers: A Local History of the Chicano Movement, 1966–1981*. Austin: University of Texas Press.

Moore, Joan. 1978. *Homeboys: Gangs, Drugs, and Prison in the Barrios of Los Angeles*. Philadelphia, PA: Temple University Press.

Moore, Joan, Diego Vigil, and Robert Garcia. 1983. "Residence and Territoriality in Chicano Gangs." *Social Problems* 31 (2): 182–194. DOI:10.2307/800210.

Morales, Gabriel, and Juan Santana. 2014. *Don't Mess With Texas! Gangs in the Lone Star State*. South Carolina: Createspace: Independent Publishing Platform.

Moreno, Mark E. 2006. "Mexican American Street Gangs, Migration, and Violence in the Yakima Valley." *Pacific Northwest Quarterly* 97 (3): 131–138.

Morrill, Robert. 2008. *The Mexican Mafia, La Eme: The Story*. San Antonio, TX: Mungia Printers.

Ornstein, J. 1983. "Linguistic and Social Aspects of Pachuco Caló: A Bilingual Variety of the U.S.–Mexico Border." In *Proceedings of the Thirteenth International Congress of Linguistics*, edited by S. Hattori et al., 832–836. Tokyo: Gakushuin University.

Pyrooz, David. 2022. "The Residue of Imprisonment: Prisoner Reentry and Carceral and Gang Spillover." SCCJ Speaker Series, April 15.

Pyrooz, David C., and Scott H. Decker. 2019. *Competing for Control: Gangs and the Social Order of Prisons*. Cambridge, UK: Cambridge University Press.

Quinn, Katherine, Jennifer L. Walsh, and Julia Dickson-Gomez. 2019. "Multiple Marginality and the Variation in Delinquency and Substance Abuse among Adolescent Gang Members." *Substance Use and Misuse* 54 (4): 612–627.

Rios, Victor M. 2017. *Human Targets: Schools, Police, and the Criminalization of Latino Youth*. Chicago, IL: University of Chicago Press.

Rodriguez, Luis. 1993. *Always Running: La Vida Loca: Gang Days in L.A.* New York: Atria Books.

Shermer, Michael. 2016. "Is Social Science Politically Biased?". *The Scientific American*, 314 (3): 316–373.
Spergel, Irving A. 1990. "Youth Gangs: Continuity and Change." *Crime and Justice* 12: 171–275.
Stoll, David. 2017. "Gang Wars of Central America: What Anthropologists Have to Say." *Latin American Politics and Society* 59 (4): 121–131. DOI:10.1111/laps.12036.
Tannenbaum, Frank. 1938. *Crime and the Community*. New York, Columbia University Press.
Tapia, M. 2014. "Latino Street Gang Emergence in the Midwest: Strategic Franchising or Natural Migration?" *Crime and Delinquency* 60: 592–618.
Tapia, Mike. 2017. *The Barrio Gangs of San Antonio, 1915–2015*. Fort Worth: Texas Christian University Press.
Tapia, Mike. 2020. *Gangs of the El Paso-Juárez Borderland: A History*. Vancouver: University of British Columbia Press.
Tapia, Mike. 2023. "Gang Violence in Texas: Urban Dynamics over Time." In *Steeped in a Culture of Violence: Murder, Racial Injustice, and Other Violent Crimes in Texas, 1965–2020*, edited by B. T. Jett and K.W. Howell. College Station: Texas A&M University Press.
Thrasher, Frederic. 1927. *The Gang: A Study of 1,313 Gangs in Chicago*. Chicago, IL: University of Chicago Press.
Tita, George E., Jacqueline Cohen, and John Engberg. 2005. "An Ecological Study of the Location of Gang 'Set Space.'" *Social Problems* 52 (2): 272–299. DOI:10.1525/sp.2005.52.2.272.
Todak, Natalie. 2017. "The Decision to Become a Police Officer in a Legitimacy Crisis." *Women & Criminal Justice* 27 (4): 250–270.
Useem, Bert, and Obie Clayton. 2009. "Radicalization of U.S. Prisoners." *Criminology & Public Policy* 8 (3): 561–592. DOI:10.1111/j.1745-9133.2009.00574.x.
Valdez, Avelardo. 2003. "Toward a Typology of Contemporary Mexican American Youth Gangs." In *Gangs and Society: Alternative Perspectives*, edited by Louis Kontos, David Brotherton and Luis Barrios, 12–40. New York: Columbia University Press.
Valdez, A., and Rene Enriquez. 2011. *Urban Street Terrorism: The Mexican Mafia and the Sureño Trece*. Santa Ana, CA: Police and Fire Publishing.
Vigil, James Diego. 1980. *From Indians to Chicanos: The Dynamics of Mexican American Culture*. Prospect Heights, IL: Waveland Press.
Vigil, James Diego. 1988 a. *Barrio Gangs: Street Life and Identity in Southern California*. Austin: University of Texas Press.
Vigil, James D. 1988 b. "Group Processes and Street Identity: Adolescent Chicano Gang Members." *Ethos* 16 (4): 421–445. doi:10.1525/eth.1988.16.4.02a00040.
Vigil, James D. 2010. *A Rainbow of Gangs: Street Cultures in the Mega-City*. Austin: University of Texas Press.
Vigil, James D. 1999. "Streets and Schools: How Educators Can Help Chicano Marginalized Gang Youth." *Harvard Educational Review* 69 (3): 270–288.
Vigil, James D. 2007. *The Projects: Gang and Non-Gang Families in East Los Angeles*. Austin: University of Texas Press.
Vigil, James D. 2020. *Multiple Marginality and Gangs: Through a Prism Darkly*. New York: Lexington Press.
Vigil, James Diego, and John M. Long. 1990. "Emic and Etic Perspectives on Gang Culture: The Chicano Case." In *Gangs in America*, edited by C. Ronald Huff, 55–68. Newbury Park, CA: Sage.
Vigil, James D., and Joan Moore. 1987. "Chicano Gangs: Group Norms and Individual Factors Related to Adult Criminality." *Aztlan* 18 (2): 27–44.

Weide, Robert D. 2021. "The Legacy of James Diego Vigil." In *Routledge International Handbook of Critical Gang Studies*, edited by David Brotherton and Rafael Gude, 691–705.

Weide, Robert D. 2022. *Divide and Conquer: Race, Gangs, Identity, and Conflict*. Philadelphia, PA: Temple University Press.

Zatz, Marjorie S. 1987. "Chicano Youth Gangs and Crime: The Creation of a Moral Panic." *Contemporary Crises* 11 (2): 129–158. DOI:10.1007/bf00728588.

SECTION 6
RESPONDING TO GANGS

CHAPTER 38

CLINICAL INTERVENTION FOR GANG-INVOLVED YOUTH
Toward an Empirically Validated Model

PAUL BOXER, JOANNA KUBIK, AND
STEPHANIE MARCELLO

IMAGINE you are a clinician or clinical case manager affiliated with the juvenile justice system and presented with two hypothetical new cases for service and treatment planning. Both clients (or patients, depending on your setting) are boys; both are in the middle adolescent age range (about 14–17 years of age); both are members of minoritized racial/ethnic communities; and both appear to exhibit personal, historical, environmental, and developmental risk factors commonly associated with antisocial behavior. These risk factors run the gamut from high levels of emotional lability and cognitive impulsivity, to early maltreatment and other trauma, to negative peer influence and serious family conflict (Borum and Verhaagen 2006). Now imagine that these two cases are alike in all these very important ways, but different in terms of one critical source of risk: one youth is gang affiliated, whereas the other is not.

Gang involvement could be construed as simply another risk factor for violent behavior, violent victimization, arrest, and related health and social challenges—after all, the data have been clear for decades showing that gang affiliation is associated with increases in all sorts of antisocial acts and associated negative outcomes (e.g., Augustyn, Thornberry, and Krohn 2014; Gordon et al. 2014; Lenzi, et al. 2019). Yet from the standpoint of developing an effective strategy for helping a juvenile, gang involvement (or "affiliation" or "membership") can represent a significant barrier to the delivery of successful treatment. For example, gang membership has been shown to substantially reduce the positive impact of some of the most effective treatments available for antisocial youth, such as multisystemic therapy (Boxer 2011; Boxer et al. 2015a).

With respect to the hypothetical scenario in which treatment plans must be developed for two juveniles in the justice system, more or less evenly matched in every way save for gang affiliation, the current state of the science is quite challenging: For the youth who is not involved in gang activity, several highly effective treatment options are available—for example, individually focused cognitive-behavioral treatments for anger, group-based social-cognitive psychoeducational programs for aggression, and home- and community-based behavioral-ecological interventions for reducing delinquency (Boxer and Goldstein 2012; Kemp, Boxer, and Frick 2020; McCart and Sheidow 2016). For the youth who is otherwise highly similar but affiliated with a gang, the prospects for evidence-based and effective treatment are less bright.

Despite a large literature on interventions targeting the variety of problem behaviors and co-occurring conditions associated with gang involvement, researchers and interventionists have yet to put forward an evidence-based strategy for helping individual gang-affiliated youth avoid recidivism, reduce their risks for problem behavior and victimization, or experience reductions in posttraumatic stress or related mental health symptoms. This is not for lack of trying. Indeed, in recent years several efforts have been launched to identify a best-practice approach to helping gang-affiliated youth. This has included federally funded efforts to examine whether top-shelf, well-established programs such as multisystemic therapy (Boxer 2011; Boxer et al. 2015a, 2017) and functional family therapy (Thornberry et al. 2018) are effective for gang-affiliated youth. This also has included some observations shared from interventions delivered in communities and clinics (Branch 1997). Further, toward the broader goal of helping gang-involved youth, gang scholars operating from lifespan or life-course developmental frameworks increasingly have been identifying experiences and processes associated with late adolescent and young adult decisions to exit gangs and gang life—both "push" (internal factors associated with gangs directly) and "pull" (external factors associated with life outside of gangs) forces that lead youth and young adults to desire a gang-free existence (Decker, Melde, and Pyrooz 2013; Densley 2018).

Taken together, findings and concepts from the intervention literature combined with observations from the developmental literature offer a compelling vision for how clinical treatments for gang-affiliated youth and young adults could be optimized. In this chapter, we first consider best-practice treatments for aggressive youth more generally, then discuss how these treatments have been examined in relation to gang-affiliated youth. Next, we connect this work to insights from more recent analyses of data from our own studies and bridge this work to the expanding lifespan and life-course literature on gang desistance and offer a novel, integrative approach to working with individual gang members in treatment.

Treatments for Aggressive Youth

Aggressive youth, particularly those involved in severe and persistent aggression, are notoriously difficult to treat—but effective approaches have been identified (Boxer and Goldstein 2012; Kemp et al. 2020). These approaches target the wide variety of risk factors and sustaining mechanisms for aggressive behavior in a manner aligned with best-practice clinical intervention modalities. It should be noted that in most respects, the behaviors exhibited by gang-involved youth that warrant treatment might not be much different in *kind* from the behavior that would be treated in a more general population of aggressive and violent youth.

Indeed, gang-involved youth and their peers who also are engaged in problem behavior but who are not gang members have quite a bit in common. Gang-involved youth tend to exhibit a variety of problem behaviors and related mental health symptoms that on the surface do not appear all that different from those shown by non-gang youth exhibiting antisocial behaviors. Along with violent or non-violent offending, these symptom profiles include posttraumatic stress reactions, substance use and abuse, and internalizing syndromes such as anxiety and depression.

Gang-involved youth and non-gang youth also tend to have similar profiles of personal and historical risk factors such as high impulsivity and sensation seeking, family conflict, and economic strain (Boxer et al. 2015b; Broidy et al. 2003; Dodge et al. 2008; Kubik, Docherty, and Boxer 2019; Thornberry et al. 2003). Yet when it comes to intervention, gang involvement represents a significant point of departure from these similarities. First of all, as the available evidence thus far suggests, only modest efforts have gone toward applying best-practice models of intervention for aggression and related problem behaviors in gang-involved youth. Second, gang-involved youth might simply not be as amenable to such models as are uninvolved but otherwise highly antisocial youth (Boxer 2019a).

The research literature illuminating effective interventions for aggression and violence has been consistent and coherent for decades and revolves around three basic premises (Boxer and Frick 2008a, 2008b; Boxer and Goldstein 2012; Kemp et al. 2020) generally validated through well-controlled treatment studies (McCart and Sheidow 2016):

1. *Individually focused treatment within a general cognitive-behavioral framework that targets the cognitive and emotional underpinnings of aggressive behavioral choices as well as the control of reactive impulses that can result in aggression.* This aspect of best-practice treatment relies on well-established clinical models of intervention for aggression that teach youth a variety of basic arousal control skills such as deep breathing and responding to early physiological signs of arousal. These strategies also challenge youth to think about their behavioral choices in more positive and constructive ways. It is worth noting that meta-analyses have shown that cognitive-behavioral therapy generally is an effective treatment modality for justice-involved youth (Lipsey 2009).
2. *Family-centered treatment within a general behavioral framework that addresses communication between caregivers and youth, caregiver disciplinary and monitoring practices, and caregiver accountability in managing youth behavior.* This element of a best-practice approach works explicitly with caregivers on using clear communication, setting developmentally appropriate limits, and implementing developmentally appropriate rewards and punishments for target behaviors. Indeed, family involvement has often been identified as a necessary condition for the effective psychosocial treatment of adolescents (Dishion and Kavanaugh 2005).
3. *Ecologically oriented treatment within a general behavioral framework that connects youth and their families to positive, prosocial community activities and supports; increases youths' social capital in their communities; and creates broader community accountability for youth behavior.* In this category of intervention, assets within the broader social ecology are leveraged in support of immediate and sustained positive change for youth by improving or creating relationships with positive role models, replacing problematic behavioral habits and activities (e.g., spending time on the street with negative peers) with new activities (e.g., joining an afterschool sports program). The equifinality (or multicausality) of youth offending and problem behavior generally underscores the importance of a broad ecological approach to intervention (Guerra et al. 2008).

These three categories of intervention targets could be considered the "starting points" for effective interventions with aggressive, antisocial youth. In recent years, researchers have begun to investigate whether evidence-based intervention packages following these basic premises can be applied to serving gang-involved youth specifically.

Applying a Best-Practice Intervention Model to Gang-Involved Youth

Referring back to the hypothetical scenario of two justice-involved youth in need of treatment and matched in every way except for gang involvement—what is it about gang involvement that differentiates these two juveniles in a manner that significantly impacts the prognosis for successful treatment? And how can our contemporary literature on gangs be leveraged toward a more specific intervention approach? To date, there have been only two known attempts to study and potentially validate the use of a recognized best-practice intervention for high-risk, antisocial youth for serving gang-involved youth.

One effort, led by Thornberry, Gottfredson, and colleagues, examined the utility of functional family therapy (FFT; Gottfredson et al. 2018; Thornberry et al. 2018). FFT is an intensive family-focused program that has been assigned top ratings by national evaluative authorities—that is, it is a "certified model plus" (Blueprints for Healthy Youth Development) and "effective—more than one study" (CrimeSolutions.gov). These ratings imply that FFT has undergone scrutiny through randomized controlled trials that have shown sustained positive impacts and utility across multiple independent research teams.

FFT is an intensive treatment program ranging from about 10 sessions in mild cases to up to 30 sessions in more challenging cases delivered over a three-month span in outpatient clinic settings or family homes. FFT targets family processes in the service of youth behavior change, with an explicit focus on improving parent–youth communication, conflict management, and joint problem solving. FFT therapists work to promote parents' efficacy in relating to their youth as well as to community agents in promoting advocacy for needs as well as lasting behavior change. FFT therapists maintain small caseloads (8–12 cases for full-time staff) and primarily engage with youth and caregivers to deliver the intervention.

In studying whether FFT can help gang-involved youth, the research team worked in tandem with a municipal court to implement a randomized controlled trial of a modified version of FFT, called FFT for gangs or FFT-G. FFT-G employed the basic FFT approach described above with enhancements for working with gang-involved youth and their families. Additional program elements involved training for therapists on the nature of gangs, greater focus in treatment on peer relationships and influences associated with problem behavior, more attention to criminogenic risk processes, even more intensive case supervision, and general case oversight from a national expert consultant rather than a local supervisor (Slothower and Fader 2017). Gang involvement was gauged via assessment conducted following random assignment to FFT-G or treatment-as-usual (family therapy treatment program).

Youth responded to three items tapping levels of gang involvement: whether the youth was previously a gang member, whether the youth was currently a gang member, or whether the youth had close friends in a gang. Youth who provided a positive response to any of those three items were considered "high risk" for gang involvement; youth who responded negatively to all three were considered "low risk." Outcome analyses suggested that high-risk youth in the FFT-G condition were significantly less likely to be re-arrested after 18 months post-treatment than were high-risk youth in the FTTP condition (28% versus 43%). No significant differences were observed for low-risk youth (FFT-G: 41%, FTTP: 50%). Although the results of the FFT-G study are certainly promising, the construction of the "gang risk" designation means that it is difficult to discern whether the intervention was specifically effective for gang-affiliated youth.

The second effort to examine the impact of a best-practice treatment on gang-involved youth has been researching multisystemic therapy (MST), led by our team (Boxer 2011; Boxer et al. 2015a, 2017). For the treatment of aggression, violence, substance abuse, and other forms of serious problem behavior, MST has also received top ratings from evaluative authorities based on studies of its short- and long-term effects—"certified model plus" (Blueprints for Healthy Youth Development) and "effective—more than one study" (CrimeSolutions.gov).

In MST, therapists with caseloads capped at five meet intensively with youth, their primary caretakers, and selected community agents over an average of about four months of service (see Henggeler et al. 2009 for detailed information). Interventions are delivered only in natural settings (not therapist offices) and are almost exclusively behavioral in nature (e.g., rewarding youth for positive behavior; teaching caregivers constructive communication and management skills) and based in the youth's natural social ecology. MST therapists engage youth individually as well as with their caregivers and, as needed, school officials, law enforcement or court officials, and other adults who might be involved in the youth's treatment such as afterschool program directors, supportive employers, or coaches. Along with small caseloads, MST therapists receive multiple levels of administrative and clinical supervision and maintain constant efforts to link youth and their families to community supports.

Studies of MST outcomes have consistently found that positive changes in family relations and peer affiliations account for success (e.g., Huey et al. 2000). This is consistent with theory and research on the development of aggressive and antisocial behavior generally, and with implications for gang members specifically. As discussed, gang-involved youth are heavily exposed to the problem behaviors of their peers and can come from very difficult or fractured family backgrounds (e.g., Thornberry et al. 2003). Huey et al.'s (2000) findings, considered within the broader literature along with the intensive nature and robust outcomes of the MST intervention protocol, set a strong basis for considering MST as a first-line approach for gang-involved youth.

In a series of studies, our team found mixed evidence of the effectiveness of MST when applied to gang-involved youth. Using clinical administrative data, Boxer (2011) reported that the effectiveness of MST treatment was diminished for youth who began services with "negative peer involvement" ($n = 124$) or "gang involvement" ($n = 24$) as primary presenting problems. Outcomes were indicated as to whether the youth completed treatment successfully (i.e., all treatment goals met). Unsuccessful treatments resulted in premature case closures due to a lack of family engagement, a new arrest during the course of treatment, placement outside the family home due to behaviors during treatment, or probation revocation due to behaviors during treatment. Among youth who entered treatment with negative peer involvement as a presenting issue, 74% completed treatment successfully—in comparison, 86% of youth who entered treatment without negative peer involvement as a presenting issue completed treatment successfully. Even starker, among youth who entered treatment with gang involvement, only 63% completed treatment successfully compared to the success rate of 85% among youth without gang involvement.

In a subsequent prospective study, Boxer et al. (2015a) applied a multi-model assessment of gang involvement (see Boxer et al. 2015b) and collected data on 421 youth referred consecutively over a 13-month period to MST services by local justice authorities. By integrating self-reports with therapist observations, Boxer et al. (2015b) identified 94 (22%) gang-involved youth. Self-reports were similar in kind to Thornberry et al.'s (2018) "gang risk" variable and included ratings of current (at the time of intake) gang affiliation, former but not current affiliation, and involvement in gang fighting. Therapist indicators included gang involvement mentioned as a problem at intake or identified as an ongoing "driver" (correlate) of problem behavior during the first couple of weeks of treatment. Over the short term, we again observed that youth who were gang involved completed treatment successfully at a rate meaningfully lower (69%) than did youth who were not gang involved (78%). The success differential increased when more specific gang identifiers were used. For example, when only the self-reported survey item indicating current (at the time of intake) gang affiliation was used, the success rate for gang-involved youth was only 38% (Boxer et al. 2015a).

Observations from our 2011 and 2015 studies suggest the idea that gang involvement interferes directly with the effective delivery of intervention services. But what about longer-term effects? Boxer et al. (2017) followed the 2015 sample for one-year post-treatment—with a 12-month "clock" that began on the date of discharge whether treatment closed successfully or not. For this follow-up, the researchers collected data from treatment site supervisors indicating whether and how often youth were arrested during the 12-month time frame. In this analysis, no significant differences were observed between gang-involved and uninvolved youth in arrests—a greater proportion of gang-involved youth were arrested (35%) compared to uninvolved youth (29%), but these rates were not statistically significantly different. A similar pattern was observed for violent arrests in particular—18% for gang-involved youth compared to 13% for uninvolved youth. Even when controlling covariates of gang involvement (e.g., risk taking, peer deviance), examining arrest counts, and analyzing time-to-arrest, no statistically significant differences emerged between gang-involved and uninvolved youth in terms of arrests during the year following MST treatment.

Of course, part of the challenge in documenting significant differences between gang-involved and uninvolved youth with respect to arrests is sample size. Overall, the arrest rate for the full sample of youth who received MST in the 2017 study was 30%—this rate on its own is already quite a bit lower than typical estimates of juvenile recidivism. While there is no consistent national standard for estimating juvenile recidivism, estimates have ranged from a low of about 40% (Aizer and Doyle 2013) to a high of 76% (Durose, Cooper, and Snyder 2014). In this context a recidivism rate of 30% suggests a general preventive effect, which seemed to apply to gang-involved youth just as well as uninvolved youth.

However, this relatively low arrest rate poses challenges to statistical analyses of gang effects, and in this context, it might be instructive to consider some concrete numbers with respect to the specific gang identification measures available. For example, when indicating gang involvement via the self-reported indicator of current (at intake) gang membership, arrest rates are not different statistically but quite different practically. For youth who denied current gang involvement at intake, the arrest rate during the year post-treatment was 29%—similar to the overall trend for the full sample. However, for the 21 young people who indicated at intake that they were members of a gang at that time, the arrest rate was 43%. This rate, in tandem with the short-term treatment success rate for self-rated gang members of only 38%, raises the possibility that there is something especially problematic about active gang membership. Indeed, post hoc analyses of differences in various background factors at treatment intake support this notion (Boxer 2019b): Current gang members entered treatment with significantly higher levels of involvement in both minor and serious delinquency with respect to both frequency and variety; greater risk-taking propensity; more negative attitudes toward education; higher rates of violent victimization; lower levels of caregiver knowledge of behavior and whereabouts; and greater exposure to peer delinquency.

Thus, whereas our overall multi-modal gang involvement indicator allowed us to maximize statistical power for inferences about the impact of any behavioral or social tie to gang activity on MST outcomes, similar to Thornberry et al. (2018), this indicator masked the potentially important probative value of focusing on self-reports of gang membership. But based on relatively recent lifespan research on gang involvement, leaving out consideration of explicit gang membership during treatment might be a particularly problematic oversight.

Is Gang Exit a Necessary Element of Successful Intervention?

In the American documentary film *Heart of Stone* (Braff and Kruvant 2009), a critical dichotomy is set forth. The film documents the impact of an urban high school principal's efforts to reduce violence and improve positive outcomes in his school, and gangs are a major influence in the lives of many of his students. Early in the film we hear from the local police director, who asserts in no uncertain terms that he is perfectly willing and able to assist any youth who wants to work on avoiding trouble—unless the youth is gang involved. The police director states plainly that the police will not work with gang members. This point is then cast in stark contrast with the principal's approach for the remainder of the film: The principal is shown to partner with active gang members in his student body, cajoling them into focusing on their studies and graduating from high school while resolving conflicts constructively and keeping violence out of the school.

In reality, of course, gang membership is not actually an either/or proposition. Following Pyrooz (2013; also see Boxer 2019a), although a youth might claim member status in a gang, this might represent very tangential affiliation through peer networks or heavily embedded active participation. Gang membership might mean the very recent affiliation of a lower-ranking younger member or the longtime affiliation and centrality of a highly placed older leader. For some youth, gang membership might be short term and fleeting while others remain involved over several years (Pyrooz, Sweeten, and Piquero 2013). Entry, exit, and re-entry into gangs can be tracked to increases, decreases, and re-increases in offending behavior and victimization (Augustyn and McGloin 2021; Melde and Esbensen 2013; Pyrooz, Decker, Webb 2014). Youth at high risk for problem behavior certainly enter (self-select) into gangs in part because of the well-understood natural developmental tendency for youth to affiliate with like-minded (or like-behaved) peers (Patterson, DeBaryshe, and Ramsey 1989). But gang affiliation or membership also serves as a risk factor that facilitates engagement in more frequent and more violent offending behavior (Dishion, Véronneau, and Myers 2010; Thornberry et al. 2003).

These observations are aligned with developmental studies showing that youth tend to increase their engagement in problem behavior of all kinds through *deviancy training* (Dishion et al. 1996) or *peer contagion* (Dishion and Tipsord 2011) processes in which peer group dynamics such as status and leadership are driven by group contingencies that incentivize aggressive, oppositional, and related challenging behaviors. Evidence for the impact of peer contagion mechanisms in the context of intervention has emerged through studies showing that reducing negative peer affiliations reduces involvement in problem behavior (Huey et al. 2000) and that aggregating antisocial youth in group-based intervention can exacerbate rather than lessen problem behavior (Dishion, McCord, and Poulin 1999).

One developmental process increasingly identified among gang-involved adolescents and young adults is the relatively natural transition out of gang activity during the transition to adulthood, in tandem with developmentally normative shifts in social and familial roles (Decker, Pyrooz, and Moule 2014). This loosely parallels the oft-noted age-crime curve (Loeber and Farrington 2014), in which offending behavior tends to increase from late childhood into a peak during mid- to late adolescence, and then gradually declines thereafter. The bottom line here is that the normative tasks of the transition to adulthood years—identifying stable employment, forming a family, completing education, and securing financial independence—mostly demand desistance from a criminogenic lifestyle. Given that involvement in crime is the major factor differentiating a gang from any other group of young people organized around some shared identity (as in a sports team or activity club), it makes sense that gang affiliation and involvement in young adulthood would show a trend similar to the age-crime curve.

Then again, although extant research suggests that exiting gangs aligns with normative tasks in the transition to adulthood as well as the age-crime curve, it is a complex process that appears to require a good deal of both internal pressure and external incentive. In addition, unlike the largely positive events that characterize the "turning points" (Ronka, Oravala, and Pulkkinen 2002) driving more normative shifts in antisocial trajectories through the transition out of adolescence and into adulthood, the process of gang exit relies on a mix of both positive and negative events and forces (Roman, Decker, and Pyrooz 2017). Further, gang exits represent more than simple behavioral changes away from gang activity, violence, and other criminality—they indicate meaningful changes in social roles and identity (Decker et al. 2014).

Roman et al. (2017) examined results across three large studies of gang disengagement to understand categorically the reasons that former gang members provide about their rationales for gang exit—looking across specific examples and stated reasons to identify both "push" and "pull" factors leading to exit. *Push factors* are largely adverse experiences or negative potential consequences of gang activity, such as injury or arrest, that push gang members out of gang life; *pull factors* are generally positive social, personal, or economic incentives that pull gang members out of gang life. Following Roman et al. (2017), many group-based approaches to dealing with gangs incorporate a number of specific intervention tactics designed to address pushes and pulls—for example, focused deterrence models that threaten significant legal consequences (push) or connecting gang members to social service supports (pull). Hospital-based violence prevention models connect to gang members victimized by violence (push) to offer treatment and sustained social service outreach (pull).

According to Roman and colleagues, individually focused treatment models (such as MST) certainly can address pushes and pulls as well. But, of course, although some individual treatments are effective for reducing violent and non-violent offending, results, as described above, have thus far been mixed in recent evaluations of top-shelf programs implemented specifically with gang members. Moreover, interventions for gangs as a whole generally have targeted offending behaviors (violence and especially gun violence) without necessarily preconditioning any intervention efforts on individuals leaving their gangs. It does seem, based on the existing lifespan-oriented research on gang exits, that leaving a gang should indeed be considered a critical prerequisite for the delivery of successful treatment services. Yet there is very little in the extant intervention literature offering guidance regarding whether and how that can happen—or be made to happen. This gap exists despite the fact there is now a reasonably sized literature on interventions that target gangs and gang members.

The Broader Landscape of Interventions for Gangs: Approaching an Integrated Model

Interventions into gang activity are not new. There have been programmatic efforts going back decades to address youth gangs and gang violence through group- and community-level (as opposed to individual- and family-level) strategies and tactics (Huey, Lewine, and Rubenson 2016; Kubik and Boxer 2022; OJJDP 2009; Rubenson et al. 2020). In recent meta-analytic work on gang programs, Huey et al. (2016) examined the outcomes of 38 controlled evaluations and discovered that only 42% of studies reported positive (ameliorative) effects on antisocial behavior (e.g., fewer arrests) and only 21% reported positive effects on gang-related outcomes (e.g., lower likelihood of gang joining). In line with the clinical intervention literature highlighting the prospects of peer contagion in group interventions, Huey et al. (2016) also found that 45% of studies showed null or adverse effects on antisocial behavior and 42% reported null effects on gang-related outcomes.

In follow-up work incorporating more recent studies, Rubenson et al. (2020) meta-analyzed 41 controlled evaluations of gang programs and discovered that adverse outcomes were significantly linked to law enforcement engagement. That is, adverse outcomes were more likely when law enforcement officials such as police officers were engaged in programming as service providers—though it was not clear whether law enforcement involvement was problematic due to participant reactance to official authority or increased detection of offending behavior due to closer law enforcement monitoring. Still, one fundamental observation from both Huey et al. (2016) and Rubenson et al. (2020) was consistent: Evaluation studies overall showed mixed effectiveness and inconsistent approaches to design and assessment. In addition, though many programs have been shown to be effective, many have not, and inconsistencies over time and across program targets have led to a contemporary situation where a variety of name-branded packages and generalized models have shown mixed results with no clear standard-bearer.

So where does this leave us? In thinking about an approach to intervention with gang-involved youth that integrates insights from the developmental and clinical intervention literatures, several key tenets emerge.

First, it should be emphasized that gang-involved youth represent more challenging "versions" of youth who are engaged in problem behavior but who are not gang involved. It is certainly the case that gang-involved youth are engaged in higher levels of violent and non-violent antisocial behavior and possess a greater and more intense array of personal and social-contextual risk factors (Boxer et al. 2015a). The best-practice literature that has developed around programs serving youth who show high and persistent levels of serious problem behavior, including violent offending and substance abuse, is very clear. As discussed earlier, **a three-pronged approach leveraging individual behavioral and cognitive-behavioral tactics, substantive and behaviorally oriented caregiver/family engagement, and meaningful linkages to the broader ecology is the basic premise or starting point for effective intervention** with such youth (Boxer and Goldstein 2012). Despite some variability in outcomes and the obvious need for more research, programs in this framework (MST and FFT) have been shown to help gang-involved youth to some degree.

Second, the lifespan research on youth and young adults entering and exiting gangs indicates that **leaving a gang should be considered an important criterion for success in any intervention for gang-involved youth—and perhaps even a requirement for starting treatment**. This observation is bolstered by our work on MST showing clear differences in risk factors assessed at intake, as well as short- and long-term program outcomes for youth who self-identified as active and current gang members at the start of treatment. Yet there is no empirically based guidance on how exactly to encourage youth to leave their gangs in any sort of systematic, replicable manner.

Some of the recent guidance that is available has been solicited directly from youth. Sharkey et al. (2015) collated data collected via open-ended, anonymous interviews with 58 adolescent boys in a minimum-security camp for youth on probation. All boys were selected by virtue of being either in gangs or in close association with gangs, and all responded to questions on how adults could help youth leave gangs. Interestingly, though perhaps not surprisingly, youth offered responses aligned quite well with the "push" and "pull" factors summarized in Roman et al. (2017), such as promoting future aspirations around life, school, and higher education; highlighting the negative impact of gangs; and offering a variety of meaningful ways for families to get involved in the process.

Third and finally, if we recognize the limitations of best-practice treatments with respect to serving active gang members while acknowledging the need to encourage those gang members to leave their gangs, we can easily see the need for a strategy that incorporates tactics targeting gang exit. But what tactics? Therapists working to help individual gang members will need to **aid their clients in identifying, understanding, and leveraging both push and pull factors that can function to spark motivation to change.**

Motivational interviewing (MI) is a person-centered counseling style for addressing the common problem of ambivalence about change. MI is about evoking that which is already present, not installing what is missing. It is not a technique, but rather a set of integrated interviewing skills. Listening is fundamental in MI. MI has demonstrated effectiveness with justice-involved populations (McMurran 2009; Stein et al. 2020). MI uses open-ended questions to invite individuals to "tell their story" in their own words without leading them in a specific direction. The MI practitioner offers affirmations or statements that recognize the strengths of the individual and acknowledges behaviors that lead in the direction of positive change. MI uses reflective listening as a communication strategy to try to understand the individual's ideas and offer the idea back to them, to confirm the idea has been understood correctly. The practitioner provides summaries throughout to ensure an understanding of the individual's perspective. The practice of MI supports individuals in their self-identified goals to facilitate change and recovery and understands that ambivalence is common when someone is looking to make a change (see Miller and Rollnik 2012).

Formative research is needed to render MI appropriate for intervention with gang-involved youth, but as a generalized strategy that has shown effectiveness for a variety of challenging clinical conditions it holds promise.

Conclusion

Given the current state of basic and applied science related to interventions for gang-involved youth, what should be done about our hypothetical justice-involved gang-affiliated client? The boy resembles his hypothetical unaffiliated peer in every way related to other personal and contextual risk factors. Based on that information, he should be engaged as soon as possible in a best-practice, evidence-based intervention like Multisystemic therapy or functional family therapy—or similarly cast programs that have shown efficacy for addressing problem behavior (McCart and Sheidow 2016). However, that comes with a caveat: His outcomes through treatment would be optimized if he is first supported to exit his gang. Even if he is on the younger side, and thus not yet oriented toward the developmental tasks of the transition from adolescence to adulthood, the boy could be made aware of the dangers of remaining gang involved and the benefits of gang exit. The boy might not feel ready or believe that he is capable of exiting his gang—but a therapist trained in motivational interviewing techniques would be able to help him prepare for what could amount to a significant change in his lifestyle and peer networks.

References

Aizer, A., and J. J. Doyle. 2013. *Juvenile Incarceration, Human Capital, and Future Crime: Evidence from Randomly Assigned Judges*. Working paper of National Bureau of Economic Research. DOI: 10.3386/w19102.

Augustyn, M. B., and J. M. McGloin. 2021. "Reconsidering the 'Gang Effect' in the Face of Intermittency: Do First- And Second-Time Gang Membership Both Matter?" *Criminology* 59: 419–453.

Augustyn, M. B., T. P. Thornberry, and M. D. Krohn. 2014. "Gang Membership and Pathways to Maladaptive Parenting." *Journal of Research on Adolescence: The Official Journal of the Society for Research on Adolescence* 24: 252–267.

Borum, R., and D. Verhaagen. 2006. *Assessing and Managing Violence Risk in Juveniles*. New York: Guilford.

Boxer, P. 2011. "Negative Peer Involvement in Multisystemic Therapy for the Treatment of Youth Problem Behavior: Exploring Outcome and Process Variables in 'Real-World' Practice." *Journal of Clinical Child and Adolescent Psychology* 40: 848–854.

Boxer, P. 2019a. "Interventions for Gang-Affiliated Youth." In *Oxford Research Encyclopedia of Criminology and Criminal Justice*. Oxford, UK: Oxford University Press. DOI:10.1093/acrefore/9780190264079.013.526.

Boxer, P. 2019b. *Risk Variation among Current, Former, and Non-Members of Youth Gangs: More Validity Evidence for Self-Nominations*. Presentation at the Biennial Meeting of the Society for Research in Child Development, Baltimore, MD.

Boxer, P., M. Docherty, M. Ostermann, J. Kubik, and B. Veysey. 2017. "Effectiveness of Multisystemic Therapy for Gang-Involved Youth Offenders: One-Year Follow-Up Analysis of Recidivism Outcomes." *Children and Youth Services Review* 73: 107–112.

Boxer, P., and P. J. Frick. 2008a. "Treating Conduct Disorder, Aggression, and Antisocial Behavior in Children and Adolescents: An Integrated View." In *Handbook of Evidence-Based Therapies for Children and Adolescents*, edited by R. Steele, M. Roberts and T. D. Elkin, 241–259. New York: Sage.

Boxer, P., and P. J. Frick. 2008b. "Treatment of Violent Offenders." In *Treating the Juvenile Offender*, edited by R.D. Hoge, N.G. Guerra and P. Boxer, 147–170. New York: Guilford.

Boxer, P., and S. E. Goldstein. 2012. "Treating Juvenile Offenders: Best Practices and Emerging Critical Issues." In *Handbook of Juvenile Forensic Psychology and Psychiatry*, edited by E. Grigorenko, 323–340. New York: Springer.

Boxer, P., J. Kubik, M. Ostermann, and B. Veysey. 2015a. "Gang Involvement Moderates the Effectiveness of Evidence-Based Intervention for Justice-Involved Youth." *Children and Youth Services Review* 52: 26–33.

Boxer, P., B. Veysey, M. Ostermann, and J. Kubik. 2015b. "Measuring Gang Involvement in a Justice-Referred Sample of Youth in Treatment." *Youth Violence and Juvenile Justice* 13: 41–59.

Branch, C. W. 1997. *Clinical Interventions with Gang Adolescents and Their Families*. Boulder, CO: Westview.

Braff, Z., and B. T. Kruvant. 2009. *Heart of Stone*. South Orange, NJ: Good Footage Productions.

Broidy, L. M., D. S. Nagin, R. E. Tremblay, J. E. Bates, B. Brame, K. A. Dodge, D. Fergusson, J. L. Horwood, R. Loeber, R. Laird, et al. 2003. "Developmental Trajectories of Childhood Disruptive Behaviors and Adolescent Delinquency: A Six-Site, Cross-National Study." *Developmental Psychology* 39: 222–245.

Decker, S. H., C. Melde, and D. C. Pyrooz. 2013. "What Do We Know about Gangs and Gang Members, and Where Do We Go from Here?" *Justice Quarterly* 30: 369–402.

Decker, S. H., D. C. Pyrooz, and R. K. Moule Jr. 2014. "Disengagement from Gangs as Role Transitions." *Journal of Research on Adolescence* 24 (2): 268–283.

Densley, J. A. 2018. "Gang Joining." In *Oxford Research Encyclopedia of Criminology and Criminal Justice*. Oxford, UK: Oxford University Press.

Dishion, T., and K. Kavanaugh. 2005. *Intervening in Adolescent Problem Behavior: A Family-Centered Approach*. New York: Guilford.

Dishion, T. J., J. McCord, and F. Poulin. 1999. "When Interventions Harm. Peer groups and Problem Behavior." *American Psychologist* 54 (9): 755–764.

Dishion, T.J., K. M. Spracklen, D. Andrews, and G. R. Patterson. 1996. "Deviancy Training in Male Adolescent Friendships." *Behavior Therapy* 27: 373–390.

Dishion, T. J., and J. M. Tipsord. 2011. "Peer Contagion in Child and Adolescent Social and Emotional Development." *Annual Review of Psychology* 62: 189–214.

Dishion, T., M. Véronneau, and M. Myers. 2010. "Cascading Peer Dynamics Underlying the Progression from Problem Behavior to Violence in Early to Late Adolescence." *Development and Psychopathology* 22 (3): 603–619.

Dodge, K. A., M. T. Greenberg, P. S. Malone, and Conduct Problems Prevention Research Group. 2008. "Testing an Idealized Dynamic Cascade Model of the Development of Serious Violence in Adolescence." *Child Development* 79: 1907–1927.

Durose, Matthew R., Alexia D. Cooper, and Howard N. Snyder. 2014. "Recidivism of Prisoners Released in 30 States in 2005: Patterns from 2005 to 2010." US Department of Justice, Office of Justice Programs, Bureau of Justice Statistics.

Gordon, R. A., H. L. Rowe, D. Pardini, R. Loeber, H. R. White, and D. P. Farrington. 2014. "Serious Delinquency and Gang Participation: Combining and Specializing in Drug Selling, Theft, and Violence." *Journal of Research on Adolescence* 24: 235–251.

Gottfredson, D. C., B. Kearley, T. P. Thornberry, M. Slothower, D. Devlin, and J. J. Fader. 2018. "Scaling-Up Evidence-Based Programs Using a Public Funding Stream: A Randomized Trial of Functional Family Therapy for Court-Involved Youth." *Prevention Science: The Official Journal of the Society for Prevention Research* 19 (7): 939–953.

Guerra, N., K. Williams, P. Tolan, and K. Modecki. 2008. "Theoretical and Research Advances in Understanding the Causes of Juvenile Offending." In *Treating the Juvenile Offender*, edited by R. Hoge, N. Guerra and P. Boxer, 33–53. New York: Guilford.

Henggeler, S. W., S. K. Schoenwald, C. M. Borduin, M. D. Rowland, and P. B. Cunningham. 2009. *Multisystemic Therapy for Antisocial Behavior in Children and Adolescents*, 2nd ed. New York: Guilford Press.

Huey, S. J., S. W. Henggeler, M. J. Brondino, and S. G. Pickrel. 2000. "Mechanisms of Change in Multisystemic Therapy: Reducing Delinquent Behavior through Therapist Adherence and Improved Family and Peer Functioning." *Journal of Consulting and Clinical Psychology* 68: 451–467.

Huey, S. J., G. Lewine, and M. Rubenson. 2016. "A Brief Review and Meta-Analysis of Gang Intervention Trials in North America." In *Gang Transitions and Transformations in an International Context*, edited by C. L. Maxson and F. A. Esbensen, 217–233. New York: Springer.

Kemp, E. C., P. Boxer, P. J. Frick, and P. J. Frick. 2020. "Treating Conduct Problems, Aggression, and Antisocial Behavior in Children and Adolescents." In *Handbook of Evidence-Based Therapies for Children and Adolescents*, edited by R. Steele and M.C. Roberts, 203–218. New York: Springer.

Kubik, J., and P. Boxer. 2022. "Preventing and Reducing Gang Membership." In *Psychology of Gang Involvement*, edited by J. L. Wood, J. S. Mallion, and S. Frisby-Osman, 118–129. New York: Routledge.

Kubik, J., M. Docherty, and P. Boxer. 2019. "The Impact of Childhood Maltreatment on Adolescent Gang Involvement." *Child Abuse and Neglect* 96: 104096.

Lenzi, M., J. D. Sharkey, A. Wroblewski, M. J. Furlong, and M. Santinello. 2019. "Protecting Youth from Gang Membership: Individual and School-Level Emotional Competence." *Journal of Community Psychology* 47 (3): 563–578.

Lipsey, M. W. 2009. "Meta-Analytic Overview." *Victims and Offenders* 4: 124–147.

Loeber, R., and D. P. Farrington. 2014. "Age-Crime Curve." In *Encyclopedia of Criminology and Criminal Justice,* edited by G. Bruinsma and D. Weisburd, 12–18. New York: Springer.

McCart, M. R., and A. J. Sheidow. 2016. "Evidence-Based Psychosocial Treatments for Adolescents with Disruptive Behavior." *Journal of Clinical Child and Adolescent Psychology* 45: 529–563.

McMurran, M. 2009. "Motivational Interviewing with Offenders: A Systematic Review." *Legal and Criminological Psychology* 14: 83–100.

Melde, C., and F. A. Esbensen. 2013. "Gangs and Violence: Disentangling the Impact of Gang Membership on the Level and Nature of Offending." *Journal of Quantitative Criminology* 29 (2): 143–166.

Miller, W. R., and S. Rollnick. 2012. *Motivational Interviewing,* 3rd ed. New York: Guilford Press.

Patterson, G. R., B. D. DeBaryshe, and E. Ramsey. 1989. "A Developmental Perspective on Antisocial Behavior." *American Psychologist* 44 (2): 329–335.

Pyrooz, D. C. 2013. "Gangs, Criminal Offending, and an Inconvenient Truth: Considerations for Gang Prevention and Intervention in the Lives of Youth." *Criminology and Public Policy* 12: 427–436.

Pyrooz, D. C., S. H. Decker, and V. J. Webb. 2014. "The Ties That Bind." *Crime and Delinquency* 60: 491–516.

Pyrooz, D. C., G. Sweeten, and A. R. Piquero. 2013. "Continuity and Change in Gang Membership and Gang Embeddedness." *Journal of Research in Crime and Delinquency* 50: 239–271.

Roman, C. G., S. H. Decker, and D. C. Pyrooz. 2017. "Leveraging the Pushes and Pulls of Gang Disengagement to Improve Gang Intervention: Findings from Three Multi-Site Studies and a Review of Relevant Gang Programs." *Journal of Crime and Justice* 40 (3): 316–336.

Ronka, A., S. Oravala, and L. Pulkkinen. 2002. "'I Met This Wife of Mine and Things Got onto a Better Track.' Turning Points in Risk Development." *Journal of Adolescence* 25: 47–63.

Rubenson, M. P., K. Galbraith, O. Shin, C. R. Beam, and S. J. Huey. 2020. "When Helping Hurts? Toward a Nuanced Interpretation of Adverse Effects in Gang-Focused Interventions." *Clinical Psychology: Science and Practice* 28: 29–39.

Sharkey, J., S. W. F. Stifel, and A. M. Mayworm. 2015. "How to Help Me Get Out of a Gang: Youth Recommendations to Family, School, Community, and Law Enforcement Systems." *OJJDP Journal of Juvenile Justice* 4: 64–83.

Slothower, M., and J. J. Fader. 2017. "Functional Family Therapy for Gang Populations (FFT-G): Program, Implementation, and Costs." Paper presented at the annual meeting of the American Society of Criminology, Philadelphia, PA.

Stein, L., R. Martin, M. Clair-Michaud, R. Lebeau, W. Hurlbut, C. W. Kahler, P. M. Monti, and D. Rohsenow. 2020. "A Randomized Clinical Trial of Motivational Interviewing Plus Skills Training vs. Relaxation Plus Education and 12-Steps for Substance Using Incarcerated Youth: Effects on Alcohol, Marijuana and Crimes of Aggression." *Drug and Alcohol Dependence* 207: 107774.

Thornberry, T., B. Kearley, D. C. Gottfredson, M. P. Slothower, D. N. Devlin, and J. J. Fader. 2018. "Reducing Crime among Youth at Risk for Gang Involvement: A Randomized Trial." *Criminology and Public Policy* 17: 953–989.

Thornberry, T., M. Krohn, A. Lizotte, C. Smith, and K. Tobin. 2003. *Gangs and Delinquency in Developmental Perspective.* Cambridge, UK: Cambridge University Press.

CHAPTER 39

NO PUBLIC BENEFIT
The Placentia Gang Injunction Opposition Campaign

SEAN GARCIA-LEYS AND JESSE ENGEL

HISTORICAL PROLOGUE

Los Angeles—1987

Violent crime in the city was approaching its all-time high.[1] Members of the Playboy Gangster Crips ran a street-corner drug market in a neighborhood the police called Cadillac/Corning (Muñiz 2015).[2] In many ways it was just like hundreds of other corners in Los Angeles. However, this corner was situated on a boundary between the mostly white neighborhoods to the north and west, and the mostly Black neighborhoods to the south and east. The dealers were mostly Black, the buyers mostly white. Law enforcement paid little attention to the corner until one day in 1986 when a young, white, college student was killed over a drug deal gone wrong. Soon after, Cadillac/Corning became a top priority. The city attorney, "John," had been assigned to that neighborhood.[3] Following the murder, John was given permission to try a new strategy—a "gang injunction."

John had spent a year observing the Playboy Gangster Crips, often from an unmarked car, learning how the gang had developed a well-designed, essentially drive-through drug sales operation. With lookouts placed at either end of the block, and resupply ordered via pager in small amounts as needed, police were unable to do anything more than bust a few low-ranking members for relatively small crimes—nothing that even slowed the operation down.

John imagined a novel approach to the problem.[4] If he could get a judge to issue a court order against the gang itself instead of just its individual members, he could attack the operation as a whole instead of the individual people, who were really just replaceable pieces. By doing that, maybe he could shut the entire operation down. It was a radical idea. The US criminal justice system is founded on the notion that criminal behavior is the result of morally deficient individuals, and so individual people should be punished for their personal acts regardless of environment or group membership. Even more, California's court system is divided into separate civil and criminal systems with different rules and requirements, and there was a presumption that drug dealing belonged in the criminal courts. The kind of court order John imagined—an order prohibiting a person or organization from certain future actions—would be a civil, not criminal procedure.

Despite its novelty, John's idea was approved by the city attorney and John went to work. He sued the Playboy Gangster Crips,[5] arguing the gang was an organization amenable to suit in civil court, just like a business. He argued that the gang created a "public nuisance," which California law described as anything that interferes with others' "comfortable enjoyment of life or property."[6] According to John, just as a judge can order a factory located near residences to stop making loud noises at night, so can a judge order a gang to stop selling drugs on a street corner. The judge in the case agreed, and Playboy Gangster Crips became the first gang subject to a gang injunction.

John asked the court for an injunction that prohibited any members of the gang from being out on the block after a curfew. The requested order also prohibited gang members from engaging in otherwise lawful activities like being in public with each other, wearing clothes that identified them as dealers, and more. The court agreed to order the injunction, but after hearing from civil rights lawyers from the American Civil Liberties Union (ACLU), the court limited the activities prohibited by the injunction to only already-criminal activities. No constitutionally protected activities would be prohibited. Though it was unclear whether further prohibiting already-criminal activities would have any practical effect at all, the suit was declared a victory by the Los Angeles City Attorney's office, who then sought more injunctions (Feldman 1987). As a tool to stop drug dealing, the injunctions could never be more than "whack-a-mole," with users simply finding new suppliers and dealers finding new places to sell. But to the people who found it unacceptable that a drug operation could brazenly continue to operate after the killing of a white college student, it was a victory worth repeating. Over the following three decades, gang injunctions proliferated and tens of thousands of people across California became subject to one of over 150 gang injunctions.[7]

INTRODUCTION

Fullerton, Orange County—July 2022

This chapter will explore two of these gang injunctions. Specifically, this chapter will provide a first-person narrative of the successful opposition to two gang injunctions in the City of Placentia in Orange County, California, from the perspective of this chapter's primary author, Sean Garcia-Leys, a civil rights attorney who has litigated several lawsuits related to gang injunctions. The next section will discuss the benefits and harms of gang injunctions and their growth and decline in California as the governing law has evolved, before turning to the events in Placentia that ultimately led to the dismissal of the gang injunctions there. The final section will offer the authors' reflections on the events and their implications.

This chapter challenges the common assumption that criminal gang injunctions' effectiveness and their effects on civil liberties are determined by whether prosecutors win a judicial order and by officers' enforcement of that order. Working closely with alleged gang members and community advocates showed us that the injunction and its enforcement can be less impactful than the response to the injunction by defendants and the community. In part, this is because the actual effects of a gang injunction court order are less than one might expect, since so many of the defendants added to a gang injunction are already on probation or parole with "gang terms" nearly identical to the terms of most gang injunctions. But this is also because defendants and their communities are important actors, and their actions are often overlooked. This chapter will describe a model collaboration between defendants, community members, criminal justice organizers, and pro bono lawyers that stopped two injunctions and led to an "unprecedented" reduction in gang crime (Emery 2018). While prosecutors claimed that the reduction in crime came from the injunction and its enforcement, the narrative presented in this chapter suggests credit for the reduction is better attributed to efforts at social integration and peacemaking led by the defendants and their community.

The Proliferation and Diminishment of California Gang Injunctions

California—1987–2022

Over the 30 years following the Playboy Gangster Crips injunction, gang injunctions became a common tool for California law enforcement agencies. Additionally, injunctions spread to several other states (O'Deane 2012) and to Britain (Carr, Slothower, and Parkinson 2017). At least one other country, New Zealand, is currently discussing adopting them as a gang suppression strategy (Cheng 2021). In 2015, California had gang injunctions in place against over 150 gangs, impacting tens of thousands of people.[8]

Two California court cases allowed for this explosion of gang injunctions. In 1997, the Supreme Court of California decided the *Acuna* case, giving the Court's approval to the prohibition of constitutionally protected activities so long as those activities are enmeshed with the gang's criminal activities.[9] Then in 2007 a state appellate court decided *Colonia Chiques*, which reasoned in favor of allowing prosecutors to name only the gang as the defendant in a lawsuit.[10] Without requiring prosecutors to name individual gang members as part of the lawsuit, police and prosecutors could then bind anyone to an injunction whom they suspected of gang membership merely by telling them they were on the injunction and giving them a copy of the court papers. This practically limitless discretion resulted in a broad application of the injunctions. According to one of my clients, two LAPD officers once drove through the Jordan Downs housing project in the Watts neighborhood of Los Angeles, throwing stacks of court documents out the window at people walking down the street saying, "you're on the injunction . . . you're on the injunction . . ." The potential for overbroad application of gang injunctions resulting from this unfettered discretion was compounded by police's ambiguous ideas of who was a "gang member." Lacking a rigorous definition, law enforcement tended to rely on stereotypes rooted more in California's 150 years of racist oppression of Black and Mexican-American "zoot suiters" and "bandidos" than in anything rooted in the work of Frederic Thrasher or of contemporary academic scholars, much less definitions based on solid, gang-specific evidence (Trujillo 1974). As a result, thousands of people across California became subject to a gang injunction without having either a day in court or legal representation.

Another result of suing a gang as an organization, as opposed to suing individual gang members, is that nobody will typically show up to oppose the lawsuit and the prosecutors can ask for nearly anything and get it. So, where gang injunctions had begun covering only one block or one corner, by 2015 some gang injunctions encompassed the greater part of entire cities.[11] Similarly, the terms of the injunctions expanded from prohibiting only criminal activities or activities clearly connected to those activities to everyday activities like going to a fast-food drive-through after dark, wearing anything with a certain color, going to the neighborhood laundromat if another suspected gang member was already there washing their clothes, having family parties at the park, or having a cell phone (Caldwell 2010). One of my clients was arrested for taking his trash out to the curb after curfew, another for talking to his brother-in-law on his back porch.

Initial studies as to the effectiveness of these injunctions were mixed (American Civil Liberties Union 1997; Grogger 2002; Maxson, Hennigan, and Sloane 2005). A more recent study attributes reductions in crime from 5% to 35% to gang injunctions (Ridgeway et al. 2018). However, another recent study on the effect of gang injunctions on housing prices attributes to gang injunctions a decrease in the price of homes sold in the injunctions' safety zones, suggesting that the social costs of gang injunctions may offset their crime reduction benefit (Owens, Mioduszewski, and Bates 2020). Yet another study found that gang injunctions led to a more complex and embedded structure of conflict between gangs (Bichler, Norris, and Ibarra 2020). The seemingly contradictory findings of these studies highlight the danger of drawing conclusions from the available data given the difficulty in isolating the effects of gang injunctions from other variables.

While the effects of gang injunctions on crime or property values are difficult to isolate and measure, their racial disproportions are not. I know of exactly zero gang injunctions in California ever ordered against a gang with a predominately white membership. Nor is the criticism that gang injunctions are racist limited only to the ethnicity of who is made subject to them. Gang injunctions' entire approach is frequently decried by civil rights advocates as one of the most overtly racist aspects of law enforcement. Injunction terms are remarkably like the "Black codes" of reconstruction-era America, laws enacted to specifically restrict the freedoms of only Black people (Stewart 1998). The injunctions' curfew provisions allowed police to treat enjoined neighborhoods like "sundown towns," towns from America's Jim Crow era where Black people knew to be off the streets by sundown or risk police violence. And in keeping with the history of the first injunction, many injunctions were not brought in places where gang violence was at its worst; injunctions were brought instead in areas where there were predominately white neighborhoods bordering neighborhoods whose residents were predominately people of color (Muñiz 2015).

Accordingly, there has been pushback from community organizers and civil liberties advocates. Community organizations in some cities, including CORE in Oxnard, Chicanxs Unidxs in Santa Barbara and Orange County, and the Stop the Injunctions Coalition in Oakland, attempted to rebrand injunctions as tools of gentrification, not public safety (Barajas 2007; Stop the Injunctions Coalition 2017; Spady et al. 2021). By doing so, they succeeded in stopping or dissolving several injunctions. In 2013, lawyers from the ACLU with pro bono attorneys from the law firm Munger, Tolles, and Olson won the *Vasquez*

v. *Rackauckas* case, a federal lawsuit that resulted in a rule that no one could be enjoined without at least being offered a day in court first.[12] This was a sea change in the law because it eventually led to nearly everyone in the state being removed from the injunctions' enforcement lists as very few people had ever been offered a day in court. Faced with having to start over, create new enforcement lists, and offer individualized hearings to each person on the lists, many law enforcement agencies decided to simply abandon their gang injunction programs, including all of the law enforcement agencies in Los Angeles County.[13] Other agencies, however, have decided to continue their gang injunction programs and have begun offering individualized hearings. While it is unclear how many of California's injunctions are still enforced in 2022 and how many people are subject to them, the number is undoubtedly much smaller than it was before the *Vasquez v. Rackauckas* decision. See Figure 39.1 for a timeline of significant decisions concerning injunctions.

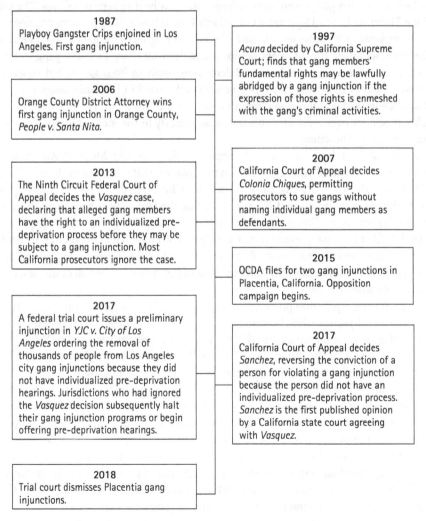

FIGURE 39.1 Timeline of Significant Decisions Concerning Civil Gang Injunctions

The Plas And La Jolla Neighborhood Gang Injunctions

Origins of the Lawsuits

Placentia, Orange County—September 2015

Just south of Los Angeles, in Orange County, District Attorney Tony Rackauckas did not abandon his gang injunctions after the *Vasquez* decision. Instead, he continued to push for more. In 2015, the Orange County District Attorney (OCDA) filed suit against two rival gangs in the City of Placentia—Plas and La Jolla.[14]

The Plas and La Jolla neighborhoods, or *varrios*, were not unusually dangerous and members of the two gangs were only infrequently involved in serious crimes. The OCDA and the Placentia Police Department could attribute 0 homicides, 0 attempted homicides, and just 22 assaults, 9 robberies, 4 vehicle thefts, and 3 fights to the gangs' 70–110 estimated active members over the 5.5 years before the district attorney filed the gang injunction suits.[15] There were a few notoriously violent individuals in both gangs, but nearly all of them were already in prison. A few people who had started in Placentia gangs as teenagers had become important figures in Orange County's drug trade, but they had been out of the neighborhood for over a decade. This injunction clearly fit the mold of injunctions as gentrification, not public safety.

The Plas and La Jolla *varrios* both began as Mexican and Mexican-American farm worker camps a hundred years earlier when the area was still mostly citrus farms (González 1994). When the citrus farms were turned into housing developments, mostly white neighborhoods grew up around the *varrios*, while the two *varrios* kept their character as Mexican-American, or Chicano, neighborhoods. Unsurprisingly to many, not long after the OCDA filed for a gang injunction, the City of Placentia began an attempt to revitalize part of the Plas *varrio* as "Old Town Placentia" (City of Placentia 2017). It appeared that the city's leaders wanted the character and nostalgia of the *varrio* but not all of the descendants of the people who created it.

Like most gang injunction proceedings, the Plas and La Jolla injunctions began in secret. The OCDA filed papers with the court that listed about 50 people, two dozen from each gang, as alleged gang members, but did not notify them about the lawsuit. While serving notice of a lawsuit to the other parties is usually among the very first steps of the process, prosecutors filed briefs with the court warning that if any gang members found out about the injunction prematurely, it could put police officers' lives at risk. This ensured prosecutors would have no opposition in court at the cases' first hearings. Without opposition, there was no one to question how the case should proceed, whether these gangs were actually organizations that could be sued under the law of civil procedure, or to point out that the OCDA's claim that giving notice to the defendants would threaten the safety of police was exaggerated and lacked evidence. After this initial process took place in secret and the OCDA had quietly worked out the initial procedure with the court, the OCDA then began the next step of serving the lawsuit to alleged gang members.

On the morning of September 30, 2015, Placentia Police Department officers fanned out across the city with copies of the 500-page court file looking for around 50 of the alleged gang members. The people they sought were nearly all young men, though they included one juvenile, one woman, and a few people over 30 years of age. Nearly all had been previously convicted for gang-related crimes, though not all for felonies. Police found some of the people they were looking for drinking in local parks. Others were found at their homes. A few were found at McDonald's, where some would go to charge their phones. Many were served in jail, where they had been recently arrested for misdemeanors, or were doing time for minor offenses, or waiting for trial. Police acted professionally, but the people served described the officers' unusually friendly demeanor and good moods as suggesting the officers were enjoying the moment. Officers chatted with some of the people being served, explaining to them what the papers meant. Some of the alleged gang members asked if there would be a warrant for their arrest if they didn't show up in court. The police explained that it was a civil suit against the gang, so they didn't have to do anything if they didn't want to, although the police failed to mention that would make the court's issuance of the injunction a foregone conclusion. Typically, that's exactly what would have happened: No one shows up to the court hearing and the court orders the injunction as a matter of routine.

But that morning, a few of the young men from Plas got together and decided they wanted some advice from someone they trusted more than the police. They visited one of the *varrio*'s mothers, Theresa Smith, a woman who lived a few blocks from the park and who was well known and respected in the neighborhood. Several years earlier, police shot and killed Theresa's son, Caesar Cruz, as he was getting out of his car during a pretextual traffic stop (Saavedra 2019). Since then, she had become a powerful voice in the community and an advocate on the national stage (Morrison 2019). "Mommie Theresa" supported mothers grieving the police killings of their children and she worked with sympathetic law enforcement officers and elected officials on policy reforms that could reduce police killings.

Two of the young men knocked on Theresa's door and asked if they could talk to her. She let them in, and they showed her the papers the police had given them and explained to her what had happened. Theresa immediately knew what the papers were. Though she was not an expert in gang injunctions, Theresa had worked closely with Belinda Escobosa, one of the ACLU lawyers who had won the *Vasquez* case. Theresa asked the young men if they wanted her help and if she had their permission to start making phone calls to get more people involved. They said yes.

Among Theresa's first calls was one to Belinda at the ACLU. At the same time, word of the injunction began reaching other activists, including Susan Luévano, one of the leaders of a local community organization Chicanxs Unidxs (San Román 2016), and Dolores Canales, an activist who worked to end solitary confinement in California prisons and who was also the mother of a man who had grown up in Plas and was currently serving time in Pelican Bay prison (Brazil 2020). Through these women and the young men who had been served the papers, word travelled through the community that something was going to be done about the injunction. As the message rippled through the neighborhoods, word came back that several young men in La Jolla had also been served. Conversations began about whether the young men of the two *varrios* could put their rivalries aside to fight the injunction together.

The Communities Organize

Sean Garcia-Leys' Account—September–November 2015

During that fall of 2015, I was a law student externing at the local ACLU office with Belinda and was acquainted with Theresa Smith. Law was my third career after working in labor and community organizing and then teaching in inner-city high schools. My work as a teacher led directly to involvement with issues related to street gangs. Many of my former students were gang members, and I frequently partnered with gang intervention workers to keep my students safe and socially integrated. I lived in the neighborhoods where I taught, including neighborhoods in Watts and East Los Angeles where gangs were deeply woven into the fabric of the communities. When I decided to leave teaching, I knew I wanted to continue to help these young people. I enrolled in law school with the goal of keeping kids like them out of the criminal justice system.

But my connection to gangs had begun even before teaching. I had grown up in Los Angeles myself and attended public schools during a time when gangs were omnipresent. I had lived not far from the Cadillac/Corning neighborhood that was the site of the first gang injunction. In my early 20s I was a lot like the college student whose murder led to that first injunction—white, from the neighborhood just west of that corner, college educated, and using drugs I bought from local gang members.

I also knew something about gang injunctions because, while teaching and living in Watts, my roommate had been in a gang but was then working as a gang interventionist. A few months after he moved in, he told me that he was on a gang injunction. I had no idea. The way he explained it to me, it gave police permission to stop him whenever he was in his old neighborhood and that he could be arrested for going there at night or visiting his brother or any of his old friends.

By the time Theresa called the ACLU looking for help, I had learned much more about gang injunctions. My ACLU externship involved researching injunctions and creating popular education materials regarding them. I had learned that one of the hurdles faced by people challenging injunctions was that prosecutors nearly always succeeded in pushing through the first phases of the court process quickly and without anyone showing up in opposition. After all, who is going to show up in court and say they represent a "criminal street gang"? As a result, when people later challenged the injunctions, judges ruled that many of the issues they wanted to raise had already been decided when the gang failed to appear and would not be reconsidered. This time, we had a chance to fight from the first day and avoid that result. I immediately volunteered to drop everything to work on the case.

After a quick flurry of phone calls and emails between the community mothers, activists, and the ACLU, there was consensus that we should immediately call a community meeting and invite the people targeted by the injunction, their families, community activists, and concerned members of the impacted people's communities. I was put in charge of finding a place to meet. I pulled up a map of the neighborhoods and saw that Cal State University Fullerton sat just outside the two proposed injunction zones. I cold-called Professor Alexandro Gradilla, head of their Chicano Studies Department, explained what we were doing, and asked if he could get us a room. He said yes. The mothers of the community and the young men who first approached Theresa did the outreach to get people to the meeting.

A few days later we met in a room at the university. It was a narrow room with a projector screen at one side and rows of chairs facing it. There was space for around 100 people. The first meeting was reasonably well attended for such short notice. There were a half dozen young men targeted by the Plas injunction and one targeted by the La Jolla injunction. There were another dozen family members and a dozen community activists. Altogether, there were about 30 of us at the meeting. My ACLU supervisor, Caitlin Sanderson, and I gave presentations with slide shows explaining what was happening from a legal perspective. We then held an open discussion. While the young men targeted for the injunction were mostly silent, several had parents or sisters who spoke out. The activists there all committed to making the fight against the injunction a priority. It was decided we would try to bring together the two neighborhoods and ask them to set aside old rivalries, and that the ACLU would take the lead on the legal response while the community mothers and activists would take the lead on grassroots organizing. Soon after, I received a letter supporting our organizing from an incarcerated former Plas member. I interpreted that as a good sign that the two targeted gangs would be willing to end their rivalry.

Our second meeting, a week or so later, was much larger with over 100 people. We were again at Cal State Fullerton, but this time in a large multi-purpose room. There were maybe a dozen of the alleged gang members targeted by the injunction, again mostly from Plas, but dozens more family members and criminal justice advocates from as far away as Los Angeles and San Diego, in addition to the Orange County activists. This time there were reporters, too. We ran the meeting as democratically and consensus based as possible. We decided that reporters were not welcome at the meeting, and they were asked to wait outside but could interview a few people who volunteered to talk to them in the hallway. One of the LA activists who had been fighting injunctions there, Kim McGill from the Youth Justice Coalition, was asked to facilitate the meeting. The ACLU was asked to continue to lead the legal work and committees were formed for organizing and media work. The different activist groups all offered their support, but it was agreed that impacted people and Placentia residents would ultimately lead the work and the activists would step back unless asked for help.

The legal plan we proposed, which was accepted at the meeting, was that as many of the people targeted by the injunction as possible should appear at the first public hearing so that the district attorney couldn't later claim they had been offered an opportunity to say they were not gang members but chose not to show up. The ACLU would not represent anyone in particular, but would request to be appointed *amicus curiae*, or "friend of the court," so as not to be limited to representing any one person's interests. The organizing committee would make sure that as many of the targeted people as possible would be in attendance, and the legal team would prepare the *amicus* argument.

The Opposition Moves to the Courtroom

Santa Ana and Placentia, Orange County—November–December 2015

On November 16, 2015, the court held its first public hearings on the injunctions. About 40 of us and about 20 uniformed police officers arrived at a courtroom on the fifth floor of the Central Justice Center, a high-rise courthouse in Santa Ana about 10 miles south of Placentia. The courtroom only held about 50 people. About a dozen of the 30 or so people targeted by the Plas injunction were there. The OCDA had asked to have the two injunction hearings separated by several hours to minimize the possibility that rival gang members would be in the building at the same time, but neither the prosecutors nor the court had anticipated any part of the community response we organized. When the courtroom doors opened, literal pushing and shoving between community members and police ensued as Kim McGill demanded that impacted people and families receive priority seating. Eventually, with a packed courtroom and most police left standing in the hall, the hearing commenced.

We coached all of the young men what to say immediately before the courtroom doors opened. Caitlin from the ACLU was prepared to make the ACLU's request to be part of the proceedings as *amicus curiae*. However, our preparations all proved unnecessary. Judge Wilson, who at that point had already held dozens of hearings in other injunction cases where only prosecutors were present, saw all of us and announced that there would be no hearing because, for the first time, he had decided that gang injunction cases were too "complex" for his department—that is, they involved too many parties. He announced he was officially transferring the case to Judge Dunning in the complex courthouse. The OCDA's prosecutors, but especially the police officers, were visibly frustrated by the decision. While we didn't know whether Judge Wilson's decision to move the case to the complex court would matter or not in the end, based solely on the police and prosecutors' looks of frustration we knew we had just had our first victory in this campaign.

Following that first public hearing, community meetings continued. Though reaching as many people as possible meant we had to hold a few separate meetings just for the La Jolla neighborhood, the truce held between the two gangs and many of the gang members chose to stop engaging in petty nuisance crimes while fighting the injunctions. Meanwhile, the legal team continued to work on the most immediate legal issue: Who had the right to argue against the gang injunction? Following their usual protocol, the OCDA hadn't named any individual people as defendants. Rather, prosecutors named only the two gangs as defendants, alleging they were "unincorporated associations" who could be sued in their own names. In the body of their complaint, the OCDA listed the people they said were active participants of the gang who would be bound by the injunction once the court ordered it, but prosecutors also argued that being named in a proposed enforcement list was not the same as being named a defendant and the listed people were not actual parties to the case. Thus, if any of the alleged gang members showed up in court and asked to argue against the injunction, they would likely be asked if they were there to represent themselves or the gang. Since it would be unauthorized practice of law for a non-lawyer member of any organization, even a gang, to represent the organization in court, to say nothing of the potential liability of claiming to be an agent of a criminal street gang, the alleged gang member would have to say that they were there to represent only themselves. Neither could Belinda nor Caitlin say they were there to represent the gang because it is unethical for a lawyer to knowingly represent a criminal organization. While Belinda and Caitlin could have argued that the gangs were not criminal organizations, that argument was likely to fail and could potentially expose them to professional, civil, and criminal liability if they lost. On the other hand, if an alleged gang member or attorney stated they represented only an individual and not the gang, the OCDA would point out that the individual was not named as a party to the suit and so had no right to appear in the case. Though the impossibility of defending oneself would seem to present an obvious due process violation, there was no published court opinion on this point, and Orange County trial court judges have always sided with prosecutors on this issue.

Our response to this Kafkaesque dilemma was twofold. First, a judge could choose to hear arguments from anyone the judge agreed to make *amicus curiae*. Caitlin, Belinda, and I prepared a written request asking that the new judge appoint the ACLU as *amicus* and wrote a legal brief arguing that the gang injunction was constitutionally deficient and would be ineffective. Second, each of the alleged gang members could ask the court to be made parties through a process called "intervention." But this process was not simple, and in all practicality it needed to be done by a lawyer. Also, codefendants in cases like this are typically expected to each be represented by a separate lawyer or law firm to prevent attorneys from having conflicting duties to their different clients.

To solve this, I went to two of my law school professors at University of California Irvine (UCI) Law School, Sameer Ashar and Annie Lai. Sameer and Annie ran the school's Immigrant Rights Clinic and were quick to understand how gang injunctions in Orange County exclusively targeted Mexican-American neighborhoods, which were as much immigrant communities as Chicano communities. They agreed to add the Immigrant Rights Clinic to the legal team.

With Sameer and Annie's help, and the help of two fellow UCI law students, Christyn Richardson and Meigan Thompson, I led the work to hold a one-day "law clinic" on intervention. Law school clinics are typically events where a group of law students meet one-on-one with people who need legal services and teach them how to meet that need themselves. The students help the clients fill out legal forms and then help the clients through the process of filing the forms with the court. All of this is done under the supervision of a practicing lawyer who will sometimes agree to more fully represent the client if an issue comes up of particular importance. But, for most instances, the clinic just gives information or advice and the clients are officially unrepresented. We decided this approach was the best way to get each of the targeted people to file a motion to intervene. It made it possible for each person to become a party to the case without having to recruit dozens of pro bono lawyers or risk conflicts between clients.

With the help of the organizing committee, which at that point consisted of the community mothers, one or two local activists, and Josh Correa, pastor at the local Well of Life church, we held our one-day law clinic. Christyn, Meigan, and I, with the help of Sameer, Annie, and Caitlin, drafted all the papers needed to intervene. Each of the clients would only need to have the process explained to them, put their names and addresses on the papers, and authorize us to file them with the court. If successful, each of the intervenors would then be allowed to challenge every aspect of the gang injunction beginning at the next hearing.

We invited everyone who's name was anywhere in either lawsuit to show up on December 2 to the Well of Life church for help officially intervening in the case. Our community partners and the families of the impacted people fanned out, finding people at home, at the park, at McDonald's, or playing video games at their *primo's* house and gave them rides to the church. For people who were incarcerated, we reached out to their family members to come. Once there, I had prepared all the legal papers they needed to file for intervention, but with blanks for the names and addresses. About a quarter of the people whose names appeared in the injunction filings came to the clinic or had family members who came to the clinic. We also helped the family members of incarcerated men write letters arguing that it was unconstitutional to enjoin them when they couldn't defend themselves because they were in jail or prison. Once we filed all of the clinic papers and the ACLU filed their *amicus* papers, we were ready for the first hearings in the new court.

By doing this work, I got to know each of the people targeted by the injunction, either personally or through their families and their criminal records. Though accused by prosecutors of being the most violent criminals in the county, I found most of the targeted people whom I met in person to be no different than the hundreds of students I had taught when I was a teacher. They were generally kind people, resilient despite being socially marginalized, but a little lost about where they fit into their world and generally without serious plans for the future. They were quiet around me at first, but when they relaxed they joked and played with each other like 10-year-old boys. There were a few exceptions. One was a very serious young man in his early 20s whose girlfriend was pregnant, and he was committed to having his tattoos, especially the ones on his face, laser removed so he could be a reliable father. One young man was developmentally disabled and was often manipulated by both gang members and police, as he would generally do whatever he was asked regardless of who asked him. One was a middle-aged man who had recently been released from prison after a several-year sentence for his involvement in countywide drug sales. He was also trying to be a reliable father and thought it was ridiculous for the OCDA to group him in with the rest of the targeted people, all of whom were at least 10 years younger and seemed like children to him. Of the dozens of people I met, only one was actively gang banging in the *varrio* and would not deny current gang participation in court.

What I discovered from meeting them or learning about them through their families or from police testimony or from reading criminal case documents was that nearly every single one of the 50 or so people whom the prosecutors sought to enjoin fell into one of two roughly evenly sized groups. The first group was people who had been involved with the gang, some seriously and some peripherally, but who were no longer actively part of the gang. They weren't "putting in work" anymore, if they ever did. Many of them were starting families or careers and, as time has now proven, no longer posed any threat to the community. The second group of people were, at that time, actively involved in gang crime. But nearly all those people were already in jail or prison. And for those who were not incarcerated, or were cycling in and out of jail, all were already subject to probation agreements nearly identical to the terms of the gang injunction. There was literally not a single person targeted by the injunction who presented a threat to the community that could be solved by a new court order.

The First Court Hearing in Complex Court

Santa Ana, Orange County—January 19, 2016

As the day of the second public hearing came, it was clear that the police were not going to be outnumbered by the community a second time. Judge Dunning's courtroom was across the parking lot from the Central Justice Center in a one-story building with only three courtrooms. Though courthouses are the sheriff's jurisdiction, the place was swarming with Placentia police officers and armed OCDA investigators. The staff parking lot was filled with police cars, and officers were going in and out through the back door of the courthouse. I saw one officer trying to double park in the staff parking lot almost hit a woman entering the courthouse through the staff entrance. This time, there were about 30 of us and at least that many law enforcement officers.

Judge Dunning's courtroom was much larger than Judge Wilson's, holding at least a hundred people. Two prosecutors, Caitlin, Sameer, and I appeared at the tables on the other side of the bar while the rest of our group stayed in the audience. There were no other cases to be heard in that courtroom that morning. Judge Dunning entered the courtroom and I recognized her as the woman who was almost hit by the police SUV in the staff lot. She called the case and the lawyers stated their appearances. Judge Dunning duly noted the attendance of everyone in the audience and was careful to address them as well as the lawyers. She said that she recognized there were a large number of people representing themselves. She also said she believed that prosecutors could be trusted to know criminal law but were often unfamiliar with civil procedure. In light of everyone's unfamiliarity with her court, she promised to be considerate and help everyone through the process.

As the first order of business, she considered letters from people incarcerated asking that they be exempted from the injunction until their release. Judge Dunning found the letters were not properly made motions and could not consider them. Next, she granted all the motions to intervene, but asked for some corrections to be made and for them to be refiled. Third, she rejected the ACLU's *amicus* brief. At that stage of the proceedings, Judge Dunning explained, she was being asked merely to decide whether to order a preliminary injunction for the year or so it was expected to take to finally decide the case. Judge Dunning stated that for reasons she was about to explain, she was not going to issue the preliminary injunction and so did not need the help of an *amicus* at that time. That brought her to the OCDA's request for a preliminary injunction. Judge Dunning pointed to the *Vasquez* case and stated no one could have their rights abridged by a gang injunction until they had an individualized hearing. Prosecutors must first prove by clear and convincing evidence that the individuals they seek to enjoin were active gang participants. Since at that point the OCDA had yet to prove anything about any individuals in a contested hearing, there was no point in ordering a preliminary injunction. With that decision, Judge Dunning concluded the hearing. Though some of the technical decisions were against us, the ultimate conclusion was definitely a good start for us—no one was enjoined despite the OCDA's request.

All of us involved in fighting the case then began preparing to meet across the hall with the community members to explain what had happened when Judge Dunning asked the attorneys to meet in her chambers. We had no idea what this was about. I had never been in a judge's chambers and was completely unsure of what was happening. Judge Dunning's clerk led the prosecutors and Caitlin and Sameer through the courtroom's back door, and I followed. Judge Dunning's chambers was a large, unwindowed office. There were chairs set out before her desk. As soon as we were all seated, she let us know why we were back there. She had hidden it up until that point, but she was furious at the prosecutors' armed occupation of her courthouse and the parking lot. She let them know in no uncertain terms that they were parties to a civil case where everyone would be treated equally. If they wanted police there, then the police could come through the front door, metal detectors and all, just like anyone else. Clearly misreading the situation, the prosecutors argued that the police were needed for safety and that it would be too onerous for each of them to go through the metal detectors at the entrance. Judge Dunning was having none of it. Her courtroom, she said, was protected by sheriff deputy bailiffs who were more than capable of protecting everyone, despite the prosecutor's apparent lack of faith in their abilities. And if prosecutors felt something more was needed, they could ask and more bailiffs could be scheduled if needed. But prosecutors should expect no special privileges!

Having said practically nothing at all, Caitlin, Sameer, and I then left Judge Dunning's chambers feeling like, for the first time in Orange County, we may have a judge who wasn't going to just rubber stamp whatever the OCDA wanted. We headed across the hall with a little bit of giddy optimism to explain to everyone exactly what had happened that morning.

The Ocda's Case Unravels

Santa Ana and Placentia, Orange County—January–July 2016

From there we continued doing everything we could to stop the injunction. We continued the community meetings. The peace held between Plas and La Jolla and gang crime in the neighborhood continued to stay relatively low. The Well of Life church intervened in the case to argue the injunction would backfire and interfere with community-based gang intervention programs like the one they ran. The grassroots activists circulated a petition around the neighborhoods stating residents didn't want the stigma of being called a gang injunction zone. My externship with the ACLU ended, but I continued to work on the case as a member of the UCI Immigrant Rights Clinic. The ACLU also stayed involved in the case, agreeing to take the young man who was developmentally disabled in a limited scope representation to argue that he was entitled to a court-appointed attorney on the basis of his disability. We at the Immigrant Rights Clinic decided to take a handful of clients directly to try to have the case thrown out on the basis that prosecutors had sued the gangs as "unincorporated associations" under the Corporations Code, but that category only applied to organizations formed for a lawful purpose. While the argument turned on legal technicalities, everyone also understood that a gang is not a corporation and shouldn't be treated like one by the courts.

There was another hearing on April 14. Under Sameer's supervision, I argued that gangs were not amenable to suit under the Corporations Code, but Judge Dunning denied our motions. But at the same time, she also made it clear that she was concerned it would be unconstitutional to hold individualized hearings for anyone incarcerated.

Then, on May 12, the court held the first individualized hearing where it would be decided whether to enjoin someone. The OCDA had asked for Chemo Ortega[16] to be the first person the court would consider. I had met with Chemo to offer to find him a lawyer, but he told me he didn't want help and that he would represent himself. Chemo had been gang involved and had only recently began transitioning out of the gang. Police had plenty of evidence of his past gang involvement and no one had any good ideas as to what evidence could possibly prove a person had recently left a gang. He seemed to think there was no chance for him to win, so he didn't want to even fight it.

When his hearing began, Chemo hadn't shown up. I was the only person from the legal team present. Since Chemo had declined my help, I was sitting in the audience. That left the police and prosecutors to present an entirely one-sided case, which they did. Prosecutors called up one police officer after another, with a slide show to support their testimony. There was no one to make objections, no one to cross-examine the officers, no opposing witnesses to give context or opposing accounts. The police testified as to each of Chemo's arrests, deconstructed his Facebook account, and showed every photo they could find that showed Chemo with other alleged gang members, throwing gang signs, or wearing gang clothes, regardless of how old the photos were. Prosecutors particularly singled out a hat that Chemo frequently wore with a diamond embroidered on the front. While the diamond was the logo for a brand popular with skaters across southern California, a diamond was also the symbol for the La Jolla neighborhood. Police claimed that, no matter if thousands of people wore that same hat elsewhere, if a Chicano youth in Placentia wore it that was proof he was a gang member. While much of the prosecutor's evidence, such as the photos of Chemo throwing gang signs, was valid evidence of Chemo's past gang involvement, much of it was exaggerated or mistook community or ethnic pride for gang admission, and it didn't deal with the relevant legal standard of gang *participation* as opposed to gang *membership*. More importantly, all of it was old, but there was no testimony as to how long gang membership typically lasts and how recent evidence must be to avoid being considered legally "stale" and inadmissible.

When the prosecution was done, Judge Dunning asked for a recess. While she was gone, Chemo finally arrived. I was sitting in the back of the audience and was the first to see him walk in. I almost couldn't believe it, but he was wearing the very same hat that police had said proved he was a gang member. I quickly pulled him aside and took the hat. He later told me that the hat was one of the only things his father had ever given him and it was a prized possession. I explained to him what had happened so far. I told Chemo if he wanted help, he could ask the judge for more time and I'd arrange a lawyer for him (as a law student still, I couldn't offer to be his lawyer myself). When Judge Dunning called the court back into session Chemo walked to the defendant's table by himself. He asked for time to find a lawyer, but Judge Dunning refused. Judge Dunning asked Chemo if he had anything to say in his defense. Looking defeated, he simply said, "no."

It seemed like that would be it, but then Judge Dunning turned to the prosecutors to ask a question. Wasn't Chemo on probation with gang terms? The prosecutor said he was. In that case, Judge Dunning said, if Chemo is actively participating in the gang, as prosecutors claimed, then wasn't Chemo in violation of his probation terms? Shouldn't prosecutors have made this case to the criminal judge overseeing Chemo's probation? It seemed to her, said Judge Dunning, that prosecutors were arguing in her court that Chemo was an active gang participant, while simultaneously allowing the criminal court to believe Chemo was adhering to the terms of his probation. Considering that, Judge Dunning said she wanted a written brief from the prosecutors on the issue of Chemo's probation. Another hearing was scheduled for July. We had another chance.

During those following months, I graduated law school and began studying for the bar exam. Two law students from the class behind me, Althea Omdahl and Tryphena Liu, took over the case for the summer while I continued to join strategy sessions and act as a liaison to the community and to Chemo. Just finding Chemo turned out to be a challenge. Whenever we could find him, he would tell us he wanted our help, but it was obvious that he had become even more hopeless and had taken to avoiding thinking about the whole thing. We'd set appointments to meet and he wouldn't show up. We began dropping by his house, hoping to find him there, but were only able to leave messages for him with his family. When the day of his second hearing came, we had yet to have even a single meeting with him to discuss his case and hadn't even gotten a signature on a representation agreement. Nonetheless, the Immigrant Rights Clinic filed a brief on his behalf, not knowing if it would be accepted by the court or not. More positively, however, the OCDA asked the court to temporarily cancel all other individualized hearings. Everyone scheduled for a hearing was also on probation with gang terms.

On July 6, we returned to Judge Dunnings' courtroom for Chemo's hearing with no signed papers making us his attorney. What's more, Chemo wasn't there, again. Sameer and Annie, with Althea and Tryphena, attempted to appear on Chemo's behalf, but when Sameer had to admit that we had no signed representation agreement and no idea where Chemo was, Judge Dunning told him that he could not appear on Chemo's behalf. The OCDA then made their argument for why Chemo's probation should not prevent the court from enjoining him. With Chemo not there, no one was allowed to argue against them. Nevertheless, Judge Dunning gave her decision—no one subject to a probation with gang terms could be enjoined. Though Judge Dunning had denied admitting Althea's and Tryphena's legal brief, Judge Dunning stated that she had come to the same conclusion in her own consideration of the legal issues. The prosecutor objected and pressed Judge Dunning on her decision. The prosecutor pointed out that no other judge had taken probation into consideration in any other gang injunction proceeding. What's more, the prosecutor said, is that if people on probation can't be enjoined, and it seemed unlikely that Judge Dunning would enjoin people who were already incarcerated, it was entirely likely that there was not a single person who could be enjoined. Nearly every one of the 50 or so people the OCDA sought to enjoin in the two injunctions were incarcerated or on probation or parole, and the few who weren't had a good chance of beating their case, so long as they had an attorney to help them. Judge Dunning responded to the prosecutor's concern by simply looking at her as if to say, "and so?" The prosecutor had nothing left to say.

We left the courtroom feeling fairly certain, to everyone's surprise, that we had just beat the injunction.

Injunctions Dismissed

Placentia, Orange County—2018

We were, in fact, right. But it would take two more years before the case actually ended. Following the hearing where Judge Dunning denied the OCDA's request to enjoin Chemo, prosecutors cancelled all the scheduled active participation hearings. Then, about every six months, they would ask for a continuance without taking any action. One day, sitting in my new office, having graduated and become a practicing public interest lawyer, I received an email alert that there had been new filings in the case. I downloaded the filings and was happy to see they were motions by the OCDA to dismiss the case. I began getting phone calls from reporters who knew I had stayed on the case, and one shared with me a press release on the dismissal motion from the district attorney's office. The gang injunction, the OCDA wrote, had been so effective it was no longer needed. Laughing, I reminded the reporters that no one had ever been made subject to the injunction, so there was no way anyone should take that explanation seriously. The truth was that the OCDA had given up after two years of trying and failing to find some way that they could argue the injunction would actually help the community. They simply couldn't prove a public benefit.

By that time, all the organizing on the issue had died out, though the peace between gangs had held and gang crime in Placentia had remained low. I was still in touch with Theresa and the community mothers and organizers, and with Sameer and Annie by email, and we all shared the news that way. Belinda and Caitlin had both left the ACLU. Caitlin had moved to Germany. I had stayed in touch with many of the alleged gang members over social media and let them know the good news. I was also able to take stock of what had happened with these young men and women in the intervening years. While I didn't methodically collect data on each of them, from talking to them it was clear that we were pretty close to 100% correct in our original categorization of them as either people engaged in crime and destined for prison or people successfully maturing out of the gang.

Unfortunately, this wasn't the successful end of the larger campaign to end gang injunctions in Orange County. Judge Dunning retired and the other Orange County gang injunction cases were transferred to judges who were more willing to accept the OCDA's arguments without questioning them. However, while the OCDA continues to enforce the 13 injunctions that were in effect before they sought the injunctions against Plas and La Jolla, they have sought no new injunctions in the five years since then.

Lessons Learned

Fullerton, Orange County—June 2022

Now, four years after the cases were dismissed, I can reflect on the Placentia gang injunction campaign from my office at the Peace and Justice Law Center in Fullerton, about a mile from the park where the Plas defendants used to hang out. Gang activity has remained low in Placentia. In fact, there is currently a countywide gang truce and many of the county's gang members have agreed to stop their nuisance behaviors in order to stop attracting law enforcement attention and to stop providing law enforcement with easy justifications for street corner detentions, arrests, and prosecutions. Though there has been little public discussion or analysis of the truce, gang graffiti and loitering, the most visible nuisance activities, appear to have dramatically decreased across Orange County. When I've discussed the current peace with currently active gang members, they name one of the people who worked behind the scenes on the peace between Plas and La Jolla as the truce agreement's architect. It is impossible to know how long this peace will last or to what degree the Placentia campaign may have influenced it, but for the moment the truce appears to be more effective at ending the public nuisance presented by gang activity than the county's gang injunctions were.

At the same time, gang injunctions have nearly disappeared in California. Soon after the Placentia campaign wound down, I joined the legal team suing the City of Los Angeles in the *Youth Justice Coalition* case.[17] Our lawsuit asked a federal trial court to require the city to obey the *Vasquez* ruling that law enforcement agencies may not enforce a gang injunction against any individual if that person had not been offered an individualized pre-deprivation hearing. Soon after we filed that lawsuit, the city looked at its enforcement lists and decided on its own that over 7,000 people should be removed from the lists. But that was insufficient for the court, and the court ordered the city to stop enforcing the injunctions even against the remaining 2,000-plus individuals until the *Vasquez* rule was implemented. The rest of Los Angeles' jurisdictions immediately followed and ceased enforcement. After some subsequent litigation, Ventura County dropped their two gang injunctions. San Diego and others followed. Los Angeles has so far decided not to attempt to restart enforcement. While Orange County and a few others continue to enforce injunctions, the enforcement lists are much smaller. Orange County's enforcement lists have gone from thousands to hundreds, and only a few dozen people are offered hearings and added every year, nearly all of them already subject to probation agreements with terms nearly identical to the injunctions. Though gang crime is up across much of California, and crime is up nationally, there did not appear to be an immediate increase in gang crime in the areas where injunction enforcement ended, and I have not heard anyone attribute the current increase in gang violence to the end of injunction enforcement.

From this vantage, there are two lessons learned in the Placentia campaign that appear to have proved correct over time. The first is that police and prosecutors cannot be trusted to limit themselves to only strategies that serve the interest of public safety; oversight is needed. The second is that grassroots, multisector alliances rooted in the lived experiences of impacted people have tremendous potential to not only defend civil liberties, but also to reduce crime and violence.

Looking back at the way this case finally ended, the futility of the Placentia injunctions is obvious. Every single person the OCDA wanted to enjoin in both of these gang injunctions was either already caught up in the criminal justice system through traditional criminal law enforcement or didn't deserve to be enjoined at all. That's been the same with every one of the dozen injunctions I've been involved in since. But what also impresses me, having now pointed out the redundancy of gang injunction orders to police and prosecutors in four different California counties, is how little the effects of the actual injunction order matter to most police. While prosecutors will sometimes admit in private, and have sometimes had to admit in court, that they cannot make a case for an injunctions' public benefit if one looks to see the effect of the injunction on each individual alleged gang member, police seem not to care. What is important to these police officers is just that an injunction exists on paper. Which, of course, begs the question of what police actually do with these injunctions.

While I know of no studies of gang injunctions' effect on police behavior, I have had enough conversations with people affected to know that many police believe gang injunctions create de facto Fourth-Amendment-free-zones. In other words, injunctions suspend the usual restrictions against unreasonable searches and seizures. If someone looks like a gang member in an injunction safety zone, an officer has reasonable suspicion to stop that person to see if they are on the injunction. Once the officer has reasonable suspicion, the officer can do a pat-down search for officer safety. The officer can call for gang unit backup. The officer can make the suspected gang member or gang members sit on the curb for the hour that it might take for the gang unit to show up. And even if the officer finds out the young men are not on the injunction list (which the officer may have already known), the officer can then fill out gang identification cards and file them away to "build book" against the young men to use if they are ever charged with a crime in the future. I also know from talking to these young people that police frequently lie to them about what a gang injunction means. Officers will tell groups of young men they come across while on patrol that it is illegal for them to be out in public because they are in a gang injunction zone. While that's a gross exaggeration, many of the young men believe it and act accordingly. Whether this is unconstitutional harassment, effective gang suppression, or merely police officers attempting to demonstrate their power is outside the scope of this chapter, but either way I suspect it is the real reason behind police officers' support for gang injunctions.

Considering that police and prosecutors, when left to their own devices, push these kinds of gang suppression strategies even when the strategies' expressed objectives are entirely redundant of other enforcement mechanisms, it is clear that communities and civil liberties advocates need to be watchdogs of the police, as we were in this case. But I would even go further to say that communities have the potential to not only oppose bad strategies, but to develop and implement more effective strategies. It is the community's knowledge of what the community needs that should drive public safety strategies. In Placentia, not only did our campaign successfully defeat the injunctions, it also led to a dramatic decrease in gang crime and violence even though the gang injunctions were never implemented. Admittedly, it was the gang injunctions that created the conditions for our campaign's success at reducing crime and violence. After all, it was the gang injunctions that were the impetus for the community organizing that led to the peace and to community support for people exiting the gangs. Still, I would not describe the effect of the injunction as deterrence because the crime and violence reduction would not have happened if not for the community-wide response, and the reduction continued after the threat of the injunction had passed. Also, there were other, more universal, conditions at play as well—dissatisfaction with the costs of crime and violence, becoming a parent, shame at the harm people had caused their community, the sense of well-being that comes from social integration—these also were impetuses for peace. Certainly, conditions have to be right for communities to self-organize, as they were in this case, but that is true of all crime and violence reduction strategies.

Relatedly, this campaign also demonstrates what element within the community needs to lead. Communities are not homogenous. Leadership should come from those who are most likely to be impacted by crime and violence. No one is more at risk for becoming a victim of gang violence than a gang member. And while gang members on their own cannot be trusted to develop policing strategies that are in the public's best interest, when working alongside their mothers and families, faith leaders, community activists, and direct service providers, even hardcore gang members can be an integral part of a group capable of remarkable public safety gains. In this case, it was only the active and alleged gang members and the people closest to them who could look over the enforcement list, picture each of the people who would be enjoined, and immediately know that the injunction was unnecessary. But not only were they able to see that the injunction wouldn't work, they were also able to offer solutions. It was they who organized the two gangs to stop their rivalry and decrease their public nuisance activities.

However, it is exactly this part of the community that is typically overlooked when law enforcement agencies look for partners for advancing public safety. I have never been to a "coffee with a cop" or a community discussion convened by police where gang-involved men, their families, and the people who work with them are accepted as valued representatives of the community.[18] Instead the community is typically represented by the community members who are least involved with gangs, whose perceptions are most shaped by the distortions of television news and other media, and who are therefore least knowledgeable, most scared, and least likely to hold law enforcement accountable. Community policing can only work when the people in the community most impacted by the criminal justice system are partners.

By sharing these reflections, I do not mean to suggest that what happened in Placentia is a model for everywhere, or that community organizing is a panacea, or that there is no place for gang suppression. As I described earlier in this chapter, Placentia had issues with gangs, but they were not as serious as the issues faced by many large urban centers. Likewise, Orange County as a whole is unique in many ways that have made the current peace possible—few interethnic gang rivalries and a history of racial and economic segregation that has placed many gangs in small, non-contiguous *varrios* that are surrounded by more affluent white neighborhoods. Still, the Placentia campaign shows that impacted people, with the support of allies, can contribute to both the advancement of civil liberties and to public safety, and can do so effectively and simultaneously.

Notes

1. Statistics from the California Department of Justice's Open Justice Portal show that violent crime incidents had just topped 100,000 for the county in one year for the first time. Violent crime incidents peaked at just over 150,000 incidents in 1993. For comparison, violent crime incidents for 2021 were just over 50,000. https://openjustice.doj.ca.gov/exploration/crime-statistics/crimes-clearances.
2. The account of the Playboy Gangster Crips injunction in this prologue is sourced primarily from Muñiz (2015, 33–55).
3. The city attorney is given only the pseudonym "John" in Muñiz's book.
4. Previously, there had been civil nuisance abatement suits aimed at specific addresses where gangs had been active in Los Angeles. As a remedy in these suits, courts typically ordered property owners to evict whoever was responsible for the gang activity happening on their property. Also, there had been one injunction aimed at graffiti abatement that named three gangs instead of property owners (*People v. Dogtown, Primera Flats, and 62nd Street East Coat Crips*, Super. Ct. Los Angeles, 1982, no. C418875). However, the remedy sought in that case was merely that defendants must participate in a graffiti cleanup effort. The Playboy Gangster Crips injunction was the first case to seek an ongoing injunction that would disrupt a gang's core criminal activities.
5. *City of Los Angeles v. Playboy Gangster Crips* (Super. Ct. Los Angeles, 1987, no. WEC118860).
6. California Civil Code § 3479.
7. There is no official tally of the number of gang injunctions or the number of people who have been made subject to them. However, attempts to catalog the number of injunctions in California have found well over 150 injunctions. Also, litigation against the City of Los Angeles revealed that there were approximately 10,000 people enjoined by that one city's gang injunctions alone.
8. See endnote 7.
9. *People ex rel. Gallo v. Acuna*, 1997, 14 Cal. 4th 1090.
10. *People ex rel. Totten v. Colonia Chiques*, 2007, 156 Cal. App. 4th 31.
11. Compare, for example, the safety zone in *People ex rel. Gallo v. Acuna*, which covered one intersection, to the injunction safety zones in the cities of Orange Cove (Decker, Pyrooz, and Densley 2022), or Long Beach (*People v. North Side Longos and Sureños*, Super. Ct. Los Angeles, 2010, no. NC054794), which cover most of the cities' square miles.

12. *Vasquez v. Rackauckas*, 9th Cir., 2013, 734 F.3d 1025.
13. Agencies did not immediately cease enforcement of gang injunctions when the Ninth Circuit Court of Appeal issued the *Vasquez v. Rackauckas* decision. It was not until two subsequent decisions that relied on *Vasquez*, *People v. Sanchez*, 2017, 18 Cal. App. 5th 727 and *Youth Justice Coalition v. City of Los Angeles*, C.D. Cal., 2017, 264 F. Supp. 3d 1057, that most California law enforcement agencies voluntarily ceased enforcement of injunctions against people who were not offered an individualized hearing.
14. *People v. La Jolla*, Super. Ct. Orange County, 2015, no. 30-2015-00810734; *People v. Plas* Super. Ct. Orange County, 2015, no. 30-2015-00810781.
15. These statistics were presented to the court as part of the Memorandum in Support of Preliminary Injunction filed in each case (*People v. La Jolla*, Super. Ct. Orange County, 2015, no. 30-2015-00810734; *People v. Plas* Super. Ct. Orange County, 2015, no. 30-2015-00810781). Because the OCDA's memorandums list numbers of people not numbers of incidents, and because some of the incidents involved more than one person, the number of incidents must be fewer than the numbers listed, perhaps far fewer.
16. Chemo Ortega is not this client's real name. He has given permission to share his story anonymously.
17. *Youth Justice Coalition v. City of Los Angeles*, C.D. Cal., 2017, 264 F. Supp. 3d 1057.
18. Some arguable exceptions to this are the Watts Gang Taskforce, the Southern California Ceasefire Committee, and the Los Angeles Police Department's Community Safety Partnership program. While each of those forums do respect the voices of gang-involved people, in each of those cases the group was convened by community members or partners serving as intermediaries between the community and police, and not unilaterally by the police.

References

American Civil Liberties Union. 1997. *False Premises, False Promises: The Blythe Street Gang Injunction and Its Aftermath*. Los Angeles.

Barajas, Frank. 2007. "An Invading Army: A Civil Gang Injunction in a Southern California Chicana/o Community." *Latino Studies* 5: 393–417.

Brazil, Ben. 2020. "Dolores Canales Fights for an End to Solitary Confinement." *Daily Pilot*, August 20.

Bichler, Gisela, Alexis Norris, and Citlalik Ibarra. 2020. "Evolving Patterns of Aggression: Investigating the Structure of Gang Violence during the Era of Civil Gang Injunctions." *Social Sciences* 9 (11): 203.

Caldwell, Beth. 2010. "Criminalizing Day-to-Day Life: A Socio-Legal Critique of Gang Injunctions." *American Journal of Criminal Law* 37: 249.

Carr, Richard, Molly Slothower, and John Parkinson. 2017. "Do Gang Injunctions Reduce Violent Crime? Four Tests in Merseyside, UK." *Cambridge Journal of Evidence-Based Policing* 1 (4): 195–210.

Cheng, Derek. 2021. "ACT Party Law and Order Proposal to 'Require' Good Behaviour from Gang Members." *NZ Herald*, July 19.

City of Placentia. 2017. "Old Town Revitalization Plan." https://www.placentia.org/726/Old-Town-Revitalization-Plan.

Decker, Scott H., David C. Pyrooz, and James A. Densley. 2022. *On Gangs*. Philadelphia, PA: Temple University Press.

Emery, Sean. 2018. "DA's Office Moves to Dismiss Gang Injunctions Aimed at Rival Placentia Crews." *OC Register*, March 8.

Feldman, Paul. 1987. "Judge OKs Modified Measures to Curb Gang." *Los Angeles Times*, December 12.

González, Gilbert G. 1994. *Labor and Community: Mexican Citrus Worker Villages in a Southern California County, 1900-1950*. Champaign, IL: University of Illinois Press.

Grogger, Jeffrey. 2002. "The Effects of Civil Gang Injunctions on Reported Violent Crime: Evidence from Los Angeles County." *Journal of Law and Economics* 45: 69–90.

Maxson, C. L., K. Hennigan, and D. Sloane. 2005. "'It's Getting Crazy Out There': Can a Civil Gang Injunction Change a Community?" *Criminology and Public Policy* 4 (3): 577–605.

Morrison, Aaron. 2019. "I'm Not Going Anywhere Until They Stop Killing People." *The Appeal*, March 13.

Muñiz, Ana. 2015. *Police, Power, and the Production of Racial Boundaries*. Berlin, Germany: De Gruyter.

O'Deane, Matthew. 2012. *Gang Injunctions and Abatement: Using Civil Remedies to Curb Gang-Related Crimes*. New York: Routledge.

Owens, Emily, Michelle D. Mioduszewski, and Christopher J. Bates. 2020. "How Valuable are Civil Liberties? Evidence from Gang Injunctions and Housing Prices in Southern California." *UCI Center for Population, Inequality, and Policy Working Papers Series*. Paper No. 20203.

Ridgeway, Greg, Jeffrey Grogger, Ruth Moyer, and John MacDonald. 2018. "Effect of Gang Injunctions on Crime: A Study of Los Angeles from 1988-2014." *Penn Criminology Working Papers Collection*. Paper No. 2018-3.0.

Saavedra, Tony. 2019. "Secret Files Reveal Details of Police Shooting That Helped Trigger 2012 Anaheim Rioting." *OC Register*, June 23.

San Román, Gabriel. 2016. "Chicanos Unidos Celebrates 10 Years of Organizing OC's Raza!" *OC Weekly*, September 30.

Spady, James, Alexander Scott, Susan Luévano, Gabriela Hernandez, and Carolyn Torres. 2021. "Chicanx Histories of the Present: A Praxis Against Gang Injunctions in Orange County, California, 2008–2016." *Radical Americas* 6 (1): 18.

Stewart, Gary. 1998. "Black Codes and Broken Windows: The Legacy of Racial Hegemony in Anti-Gang Civil Injunctions." *Yale Law Journal* 107 (7): 2249–2279.

Stop the Injunctions Coalition. 2017. "We Won! A Full Victory Against Gang Injunctions!" https://stoptheinjunction.wordpress.com/.

Trujillo, Larry D. 1974. "La Evolución del 'Bandido' al 'Pachuco': A Critical Examination and Evaluation of Criminological Literature on Chicanos Issues." *Criminology* 9 (2): 43–67.

CHAPTER 40

"SOMEBODY'S WATCHING ME"
Surveying Police Surveillance of Gangs

MATTHEW VALASIK AND
P. JEFFREY BRANTINGHAM

STREET gangs remain one of the most debated issues in the field of criminology. There often seems to be little academic agreement on fundamental questions ranging from the definition of gangs to the nature and prevalence of delinquent or criminal behavior by gang associates[1] (Curry 2015; Goeury 2022; Moore and Stuart 2022; Pyrooz and Mitchell 2015; Sullivan 2005; Van Hellemont and Densley 2021; Van Hellemont and Mills 2022). Even more contentious are questions surrounding how society responds to street gangs, particularly their policing (Barrows and Huff 2009; Brunson et al. 2015; Caudill et al. 2017; Decker 2003; Durán 2009; Fraser and Atkinson 2014; Goeury 2022; Howell 2022; Katz and Webb 2006; Klein 1998, 2004, 2009; Valasik and Reid 2021; Wolf 2017). On the one hand, there is great concern within communities saddled with chronic gang problems that not enough is being done to prevent youth from joining gangs and to hold gangs accountable for their actions (Bloch and Meyer 2019; Brunson et al. 2015; Leovy 2015; Murch 2015). On the other, there is great concern that heavy-handed policing tactics and mass incarceration serve to reinforce rather than undermine gangs (Brotherton 2015; Fraser and Atkinson 2014; Huebner, Varano, and Bynum 2007; Jackson and Rudman 1993; Klein 1998; Lessing 2017; Swaner 2022). Sometimes these twin criticisms are leveled at the same time through claims that communities are being both over- and underpoliced (Boehme, Cann, and Isom 2022; Martinez 2015; Murch 2015; Rice and Lee 2015; Rios 2011; Zatz and Portillos 2000).

Further exacerbating the tension between these views is the increased use by law enforcement agencies of new technology as tools to counter serious and violent crime (Ferguson 2022; Gettinger 2017; Merola and Lum 2013, 2014; Saulnier and Thompson 2016). In particular, public perception about the use and potential abuse of novel "surveillance" technology by law enforcement agencies produces conflicting narratives (Ackerman 2021; Ryan-Mosley and Strong 2020). There is clear apprehension surrounding the use of "big data" to help determine where and when to deploy limited police resources (Ackerman 2021; Bakke 2018; Bartosiewicz 2015; Benbouzid 2019; Zhu 2016). This apprehension grows even more when the subject of "big data" involves policing street gangs (Brayne 2020; Densley and Pyrooz 2020; Howell 2022; Pittman 2020; Van Hellemont and Densley 2021). Yet it is also clear that "predictive policing, and big data surveillance, is not new: it is simply an extension of what has been long-practiced" (Minocher and Randall 2020, 1121).

While there needs to be greater transparency, routine audits, and standardized and systematic processes followed in how big data, computer algorithms, machine learning, and predictive modeling are used in policing gangs, there remains a disconnect between the promise of data-driven policing of gangs and the reality of policing of gangs (see Davis et al. 2022). The potential for corruption and misconduct in anti-gang policing (Domanick 2016; Kaplan 2009; LAPD 2020), specifically, and decentralized specialized police units (Fenton 2021; Woods and Soderberg 2020), generally, is a persistent risk without accountability and oversight. The moral panic that "surveillance" technology and data-driven policing represent are a severe threat to the privacy and security of the general public (e.g., Richardson et al. 2019) serves mostly to promote a "myth of big data surveillance as a new, nearly cataclysmic threat to public well-being" that must be dismantled (Minocher and Randall 2020, 1109). There are certainly problems with data or technology used in support of anti-gang policing. But, as Densely and Pyrooz (2020) point out, "the opposite of bad data is not no data, but good data" (24). There is value in collecting *good* information on gangs and gang associates and using this in *transparent* and *accountable* ways to aid in criminal investigations and prevent neighborhood violence.

The goal of this chapter is twofold: (1) discuss how gangs are policed using traditional and data-driven approaches and (2) temper fears that police spend all of their time actively surveilling the populace, violating our Fourth Amendment rights, and invading our privacy (see Ferguson 2021, 2022). While data-driven policing is fashionable, both in conventional and anti-gang policing, much like other notable policing approaches (e.g., community policing), its adoption and implementation remain an uneven process throughout law enforcement jurisdictions in the United States. For instance, out of approximately 18,000 police jurisdictions nationwide, only 187 police agencies (1.03%) report using some type of predictive policing software, one of the lesser forms of data-driven policing, compared to 3,163 police agencies (17.6%) that use body-worn cameras, the most used form of data-driven policing (Atlas of Surveillance 2022).[2] The result is a patchwork of systems and processes that are hard to reconcile with the notion of a panoptic surveillance state (Brayne 2020; Hennigan and Sloane 2013; McQuade 2019). Similarly, the use of traditional surveillance methods, such as wiretaps and even easily scoured social media posts on platforms such as Twitter, Instagram, and TikTok, is generally done in support of ongoing criminal investigations (see Berlusconi 2013; Patton et al. 2017). Such tools are generally not used proactively by law enforcement, largely due to limited access, lack of training, and knowledge about social media (LexisNexis 2012). Thus, the policing of gangs, gang associates, and gang violence, historically and presently, remains overwhelmingly reactive and geographical in nature (Bloch 2020, 2021; Bloch and Phillips 2021; Muñiz 2015; Valasik and Tita 2018; Valasik and Torres 2020; Weisel and Shelley 2004). As a result, this chapter will focus on the Los Angeles Police Department, which, for better or worse, is one of the leaders in policing street gangs (Bloch and Phillips 2021; Brayne 2020; Gascón and Rousell 2019; Klein 1998, 2009; Tita et al. 2003; Valasik, Reid, and Phillips 2016). Overall, this chapter seeks to balance some of the hyperbole that has emerged around data-driven anti-gang policing (Brayne 2020, 119; see Ferguson 2017, 2021, 2022) with a sober portrait that focuses on the mundane nature of police work and how the basic data gathered about gangs and gang associates are used in practice.

SURVEILLANCE, INTELLIGENCE GATHERING, OR INVESTIGATING

Before discussing the traditional and data-driven approaches employed by law enforcement agencies to police street gangs, it is necessary to identify a few concepts that get obfuscated in the literature and the critiques of anti-gang policing operations. These indistinct terms are "surveillance," "intelligence gathering," and "investigation.[3]"

The first term is routinely used by scholars but rarely defined. Here, we define "surveillance" as the continuous observation of a place, person, group, object, or activity. Such activities can range from physical observations to digital monitoring of conversations (voice, video, or text), metadata, and geolocation. Surveillance can be either active, explicit observation, or passive/reactive (post hoc) monitoring. Relatedly, surveillance can be *directed*, focusing on "people and places deemed suspicious," or undirected, "gather[ing] information on everyone, rather merely those under suspicion," referred to as dragnet surveillance (Brayne 2020, 14).

A related concept is "intelligence gathering." In the realm of policing, intelligence gathering is regarded as the collection of information to identify individuals or groups. The implicit purpose of intelligence gathering is to monitor, anticipate, or prevent possible criminal activity (see Katz and Webb 2006; Katz, Webb, and Schaefer 2000; Valasik et al. 2016). Brayne's (2018, 2020) category of directed surveillance conceptually overlaps with the definition of intelligence gathering; however, her definition is centered on the data-driven aspects of predictive policing, place or person based, and not on the traditional understanding of surveillance as the continued observation of persons, places, or activities. Intelligence gathering can be discontinuous and does not rely solely on continuous observation, such as talking to an informant.

The last interconnected concept is "investigation," broadly defined as the process of studying by close observation or systemic inquiry. For law enforcement, a criminal investigation is a formal examination to ascertain facts of illegal activity, usually conducted by police detectives in investigative units. For police, investigation differs from intelligence gathering only in the sense that the former is directed toward building legal cases around crimes that have already occurred, while the latter is directed toward future risks (see Ratcliffe 2016).

It is necessary to connect these entangled terms with the various approaches to anti-gang policing. Anti-gang policing remains predominantly reactive in nature, focused on the investigation of documented criminal activity. To the extent that police take a forward-looking approach to gangs, it mostly involves (opportunistic) gathering of intelligence (e.g., field interview cards, territorial mapping) that might—but mostly does not—prove useful for future investigations. The reactive stance in anti-gang policing is not only seen in how anti-gang units operate, but also in the details of anti-gang legislation (e.g. 1988 California Street Terrorism Enforcement and Prevention Act, or STEP Act), civil gang injunctions, gang databases, and gang prosecutions, all of which are enacted or operate in response to ongoing gang-related issues in an area (Allan 2004; Barrows and Huff 2009; Bjerregaard 2015; Pyrooz, Wolfe, and Spohn 2011). Undirected surveillance activities such as checking license plates against a database by anti-gang (and all other) police units are undertaken to facilitate ongoing criminal investigations (looking for outstanding warrants, etc.). Otherwise, anti-gang policing passively observes places, persons, groups, or objects in response to criminal activity, such as a homicide, in the hopes of arresting a suspected offender. The objective of anti-gang policing surveillance is simply the production of legally actionable intelligence that could be used to arrest an offending gang associate or facilitate the prosecution of an offending gang associate (see Anderson et al. 2009; Caudill et al 2017; Pyrooz et al. 2011; Walker and Cesar 2020).

Traditional Surveying of Gangs

The initial response to street gangs by law enforcement is to use pre-existing resources (i.e., patrol, investigations, community relations) to distribute the responsibility for specific aspects of gang control (i.e., intelligence, prevention, enforcement, and follow-up investigation) among established departmental units (Dunn 2007; Huff and McBride 1993; Katz and Webb 2006; Needle and Stapleton 1983; Weisel, Painter, and Kusler 1997). Yet in jurisdictions where gangs and gang-related violence are more prevalent, there is a greater likelihood that a police agency will develop a specialized anti-gang unit (Huff and McBride 1993; Needle and Stapleton 1983; Weisel and Shelley 2004). The emergence of specialized anti-gang units was seen as a way to increase both the efficiency and effectiveness of the response to gang-related crime. The thought was that specialized anti-gang units would lead to better coordination with the community in preventing gang-related violence (Braga 2015; Weisel and Shelley 2004).

The organizational configurations of these units are quite varied, ranging on a spectrum from being fully centralized and integrated, with a robust chain of command, to decentralized and decoupled, with limited connections to other departmental units and lacking measures of accountability (Katz and Webb 2006: Weisel and Shelley 2004). The organizational disposition and operational procedures of anti-gang units also tend to reflect the differing perceptions of the level and type of gang issue recognized by the agency (Katz 2001; Rostami, Melde, and Holgersson 2015; Weisel and Shelley 2004). For instance, in Los Angeles County, the two largest law enforcement agencies, the Los Angeles Police Department (LAPD) and the Los Angeles Sheriff's Department (LASD), developed quite distinctive anti-gang units based on contrasting philosophies. Originally, the LAPD's anti-gang squads, called CRASH (Community Resources Against Street Hoodlums) units, focused on "total suppression" with pairs or groups of uniformed officers who, according to authorities on the matter, "harass gang members wherever they find them, at the same time collecting intelligence on gang activities" (Freed 1986, 1). By contrast, the LASD emphasized "targeted suppression," with plainclothes deputies selecting the most criminally active gangs to concentrate their resources on while disregarding minor transgressions of non-targeted gang associates (Klein 1998).

LAPD's CRASH was originally highly centralized, being staged out of three of LAPD's four bureaus (i.e., South, West, Central, and Valley). Mimicking the LASD, CRASH was later decentralized to each of LAPD's 12 divisions (Freed 1986).[4] The shifting of CRASH units away from administrative centers produced a host of unintended consequences. CRASH units were essentially decoupled from the daily operations and direct oversight of their local stations. This allowed CRASH officers more latitude in generating gang intelligence and greater flexibility in surveillance, but it also limited the amount of collaboration with other departmental units and hindered the sharing of information (Herbert 1997; Klein 2004). The cloistered environment of specialized CRASH units encouraged the emergence of organizational structures and behaviors mirroring what they were tasked with policing (Faturechi 2012), culminating in the LAPD's infamous Rampart Scandal[5] (Domanick 2016; Kaplan 2009; Klein 2004; Rice et al. 2006). Similar outcomes are seen with the Gun Trace Task Force in Baltimore (Fenton 2021; Woods and Soderberg 2020) and the LASD's culture of secret subgroups (Peterson et al. 2021).

In March 2003, the LAPD launched its present-day anti-gang unit structure, the Gang Impact Team (GIT). GIT is a full-spectrum approach to gang enforcement through collaboration and coordination, bringing together officers and detectives from the Gang Enforcement Detail, Narcotics Enforcement Detail, Community Law Enforcement and Recovery Unit, and the Gang and Narcotics Division (LAPD 2004, 2015). The primary responsibility of GITs is the collection and circulation of intelligence, followed by implementing strategies to reduce gang-related crime, maintaining both intra- and interdepartmental and agency relationships, and collaborating with the broader community (LAPD 2015; Valasik et al. 2016). According to the GIT mission statement, the unit has two primary components: uniformed officers and an investigatory section. Uniformed gang officers using marked patrol cars (lacking mounted light bars on their roofs) are responsible for intelligence gathering and making arrests, including probation searches of gang associates and civil gang injunction arrests (Hennigan and Sloane 2013; Valasik 2014). The intelligence collected is on the gang, its membership, and any noticeable gang activity. This gang intelligence is then disseminated to patrol and other investigatory units in the division and other LAPD community policing areas. Gang detectives in the investigatory section are responsible for following up on gang-related crimes and further reviewing these incidents (LAPD 2015).

Despite the strides that have been made by the LAPD to increase the accountability of their anti-gang units (e.g., removal of autonomy, direct oversight, implementing body-worn cameras), individuals still compose these units, meaning that they are not infallible. Misconduct, negligence, and corruption remain concerns that require continuous attention and thorough accountability (see Domanick 2016; LAPD 2020).

Collection and Use of Gang Intelligence: The Field Information Card

Anti-gang units' principal function is to gather intelligence on gangs, their associates, and their activities to guide enforcement activities and strategic planning (Klein 1995; Valasik et al. 2016). The most readily discussed artifact of gang policing is the creation and maintenance of gang databases, which are then used at the local, state, regional, or federal levels (Barrows and Huff 2009; Bloch 2020; Densley and Pyrooz 2020; Fraser and Atkinson 2014; Huff and McBride 1993; Jacobs 2009; Kennedy 2009; Klein 2009; McQuade 2019; Muñiz 2022; Petering 2015; Pittman 2021; Short 2009; Spergel 2009; Vila and Meeker 1997). Despite questions about the quality and accuracy of gang databases (Chesney-Lind et al. 1994; Densley and Pyrooz 2020; Huff and Barrows 2015; Pyrooz and Sweeten 2015; Spergel 1995), their use by law enforcement agencies, prosecutors' offices, and correctional staff to identify and prosecute gang associates remains commonplace (see Caudil et al. 2017; Pyrooz, Decker, and Owens 2020). It is important to understand, therefore, how the information in gang databases is populated.

The most common source of information in gang databases is the collection of gang intelligence through field interviews (FI). FI cards are used by law enforcement agencies for a variety of investigative reasons, such as interviewing witnesses at a crime scene; however, their regular use to gather gang intelligence by chronicling affiliations of gang associates and their public relationships with other gang associates and non-gang individuals is where most castigation is centered (Brayne 2020; Jackson and McBride 1983; Katz 2003; Katz and Webb 2006; Leovy 2015; O'Deane 2008; Rios 2011; Valasik 2014; Valasik et al. 2016). Ethnographic research by Vigil (2007) finds that police frequently monitor gangs with "officers stopping and questioning gang members to fill in [FI] cards even if no crime was committed so that the cards can later be used as evidence in courts to show gang affiliation"[6] (21; see also Brayne 2020, 65). While every encounter between police and a civilian should produce a FI card, given police discretion this is likely not the case. The expectation (rightly or wrongly) is that FI cards are routinely completed when officers encounter gang members to chronicle their ongoing gang activity.[7] This makes FI cards an important and valuable resource for investigating and prosecuting gang-related crimes (Katz 2006; Klein 2009). As such, FI cards' "importance cannot be overstated" as they have the ability to link individuals over space and time through repeated interactions with police (Brayne 2020, 64).

Yet the assumptions that critics of this form of gang intelligence raise focus exceedingly on FI cards being the foundational component of data-driven policing (see Brayne 2020). The process of an officer manually filling out a FI card on a gang associate and that information showing up in an electronic gang database or being queried by some other data-driven approach is not as instantaneous or fastidious as it gets portrayed in the literature (see Brayne 2020; Ferguson 2017).[8] A critical defect that Brayne (2020) glosses over in her discussion about FI cards as the "fundamental building blocks" of many data-driven policing strategies is the fact that they "have to be manually entered into databases" (64).

Research asserts that gang intelligence is reliably collected with officers being able to accurately identify criminally active gang associates (Katz et al. 2000). Yet even if a FI card is collected on an individual, an error can still be introduced into the system. First, when a police officer encounters a gang associate and completes a FI card by hand, the information collected may be inaccurate, recorded incorrectly (e.g., misspelled), placed in the wrong field, or may be illegible.

Second, when a FI card is entered into a gang database the same set of errors could be introduced secondarily or the initial errors will not be addressed when being archived. Even worse, an eligible FI card meeting the required criteria for inclusion may never be entered into the database (LAPD 2020). Given the likelihood that the individuals entering the FI into a database do not wish to be held accountable for any mistakes, even if fixing initial errors produces a more accurate and reliable database, it is more reasonable to expect that any errors in the database are the result of an officer not producing a clean FI at the point of contact with the gang associate. Van Gennip et al. (2018) highlight some of these issues with FIs having been entered with "misspellings, different ways of writing names, and even address changes over time" that "can all lead to duplicate entries in the database for the same person" which "bloat the storage size of the database" and "make analyses of the data much more complicated, much less accurate, and may render many forms of analyses impossible, as the data are no longer a true representation of the real world" (109–110). It is no surprise, then, that audits of gang databases identify "instances of questionable data entries related to individuals' birthdates, criteria dates, purge dates, and individuals' location information" (California State Auditor 2016, 17). For example, the California State Auditor (2016) uncovered that "42 individuals in CalGang whose birthdates indicated that they were less than one year old at the time their information was entered, 28 of whom were entered into the system in part because they admitted to being gang members." The problem here is not that law enforcement officers are accusing infants of being gang members but that "flawed documentation; inadequate or inconsistent quality control . . .; or ineffective auditing" is the culprit of such errors (Huff and Barrows 2015).

Finally, officer negligence, or worse, the falsification of an individual's information to meet the criteria required to be entered into a gang database, may transpire (LAPD 2020). The inconsistent collection of information by officers, whether due to inadequate training, prejudice, bias, or other nefarious reasons, is extremely disconcerting (LAPD 2020). All in all, police agencies that rely on FI cards as part of their anti-gang policing strategy must not only have robust training on the collection, intended use, and archiving of such gang intelligence, but must also maintain a qualified support staff of analysts to regularly audit, document, and correct errors.

Data quality within gang databases is likely to have downstream effects on data-driven police systems (in addition to issues of trust in the police or violating individuals' civil liberties). The "need for stronger controls over the processes for entering, evaluating, and auditing the data" produced from FI cards is imperative for the functioning of data-driven systems (California State Auditor 2016, 39; LAPD 2020). This is particularly the case for both focused deterrence programs and person-based predictive policing systems, such as chronic offender lists, which rely on accurate and legible record keeping (see Braga 2015; Brayne 2020; Ferguson 2017). However, the present reality when it comes to policing gangs is that the use and reliance on data-driven systems remains more symbolic than instrumental. Most filled-out FI cards are stored in a locked filing cabinet within a secured room at a police station where they stay until they are needed for a gang-related investigation or prosecution. Police officers are generally averse to data entry, as readily depicted in the first episode of *The Wire* (2002), and the notion that they are now "data-entry experts, interpreters, and technicians" is misdirected (Ferguson 2017, 104). While the information provided on FI cards has the potential to create networked sociograms linking gang associates, or geolocating where gang associates reside or hangout, as Ferguson (2017, 102) and Brayne (2020, 67, 111) caution, anti-gang units do not typically use the data from FI cards for this purpose, let alone proactive, continuous surveillance. Rather, gang databases are used primarily to aid detectives in closing criminal investigations, identifying suspects and their affiliations, and facilitating prosecutors in convicting offenders. The potential impact of errors and inconsistencies on FI cards (and the inclusion of those errors into gang databases) on investigations, arrests, and prosecutions remains a concern, nonetheless.

Given that an anti-gang unit's principal responsibility is the collection and dissemination of gang intelligence (i.e., FI cards), if anti-gang units were surveilling gang associates through data-driven systems, then an officer's experience level in the unit should not impact their ability to collect gang intelligence. Any officer should be able to identify individuals who are gang associates and suppress gang activity through enforcement capabilities given access to data-driven reports, bulletins, maps, social networks, and lists of individuals (e.g., chronic offender lists) of elevated concern. Yet Valasik et al. (2016) reveal that this is not the case. They find that the temporary shutdown of an anti-gang unit produced a significant, permanent decline in the number of FIs collected involving a gang associate by newly assigned anti-gang unit officers. A reduction that, over the course of a year, was unable to return to earlier levels prior to the disbandment. Additionally, there was a "dramatic permanent decline in gang arrests," and after one year neither the reconstituted anti-gang unit nor the division as a whole "had returned to their pre-intervention levels of gang suppression" (Valasik et al. 2016, 103).

These findings run counter to arguments that the LAPD's anti-gang units are actively surveilling gang associates, let alone are able to locate and identify these individuals at will. Anti-gang units' supportive role of providing accurate and actionable gang intelligence, which is imperative in solving gang-related crimes, such as homicides and drive-by shootings (Katz 2003, 504), is reliant on veteran officers in the unit, with their years of expertise and street knowledge to be effective and "yield distinct advantages to a department" (Klein 2004, 179).

FI cards remain an intelligence-gathering instrument, with anti-gang units engaged in reactive investigations surrounding a criminal incident or a suspect, focusing on past criminal events and potential suspects (Brodeur 2010). Policing gangs is rarely proactive in nature, such as preventing a gang associate from carrying out retaliatory violence. Despite advances in digital surveillance and the ability to sift through social media posts, law enforcement's use of such techniques is greatly limited to only a handful of jurisdictions. In application, the territorial nature of street gangs means that policing them remains very much geographical in its approach, not technological (Bloch 2020; Bloch and Phillips 2021; Valasik and Torres 2020).

Data-Driven Policing of Gangs in the Twenty-First Century

Given the track record of policing in America, there is genuine concern that data-driven policing methods may exacerbate racial biases or infringe on civil liberties (Brayne 2020; Ferguson 2017, 2021, 2022; Jefferson 2017). For instance, this could emerge with data-driven policing approaches that identify potential at-risk offenders, and broadly or more narrowly target gang associates before the commission of a crime through criminal profiling (Degeling and Berendt 2018). This overzealous scrutiny of targeted individuals by law enforcement, looking for a criminal code violation to support an arrest, further diminishes trust in the police and only fuels legal cynicism in the community (Martinez 2016). That being said, such data-driven methods are not that different from well-received, evidence-based "pulling levers" of focused deterrence programs, such as Operation Ceasefire, which focus their interventions on gang associates who are participating in violence and intimidating local communities (see Braga 2015).

A similar concern is often raised for place-based forecasting, which predicts a time and location where a crime is likely to occur by introducing a law enforcement officer into an area where they have an increased opportunity to exercise racial bias (Brayne 2020; Ferguson 2017). Lum and Isaac (2016) demonstrated the potential for racially biased results after conducting a simulation study of place-based forecasting with drug arrests as the outcome variable. While Lum and Isaac (2016) make several problematic assumptions, including both the framing of a data-generating process that guarantees their result and the use of an inappropriate outcome variable,[9] their gambit is successful in demonstrating that attention needs to be paid to whether placed-based predictive policing approaches produce biased outcomes.

A randomized controlled trial, however, revealed that despite there being more arrests in forecasted areas there are no significant differences in the proportions of arrests between whites, Blacks, or Latinos in treatment or control conditions (Brantingham et al. 2018). Brantingham et al. (2018) concluded that place-based forecasting did not contribute to racial bias in arrests. Research has revealed that increased police activity in documented hotspots does not negatively impact community perceptions of disorder, violent or property crime, perceived safety, satisfaction with police, or procedural justice, suggesting that the use of similarly related data-driven approaches would not automatically impact community residents in a deleterious manner (Ratcliffe et al. 2015). Benbouzid (2019) contends that such forecasting "is less a tool about the anticipation of crime a[nd] more like a dosage machine of safety in the continuity of Compstat" (11), which has been viewed as a successful crime reduction device that has become widely adopted by police agencies across the globe (Bratton and Malinowski 2008; Vito, Reed, and Walsh 2016; Weisburd et al. 2003; White 2014; Zimring 2012).

Degeling and Berendt (2018) stress that each data-driven policing approach relies on different theories and have unique assumptions that guide the forecasting algorithm. As such, it is necessary to be aware of this before evaluating a particular approach. Critics often conflate the methods for predicting potential offenders with those for predicting crime locations to suit arguments against the use of data-driven policing (Moses and Chan 2016; Perry 2013).

It is also important to keep in mind that the information systems that data-driven policing rely on tend to be "a patchwork of legacy systems, each brought on at different times, used by different people in different divisions, and [are] often unable to operate in tandem or communicate from one platform to another" (Brayne 2020, 33). Brayne (2020) also notes that the "data use and integration are nowhere near seamless," with usage varying by an officer's role, their unit, and the division they are assigned to (33). It becomes clear that data-driven information systems are "not so much Orwellian as Kafkaesque ... rather than being efficient and omniscient systems of total surveillance, they are buried under the weight of their own bureaucracy and inefficiency" (Bohigian 2022, 390).

The Reality versus the Possibilities of Data-Driven Policing

There is a big difference between the promise of data-driven systems and the reality. While there is much hysteria about data-driven surveillance by police in the news media, most use of data is not much different from the use of a search engine on the web. At most, police have been able to connect previously siloed data systems, such as FI cards, criminal rap sheets, license plates, traffic citations, and so on and facilitate searches of that information from a common interface (Brayne 2020). The results of such queries may be beneficial, or they could be of no use. It still requires a trained police officer to ascertain which information is worthwhile; the software just allows for the investigating to be performed in a timelier manner. Just as Valasik et al. (2016) observe that the expertise and street knowledge of veteran anti-gang unit officers is crucial in producing gang intelligence and suppressing gang activity, it is not the datasets that matter per se, but having a qualified individual able to synthesize the information that is being presented and interpret conclusions.

While data-driven policing does allow for "the proliferation of digitized records, mak[ing] it possible to merge data from previously separate institutional sources into an integrated, structural system in which disparate data points are displayed and searchable in relation to one another, and in which individuals can be cross-referenced across databases," this process is far from an automatic, all-knowing endeavor that allows police officers to actively surveilling the populace (Brayne 2020, 53). For instance, this lack of automation was documented by Uchida and Swatt (2013) in LAPD's Newton Community Policing Area during Operation LASER. A special crime intelligence detail (CID) was constructed specifically to conduct a daily review of not just FI cards but all "citations, release from custody forms, crime reports, and arrest reports" to create a potential candidate pool of "chronic offenders" that CID would then conduct "more in-depth analyses of those individuals to confirm that they have been appropriately targeted" (292). Furthermore, Brayne (2020) notes that "most staffers . . . use it [data-driven systems] for simple queries," such as a license plates, phone numbers, or suspect demographic characteristics (42). The information that gets provided still needs to be examined, with some of the data being useful and other pieces not being helpful. It is not easy or automatic in any sense; it just facilitates the criminal investigative process.

Brayne (2020) raises concerns about using such systems in relation to anti-gang policing. When police collect a FI card for a gang associate, any individuals who are present will have their information collected in the "Persons with Subject" field or the narrative section, thereby making it look like these individuals are also affiliated with a gang (Brayne 2020, 111). While this is a valid concern, the reality is that there is only a limited amount of space on the index-sized FI cards. Name, date of birth, sex, gang moniker, and affiliation have explicit fields of entry and only four lines for a narrative. This greatly limits the viability of FI cards as the lynchpin to uncovering a gang's social network. Additional data would be required to get a true sense of the structure of a gang, such as co-arrests (see Ciomek, Braga, and Papachristos 2020; Faust and Tita 2019; Papachristos, Braga, and Hureau 2012). At best, FI data could reveal the public patterns of connections among gang associates (see Valasik 2014). In the end, FI cards are primarily used to document criminal gang activity for future prosecutions and are not designed to be used as the building blocks of data-driven policing (see Valasik et al. 2016).

Brayne (2020) asserts that these associating individuals observed at a stop will be "gathered up in . . . the 'secondary surveillance network'" by the sole fact that they have a social connection to a gang associate (111). This is an appropriate concern, though the issue is with the resulting intelligence rather than surveillance per se. It is important to remember that without rigorous processes of entering, assessing, and scrutinizing the data being entered into the database the data-driven system is using, there will be issues with what is being outputted to officers (see LAPD 2020). For instance, with person-based forecasting, the creation of chronic offender lists is troublesome as they focus law enforcement's attention on individuals who have already become ensnared in the criminal justice system, either unintentionally or by design. As the actions of these individuals become scrutinized more intensely it is more likely that overzealous policing will result in violating an individual's civil liberties or exposing a criminal infraction (e.g., traffic violation, jaywalking) that could result in an arrest. This is the principal reason why data-driven policing person-based forecasting is problematic—the targeting of individuals before they have violated the law.

Place-Based Approaches as the Alternative

Data-driven policing through place-based approaches are similar to hotspot policing with traditional heat maps based on prior criminal activities. The goal in both cases is to provide a rational basis for limiting attention to the places where and when a crime is most likely to transpire to better allocate limited police resources. People forget that crime heat maps are also generated by algorithms. The only difference with more recent forms of place-based data-driven approaches is that the algorithms used now are often (though not always) more behaviorally realistic and, more importantly, are generally able to adjust more quickly as crime patterns change. The logic is that just because an area experienced an uptick in criminal activity at a prior point in time does not necessarily mean it will continue to experience the same criminal activity in the future. Data-driven policing helps to provide a more nuanced and accurate expectation of where crimes are likely to occur. There are generally two broad placed-based approaches: place-based forecasting and risk terrain modeling (RTM).

Space has always been important in understanding patterns of crime, but particularly gangs and gang-related violence (Brantingham et al. 2012; Papachristos and Hughes 2015; Tita, Cohen, and Engberg 2005; Tita and Radil 2011; Valasik and Tita 2018). Theory suggests that place-based forecasting is most effective at predicting property crimes such as car theft, burglary, or theft from a motor vehicle, with their high level of occurrence and relatively high rate of reporting (Brayne 2020; Mohler et al. 2015; Ratcliffe et al. 2021; Taylor and Ratcliffe 2020). It is expected that violent crime, with its lower levels of occurrence and reporting (e.g., assault, homicide, rape) is not as effectively estimated through place-based forecasting (Brayne 2020).[10] Police agencies, therefore, tend to focus more of their attention on the suspects and victims of violence through person-based predictions rather than place-based approaches (see the discussion below).

That being said, gang-related violence is not random, but tends to cluster in particular areas (Papachristos, Hureau, and Braga 2012; Smith et al. 2012) and remains stubbornly concentrated over time (Papachristos 2013; Valasik et al. 2017). Though his argument is cliché, Ferguson (2017) concedes that both the theory around place-based predictions and its application should "forecast with some accuracy" since "the combination of territoriality and predictably means that future gang violence" is confined to a very limited area of the urban environment (71) (see Valasik 2018). Furthermore, contrary to Ferguson's (2017) equivocating that the underreporting of crime produces data issues in criminal forecasting, he fails to point out that the Department of Justice report informing his argument does not include homicide in the violent victimization measure (see Langton et al. 2012). Homicide has long been considered to be fully and reliably accounted for in official crime reports (Messner 1984; Skogan 1977). Specifically, looking at gang-related crime, research has shown "that police reports of gang measures—specifically homicide—meet the measurement requirements necessary to be used reliably and validly" and that "police reports of gang crime are not fraught with measurement error so as to be unsuitable for meaningful analysis" (Decker and Pyrooz 2010, 370). Therefore, using measures of gang-related violence, particularly homicide, would be more than appropriate for criminal forecasting.

RTM differs from other place-based forecasting methods in moving beyond event histories. RTM merges concepts from spatial analysis and environmental criminology, identifying statistically significant features of the built environment, social and physical landscapes, and their interactions about an outcome incident (i.e., gang-related homicides, gang-related assaults) to determine an area's level of spatial vulnerability or risk (Caplan and Kennedy 2016). Using RTM to examine gang-related violence, homicides, and assaults, Valasik (2018) revealed that this data-driven approach can produce accurate forecasts. He found that areas spatially vulnerable to experiencing a gang-related homicide contend with concentrations of gang associates' residences and gang "set space" locations (well-known gang hangouts). Areas at risk of gang-related assaults are in close proximity to where gang associates are observed loitering by police while also being influenced by both environmental (i.e., metro rail stops) and social landscape (i.e., residential concentrations of local gang associates) features (Valasik 2018).

RTM differs from place-based forecasting in that it can identify the environmental risk factors associated with a type of crime and assess their spatial influence on an area's vulnerability to experiencing that type of crime in the future (Davis et al. 2022). Additionally, RTM does not require the inclusion of prior criminal incidents to identify areas spatially vulnerable to crime, which may temper the concern that police officer bias drives crime forecasts. Ultimately, Ferguson (2017) does concede that "as long as crime continues to happen in particular places, understanding those places and the environmental risk associated with those places is a clear measure of progress" (83).

Conclusion

An exaggerated paranoia exists that novel technologies (e.g., data-driven systems) are being used to actively surveil citizens and invade their privacy. While this paranoia may be spot on at the federal level, it is the exception not the rule for local law enforcement agencies (see Ackerman 2021). This overestimation is particularly salient in regard to the policing of street gangs (see Brayne 2020; Howell 2022; Pittman 2021). The goal of this chapter was to provide an even-handed discussion of the realities of anti-gang policing under data-driven systems compared to fashionable theoretical argumentation on the potential "legal implications of big data policing" (Brayne 2020, 119; see Ferguson 2017, 2021, 2022). In particular, it was to show that the policing of street gangs remains an anachronistic practice of traditional police work.

It is important to keep in mind that just because law enforcement has access to data-driven approaches, it does not necessarily mean that any privacy, civil liberties, or Fourth Amendment protections are being violated. Brayne (2020, 134) notes that just because a data-driven system "increases the opportunities" for impropriety, it does not mean such improprieties are taking place. She did not observe any during her fieldwork with the LAPD. The rhetoric surrounding how police bias and discretion contaminate data-driven anti-gang policing masks the mundane and longstanding practices of law enforcement officers. This is not to say that data-driven anti-gang policing is infallible. There is always a human component to policing, and officer discretion will always be an unsettled part of the process (see Brantingham et al. 2018; Brayne 2020; Ferguson 2017). As such, there needs to be an ongoing effort to ensure transparency and robust standardization procedures for the systematic collection and entry of data. In addition, there should be routine evaluation and auditing of data-driven systems (see Davis et al. 2022; LAPD 2020).

A driving assumption by Brayne (2020) and Ferguson (2017) is that data-driven policing results in officers being proactive in their duties. Research regularly reveals that the most prevalent forms of proactive policing are traffic enforcement and random patrol, driving around a designated geographic area in an attempt to deter potential crime (see Lum et al. 2020; Weisburd and Eck 2004). Furthermore, Wu et al. (2022) highlight that even when police are tasked with targeting areas with elevated levels of crime such targeting is "often short-lived and ineffective" (358). These findings highlight the difficulty of securing officer support and buy-in when introducing novel technology and approaches (Brayne 2020). For instance, while in attendance at LAPD's 1st Annual Foothill Crime Fighters Conference on February 3, 2013, officers were allowed to anonymously share their thoughts and feelings about data-driven systems being used in the division. While there was a range of responses, many of them were not supportive of the new approaches. It is no surprise then that data-driven anti-gang initiatives remain inconsistently implemented within and across jurisdictions (see Brayne 2020; Hennigan and Sloane 2013).

In the end, the jurisdictional complexity of policing fails to produce the perceived "seamless information sharing environment envisioned" by scholars and instead results in a "series of overlapping and often conflicting programs" (McQuade 2019, 78). Furthermore, law enforcement's use of both conventional (i.e., wiretaps) and digital (e.g., social media platforms) surveillance techniques remain a predominantly reactive endeavor to facilitate a criminal investigation (see Berlusconi 2013; Patton et al. 2017). The handful of large police agencies that can direct resources for more proactive surveillance of social media platforms remains limited. The vast majority of police jurisdictions lack training, have limited access, and are without a knowledge base about social media (LexisNexis 2012). As such, anti-gang policing remains relatively anachronistic, geographically targeting areas where gang associates are most likely to be loitering (e.g., residences, gang set space) and not technologically guided through data-driven systems. Anti-gang policing results primarily in the accustomed collection of intelligence (i.e., FI cards). This intelligence is not the driving component of a data-driven surveillance system, but rather is used to aid in the arrest and prosecution of offending gang associates (see Anderson et al. 2009; Caudill et al. 2017; Pyrooz et al. 2011; Valasik et al. 2016; Walker and Cesar 2020).

Notes

1. It is necessary to acknowledge the potential breadth of individuals who are identified as being part of a gang, due to the complexities of gang life or law enforcement's discretion in identifying constituents. The term "gang associate" is used in this chapter, instead of gang member, to identify individuals who are perceived as, labeled as, or self-reported as an actual gang member (see Rios 2017; Stuart 2020).
2. It is important to remember that data-driven policing is not squarely a gang-focused strategy, so these numbers are a rather generous estimate to the use of data-driven techniques to surveil street gangs. Studies to date on the use of data-driven policing remain in only a handful of very large police jurisdictions that have resources to commit to such endeavors, such as the Los Angeles Police Department, Chicago Police Department, New York Police Department, and the Metropolitan Police Department (London) (Brayne 2020; Densley 2013; Patton et al. 2017; Stuart 2020).
3. The definitions used in this chapter are synthesized from Dictionary.com, Merriam-Webster Dictionary, and Britannica Dictionary.
4. Note that today there are 21 geographically distinct divisions or community policing areas that makeup the LAPD's jurisdiction boundaries.
5. On August 25, 1998, LAPD gang CRASH unit officer Rafael Pérez was arrested and eventually convicted for stealing 8 pounds of cocaine from an LAPD evidence locker. Pérez accused other CRASH officers of police misconduct, including planting evidence, false imprisonment, illegal search and seizures, unprovoked beatings, perjury, bank robbery, stealing and selling narcotics, framing suspects, assault, murder, and concealing a crime (Domanick 2016; Reese 2005; Rice et al. 2006). The fallout from the Rampart Scandal resulted in the LAPD entering into a consent decree with the US Department of Justice, requiring dozens of reforms including the abolishment of CRASH units and the development of new management procedures with stringent checks and balances designed to inhibit the possibility of future corruption (Chemerinsky 2000; Stone, Foglesong, and Cole 2009). Also, over 150 individuals had their convictions overturned and were released from prison, with at least $125 million being dispensed in settlements (Klein 2004).
6. The LAPD Department Manual (Line Procedures 4/269.20) defines the indicators for gang membership as when an individual meets at least two of the following criteria: admits to being a gang associate, arrested for offenses consistent with gang activity, been identified as a gang associate by a reliable source, observed associate with documented gang associates, observed brandishing gang symbols/hand signs, observed frequenting gang areas, observed wearing gang dress, or has gang tattoos.
7. As of 2020, it is explicit LAPD policy that contacts with gang associates should not produce an FI unless the individual has knowledge of or has been involved in criminal activity or is a parolee/probationer or an arrestee.
8. If the stop involves a gang associate, additional information is collected documenting their gang membership (tattoos, attire, etc.) and the observed gang activity. "Upon supervisory review and approval of the FI Card containing gang-related information, it shall be routed to the Area GIT [gang unit] where the FI Card was completed for review and verification. Only a GIT officer shall complete a CAL/GANG Card if the criterion for a gang member or gang affiliate has been met. After completing the CAL/GANG Card or if a card already exists, the Area G-CAD [gang crime analyst division] shall enter the new information into the CAL/GANG System within three working days. The FI Card shall then be routed through the Area Records Unit for normal processing" (LAPD 2012).

9. Drug-related crimes, compared to other property and violent crimes (e.g., robbery, burglary, assault) are some of the most proactively enforced by police, which sets up divergence in police practices that could account for the biased results (Lynch et al. 2013). Most crime detection by police remains reactive in nature and dependent on the local citizenry (Black 1970).
10. Unpublished analyses suggest that this contrast is too simplistic. Analyses of predictive accuracy show in general that robbery tends to be the most predictive of all crimes, beating property crimes like burglary by a substantial margin. One possible explanation for this finding is that potential robbery targets (e.g., convenience stores) are far less numerous than burglary targets, and therefore repeat victimization is easier to predict for robbery.

References

Ackerman, Spencer. 2021. *Reign of Terror: How the 9/11 Era Destabilized America and Produced Trump*. New York: Penguin.

Allan, Edward L. 2004. *Civil Gang Abatement: The Effectiveness and Implications of Policing by Injunction*. El Paso, TX: LFB Scholarly Publishing.

Anderson, John, Mark Nye, Ron Freitas, and Jarrett Wolf. 2009. *Gang Prosecution Manual*. Washington: US Department of Justice, Office of Justice Programs, Office of Juvenile Justice and Delinquency Prevention.

Atlas of Surveillance. 2020. Electronic Frontier Foundation. https://atlasofsurveillance.org/.

Bakke, Erik. 2018. "Predictive Policing: The Argument for Public Transparency." *NYU Annual Survey of American Law* 74: 131.

Bartosiewicz, Petra. 2015. "Beyond the Broken Window." *Harper's Magazine*, 56.

Barrows, Julie, and C. Ronald Huff. 2009. "Gangs and Public Policy: Constructing and Deconstructing Gang Databases." *Criminology and Public Policy* 8 (4): 675–703.

Benbouzid, Bilel. 2019. "To Predict and Manage: Predictive Policing in the United States." *Big Data and Society* 6 (1).

Berlusconi, Giulia. 2013. "Do All the Pieces Matter? Assessing the Reliability of Law Enforcement Data Sources for the Network Analysis of Wire Taps." *Global Crime* 14 (1): 61–81.

Bjerregaard, Beth E. 2015. "Legislative Approaches to Addressing Gangs and Gang-Related Crime." In *The Handbook of Gangs*, edited by Scott Decker and David Pyrooz, 345–368. Chichester, UK: Wiley.

Black, D. J. 1970. "The Social Organization of Arrest." *Stan. L. Rev.* 23, 1087.

Bloch, Stefano. 2020. "Broken Windows Ideology and the (Mis) Reading of Graffiti." *Critical Criminology* 28 (4): 703–720.

Bloch, Stefano. 2021. "Police and Policing in Geography: From Methods, To Theory, to Praxis." *Geography Compass* 15 (3): e12555.

Bloch, S., and D. Meyer. 2019. "Implicit Revanchism: Gang Injunctions and the Security Politics of White Liberalism." *Environment and Planning D: Society and Space* 37 (6): 1100–1118. https://doi.org/10.1177/0263775819832315

Bloch, Stefano, and Susan A. Phillips. 2021. "Mapping and Making Gangland: A Legacy of Redlining and Enjoining Gang Neighborhoods in Los Angeles." *Urban Studies* 59 (4): 750–770.

Boehme, Hunter M., Deanna Cann, and Deena A. Isom. 2022. "Citizens' Perceptions of Over- and Under-Policing: A Look at Race, Ethnicity, and Community Characteristics." *Crime and Delinquency* 68 (1): 123–154.

Bohigian, S. 2022. "'Not So Much Orwellian as Kafkaesque': The War on Crime, Information Sharing Systems, and the Limits of Criminal Justice Modernization and Surveillance in Los Angeles County." *Journal of Urban History* 48 (2): 381–398. https://doi.org/10.1177/00961 44220944130.

Braga, Anthony A. 2015. "Police Gang Units and Effective Gang Violence Reduction." In *The Handbook of Gangs*, edited by Scott Decker and David Pyrooz, 309–327. Chichester, UK: Wiley.

Brantingham, P. Jeffrey. 2017. "The Logic of Data Bias and Its Impact on Place-Based Predictive Policing." *Ohio St J Crim L* 15: 473.

Brantingham, P. Jeffrey, George Tita, Martin Short, and Shannon Reid. 2012. "The Ecology of Gang Territorial Boundaries. *Criminology* 50 (3): 851–885.

Brantingham, P. Jeffrey, Matthew Valasik, and George O. Mohler. 2018. "Does Predictive Policing Lead to Biased Arrests? Results from a Randomized Controlled Trial." *Statistics and Public Policy* 5 (1): 1–6.

Bratton, William, and Sean Malinowski. 2008. "Police Performance Management in Practice: Taking COMPSTAT to the Next Level." *Policing: A Journal of Policy and Practice* 2 (3): 259–265.

Brayne, Sarah. 2018. "The Criminal Law and Law Enforcement Implications of Big Data." *Annual Review of Law and Social Science* 14: 293–308.

Brayne, Sarah. 2020. *Predict and Surveil: Data, Discretion, and the Future of Policing*. New York: Oxford University Press.

Brodeur, Jean-Paul. 2010. *The Policing Web*. Oxford, UK: Oxford University Press.

Brotherton, David. 2015. *Youth Street Gangs: A Critical Appraisal*. New York: Routledge.

Brunson, Rod K., Anthony A. Braga, David M. Hureau, and Kashea Pegram. 2015. "We Trust You, but Not That Much: Examining Police–Black Clergy Partnerships to Reduce Youth Violence." *Justice Quarterly* 32 (6): 1006–1036.

California State Auditor. 2016. *The CalGang Criminal Intelligence System*. Sacramento, CA.

Caplan, Joel, and Leslie Kennedy. 2016. *Risk Terrain Modeling: Crime Prediction and Risk Reduction*. Berkeley: University of California Press.

Caudill, Jonathan W., Chad R. Trulson, James W. Marquart, and Matt DeLisi. 2017. "On Gang Affiliation, Gang Databases, and Prosecutorial Outcomes." *Crime and Delinquency* 63 (2): 210–229.

Chemerinsky, Erwin. 2000. "An Independent Analysis of the Los Angeles Police Department's Board of Inquiry Report on the Rampart Scandal." *Loyola of Los Angeles Law Review* 34: 545.

Chesney-Lind, Meda, Anna Rockhill, Nancy Marker, and Howard Reyes. 1994. "Gangs and Delinquency." *Crime, Law and Social Change* 21 (3): 201–228.

Ciomek, Alexandra M., Anthony A. Braga, and Andrew V. Papachristos. 2020. "The Influence of Firearms Trafficking on Gunshot Injuries in a Co-Offending Network." *Social Science and Medicine* 259: 113–114.

Curry, G. David. 2015. "The Logic of Defining Gangs Revisited." In *The Handbook of Gangs*, edited by Scott Decker and David Pyrooz, 7–27. Chichester, UK: Wiley.

Davis, Jeremy, Duncan Purves, Juan Gilbert, and Schuyler Sturm. 2022. "Five Ethical Challenges Facing Data-Driven Policing." *AI and Ethic* 2: 185–198.

Decker, Scott H, ed. 2003. *Policing Gangs and Youth Violence*. Belmont, CA: Wadsworth/Thomson Learning.

Decker, Scott, and David Pyrooz. 2010. "On the Validity and Reliability of Gang Homicide: A Comparison of Disparate Sources." *Homicide Studies* 14 (4): 359–376.

Degeling, Martin, and Bettina Berendt. 2018. "What Is Wrong about Robocops as Consultants? A Technology-Centric Critique of Predictive Policing." *AI and Society* 33 (3): 347–356.

Densley, James. 2013. *How Gangs Work: An Ethnography of Youth Violence*. London: Palgrave Macmillan.

Densley, James A., and David C. Pyrooz. 2020. "The Matrix in Context: Taking Stock of Police Gang Databases in London and Beyond." *Youth Justice* 20 (1–2): 11–30.

Domanick, Joe. 2016. *Blue: The LAPD and the Battle to Redeem American Policing*. New York: Simon and Schuster.

Dunn, William. 2007. *The Gangs of Los Angeles*. Bloomington, IN: iUniverse.

Durán, Robert J. 2009. "Legitimated Oppression: Inner-City Mexican American Experiences with Police Gang Enforcement." *Journal of Contemporary Ethnography* 38 (2): 143–168.

Faturechi, Robert. 2012. "Secret Clique in LA County Sheriff's Gang Unit Probed." *Los Angeles Times*, April 20.

Faust, Katherine, and George E. Tita. 2019. "Social Networks and Crime: Pitfalls and Promises for Advancing the Field." *Annual Review of Criminology* 2: 99–122.

Fenton, Justin. 2021. *We Own This City: A True Story of Crime, Cops, and Corruption*. New York: Random House.

Ferguson, Andrew Guthrie. 2017. *The Rise of Big Data Policing*. New York: New York University Press.

Ferguson, Andrew Guthrie. 2021. "Surveillance and the Tyrant Test." *Georgetown Law Journal* 110: 205.

Ferguson, Andrew Guthrie. 2022. "Persistent Surveillance." *Alabama Law Review* 74: 1–64.

Fraser, Alistair, and Colin Atkinson. 2014. "Making Up Gangs: Looping, Labelling and the New Politics of Intelligence-Led Policing." *Youth Justice* 14 (2): 154–170.

Freed, D. 1986. "Policing Gangs: Case of Contrasting Styles: Strides Made by Sheriff's Dept. Cast a Pall on Methods Used by the L.A. Police Dept." *Los Angeles Times*, January 19.

Gascón, Luis Daniel, and Aaron Roussell. 2019. *The Limits of Community Policing: Civilian Power and Police Accountability in Black and Brown Los Angeles*. New York: New York University Press.

Gettinger, Dan. 2017. "Public Safety Drones." Center for the Study of the Drone at Bard College.

Goeury, Hugo. 2022. "The Birmingham School and Critical Gang Studies." In *Routledge International Handbook of Critical Gang Studies*, edited by David Brotherton and Rafael Gude, 29–44. New York: Routledge.

Hennigan, Karen M., and David Sloane. 2013. "Improving Civil Gang Injunctions: How Implementation Can Affect Gang Dynamics, Crime, and Violence." *Criminology and Public Policy* 12 (1): 7–41.

Herbert, Steve. 1997. "Territoriality and the Police." *The Professional Geographer* 49 (1): 86–94.

Howell, Babe. 2022. "Gang Narratives and Race-Based Policing and Prosecution in New York City." In *Routledge International Handbook of Critical Gang Studies*, edited by David Brotherton and Rafael Gude, 177–193. New York: Routledge.

Huebner, Beth M., Sean P. Varano, and Timothy S. Bynum. 2007. "Gangs, Guns, and Drugs: Recidivism among Serious, Young Offenders." *Criminology and Public Policy* 6 (2): 187–221.

Huff, C. Ronald, and Julie Barrows. 2015. "Documenting Gang Activity." In *The Handbook of Gangs*, edited by Scott H. Decker and David C. Pyrooz. Chichester, UK: Wiley.

Huff, C. Ronald, and Wesley D. McBride. 1993. "Gangs and the Police." In *The Gang Intervention Handbook*, edited by A. P. Goldstein and C. R. Huff, 401–415. Champaign, IL: Research Press.

Jackson, Patrick, and Cary Rudman. 1993. "Moral Panic and the Response to Gangs in California." In *Gangs: The Origins and Impact of Contemporary Youth Gangs in the United States*, edited by Scott Cummings and Daniel Monti, 257–275. Albany: State University of New York Press.

Jackson, Robert K., and Wesley D. McBride. 1983. *Understanding Street Gangs*. Custom Publishing Company.

Jacobs, James B. 2009. "Gang Databases: Context and Questions." *Criminology and Public Policy* 8: 705.

Jefferson, Brian Jordan. 2017. "Predictable Policing: Predictive Crime Mapping and Geographies of Policing and Race." *Annals of the American Association of Geographers* 108 (1): 1–16.

Kaplan, Paul J. 2009. "Looking through the Gaps: A Critical Approach to the LAPD's Rampart Scandal." *Social Justice* 36 (1): 61–81.

Katz, Charles M. 2001. "The Establishment of a Police Gang Unit: An Examination of Organizational and Environmental Factors." *Criminology* 39 (1): 37–74.

Katz, Charles M. 2003. "Issues in the Production and Dissemination of Gang Statistics: An Ethnographic Study of a Large Midwestern Police Gang Unit." *Crime and Delinquency* 49 (3): 485–516.

Katz, Charles M., Edward R. Maguire, and Dennis W. Roncek. 2002. "The Creation of Specialized Police Gang Units: A Macro-Level Analysis of Contingency, Social Threat and Resource Dependency Explanations." *Policing: An International Journal of Police Strategies and Management* 25 (3): 472–506.

Katz, Charles M., and Vincent J. Webb. 2006. *Policing Gangs in America*. Cambridge, UK: Cambridge University Press.

Katz, Charles M., Vincent J. Webb, and David R. Schaefer. 2000. "The Validity of Police Gang Intelligence Lists: Examining Differences in Delinquency between Documented Gang Members and Nondocumented Delinquent Youth." *Police Quarterly* 3 (4): 413–437.

Kennedy, David M. 2009. "Gangs and Public Policy: Constructing and Deconstructing Gang Databases." *Criminology and Public Policy* 8: 711.

Klein, Malcolm W. 1995. *The American Street Gang: Its Nature, Prevalence, and Control*. Oxford, UK: Oxford University Press.

Klein, Malcolm W. 1998. "The Problem of Street Gangs and Problem-Oriented Policing." In *Problem-Oriented Policing: Crime-Specific Problems, Critical Issues, and Making POP Work*. Washington, DC: Police Executive Research Forum.

Klein, Malcolm W. 2004. *Gang Cop: The Words and Ways of Officer Paco Domingo*. Lanham, MD: Rowman Altamira.

Klein, Malcolm W. 2009. "Street Gangs Databases: A View from the Gang Capitol of the United States." *Criminology and Public Policy* 8: 717.

Langton, Lynn, Marcus Berzofsky, Christopher P. Krebs, and Hope Smiley-McDonald. 2012. *Victimizations not Reported to the Police 2006–2010*. Washington, DC: US Department of Justice, Office of Justice Programs, Bureau of Justice Statistics.

Leovy, Jill. 2015. *Ghettoside: A True Story of Murder in America*. London: One World.

Lessing, Benjamin. 2017. "Counterproductive Punishment: How Prison Gangs Undermine State Authority." *Rationality and Society* 29 (3): 257–297.

LexisNexis. 2012. "Role of Social Media in Law Enforcement Significant and Growing." *Business Wire*. https://www.businesswire.com/news/home/20120718006055/en/Role-of-Social-Media-in-Law-Enforcement-Significant-and-Growing.

Los Angeles Police Department (LAPD) (2022), "LAPD Manual", available at: www.lapdonline.org/lapd_manual/ (accessed 28 May 2022).

Los Angeles Police Department (LAPD). 2004. *Los Angeles Police Department Plan of Action: For the Los Angeles That Is and the Los Angeles That Could Be*. Los Angeles, CA: Los Angeles Police Foundation.

Los Angeles Police Department (LAPD). 2015. *Gang Impact Team (GIT) Orders and Policies Reference Guide*. Los Angeles, CA: Gang Coordinator's Office, Operations Central Bureau.

Los Angeles Police Department (LAPD). 2020. *Review of CALGANG Database Entries by the Metropolitan Division and the Gang Enforcement Details*. Los Angeles, CA: Chief of Police.

Lum, Cynthia, Christopher S. Koper, Xiaoyun Wu, William Johnson, and Megan Stoltz. 2020. "Examining the Empirical Realities of Proactive Policing through Systematic Observations and Computer-Aided Dispatch Data." *Police Quarterly* 23 (3): 283-310.

Lum, Kristian, and William Isaac. 2016. "To Predict and Serve?" *Significance* 13 (3): 14-19.

Lynch, M., M. Omori, A. Roussell, and M. Valasik. 2013. "Policing the 'Progressive' City: The Racialized Geography of Drug Law Enforcement." *Theoretical Criminology* 17 (3): 335357. https://doi.org/10.1177/1362480613476986

Martinez, Cid. 2016. *The Neighborhood Has Its Own Rules*. New York: New York University Press.

McQuade, Brendan. 2019. *Pacifying the Homeland: Intelligence Fusion and Mass Supervision*. Berkeley: University of California Press.

Merola, L. M., Lum, C., Cave, B., & Hibdon, J. 2014. "Community Support for License Plate Recognition. *Policing: An International Journal of Police Strategies & Management* 37 (1): 30-51.

Merola, Linda M., and Cynthia Lum. 2014. "Predicting Public Support for the Use of License Plate Recognition Technology by Police." *Police Practice and Research* 15 (5): 373-388.

Messner, Steven F. 1984. "The 'Dark Figure' and Composite Indexes of Crime: Some Empirical Explorations of Alternative Data Sources." *Journal of Criminal Justice* 12 (5): 435-444.

Minocher, Xerxes, and Caelyn Randall. 2020. "Predictable Policing: New Technology, Old Bias, and Future Resistance in Big Data Surveillance." *Convergence* 26 (5-6): 1108-1124.

Mohler, G. O., M. B. Short, Sean Malinowski, Mark Johnson, George Tita, Andrea Bertozzi, et al. 2015. "Randomized Controlled Field Trials of Predictive Policing." *Journal of the American Statistical Association* 110 (512): 1399-1411.

Moore, Caylin Louis, and Forrest Stuart. 2022. "Gang Research in the Twenty-First Century." *Annual Review of Criminology* 5: 299-320.

Moses, Lyria, and Janet Chan. 2016. "Algorithmic Prediction in Policing: Assumptions, Evaluation, and Accountability." *Policing and Society* 28 (7): 806-822.

Muñiz, Ana. 2015. *Police, Power, and the Production of Racial Boundaries*. New Brunswick, NJ: Rutgers University Press.

Muñiz, Ana. 2022. "Gang Phantasmagoria: How Racialized Gang Allegations Haunt Immigration Legal Work." *Critical Criminology* 30 (3): 1-17.

Murch, Donna. 2015. "Crack in Los Angeles: Crisis, Militarization, and Black Response to the Late Twentieth-Century War on Drugs." *Journal of American History* 102 (1): 162-173.

Needle, Jerome, and William Vaughan Stapleton. 1983. *Police Handling of Youth Gangs*. US Department of Justice, Office of Juvenile Justice and Delinquency Prevention, National Institute for Juvenile Justice and Delinquency Prevention.

O'Deane, Matthew. 2008. *Gang Investigator's Handbook: A Law Enforcement Guide to Identifying and Combating Violent Street Gangs*. Boulder, CO: Paladin Press.

Papachristos, Andrew V. 2013. "48 Years of Crime in Chicago: A Descriptive Analysis of Serious Crime Trends from 1965 to 2013." Yale, Institution for Social and Policy Studies, Working Paper.

Papachristos, Andrew, and Lorine Hughes. 2015. "Neighborhoods and Street Gangs." *The Handbook of Gangs*, edited by Scott H. Decker and David C. Pyrooz, 98–117. Chichester, UK: Wiley.

Papachristos, Andrew V., Anthony A. Braga, and David M. Hureau. 2012. "Social Networks and the Risk of Gunshot Injury." *Journal of Urban Health* 89 (6): 992–1003.

Patton, Desmond Upton, Douglas-Wade Brunton, Andrea Dixon, Reuben Jonathan Miller, Patrick Leonard, and Rose Hackman. 2017. "Stop and Frisk Online: Theorizing Everyday Racism in Digital Policing in the Use of Social Media for Identification of Criminal Conduct and Associations." *Social Media + Society* 3 (3).

Petering, Robin. 2015. "The Potential Costs of Police Databases: Exploring the Performance of California's Gang Database (CalGang)." *Journal of Forensic Social Work* 5 (1–3): 67–81.

Peterson, Samuel, Dionne Barnes-Proby, Kathryn E. Bouskill, Lois M. Davis, Matthew L. Mizel, Beverly A. Weidmer, Isabel Leamon et al. 2021. *Understanding Subgroups within the Los Angeles County Sheriff's Department*. Santa Monica, CA: RAND Corporation.

Pittman, Lauren M. 2021. "Constructing a Compromise: The Current State of Gang Database Legislation and How to Effectuate Nationwide Reform." *Iowa Law Review* 106: 1513.

Pyrooz, David C., Scott H. Decker, and Emily Owens. 2020. "Do Prison Administrative and Survey Data Sources Tell the Same Story? A Multitrait, Multimethod Examination with Application to Gangs." *Crime and Delinquency* 66 (5): 627–662.

Pyrooz, David C., and Meghan M. Mitchell. 2015. "Little Gang Research, Big Gang Research." In *The Handbook of Gangs*, edited by Scott H. Decker and David C. Pyrooz, 28–58. Chichester, UK: Wiley.

Pyrooz, David C., and Gary Sweeten. 2015. "Gang Membership between Ages 5 and 17 Years in the United States." *Journal of Adolescent Health* 56 (4): 414–419.

Pyrooz, David C., Scott E. Wolfe, and Cassia Spohn. 2011. "Gang-Related Homicide Charging Decisions: The Implementation of a Specialized Prosecution Unit in Los Angeles." *Criminal Justice Policy Review* 22 (1): 3–26.

Ratcliffe, Jerry H. 2016. *Intelligence-Led Policing*. New York: Routledge.

Ratcliffe, Jerry H., Ralph B. Taylor, Amber Perenzin Askey, Kevin Thomas, John Grasso, Kevin J. Bethel, Ryan Fisher, and Josh Koehnlein. 2021. "The Philadelphia Predictive Policing Experiment." *Journal of Experimental Criminology* 17 (1): 15–41.

Reese, Renford. 2005. *Leadership in the LAPD: Walking the Tightrope*. Durham, NC: Carolina Academic Press.

Rice, Constance L., Jan Handzlik, Laurie Levenson, Stephen Mansfield, Carol Sobel, and Edgar Twine. 2006. *Rampart Reconsidered: The Search for Real Reform Seven Years Later*. Los Angeles: Rampart Review Panel.

Rice, Constance, and Susan K. Lee. 2015. *Relationship-Based Policing Achieving Safety in Watts*. Washington, DC: Advancement Project.

Richardson, Rashida, Jason M. Schultz, and Kate Crawford. 2019. "Dirty Data, Bad Predictions: How Civil Rights Violations Impact Police Data, Predictive Policing Systems, and Justice." *NYU Law Review* 94: 15.

Rios, Victor M. 2011. *Punished: Policing the Lives of Black and Latino boys*. New York: New York University Press.

Rios, Victor M. 2017. *Human Targets: Schools, Police, and the Criminalization of Latino Youth*. Chicago, IL: University of Chicago Press.

Rostami, Amir, Chris Melde, and Stefan Holgersson. 2015. "The Myth of Success: The Emergence and Maintenance of a Specialized Gang Unit in Stockholm, Sweden." *International Journal of Comparative and Applied Criminal Justice* 39 (3): 199–217.

Ryan-Mosley, T., and J. Strong. 2020. "The Activist Dismantling Racist Police Algorithms." *MIT Technology Review*, June 5.

Saulnier, Alana, and Scott N. Thompson. 2016. "Police UAV Use: Institutional Realities and Public Perceptions." *Policing: An International Journal of Police Strategies and Management* 39 (4): 680–693.

Short, James F. 2009. "Gangs, Law Enforcement, and the Academy." *Criminology and Public Policy* 8: 723.

Skogan, Wesley G. 1977. "Dimensions of the Dark Figure of Unreported Crime." *Crime and Delinquency* 23 (1): 41–50.

Smith, L. M., Bertozzi, A. L., Brantingham, P. J., Tita, G. E., & Valasik, M. 2012. Adaptation of an ecological territorial model to street gang spatial patterns in Los Angeles. *Discrete and Continuous Dynamical Systems* 32 (9), 3223-3244.

Spergel, Irving A. 1995. *The Youth Gang Problem: A Community Approach*. Oxford, UK: Oxford University Press.

Spergel, Irving. 2009. "Gang Databases—To Be or Not to Be." *Criminology and Public Policy* 8: 667.

Stone, Christopher, Todd S. Foglesong, and Christine M. Cole. 2009. *Policing Los Angeles under a Consent Degree: The Dynamics of Change at the LAPD*. Cambridge, MA: Program in Criminal Justice Policy and Management, Harvard Kennedy School.

Stuart, Forrest. 2020. *Ballad of the Bullet*. Princeton, NJ: Princeton University Press.

Sullivan, Mercer L. 2005. "Maybe We Shouldn't Study 'Gangs': Does Reification Obscure Youth Violence?" *Journal of Contemporary Criminal Justice* 21 (2): 170–190.

Swaner, Rachel. 2022. "'We Can't Get No Nine-to-Five': New York City Gang Membership as a Response to the Structural Violence of Everyday Life." *Critical Criminology* 30: 95–111.

Taylor, Ralph B., and Jerry H. Ratcliffe. 2020. "Was the Pope to Blame? Statistical Powerlessness and the Predictive Policing of Micro-Scale Randomized Control Trials." *Criminology and Public Policy* 19 (3): 965–996.

Tita, George, K. Jack Riley, Greg Ridgeway, Clifford A. Grammich, and Allan Abrahamse. 2003. *Reducing Gun Violence: Results from an Intervention in East Los Angeles*. Santa Monica, CA: Rand Corporation.

Tita, George, Jacqueline Cohen, and John Engbert. 2005. "An Ecological Study of the Location of Gang 'Set Space'." *Social Problems* 52 (2): 272–299.

Tita, George, and Steven Radil. 2011. "Spatializing the Social Networks of Gangs to Explore Patterns of Violence." *Journal of Quantitative Criminology* 27: 521–545.

Uchida, Craig D., and Marc L. Swatt. 2013. "Operation LASER and the Effectiveness of Hotspot Patrol: A Panel Analysis." *Police Quarterly* 16 (3): 287–304.

Valasik, Matthew Aaron. 2014. *"Saving the World, One Neighborhood at a Time": The Role of Civil Gang Injunctions at Influencing Gang Behavior*. Irvine: University of California.

Valasik, Matthew, Michael S. Barton, Shannon E. Reid, and George E. Tita. 2017. "Barriocide: Investigating the Temporal and Spatial Influence of Neighborhood Structural Characteristics on Gang and Non-Gang Homicides in East Los Angeles." *Homicide Studies* 21 (4): 287–311.

Valasik, Matthews. 2018. "Gang Violence Predictability: Using Risk Terrain Modeling to Study Gang Homicides and Gang Assaults in East Los Angeles." *Journal of Criminal Justice* 58: 10–21.

Valasik, Matthew, and Shannon E. Reid. 2021. "Classifying Far-Right Groups as Gangs." *Contexts* 20 (4): 74–75.

Valasik, Matthew, Shannon E. Reid, and Matthew D. Phillips. 2016. "CRASH and Burn: Abatement of a Specialised Gang Unit." *Journal of Criminological Research, Policy and Practice* 2 (2): 95–106.

Valasik, Matthew, and George Tita. 2018. "Gangs and Space." In *The Oxford Handbook of Environmental Criminology*, edited by Gerben Bruinsma and Shane Johnson, 839–867. Oxford, UK: Oxford University Press.

Valasik, Matthew, and Jose Torres. 2020. "Civilizing Space or Criminalizing Place: Using Routine Activities Theory to Better Understand How Legal Hybridity Spatially Regulates 'Deviant Populations.'" *Critical Criminology* 30: 1–21.

Van Gennip, Yves, Blake Hunter, Anna Ma, Daniel Moyer, Ryan de Vera, and Andrea L. Bertozzi. 2018. "Unsupervised Record Matching with Noisy and Incomplete Data." *International Journal of Data Science and Analytics* 6 (2): 109–129.

Van Hellemont, Elke, and James Densley. 2021. "If Crime Is Not the Problem, Crime Fighting Is No Solution: Policing Gang Violence in the Age of Abolition." *Journal of Aggression, Conflict and Peace Research* 13 (2/3): 136–147.

Van Hellemont, Elke, and Michael Mills. 2022. "Cultural Criminology and Gangs: Street Elitism and Politics in Late Modernity." In *Routledge International Handbook of Critical Gang Studies*, edited by David Brotherton and Rafael Gude, 111–121. New York: Routledge.

Vigil, James Diego. 2007. *The Projects: Gang and Non-Gang Families in East Los Angeles*. Austin: University of Texas Press.

Vila, Bryan, and James W. Meeker. 1997. "A Regional Gang Incident Tracking System." *Journal of Gang Research* 4 (3): 23–36.

Vito, Gennaro, John Reed, and William Walsh. 2016. "Police Executives' and Managers' Perspectives on Compstat." *Police Practice and Research* 18 (1): 15–25.

Walker, D'Andre, and Gabriel T. Cesar. 2020. "Examining the 'Gang Penalty' in the Juvenile Justice System: A Focal Concerns Perspective." *Youth Violence and Juvenile Justice* 18 (4): 315–336.

Weisburd, David, and John E. Eck. 2004. "What Can the Police Do to Reduce Crime, Disorder, and Fear?" *Annals of the American Academy of Political and Social Science* 593 (1): 42–65.

Weisburd, David, Stephen Mastrofski, Ann Marie McNally, Rosann Greenspan, and James Willis. 2003. "Reforming to Preserve: Compstat and Strategic Problem Solving in American Policing." *Criminology and Public Policy* 2 (3): 421–456.

Weisel, Deborah Lamm, Ellen Painter, and Carolyn Robison Kusler. 1997. *The Police Response to Gangs: Case Studies of Five Cities*. Washington, DC: Police Executive Research Forum.

Weisel, Deborah Lamm, and Tar O'Connor Shelley. 2004. *Specialized Gang Units: Form and Function in Community Policing*. Washington, DC: National Institute of Justice.

White, M. D. 2014. "The New York City Police Department, Its Crime Control Strategies and Organizational Changes, 1970-2009." *Justice Quarterly* 31 (1), 74–95.

Wolf, Sonja. 2017. *Mano dura: The Politics of Gang Control in El Salvador*. Austin: University of Texas Press.

Woods, Baynard, and Brandon Soderberg. 2020. *I Got a Monster: The Rise and Fall of America's Most Corrupt Police Squad*. New York: St. Martin's Publishing Group.

Wu, X., Koper, C. & Lum, C. 2022. Measuring the Impacts of Everyday Police Proactive Activities: Tackling the Endogeneity Problem. *J Quant Criminol* 38, 343–363. https://doi.org/10.1007/s10940-021-09496-8

Zatz, Marjorie S., and Edwardo L. Portillos. 2000. "Voices from the Barrio: Chicano/a Gangs, Families, and Communities." *Criminology* 38 (2): 369–402.

Zhu, Olivia. 2016. "What Everyone Is Getting Wrong about Predictive Policing." *Quarks Daily*, 3.

Zimring, Franklin. 2012. *The City That Became Safe: New York's Lessons for Urban Crime and Its Control*. Oxford, UK: Oxford University Press.

CHAPTER 41

POLICING GANGS
Five Reasons Why Traditional Strategies Fail

MADELEINE NOVICH

The national discourse on policing, following the murder of George Floyd by a Minneapolis police officer, has sparked a historic protest and reform movement that remains ongoing. At its core is a call for national recognition of systemic racism and radical policing reform, issues that continue to present in how police attempt to control and combat gangs. Following the dramatic rise in gang membership and gang-related problems over the past two decades, American police departments formed task forces or developed specialized gang units (Curry, Decker, and Pyrooz 2014; Katz and Webb 2006; Perna 2015). Task forces, which tend to be temporary and interagency (i.e., local, state, and/or federal), are typically created in response to a flare-up in violence (Perna 2015). Gang units, on the other hand, tend to be within a single agency and permanent. Between 2004 and 2007, 365 of America's largest police forces established gang units, and more than 4,300 officers were employed to address gang-related problems (Langton 2007). These units are solely focused on gang control efforts, deploying officers to deal specifically with gang members and gang problems (Klein 1995; Langton 2007).

Often reactive in nature, the officers' priorities are to respond to gang-related street crimes like drive-by shootings, assaults, vandalism, and drug sales (Klein 1995; Langton 2007). While gang activity and local gang problems differ across geographic settings, and despite there being no uniformly agreed-upon definition of a gang (see Langton 2007), police responses and strategies to mitigate gang crime typically do not vary widely (Katz and Webb 2006; Curry et al. 2014). Instead of bespoke approaches based on unique contextual challenges, gang suppression efforts were developed via a mimetic process that includes variations of aggressive enforcement practices premised on zero-tolerance policing (Webb and Katz 2014). Task force and gang unit officers typically engage in the following four functions: intelligence, enforcement/suppression, investigations, and prevention (Webb and Katz 2014; Langton 2007) with the bulk of their efforts focused on intelligence, investigation, and suppression (Curry et al. 2014; Klein 1995; Langton 2007).

While the goals of these efforts, which are solving gang crimes, reducing community violence, and incarcerating gang-involved offenders are admirable, the actual mechanics of these practices result in the opposite of what police are attempting to achieve. Face-to-face interactions with police are commonly viewed extremely negatively by gangs and community members. Marked by perceptions of distrust, disrespect, and racial profiling, these encounters inhibit relationship-building. Second, the increased scrutiny, coupled with lengthy gang-related sentencing policies, results in high rates of incarceration. Both the experience of prison and the collateral consequences of incarceration contribute to new or continued gang membership. Alternatively, an emphasis on other, non-police-focused efforts, like early intervention or community programming, may be more effective when dealing with gangs and their members. This suggests that defunding the police and moving away from punitive-focused strategies and, instead, allocating resources to community programs may be a better solution.

Gang Task Force Functions

To fully understand how and why traditional policing is problematic, it is important to outline exactly what police do. Gang task force and gang unit officers, regardless of geographic location and size and dynamics of the gang problem, typically engage in four primary functions: intelligence gathering, suppression and enforcement, reactive investigation, and public education. They typically adopt the perspective that gang members are violent, out of control, and in need of aggressive suppression tactics (Klein 1995).

Intelligence Gathering

Intelligence gathering is the most common function (Langton 2007). These activities can consume up to 83% of a gang task force officers' daily responsibilities (Klein 1995). Intelligence is viewed as crucial, because officers believe that they can "develop personal relationships with gang members for the purpose of establishing a thorough intelligence network" (Webb and Katz 2014, 473). The ultimate goal of intelligence gathering is to help solve gang-related crime and become a centralized hub of intelligence on gangs and gang members. Using what is commonly understood as "saturation patrols" (Fritsch, Caeti, and Taylor 1999), officers attempt to build databases by collecting and digitally storing information on known and suspected gang members (Curry et al. 2014; Langton 2007). The information often includes images of their graffiti along with pictures and identifying details (i.e., tattoos) taken with or without the individual's consent during routine stops or stop and frisks, from a distance, or scraped from social media profiles like Facebook and Twitter (Real Search Action Research Center 2012; Behrman 2015). In the age of technology and viral media content, police increasingly rely on videos from YouTube and images from gang members' social media accounts or personal websites to populate and enhance gang databases and provide important and compelling evidence for court cases. This includes pulling details on "nicknames, tattoos, schools, addresses, and known associates" (Behrman 2015, 321).

However, database building and usage are extremely controversial, especially concerning how people are included, how they appeal for removal, the overrepresentation of minorities, and the consequences of being placed in a gang database (Durán 2013; Muñiz 2014; Densley and Pyrooz 2020; Trujillo and Vitale 2019). Gang databases have sparked hotly contested discussions surrounding "big data" and intelligence-led policing (Ferguson 2017; Ratcliffe 2016). Despite officer reliance on them, their actual effectiveness remains debatable given the likelihood that the databases include faulty or inaccurate information (Densley and Pyrooz 2020). Regardless of these issues, major police departments, like the NYPD, have doubled-down on efforts to grow their gang units and aggressively populate their databases to build large-scale conspiracy cases against suspected gang members (Trujillo and Vitale 2019). In doing so, they hope to target and dismantle both large, established gangs as well as smaller, loosely affiliated "crews" (Chalfin, LaForest, and Kaplan 2021; Trujillo and Vitale 2019). Given that the bulk of task force and gang unit officer time and efforts are focused on intelligence, this suggests "that most gang units focused more on developing specialized knowledge about area gangs, gang members, and gang activities than on developing specialized tactics for neutralizing gang activities" (Langton 2007, 5).

Suppression and Enforcement

These activities are the second most common responsibilities performed by gang task force officers (Webb and Katz 2014). These strategies are the most visible to the public, taking the form of directed patrol in gang territories, housing complexes, parks, and parking lots (Webb and Katz 2014). This can also include truancy and curfew enforcement as well as crackdowns (i.e., gang raids) (Fritsch et al. 1999). Indeed, gang raids, which are a common law enforcement strategy, are typically high-profile, coordinated events among various law enforcement agencies. They are characterized by extremely aggressive police behavior with the intent to "sweep" areas and result in high rates of arrests (Trujillo and Vitale 2019). For example:

In 2014, the NYPD, in collaboration with the Manhattan District Attorney's Office, launched a massive gang raid in West Harlem. Hundreds of armed police officers swarmed the Manhattanville and Grant Houses, as well as surrounding buildings, in a coordinated pre-dawn operation. The West Harlem sweep was the largest gang takedown in New York City's history at the time and led to two indictments of 103 mostly young Black and Latinx individuals. (Trujillo and Vitale 2019, 4)

These raids have been described as "violent, dangerous and traumatic experiences" for all who experience them, as police use "assault rifles, battering rams, flash grenades and helicopters" (Trujillo and Vitale 2019, 5). While a round-up intends to reduce crime and violence, and that is the case in some studies (Chalfin et al. 2014), other studies caution that poorly executed suppression strategies can increase gang cohesion and damage police–community relations (Greene and Pranis 2007; Decker and Curry 2003; Fritsch, Caeti, and Taylor 2003).

In addition to raids, officers often engage in the routine stopping of individuals they believe to be gang involved, patrolling gang neighborhoods, going undercover, or making arrests (Langton 2007). The police describe these responsibilities as twofold; keeping "an eye on gang members and gang activity, and at the same time [providing] them with the opportunity to develop personal relationships with gang members" (Webb and Katz 2014, 473). While the time spent on this function varies greatly across departments, suppression activities are generally seen as the most valuable and visible among the officers (Webb and Katz 2014; Langton 2007). Suppression, which is grounded in deterrence theory, is believed to reduce gangs and gang involvement. The "swifter, severer, and more certain punishment will lead to a reduction of gang-related activity by those currently in gangs, as well as to a reduction in the number of individuals wishing to participate in gangs and gang behavior in the future" (Webb and Katz 2014, 470). How true this is, however, remains a subject of debate (Greene and Pranis 2007; Decker and Curry 2003).

Reactive Criminal Investigations

The third function of gang task force officers involves criminal investigations. Gang unit officers, often in tandem with other non-gang task force officers, help solve gang-related crimes (Webb and Katz 2014). This is also referred to as providing support to other departments (see Langton 2007). The officers are called in, due to their extensive knowledge of gang-related intelligence and acute familiarity with local gang members, to investigate a range of crimes, including serious violent felonies, narcotic offenses, and graffiti (Langton 2007). Also, the officers believe that participation in these investigations grant them access to additional timely and salient intelligence on the gangs in their jurisdiction (Webb and Katz 2014). While investigations are found to be important and valuable, these duties often did not make up the bulk of the officers' time (Webb and Katz 2014).

Prevention

The fourth and least performed task is more common among larger gang units than smaller ones (Langton 2007). The goal is to spread awareness of the gang problem and gain support for the gang task force as a legitimate unit among the public (Webb and Katz 2014). These often take the form of public education seminars or presentations at schools that inform at-risk youth and parents about the harms of gang membership. It also includes handing out gang prevention literature to schools, parents, and community members (Langton 2007). The officers also participate in activities designed to keep youth from joining gangs "such as mentoring programs, social skills and leadership training, drug prevention groups, and self-esteem building programs" (Langton 2007). One of the primary goals of prevention is to promote awareness of the gang task force and convince the public of its need and effectiveness (Webb and Katz 2014). Despite the perceived value of this function, few officers believe it should be the responsibility of the gang task force unit (Webb and Katz 2014).

Functions as Traditional Policing Practices

These four functions define *traditional gang policing practices* regardless of gang units' unique urban, suburban, or rural context and the size of the local gang problem. The relative impact of these practices remains somewhat unclear, however (Greene and Pranis

2007). This may be because there is no agreement about the best course of action. For example, some law enforcement officials believe gang crime can be neutralized by removing the leaders; others argue that leadership is fluid and the members can replace incapacitated members as quickly as they are removed (Greene and Pranis 2007). Some strategies suggest that targeting the "OGs" will make the most impact because they cause the greatest amount of harm while others argue that focusing on the newer, younger members will hinder the gangs' ability to thrive and proliferate (Greene and Pranis 2007).

An analysis of violence reduction following gang task force efforts remains mixed. Some research suggests that multi-modal, deterrence-focused programs like Boston's Operation Ceasefire can be very effective in gang desistance and gun violence reduction (Braga, Bureau, and Papachristos 2014). Other research, however, suggests that replicating it effectively in other cities has been challenging (Greene and Pranis 2007). Similarly, some research suggests that aggressive suppression efforts, like gang takedowns, are impactful in both long- and short-term violence reduction efforts (Chalfin et al. 2021; Ratcliffe, Perenzin, and Sorg 2017). However, other research suggests the opposite (Decker and Curry 2003; Fritsch et al. 1999). Indeed, a meta-analysis of gang enforcement efforts from 17 jurisdictions found few examples of success but many examples of failure. Their analysis identified several problems, including a "lack of correspondence between the problem . . . and law enforcement responses . . ., resistance on the part of key agency personnel on collaboration or implementation of the strategy as designed, [and] a tendency for any reductions in crime or violence to evaporate quickly often before the end of the intervention period" (Greene and Pranis 2007, 7).

Civil gang injunctions, which are a popular strategy, place restrictions on individuals from wearing certain colors, residing in/occupying certain geographic spaces, engaging in illegal behavior, and limiting whom one can interact with, but they also have had mixed outcomes. Some research suggests that they are a powerful tool with long-lasting violence reduction results (Ridgeway et al. 2019), while other studies caution against their use due to their ambiguous impact on violence reduction (Maxson, Hennigan, and Sloane 2003) and legalized control of minority communities (Muñiz 2014). Evidence is mixed on the realized impact of aggressive policing strategies. As such, it behooves scholars to take a critical look at how traditional policing strategies may fail, even when they seemingly win.

How Traditional Gang Policing Fails

Based on a survey of traditional gang policing literature, it can be argued that meaningful policing relies on two primary assumptions: (1) that intelligence gathering will establish a robust intelligence network that will help reduce gang problems via community insight and involvement, and (2) that aggressive enforcement will reduce gang participation and related crime through incapacitation and deterrence. However, these assumptions are problematic, and these practices arguably reduce police effectiveness overall and actually contribute to the gang problem.

Intelligence Gathering Does Not Establish the Desired Network

Gang task force officers believe that relationship-building with gang members will help them establish "a thorough intelligence network" (Webb and Katz 2014, 473). Research suggests that gang units are effective in collecting intelligence information and are necessary for dealing with local gang issues (Valasik, Reid, and Phillips 2016). Further, evidence suggests that disbanding gang units can lead to a considerable decline in intelligence and suppression efforts (Valasik et al. 2016). As such, well-established gang units hope that this intelligence network will loop them into information relating to gang crime, gang members, and possible future gang activity. This would, ideally, enable them to curb gang-related violence, monitor suspected members, and prevent gang violence from happening. While this makes sense abstractly, for this to be successful it hinges on adequate and reliable citizen participation. This is known as "co-production": "Producing public safety is a coproduction process, wherein police and citizens, and other organizations working with the police, all contribute to the outcome" (Taylor 2006, 106).

However, citizens' willingness or unwillingness to work with law enforcement often stems from favorable or unfavorable perceptions of police behavior (Taylor 2006). Research indicates that citizens comply with legal authorities when they are perceived as legitimate actors of the state (Murphy and Cherney 2012; Sunshine and Tyler 2003; Tyler 1990). Legitimacy, defined as "a property of an authority that leads people to feel that the authority or institution is entitled to be deferred to and obeyed" (Sunshine and Tyler 2003, 514), is earned through positive face-to-face encounters marked by respectful interpersonal treatment, perceptions of trust and fairness, and an individual's ability to participate in their exchange (see Tyler 1990). The culmination of these factors results in the police being perceived as "procedurally just" and therefore legitimate and worthy of citizen compliance (Tyler 1990). Indeed, research suggests that law enforcement could establish a symmetrical and mutually beneficial relationship between both parties—citizens and police—by acting in a procedurally just manner (Tyler 1990; Tyler and Huo 2002).

However, there is a paradoxical problem with this approach. Information is typically gathered via stop and frisk or aggressive policing strategies—which disproportionately impact communities of color. Of late, to mitigate racial profiling and racial violence, many police departments have adopted community policing models aimed at improving police–citizen relations (Brunson et al. 2015). The goals of community policing are to involve the local community in defining problems, include them in problem solving, and cultivate relationships between local businesses and neighborhood leaders. In doing so, the hope is there will be a vested interest in collaborating with law enforcement.

The community policing framework can be used to inform or modify traditionally aggressive policing tactics like stop and frisk (Rios, Prieto, and Ibarra 2020). For example, to best interact with community members and gang-involved persons, officers may include procedural justice as part of their face-to-face policing efforts. They might, for instance, allow individuals to participate in their stop and attempt to be respectful when engaging with someone they encounter.

However, Rios et al. (2020) recently identified how challenging this can be. Their recent study examined how police both used courtesy and respect and stop and frisk when engaging with a criminalized population. Though the officers expressed a desire to gather intelligence or support gang members with gang desistance, they traditionally used stop and frisk to initiate the exchange (Rios et al. 2020). These practices, which were understood as racially motivated points of contact, were viewed negatively, which undermined their legitimacy and alienated them from the communities they were attempting to connect with. This, the scholars argue, results in a paradoxical policing approach best understood as "the legitimacy policing continuum" (Rios et al. 2020, 59). This is where officers are attempting to present both courteous interpersonal treatment and unequivocal domination. The strategies examined by Rios et al. (2020) are arguably among the better policing practices to garner support and legitimacy, even though they fail to do so. Given that the majority of officers do not attempt to incorporate community policing, it is perhaps not surprising that the majority of intelligence gathering face-to-face interactions are markedly more negative and perpetuate the opinion that police are distrustful, racially biased, and disrespectful (Novich and Hunt 2016).

Distrust due to Racially Motivated Police Behavior

As noted above, law enforcement engages in intelligence gathering to catalog gang members in a database for effective enforcement. However, current police strategies not only render intelligence gathering ineffective but is damaging to community relations (Durán 2013; Rios et al. 2020). This is largely because gang task force officers are viewed as prejudicial, a key failing in terms of acting procedurally just and establishing legitimacy (Tyler 2006). Extensive research indicates that gang task force officers use tactics that employ racial profiling to populate their databases. This includes making directed stops and using the controversial policy of stop, question, and frisk (Densley and Pyrooz 2020; Rios et al. 2020). The "saturation patrols" routinely target minority males, both adults and juveniles, based on their racial/ethnic identity (Durán 2009; Miller 1995; Stewart et al. 2009). Officers focus efforts on young Black and Latino males and omit or ignore young white men and women (Gau and Brunson 2015; Durán 2009; Novich and Hunt 2018). These numbers are reflected in national statistics, which indicate that approximately 81% of all gangs are people of color and 93% are male (National Gang Center 2022). These numbers are complicated (Densley and Pyrooz 2020). Black and Latino youth are more likely to self-report as gang members when compared to their white counterparts (Densley and Pyrooz 2020). However, law enforcement certainly underestimates and misidentifies individuals, focusing on men of color with tattoos wearing chic urban attire (Durán 2009; Miller 1995; Pyrooz and Sweeten 2015).

This method of policing has been interpreted as legitimated profiling—where citizens believe officers are allowed to stop individuals based on their race, clothing, age, and demographic status, regardless of if the person is following the law at the time of the exchange (Durán 2013). The perceived racial profiling creates confusion, feelings of harassment, and anger among community members, eroding trust and confidence in law enforcement (Durán 2013; Gau and Brunson 2015). For example, a study by Novich and Hunt (2018) examined interactions between gang-involved youth and police. The scholars found that the gang members understood and validated when an officer stopped them while actively involved in criminal behavior, but they openly perceived information-gathering-type stops as being "fucked with," "harassed," or "messed with by the police" (Novich and Hunt

2018). Their negative reactions went so far as to question police legitimacy, like Erica, who remarked after being stopped "for no reason," "I think the police don't be doing their job. They just be trying to mess with ... young people like us, like just arrest you for no reason" (Novich and Hunt 2018, 59).

While these policing initiatives are designed to increase public safety and mitigate gang crime, they ultimately do more harm than good (Rios et al. 2020). The increased police visibility leads to amplified concerns of police harassment (Brunson 2007; Gau and Brunson 2015) and heightened levels of trauma and anxiety among urban youth (Geller et al. 2014), and it negatively impacts experiences of procedural justice, perceptions of legitimacy, and compliance (Gau and Brunson 2015; Novich and Hunt 2018). Moreover, misidentification and lack of an individual's ability to clarify their gang status leads to unreliable and inaccurate databases. As Durán (2009) aptly noted, "the actual practice of gang enforcement included: (1) racialized profiles, (2) fabricated intelligence, and (3) suppression of marginalized communities. The problem became not that of law ... but rather the enforcement of laws" (264). Racially biased police behavior, therefore, undermines attempts at coproduction and alienates individuals whom officers hope would serve as key informants in their "intelligence network."

Negative Perceptions of Police due to Disrespectful Exchanges

To make matters worse, experiences of racially motivated police behavior are commonly compounded by perceptions and experiences of disrespect during face-to-face intelligence-gathering encounters. Disrespectful behavior can come in several forms, but most commonly it is reported as disproportional or inappropriate use of force (Brunson 2007; Novich and Hunt 2016). This can range from being handcuffed too tightly (Kleinig 2014; Novich and Hunt 2018), being pushed against the ground or a wall (Novich and Hunt 2016), having a weapon drawn, or in the most extreme circumstances, shootings (Chevigny 1995). One study examined police–gang member interactions and found it was common for gang members, regardless of gender or age, to experience being thrown, slammed, grabbed, shoved, beaten, or handled roughly by officers (Novich and Hunt 2016). Dennis, for example, a participant in Novich and Hunt's (2016) study, recalled his violent interaction with police: "They had me in handcuffs tight as fuck. So tight that you could see the marks around my wrists and they had me in the car scuffed up" (4).

Disrespectful police behavior also takes the form of verbal abuse. This includes being sworn at or called names or speaking in a way perceived as rude, demeaning, or threatening (Durán 2009; Nichols 2010; Fratello et al. 2013; Novich and Hunt 2016). Melanie, for instance, recalled when police arrested her: "Some motherfuckers came from behind. I don't know where they came from. . . . I was shaking so hard. . . .Them motherfuckers choked me out ... calling me bitches and all that shit" (Novich and Hunt 2016, 5). Though gang members understand they have an increased likelihood of encountering police, they strongly feel that disrespect is unnecessary. Diego, a Latino gang member, explained:

I respect [gang task force and narcotics police], but if they want to come disrespecting, I don't give a fuck if you are a cop. That's my family. You can't come over here and disrespect them. I don't care if you got a badge, we are all human.... Don't come disrespecting just because you got a fucking badge and you are going to come pushing around and shit. You going to come and respect the family. (Novich and Hunt 2016, 4)

Furthermore, these public displays of disrespect have widespread negative effects among the communities in which they occur (Rosenbaum et al. 2005; Weitzer and Tuch 2004). In addition to damaging relationships with gang members, disrespect impacts those who might be sympathetic to policing efforts. This includes the family, friends, and community leaders that the police hope to reach during prevention initiatives. Given the ubiquity of cell phone technology, instances of aggressive police behavior are now recorded and spread virally through social media outlets like Instagram, Facebook, and Twitter. Recent research measured the impact of viral videos of police misconduct and found that they disproportionately impact young communities of color by contributing to feelings of fear, concerns of victimization, trauma, and emotional distress (Novich and Zduniak 2021). This suggests that witnessing aggressive police behavior can profoundly impact perceptions and feelings toward law enforcement. While gang task force officers may attempt to interact discreetly with gang members, street gang activity is highly visible, and most attempts to control them occur in public spaces. Thus police behavior is not limited to just the two parties, and negative, visible interactions can have rippling, damaging effects that permeate throughout entire communities (Novich and Zduniak 2021).

Aggressive Policing May Not Reduce Gang Problems or Membership

Perhaps these pitfalls could be overlooked if the traditional policing strategies were found to be effective in gang suppression and crime control. Traditional policing strategies, premised on deterrence theory, suggest that heavy surveillance, aggressive enforcement and sweeps, and rapid and certain punishment will lead to a reduction in gang members engaging in crime (Klein 1995). The specific-deterrence model posits that gang members arrested will be physically removed from society and no longer have opportunities to offend—especially if they are incarcerated for extensive periods. These aggressive responses then send a powerful general deterrent to other gang members or potential gang members. The assumption is that these would-be offenders would respond rationally by weighing the cost of gang involvement and gang-related crime with the benefits of gang membership. By making the punishments so painful, law enforcement hopes the gang members and prospective gang members would willingly withdraw from gang activity (Hennigan and Sloane 2013; Klein 1995).

The inherent problem, as Klein (1995) pointed out, is that these policies and practices do not account for the "calculus of the gang members' perceptions, values, and entrapment in the social psychology of the group process... Successful deterrence does not inhere only in the actions of the suppressors but also in the reactions of the suppressed" (160). In line with social identity theory and the nuances of intergroup dynamics, a profound social identity with a gang makes individuals less concerned about the personalized costs associated with gang crime and violence. This may be due to the normative nature of crime and punishment within gang culture (Hennigan and Spanovic 2012). Group identity, especially among gangs, is a powerful driving force in behavior, and there may be little police or sanctions can do to truly impact desistance. For example, civil gang injunctions (CGIs), designed to control individual behavior, can actually promote greater cohesion among the group (Hennigan and Sloane 2013). Although enforcement of CGIs can inhibit public gatherings and attempt to mitigate social gatherings, evidence suggests that they may do little to decrease the frequency with which youth associate (Hennigan and Sloane 2013).

Further, an individual's decision to participate in a gang is often nuanced. Women, for example, typically join gangs because they come from violent or neglectful homes, have family and friends who are gang involved, or live in low socioeconomic neighborhoods with widespread gang activity (Miller 2001). They decide to participate because they are seeking belonging or a desire to be in a "safe" space away from physical and sexual abuse. The young women "perceive these groups as capable of meeting a variety of needs in their lives, both social and emotional, and sometimes economic" (Miller 2001, 62). In other words, gang membership may be perceived as the best available option for self-preservation and worth the risk of severe punishment, assuming they are aware of the consequences. Regardless, boiling it down to a simple cost–benefit ratio dismisses the gravity of their reality and demonstrates a blatant misunderstanding about why gang membership is viewed as valuable among its members.

Given this, it is perhaps unsurprising that research shows that aggressive tactics may not reduce violence nor encourage desistance (Klein 1995). For example, Klein (1995) studied the impact of an extremely aggressive and well-funded sweep called Operation Hammer. This massive anti-gang police sweep employed over 1,000 police officers and, over the course of several days, arrested everyone who had outstanding warrants, issued new traffic citations, arrested individuals who exhibited gang-related behaviors, and arrested additional individuals based on observed criminal behavior (Klein 1995). A total of 1,453 arrests were made, but of those 1,350 were released without charges and nearly half were found to be non-gang related (Klein 1995). In the end, there were only 60 felony arrests, with charges filed on 32 arrests (Klein 1995). Despite this effort being exceptionally inefficient, the process was repeated several more times—to the same effect. Operation Hammer was supposed to send a powerful message of deterrence, and given its extreme nature, it was potentially in the best position to do so. However, it likely resulted in "good laughing material" among gang members and increased cohesion among their groups (Klein 1995, 163).

To be fair, not all aggressive policing practices are ineffective. There is evidence to suggest that "pulling levers" programs, like the Boston Ceasefire Project, can be successful in reducing gang violence and participation (see Braga, Kennedy, Waring, and Piehl 2017; Braga, Hureau, and Papachristos 2014; Braga et al. 2017). These policies "pull every lever" to mitigate gang violence. This includes focused policing on gang activity, reaching out to gang members, and including community members in the fight against gang violence. Inspired by the outcome in Boston, these programs have been replicated in cities across America, including Baltimore (Webster et al. 2013), Chicago (Papachristos, Meares, and Fagan 2007), Newark (Boyle et al. 2010), and Phoenix (Fox et al. 2015)—to varying degrees of success. More recently, Chalfin et al. (2021) examined the impact of "precision policing" on gun crime, whereby police focused on a small number of gang-related individuals thought to be responsible for the greatest amount of violence. Their New York City–based study revealed that, following a series of "gang takedowns" in conjunction with lengthy charges, "gun violence in and around public housing communities fell by one-third in the first year . . .

[which] imply that gang takedowns explain nearly one-quarter of the decline in gun violence in New York City's public housing communities over the last eight years (Chalfin et al. 2021, 1047)." Reducing gun violence is no doubt a win for law enforcement and the communities. However, while the immediate outcome is positive there may be questionable long-term benefits and unintended consequences relating to incarceration that might perpetuate gang participation and foster a stronger gang identity (Pyrooz, Gartner, and Smith 2017).

Aggressive Policing and Arrests Lead to More Gang Members

As noted above, aggressive policing like these sweeps increases the gang members' likelihood of arrest and incarceration (Curry et al. 2014). Incarceration is generally a net negative for tackling the gang problem because of how ubiquitous gangs are in prison (Pyrooz et al. 2017). First, prison may cause non-gang members to join a gang—increasing the overall total number of members (Pyrooz et al. 2017). For example, Pyrooz and Decker (2019) found that half of the self-reported prison gang members in their study joined a gang for the first time following incarceration. This may be due to at-risk individuals entering a hostile environment where gangs are rampant and violent and joining may be beneficial for self-preservation (Hunt et al. 1993). Indeed, Pyrooz et al. (2017) were able to establish a causal link between prison and gang involvement. After examining longitudinal data on incarcerated, non-gang offenders, the authors found that "incarceration—particularly in jails and prisons—leads to a greater likelihood of participation in gangs during periods of incarceration than when on the street" (294).

For current gang-involved individuals, prison can strengthen ties among its members and their groups (Curry et al. 2014; Huebner, Varano, and Bynum 2007; Pyrooz et al. 2017). As Pyrooz et al. (2017) noted, gang members are not "entering institutions as isolated 'new fish' . . . an incarcerated gang member might find himself embedded—for better or for worse—within the company of fellow gang members, gang allies, or gang rivals" (294). Coupled with the complex practices and policies within the prison and the clash between the two, gang members may become even more entrenched with their groups. There is also evidence to suggest that older gang members may continue to lead their respective gangs while incarcerated, suggesting that removal from the street does not necessarily mean removal from gang involvement (Curry et al. 2014). Prison, given how common it is among gang members, may also be viewed as a "natural extension of gang life" and thus a normalized part of the gang experience (Pyrooz et al. 2017; Levitt and Venkatesh 2000; see also Western 2006). It is thus not something to be feared and instead may even be viewed as a "rite of passage" (Moore 1978; Green 2016).

Finally, when they are released back into society, of which many are, gang members face challenges that contribute to continued gang involvement (Curry et al. 2014; Huebner et al. 2007). For example, it can be extremely difficult to find legitimate employment post-release that pays well and provides opportunities for growth and tenure (Western 2006). They face the stigma of a record, which impacts their marriageability and peer network (Western 2006). If they were married, incarceration increases the likelihood of emotional trauma, stress, and subsequent divorce, which leads to high rates of family disruption (Western 2006). Incarceration lowers their likelihood of forming prosocial attachments that help with pathways out of these groups. This, coupled with strong gang ties, makes it uniquely challenging for them to desist (Huebner et al. 2007). Thus, experience and time spent in a carceral institution do the opposite of what law enforcement intends. It does not serve as a deterrent to gang involvement and gang crime. Instead, the collateral consequences of incarceration are it creates new gang members, fosters greater gang connections while in prison, and has minimal impact on one's gang involvement during and post-incarceration.

Reassessing Current Strategies

Gang formation, membership, and crime are complex. It is a side effect of profound foundational issues relating to social, economic, familial, and neighborhood problems (Decker and Curry 2000; Krohn and Thornberry 2008). It is also a response to proximate causes, including existing gang threats, street values of violence, and limited legitimate outlets (Decker and Curry 2000). Individuals who join gangs are more likely to have formed weak attachments to parents and school; have histories of trauma, neglect, and drug abuse; and come from impoverished homes (Krohn and Thornberry 2008; Miller 2001). In the wake of a broken past, gangs become attractive alternatives. They are viewed, albeit often wrongly, as pseudo-families that can provide safety, belonging, support, and often access to basic needs like housing, money, and food (Miller 2001).

When gang members have the opportunity to desist or change their trajectory, it may be because they have formed strong relationships with non-gang-involved individuals—like spouses or children (Pyrooz and Decker 2011). They may have returned to school or found a job that provides economic stability and prosocial networks (Pyrooz and Decker 2011; Moloney et al. 2009). They may have aged out or decided to distance themselves from the violence (Pyrooz and Decker 2011). The decision to disengage and stop offending is generally not because they fear punishment or have gone to prison. While responding to gangs and related crime is no doubt necessary given the seriousness and violence among these groups, it behooves law enforcement to acknowledge that their current practices may not only be ineffective but might actually be contributing to gang perpetuation. The complex nature of gangs requires a nuanced solution beyond brute force. As Decker and Curry (2000) note:

The successful design of gang intervention strategies depends on the solid understanding of at least five specific domains of information: (1) the prevalence of gangs; (2) the mechanisms and nature of the spread of gangs and gang membership; (3) the role of the gang in generating crime, especially violence; (4) gang processes, including recruitment, leaving the gang, and forming relationships within the gang; and (5) relationships between gangs, gang members, and social institutions such as schools, families, and law enforcement. (130)

Traditional policing practices, unfortunately, do little to address gang violence and involvement. Though outwardly visible, law enforcement's reactive nature is just that—publicly responding to, but not fixing, gang problems. While their goals of intelligence and suppression are understandable, the mechanics result in alienation among the populations they are trying to collaborate with. Aggressive police practices lead community and gang members to view them negatively and contribute to perceptions of distrust, disrespect, and racial profiling. These encounters damage the "personal relationship" necessary for successful co-production. Further, the amplified scrutiny often results in incarceration, which increases gang membership and deepens gang ties while simultaneously hindering personal growth and capping legitimate pathways to desistance (Densley and Pyrooz 2019).

Given this, it may be time to explore alternatives that might impact the gang problem. While there is no single solution, perhaps a more effective approach is a nationwide, multimodal early intervention strategy. These interventions would address underlying risk factors that would make gangs less necessary and less attractive (Howell 2013). Several options could be included. For instance, school is often an opportunity to identify at-risk youth early on. Allocating funding for mental health professionals in school settings would likely help locate children who may need additional services and coordinate the services accordingly (Howell 2013). Bolstering staff can also increase the likelihood of home visits and early recognition of individuals in need. This may be particularly useful for young women, who disproportionately experience trauma, abuse, and neglect (Miller 2001). Another approach could be to invest in more robust school-based programming. Developing free after-school programming, for instance, designed to improve academics, has several benefits such as socioemotional health, academic success (Posner and Vandell 1994), and delinquency reduction (Gottfredson et al. 2004). For example, Posner and Vandell (1994) measured the impact of formalized after-school programming and found that children in these programs spent more time on academics and enrichment lessons and less time watching TV and playing unsupervised with other children. These programs are also positively correlated with stronger academic outcomes, peer relations, and emotional adjustments. Another module could be greater investment in community-based organizations that provide at-risk youth with safe, supportive, and nurturing environments, like the 4-H clubs, GRASP, and Scouts (Taylor and Smith 2013). For older at-risk individuals, increasing access to organizations that provide training and skill building that leads to stable and meaningful employment would also be helpful. These are strategies that address and counteract the socioemotional and economic attractiveness of gangs (Taylor and Smith 2013).

Law enforcement could also be involved in community-based programming like the Boys and Girls Club of America (Langton 2007; Taylor and Smith 2013). This may allow law enforcement to engage in true community-based relationship-building instead of straddling respectful but aggressive reactive policing (Rios et al. 2020). While this is certainly not an exhaustive list of what could and should be done, it highlights that there are impactful policing alternatives that can move the needle in the right direction. If funding is an issue, perhaps this is where policymakers look to "defund the police" and reallocate some of those resources. By investing in our at-risk youth, both on a micro and macro level, we can change their trajectories and build communities premised on values of emotional support, mental health, and future stability.

REFERENCES

Boyle, Douglas J., Jennifer L. Lanterman, Joseph E. Pascarella, and Chia-Cherng Cheng. 2010. "The Impact of Newark's Operation Ceasefire on Trauma Center Gunshot Wound Admissions." *Justice Research and Policy* 12 (2): 105–123.

Braga, Anthony, David M. Hureau, and Andrew V. Papachristos. 2014. "Deterring Gang-Involved Gun Violence: Measuring the Impact of Boston's Operation Ceasefire on Street Gang Behavior." *Journal of Quantitative Criminology* 30 (1): 113–139.

Braga, Anthony A., David M. Kennedy, Elin J. Waring, and Anne Morrison Piehl. 2001. "Problem-Oriented Policing, Deterrence, and Youth Violence: An Evaluation of Boston's Operation Ceasefire." *Journal of Research in Crime and Delinquency* 38 (3): 195–225.

Braga, A. A., Kennedy, D. M., Waring, E. J., & Piehl, A. M. 2017. "Problem-oriented Policing, Deterrence, and Youth Violence: An Evaluation of Boston's Operation Ceasefire." In *Gangs*, 513–543. Routledge.

Brunson, Rod K. 2007. "Police Don't Like Black People: African-American Young Men's Accumulated Police Experiences." *Criminology and Public Policy* 6 (1): 71–102.

Brunson, Rod K., Anthony A. Braga, David M. Hureau, and Kashea Pegram. 2015. "We Trust You, But Not That Much: Examining Police–Black Clergy Partnerships to Reduce Youth Violence." *Justice Quarterly* 32 (6): 1006–1036.

Chalfin, Aaron, Michael LaForest, and Jacob Kaplan. 2021. "Can Precision Policing Reduce Gun Violence? Evidence from 'Gang Takedowns' in New York City." *Journal of Policy Analysis and Management* 40 (4): 1047.

Chevigny, Paul. 1995. *Edge of the Knife: Police Violence in the Americas*. New York: New Press.

Curry, G. David, Scott H. Decker, and D. C. Pyrooz. 2014. *Confronting Gangs: Crime and Community*. New York: Oxford University Press.

Decker, Scott H., and G. David Curry. 2000. "Responding to Gangs Comparing Gang Member, Police, and Task Force Perspectives." *Journal of Criminal Justice* 28 (2): 129–137.

Decker, Scott H., and G. David Curry. 2003. "Suppression without Prevention, Prevention without Suppression: Gang Intervention in St. Louis." In *Policing Gangs and Youth Violence*, edited by Scott H. Decker, 191–213. Belmont, CA: Wadsworth.

Densley, James A., and David C. Pyrooz. 2019. "A Signaling Perspective on Disengagement from Gangs." *Justice Quarterly* 36 (1): 31–58.

Densley, James A., and David C. Pyrooz. 2020. "The Matrix in Context: Taking Stock of Police Gang Databases in London and Beyond." *Youth Justice* 20 (1–2): 11–30.

Durán, Robert J. 2009. "Legitimated Oppression: Inner-City Mexican American Experiences with Police Gang Enforcement." *Journal of Contemporary Ethnography* 38 (2): 143–168.

Duran, Robert. 2013. *Gang Life in Two Cities: An Insider's Journey*. New York: Columbia University Press.

Ferguson, Andrew Guthrie. 2017. *The Rise of Big Data Policing*. New York: New York University Press.

Fratello, J., A. Rengifo, and J. Trone. 2013. *Coming of Age with Stop and Frisk: Experiences, Self-Perceptions, and Public Safety Implications*. New York: Vera Institute of Justice Center on Youth Justice.

Fox, Andrew M., Charles M. Katz, David E. Choate, and E. C. Hedberg. 2015. "Evaluation of the Phoenix TRUCE Project: A Replication of Chicago CeaseFire." *Justice Quarterly* 32 (1): 85–115.

Fritsch, Eric J., Tory J. Caeti, and Robert W. Taylor. 1999. "Gang Suppression through Saturation Patrol, Aggressive Curfew and Truancy Enforcement: A Quasi-Experimental Test of the Dallas Anti-Gang Initiative." *Crime and Delinquency* 45 (1): 122–139.

Fritsch, Eric J., Tory J. Caeti, and Robert W. Taylor. 2003. "Gang Suppression through Saturation Patrol and Aggressive Curfew and Truancy Enforcement: A Quasi-Experimental Test of the Dallas Anti-Gang Initiative." In *Policing Gangs and Youth Violence*, edited by Scott H. Decker, 122–139. Belmont, CA: Wadsworth.

Gau, Jacinta M., and Rod K. Brunson. 2015. "Procedural Injustice, Lost Legitimacy, and Self-Help Young Males Adaptations to Perceived Unfairness in Urban Policing Tactics." *Journal of Contemporary Criminal Justice* 31 (2): 132–150.

Geller, Amanda, Jeffrey Fagan, Tom Tyler, and Bruce G. Link. 2014. "Aggressive Policing and the Mental Health of Young Urban Men." *American Journal of Public Health* 104 (12): 2321.

Gottfredson, D. C., S. A. Gerstenblith, D. A Soulé, S. C. Womer, and S. Lu. 2004. "Do After School Programs Reduce Delinquency?" *Prevention Science* 5 (4): 253–266.

Green, Edward L. W. 2016. *The Weight of the Gavel: Prison as a Rite of Passage*. Lawrence: University Press of Kansas.

Greene, Judith, and Kevin Pranis. *Gang Wars: The Failure of Enforcement Tactics and the Need for Effective Public Safety Strategies*. Washington, DC: Justice Policy Institute.

Hennigan, Karen M., and David Sloane. 2013. "Improving Civil Gang Injunctions: How Implementation Can Affect Gang Dynamics, Crime, and Violence." *Criminology and Public Policy* 12 (1): 7–41.

Hennigan, Karen M., and Marija Spanovic. 2012. "Gang Dynamics through the Lens of Social Identity Theory." In *Youth Gangs in International Perspective*, edited by Finn-Aage Esbensen and Cheryl L. Maxson, 127–149. New York: Springer.

Howell, James C. 2013. "Why Is Gang-Membership Prevention Important?" In *Changing Course: Preventing Gang Membership*. Washington DC: Department of Justice.

Huebner, Beth M., Sean P. Varano, and Timothy S. Bynum. 2007. "Gangs, Guns, and Drugs: Recidivism Among Serious, Young Offenders." *Criminology and Public Policy* 6 (2): 187–222.

Hunt, Geoffrey, Stephanie Riegel, Tomas Morales, and Dan Waldorf. 1993. "Change in Prison Culture: Prison Gangs and the Case of the Pepsi Generation." *Social Problems* 40 (3): 398–409.

Katz, Charles, and Vincent Webb. 2006. *Policing Gans in America*. Cambridge, UK: Cambridge University Press.

Klein, Malcolm W. 1995. *The American Street Gang. Its Nature, Prevalence, and Control*. New York: Oxford University Press.

Kleinig, John. 2014. "Legitimate and Illegitimate Uses of Police Force." *Criminal Justice Ethics* 33 (2): 83–103.

Krohn, M. D., and T. P. Thornberry. 2008. "Longitudinal Perspectives on Adolescent Street Gangs." In *The Long View of Crime: A Synthesis of Longitudinal Research*, edited by A. M. Liberman, 128–160. New York: Springer.

Langton, Lynn. 2007. *Gang Units in Large Local Law Enforcement Agencies*. Washington DC: US Department of Justice, Bureau of Justice Statistics.

Maxson, Cheryl, Karen Hennigan, and David Sloane. 2003. "For the Sake of the Neighborhood: Civil Gang Injunctions as a Gang Intervention Tool in Southern California." In *Policing Gangs and Youth Violence*, edited by Scott H. Decker, 239–266. Belmont, CA: Wadsworth.

Miller, Jody. 1995. "Struggles Over the Symbolic: Gang Style and the Meanings of Social Control." In *Cultural Criminology*, edited by Jeff Ferrell and Clinton Sanders, 213–234. Boston, MA: Northeastern University Press.

Miller, Jody. 2001. *One of the Guys: Girls, Gangs, and Gender*. Oxford, UK: Oxford University Press.

Moloney, Molly, Kathleen MacKenzie, Geoffrey Hunt, and Karen Joe-Laidler. 2009. "The Path and Promise of Fatherhood for Gang Members." *British Journal of Criminology* 49 (3): 305–325.

Moore, Joan. 1978. *Homeboys: Gangs, Drugs, and Prisons in the Barrios of Los Angeles*. Philadelphia, PA: Temple University Press.

Muñiz A. 2014. "Maintaining Racial Boundaries: Criminalization, Neighborhood Context, and the Origins of Gang Injunctions." *Social Problems* 61: 216–236.

Murphy, Kristina, and Adrian Cherney. 2012. "Understanding Cooperation with Police in a Diverse Society." *British Journal of Criminology* 52 (1): 181–201.

National Gang Center. 2022. https://www.nationalgangcenter.gov.

Nichols, A. 2010. "Dance Ponnaya, Dance! Police Abuses Against Transgender Sex Workers in Sri Lanka." *Feminist Criminology* 5 (2), 195–222.

Novich, Madeleine, and Geoffrey Hunt. 2016. "'Get Off Me': Perceptions of Disrespectful Police Behaviour among Ethnic Minority Youth Gang Members." *Drugs: Education, Prevention and Policy* 24 (3): 248–255.

Novich, Madeleine, and Geoffrey Hunt. 2018. "Trust in Police Motivations during Involuntary Encounters: An Examination of Young Gang Members of Colour." *Race and Justice* 8 (1): 51–70.

Novich, Madeleine, and Alyssa Zduniak. 2021. "Violence Trending: How Socially Transmitted Content of Police Misconduct Impacts Reactions toward Police among American Youth." In *The Emerald International Handbook of Technology Facilitated Violence and Abuse*, edited by J. Bailey, A. Flynn, and N. Henry, 271–288. Bingley, UK: Emerald Publishing Limited.

Papachristos, Andrew V., Tracey L. Meares, and Jeffrey Fagan. 2007. "Attention Felons: Evaluating Project Safe Neighborhoods in Chicago." *Journal of Empirical Legal Studies* 4 (2): 223–272.

Perna, N. 2015, November 24. "5 Requirements for a Successful Gang Task Force." Police1. https://www.police1.com/chiefs-sheriffs/articles/5-requirements-for-a-successful-gang-task-force-kYttSwGDqFOsL6RO/.

Posner, J. K., and Vandell, D. L. 1994. "Low-Income Children's After-School Care: Are There Beneficial Effects of After-School Programs?" *Child Development* 65 (2): 440.

Pyrooz, D. C., and S. H. Decker. 2011. "Motives and Methods for Leaving the Gang: Understanding the Process of Gang Desistance. *Journal of Criminal Justice* 39 (5): 417–425. https://doi.org/10.1016/j.jcrimjus.2011.07.001

Pyrooz, David C., and Scott H. Decker. 2019. *Competing for Control: Gangs and the Social Order of Prisons*. Cambridge, UK: Cambridge University Press.

Pyrooz, David C., Nancy Gartner, and Molly Smith. 2017. "Consequences of Incarcerations for Gang Membership: A Longitudinal Study of Serious Offenders in Philadelphia and Phoenix." *Criminology* 55 (2): 273–306.

Pyrooz, David C., and Gary Sweeten. 2015. "Gang Membership between Ages 5 and 17 Years in the United States." *Journal of Adolescent Health* 56 (4): 414–419.

Ratcliffe, Jerry H. 2016. *Intelligence-Led Policing*. New York: Routledge.

Ratcliffe, J. H., Perenzin, A. and Sorg, E. T. 2017. "Operation Thumbs Down: A Quasi-Experimental Evaluation of an FBI Gang Takedown in South Central Los Angeles." *Policing: An International Journal* 40 (2): 442–458.

Real Search Action Research Center (RARC). 20e12. *Tracked and Trapped: Youth of Color Gang Databases and Gang Injunctions*. Youth Justice Coalition.

Ridgeway, Greg, Jeffrey Grogger, Ruth Moyer, and John MacDonald. 2019. "Effect of Gang Injunctions on Crime: A Study of Los Angeles from 1988-2014." *Journal of Quantitative Criminology* 35: 517–541.

Rosenbaum, Dennis P., Amie M. Schuck, Sandra K. Costello, Darnell F. Hawkins, and Marianne K. Ring. 2005. "Attitudes toward the Police: The Effects of Direct and Vicarious Experience." *Police Quarterly* 8 (3): 343–365.

Steven D. Levitt, Sudhir Alladi Venkatesh. 2000. "An Economic Analysis of a Drug-Selling Gang's Finances." *The Quarterly Journal of Economics* 115 (3): 755–789.

Stewart, Eric A., Eric P. Baumer, Rod K. Brunson, and Ronald L. Simons. 2009. "Neighborhood Racial Context and Perceptions of Police-Based Racial Discrimination among Black Youth." *Criminology* 47 (3): 847–888.

Sunshine, Jason, and Tom R. Tyler. 2003. "The Role of Procedural Justice and Legitimacy in Shaping Public Support for Policing." *Law and Society Review* 37 (3): 513–548.

Taylor, Ralph B. 2006. "Critic Incivilities Reduction Policing, Zero Tolerance, and the Retreat from Coproduction: Weak Foundations and Strong Pressures." *Innovations in Policing*, January: 98–114.

Taylor, Carl S., and Pamela R. Smith. 2013. "The Attraction of Gangs: How Can We Reduce It?" In *Changing Course: Preventing Gang Membership*, edited by Thomas Simon, Nancy Ritter, and Reshma Mahendra, 19–30. Washington DC: Department of Justice.

Trujillo, J., and Alex Vitale. 2019. *Gang Takedowns in the de Blasio Era: The Dangers of "Precision Policing".* The Policing and Social Justice Project, Brooklyn College.

Tyler, Tom R. 1990. *Why People Obey the Law*. New Haven, CT: Yale University Press.

Valasik, Matthew, Shannon E. Reid, and Matthew D. Phillips. 2016. "CRASH and Burn: Abatement of a Specialised Gang Unit." *Journal of Criminological Research, Policy and Practice* 2 (2): 95–106.

Webb, V. and C. Katz. 2014. "A Study of Police Gang Units in Six Cities." In *The Modern Gang Reader*, edited by C. Maxson, A. Egley, J. Miller and M. Klein, 4th ed. New York: Oxford University Press.

Webster, Daniel W., Jennifer Mendel Whitehill, Jon S. Vernick, and Frank C. Curriero. 2013. "Effects of Baltimore's Safe Streets Program on Gun Violence: A Replication of Chicago's CeaseFire Program." *Journal of Urban Health* 90 (1): 27.

Weitzer, Ronald, and Steven A. Tuch. 2004. "Race and Perceptions of Police Misconduct." *Social Problems* 51 (3): 305–325.

Western, Bruce. 2006. *Punishment and Inequality in America*. New York: Russell Sage Foundation.

CHAPTER 42

DEFUND THE POLICE?
Considerations for Reducing Gang Violence

ANTHONY A. BRAGA, JOHN M. MACDONALD, AND GEORGE TITA[1]

THE year 2020 was uniquely terrible for public safety in many cities in the United States. The unprecedented challenge posed by the COVID-19 pandemic caused police departments to change their day-to-day operations to ensure they were engaging critical public health precautions while still providing policing services to the public. In many jurisdictions, police department resources were further strained by managing racial justice protests in the wake of the brutal death of George Floyd at the hands of Minneapolis police officers on May 25, 2020. These protests spawned a new movement for calls to "defund the police" that were coupled with modest police budget decreases in some cities such as Los Angeles, Minneapolis, and New York City (e.g., Gross and Eligon 2020; Levintova 2020; Mays 2020). While the debate continues regarding underlying causes, gun violence spiked in many US cities during the summer of 2020.

In 2020, the number of homicides in the United States rose by 30%, an annual rise not seen in more than six decades (Lopez 2022). The 2020 rise in homicides was followed by a 7% rise in 2021 (Elinson 2022). While there is a lack of detailed nationwide data to characterize the dynamics of the current rise in homicide, two things suggest a similarity between the peak period of the early 1990s and the current rise in homicides. First, the recent increases are concentrated in economically disadvantaged racial and ethnic minority communities (Schleimer et al. 2021). Second, the recent increases were a result of murders committed with a firearm. The proportion of homicides committed with a firearm is larger today than it was in the early 1990s.[2] In two cities with data sufficient to analyze the current trends—Oakland, California, and Baltimore, Maryland—the majority of 2020 homicides were generated by and against gangs, drug selling crews, and other criminally active groups of offenders (Barao and Braga 2021; Crime and Justice Policy Lab 2021). These facts suggest the important roles played by place dynamics, subgroups of active offenders, and guns in fueling the recent surge in homicides. The skewed distribution of where, how, and who is responsible for driving the rise in homicides implies that a small change in marginal deterrence among the right groups in the right places generates an outsized effect on gun violence in many cities.

"Defund the police" is a slogan that generally represents the diversion of funds away from police departments and toward non-policing public safety programs such as heightened social service and opportunity provision for at-risk youth, enhanced mental health counseling, improved health care, and strengthening the prevention work of community-based organizations. These demands for the reallocation of funds can range from modest proposals to reduce the harms associated with aggressive policing strategies by bolstering community public safety capacities to stronger calls for defunding as the first step toward eventual police abolition (McDowell and Fernandez; Vitale 2017). Activist groups, such as Black Lives Matter, and some politicians, such as progressive lawmakers in the Democratic Party, publicly support the "defund the police" movement (Rodriguez 2020). However, amid mounting concerns over increasing violence, a 2021 Pew Research poll suggests 85% of Americans want police funding to either stay the same or increase (Parker and Hurst 2021). And, despite Black Americans' persistently lower ratings of confidence and trust in the police relative to white Americans (e.g., Weitzer and Tuch 2006), 76% of Black Americans surveyed wanted police funding to either stay the same or increase (Parker and Hurst 2021).

There are no systematic studies of the impact of the "defund the police" movement on the rise in serious urban violence. Given that cities have not actually defunded police, a more appropriately framed examination involves assessing what happens when cities experience "de-policing." The withdrawal from proactive activities limits police effectiveness in controlling high-risk people within places where crime is concentrated. Homicide has been observed to increase when anti-policing sentiment results in local police departments engaging in "de-policing" (Devi and Fryer 2020; Kim 2023). In communities characterized by low levels of trust and confidence in social institutions, de-policing can further erode citizen willingness to cooperate with homicide investigations and promote citizens "policing themselves" by taking the law into their own hands (LaFree 1998; Leovy 2015). This can again lead to the unintended consequence of increasing incidents of gun violence.

Careful and precise police focus on the small and knowable proportion of local community members involved in gangs and criminally active groups can better position cities to manage homicide problems (Chalfin et al. 2021; Braga and Kennedy 2021). However, if this small population of very risky individuals is not appropriately managed by the police and their partners, rapid and steep increases in fatal and non-fatal shootings can result as cycles of retaliatory violence spin out of control (Blumstein 1995; Cook and Laub 2002; Braga 2003) with the potential to spread out to other sections of cities (Zeoli et al. 2014).

The potential for gun violence to spread among a subset of active offenders (e.g., Papachristos, Wildeman, and Roberto 2015) has gone largely unappreciated in popular press accounts of the current homicide increase. The police are the primary absorbing barrier to continued violence by armed offenders in many disadvantaged neighborhoods. The "gambler's ruin" problem, a statistical concept drawn from theoretical considerations of gambling patterns (e.g., Epstein 1995), provides a clear application to the problem of gang or group violence. If the absorbing barrier to the spiral of retaliatory violence is lowered by even a small amount by relaxed management of high-risk individuals and places, the chance that violence will spiral out of control exceeds the chance that it will not. The blackjack player in a casino that continues to stay at the table when the odds of losing exceed those of winning will eventually meet their financial ruin, even if they are lucky to win a few hands. Similarly, it is not difficult to imagine that a small increase in "de-policing" of a group of high-risk offenders will quickly lead to a surge in shootings.

It is important to note at the outset that we do not believe policing is the only available response to gang violence. Cities should have a portfolio of primary, secondary, and tertiary prevention programs that draw on salient public health and social welfare evaluation evidence to guide a comprehensive effort to address gang problems (Braga, Kennedy, and Tita 2002). Policing is a complement to these approaches, not a competitor. Nevertheless, we feel strongly that the police are a key element of this broader approach and, with appropriate criminal justice, social service, and community-based partners in place, a powerful prevention mechanism to address sudden spikes in gang-involved gun violence. The removal of the police from a comprehensive response to outbreaks of gang shootings through "abolition-or-bust" approaches greatly jeopardizes public safety. Decreasing available police resources through more modest "defund" efforts, as well as police decisions to step away from proactive strategies in the face of public disapproval, facilitates continued gang shootings that cause recurring harm to economically disadvantaged, mostly minority communities. In this chapter, we consider how the current "de-policing climate" undermines focused deterrence, ignores how a small subset of offenders create larger risks of increased violence, and hampers the development of evidence-based policing strategies that act as an absorbing barrier that prevents violence from spiraling out of control.

We begin by summarizing the literature that demonstrates a subpopulation of gangs and active offenders with extensive criminal justice system experience are responsible for a large share of the gun violence in cities. We then briefly describe focused deterrence and the theory and empirical evidence supporting its effectiveness in curbing gun violence. Next we present our concerns about how the current climate hinders the effective implementation of focused deterrence. We then conclude by noting that alternative responses to gun violence that fail to acknowledge well-established demographic and situational characteristics of gun violence run the risk of contributing to systemic harm in the most economically disadvantaged communities. Just as the architects of aggressive policing strategies should bear some responsibility for the collateral and downstream consequences associated with overly harsh policing in disadvantaged minority communities, we argue that advocates for alternative systems have a responsibility to demonstrate the efficacy of a non-policing approach and have some stake in the downside consequences of programs they suggest if they prove not to work.

Most Gun Violence is Driven by Gangs and Groups of Co-Offenders

Gun violence is usually concentrated among groups of serious offenders, and conflicts between street gangs have long been noted to fuel much of the serious street violence in major cities (Miller 1975; Braga 2004; Howell and Griffiths 2016). Moreover, relative to non-gang delinquent youth offending patterns, youth involvement in gangs leads to elevated levels of criminal behavior, especially violent offending (Thornberry et al. 2003; Pyrooz et al. 2016). In some cities, such as Baltimore, the violent street scene is characterized by various criminal groups ranging from small informal networks of drug sellers and street robbery crews to more formal gangs to larger drug trafficking organizations (Braga et al. 2002). Dealing with group-related violence is a challenge for most US police departments. City-level studies have found gang-related motives in more than one-third of homicides in Chicago (Block and Block 1993), half of the homicides in Los Angeles' Boyle Heights area (Tita et al. 2003), and nearly two-thirds of Oakland homicides (Braga et al. 2019). A study of more than 20 cities generally found that, on average, less than 1% of a city's population was involved in gangs, drug crews, and other criminally active groups, but they were connected to over 50% of a city's shootings and homicides (Lurie 2019).

Even in cities where gang-on-gang conflict is less prominent, high-risk co-offending networks are central to gun violence problems. In Newark, New Jersey, an analysis of homicide data for 2009–2012 found that while only 16% were the result of disputes between gangs, most homicides (60%) involved gang members (Papachristos, Braga, et al. 2015). Newark's 4th Precinct was home to some 47 sets of gangs and criminally active groups that represented less than 2% of the area's population but were involved in almost 69% of the murders in that area. Nearly one-third of all shootings in Newark occur in a co-offending network that contains less than 4% of the city's total population. Being a gang member in this risky social network increased an individual's risk of being shot by 344%, and being a non-gang member who is socially connected to a gang member increased an individual's risk of being shot by 94%. In St. Louis, the age-adjusted homicide mortality rate among gang populations was 950 per 100,000—a rate that was three times greater than homicide mortality rates among young Black males in the city (Pyrooz et al. 2020).

Rates of non-fatal and fatal shootings within such co-offending networks are considerably higher than city-level rates or even the highest crime neighborhoods. In Chicago, for example, 70% of all fatal and non-fatal gunshot injuries occurred in identifiable networks composed of individuals arrested in previous years who made up less than 6% of the city's total population; the rate of gun homicide in the network was more than nine times higher than the city average (Papachristos, Wildeman, and Roberto 2015). Conflicts among Cape Verdean gangs were a prominent feature of a resurgence of Boston gang violence in the mid-2000s (Braga, Hureau, and Winship 2008). Social network analysis revealed that 85% of total shootings in a Cape Verdean neighborhood were concentrated among a co-offending network of 763 individuals connected to 10 gangs who represented less than 3% of the resident population of that neighborhood; what is more, each "handshake" an individual was closer to a gunshot victim in the network increased their personal risk of gunshot injury by 25% (Papachristos, Braga, and Hureau 2012).

"Cafeteria-style offending," where individuals take advantage of a range of criminal opportunities that arise from specific situations and through social connections, is a central aspect of gangs and gang dynamics (e.g., Klein 1995). For instance, a study of 2016–2017 Oakland homicides found that 72% of these homicides had gang members involved as offenders, victims, or both (California Partnership for Safe Communities 2018). This study further revealed that 76% of victims and suspects were previously known to the criminal justice system. These "criminal justice known" individuals had, on average, 12 prior arrests for a variety of armed and unarmed violent, drug, property, and disorder offenses. More than two-thirds were previously convicted felons, more than a third were on active probation supervision at the time of the homicide event, and more than two-thirds had spent time incarcerated before the homicide occurred.

Given that a high percentage of likely shooters are involved with the criminal justice system, they are quite likely to have warrants against them or violate probation or parole conditions. In principle, they face a credible threat of being arrested and sanctioned.[3] Policies and practices that seek to reduce sanctions in the entire population neglect to appreciate the heterogeneity in offending and how these changes could affect high-rate offenders in the high-risk tail of the distribution, and that changes at the margin for the general population will vastly underestimate the potential for violence to increase. This point is not merely conceptual, as it connects back to basic principles in mathematics around Jensen's inequality, such that in a non-linear distribution (e.g., convex function), the linear transformation will be less than the actual point along the upper tail of the distribution (McShane 1937). The effect of deterrence for the average offender in the population is not equivalent to those at the extreme of the offending distribution. Following this same principle of inequality, evaluation evidence suggests efforts focused on increasing the risks of sanctions on a subgroup of active offenders create outsized gun violence reduction benefits.

FOCUSED DETERRENCE

Focused-deterrence strategies, sometimes called "pulling levers" policing programs, are often framed as problem-oriented exercises in which specific recurring crime problems are analyzed, and responses are highly customized to local conditions and operational capacities (Braga and Kennedy 2021). There are three main variations of focused deterrence: group violence intervention, drug market intervention, and individual offender programs. The group violence intervention attempts to halt persistent gun violence generated by gangs and other criminally active groups. These strategies seek to change offender behavior by understanding underlying violence-producing dynamics, the conditions that sustain recurring violence problems, and implementing a blended set of actions from law enforcement, social services, and community members who can exert informal social controls through their social networks and community standing. Focused-deterrence operations have tended to follow this basic framework:

- Selection of a particular crime problem, such as serious gun violence
- Pulling together an interagency enforcement group, typically including police, probation, parole, state and federal prosecutors, and sometimes federal enforcement agencies
- Conducting research, usually relying heavily on the field experience of front-line police officers, to identify key offenders, groups of offenders, such as street gangs and drug crews, and characterizing the context of their criminal behaviors
- Framing a special enforcement operation directed at those offenders and their co-offenders and designing all legal tools (or levers) to sanction groups of offenders in ways that reduce the chances they will continue to commit serious violence
- Matching enforcement operations with parallel social services and moral voices of affected communities to those same offenders and groups
- Communicating directly and repeatedly with offenders and their co-offending groups to let them know they are under particular scrutiny, what criminal acts will receive special attention when that has happened to particular offenders and groups, and what they can do to avoid enforcement action (Kennedy 2019)

Focused-deterrence programs attempt to promote legitimacy by ensuring that crime control efforts are focused on the safety and well-being (including preventing contact with the criminal justice system) of group members and others at high risk of violence. Focused deterrence is not an indiscriminate increase in sanction severity—it is focused on those believed to be responsible for a disproportionate share of gun violence in communities. When implemented as designed, focused deterrence responds to triggering events, such as a gun homicide committed by a specific gang, and the rationale supporting subsequent enforcement actions is transparent to community members and offenders alike. Effective focused-deterrence interventions involve community stakeholders in the design and implementation of the program. Contacts between offenders and the authorities are conducted through focused deterrence sessions in a procedurally just way that offers credible threats of sanctions and help and assistance to offenders who are willing to desist from violent offending (Kennedy 2011).

Theory

Deterrence is affected by offender perceptions of sanction risk and certainty of detection (Nagin 2013). The effective communication of the risks of punishments to relevant audiences is an important step in generating deterrence (Zimring and Hawkins 1973). Focused-deterrence/pulling levers strategies attempt to prevent crime by directing deterrence messages to individuals identified as being at especially high risk of offending with, or being victimized by, a firearm. In addition to sanctions, the messaging also includes the potential benefits of available services (e.g., tattoo removal, employment, drug counseling) to improve their life trajectories and makes normative appeals to halt behavior that traumatizes communities.

Focused deterrence relies on group notification meetings (i.e., call-ins, forums) and customized individual notifications from criminal justice officials to inform offenders that criminal behavior will be responded to with certain and swift consequences. Direct communications, coupled with swift and certain sanctions for violating established behavioral norms, influence offender perceptions of apprehension risk. Face-to-face meetings with offenders are an important first step in altering their perceptions about sanction risk (Nagin 2013). Direct communications and affirmative follow-up responses are the types of new information that may cause offenders to reassess the risks of continuing their criminal behavior (in this case, shooting at rivals) (McGarrell et al. 2006).

Focused-deterrence strategies make the prospect of sanctions more legitimate by bringing in individual norms, values, and informal social control (Kennedy 2011). Legitimacy represents more than mere public support; rather it represents the willingness of the public to recognize and voluntarily defer to official authority (Beetham 1991). Research suggests that the way police treat citizens directly and measurably influences citizen perceptions of the police (Tyler 2006; Reisig, Bratton, and Gertz 2007). Police are viewed as legitimate authorities when citizens perceive that the police treat citizens with respect and make their decisions to use authority fairly (Tyler 2006). Punishments are deemed illegitimate when they are excessive, poorly motivated, and not well aligned with individual and community norms (Kennedy, Kleiman, and Braga 2017). Sanctions should be consistent with community and individual norms rather than threats wielded by external and possibly hostile authorities. Focused deterrence builds on concepts of police legitimacy and procedural justice when communicating with offenders and engaging community partners. Call-ins with groups of violent offenders and custom notifications with individual offenders are designed to inform them they were selected for intervention by virtue of their serious violent behavior rather than their status (such as gang member or drug seller); the partnership then expresses concern for the well-being of the community and of the offenders themselves and provides offenders a clear choice by offering help and promising sanctions for continued violence in a respectful and business-like manner (Braga and Kennedy 2021).

Community-based organizations and resident groups can be potent crime prevention partners for law enforcement agencies (Sampson, Raudenbush, and Earls 1997; Sharkey 2018). Focused-deterrence programs seek to stimulate informal social controls to reduce both offending and punishment rates. These programs customarily include relevant community-based organizations in the larger crime reduction partnership to deliver key intervention actions. Using Boston as an example, key community partners have included activist Black clergy groups (such as the Ten Point Coalition and Black Ministerial Alliance), street outreach workers (such as those employed by Roca and the Boston Centers for Youth and Families), and local non-profits focused on providing mental health services (such as the YMCA's YouthConnect program) and improving education and employment opportunities (such as STRIVE Boston and Youth Options Unlimited). Community-based organizations are included in numerous program activities such as upfront conversations on selecting violent gangs for intervention, the development and execution of communication campaigns with groups and individuals, mobilizing community anti-violence voices through neighborhood "peace walks" and community cookouts, and connecting specific high-risk youth with services and opportunities (Braga and Kennedy 2020). The list of partners in Los Angeles is similar, with Homeboy Industries/Father Gregory Boyle and Mothers of East Los Angeles/Father John Moretta of Resurrection Parish playing important roles in legitimizing efforts in the community and offering "carrots" for desistance from participating in gun violence (Tita et al. 2003).

Evaluation Evidence

An ongoing systematic review shows the positive impact of focused-deterrence programs on serious violence. The most recent iteration of the systematic review identified 24 quasi-experimental evaluations of focused-deterrence programs (Braga, Weisburd, and Turchan 2018). These studies evaluated focused-deterrence programs implemented in small, medium, and large cities. Except for an evaluation of a focused-deterrence program implemented in Glasgow, Scotland, all included studies were in the United States. Twelve evaluations tested the impacts of gang and group intervention programs on violence, nine evaluations considered the effects of focused deterrence on crime problems connected to street-level drug markets, and three evaluations appraised crime reductions generated by focused-deterrence programs targeting individual repeat offenders. The systematic review examined studies published after 2000, with half released after 2013.

Nineteen of the 24 focused-deterrence evaluations (79.2%) included in the review reported at least one significant crime control effect (Braga et al. 2018). A meta-analysis of the program impacts found moderate reductions in targeted crime problems associated with focused-deterrence programs, with the largest impacts produced by the gang and group violence reduction programs. The program evaluation evidence on the impacts of focused deterrence on targeted crime problems continues to grow. Completed after the latest version of the systematic review, quasi-experimental evaluations of focused deterrence in two very challenging urban environments—Oakland (Braga et al. 2019) and Philadelphia (Roman et al. 2019)—reported statistically significant reductions in shootings in areas with targeted gangs relative to matched comparison areas with untreated gangs.

The rigor of the gang and group violence reduction focused-deterrence evaluations has steadily improved over time with contemporary quasi-experimental designs using more sophisticated methods, such as propensity score matching and synthetic controls, to ensure comparable treatment and control groups (Braga et al. 2018). These more rigorous quasi-experimental evaluations estimate smaller but still meaningful statistically significant reductions in crime and violence.[4] The absence of randomized experiments on gang and group violence reduction focused deterrence, however, means there is limited causal evidence of the impact of these programs on violent crime (e.g., National Research Council 2018). Three randomized controlled trials of the individual offender strategy have been completed. Hamilton, Rosenfeld, and Levin (2018) found that parolees and probationers who were invited to attend the focused-deterrence notification meeting were less likely to be arrested over the following 17 months relative to those who did not attend the meeting. In an unpublished report, Sharkey (2014) found individuals who were called in to attend the notification forums were substantially less likely to violate their parole, and this effect was driven primarily by reductions in violations due to absconding. However, the program did not affect individual arrest rates or neighborhood-level gun violence. Ariel, Englefield, and Denley (2019) reported arrests decreased by 21% among prolific offenders who were randomized to a policing program comprising preemptive engagements by a police officer offering both carrots (desistance pathways) and sticks (increased sanction threats) relative to a control group that receive no additional attention.

Despite the continued need for stronger evaluations, a policy consensus is emerging on the crime control value of focused-deterrence strategies. For instance, a US Agency for International Development meta-review of 43 systematic reviews, which considered over 1,400 studies of community-violence prevention programs, concluded that focused deterrence had the largest direct impact on violence of all the interventions reviewed (Abt and Winship 2016). Likewise, Public Safety Canada, which is that country's Department of Public Safety and Domestic Preparedness, published a systematic review and meta-analysis of street gang violence control strategies and concluded focused-deterrence programs were the most consistently effective responses to gang-related delinquency (Wong et al. 2012).

How the Current Climate Undermines Focused Deterrence

Policing reforms that reduce unintended harms and promote better relations with economically disadvantaged racial and ethnic minority communities are sorely needed. Strained relationships between police and the citizens they serve in minority communities are rooted in a long history of racial discrimination in the United States and aggressive law enforcement practices associated with racial disparities (e.g., Muhammad 2010). The deficient implementation of focused deterrence could exacerbate poor police–community relations and generate collateral harms, such as increased racial disparities, through increased surveillance and harsh enforcement if these strategies are not appropriately focused (Griffiths and Christian 2015). When properly implemented, these strategies may reduce incarceration because they focus on a small number of highly active offenders rather than the indiscriminate application of aggressive enforcement to large areas. Its operating principle is to change offender behavior rather than simply remove offenders from the streets (Braga and Kennedy 2021).

Efforts that encourage police departments to be more focused in their use of enforcement actions, limit the use of force, enhance community and problem-oriented policing efforts, and ensure procedurally just police contacts are needed in disadvantaged minority neighborhoods suffering the bulk of gun violence problems. However, reform agendas can be pursued and implemented without disrupting the crime control capacity of police departments. For instance, a recent multi-city randomized experiment revealed that the infusion of procedural justice principles into hotspot policing resulted in stronger crime control gains and improved community perceptions of the police in treated places relative to standard hotspot policing in control places (Weisburd et al. 2022).

Focused deterrence was one of many programs developed after the passage of the Violent Crime Control and Law Enforcement Act of 1994 (also known as the 1994 Crime Bill). Drafted by then-Senator Joseph Biden and signed by President Bill Clinton, this 1994 Crime Bill was a response to the growing criticism that the Democratic Party was "soft on crime." The seminal Boston Gun Project and its resultant Operation Ceasefire intervention was developed in the mid-1990s in the context of an unprecedented increase in youth gun violence and an encouraging period of experimentation with new community and problem-oriented policing programs. Therefore, at least at first glance, it appears that Boston's response to gun violence was formulated in an environment that differs significantly from today's calls to defund or even abolish local law enforcement (these demands seem to be abating with President Biden's recent call to "fund the police" in his 2022 State of the Union speech). What remains the same is the need to halt gun violence in most major cities and in particular the most economically disadvantaged neighborhoods in these cities suffering from the highest rates of homicides.

Focused deterrence developed from on-the-ground trial and error collaborations between law enforcement, social service agencies, and community groups shaped into an evidence-based gun violence reduction strategy that promotes improved police–community relations (Kennedy 2011; Meares 2009; Brunson 2015). Focused deterrence, when done correctly, is supported by a robust community partnership that benefits the most impacted neighborhoods suffering from elevated rates of gun violence. Unfortunately, the current climate and debasement of the police undermines the effective implementation of focused deterrence in at least four key ways.

It Limits Community Collaborations

Putting together a working group of representatives from relevant criminal justice, social service, and community-based organizations who can bring varied incentives and disincentives to influence targeted offender behavior is a key early operational step. Beyond criminal justice partners, Boston's Operation Ceasefire working group included street outreach workers and Ten Point Coalition activist Black clergy. In Los Angeles, the Ceasefire partnership enjoyed active participation from the same set of criminal justice system actors enjoyed in Boston. The community partners include representatives from the street-level gang intervention workers, medical staff from a local hospital, and members of the local clergy, including Father Gregory Boyle of Homeboy Industries, whose efforts to reduce violence in the local community have garnered national attention (Tita et al. 2003).

How likely are community members, street outreach workers, and social service providers to be supportive and involved in focused-deterrence programs in a climate supportive of defunding the police? Distrust between police and the community is nothing new. Los Angeles in the early 1990s serves as a concerning reminder. The March 3, 1991, videotaped beating of Rodney King by Los Angeles Police Department (LAPD) police officers "went viral" before the age of social media. The subsequent acquittal of LAPD officers charged in the beating sparked the 1992 Los Angeles urban riots and calls for police reform. The RAND Corporation was able to work with the LAPD and partnering organizations to launch a focused-deterrence strategy in 2000. However, a massive corruption scandal discovered in the anti-gang units of the Rampart police division during the late 1990s led to federal litigation and nine years of oversight under a consent decree. While the cloud of the scandal hovered over the project, community and social service partners remained invested as they recognized that partnering with the police was the only way that violence would diminish in their neighborhoods.

The RAND Corporation noted impressive short-term gang violence reductions between two warring gangs operating in the Hollenbeck neighborhood in its impact evaluation of the Los Angeles Ceasefire intervention (Tita et al. 2003). The RAND evaluation noted that violent crimes, gang crimes, and gun crimes were substantially reduced among the two gangs over a six-month pre-post period in treated census block groups relative to comparison census block groups matched through propensity score models. The RAND evaluation also suggested spillover deterrence impacts, as slightly larger reductions in these crimes were evident among four non-targeted rival gangs in surrounding census block groups during the same period. The evaluators suggested that these diffusion effects may have been generated by diminished conflicts between the targeted gangs and their socially connected rivals (Tita et al. 2003).

The 2002 hiring of Chief William Bratton ushered in an era of reform at the LAPD by embracing community policing and implementing a more focused COMPSTAT Plus crime management accountability model. In contrast to COMPSTAT models that focus on field interrogations, arrests, and tactical units to control crime, COMPSTAT Plus focused on a more holistic assessment of the quality of arrests, police investigations, and clearance rates for crimes under the guidance of LAPD area commanders. The LAPD eventually emerged out of this era of reform with increased public approval for the performance of the police among Black and Hispanic residents (Fagan and MacDonald 2013). Indeed, some 83% of Los Angeles residents, including 76% of Black and 68% of Hispanic residents, respectively, expressed strong approval for the LAPD in 2009 (Stone, Foglesong, and Cole 2009). This is just one example where out of a period of scandal and reform the police emerged to be more professional and held in higher regard by minority communities. In the wake of these reforms, the National Network for Safe Communities collaborated with the LAPD under the leadership of Chief Charles Beck to implement focused deterrence again in the early 2010s.

Los Angeles experienced 397 murders in 2021, an increase of almost 12% from 355 in 2020, which was a 54% increase from the 258 in the pre-pandemic year of 2019 (Regardie 2022). Like in other cities, abolishing and defunding the police were rallying cries of protestors during the summer of 2020 and sharply critical assessments of the LAPD persist today. The reality, however, is that police budgets were not slashed, though we do not discount that changes in morale among sworn officers might have had an impact via de-policing, including evidence from cities like Denver where police stops fell dramatically in the post-Floyd months (Pyrooz, Nix, and Wolfe 2021). If the City of Los Angeles implements focused deterrence once again to address its current gun violence crisis, will community and social service partners be willing to collaborate with the LAPD on these efforts given the current climate? Will the LAPD feel empowered to re-engage the community and embrace proactive enforcement against gangs as required in focused deterrence? It seems possible that bridges between the police, community, and social service stakeholders will need to be rebuilt. And, if the LAPD is not likely to engage in appropriate proactive tactics and community members are reluctant to partner, more young minority males will continue to suffer fatal and non-fatal gunshot injuries as gang conflicts remain unchecked.

It Encourages Unfocused and Indiscriminate Tactics

Cities that implement focused-deterrence programs must conduct upfront and ongoing analyses of gun violence problems. This process is vital in identifying the etiology of gun violence and to determine what factors are modifiable through intervention. For instance, by determining who is responsible for homicide and the role that gangs and criminally active groups play in retaliatory violence, one can design a focused-deterrence intervention with relevant stakeholders that is customized to the particular context. Identifying the etiology of gun violence requires crime incident reviews and group audits where academics and practitioners work together to develop detailed qualitative and quantitative insights on the nature of events and the role of criminally active groups and gangs in perpetrating these incidents.

Boston, Los Angeles, and other jurisdictions often included gang outreach workers, service providers, and community organizers in the assessment reviews. Community partners often provide insights not known to the police regarding antecedent events, the degree to which a particular event might span retaliation, and the risk of reprisal or victimization of particular gang members. Partner participation serves as an important "check and balance" to police perceptions of events and the participants. Such collaboration also increases transparency in law enforcement actions, safeguarding against focused-deterrence interventions from expanding beyond the individuals and groups most at-risk for generating a recurring pattern of gun violence in communities. Discussions between police, social service providers, and community activists can also "humanize" the subjects of focused intervention through discussion of their life experiences and challenges that can shape a conversation, ultimately recognizing that services and opportunities may be a better route for behavioral change for specific youth rather than harsher sanctions (Kennedy 2011; Braga and Kennedy 2021).

A political climate that demoralizes the police profession makes it much less likely that street outreach workers, social service providers, and community organizers will be willing to participate. In Baltimore in 2020, two local street outreach organizations declined to participate in audits that involved the Baltimore Police Department. Braga and colleagues needed to hold separate reviews. The street outreach worker review was not overly fruitful, as the participants did not provide any specific information that could be helpful to law enforcement. While the combined results of the two reviews did provide a rich snapshot of gang and group violence in the city's Western District, there were no productive police–community conversations about actual group members, and no shared understanding developed of risks posed by specific people in identified groups.

Focused deterrence requires precise information on risky people and violent relationships. Without such information, police have to control gun violence armed with only blunt insights (like time and place) that exposes a much wider range of people to traditional law enforcement tactics, such as stop and frisk. Thus, calls to eliminate police gang databases (e.g., Smith, Owusu, and Borden 2022) may result in more indiscriminate enforcement of gang members by the police. The criteria for inclusion in police gang databases certainly deserve scrutiny so that uninvolved youth are not included (Densley and Pyrooz 2020). However, in the absence of carefully constructed, systematic intelligence on gangs and their members, police will have little guidance on which individuals are worthy of focused deterrence (Densely and Pyrooz 2018; Winship and Braga 2022). This could result in overpolicing tactics, such as street sweeps, which unfairly target all youth in an impacted community (e.g., "Operation Hammer" in South Los Angeles in 1985 [Davis 1988] and the takedown of the "Bronx 120" in New York City in 2016 [Howell and Bustamante 2019]).

It Undermines Swiftness and Certainty in Sanctions

Focused deterrence requires the swift and certain delivery of sanctions to increase offender perceptions of apprehension risk that, in turn, decrease violent gun behaviors. Effective applications of focused deterrence rely on comprehensive and precise enforcement responses to outbreaks of gang violence. To stop shootings from spiraling out of control there needs to be clear and direct communication with violent offenders so that their actions will receive the full attention of the criminal justice system. Police can take advantage of the chronic and varied offending of gangs to make arrests for myriad offenses. Prosecutors can prioritize charges against chronic offenders to ensure they receive certain penalties. Probation and parole officers can ensure that gang members under community supervision are abiding by their release conditions and can revoke community supervision for those involved in groups who persist in committing violent offenses.

It is important to note here that the mobilization of the criminal justice system to hold gang members accountable is driven by their serious violent behavior. The rationale is not to further criminalize behaviors to keep disadvantaged young people ensnared in the criminal justice system. Rather, enforcing the law and addressing violations of community supervision is intended to disrupt opportunities for a very risky young person to be killed or commit a killing. Both ends result in far greater harm to the community and the individuals involved. Failure to engage available enforcement options against those committing shootings undermines the key deterrence mechanism of focused deterrence.

Focused deterrence works best when members of the interagency working group communicate enforcement threats to violent groups. If the deterrence message is no longer credible and promises of consequences for continued acts of violence go unmet, offenders will perceive that their actions will bear no costs.

A related problem involves well-intentioned bail reform efforts. Gang violence involves fast-moving dynamics. Removing a high-risk person from the street promptly, even for a night, can save lives. Higher bail amounts for violent offenders help ensure that individuals arrested and charged with gun violence are not back on the street before a criminal court trial. Preventive detention for high-risk individuals provides some measure of temporary incapacitation. No bail, low bail, and bailouts by non-profits are not appropriate for this high-risk group. In short, there need to be policies that prevent gang members from being eligible for bail reform benefits when their group is actively engaged in shootings.

When it comes to high-risk run offenders, prosecutors also need to press forward with charges including lesser offenses like illegal drug possession, larceny, and disorder. No prosecution edicts should be suspended when a specific gang is engaged in shootings. As we noted above, there is an accumulated daily risk of violence that occurs when a gang is actively involved in violence, such that incremental decisions to hold gang members accountable for criminal behavior have a multiplying effect. The increased risk for violence for high-risk offenders is similar to the gambler's ruin problem (Coolidge 1909), where successive plays of cards with the odds stacked toward the house will ensure with complete certainty eventual financial ruin.

It May Result in Harsher Sanctions

Offenders tend to overvalue available and immediate rewards and discount distal and uncertain punishments in the future. As such, increasing the severity of punishment is not a good substitute for swiftness and certainty in deterrence-based crime prevention strategies. Offenders are often risk averse and may prefer outcomes with low uncertainty in the present versus those in the future. As a result, a certain but minor punishment in the present will generate much higher deterrence than a more severe one that is in the distant future. As Beccaria (1764/1872) noted, "the certainty of being punished, however lightly, always makes a stronger impression than the fear of another worse punishment ... [as] hope ... tends to keep the thought of greater evils remote from us" (107). Increasing punishment severity in the future is counterproductive relative to a more certain punishment in the present. James Q. Wilson (1975) observed that severity makes swiftness and certainty not as feasible, as harsh sanctions (such as long prison sentences) are expensive and difficult to impose consistently. Harsh punishments are not swift and certain because they have layers of procedural protections to avoid miscarriages of justice against the accused.

Focused-deterrence strategies economize on the severity of sanctions by imposing punishments that are only as harsh as needed to change specific individual behaviors (Kennedy 2008). For some gang members, this could be as simple as changing the conditions of their probation so they can't be hanging out with particular people in specific spaces, and backing that up with community visits by probation officers. For other gang members, arrests and prosecution of lower-level offenses that disrupt their illicit income could serve as a meaningful deterrent. For still others, harsher penalties offered by federal prosecution may be necessary. The adoption of felon-in-possession and drug-dealing cases by federal prosecutors can preserve the swiftness and certainty required by focused deterrence.

Focused-deterrence strategies will be challenged to generate crime reduction impacts when implemented in a local environment characterized by a demoralized police department and progressive prosecution policies that do not make exceptions to hold violent gang offenders accountable for lesser crimes. In these contexts, the interagency working group seems likely to rely on federal law enforcement to change offender perceptions of sanction risks. Not only do federal punishments usually involve longer sentences, but people convicted of federal crimes are not eligible for parole and serve their sentences far away from their families and friends. In Baltimore, former State's Attorney Marilyn Mosby pledged to support the city's focused-deterrence strategy. However, it remained unclear to working group members whether her office would adopt appropriate cases against violent group members. As a result, the first two enforcement actions against violent groups in the Western District involved federal law enforcement agencies with resulting cases prosecuted by the US Attorney's Office.

CONCLUSION

The path forward for an effective response to gang violence is to recognize the skewed distribution of active offenders that generate a disproportionate share of gang-involved gun violence, that public safety responses need to be tailored to the non-linear relationship between sanctions and offenders, and that a focused and precise effort to hold high-rate offenders accountable for their actions will generate outsized benefits at reducing gun violence. A focused-deterrence approach supported by input from the communities afflicted by gun violence has the benefit of minimizing sanctions to those only necessary to maintain public safety in a way that is consistent with community values and norms. Rather than projecting desires, rhetoric, and hope for what might work, focused deterrence is supported by empirical evidence and is logically consistent with basic facts of urban gun violence. We agree with calls to prevent serious gang violence by making strong investments in schools, families, and neighborhoods. However, as we wait for those investments to be made and take root in affected communities, cities need strategies now that better manage outbreaks of gang shootings and reduce the recurring trauma of fatal and non-fatal gun injuries.

The defund police movement offers few evidence-based ideas to deal with gang violence. Their primary recommendation—violence interrupters and gang outreach workers—has a very mixed evidence base characterized by a prevalence of null and backfire effects on serious violence (e.g., Hureau et al. 2023; Klein 1995). Other suggestions don't seem well suited to deal with the immediacy of addressing emergent retaliatory gun violence among gangs. Mental health professionals are vital in managing emotional trauma at the shooting scenes, but there is a lack of scientific evidence to support the position that their presence will help stave off retaliatory violence. Instead, the beneficial effects of mental health counseling seem likely to be felt over a longer period. Furthermore, the tragic murders of street intervention specialists in Los Angeles (Elinson 2021) and Baltimore (Jackson 2021) highlight the level of danger in these situations. Social workers often note that police presence is required before they will respond to the aftermath of a shooting scene (Struhl and Gard-Murray 2022). We believe this again highlights the need to coordinate law enforcement and community-based responses to these violent situations. Such responses require careful planning and scaling such that staff is available around the clock to attend to the thousands of shootings in major cities each year (e.g., Los Angeles had 397 homicides and 1,459 shooting victims in 2021).

The evidence on community-based non-profits that can be an alternative to police in controlling serious gun violence is limited (but see Sharkey 2018; Brantingham, Tita, and Hertz 2021). There are some examples of business improvement districts that have been shown to help control crime—but they employ private security. Place-based programs like efforts to green vacant lots, repair abandoned housing, and other situational crime prevention efforts (MacDonald, Branas, and Stokes 2019) are not likely to be effective if police are not active in holding high-risk offenders accountable. Place-based programs require personnel to attend to serious crime when it is present. Other programs that defund movement advocates mention, like investing in education, take years to pay off. Diverting funds to primary prevention will not provide any immediate crime control benefits to a surge in gun violence in a community. The evidence when police actually go on strike (Sherman 1995) or pull back (Devi and Fryer 2020) shows that violence surges quickly. Defunding the police without an alternative public safety apparatus that can attend to high-risk offenders and their groups will likely lead to private police in affluent areas, who are less accountable and where there is little case law or statutes in place to regulate their behavior. This is not a good path for an egalitarian democracy where public safety should be a basic right of citizenship.

Recently, residents of Minneapolis were presented with the opportunity to shutter its police department and replace it with a more general "public safety" department. By a wide margin the policy change failed, chiefly because of a lack of support among Black residents. Why? In the words of Minneapolis civil rights attorney Nakima Levy Armstrong (2021), "black voters want better policing, not posturing by progressives." Residents of minority neighborhoods bear the brunt of gun violence and, if these various defund the police movement alternatives fail, will continue to lose loved ones. Many of the loudest voices in favor of defunding the police do not live in impacted communities. One might argue that these voices don't have any "skin in the game" when offering suggestions on dealing with complex problems such as gang-involved gun violence. Moving forward, public policy would be better served by paying close attention to scientific evidence and the views of actual stakeholders who live in troubled neighborhoods.

Notes

1. Authors are listed in alphabetical order. Anthony A. Braga is the Jerry Lee Professor of Criminology and director of the Crime and Justice Policy Lab at the University of Pennsylvania. John M. MacDonald is professor of Criminology and Sociology at the University of Pennsylvania. George Tita is professor of Criminology, Law and Society at the University of California, Irvine.
2. For instance, Federal Bureau of Investigation Supplementary Homicide Reports show that 76.6% of homicides were committed with firearms in 2020 (16,527 of 21,570) as compared to only 64.2% of homicides in 1990 (15,058 of 23,438) (Puzzanchera, Chamberlin, and Kang 2021).

3. The extent to which the extensive criminal histories of a majority of homicide offenders and homicide victims are influenced by systematic racism in the criminal justice system, biased and selective enforcement by police departments, or the unfair labeling of minority youth as deviant remains an empirical question. Nevertheless, this continued high rate of offending and ongoing criminal justice involvement provides an important opportunity to disrupt fast-moving street gang dynamics that could ultimately lead to their death or the death of others. For the involved gang members, their loved ones, and the community at large, it seems preferable for likely shooters to be sanctioned and alive rather than being killed or killing someone else.
4. The systematic review meta-analysis reported that the quasi-experimental evaluations with unmatched control groups were associated with a much larger statistically significant .703 standardized mean difference effect size relative to quasi-experimental evaluations with matched control groups that were associated with a statistically significant .194 standardized mean difference effect size (Braga et al. 2018).

References

Abt, Thomas, and Christopher Winship. 2016. *What Works in Reducing Community Violence.* Washington, DC: United States Agency for International Development.

Ariel, Barak, Ashley Englefield, and John Denley. 2019. "'I Heard It Through the Grapevine': A Randomized Controlled Trial on the Direct and Vicarious Effects of Preventative Specific Deterrence Initiatives in Criminal Networks." *Journal of Criminal Law and Criminology* 109 (4): 819–867.

Armstong, Nakima Levy. 2021. "Black Voters Want Better Policing, Not Posturing by Progressives." *New York Times,* November 9. https://www.nytimes.com/2021/11/09/opinion/minneapolis-police-defund.html.

Barao, Lisa M., and Anthony A. Braga. 2021. *Oakland Violence Problem Analysis, 2019–2020.* Unpublished report submitted to the City of Oakland. Philadelphia, PA: Crime and Justice Policy Lab, University of Pennsylvania.

Beccaria, Cesare. 1764/1872. *On Crimes and Punishment.* Albany, NY: W.C. Little & Co.

Beetham, David. 1991. *The Legitimation of Power.* Atlantic Highlands, NJ: Humanities Press International.

Block, Carolyn R., and Richard Block. 1993. *Street Gang Crime in Chicago.* Washington, DC: National Institute of Justice, US Department of Justice.

Blumstein, Alfred. 1995. "Youth Violence, Guns, and the Illicit-Drug Industry." *Journal of Criminal Law and Criminology* 86 (1): 10–36.

Brantingham, P. Jeffrey, George E. Tita, Denise Hertz. 2021. "The Impact of the City of Los Angeles Mayor's Office of Gang Reduction and Youth Development (GRYD) Comprehensive Strategy on Crime in the City of Los Angeles." *Justice Evaluation Journal* 4 (2): 217–236.

Braga, Anthony A. 2003. "Serious Youth Gun Offenders and the Epidemic of Youth Violence in Boston." *Journal of Quantitative Criminology* 19 (1): 33–54.

Braga, Anthony A. 2004. *Gun Violence Among Serious Young Offenders.* Washington, DC: US Department of Justice, Office of Community Oriented Policing Services.

Braga, Anthony A., David Hureau, and Christopher Winship. 2008. "Losing Faith? Police, Black Churches, and the Resurgence of Youth Violence in Boston." *Ohio State Journal of Criminal Law* 6 (1): 141–172.

Braga, Anthony A. and David M. Kennedy. 2021. *A Framework for Addressing Violence and Serious Crime: Focused Deterrence, Legitimacy, and Prevention*. New York: Cambridge University Press.

Braga, Anthony A., David M. Kennedy, and George Tita. 2002. "New Approaches to the Strategic Prevention of Gang and Group-Involved Violence." In *Gangs in America*, edited by C. Ronald Huff, 271–286. Thousand Oaks, CA: Sage Publications.

Braga, Anthony A., David L. Weisburd, and Brandon Turchan. 2018. "Focused Deterrence Strategies and Crime Control: An Updated Systematic Review and Meta-Analysis of the Empirical Evidence." *Criminology & Public Policy*, 17 (1): 205–250.

Braga, Anthony A., Gregory Zimmerman, Lisa Barao, Chelsea Farrell, Rod Brunson, and Andrew V. Papachristos. 2019. "Street Gangs, Gun Violence, and Focused Deterrence: Comparing Place-Based and Group-Based Evaluation Methods to Estimate Direct and Spillover Deterrent Effects." *Journal of Research in Crime and Delinquency* 56 (4): 524–562.

Brunson, Rod. 2015. "Focused Deterrence and Improved Police-Community Relations: Unpacking the Proverbial 'Black Box.'" *Criminology & Public Policy* 14 (3): 507–514.

California Partnership for Safe Communities. 2018. *Oakland Violence Problem Analysis, 2017–2018*. Unpublished report submitted to the City of Oakland. Oakland: California Partnership for Safe Communities.

Chalfin, Aaron, Benjamin Hansen, Emily Weisburst, and Morgan Williams Jr. 2021. "Police Force Size and Civilian Race." *American Economic Review: Insights* 4 (2): 139–158.

Cook, Philip J. and John Laub. 2002. "After the Epidemic: Recent Trends in Youth Violence in the United States." *Crime and Justice* 29: 1–37.

Coolidge, Julian. 1909. "The Gambler's Ruin." *Annals of Mathematics* 10 (4): 181–192.

Crime and Justice Policy Lab. 2021. *Group Violence Reduction Strategy: Initial Findings from the Western District Problem and Opportunity Analysis*. Unpublished report submitted to the City of Baltimore. Philadelphia, PA: Crime and Justice Policy Lab, University of Pennsylvania.

Davis, Michael. 1988. "Los Angeles: Civil Liberties between the Hammer and the Rock." *New Left Review* 170: 37–60.

Densley, James, and David Pyrooz. 2018. "Is Gang Activity on the Rise? A Movement to Abolish Gang Databases Makes It Hard to Tell." *Salon*, July 17. https://www.salon.com/2018/07/17/is-gang-activity-on-the-rise-a-movement-to-abolish-gang-databases-makes-it-hard-to-tell_partner/.

Densley, James, and David Pyrooz. 2020. "The Matrix in Context: Taking Stock of Police Gang Databases in London and Beyond." *Youth Justice* 20 (1-2): 11–30.

Devi, Tanaya, and Roland G. Fryer Jr. 2020. "Policing the Police: The Impact of 'Pattern-or-Practice' Investigations on Crime." NBER Working Paper. https://www.nber.org/papers/w27324.

Elinson, Zusha. 2021. "Los Angeles Gang-Intervention Worker Is Killed." *Wall Street Journal*, September 9. https://www.wsj.com/articles/los-angeles-gang-intervention-worker-is-killed-11631192400.

Elinson, Zusha. 2022. "Murders in U.S. Cities Were Near Record Highs in 2021." *Wall Street Journal*, January 6. https://www.wsj.com/articles/murders-in-u-s-cities-were-near-record-highs-in-2021-11641499978.

Epstein, Richard. 1995. *The Theory of Gambling and Statistical Logic*. New York: Academic Press.

Fagan, Jeffrey, and John MacDonald. 2013. "Policing, Crime, and Legitimacy in New York and Los Angeles: The Social and Political Contexts of Two Historic Crime Declines." In *New York and Los Angeles: The Uncertain Future*, edited by David Halle and Andrew Beveridge, 243–299. New York: Oxford University Press.

Griffiths, Elizabeth, and Johanna Christian. 2015. "Considering Focused Deterrence in the Age of Ferguson, Baltimore, North Charleston, and Beyond." *Criminology & Public Policy* 14 (3): 573–581.

Gross, Jenny, and John Eligon. 2020. "Minneapolis City Council Votes to Remove $8 Million from Police Budget." *New York Times*, December 12. https://www.nytimes.com/2020/12/10/us/minneapolis-police-funding.html.

Hamilton, Benjamin, Richard Rosenfeld, and Aaron Levin. 2018. "Opting Out of Treatment: Self-Selection Bias in a Randomized Controlled Study of a Focused Deterrence Notification Meeting." *Journal of Experimental Criminology* 14 (1): 1–17.

Howell, Babe, and Priscilla Bustamante. 2019. "Report on the Bronx 120 Mass 'Gang' Prosecution." *Bronx 120 Report*. https://papers.ssrn.com/sol3/papers.cfm?abstract_id=3406106.

Howell, James, and Elizabeth Griffiths. 2016. *Gangs in America's Communities*. Thousand Oaks, CA: Sage.

Hureau, David M., Anthony A. Braga, Tracey Lloyd, and Christopher Winship. 2023. "Streetwork at the Crossroads : An Evaluation of a Street Gang Outreach Intervention and Holistic Appraisal of Streetwork Research Evidence." *Criminology* 61 (4): 676 -711.

Jackson, Phillip. 2021. "'He Loved Cherry Hill': Slain Baltimore Safe Streets Worker Turned His Life around While Improving His Community, Friends Remember." *Baltimore Sun*, July 8. https://www.baltimoresun.com/news/crime/bs-md-ci-cr-shooting-funeral-20210708-otfvueoqnzdflfln5baqkshyn4-story.html.

Kennedy, David M. 2008. *Deterrence and Crime Prevention: Reconsidering the Prospect of Sanction*. London: Routledge.

Kennedy, David M. 2011. *Don't Shoot*. New York: Bloomsbury.

Kennedy, David M. 2019. "Policing and the Lessons of Focused Deterrence." In *Police Innovation: Contrasting Perspectives*, edited by David Weisburd and Anthony A. Braga, 205–226. New York: Cambridge University Press.

Kennedy, David M., Mark Kleiman, Anthony A. Braga. 2017. "Beyond Deterrence: Strategies of Focus and Fairness." In *Handbook of Crime Prevention and Community Safety*, edited by Nick Tilley and Aiden Sidebottom. New York: Routledge.

Kim, Dae-Young. 2023. "Did De-policing Contribute to the 2020 Homicide Spikes?" *Police Practice and Research*, DOI: 10.1080/15614263.2023.2235056

Klein, Malcolm. 1995. *The American Street Gang: Its Nature, Prevalence, and Control*. New York: Oxford University Press.

LaFree, Gary. 1998. *Losing Legitimacy: Street Crime and the Decline of Social Institutions in America*. Boulder, CO: Westview Press.

Leovy, Jill. 2015. *Ghettoside: A True Story of Murder in America*. New York: Penguin Random House.

Levintova, Hannah. 2020. "Here's Where the Movement to Defund Police Is Gaining Momentum." *Mother Jones,* June 6. https://www.motherjones.com/politics/2020/06/heres-where-the-movement-to-defund-police-is-gaining-momentum/.

Lopez, German. 2020. "Examining the Spike in Murders." *New York Times*, January 18. https://www.nytimes.com/2022/01/18/briefing/crime-surge-homicides-us.html.

Lurie, Stephen. 2019. "There's No Such Thing as a Dangerous Neighborhood." CityLab, February 25. https://www.citylab.com/perspective/2019/02/broken-windows-theory-policing-urban-violence-crime-data/583030/.
MacDonald, John, Charles Branas, and Robert J. Stokes. 2019. *Changing Places: The Science and Art of New Urban Planning.* Princeton, NJ: Princeton University Press.
Mays, Jeffery C. 2020. "Who Opposes Defunding the N.Y.P.D.? These Black Lawmakers." *New York Times*, August 10. https://www.nytimes.com/2020/08/10/nyregion/defund-police-nyc-council.html.
McDowell, Meghan, and Luis Fernandez. 2018. "'Disband, Disempower, and Disarm': Amplifying the Theory and Practice of Police Abolition." *Critical Criminology* 26 (3): 373–391.
McGarrell, Edmund, Steven Chermak, James Wilson, and Nicholas Corsaro. 2006. "Reducing Homicide through a 'Lever-Pulling' Strategy." *Justice Quarterly* 23 (2): 214–229.
McShane, Edward J. 1937. "Jensen's Inequality." *Bulletin of the American Mathematical Society* 43 (8): 521–527.
Meares, Tracey. 2009. "The Legitimacy of Police among Young African American Men." *Marquette Law Review* 92 (4): 651–666.
Miller, Walter. 1975. *Violence by Youth Gangs and Youth Groups as a Crime Problem in Major American Cities*, Washington, DC: US Government Printing Office.
Muhammad, Khalil Gibran. 2010. *The Condemnation of Blackness: Race, Crime, and the Making of Modern Urban America.* Cambridge, MA: Harvard University Press.
Nagin, Daniel. 2013. "Deterrence in the Twenty-First Century." *Crime and Justice* 42: 199–263.
National Research Council. 2018. *Proactive Policing: Effects on Crime and Communities.* Washington, DC: The National Academies Press.
Papachristos, Andrew V., Anthony A. Braga, and David M. Hureau. 2012. "Social Networks and the Risk of Gunshot Injury." *Journal of Urban Health* 89 (6): 992–1003.
Papachristos, Andrew V., Anthony A. Braga, Eric Piza, and Leigh Grossman. 2015. "The Company You Keep? The Spillover Effects of Gang Membership on Individual Gunshot Victimization in a Co-Offending Network." *Criminology* 53 (4): 624–649.
Papachristos, Andrew V., Christopher Wildeman, and Elizabeth Roberto. 2015. "Tragic, but Not Random: The Social Contagion of Nonfatal Gunshot Injuries." *Social Science & Medicine* 125: 139–150.
Parker, Kim, and Kiley Hurst. 2021. "Growing Share of Americans Say They Want More Spending on Police in Their Area." Pew Research Center, October 26. https://www.pewresearch.org/fact-tank/2021/10/26/growing-share-of-americans-say-they-want-more-spending-on-police-in-their-area/.
Puzzanchera, Charles, G. Chamberlin, and W. Kang. 2021. "Easy Access to the FBI's Supplementary Homicide Reports: 1980–2020." https://www.ojjdp.gov/ojstatbb/ezashr/.
Pyrooz, David C., Ryan K. Masters, Jennifer J. Tostlebe, and Richard G. Rogers. 2020. "Exceptional Mortality Risk among Police-Identified Young Black Male Gang Members." *Preventive Medicine* 141: 106269. https://doi.org/10.1016/j.ypmed.2020.106269.
Pyrooz, David C., Justin Nix, and Scott Wolfe. 2021. "Understanding Denver's Devastating Rise in Homicides in 2020, the Largest in at Least 5 Years." *The Denver Post*, February 24. https://www.denverpost.com/2021/02/24/denver-crime-rate-homicide-shooting-property-crime-police.

Pyrooz, David C, Jillian J. Turanovic, Scott H. Decker, and Jun Wu. 2016. "Taking Stock of the Relationship between Gang Membership and Offending: A Meta-Analysis." *Criminal Justice and Behavior* 43 (3): 365–397.

Regardie, Jon. 2022. "New Crime Stats Revealed: Homicides in Los Angeles Soared in 2021." *Los Angeles Magazine,* January 17. https://www.lamag.com/citythinkblog/new-crime-stats-revealed-homicides-in-los-angeles-soared-in-2021/.

Reisig, Michael, Jason Bratton, and Marc Gertz. 2007. "The Construct Validity and Refinement of Process-Based Policing Measures." *Criminal Justice and Behavior* 34 (8): 1005–1028.

Rodriguez, Eddy. 2020. "Which Lawmakers Support Defunding the Police?" *Newsweek,* June 12. https://www.newsweek.com/which-lawmakers-support-defunding-police-1510556.

Roman, Caterina, Nathan Link, Jordan Hyatt, Avinash Bhati, and Megan Forney. 2019. "Assessing the Gang-Level and Community-Level Effects of the Philadelphia Focused Deterrence Strategy." *Journal of Experimental Criminology* 15 (4): 499–527.

Sampson, Robert, Stephen Raudenbush, and Felton Earls. 1997. "Neighborhoods and Violent Crime." *Science* 277: 918–924.

Schleimer, Julia P., Shani A. Buggs, Christopher D. McCort, Veronica A. Pear, Alaina De Biasi, Elizabeth Tomsich, Aaron B. Shev, Hannah S. Laqueur, and Garen J. Wintemute. 2022. "Neighborhood Racial and Economic Segregation and Disparities in Violence during the COVID-19 Pandemic." *American Journal of Public Health* 112 (1): 144–153.

Sharkey, Patrick. 2014. *Evaluation of the New York State Gun Violence Reduction Program.* Unpublished report. New York: Crime Lab New York.

Sharkey, Patrick. 2018. *Uneasy Peace: The Great Crime Decline, the Renewal of City Life, and the Next War on Violence.* New York: W.W. Norton.

Sherman, Lawrence W. 1995. "The Police." In *Crime,* edited by James Q. Wilson and Joan Petersilia, 327–348. San Francisco, CA: ICS Press.

Smith, Sandra Susan, Felix Owusu, and Stacey Borden. 2022. "Boston's Gang Database Should Be Dismantled." *Boston Globe,* January 31. https://www.bostonglobe.com/2022/01/31/opinion/bostons-gang-database-should-be-dismantled/.

Stone, Christopher, Todd Foglesong, and Christine M. Cole. 2009. *Policing Los Angeles Under a Consent Decree: The Dynamics of Change at the LAPD.* Cambridge, MA: Kennedy School of Government, Harvard University.

Struhl, Benjamin, and Alexander Gard-Murray. 2022. *Fulfilling the Promise of Public Safety: Some Lessons from Recent Research.* Philadelphia, PA: Crime and Justice Policy Lab, University of Pennsylvania.

Thornberry, Terence P., Marvin D. Krohn, Alan J. Lizotte, Carolyn A. Smith, and Kimberly Tobin. 2003. *Gangs and Delinquency in Developmental Perspective.* New York: Cambridge University Press.

Tita, George, Kevin Riley, Greg Ridgeway, Clifford Grammich, Allan Abrahamse, and Peter Greenwood. 2003. *Reducing Gun Violence: Results from an Intervention in East Los Angeles.* Santa Monica, CA: RAND Corporation.

Tyler, Tom. 2006. *Why People Obey the Law.* 2nd ed. Princeton, NJ: Princeton University Press.

Vitale, Alex. 2017. *The End of Policing.* Brooklyn, NY: Verso.

Weisburd, David, Cody W. Telep, Heather Vovak, Taryn Zastrow, Anthony A. Braga, and Brandon Turchan. 2022. "Reforming the Police through Procedural Justice Training: A Multi-City Randomized Trial at Crime Hot Spots." *Proceedings of the National Academy of Sciences* 119 (13): e2118780119.

Weitzer, Ronald, and Steven Tuch. 2006. *Race and Policing in America*. New York: Cambridge University Press.

Wilson, James Q. 1975. *Thinking about Crime*. New York: Basic Books.

Winship, Christopher, and Anthony A. Braga. 2022. "Reform Boston's Gang Database, Don't Dismantle It." *Boston Globe,* January 24. https://www.bostonglobe.com/2022/02/24/opinion/reform-bostons-gang-database-dont-dismantle-it/.

Wong, Jennifer, Jason Gravel, Martin Bouchard, and Carlo Morselli. 2012. *Effectiveness of Street Gang Control Strategies: A Systematic Review and Meta-Analysis of Evaluation Studies*. Ottawa, ON: Public Safety Canada.

Zeoli, April, Jesenia Pizarro, Sue Grady, and Christopher Melde. 2014. "Homicide as Infectious Disease: Using Public Health Methods to Investigate the Diffusion of Homicide." *Justice Quarterly* 31(3): 609–632.

Zimring, Franklin, and Gordon Hawkins. 1973. *Deterrence: The Legal Threat in Crime Control*. Chicago, IL: University of Chicago Press.

CHAPTER 43

MAKING SENSE OF THE MODELS
Continuities and Differences across Prominent Gang/Group Gun Violence Intervention Models

JESSE JANNETTA, PAIGE S. THOMPSON, AND LILY ROBIN

THE alarming increases in gun violence across the United States that began with the onset of the COVID-19 pandemic, coupled with the increased attention to reducing the harms caused by policing arising from the mass protests after the murder of George Floyd, have created a renewed demand for solutions to community gun violence. In particular, there have been fervent calls from community members and stakeholders alike urging solutions to this type of violence that go beyond broad-based suppression strategies—though they have also occasioned new calls for those as well (Reny and Newman 2021). This chapter seeks to contribute to the discourse around available approaches to doing so by drawing out points of comparison and contrast among the most prominent gun violence intervention strategies addressing group or gang gun violence: focused deterrence, public health models, and the Spergel Model of Gang Intervention and Suppression/OJJDP Comprehensive Gang Model (hereafter referred to as the Comprehensive Gang Model). We focus on these approaches because evaluations of them constitute the sizable majority of the research literature on interventions to address youth gang violence that go beyond suppression and broad-based enforcement, and they serve as important reference points for anti-violence practice due to their prevalence and national organizations endorsing them and advancing guidance on implementing them.

In speaking to these questions, we build this chapter through work the Urban Institute completed in 2022, with support from the National Institute of Justice and the Office of Juvenile Justice and Delinquency Prevention and guided by a multidisciplinary panel of experts, to develop a research-based practice guide that local governments, law enforcement agencies, and organizations intervening in community violence can use to prevent and reduce gun violence committed by youth approximately ages 10 to 25 involved in gangs/groups (Jannetta et al. 2022).[1] To inform recommendations in the guide, Urban researchers conducted a *literature synthesis* on the efficacy (with respect to rates of violence, gun violence, and future criminal legal system involvement) and implementation of youth gang/group and gun violence reduction strategies (Matei et al. 2022) and an *environmental scan* of youth gang/group interventions across the nation, which included interviews with 105 stakeholders and staff of 14 youth gang/group and gun violence interventions about the design, development, funding, and sustainability of their interventions (Ervin et al. 2022). Criteria for inclusion in the literature synthesis and environmental scan were programs or interventions that focused on reducing gun violence committed by youth in the age range, including both those working only with youth and those primarily but not exclusively doing so. The project's focus was on efforts designed to provide an immediate response to acute gun violence problems, as opposed to those that address risk factors associated with violence more broadly or over a longer time horizon.

This chapter begins with a section describing the three prominent intervention models. The second section will provide a brief overview of what the evidence suggests about the efficacy of each model. The third section will cover the significant overlap in activity components and implementation considerations across the three models. Finally, the fourth section will offer insight into the key features of each model that differentiate them from one another. Specifically, this section will identify differences related to each model's locus of intervention and degree of focus on gangs/groups and the role of enforcement and sanctions.

INTERVENTION PROGRAM MODELS

Program models are helpful in that they show you how different pieces fit together, how they relate to a specific theory or understanding of how violence works, and provide a standard for fidelity. That said, in our work developing the practice guide, we encountered a field in which these program models are important organizing principles guiding action against violence, but also a field in which there is considerable overlap and hybridization across models at the local level. In recognition of this, our practice guide highlighted common practices shared by effective anti-violence programs across model types. An important finding from our project's environmental scan is that these models can and do coexist in many places, with differing degrees of harmony or friction. For example, public health approaches and focused deterrence interventions have operated simultaneously in cities included in our environmental scan such as Baltimore and Oakland. In light of this reality, understanding the differences between the models is less a question of whether one model is "better" than another than of grasping the different assets, theories of change, and mechanisms each brings to the work. This approach de-emphasizes the sometimes intense rhetorical competition between prominent models (and their proponents) for attention, funding, and political support in policy debates.

But before doing that, we briefly describe the three main program models of focus: the focused deterrence model, the public health model, and the Comprehensive Gang Model.

Focused Deterrence

The focused deterrence model grew out of Boston's Operation Ceasefire in the mid-1990s (Kennedy et al. 2001) and has evolved through substantial replication and iteration since then. In focused deterrence interventions targeting gun violence, partners engage members of groups actively engaged in gun violence, identified via analysis generally combining quantitative data and local knowledge of group dynamics, and communicate a multipart message intended to convince the group and its members to desist from gun violence. Communication of the message often occurs during "call-in" meetings held for people in groups that are involved in active conflicts in the community where they are informed that the entire group is at risk of sanctions if members of that group persist in engaging in gun violence. The purpose of these call-ins is to have attendees disseminate the message throughout the group; the attendees may not themselves be the group members most at risk of involvement in gun violence. Message delivery can also be done in one-on-one meetings ("custom notifications") with particularly high-risk people.

Focused deterrence interventions involve a partnership of law enforcement, community members, and service providers who have a common goal of reducing violence in their communities yet have distinct roles in working toward that goal. Law enforcement identifies the groups engaged in violence and communicates to them both the consequences of continuing violence and the benefits of peaceful actions. This is done to secure voluntary compliance from group members before implementing enforcement measures and delivering sanctions. If a group continues to engage in gun violence after being warned, law enforcement conducts coordinated enforcement actions against members of the group for any illegal activity in which they may be involved. Community members involved in focused deterrence message communication include surviving family and friends of victims of violence, former gang/group members, and community leaders. Their role is to articulate the moral necessity of stopping gun violence, highlighting the individual and community-level toll of violence while also emphasizing support for gang/group members who decide to leave the violence behind. Outreach service providers provide support for life changes that reduce individual risk of involvement in violence, helping group members achieve their goals and sustain their commitment to non-violence (National Network for Safe Communities 2020). The robustness of service provision and support can vary considerably in focused deterrence efforts; some have robust outreach, case management, and service connection components, whereas others have more modest service provisions involving referrals to community-based organizations.

Community-Based and Hospital-Based Public Health Approaches

The public health model for preventing gun violence is built on the understanding that the spread of violence has epidemiological properties, including transmission via exposure (National Research Council 2013). Community-based public health approaches to gun violence reduction generally include reactive approaches to instances of violence (e.g., violence interruption to head off retaliation stemming from a shooting) and more proactive approaches to reducing the risk of violence through means such as outreach and engagement of individuals at high risk of involvement and changing community norms around violence.

The predominant public health approach to gun violence is Cure Violence, which emerged from Chicago in the early 2000s, and whose model and technical assistance have been important influences on public health interventions beyond Cure Violence replications. Sowing the seeds for longstanding confusion around focused deterrence and public health approaches, the intervention that became Cure Violence was initially called Chicago Ceasefire. Cure Violence operates in three primary ways to stop the spread of violence: directly interrupting it via preventing retaliatory shootings and mediating active conflicts between groups, identifying people at highest risk of perpetrating violence and engaging with them to change their thinking, and working to change group norms regarding violence (Butts et al. 2015). Professionals called "violence interrupters" are responsible for the direct interruption of violence transmission, and outreach workers are responsible for the engagement of high-risk individuals. Employing credible messengers to carry out both roles is a principle of Cure Violence, as is ongoing data analysis to monitor implementation fidelity and identify any changes in violence dynamics (Cure Violence Global 2019). Notably, in contrast with the Comprehensive Gang Model and the focused deterrence model, public health models do not incorporate suppression or other enforcement components.

Hospital-based violence intervention programs (HVIPs) are another prominent type of public health intervention to address gun violence. In some cases, HVIPs are a component of community-based public health interventions with the hospital as a setting to carry out similar activities to those occurring elsewhere in the community. In other cases, HVIPs are housed administratively within hospital trauma centers as standalone programs. In either case, these interventions are based on the notion that violence is recurrent and that someone hospitalized after a shooting or similar violent incident is at high risk for further victimization, that the shooting could be the occasion for further retaliatory violence, but also that assisting someone who has experienced this kind of trauma in the hospital can be a unique opportunity to engage them in services and supports (NNHVIP 2019). Intervention staff meet with potential clients in the hospital, assess their risk/need factors, plan with them and their families for discharge and safety, and connect them to critical services and supports.

Comprehensive Gang Model

The Comprehensive Gang Model was developed in an effort led by Irving Spergel, drawing largely on social disorganization theory, to create a composite approach to addressing youth gangs by drawing on a comprehensive assessment of agency and group efforts to respond to gang/group problems initiated in the late 1980s (OJJDP 2009; National Gang Center 2010). It is based on the premise that violence committed by people affiliated with gangs is a result of social disorganization and provides a framework for coordinating a collaborative multidisciplinary response that leverages community resources, builds capacity, and improves the efficacy of service delivery. The collaborative model focuses on the partnership of law enforcement agencies, social service agencies, and grassroots and faith-based organizations. The model's framework is highly adaptive and has multidisciplinary and cross-system case management, services, and outreach at its core. It is intended to reduce serious and entrenched youth gang crime and violence by creating and equipping a community that is well suited to conduct effective violence prevention, intervention, and suppression through five main strategies: community mobilization, opportunities provision, social intervention, suppression, and organizational change. The model includes suppression and intervention activities for identified gang members already involved in serious and chronic crime and prevention activities for youth who are likely to have such involvement in the future.

EVIDENCE OF EFFECTIVENESS

The three program models under discussion in this chapter were predominant among the original studies and prior literature syntheses we reviewed as part of the research-based practice guide project. Summarizing this research base is challenging because of variation in methods, outcomes, and the overall mixed nature of the impact findings in the aggregate, and often within a single study (Matei et al. 2022).

Focused deterrence has the most extensive evidence base of the three models, and the preponderance of evidence on focused deterrence interventions indicates they are effective at reducing crime and violence, with statistically significant effects found across multiple studies looking at outcomes related to violence such as fatal and non-fatal shootings, shooting behavior, shooting victimization, violent offending, and homicides (Matei et al. 2022; Braga, Weisburd, and Turchan 2018; Braga and Weisburd 2012; Petrosino et al. 2015). Our literature synthesis identified 15 original studies within scope that examined focused deterrence interventions, covering 10 interventions. For three of those 10 interventions[2] only positive findings (e.g., decreases in outcomes such as gang/group involvement and violent crime) were reported. For the other seven, findings were mixed, meaning there were both statistically significant positive and null findings reported; none of the studies found statistically significant negative impacts (e.g., increases in outcomes such as gang/group involvement and violent crime). We identified 23 relevant prior literature syntheses and reviews, 18 of which addressed focused deterrence interventions. These reviews, which were usually more inclusive than our synthesis (particularly due to our project's specific focus on interventions for youth), consistently identified focused deterrence interventions as effective. Quasi-experimental designs and matched comparison groups have become more prevalent in focused deterrence studies in recent years, which have resulted in a substantial decrease in the average mean effect size across focused deterrence studies (Braga et al. 2018). Mean effect sizes appear to be greater for focused deterrence interventions addressing groups/gangs than for those targeting high-risk individuals or drug markets (Braga et al. 2018).

The evidence base of public health models is more mixed, as is the evidence base for the Comprehensive Gang Model. Over half of the interventions of each type examined by original studies coded in our literature synthesis found statistically significant reductions in outcomes such as fatal and non-fatal shootings, violent crime, homicides, and gang/group involvement, with considerable variation in effect size across studies. Our literature synthesis identified 14 original studies within scope that examined public health interventions, covering nine interventions. For three of those interventions, only positive findings were reported, five had mixed findings, with one finding largely negative statistically significant impacts (Wilson and Chermak 2011). Fewer of the prior literature reviews and syntheses covered public health interventions (11 of 23) than focused deterrence interventions, and these generally confirmed that some had positive results, but many had mixed results.

The research findings on the Comprehensive Gang Model are more mixed; of the six interventions addressed by the 11 original studies we coded, there were mixed results for five (including both null and negative findings alongside positive results) and solely positive findings for one. Twelve prior literature reviews and syntheses covered the Comprehensive Gang Model, also citing mixed results. Public health and Comprehensive Gang Model studies that found mixed effects often found that positive impacts existed in some intervention sites but not others (e.g., Butts et al. 2015; Cahill et al. 2008). For the Comprehensive Gang Model in particular, implementation fidelity emerged as a critical precondition for generating impact (Howell and Howell 2019), which is perhaps unsurprising given the complexity and comprehensiveness of this intervention model.

The empirical evidence on HVIPs fell outside the scope of the literature synthesis, but extant research on HVIPs has demonstrated effectiveness in terms of reducing violent reinjury among participants, and some evidence of reducing future criminal legal system involvement, including for violence (Becker et al. 2004; Bonne and Dicker 2020; Evans and Vega 2018; Juillard et al. 2016; Purtle et al. 2013; Strong et al. 2016).

While this extant research base provides promising evidence about what all three models can achieve in reducing gun violence, there are substantial shortcomings in terms of methodological rigor that must be addressed if the research community is to consider any of them "proven." Randomized controlled trials and other research designs supporting strong causal inference about these models are nearly absent from the research literature. This is largely due to the difficulties in deploying such methodologies for interventions that, when done properly, are based on problem analysis and focus intentionally on the highest risk places, groups, and individuals. When implemented at scale, they tend to operate across an entire city or similar jurisdictions. When they are not implemented at that scale due to factors like resource limitations or a need to start a smaller scale in the early implementation stages, initial areas are usually selected precisely because they are not like other parts of the city or jurisdiction. Truly comparable counterfactuals are thus difficult to establish, but a research base including more rigorous tests of impact would provide greater confidence in the promising findings to date, ensure those findings stand up to scrutiny, and support the long-term sustainability of effective violence reduction interventions.

An important caveat on looking comparatively at the evidence base for these program models is that there is tremendous heterogeneity and innovation *within* these model approaches. All the initiatives included in the environmental scan that had been in operation for five or more years reported significant changes in their programs. With variance in model approaches across places and over time within places, the question arises of what we are capturing and what we are missing by aggregating studies of these interventions at particular points in time when the interventions in the field are constantly evolving.

Emergent Models

The environmental scan captured several emerging models that have not yet been subject to the level of research attention that the three prominent models covered in this chapter have, but they still represent promising new directions in mitigating gang/group gun violence. Some of these emergent frameworks can be incorporated into more established models, as the Los Angeles Gang Reduction and Youth Development (GRYD) program has done with trauma-informed care approaches (Dierkhising 2020). Others, however, are new standalone approaches.

Perhaps the most prominent of the emergent standalone approaches is Advance Peace. Initially developed in 2010 in Richmond, California, under the auspices of the city's Office of Neighborhood Safety, Advance Peace seeks to reduce urban gun violence by engaging with the people most impacted by cyclical and retaliatory gun violence. Advance Peace works to identify the people most at risk of involvement in gun violence and engage them via formerly incarcerated street outreach workers called Neighborhood Change Agents (NCAs; Corburn and Fukutome 2019). Advance Peace participants become part of an 18-month intensive fellowship program, which includes frequent supportive engagement with NCAs, life planning, mentorship, service connection, travel and internship opportunities stipends, and varied forms of social connection and support. Unlike the Cure Violence model, outreach and service referrals are combined roles carried out by the same individuals (Corburn, Boggan, and Muttaqi 2020).

Advance Peace builds on and also differentiates itself from focused deterrence and public health approaches in ways that are important in themselves and illuminate the distinctions between these more established and researched models (Corburn et al. 2020). It was also identified by researchers at John Jay College of Criminal Justice as one of the most established versions (along with Cure Violence) of what they called "Community Violence Interventions at the Roots (CVI-R)," community-centered grassroots strategies that operate separately from law enforcement or traditional human services (Pugliese et al. 2022). For these reasons, we discuss Advance Peace alongside the three main models at several points in the next sections of this chapter.

Key Similarities

One of the notable findings across the literature synthesis and environmental scan was the extent of overlap in activity components across interventions based on the three main program models, as well as with emergent models like Advance Peace. This degree of commonality is indicated in Table 43.1, which provides a summary of the prevalence of each activity in the original studies reviewed in the synthesis of relevant literature, by program model type. The knowledge base of effective practice cross-cuts the models, and the convergence on similar core components from different starting points should perhaps increase our confidence in the value of these components.

Table 43.1 Activities Appearing in the Coded Original Studies, by Model

Activity	Focused Deterrence (*n*=15)	Public Health (*n*=14)	CGM (*n*=11)
Case management/services	✔	✔✔	✔
Conflict mediation	✔	✔✔	✔
Credible messengers		✔	
Employment assistance	✔	✔	✔
Enhanced enforcement	✔✔		✔✔
Enhanced surveillance	✔✔		✔✔
Faith-based activities	✔	✔	
Hospital-based intervention		✔	
Outreach workers	✔	✔✔	✔✔
Public perception campaigns	✔	✔✔	✔✔
Reducing the gun supply	✔	✔	

Note: Double checkmarks indicate activities that were more prominently mentioned in the literature.

The literature synthesis indicated five activities were present across all the intervention models: (1) *case management/services* to address a variety of needs including education, employment, and behavioral health; (2) *conflict mediation* to de-escalate situations that could evolve toward gun violence; (3) *employment assistance*, sometimes including stipends; (4) the employment of *outreach workers* that work directly with gang/group-involved youth and offer mentorship and connection to services; and (5) *public perception campaigns* such as public service announcements that communicate messages calling for the gun violence to stop. However, the environmental scan revealed greater nuance across interventions and model types. Case management and connections to services (including employment services) were a component of every one of the 14 interventions included in the environmental scan, and outreach workers were a feature of interventions across model types in the environmental scan. Conflict mediation was not a component of the focused deterrence interventions included in the environmental scan, although in some cities they worked alongside other organizations that engaged in mediation work. Public perception campaigns were less prevalent in the focused deterrence interventions included in the environmental scan.

The environmental scan elevated the use of *incident response*. Incident response involves sending community violence intervention staff, such as violence interrupters, to shooting scenes to reduce the likelihood of further violence by doing activities such as controlling rumors or identifying people who might be motivated to retaliate and seeking to eliminate that possibility. While the literature noted the use of outreach workers and conflict mediation broadly, the specific activity of incident response was notably present across all models in the environmental scan. *Community events* were also a feature of environmental scan interventions associated with all three model types (though less common among focused deterrence interventions) and took the form of cookouts, parades, raffles, talent shows, block parties, holiday parties, and school supply giveaways. They served a variety of goals, including building relationships with the community, providing residents with material resources (e.g., clothing, food, gift cards, diapers, toiletries, personal protective equipment during the COVID-19 pandemic), connecting community members to services (e.g., mental health services, grief counseling, anger management, legal services), and sharing information specifically about violence and resources available to address it. The absence of this activity in the literature synthesis is perhaps due to its scope explicitly not including prevention activities, of which community events are often a component.

It's also possible that the difference here between the literature synthesis and environmental scan findings may be a matter of clarity and specificity of definitions. Some of the incident response work, like violence interruption, could be seen as a form of conflict mediation, and community events in some interventions serve as a means to spread the messages from the public perception campaigns.

Only two activities, *credible messengers* and *hospital-based interventions*, were mentioned in studies of only one model type—public health. This is a substantial difference from what we found in the environmental scan, in which credible messengers and hospital-based intervention were mentioned as components of multiple interventions associated with each model. There are several potential explanations for this difference, including that the research literature was not attentive to the presence of these components, that as the field has evolved these components have become either more present or more explicitly named in a variety of interventions, or that practitioners in the field define what constitutes activities that are part of the intervention more broadly than do researchers examining them. Certainly, the employment of people trusted by gang/group-affiliated youth who have a history of involvement in gangs/groups or gun violence and a connection to the community have been part of interventions to reduce youth gang/group and gun violence for many years, whereas the specific terminology of calling them "credible messengers" has become more widespread in recent years.

Environmental scan findings suggested that direct work with communities to identify anti-violence strategies was more prevalent in public health interventions, and providing recreational and educational programming to youth was more associated with the Comprehensive Gang Model.

Probably the most notable difference in activities, present in both the literature synthesis and the environmental scan, is that *enhanced surveillance* and *enhanced enforcement* were prominent components of focused deterrence and Comprehensive Gang Model interventions, and very much not so for public health models, something we will delve into in the next section. Enhanced enforcement activities included targeted arrests, expedited prosecution, and punitive sanctions, and enhanced surveillance activities included focused law enforcement surveillance on people with ties to groups in prioritized areas and heightening community supervision after conviction for people with ties to gangs/groups suspected of committing acts of gun violence.

In addition to overlap in activities across program models, there are common implementation considerations across them. The importance of collaborating with the community and building community trust was noted across all three model types in the literature synthesis and environmental scan. Community members have unique insight into the challenges and assets of their communities, and that knowledge is imperative to building a successful intervention regardless of model type. However, community knowledge cannot be accessed and no model can be successful or sustained without community support. Just as trust with the community as a whole is important, building trusting relationships with young people served by interventions is also critical to success. Regardless of model type, young people must trust the intervention and intervention staff that are engaging with them for intervention activities to be successful.

Data-driven problem analysis at the start of an intervention and continually monitoring data and adjusting goals as necessary was another shared implementation consideration across model types. Focused deterrence models must identify the people and places at the highest risk of gun violence. The five core strategies of the Comprehensive Gang Model must be tailored to the specific local problem and needs. Public health models rely on clear identification and understanding of risks and needs to guide the interruption of violence transmission and engagement with people most at risk of future involvement in violence. For some public health interventions included in the environmental scan, consistently obtaining quality data from law enforcement was a challenge, and they relied more on data from hospitals and public health systems to understand risk and violence trends.

Interventions across all model types typically include partnerships with stakeholders across several organizations. These partnerships tend to be more successful when there is a clear and agreed-upon intervention goal that is understood across partners, partner roles are clearly defined and distinct, and there are formalized methods of communication and collaboration.

Finally, sustainability is an implementation concern that was noted in almost every intervention across the literature synthesis and environmental scan. All interventions with partnerships across agencies, regardless of model type, can be impacted by staff turnover and leadership changes. Identifying and sustaining funding over time was also noted as a challenge common to interventions associated with all three models.

Key Differences

A critical lesson of the youth gun and gang/group violence literature synthesis and environmental scan is the degree to which a focus on different models masks similarities in the component activities of interventions associated with those models. Having grounded our discussion in the continuities across these models, we turn now to a discussion of some of the important distinctions between them.

Grounding Theory

The three prominent program models build their efforts on slightly different etiologies of gun violence. These understandings are not necessarily contradictory, but they do give rise to important differences in focus and emphasis.

Many of the key interventions, and certainly the public health and focused deterrence approaches (as well as Advance Peace), operate from the insight that a relatively small and identifiable number of people are at the core of much community gun violence. Public health- and focused deterrence-built strategies from this insight intervene in how violence spreads based on social dynamics like intergroup conflict and retaliation. Social connections expand the risk factors for violence from the individual to the group level. Group affiliation situated in conflict networks creates friction that can escalate to violence, and violence committed by a member of one group against another can ripple out as the group is the target of retaliation rather than the individual perpetrator. In the environmental scan, we found that the idea of violence as a "disease" or a "pathogen/virus" transmitted through social groups is common across these interventions, though the ideas may be articulated differently (Ervin et al. 2022). The group-based messaging of focused deterrence also relies on group transmission—the combined message of enhanced sanction threat, community moral voice, and the offer of support is intended to spread through the group starting with call-in attendees of custom notification participants.

The focus on social dynamics in these models is evident in conflict mediation and violence interruption components of public health models, the group call-in meetings and coordinated enforcement components of focused deterrence, and the importance of addressing community norms in both. All of these directly intervene in social processes that can fuel gun violence or mobilize social counterprocesses that make such violence less likely. These counterprocesses can happen within the groups engaged in violence (e.g., motivating group members to de-escalate due to the heightened collective sanctions threat in focused deterrence) or from without (e.g., mobilizing community norms against gun violence to make moral claims on people at high risk of committing violence).

The mechanism by which the interventions disrupt these violence dynamics is where differences between focused deterrence and public health approaches become more evident. As the name implies, focused deterrence interventions seek to deter groups, and individuals in them, from engaging in further violence by increasing the level of specific enforcement risk to them. Public health models try to interrupt cycles of violence through direct engagement with individuals at moments when the likelihood of retaliatory shootings is particularly high (e.g., in the immediate aftermath of a shooting) and conflict mediation between groups as conflicts emerge and intensify. But in observing activities in the field, these distinctions may be more of a matter of emphasis. Many focused deterrence efforts include street outreach components that involve violence interruption, and interventionists working in public health models interviewed for the environmental scan sometimes noted the importance of communicating to their clients or prospective clients that they were under enhanced sanctions risk, even though those sanctions were not related to the public health intervention itself.

The Comprehensive Gang Model is not as narrowly focused on gun violence in the immediate term as these other models. The grounding of the Comprehensive Gang Model in social disorganization theory, which is about the connection between neighborhood ecological factors and future criminal activity, is part of what accounts for its comprehensiveness. The model is attentive to changing the place-based dynamics that are feeding gang activity and associated violence. Intervention and suppression strategies in the Comprehensive Gang Model are focused on a population that overlaps with those of public health and focused deterrence approaches. However, the Comprehensive Gang Model includes prevention-focused components that are more broadly targeted (i.e., far more youth are *at risk* of involvement in gangs and gang-related violence than youth who become part of the high-risk population) and bears fruit in violence reduction on a longer timeline. The comprehensiveness of the Comprehensive Gang Model and the focus on social intervention and opportunities provision relevant to youth can serve as a platform for building more specific theories. For example, the Los Angeles GRYD program is integrating an Activating Intentional Youth Development Approach to guide engagement with youth in prevention programming (Larson and Herz 2020).

Locus of Intervention/Degree of Focus on Gangs/Groups

Work to reduce gun violence related to gangs/groups can focus on individuals, gangs/groups, families and communities, or neighborhoods. Interventions in the field are often addressing violence at a combination of these levels, and the models we are discussing interact with them in different ways.

One large distinction among these models is how they relate to gangs/groups. The Comprehensive Gang Model is by far the most focused on gangs, and the only one that includes reducing gang affiliation as a specific goal. For the other models, gangs (or other groups or street organizations) are of interest only insofar as they are actively involved in gun violence problems. They do not make reducing gang/group involvement and gang/group joining as such primary goals, though they may be considered intermediate outcomes related to reducing shootings.

Focused deterrence interventions targeting gun violence tend to eschew the term "gang" in favor of "group," on the understanding that many of the social entities that are the locus of the intervention are much smaller and looser networks than connoted by the term "gang" (National Network for Safe Communities 2020). Additionally, focused deterrence models engage groups guided by their degree of involvement in gun violence. A group that does not engage in gun violence, or only very rarely, would not rise to the top of the list for interventions and would not become subject to focused deterrence attention, regardless of other criminal or problematic conduct in which group members might be involved. Gang involvement is recognized by public health interventions as a factor indicating someone is in the high-risk population of focus. It is one of seven criteria used for the purpose, any four of which make someone appropriate for Cure Violence engagement (Butts et al. 2015). However, recent Cure Violence materials do not mention gangs directly, although they do include "group conflict" and "formation of a new group" among the situations that are likely to result in violent acts (Cure Violence 2019).

By contrast, Advance Peace emphasizes the individual focus of its approach and differentiates itself from focused deterrence by the lack of importance attached to affiliation with "street organizations" (Corburn et al. 2020). The program's theory of change is to "End cyclical & retaliatory urban gun violence by investing in the development, health, and healing of highly influential individuals at the center of urban gun violence" and emphasizes that affiliation with any gang or group is not necessary to participate in program components like the Peacemaker Fellowship (Corburn et al. 2020). However, it is possible making this distinction overstates the differences between the models. Even models like focused deterrence that directly focus on groups also attend to individual attributes that guide focus. Further, the increasing prevalence of individual custom notifications as a mechanism to deliver the focused deterrence message in addition to group call-ins bridges the gap between group and individual as the locus of intervention.

Geography is another important locus of intervention, as gun violence is a highly concentrated phenomenon. Additionally, organizing interventions geographically is important for building local knowledge of social dynamics among outreach workers and building service networks. For instance, public health models require the interventionists to know who is affiliated with whom and to build relationships and lines of communication with them so that when a shooting incident occurs they have a good sense of who might retaliate and how to reach them. Essentially all the Comprehensive Gang Model, focused deterrence, and public health interventions included in the environmental scan had geographical areas of focus, though this was in some cases experienced as a frustrating constraint when violence dynamics, gang/group networks, or social connections straddled program service areas and city/county boundaries. Advance Peace is less geographically organized, operating on a citywide basis owing to its strong focus on individuals and not including work on community norms around violence, attention to which inherently moves interventions to a geographical focus. The Comprehensive Gang Model is focused on reducing gang violence, but also aims to change community conditions to mitigate system failures and community dysfunctions that contribute to gang/group problems.

A more specific form of geographical focus is engaging with norms and narratives that support or counter violence in communities. Public health models seek explicitly to "change community norms that allow, encourage and exacerbate violence in chronically violent neighborhoods to healthy norms that reject the use of violence" (Cure Violence 2019). In the Comprehensive Gang Model, primary prevention strategies that focus on the entire population of high-crime, high-risk communities play a role in dealing with community-wide dynamics. Focused deterrence is also attentive to community norms and narratives, engaging with them as part of the integrated message delivered via call-ins and custom notifications. In the focused deterrence concept, effective use of community norms and narratives against violence to influence the behavior of group members is closely tied to building trust between communities and law enforcement: "Community norms against violence and crime (informal social control), freed to emerge as tensions with law enforcement ease, can carry much of the burden of crime prevention" (National Network for Safe Communities 2016). Consistent with its tight focus on high-risk individuals, Advance Peace does not seek to affect community norms around violence (Corburn et al. 2020).

Another key distinction related to the locus of intervention is the focus on age range. The Comprehensive Gang Model is explicitly focused on youth and young adults, with the prevention aspect of the model making this necessary. Because they incorporate prevention and intervention, Comprehensive Gang Model interventions often need to establish separate service pathways for each, with prevention services having a younger service population than intervention. While their intervention logic does not imply a top age for engagement, public health interventions are usually focused on people younger than 30 (Butts et al. 2015), and focused deterrence and HVIPs may define engagement populations by age due to local plans or external factors such as funding sources.

Our project focused on youth gun violence associated with gangs/groups, and many interventions in the field focus on juvenile and young adult populations as drivers of gun violence. This premise was challenged by what we heard from partners in several interventions covered in our environmental scan, spanning public health, focused deterrence, and hospital-based violence intervention, who reported finding the average ages of shooting perpetrators and victims were closer to 30 than the defined service population of mid-20s or younger, and therefore needing to adjust their criteria to allow for working with that age range (Ervin et al. 2022). This echoes findings from analyses of characteristics of shooting perpetrators and victims in cities such as Oakland (Muhammad 2018) and Washington, DC (National Institute for Criminal Justice Reform 2021).

Role of Enforcement

Probably the most difficult and sensitive issue facing efforts to address gang/group-related gun violence is the role of law enforcement in the partnerships specifically, and how enforcement activities relate to the other components generally. All the models under discussion here incorporate messages of care and support for people most at risk of shooting and being shot, and all therefore must calibrate how that relates to surveillance and enforcement from police and other justice agencies. This calibration is required regardless of whether enforcement activities are part of the model (as with focused deterrence and the Comprehensive Gang Model) or external to it (as with public health, HVIP, and Advanced Peace). An Oakland Ceasefire stakeholder described how that message was braided together in their focused deterrence efforts: "Message always is we want you to be alive, free, and successful but you're also on law enforcement's radar." How the models navigate the tensions inherent in this statement is a major differentiator among them.

This issue is particularly intense for focused deterrence due to how central targeted enforcement is to how the model works. Not only is the threat of targeted enforcement actions a central pillar of the focused deterrence messaging, but that messaging in call-in meetings can rely on prior enforcement actions to impress upon attendees the seriousness of the risk they face if their group does not desist from violence (Fontaine et al. 2017). In this sense, focused deterrence depends on at least some enhanced enforcement activity for its success in a way the other models do not. The nature of the relationship between the types of enforcement done, direct messaging of enhanced risk, and the logic of addressing gun violence through changing group dynamics in focused deterrence models can cause some confusion. In a recent example, Howell (2018) characterized focused deterrence as instituting "a zero-tolerance policy for any law-breaking activity on the part of identified individuals," who are notified "that they are subject to long prison sentences for any subsequent offenses, probation or parole violations." As David Kennedy (2019) noted in a response essay, this misframes the role of enforcement. Parsing this misframing helps tease out how enforcement operates in focused deterrence—what causes enhanced enforcement to occur is group engagement in gun violence specifically (not individual engagement in any lawbreaking or misconduct), enforcement actions focus on group members rather than being individualized (to affect group behaviors and incentives), and the enforcement can deliver consequences for an array of offense and supervision violations not related to gun violence because once an enforcement action is triggered by gun violence coming from the group, law enforcement can use "a wide menu of options for delivering sanctions to the entire group" that exists due to their involvement in a range of misconduct (National Network for Safe Communities 2020). In a focused deterrence strategy delivered with fidelity, what there is zero tolerance for is groups engaging in gun violence, and only this behavior results in enforcement and sanctions beyond what is routine.

If the multipart focused deterrence message is to be delivered and the promise of both support for those who seek it and consequences for continued engagement in violence is to be fulfilled, these interventions must build and sustain working trust between police and communities so that they jointly own the work and each plays their roles. Research and writing on focused deterrence emphasize that success hinges on strong partnerships between the community and law enforcement. However, people in communities where violence is most prevalent have a substantial history of distrust of police (Fontaine et al. 2019), and that distrust is an ongoing challenge to manage in focused deterrence interventions. For this reason, focused deterrence often involves explicit efforts to improve relationships between police and communities where violence is concentrated (Muhammad 2018). This joining of goals is perhaps most evident in the National Initiative of Building Community Trust and Justice, which in most sites tied the trust-building and legitimacy enhancement work with focused deterrence efforts (Jannetta et al. 2019). This aspect of the work has given rise to the police–community reconciliation approach developed by the National Network for Safe Communities (Kuhn and Lurie 2018), which emphasizes the need to address the serious historical and current harms of racialized policing in order to do this trust-building and support sustained success in reducing gun violence. However, the effectiveness of these interventions has yet to be proven, and one of the National Initiative test sites was Minneapolis, where it was insufficient to prevent the murder of George Floyd and the subsequent unrest (Jannetta 2020). Absent advances in police accountability in particular, the prospects for sustaining the trust and relationships necessary for long-term co-production of safety are highly uncertain.

While the role of enforcement is not as central to the Comprehensive Gang Model as it is to focused deterrence, suppression is one of its five strategies. Suppression is defined in the Comprehensive Gang Model to include both formal and informal social control, involving monitoring of gang-involved youth by criminal and juvenile justice agencies and by schools and community organizations (National Gang Center 2010), but suppression work as defined also involves "identifying the most dangerous and influential gang members and removing them from the community" (National Gang Center 2010). Important for understanding the role of enforcement in the Comprehensive Gang Model is that, as a comprehensive model, it tends to have more differentiation in service populations, with separately defined service populations for prevention, intervention, and suppression components. This is unlike focused deterrence, public health, and Advance Peace, in which a single population is the focus for both positive engagement and enforcement attention (whether the latter is within or outside the program itself).

Public health models do not name police as a core partner in the same way as focused deterrence and the Comprehensive Gang Model does, and Advance Peace "does not work alongside law enforcement to communicate its messages against violence" (Corburn et al. 2020). Our environmental scan found variation in the relationship between public health interventions and law enforcement, from minimal communication and coordination to having police serve on hiring panels for interventionists. While enforcement activities were not part of any of the public health interventions included in the scan, interventionists were well aware that the people they were serving or seeking to engage in the program were under enhanced scrutiny from law enforcement, and several noted that clearly communicating this to program participants was important.

Regardless of whether enforcement has a place within these program models, law enforcement is a presence in the places where they operate and in the lives of the people they are engaging. Thus, efforts that do not include law enforcement usually had some working understanding with the police, often involving strict rules about information sharing and coordination at leadership levels (not on the street), to facilitate the work on the ground (Ervin et al. 2022; Jannetta et al. 2022). Views of interventionists and police on how this relationship should and did work varied considerably, from a mutual understanding of "they have their job and we have ours" to descriptions of harassment of interventionists by some police officers. A common sentiment was that securing and maintaining support from law enforcement for public health and Advance Peace interventions was important because of the power and influence law enforcement has. At the same time, the very experience that gives interventionists credibility with people at the highest risk of shooting and being shot can make them suspect in the eyes of law enforcement, which can in turn lead to suspicion, interference, and harassment in the streets.

Stakeholders in several focused deterrence and Comprehensive Gang Model efforts included in the environmental scan described a departure from broad enforcement tactics like sweeps. In their estimation, this was possible because law enforcement is involved in the efforts, which creates a different kind of platform to influence their tactics, orientation, and culture. A potential benefit of having enforcement as part of these interventions is that it ties the use of enforcement to broader strategies and *may* discipline its use. In theory, the narrower focus of focused deterrence relative to business-as-usual enforcement approaches can lead to lower overall enforcement burdens on communities where gun violence is concentrated. However, it is not clear to what degree this happens in practice—research on focused deterrence models has been largely silent on the question of whether they entail lower overall levels of police contact, arrest, prosecution, or incarceration. All of the models under discussion here can be a substitute for broad-brush enforcement tactics, but they can just as easily be a complement if law enforcement and local government leadership choose.

Conclusion

Looking at the state of anti-violence evidence and practice, there is much that is heartening and much that is challenging. To start with the challenges, there is still much we need to know. Using more rigorous methods to make stronger causal claims about the effectiveness of all the prominent models and programs than the largely quasi-experimental current evidence allows is one area of focus, as is seeking opportunities to address imbalances in the level of evaluation resources devoted to strategies led by police relative to those that are not (John Jay College Research Advisory Group on Preventing and Reducing Community Violence 2020). Working across research and practitioner worlds to better define and deliver implementation fidelity so that the quality and impact of the typical version of these models approaches the standard of the best of them is another area of focus. More implementation-focused and comparative evaluations might also shed light on the relationship between program activities and impact on violence, and on how these models can complement one another. Greater attention to how these interventions relate to police contact, arrest, and incarceration is another important area.

Turning to what is heartening, we know substantially more than we did a few decades ago about what these approaches that go beyond suppression and broad-based enforcement can accomplish and what strong practice looks like, with points of convergence across prominent and emergent models as guides to what needs to be part of effective anti-violence work. To name some key points, the work needs to be driven by analysis that combines data and ground-level knowledge of local dynamics, to meet young people and others at high risk of shooting and being shot with trust-building engagement and positive supports, to work proactively to interrupt conflicts and other violence transmission vectors, and to build broad partnerships to mobilize the wide range of community and government forces necessary to mitigate a problem as complex as gun violence. More specifically, a reasonably stable and workable relationship between law enforcement and community aspects of antiviolence work is needed. This has always been challenging to achieve, more so in recent years, and will be a constant battle unless and until policing can deliver equitable service and protection to all communities, including supporting community-led work to shoulder more of the work of community protection.

Notes

1. Our project publications use the terms "gang" and "group" together, as some prominent organizations in the youth gun violence prevention field prefer the term "group" because their interventions often deal with collections of people that do not meet the statutory or vernacular definition of gangs. We also approach the use of the term "gang" with caution, in recognition of concerns about the detrimental labeling effects of the term "gang" raised by many environmental scan practitioner interview respondents.
2. Some interventions were subject to multiple studies, and in our literature synthesis we reported summary results by the intervention rather than the study.

References

Becker, Marla G., Jeffery S. Hall, Caesar M. Ursic, Sonia Jain, and Deane Calhoun. 2004. "Caught in the Crossfire: The Effects of a Peer-Based Intervention Program for Violently Injured Youth." *Journal of Adolescent Health* 34 (3): 177–183. https://pubmed.ncbi.nlm.nih.gov/14967340/.

Bonne, Stephanie, and Rochelle A. Dicker. 2020. "Hospital-Based Violence Intervention Programs to Address Social Determinants of Health and Violence." *Current Trauma Reports* 6 (1): 23–28. https://doi.org/10.1007/s40719-020-00184-9.

Braga, Anthony A., and David L. Weisburd. 2012. "The Effects of Focused Deterrence Strategies on Crime: A Systematic Review and Meta-Analysis of the Empirical Evidence." *Journal of Research in Crime and Delinquency* 49 (3): 323–358. https://doi.org/10.1177/0022427811419368.

Braga, Anthony A., David Weisburd, and Brandon Turchan. 2018. "Focused Deterrence Strategies and Crime Control: An Updated Systematic Review and Meta-Analysis of the Empirical Evidence." *American Society of Criminology* 17 (1): 205–250. https://doi.org/10.1111/1745-9133.12353.

Butts, Jeffrey A., Caterina Gouvis Roman, Lindsay Bostwick, and Jeremy R. Porter. 2015. "Cure Violence: A Public Health Model to Reduce Gun Violence." *Annual Review of Public Health.* 36 (1): 39–53. https://www.annualreviews.org/doi/10.1146/annurev-publhealth-031914-122509.

Cahill, Megan, Mark Coggeshall, David Hayeslip, Ashley Wolff, Erica Lagerson, Michelle Scott, Elizabeth Davies, Kevin Roland, and Scott Decker. 2008. *Community Collaboratives Addressing Youth Gangs: Interim Findings from the Gang Reduction Program*. Washington, DC: Urban Institute. https://www.urban.org/research/publication/community-collaboratives-addressing-youth-gangs-interim-findings-gang-reduction-program.

Corburn, Jason, DeVone Boggan, and Khaalid Muttaqi. 2020. *Advance Peace and Focused Deterrence: What Are the Differences?* Berkeley and Richmond, CA: Advance Peace & UC Berkeley. https://www.advancepeace.org/wp-content/uploads/2020/08/ap-focused-deterrence-v1-1.pdf.

Corburn, Jason, and Amanda Fukutome. 2019. *Advance Peace Stockton: 2018–2019 Progress Report*. Berkeley, CA: UC Berkeley Institute of Urban & Regional Development. https://www.advancepeace.org/wp-content/uploads/2020/02/Advance-Peace-Stockton-2018_2019-Progress-Report-FINAL_2019.pdf.

Cure Violence Global. 2019. *The 5 Required Components of Cure Violence*. Chicago, IL: Cure Violence Global. https://1vp6u534z5kr2qmrow11t7ub-wpengine.netdna-ssl.com/wp-content/uploads/2019/12/2019.12.12-Cure-Violence-Criteria.pdf.

Dierkhising, Carly B. 2020. *Building Capacity for Trauma-Informed Care within GRYD Intervention Family Case Management (FCM) Services*. Los Angeles, CA: City of Los Angeles Mayor's Office of Gang Reduction and Youth Development (GRYD). https://www.juvenilejusticeresearch.com/sites/default/files/2020-08/GRYD%20Brief%205_Trauma-Informed%20Care%20within%20GRYD%20FCM%20services_6.2020.pdf .

Ervin, Storm, Lily Robin, Lindsey Cramer, Paige S. Thompson, Rod Martinez, and Jesse Jannetta. 2022. *Implementing Youth Violence Reduction Strategies: Findings from a Scan of Youth Gun, Group and Gang Violence Interventions*. Washington, DC: Urban Institute. https://www.urban.org/sites/default/files/2022-03/implementing-youth-violence-reduction-strategies_0.pdf.

Evans, Douglas, and Anthony Vega. 2018. *Critical Care: The Important Role of Hospital-Based Violence Intervention Programs*. New York: Research and Evaluation Center, John Jay College of Criminal Justice. https://academicworks.cuny.edu/cgi/viewcontent.cgi?article=1442&context=jj_pubs.

Fontaine, Jocelyn, Sino Esthappan, Nancy G. La Vigne, Daniel Lawrence, and Jesse Jannetta. 2019. *Views of the Police and Neighborhood Conditions: Evidence of Change in Six Cities Participating in the National Initiative for Building Community Trust and Justice*. Washington, DC: Urban Institute. https://www.urban.org/sites/default/files/publication/100706/2019.11.11_ni_community_survey_brief_final_0.pdf.

Fontaine, Jocelyn, Jesse Jannetta, Andrew Papachristos, David Leitson, and Anamika Dwivedi. 2017. *Put the Guns Down: Outcomes and Impacts of the Chicago Violence Reduction Strategy*. Washington, DC: Urban Institute. https://www.urban.org/sites/default/files/publication/92321/2017.07.31_vrs_full_report_finalized_0.pdf.

Howell, James C. 2018. "What Works with Gangs: A Breakthrough." *Criminology & Public Policy* 17 (4): 991–999. https://onlinelibrary.wiley.com/doi/10.1111/1745-9133.12398.

Howell, James C., and Megan Q. Howell. 2019. "Serious Gang Problems in the United States: What to Do?" In *Critical Issues in Crime and Justice*, 3rd ed., edited by Dan Okeda and Mary H. Maguire, 156–170. Los Angeles, CA: Sage Publications.

Jannetta, Jesse. 2020. "It Wasn't Enough: The Limits of Police-Community Trust-Building Reform in Minneapolis." *Urban Wire* (blog), June 4. https://www.urban.org/urban-wire/it-wasnt-enough-limits-police-community-trust-building-reform-minneapolis.

Jannetta, Jesse, Sino Esthappan, Jocelyn Fontaine, Mathew Lynch, and Nancy La Vigne. 2019. *Learning to Build Police-Community Trust: Implementation Assessment Findings from the National Initiative for Building Community Trust and Justice*. Washington, DC: Urban Institute. https://www.urban.org/sites/default/files/publication/100705/learning_to_build_police-community_trust_3.pdf.

Jannetta, Jesse, Rod Martinez, Paige S. Thompson, Janine Zweig, Lily Robin, Leigh Courtney, Lindsey Cramer, Storm Ervin, Andreea Matei, and Krista White. 2022. *A Research-Based Practice Guide to Reduce Youth Gun and Gang/Group Violence*. Washington, DC: Urban Institute. https://www.urban.org/sites/default/files/publication/105303/a-research-based-practice-guide-to-reduce-youth-gun-and-gang-group-violence.pdf.

John Jay College Research Advisory Group on Preventing and Reducing Community Violence. 2020. *Reducing Violence without Police: A Review of Research Evidence*. New York: Research and Evaluation Center, John Jay College of Criminal Justice, City University of New York. https://johnjayrec.nyc/2020/11/09/av2020/.

Juillard, Catherine, Laya Cooperman, Isabel Allen, Romain Pirracchio, Terrell Henderson, Ruben Marquez, Julia Orellana, Michael Texada, and Rochelle Ami Dicker. 2016. "A Decade of Hospital-Based Violence Intervention: Benefits and Shortcomings." *Journal of Trauma and Acute Care Surgery* 81 (6), 1156–1161. https://pubmed.ncbi.nlm.nih.gov/27653168/.

Kennedy, David M. 2019. "Response to 'What Works with Gangs: A Breakthrough.'" *Criminology & Public Policy* 18 (1): E1–E4. https://doi.org/10.1111/1745-9133.12438.

Kennedy, David, Anthony A. Braga, Anne M. Piehl, and Elin J. Waring. 2001. *Reducing Gun Violence: The Boston Gun Project's Operation Ceasefire*. Washington, DC: National Institute of Justice. https://www.ojp.gov/pdffiles1/nij/188741.pdf.

Kuhn, Sam, and Stephen Lurie. 2018. *Reconciliation between Police and Communities: Case Studies and Lessons Learned*. New York: John Jay College of Criminal Justice. https://nnscommunities.org/wp-content/uploads/2017/10/Reconciliation_Full_Report.pdf.

Larson, Anne, and Denise C. Herz. 2020. *Achieving Intentional Youth Development: The Use of the Activating Intentional Youth Development Approach (AIYDA) in GRYD Prevention Programming*. Los Angeles, CA: City of Los Angeles Mayor's Office of Gang Reduction and Youth Development (GRYD). https://www.juvenilejusticeresearch.com/sites/default/files/2020-08/GRYD%20Brief%206_Achieving%20Intentional%20Youth%20Development_7.2020.pdf.

Matei, Andreea, Leigh Courtney, Krista White, Lily Robin, Paige S. Thompson, Rod Martinez, and Janine Zweig. 2022. *Implementing Youth Violence Reduction Strategies: Findings from a Synthesis of the Literature on Gun, Group and Gang Violence*. Washington, DC: Urban Institute. https://www.urban.org/sites/default/files/publication/105301/implementing-youth-violence-reduction-strategies_1.pdf.

Muhammad, David. 2018. *Oakland's Successful Gun Violence Reduction Strategy*. Oakland, CA: National Institute for Criminal Justice Reform. https://nicjr.org/wp-content/uploads/2018/02/Oakland%E2%80%99s-Successful-Gun-Violence-Reduction-Strategy-NICJR-Jan-2018.pdf.

National Gang Center. 2010. *Best Practices to Address Community Gang Problems: OJJDP's Comprehensive Gang Model*. Washington DC: Office of Juvenile Justice and Delinquency Prevention. https://ojjdp.ojp.gov/library/publications/best-practices-address-community-gang-problems-ojjdps-comprehensive-gang-0.

National Institute for Criminal Justice Reform. 2021. *Gun Violence Problem Analysis Summary Report: Washington, DC*. Oakland, CA: National Institute for Criminal Justice Reform.

https://cjcc.dc.gov/sites/default/files/dc/sites/cjcc/release_content/attachments/DC%20Gun%20Violence%20Problem%20Analysis%20Summary%20Report.pdf.

National Network for Safe Communities. 2016. *Group Violence Intervention: An Implementation Guide*. Washington, DC: Office of Community Oriented Policing Services. https://nnscommunities.org/wp-content/uploads/2017/10/GVI_Guide_2016.pdf.

National Network for Safe Communities. 2020. *Group Violence Intervention: Issue Brief*. New York: National Network for Safe Communities at John Jay College of Criminal Justice. https://nnscommunities.org/wp-content/uploads/2020/08/GVI-Issue-Brief-1.pdf.

National Research Council. 2013. *Contagion of Violence: Workshop Summary*. Washington, DC: The National Academies Press. https://doi.org/10.17226/13489.

NNHVIP (National Network of Hospital-Based Violence Intervention Programs). 2019. *NNHVIP Policy White Paper: Hospital-Based Violence Intervention: Practices and Policies to End the Cycle of Violence*. Jersey City, NJ: Health Alliance for Violence Intervention (formerly NNHVIP). https://static1.squarespace.com/static/5d6f61730a2b610001135b79/t/5d83c0d9056f4d4cbdb9acd9/1568915699707/NNHVIP+White+Paper.pdf/.

OJJDP (Office of Juvenile Justice and Delinquency Prevention). 2009. *OJJDP Comprehensive Gang Model: Planning for Implementation*. Washington DC: Office of Juvenile Justice and Delinquency Prevention. https://nationalgangcenter.ojp.gov/sites/g/files/xyckuh331/files/media/document/implementation-manual.pdf.

Petrosino, Anthony, Patricia Campie, James Pace, Trevor Fronius, Sarah Guckenburg, Michael Wiatrowski, and Lizette Rivera. 2015. "Cross-Sector, Multi-Agency Interventions to Address Urban Youth Firearms Violence: A Rapid Evidence Assessment." *Aggression and Violent Behavior* 22: 87–96. https://doi.org/10.1016/j.avb.2015.04.001.

Pugliese, Katheryne, Paul Odér, Talib Hudson, and Jeffrey A. Butts. 2022. *Community Violence Intervention at the Roots (CVI-R): Building Evidence for Grassroots Community Violence Prevention*. New York: Research and Evaluation Center, John Jay College of Criminal Justice. https://johnjayrec.nyc/2022/06/03/cvir2022/.

Purtle, Jonathan, Rochelle Dicker, Carnell Cooper, Theodore Corbin, Michael B. Greene, Anne Marks, Diana Creaser, Dreic Topp, and Dawn Moreland. 2013. "Hospital-Based Violence Intervention Programs Save Lives and Money." *Journal of Trauma and Acute Care Surgery* 75 (2): 331–333. https://pubmed.ncbi.nlm.nih.gov/23887566/.

Reny, Tyler T., and Benjamin J. Newman. 2021. "The Opinion-Mobilizing Effect of Social Protest against Police Violence: Evidence from the 2020 George Floyd Protests." *American Political Science Review* 115 (4): 1499–1507. doi:10.1017/S0003055421000460.

Strong, Bethany L., Andrea G. Shipper, Katherine D. Downton, and Wendy G. Lane. 2016. "The Effects of Health Care–Based Violence Intervention Programs on Injury Recidivism and Costs: A Systematic Review." *Journal of Trauma and Acute Care Surgery* 81 (5): 961–970. doi: 10.1097/TA.0000000000001222.

Wilson, Jeremy M., and Steven Chermak. 2011. "Community-Driven Violence Reduction Programs: Examining Pittsburgh's One Vision One Life." *Criminology & Public Policy* 10 (4): 993–1027. https://doi.org/10.1111/j.1745-9133.2011.00763.x

Appendix: Coded Studies

Our review of the literature on interventions to address youth gun violence connected to gangs/groups covered both original studies (an empirical evaluation of a single intervention) and literature syntheses (a synthesis of findings from multiple empirical evaluations). Studies that met our criteria for inclusion and coded are listed in this appendix.

Original Studies

Arbreton, Amy J. A., and Wendy S. McClanahan. 2002. *Targeted Outreach: Boys & Girls Clubs of America's Approach to Gang Prevention and Intervention*. Philadelphia, PA: Public/Private Ventures.

Braga, Anthony A., Robert Apel, and Brandon C. Welsh. 2013. "The Spillover Effects of Focused Deterrence on Gang Violence." *Evaluation Review* 37 (3–4): 314–342.

Braga, Anthony A., David M. Hureau, and Andrew V. Papchristos. 2014. "Deterring Gang-Involved Gun Violence: Measuring the Impact of Boston's Operation Ceasefire on Street Gang Behavior." *Journal of Quantitative Criminology* 30 (1): 113–139.

Braga, Anthony A., David M. Kennedy, Elin J. Waring, and Anne Morrison Piehl. 2001. "Problem-Oriented Policing, Deterrence, and Youth Violence: An Evaluation of Boston's Operation Ceasefire." *Journal of Research in Crime and Delinquency* 38 (3): 195–225.

Braga, Anthony A., Anne M. Piehl, and David Hureau. 2009. "Controlling Violent Offenders Released to the Community: An Evaluation of the Boston Reentry Initiative." *Journal of Research in Crime and Delinquency* 46 (4): 411–436.

Braga, Anthony A., Glenn L. Pierce, Jack McDevitt, Brenda J. Bond, and Shea Cronin. 2008. "The Strategic Prevention of Gun Violence Among Gang-Involved Offenders." *Justice Quarterly* 25 (1): 132–162.

Brantingham, P. Jeffrey, Nick Sundback, Baichuan Yan, and Kristine Chan. 2017. *GRYD Intervention Incident Response and Gang Crime: 2017 Evaluation Report*. Los Angeles: University of California.

Cahill, Megan, Mark Coggeshall, David Hayeslip, Ashley Wolff, Erica Lagerson, Michelle Scott, Elizabeth Davies, Kevin Roland, and Scott Decker. 2008. *Community Collaboratives Addressing Youth Gangs: Interim Findings from the Gang Reduction Program*. Washington, DC: Urban Institute.

Cahill, Megan, and David Hayeslip. 2010. *Findings from the Evaluation of OJJDP's Gang Reduction Program Juvenile Justice Bulletin*. Washington, DC: US Department of Justice, Office of Juvenile Justice and Delinquency Prevention.

Cahill, Megan, Jesse Jannetta, Emily Tiry, Samantha Lowry, Miriam Becker-Cohen, Ellen Paddock, Maria Serakos, Loraine Park, and Karen Hennigan. 2015. *Evaluation of the Los Angeles Gang Reduction and Youth Development Program: Year 4 Evaluation Report*. Washington, DC: Urban Institute.

Campie, Patricia, Anthony Petrosino, Trevor Fronius, and Nicholas Read. 2017. *Community-Based Violence Prevention Study of the Safe and Successful Youth Initiative: An Intervention to Prevent Urban Gun Violence*. Washington, DC: US Department of Justice, Office of Justice Programs.

Decker, Scott H., and David C. Pyrooz, eds. 2015. *The Handbook of Gangs*. New York: Wiley.

Delaney, Christopher. 2006. *The Effects of Focused Deterrence on Gang Homicide: An Evaluation of Rochester's Ceasefire Program*. Rochester, NY: Rochester Institute of Technology.

Fontaine, Jocelyn, Jesse Jannetta, Andrew Papachristos, David Leitson, Anamika Dwivedi. 2017. *Put the Guns Down: Outcomes and Impacts of the Chicago Violence Reduction Strategy*. Washington, DC: Urban Institute.

Fox, Andrew M., David E. Choate, Charles M. Katz, Chirin Marvastian, and Eric C. Hedberg. 2012. *Final Evaluation of the Phoenix TRUCE Project: A Replication of Chicago CeaseFire*. Phoenix: Center for Violence Prevention and Community Safety, Arizona State University.

Fritsch, Eric J., Tory J. Caeti, and Robert W. Taylor. 1999. "Gang Suppression through Saturation Patrol, Aggressive Curfew, and Truancy Enforcement: A Quasi-Experimental Test of the Dallas Anti-Gang Initiative." *Crime & Delinquency* 451: 122–139.

Gorman-Smith, Deborah, and Franklin Cosey-Gay. 2014. *Residents' and Clients' Perceptions of Safety and CeaseFire Impact on Neighborhood Crime and Violence*. Chicago, IL: School of Social Service Administration, University of Chicago.

Henry, David B., Shannon Knoblanch, and Rannveig Sigurvinsdottir. 2014. *The Effect of Intensive CeaseFire Intervention on Crime in Four Chicago Police Beats: Quantitative Assessment*. Chicago, IL: McCormick Foundation, University of Chicago, and University of Illinois.

Huff, C. Ronald, and Kenneth S. Trump. 1996. "Youth Violence and Gangs: School Safety Initiatives in Urban and Suburban School Districts." *Education and Urban Society* 28 (4): 492–503.

McClanahan, Wendy S., Tina J. Kauh, Alice Elizabeth Manning, Paola Campos, and Chelsea Farley. 2012. *Illuminating Solutions: The Youth Violence Reductions Partnership*. Philadelphia, PA: Public/Private Ventures.

McDaniel, Dawn Delfin. 2010. *Reducing Gang Involvement Through Employment: A Pilot Intervention*. Dissertation, University of Southern California.

McDevitt, Jack, Scott H. Decker, Natalie Kroovand Hipple, Edmund F. McGarrell, John Klofas, and Tim Bynum. 2007. *Project Safe Neighborhoods: Strategic Interventions*. Washington, DC: US Department of Justice, Office of Justice Programs.

McGarrell, Edmund F., Steven Chermak, Jeremy M. Wilson, and Nicholas Corsaro. 2006. "Reducing Homicide through a "Lever-Pulling" Strategy." *Justice Quarterly* 232 (2): 214–218.

McGarrell, Edmund F., Nicholas Corsaro, Chris Melde, Natalie Hipple, Jennifer Cobbina, Timothy Bynum, and Heather Perez. 2013. *An Assessment of the Comprehensive Anti-Gang Initiative: Final Project Report*. Washington, DC: National Institute of Justice.

McGarrell, Edmund F., Natalie Kroovand Hipple, Nicholas Corsaro, Timothy S. Bynum, Heather Perez, Carol A. Zimmermann, and Melissa Garmo. 2009. *Project Safe Neighborhoods— A National Program to Reduce Gun Crime: Final Project Report*. Washington, DC: US Department of Justice, Office of Justice Programs.

Papachristos, Andrew V., and David S. Kirk. 2015. "Changing the Street Dynamic: Evaluating Chicago's Group Violence Reduction Strategy." *Criminology & Public Policy* 14 (3): 525–558.

Picard-Fritsche, Sarah, and Lenore Cerniglia. 2013. *Testing A Public Health Approach to Gun Violence: An Evaluation of Crown Heights Save Our Streets, A Replication of the Cure Violence Model*. Washington, DC: Center for Court Innovation.

Pyrooz, David, Elizabeth Weltman, and Jose Sanchez. 2019. "Intervening in the Lives of Gang Members in Denver: A Pilot Evaluation of the Gang Reduction Initiative of Denver." *Justice Evaluation Journal* 2 (2): 139–163.

Sierra- Arévalo, Michael, Charette Yanick, and Andrew V. Papachristos. 2016. "Evaluating the Effect of Project Longevity on Group-Involved Shootings and Homicides in New Haven, Connecticut." *Crime & Delinquency* 63 (4): 446–467.

Skogan, Wesley G., Susan M. Hartnett, Natalie Bump, and Jill Dubois. 2008. *Evaluation of CeaseFire-Chicago*. Washington, DC: US Department of Justice, Office of Justice Programs.

Spergel, Irving A., Kwai Ming Wa, and Rolando Villarreal Sosa. 2001. *Evaluation of the Bloomington-Normal Comprehensive Gang Program*. Chicago, IL: University of Chicago, School of Social Service Administration.

Spergel, Irving A., Kwai Ming Wa, and Rolando Villarreal Sosa. 2002. *Evaluation of the Mesa Gang Intervention Program*. Chicago, IL: University of Chicago, School of Social Service Administration.

Spergel, Irving A., Kwai Ming Wa, and Rolando Villarreal Sosa. 2003. *Evaluation of the Riverside Comprehensive Community-Wide Approach to Gang Prevention, Intervention, and Suppression*. Chicago, IL: University of Chicago, School of Social Service Administration.

Spergel, Irving A., Kwai Ming Wa, and Rolando Villarreal Sosa. 2004. *Evaluation of the San Antonio Comprehensive Community-Wide Approach to Gang Prevention, Intervention, and Suppression*. Chicago, IL: University of Chicago, School of Social Service Administration.

Spergel, Irving A., Kwai Ming Wa, and Rolando Villarreal Sosa. 2004. *Evaluation of the Tucson Comprehensive Community-Wide Approach to Gang Prevention, Intervention, and Suppression*. Chicago, IL: University of Chicago, School of Social Service Administration.

Spergel, Irving A., Kwai Ming Wa, and Rolando Villarreal Sosa. 2006. "The Comprehensive, Community-Wide, Gang Program Model: Success and Failure." In *Studying Youth Gangs*, edited by James F. Short and Lorine A. Hughes, 203–224. Lanham, MD: AltaMira Press.

Spergel, Irving A., Kwai Ming Wa, Susan Grossman, Ayad Jacob, Sungeun Ellie Choi, Rolando V. Sosa, Elisa M. Barrios, Annot Spergel, Laura Anderson, Louis Arata, et al. 2003. *The Little Village Gang Violence Reduction Project in Chicago*. Washington, DC: US Department of Justice, Office of Justice Programs.

Strutner, Stephanie. n.d. *IGNITE Youth Alliance Impact Report: Comprehensive Gang Model, Fort Pierce, FL, 2014–2018*. Port St. Lucie, FL: Roundtable of St. Lucie County.

Tita, George, K. Jack Riley, Greg Ridgeway, Clifford Grammich, Allan F. Abrahamse, and Peter W. Greenwood. 2003. *Reducing Gun Violence: Results from an Intervention in East Los Angeles*. Washington, DC: RAND Corporation.

Totten, Mike, and Sharon Dunn. 2011. *Final Evaluation Report for the North Central Community Association Regina Anti-Gang Services Project*. Gatineau, QC: Totten and Associates.

Wallace, Danielle, Andrew V. Papachristos, Tracey Meares, and Jeffrey Fagan. 2016. "Desistance and Legitimacy: The Impact of Offender Notification Meetings on Recidivism among High-Risk Offenders." *Justice Quarterly* 33 (7): 1237–1264.

Webster, Daniel W., Jennifer Mendel Whitehill, Jon S. Vernick, and Frank C. Curriero. 2013. "Effects of Baltimore's Safe Streets Program on Gun Violence: A Replication of Chicago's CeaseFire Program." *Journal of Urban Health* 90 (1): 27–40.

Webster, Daniel W., Jennifer Mendel Whitehall, Jon S. Vernick, and Elizabeth M. Parker. 2012. *Evaluation of Baltimore's Safe Streets Program: Effects on Attitudes, Participants' Experiences, and Gun Violence*. Baltimore, MD: Johns Hopkins Bloomberg School of Public Health.

Wilson, Jeremy M., and Steven Chermak. 2011. "Community-Driven Violence Reduction Programs: Examining Pittsburgh's One Vision One Life." *Criminology & Public Policy* 10 (4): 993–1027.

Wilson, Jeremy M., Steven Chermak, and Edmund F. McGarrell. 2011. *Community-Based Violence Prevention: An Assessment of Pittsburgh's One Vision One Life Program*. Santa Monica, CA: RAND Corporation.

Literature Syntheses

Abt, Thomas, and Christopher Winship. 2016. *What Works in Reducing Community Violence: A Meta-Review and Field Study for the Northern Triangle*. Bethesda, MD: Democracy International, Inc.

Braga, Anthony A., and David L. Weisburd. 2011. "The Effects of Focused Deterrence Strategies on Crime: A Systematic Review and Meta-Analysis of the Empirical Evidence." *Journal of Research in Crime and Delinquency* 49 (3): 323–358.

Braga, Anthony A., David Weisburd, and Brandon Turchan. 2018. "Focused Deterrence Strategies and Crime Control: An Updated Systematic Review and Meta-Analysis of the Empirical Evidence." *Criminology & Public Policy* 17 (1): 205–250.

Butts, Jeffrey A., Caterina Gouvis Roman, Lindsay Bostwick, and Jeremy R. Porter. 2015. "Cure Violence: A Public Health Model to Reduce Gun Violence." *Annual Review of Public Health* 36: 39–53.

Decker, Scott H., and Reed L. Winifred. 2002. *Responding to Gangs: Evaluation and Research*. Washington, DC: US Department of Justice, Office of Justice Programs.

Development Services Group, Inc. 2010. *Community- and Problem-Oriented Policing*. Washington, DC: Office of Juvenile Justice and Delinquency Planning.

Development Services Group, Inc. 2014. *Gang Prevention*. Washington, DC: Office of Juvenile Justice and Delinquency Prevention.

Development Services Group, Inc. 2016. *Gun Violence and Youth*. Washington, DC: Office of Juvenile Justice and Delinquency Prevention.

Ericson, Nels. 2001. *Public/Private Ventures' Evaluation of Faith-Based Programs*. Washington, DC: US Department of Justice, Office of Justice Programs, Office of Juvenile Justice and Delinquency Prevention.

Giffords Law Center. 2017. *Investing in Intervention: The Critical Role of State-Level Support in Breaking the Cycle of Urban Gun Violence*. San Francisco, CA: Giffords Law Center.

Howell, James C. 2000. *Youth Gang Programs and Strategies*. Washington, DC: US Department of Justice, Office of Juvenile Justice and Delinquency Prevention.

Howell, James C., and Megan Q. Howell. 2019. "Serious Gang Problems in the United States: What to Do?" In *Critical Issues in Crime and Justice*, 3rd ed., edited by Dan Okeda and Mary H. Maguire, 156–170. Los Angeles, CA: Sage Publications.

Howell, James C., and Michelle A. Young. 2013. "What Works to Curb U.S. Street Gang Violence." *The Criminologist* 38 (1): 39–41.

Jannetta, Jesse, Megan Denver, Caterina J., Roman, Nicole P. Svajlenka, Martha Ross, and Benjamin Orr. 2010. *The District of Columbia's Mayor's Focused Improvement Area Initiative: Review of the Literature Relevant to Collaborative Crime Reduction*. Washington, DC: Urban Institute

Klein, Malcolm W., and Cheryl L. Maxson. 2006. *Street Gang Patterns and Policies*. New York: Oxford University Press.

Meares, Tracey, Andrew V. Papachristos, and Jeffery Fagan. 2009. *Homicide and Gun Violence in Chicago: Evaluation and Summary of the Project Safe Neighborhoods Program*. Washington, DC: US Department of Justice, Office of Justice Programs.

National Crime Prevention Centre. 2007. *Addressing Youth Gang Problems: An Overview of Programs and Practices*. Ottawa, ON: National Crime Prevention Centre.

Petersen, Rebecca D., and James C. Howell. 2013. "Program Approaches for Girls in Gangs: Female Specific or Gender Neutral?" *Criminal Justice Review* 38 (4): 491–509.

Petrosino, Anthony, Patricia Campie, James Pace, Trevor Fronius, Sarah Guckenburg, Michael Wiatrowski, and Lizette Rivera. 2015. "Cross-Sector, Multi-Agency Interventions to Address Urban Youth Firearms Violence: A Rapid Evidence Assessment." *Aggression and Violent Behavior* 22: 87–96.

Roman, Caterina G., Scott H. Decker, and David C. Pyrooz. 2017. "Leveraging the Pushes and Pulls of Gang Disengagement to Improve Gang Intervention: Findings from Three Multi-Site Studies and a Review of Relevant Gang Programs." *Journal of Crime and Justice* 40 (3): 316–336.

Short, James F. 2008. "Book Review of Spergel, I. A. 2007. *Reducing Youth Gang Violence: The Little Gang Project in Chicago.*" *Social Service Review* 821: 153–157.

Wong, Jennifer S., Jason Gravel, Martin Bouchard, Carlo Morselli, and Karine Descormiers. 2012. *Effectiveness of Street Gang Control Strategies: A Systematic Review and Meta-Analysis of Evaluation Studies.* Ottawa, ON: Public Safety Canada.

Index

For the benefit of digital users, indexed terms that span two pages (e.g., 52–53) may, on occasion, appear on only one of those pages.

Tables and figures are indicated by *t* and *f* following the page number

A World of Gangs (Hagedorn), 171*t*, 265–66, 723–24, 726–27
Advance Peace, 876, 879–80, 881–82, 883, 884–85
Africa
    African Americans in gangs, 159–60, 174, 243–44, 278
    African slaves, 352–57
    Characteristics in Africa Conducive to Gangs, 502–9
    Gangs in Africa, 400–1, 500–1
        South Africa, 264, 274, 500, 503, 505, 643–44
    Gangs in the African, South Asian, and Caribbean context, 151–58, 170–72
Alexander, Ava, 8, 470
Almighty Latin King and Queen Nation (ALKQN), 272, 275, 667–68
American gangs, 17, 18–19, 258–59, 703–4
anomie theory, 178–79
anti-gang and gang crime legislation, 2, 94–96, 97, 226, 228, 329, 522–23, 532–33, 680, 810–14, 815–16, 818–19, 820–21, 841, 858
    Anti-Gang Initiative (CAGI), 211, 226
Arizona Arrestee Drug Abuse Monitoring Program, 684–85, 689
Asia, 258, 401–2, 500, 660–61
    Asian gangs, 107, 151*t*, 174 (*see also* Africa: Gangs in the African, South Asian, and Caribbean context)
    characteristics in Asia conducive to gangs, 502–6
Aspholm, Roberto, 10, 714, 750
Australia
    gangs in Australia, 178, 401, 643–44

Barrio Gangs (Vigil), 168*t*, 718, 753, 754, 761–62
Barrio 18 (18th Street), 128, 330–32, 341–42, 662, 667
"big data" policing, 11, 809–10, 820–21, 834
Biondi, Karina, 331
Blackstone Rangers, 603–4
bloods, 18–19, 78, 93, 94–95, 127, 360, 382, 521–22, 567–68, 569, 703–4
Bloch, Stefano, 5, 122
Blueprints for Healthy Young Development, 775, 776, 777
Boston, 60–61, 62, 65, 67, 75, 76–77, 80–81, 250, 259, 607, 716, 841–42, 855, 857, 859
    Boston Gun Project, 76, 77–78, 80, 81, 82–83, 857
    gangs in, 82–83, 379–80, 396, 601, 677, 852
    Operation Ceasefire, 75, 171*t*, 229, 246, 836, 841–42, 857–58, 872
Bouchard, Martin, 4, 36
Boxer, Paul, 10, 773
Boys and Girls Club of America (BGCA), 686, 708–9, 844
Braga, Anthony, 11, 849
Brantingham, Jeffrey, 8, 518, 809
Broidy, Lisa, 7, 395
Bubolz, Bryan, 4–5, 106
Bucerius, Sandra, 6, 287, 290*t*

cafeteria-style offending, 852
Cahill, Meagan, 5–6, 235
CalGang database, 83, 249, 814–15
California, 10, 16–17, 94, 96, 97–98, 99, 262, 290*t*, 382, 519–20, 566, 584, 735–37, 749, 787, 849, 852. *See also* CalGang database

California (*cont.*)
  gangs in, 79, 124, 168t, 180, 237, 246, 381, 401–2, 638–40, 643–46, 648, 650, 652, 659, 665, 761, 764–65
  Street Terrorism Enforcement and Prevention (STEP), 95–96
Canada, 60–61, 184, 288, 622, 856
  gangs in, 6, 49, 312, 643–44
Caribbean, 6–7, 330–31, 351, 502, 506, 622
  gangs in, 351, 500, 659 (*see also* Africa: Gangs in the African, South Asian, and Caribbean context)
Carlton, Mary Poulin, 5, 207
Carson Dena, 10
cartels, 330–31, 503–4, 506, 721, 723–63
causes and correlates of Delinquency Research, 5, 140–41, 181–82, 223, 224–25, 733
Cesar, Gabriel, 9, 560
change point detection (CPD) approach, 5, 142, 145, 146, 147, 147f, 149, 150–59
Chen, Susan, 8, 470
Chicago, 60–61, 62, 65, 66, 67, 75, 76–77, 78, 82, 124, 159–60, 161, 225–26, 251, 396, 433, 624, 628, 677, 721–22, 723–24, 755, 841–42, 851–52
  Chicago's Black Disciples, 604
  Chicago School, 68, 124, 159–60, 161, 178–79, 270, 273, 444, 448–49, 722, 745
  gangs in, 16–17, 18–19, 56, 61, 64, 77–78, 81, 92, 122–23, 160t, 171t, 246, 259, 264, 272, 274, 378, 384–86, 400, 604, 660–61, 662–63, 667–68, 681–82, 683, 719, 725
  Gangster Disciples (Chicago), 681–82
Chicano/a gangs, 107, 126, 400, 717, 748, 753, 757–58, 759–60, 761–62, 764–65
China, 24, 353, 503
  Hong Kong, 259, 271, 506–7
City Gangs (Miller), 377, 396
civil gang injunctions (CGI's), 10, 129–30, 168–70, 380, 532–33, 735–36, 811–12, 813, 836, 840–41
code of the street, 377–78, 382, 386, 400–1, 484–85, 644
communication, 55, 56, 321, 445–46, 458–59, 602, 621–22, 759, 776, 777, 783, 854, 855, 860, 872, 879, 881–82
  non-verbal, 78, 384

  technology and social media, 27–29, 82–83, 387, 618, 623, 628, 667, 668
Community-Oriented Policing Services (COPS), 208, 686. *See also* anti-gang initiative
Community Resources Against Street Hoodlums (CRASH), 531–32, 812–13
Competing for Control (Decker), 649
Comprehensive Gang Model, 5, 11, 210–11, 225–28, 237, 687, 870, 873–75, 878, 879, 880–85
COMPSTAT, 817, 858–59
concentrated disadvantage, 463, 757
Cosa Nostra, 37, 42, 43, 262
Covey, Herb, 8, 499
crime and delinquency, 8, 55, 151t, 213t, 464, 519–20, 677, 697–98
  gang violence, 25, 54, 55, 74, 89–90, 94–95, 99–100, 110, 116, 127–28, 172, 173t, 180, 185, 186, 207, 210, 211, 213t, 221, 223, 227–28, 229–30, 235, 272–73, 274, 304, 316–17, 320, 321, 330–31, 332, 333t, 343, 351, 386, 396, 401–2, 404, 503, 505, 521, 546, 548, 554–55, 564, 568, 582, 585, 618–19, 621, 622, 623, 625, 629, 666–67, 680, 682–83, 687, 703–4, 705, 719, 735, 749, 781, 790, 803–4, 805, 810–11, 819–20, 837, 841–42, 843–44, 849, 870
  gun violence, 11, 54, 174–75, 250–51, 618, 620, 621–22, 623–25, 719, 781, 836, 841–42, 849–70
Crips, 18–19, 78, 93, 94–95, 124, 127, 360, 382, 384–85, 521–23, 659, 667, 703–4, 787, 788, 789
critical race theory, 9, 618
Crutchfield, Robert, 709
culture-as-products, 7, 375–76, 376t, 383–88
culture-as-toolkit, 7, 375–76, 376t, 380–83
culture-as-values, 7, 375, 376–83, 388, 389
Cure Violence model (initially Chicago Ceasefire), 229, 251, 709, 873

Decker, Scott H., 3–4, 10, 15, 228, 230, 263, 561, 649, 677
Delinquent Boys: The Culture of the Gang (Cohen), 160t, 161, 178–79
Densley, James, 1

Denver, 224–25, 450, 677
Denver Youth Survey (DYS), 181–82, 224–25, 697–98
depersonalization, 4–5, 107, 112–13
deprivation theory, 638
Descormiers, Karine, 4, 36
Deuchar, Ross, 8, 543
deviant groups, 4, 22–23
differential association, 166–68, 170, 477–78
disengagement/desistance, 4–5, 8, 9–26, 107, 110–17, 401–2, 406, 458–61, 462, 463, 481, 564, 569–70, 599, 600, 602, 608, 678, 682, 684–85, 689–90, 701–2, 774, 780–81, 836, 837–38, 843
  emotional, 479
  moral, 431–32, 483
Doyle, Caroline, 331
drive-by shooting, 388, 520–21, 764–65, 816, 832
drug dealing, 37, 40, 44, 82–83, 89–90, 126, 295, 531, 552–53, 718, 719, 720, 724, 787–88
drug trafficking, 43, 79, 84, 180, 223, 500, 506, 509–10, 688, 719, 851–52
drug use, 25, 59, 63, 180–81, 321, 335, 377, 501–2, 510, 601, 627, 684, 689, 718, 747, 748
duration of gangs, 22, 356, 499–500

educational pipeline, 9, 578
  school-to-prison pipeline, 579–82
Egley, Arlen, 5–6, 235
El Rukins, 603–4, 609
Elsaesser, Caitlin, 9, 618
emerging gang city, 677, 678–80
Engel, Jesse, 10, 787
enhancement effect/ hypothesis, 7–8, 58–59, 62, 414, 434, 445, 449, 454, 460–61, 471, 475–76, 640, 682
Esbensen Finn-Aage, 10, 677, 696
ethnicity, 17, 19, 91, 106, 174, 177, 186, 239, 243–44, 278, 293–94, 404–5, 478, 510, 578–79, 580, 583, 645, 659, 701–2, 706, 755, 764, 790
Eurogang, 15, 140–41, 170, 182–83, 511, 622, 696–97, 703–5, 732, 733, 736–37, 739–40
  definitions, 3–4, 15, 40, 75, 143, 331–32, 705–6
  expert survey, 360, 363

Europe, 1, 8, 15, 159–60, 271, 279, 288, 352–53, 354, 499, 502, 503, 508–9, 544, 622, 651, 659, 664, 704, 708, 740. *See also* Eurogang
  gangs in, 170, 401–2, 504, 506–7, 510, 660–61, 663, 667, 703–4, 736–37 (*see also* Eurogang)
extremist groups, 175, 248, 503–4, 506–7, 682, 685

Facebook, 623–24, 800–1, 833, 840. *See* communication
facilitation effect/ hypothesis, 58–59, 62, 209, 414, 433–34, 455, 471, 640
familial nature of gangs, 96–97, 98, 112, 302, 341, 560–61, 568, 583–84
Federal Bureau of Investigation (FBI), 76, 77, 82, 84, 336, 664–65, 689
  National Gang Assessment, 79
  National Gang Intelligence Center (NGIC), 79, 180, 224
female gang members, 6, 110–11, 163, 223, 244, 272, 288, 293–94, 331, 332, 337–38, 341–42, 344, 396, 397, 399, 400, 403, 405, 500, 568, 720–21, 732–33, 746–47, 748, 749
Fernandez Tiffany, 9, 560
focused deterrence, 11, 74, 75, 174–75, 185, 250, 780–81, 849, 870, 872–73, 874, 879–80, 881, 882–84, 885
Fraser, Alistair, 6, 259, 269
Freng, Adrienne, 6, 10, 312, 707
functional family therapy (FFT), 10, 186, 213t, 228–29, 566–67, 774, 776, 782, 783
  FFT-G, 228–29, 567, 776–77

gang affiliation, 98, 99–100, 108, 122, 209, 378–79, 382–83, 430, 508, 525–26, 602–3, 612–13, 638–39, 681–82, 689, 706, 773–74, 778, 779–80, 814, 881
gang assessments, 97–98, 174–75, 181, 227, 444, 689
gang characteristics, 19, 23, 68, 239, 242, 244, 315–16, 519–20, 705
gang cliques, 8, 519, 523–26, 530–33, 531f, 534, 663–64, 734
gang culture, 7, 81, 127, 262, 276, 316–17, 318–19, 375, 400, 507, 510, 546–47, 549, 605–6, 607, 608–9, 622, 625, 630–31, 665–66, 667, 749, 840–41

gang databases, 97–98, 116–17, 248–49, 277, 295–96, 811–12, 813–16, 833–34, 860. *See also* CalGang database
gang desistance. *See* desistance/disengagement
gang dynamics, 4, 7, 58, 65, 82–83, 271, 272, 274, 275, 295, 456, 659, 683, 718–19, 726, 747, 748, 852
gang embeddedness, 108, 110, 113–14, 115, 186, 552, 554, 685
gang enhancements, 98, 682
gang formation, 6, 60, 92, 93, 126, 187, 360, 375, 501, 502, 504–5, 508–9, 510–11, 756–58, 763, 843
gang graffiti, 124, 125, 803
gang interventions, 69, 110–11, 244–45, 247, 250–51, 383, 571, 687
Gang Reduction Program (GRP), 226
Gang Resistance Education and Training (G.R.E.A.T.), 5, 41, 159–60, 182, 184, 185, 228, 321, 566, 588, 696–97, 698–702, 703, 705–6, 707–9, 739–40
gang structure, 78, 227–28, 275, 320, 385–86, 402–6, 554, 639, 734–35
gang units, 168–70, 174–75, 181, 522–23, 531–33, 584, 811–12, 813–14, 815–16, 832, 834, 835–36, 837, 858
Gangs and Delinquency in Developmental Perspective (Thornberry), 182
gangs and politics, 10, 16–18, 126, 174, 187, 244–45, 269, 271, 272, 273–76, 278–79, 295, 338, 356, 359, 361, 363, 506–7, 550, 663, 738, 760
Garcia-Leys, Sean, 10, 788, 794
girls. *See* female gang members
Girn, Alysha, 4, 36
globalization, 8, 151*t*, 170, 272, 273, 501, 507, 659, 660, 663, 664, 666–68, 715, 722, 723
Going Down to the Barrio (Moore), 749, 750
Google Ideas, 679*f*, 681, 682, 684, 685
Gottfredson, Denise, 229, 709, 776
governance theory of prison gangs, 9, 638, 639–40, 642–43, 644–46, 649–50
Gravel, Jason, 5, 139
group process, 1, 7, 21, 36, 55–56, 58–59, 61–62, 63–69, 91–92, 108, 127, 161–63, 164*t*, 170, 178–79, 186, 402, 404–5, 416–24, 456–58, 561, 562–63, 601, 609–10, 611–12, 618–19, 640, 678, 680, 682–84, 724, 747, 840–41
group violence intervention, 74, 75, 174–75, 185, 229, 250, 853
Gutiérrez Rivera, Lirio, 331
Gypsy Jokers, 258, 262

Hagedorn John, 10, 19, 151*t*, 168*t*, 171*t*, 264, 265–66, 270, 376*t*, 384–85, 582–83, 604, 664, 677, 714, 750, 758
Hallsworth, Simon, 17–18, 19, 276
Harding, Simon, 8, 543
hate groups, 175, 248, 603, 609
Hawkins, Darnell, 709
hierarchy, 45, 47, 76, 110–11, 114, 320, 356, 385–86, 404, 518–19, 550, 551, 606, 645
hispanic gangs, 315–16. *See also* Latino gangs
Hollenbeck, 523–26, 528–34, 531*f*, 858
Homeboy Industries, 329, 764, 855, 857–58
Homeboys: Gangs, Drugs, and Prisons in the Barrios of Los Angeles (Moore), 164*t*, 718, 748
Honor and the American Dream (Horowitz), 718
Horowitz, Ruth, 163, 290*t*, 298–99, 300, 301, 302, 378, 400, 607, 718
Howell, James, 5–6, 230, 235
Huerta, Adrian, 9, 577
Huff, Ron, 2, 168*t*, 243, 677, 684, 738
Hughes, Lorine, 7, 395
human trafficking, 76, 84, 509
Hureau, David, 4, 54

identity salience, 4–5, 107, 110–11, 112–13, 114
Illinois, 79, 225–26, 638–40, 643–44, 718, 721–22, 725, 750. *See also* Chicago
immigrant, 16–17, 107–8, 293–94, 384–85, 478, 504, 510, 722, 763. *See also* Immigrant Rights Clinic; transnational gangs
Immigrant Rights Clinic, 797, 800, 801–2
immigration, 1–2, 81, 159–60, 295, 504, 508–9, 510, 659, 689–90
immigration policy-deportations, 274, 295, 360, 510, 659, 664–66
importation theory, 638–39
India, 139, 187, 352, 353, 503, 643–44, 647
indigenous communities, 178, 474
gangs in, 6, 312, 384–85

informal-diffuse perspective, 45–46, 683
initiation into gangs, 41, 77, 93, 108, 320, 474, 475–76, 562, 746
　female gang members, 292–93, 379
instrumental-rational perspective, 37–38, 45–46, 683
International Self-Report Delinquency (ISRD), 24, 739–40
Internet, 3–4, 30, 262, 386, 406, 763. *See also* communication; Facebook
　gangs using, 8, 16, 26–28, 127–28, 508, 645, 667, 682
　Internet BANGING, 27, 173*t*, 386, 621–22
intervention strategies, 225, 229–30, 683, 843, 870. *See also* gang interventions

jails. *See* prison and jails
Jannetta, Jesse, 11, 870
joining a gang, 7–8, 9, 43, 60, 63, 107, 170, 174, 185, 242, 251, 317–19, 321, 395, 413, 414–16, 424–25, 428–32, 433–35, 450–51, 453–55, 462, 471, 474–75, 479, 518, 560–61, 562, 563, 564–67, 570–71, 580, 651–52, 683, 736, 781, 842
José Méndez, María, 6, 329

Kane, Candice, 230, 709
Kelley, Barbara Tatem, 5, 207
Kennedy, David, 4, 74, 883
Kerig, Patricia, 8, 470
Klein, Malcom, 3–4, 10, 15, 80–81, 161–63, 164*t*, 168*t*, 170, 171*t*, 178–79, 180, 565
Kubik, Joanna, 10, 773
Kubiniec, Haleigh, 9, 599

labor market, 93, 397, 398, 747, 750–51
Latin America and Caribbean, 24, 329–31, 332–35, 336, 345, 507, 647–48, 651, 661, 666
　Belize, 330–31, 351–52, 358–59, 360–61, 362–64, 659, 665
　Colombia, 330–31, 333*t*, 503
　Ecuador, 275, 330–31, 506, 643–44, 668
　El Salvador, 81, 295, 330–32, 333*t*, 340, 341–42, 343, 500, 503, 505–6, 605–6, 611, 643–44, 662, 665, 667, 668
　Guatemala, 274, 330–32, 333*t*, 337, 338, 343, 344–45, 502, 503, 643–44, 662, 665
　Honduras, 330–32, 333*t*, 340, 342, 360, 500, 502, 503, 643–44, 662, 668
　Mexico, 330–31, 502, 504–5, 507, 523, 643–44, 733
Latin Kings, 56, 77–78, 127, 525–26, 603–4, 659, 667, 668
Latino gangs, 174, 534, 724, 764–65
Lauger, Tim, 9, 599
leadership in gangs, 18, 45–46, 48–49, 76, 82, 84, 127, 292–93, 320, 519–20, 603–4, 760, 835–36
Lee, Sou, 4–5, 106
Levenson, Deborah, 331
Leverso, John, 1, 54
life course, 7, 9, 106, 151*t*, 174, 225, 272, 401–2, 414, 415, 416–24, 434, 458, 560, 562, 564–66, 570–71, 678
　school life course, 578
London, 722
　gangs in, 42, 186, 276, 401–2, 553, 554–55
Lopez-Aguado, Patrick, 4, 89
Los Angeles, 17, 60–61, 77, 78, 81, 94–95, 123, 124, 125, 151*t*, 251, 259, 274, 569–70, 682, 720–21, 733, 735, 745, 749–50, 764, 787–88, 789–91, 849, 851–52, 855, 858, 859, 862–63
　gangs in, 8, 18–19, 65, 76–77, 78, 94, 126, 384–85, 400, 660–61, 662, 667, 680, 703–4, 717, 753, 794 (*see also* Hollenbeck)
　Gang Reduction and Youth Development (GYRD), 876
　LAPD, 11, 18, 83, 94–95, 520, 523, 525–26, 531–32, 789–90, 810–11, 812–13, 816, 818, 821, 858–59
loyalty
　gangs, 45–46, 78, 108–9, 395–96, 397, 457, 545–46, 553, 563, 568, 760, 762

MacDonald, John, 11, 849
Mafia, 21–22, 42, 81, 143, 264, 723–24
Maguire, Edward, 6–7, 351
Mara Salvatrucha (MS-13), 78, 84, 127, 330–32, 341–42, 509–10, 521–22, 659, 662–63, 667, 765
Maras, 93, 172, 274, 331–32, 506, 507, 509–10. *See also* Mara Salvatrucha
Marcello, Stephanie, 10, 773

marginalization, 6, 107–8, 126, 163, 174, 295, 312, 318, 319, 323, 329, 376–77, 379–80, 382, 397, 471, 478, 480–81, 484, 501, 504, 508, 510, 511, 546–47, 548, 554, 578–79, 621, 659, 661–62, 665, 666, 706, 753, 754–55, 756–57, 761
Marijuana, 294–95, 335, 506, 510, 610, 748
marriage, 114, 293–94, 300, 378–79, 426, 459, 461–62, 588, 684, 842–43
masculinity, 7, 110–11, 272–73, 293–94, 298–99, 336–37, 340–41, 343, 377, 378–79, 382–83, 395–97, 398–402, 403–6, 450, 481, 548–49, 568, 569, 570–71, 600–1, 602, 607, 639, 685
Maxson, Cheryl, 10, 18–19, 163, 704, 705, 732
Melde, Chris, 10, 702
Mendez, Lucybel, 8, 470
mental health and gangs, 8, 151t, 174, 314–15, 317, 342–43, 359, 426, 470, 578, 582, 591, 623, 774–75, 850, 862–63, 877–78
Mexican Mafia, 521–22, 643, 749, 764–65
Miguel Cruz, José, 9, 659
Miller, Jody, 290t, 379, 397, 399, 677, 690
Miller, Walter, 10, 178–79, 210, 223, 230, 236, 396, 399
mobilizing events, 683
Moore, Caylin, 7, 375
Moore, Joan, 10, 123, 163, 164t, 168t, 290t, 717, 751, 754, 757, 760–62
Moore, John, 230
moral disengagement. *See* disengagement
moral panics, 4, 93, 96–97, 295, 749, 757
Moreno, Mark E., 10, 753
motorcycle gangs, 22, 42, 43, 76, 82–83, 84, 143, 247–48
Moule, Rick, 10, 677
multisystemic therapy (MST), 10, 186, 566–67, 773, 774, 777–79, 781, 782, 783

National Assessment of Law Enforcement Anti-Gang Information Resources, 223–24
National Crime Agency, 553
National Crime Prevention Council, 703
National Gang Center, 180, 222, 238, 239, 245–47, 250
National Institute of Justice (NIJ), 5–6, 80–81, 180–81, 207–10, 211, 212, 213t, 221–22, 224, 227–30, 236, 246–47, 499–500, 696–97, 699, 700, 702, 870–71

National Longitudinal Study of Adolescent to Adult Health, 182, 474
National Longitudinal Survey of Youth (NLSY), 182, 235, 242, 433, 565
National Youth Gang Center (NYGC), 180, 210–11, 224, 238, 239
National Youth Gang Survey (NYGS), 82, 210–11, 221, 224, 235, 689
networks
  criminal, 82–83, 173t, 211, 356, 507, 662–63, 664–65
  gang, 4, 47–48, 54, 55, 56–57, 58–59, 60–61, 65, 66–67, 68–69, 74, 76, 91, 92, 96–98, 100, 151t, 186, 209, 213t, 246, 251, 322, 355–56, 404, 523, 599–600, 606–7, 643, 644, 761–62, 779–80, 881–82
New York City, 81, 262, 397, 841–42, 849, 860
NYPD, 79, 80–81, 834
Novich, Madeleine, 11, 832

Office of Justice Programs (OJP), 5, 179, 180, 207–8, 210, 212, 221–22, 229–30
Office of Juvenile Justice and Delinquency Prevention (OJJDP), 179, 180, 181–82, 207–8, 210–11, 213–20t, 221, 222, 223–30, 235, 238, 245–46, 687, 697–98, 870–71
Operation Hammer, 841, 860
Operation LASER, 818
organized crime, 4, 21–22, 41, 42, 43, 45–46, 47, 48–49, 76–77, 82–83, 84, 174, 227–28, 262, 265, 356, 364, 499–500, 505–6, 546–49, 554–55, 666, 668, 677, 681–82, 685, 715, 722, 723–24

Pandillas, 331–32, 503
Papachristos, Andrew, 4, 54, 709
Pathways to Desistance, 182, 474, 475
patriarchal bargain, 302
Patton, Desmond, 9, 618
peer groups, 4, 36, 37–39, 39t, 40–41, 42, 43, 44, 45, 46–48, 49, 62, 109–10, 292–93, 318–19, 377, 415, 424–25, 454, 462, 550, 718–19
persistence in gangs, 4–5, 107, 109–10, 112–13, 518–19
People and Folks (Hagedorn), 714, 717, 718–19, 720–21, 725, 726–27, 750
People ex rel. Gallo v. Acuna, 789–90, 791f

Peterson, Dana, 10, 696
Philadelphia, 65, 270, 377–78, 567, 734, 855–56
    gangs in, 66, 258, 417t
Phoenix, 397–98, 417t, 677–78, 682, 699, 841–42
Pittsburgh, 181–82, 224–25, 417t, 697–98
policing
    gang suppression, 10, 11, 17, 18, 172, 174–75, 179, 224, 225–26, 227, 237, 249, 666, 687, 749, 763, 789, 805, 806, 812, 816, 832, 833–34, 836, 837, 839, 840, 870, 873–74, 880–81, 885–86 (see also Comprehensive Gang Model)
    mano dura, 278, 329, 330
    See also gang units
politicization and radicalization, 8, 100–1, 213t, 274, 506–7
poverty, 270, 276, 314–15, 354, 358, 359, 376–80, 376t, 387–88, 396, 402, 501, 502, 541–674, 716–17, 746–47, 754–55
Power on the Inside (Roth), 259
prison and jails, 96, 151t, 166, 174, 185, 638, 842
    gangs in, 9, 76, 126, 151t, 239, 247–48, 259, 262, 264, 303, 317, 322, 506, 638, 682, 684, 723–24, 754–55, 759, 762, 764–65
probation and parole, 99–100, 227–28, 473, 688, 716, 777–78, 782, 788–89, 798, 801–2, 803–4, 813, 852–53, 856, 860, 861–62, 883
Project Safe Neighborhoods (PSN), 211, 226, 229–30
public health model, 251, 870, 871, 872–73, 874–75, 878, 879, 880, 881–82, 884
public schools, 59, 432–33, 579–80, 582, 724. See also St. Louis Public Schools' Anti-Drug, Anti-Gang Task Force
"pull" and "push" forces, 9, 209, 424–25, 458, 471, 569, 684–85, 780–81
Pyrooz, David, 10, 649, 677

qualitative methods, 23, 122, 260, 362, 612–13
quantitative methods, 23, 359, 687–88
quintessential group process, 63
quintessential population heterogeneity perspective, 424

race and ethnicity
    racialization, 9, 93, 94, 95–96, 98–100, 126, 269, 270, 274, 277, 278, 295, 314–15, 335, 579, 584, 725, 839, 883–84

racism, 6, 56, 68–69, 269, 273, 295, 312–13, 319, 323, 400–1, 403, 413–14, 502, 561–62, 640, 648, 723, 747, 758, 832
Racketeer Influenced and Corrupt Organizations Act (RICO), 127, 759
Ranum, Elin Cecilie, 331
rational choice theory, 7–8, 444, 445–60, 462
recidivism, 151t, 174, 228–29, 314–15, 322, 567, 648, 774, 778
recruitment, 48, 151t, 304, 316–17, 318, 463, 506–7, 520, 577, 684, 843
reflected appraisals, 4–5, 107, 109, 110–11, 112–13
Reid, Shannon, 10, 732
relational perspective, 4, 56–57
religion and gangs, 9, 599
Reséndiz Rivera, Nelly Erandy, 331, 333t
respect in gangs, 43, 63–64, 80, 96–97, 107–8, 109, 264, 319, 320, 378, 384, 395, 450–51, 452–53, 459–60, 551, 552, 568, 583, 584, 649–50, 667, 687
responses to gangs, 224, 225, 251
retaliation/ retaliatory violence, 74–75, 77, 79–80, 229, 250–51, 320, 321, 382, 484, 520, 549, 553, 604, 680, 683, 816, 850, 859, 862–63, 872–73, 876, 879–80, 881
risk factors for gang membership, 171t, 226, 227–28, 246, 251, 317–18, 319, 321, 415, 429, 433, 434, 461, 474, 475–76, 477–82, 501–2, 503–4, 555, 560, 566, 775
Robin, Lily, 11, 870
Rochester Youth Development Study (RYDS), 181–82, 224–25, 697–98
Rodriguez, Nancy, 690, 709
Rosen, Jonathan, 9, 659
Roth, Mitchel, 6, 256
Ruiz, Pamela, 331
Rural Gang Initiative, 225–26

Sampó, Carolina, 331
Sanchez, Jose, 7, 413, 678
Santacruz Giralt, María Lizet, 331, 333t
Saunders-Hastings, Katherine, 331, 333t, 343
school and gangs. See also public schools
    expulsion, 577–78, 579–80
    school failure, 414–15
    school shootings/ violence, 151t, 580
Schwarze, Tilman, 6, 269

secrecy, 45–46, 47, 139, 499–500
selection effect/ hypothesis, 58–59, 415, 424, 425, 426, 428–30, 431, 432, 651–52
self-actualization, 562–63, 564, 565, 567, 568
self-control, 109–10, 415–25, 417*t*, 433, 626, 644
self-report, 26, 41–42, 43, 49, 79, 224–25, 235, 240–41, 242, 243–44, 378, 386, 395, 417*t*, 432–33, 470–71, 475, 563, 566, 577, 584, 661, 689, 698, 704, 705, 778–95, 838, 842. *See also* International Self-Report Delinquency (ISRD)
serious violence, 79, 554–55, 611–12, 853, 855, 862–63
set space, 124, 127, 820, 821
sexism, 273, 293–94, 299–300, 302, 398
sexual violence, 272–73, 299–300, 339, 342, 448, 819
Short, Jim, 10, 18–19, 435
shot caller, 116, 645–46
signaling theory, 108, 415, 458–59, 460, 683, 685
Singapore, 417*t*, 643–44
sisterhood, 341, 397, 564
Skarbek, David, 9, 638
Slum, 275, 359, 379–80, 413, 505, 662, 722–23
social bond theory, 415
social capital, 543, 562, 775
social capital theory, 8, 543, 546
social construction of gangs, 4, 89, 720–21
social dynamics, 209, 879–80, 881–82
social disorganization, 318, 376–77, 376*t*, 471, 501, 757, 873–74, 880–81
social intervention, 225, 226, 687, 873–74, 880–81
social learning, 151*t*, 166–68, 170, 415, 477–78
social media. *See* communciation
social network analysis, 185, 186, 852
socioeconomic status, 17, 414–15, 578–79, 626
Spergel, Irving, 10, 178–79, 223–24, 225, 230, 687, 873–74. *See also* Comprehensive Gang Model
St. Clair, Hannah, 6, 312
St. Louis, 677–80, 682, 684–85, 686–87, 852
 gangs in, 264–65, 397, 532, 677, 680
 Gang Studies and Safe Futures, 685–86, 687, 688

Homicide Project, 686
 Public Schools' Anti-Drugs and Anti-Gangs Task Force, 680, 686, 688
 Mayor's Task Force on Gangs and Drugs, 680, 686
strain theory, 415
street capital, 8, 402, 405, 543
Street Corner Society (Whyte), 64, 160*t*, 161
Street Gangs and Street Workers (Klein), 161–63, 164*t*, 718
street orientation, 3–4, 19, 27, 28
street work, 225, 734
structure and organization. *See* gang structure
Stuart, Forrest, 7, 375
subcultural theory, 402–3
subjective expected utility, 7–8, 445–46, 447, 463
suppression. *See* policing
symbolic interactionism, 4–5, 107, 114–15
symbols, 9, 55, 91, 97, 112, 240, 248, 320, 384–85, 400, 401, 481, 518, 519–20, 600, 609–10, 660, 662, 666, 667, 703–4, 719, 747

tattoos, 78, 116, 330, 384, 401–2, 484, 590, 645, 662–63, 759, 798, 833, 838
Tapia, Mike, 10, 263, 753
territoriality, 5, 20, 29, 124, 151*t*, 355, 519–20, 660, 666–68, 819–20
terrorism and terrorists, 151*t*, 175, 212, 332, 448, 509, 533, 603–4, 629, 666, 682
The American Street Gang (Klein), 179
The Gang: A Study of 1,313 Gangs in Chicago (Thrasher), 1, 122–23, 140–41, 160–61, 160*t*, 258, 375, 719
The Insane Chicago Way (Hagedorn), 723–24, 726–27
the Molls, 396
The Social Order of the Slum (Suttles), 161–63
thick theory, 9, 641–42, 642*t*
thin theory, 642*t*, 642–43
Thomas, Kyle, 7–8, 444
Thompson, Paige, 11, 870
Thornberry, Terence, 151*t*, 171*t*, 224–25, 228–29, 230, 414, 434, 471, 776, 778
Thrasher, Frederic, 97, 265–66, 270, 719, 789–90
Tita, George, 11, 849

tomboy, 292–93, 396, 720–21
Tostlebe, Jennifer, 7, 413, 678
Transgang Project, 511, 663
transnational gangs, 9, 127, 659
Trinidad and Tobago, 351–52, 353, 355, 357–59, 360, 362–64, 622–23
turf, 41, 56, 77, 78, 79, 80, 125, 240, 248, 275, 320, 356, 548–49, 552–53, 685–87, 762, 764
turning points, 140–42, 145, 146–49, 150–75, 180, 181, 461–62, 560–61, 562, 684, 685, 738, 780
Twitter, 248, 385, 386, 623–24, 628, 810–11, 833, 840
typologies of gangs, 19, 42, 756–57

underclass, 125–26, 377–78, 721, 726–27, 755, 757, 759–60, 762–63, 764, 765–66
Understanding Street Culture (Ilan), 402
unified theory, 415
Uniform Crime Report (UCR), 77, 241, 677
University of Missouri- St. Louis, 677–78, 696–97
Urbanik, Marta-Marika, 6, 287
urbanization, 8, 274, 501, 504–5, 661, 722–23
U.S. Department of Justice (DOJ), 5, 77–78, 84, 207–8, 221–22, 229, 235, 236, 819–20

Valasik, Matthew, 8, 518, 809
Van Damme, Ellen, 6, 290–91*t*, 329
Vandenbogaerde, Ellen, 331
verbal duels, 400

Vice Lords, 164*t*, 264, 265, 604, 643, 718, 722
victimization, 9, 17, 37, 54, 58–59, 62, 67, 74, 76–77, 81, 93, 108, 109–10, 112, 116, 151*t*, 170, 174, 208–9, 213*t*, 317, 337–38, 397–98, 403–4, 446, 450, 452–53, 458, 459, 471, 472, 477, 479, 480–83, 484, 485, 560, 562, 563, 566, 567, 569, 570–71, 577, 585, 586–87, 599–600, 644, 684–85, 774, 778–80, 874
    females, 339, 341–42
    online, 626, 840
Vigil, Diego, 10, 163, 568, 577–78, 718, 744, 753

Walker, D'Andre, 9, 560
wannabes, 113, 417*t*, 720
war on drugs, 180, 181, 274, 531–32, 666
war on gangs, 151*t*, 276, 722, 725
Weerman, Frank, 3–4, 15
Weisel, Deborah, 683
Werlau, Maria, 331
Woltz, Kaitlyn, 9, 638
women and gangs. *See* female gang members
Wyrick, Phelan, 5, 207

youth gangs, 151*t*, 164*t*, 168*t*, 171*t*, 180, 223, 225, 227–28, 236–37, 238, 239, 240, 247–48, 259, 278, 316, 470–71, 475–76, 660–61, 756–57, 781, 873–74
Youth Gangs in International Gang Transitions (Esbensen and Maxson)
YouTube, 385, 623, 833